MARKETING RESEARCH

MARKETING RESEARCH

TWELFTH
EDITION

David A. Aaker

E. T. Grether Professor Emeritus of Marketing and Public Policy
University of California, Berkeley

V. Kumar

Regents Professor
Richard and Susan Lenny Distinguished Chair & Professor in Marketing,
Director of the Marketing Ph.D. Program, and
Executive Director, Center for Excellence in Brand and Customer
Management, Georgia State University;
Chang Jiang Scholar, Huazhong University of Science and Technology,
China;
Lee Kong Chian Fellow, Singapore Management University, Singapore;
and ISB Senior Fellow, Indian School of Business, Hyderabad, India

Robert P. Leone

J. Vaughn and Evelyne H. Wilson Chair and
Professor of Marketing
Neeley School of Business, Texas Christian University

George S. Day

Geoffrey T. Boisi Professor of Marketing, and
Co-Director of the Mack Institute for Innovation Management,
Wharton School, University of Pennsylvania

VICE PRESIDENT & DIRECTOR	George Hoffman
EXECUTIVE EDITOR	Lise Johnson
DEVELOPMENT EDITOR	Jennifer Manias
ASSOCIATE DEVELOPMENT EDITOR	Kyla Buckingham
SENIOR PRODUCT DESIGNER	Allison Morris
MARKET SOLUTIONS ASSISTANT	Amanda Dallas
SENIOR DIRECTOR	Don Fowley
PROJECT MANAGER	Gladys Soto
PROJECT SPECIALIST	Nichole Urban
PROJECT ASSISTANT	Anna Melhorn
EXECUTIVE MARKETING MANAGER	Christopher DeJohn
ASSISTANT MARKETING MANAGER	Puja Katariwala
ASSOCIATE DIRECTOR	Kevin Holm
SENIOR CONTENT SPECIALIST	Nicole Repasky
PRODUCTION EDITOR	Bharathy Surya Prakash
PHOTO RESEARCHER	MaryAnn Price

This book was set in 10/12 Times LT Std Roman by SPi Global and printed and bound by Strategic Content Imaging.

Founded in 1807, John Wiley & Sons, Inc. has been a valued source of knowledge and understanding for more than 200 years, helping people around the world meet their needs and fulfill their aspirations. Our company is built on a foundation of principles that include responsibility to the communities we serve and where we live and work.

In 2008, we launched a Corporate Citizenship Initiative, a global effort to address the environmental, social, economic, and ethical challenges we face in our business. Among the issues we are addressing are carbon impact, paper specifications and procurement, ethical conduct within our business and among our vendors, and community and charitable support. For more information, please visit our website: www.wiley.com/go/citizenship.

ISBN: 978-1-119-23872-0 (PBK)
ISBN: 978-1-119-22201-9 (EVALC)

Library of Congress Cataloging-in-Publication Data:

Names: Aaker, David A., author.
Title: Marketing research / David A. Aaker, V. Kumar, Robert P. Leone, George
  S. Day.
Description: Twelfth edition. | Hoboken, NJ : John Wiley & Sons, Inc., [2016]
  | Includes bibliographical references and index.
Identifiers: LCCN 2015039978 (print) | LCCN 2015042858 (ebook) | ISBN
  9781119238720 (pbk. : alk. paper) | ISBN 9781119236085 (epub)
Subjects: LCSH: Marketing research.
Classification: LCC HF5415.2 .A14 2016 (print) | LCC HF5415.2 (ebook) | DDC
  658.8/3--dc23
LC record available at http://lccn.loc.gov/2015039978

Printing identification and country of origin will either be included on this page and/or the end of the book. In addition, if the ISBN on this page and the back cover do not match, the ISBN on the back cover should be considered the correct ISBN.

10 9 8 7 6 5 4 3 2 1

Dedicated with love
To my wife, Kay

To my parents, Patta and Viswanathan
my family—Aparna, Prita, Anita, Rohan, and Ryan
my sister Shanti, and her family, Prasad, Amritha and Deepa,
my uncle, Kannan
and, my in-laws, Dr. Lalitha and Ramamurthy

To my wife, Teresa and
my daughters—Amy and Casey

To my wife, Alice

PREFACE

The role of marketing research in organizations across the globe has continued to become more important as more and more data become available to marketers from an ever-increasing number of sources. Understanding how to get marketing insights from these data is what companies need in order to achieve marketing and financial success. Ever since companies started to collect primary data through consumer surveys to help them plan marketing activities, the field of marketing research with respect to the data requirements has come a long way. The nature and type of data being collected now also include not only store scanner data but also consumer home shopping panels and data from social media. Now more than ever companies have the ability to collect a wide range of customer information pertaining to attitudes, behaviors, and demographics. Ably supported by the growth in data storage and retrieval techniques (ranging from small databases to huge data farms), the area of marketing research has grown by leaps and bounds over the past decades. This growth has been accentuated by the declining data storage costs and the growing expanse of the Internet medium. These developments have enabled companies to invest in data now more than ever. These forces, coupled with the technology trends and the emergence of a global marketplace, require managers to take cognizance of the important role of marketing intelligence. Further, the customer-level interactions on the Internet and the emergence of social networking as an important medium of marketing add a new dimension to traditional marketing research intelligence. This new edition of *Marketing Research* brings to the forefront the relevance of marketing intelligence.

If we can compare marketing to a long train with multiple compartments, then marketing research would justly claim the dual roles of the engine that powers the train and the links that connect the individual compartments to form a cohesive functional unit. In other words, marketing research is pervasive—the *brain* and the *brawn* of any marketing organization. Having said this, we realize that marketing research is a complex subject and therefore has to be introduced to the student one compartment at a time before the entire train can be visualized. We also realize the danger in this approach. The student can get overly excited or, even worse, overwhelmed by the individual units so that he or she fails to see the proverbial "big picture"—the overarching framework, the subtle but essential interactions between units, and the ultimate purpose, namely, how marketing research can help organizations achieve their goals.

This revised edition takes a "macro–micro–macro" approach toward communicating the intricacies of marketing research and its usefulness to the marketing organization. The first two chapters provide an overview of the marketing research process in order for the student to see the "big picture." The chapters that follow then discuss in detail the individual components. The chapters have benefitted significantly from updates with respect to newer and more recent business examples and industry statistics. Further, the concepts introduced and discussed in the text have been harmoniously tied to popular industry practices for easy understanding. While maintaining the strengths of previous editions, this edition focuses on the recent trends in marketing intelligence. Specific importance has been given to the concepts such as Customer Lifetime Value, Share of Wallet, Brand Equity, Mobile Marketing, and the increasing role of Social Media Marketing. Topics of less interest and relevance to the practice of marketing and marketing research have been eliminated. Some of the cases and problems have been moved to Wiley's Web content for the book while some of the more dated cases have been removed and replaced with more current cases.

We begin with a macro-level treatment of what marketing research is, where it fits within an organization, and how it helps in managerial decision making. Here, we also discuss the marketing research industry, with a brief treatment of both suppliers and users.

The body of the text takes a micro-level approach, detailing each and every step of the marketing research process. In describing the marketing research process, a decision-oriented perspective has been adopted to help students, who are future managers and researchers, make better decisions. Detailed discussions of the process, with numerous examples from the industry, characterize this micro phase.

Finally, we wrap up with a macro-level treatment of the applications of marketing research. Here we address the traditional 4P research, as well as contemporary issues such as brand equity, customer satisfaction research, and emerging issues that continue to fascinate marketers, such as e-commerce, direct marketing, database marketing, and relationship marketing, while taking care to incorporate some of the latest research and developments in these fields.

Objectives of This Text

Our overall objectives in writing this text continue to be the following:

1. To emphasize the role of marketing research in today's world and to focus on the techniques and steps that show how a company can gather marketing intelligence and use this information to generate insights that can be used in strategic decision making.

2. To communicate in an interesting and informative manner the essence of marketing research to "future managers" and "future researchers." Both groups need to know when marketing research can and should be used, what research alternatives exist, how to recognize effective and ineffective research, and how to interpret and apply the results.

3. To illustrate the usefulness of the Internet, online marketing research, and other advances in technology in collecting data and show real-world applications.

4. To emphasize the current developments in marketing research, such as the distinction between domestic and international market research, the emphasis on customer value management, and the influence of social media.

5. To use examples, applications, and illustrations throughout the book, in an effort to tie the material to the real world and thus provide interest and better understanding to the student.

6. To discuss the fastest growing applications of marketing research, e-commerce, direct marketing, database marketing research, customer relationship management, and social networking and their impact on businesses.

7. To provide a clear and comprehensive treatment of data analysis topics. Each chapter includes simple numerical examples to help students get a hands-on feel for the material.

8. To provide a thorough coverage of the most advanced and current marketing research methodologies, pointing out their limitations as well as their potential for enhancing research results.

New to This Edition

Consistent with these objectives, the 12th edition has undergone some critical changes. The more prominent of these include the following:

1. The chapter objectives have been clearly detailed on the first page of each chapter in order to clearly communicate what is to be covered in the chapter.

2. The chapter on *Qualitative Methods* has been revised to include a richer discussion on focus groups and observational research.

3. Chapter 1 (*A Decision-Making Perspective on Marketing Intelligence*) has undergone major updates that serve as a good example to indicate the level and nature of additions made throughout this edition. The updates are in the form of new company examples, and updated company and market statistics.

4. Chapter 2 (*Marketing Research in Practice*) provides an updated picture of the global marketing research industry. It includes the latest findings in this area and lists the Top 25 Global Research Organizations in the marketing research industry.

5. Chapter 7 (*Marketing Research on the Internet*) also contains important updates to this edition. The chapter now has up-to-date numbers and statistics with respect to the Internet, and how marketing research is being conducted on the Internet. New material such as Amazon's Mechanical Turk (or MTurk) and new industry trends have also been added.

6. The examples contained in the Marketing Research in Action throughout the book have been updated with relevant content changes.

7. Statistics and other trend information have been updated.

8. New cases and study questions have been added and dated cases have been removed.

9. The text has also benefitted from additions and updates to new and emerging topics of lifetime value, measuring the effectiveness of social media campaigns and understanding the value of word-of-mouth marketing.

10. The web address www.wiley.com/college/aaker can be used for accessing information pertaining to the textbook and its contents.

Features of the Book

1. The text communicates the essence of marketing research in an interesting and informative manner to future managers and future researchers. Both groups need to know when marketing research can and should be used, what research alternatives exist, how to recognize effective and ineffective research, and how to interpret and apply the results.

2. The Cases and Part Cases are positioned appropriately at the end of chapters and text parts to stimulate interest, add realism to the marketing research curriculum, and help develop decision-making skills. These cases cover a wide range of products and organizations.

3. The chapter on *A Decision-Making Perspective on Marketing Intelligence* attempts to enlighten the readers of the importance and means of accessing data from multiple sources and delivering to end-users for analysis.

4. The chapter on *Marketing Research on the Internet* links the reader with the world of marketing research to keep abreast with the emerging trends and changes in the marketplace.

5. Discussion of the international element of marketing research has been continued. Particularly, an effort has been made to provide a clear distinction between the domestic and international marketing research processes and prepare the users of this text to face the challenges of multinational research.

6. The chapter on *New Age Strategies* reiterates the fact that understanding of the customer is the key to marketing success. The chapter focuses on the tools provided by marketing

intelligence for better knowledge of customer profiles. The chapter also focuses on e-commerce, database marketing, relationship marketing, and social networking. The growth in e-commerce is phenomenal, and the firm's ability to identify individuals and market to them is an important task. Database marketing is currently one of the most important tools for businesses facing the challenges of the twenty-first century. As firms shift their resources more toward targeted marketing, the discussion in this chapter becomes more valuable.

7. Marketing Research in Action sections in various chapters have been updated to focus on the real-world applications of Marketing Research.

8. Each chapter also includes Learning Objectives, a Chapter Summary, and Questions and Problems.

Organization of the Text

The book is organized to reflect the "macro–micro–macro" approach toward imparting marketing research training to the student. The text consists of five parts. Parts I and V deal with the "macro" aspects of marketing research; Parts II–IV deal with the micro aspects.

Part I, consisting of four chapters, deals with the nature and scope of marketing intelligence and marketing research. Here, the overall framework of marketing research is presented, and where and how marketing research fits in with the other aspects of marketing is explained. The nature of the research industry and suppliers is also discussed here.

Part II, consisting of Chapters 5 through 15, deals extensively with the various aspects of data collection. This part is further divided into four sections, one section devoted to each of the three fundamental types of marketing research: exploratory, descriptive, and causal. The final section addresses the issue of sampling.

Part III, consisting of three chapters, discusses the fundamental aspects and techniques in data analysis. These include basic analysis issues such as data editing, coding, and simple techniques such as hypothesis testing, chi-square analysis, and the analysis of variance.

Part IV is devoted exclusively to advanced and more sophisticated data analysis techniques such as correlation and regression analysis, discriminant analysis, factor analysis, cluster analysis, conjoint analysis, and multidimensional scaling. This part consists of four chapters, the last chapter dealing with the aspects of presenting the research results.

In **Part V,** the student is exposed to the measures, metrics, and strategies of marketing intelligence. This section has three chapters and provides the student with a comprehensive picture of marketing research, highlighting how the marketing-mix measures, the brand and customer metrics, and the new-age strategies fit into the application of marketing intelligence.

Supplements to the Text

- All relevant information pertaining to the textbook and its contents can be accessed from this website—www.wiley.com/college/aaker. This website will periodically update information that is relevant for keeping the text up to date.

- An Instructor's Manual will accompany this text. This manual provides solutions to end-of-chapter Questions and Problems and discusses all the test cases in greater detail. Exam questions are arranged by chapter and include multiple-choice and true/false questions. An example of a course syllabus is presented, and many suggestions for the organization of the course are provided. This resource can be found on the Instructor Companion site.

- A test bank has been added to the website, which provides sample test questions in each chapter.

- PowerPoint presentations of selected material from each chapter are available.

- Data sets that contain data for end-of-chapter cases and statistical analysis are available. SPSS®-interpreted examples are also available.

- The website also contains detailed information on the mini-project designed for students mentioned at the end of the eighth chapter.

- End-of-chapter questions are also available on the website.

- New Marketing Research Video Series: Brand new interview-style video clips of top marketing research companies. Each video, six to eight minutes in length, presents interviews with key personnel to discuss how they apply the major concepts of marketing research to their business. The Wiley Marketing Research Video Series can be accessed on the Instructor and Student Companion websites.

Acknowledgments

Many debts have been accumulated over the years during which 12 editions of this book have taken shape. We are especially grateful to our students, who gave us feedback from the consumer's perspective and whose field research projects provided many of the illustrations and problems; to our colleagues, who stimulated us and brought new ideas and approaches to our attention; and to our clients, who gave us many opportunities to put ideas into practice and thus broaden our understanding of marketing research as it is currently practiced. It has been a continuing pleasure to associate with a class publisher, John Wiley & Sons, and to work with a number of Wiley editors over the years—most recently, Gladys Soto and her team.

We also would like to express thanks to Bharath Rajan, A. J. Radcliffe, Christin Woods, Madhuri Puttaswamy, and Prakash RaviChandar for their efforts toward the production of the 12th edition.

Finally, we wish to express our sincere appreciation to our families and friends for their constant support, encouragement, and sacrifices during the creation of this book.

DAVID A. AAKER
V. KUMAR
ROBERT P. LEONE
GEORGE S. DAY

BRIEF CONTENTS

CONTENTS

PART II   DATA COLLECTION

SECTION A: SECONDARY AND EXPLORATORY RESEARCH

SECTION C: CAUSAL RESEARCH

13 EXPERIMENTATION 314

SECTION D: SAMPLING

14 SAMPLING FUNDAMENTALS 345

15 SAMPLE SIZE AND STATISTICAL THEORY 373

PART III   DATA ANALYSIS

16 FUNDAMENTALS OF DATA ANALYSIS   397

17 HYPOTHESIS TESTING: BASIC CONCEPTS AND TESTS OF ASSOCIATIONS   417

18 HYPOTHESIS TESTING: MEANS AND PROPORTIONS   436

PART IV   SPECIAL TOPICS IN DATA ANALYSIS

19   CORRELATION ANALYSIS AND REGRESSION ANALYSIS   462

20   DISCRIMINANT, FACTOR, AND CLUSTER ANALYSIS   492

21   MULTIDIMENSIONAL SCALING AND CONJOINT ANALYSIS   534

25 NEW AGE STRATEGIES 639

APPENDIX A 677

GLOSSARY 703

INDEX 721

A Decision-Making Perspective on Marketing Intelligence

1

LEARNING OBJECTIVES

- Describe the concept of business intelligence.
- Describe the need and use of marketing intelligence in an organization.
- Describe how marketing intelligence fits in the bigger scheme of the marketing environment.
- Explain the role of marketing intelligence in decision making.
- Discuss the factors that affect marketing intelligence decisions.
- Describe how and when marketing research is used.
- Discuss the implication of ethical issues in gathering marketing intelligence.
- Discuss the ethical responsibilities and rights of the respondent in marketing research.
- Explain the impact international trade has had on marketing research.

An Overview of Business Intelligence

As they manage their businesses and compete in a global market, decision makers face many questions every day. *Is the business healthy? Who are my best customers? How can I attract new customers? What supplier should I choose? Are we using the right marketing mix?*

Effectively managing the performance of the business means knowing what questions to ask and having the facts readily at hand to answer them. This is what business intelligence (BI) delivers. BI, at its core, is the ability to access data from multiple sources within an enterprise and deliver it to business users for analysis.[1] BI bridges the gap between disparate operational systems and data-hungry end users. It connects people to their business. It creates an information environment that makes it easy for people to get the reports they need in the context of their day-to-day activities. It provides an accessible means of analyzing the business and getting to the bottom of what's behind trends and anomalies. And, it offers a reliable barometer of how well the business is performing. The following examples give a flavor of the possibilities BI offers.

Georgia Aquarium[2]

Studies performed at the Georgia Aquarium in 2013, located in Atlanta, have tremendously validated the need for marketing research. Despite being the world's largest aquarium, attendance had dropped over the years, prompting board members to look for the reasoning behind this.

Researchers were brought in to identify ways to bring more attendance to the facilities. The project involved assessing the various constraints that existed within the aquarium and how they could resolve certain issues. The primary focus was placed on understanding the customers that visit Georgia Aquarium, how to attract the right ones, and what can be done to make sure they return for future visits.

A group of researchers began the study by identifying the top 50 zip codes of the aquarium's visitors as well as the top 50 zip codes of the season-pass holders. Combining the data, the researchers assessed what were the common traits in the two groups (i.e., demographics) and targeted other zip codes comprised of individuals with similar characteristics. After identifying this market as young individuals located in areas where new homes and apartments were being developed, a decision was made for an increase in media spending from $2 to $2.7 million. The locations where advertisements were placed changed, with billboard signs being posted in areas with heavy traffic, and commercial ad's being displayed during the airing of the most popular cable television shows.

After the plan was implemented in 2013, Georgia Aquarium has seen a $700,000 investment turn into an $8 million increase in revenue, with attendance increasing by 10 percent. This strategy incorporated by Georgia Aquarium, combining data analytics and market research, proved formidable in developing methods to attract future customers.

Erlanger (Ky.) Police Department[3]

In a novel attempt at fighting crime, the Erlanger, Kentucky, police department has developed a portal that helps its officers to track and solve crimes. Developed in September 2008, the portal combines concepts from BI searching and mapping. This Web-based BI portal allows patrol officers to enter data—or even pieces of data such as a few numbers from a license plate—into a simple search interface and retrieve information from their own databases and those of neighboring towns. This solution was developed to address the long-standing need for an unified communications network bridging the fire and police departments. Specifically, the Erlanger Police Department wanted to tap into the records management systems of 19 separate government agencies in order to search and analyze information about suspects, reported incidents, arrests, and crimes.

In order to develop this software, the department bought a readily available software that has geomapping and BI features and added an open-source search, which compiles structured and unstructured data references into an index that can easily be searched by an appliance. This final software categorized search results to give users a better context and relevancy for search queries. This Web-based software combined real-time crime data from multiple agencies with crime records and incident reports stretching back five years to link information about suspects, incidents, and arrests.

This software was able to completely search the records management systems and create maps and information that helped officers perform their duties. This software enabled officers to see over the last 24 hours where calls have occurred and compared crime statistics against previous and current year's data. The department believes that the software's success will be judged in part by whether the department can continue to handle the 5–10 percent annual increase in calls to the communications center while maintaining its recent 1–2 percent annual rate of increase in crimes solved—all without having to add more personnel.

Recent Trends in Business Intelligence

Business intelligence tools and systems play a key role in the strategic planning process of a firm. These systems allow the firm to gather, store, access, and analyze corporate data to aid in decision making. Historically, such data were available to only a limited number of individuals in a

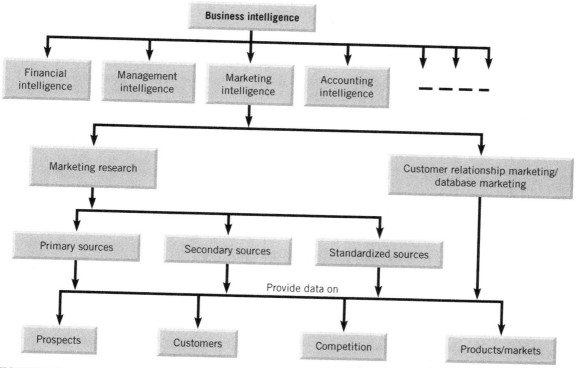

FIGURE 1.1
Typical Areas Under the Umbrella of Business Intelligence.

firm. However, the increased use of cloud storage by many firms makes these data available to units throughout the organization. The science of BI is being utilized by specialists in different business fields today. Business intelligence comprises several components—financial intelligence, marketing intelligence, accounting intelligence, and management intelligence among others, as shown in Figure 1.1. Financial intelligence provides consultancy, forward-looking financial accounting and procurement systems, strategic BI, and support. To quote the words of an industry executive, "Financial intelligence works by empowering the CFO to make critical and successful decisions, giving the CIO current yet reliable technology and the CEO quality time to think strategically." Accounting and management intelligence incorporate the tools and techniques of the respective fields. In this book, we are interested in the marketing intelligence component of BI.

Introduction to Marketing Intelligence

According to American Marketing Association, marketing is defined as the activity, set of institutions, and processes for creating, communicating, delivering, and exchanging offerings that have value for customers, clients, partners, and society at large.[4] The marketing concept does not focus on one aspect of marketing or only units within the firm but recognizes the roles of non-marketers in the marketing process such as customers, vendors, or external agencies who regulate marketing.

While marketing centers around satisfying customer needs, an organization must have systems in place to understand and monitor customer needs. Marketing intelligence helps organizations in this process and focuses on gathering customer-level information that would assist in business decision making and policy analysis.

What Is Marketing Intelligence?

Marketing intelligence (MI) is *"the process of acquiring and analyzing information in order to understand the market (both existing and potential customers); to determine the current and future needs and preferences, attitudes and behavior of the market; and to assess changes in the business environment that may affect the size and nature of the market in future."*[5]

Marketing intelligence has the capacity to be at the forefront in contributing to the development of a business environment through strategic research; risk and policy analysis; credit-rating documentation; storage, publication; reporting; and communication of reliable, timely, and objective business information. It incorporates information from customer analysis and industry analysis as well as general market conditions.

In other words, marketing intelligence calls for understanding, analyzing, and assessing the internal and external environment related to a company's customers, competitors, markets, and industry to enhance the decision-making process. This would require the integration of competitive intelligence, marketing research, market analysis, and business and financial analysis information.[6]

Components of Marketing Intelligence

Marketing intelligence primarily focuses on creation and management of profitable long-term relationships with customers with an emphasis on the use of information and communication technologies in researching, selecting, entering, and competing in global markets. As shown in Figure 1.1, the various components of marketing intelligence can be included under two main areas—marketing research and customer relationship marketing/database marketing.

Marketing research focuses primarily on the collection and use of information on customers and their needs for designing marketing programs. Marketing data can be collected from primary, secondary, and standardized sources. Data analysis in marketing research uses the data on prospects, customers, competition, products, and markets, while incorporating marketing concepts, methods, and quantitative tools, to make meaningful decisions with regard to marketing campaigns, resource allocation, and the managerial planning process. Customer relationship management/database marketing integrates information on customer buying behavior and motivation obtained from a firm's database and market research. This information aids the firm to manage the offers made to its customers (both current and new products and services), in order to acquire new customers, and satisfy and retain existing customers in a profitable manner.

Need for Marketing Intelligence

Marketing research plays a critical part in a marketing intelligence system. It aids in improving management decision making by providing relevant, accurate, and timely information. The following examples provide a flavor of marketing research in action.

- When Apple Inc. launched the iPad in early 2010, Steve Jobs (then CEO of the company) described it as the company's most advanced technology at an unbelievable price. The company experienced a tremendous level of sales, and by April of 2011 had sold over 15 million units. This exceeded the number of iPhones sold in the first year, and exceeded the sales of all other tablets put together. The rationale behind their dominant position in the tablet market can largely be attributed to their surprise launch, catching competitors flat-footed. In comparison to previous launches, this was one of the greatest routings in the history of consumer electronics. Apple has been able to capitalize on the successful design of the iPad and has further exercised their stronghold on innovation.

- Sephora makeup has taken the extra initiative in providing its sales personnel with up-to-date information on its products, allowing them to educate customers as well as give them an actual testing of the product. By signing up for *Beauty Insider*, their loyalty membership program, customers are provided with a card that allows them to enter a profile, allowing sales personnel the opportunity to gain information on customers buying behavior and preferences.[7]

- The Tesla Roadster was introduced in July 2006. The car was positioned in a unique way in the automobile industry, as it was the first highway-capable all-electric vehicle that was produced in large quantity in the United States. In addition to a strong presence in the United States, Tesla has been able to market the Roadster in over 30 countries, with several drivers qualifying for government incentives in certain countries. Their position in the market has been sustained largely due to their innovativeness, their ability to take advantage of a market that values energy efficiency and their capability regarding opening and operating company-owned stores rather than through franchise dealerships.

All these examples point to the need for marketing intelligence because of the following:

- Producers have little direct contact with consumers (geographical distance and channel layers).

- Channels have little knowledge about customer attitudes, preference, and changing tastes.

- Firms need to understand the competition without spying on them.

- Management goals involve sales targets and market share achievement.

- There is a need to identify successful new product developments early in the process to ensure growth and revenue maximization by finding a balance between costs and prices of products.

- The future is uncertain, yet, businesses do need to anticipate the future. The need is to look at least 5–10 years in advance. Pharmaceutical companies do it on a regular basis because they have to plan for what happens when a particular patent expires.

Table 1.1 lists the various areas where marketing intelligence is applied.

Traditional forecasting involves extrapolating from the present. The problem with this approach is that the further forward one goes, the greater the error—thus, the greater the risk of a mistake. Three examples illustrate the problem of anticipating the future.

In 1943, Thomas Watson, then chairman of IBM, forecasted a world market for about five computers. In 1970, Ken Olsen, founder of Digital Equipment Corporation, said no one needed to have a personal computer at home. In 1981, Microsoft's founder Bill Gates said that 640 K would be enough memory for anyone.

According to AWARE, a marketing intelligence services company, Scenario Planning is a technique that overcomes these problems. It is a methodology that allows practitioners to prepare for the future by looking at trends in the present and mapping how these interrelate with each other. From this study, a number of scenarios picturing possible future worlds are drafted, along with a description of how these futures could arise. Businesses then plan around these—with contingency plans for undesirable elements. Key change indicators are monitored and used to gauge how events are turning out.

Companies using the technique have reported remarkable successes—the oil company Shell, for example, predicted the Oil Crisis of the 1970s, and the changes that took place prior to and immediately after the fall of the Soviet Union in the early 1990s.

The different functions under marketing intelligence are all interrelated in the sense that the data collected using various techniques in marketing research are then analyzed and interpreted to improve the efficient management of customer–firm relationships, and the knowledge and

Table 1.1 Domains of Marketing Intelligence

- **Product decisions**
  Marketing intelligence helps in making decisions on investing in new products and in optimizing product specifications or offerings to target customer groups.

- **Customer segmentation decisions**
  Marketing intelligence gives an opportunity for companies to study the impact of advertisements—before and after advertising. Based on research and audience composition, marketing intelligence gives companies the flexibility to choose advertising media. Finally, MI also gives companies enough information for selection of target segments.

- **Brand and pricing decisions**
  Marketing intelligence helps decision makers in building brand equity and consciousness among the targeted customer segments. Gathering marketing intelligence also helps capture popular perceptions and changing trends, tastes, and lifestyles.

- **Keeping stakeholders happy**
  Understanding stakeholder needs and responding to them keeps all stakeholders—customers, channels, and suppliers—satisfied. A satisfied customer is a profitable customer.

- **Market estimation, competitive benchmarking, and distribution**
  Marketing intelligence also helps in quantitative analysis of market forces—estimating size of the market, quantitative and behavioral analysis of the market, and forecasting future trends/needs. Marketing intelligence also helps in market share analyses.

  In short, the domains of marketing intelligence application appear vast and include identifying marketing opportunities to build profitable businesses; developing and using marketing intelligence; designing the marketing mix; acquiring and retaining customers; and planning, organizing, evaluating, and controlling market performance.

  Judicious gathering of marketing intelligence helps companies to walk up the marketing thinking ladder by explaining how to grasp and outperform consumer value migration and hence to make more money by adding more value to existing brands. Outcome is simply more consumer-oriented businesses.

experience created from these fields can be used to effectively manage new product development and marketing. Customer relationship marketing and database marketing will be covered briefly in the last chapter. But the primary focus of this book is the marketing research arm of marketing intelligence.

Marketing Research

Any marketing organization should have a marketing intelligence system in place that helps them obtain information on consumer needs and gathers marketing intelligence that will help them understand how to satisfy these needs efficiently. Each decision a company makes poses unique needs for information gathered through marketing research, and relevant strategies can be developed based on the information gathered through marketing research. These strategies help companies in designing and implementing specific marketing campaigns, for example, multicultural marketing campaigns (MCM).

For instance, a survey by the Association of National Advertisers, New York, in 2012, found that newer media platforms are being increasingly funded. Nearly 56 percent of those surveyed stated that funding for newer media platforms has shifted from traditional (general market) media as well as the budget for marketing communications. Tools such as mobile, social media, and location-based applications are being used to target multicultural audiences. In addition, blogging has become a primary source of communication, primarily with Hispanic audiences. The survey found search engine's served as the most favored media vehicle for reaching multicultural audiences (70 percent), followed closely by social media (67 percent), mobile (64 percent), twitter (48 percent), webinars (48 percent), blogs (44 percent), and video-on-demand (38 percent). These findings have had important implications in how to target the customer for different multicultural segments.

Conquering Latino Homes

Hispanics account for nearly 17 percent of the U.S. population and are about 54 million strong.[8] According to the Census Bureau, the demographic grew 53 percent from 2000 to 2013, making it the fastest growing demographic in the United States. The 2013 Pew Hispanic Center survey indicates that 95 percent of Hispanic adults with family incomes of $50,000 go online at least occasionally. The study also found education to be a key factor in Internet usage. For instance, those who have no high school diploma are least likely to go online (58 percent). Among those with a high school diploma, 85 percent go online at least occasionally. And among those with some college education, 91 percent go online. Among Internet users, 31 percent are English dominant, and 41 percent are bilingual. Furthermore, the study found that 76 percent Hispanic Internet users access the Internet on a cellphone, tablet, or other mobile handheld device at least occasionally.[9] This demographic holds much promise to marketers and advertisers in terms of revenue and has been receiving increased attention over the years (see Table 1.2).

The Hispanic market contributes more than $1.2 trillion toward purchasing power of the multicultural population. Due to the popularity of the Hispanic market, advertisement spending aimed at this demographic has steadily increased. A Nielsen Report showed that advertisement spending in the United States directed toward Hispanics increased by 11.1 percent from 2011 to 2012. Marketers reportedly spent in excess of $8 billion dollars, up from $3 billion in 2003. The study further reported that television marketing covered 50 percent of their total spending and is continuing to grow much faster than the average rate. Digital advertisement spending has also been heavily directed toward Hispanic audiences, with desktop and mobile spending increasing 15 percent in 2011. At the time of the report, it was estimated that nearly 70 percent of Hispanic users use some form of social networking on a monthly basis, ranging from Twitter, to Facebook, to LinkedIn.

During the 2014 Soccer World Cup, companies viewed this as a tremendous business opportunity to target new audiences, primarily Hispanics. Companies such as Gatorade, Hyundai, and Chips Ahoy began running several ads in English and in Spanish. The addition of ESPN Deportes to the ESPN network has provided a tremendous boost to the U.S. English broadcast. Popular beer distributor Corona began to further their push toward Hispanic customers by releasing bilingual commercials. The rationale behind this lies in the ever-growing multicultural personalities present within millennials. The Voice of Hispanic Marketing reports that Hispanics now make up 17 percent of the U.S. population, and going forward, it is expected that the collective amount spent in advertising will continue to increase.[10]

Advertisers are now making ads that depict cultural integration and generate product awareness. The pioneer in this effort is Sears, which came up with the "Solo Para Ti" (Just for You) campaign on Spanish-speaking television. Imagine The ROI of Sears in 2050 when the Hispanic population represents 25 percent of the total U.S. population! Marketing Research in Action 1.1 provides the initiative made by J.C. Penney, Co., in targeting Hispanic consumers.

Table 1. 2   Changing U.S. Demographics

Segment	2013	2012	2011	2010	2009
Hispanic or Latino	51,786,591	50,545,275	49,215,563	47,727,533	45,476,938
Not Hispanic or Latino	259,750,003	258,593,436	257,388,209	256,237,739	255,984,595
Total	**311,536,594**	**309,138,711**	**306,603,772**	**303,965,272**	**301,461,533**

Source: "Hispanic or Latino Origin By Specific Origin," U.S. Census Bureau, 2005–2009 American Community Survey.

Marketing Research in Action 1.1

■ J.C. PENNEY TARGETS HISPANIC CONSUMERS

J.C. Penney's latest marketing push has targeted Hispanic women. A 2012 report showed that J.C. Penney ranks fifth among retailers with regard to spending in Hispanic media. During the 2014 Soccer World Cup, the company launched a campaign that targeted Latinos, who have been identified by company executives as its "North Star." The rationale behind the campaign was that Latina women make up a larger percentage of World Cup viewers than non-Hispanic men. Given the increasingly growing role of Latina customers in the general market, marketing leaders at J.C. Penney see Latina women as a key component to rebuilding the brand and products offered.

In 2014, Hispanics made up 9 percent of J.C. Penney's customer base, but accounted for double-digit percentage of the company's store sales. In addition, the company is named more often by Latina women as the store they shop at most frequently. As of 2014, J.C. Penney had over 180 stores located in areas where sales from Hispanics are higher than average. Further actions have been taken to provide an enjoyable shopping experience for these Hispanic customers including: bilingual signage and the playing of Latin music throughout stores.

Furthermore, the assistance of social media has provided a large platform for J.C. Penney to further their push toward the Hispanic market. Online retailing is currently a primary source of shopping for customers, and the company has launched a new Hispanic Facebook page to improve interactions between the company and customers. In addition, J.C. Penney has increased their efforts toward creating products and incentives for the Hispanic customer in the form of a revamped rewards program, various lines of cookware, with newer products expected to be released in the near future.

Moving forward, company leaders believe that it is essential to take advantage of the strong position J.C. Penney currently maintains with its Latina customers. Within the demographic, it has been noticed that targeting older and lower-income individuals would be to the company's benefit, in addition to re-gaining the business of their previously loyal customers. As their most important customer, catering to the desires of Hispanics will allow J.C. Penney to rebuild their brand and gain a competitive edge.

Source: Adapted from "Natalie Zmuda June 9, 2014, "J.C. Penney Aims Marketing Squarely at Latinas" at http://adage.com/article/cmo-strategy/j-c-penney-aims-marketing-squarely-latinas/293602/ and Jeri Smith, on August 22, 2013, "J.C. Penney's Turnaround: Focus on Hispanics, Social Media" at http://www.mediapost.com/publications/article/207001/jcpenneys-turnaround-focus-on-hispanics-social.html?edition= , Retrieved on April 21, 2015.

A.C. Nielsen has used its Homescan system to analyze Hispanic consumer habits. Homescan recruits residents of some 500 Latino households who will keep track of their store purchases and scan the bar codes into *la maquinita*, or the little machine. Early findings show that Latino households outspend general market households in many product categories. For example, the average Hispanic household in the survey spent 67 percent more on carbonated soft drinks than did the average non-Hispanic household, 89 percent more on fruit drinks, 39 percent more on cereal, and 41 percent more on toilet paper.

Virtually every private- and public-sector organization encounters the same pressures for more and better information about its ever-changing markets. Whether the organization serves customers in competitive market environments or clients in a public-sector enterprise, it is necessary to understand and satisfy the changing needs of diverse groups of people.

Marketing research is the function that links the consumer, customer, and public to the marketer through information—information used to identify and define marketing opportunities and problems; generate, refine, and evaluate marketing actions; monitor marketing performance; and improve understanding of marketing as a process. Marketing research specifies the information required to address these issues, designs the method for collecting information, manages and implements the data collection process, analyzes, and communicates the findings and their implications.

American Marketing Association
Official Definition of Marketing Research

This definition highlights the role of marketing research as an aid to decision making. An important feature is the inclusion of the specification and interpretation of needed information. Too often, marketing research is considered narrowly as the gathering and analyzing of data for someone else to use. Firms can achieve and sustain a competitive advantage through the creative use of market information. Hence, marketing research is defined as an information input to decisions, not simply the evaluation of decisions that have been made. Market research alone, however, does not guarantee success; the intelligent use of market research is the key to business achievement. A competitive edge is more the result of how information is used than of who does or does not have the information.[13]

Role of Marketing Research in Managerial Decision Making

Marketing decisions involve issues that range from fundamental shifts in the positioning of a business or the decision to enter a new market to narrow tactical questions of how best to stock a grocery shelf. The context for these decisions is the market planning process, which proceeds sequentially through four stages: situation analysis, strategy development, marketing program development, and implementation. This is a never-ending process, so the evaluation of past strategic decisions serves as an input to the situation assessment. Figure 1.2 suggests some elements of each stage. During each stage, marketing research makes a major contribution to clarifying and resolving issues and then choosing among decision alternatives. The following sections describe these steps in more detail and describe the information needs that marketing research satisfies.

Situation Analysis

Effective marketing strategies are built on an in-depth understanding of the market environment of the business and the specific characteristics of the market. The depth of these information needs can be seen from the list in Table 1.3, which shows the requirements of a major consumer packaged-goods manufacturer.

FIGURE 1.2
Marketing Planning Process.

Table 1.3   Scope of Situation Assessment for a Consumer Goods Manufacturer

1. Market environment
   a. Technologies? How else will customers satisfy their needs?
   b. Economic trends? Disposable income?
   c. Social trends? What are the trends in age, marital status, working women, occupations, location, and shifts away from the center city? What values are becoming fashionable?
   d. Political and regulatory? New labeling and safety requirements.

2. Market characteristics
   a. Market size, potential, and growth rate?
   b. Geographic dispersion of customers?
   c. Segmentation: How many distinct groups are there? Which are growing?
   d. Competition: Who are the direct rivals? How big are they? What is their performance? What is their strategy, intention, and likely behavior with respect to product launches, promotions, and the like?
   e. Competitive products? Their nature and number?
   f. Channel members? What is the distribution of sales through supermarkets and other outlets? What are the trends? What are they doing to support their own brands?

3. Consumer behavior
   a. What do they buy? A product or service? A convenience, shopping, or specialty good? A satisfaction . . .?
   b. Who buys? Everybody? Women only? Teenagers (i.e., demographic, geographic, and psychographic classification)?
   c. Where do they buy? Will they shop around or not? Outlet types?
   d. Why do they buy? Motivations, perceptions of product and needs, influences of peers, prestige, influence of advertising, media?
   e. How do they buy? On impulse? By shopping (i.e., the process they go through in purchasing)?
   f. When do they buy? Once a week? Every day? Seasonal changes?
   g. Anticipated change? Incidence of new products, shifts in consumers' preferences, needs?

The macroenvironment includes political and regulatory trends, economic and social trends, and technological trends. Marketing researchers tend to focus on those trends that affect the demand for products and services. For example, the most important influences on the demand for consumer packaged-food products over the last decade were as follows:

- Demographic shifts, including a record number of aging adults who were increasingly affluent and active.

- Rapid changes in family structure as a result of delayed marriages, blended families, fewer children and a high divorce rate.

- Shifts in values as consumers became preoccupied with their own economic and emotional well-being.

These trends resulted in increased concerns about the quality of food, nutritional value, personal fitness, and "naturalness." Equally influential were shifts in food consumption patterns toward "grazing" or snacking, and more away-from-home eating.

Understanding the customers—who they are, how they behave, why they behave as they do, and how they are likely to respond in the future—is at the heart of marketing research. Increasingly, marketing researchers are being asked to turn their talents to understanding the behavior and intentions of consumers. Marketing Research in Action 1.2 depicts how eating and drinking habits among Italians have made Nestle in Italy see a new market to promote their bottled water.

A major responsibility of the marketing research function is providing information that will help detect problems and opportunities and then, if necessary, learning enough to make decisions as to what marketing program would result in the greatest response. An opportunity might be presented by the sense that customers are increasingly dissatisfied with existing products.

Marketing Research in Action 1.2

■ MARKET ON THE GO

While eating and drinking on the street may seem a normal behavior in the United States, it could mean violating two fundamental rules in Italy—looking good and eating well. Italians are often taught that eating or drinking while walking causes indigestion, with the exception of a gelato or a slice of focaccia being the only food they could enjoy on the street. Italian children too are taught not to eat or drink anywhere but at the table. This rule is so strictly adhered to, that many shops and businesses still close for 2 hours between 12:30 and 2:30 in the afternoon so people can enjoy a leisurely meal. This is also reflected in licensing laws that do not permit sales of food or drinks at places such as newsstands.

Italians have always believed in the curative properties of mineral waters, with some small towns making public fountains out of spring water. According to International Bottled Water Association, a U.S.-based trade association representing the bottled water industry, per capita consumption of bottled water in Italy was 53.3 gallons in 2007—third in the world after United Arab Emirates and Mexico, as compared to the 29.3 gallons in the United States during the same year. Italy is among the leading producers, exporters, and consumers of mineral water in the world with over 250 brands of Italian mineral water on the international market and over 600 brands sold domestically. However, Italians drink just 12 liters a year on the move, half of what Americans do.

Nestle SA, a major player in the bottled-water business, is now trying to build a new market by changing Italian habits. They have designed a new bottle top with a membrane to prevent leaking into handbags. To encourage the consumption of bottled water outside, Nestle distributes their water at soccer games and aerobic sessions.

To promote the "on the go" behavior, Nestle is trying to persuade Italians to drink more bottled water away from the table through its new offerings. To cater to the young women segment, they have launched a brand named Acqua Panna. The TV commercials for this squeezable hourglass-shaped 75 cl (25.4 oz.) bottle, known as Panna 75, feature a fashionable cartoon character named Lulu who carries a purse containing Acqua Panna, tipped over to show that it does not leak.

Nestle researchers also found that Italian mothers believe that fizzy drinks and ice are not good for kids. For this, they came up with a brand of still water called Issima—denoting an Italian suffix used in superlatives—in 11.2 oz. bottles. The marketers at Nestle arranged for free samples to be handed out to mothers and explained that the squeezable bottle fits neatly in lunch boxes, and is neither fizzy, nor cold, nor a soda. Nestle's promotion activities for Issima included conducting contests for kids on its Issima website with prizes such as radios and flashlights, launching a website that lets kids play a game following the adventures of Issimo—a skateboarding cartoon character—and signing a deal with Autogrill, Italy's largest roadside restaurant chain to include Issima in its kids' meals.

Source: Originally published by D. Ball, "Italian Challenge: Water Everywhere, but Not to Go," The Wall Street Journal, May 23, 2005, p. A.1, and printed with permission. Some statistics have been updated and adapted since then.

Marketing research could be asked to detect the dissatisfaction, perhaps determine how many people are dissatisfied, and learn the level and nature of that dissatisfaction.

Various research approaches are used to analyze the market. Perhaps the simplest is to organize information already obtained from prior studies, from magazine articles that have been printed, and from customers' comments to a firm's sales representatives. This is called **secondary data**. Another approach is to have small groups of customers, called **focus groups**, discuss their use of a product. Such discussion groups can provide many ideas for new marketing programs. When it is necessary to understand it in greater depth, a survey is often employed. For example, to understand the competitive position of Quebec in the tourism market, a survey was conducted to determine the benefits sought by visitors and nonvisitors, as well as the risks they perceived.

Marketing Research in Action 1.3

■ RESTRUCTURING AND REJUVENATING MCDONALD'S

With more than 36,000 stores in 100 countries, McDonald's is the world's largest fast food chain. Despite a whopping $96.91 billion market value, McDonald's sales had been stagnant for several years and dipped 2.3 percent in the first quarter of 2015. This has spurred an initiative toward innovation that will provide newer and better alternatives for their customers. The company plans to roll out a "Create Your Taste" burger option in over 2,000 of its locations sometime in 2015, which will allow customers to use a touch screen to build their own burgers by choosing from a list of buns, toppings, and sauces. After selecting their desired ingredients, customers will sit down and wait for approximately 7 minutes for a server to bring their burger to the table.

The primary reason for restructuring their service approach is to trigger an increase in business, primarily from young customers. During the 2000's, McDonald's saw a tremendous increase in its share price jumping from $12 in 2003 to $100 in 2011. However, recent struggles have caused a dip in performance, primarily in the United States. The presence of other fast food chains, such as Burger King and Subway, have taken business away from McDonalds. Going forward, the company continues to expand its menu and hopes the focus on value, consistency, and convenience will serve as an effective tool for consistently bring in customers.

Source: Adapted from The Economist January 9, 2015, "That World's Largest Fast-Food Chain is Floundering." Retrieved on April 22, 2015 from http://www.businessinsider.com/the-worlds-largest-fast-food-chain-is-floundering-2015-1.

The results identified a large group who felt highly insecure in new and/or foreign environments and were not attracted by the appeals of uniqueness in culture, traditions, and architecture that Quebec used to differentiate its product. Marketing Research in Action 1.3 is a prime example of a company repackaging and tailoring its product range based on customer preferences and demand.

Strategy Development

All businesses have strategies, which are the methods used to make and sell products or perform services. Often, strategies are determined by a company's reaction to events beyond its control rather than by solid marketing intelligence and strategic planning. But, the question asked is why do firms plan? The answer is simple: competitive advantage.[14]

Several factors contribute to organizational growth in both size and complexity. Decision making gets more and more complex as the size of the business and market share increases, and vice versa when the business size and market share decreases. This implies a critical need for strategic focus—focusing on customer/competitive analysis. Both elements are critically dependent on rigorous marketing intelligence.[15]

In order for companies to maximize opportunity, they must first assess their strategic position. Only then will management be able to decide where and how the company should position itself. Evaluations of past performance, marketing strengths and weaknesses, reputation for quality products, utilization issues, and mission need to be addressed. All of these issues can be addressed by strategic planning and good marketing intelligence.[16]

During the strategy development stage, the management team of the business decides on answers to three critical questions. Marketing research provides significant help in finding the answers to these questions.

1. *What business should we be in?* Specifically, what products or services should we offer? What technologies will we utilize? Which market segments should we emphasize? What channels should we use to reach the market? These are far-reaching choices that set the context for all subsequent decisions.

These questions have become especially compelling in markets that are mature and saturated, including not only most packaged goods but also household appliances, automobiles, and services such as banking and air travel. One sure route to growth in this competitive environment is to create highly targeted products that appeal to the tastes of small market segments. Research supports this search for niches with large-scale quantitative market studies that describe buying behavior, consumer beliefs and attitudes, and exposure to communications media. Large samples are needed to delineate the segments, indicate their size, and determine what the people in each segment are seeking in a product.

2. *How will we compete?* Next the management team has to decide why the business is better than the competition in serving the needs of the target segment, and what has to be done to keep it in front. Competitive superiority is revealed in the market as either differentiation along attributes that are important to target customers or the lowest delivered cost position. Otis Elevator is able to dominate the elevator business by using information technologies to provide superior service response and preventive maintenance programs that reduce elevator breakdowns—attributes that customers appreciate.

Marketing research is essential for getting answers to three key questions about differentiation: What are the attributes of the product or service that create value for the customer? Which attributes are most important? How do we compare to the competition? For example, every movie has a dozen different story lines, and Joseph Helfgot, a sociologist turned Hollywood market researcher, says he knows which one you want to hear. Helfgot is the one who tells studio executives how to sell their movies and sink-or-swim release schedules. Consider *The Silence of the Lambs*. Is it about a gruesome serial murderer? Or a feisty FBI ingenue? Or a brilliant psychotic helping the FBI catch a like-minded fiend? None of the above, Helfgot found out. Audiences were interested in hearing a story about the bizarre relationship between Jodie Foster, an FBI academy graduate, and imprisoned serial killer Hannibal Lecter—played by Anthony Hopkins—who helped her solve the murders. That became the focus of the publicity campaign for what turned out to be a blockbuster hit. With marketing costs accounting for up to a third of movie budgets and with competition for space in movie theaters becoming increasingly fierce, studios have come to rely on whatever information science can provide to help sell their movies.

The attributes of value go well beyond physical characteristics to encompass the support activities and systems for delivery and service that make up the augmented product. In the lodging market, the key attributes are honoring reservations on time and providing good value for the money, quality and amenities of the guest rooms. Each market has unique attributes that customers employ to judge the competitive offerings, which can be understood only through careful analysis of usage patterns and decision processes within that market. This knowledge comes from informed sources and in-depth customer surveys.

An understanding of competitive advantage also requires detailed knowledge of the capabilities, strategies, and intentions of present and prospective competitors. Marketing research contributes here in two ways: identifying the competitive set, and collecting detailed information about each competitor. Some ways of undertaking competitive intelligence work are discussed later in the book. Marketing Research in Business 1.4 talks about how marketing research helped a speech-recognition software provider find his market.

3. *What are the objectives for the business?* An objective is a desired performance result that can be quantified and monitored. There are usually objectives for revenue growth, market share, and profitability. Increasingly, firms are adopting objectives for service levels (e.g., speed of response to quotations) and customer satisfaction. Marketing research is needed to establish both the market share and the level of customer satisfaction. Sometimes, share information—we have x percent of the y market—is readily available from secondary sources, but it may not be if the served market is different from the standard definition or if share is defined in dollar sales terms rather than unit volume.

Marketing Research in Action 1.4

■ UNDERSTANDING A SPECIALIZED MARKET

Despite opening in the 1970's, the LACTAID brand has continuously looked for ways to improve and evolve their products. The brand has showcased their products as an alternative for those affected individuals to still enjoy farm produced dairy products. Having originally focused on milk, the company has added several other products to their catalog including ice cream, cottage cheese, chocolate milk, and eggnog. Well into its fourth decade of business, the company has experienced a steady increase in performance nearly doubling from 2007 to 2012, resulting in over $900 million in sales in the United States and Europe. The latest push has involved launching a new LACTAID list of dietary enzyme supplements, which will assist individuals that are lactose intolerant in breaking down the lactose found in dairy foods.

The primary reasons for growth in the lactose-free market can be attributed to two primary causes: technological improvements, and an increased level of self-awareness and diagnosis toward the lactose-intolerance condition. LACTAID has consistently worked to ensure that their products taste good, which lactose-free products were traditionally not known for. In Europe and the United States, the level of self-diagnosis has increased over the years, providing ample business opportunity for a company such as LACTAID. While there are still untapped markets, such as Asia, for LACTAID to explore, the primary reason for avoiding those places is due to the lack of dairy consumption as a whole, in comparison to the United States and Europe. However, going forward, marketers believe that there is potential for LACTAID to carve a place in the market for itself in every country around the globe.

Source: Adapted with permission from M. Astley, "Self-diagnosed lactose intolerance driving lactose-free dairy sales-analyst," Dairy Reporter, 14 June 2012.

Marketing Program Development

Programs embrace specific tasks, such as developing a new product or launching a new advertising campaign (see Marketing Research in Action 1.4). An action program usually focuses on a single objective in support of one element of the overall business strategy. This is where the bulk of ongoing marketing research is directed. An idea of the possibilities of and needs for research can be gathered from Table 1.4, which describes some of the representative program decisions that utilize information about market characteristics and customer behavior.

To illustrate some of the possible research approaches that are employed, we will focus on the series of market research studies that were conducted to help Johnson Wax Company successfully introduce Agree Creme Rinse in 1977 and Agree Shampoo in 1978. The story begins with a major market analysis survey of hair-care practices that was conducted in the early 1970s. The study showed that there was a trend away from hair sprays, but a trend toward shampooing hair more frequently and a growing concern about oily hair. This led to a strategic decision to enter the shampoo and creme rinse market with products targeted toward the oiliness problem. This decision was supported by other studies on competitive activities in the market and on the willingness of the retailers to stock new shampoos.[17]

A total of 50 marketing research studies conducted between 1975 and 1979 supported the development of these two products. A series of focus group discussions was held to understand the oiliness problem and people's perceptions of existing shampoo products. The firm was particularly interested in learning about teenagers, since most of its products were sold to

Table 1.4 Developing the Marketing Program—Representative Decisions That Draw on Marketing Research

1. Segmentation decisions
   Which segment should be the target?
   What benefits are most important for each segment?
   Which geographic area should be entered?

2. Product decisions
   What product features should be included?
   How should the product be positioned?
   What type of package is preferred by the customers?

3. Distribution decisions
   What type of retailer should be used?
   What should be the markup policy?
   Should a few outlets be employed or many?

4. Advertising and promotion decisions
   What appeals should be used in the advertising?
   In which vehicles should the advertising be placed?
   What should the budget be?
   What sales promotion should be used, and when should it be scheduled?

5. Personal selling decisions
   What customer types have the most potential?
   How many salespeople are needed?

6. Price decisions
   What price level should be changed?
   What sales should be offered during the year?
   What response should be made to a competitor's price?

7. Branding decisions
   What should be the name, symbol, logo, and slogan that will be associated with the product?
   What is the position that the brand should adopt vis-à-vis the competition?
   How can brand loyalty be increased?

8. Customer satisfaction decisions
   How should customer satisfaction be measured?
   How often should it be measured?
   How should customer complaints be handled?

homemakers. One goal of these focus groups was to get ideas for a copy theme. Subsequently, more focus groups were held to get reactions to the selected advertising theme, "Helps Stop the Greasies." Several tests of advertising were employed in which customers were exposed to advertisements, and their reactions were obtained. In fact, more than 17 television commercials were created and tested.

More than 20 of the studies helped to test and refine the product. Several blind comparison tests were conducted, in which 400 women were asked to use the new product for two weeks and compare it to an existing product. (In a **blind test**, the products are packaged in unlabeled containers and the customers do not know which contains the new product.)

Several tests of the final marketing program were conducted. One was in a simulated supermarket where customers were asked to shop after they had been exposed to the advertising. The new product, of course, was on the shelf. Another test involved placing the product in an actual supermarket and exposing customers to the advertising. Finally, the product was introduced using the complete marketing plan in a limited test area involving a few selected communities including Fresno, California, and South Bend, Indiana. During the process, the product, the advertising, and the rest of the marketing program were being revised continually. The effort paid handsome dividends: Agree Creme Rinse took a 20 percent share of the market for its category and was number one in unit volume, and Agree Shampoo also was introduced successfully. In the 1980s, Gillette introduced Mink Difference Shampoo, containing mink oil, for the older market, and for the younger segment, Silkience, a self-adjusting shampoo that provided differential conditioning depending on the user's hair type.

Implementation

The beginning of the implementation phase is signaled by a decision to proceed with a new program or strategy and by the related commitments to objectives, budgets, and timetables. At this point, the focus of marketing research shifts to such questions as

Did the elements of the marketing program achieve their objectives?

How did sales compare with objectives?
In what areas were sales disappointing? Why?
Were the advertising objectives met?
Did the product achieve its distribution objectives?
Are any supermarkets discontinuing the product?

Should the marketing program be continued, revised, or expanded?

Are customers satisfied with the product?
Should the product be changed? More features added?
Should the advertising budget be changed?
Is the price appropriate?

For research to be effective at this stage, it is important that specific measurable objectives be set for all elements of the marketing program. Thus, there should be sales goals by geographic area; distribution goals, perhaps in terms of the number of stores carrying the product; and advertising goals, such as achieving certain levels of awareness. The role of marketing research is to provide measures against these objectives and to provide more focused studies to determine why results are below or above expectations.

Often underlying this phase of marketing management is uncertainty about the critical judgments and assumptions that preceded the decision. For example, in the first half of 1996, Compaq, IBM, Dell, and Gateway all launched new products in the personal computer market. Compaq introduced its Presario line of personal computers, designed to target specific groups of consumers.[18] Prior to this, most companies targeted only one brand of PC toward the home segment. One reason was a fundamental assumption about whether customers use computers for purposes other than traditional computing tasks. In response to this uncertainty, the companies undertook research studies to measure the acceptability of new product entries and maintaining computer usage at home.

There is overlap among the phases of the marketing process. In particular, the last phase, by identifying problems with the marketing program—and perhaps opportunities as well—eventually blends into the situation analysis phase of some other follow-up marketing program.

Factors that Influence Marketing Research Decisions

Marketing research is not an immediate or an obvious path to finding solutions to all managerial problems. A manager who is faced with a particular problem should not instinctively resort to conducting marketing research to find a solution to the problem. A manager should consider several factors before ordering marketing research and conduct a value analysis to answer the simple question—will the reduction in risk be greater than the cost?—which includes the time delay associated with waiting to make the decision. In many situations, it is best not to conduct marketing research. Hence, the primary decision to be made is whether or not market research is called for in a particular situation. The factors that influence this initial decision include the following.

Relevance

Research should not be conducted to satisfy curiosity or confirm the wisdom of previous decisions. Relevance comes through support of strategic and tactical planning activities, that is, by anticipating the kinds of information that will be required. This information is the backbone of the ongoing information system. As new circumstances arise and decision alternatives become more specific, research projects may be undertaken. Throughout the planning of these projects, the focus must be constantly on decisions.

Type and Nature of Information Sought

The decision whether to conduct marketing research depends on the type and nature of the information sought. If the information required for decision making already exists within the organization, in the form of results of a study conducted for a different problem or in the form of managerial experience and talents, marketing research is not called for. Under these circumstances, further research would be redundant and a waste of money. For example, Procter & Gamble, using its prior knowledge of the U.S. coffee market, launched Folger's Instant Coffee nationally, after some preliminary research. The same is true for many organizations that have accumulated rich experience in a particular market and already possess the information required to solve a certain problem.

Timing

Research decisions are constrained by the march of events. Often, these decisions are fixed in time and must be taken according to a specified schedule, using whatever information is available. If a new product is to be launched in the spring, all the research-based decisions on price, product formulation, name, copy appeals, and other components must be conducted far in advance. One role of the planning system is to schedule needed market research so that it can be conducted in time to influence decisions. The formulation of responses to competitive actions puts the greatest time pressure on researchers, for the results are always wanted "yesterday." There are, of course, many situations where the timing of decisions is contingent upon the research results. Even so, there is still time pressure stemming from the recognition that failure to take corrective action or pursue an opportunity as quickly as possible will result in opportunity costs.

Availability of Resources

Though the need for resources to be available may appear to be obvious, in several instances managers have called for marketing research without properly understanding the amount of resources available—including both financial and human resources. Lack of funds can result in improper and inefficient execution of a marketing research project. The results of such research often will be inaccurate. Again, if funds are available to conduct proper research but are insufficient to implement the results of the research, the marketing research is made useless. Also, the availability of a talent pool is a critical issue in deciding whether or not to conduct extensive marketing research. This is particularly so when the research is being conducted by an external source. When poorly qualified researchers are hired, the weaknesses in their training and lack of insight produce unimpressive and often inapplicable results.

Cost–Benefit Analysis

Before conducting marketing research, a prudent manager should perform a cost–benefit analysis to determine the value of the information sought through the research. Willingness to acquire additional decision-making information by conducting marketing research depends on a manager's perception of the risk associated with making the wrong decision. This is weighed against the incremental quality and value of the information vis-à-vis its cost and the time it would take to conduct the research. Hence, before conducting marketing research, it is necessary to have some estimate of the value of the information being sought. Such an estimate will help determine how much, if anything, should be spent on the research and what type of research should be done.

Use of Marketing Research

Although research is conducted to generate information, managers do not readily use the information to solve their problems. The factors that influence a manager's decision to use research information are (1) research quality, (2) conformity to prior expectations, (3) clarity of presentation, (4) political acceptability within the firm, and (5) challenge to the status quo.[19] Researchers and managers agree that the technical quality of research is the primary determinant of research use. Also, managers are less inclined to utilize research that does not conform to prior notions or is not politically acceptable.[20] Some researchers argue that the use of information is a function of the direct and indirect effects of environmental, organizational, informational, and individual factors.[21] However, a researcher should not alter the findings to match a manager's prior notions. Furthermore, managers in consumer organizations are less likely to use research findings than their counterparts in industrial firms.[22] This is due to a greater exploratory objective in information collection, a greater degree of formalization of organizational structure, and a lesser degree of surprise in the information collection.

Does Marketing Research Guarantee Success?

It is easier to conduct research and generate information than to understand the consequences of the information. Many companies with excellent marketing research experience have failed in their efforts to capture the actual needs of the consumers. For example, Coca-Cola conducted numerous studies before introducing New Coke. The study results revealed that New Coke tasted better than the original Coke, yet the product failed in the marketplace because of consumers' strong emotional/loyalty attachment to the original Coke.[23] Realizing that the market needed a low-calorie beer, Gablinger introduced the first low-calorie beers. However, the poor taste of the beer led to its downfall. Later, Anheuser-Busch and Miller Brewing achieved great success by emphasizing the benefits of good taste and a less filling product (rather than fewer calories, although what the market wanted was a low-calorie beer).[24] Findings in international markets have shown that a product should be priced in a manner in which the customer will realize the value received and that the price should be within reach of the target market. This was observed in the case of Warner–Lambert's launch of its five-unit pack of Bubbaloo bubble gum in Brazil.

Despite bubble gum representing a majority of the overall gum sector in Brazil, the product failed. The reason was the high price with respect to the target market. The company then re-launched the gum as a single-unit pack and revised the price within the range of the target segment. This price revision stabilized the brand and helped improve sales.[25]

Ethics in Marketing Research

Ethics refers to moral principles or values that generally govern the conduct of an individual or group. Researchers have responsibilities to their profession, clients, and respondents and must adhere to high ethical standards to ensure that both the function and the information are not brought into disrepute. The Marketing Research Association, Inc. (Chicago, Illinois) has instituted a code of ethics that serves as a guideline for marketing ethical decisions. Marketing Research in Action 1.5 shows the Code of Professional Ethics and Practices instituted by the Marketing Research Association.[26] The Council of American Survey Research Organization (CASRO) has also established a detailed code of marketing research ethics to which its members adhere.[27] Usually, three parties are involved in a marketing research project: (1) the client who sponsors the project, (2) the supplier who designs and executes the research, and (3) the respondent who provides the information. The issue of ethics in marketing research involves all three players in a research project. In a recent case, both the sponsor's and the supplier's ethics were found to be in question. Marketing Research in Action 1.6 provides the details of the case.

Marketing Research in Action 1.5

■ CODE OF ETHICS OF MARKETING RESEARCH ASSOCIATION

The Code of Professional Ethics and Practices

1. To maintain high standards of competence and integrity in marketing and survey research.

2. To maintain the highest level of business and professional conduct and to comply with Federal, State and local laws, regulations, and ordinances applicable to my business practice and those of my company.

3. To exercise all reasonable care and to observe the best standards of objectivity and accuracy in the development, collection, processing and reporting of marketing, and survey research information.

4. To protect the anonymity of respondents and hold all information concerning an individual respondent privileged, such that this information is used only within the context of the particular study.

5. To thoroughly instruct and supervise all persons for whose work I am responsible in accordance with study specifications and general research techniques.

6. To observe the rights of ownership of all materials received from and/or developed for clients, and to keep in confidence all research techniques, data and other information considered confidential by their owners.

7. To make available to clients such details on the research methods and techniques of an assignment as may be reasonably required for proper interpretation of the data, providing this reporting does not violate the confidence of respondents or clients.

8. To promote the trust of the public for marketing and survey research activities and to avoid any procedure that misrepresents the activities of a respondent, the rewards of cooperation or the uses of data.

9. To refrain from referring to membership in this organization as proof of competence, since the organization does not so certify any person or organization.

10. To encourage the observance of principles of this code among all people engaged in marketing and survey research.

Visit http://www.marketingpower.com/Pages/default.aspx for more information on this organization.

Source: Reprinted by permission of the Marketing Research Association, Inc., Chicago, IL.

Marketing Research in Action 1.6

■ FORMER MICROSOFT EMPLOYEE LEAKS CODE

In the midst of releasing Windows 8, Microsoft was faced with a predicament that commonly occurs in the tech-world. An employee, Alex Kibkalo was accused of leaking the code used to create Windows 8 to a blogger in France, which he attributes to doing because of a poor performance evaluation from the company. The transferring of this information had a circular effect, in that the blogger, who received the code, passed it along to a Microsoft employee who then passed it on to a company executive. This prompted the company to take a further look and led to the arrest of Kibkalo who is now facing federal charges on the basis of stealing trade secrets.

Source: Adapted from "Ex-Microsoft Employee Arrested for Giving Out Windows 8 Code" by Jon M. Chang on March 20, 2014, from http://abcnews.go.com/blogs/technology/2014/03/ex-microsoft-employee-arrested-for-giving-out-windows-8-code/.

The Respondent's Ethics and Rights

A respondent who of his or her own free will agrees to participate in a marketing research project has the ethical obligation to provide the supplier, and hence the client, with honest and truthful answers. The respondent can abstain from answering a sensitive question, but falsifying the answer is ethically improper.

Any respondent who participates in a research project has the following rights:

- The right to privacy.
- The right to safety.
- The right to know the true purpose of the research.
- The right to the research results.
- The right to decide which questions to answer.

The Sponsor's Ethics

The sponsor, or the research client, has to abide by a number of ethical or moral rules and regulations when conducting a research study. The more common sources of ethical problems in the client establishment stem from the following sources.

Overt and Covert Purposes

Most researchers have encountered situations where the main purpose of their efforts was to serve someone's organizational goals. Thus, research can be used to postpone an awkward decision or to lend respectability to a decision that has been made already. A related purpose is to avoid responsibility. When there are competing factions, the manager who must make a difficult choice looks to research to guide the decision. This has the further advantage that if the decision is later proven wrong, the manager can find someone else to blame.

Sometimes, a covert purpose will open the way to ethical abuses that present difficult dilemmas to researchers. The most serious abuses are created when there is subtle (or not so subtle) pressure to design research to support a particular decision or enhance a legal position.

Dishonesty in Dealing with Suppliers

A few client companies have been known to indulge in "picking the brains" of research suppliers by asking them to submit elaborate bids that detail the research design and methodology the supplier would adopt in conducting the research. Later, the client firm uses these ideas and conducts the research on its own. Another technique that client firms sometimes use is to make a false promise of future contracts in an effort to obtain a low price for the current project.

Misuse of Research Information

The client firm should not misuse information gathered through marketing research projects. For example, databases about consumer preferences are used in target marketing to identify the people who are most likely to buy or use a product. Netflix Inc., a provider of on-demand Internet streaming media, is available to viewers in different parts of the world and a flat rate DVD-by-mail in the United States. Netflix maintains an extensive personalized video recommendation system based on customer views, ratings, and reviews. In 2011, two Virginia residents filed a suit against Netflix citing that after signing for a new account Netflix had retained information on their DVD and streaming videos as well as their personal contact information. According to the federal Video Privacy Protection Act (VPPA), video rental companies are forbidden from disclosing any personal information or information on the genres of videos the customer had rented in the past. VPPA requires rental companies to delete personal data and rental histories after an account has been closed for a certain period of time. This resulted in an approximate cost of $9 million settlement of the law suit.[28] Marketing Research in Action 1.7 provides the current legislative scenario regarding disposal of data.

Too often researchers find themselves dealing with demands by sales or other personnel for access to results and the names and telephone numbers of respondents. The intention, of course, is to use the research study for the entirely different—and usually unethical—purpose of generating sales leads. The only time this is acceptable is when the interviewer asks specifically whether the respondent will accept a follow-up sales call, or would like more information, and acts precisely on the respondent's answer.

Disguising Selling as Research

Sadly, there are a number of situations where the research study is simply a disguise for a selling pitch. Many people have received phone calls, ostensibly to ask some research questions, that lead only to a canned sales message for life insurance, an encyclopedia, or a mutual fund. This is not only unethical behavior because it has no merits on its own, it is also a serious abuse of respondent rights. Not surprisingly, respondents are more suspicious after a few of these encounters and may refuse to participate in any research study.

The Supplier's Ethics

The more common ethical issues for the research supplier are as follows:

- *Violating client confidentiality.* Disclosing any information about the client that the supplier has gathered from the research project amounts to a violation of client confidentiality.

Marketing Research in Action 1.7

■ DATA DISPOSAL

CMOR (Council for Marketing and Opinion Research) is an organization that deals with state and federal legislation that affects market and opinion research. Some of its tasks include monitoring telephone solicitation bills, electronic monitoring legislation, data privacy, consumer list legislation, caller ID/call blocking, and political telemarketing.

According to CMOR, personal or client information discarded in the trash, any data stored on discarded or donated computer technology (such as hard drives and thumb drives), any data stored on devices that are thrown away or donated to charity, is legally and effectively open to anyone. Furthermore, electronic data kept beyond its usefulness invites mischief or accidental breach. Some of the reasonable measures could include establishing and complying with policies to:

- Burn, pulverize, or shred papers and destroy or erase electronic files or media containing personal data so that the information cannot be read or reconstructed. This includes any items destined for recycling, charity, or some other form of use;
- Only maintain data as long as necessary;
- Audit your organization's data holdings on a regular basis and keep track of what data is disposed when—and how;
- Conduct due diligence and hire a document destruction contractor to dispose of material specifically identified as personal data.

Some of the due diligences that can be adopted by researchers are as follows:

- Reviewing an independent audit of a disposal company's operations and/or its legal compliance;
- Obtaining information about the disposal company from several references;
- Requiring that the disposal company be certified by a recognized trade association;
- Reviewing and evaluating the disposal company's information security policies or procedures.

For more information on CMOR, go to www.cmor.org.
Source: http://www.mra-net.org/ga/documents/bestpractices/datadisposal_mra_best_practices.pdf.

- *Improper execution of research.* Suppliers are required to conduct marketing research projects in an objective manner, free from personal biases and motives. Improper execution also includes using biased sampling, ignoring relevant data, or misusing statistics, all of which lead to erroneous and misleading results. Marketing Research in Action 1.5 gives a brief listing of federal and state legislation that affects market and opinion research.

Abuse of Respondents

Abuse of respondents is perhaps the most frequent and controversial problem that crops up regarding ethics in conducting research. Any form of violation of a respondent's rights amounts to unethical treatment or abuse of the respondent.

International Marketing Research

The increase in international trade and the emergence of global corporations resulting from increased globalization of business have had a major impact on all facets of business, including marketing research. The increase in global competition, coupled with the formation of regional trading blocs such as the European Community (EC) and the North American Free Trade Agreement (NAFTA), have spurred the growth of global corporations and the need for international marketing research. The need to collect information relating to international markets, and to monitor trends in these markets, as well as to conduct research to determine the appropriate strategies that will be most effective in international markets, is expanding rapidly. For example, Panda Express, a fast casual American-based Chinese restaurant serving American-Chinese cuisine, opened its first store in Mexico City on September 3, 2011, due to the growing demand for diversified taste palette among mature consumers. However, to understand the market first, Panda Express partnered with master franchiser Grupo Gigante for its development and operations in Mexico. Panda Express achieved success in this venture by developing deep relationships with the Grupo Gigante team. Research revealed that awareness of Panda Express items is quite high among Mexican consumers and that they place a great deal of emphasis on American products (which are better from the consumers' perspective). The popularity allowed Panda Express to move into Mexico seamlessly. As of March 2015, there are 18 outlets in Mexico and plans on opening 10 more by the end of the year.[29]

The marketing research industry in the United States is increasingly growing into an international industry, with more than one-third of its revenues coming from foreign operations. The increase in the importance of global business has caused an increase in awareness of the problems related to international research. **International marketing research** can be defined as marketing research conducted either simultaneously or sequentially to facilitate marketing decisions in more than one country.[30] As such, the basic functions of marketing research and the research process do not differ in domestic and multicountry research; however, the international marketing research process is much more complicated and the international marketing researcher faces problems that are different from those of a domestic researcher. Marketing Research in Action 1.8 talks about Coca-Cola's foray and experience in the Chinese market.

Throughout this book, we will be discussing the international aspect of the marketing research process, and, when applicable, we will be highlighting the differences between domestic and international research.

Marketing Research in Action 1.8

■ KFC'S SUCCESS IN AN EMERGING MARKET—CHINA

Due to the saturation in the home market, KFC started exploring international expansion options. When it entered China, KFC transformed their business model to suit the local market. The renewed format now posed formidable barriers to new entrants and served as a good example for other companies on adapting and replicating in an emerging market.

KFC understood that food was the heart of Chinese culture, and great flavors and ambience were required to win the Chinese consumers over. Unlike in the United States, KFC was not set up as a fast food chain in China, but as a restaurant that served a variety of foods and traditional dishes appealing the Chinese customers. KFC's menu in China contained 50 items as compared to 29 in America. Furthermore, KFC customized its recipes based on different regions in China. The KFC bestseller breakfast in China is a Chinese authentic rice porridge called congee that is hard to make at home.

KFC also developed a logistics network and warehouses to connect to the rural parts of China. An excellent customer service concept was promoted, unfamiliar in China after decades of communism, by training employees with basic people skills.

These changes by KFC reinforce their customer-focused outlook and their interest in the Chinese market. Their strategy has clearly worked for them to establish a long-term presence in China.

Source: David Bell and Mary Shelma, "KFC's Radical Approach to China," Harvard Business Review, November, 2011.

The task of marketing research is to find a sizable segment with homogeneous tastes. The growing presence of an international market in the United States has been influenced by both domestic and foreign markets. In the domestic arena, ethnic groups range from Chinese to Turkish, each lending a piece of its culture to the U.S. market. Within each ethnic group, the product preference is diverse. These facts present a challenge to marketing research to find a homogeneous group among the "melting pot" of international products. Complicating matters is the rise in foreign manufacturers selling their goods in the United States.

SUMMARY

Marketing research links the organization with its market environment. It involves the specification, gathering, analysis, and interpretation of information to help management understand that particular market environment, identify its problems and opportunities, and develop and evaluate courses of marketing action. The marketing management process involves situation analysis, strategy development, and marketing program development and implementation. Each of these areas includes a host of decisions that need to be supported by marketing research information. Marketing research, to be effective, should be relevant, timely, efficient, accurate, and ethical.

QUESTIONS AND PROBLEMS

1.1 How might the following use marketing research? Be specific.

(a) A small sporting goods store

(b) Continental Airlines

(c) Ohio State University

(d) Houston Astros baseball team

(e) Sears Roebuck

(f) A major television network (CBS, NBC, or ABC)

(g) Compaq Computers

(h) A museum in a major city

(i) A shopping mall in downtown Houston

1.2 How might marketing research be used to support each of the steps in Figure 1.1 that describes the marketing planning process? For example, how could it help select the served market segment?

1.3 What are some ethical problems that marketing researchers face in designing and conducting field studies?

1.4 In some companies, both strategic planning and marketing research functions report to the same executive and may be more or less integrated. What are the advantages of locating the research function in this part of the organization? What arguments could be made in opposition to this arrangement?

1.5 Most companies have entire marketing research studies, or portions of entire studies, such as interviewing, done by outside suppliers. What factors will determine whether a firm decides to "make versus buy"—that is, to contract out most or all of a study or conduct it themselves?

1.6 How does marketing research directed toward strategy development differ from that directed toward marketing program development?

1.7 Fred Burton, the owner of a small tennis club in Wichita, Kansas, feels that a demand exists for indoor courts that presently is not being served. He is considering employing a marketing research company to conduct a study to ascertain whether a market exists for the indoor facilities.

(a) What factors should Mr. Burton consider before ordering market research to be conducted?

(b) What are the possible pitfalls that the marketing research company must avoid while conducting the study?

(c) After obtaining the market research recommendations, Mr. Burton decides not to use the information generated by the market research study. What factors could have influenced his decision not to use the research information?

1.8 Linda Phillips, an engineering student, has designed an innovative piece of equipment to help the physically disabled to communicate. The equipment incorporates a system of electronic signals emitted with a slight turn of the head. She feels that this product could have commercial success if marketed to health-care organizations, but she has had no past experience in marketing management and does not know how to undertake the market planning and evaluation process. Acting as Ms. Phillips's marketing consultant, suggest a course of action to help her bring this innovative product to its market.

1.9 Despite the presence of a written code of ethics, why are some marketing ethical problems hard to cure? Discuss this from both the sponsor and supplier points of view.

END NOTES

1. http://www-01.ibm.com/software/data/cognos/products/bi_whitepaper.pdf.

2. "Boosting Demand in the 'Experience Economy'." *Harvard Business Review*, 93.1/2, 2015, pp. 24–26.

3. H. Havenstein, "Better BI: Erlanger (Ky.) Police Department," *Computerworld*, September 1, 2008.

4. L. A. Keefe, "Marketing Defined," *Marketing News*, January 15, 2007, pp. 28–29.

5. S. L. Cornish, "Product Innovation and the Spatial Dynamics of Market Intelligence: Does Proximity to Markets Matter?" *Economic Geography*, 73, (2), April 1997, pp. 147.

6. M. Huster, "Marketing Intelligence: A First Mover Advantage," *Competitive Intelligence Magazine, Washington*, 8(2), March/April 2005, p.13.

7. M. Langie, "Personalization Success: Why Sephora and Leading Brands Thrive, October 8, 2014," http://blogs.adobe.com/digitalmarketing/digital-marketing/personalization-success-sephora-leading-brands-thrive/.

8. "Annual Estimates of the Resident Population by Sex, Race, and Hispanic Origin for the United States, States, and Counties: April 1, 2010 to July 1, 2013," U.S. Census Bureau, Population Division, Release Date: June 2014.

9. M. H. Lopez, A. Gonzalez-Barrera and E. Patten, "Closing the Digital Divide: Latinos and Technology Adoption" March 7, 2013, http://www.pewhispanic.org/2013/03/07/ii-internet-use-3/.

10. K. Monllos, "Here's Why Brands Are Speaking Spanish in General Market Ads," *Adweek*, June 24, 2014.

11. "His and Her Toothpaste," *Wall Street Journal*, September 5, 2002.

12. Adapted and updated from R. Nakashima, "Turning Renters into Buyers," *The Hartford Courant*, June 28, 2005.

13. Adapted from P.V. Barbara and G. Zaltman, *Hearing the Voice of the Market*. Cambridge, MA: Harvard Business School Press, 1991.

14. G. S. Day, "Evaluating Business Strategies," *Strategic Planning Management*, Spring 1984.

15. D. C. Bernhardt, "'I Want It Fast, Actual, Actionable'—Tailoring Competitive Intelligence to Executive's Needs," *Long Range Planning*, 27(1), Feb 1994, p. 12.

16. B. Jaworski and L. G. Wee, "Competitive Intelligence and Bottomline Performance," *Competitive Intelligence Review*, 3(4), 1993, pp. 23–27.

17. "Key Role of Research in Agree's Success Is Told," *Marketing News*, January 12, 1979, p. 14.

18. D. Silverman, "Compaq Unveils Revised Presarios," *Houston Chronicle*, July 16, 1996, p. 1D.

19. R. Deshpande and S. Jeffries, "Attitude Affecting the Use of Marketing Research in Decision Making: An Empirical Investigation, in Kenneth L. Bernhardt et al. eds., *Educator's Conference Proceedings, Series 47*, Chicago: American Marketing Association, 1981, pp. 1–4.

20. R. Deshpande and G. Zaltman, "Factors Affecting the Use of Market Research Information: A Path Analysis," *Journal of Marketing Research*, 19, February 1982, pp. 14–31; R. Deshpande and G. Zaltman, "A Comparison of Factors Affecting Researcher and Manager Perceptions of Market Research Use," *Journal of Marketing Research*, 21, February 1982, pp. 32–38; M. Hu, "An Experimental Study of Managers and Researchers Use of Consumer Research'" *Journal of Academy of Marketing Science*, Fall 1986, pp. 44–51; and H. Lee, F. Acito, and R. Day, "Evaluation and Use of Marketing Research by Decision Makers: A Behavioural Simulation," *Journal of Marketing Research*, 24, May 1987, pp. 187–196.

21. A. Menon and P. R. Varadarajan, "A Model of Marketing Knowledge Use Within Firms," *Journal of Marketing*, 56, October 1992, p. 61.

22. R. Deshpande and G. Zaltman, "A Comparison of Factors Affecting Use of Marketing Information in Consumer and Industrial Firms," *Journal of Marketing Research*, 24, February 1987, pp. 114–118.

23. B. D. Gelb and G. M. Gelb, "Coke's Lesson to the Rest of Us," *Sloan Management Review*, Fall 1986.

24. R. D. Hisrich and M. P. Peters, *Marketing Decisions for New and Mature Products*. New York: Macmillan, 1991, p. 427.

25. P. Cateora and J. Graham (2007), "International Marketing," 13th edition, McGraw-Hill Irwin, pp. 533–534.

26. *"Code of Ethics of Marketing Research Association."* Chicago, IL: Marketing Research Association, Inc.

27. "CASRO Code of Standards for Survey Research," *The Council of American Survey Research Organizations, Annual Journal*, 1992, pp. 19–22.

28. "Netflix pays $9 million to settle privacy violation lawsuit," *Cnet Magazine*, February 13, 2012.

29. "Panda Express says to build over 250 restaurants in Mexico by 2021," *Reuters*, March 5, 2014.

30. V. Kumar, International Marketing Research, Prentice-Hall, NY, 2000.

Case 1-1 ‖ Preteen Market—The Right Place to Be In for Cell Phone Providers?

Do parents of preteens envision a need for equipping their children with cell phones? This seems to be the million-dollar question facing cell phone makers like Firefly who view the preteen market as offering more growth opportunities than the senior market. The preteen market is unique in that the ultimate customer, the child, does not make the purchase decision. On one side of this indirect target market are parents with hectic or variable schedules and those who are more harried or worried about their children's safety. On the other side are parents who are skeptical about the misuse of cell phones by the kids themselves or others and those who consider a kid cell phone as an unnecessary investment especially considering the fact that kids are usually under some supervision or the other, not to mention their tendency to lose personal belongings.

Cell phone makers are following the trend set by other industries such as food companies and retailers in targeting the preteen market. Firefly launched its phones in February 2005 priced at $199 offering 12 months or 1,200 minutes of phone service—whichever comes first. The Firefly phone has a number of safety features that make it simpler to use than a conventional phone but harder to abuse. It does not have a numerical keypad. Instead, parents can program up to 20 phone numbers into the device which cannot be changed without a password. Parents can also program the phone in such a way that it only accepts calls from certain numbers.

Firefly is not the only wireless carrier targeting the preteen market. Some providers offer regular cell phones at a steep discount for family plans. Wherify, a preteen phone specialist, is offering a kid phone that comes with a global positioning system locator—so parents can better track their offspring. Mattel Inc. is launching a phone with a Barbie theme.

While equipping 8- to 12-year-olds with cell phones makes it easier for parents and children to get a hold of each other and coordinate activities, parents have other issues to grapple with. Many schools do not allow students to bring cell phones to classrooms. According to one University of Chicago child psychiatrist, most 8- to 12-year-olds do not need a cell phone. So the challenge for Firefly and their competitors is "At what age do kids really need a phone?" and "Is the preteen market really worth going after?"

Questions for Discussion

1. Do you think preteens offer good market potential for cell phone companies?

2. While designing products for this market, what are the issues faced by the service providers?

Source: Adapted with permission from Mike Hughlett, "Target: Teens—Cell Phone Company Going After the Preteen Market," *Chicago Tribune*, April 12, 2005.

Case 1-2 ‖ Best Buy on a Segmentation Spree

With $24.5 billion in 2005 sales, Best Buy Co. is the nation's largest seller of consumer electronics. Its spacious store and large inventory has helped it to increase market share, even as its rivals such as Circuit City Stores Inc. and Sears, Roebuck & Co., have struggled. In fiscal 2004 that ended in February, Best Buy reported net income of $570 million. Though up from $99 million during the 2003 fiscal period, it was still below the $705 million it earned in fiscal 2002.

Best Buy estimates that nearly 20 percent of its 500 million visitors each year are undesirable and wants to get rid of these customers. Behind this approach is Best Buy's chief executive officer, Brad Anderson. While most chains use their marketing budgets primarily to maximize customer traffic in the view that more visitors will lift revenue and profit, Best Buy uses it to shun its unwanted customers. This would mean dumping nearly 100 million of their unprofitable customers. A variation of this approach is being used in the financial-services

industry, wherein attention is lavished on the best customers and the unprofitable customers are penalized with fees for using ATMs or tellers or for obtaining bank records.

From Best Buy's 1.5 million daily customers, Mr. Anderson wants to separate the "angels" from the "devils." Angels are customers who boost profits by snapping up high-definition televisions, portable electronics, and newly released DVDs without waiting for markdowns or rebates. The devils are Best Buy's worst customers. They buy products, apply for rebates, return the purchases, and then buy them back at returned-merchandise discounts. They load up on "loss leaders," then flip the goods at a profit on eBay, slap down rock-bottom price quotes from websites and demand that Best Buy make good on its lowest-price pledge. At dozens of websites such as fatwallet.com, slickdeals.net, and techbargains.com, the devil customers trade electronic coupons and tips from former clerks and insiders, hoping to gain extra advantages against the stores.

Best Buy has rolled out its angel–devil strategy in about 100 of its 670 stores. It is examining sales records and demographic data and devouring databases to identify good and bad customers. To lure the high-spenders, it is stocking more merchandise and more appealing service options. To keep the undesirables away, the company is cutting back on promotions and sales tactics that tend to draw them. However, the risk attached to such an exercise is significant. The pilot stores have proved more costly to operate and since different pilot stores target different types of customers, they threaten the company's economies of scale.

After a series of analyses, Best Buy concluded that most of its business came from five distinct customer groups: upper-income men, also referred internally as "Barrys"—who tend to be enthusiasts of action movies and cameras; "Jills"—who are suburban mothers; busy but usually willing to talk about helping their families; small-business owners; "Buzzes"—technology enthusiasts, also known as early adopters and interested in buying and showing off the latest gadgets. Mr. Anderson decided that each store should study the demographics of the local market and realign themselves by stocking merchandise accordingly. Armed with this information, Best Buy began working on ways to avoid unprofitable customers. They just could not bar them from entering their stores. But in summer 2004, they took steps to put an end to one of the biggest problems. They enforced a restocking fee of 15 percent of the purchase price on returned merchandise. To discourage customers who return items with the intention of repurchasing them at an "open box" discount, they are experimenting with reselling them over the Internet, so that the goods do not reappear in the stores where they were originally purchased. In July 2004, they cut ties with fatwallet.com, an online affiliate that collected referral fees for delivering customers to Best Buy's website, for revealing information about Best Buy's planned Thanksgiving Weekend sale.

Training of store clerks plays a vital role in identifying desirable customers by concentrating on their shopping preferences and behavior. Staffers use quick interviews to identify profitable customers. For instance, if a customer says his family has a regular "movie night," he is a prime candidate for home-theater equipment. Likewise, shoppers with large families are shown larger appliances and time-saving products. The company attempts to entice the Barrys and Jills by providing services like a "personal shopper," to locate unusual items, alert them on preferred items, and coordinate service calls.

Best Buy's Westminster, California, store is one of 100 using this technique. It targets upper-income men with a wide range of pricey home-theater systems and small-business owners with network servers and office PC solutions. During DVD releases, the store clerks identify promising customers and guide them into a back room that displays $12,000 high-definition home-theater systems. The room has easy chairs, a leather couch, and a basket of popcorn to simulate a theater atmosphere. At stores popular with Buzzes, Best Buy is setting up video game sections furnished with leather chairs and players hooked to giant plasma-screen televisions. Mr. Anderson says early results indicate pilot stores performed far better than conventional stores, following which the company began converting another 70 stores.

Best Buy intends to customize the rest of its stores over the next three years. With customization of stores, stock maintenance becomes crucial as it could topple the sales and customer goodwill. Periodic design changes and customizations cause the costs to go up, but Mr. Anderson says that as stores share the successful ideas for acquiring customers, the average cost per store should fall.

Questions for Discussion

1. What benefits can Best Buy hope to gain from its customer segmentation tactics?

2. Do you think Best Buy is making adequate use of marketing intelligence practices for its business decisions?

Source: Adapted with permission from Gary Mc Williams, "Analyzing Customers, Best Buy Decides Not All Are Welcome," *The Wall Street Journal*, November 8, 2004, p. A.1.

Case 1-3 | **Ethical Dilemmas in Marketing Research**[1]

The following scenarios present a set of ethical dilemmas that might arise in marketing research. Your assignment is to decide what action to take in each instance. You should be prepared to justify your decision. Bear in mind that there are no uniquely right answers: Reasonable people may choose different courses of action.

1. You are the market research director of a pharmaceutical company, and the executive director suggests to you that company interviewers telephone physicians under the name of a fictitious market research agency. The purpose of the survey is to help assess the perceived quality of the company's products, and it is felt that the suggested procedure will result in more objective responses.

What action would you take?

2. You are employed by a marketing research firm and have conducted an attitude study for a client. Your findings indicate that the product's marketing efforts are not effective. This finding is badly received by the client's product management team. They request that you omit that data from your formal report, which you know will be widely distributed, on the grounds that the oral presentation was adequate for their needs.

What do you do?

3. You are a study director for a research company undertaking a project for a regular client of your company. A study you are working on is about to go into the field when the questionnaire you sent to the client for final approval comes back drastically modified. The client has rewritten it, introducing leading questions and biased scales. An accompanying letter indicates that the questionnaire must be sent out as revised. You do not believe that valid information can be gathered using the revised instrument.

What action would you take?

4. A well-respected public figure is going to face trial on a charge of failing to report his part ownership of certain

regulated companies while serving as a Canadian provincial minister. The defense lawyers have asked you, as a market research specialist, to do a research study to determine the characteristics of people most likely to sympathize with the defendant and hence to vote for acquittal. The defense lawyers have read newspaper accounts of how this approach has been used in a number of instances.

What action would you take?

5. You are the market research director for a large chemical company. Recent research indicates that many of your company's customers are misusing one of its principal products. There is no danger resulting from this misuse, though customers are wasting money by using too much of the product at one time. You are shown the new advertising campaign by the advertising agency. The ads not only ignore this problem of misuse, they actually seem to encourage it.

What action would you take?

6. You show up your first day for a summer internship to meet your supervisor and get your first assignment. She gives you a questionnaire with specific marketing planning questions and tells you that she would like you to contact the company's main three competitors and tell them you are a student doing a study on the industry and get the answers to the questions. She says you should not tell them you are working for the company over the summer and adds "there is nothing wrong with not telling them—omitting the fact is not really lying." You ask her what you should do if they ask, and she says 'just tell them you are a student working on a paper and you don't want to get a poor grade on the assignment."

What action would you take?

[1] These vignettes were provided through the courtesy of Professor Charles Weinberg, University of British Columbia, and are reproduced with his permission.

Marketing Research in Practice

2

LEARNING OBJECTIVES

- Discuss briefly the practice of marketing research.
- Discuss the concept of information systems and decision support systems.
- Discuss marketing decision support systems.
- List the various suppliers of marketing research information and the types of services offered by them.
- Discuss the criteria used to select suppliers.
- Explain the impact international trade has had on marketing research.
- Describe the career options available in the marketing research industry.

In practice, a marketing research department's goal can be grouped into three major categories[1]: programmatic, selective, or evaluative. **Programmatic research** is performed to develop marketing options through market segmentation, market opportunity analysis, or consumer attitude and product usage studies. **Selective research** is done to test different decision alternatives such as new product concept testing, advertising copy testing, pretest marketing, and test marketing. **Evaluative research** is carried out to evaluate performance of programs, including tracking advertising recall, corporate and brand image studies, and measuring customer satisfaction with the quality of the product and service. As the number of products and types of services introduced into the market increase, the need for marketing research explodes and the future of marketing research appears to be both promising and challenging.[2]

Unquestionably, marketing research is a growth industry. In the last decade, real expenditures on marketing research (i.e., after adjusting for inflation) are more than doubled. This is largely a consequence of economic and social changes that have made better marketing an imperative.

With marketing the new priority, marketing research is the rallying cry. Companies are frantically trying to get their hands-on information that identifies and explains the needs of powerful new consumer segments now being formed. Kroger Co., for example, holds more than 250,000 consumer interviews a year to define consumer wants more precisely. Some companies are pinning their futures on product innovations, others are rejuvenating time-worn but proven brands, and still others are doing both.[3]

Not only are the companies that always did marketing research doing a great deal more, but the breadth of research activities also continues to expand.

- Senior management is looking for more support for its strategic decisions; therefore, researchers are doing more acquisition and competitor studies, segmentation and market structure analyses, and basic strategic position assessments.

- Other functions, such as the legal department, now use marketing research evidence routinely. Corporate Affairs wants to know shareholders', bankers', analysts', and employees' attitudes toward the company. The service department continuously audits service delivery capability and customer satisfaction.

- Entire industries that used to be protected from the vagaries of competition and changing customer needs by regulatory statutes are learning to cope with a deregulated environment. Airlines, banks, and financial-services groups are looking for ways to overcome product proliferation, advertising clutter, and high marketing costs brought on by more sophisticated customers and aggressive competitors.

In this chapter, we will look at how companies use the information gathered by marketing research, at the various ways they obtain this marketing research information, and at the career opportunities available in the marketing research industry.

Information Systems, Decision Support Systems, and Marketing Research

An **information system** (IS) is a continuing and interacting structure of people, equipment, and procedures designed to gather; sort; analyze; evaluate; and distribute pertinent, timely, and accurate information to decision makers. While marketing research is concerned mainly with the actual content of the information and how it is to be generated, the information system is concerned with managing the flow of data from many different projects and secondary sources to the managers who will use it. This requires databases to organize and store the information and a **decision support system** (DSS) to retrieve data, transform it into usable information, and disseminate it to users.

Databases

Information systems contain three types of information. The first is recurring day-to-day information, for example, the market and accounting data that flow into the organization as a result of market analysis research and accounting activities. Automobile firms use government sources for monthly data on new-car sales by brand and geographic area. In addition, surveys are conducted yearly to determine the ages and types of automobiles currently being driven, the lifestyles of the drivers (their activity and interest patterns), their media habits, and their intentions to replace their cars. The accounting department submits sales and inventory data for each of its dealers on a continuing basis, to update and supplement the information system.

A second type of information is intelligence relevant to the future strategy of the business. Automobile firms, for example, collect reports about new sources of fuel to power automobiles. This information might come from scientific meetings, trade organizations, or perhaps from government reports. It also might include information from salespersons or dealers about new-product tests being conducted by competitive firms. Intelligence is difficult to develop because it usually involves diverse and changing sets of topic and information sources and is rarely collected systematically.

A third input to the information system is research studies that are not of a recurring nature. The potential usefulness of a marketing research study can be multiplied manifold if the information is accessible instead of filed and forgotten. However, the potential exists that others may use the study, although perhaps not in the way it was originally intended.

Decision Support Systems (DSS)

Databases have no value if the insights they contain cannot be retrieved. A DSS not only allows the manager to interact directly with the database to retrieve what is wanted but also provides a modeling function to help make sense of what has been retrieved.

A common example of a DSS in action is that used by many industrial salespeople—especially those selling products that require significant customization. The salesperson frequently will be asked whether or not the price and delivery time of a unique product configuration will meet or exceed a competitor's promises. Without leaving the customer's office, the salesperson can plug a laptop computer into a phone jack and begin communicating with a database stored in the company's main computer memory. The salesperson types in the product configuration and desired delivery data, and these requirements are compared to the costs, inventory, and assembly time contained in the databank. In a matter of minutes, the salesperson can propose a price and delivery date—and perhaps close the sale.

Each firm has to develop or adapt models to support its own decision problems. For example, Avon Products, Inc., the door-to-door cosmetics firm, has unique problems as the result of a part-time sales force of almost 400,000 representatives theoretically covering half of the 80 million households in North America. This sales force carries a large product line that each year adds 1,600 new or reformulated products. The following computer models were added to their DSS to help cope with these problems[4]:

- A sales force turnover model, which revealed that the most significant variable influencing the turnover rate, was the level of the appointment fee that representatives pay for initial materials.

- An order model that explains the components of the average order and isolates the actionable variables, such as the size and timing of the catalog and the gift incentives.

- A procurement model that helps determine how much of a new product to buy, when to purchase it, and the risks involved.

Applying Information Systems to Marketing Research

Often, the process of developing and using models and information systems reveals gaps in the databank that have to be closed. These emergent needs for information become a marketing research problem; for example,

- Performance (sales, market share, contributions, and patronage) may be unsatisfactory relative to objectives. Perhaps the condition can be traced to a specific geographic area, but the underlying reasons still must be sought before action can be taken.

- A competitor may launch a new product or employ a new advertising appeal, with unknown consequences for the firm's competitive position.

- An unavoidable increase in costs puts pressures on profitability (or, in the case of a transit system, for example, increases subsidy requirements to an unacceptable level). Various possible increases in prices (or fares) must be evaluated.

- An upsurge in interest in health and nutrition may suggest to a snack company a new product line directed toward responding to this interest. Concept testing might be a first step in exploring this opportunity.

Given the sometimes chaotic and usually uncertain nature of most market environments, a large number of problems and some opportunities can emerge. Few will ever be given formal

Marketing Research in Action 2.1

■ THE FOURTH WAVE IN MARKETING RESEARCH

Much of the initial interest in marketing research came about during the transition from a sales-oriented to a marketing-oriented business environment. In the First Wave, seat-of-the-pants decision making progressed to a data-based decision. But, with more data available, a large problem arose: A handful of data was helpful; a truckload was not necessarily better. So, in the Second Wave, the progression was from data-based decision to information-based decision making. Rather than review a multitude of individual facts, the role of marketing research evolved to manipulate data to summarize the underlying patterns. Unfortunately, much of the criticism of marketing research today is a result of this excessive focus on methodology and statistics. The problem with marketing research was not that it was centered on incompetent analysis, but the lack of a decision-maker's perspective and the inability to provide actionable insights consistently once the data were analyzed correctly.

In the Third Wave, we progressed from information-based decision making to system-based decision making. The Third Wave involved a number of developments centered on automated decision systems (ADS) that put the power of marketing information directly into the hands of nontechnical decision makers. It was a three-way marriage between marketing analysis, computer and information technologies, and the formal marketing planning process.

The team approach, including marketing researchers, systems engineers, and marketing management, provided the synergy needed to build useful computer-based systems that helped managers through the marketing planning and evaluation process. Through pooling expertise and applying information technologies, the full potential of marketing information was realized in the Third Wave.

Finally, in the Fourth Wave, the emergence of e-commerce and large customer databases has motivated organizations to move from an aggregate-level summarization of data (in order to uncover the underlying patterns as in the Second Wave) to a manipulation of data on an individual-by-individual basis. A majority of organizations currently are leveraging the technology developed during the Third Wave and the rich information they have about each individual customer, to tailor both their product/service and marketing messages on an individual customer basis. Also called mass-customization, this strategy develops relations with every customer that an organization possesses and finally allows managers to assess the lifetime value of every individual customer to the organization.

Source: Adapted from Kumar, Aaker, and Day, Essentials of Marketing Research, *2nd ed., John Wiley & Sons, Inc., 2002; and "Third Wave of Marketing Research on the Horizon,"* Marketing News, *March 1, 1993, p. 6.*

consideration. There may be no further need for clarification, the implications may not appear serious, or the response may appear evident in the judgment of the decision maker. Our interest is in those problems or opportunities that need to be clarified, whose consequences are uncertain, or that involve the development of new programs, products, or services.

The information system serves to emphasize that marketing research should not exist in isolation as a single effort to obtain information. Rather, it should be part of a systematic and continuous effort by the organization to improve the decision-making process. Marketing Research in Action 2.1 describes the "fourth wave" in marketing research, telling how marketing research has progressed from the rudimentary to the sophisticated.

Marketing Decision Support Systems

A typical marketing manager regularly receives some or all of the following data: factory shipments or orders; syndicated aggregate (industry) data services; sales reports from the field sales force; consumer panel data; scanner data; demographic data; and internal cost and budget data.

These data may also come in various levels of detail and aggregation. Often, they use different reporting periods and incompatible computer languages. Add to this sales estimates about competing brands and advertising, promotion, and pricing activity, and there is a data explosion.

Managers don't want data. They want, and need, decision-relevant information in accessible and preferably graphical form for (1) routine comparisons of current performance against past trends on each of the key measures of effectiveness, (2) periodic exception reports to assess which sales territories or accounts have not matched previous years' purchases, and (3) special analyses to evaluate the sales impact of particular marketing programs and to predict what would happen if changes were made. In addition, different divisions would like to be linked to enable product managers, sales planners, market researchers, financial analysts, and production schedulers to share information.

The purpose of a **marketing decision support system** (MDSS) is to combine marketing data from diverse sources into a single database that line managers can enter interactively to quickly identify problems and obtain standard periodic reports, as well as answers to analytical questions.

Characteristics of an MDSS

A good MDSS should have the following characteristics:

1. *Interactive*: The process of interaction with the MDSS should be simple and direct. With just a few commands, the user should be able to obtain the results immediately. There should be no need for a programmer in between.

2. *Flexible*: A good MDSS should be flexible. It should be able to present the available data in either discrete or aggregate form. It should satisfy the information needs of the managers in different hierarchical levels and functions.

3. *Discovery oriented*: The MDSS should not only assist managers in solving the existing problems but also help them to probe for trends and ask new questions. The managers should be able to discover new patterns and be able to act on them using the MDSS.

4. *User friendly*: The MDSS should be user friendly. It should be easy for the managers to learn and use the system. It should not take hours just to figure out what is going on. Most MDSS packages are menu driven and are easy to operate.

A typical MDSS is assembled from four components (see Figure 2.1).

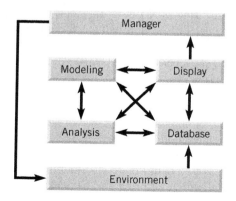

FIGURE 2.1
The Four Components of an MDSS.

Database

The database contains data from all sources, stored in a sufficiently disaggregated way so that it can be analyzed by product item, sales district, trade account, or time period. The best systems have databases that can be easily updated with new information and have sufficient flexibility that data can be readily analyzed in new ways. Since most analyses deal with a subset of a larger database, the supporting software should permit random access to any and all data to create appropriate subsets.

Reports and Displays

The capabilities of an MDSS range from simple ad hoc tables and reports to complex plots, charts, and other graphic displays. Any report or display can include calculations such as variances and running totals, or the results of statistical procedures found in the system. Typical reports produced with an MDSS include status reports that track current trends, exception reports on troubled brands and markets, and variance reports showing budget and actuals for sales and profits. The report in Figure 2.2 answers the question: "In which regions is the Mama Mia brand not keeping up with the industry trend?" Figure 2.2 shows that product category sales were up 5.8 percent, whereas Mama Mia sales were up only 2.0 percent. On a more detailed level, product category sales were up 13.1 percent in Cleveland and 1.7 percent in Miami, while Mama Mia sales rose 6.5 percent in Cleveland and fell 0.3 percent in Miami.

Analysis Capabilities

Analysis capabilities are used to relate the data to the models, as well as to clarify relationships, identify exceptions, and suggest courses of action. These capabilities should include the ability to make calculations such as averages, lags, and percentage changes versus a previous period and to conduct seasonal analyses and standard statistical procedures such as regression, correlation, and factor analysis. These procedures will be covered in subsequent chapters of this book.

Models

Models represent assumptions about how the world works, and specifically how brand sales, shares, and profits respond to changes in elements of the marketing mix. Models are used to test alternative marketing programs, answer "what if" questions, and assist in setting more realistic objectives. For example, managers want help with such questions as: What is the impact on profitability of achieving wider distribution? What is the optimal call level for each sales representative for each account and prospect? What objectives should be set for coupon redemption and the profitability of promotion programs? The models used to address these questions can range from forecasts to complex simulations of relationships among marketing, economic, and other factors.

Using an MDSS offers the organization a number of advantages. It results in substantial cost savings because it helps in making better and quicker decisions. The presence of MDSS forces the decision maker to view the decision and information environment within which he or she operates; hence, it leads to a better understanding of the decision environment. Since managers can now retrieve and utilize information that was never accessible before, it results in the enhancement of decision-making effectiveness. Using an MDSS results in better quality and quantity of data being collected and hence increases the value of the information to managers.

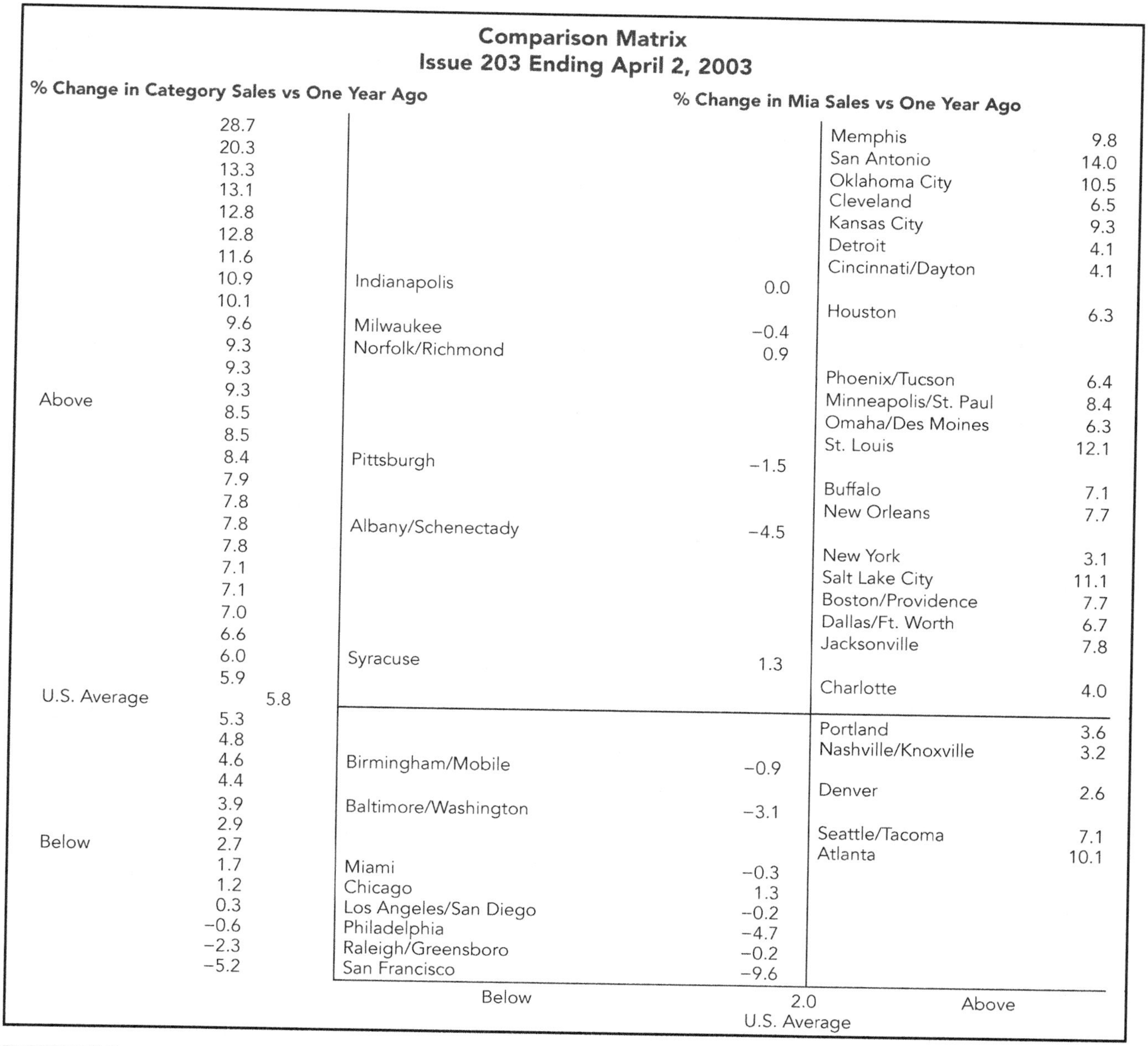

Comparison Matrix
Issue 203 Ending April 2, 2003

% Change in Category Sales vs One Year Ago   **% Change in Mia Sales vs One Year Ago**

Category %	City	Mia %		City	Mia %
28.7				Memphis	9.8
20.3				San Antonio	14.0
13.3				Oklahoma City	10.5
13.1				Cleveland	6.5
12.8				Kansas City	9.3
12.8				Detroit	4.1
11.6				Cincinnati/Dayton	4.1
10.9	Indianapolis	0.0			
10.1				Houston	6.3
9.6	Milwaukee	−0.4			
9.3	Norfolk/Richmond	0.9			
9.3				Phoenix/Tucson	6.4
9.3				Minneapolis/St. Paul	8.4
9.3				Omaha/Des Moines	6.3
8.5				St. Louis	12.1
8.5					
8.4	Pittsburgh	−1.5		Buffalo	7.1
7.9				New Orleans	7.7
7.8					
7.8	Albany/Schenectady	−4.5		New York	3.1
7.8				Salt Lake City	11.1
7.1				Boston/Providence	7.7
7.1				Dallas/Ft. Worth	6.7
7.0				Jacksonville	7.8
6.6					
6.0	Syracuse	1.3			
5.9				Charlotte	4.0

Above (left axis label, spanning upper rows)

U.S. Average 5.8

Category %	City	Mia %		City	Mia %
5.3				Portland	3.6
4.8				Nashville/Knoxville	3.2
4.6	Birmingham/Mobile	−0.9			
4.4				Denver	2.6
3.9	Baltimore/Washington	−3.1			
2.9				Seattle/Tacoma	7.1
2.7				Atlanta	10.1
1.7	Miami	−0.3			
1.2	Chicago	1.3			
0.3	Los Angeles/San Diego	−0.2			
−0.6	Philadelphia	−4.7			
−2.3	Raleigh/Greensboro	−0.2			
−5.2	San Francisco	−9.6			

Below (left axis label, spanning lower rows)

Bottom axis: Below   2.0 U.S. Average   Above

FIGURE 2.2
Comparison of Brand Performance with Industry Trend.

Gaining Insights from an MDSS

When an over-the-counter (OTC) drug manufacturer suffered a decline in national unit market share for its drug "Alpha," management turned to an MDSS for insights. They suspected that the losses would be traced to actions of the two main competitors. "Beta" was a private-label competitor that was sold at half the price of Alpha. The other competing brand, "Delta," was produced and marketed by another division of the same company, following a rather similar strategy. Initial data from the DSS seemed to confirm management's initial suspicions. Alpha's share had dropped from 5.0 to 2.5 percent, and Delta's share had more than doubled from 2.0 to 4.5 percent. However, subsequent analysis of the database showed that this information was misleading.

The premise of the further analysis was that any competitive effects should be evident at the regional as well as the national level. To test this possibility, the market share changes of Alpha were related to share changes of Beta and Delta, by region, for a six-month period.

The results, shown in Figure 2.3, confirmed the adverse effects of Beta on Alpha. In almost every region, a share decrease for Alpha was associated with a share increase for Beta. A different picture emerged, however, when a similar analysis (shown in Figure 2.4) was done with

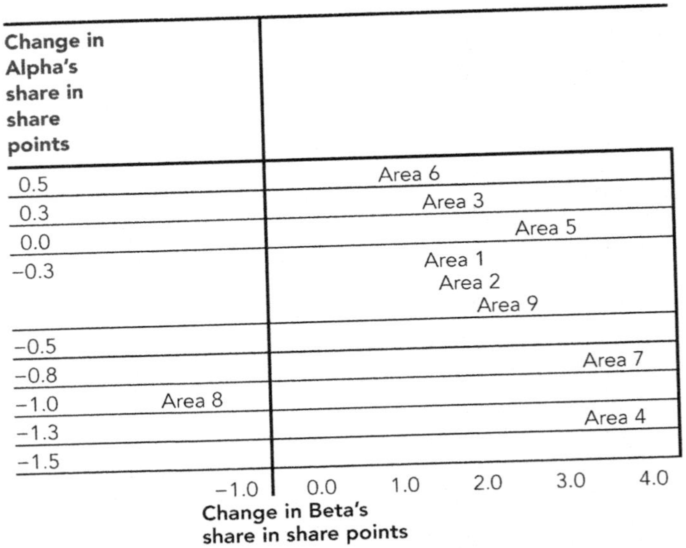

FIGURE 2.3
Regional Market Share Changes—Alpha and Beta.

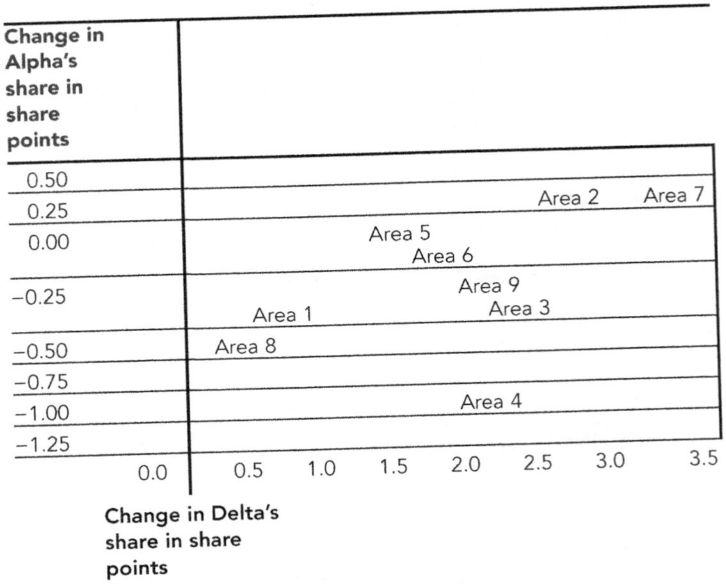

FIGURE 2.4
Regional Market Share Changes—Alpha and Delta.

Delta. In the regions where Alpha's share had decreased the least, Delta's share had increased the most. Conversely, Alpha's share had decreased the most in those regions where Delta had gained the least share. Clearly, Delta was not the source of Alpha's problems; more likely, Delta was helping Alpha by combining the two brands' sales force efforts. This analysis prevented a potentially damaging interdivisional dispute and helped focus management's attention on the proper target competitor.

Suppliers of Information

In general, managers can acquire the necessary information for decision making from two basic types of sources:

1. The corporate or in-house marketing research department.

2. External suppliers.

Usually, managers use a mix of in-house and external approaches to solve a certain problem. Both can feed information directly to their clients, who are users with decision-making needs. More often, the outside suppliers get their direction and provide information to an inside research group. These inside suppliers translate the problems of their clients into specific information requirements, decide how the information will be collected and by whom, and then interpret the findings. Figure 2.5 shows the interaction among the participants in a marketing research activity.

The purpose of this section is to discuss briefly the nature and attributes of the providers of marketing research services, the types of services they provide, and the factors that influence the choice of a suitable supplier for a given situation. Figure 2.6 gives a concise summary of the different types of information suppliers within the marketing research industry.

Corporate/In-House Marketing Research

The location of the marketing research department within an organization and the strength of the department vary from firm to firm and to a very great extent depend on the requirements for information and the organizational structure of the firm. Some firms have a single centralized research department, housed in the corporate headquarters, which provides the information required to the various business units scattered geographically and/or functionally. The other

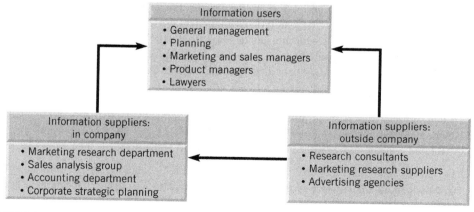

FIGURE 2.5
Participants in Marketing Research Activities.

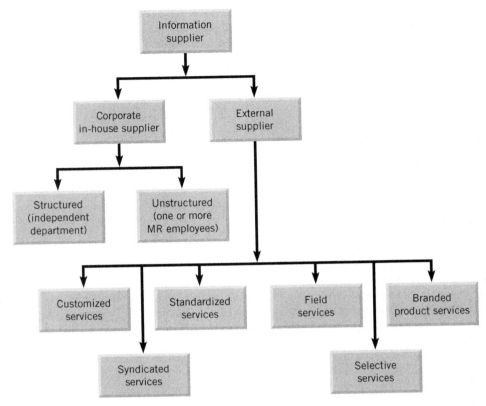

FIGURE 2.6
Information Suppliers and Services.

extreme is the completely decentralized operation, wherein each business unit or geographic unit has its own research department. The type of structure adopted depends on the amount of information required, the frequency with which it is required, the uniqueness of the information, and the time available to collect it. In most major organizations, especially in multinational corporations, a mix of both these structures can be found.

Not all organizations (regardless of size) have an in-house research establishment. Even among those that have an in-house research department, it is not unusual to seek the assistance of external suppliers. Virtually all research users at some time use the services of outside research specialists. Their role may be limited to raw-data collection, depending on the research approach, questionnaire, and sampling method provided by the client. At the other extreme, the client may assign the entire problem to an outside consultant who is responsible for every step to the completed report and action recommendations. Other possibilities are to bring in outside specialists for special problems (such as a sampling expert to draw a complex sample) or to employ services that have special facilities or data.[5]

Many related considerations influence the decision to go outside:

1. Internal personnel may not have the skills or experience. Few but the largest companies have specialists in all areas from psychologists able to conduct focus group interviewing to electronics engineers with MBAs who have studied the telecommunications equipment market.

2. Outside help may be called in to boost internal capacity in response to an urgent deadline.

3. It may be cheaper to go outside. Specialists who have encountered similar problems with other clients probably are more efficient in dealing with the problem, and because they are not on the staff there is no risk of underutilization of their time.

4. Shared cost and multiclient studies coordinated by an outside supplier offer considerable savings possibilities. Multiclient studies are feasible when several organizations have related needs for information about a major topic, such as the future of electronic funds transfer systems. Each client pays an agreed share of the total cost. The ultimate in shared-cost studies are the large standardized data collection services, such as store audits of product sales activity or omnibus surveys, which combine questions from several clients.

5. Often, outside suppliers have special facilities or competencies (an established national interviewing field force, conference rooms with one-way mirrors, banks of telephone lines, or test kitchens) that would be costly to duplicate for a single study.

6. Political considerations may dictate the use of an outside research specialist whose credentials are acceptable to all parties in an internal policy dispute. Research people within the organization may be well advised to avoid being on one side or the other of a sensitive issue.

7. Marketing research is used increasingly in litigation or in proceedings before regulatory or legislative bodies. The credibility of the findings generally will be enhanced if the study is conducted by a respected outsider. Also, this kind of research often is subjected to critical questioning or cross-examination and is likely to stand up only if designed to high standards, which may exceed those used within the organization for routine decision-making purposes.

External Suppliers of the Research Industry

The marketing research industry consists of several hundred research firms, ranging from small, one-person operations to large corporations having operations in multiple countries. Table 2.1 lists the top 25 Global research firms and their annual revenues for the year 2013. The table also gives an estimate of the total revenue from outside the parent country.

According to Laurence Gold, author of *The 2014 AMA Gold Global Top 25 Report*, through mergers and acquisitions, the Global marketing research industry is becoming even more worldly and cosmopolitan. As can be seen from the table, the total revenue of the top 25 firms exceeded $21 billion, and more than one half of this revenue is estimated to come from operations outside the parent country.[6] The total revenue in 2013 represents a 3.3 percent growth over 2012. After adjusting for worldwide inflation, the real growth was 2.0 percent, indicating a flat growth rate over the last five years.

In 2013, only three of the Top 25 firms did not have revenue contributions from outside their home countries. As a group, the Top 25 firms had 122,310 full-time research employees in 2013, an increase from 103,136 in 2010.[7]

Figure 2.7 provides the growth in research spending only within the United States between 1991 and 2010. While there was negative growth in 2009, 2010 shows that spending has come back as the overall economic environment improves.

Table 2.1   Top 25 Global Research Organizations

U.S. ranks 2013	U.S. ranks 2012	IMR firms	Parent country	Global research revenue ($, in millions)	Percent of global revenue from outside home country (%)
1	1	Nielsen Holdings N.V.	U.S.	$6,045.0	47.2%
–	9#	Arbitron Inc.	U.S.	476.0	1.3
2	2	Kantar*	U.K.	3,389.2	71.9
3	5	IMS Health Holdings Inc.	U.S.	2,544.0	63.2
4	3	Ipsos SA	France	2,274.2	93.1
5	4	GfK SE	Germany	1,985.2	70.0
6	6	Information Resources Inc.	U.S.	845.1	40.4
7	8	Westat Inc.	U.S.	582.5	3.2
8	–	dunnhumby Ltd.	U.K.	453.7	46.5
9	7	INTAGE Holdings Inc.**	Japan	435.5	5.6
10	10	The NPD Group Inc.	U.S.	287.7	29.7
11	11	comScore Inc.	U.S.	286.9	29.3
12	15	J.D. Power and Associates*	U.S.	258.3	33.1
13	13	IBOPE Group	Brazil	231.1	22.4
14	14	ICF International Inc.	U.S.	225.3	23.7
15	13	Video Research Ltd.**	Japan	204.0	–
16	19	Symphony Health Solutions	U.S.	198.7	1.1
17	16	Macromill Inc.	Japan	184.7	10.9
18	17	Maritz Research	U.S.	177.6	21.8
19	18	Abt SRBI Inc.	U.S.	172.8	9.9
20	–	Decision Resources Group	U.S.	150.3	28.1
21	20	Harris Interactive Inc.	U.S.	139.7	38.4
22	24	ORC International	U.S.	122.0	32.9
23	22	Mediametrie	France	106.1	14.0
24	25	Yougov plc	U.K.	101.4	70.3
25	21	Lieberman Research Worldwide	U.S.	100.3	32.2
		TOTAL		**21,501.3**	**55.0**

Source: Adapted from "The 2014 AMA Gold Global Top 25 Report", by Laurence N. Gold, *Marketing News*, August 2014, pp. 34–72.

Notes: #Arbitron Inc. was acquired by Nielsen Holdings N.V.

*Estimated by Top 25 author;

**For fiscal year ended March 2014.

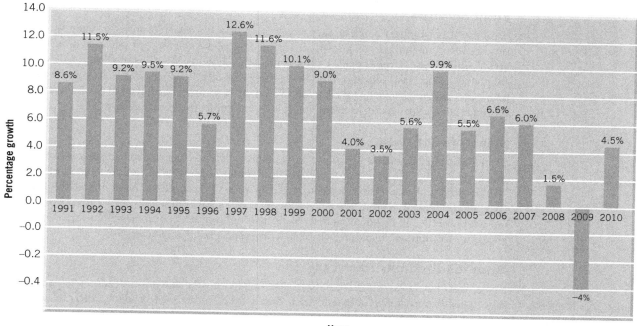

FIGURE 2.7
Growth in Research Spending Within the United States.
Source: J. Honomichl, "Top 50 Report," *Marketing News,* June 30, 2011, p. 13.

Type and Nature of Services

External suppliers that collectively comprise the marketing research industry can be further classified into six different groups, depending on the type and nature of the services they provide. Based on Figure 2.6, the major types of services provided by external suppliers of information are discussed in the paragraphs that follow.

Customized Services

Firms that specialize in customized services work with individual clients to help them develop and implement a marketing research project from top to bottom. They work with management on any given problem and go through the entire research process, including analyzing and presenting the final results.

Syndicated Services

Syndicated services are companies that routinely collect information on several different issues and provide it to firms that subscribe to their services. The Nielsen Television Index, which provides information on audiences viewing different TV programs, is an example of such services. These suppliers also provide information on retail sales, household purchasing patterns, and so on, which they collect through scanner data.

Standardized Services

Standardized services are market research projects conducted in a standard, prespecified manner and supplied to several different clients. The Starch Readership Survey is a typical example of such a service; it provides clients information regarding the effectiveness of print advertisements, in the form of Starch scores.

Field Services

Field services suppliers concentrate on collecting data for research projects. They specialize in various survey techniques such as mail surveys, telephone surveys, or personal surveys. These organizations range from small, one-person establishments to large, multinational, wide-area telephone service (WATS)-line interviewing services, and have extensive facilities for personal interviews in homes and shopping malls. Some of these firms specialize in qualitative data collection methods such as focus group interviews and projection techniques.

Selective Services

Some companies specialize in just one or two aspects of marketing research, mainly concerned with data coding, data editing, or data analysis. These generally are small firms, sometimes referred to as "lab houses," with expertise in sophisticated data analysis techniques. The proliferation of software for marketing research projects has led to an increase in such lab houses. Any enterprising individual with expertise in computer and sophisticated multivariate analysis techniques can acquire the necessary software packages and establish a firm specializing in data analysis.

Branded Products Services

Some firms have developed specialized data collection and analysis procedures to address specific types of research problems, which they market as branded products. PRIZM, a Claritas Corporation product that forms clusters of the population on the basis of lifestyle and Zip Code classifications, is an example of one such branded product. Using this technique, the entire U.S. population is divided into 40 clusters. Author Michael J. Weiss, in his popular book, *Clustering of America*, New York, NY: Harper & Row Publishers (1988), provides a vivid portrait of the nation's 40 neighborhood types—their values, lifestyles, and eccentricities.

Criteria for Selecting External Suppliers

Once the decision has been made to go outside, there remains the question of which consultant or supplier to retain. What criteria should a firm adopt in selecting an external research supplier? Several academic scholars have conducted research studies to identify the factors that are important in the selection of external suppliers. A crucial factor in the choice is the judgment as to whether the supplier or consultant actually can deliver the promised data, advice, or conclusions. This judgment should be made only after the following steps have been followed:

1. A thorough search for names of people and companies who have acknowledged expertise in the area of the study.[8]

2. Selection of a small number of bidders on the basis of recommendations of colleagues or others who have had similar needs.

3. Personal interviews with the person who would be responsible for the project, asking for examples of work on similar problems, their procedures for working with clients, and the names of previous clients who could provide references.

4. A check of the references of each potential supplier, with special attention to comments on their depth of competence and expertise, their creativity in dealing with problems, and the quality and adequacy of resources available.

Selection is made on the basis of how well the problem and objectives have been understood,[9] comments by the references, and whether the quoted price or fee is a good value in light of the research approach that is proposed. Seldom is the lowest quotation the best value. To minimize the problem of comparability, all bidders should respond to the same study specifications.[10]

Career Opportunities in Marketing Research

Marketing research offers several promising career opportunities,[11] depending on one's level of education, experience, interests, and personality. Interesting and exciting careers are available both within research supplier organizations—typically, external suppliers of marketing research services such as A.C. Nielsen, Information Resources, Inc. (IRI), J.D. Power and Associates, and so on—and within companies that have their own research department. A brief description of marketing research jobs, the required level of education, the real level of experience, and the average annual compensation are provided in the Appendix of this chapter.

Demand is outstripping the research industry's supply of high-level data analysts, also known as marketing research methodologists. The marketing research methodologist is an individual who has a balanced and in-depth knowledge of the fields of statistics, psychometrics, marketing, and buyer behavior and applies that knowledge to describe and infer causal relationships from marketing data. Typically, today's marketing research methodologist has specialized in one of the fields mentioned at the master's and doctorate level. They will have to acquire considerable knowledge in the related fields through additional coursework, targeted in-depth readings, and ongoing communication and interaction with peer-level specialists. However, some well-known methodologists emerged from the engineering and hard science disciplines while others migrated from political science, sociology, agricultural science, geology, and anthropology. A well-rounded research methodologist would include the following coursework in his or her program of study:

- Probability and statistics

- Multivariate statistics

- Human psychology

- Organizational psychology

- Psychometric measurement

- Marketing research

- Sociology

- Buyer behavior

- Microeconomics

- Marketing management

- Business communications

- Social media marketing

The need for advanced analytical techniques has been accelerating for the last several years as both research companies and corporate research departments become more familiar with the power and utility of newer methodologies. A sharp dissonance between supply and demand is fostering:

1. Erroneous execution and delivery of advanced analyses by unqualified research analysts.

2. Failure to recommend advanced methodologies by independent research organizations and consultants.

Therefore, marketing researchers must work with other interested parties to remedy the situation and offer support for the marketing methodologist position. The specialty of the marketing research methodologist will assume an ever-increasing role in the business of marketing research.[12]

SUMMARY

The focus of marketing research has shifted from ad hoc methods to collecting data and helping managers make informed, knowledgeable decisions. The MDSS is the latest in a series of developments that help marketing managers use the information they obtain in a more meaningful manner. Marketing research is a key component of the MDSS because it provides one of the main inputs into the system. Marketing research can either be done in house or bought from outside suppliers. A number of market research companies provide many services, both syndicated and customized.

QUESTIONS AND PROBLEMS

2.1   **(a)** How do marketing information systems aid marketers in their decision making?

(b) What types of information can be obtained from marketing information systems?

2.2   What are the inherent characteristics of an effective marketing decision support system?

2.3   A marketing manager needs to find the causes for the decline in market share of his or her company's product. The manager decides to conduct marketing research.

(a) How should he or she go about finding a supplier of research services?

(b) Suppose the manager decides to introduce the product in Europe. A study needs to be conducted to assess the acceptance of the product in various markets. What criteria should the manager use in selecting a research supplier?

2.4   Identify three examples of identification of market opportunities or marketing problems from recent secondary data sources.

END NOTES

1. S. Seggev, "Listening Is Key to Providing Useful Marketing Research," *Marketing News*, January 22, 1982, p. 6.

2. K. R. Wade, "The When/What Research Decision Guide," *Marketing Research: A Magazine of Management & Applications*, 5, Summer 1993, pp. 24–27.

3. "Marketing: The New Priority," *Business Week*, November 21, 1983, p. 96.

4. C. Miller, "Computer Modelling Rings the Right Bell for Avon," *Marketing News*, May 9, 1988, p. 14.

5. P. Boughton, "Marketing Research Partnerships: A Strategy for the '90s," *Marketing Research: A Magazine of Management and Applications*, 4, December 1992, pp. 8–13.

6. L. N. Gold, "The 2014 AMA Gold Global Top 25 Report," *Marketing News*, August 2014, pp. 34–72.

7. L. N. Gold, "The 2014 AMA Gold Global Top 25 Report," *Marketing News*, August 2014, pp. 34–72.

8. Useful sources are *Greenbook: International Directory of Marketing Research Houses and Services*, New York: American Marketing Association, annual; *Consultants and Consulting Organizations Directory*, Detroit: Gale Research Co., triennial with annual supplements; and *Bradfords Directory of Marketing Research Agencies in the U.S. and Around the World*, Fairfax, VA: Bradford Publishing Co., 1984. A list of the top 300 companies that specialize in focus-group interviewing techniques appears in the January issues of *Marketing News*.

9. *Marketing News* provides a directory of software for marketing research application.

10. R. D. Speer, "Follow These Six Steps to Get Most Benefit from Marketing Research Consultant Project," *Marketing News*, September 18, 1981, pp. 12–13. *Marketing News* publishes a directory of international marketing research firms on a regular basis.

11. T. C. Kinnear and A. R. Root, *Survey of Marketing Research* Chicago American Marketing Association, 1996; C. McDaniel and R. Gates, *Contemporary Marketing Research*. Minneapolis, MN: West Publishing Co., 26. *Marketing News* on a regular basis publishes a directory of marketing research firms located within research users such as Coca-Cola, AT&T, etc., in their in-house research department.

12. W. D. Neal, "The Marketing Research Methodologist," *Marketing Research*, 10(1), Spring 1998, pp. 21–25.

APPENDIX

Marketing Research Jobs

Please visit http://www.drvkumar.com/MR12 to get more information on the type of marketing research jobs available.

The Marketing Research Process

3

LEARNING OBJECTIVES

- Describe the various stages of the marketing research process.
- Discuss the importance of the problem/opportunity identification stage of the research process.
- Discuss the issues related to hypotheses development.
- Explain the concept of value of information and its role in deciding when marketing research is beneficial.
- Discuss how the research purpose and the research objectives are developed.
- Describe the international marketing research process.

How is the market research project conceived, planned, and executed? The answer, in part, is through a research process, consisting of stages or steps that guide the project from its conception through the final analysis, recommendation, and ultimate action. The **research process** provides a systematic, planned approach to the research project and ensures that all aspects of the research project are consistent with each other. It is especially important that the research design and implementation be consistent with the research purpose and objectives. Otherwise, the results will not help the client.

The research process is described in this chapter and in Chapter 4. This chapter provides an overview of the research process, a discussion of the research purpose and research objectives, and a consideration of the value of research information. Negative findings are as valuable as positive ones. In fact, they are often more revealing, as they provide valuable insight into customers' psyches. Today, the research process has evolved to encompass decision making. This combined process transforms mundane marketing research to marketing intelligence. Chapter 4 gives an overview of the research design and its implementation. Altogether, these two chapters are the foundation for the rest of the book.

Overview of the Marketing Research Process

Research studies evolve through a series of steps, each representing the answer to a key question.

1. *Why should we do research?* This establishes the research purpose as seen by the management team that will be using the results. This step requires understanding the decisions to be made and the problems or opportunities to be diagnosed.

2. *What research should be done?* Here the management purpose is translated into objectives that tell the managers exactly what questions need to be answered by the research study or project.

3. *Is it worth doing the research?* The decision has to be made here about whether the value of the information that will likely be obtained is going to be greater than the cost of collecting it.

4. *How should the research be designed to achieve the research objectives?* Design issues include the choice of research approach—reliance on secondary data versus conducting a survey or experiment—and the specifics of how to collect the data. Chapter 4 deals with how to approach these issues.

5. *What will we do with the research?* Once the data have been collected, how will it be analyzed, interpreted, and used to make recommendations for action?

The necessary steps are linked in a sequential process (see Figure 3.1). Although the steps usually occur in this general order, we must emphasize that "early" decisions are always made by looking ahead to "later" decisions. The early decisions are constantly being modified to account for new insights and possibilities presented by later decisions. Also, the steps do not function in isolation. Rather, they are embedded in the ongoing planning process of the business, which culminates in the development of strategies, programs, and action. This planning process provides the purposes of the research. In turn, planning is supported by the information system, which (1) anticipates the type of information required by decision makers and (2) organizes data that have been collected to ensure their availability when needed.

The development of a research purpose that links the research to decision making and the formulation of research objectives that serve to guide the research are unquestionably the most important steps in the research process. If they are correct, the research stands a good chance of being both useful and appropriate. If they are bypassed or wrong, the research almost surely will be wasteful and irrelevant. These aspects of research, too often neglected by managers, will be discussed in detail in this chapter. Chapter 4 deals with research design; the chapters in Part II discuss the various methods to collect data; and the chapters in Part III of the book deal with analysis and interpretation of the data.

The Preliminary Stages of the Marketing Research Process

Step 1—Research Purpose

Research problems are more likely to be poorly defined, only partially understood, and missing possible decision alternatives that should be analyzed. Defining problems accurately is a combination of data and judgment that demands real thought and effort. Problems, opportunities, and "nonproblem" situations are closely related to structure. Altogether they make up a family of gaps. The concept of analyzing the gaps as problems is based on the following:

1. *Recognizing/understanding a problem.* A problem is a gap between what was supposed to happen and what did happen between our objective and our accomplishment. Three elements are required to recognize a problem:

   - Something must be expected to happen.

   - Feedback must be received on what actually happens.

   - Expectations and feedback must be compared.

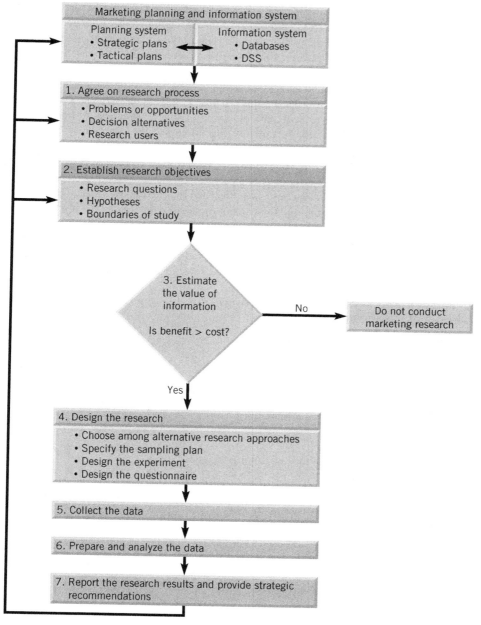

FIGURE 3.1
The Marketing Research Process.

2. *Knowing where and when the gap or problem occurred.* Once a problem is defined, it is easier to approach the cause and solution to the gap(s), in accordance with the level of detail of the analysis. In the end, problem definition is and will always be a creative act, a balance between thorough research and intuition. Problem definition is best thought of as a solution definition—the selection of a domain is likely to be rich in ideas to solve the problem. Problem definition is a creative act. The payoff from good marketing definition is enormous—nothing else we do has so much leverage on profit.[1]

Seldom will research problems come neatly packaged with obvious information requirements, clear-cut boundaries, and pure motives on the part of the decision makers. Launching a research study with such shaky inputs is a recipe for producing unusable findings and unhappy clients. It is in the best interest of both the researcher and the managers paying for the research to be sure that the research purpose is fully understood. One of the hallmarks of a competent researcher is the ability to get to the heart of the management problem.

Consider the seemingly straightforward request by the chairperson of an association of community merchants for a research project. The objective of this project was to help reduce the propensity of residents in the community to do their shopping in two nearby communities. Clearly, the purpose of the research was to identify and evaluate various ways to increase the local merchants' share of shopping by residents.

Further probing, however, revealed that the statement of the problem was at least partially inaccurate. Only late in the research process was it learned by the researcher that the chairperson was having real difficulty convincing the other local merchants that there was a serious enough outflow of local trade to warrant joint action to reverse the flow. This certainly changed the purpose of the research. Now the researcher would have to measure the level of retail trade outflow, in addition to finding the reasons for the outflow. This required a major change in the research design but had the change not been made the results would have been of little value to the client.

The **research purpose** comprises a shared understanding between the manager and the researcher, which are as follows:

1. Problems or opportunities to be studied

   - Which problems or opportunities are anticipated?

   - What is the scope of the problems and the possible reasons?

2. Decision alternatives to be evaluated

   - What are the alternatives being studied?

   - What are the criteria for choosing among the alternatives?

   - What is the timing or importance of the decision?

3. Users of the research results

   - Who are the decision makers?

   - Are there any covert purposes?

Problem or Opportunity Analysis

In analyzing problems or studying opportunities, identifying loyal customers and doing targeted marketing are very important. Marketing Research in Action 3.1 reiterates the importance of market research and data-based marketing in creating "top of mind awareness" of products.

Research often is motivated by a problem or opportunity. The fact that sales are below expectations in the East might be a problem requiring research. The fact that people are consuming fewer sweets might be a problem or a potential opportunity for a candy company. Increased leisure time might be viewed as an opportunity by a recreation-oriented organization. In such cases, the research purpose should specify the problem or opportunity to be explored. Identifying and defining the problem or opportunity is a crucial first step in the marketing research process. Especially in situation analysis contexts, exploratory research is needed to identify problems and opportunities. What sales areas are showing weak performance? What segments represent opportunities

Marketing Research in Action 3.1

■ WHAT DO TODAY'S BUYERS WANT?

Today's buyers have created challenges for all businesses. They are

- Skeptical—their trust has been broken by every industry.
- Cautious—they take a lot of time to weigh decisions.
- Tired of selling and sales pressure—they are weary of spam and telephone sales.
- Busy—they want everything quick and easy.
- Confused—they are bewildered with the variety of offers.

Source: findmorebuyers.com/page.cfm/11, January 2003.

Today's buyers have access to information because of the Internet, and they can make better decisions because of the global market available for choice. Marketers have to create a "top of mind awareness" of their products. To do this, they have to constantly inform buyers about their products without irritating them. This means they have to identify their most loyal customers and do a great deal of targeted marketing. This is possible only through marketing research and data-based marketing.

Once marketers have identified their customers, it's very easy to find buyers with a similar profile and generate loyal, profit-generating customers.

Marketing Research in Action 3.2

■ BEST BUY GOES LEAN

Best Buy, with intense competition from competitors, has slashed capital spending for its 2009 budget by half along with buy outs and layoffs. Given Best Buy's emphasis on its personnel, the suggestion of layoffs demonstrates a change in long-held priorities.

Best Buy faces intense competition mainly from retailers such as Wal-Mart, Target, and Costco coming after mainstay businesses including television, digital cameras, and gaming. For instance, television shoppers at Best Buy are going

for less expensive sets, especially for their second or third TVs. Further, consumers replacing their TVs are settling for 34-inch screens from 42-inch screens. Best Buy's competitors use fewer employees to run the electronics business throughout and continue to figure out ways to sell electronics right off the rack rather than through a sales clerk.

By becoming leaner, Best Buy is preparing itself for a competitive reality where consumers are becoming more concerned about spending, and where discounters and warehouse clubs are the major competition.

Source: M. Duff, "Best Buy Goes Leaner As Customers Waver, Competitors Press," BNET Retail, December 19, 2008.

because they are dissatisfied with current products or because they are underusing the product? Even in exploratory research, however, it will be helpful to identify the nature of the problem or opportunity that is motivating the research. Further, the goal should be to move from exploratory research to research more focused on a decision. Marketing Research in Action 3.2 illustrates the process of changing marketing approach by reacting to market situations.

The manager needs to make certain that the real problem is being addressed. Sometimes the recognized problem is only a symptom, or perhaps merely a part of a larger problem. A sobering illustration of this is the plight of Compton Corp.,[2] a manufacturer of capital equipment costing between $10,000 and $25,000. The company was dominant in its market, with a share as large as the next two biggest competitors. All the companies sold their equipment through a network of independent distributors, each of which sold the products of at least two competitors. For several years, this market leader had been losing share. In an attempt to reverse the trend, the company changed advertising agencies. When the new agents funded a study of end users, they found to their surprise that the previous agency had done a superb job of creating awareness and favorable attitudes. However, many of the equipment purchasers who favored Compton were actually buying the competing brands. This problem had little to do with the performance of the advertising agency. A new study, oriented toward the distributors, found that Compton's distributor-relations program was very weak relative to its competitors. One competitor emphasized sales contests, another offered cash bonuses to salespeople, and a third was particularly effective with technical sales assistance directed to difficult accounts. Not surprisingly, these factors influenced the distributors when they were asked for advice, or when the prospective purchaser did not have a firm commitment to Compton equipment.

In this case, the real problem ultimately was isolated, but only after much time and energy had been directed toward the wrong problem. When defining the problem, it is important to think broadly about the possible causes or influential variables. This may justify a separate exploratory research study. Further, what appears to be a genuine problem or opportunity may not be researchable. For example, if a company that manufactures washing machines is interested in determining the replacement rates for all machines sold within the last three years, it may not be worthwhile to pursue the issue. Since most household washing machines have a life span ranging from five to 10 years, the problem of identifying the replacement rate for working machines sold within the last three years may be a nonresearchable problem.

Decision Alternatives

For research to be effective, it must be associated with a decision. Marketing research is committed to the principle of utility. In general, if research is not going to have an effect on decisions, it is an exercise in futility. The researcher should always be sensitive to the possibility that either there are no decision alternatives—and therefore no decision—or that the research findings will not affect the decision, usually because of resource or organizational constraints. In such circumstances, the research will have no practical value and probably should not be conducted.

When a decision potential does exist, it is important to identify it explicitly because the research then can be designed for maximum effectiveness. For example, researchers frequently are asked to assess the potential of a market that is not familiar to the company. But what are the decisions the manager faces? Is the manager thinking of acquiring a company serving that market? Has the lab produced a new product that might be sold as a component to the industry serving that market? The answers will have a significant influence on the design of the research.

A most useful way to clarify the decision motivating the research is to ask (1) What alternative actions are being considered? (2) What actions would be taken, given the various feasible outcomes of the research? This line of questioning can be very enlightening for the decision maker, as well as for the researcher, in terms of clarifying exactly what the research can accomplish. The story in Marketing Research in Action 3.3 illustrates how both can learn from a focus on decisions.

Sometimes the decision involved is highly specific. A copy test is used to select a copy alternative. A concept test is employed to determine if a concept should be developed further. Sometimes the decision can be very general. What markets should be the primary targets of our organization? Should our marketing program be changed? It is desirable to be as specific as possible, because the research purpose then will be more effective in guiding the development of the research design. However, even if the decision is necessarily general, it needs to be stated clearly.

Criteria for Choosing Among Alternatives

It is essential for the researcher to know how the decision maker will choose among the available alternatives. Suppose a product manager is considering three possible package redesigns for a health-care product with declining sales. This would seem to be a straightforward research

Marketing Research in Action 3.3

◼ POLITICAL CAMPAIGN RESEARCH

The meeting between Hugh Godfrey and two project directors from Pollsters Anonymous, a well-known survey research company, had taken a surprising turn. Here were two researchers suggesting that no research be undertaken.

Godfrey was campaign manager for John Crombie, a university professor and erstwhile Democratic challenger of the Republican incumbent for the local House of Representatives seat. He and his candidate were anxious to undertake a program of research. They thought it would be a good idea to take surveys in May and September (five months and six weeks prior to the election) of voter awareness of the candidate, attitudes toward him, issue salience, and intentions to vote. The results would be helpful in clarifying the candidate's position and deciding on media expenditures. Positive results would be useful in soliciting campaign contributions, which loomed as a big problem.

During the meeting the researchers had asked what Godfrey expected to find. He was sure that the initial survey would reveal low awareness and would confirm other information he had that there was a low level of voter registration among Democrats in the area. The next question was whether any foreseeable results would persuade him not to spend all his available resources on a voter registration drive. He also admitted that the preliminary estimate of $6,000 for a May survey was a large chunk of his available funds. In fact, he was thinking, "With the money I would spend on the survey, I could hire enough canvassers to get at least 1,500–2,000 registrations."

undertaking, as the decision alternatives are completely specified. However, the product manager could use some or all of the following criteria to choose the best of the three alternative packages:

1. Long-run sales
2. Trial purchases by users of competing brands
3. Amount of shelf space assigned to the brand
4. Differentiation from competitive packages
5. Brand-name recognition

The researcher and decision maker need to discuss all possible criteria in advance, and choose those that are appropriate. If the criterion for comparison is long-run sales results, the research approach will be much more elaborate than if the choice is based simply on brand-name recognition.

Timing and Importance

Timing and importance are always pivotal issues in the research process. How crucial is the decision? If the wrong decision is made, what will be the consequences? Obviously, the decision to "go national" with a new government program represents a much larger commitment than the decision to pursue a new program idea a bit further. Other questions concern the timing of the decision. What is the time pressure on the decision? Is information needed quickly, or is there time to develop an optimal research design?

Research Users—Decision Makers

When the research results will be used to guide internal problem solving, the researcher must know the objectives and expectations of the actual decision makers. The bigger the problem, the more difficult this becomes, for not only are a large number of people likely to be involved, but the contact person may simply be acting as a liaison whose interpretation of the problem and the need for research may be secondhand. The major benefit from making an effort to reach all the decision makers is that the research purpose is likely to be specified more adequately. These contacts also will tell the researcher (especially an outside supplier who is called in to undertake the work) a good deal about the resources that are available to deal with the problem. This is very helpful in developing a realistic proposal.

Increasingly, marketing research is entering the public domain, which introduces a new set of users who frequently have very different criteria for evaluating research results. For example:

- A public utility presents a research study to a regulatory body in support of a request for a rate change or the introduction of a change in service level.

- An industry trade association conducts research designed to influence proposed legislation or trade regulations. The Direct Mail Marketing Association has sponsored a study of mail-order buyers in response to a proposed Federal Trade Commission order that would require sellers to offer a refund if they could not ship the ordered goods within a month.

- A regional transit agency wants to build public support for the continuation of an experimental program involving "dedicated" bus lanes (part of a road or highway on which no automobile traffic is permitted). The research demonstrating the effectiveness of the program is to be presented to various public bodies and citizen groups.

In most cases, the research in the above examples will be used to support a decision alternative. However, examination of the results often is conducted in an adversarial setting, which means more criticism of shortcomings and necessitates a higher quality of research.

Overt and Covert Purposes

It would be naive to presume that research is always conducted to facilitate rational problem-solving activity or that the decision maker always will be willing or able to share reasons for initiating the research. As discussed in Chapter 1, there are times when the main purpose of marketing research is to serve someone's organizational goals or for other unethical purposes. None of these abuses can be condoned. Often they are specifically prohibited by industry codes of ethics. When they are not, one's moral standards become the compass for deciding what is right.

Step 2—Research Objective

The research objective is a statement, in as precise terminology as possible, of what information is needed. The research objective should be framed so that obtaining the information will ensure that the research purpose is satisfied.

Research objectives have three components. The first is the *research question*. It specifies the information the decision maker needs. The second and third elements help the researcher make the research question as specific and precise as possible. The second element is the *development of hypotheses* that are basically alternative answers to the research question. The research determines which of these alternative answers is correct. It is not always possible to develop hypotheses, but the effort should be made. The third is the *scope* or boundaries of the research. For example, is the interest in current customers only or in all potential customers?

Research Question

The research question asks what specific information is required to achieve the research purpose. If the research question is answered by the research, then the information should aid the decision maker.

An illustration comes from a company in the toiletries and cosmetics business, which was interested in acquiring a smaller firm with an apparently complementary product line. One anticipated benefit of the acquisition was the opportunity to eliminate one of the sales forces. The purpose of the research was to assess whether the company could use its existing sales force to distribute the products of the acquired company. The corresponding research objective was to determine how much the retail distribution patterns of the two companies overlapped. There was some preliminary evidence suggesting (i.e., hypothesizing) that distribution coverage would differ by geographic area and store type. The resulting study found that there was very little overlap because the acquiring company emphasized major metropolitan areas, whereas the other company was represented largely in smaller cities and suburbs.

It is possible to have several research questions for a given research purpose. Thus, if the purpose is to determine if a specific advertisement should be run, the following research questions could be posed:

- Will the advertisement be noticed?

- Will it be interpreted accurately?

- Will it influence attitudes and lead to an increase in sale?

These questions correspond to the criteria used to evaluate the advertising alternatives. Similarly, if the purpose is to determine how to improve the services of a bank, possible research questions might be the following:

- What aspects of the current service are customers most pleased with, and with which are they most dissatisfied?

- What types of customers use the various services?

- What benefits do people seek from banks?

Each of these questions should pass the test of being relevant to the purpose. For example, if customer types are identified that use a service such as traveler's checks, it may be possible to modify that service to make it more convenient or attractive to them.

Sometimes the researcher can select a major objective and some supporting objectives. An example is a study conducted for the U.S. Department of Defense to address the problem of declining strength of the National Guard and the reserve components such as the Army Reserve.[3] The research purpose was to determine what job characteristics (product dimensions) would increase the enlistment levels and the reenlistment levels of various demographic types. Job characteristics such as salary, fringe benefits, educational opportunity, travel, job image, and hair regulations were among the possible policy variables that could be adjusted. The overall objective of the study, to examine motivation factors in enlistment and reenlistment, led to several supporting objectives. The first of these was to measure young people's propensity to serve (or reenlist). The second was to determine current perceptions of the reserve in terms of 12 key attributes. The third was to determine the relative importance of the 12 key job attributes that could provide the basis for influencing young men and women to join and remain in the service.

The researcher will always try to make the research question as specific as possible. Suppose the research question as to which customer types use the various bank services could be replaced by the following research question: What are the lifestyle and attitude profiles of the users of credit cards, automatic overdraft protection, and traveler's checks? This increase in specificity would aid the researcher in developing the research design by suggesting whom to survey and what questions to include. The role of the research objective is to provide guidance to the research design. The more specific the research question is, the more practical guidance will be provided.

When a research question is set forth, it is sometimes difficult to realize that the question can and should be made more specific. The remaining two elements of the research objective—hypothesis development and the research boundaries—provide exercises to help the researcher make the research question more specific.

Hypothesis Development

A **hypothesis** is a possible answer to a research question. The researcher should always take the time and effort to speculate as to possible research question answers that will emerge from the research. In doing so, the fact that everyone already knows the answer sometimes becomes apparent. More often, the effort will add a considerable degree of specificity to the research question.

A hypothesis could speculate that sales are down in the Northeast because the level of competition has been abnormally high there during the past two months. Such a hypothesis provides considerable detail to a research question that asks what the problem is in the Northeast. It guides the research by ensuring that competitive promotions are included in the research design. One important role of a hypothesis is to suggest variables to be included in the research design—in this case, competitive promotion.

A research problem might be to estimate the demand for a new product. The hypothesis that the product will do well in the North but not in the South adds the concept of geographic location to the problem. It suggests that the sampling plan should include people from both regions. If the hypothesis suggests that the product will not do well in the South because it is not compatible with the Southern lifestyle, it becomes evident that the research should measure not only purchase intentions, but also how the product would be used.

Normally, there will be several competing hypotheses, either specified or implied. If all the hypotheses were known in advance to be true, there would be little reason to conduct the research. Thus, one objective of research is to choose among the possible hypotheses. A good illustration of the role of competing hypotheses is the problem faced recently by a satellite television company. A satellite TV company picks up TV and radio signals and "pipes" the high-quality signals directly into subscribers' homes via satellite. This company provided service to 75 percent of the households within its total service area. The problem facing the company was that there were several areas where the penetration rate was far below average. The population in these areas represented about 15 percent of the total service area. Bringing these areas closer to the average would improve profitability significantly. Before remedial action could be taken, however, it was necessary to establish the reasons for the low penetration. Various reasons were suggested by management, including the following:

1. Good television reception is available.

2. There is a very large transient population.

3. Residents have had poor previous experience with satellite service.

4. The price is too high, given the incomes in the area.

5. The sales force coverage has been inadequate.

6. A large percentage of the residents of the area are in age or social class groups that watch little television.

The challenge for the researcher is to devise a research approach that will gather information that can test each of these hypotheses. Hypotheses are not appropriate for all situations. As the upcoming discussions on exploratory research in Chapter 4 will make clear, there may be insufficient information for developing hypotheses. There are also times when the most reasonable hypothesis statement is simply a trivial restatement of the research question. For example:

RESEARCH

Question: Will the advertisement attract attention?

Hypothesis: It will attract attention.

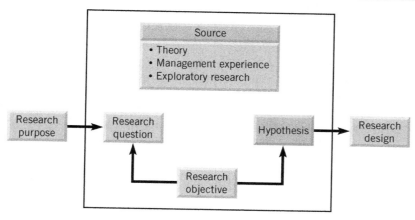

FIGURE 3.2
Hypothesis Development.

In such cases, the hypothesis will not add anything to the research and should simply be omitted. Hypothesis development should not be viewed as an item on a checklist to be quickly satisfied, but rather as an opportunity to communicate information and to make the research question more specific.

How does the researcher generate hypotheses? The answer is that whatever information is available is used to speculate on which answers to the research questions are possible and which are likely. The researcher can use three main sources of information to develop hypotheses, as illustrated in Figure 3.2. First, the researcher can draw on previous research efforts; in fact, it is not uncommon to conduct exploratory research to generate hypotheses for future large-scale research efforts. The research purpose might be deciding whether to conduct the large-scale studies.

A second source of hypotheses is theory from such disciplines as psychology, sociology, marketing, or economics. Thus, economic theory might suggest the importance of price in explaining a loss of retail sales. Marketing theory could indicate that distribution is important in predicting new-product acceptance. The use of attitude as a measure of advertising impact might be suggested by psychological theory.

A third and perhaps the most important source of hypotheses is the manager's experience with related problems, coupled with a knowledge of the problem situation and the use of judgment. This source is illustrated by the manufacturer who has discovered an unusual increase in selling costs. Past experience with similar problems, plus a preliminary investigation into the reasons for the problem, point to an increase in the proportion and number of small orders received. The tentative hypothesis is: Small orders (suitably defined) have increased in both number and proportion, and this increase, coupled with a higher cost of processing these orders, has raised selling costs. The research could then be directed at the questions of (1) the extent of increase in small orders (and the reasons for the increase) and (2) the additional unit costs involved in processing orders of different sizes.

Research Boundaries

Hypothesis development helps make the research question more precise. Another approach is to indicate the scope of the research or the **research boundaries**. Is the interest in the total population restricted to men, or to those on the West Coast? Is the research question concerned with the overall attitude toward the proposed new automobile, or is it necessary to learn customer attitudes about trunk space, handling, gas economy, styling, and interior appearance?

Much of the dialog between the researcher and the decision maker will be about clarifying the boundaries of the study. For example, a manager may wish to study the effects of the European Union's core industrial policy inspired by the Treaty on European Union, which came into force in 1993.[4] During the process of hypothesis development, the possible effects may be isolated. This still leaves a number of areas of ambiguity. What is meant by "condition"—profitability, competitive position in world markets, labor relations? How is the "industry" to be defined? What geographic areas are to be considered? What time period is to be appraised?

A final question of research scope regards the desired precision or accuracy of the results. This will, of course, depend on the research purpose. If a multimillion-dollar plant is to be constructed on the basis of the research results, a high degree of accuracy will be required. If, however, the decision involves the investment of a small sum in research and development on a new product idea, then a crude judgment as to the potential of the product would be acceptable.

Step 3—Estimating the Value of Information

Before a research approach can be selected, it is necessary to have an estimate of the value of the information—that is, the value of obtaining answers to the research questions. Such an estimate will help determine how much, if anything, should be spent on the research.

The value will depend on the importance of the decision as noted in the research purpose, the uncertainty that surrounds it, and the influence of the research information on the decision. If the decision is highly significant in terms of the investment required or in terms of its effect on the long-run success of the organization, then information may have a high value. However, uncertainty that is meaningful to the decision also must exist if the information is to have value. If the outcomes are already known with certainty, or if the decision will not be affected by the research information, the information will have no value.

To illustrate and expand on these concepts, consider the simplified examples in Figure 3.3. In case A, the decision to introduce a new product is shown as a decision tree. The first two branches represent the decision alternatives—to introduce the product or to decide not to introduce it. The second branch represents the uncertainty. Our descriptive model indicates that if the product is successful, a profit of $4 million will result. The indication is that there is a probability of 0.6 (obtained from prior experience) that the product will be successful. However, if the product is not successful, the profit will be only $1 million, an event that will occur with probability 0.4.

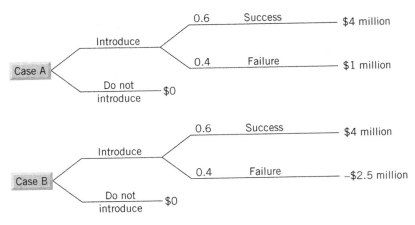

FIGURE 3.3
Illustrative Decision Models.

These subjective probabilities have been calculated based on prior knowledge of the situation. How much should we be willing to pay for perfect information in this case? If someone could tell us, in advance and with certainty, whether the product would be successful, how much would we pay for that information? The correct answer is nothing! The fact is that our decision would be the same regardless of the information. We would introduce the product, for even if the product were not well accepted, we would still make the $1 million. In this case, not only is the decision insignificant to the organization, it is nonexistent. There is only one viable alternative. Without alternatives there is no decision contest, even if uncertainty exists; therefore, there is no need for additional information.

In case B, the estimate is that if the product is not successful, a loss of $2.5 million will occur. Since the expectation of the new product's eventual performance is still, on balance, positive, the product would be introduced.[1] In this case, however, perfect information now would have value. If we knew in advance that the product would not be accepted, we would decide against introducing it and save $2.5 million. Since our best estimate of the probability of the product not being accepted is .4, the value of the information would be .4 times $2.5 million, or $1 million. Thus, if this decision contest could be repeated many times, perfect information would save us $2.5 million about 40 percent of the time and would save us nothing (since it would not alter our decision) about 60 percent of the time. On average, it would save us $1 million. By spending money on research, we might improve our knowledge of how the product will be accepted. But market research is unlikely to be as good as perfect information, and therefore, its value will be less than $1 million. Obviously, if the cost associated with an unsuccessful product were lower, or if the probability of an unsuccessful product were smaller, the value of information would be less. (The online Appendix to this chapter extends this example to include the possibility of using a concept test to predict whether or not the product will succeed. A method is developed to determine the value of the concept test to the decision maker.)

Planning a New HMO

To see how a research purpose and a set of research objectives are developed, let us join a meeting that took place at the Fraser General Hospital in September 2002.

The five doctors had a dilemma. They had spent a useful morning confirming that their hospital had the resources to operate a health maintenance organization (HMO). These resources were substantial, as would be expected in a big teaching and research hospital with a strong regional reputation. The concept of an HMO is explained briefly in Marketing Research in Action 3.4.

Leading HMOs are experimenting with the demi-science called "alternative medicine," hoping to cure ills when regular medicine fails. This is a startling trend. Many doctors still view some alternative methods with great skepticism—the word "quackery" is bandied about—and HMOs have a reputation for shunning all except the most reliable treatments. While most HMOs already offer chiropractic coverage, a number are adding acupuncturists and massage therapists, along with practitioners called naturopaths who use herbal remedies, relaxation therapies, yoga, and more. The health plans are offering to cover this care just as they do treatment by cardiologists and pediatricians.

The September 10, 2002, meeting was one in a long series of informal talks, investigations, and efforts to build support for the idea within the hospital. These efforts had brought the doctors to a critical point: Their problem was how to determine whether there was enough market demand in the region to support another HMO. Although each member of the planning group was

---

[1]The expected value of introducing the product would be $0.6(4M) + 0.4(-2.5M) = 1.4M$.

Marketing Research in Action 3.4

■ WHAT IS AN HMO?

There are two basic kinds of health coverage. The HMO is the best example of the prepaid group-practice type. This involves fixed monthly payments directly to a group of doctors or a clinic that is then responsible for all the health needs covered by the plan. The other type of coverage is the insurance type, which involves a company that collects premiums from subscribers, who can go to any clinic or doctor they choose. The insurance company pays for the services covered by the policy. In both cases, there may be limits to the coverage of such items as hospitalization, drugs, and office visits. The big drawback of the HMO is restriction of the choice of physicians and hospitals to those affiliated with the HMO. Generally, the total annual cost of an HMO to the consumer is lower than for group insurance plans. One reason is that the flat-fee formula discourages doctors from hospitalizing patients for longer than necessary. Also, the emphasis on preventative care produces fewer seriously ill patients.

---

convinced of the prospective benefits to the community, the hospital teaching program, and the bed utilization rate, they knew they needed persuasive evidence before the hospital trustees would provide start-up funds. After all, the trustees were even reluctant to approve funds for initial planning. What would it take before they would approve an initial investment in excess of $400,000?

The trustees were not the only hurdle. Each of the doctors in the HMO planning group knew at least one colleague who was openly skeptical because of the presence of competitive health-care programs. There was a well-established HMO about 8 miles away, plus several clinics operating on a fee-for-service basis. Many of the clinic doctors had privileges at the Fraser General Hospital.

At lunch, the planning group was joined by Herb Ellis, a partner in a local research and consulting firm. He had been invited by one of the doctors who knew him socially. During lunch, the doctors enthusiastically described the HMO concept, what it meant to subscribers—especially those on low incomes—and some of the innovations, such as consumer inputs to operations and procedures.

After lunch, John Akitt, a surgeon and the originator of the HMO proposal, reviewed some of the tentative decisions that would influence the market analysis. First, they intended to offer fairly comprehensive services from the beginning, including internal medicine, pediatrics, surgery, orthopedics, obstetrics, and gynecology. However, they were not sure whether they should also offer dentistry and optometry at an additional fee. Such an array of services was felt to be competitively necessary, but when combined with a high doctor–enrolled patient ratio to ensure a high service level, the result was very high fixed costs.

All the doctors agreed that one way to keep initial costs down was to concentrate on larger employer groups. This meant that a two-stage marketing effort would be required—first to get the employer to agree to offer the HMO plan as a subsidized benefit and then to persuade the employees to switch from their present health-care plan. The largest employer in the vicinity was the state university, 2 miles away, with over 13,000 faculty, staff, and married students who could join a health plan. The university's vice president of finance appeared committed to offering the HMO plan. There were three other large employers nearby, representing an additional 20,000 possible enrollees. However, they had been much less enthusiastic about offering the Fraser Hospital HMO as a benefit, and implied that they would not consider it until it had been operating successfully for a few months. This was upsetting to the doctors, for a sizable enrollment base had to be generated quickly if the HMO was to achieve its objectives. Still, if there was a significant adoption of the HMO within the university, they felt they could get close to the break-even target in the short run.

As the discussion progressed, Ellis realized that the extent and rate of acceptance of the HMO would depend on the marketing effort and the fee level. Marketing was a real problem, since solicitation of patients was, strictly speaking, unethical. This probably did not prevent personal selling and other communications efforts to explain the differences between fee-for-service and HMO plans. Pricing seemed to be a big factor; the prepaid feature of the HMO meant that prospective enrolled would see a bigger monthly salary bite, although over the long run total health costs would be lower. Since a large proportion of costs were fixed, a high enrollment target could help to lower fees. Otherwise, to lower fees, it would be necessary to reduce services, which would make the HMO less attractive. Without knowledge of the price sensitivity of the market, it would be hard to establish a fee structure. But who was the target market? On this the doctors had many conflicting opinions and the meeting became quite heated. Was the HMO concept most attractive to young families, older families with or without children, or enrollees in the competitive HMO? No one was sure just how big an area an HMO could serve. Although some existing HMOs attracted only people within a 10-mile radius of the hospital, there was a feeling that convenience and driving time were more important than distance.

At this point, Herb Ellis felt that he had some understanding of the doctors' marketing problems. Rather than discuss research approaches, he asked for another meeting at which specific research purposes and objectives could be discussed. These would be the basis for a research proposal. He already knew that a big constraint on his planning would be the available budget. There was no way that more than $10,000 could be found to finance marketing research, no matter what the economic value of the research information to the hospital.

Prior to his second meeting with the planning committee, Herb Ellis did some background reading on the HMO concept, talked to several doctors in private practice, and informally interviewed four members of the competitive HMO. With this background, he was ready to discuss preliminary research purposes and objectives, which could be used to guide the design of the study.

During the second meeting with the hospital planning committee, quick agreement was reached that the primary purpose of the study was to address the decision as to whether the proposal for an HMO should be pursued to the point of making major investments in its implementation. The following research objective consists of the research question and a statement of the study scope.

RESEARCH

Question: What is the demand for the new HMO?

Scope: Limited to students, staff, and faculty of the university.

The study was limited to university students, staff, and faculty for several reasons. First, the university administration was favorably disposed toward the plan, giving it the best chance of success in that environment. If support from that group was not in evidence, then the prospects would be dim in other organizations. Second, the budget limitation made it unlikely that any worthwhile research could be conducted with more than one organization. No geographic limits were placed on the study as it was thought that distance from the home to the HMO would have only a weak influence on individual interest in the proposed HMO.

Much more time was spent on developing the supporting purposes and objectives, with Ellis constantly challenging the usefulness of each proposed purpose and objective. Because of the tight budget constraint, he was fearful that overly ambitious objectives would be difficult to achieve with the alternative research designs he had in mind. Finally, the following set of supporting purposes and objectives was developed.

RESEARCH

Purpose: What target market segments should the HMO emphasize?

Objective: Identify the market segments most interested in the proposed HMO. Estimate their probable rate of utilization of medical services from their past medical experience.

Purpose: What services should be provided at what price level?

Objective: Identify the attributes or characteristics of health plans that would have the greatest influence on an individual's choice among alternatives.

During the meeting, a number of hypotheses were advanced as to who was most likely to be interested in the plan. Of course, they would have to express strong interest in the plan as described to them. In addition, good prospects would be those who were dissatisfied with the coverage or quality of their present plan, did not have a long-standing relationship with a family doctor, had favorable attitudes toward the Fraser General Hospital, and were not enrolled in other plans through their spouses. At the end of the meeting, the chairperson indicated a need for a proposal in time for the trustees' meeting on October 3. If the proposal was approved, they would need the results of the study no later than the first week in February.

The International Marketing Research Process

As we mentioned in Chapter 1, the basic functions of marketing research and the various stages in the research process do not differ between domestic and international research. The international marketing research (IMR) process, however, is much more complicated than the domestic research process. IMR is more complicated because of the necessity to ensure construct, measurement, sampling, and analysis equivalence before any cross-cultural study is conducted. A thorough research of the proposed international market is very important before launching a new product or service. Although it is complex, it can be an extremely beneficial process. To avoid high-profile mistakes in IMR, there are some considerations to be made:

1. Profile your target customers and clients.

2. Interview target segments to assess how well they match your preconceived ideas.

3. Hire local researchers who know the costs and methods that are workable in local markets.

4. Use a variety of methods to get a well-rounded picture of these proposed markets, the best approach being a combination of qualitative and quantitative methods that provides picture references, strength, beliefs, and anecdotes.

5. Look at the findings and analyze what must be done differently, abroad or internationally, in comparison with current domestic marketing activities.[5]

Thus, while conducting IMR, one should be aware of the complicated cultural differences in differing regions of the world. This complication stems from operating in different and diverse environmental contexts, ranging from the technologically advanced and stable United States to mature Western European markets, to the fast-changing environments in newly industrialized countries such as Hong Kong (part of China) and South Korea, to developing economies such as India and Brazil, to transforming economies such as the former Soviet Union and Eastern Europe, and to less developed countries on the African continent. Marketing Research in Action 3.5 illustrates the differences between the United States and Canada.

Marketing Research in Action 3.5

▨ ARE CANADIANS OUR COUSINS UP NORTH?

The United States and Canada are not only geographically neighbors but are also each other's largest trading partner. FTA, NAFTA, and interfirm trade explain most of the increasing trade between the two countries. Nearly 90 percent of the total Canadian population lives within 100 miles of the U.S. border. So, can a U.S.-based manufacturer treat the Canadian market as a mere extension of the domestic markets? Absolutely not! Despite their proximity and close ties, important differences exist between the two countries. These include demographic, economic, and cultural differences. For starters, as of June 2008, the Canadian population is about 33,212,696 (Canada Stats), or roughly about 11 percent of the U.S. population 303,824,640 (U.S. Census) for the same period. Interestingly, over 65 percent of the population is accounted for by two provinces—Ontario and Quebec. Ontario has a socialist government, which is pro-labor and imposes more restrictions on business than the provincial governments or the United States. The costs of doing business are, in general, higher in Canada. Bilingual labeling is required. Personal and corporate income taxes are higher, as are transportation and distribution costs and interest rates. Apart from these macro-level differences, there are differences in the way business is done. For example, offering a sales promotion, like a contest, entails special legal requirements that may vary from province to province.

The cultural differences are as important as the demographic, economic, political, and legal differences. More than 80 percent of the Quebec population uses French as its first language, and Quebec nationals are committed to sovereignty status. Canadians are extremely sensitive to environmental issues, and even municipal governments have strict local environmental ordinances. To make matters even more difficult, Canada uses the metric system!

Source: Updated and adapted from "Do Your Homework Before You Start Marketing in Canada," Marketing News, September 14, 1992.

Framing Research Questions in an International Environment

Problems may not always be couched in the same terms in different countries or cultural contexts. This may be due to differences in socioeconomic conditions, levels of economic development, or differences in any of the macroenvironmental factors.

Several academic scholars have identified and have pointed out the major reason for the failure of businesses and marketing research projects in a foreign environment. The result has been the *self-reference criterion* (SRC) adopted by researchers in defining the problem in a foreign country. SRC assumes that the environmental variables (cultural and others) that are prevalent in the researcher's domestic market are also applicable to the foreign country. This is a major cause for the failure of research projects, since defining the problem is the most crucial step in the marketing research process.

One of the most frequent objectives of IMR is **foreign market opportunity analysis**.[6] Marketing Research in Action 3.6 is a good example of international marketing research. When a firm launches international activities, information can be accumulated to provide basic guidelines. The aim is not to conduct a painstaking and detailed analysis of the world, but to gather information on questions that will help management narrow the possibilities for international marketing activities. Possible questions that an international marketing researcher might ask to achieve this objective include the following:

- Do opportunities exist in foreign markets for the firm's products and services?

- Which foreign markets warrant detailed investigation?

Marketing Research in Action 3.6

■ PILLSBURY PRESSES FLOUR POWER IN INDIA

The Pillsbury Doughboy has landed in India to pitch a product that he had just abandoned in America: plain old flour. Pillsbury's recent products sold in the United States have diversified from plain flour to frozen cookie dough and microwave pizzas. In India, however, selling packaged flour is almost revolutionary. This is due to the fact that most Indian housewives still buy raw wheat in bulk. They then clean it by hand, store it in huge metal hampers, and regularly carry some to a neighborhood mill, where it is ground between two stones.

Pillsbury is onto a potentially huge business. India consumes about 74 million tons of wheat a year (July 2001 est.), second only to China. (The United States consumes about 33 million tons, U.S. Census July 2001 est.) Much of India's wheat ends up as *roti*, a flat bread prepared on a griddle that accompanies almost every meal. In a nation where people traditionally eat with their hands, *roti* is the spoon. Nevertheless, less than 1 percent of all whole wheat flour is sold prepackaged. India's climatic extremes and bad road conditions make it difficult to maintain freshness from mill to warehouse, let alone on store shelves.

Starting a flour operation meant turning back the clock for Pillsbury. Though it was born as a U.S. flour-milling company 130 years ago, it exited from that business in the early 1990s to focus on products such as frozen baked goods and ice cream. Pillsbury thought of introducing high-value products when it first explored India. But it quickly learned that most Indians don't have enough disposable income for such fare. Pillsbury is betting that flour will generate enough sales volume to compensate for the razor-thin margin. Marketing managers climbed into the attics where housewives store their wheat and accompanied them to their tiny neighborhood flour mills. Pillsbury had hoped to establish contracts with existing mills, but inspectors found hygiene and safety at some properties to be compromising.

Many focus groups and lab tests later, Pillsbury came up with its packaged wheat blend, Pillsbury Chaki Fresh Atta. Responding to consumers' biggest concern, Pillsbury pitches the flour with a promise that *rotis* made from it will stay soft "for 6 hours." The company declines to say what ingredients keep the flour tasting fresh, though it says there are no artificial preservatives. The packaging is made of a robust plastic laminate that costs about two and a half times as much as the paper wrappers typically used in the United States.

According to recent studies, the size of the Indian food industry is estimated at $69.4 billion, of which the processed food industry accounts for $22 billion. The total Indian market for food processing equipment amounted to $1.2 billion in 1999–2000 and is estimated to increase to over $2 billion by 2005, with a predicted average annual growth rate of 15–18 percent over the next two years. The market is still minuscule, and gains will largely depend on how quickly Indian housewives embrace convenience. Several local companies familiar with Indian tastes have launched branded flour in recent years, only to flounder.

Source: Updated from article by M. Jordan, The Wall Street Journal, May 5, 1999, p. B1.

- What are the major economic, political, legal, and other environmental facts and trends in each of the potential countries?

- What mode of entry does the company plan to adopt to enter the foreign market?

- What is the market potential in these countries?

- Who are the firm's present and potential customers abroad?

- What is the nature of competition in the foreign markets?

- What kind of marketing strategy should the firm adopt?

Marketing Researach in Action 3.7 describes how the environment affects marketing a product, thereby emphasizing the need for market research before product introduction.

Marketing Research in Action 3.7

◼ TWO OF A KIND? ENVIRONMENTAL DIFFERENCES BETWEEN THE UNITED STATES AND THE UNITED KINGDOM

Lewis W. Griptight, Co., a baby products company based in the United Kingdom, experienced success with its new Kiddiwinks line of infant and toddler accessories and decided to introduce it to their counterpart, Binky-Griptight division, in the United States. Since American mothers prefer their kids to be well-groomed, a grooming set was added to the U.S. line.

Both U.S. and U.K. customers agree on the importance of safety and reject glass bottle products, despite their environmentally friendly and hygienic features. Despite the similarities, extensive marketing research discovered some subtle environmental differences between the United States and the United Kingdom. These differences (cultural and legal) made a huge impact on the way the product was introduced in the United States (and may trigger major changes in the British line).

One cultural difference concerned naming the product. Kiddiwinks, the British line, means "children" to consumers in Britain, but is meaningless to U.S. consumers. To prepare the product for the U.S. market, the company named the U.S. line "Binkykids" because of the consumers' high recognition and association of the Binky name with pacifiers.

Another difference dealt with cultural perception of kids' products and led to dramatic changes in color and packaging graphics. Conservative British mothers view kids' items as medical products and therefore prefer the symbolic white packaging of Kiddiwinks products. The Binkykids package, on the other hand, was given a more stylish look and "prominently features the line's signature green and lilac colors." Although American moms are very safety conscious, they still favor a more "flamboyant" or a "cute and cuddly" look.

A third difference related to safety regulatory matters. U.S. consumers like innovative products and Binky-Griptight introduced a pacifier, their flagship product, that plays lullabies when sucked on. However, this product would require redesign in the United Kingdom because of safety regulations.

For more interesting articles on marketing research go to http://www.marketingpower.com/ResourceLibrary/Pages/default.aspx.
Source: C. Miller, "Kiddi Just Fine in the U.K., but Here It's Binky," Marketing News, August 28, 1995, p. 8.

SUMMARY

The research process consists of a series of stages or steps that guide the research project from conception through to final recommendations. An overview of the domestic marketing research and the IMR processes was presented. This chapter discussed the research purpose and the research objective in detail. Chapter 4 will provide a discussion of the research design and implementation stages. Altogether, the two chapters will provide a structure for the rest of the book.

The specification of the research purpose involves, first, the identification of the decision involved, its alternatives, and the importance of its timing. Sometimes the decision is as general as: "Should our marketing program be changed?" In such cases, it is also useful to specify the problem or opportunity that is motivating the research or the environmental surveillance objective. The

purpose statement also should consider who the research users are. There are times when identifying the research users and understanding their decisions and motives can significantly improve the effectiveness of the research.

The research objective involves the identification of the research questions. The answer to an appropriate research question should be relevant to the research purpose, and the question should be as specific as possible. In particular, hypotheses should be developed whenever possible. The research boundaries specification is also part of the research objective statement.

Even at the early stages of research conceptualization, it is useful to consider what value the resulting information is likely to have. This exercise may lead to a decision to forgo the research, or at least make a judgment about the appropriate scale of the research project.

QUESTIONS AND PROBLEMS

3.1 Jim Mitchell, a high-profile businessperson, is considering running for state governor against a two-term incumbent. Mitchell and his backers do not want to enter the race unless there is a reasonable chance of winning. What are some research questions and hypotheses that, if answered, could help him make the decision?

3.2 At the beginning of Chapter 1, there are two examples of management information needs: Georgia Aquarium and Erlanger (Ky.) Police Department. Review each of these situations and develop an appropriate set of research purposes and objectives.

3.3 In the United Kingdom, cars are polished more frequently when the owners do not have garages. Is the lack of a garage a good variable for predicting sales of car polish? Are there other hypotheses that might explain this finding?

3.4 Can you think of additional research objectives for the HMO study?

3.5 You have been retained by a manufacturer of major appliances to investigate the probable color preferences for stoves and refrigerators in the coming year. What is the purpose of the research? Are there different purposes that might require different research approaches?

3.6 The president of a small chain of women's clothing stores was concerned about a four-year trend of decreasing profits. The stores have been characterized as being rather conservative over the years with respect to their product line, store decor, and advertising. They have consistently avoided trendy clothes, for example. Their market is now becoming extremely competitive because several aggressive fashion stores are expanding and are aiming at the young, fashion-conscious buyer. As a result of this competition and the disappointing profit trend, the president is considering making the product line appear less conservative and more oriented toward the young buyer. Before making such a risky change, the president feels it prudent to conduct some marketing research to learn the exact status of his chain. What should be the research purpose? Compose a set of research questions that would be helpful.

3.7 Explain the role of an information system. How would the possible role differ for Avon Products and Johnson Wax Company? (Refer to the Agree Shampoo example in Chapter 1 for background.)

3.8 Consider the example in Figure 3.1 in the Web Appendix to this chapter. What would be the expected value of perfect information if the loss would be $1 million instead of $2.5 million? How about if the loss would be $10 million instead of $2.5 million? What would it be if the probability of failure would be .2 instead of .4? Explain in words what is meant by the expected value of perfect information and what its implication is.

3.9 Consider the example in Figure 3.1 in the Web Appendix to this chapter. Determine the value of research information under the following situations:

(a) $Pr(Neg \mid F) = .9$ and $Pr(Pos \mid F) = .1$ and all else remains the same.

(b) $Pr(Pos \mid S) = .7$ and $Pr(Neg \mid S) = .3$ and all else remains the same.

(c) $Pr(Pos \mid S) = .9$, $Pr(Neg \mid S) = .1$, $Pr(Neg \mid F) = .9$, $Pr(Pos \mid F) = .1$.

3.10 ExoArt, Inc., a small U.S.-based manufacturer of exotic jewelry, feels that a market exists for its product in foreign markets. However, the company's managers have no experience in the international environment and do not know how to proceed in forming a marketing strategy for international markets. They have decided to contact a marketing research firm to help with the process. The researchers recommend a "foreign market opportunity analysis" as a starting point for the company's internationalization.

(a) What is the aim of a foreign market opportunity analysis?

(b) Which questions might a researcher ask to gather information for the analysis?

(c) What is the most probable cause of failure for a business or marketing research project in a foreign environment?

3.11 **(a)** Are there any differences between the basic functions of marketing research in a domestic environment and those in an international environment?

(b) Why is the international research process considered more complicated than the domestic research process?

3.12 Crystal-Clear Lens, Inc., a newly formed mail-order contact lens company, has struggled to obtain break-even sales after five years in the eyewear market. The company's founders felt that a high demand would exist for mail-order supply as a low-cost alternative to purchasing lenses at optical outlets. These retail outlets usually are within close geographic proximity to an affiliated optician. This allows customers to have their eyesight examined by the optician and then take the prescription to the optical outlet to purchase their eye-glasses or contact lens. Many retail outlets offer coupons that refund the cost of the eye examination upon the purchase of contact lenses and offer several free follow-up visits after the sale to check that the prescription has been made up correctly. The mail-order process requires customers to send in their prescription after the eye examination, whereupon the contact lenses will be supplied within two weeks of receipt of the order. The managers at Crystal-Clear Lens, Inc., have employed you as their marketing research consultant, to determine the reasons for the low sales.

(a) What would be the research purpose of this study?

(b) How does the research purpose differ from the research objective? Illustrate this difference in terms of the Crystal-Clear Lens example.

(c) What specific information would be required to achieve the research purpose? (That is, state the research question.)

(d) State some preliminary hypotheses to answer the research question.

END NOTES

1. L. D. Gibson, "Defining Marketing Prolems—Don't Spin Your Wheels Solving the Wrong Puzzle," *Marketing Research*, 10(1), Spring 1998, pp. 5–12.

2. Adapted from I. D. Canton, "Do You Know Who Your Customer Is?" *Journal of Marketing*, April 1976, p. 83.

3. "Conjoint Analysis of Values of Reserve Component Attitudes," a report prepared for the Department of Defense by Market Facts, Chicago, November 1977.

4. Europa: http://europa.eu/.

5. A. L. Stewart-Allen, "Do Your International Homework First," *Marketing News*, 33(1), January 4, 1999, p. 25.

6. Adapted from R. M. Czinkota and I. A. Ronkainen, *International Marketing*, 3rd ed., Orlando, FL: Dryden Press, 1993.

Case 3-1 | **A VideOcart Test for Bestway Stores**

The executives of Bestway Stores were intrigued with a proposal they had received from Information Resources, Inc., the developer of the VideOcart, to participate in a market test of the new point-of-sale technology. They were debating whether to agree to let IRI conduct a test in 3 of their 300 stores. Their reasons for doing it were not because they especially wanted to help IRI, but rather to learn about the benefits and shortcomings of this approach to in-store displays as a possible competitive weapon. As an input to the decision, the marketing research department was asked to design a study that would assess the desirability of deploying the new display technology in all their stores once the test was finished. The test was to last about 12 months.

How Does a VideOcart Work?

Here is what a consumer would find:

After a long day at work, you rush to the supermarket to pick up dinner. As you wheel a grocery cart down the aisle, an ad for Brand X coffee flashes on a liquid-crystal screen perched on your cart's handlebar. The ad reminds you that you need coffee, so you drop a can of Brand X into your cart and push on to the next aisle.

Much of what the Bestway Stores' management knew about the VideOcart came from a press conference. They learned that IRI would beam a commercial via satellite to a pick-up dish at each store. The signal would be sent out by a low-power FM transmitter to each cart and then stored in the memory of a computer located in the handlebar of the cart.

According to an IRI spokesperson,

The ads will be shown at breaks in an information and entertainment program for consumers and won't interrupt the program. The sequence of the ads shown will be determined by the route of the cart through the store.

As a shopper pushes a VideOcart down the aisles, the manufacturer's ads for brands on the shelves being passed at that moment will be "triggered" at a rate of about two per aisle (about 32 per store) and appear on the flat, 6-in. by 8-in. liquid-crystal display mounted on the handles of the cart. Tie-in promotion ads also will be able to be used—for instance, a hotdog bun ad when the cart is near the hot dogs.

Only about 15 percent of VideOcart's display time will be devoted to ads. The rest will be a friendly medium in which to display ads, including a continually changing video newsmagazine, news to create a new shopping experience, store specials and maps, trivia questions, and videogames to play while waiting to check out.

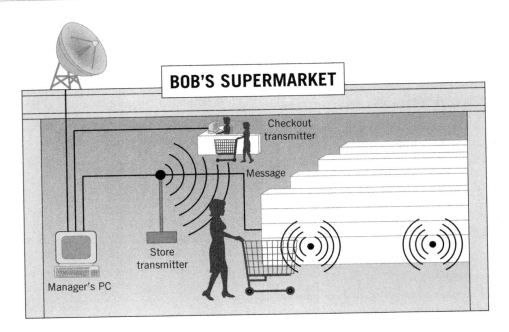

The video seen on the screen isn't television but will use attention-getting graphics created on a personal computer.

The Test of the VideOcart

Besides gathering sales data, the test markets will be used to perfect consumer programming and fine-tune the technology. IRI also will be checking on factors such as the ideal length of ads, shopper interest in games and information, how the shopper interacts with the unit, and opportunities for the grocers to contribute programming. VideOcart's computer capabilities also will offer supermarkets some advantages, including sounding an alarm if a cart is taken too far from the store, as in an attempt to steal it. The stores also could use VideOcart to transmit information such as the shortest checkout line, the next number up at the deli counter, or that a red Ford in the parking lot has its lights on.

We will put the needed equipment into the supermarkets—including a satellite dish on the roof—at no cost to the retailers and eventually will pay the supermarkets a royalty four to six times greater than they're now receiving from other shopping cart ads. We're not asking for an exclusive in the supermarkets, but we're out to make that other type of shopping cart ad irrelevant.

The VideOcarts will be designed to be weatherproof and childproof. The retailers will have to recharge the batteries on the carts each night.

The carts should be equipped for under $500 per cart. The average supermarket has about 100 carts and IRI would turn about 75 of them into VideOcarts, which we expect shoppers will seek out because they'll make shopping efficient and fun.

VideOcart will offer excellent media efficiency compared to other alternatives. Once national, the medium will reach 60 percent of all shoppers in a week at the cost per thousand of a free-standing newspaper insert—$4–$5 per thousand households.

VideOcart ads will be able to be created in a few hours and somewhat inexpensively using microcomputer graphics software. The learning curve to master the technology should be short and IRI will provide technical support and counsel.

THE ASSIGNMENT

The marketing research manager pondered about this project and wondered what really had to be learned to draw up a statement of purpose. With this in hand, the design of the research would be a lot easier. Time was short, for management needed to know how the research manager was going to get usable information. If it looked too difficult or expensive, they might not agree to a test in their stores.

| Philip Morris Enters Turkey

Under regulatory and legal fire in the United States, tobacco companies have been staking their financial futures in developing countries. In the seven years since Turkey abolished price controls that had propped up its state-owned tobacco company, Philip Morris has gotten millions of Turks to cast aside local cigarettes in favor of its Marlboro, Parliament, and L&M brands. For Philip Morris—which saw international tobacco profits grow 60 percent to $4.6 billion last year from 1994—nowhere has that push been more successful than in Turkey. In the nation that inspired the phrase "smokes like a Turk," 43 percent of the 62.9 million population smokes, according to government estimates, compared to 25 percent in the United States. Meantime, cigarette consumption in Turkey has increased at an annual rate of about 4.76 percent since 1992, making this one of the fastest-growing markets in the world. Philip Morris has watched its share of the Turkish cigarette market mushroom, to 23 percent in 1997 from 15 percent in 1995, while Tekel, the government-owned tobacco company, has seen its hold drop to 70 percent from 82 percent over the same period, according to figures provided by the Turkish government. Third-ranked R.J. Reynolds, with its Winston and Camel brands, says its share has grown to 7.3 percent from 2.9 percent.

Turkish smokers got their first taste of Philip Morris brands in the 1970s, when smuggled, tax-free American cigarettes began flooding local bazaars. But it wasn't until the early 1980s that the company was allowed to sell cigarettes in Turkey. Eager to raise Turkey's status in the West, then–Prime Minister Turgut Ozal decided to turn his rural country into a model of free enterprise. One of his targets: Tekel, the creaky state monopoly that has held exclusive rights to sell tobacco, salt, and liquor to Turks since the waning days of the Ottoman Empire.

How could Mr Ozal prod Tekel into the modern age? He announced in 1984 that foreign tobacco merchants would be allowed in Turkey for the first time since the days of the sultans.

But there was a catch: Tekel would continue to price and distribute all cigarettes both foreign and domestic. That advantage came in especially handy when Tekel in 1988 launched Tekel 2000, a cigarette blended with American tobacco leaves that it designed to compete with Marlboro. Priced about 25 cents lower than a standard 20-cigarette pack of Marlboros at the time, Tekel 2000 quickly won a quarter of the market.

Arguing that it couldn't survive in Turkey unless it had the right to price and distribute its own products, Philip Morris leveraged the one thing it had that the government badly wanted: millions of dollars to invest in the country. And it wouldn't invest that money unless Tekel gave up control.

Tekel eventually relented, and in May 1991, Philip Morris got the right to market, price, and distribute its own cigarettes, conditioned on a number of factors, including building its own factory. Philip Morris announced a joint venture with Sabanci Holding Inc., a local company, and poured $100 million to start construction of a factory in the southwestern city of Torballi. The factory opened in 1993; Philip Morris eventually expanded it into a $230 million facility capable of cranking out more than 28 billion cigarettes annually.

Supporting the idea that Philip Morris adjust its cigarette blends is a confidential 1992 report, titled "PM's Global Strategy: Marlboro Product Technology," conducted by researchers at rival B.A.T. Industries PLC's Brown & Williamson unit. "When Marlboro has been introduced into a market there is no evidence that initial offerings may be closer to that market's traditional taste," concludes the report that documents different Marlboro formulations in countries including Brazil, Britain, and Germany. "Over time PM will alter the product and introduce product technology more consistent with an overall Marlboro sensory character."

Philip Morris says it doesn't comment on speculation by competitors. The company says it strives "to ensure that Marlboros are as consistent as possible worldwide," but adds that some variation results from local regulations that limit constituents like tar or require the use of locally grown tobaccos. Beyond the taste difference, Tekel couldn't keep up when Marlboro's prices were cut. Although they still maintain Tekel 2000 was a success, Tekel executives announced that they want to sell the brand to a foreign competitor. Where Philip Morris really bested rivals is in marketing and distribution.

Questions for Discussion

1. Obtain information on the current consumption pattern of cigarettes in Turkey. How has this changed in the last 10 years? What kind of research should Philip Morris be doing to gain market share in Turkey?

2. What kind of information should Philip Morris obtain to decide on a marketing and distribution strategy in Turkey? How can Philip Morris obtain this information?

3. Is it ethical for Philip Morris to overtly alter the taste of its cigarettes over a period of time for its own profit?

Source: This case was prepared by V. Kumar and Rajkumar Venkatesan for the purpose of classroom discussion from "How Philip Morris Got Turkey Hooked on Marlboro," *Wall Street Journal*, September 1998.

Appendix for this Chapter is available on the Web.

Additional Case for this Chapter is available on the Web:

| Sperry/MacLennan Architects and Planners

4

Research Design and Implementation

LEARNING OBJECTIVES

- Discuss the definition and purpose of research design and describe the different types of research designs.
- Identify the appropriate data collection method for a given research design.
- Describe and briefly discuss the various sources of errors in a design.
- Discuss the concepts of budgeting and scheduling a project.
- Describe the elements of a research proposal.
- Describe the added complexities of designing a research process for international marketing decision making.
- Discuss the issues in international marketing research design.

A **research design** is the detailed blueprint used to guide a research study toward its objectives.

The process of designing a research study involves many interrelated decisions. The most significant decision is the choice of **research approach** because it determines how the information will be obtained. The chosen research should be flexible enough to accommodate decision-making systems that, in turn, would contribute to valuable marketing intelligence tools. Typical questions at this stage are as follows: Should we rely on secondary sources such as the Census? Which is more appropriate, an exploratory approach with group discussions or a survey? Is a mail, telephone, fax, or personal interview survey better for this problem?

Tactical research decisions are made once the research approach has been chosen. Here the focus is on the specific measurements to be made or questions to be asked, the structure and length of the questionnaire, and the procedure for choosing a sample to be interviewed. These tactical decisions are also constrained by time and budget availability, so before a study can be implemented, the estimated costs must be compared to the anticipated value.

To design something also means to ensure that the pieces fit together. The achievement of this fit among objectives, research approach, and research tactics is inherently an iterative process in which earlier decisions are constantly reconsidered in light of subsequent decisions. This may mean a revision of the research objectives as new insights are gained into the complexities of the population to be sampled, or a reassessment of the research approach in light of realistic cost estimates. Consequently, few researchers find that they have designed their research studies in the neat and linear fashion that is implied by Figure 4.1; however, this figure is a useful overview of major research design topics to be introduced in this chapter. Also in this chapter, we will discuss the research proposal as a vehicle for summarizing significant decisions made during the research design process.

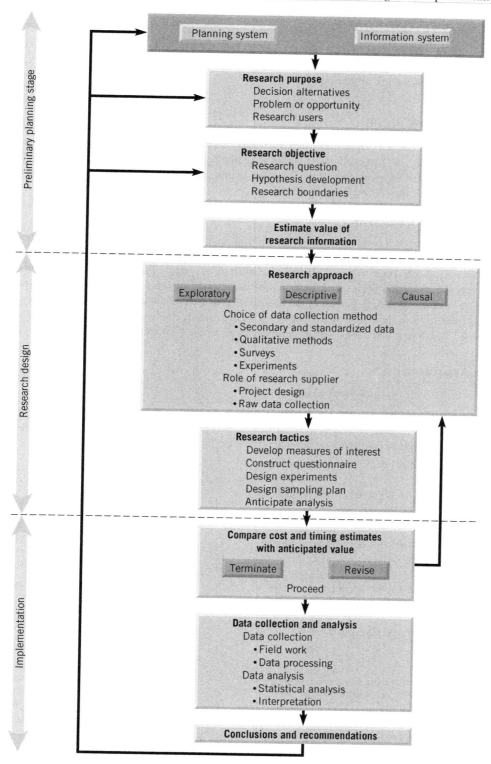

FIGURE 4.1
The Research Design Process.

Research Approach

The choice of a research approach depends on the nature of the research that one wants to do. In this section, the various types of research approaches, data collection methods, and the factors affecting their choice are discussed.

Types of Research

All research approaches can be classified into one of three general categories of research: exploratory, descriptive, and causal. These categories differ significantly in terms of research purpose, research questions, the precision of the hypotheses that are formed, and the data collection methods that are used.

Exploratory Research

Exploratory research is used when one is seeking insights into the general nature of a problem, the possible decision alternatives, and relevant variables that need to be considered. Typically, there is little prior knowledge on which to build. The research methods are highly flexible, unstructured, and qualitative, for the researcher begins without firm preconceptions as to what will be found. The absence of structure permits a thorough pursuit of interesting ideas and clues about the problem situation.

Exploratory research hypotheses are often vague and ill defined, or they do not exist at all. Table 4.1 illustrates this point with three examples. In the first example, the research question

Table 4.1　Three Research Approaches

Research purpose	Research question	Hypothesis
Exploratory research		
1. What new product should be developed?	What alternative ways are there to provide lunches for school children?	Boxed lunches are better than other forms.
2. What product appeal will be effective in advertising?	What benefits do people seek from the product?	The constructs are unknown.
3. How can our service be improved?	What is the nature of any customer dissatisfaction?	An image of impersonalization is a problem.
Descriptive research		
4. How should a new product be distributed?	Where do people now buy similar products?	Upper-class buyers use specialty stores, and middle-class buyers use department stores.
5. What should be the target segment?	What kinds of people now buy the product, and who buys our brand?	Older people buy our brand, whereas the young married are heavy users of competitors'.
6. How should our product be changed?	What is our current image?	We are regarded as being conservative and behind the times.
Causal research		
7. Will an increase in the service staff be profitable?	What is the relationship between size of service staff and revenue?	For small organizations, an increase in 50 percent or less will generate marginal revenue in excess of marginal costs.
8. Which advertising program for public transit should be run?	What would get people out of cars and into public transit?	Advertising program A generates more new riders than program B.
9. Should a new budget or "no frills" class of airfare be introduced?	Will the "no frills" airfare generate sufficient new passengers to offset the loss of revenue from existing passengers who switch from economy class?	The new airfare will attract sufficient revenue from new passengers.

Marketing Research in Action 4.1

◼ ONLINE RESEARCH COMMUNITIES

Traditional marketing research is of late increasingly spilling over into cheaper and noninvasive media such as the Internet. Companies such as Kraft Foods and Coca-Cola have created private online research communities to collect data on consumer shopping behavior. Other companies like Dell and MarketFoods have "democratized" innovation through active interaction and participation of consumers in online forums. These online communities are increasingly being viewed as collective and outsourced research and development hubs where consumer problems surface and innovative solutions are brainstormed.

asks what alternative ways there are to provide lunches for school children. It was precipitated by information suggesting problems with existing school lunch programs. In this case, there simply is no information that would suggest even the most tentative of hypotheses. In the second example, the research question is to determine what benefits people seek from the product. Since no previous research considered consumer benefits, it is difficult even to provide a list of them. In the third example, the hypothesis is advanced that a root cause of customer dissatisfaction is an image of impersonalization. However, this hypothesis is extremely tentative and provides at best only a partial answer to the research question.

Exploratory research is also useful for establishing priorities among research questions and for learning about the practical problems of carrying out the research. Marketing Research in Action 4.1 illustrates how various companies are using online surveys to conduct exploratory research to gain insight into consumers' lifestyles.

A variety of productive exploratory approaches will be discussed in Chapters 5 through 8, including literature reviews, individual and group unstructured interviews, and case studies.

Descriptive Research

Descriptive research embraces a large proportion of marketing research. The purpose is to provide an accurate snapshot of some aspect of the market environment, such as:

- The proportion of the adult population that supports the United Way.

- Consumer evaluation of the attributes of our product versus competing products.

- The socioeconomic and demographic characteristics of the readership of a magazine.

- The proportion of all possible outlets that are carrying, displaying, or merchandising our products.

In descriptive research, hypotheses often will exist, but they may be tentative and speculative. In general, the relationships studied will not be causal in nature. However, they may still have utility in prediction.

In the fourth example in Table 4.1, the research question concerns where people buy a particular type of product. One hypothesis is that upper-class families buy this type of product in specialty stores and middle-class families use department stores. There is no explicit cause–effect relationship. The question is simply to describe where people buy. With this hypothesis it is clear that if data are gathered, it will be important to include indicators of social class and to be prepared to analyze the data with respect to stores classified as specialty and department stores. Thus, the development of the hypothesis provides guidance to the researcher by introducing more detail to the research question. Similarly, in the sixth example, the hypothesis suggests that when image is being measured, it is necessary to include measures of innovativeness. Marketing Research in Action 4.2 provides an example of the outcome of descriptive research.

Causal Research

When it is necessary to show that one variable causes or determines the values of other variables, a causal research approach must be used. Descriptive research is not sufficient, for all it can show is that two variables are related or associated. Of course, evidence of a relationship

Marketing Research in Action 4.2

■ DOES COLOR MATTER?

In the soft-drink industry, Coke gave rise to Cherry Coke and Diet Coke. If flavor makes a difference in the drink, can colors do the same for cars? Research experts and color experts strongly agree. For new-car buyers, color and appearance are nearly as important as price. Automakers need to predict which color will be "hot" in the future and change 30 percent of their color offerings based solely on sales trends and the opinions of color experts. Since color is a subjective issue, consumers can't foretell their color choice far in advance of a purchase decision and tend to be trend-conscious.

Cooper Marketing Group conducts a nationwide consumer color preference study annually and devised a "color lifestyle" segmentation to identify the "movers and shakers in color." The group designed a series of psychographic statements for respondents to choose from, which concerned the influence of color on purchasing decisions, and came up with three clearly defined color personalities:

- The *color-forward* consumer likes to be the first to try a "new" color and is willing to spend more for a product in a fashionable color. Color-forward people tend to be women under 30 or over 50 or men under 30; city dwellers; impulse buyers; people who make less than $35,000 per year.
- *Color-prudent* consumers will buy a "new" color only after seeing friends try it. They often put quality ahead of color when choosing products. Color-prudent people tend to be men or women age 30–50; suburban; careful shoppers; people who make more than $50,000 per year.

- *Color-loyal* consumers replace a product with another of the same color and prefer safe colors such as blue or gray rather than fashionable colors. Color-loyal people tend to be men over 60; suburban or rural; people who dislike shopping; and may fall anywhere on the income spectrum.

The color-forward group represents a small, but highly influential, consumer segment. Color-prudent shoppers make up the bulk of the market. Color-loyalists are a small, highly predictable segment because they repeatedly buy the same color. This demographic data allows automakers to examine reasons behind color trends and is useful in advertising and product positioning.

Car manufacturers try to use color to establish brand character and distinguish themselves from their cousins or competition. Colors must not only be designed with consumer preferences in mind, they must also take into account the market segment and physical characteristics of each car. For example, "muscle" cars of the 1960s had colors that even Crayola's crayons don't include—"hemmy orange," "top banana," and "plum crazy"—and are a perfect example of the value color can bring to the marketing identity of a vehicle.

Consumers rank green as the hottest shade (19.4 percent), followed by white (18.1 percent), light brown (11.8 percent), medium red (10 percent), and black (5.7 percent) as researched by Dupont Automotive Company. According to Cooper Marketing group, consulting consumers on color preferences before deciding on "hot" colors is like taking 5,000 consumers into a boardroom meeting. This research can effectively counter influential executives who simply decide against a recommended color.

For more interesting articles on marketing research go to http://www.marketingpower.com/ResourceLibrary/Pages/default.aspx.
Source: Adapted from T. Triplett, "Carmakers Driven by Quest to Find Tomorrow's Color," Marketing News, August 28, 1995, p. 38; T. Triplett, "Research Probes How Consumers Rely on Color for Their Purchases," Marketing News, July 1, 1996, pp. 1, 39.

or an association is useful; otherwise, we would have no basis for even inferring that causality might be present. To go beyond this inference, we must have reasonable proof that one variable preceded the other and that there were no other causal factors that could have accounted for the relationship.

Suppose we had evidence that territories with extensive sales coverage, as measured by the number of accounts per salesperson, had higher per-capita sales. Are there sufficient grounds for a decision to increase sales coverage in areas where sales currently are weak? The answer would depend first on whether past increases in sales coverage had led to increases in sales. Perhaps the allocation of the sales force annual budget was based on the previous year's sales. Then we might conclude that past sales increases led to an increase in sales coverage—a conclusion with dramatically different implications. Second, we would have to be sure that there were no other reasons for differences in sales between territories. Perhaps the weak sales territories had special requirements because of climate differences, and our product was at a disadvantage; or perhaps the weak territories were served by competitors with local advantages. In either case, adding more salespeople to weak sales territories would not improve sales, for the basic problems still would be present.

Because the requirements for proof of causality are so demanding, the research questions and relevant hypotheses are very specific. The examples in Table 4.1 show the level of detail that is desirable. Marketing Research in Action 4.3 describes an application of causal research.

Marketing Research in Action 4.3

◼ IS EVERYDAY LOW PRICING LEADING TO EVERYDAY LOW PROFITS?

Over the past six months, Procter & Gamble has announced that 50 percent of its volume was on "value pricing"—its name for everyday low prices (EDLP)—and that it expects to save $175 million from the shift. But a new report from Salomon Brothers offers a more sobering picture of P&G's trendline at the checkout stand. In 10 of 11 household product categories it tracked, P&G's dollar market share in supermarkets fell in 1992. The million-dollar question now facing the retail industry is, "Should supermarkets adopt the EDLP strategy? Does the EDLP strategy provide greater profits over traditional pricing strategies?"

A group of researchers from the University of Chicago conducted an experiment to find answers to these questions. The researchers manipulated prices in 19 product categories in 88 stores of Dominick's Finer Foods, Inc., based in Chicago, and patronized by an estimated 1 million people each week. Some stores used the standard pricing approach, called "high–low" in the industry. Others were converted to everyday low pricing, in which prices were reduced and kept low. In their analysis of everyday low pricing, the researchers moved prices up and down 10 percent in the key categories—which included beer, cereals, cigarettes, detergents, frozen entrees, juices, and soft drinks—and accounted for 30 percent of an average store's sales. In stores with everyday low pricing in those categories, prices were dropped an additional 10 percent. In stores with a high–low strategy, prices were raised 10 percent to test consumer response.

The result: Stores featuring everyday low pricing rang up slightly more sales but much less profit than the high–low stores. Overall, profits in the categories that used everyday low pricing were about 17 percent below what grocers would have made with the traditional high–low approach, the researchers calculate. They attribute the difference to the higher profit margins on items that aren't on sale.

To find out more about other Procter & Gamble products go to http://www.pg.com.

Source: Adapted from J. Berry, "So How Is P&G's Share? Lagging, New Study Says," Brandweek, April 19, 1993, p. 16; R. Gibson, "Broad Grocery Price Cuts May Not Pay," Wall Street Journal, May 7, 1993, pp. B1, B8.

Detective Funnel

Each of the three types of research—exploratory, descriptive, and causal—has a distinct and complementary role to play in many research studies. This is most evident in studies that are initiated with this question: Why are our sales (share, patronage, and contributions) below our objectives or below last year's performance? The first step is to use exploratory techniques to generate all possible reasons for the problem (as shown in the drawing). Thereafter, a combination of descriptive and causal approaches is used to narrow the possible causes. Hence, the research is used in exactly the same way that a detective proceeds to eliminate unlikely suspects. Descriptive research evidence is often sufficient to filter out many of the possible causes.

For example, a municipal transit company, seeking to understand why ridership has declined suddenly, can quickly dispose of weather-related factors by examining weather records to see whether the recent weather pattern has been unusual. Similarly, evidence from customer records can be used to determine whether or not telephone complaints about the quality of service have increased. Also, their surveys of customers will reveal that service frequency and fares are the two most important factors in evaluating transit service, whereas riders are indifferent to the amount and type of advertising inside buses. If fares have not risen or the costs of competitive transportation modes such as car parking or operating costs have not declined, then attention can be focused on service frequency. Whether this is the causal factor depends on whether there was a reduction in frequency that preceded the decline in ridership.

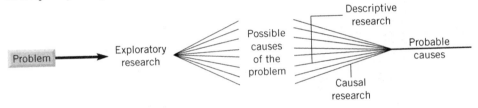

Data Collection Methods

The research designer has a wide variety of methods to consider, either singly or in combination. They can be grouped first according to whether they use secondary or primary sources of data. **Secondary data** are already available because they were collected for some purpose other than solving the present problem. Included here are (1) the existing company information system; (2) databanks of other organizations, including government sources such as the Census Bureau or trade association studies and reports; and (3) syndicated data sources, such as consumer purchase panels, where one organization collects reasonably standardized data for use by client companies. These secondary sources are discussed in Chapters 5 and 6. **Primary data** are collected especially to address a specific research objective. A variety of methods, ranging from qualitative research to surveys to experiments, may be employed. These methods are described in more detail in Table 4.2. Some methods are better suited to one category of research than another.

Because different methods serve different purposes, a researcher often will use several in sequence, so the results from one method can be used by another. For example, in investigating the potential for a new frozen dessert product, a researcher may begin by consulting secondary sources, such as Census statistics or industry trade association statistics, or by studying the performance of similar products that have been launched into the same market. Then qualitative research would be used to gain insights into the benefits sought by customers and into sources of dissatisfaction with the existing products. These tentative insights could be confirmed by telephone survey interviews of a representative sample of potential buyers. Finally, a controlled store experiment might be used to test the appeal of different packages. Data collection methods also

Table 4.2   Relationship between Data Collection Method and Category of Research

Data collection method	Category of research		
	Exploratory	Descriptive	Causal
Secondary sources			
Information system	a	b	
Databanks of other organizations	a	b	
Syndicated services	a	b	b
Primary sources			
Qualitative research	a	b	
Surveys	b	a	b
Experiments		b	a

a = Very appropriate method. b = Somewhat appropriate method.

vary depending on the managerial style and the culture of the organization. Marketing Research in Action 4.4 describes a method the Japanese use to collect data.

Choosing a Research Approach for the HMO Study

Seldom is a data collection method perfectly suited to a research objective. A successful choice is one that has the greatest number of strengths and the fewest weaknesses relative to the alternatives. Often, this is achieved by combining several methods to take advantage of their best features and minimize their limitations. This was what Herb Ellis had to do to get the amount of

Marketing Research in Action 4.4

▇ DATA COLLECTION—THE JAPANESE WAY

Cultural and individual preferences play a major role in determining the research technique and the method of data collection adopted for a given research project. U.S. managers, in general, prefer gathering large quantities of data through surveys, which provides numbers that can be manipulated statistically. In contrast, managers in Japan prefer the "soft" approach. For example, when Sony conducted a market survey to determine consumers' preference for a lightweight portable cassette player, results showed that consumers would not buy a tape player that did not have the recording function. Regardless of these results, Sony's chairman Akio Morita went ahead with his plans for introducing the Walkman, and the rest is history.

Sony's disdain for surveys and other scientific research tools that U.S. managers believe in is shared by other large Japanese consumer goods manufacturers such as Matsushita and Toyota. Of course, Japanese corporations do want accurate and useful information about their markets; they just go about it differently. Japanese-style market research relies heavily on two kinds of information: "soft data" obtained from visits to dealers and other channel members; and "hard data" about shipments, inventory levels, and retail sales. Japanese managers believe that these data better reflect the behavior and intentions of flesh-and-blood consumers.

For an article on Japanese data collection methods go to http://hbsp.harvard.edu/product/articles.
Source: Adapted from K. J. Johansson and I. Nonaka, "Market Research the Japanese Way," Harvard Business Review, May–June 1987, p. 16.

information required by the research objectives and still remain within the budget limit (see Chapter 3 for a discussion of HMOs).

From the beginning, it was clear that the overall research approach would involve preliminary qualitative research followed by a survey, to expose the concept of a health maintenance organization to a large representative sample and test the specific hypotheses. Ellis proposed to conduct two focus groups to establish the vocabulary used by the target respondents and the attributes they used to evaluate a health plan, as well as explore their knowledge and expectations of health plans and their reasons for past or prospective changes. The problem was deciding the kind of survey to conduct.

The principal survey options were mail questionnaires and personal or telephone interviews. Each, however, had a serious drawback. Personal interviews using trained interviewers were simply too costly and would have been feasible only with a sample that was too small to identify adequately the differences among the three segments. Telephone interviews would have been difficult to conduct, both because of the length of the questionnaire and the evident need for multiple-category questions, which are awkward to communicate orally. The questionnaire could have been administered by mail, but experience suggested that the response rates would be low unless substantial incentives and follow-ups were used.

The solution was a self-administered questionnaire, with door-to-door delivery and pickup by untrained survey assistants. The advantage of the telephone in reaching large samples economically was utilized both to establish contact and then to get agreement to participate. During the initial phone call, arrangements were made to deliver and pick up the questionnaire. Before the pickup, a reminder phone call was made to ensure that the questionnaire had been completed. In some instances the respondent was given a stamped, addressed envelope so the questionnaire could be returned by mail.

The research approach was successful in achieving a high response rate at a low cost per completed interview. The key to success was in matching the approach to the objectives of the study and the characteristics of the population, notably, the presence of an up-to-date listing, the limited geographic area to be covered, and the participants' inherent interest in the subject of the survey.

Research Tactics and Implementation

Once the research approach has been chosen, **research tactics** and **implementation** follow: the specifics of the measurements, the plan for choosing the sample, and the methods of analyses must be developed.

Measurement

The first step is to translate the research objective into information requirements and then into questions that can be answered by anticipated respondents. For example, one of the objectives in the HMO study is to estimate probable demand for the proposed HMO. This means that information will be needed on (1) the respondents' overall evaluation of the proposed HMO, (2) their preference for the proposed HMO relative to their present health plan, and (3) their likelihood of adopting the new plan if it becomes available. As we will see in Chapters 10–12, there are many ways to ask questions to obtain this kind of attitudinal information.

Once the individual questions have been decided, the measuring instrument has to be developed. Usually this instrument is a questionnaire, but it also may be a plan for observing behavior or recording data. The researcher designing an effective questionnaire must be concerned with how questions on sensitive topics such as income can be asked, what the order of the questions should be, and how misinterpretations can be avoided.

Sampling Plan

Most marketing research studies are limited to a sample or subgroup of the total population relevant to the research question, rather than a census of the entire group. The sampling plan describes how the subgroup is to be selected. One approach is to use probability sampling, in which all population members have a known probability of being in the sample. This choice is indicated whenever it is important to be able to show how representative the sample is of the population. Other critical decisions at this stage are the size of the sample, as this has direct implications for the project budget, and the means of minimizing the effect on the results of sample members who cannot be reached or who refuse to cooperate.

Anticipating the Analysis

When one is bogged down in the details of tactical research problems, it is easy to lose sight of the research objectives. Before actual data collection begins, the researcher must be alert to the possibility that the data will be inadequate for testing the hypotheses or will be interesting but incapable of supporting action recommendations. Once the data have been collected, it is too late to lament, "Why didn't we collect data on that variable?" or "Why didn't we foresee there wouldn't be enough respondents to test that hypothesis?"

With these concerns in mind, the researcher should plan in advance how each of the data items is to be analyzed. One useful device is to generate fictional (simulated) data from the questions in the measurement instrument. These simulated data can be analyzed to ensure that the results address the objectives. For example, a great deal of preliminary data analysis consists of cross-tabulating one question with a second question. Each of the anticipated tables should be reviewed in terms of its relevance to the research question. Any shortcomings identified now will help guide the changes to the questionnaire before it is sent into the field.

Analysis of Value versus Cost and Time Involved

At this stage of the design, most of the cost has yet to be expended, but the research is now completely specified and a reliable cost estimate should be available. Thus, a more detailed cost–benefit analysis should be possible to determine if the research should be conducted as designed or if it should be conducted at all.

One component of cost to be considered is the time involved. A research study can take six months or more. It may be that such a time period will delay a decision, thus creating the risk that a set of attractive conditions will be missed. For example, if the research designed to test a new product takes too long, a competitor may preempt the market with its own version of the product.

The analysis can conclude that either the research design is cost effective and should proceed or that it is not and should be terminated. Usually, instead of termination, consideration will be given to a revised research design that will be less costly. Perhaps a smaller sample could be used, or a laboratory experiment substituted for a field experiment. Throughout the whole research process, new information is uncovered that may make it useful to alter the purpose, the research question, the research approach, or some aspect of tactics. Indeed, it is much more accurate to think of the research process as a series of iterations and reconsiderations rather than an ordered sequence of well-defined steps. Marketing Research in Action 4.5 illustrates how firms are going after more budgets for marketing research.

Errors in Research Design

The usefulness of a research project depends on the overall quality of the research design and on the data collected and analyzed based on the design. Several potential sources of error can affect the quality of a research process. The errors can influence the various stages of the research process and result in inaccurate or useless research findings. Errors specific to each stage of the research process are mentioned in subsequent chapters. In Figure 4.2, we present an overview of the various types of errors that can affect a research design, with a brief description of each type. For a detailed description of the different types of errors, refer to the Appendix at the end of this chapter.

Budgeting and Scheduling the Research Project

Decisions regarding the allocation of resources—time, money, and human resources—form an important part of the planning for a research project. In any organization, there are constraints and limitations on the availability and use of resources. Given these constraints, budgeting and scheduling activities ensure that the resources are used effectively and efficiently. The cost–benefit analysis that precedes the research design phase gives management a preliminary idea of the value of a marketing research project. By comparing the expected research information with its anticipated costs—both time and money—management can decide whether a particular project

---

Marketing Research in Action 4.5

■ IT PAYS TO BE PRODUCTIVE

A 2007 survey by Aberdeen, a research and market intelligence company, revealed that Best-in-Class companies (those performing in the top 20 percent of all survey respondents) have instituted marketing performance strategies to showcase marketing's value to the organization and improve management's view to marketing decisions. Moreover, 33 percent of all companies surveyed recognize "proof of results for justification of next year's marketing budget" as a key driver for the adoption of new performance measurement capabilities.

Best-in-Class organizations showed significant performance improvements in comparison to Industry Average and Laggard companies in several areas over the previous 12 months. Specifically, the Best-in-Class companies achieved:

- A 9% mean increase in Return on Marketing Investment (ROMI) in the past 12 months.
- A 12% mean increase in new leads into the sales pipeline in the past 12 months.
- A 11% mean increase in customer cross-sell/up-sell opportunities in the past 12 months.
- A 10% mean increase in customer retention rate in the past 12 months.

The key to success for marketing organizations rests in improving marketing performance and identifying the drivers and detractors for performance. Further, with marketing performance becoming a key indicator for budget allocation, companies are now involved in identifying novel methods to make marketing activity more effective, efficient, and profitable.

Source: "Best-in-Class Companies Improve Marketing Performance Through Measurement Capabilities," Market Wire, BNET Publications, November 2007.

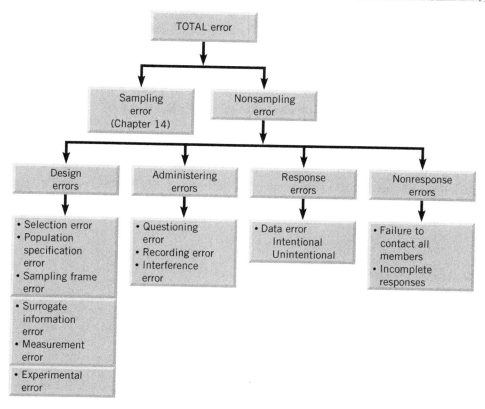

FIGURE 4.2
Errors in Research Design.

is worth conducting. After deciding that the benefits exceed the costs, we enter into the blueprint stage or the research design stage.

Two common approaches to budgeting for a marketing research project are estimating the dollar costs associated with each research activity or determining the activities to be performed, in hours, and then applying standard cost estimates to these hours. The former approach typically is used when a marketing research project is relatively unusual or expensive. The latter approach is used for routine marketing research projects or when the researcher has considerable knowledge of research activity costs.

Since certain research activities (most notably data analysis) cannot be initiated before other activities (data collection) are completed, research activities must be closely coordinated for a research project to be completed on time and within budget. Scheduling makes certain that appropriate personnel and resources are available to carry out the necessary research activities, so that the entire research process is completed as economically and efficiently as possible. One approach to scheduling is an activity flowchart, a schematic representation, or diagram that sequences the required research activities.

Scheduling helps marketing researchers answer a vital question: Who is responsible for accomplishing what research activity within what time period? This is a critical question for any marketing research project, for it not only allocates a person to a task but also provides a time frame within which the task is to be accomplished. Essentially, it identifies the personnel accountable for a particular task.

Several creative managerial techniques can be used for scheduling a research project. The most often used of these techniques are (1) the critical path method (CPM), (2) the program evaluation and review technique, (3) GANTT charts, and (4) graphical evaluation and review techniques.

The **critical path method** is a network approach that involves dividing the marketing research project into multiple components and estimating the time required to complete each component/activity. The **program evaluation and review technique** (PERT) is a probability-based scheduling approach that recognizes and measures the uncertainty of project completion times. **GANTT** charts are a form of activity flowchart that provide a schematic representation incorporating the activity, time, and personnel requirements for a given research project. An illustration of the use of a GANTT chart for a marketing research project is given in Figure 4.3. **Graphical evaluation and review techniques** (GERT) are essentially a second-generation PERT approach to scheduling, in which both the completion probabilities and activity costs to be built into a network representation are considered.

Research Proposal

A **research proposal** describes a plan for conducting and controlling a research project. While it has an important function as a summary of the major decisions in the research process, it is useful for a number of other reasons as well. Administratively, it is the basis for a written agreement or contract between the manager and researcher, as well as a record of what was agreed upon. As such, it provides a vehicle for reviewing important decisions. This helps ensure that all parties are still in agreement on the scope and purpose of the research and reduces later misunderstandings. Frequently, proposals are used to make a choice among competing suppliers and to influence positively the decision to fund the proposed study. For these latter purposes, a proposal should be

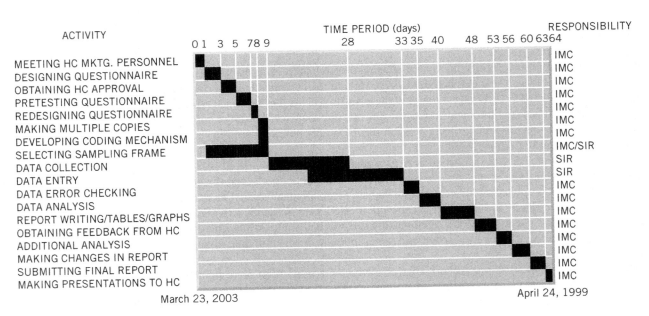

FIGURE 4.3
GANTT Chart for the 2003 Cingular Wireless.

viewed as a persuasive device that demonstrates the researcher's grasp of the problem and ability to conduct the research and also highlights the benefits of the study.

Like other communications, the structure and coverage of a proposal must be tailored to the situation. However, the following content outline has been used widely, as it ensures that likely questions will be anticipated.

Basic Contents of a Proposal

Executive summary: A brief overview of the contents of the proposal. This may be the only part some people read, so it should be sufficient to give them a basic understanding of the proposal.

Research purpose and objective: A description of the management problem, defining the information to be obtained in terms of research questions to be answered. This information must be related explicitly to the management problem.

Research design: Presents the important features of the research methods to be used, with justification of the strengths and limitations of the chosen method relative to the alternatives. All aspects of the research that might be elements of a contract should be discussed, such as sample size, quality control procedure, data collection method, and statistical analysis. Details of questionnaire format, sample selection procedures, and so forth should be confined to an appendix.

Time and cost estimates: All negotiated aspects, including total fees, payments, provisions, treatment of contingencies such as the clients' decision to expand or cancel the study, and the schedule for submission of interim, draft, and final reports.

Appendixes: Any technical matters of interest to a small minority of readers should be put at the back end of the proposal.

An example of a research proposal is given in Marketing Research in Action 4.6.

Designing International Marketing Research

As we explained earlier in Chapters 1–3, international marketing research is conducted to aid in marketing decisions in more than one country. Designing a research process for international marketing decision making is considerably more complex than designing it for a single country. Conducting research in different countries implies much greater attention to issues such as:

1. Understanding the nature and type of information sought

2. Defining the relevant unit of analysis

3. Formulating problems, variable specifications, and categories

4. Identifying and selecting sources of information

5. Availability and comparability of data

6. Achieving equivalence of samples and measures across countries and cultures

7. Identifying the degree of centralization of the research

8. Coordinating research across countries

9. Finding errors in the research design

10. Learning the cost of conducting research in multiple countries

Marketing Research in Action 4.6

■ A RESEARCH PROPOSAL TO CRYSTAL BANK

Research Purpose

The purpose of the study is to analyze various issues pertaining to the credit needs of consumers living in certain areas of Austin that have branches of Crystal Bank. Crystal Bank is focused on improving customer satisfaction and wishes to undertake a study to continue doing so. Specifically, the research objectives are to

- Gauge consumer sentiment on the services provided by various financial institutions;
- Identify areas of improvement among the services provided by the financial institutions;
- Determine the type of loans most requested for/needed by the consumers;
- Identify the important and attractive attributes of the different types of loans;
- Determine the types of lending institutions most popular with the consumers;
- Identify the important characteristics that make a lending institution attractive to the consumers; and
- Provide a demographic profile of the consumers.

Research Design

The survey research will be conducted by mailing a questionnaire to a total of 300 consumers living in the areas served by each of the 15 Austin area branches of Crystal Bank. The questions cover a wide range of issues including

- Identifying the types of accounts operated by the consumer, whether he or she is happy with the services;
- Obtaining likelihood of the respondent applying for a specific type of loan in the next 12 months;
- Determining the characteristics of the loan application and loan repayment that are important to the respondent;
- Identifying characteristics of the lending institutions which influence the respondent's choice; and
- Finally, it will seek demographic and lifestyle information about the respondents.

Sample Research Questions

Do you currently deal with a financial institution?

Yes   No

If Yes, what type of financial institutions do you deal with? (Check all that apply)

Savings and Loan   Bank

Credit Union   Other (Please specify _____)

Have you applied for any loan in the past five years?

Yes   No

If Yes, where did you apply for the loan? (Check all that apply)

Savings and Loan   Credit Union

Mortgage Company   Bank

Other (Please specify _____)

What type of loans did you apply for? (Check all that apply)

Home purchase   Automobile

Home repair/remodeling   Educational

Major appliance purchase   Personal

Other (Please specify _____)

Rank the following factors in decreasing order of importance, which will influence your choice of lending institution in applying for any loan. (1—Most important; 2—Second most important, and so on)

_____ Institution reputation   _____ Location of the institution

_____ Present relationship with the   _____ Level of service provided
institution

_____ Other (Please specify _____)

Sample Selection

The sampling procedure employed for the project will be stratified sampling, a technique widely used in such surveys. Stratified sampling ensures representation of consumers living near each of the 15 locations of Crystal Bank. The quality of the mailing list will determine the successful implementation of stratified sampling.

Data Collection

Telephone surveys will be used to gather information.

Statistical Analysis

Based on the type of scaled response, appropriate statistical methods will be used and inferences made. However, given the type of scales which will be used, a substantial part of the analysis will focus on frequencies, relative frequencies, and cross-tabulations.

Project Report

A written report will be submitted, and an oral presentation of the findings can be made by our firm.

Project Cost and Schedule

The project will be completed within a period of 12 weeks from the time the information requirements are provided by Crystal Bank to our firm. However, this is dependent on the assumption that the data collection process will be completed within a four-week period. The cost of the project is expected to be $10,000.00.

Marketing Research in Action 4.7 gives a brief synopsis of the pitfalls a researcher can encounter while conducting international marketing research.

Issues in International Research Design

Regardless of the basic research design selected (exploratory, descriptive, or causal), researchers need to be familiar with and experienced in handling several issues or problems unique to the conduct of marketing research within and across countries and cultural groups. Three issues

Marketing Research in Action 4.7

▉ A PRACTITIONER'S VIEW OF THE KEY PITFALLS IN CONDUCTING INTERNATIONAL RESEARCH

The key pitfalls to avoid when conducting an international marketing research project are as follows:

1. *Selecting a domestic research company to do your international research:* Only a handful of domestic research companies are both dedicated to and expert in international research. It is important that international projects be coordinated by a team whose sensitivity and knowledge of foreign markets will ensure a well-executed study. Emphasis should be placed on selecting a research company with a solid reputation and extensive experience in the design, coordination, and analysis of global research.

2. *Rigidly standardizing methodologies across countries:* Attempting to be consistent with a methodological approach across countries is desirable but, among other things, two key questions need to be asked in order to determine whether a particular methodology will yield the best results: (1) Does the culture lend itself to that methodology? For example, relationships in Latin America are based on personal contact. Hence, when

conducting business-to-business surveys, personal interviews, though expensive, are more efficient than telephone interviews. (2) Does the local infrastructure hinder the use of that methodology? For example, telephone surveys are very common in the United States, but in Russia, the telephone system is notoriously inefficient. For example, the Moscow office for *The Economist* conducted an informal study to determine how ineffective the phone system is. The office kept a log of international calls made in a 30-day period. A total of 786 calls were attempted, of which 754 resulted in no connection, 6 calls were cut off halfway through, and 2 were wrong numbers. Also, the cost of using this inefficient system is exorbitant. To install the phone costs $2,865; one year's service costs $485, and a 1-minute call from Moscow to London costs $3.30.[1]

3. *Interviewing in English around the world:* When conducting business-to-business research, even if the executives in the foreign country speak English, interviewing in English might result in inaccurate responses. Are the subjects comprehending the questions accurately and fully, or are there nuances to the question that are not being understood? Are their answers to open-ended questions without detail and richness due

to their apprehension about responding in a non-native language? Moreover, has their attention been diverted to a consideration of accents (theirs and/or the interviewer's) rather than the research questions at hand? Hence, even though translating the questionnaire may be costly and time consuming, it results in more accurate responses.

4. *Setting inappropriate sampling requirements:* Several country-specific variables influence the selection of appropriate sampling procedures in multicountry marketing research. For example, although random sampling is statistically the most reliable technique to use, it may be impractical in a given foreign market. Reasons may include the fact that in many of the less developed countries the literacy rate is very low. Hence, when sampling for surveys that require the respondent to be literate, random sampling might not work.

5. *Lack of consideration given to language:* Translations into the appropriate local languages need to be checked carefully. When possible, a quality control procedure of "back-translation" should be followed. The prime consideration is to ensure translation of the questionnaire so that there is equivalent meaning and relevance in all the countries where the project is being conducted.

6. *Lack of systematic international communication procedures:* One of the biggest problems of international research is communicating clearly with the local research companies. Do they understand the objectives of the study? Do they understand the sampling criteria? And do they understand what is expected from them? All too often, assumptions are made concerning the above issues that lead to major problems in the study's execution.

7. *Misinterpreting multicountry data across countries:* Analysis of the study's data must focus on the international market from which the data were gathered. Survey comparisons across countries should be made with the understanding of how the particular countries may differ on many key factors, including local market conditions, the maturity of the market, and the local competitive framework for the study category.

8. *Not understanding international differences in conducting qualitative research:* When conducting qualitative research such as focus groups, group discussions, and in-depth interviews, the researcher must be aware of the importance of culture in the discussion process. Not all societies encourage frank and open exchange and disagreement among individuals. Status consciousness may result in situations in which the opinion of one is reflected by all other participants. Disagreement may be seen as impolite, or certain topics may be taboo.[2] Also, in some countries, such as parts of Asia, mixed-sex and mixed-age groups do not yield good information in a consumer group discussion. Younger people, for example, often defer to the opinions of older people. If groups cannot be separated by age and sex, one-to-one interviews should be done.

For more information on CASRO go to http://www.casro.org.

Source: Adapted from D. Chandler, "8 Common Pitfalls of International Research," The Council of American Survey Research Organizations Journal, 1992, p. 81.

critical to international research design are (1) determining information requirements, (2) determining the unit of analysis, and (3) achieving equivalence of construct, measurement, sample, and analysis.[3]

Determining Information Requirements

In determining the information required for international marketing research, a primary consideration is the specific level and type of decision for which the research is being conducted. In general, the types of decisions fall into two broad categories—strategic decisions and tactical decisions. These two types differ significantly in their information requirements and the level in the organization structure where the decision making is done.

Global *strategic decisions* are made mostly at corporate headquarters, and they normally concern issues pertaining to foreign market selection, market entry, mode of entry, market expansion strategies, and decisions related to global standardization versus local adaptation of marketing-mix strategies. Such decisions involve the entire organization and determine the overall allocation of company resources across country markets. If a firm is involved in more than one product category, the decisions involve not only country markets but also product markets within countries. The information required for global strategic decisions is governed by the company's overall objectives and has implications pertaining to the company's long-term survival.

Tactical decisions, on the other hand, are concerned with micro-level implementation issues, and the information required for tactical decision making is obtained mostly from primary data. These decisions are concerned primarily with marketing-mix strategies in country/product markets—for example, what type of advertising copy would be effective in a given culture. The decisions are made at the functional or subsidiary level rather than at the corporate level.

Unit of Analysis

In conducting marketing research in more than one country, another major issue to be sorted out is at what level the analysis is to be done. Should it be done at (1) the global level, considering all countries simultaneously (a very complicated and seldom undertaken unit of analysis); (2) the regional level, considering groups of countries as being relatively homogeneous in terms of macroenvironmental factors (e.g., the European Union and the North American Free Trade Agreement countries can be considered regional trading blocs); (3) the country level, where each country is taken as a separate unit; or (4) similar segments across countries (a recent trend that is gaining popularity). In this last type of analysis, the researcher targets homogeneous segments having similar tastes and preferences, across countries.

Construct, Measurement, Sample, and Analysis Equivalence

While conducting research across national boundaries, it is important for the researcher to be able to compare data across countries. Hence, examining the various aspects of data collection processes and establishing their equivalence becomes a necessity. The following example illustrates the importance of equivalence issues in international marketing research. Initial data from a study conducted in Europe suggested that the percentage of Belgian women taking baths was far higher than for any other nationality. However, a closer look at the data revealed that the time period was not comparable. While women in Belgium were asked if they had taken a bath in the last seven days, in all other countries the question had been, "Have you had a bath in the last three days?"[4]

Construct equivalence deals with how both the researcher and the subjects of the research see, understand, and code a particular phenomenon. The problem confronting the international researcher is that, because of sociocultural, economic, and political differences, perspectives may be neither identical nor equivalent. The international researcher is constantly faced with the self-reference criterion problem and its implications in formulating a research design. Construct equivalence is concerned with the question: "Are we studying the same phenomenon in countries X and Y?" For example, in the United States, bicycles are used predominantly for recreation; in the Netherlands and various developing countries, they provide a basic mode of transportation. This implies that the relevant competing product set must be defined differently. In the United States, it will include other recreational products, whereas in the Netherlands, it will include alternative modes of transportation.

Measurement equivalence deals with the methods and procedures the researcher uses to collect and categorize essential data and information. Construct and measurement equivalence are highly interrelated. Measurement is the operationalization of the constructs to be used. Measurement equivalence is concerned with the question: "Are the phenomena in countries X and Y measured the same way?" For example, while Americans measure distance in miles, in most of the other countries of the world, it is measured in kilometers.

Because of sociocultural, economic, and political differences among or between countries, the international researcher faces two problems not encountered by the domestic researcher: (1) identifying and operationalizing comparable populations and (2) selecting samples that are simultaneously representative of other populations and comparable across countries. **Sampling equivalence** is concerned with the question: "Are the samples used in countries X and Y equivalent?" For example, children in the United States are legitimate respondents, because they exercise substantial influence in the purchase of cereals, toys, desserts, and other items, whereas in Asian cultures, it is the parent who decides most of these issues.

Regarding *analysis equivalence*, respondents from different countries have a tendency to choose either extreme scale points or middle values based on their cultural habits. Therefore, it may not be appropriate to compare the means of different scale items across countries; rather, some measure of deviation from the norm should be established. In other words, standard deviations may be better measures for comparison purposes.

Apart from these issues, other aspects of the research process, such as identifying sources of data, availability, and comparability of data from different countries, problems associated with primary data collection across countries, and so forth, add to the complexity of the international research process. Also, these issues add to the nonrandom error component of the research process. These issues will be dealt with in greater detail in subsequent chapters.

SUMMARY

In this chapter, the focus has shifted from the manager's problems and information needs—as expressed in the research purpose and objectives—to the strategic and tactical decisions that will achieve the objectives of the research approach. The various research approaches include qualitative research, surveys, observation, and experimentation. Tactical research design decisions include the choice of a research supplier, questionnaire development, the design of the experiment, the sampling plan, and the anticipation of data analysis. Implementation involves a final cost–benefit check, plus data collection, data analysis, and the development of conclusions and recommendations. Also, issues relevant to the design of international marketing research projects are discussed in this chapter.

An important distinction can be made among exploratory, descriptive, and causal research. Exploratory research, which tends to involve qualitative approaches such as group interviews, is usually characterized by ill-defined or nonexistent hypotheses. Descriptive research, which tends to use survey data, is characterized by tentative hypotheses that fall short of specifying causal relationships. Causal research, which tends to rely on experimentation, involves more specific hypotheses involving causal relationships. Possible sources of errors in research designs are presented, and the concepts of budgeting and scheduling a research project are discussed in some detail.

The major decisions during the research process are summarized in the research proposal. This step is essential to ensuring that the manager's problems have been translated into a research study that will help obtain relevant, timely, and accurate information—and not cost more than the information is worth.

QUESTIONS AND PROBLEMS

4.1 Is a research design always necessary before a research study can be conducted?

4.2 In what ways do exploratory, descriptive, and causal research designs differ? How will these differences influence the relative importance of each research approach at each phase of the marketing program development process described in Chapter 1?

4.3 What alternative research approaches should Herb Ellis consider for the HMO study? What are the strengths and weaknesses of the possible approaches?

4.4 A manufacturer of hand tools uses industrial supply houses to reach its major markets. The company is considering a new, automatic inventory-control procedure. How would you proceed with an exploratory study in advance of a larger study of the dealers' reactions to this new procedure?

4.5 What problems can you foresee in a test of the hypothesis that federal food stamps issued to low-income individuals are being used to supplement food budgets rather than replace former spending on food?

4.6 The problem of a large satellite TV company was described in Chapter 3 in the Hypothesis Development section. A number of hypotheses were offered by management to account for the poor penetration in several areas comprising 15 percent of the population of the total service area. If you were the researcher assigned to study this problem, how would you proceed? Specifically is the statement of purpose of the research adequate? What alternative research designs should be considered? Will one design be adequate to test all the hypotheses?

4.7 Smith Computers, Inc., a U.S.-based manufacturer of personal computers, has developed a microcomputer using the Pentium microchip technology, but at a fraction of the cost of its competitors. The company has an in-house marketing research department, and a study has been ordered to assist in developing the marketing program for this product.

(a) Which type of research would be most appropriate for this study?

(b) What are the possible errors that could be made in designing the research project?

(c) Scott Peters, the head of the marketing research department, must prepare a research proposal. Suggest a content outline that will ensure that all likely questions will be addressed.

(d) Peters has also been given the task of identifying foreign market opportunities for this product. What critical issues must be considered in formulating the research design?

4.8 What possible problems might be encountered by a domestic research company in conducting an international research study?

4.9 (a) How is a cost–benefit analysis useful to the management in deciding whether or not to conduct a marketing research study?

(b) What are the two approaches to budgeting for a market research project?

(c) For what situation is each approach most suitable?

4.10 Sugar Land Creamery is planning to launch a new flavor of ice cream and wants to get a "snapshot" of the potential market. The ice cream has a coconut-white chocolate flavor with mixed-in pistachios and is aimed at the premium market. What type of research design is appropriate? Develop the research purpose, research questions, and hypothesis.

END NOTES

1. "Hung Up," *The Economist*, July 20, 1991, p. 50.

2. R. M. Czinkota and A. R. Ilkka, *International Marketing*, 3rd ed. Orlando, FL: The Dryden Press, 1993, pp. 550, 551.

3. V. Kumar, *International Marketing Research*, Englewood Cliffs, NJ: Prentice-Hall, 2000.

4. C. Min-Han, B.-W. Lee, and K.-K. Ro, "The Choice of Survey Mode in Country Image Studies," *Journal of Business Research*, 29, February 1994, pp. 151–152.

APPENDIX

Errors in Research Design[1]

The total error in a research study is the difference between the true mean value (within the population) of the variable being studied and the observed mean value obtained through the research study. This error has two main components:

Sampling Error	Sampling error is the difference between a measure obtained from a sample representing the population and the true measure that can be obtained only from the entire population. This error occurs because no sample is a perfect representation of a given population, unless the sample size equals the population. This issue will be dealt with in greater detail in Chapters 14 and 15.
Nonsampling Error	Nonsampling error includes all other errors associated with a research project. There may be several different reasons for these errors, which can be broadly classified into four groups: (1) design errors, (2) administering errors, (3) response errors, and (4) nonresponse errors.

[1]Figure 4.2 provides a schematic diagram of the various types of errors possible in a research study.

Design Errors	Design errors, also called researcher-induced errors, are mainly due to flaws in the research design. There are several different types of design errors.
Selection Error	Selection error occurs when a sample obtained through a nonprobability sampling method is not representative of the population. For example, if a mall interviewer interested in shopping habits of the visitors to the mall avoids interviewing people with children, he or she is inducing a selection error into the research study.
Population Specification Error	Population specification error occurs when an inappropriate population is chosen from which to obtain data for the research study. For example, if the objective of a research study is to determine what brand of dog food people buy for their pets, and the research draws a sample from a population that consists predominantly of cat owners, a population specification error is induced into the study.
Sampling Frame Error	A sampling frame is a directory of population members from which a sample is selected. A sampling frame error occurs when the sample is drawn from an inaccurate sampling frame. For example, if a researcher interested in finding the reasons why some people have personal computers in their homes selects the sample from a list of subscribers to PC World, he or she is inducing a sample frame error into the study.
Surrogate Information Error	Surrogate information error is the difference or variation between the information required for a marketing research study and the information being sought by the researcher. The famous (or rather infamous) New Coke taste tests are a classic example of surrogate information error. The researchers in that case were seeking information regarding the taste to New Coke versus Old Coke, but the study should have determined consumer's attitudes toward a change in the product and not just their taste preferences.
Measurement Error	Measurement error is the difference or the variation between the information sought by a researcher for a study and the information generated by a particular measurement procedure employed by the researcher. Measurement error can occur at any stage of the measurement process, from the development of an instrument to the data analysis and interpretation stage. For example, if a researcher interested in the individual income of the respondent words the question as annual household income, a measurement error is being induced into the research study.
Experimental Error	An experiment is designed to determine the existence of any causal relationship between two variables. Any error caused by the improper design of the experiment induces an experimental error into the study.
Data Analysis Error	Data analysis error can occur when the data from the questionnaires are coded, edited, analyzed, or interpreted. For example, incorrect coding of data or a wrong use of a statistical analysis procedure can induce a data analysis error into the study.
Administering Errors	All errors that occur during the administration of a survey instrument to the respondents are classified as administering errors. They are caused by mistakes committed by the person administering the questionnaire. They may be caused by three major factors.
Questioning Error	This error arises while addressing questions to the respondents. If the interviewer does not word the question exactly as designed by the researcher, a questioning error is induced.
Recording Error	This error arises from improperly recording the respondent's answers. If the interviewer misinterprets the response or hears it inaccurately, this induces a recording error into the study.
Interference Error	This error occurs when an interviewer interferes with or fails to follow the exact procedure while collecting data. For example, if the interviewer fabricates the responses to a survey, it induces an interference error.

(continued)

Response Errors	Response errors, also called data errors, occur when the respondent—intentionally or unintentionally—provides inaccurate answers to the survey questions. This might be due to the respondent's failing to comprehend the question or it may be due to fatigue, boredom, or misinterpretation of the question. Response errors can occur when a respondent who is unwilling or embarrassed to answer a sensitive question provides an inaccurate or false response.
Nonresponse Errors	Nonresponse errors occur if (1) some members of a sample were not contacted, and hence their responses were not included in the study; or (2) some of the members contacted provide an incomplete or no response to the survey instrument. The primary reasons for this error occurring include the unwillingness of respondents to participate in the study and the inability of the interviewer to contact the respondents.

Case 4-1 | Reynolds Tobacco's Slide-Box Cigarettes

There is *a* tendency for management to think of marketing research as an expense, perhaps a necessary expense, but an expense nevertheless. With corporate attention being focused more and more on the bottom line, one question is often asked: "What is the impact of current or potential new activities on profit?" This case focuses on how marketing research can aid in decision making and enhance the bottom line.

To give you some basic understanding of the business situation, the cigarette industry is very mature. Many big opportunity areas for product differentiation have already been thoroughly explored and mined by the major manufacturers. There are different product attributes, ranging from different flavors(menthol and nonmenthol), to different "tar" levels (full flavor, light/low "tar," ultralow "tar"), to different lengths (king size to 120 mm), and even different circumferences (superslims to wide circumference). Imagery is another means of differentiating products, so there are upscale cigarettes, masculine cigarettes, feminine cigarettes, and so on. Finally, price is another important dimension differentiating brands. Combining all these methods of differentiating products results in literally hundreds of types of cigarettes available to smokers, ranging from superslim, ultralow-tar 120s in a box to traditional nonfilter 70-mm cigarettes.

With this in mind, you would think that there are few new ideas under the sun for tobacco manufacturers. That may be, but ideas that have the potential to draw business from competition and increase one company's share of the market are constantly being examined.

One such new idea was a brand that R.J. Reynolds Tobacco Co. (RJR) had in test market. This new brand was developed to capture Marlboro smokers with imagery that was more sociable and had more appeal to both male and female adult smokers than Marlboro's traditional solitary cowboy image. From a product standpoint, the new brand's smoothness was emphasized in contrast to the rich flavor emphasized in Marlboro advertising. Marlboro's conventional crush-proof box has always been a key feature of the brand. Rather than offering the new brand in an identical packaging configuration, Reynolds Tobacco's R&D department developed a slide-box, a unique configuration that operated something like a matchbox. This feature was intended as yet another point of difference to attract Marlboro smokers to the new brand.

Concept product test results of the new brand (Table 4.3) in a conventional crush-proof box, versus the slide-box, indicated that the slide-box would enhance the new brand's appeal among prospect smokers.

When Reynolds management saw these results, they said, "If this slide-box is better than the conventional crush-proof box, we shouldn't just limit it to a new brand that may or may not make it out of the test market. To really capitalize on the apparent appeal of the slide-box, we should put it on our established products." The direction to put it on established brands is not as clear as it may sound at first blush. There were several questions to be resolved: Which brands? Which styles of which brands? Should the slide-box replace any current conventional crush-proof box, or should it be an additional offering? How would a slide-box launch fit in with other planned programs? How big an announcement should this be? (All media forms? Point-of-sale advertising only?) Should pack graphics be redesigned to emphasize the change, or should they just be translated from existing graphics? How much volume would the slide-box generate and, therefore, how much new equipment would need to be purchased?

Given the excitement over this proposition, tentative plans were made regarding which brands would use the

Table 4.3 Concept Product Test Results

	Conventional crush-proof box	Slide-box
Positive purchase interest	56[a]	64
Intended frequent use	<u>59</u>[a]	<u>68</u>
As usual brand	20	24
Occasionally	39	44
Package increased purchase interest	<u>51</u>[a]	<u>73</u>
Increased a lot	27	53
Increased a little	24	20
Overall positive taste rating	72[a]	80

[a]Significant at 80% confidence level or greater.

slide-box, volume projections were calculated, and equipment was ordered. The long equipment lead time provided time to resolve some of the key questions surrounding the slide-box. The most critical question was which brand or brands should use the slide-box. The issue here was one of image compatibility, that is, whether the inherent image of the slide-box was compatible with the current or desired image of the brand. Another critical question was what was its source of appeal. If it was indeed a better package, what were specific benefits that could be advertised to prospect smokers?

A good deal of what marketing researchers do is implement standardized methodologies to answer recurring marketing questions: How does a product compare to competition? How effective is this new ad campaign? How appealing is this premium? The issues and questions surrounding the slide-box were new, so the marketing research department developed a custom research design that they felt would generate required consumer input on the slide-box.

The research was designed with two objectives. The first objective was to determine which of RJR's major established brands has an image consistent with the image projected by the slide-box; and the second objective was to determine the degree of interest in this new slide-box packaging among each of these brands' prospect smoker groups. In designing the study, they knew that they needed to analyze the data by each brand's prospect group. So they designed the sample in two phases. First, a large random sample of adult smokers was drawn. Then additional interviews were conducted to give them large enough bases of specific types of smokers. As a result, the sample for the study consisted of 767 adult smokers, 600 of whom were

selected randomly, and an additional 167 interviews to fill out specific prospect group quotas.

Given the sample size and the fact that RJR wanted representation across the country, the marketing research department conducted personal interviews in 20 geographically dispersed markets during June 1991. The biggest challenge in designing this research was to evaluate the image of the packaging itself without allowing any influence of the image of any brand. Hence, they showed smokers a sample of the packaging without any graphics. Further, since they wouldn't be able to evaluate people's responses to the slide-box packaging in a vacuum, they also showed them prototypes of current packaging, that is, conventional crush-proof box and soft pack, also without any graphics. This provided benchmarks to help them interpret the results.

They agreed that there are two aspects of packaging on which the packs should be evaluated: benefits of the packaging itself (such as protecting the contents and being easy to open or close), and the image of the types of smokers who would use such packaging (such as white-collar versus blue-collar). They showed respondents prototypes of each of the three types of packaging attributes and user imagery. Importantly, each smoker interviewed was given a fresh prototype and allowed to open it. After they had obtained this information, they then had each of the brands in their study rated on these same user characteristics.

Finally, they asked the smokers in their study directly how appropriate the three types of packages were for the brands of cigarettes included in their study. The order in which all packs and brands were presented was rotated to avoid any order bias. The results of the overall evaluation of packs are given in Table 4.4.

The outcomes of the perception studies are illustrated in Figures 4.4–4.6.

The researchers found that the slide-box had functionality problems as compared to the conventional crush-proof box. It was seen as having cosmetic advantages, such as being attractive, modern, being in its own case, and having an edge over the conventional crush-proof box. And, once opened, hard to keep closed. Thus, the cigarettes were more apt to fall out. The slide-box was also seen as less convenient to use. And importantly, the slide-box was perceived to be more gimmicky than the conventional crush-proof box. It is important to note that although these problems were pervasive, in that all target

Table 4.4   Overall Evaluation of Packs

	Slide-box pack (%)	Conventional crush-proof box (%)	Soft pack (%)
Favorable	60	70	42
Unfavorable	26	8	26

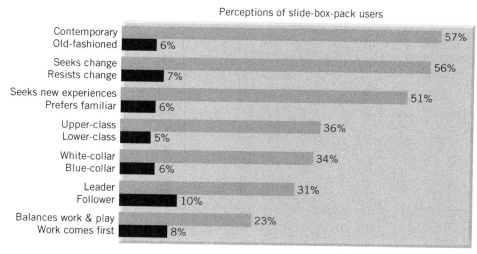

FIGURE 4.4
Perceptions of Slide-Box-Pack Users.

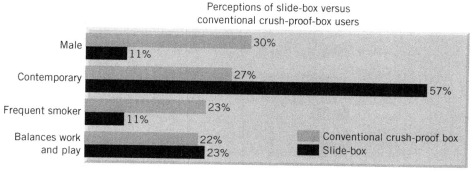

FIGURE 4.5
Perceptions of Slide-Box versus Conventional Crush-Proof-Box Users.

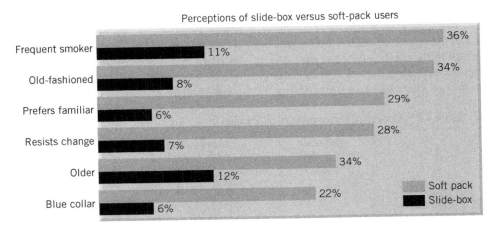

FIGURE 4.6
Perceptions of Slide-Box versus Soft-Pack Users.

Table 4.5   Appropriateness of Packs of Cigarette Brands

	Percent saying extremely/very appropriate				
	Established brand A	Established brand B	Established brand C	Established brand D	Most often brand
Slide-box	32	47	49	39	48
Conventional crush-proof box	55	64	51	62	73
Soft pack	61	44	39	55	44

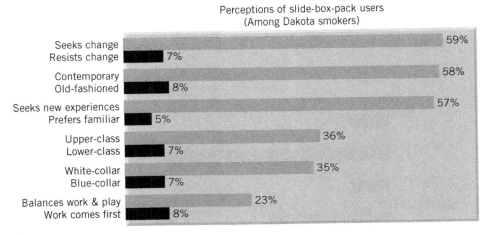

FIGURE 4.7
Perceptions of Slide-Box-Pack Users (among New Brand Smokers).

groups felt this way, it was conceivable that these pack problems might go away as smokers became more experienced with using this configuration.

It was also important that the user image of the slide-box was, with one exception, not felt by respondents to be compatible with the user imagery of the brands for which the pack was being considered. The analysis found that only one of the established brand's prospect group was most likely to find the slide-box as appropriate for the brand as the conventional crush-proof box and to believe that brand's smokers and slide-box users share many similar characteristics. Both groups were pictured as white-collar, upper-class women seeking changes and new

experiences. The only inconsistency was that respondents perceived the slide-box user as European. Their image of the slide-box user was more consistent with their image of their current brand than their image of the conventional crush-proof-box user.

The results of the appropriateness of packs of cigarette brands are presented in Table 4.5.

The new brand was not included in this national study, as it was only in test market at this time. However, the new brand's prospect group did not rate the slide-box as highly overall as they rated the conventional crush-proof box. Figure 4.7 provides the differences in perception of slide-box-pack users among the new-brand smokers.

Questions for Discussion

1. Why are the results of the second study different from the first?

2. Based on these findings, what is your recommendation to the company?

Source: This case was adapted with permission from a case originally written by H. D. Murphy and M. E. Brownell, "How Research Can Save Your Company Time and Money!: A Case Study," *The Council of American Survey Research Organizations Annual Journal*, 1992, pp. 107–112.

Cases for Part I

Nature and Scope of Marketing Research

Case I-1 ||| Clover Valley Dairy Company

In the fall of 1978, Vince Roth, General Manager of the Clover Valley Dairy Company, was considering whether a newly developed multipack carrier for yogurt was ready for market testing and, if so, how it should be tested.

Since 1930, the Clover Valley Dairy Company had sold, under the trade name Valleyview, milk, ice cream, and other milk by-products—such as yogurt, cottage cheese, butter, skim milk, buttermilk, and cream—in Camden, New Jersey. The raw milk was obtained from independent farmers in the vicinity of Camden and was processed and packaged at the Clover Valley Dairy.

Clover Valley's sales had grown steadily from 1930 until 1973 to an annual level of $3.75 million. However, between 1973 and 1977, a series of milk price wars cut the company's sales to $3.6 million by 1977. During this time, a number of other independent dairies were forced to close. At the height of the price wars, milk prices fell to 75 cents per half-gallon. In the spring of 1977, an investigation of the milk market in Camden was conducted by the Federal Trade Commission and by Congress. Since then, prices had risen so that Clover Valley had a profit for the year to date.

Clover Valley served approximately 130 grocery store accounts, which were primarily members of a co-operative buying group or belonged to a 10-store chain that operated in the immediate area. Clover Valley no longer had any major chain accounts, although in the past they had sold to several. Because all three of the major chains operating in the area had developed exclusive supply arrangements with national or regional dairies, Clover Valley was limited to a 30 percent share of the Camden area dairy product market.

Although Clover Valley had a permit to sell its products in Philadelphia, a market six times the size of Camden, management decided not to enter that market and instead concentrated on strengthening their dealer relationships. In addition, it was felt that, if a price war were to ensue, it might extend from Philadelphia into the Camden area.

With the healthier market and profit situation in early 1978, Clover Valley began to look for ways to increase sales volume. One area that was attractive because of apparent rapid growth was yogurt. During the previous three years, management had felt that this product could help to reverse Clover

Valley's downward sales trend, if given the correct marketing effort. However, the financial problems caused by the loss of the national grocery chains and the price war limited the firm's efforts. As a result, Mr Roth felt that Clover Valley had suffered a loss of share of yogurt sales in the stores they served.

Since 1975, Mr Roth had been experimenting with Clover Valley's yogurt packaging with the hope that a new package would boost sales quickly. All dairies in Clover Valley's area packaged yogurt in either 8-oz or 1-lb tubs made of waxed heavy paper. Clover's 8-oz tub was about 5 in. high and $2\frac{1}{2}$ in. in top diameter, tapering to $1\frac{3}{4}$ in. at base.

The first design change to be considered was the use of either aluminum or plastic lids on the traditional yogurt tubs. However, these were rejected because the increased costs did not seem to be justified by such a modest change. Changing just the lid would not make their tubs appear different from their competitor's tubs, it was felt.

By 1976, Mr Roth had introduced a completely different package for Clover Valley's yogurt. The 8-oz tubs were replaced by 6-oz cups, designed for individual servings. In addition, the new cups were made of plastic and had aluminum foil lids. The 1-lb tubs were unchanged. No special promotional effort was undertaken by Clover Valley, but unit sales of the new 6-oz cups were more than triple the unit sales of the old 8-oz tubs (see Exhibit 4.8). While the increased sales volume was welcomed, the new plastic cups increased unit packaging costs from 7.2 cents to 12.0 cents. This more than offset the saving of 4 cents because of the reduction in the amount of yogurt per container. Retail prices were reduced from 41 cents to 34 cents for the new 6-oz cup, while the price for the 1-lb tub remained at 75 cents. The increased sales then increased the total dollar contribution to fixed costs from yogurt by only 5 percent. (All dairies priced their yogurt to give retailers a 10 percent margin on the retail selling price. Competitor's retail prices for their 8-oz tubs remained at 41 cents.)

Exhibit I.1   Clover Valley Dairy Company: Sales Results

	1974	1975	1976	1977	1978
Unit Sales of Yogurt—8-oz Tubs (6-oz after June 1977)					
January		1,203	3,531	7,899	18,594
February		996	3,651	7,629	20,187
March		960	3,258	6,677	20,676
April		853	3,888	6,081	20,199
May		861	4,425	5,814	18,420
June		915	4,044	12,726[a]	14,424
July		978	3,546	13,422	16,716
August		1,254	3,696	15,105	16,716
September		1,212	3,561	23,601	18,657
October	1,740	1,485	4,731	23,214	
November	1,437	2,928	4,499	22,146	
December	1,347	3,528	6,177	17,916	
Unit Sales of Yogurt—1-lb Tubs					
January	3,882	3,715	3,937	3,725	2,971
February	4,015	3,596	3,833	3,510	3,232
March	4,061	3,670	3,285	3,344	2,866
April	3,573	3,405	3,333	3,503	3,392
May	3,310	3,482	3,609	3,101	2,390
June	3,252	3,376	3,366	3,537	2,094
July	3,383	3,366	2,837	3,827	2,589
August	3,721	3,307	2,616	3,103	2,384
September	3,415	3,275	2,729	2,871	2,895
October	3,276	3,450	2,816	3,028	
November	3,865	4,650	3,375	2,796	
December	4,110	3,908	3,386	3,086	

[a]6-oz tubs.

Mr Roth felt that both the change to plastic and the convenience of the smaller size were responsible for the increased sales. However, he was disappointed with the high packaging costs and began to look at ways of reducing them, without changing the package much further. He felt another package change would be too confusing to consumers. Because of the economies of scale needed to produce plastic containers, costs could be reduced if more units were produced and sold. Mr Roth felt that packaging a number of cups together would make the 6-oz cups easier to carry home, which might increase sales, and would certainly reduce packaging costs.

By 1978, work had begun on developing a multipack holder to hold six cups together. A single strip of aluminized plastic would serve both as holder and as the top for two rows of three yogurt cups. A single cup could be readily separated from the others in the pack. Dairy personnel constructed wooden models of several different cups for use with the holder and with plastic-molding experts, choosing one that would mold easily and cheaply. Eventually, some of these carriers were made to order for testing in the plant and among Clover Valley employee families.

Several problems soon became apparent. The holder did not always fasten securely to all six cups in the multipack. While the holder strip was being put on, the side walls of the cups were slightly compressed, causing some cups to crack at the edges. When consumers tried to remove one of the cups, they sometimes pulled the top from an adjacent cup. The problem was the strength of the aluminized plastic, which made it difficult to tear even when perforated.

The multipack was redesigned and again tested in the plant and by employee families. It appeared that the new package was performing satisfactorily. Negotiations with Clover Valley's carton supplier resulted in an estimated price of 8.5 cents for the first 100,000 units. Thereafter unit costs would drop to 7.5 cents per 6-oz cup.

Mr Roth decided that the best multipack carrier presently possible had been designed. His attention then turned to methods of testing the new packs for consumer acceptance. Mr Krieger, his father-in-law and president of Clover Valley, sent him the following letter concerning market testing:

Dear Vince,

Concerning the market test of the new cups and carriers, I have a few suggestions that may be helpful, although the final decision is yours. I think we should look for a few outlets where we are not competing with the other dairies, perhaps the Naval Base or Bill's Market. Actually, if we use Bill's, then the test could be conducted as follows:

1. *Give Bill a special deal on the multipacks for this weekend.*

2. *In the next two weeks, we'll only deliver the multipacks and no single cups at all.*

3. *In the third week we'll deliver both the packs and the single cups.*

4. *During the third weekend we'll have someone make a survey at the store to determine its acceptance.*

5. *Here is how it could be conducted:*

   a. *Station someone at the dairy case.*

   b. *After the shoppers have chosen either single cups or the multipacks, question them.*

   c. *If they chose the multipacks, ask them why.*

   d. *If they chose the single cups ask them why they didn't buy the packs.*

   e. *Thank them for their help and time.*

Yours,
CHARLES KRIEGER
   (signed)

Questions for Discussion

1. Should the new multipack carrier be tested?

2. If a test is judged necessary, what should be the criteria for success or failure?

3. How useful is the proposed test in addressing the management problem? What changes, if any, would you recommend?

Additional Case for this Chapter is available on the Web:

Web Case 4-1 ||| California Foods Corporation

5

Secondary Sources of Marketing Data

LEARNING OBJECTIVES

- List the various secondary data sources.
- Discuss the uses of secondary data.
- List the benefits and limitations of secondary data.
- Describe the internal sources and forms of secondary data.
- Explain the value of demographic, economic, and social statistics contained in census data.
- Explain the importance of the North American Industry Classification System.
- Discuss how to appraise secondary sources.
- Describe applications of secondary data.
- Discuss the sources of secondary data used in international marketing research.
- Explain the problems associated with secondary data in international marketing research.
- Discuss applications of secondary data in domestic and international marketing research.

The previous chapters identified many data sources. Marketing intelligence can also be gathered by linking and cross-analyzing existing database information. Many research organizations now have vast stores of information in their databases that cover customer behavior over time. These only suggest the vast array of possibilities that can literally submerge the manager and researcher in numbers. The real problem with this data explosion is not the quantity but the variability of the sources with respect to quality, availability, cost, timeliness, and relevance to the needs of the decision maker. In this chapter, we begin the task of identifying and assessing the data that answer the decision maker's specific questions.

One of the hallmarks of a competent marketing researcher is familiarity with the basic sources pertaining to the market being studied, coupled with sensitivity to their respective strengths and weaknesses. This means that time will not be lost in an aimless search for nonexistent data, and neither time nor money will be wasted on a premature decision to go into the field to obtain the data.

Figure 5.1 shows the principal sources available to a researcher who is responding to a research question or considering what data to collect in order to anticipate future information needs. This chapter deals with externally available *secondary sources*, for which the specification, collection, and

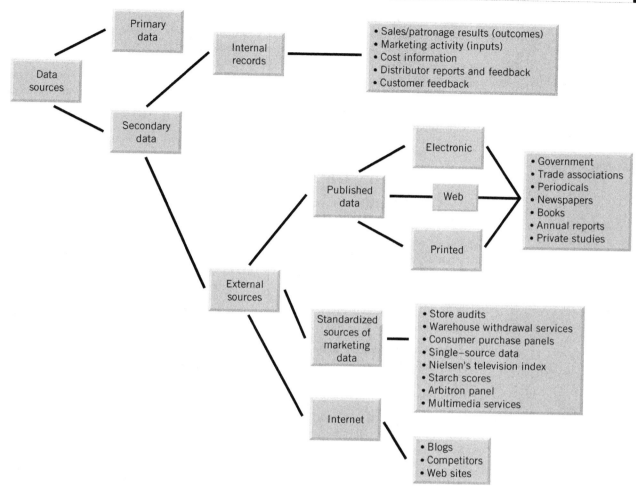

FIGURE 5.1
Sources of Secondary Data.

recording of the data were done for another purpose by someone other than the user. We will take a particularly close look at census data, because it is so fundamental to understanding all aspects of a market economy. This becomes evident when census data are used to analyze market demand. We will also look at **standardized data** (Chapter 6), which are collected especially for a set of information users with a common need. Standardized data are both purpose-specific and expensive, but still much cheaper than having each user do it singly. Often, the immediate and unique needs of a decision maker require collecting original, or **primary data**, which is the topic of the rest of the book.

Secondary Data

Secondary data are data that were collected by persons or agencies for purposes other than solving the problem at hand. They are one of the least expensive, quickest, and easiest means of access to information. Hence, the first thing a researcher should do is search for secondary data available on the topic. The amount of secondary data available is overwhelming, and researchers have to locate and utilize the data that are relevant to their research. Most search procedures follow a distinctive pattern, which begins with the most available and least costly sources. Figure 5.1 shows the various sources of secondary data. The order from top to bottom corresponds roughly to the order in which the alternative sources should be considered, or to the likelihood of that type of data being incorporated into the marketing information system. That is, almost all information systems initially are based on routinely collected internal data and expand through the inclusion of data from published and standardized sources.

Uses of Secondary Data

Secondary data can be used by researchers in many ways. In this section, we look at the various ways in which it can be used.

1. Secondary data may actually provide enough information to resolve the problem being investigated. Suppose a marketing researcher needs to know the income of households in a particular market area; all he or she has to do is to look into the appropriate Census Bureau report.

2. Secondary data can be a valuable source of new ideas that can be explored later through primary research.

3. Examining available secondary data is often a prerequisite to collecting primary data. It helps to define the problem and formulate hypotheses about its solution. It will almost always provide a better understanding of the problem, and its context frequently will suggest solutions not considered previously.

4. Secondary data are of use in the collection of primary data. Examining the questionnaires, methodology, and techniques employed by other investigators in similar studies may be useful in planning the present one. It may also suggest better methods.

5. Secondary data also help to define the population, select the sample in primary information collection, and define the parameters of primary research.

6. Secondary data can also serve as a reference base against which to compare the validity or accuracy of primary data. It may also be of value in establishing classifications or baselines that are compatible with past studies so that trends may be more readily analyzed.

Benefits of Secondary Data

The most significant benefits secondary data offer a researcher are savings in cost and time. Secondary data research often involves just spending a few days in the library or on the Internet extracting the data and reporting them. This should involve very little time, effort, and money compared to primary research. Even if the data are bought from a standardized data source, it will turn out to be cheaper than collecting primary data because the cost of data collection is shared by all those using the data.

Certain research projects may not be feasible for the firm; in such cases, recourse to secondary data will be the only solution. For example, if a firm needs some information on the entire population of the United States, it will be neither physically nor financially possible for the company to obtain it. Historical data are always secondary data. If a firm wants to obtain information on something that happened in the past, it cannot conduct primary research to obtain it.

In some cases, secondary data can be more accurate than primary data. For example, if a company wants information on the sales, profits, and so forth, of other companies, it can get more reliable and accurate information from government-released sources, trade associations, or general business sources than from the companies themselves.

Limitations of Secondary Data

Despite the many potential benefits of secondary data, they also have a number of limitations. By definition, secondary data are data that were collected in the past for purposes other than the current research. Hence, problems of fit sometimes occurs between the data required for current research and the available data. The available data may have a different unit of measurement from what is required. For example, consumer income can be measured and reported at the individual, family, or household level. Even assuming that the data use the same unit of measurement, there still may be differences in the class definitions. For example, if the problem demands classification of income of individuals in increments of $10,000 ($0–$10,000, $10,001–$20,000, etc.), it does not help the researcher if he or she gets data where it is classified in increments of $7,500 ($0–$7,500, $7,501–$15,000, etc.).

The researchers have no knowledge of how the data were collected, nor do they have any control over it. Therefore, they do not know anything about its accuracy or its bounds of error. They must make a number of assumptions before they can use it for actual analysis. It is also very difficult to evaluate the accuracy of the data already collected because one can gauge its accuracy only by assessing such research characteristics as the methodology used or evidence of conscientious work. In many cases, the secondary data may not be sufficient to meet the data requirement for the research at hand. In these cases, researchers may have to use primary research.

Secondary data may be outdated and hence cannot be used in current research. Data about attendance at theaters five years ago will probably be irrelevant to determine the type of motion pictures to be produced next spring because motion picture preferences continually change. Another problem frequently faced by researchers using secondary data is one of publication currency. The time from data collection to data publication is often long; hence, the data are outdated even when they are first available. An example is the government census, which takes three years to be published. The benefits and limitations of secondary data are summarized in Table 5.1.

Finally, when using secondary data, it is important to always go back to the original source. By doing so you can determine who collected the data, why it was collected, how it was collected, and when it was collected. The answers to these questions are important since they help you better understand the quality of the data. Also, by knowing who collected the data, you have the ability to contact that source and find out more about the study.

Table 5.1   Benefits and Limitations of Secondary Data

Benefits	Limitations
1. Low cost	1. Collected for some other purpose
2. Less effort expended	2. No control over data collection
3. Less time taken	3. May not be very accurate
4. Sometimes more accurate than primary data	4. May not be reported in the required form
5. Some information can be obtained only from secondary data	5. May be outdated
	6. May not meet data requirements
	7. A number of assumptions have to be made

Internal Sources of Secondary Data

Internal Records

A company's **internal records**, accounting and control systems, provide the most basic data on marketing inputs and the resulting outcomes. The principal virtues of these data are ready availability, reasonable accessibility on a continuing basis, and relevance to the organization's situation.

Data on *inputs*—marketing effort expended—can range from budgets and schedules of expenditures to salespeople's call reports describing the number of calls per day, who was visited, problems and applications discussed, and the results of the visit.

Extensive data on *outcomes* can be obtained from the billing records on shipments maintained in the accounting system. In many industries, the resulting sales reports are the single most important items of data used by marketing managers, because they can be related (via exception reporting methods) to plans and budgets to determine whether performance is meeting expectations. Also, they may be compared with costs in order to assess profitability.

New developments in information technology that tie customers more tightly to suppliers are improving the timeliness and depth of the sales information available to managers. For example, American Hospital Supply has supplied hospitals with computers so that hospital order entries go directly to the sales department, where they are stored in a computer and can be immediately accessed and analyzed for trends and transaction details. Salespeople at Wrangler Womenswear can connect their portable computers to the corporate computer to send and retrieve messages, enter orders, and receive up-to-date sales information.

Using Internal Data Effectively

Many diagnostic studies potentially can be undertaken with various combinations of internal and external data to address such questions as the following:

- What is the effect of marketing inputs (number of sales calls or types of distribution channels) on outcomes such as profitability and unit sales within regions or sales territories?

- Is our sales performance within key market segments or types of retailers improving or deteriorating?

- Are current sales and marketing expenditures above or below the levels set in the annual budget and sales plan?

Such insightful analyses, however, often are thwarted because of limitations in the accounting system and distortions in the data.

The first problem is that accounting systems are designed to satisfy many different information needs. As a result, the reporting formats frequently are rigid and inappropriate for marketing decisions. Often, the accounting data are too highly aggregated into summary results and are not available for key managerial units, such as geographic areas, customer types, or product types. Efforts to break down sales and profitability data by different units may involve special, time-consuming studies. It is also possible that production, sales, and profit figures are each measured in slightly different time frames, which are all at variance with external data such as bimonthly store audit data.

A second problem is the quality of the data found in the internal records. On the input side, the reports of salespeople's call activities may be exaggerated if they are being evaluated on this basis. Indeed, the well-known optimism of salespeople may unconsciously pervade all the data from this source. Accounting data are not exempt from such problems. The usual interpretation of a sales invoice is compromised if liberal return privileges are permitted or if the product is purchased at one location but delivered to or used in another. In general, whenever there is a long distribution channel, with several places where inventories can be accumulated, the data on orders received or invoices billed may not correspond to actual sales activity.

Customer Feedback

Increasingly, companies are augmenting their internal records with systematic compilations of product returns, service records, and customer correspondence, in a manner that permits easy retrieval. Responding to the voice of the customer has become critical in order to maintain or increase market share in today's competitive environment.[1] Complaint letters are being used as sources of data on product quality and service problems. One reason is the insight they can provide into the problems of small groups with unusual requirements, reactions, or problems. For example, a premarket skin abrasion test of a new talc-based bath powder uncovered no problems, but the complaint letters that poured in shortly after the reformulated product was introduced revealed serious problems among a small group with sensitive skin.

Complaint letters, however, present an incomplete and distorted picture. People who write such letters are not typical clients or customers. They are most likely to be highly educated, articulate, and fussy, with more than average amounts of free time. A letter of complaint is actually a rather infrequently used method of resolving dissatisfaction; instead, people are more likely to switch brands, shop in a different store, or complain to their friends. Manufacturers are almost completely cut off from knowledge of customer unhappiness because most complaints are voiced to retailers and there is little systematic feedback from retailers to manufacturers.

Customer Database

Many companies have started to build customer databases on their own. A customer database is raw information on the customer that can be sorted and enhanced to produce useful information. Records of frequent customers and their transactions are maintained, and the companies use this data to find out what is common among its customers. This data can also be used to find out about customers' product preferences, form of payment, and so on. Holiday Inn has created a customer database for its Priority Club members in order to track their activities and transactions with regard to the company.[2] These customer databases are now being used extensively by marketing managers for formulating relationship marketing strategies and to determine the actual value of a customer (CLV). This is discussed in greater detail in the final chapter of the book.

External Sources of Secondary Data

Published Data Sources

Published data are by far the most popular source of marketing information. Not only are the data readily available, often they are sufficient to answer the research question. For example:

- A marketing manager studying developments in the wine industry will use trade association data to learn how the total consumption of wine is broken down by type of customers, geographic area, type of wine, brand name, and distribution client. These data are available annually and sometimes quarterly, so significant trends can be isolated readily.

- A person starting a new specialty shop will use census data on family characteristics and income to support a likely location for the shop.

- Local housing planners rely on census data dealing with the characteristics of housing and households in their locality to judge the need for new housing construction or housing rehabilitation.

The prospective user of published data also is confronted with the problem of matching a specific need for information with a bewildering array of secondary data sources of variable and often indeterminate quality. What is needed first is a flexible search procedure that will ensure that no pertinent source is overlooked, and second, some general criteria for evaluating quality. These issues will be dealt with in the next two sections.

Finding Published Sources

The major published sources are the various government publications (federal, state, provincial, and local), periodicals and journals, and publicly available reports from private groups such as foundations, publishers, trade associations, unions, and companies. Of all these sources, the most valuable data for the marketing researcher come from government census information and various registration requirements. The latter encompass births, deaths, marriages, income tax returns, unemployment records, export declarations, automobile registrations, property tax records, and so on.

How should someone who is unfamiliar with a market or research topic proceed? In general, two basic rules are suggested to guide the search effort: (1) start with the general and go to the specific and (2) make use of all available expertise.[3] The four main categories are authorities, general guides and indices, compilations, and directories.

Authorities

Knowledge of pertinent sources—and of their limitations—comes from continued experience. Thus, the best starting point is someone else who has been doing research on the same subject. Trade associations and specialized trade publications are particularly useful, for they often compile government data and collect additional information from their subscribers or members.[4] If information about a specific geographic area is sought, the local chamber of commerce is a good place to begin. When the problem or topic is too large or ill defined, there is no substitute for a well-informed reference librarian.

General Guides and Indices

Within the category of guides and indices, there is a hierarchy of generality. At the top are the "guides to the guides," such as Constance Winchell's *Guide to Reference Books* (Chicago: American Library Association), *The Bibliographic Index: A Cumulative Bibliography of Bibliographies* (New York: H. W. Wilson Co.), *The Cumulative Book Index* (New York: H. W. Wilson Co.), and *Guide to Special Issues and Indexes of Periodicals* (New York: Special Libraries Association).

At the next level of reference materials are guides to general business information sources. Several important bibliographies are the *Encyclopedia of Business Information Sources*, the *Encyclopedia of Geographic Information Sources* (Detroit: National Gale Research Co.), and the *Statistical Reference Index* (Washington, D.C.: Congressional Information Service). At a third level of generality, business periodical indices (e.g., *Psychological Abstracts*, Washington, D.C.: American Psychological Association; *The Wall Street Journal*) contain references to a large number of journals, periodicals, and newspapers.

For studies of international markets, there is the *International Bibliography of Marketing and Distribution* (Munchen-Pullach: Verlag Dokumentation). Each country has its own reference guides to domestic periodicals. For example, in Canada, there is the (*Annual*) *Statistics Canada Catalogue* and the *Canadian Business Index*, and in the United Kingdom, there is the *Annual Abstract of Statistics* (London: H. M. Stationery Office). Most countries have reference guides to state and provincial jurisdictions. For example, *Canadiana* (Ottawa: National Library of Canada) includes a regular listing of provincial and municipal government publications.

Marketing researchers often overlook valuable information on trends and conditions in specific markets, which is produced by firms such as Frost and Sullivan, Predicasts, Euromonitor, Economist Intelligence Unit, Stanford Research Institute, and A. D. Little. Although these reports may be expensive, they usually are much cheaper than primary research. These reports are indexed and described in the following:

- Findex (Find/SVP) provides fully integrated research, advisory, and business intelligence services in a broad range of industries and disciplines.

- Research Alert Direct, a new line of Internet-delivered alerting services, reports deal with trends in consumer markets, attitudes, and lifestyle.

Compilations

Compilations are intermediate sources, in that they facilitate access to the original sources. This is particularly desirable with statistical information. The standard work in this area is the *Statistical Abstract of the United States* (Washington, D.C.: U.S. Bureau of the Census), which contains selections from the various censuses as well as data collected by other agencies. For example, data on the number of industrial robots installed worldwide, by country, are compiled by the U.S. International Trade Commission. General-purpose marketing statistics are published in volumes such as *Market Guide*, *Marketing Economics Guide* (New York: Marketing Economics Institute), and the *Rand McNally Commercial Atlas and Marketing Guide*. Other valuable compilations are the *Sales and Marketing Management* annual statistical issues detailing the "Survey of Buying Power," which includes industrial incomes, sales of six types of retail stores, market potential indices for states, countries, and metropolitan areas, and similar statistics for Canada.

Directories

Directories are useful for locating people or companies that could provide information. Trade directories supply a wealth of information on individual companies, including addresses, names of executives, product range, and brand names. Information on parent companies and/or subsidiaries often is provided. The *Thomas Register of American Manufacturers* (New York: Thomas Publishing Co.) lists such data on more than 150,000 manufacturing firms. There is now a Thomas Register for Europe, which is the first pan-European buying guide for manufacturers. *Who Owns Whom* (North American Edition) lists 6,500 parent companies and 100,000 domestic and foreign subsidiaries and associated companies. Some directories are narrowly focused, such as *McKitrick's Directory of Advertisers*, or the *Pulp and Paper Directory of Canada*. A number of directories, such as *World Who's Who in Finance and Industry* (Detroit: National Cole Research Co.) and *Standard and Poor's Register of Corporations, Directors and Executives* (covering the United States and Canada), provide general biographical information on individuals.

It is important to realize that only a few of the better-known sources have been described or mentioned here. Almost all of these guides, compilations, and directories are now available online. The researcher is always best advised to seek the assistance of a qualified reference librarian whenever a new area or topic is being studied.

Computer-Retrievable Databases

Even with the array of printed bibliographies, directories, and indices, a search can be very time-consuming. Recent advances in computer technology have resulted in more efficient methods of cataloging, storing, and retrieving published data. The growth in the number of databases available electronically through computers has been dramatic. Thousands of online databases are available to researchers and analysts working in almost every area of business, science, law, education, and the social sciences. These databases are easily accessible from personal computers and mobile devices. Increasingly, the interfaces developed for the user's communication with the database system is designed to be user friendly. As a result, use of these electronic information sources has expanded rapidly to facilitate almost any search for information and is no longer limited to computer specialists.

The large number of databases can be overwhelming. Databases can be classified by type of information contained or by the method of storage and retrieval. Figure 5.2 gives a comprehensive view of the classification.

Classification of Databases Based on Content of Information

Reference Databases

Reference databases refer users to articles and news contained in other sources. They provide online indices and abstracts and are therefore referred to as **bibliographic databases**. Use of these databases is a quick and efficient method for researching a subject before obtaining

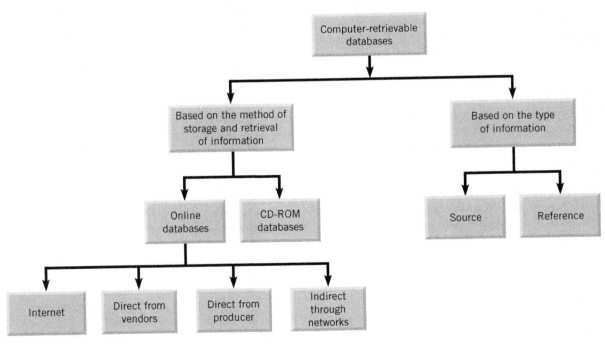

FIGURE 5.2
Classifying Computer-Retrievable Databases.

a large amount of detailed information. Reference databases provide three distinct search features:

1. They are up-to-date summaries or references to a wide assortment of articles appearing in thousands of business magazines, trade journals, government reports, and newspapers throughout the world.

2. The information is accessed by using natural-language key words, rather than author or title. For example, the word "steel" will cause the computer to retrieve all abstracts that contain that word.

3. Key words can be combined in a search for articles that cover a number of related topics.

Source Databases

Source databases provide numerical data, a complete text, or a combination of both. These include the many economic and financial databases and textual source databases that contain the complete texts of newspaper or journal articles.

As opposed to the indices and summaries in the reference database, source databases provide complete textual or numerical information. They can be classified into (1) full-text information sources, (2) economic and financial statistical databases, and (3) online data and descriptive information on companies.

Lexis-Nexis has introduced three new services. *Tracker* scans thousands of publications daily and delivers relevant news for only those topics designated by the customer. *PubWatch* allows users to scan a particular publication table of contents and select only the stories they want to read. *AM News Brief* provides news summary every day. Market research reports from more than a dozen brand names such as Data Monitor, Find/SVP, and Nielsen are also available on Nexis.

In addition to the various major databases that provide financial information about companies and stocks, such as *Standard and Poor's Compustat Services* and the *Value Line Database*, a number of online sources provide nonfinancial information about companies. Examples include the following:

Dun and Bradstreet Identifier: Over 57 million public and private companies, government agencies, and contractors, schools and universities with five or more employees, listing addresses, products, sales executives, corporate organizations, subsidiaries, industry information, and sales prospects.

Disclosure: 12,500 U.S. public companies with at least $5 million in assets. Information includes description of the business, balance sheet, cash flow, income statement, financial ratios, president's letter, and management discussion.

American Business Directory: Over 10 million companies, mainly private. Also lists government offices and professionals, such as physicians and attorneys. Includes estimates of sales and market share.

Standard and Poor's Corporate Description Plus News: 12,000 public companies, with strategic and financial information plus news. Includes business description, incorporation history, earnings and finances, capitalization summary, and stocks and bond data.

Invested Group MarkIntel: Comprises two databases, MarkIntel, which features reports authored by top-rated business publishing firms, and MarkIntel Master, which features exclusive online primary research from leading consulting and market research firms.

Data-Star: Has several individual files with full-text market research reports. Also provides a Focus Market Research which includes Data Monitor, Euromonitor, ICC Keynote Report, Investext, Frost and Sullivan, European Pharmaceutical Market Research, and Freedonia Industry and Business Report.

NTIS: The National Technical Information Service is the official source for government-sponsored U.S. and worldwide scientific, technical, engineering, and business-related information. The NTIS collection includes business and management studies as well as international marketing reports. The information is available in CD-ROMs, computer tapes and diskettes, and online.

Classification of Databases Based on Storage and Retrieval Methods

Another useful way of classifying databases is based on their method of storage and retrieval. They can be classified as online databases and CD-ROM databases.

Online Databases

Online databases can be accessed in real time directly from the producers of the databases or through a vendor. In order to access online databases, all one needs is a personal computer and Internet access. Online databases drastically reduce the time required for a search and bring data right to the desk. Use of the Internet to obtain useful marketing research information is discussed in Chapter 7.

Accessing Online Databases

Online databases are accessible both from their producers and increasingly from online information services. Most online services charge a fee for access to each database, a charge for the amount of information retrieved, and possibly supplemental charges, depending on the nature of the information or the contract arrangements. Some leading vendors of online databases are BRS (Bibliographic Retrieval Service), Knight-Ridder Information Service (formerly DIALOG), Dow Jones News/Retrieval Service, Inc., and Mead Data Central. Commercial online services such as AOL, Compuserve, and Prodigy also allow access to a number of online databases. If you are a frequent online user, the vendors offer a number of options. One way is to pay a monthly fee that entitles the user to a certain minimum usage and after that the user is charged per minute. The actual cost of each service varies from vendor to vendor.

Advantages of Online Methods

The main advantage of online methods is the scope of the information available on databases. They now cover several thousand U.S. and worldwide information sources. A second advantage is the speed of information access and retrieval. Often, much of the information is available from a computer before it is available in published form because of the time required for printing and mailing printed material. Third, commercially available search procedures provide considerable flexibility and efficiency in cross-referenced searching. For example, by using the EIS Industrial Plants database, it is possible to locate plants that simultaneously meet several criteria, such as geographic location, industry code, and market share. The future of computer-retrievable databases is exciting. Marketing Research in Action 5.1 gives an idea about the computer-retrieval databases of the future.

Marketing Research in Action 5.1

■ VIRTUAL REALITY

Virtual reality (VR) is being used for applications ranging from three-dimensional animation for games to geophysical analysis. Virtual reality is a human–computer interface that does not include keyboard and mouse; rather, the interface tracks the movement of the user's hands and head. The movements of the human body replace the clicking and typing. This not only helps to input data faster but also makes the visualization of results very convenient.

VR tools include the following:

- Visualization of all data types simultaneously in a common virtual world
- Walk-through and fly-through capabilities
- Multiattribute visualization
- Interactive real-time region growing
- Import and export of data

The benefits of these tools in data analysis are many. They allow a new user to understand the data faster and thus be productive in a limited time frame. They also allow a user to easily understand complex relationships between data types and multiattribute visualization. Because interactive real-time region growing is possible, there is improved understanding of various attributes that can affect the data. The biggest advantage is improved interdisciplinary collaboration. By integrating different data types in a common virtual work and by using large immersive screens, a group of people can share the same experience and take an active part in the work in front of the screen.

Source: "Inside Reality," http://oilit.com/2journal/2article/0007/0002.pdf, January 2003.

Limitations of Online Methods

The main limitations of the reference databases available online are their reliance on the accuracy of the author, the dependence on the journal and article selection policy of the database producer, and the idiosyncrasies of the search procedures of the different databases as well as the different database network vendors.[5]

Because the computer search is based on finding certain key words within the abstract, there is the possibility that some important information will be missed if an abstract is missing a key word. On the other hand, a lot of irrelevant data may be generated if certain key words used to limit a search are not cited in an abstract. For example, a manufacturer of minicomputers who is interested only in developments pertaining to minicomputers may not want to retrieve the entire database on computers. However, the abstract may contain the word "computer" regardless of size, and accessing information on minicomputers would also yield general computer information.

Another limitation arises from the enormous amount of information now available online. It is often quite difficult to know which of the myriad sources has the correct information most readily accessible. Finally, the researcher using online database retrieval services must weigh the benefits of the research procedure, including timeliness, speed, and scope of information retrieval, against the costs of searching and accessing computer-retrievable databases.

Census Data

The demographic, economic, and social statistics contained in great detail in **census data** are key aspects of many marketing studies, for example:

> *Company Y must decide where to locate a new shopping mall and which kinds of stores to install. These decisions will require (1) **census of population** information about the populations with access to the*

*proposed locations, (2) **census of retail trade** information about likely competitors and local wage levels, and (3) **census of construction industries** information about land development, contractors, and construction costs, available by state and metropolitan area.*

Understanding the Census

All countries conduct a mandatory enumeration of important facts about their population and the economic and social environment. The major national and international census data collection agencies and some of their major publications are the U.S. Bureau of the Census (www.census. gov/), Statistics Canada, Statistical Office of the European Communities (Social Statistics, Industrial Statistics), Great Britain Central Statistical Office (*Annual Abstract of Statistics*), Japan Bureau of Statistics (*Japan Statistical Yearbook*), and the United Nations (*Statistical Yearbook*).

The U.S. Bureau of the Census is illustrative of the scope of these undertakings. There are actually eight regular *economic censuses*, taken in the years ending with the numbers 2 and 7, and *censuses of population* and *housing*, which are taken every 10 years in the year ending with 0. The eight economic censuses compile detailed statistics on the structure and functioning of the major economic sectors: agriculture, construction industries, manufacturers, mineral industries, retail trade, service industries, transportation, and wholesale trade.

Two major innovations were introduced in the 2000 Census. One is the availability of census data on CD-ROM. For a fee, the Census Bureau provides detailed summaries of the information it obtains on CD-ROM. The bureau also sells computer software that may be used for accessing and tabulating data on the CD-ROM. The second major innovation in the 1990 Census was the introduction of the Topologically Integrated Geographic Coding and Referencing (TIGER) system. The TIGER system gives the user the ability to generate a digitized street map of the entire 3.6-million-square-mile map of the United States. Specifically, with use of the TIGER system, one can literally chart every block in every county in the United States, both topographically and demographically. Five versions of the TIGER maps are available from the federal government. These include the prototype and precensus versions, both issued in 1989; the Initial Voting Codes version, released in October 1990, which blankets the United States by election districts; and the initial and final postcensus versions, the latter released in the early part of 1991. TIGER covers 3,286 counties in the United States, including addresses from the most populated urban areas to the most rural areas. One of TIGER's most popular uses is to plot store locations.

To use census data effectively, one must be able to locate quickly the specific information relevant to the research topic. The *Index to Selected 2000 Census Reports* and the *Index to 2000 Census Summary Tapes* list all the titles of tables available from the 2000 Census in either printed or tape form. Each table is described in terms of the variable and the level of aggregation used. For example, one table may be described as "education by sex," with an indication of the level of aggregation available.

Census data can be obtained at many levels of aggregation (see Figure 5.3). The smallest identifiable unit is the **city block** bounded by four streets and some other physical boundaries. City blocks then are combined arbitrarily to form **block groups**. The block groups then are collected together to make up **census tracts**, which are generally used to approximate neighborhoods. Census tracts have populations of above 4,000 and are defined by local communities. In urban areas, census tracts are combined to form **metropolitan statistical areas** (MSAs), which are counties containing a central city with populations of at least 50,000.

The general concept of a metropolitan area is one of a large population nucleus, together with adjacent communities that are determined to have a high degree of economic and social integration with that central nucleus. A metropolitan statistical area containing a single core with a population of at least 2.5 million may be subdivided to form smaller groupings of counties referred to as **metropolitan divisions**. While a metropolitan division is a subdivision of a larger

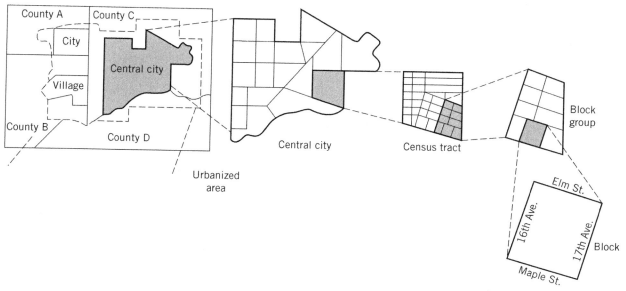

FIGURE 5.3
Geographic Subdivisions of an MSA.

metropolitan statistical area, it often functions as a distinct social, economic, and cultural area within the larger region.[6] In June 1983, the federal government replaced the old **standard metropolitan statistical area (SMSA)** designation with new definitions. To maintain comparability, data for an earlier period are revised where possible, to reflect the MSA boundaries of the more recent period. In addition to the new standard MSAs, the largest defined areas are *combined statistical areas* (CSAs), which are metropolitan complexes containing separate component areas. [There are 367 MSAs and 68,000 census tracts and 211,267 block groups in the United States (including Puerto Rico).]

Finally, the whole country is divided into four large regions (Northeast, Midwest, South, and West). In addition, census data are available by civil divisions, such as states, counties, cities, and wards. The data from the latest census can be obtained from the Census Bureaus online database called Cendata. Cendata has an efficient measuring system that leads you to the data you need.

North American Industry Classification System

The **North American Industry Classification System (NAICS)**[7] is the new standard code system to describe business establishments and industries, replacing the Standard Industrial Classification (SIC) codes. It is the first industry classification system developed in accordance with a single principle or aggregation: the principle that producing units that use similar production processes should be grouped together in the classification (see Table 5.2).

The NAICS went into effect for reference year 1997 in Canada and the United States and for 1998 in Mexico. It was developed to provide a consistent framework for the collection, analysis, and dissemination of industrial statistics. Designed by the United States, Mexican, and Canadian governments, NAICS has implications for economists, regulators, marketers, publishers, and anyone else who uses industry-based data. The most obvious use of the codes is in the 1997

Table 5.2   North American Industrial Classification System

NAICS level	NAICS code	Description
Sector	51	Information
Subsector	515	Broadcasting (except Internet)
Industry group	5151	Radio and TV
Industry	51511	Radio Broadcasting
U.S. industry	515112	Radio Stations

Source: http://www.census.gov/eos/www/naics/.

Economic Census. Of the 1,170 NAICS codes, 358 are new industries, 390 are revised from SIC, and 422 can be compared to the older SIC codes.

The system was developed by the United States, Canada, and Mexico to provide comparable statistics across the three countries. For the first time, government and business analysts will be able to directly compare industrial production statistics collected and published in the three North American Free Trade Agreement countries. NAICS also provides for increased comparability with the International Standard Industrial Classification System (ISIC, Revision 3) developed and maintained by the United Nations.

NAICS industries are identified by a six-digit code, in contrast to the four-digit SIC code. The longer code accommodates the larger number of sectors and allows more flexibility in designating subsectors. The international NAICS agreement fixes only the first five digits of the code. The sixth digit, where used, identifies subdivisions of NAICS industries that accommodate user needs in individual countries. There are 20 broad sectors in the NAICS system, up from the 10 divisions of the NAICS system.

Appraising Secondary Sources

Users of secondary sources rapidly develop a healthy skepticism. Unfortunately, there are many reasons why a forecast, historical statistic, or estimate may be found to be irrelevant or too inaccurate to be useful. Before such a judgment can be made, the researcher should have answers to the following questions:

1. *Who?* This question applies especially to the reputation of the collecting agency for honest and thorough work and the character of the sponsoring organization, which may influence the interpretation and reporting of the data. A related question is whether either organization has adequate resources to do a proper job. The problems do not end here, for the original data source (which provided the count, estimate, or other basis for the reported result) may have its own motives for biasing what it reports. A company that is pressed by a trade association, chamber of commerce, or government agency may be unwilling to report the true state of affairs or to take the time to collect the data, which may result in a biased guess.

2. *Why?* Data that are collected to further the interests of a particular group are especially suspect. Media buyers, for example, soon learn to be wary of studies of media. It is easy to choose unconsciously those methods, questions, analysis procedures, and so forth, that favor the interests of the study sponsor, and it is unlikely that unfavorable results will be exposed to the public.

3. *How?* It is impossible to appraise the quality of secondary data without knowledge of the methodology used to collect them. Therefore, one should immediately be suspicious of any source that does not describe the procedures used—including a copy of the questionnaire (if any), the nature and size of the sample, the response rate, the results of field validation efforts, and any other procedural decisions that could influence the results. The crucial question is whether any of these decisions could bias the results systematically.

The need for caution is illustrated by a study to determine the best locations for new bank branches. The researchers initially used the projections of population in different parts of the city, which were provided by the city planning commission. These ostensibly valuable data had to be discarded when it was found that the commission had arrived at their projections by subdividing on maps the areas to be developed and multiplying each area by the density of families in the already-established areas of the city. When this methodology was discovered, a proper projection was made by canvassing every real estate developer in the area regarding his or her future plans. The difference between the two projections was great, both in extent and timing of population increases.

4. *What?* Even if the available data are of acceptable quality, they may prove difficult to use or inadequate to the need. One irritating and prevalent problem is the classifications that are used. Wide variations in geographic, age, and income groupings across studies are common; for example, there is no accepted definition for the minimum number of stores in a supermarket chain.

5. *When?* There is nothing less interesting than last week's newspaper. Sooner or later, the pace of change in the world in general, and in markets in particular, renders all secondary data equally obsolete and uninteresting except to the historian. The rate of obsolescence varies with the types of data, but in all cases, the researcher should know when the data were collected. There may be a substantial lag between the time of collection and the publication of the results.

6. *Consistency?* With all the possible pitfalls in secondary data and the difficulty in identifying them fully, the best defense is to find another source that can be used as a basis for comparison. Ideally, the two sources should use different methodologies to arrive at the same kind of data. In the likely event that there is some disagreement between the two sets of data, the process of reconciliation should first identify the respective biases in order to narrow the differences and determine which set is the most credible.

Applications of Secondary Data

Secondary data are widely used for a number of marketing research problems. We have already discussed the various sources of secondary data and how to appraise them. In this section, we will look at the various applications of secondary data. Table 5.3 gives a comprehensive framework of the types of sources to be used for different applications.

Demand Estimation

Most marketing resources, especially sales effort, service coverage, and communication activity, are allocated by region, segment, or territory. The key to efficient allocation is knowledge of the potential of each segment relative to other segments. Hence, demand estimation is a key determinant of the allocation of resources. Demand can be estimated from secondary data by the methods described in the paragraphs that follow.

Table 5.3   Applications of Secondary Data

Demand estimation	Monitoring the environment
1. Census data 2. North American Industry Classification System (NAICS) 3. Trade associations data 4. Experts and authorities	1. Press releases 2. Legislation and laws 3. Industry news 4. Business and practitioner literature, such as magazines
Segmentation and targeting	**Developing a business intelligence system**
1. PRIZM 2. CLUSTER PLUS 3. DMI 4. NAICS 5. TIGER	1. Competitors' annual reports 2. Press releases 3. Blogs 4. Competitors' web pages

Direct Data Methods

Direct data methods are based on a desegregation of total industry data. The sales information may come from government sources, industry surveys, or trade associations. For example, the National Electrical Manufacturers Association reports shipments of refrigerators to retailers. Such data are useful for establishing relative market potentials only if the sales can be broken down by the organization's sales or operating territories. Fortunately, industry refrigerator shipment data are available by trading area. This permits a direct comparison of the share of company sales and industry sales in each territory.

Corollary Data Methods

One solution to the absence of industry sales data for each territory is to use another variable that is (1) available for each sales territory or region and (2) correlated highly with the sales of the product. For example, the territory demand for child-care services or baby food is correlated highly with the number of births in the area during the previous three years. Thus, the share of births in all geographic areas within the territory of interest would be a good proxy for the relative market potential within that territory.

Companies use other methods that are peculiar to their product and sales environment to forecast sales. An example of such a method is given in Marketing Research in Action 5.2. In the example, Hansen Company, a manufacturer of quick connective couplings for air and fluid power transmission systems, uses a "sales-per-employee ratio" to forecast sales.

Monitoring the Environment

One of the most important uses of secondary data is to monitor the environment in which the company is functioning. Monitoring the environment is very crucial these days because it is highly volatile and because attitudes, fashions, and fads change so often. To keep abreast of all the latest developments, a company has to be in constant touch with newspapers, general magazines, and periodicals. It has to know all the latest legislation and laws that may affect it. To know about the most recent trends in the industry, a firm has to look in the latest journals in the field. Thus, constant monitoring of the environment through surveillance of all the relevant indicators is very important to compete effectively in this dynamic environment.

Marketing Research in Action 5.2

◼ RELATIVE SALES POTENTIALS

What can be done if a reliable estimate of total industry sales is unavailable, the customers cannot provide a good estimate of their purchases of the product, and the product is used in many industries, so there are no obvious corollary variables? This was the situation confronting the Hansen Company, a manufacturer of quick connective couplings for air and fluid power transmission systems, who distributed these products through a national network of 31 industrial distributors. To be able to evaluate and control their activity, the company badly needed data on the relative performance of their distributors. Its approach was based on the only reliable data that were available to it—sales of company products, by distributor. To utilize these data, the company made the assumption that it should be possible for Hansen distributors to attain the same sales-per-employee ratio in noncustomer establishments as in customer establishments. To establish the sales-per-employee ratio that would serve as a performance standard, the following steps were taken:

1. A random sample of 178 accounts was drawn from a census of all customer accounts buying $2,000 or more from the seven best distributors (where "best" was defined in terms of perceived effectiveness of management and utilization of an up-to-date data processing system).
2. Each account was assigned to a two-digit SIC group on the basis of its principal output or activity.
3. Data on the number of employees in each account were obtained primarily from industrial directories.
4. Sales-per-employee ratios were computed for each SIC group within the set of seven distributors.

5. Sales-per-employee ratios for each SIC group were multiplied by the total employment in all establishments in each of the 31 distributor territories. The employment data came from the current edition of the County Business Patterns publication of the U.S. Census. The output of these five steps was a table for each distributor, patterned after the following table, which gives the results for distributor A.

1997 Sales Potential—Distributor A

Two-digit SIC group	1997 hansen sales per employee	Total employees	Sales potential
33	$1.56	4,113	$ 6,416
34	2.53	14,792	37,424
35	3.28	15,907	52,175
36	1.93	32,677	63,067
37	1.71	2,024	3,461
38	3.48	409	1,423
Total		69,922	$163,966

The resulting sales potential was compared with actual sales, which for distributor A amounted to $86,218 in 1997. That is, actual sales performance was 52.6 percent of sales potential. The sales performance for all distributors ranged from 125.0 percent to 15.4 percent, with an average of 50.3 percent. It is not surprising that the distributor with sales of only 15.4 percent of potential was subjected to a very careful review, which revealed that the salespeople did not really know how to sell the product to major accounts in the area.

Segmentation and Targeting

Market segmentation is common among businesses seeking to improve their marketing efforts. Effective segmentation demands that firms group their customers into relatively homogeneous groups. The NAICS and Dun's Market Identifiers (DMI) are used by companies selling industrial goods to segment their markets.

One of the latest developments with regard to segmentation for consumer products is *geocoding*, or a cluster demographic system, which identifies groups of consumers who share demographic and lifestyle characteristics. Several services now can link U.S. Census data on a Zip Code basis to lifestyles, to help marketing researchers identify the best areas in which to concentrate their efforts. Among the services are PRIZM(by Claritas) and CLUSTER PLUS (by Donnelly Marketing Information Services).

About 1,000 consumer characteristics can be used to build clusters of homogeneous groups. Demographic variables include age, marital status, size of household, and income. Marketing Research in Action 5.3 illustrates how important demographic variables are in segmentation and targeting. Behavioral characteristics include amount of TV watched, amount of white bread consumed, types of magazines read, and so on. Geographic areas range from cities and counties to Zip Codes, census tracts, and block groups.

The **Potential Rating Index Zip Markets (PRIZM)** system is based on evidence that people with similar cultural backgrounds and circumstances will gravitate naturally toward one another. Each of the 35,600 zip markets was first described according to 34 key demographic factors. These zip markets were originally clustered into 40 distinct groups which were each very homogeneous within themselves and very different from other groups. Subsequently 22 new consumer groups were added, bringing the total number of clusters to 62. The larger number of clusters reflect the increasing ethnic and economic complexity of the nation's population.[8] Claritas has also introduced workplace PRIZM, which accurately profiles a market's working population and demonstrates the difference between the area's daytime and nighttime demographics.

Since every market is composed of Zip Code areas, it is possible to estimate the sales potential of a market by zip market clusters. As an example, a power tool manufacturer was able to create

Marketing Research in Action 5.3

■ TARGETED MARKETING FOR AFRICAN-AMERICANS

African-Americans comprise about 13 percent of the population in the United States (around 39.2 million) and by 2050, this number is predicted to rise by 15 percent. With their spending on products and services being on the increasing trend, it provides enough incentive for companies to target this segment and come up with innovative ways to reach them. Marketers adopt various strategies to win over a particular segment of the market, some of which are given below:

• Segmentation—It is critical for a company to divide its target audience into segments based on ethnicity, lifestyle and other demographics like education, household income etc. Each of these segments must be analyzed in-depth and the company must look for inventive ways to reach out to them. A good example of this is the case of Nissan. Research done by the company revealed that their African-American consumers preferred to be "included" rather than "targeted." This led Nissan to embark on a series of "integrated marketing" for their Altima brand which did not directly target the African-American population but, subtly included them in the target audience. Through this initiative, Nissan saw a 14 percent increase in their sales of Altima to African-American audience and a 29 percent overall increase in African-American customer base.

• Community-based events—Another tested method of gaining attention among segments in the market is hosting community based events such as exhibitions etc. New York-based Merrill Lynch & Company Inc has conducted many of these events and benefited greatly from them. In October 2005, the firm sponsored a cultural exhibition: The Art of Architecture in Africa, and invited more than 300 prospective clients who were attended to by over 25 financial advisors from Merrill Lynch.

There has been increasing focus on the African-American consumer segment. Some of the successful industries in this initiative are automotive manufacturers, financial services, wireless providers, consumer packaged goods, and insurance companies. The key to succeed in this multicultural marketing campaign lies in a companywide commitment to ensure success, cultural sensitivity, and the ability to capture their attention and loyalty.

Source: D. L. Vence, "Mix it up," Marketing News, October 15, 2006.

a PRIZM profile of product warranty cards mailed by recent buyers. This told the manufacturer which Zip Code areas should be chosen as target markets and helped to allocate media spending and sales force effort.

Developing a Business Intelligence System

A **business intelligence system** is basically a system that contains data on the environment and the competitors. It forms an integral part of the marketing decision support system. Both primary and secondary data form a part of the business intelligence system. As has already been said, data on the environment can be obtained from a variety of sources. Data on competitors can be obtained from their annual reports, press releases, patents, and so on.

Sources of Secondary Data for International Marketing Research[9]

Secondary data are a key source of information for conducting international marketing research. This is in part due to their ready availability, the high cost of collecting primary data versus the relatively low cost of secondary data, and the usefulness of secondary data in assessing whether specific problems need to be investigated, and if so, how. Further, secondary data sources are particularly valuable in assessing opportunities in countries with which management has little familiarity, and in product markets at an early stage of market development.

A wide variety of secondary data sources are available for international marketing research. These range from sources that provide general economic, social, and demographic data for almost all countries in the world, to sources that focus on specific industries worldwide.

A host of sources of macroeconomic data are to be found, ranging widely in the number of countries or regions covered. Many of these are based on or derived from United Nations and World Bank data. The Business International, Euromonitor, and Worldcasts divisions of Predicasts also publish annual information on macroeconomic variables.

The preceding macroeconomic data sources, with the exception of Euromonitor, relate to the general business environment. They therefore do not provide much indication as to market potential for specific industries. A number of sources of industry-specific data are available. They are United Nations *Yearbooks*, publications of the U.S. Department of Commerce, *The Economist*, and the *Worldcasts*.

Numerous other sources specific to individual countries or product markets are also to be found. The U.S. Department of Commerce, for example, publishes *International Marketing Handbook*, which provides profiles and special information about doing business in various countries. Information regarding regulations, customs, distribution channels, transportation, advertising and marketing research, credit, taxation, guidance for business travelers abroad, and so forth, is compiled in their "Overseas Business Reports." Governments or other bodies frequently publish national yearbooks or statistical data books. Various private sources also publish regional and country handbooks. The World of Information, for example, publishes the *African Guide*, the *Middle East Review*, and so on.

Problems Associated with Secondary Data in International Research

Two major problems are associated with secondary data in international marketing research: the accuracy of the data and the comparability of data obtained from different countries.

Data Accuracy

Different sources often report different values for the same macroeconomic factor, such as gross national product, per-capita income, or the number of television sets in use. This casts some doubt on the accuracy of the data. This may be due to different definitions followed for each of those statistics in different countries. The accuracy of data also varies from one country to another. Data from highly industrialized nations are likely to have a higher level of accuracy than data from developing countries because of the difference in the sophistication of the procedures adopted. The level of literacy in a country also plays a role in the accuracy of the macroeconomic data collected in that country.

Comparability of Data

Business statistics and income data vary from country to country because different countries have different tax structures and different levels of taxation. Hence, it may not be useful to compare these statistics across countries. Population censuses may not only be inaccurate, they also may vary in frequency and the year in which they are collected. Although in the United States they are collected once every 10 years, in Bolivia, there was a 25-year gap between two censuses. So most population figures are based on estimates of growth that may not be accurate and comparable. Measurement units are not necessarily equivalent from country to country. For example, in Germany, the expense incurred on buying a television would be classified as entertainment expense, whereas in the United States, it would be classified as furniture expense.

Applications of Secondary Data in International Research

Secondary data are particularly useful in evaluating country or market environments, whether in making initial market-entry decisions or in attempting to assess future trends and developments. They thus form an integral form of the international marketing research process. More specifically, three major uses of secondary data are in:

1. Selecting countries or markets that merit in-depth investigation

2. Making an initial estimate of demand potential in a given country or a set of countries

3. Monitoring environmental changes

Secondary data can be used systematically to screen market potential, risks, and likely costs of operating in different countries throughout the world. Two types of generalized procedures are used. The first procedure classifies countries on two dimensions: the degree of demographic and economic mobility, and the country's domestic stability and cohesion. The second procedure calculates multiple factor indices for different countries. For example, *Business International* publishes information each year on three indices showing (1) *market growth*, (2) *market intensity*, and (3) *market size*, for countries in Western and Eastern Europe, the Middle East, Latin America, Asia, Africa, and Australia. Customized models, which are geared to specific company objectives and industry characteristics, can also be developed using secondary data.

Once the appropriate countries and markets to be investigated in depth have been determined, the next step is to make an explicit evaluation of demand in those countries or markets.[10] This is important when considering initial market entry because of the high costs and uncertainty associated with entering new markets. Management has to make an initial estimate of demand potential and also project future market trends.

Four types of data analyses are unique to demand estimation in an international context. The first and the most simplistic is lead–lag analysis. This uses time-series (yearly) data from a country to project sales in other countries. A second procedure is the use of surrogate indicators. This is similar to the use of general macroindicators but develops the macroindicators relative to a specific industry or product market. An example of a surrogate indicator is the number of childbirths in the country as an indicator of the demand potential for diapers. A third technique, which relies on the use of cross-sectional data (data from different countries), is analogous to the use of barometric procedures in domestic sales forecasting. One assumes that if there is a direct relationship between the consumption of a product, service, or commodity and an indicator in one country, the same relationship will hold in other countries to estimate the demand. The fourth and most complex forecasting model is the econometric forecasting model. This model uses cross-sectional and time-series data on factors underlying sales for a given product market for a number of countries to estimate certain parameters. Later, these models can be used to project the market demand.

A third use of secondary data in an international context is to monitor environmental changes. Monitoring environmental changes requires surveillance of a number of key indicators. These should be carefully selected and tailored to the specific product or range of products with which management is concerned. Two types of indicators are required. The first monitors the general health and growth of a country and its economy and society; the second, those of a specific industry or product market. A variety of procedures can be used to analyze the impact of environmental factors on world trends or industrial countries, and on product markets, as well as the implications for market growth and appropriate marketing strategies. These range from simple trend projections or tracking studies and the use of leading indicators to the more complex scenario evaluation studies.

SUMMARY

The theme of this chapter is the wealth of data available to marketing researchers. Many management problems can be resolved by recourse to the firm's internal records or to secondary sources such as government statistics, trade association reports, periodicals, books, and private studies. With the growing power of computers, these data are increasingly easy to access in databases. The low cost and convenience of these database sources leave no excuse for not starting a marketing research study with a thorough scan of what is already available. Invariably, the researcher will be surprised at the extent of what is already available with very little effort. Even if it is not entirely suitable, the secondary data sources can provide useful pointers on how to design a good research study.

QUESTIONS AND PROBLEMS

5.1   You are opening a new retail store that will sell personal computers and software. What secondary data are available in your area to help you decide where to locate the store? Would the same data be relevant to someone opening a convenience copying center?

5.2   A large chain of building supply yards was aiming to grow at a rate of three new yards per year. From past experience, this meant carefully reviewing as many as 20 or 30 possible locations. You have been assigned the task of making this process more systematic. The first step is to specify the types of secondary information that should be available for the market area of each location. The second step is to identify the possible sources of this information and appraise their usefulness. From studies of the patrons of the present yards, you know that 60 percent of the dollar volume is accounted for by building contractors and tradesmen. The rest of the volume is sold to farmers, householders, and hobbyists. However, the sales to do-it-yourselfers have been noticeably increasing. About 75 percent of the sales were lumber and building materials, although appliances, garden supplies, and home entertainment systems are expected to grow in importance.

5.3 For each of these products, which industry associations would you contact for secondary data? (a) Foreign convenience dinners, (b) numerically controlled machine tools, (c) irrigation pipe, (d) imported wine, (e) compact disk players, and (f) children's shoes.

5.4 Obtain data on beer consumption in your state or province for the latest available year. Calculate the per-capita consumption for this area and compare it to that for the country as a whole. What accounts for the difference?

5.5 Educational Edge, a small company with limited resources, is interested in segmenting potential markets for its erasable transparencies.

(a) Which type of data would be best suited to obtain the required information?

(b) What are the possible sources of information to aid in the segmentation decision?

(c) What are the benefits and limitations of using secondary data for this purpose?

5.6 Howard Enterprises, a small family-owned manufacturer of unique lamps, has begun to receive unsolicited inquiries about its product from foreign countries. The company has been operating exclusively in the domestic environment, but these inquiries have become numerous enough to suggest that a market for these specialty lamps may exist abroad. J. P. Howard, the company head, decided to contact Peter Franks, an old college friend of his, who is now the head of marketing research for a multinational company, to ask for his advice on how to proceed in evaluating foreign country markets. Mr Franks recommends that Howard Enterprises should select countries that merit in-depth investigation and proceed to make an initial estimate of the demand potential in these countries.

(a) Considering the limited resources that are available to Mr Howard's company, explain how secondary data can be used to help Mr Howard follow his friend's recommendation.

(b) What are the possible limitations of secondary data of which Mr Howard must be aware when conducting the marketing research?

5.7 From secondary data sources, obtain sales for an entire industry and the sales of the major firms in that industry for any year. Compute the market shares of each major firm. Using another source, obtain information on the market shares of these same firms. Are there differences? If so, why?

END NOTES

1. E. R. Kidd, "Establishing Quality Focus in a Multi-Cultural Organization," presented at the Third Congress on Competitive Strategies.

2. P. A. Francese and L. M. Renaghan, "Finding the Customer," *American Demographics*, January 1991, pp. 48–51.

3. More extensive discussion of data sources and how to locate them can be found in Lorna Daniels, *Business Information Sources*, Berkeley, CA: University of California Press, 1985; Lorna Daniels, Notes on Sources of External Marketing Data, in B. Shapiro, R. Dolan, and J. Quelch (eds.), *Marketing Management Vol. ii*, Homewood, IL: Richard D. Irwin, 1985, Appendix; Barbara E. Brown, *Canadian Business and Economics: A Guide to Sources of Information*, Ottawa: Canadian Library Association, 1984; and L. M. Fuld, *Competitor Intelligence*. New York: John Wiley, 1985.

4. A comprehensive listing of these associations can be found in the *Encyclopedia of Associations*, Detroit: National Gale Research Co., 1984; and in L. M. Fuld, *Competitor Intelligence*. New York: John Wiley, 1985.

5. An interesting compilation of reasons why a database search might not meet with success is provided in Jeff Pemberton, "Faults and Failures—25 Ways That Online Searching Can Let You Down," *Online*, September 1983.

6. http://proximityone.com/metros.htm.

7. http://www.census.gov/eos/www/naics/.

8. C. D. Valle, "They Know Where You Live—And How You Buy," *Business Week*, February 7, 1994.

9. For a more detailed discussion, see S. P. Douglas and C. Samuel Craig, *International Marketing Research*, Englewood Cliffs, NJ: Prentice-Hall, 1983.

10. V. Kumar, A. Stam, and E. A. Joachimsthaler, "An Interactive Multicriteria Approach to Identifying Potential Foreign Markets," *Journal of International Marketing*, 2(1), 1994, pp. 29–52.

Case 5-1 | Barkley Foods

Joyce Stevenson, the manager of marketing research for Barkley Foods, had just left an emergency meeting with the firm's president. An opportunity to buy an established line of gourmet (high-quality/high-priced) frozen dinners had arisen. Because there were other interested buyers, a decision had to be made within three or four weeks. This decision depended on judgments about the future prospects of the gourmet frozen dinner market and whether Barkley could achieve a competitive advantage. The marketing research group was asked to provide as much useful information as possible within a 10-day period. Although uncomfortable with the time pressure involved, Joyce was pleased that marketing had finally been asked to participate in the analysis of acquisition prospects. She had pressed for such participation and now she had to deliver.

Because of prior work on frozen fruit juices, Joyce had some knowledge of the gourmet frozen market. It was pioneered by Stouffer, who introduced the Lean Cuisine line of entrees in 1981. Since then, other firms have entered the industry with complete gourmet dinners (including Swanson's Le Menu and Armour's Dinner Classics). The distinction between entrees, dinners, and the three main types of food offered—conventional, ethnic (i.e., Benihana Restaurant Classics), or low-calorie (i.e., Weight Watchers or Light & Elegant)—define relevant submarkets. Joyce hypothesized that the gourmet frozen food buyer differs from the buyer of conventional "TV dinners" in several respects. The gourmet frozen food buyers are generally young, upper-socioeconomic-group people who probably have microwaves, are more health conscious, and are likely to be working women and others who want sophisticated cuisine but lack the time to prepare it.

Barkley Foods was a diversified food company with sales of $2.3 billion. Over 80 percent of its sales came from branded packaged food products sold nationally through grocery stores. Its largest product areas were canned tomato products, frozen orange juice, cake mixes, and yogurt. Barkley was known to have strengths in operations (product preparation), distribution (obtaining distribution and managing the shelves), and advertising. Their brands typically held a solid second-place position in the supermarket. There was no effort at umbrella brand identification, so each product area was carried by its own brand.

Joyce Stevenson had previously been in strategic planning, and reviewed the type of information and analysis that would be required to support a strategic decision like this one. She wrote down the following four sets of questions to guide the thinking of the research group:

1. Market analysis
   - What are the size, current growth rate, and projected growth rate of the industry and its relevant subsets (such as ethnic dinners) for the next five and ten years?
   - What are the important industry trends?
   - What are the emerging production technologies?
   - What are the distribution trends?
   - What are current and future success factors (a competitive skill or asset needed to compete successfully)?

2. Environmental analysis
   - What demographic, cultural, economic, or governmental trends or events could create strategic threats or opportunities?
   - What major environmental scenarios (plausible stories about the future) can be conceived?

3. Customer analysis
   - What are the major segments?
   - What are their motivations and unmet needs?

4. Competitor analysis
   - Who are the existing and potential competitors?
   - What are their current or forecasted levels of sales, market shares, and profits?
   - What are their strengths and weaknesses?
   - What strategies are they following, and how are they differentiating themselves in the market?

Questions for Discussion

1. What secondary data sources would be useful? What types of questions might be answered by each?

2. Identify one piece of information from the library that would be helpful and relevant. How did you locate it?

3. What other mechanisms would you use to gather information?

| *Case 5-2* ||| Dell in Latin America? |

Dell, which thrived while other PC makers stumbled in 1998, reported a 53 percent jump in profit and a 50 percent jump in revenue for its fiscal second quarter, which ended in July 1998. Unlike most of its rivals, Dell deals directly with customers and builds PCs only after receiving an order. However, all is not well for Dell. While Dell continues to blow away the competition and Wall Street with enormous increases in personal-computer sales, it is continually scrambling to bring in and train enough people to keep up with its orders.

The company's employment had grown 56 percent in 1997, to 20,800, and within a span of three months Dell added 225 people a week—about the same it added every six weeks in 1996. To manage this expansion, Dell has aggressively recruited experienced outsiders and tried to standardize training of new employees. It has also created a culture where managers are rewarded for seeing their divisions split into smaller units and their responsibilities cut back.

Incidentally, Dell Computer Corp. is expected to announce a major foray into Brazil, in a bid to boost its share of Latin America's fast-growing personal-computer market. Foreign companies with local production plants dominate Latin America's estimated $6.5 billion personal-computer market. Compaq Computer Corp., International Business Machines Corp., Acer Inc., and Hewlett-Packard Co. together accounted for 42 percent of desktop and notebook sales in 1997, according to IDC Latin America, a market-research firm. Dell ranked ninth with 1.2 percent of the market. At the company's annual meeting in July 1998, Vice Chairman Morton Topfer said Dell aimed to open a plant in Latin America in 1999 and noted that Latin America is key to its international expansion. The company already operates regional production plants in Malaysia, Ireland, the United States, and China.

Questions for Discussion

1. What are the issues concerning the Latin American market that Dell should address before it enters into Brazil?

2. What kind of information is needed to address the issues identified in question 1? What are the possible sources of the required information?

3. What are your recommendations to Dell regarding the steps for expanding its operations in Latin America?

Source: This case was prepared by V. Kumar and Rajkumar Venkatesan for the purpose of classroom discussion from "Dell to Build Plant to Boost Latin Presence," *Wall Street Journal*, August 18, 1998, and "Dell Scrambles to Find Enough Workers to Fuel Growth," *Wall Street Journal*, August 20, 1998.

Additional Case for this Chapter is available on the Web:

| *Web Case 5-1* ||| Eddie Bauer: Strategize with Secondary Marketing Data |

Standardized Sources of Marketing Data

6

LEARNING OBJECTIVES

- Describe the process of conducting retail store audits.
- Discuss the advantages and limitations of consumer purchase panels.
- Discuss the sources and applications of scanner data.
- Describe the value of commercial information collected from media-related standardized sources.
- Describe a framework for the various applications of standardized data sources.

Marketing intelligence is a form of business intelligence whereby data and information are analyzed and transformed for use in strategic planning and problem solving. The more specific and topical the need for information, the smaller is the likelihood that relevant secondary data will be found. The researcher then has the choice of designing a special study or taking advantage of standardized data collection and analysis procedures. The latter alternative generally exists whenever several information users have common information needs and when the cost of satisfying an individual user's need is prohibitive. These conditions are most often encountered with consumer goods sold to large, diffuse markets and repurchased at frequent intervals. A further condition—especially important for data sources such as store audits and continuous consumer panels—is that the information needs are recurrent and can be anticipated. Thus, the data supplier can enter into long-term relationships with clients and be sure of covering the heavy fixed costs. The clients get continuity of data series, which is essential for monitoring and evaluation purposes.

This chapter describes and evaluates the major syndicated sources of marketing data, including store audits, warehouse withdrawal services, consumer purchase panels, and scanner-based systems. Each source has a distinctive profile of strengths and weaknesses that reflects differences in orientation, types of measures, and their location in the distribution channel. To get a full picture of the market situation of a product category or brand, it is usually necessary to use several sources in combination. Unfortunately, when this is done the result is more often confusion rather than clarity of insight because of information overload. This is such a prevalent problem that the last section of this chapter is devoted to recently developed decision support systems that help reduce the confusion.

The use of standardized data sources has been revolutionized by **single-source data** from scanner systems. This means that all data on product purchases and causal factors, such as media exposure, promotion influence, and consumer characteristics, come from the same households. These data are being made possible through advances in information technology. Single-source data has not fully displaced other standardized sources, but it is used in conjunction with them to generate important new insights.

To understand the basic motivation for using standardized sources, consider the problems of a manufacturer of cold remedies who has to rely on factory shipment data for sales information. Management is especially interested in the reaction to a new convenience package that was introduced at the beginning of the cold season in December. By the end of January, the following information had been received from the accounting department:

Week ending	Factory shipments
December 28	12,700 cases
January 4	19,800 cases
January 11	18,200 cases
January 18	14,100 cases
January 25	11,050 cases

All the usual problems of interpreting time-series data are compounded in this example by the ambiguities in the data. For example, while the cases were shipped from the factory, there is no information concerning where or when they were sold. The peak in factory shipments during the week ending January 4 represents a substantial amount of "pipeline filling," in anticipation of sales to come in the future during the cold season, and an unknown amount of product sold for pipeline filling still remains on the shelves. Also unknown is competitive performance during this period: Did the new package gain sales at the expense of competition, or was there a loss of market share? Shipment data provide no diagnostic information, so these questions remain: How many retail stores used the special displays of the new product? Were competitors making similar or more effective offers? Was there a carryover of last year's stock in the old package? Without answers to these questions, the manager is in no position either to correct problems or to continue the strong points of the campaign.

Retail Store Audits

Every two months a team of auditors from a research firm visits a sample of stores to count the inventory on hand and record deliveries to the store since the last visit. Sales during the two-month period, for any desired classification of product category (including brands, sizes, package types, and flavors), are arrived at by computing

$$\text{Beginning inventory} + \text{deliveries} - \text{ending inventory} = \text{sales for the periods}$$

These **retail store audit** results then are projected—to arrive at nationwide and regional estimates of total sales, inventories, and so forth—and reported to the client between six and eight weeks after the end of the period. During each store visit, the auditor also may collect observable information such as shelf prices, display space, the presence of special displays, and in-store promotion activities.

Nielsen Retail Index

A.C. Nielsen Co. and Audits and Surveys provide auditing services. Nielsen's auditing services cover four major reporting groups:

1. Grocery products

2. Drugs

3. Other merchandise

4. Alcoholic beverages

Audits and Surveys deals with products, regardless of the type of retail outlet carrying the product. The data provided by these two companies are incredibly rich. Table 6.1 summarizes the information that is provided in the bimonthly report of Nielsen. A disadvantage of the audit data is that it cannot be linked to household characteristics. For additional information, visit the A.C. Nielsen website at http://ca.nielsen.com/content/nielsen/en_ca/insights/reports.html.

Consumer Purchase Panels

From store audits and warehouse withdrawal services, we can learn how much product is moving through the distribution channel. As this information is one step removed from the actual purchase transaction, we still don't know who bought, how frequently they bought, or whether the seeming stability of market shares reflects stable purchasing patterns or a great deal of switching back and forth between brands and stores in response to short-term promotional efforts. To answer these questions, we need detailed records of purchasing activity by the same people over an extended period of time. Here are two methods for collecting this data:

1. In the **home audit** approach, the panel member agrees to permit an auditor to check the household stocks of certain product categories at regular intervals. A secondary condition is that the panel member save all used cartons, wrappers, and so on, so the auditor can record them.

2. In the **mail diary method**, the panel member records the details of each purchase in certain categories and returns the completed diary by mail at regular intervals (biweekly or monthly). The detail that can be collected is illustrated for 2 of the 88 clothing, food, and personal-care products recorded by members of the American Shoppers Panel (see Figure 6.1).

Table 6.1   Contents of a Nielsen Store Audit Report

Each of the following variables can be subdivided as follows:
  a. Sales districts
  b. Size of county (A, B, C, or D)
  c. Type of store (e.g., chain versus large-medium-small independents)
  d. Thirty-two largest metropolitan markets
1. **Sales** (volume, trend, and share) on the basis of retail dollars and units, pounds or equivalent cases for total market, and major brands by sizes, flavors, types, etc., as appropriate to the category
2. **Distribution**
  a. Percentage of all stores, and all commodity sales, carrying each brand, and size
  b. Out-of-stock conditions
  c. Retail inventories
  d. Stock cover (the length of time the stocks will last, assuming current rates of sales)
  e. Source of delivery (wholesaler, rack jobbers, manufacturer, chain warehouse, or interstore transfers)
3. **Selling prices** and volume sold at each price or deal
4. **Retailer support** in terms of shelf facings, special displays, in-store advertising, and newspaper advertising
5. **Media advertising** for total market and major brands
6. **Special analyses** (illustrative)
  a. Analyses of combinations of brands stocked to determine the extent to which individual brands compete together
  b. Cumulative distribution of new products

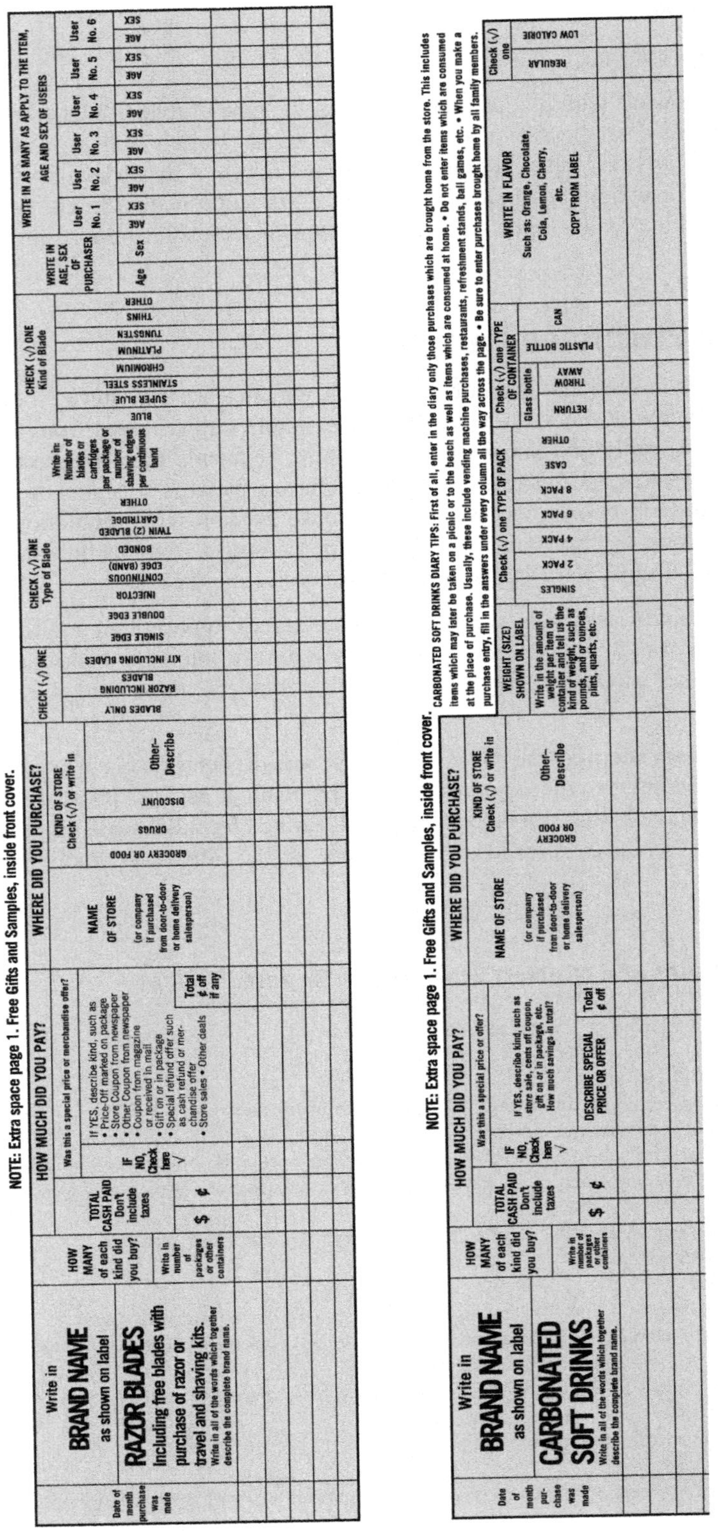

FIGURE 6.1

Illustrations of Recording Forms Used in Mail Diary Panels.

Both types of panels are used extensively in Europe, whereas in the United States and Canada, the mail diary method is dominant. When comparisons have been possible, the two methods have produced equally accurate market share and trend data.[1]

National Family Opinion (NFO) and the National Purchase Diary Panel (NPD) both operate mail diary panels.

Each month MRCA delivers a report for the preceding month, showing total consumer purchases of each brand in the category, plus sales overall, which can be converted into volume and dollar market shares. Each quarter, an analysis of purchases by regions and by type of retail outlet is provided.

The IPSOS Home Testing Institute (HTI) Consumer Panel gives you a direct link to 350,000 households (almost a million individuals) who have agreed to participate in IPSOS studies conducted by mail, phone, or the Internet. Within the panel, a core sample of 250,000 households is geographically and demographically balanced to provide an accurate picture of today's marketplace.

Advantages of Consumer Panels

The data from a panel can be analyzed as a series of snapshots—providing information on *aggregate* sales activity, brand shares, and shifts in buyer characteristics and types of retail outlets from one month to the next. However, just as a motion picture is more revealing than a snapshot, it is the ability to measure *changes in the behavior of individuals* that is the real advantage of a panel. Knowledge of the sequence of purchases makes it possible to analyze:

- Heavy buyers and their associated characteristics.

- Brand-switching rates and the extent of loyal buying. (Evidence of stable purchase activity in the aggregate usually masks a great deal of individual movement.)

- Cumulative market penetration and repeat purchase rates for new products. (The success of new products depends jointly on the proportion who have tried them once and then purchased them a second, third, or fourth time.)

A **continuous purchase panel** is an excellent vehicle for conducting quasiexperiments. A change in price, advertising copy, or package can be implemented in one panel region and the results compared with those of other panel regions where no change was made. Also, because of the lengthy relationship with members of continuous panels, there is much more opportunity to collect classification and attitudinal information to help understand the observed changes in behavior.

In comparison with interview methods, although not with audits, the continuous purchase panel has the advantage of accuracy. Several studies have found that interview respondents will exaggerate their rate of purchasing (an effect that is most pronounced for infrequently purchased products) and dramatically oversimplify brand-switching behavior. Apparently, survey respondents tend to equate their most recent brand buying behavior with their "normal" behavior—whether or not this is accurate.

Limitations of Consumer Panels

The limitations all relate to the vulnerability of panels to various biases. The first problem encountered is **selection bias** because of the high rates of refusal and the resulting lack of representativeness. It is estimated that panel recruitment rates may vary from as low as 10–15 percent when the initial contact is made by mail in the United States to 50 percent or more for personal contacts made on behalf of panels in Great Britain.

A related problem is **mortality effect**, which may mean a dropout rate in excess of 20 percent a year. Some of this is unavoidable because it is attributable to moves and illness. To reduce both the refusal and mortality rates, all panels offer some incentive for continuing participation; these include direct money payments and stamp schemes in exchange for gifts.

There is little doubt that those who refuse or drop out differ from those who participate and remain. In particular, those who are not interested in the topic are the most likely to drop out. These losses are replaced by new members with similar characteristics. This amounts to a matching procedure, but of course it is not possible to match on all important characteristics. In Chapter 9, we will examine the problem of refusals, which afflicts all forms of survey work. As a consequence, however, all panels underrepresent the very rich, the very poor, and the transitory.

Panels also are subject to a variety of *testing effects*. There is a definite tendency for new panel members to report unusual levels of purchasing because of the novelty of the reporting responsibility. This effect is so pronounced that the first month's results usually are discarded. Surprisingly, there is little evidence to suggest that there is any long-run conditioning behavior that would lead to great brand loyalty or price consciousness that would produce systematically biased data.

Finally, it should be kept in mind that usually one person does the recording of purchases. Whenever a product, such as cigarettes or toothpaste, is purchased by several members of the household, there is a good chance that some purchases will be missed. These products are also troublesome to analyze, for what appears to be brand switching simply may be the purchasing of different brands for (or by) different members of the household.

Scanner Services and Single-Source Systems

It is no understatement to say that standardized sources of marketing data for consumer goods have been revolutionized by the **universal product code (UPC)** scanner. By the end of 1992, 80 percent of the commodity value of groceries, 85 percent of the commodity value of mass merchandises, and 40 percent of the commodity value for drugs came through scanner-equipped retail stores.[2]

Within markets equipped with scanner checkouts, purchases are recorded by passing them over a laser scanner, which automatically reads the bar-coded description (the universal product code) printed on each package. This in turn activates the cash register, which relates the product code to its current price—held in computer memory—and calculates the amount due. All the pertinent data on the purchase are then stored in the computer and can be accessed instantly for analysis. In addition to price, the memory stores information on coupon use, so marketers can quickly measure consumer response to using coupons across product categories. Information about shelf space, end-of-aisle displays, use of cooperative advertising, and the like can be merged with scanner data in order to measure the impact on sales, item movement, and net contribution of each marketing effort. Advanced applications are currently available that convert pictures taken from mobile phone cameras into scan-quality files that can be used as sources of marketing information.

As mentioned earlier, the impact of scanners is being felt in the conduct of retail audits, where in-person audits will soon be obsolete, and in the growth of single-source services that track the behavior of individual households, from the TV set to the checkout counter.

Scanner-Based Audit Services

The most immediate benefits of **scanner data** are a high degree of accuracy, time savings, and the ability to study very short time periods of sales activity. To appreciate these benefits, consider the introduction of a new food product into a test market monitored by a scanner-based audit service.

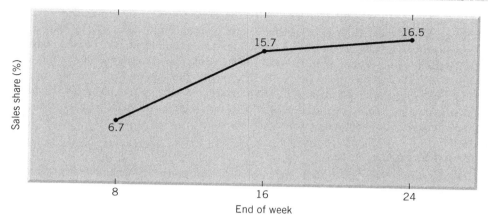

According to the standard bimonthly reports from the store audit service, there was steady progress in building the market share. During the second bimonthly period (see the above graph), share more than doubled, as retailer advertising and coupon promotions were stepped up.

The results from the third period normally would not be available for six to eight weeks. With scanning data, however, weekly reports on this product were available within two to three weeks of the period's end. These weekly reports were far more revealing, as we see from the data shown in Figure 6.2 for the same time period following the launch. The first 11 weeks followed a fairly typical new-brand cycle, with share by week 10 only half of the initial peak. Back-to-back price and coupon promotion in weeks 12 and 13 boosted shares to twice the introductory level. Shares then declined, until a further promotion in week 18. Fortunately, postpromotion shares were always higher than prepromotion shares through week 22. The sharp decline in week 23 was traced to a shortage of the most popular size of package, which was rectified during the next week.

Three scanner-based audit services provide nationally, or locally, representative results within two weeks of the end of the reporting period. Each service provides full detail on each universal product code in a product category: product description, size, price, unit movement and unit share, and dollar sales and share, as well as availability in stores, shelf-space allocation, and usage of coupons. These data can be made available in virtually any combination of stores, to look at sales by chain, geographic area, or even individual store.

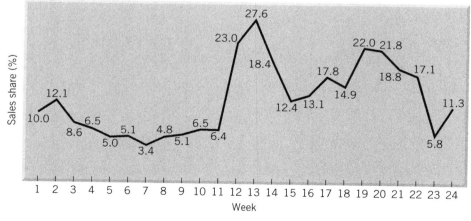

FIGURE 6.2
Weekly Results from Scanner Service.

Nielsen's SCANTRACK now appears to be the largest service, with access to over 3,000 scanner-equipped stores. Both SCANTRACK and Nielsen Food Index (NFI) reports can be accessed directly by a manager with a personal computer and a modem, who can then tap directly into the Nielsen online system. For categories such as candy, snacks, and tobacco, where a large proportion of sales are made in stores without scanners, the supermarket scanner data can be combined with in-person audit data. A.C. Nielsen tracks consumer purchasing in over 150,000 retail outlets in more than 65 countries to provide clients with the most accurate, comprehensive, and timely information about the dynamics of the marketplace.

Applying Scanner Data

Scanner data are used mainly to study the behavior of the consumer when different elements of the marketing mix are varied. They are also used to study and forecast the sales of a new product. For example, in 1991 Frito Lay, Pepsico's $4.2-billion-a-year snack-food division, tested its new multigrain snack called Sun Chips for 10 months in the Minneapolis area. The company experimented with 50 ridges and a salty, nutty flavor, and introduced the product on supermarket shelves. Using scanner data, the company discovered how many shoppers actually took home their first bag of Sun Chips in a given week and who went back a second and third time. This "depth of repeat" gives the company a much clearer sense of the product's potential.[3]

Even retailers are using scanner data. They not only purchase scanner data but also conduct their own tests.[4] They conduct a number of experiments to analyze historical demand at various pricing levels and determine the prices at which they can maximize their total contribution. One retail grocer offered Minute Rice at five different prices over a period of 16 weeks, and the sales results are graphically shown here[5]:

With costs of $0.69 per box, the store could see that profit was maximized at a price of $1.19. Lower prices did not generate sufficient incremental volume to overcome the drop in per-unit profit. This kind of analysis can now be done routinely for thousands of retail store items. This helps retailers control their operations more closely, and some feel that it will significantly enhance their power over manufacturers. Retailers with strong "store brands" have been able to capture market share from national brands by better understanding their customers' preferences and price sensitivity.

Safeway is an example of a retailer that does a lot of scanner-based research. Safeway used scanner data to test alternative placement of products within a store. Results showed, for example, that foil-packaged sauce mixes should not be displayed together but should be spread around

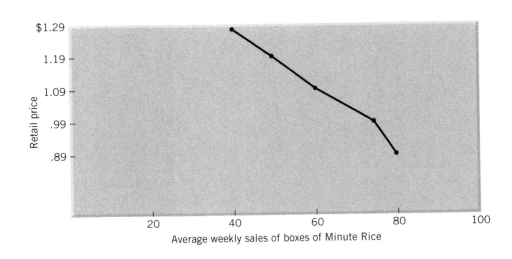

the store according to their contents (spaghetti sauce mix near bottled spaghetti sauce, gravy mix near canned gravy, etc.). In 1990, Safeway created Safeway Scanner Marketing Research Services (SSMRS). Its first product was StoreLab. Clients can test the effectiveness of off-shelf displays, shelf extenders, in-store signs, new package designs or sizes, and consumer bonus packages.[6]

A new technology called RFID may replace the bar codes. RFID utilizes a tiny silicon chip to store information; a small transmitter would then send this information to a scanner. RFID offers more benefits than a UPC, such as:

- The ability to store more information than an 11-digit bar code.

- The ability to change the information on the tag.

- The ability to transmit all the information on the chip to a scanner without a clear line of sight.

RFID tags could make grocery shopping much easier. To check out, all you would have to do is roll your loaded shopping cart past an RFID scanner. In less than a second, it would scan the information on every item in your cart. Shoppers might be able to bag the items as they are selected and walk past the RFID scanner with the items already bagged. Although instant check-out sounds like a technological benefit every shopper would appreciate right away, RFID tags on groceries are still years away. The most significant problem is the high cost of the tiny tag components; the price of a few pennies per tag means that RFID is still impractical for grocery-product manufacturers, which operate on low profit margins. So while the supermarket industry led the way in the adoption of bar codes, other industries will lead the way to the adoption of RFID tags. Supermarket shoppers can be certain that the cost of the RFID tags will steadily decrease and will eventually be less than a penny per tag. Shoppers can also be certain that supermarkets will use any technology that reduces the labor cost required to check out a customer.[7] Marketing Research in Action 6.1 illustrates the type of tracking system with bar codes. Bar codes have also facilitated the integration of physical and online transactions of products. Marketing Research in Action 6.2 shows how use of unique electronic identity (web code) helps producers, retailers, and consumers.

Marketing Research in Action 6.1

■ BAR CODES MONITOR EFFECTIVENESS OF ADS

David Kirwan of Broadwell Marketing Group has created a bar code tracking system to help clients determine which types of ads, special offers, and media mix yield the most benefit. Broadwell was founded seven years ago in a converted two-car garage and has now evolved into a full-fledged marketing and advertising services company that generated $65 million in revenues in 1998. Manufacturers have used bar code coupons to gather information about consumer buying habits at supermarkets but Broadwell has adapted it further to get immediate feedback for restaurants and other stores. This is called *intelligent marketing*. Pizza Hut has collected $24 million in yearly savings thanks to intelligent marketing. Since applying this technique in 1994, Pizza Hut has cut its coupon and direct-marketing costs by 40 percent while nearly doubling its redemption rate. They used the data collected to consolidate different regional marketing departments into one, leveraging its printing and media buying power, which cuts down promotional pitches from 650 to less than 20. Broadwell clients include about two dozen major restaurants and retail chains.

For a closer look on this article go to http://search.chron.com/chronicle/advancedSearch.do.
Source: C. Hall, Houston Chronicle, Sunday, March 7, 1999, p. 10D.

Marketing Research in Action 6.2

■ BAR CODES AND THE INTERNET

With bar codes, companies can unify the online and physical worlds. Bar codes, or any other machine-readable encoded labels, allow physical objects to send data and instructions to networks. By combining bar codes with the Internet, consumer goods companies can stamp every product with a unique electronic identity that can be read wirelessly by new scanning gadgets. Stores can take inventory faster, and more accurately, since shelves equipped with wireless receivers will instantly know when a particular kind of merchandise is gone. With the use of supply chain software and store security system, stores can track a product's location by their bar code labels, and stolen items will be identifiable anywhere. Consumers will be able to execute transactions on the Web, and they can scan special "Web codes" in advertisements or on products.

Source: D. Orenstein, "Raising the Bar," Business 2.0, August 2000.

Single-Source Systems

Single-source systems are usually set up in reasonably self-contained communities, with their own newspaper and cable TV, and are roughly representative of the country's demographics.[8]

After recruiting a test panel of community households, with small payments or coupons as inducements, the researcher monitors each home's TV viewing habits and quizzes household members periodically on what newspapers, magazines, and web sites they regularly read. This provides detailed records of exposure to programming and specific commercials.

Each panel member presents an identification card at a scanner-equipped grocery store each time a purchase is made. This card alerts the checkout terminal to send an item-by-item record of those purchases to a computer that will be included with all other panel members. Then researchers can relate the details of a household's purchase of each product to previously collected classification information about the household and any promotional stimuli to which they were exposed.

These panel households can also be individually targeted for newspaper advertising, so a marketer can experiment with different combinations of advertising copy and/or exposure, discount coupons, and in-store price discounts and promotions. The effects of these different programs can be monitored unobtrusively in the supermarket and each panel member's purchase compared with what he had purchased before the test. To control for competitive activity, the service also tracks the amount of feature, display, and couponing activity in each supermarket.

Television advertising exposure can also be controlled through the cable provider. For example, it is possible to transmit a Duncan Hines cake mix commercial only to Betty Crocker customers to find out if they can be induced to switch. The process of collecting data and providing it to manufacturers and retailers is shown in Figure 6.3.

A typical application of single-source systems is an experiment by the Campbell Soup Company. Using an index of 100 for the average household's V8 consumption, Campbell found that demographically similar TV audiences were consuming vastly different quantities of V8. In early 1987, for example, *General Hospital* audiences had a below-average 80 index, while *Guiding Light* audiences had an above-average 120 index. The results were surprising because *General Hospital* had a slightly higher representation of 25- to 54-year-old women, who were known from other research to be heavier buyers of V8. With this sort of information at hand, it becomes possible to rearrange media schedules to raise the average index.[9]

The possibilities for research are limited only by the ingenuity of the researchers.[10] Suppose the research purpose is to decide whether a product sample should be an alternative or an accompaniment to TV commercials for a child-oriented cereal. The household test panel could be divided into four matched groups and given different combinations of samples and advertising.

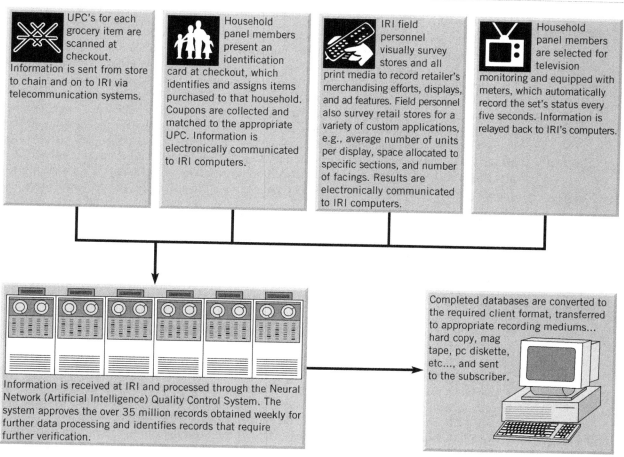

FIGURE 6.3
The Process of Scanner Data Collection by IRI.
Source: Information Resources, Inc.

Sales results could then be monitored to determine whether the group that was also exposed to advertising would be more brand-loyal in subsequent weeks.

The advantages of single-source data for this kind of market response study—compared with conventional market tests—are (1) availability of extensive pretest records, (2) immediate availability of test results, and (3) ability to compare the purchases of households receiving a specific ad during the test with their own purchases prior to the test as well as with purchases of those who were not exposed to the new product ad.

The disadvantage is that single-source systems can track purchases only at grocery stores and drugstores that are equipped with scanners. Furthermore, the test services do not know whether viewers actually are watching a television commercial when it is on, or whether they leave the room during the commercial break. Test participants who are paid volunteers might also unconsciously bias the results because they know they are sending a message to advertisers. An unresolved question is whether tests conducted in small, self-contained markets can predict nationwide results. Finally, there are significant differences in results among competing single-source services that raise questions about the quality of the findings.

Comparing Single-Source Services

One of the most advanced services is BehaviorScan, by Information Resources, Inc. (IRI).[11] It has 3,000 households wired in each of various minimarkets across the United States, from Pittsfield, Massachusetts, to Visalia, California. BehaviorScan, an electronic test marketing service, allows marketers to test new products or new marketing programs. BehaviorScan targets TV commercials in a controlled environment to specific households and tracks the effectiveness of those ads in six smaller markets. It pioneered the service and has had the most experience in conducting tests. IRI's system uses the identification card described earlier, so that details of transactions can be recorded, by household, upon presentation of the card to cashiers at participating stores. IRI also has another product called InfoScan. InfoScan is a syndicated market tracking service that provides weekly sales, price, and store-condition information on products sold in a sample of 12,000 grocery and 7,800 drug stores. The InfoScan service also includes a national sample of thousands of households whose purchases are recorded by checkout or hand-held scanners. BehaviorScan provides data about different markets, whereas InfoScan provides data on different products. Retail sales, detailed consumer purchasing information, and promotional activity are monitored and evaluated for all UPC products.

For several years, A.C. Nielsen had been testing a single-source service—Consumer Panel Services—and had 15,000 homes by 1989. In 1999, Nielsen had increased its panel size to 125,000 households. Nielsen, along with another new entrant, Scan America (a joint venture of Control Data and Selling Areas Marketing, Inc., a subsidiary of Time, Inc.) offers a very different technology. Unlike BehaviorScan participants, Nielsen families record their purchases at home by passing a penlike wand over goods bearing bar codes, keying in other information about coupons at the same time. The information is transmitted daily through a device attached to participants' television sets. Because Nielsen's system is not dependent on retailers who cooperate, it allows tracking of purchases from a wider range of stores, but it has been criticized for requiring that participants be actively involved in entering the data. Another important difference is that Nielsen can send test commercials over the air, so members of the sample do not have to be cable subscribers.[12]

Retail Measurement Services provides product movements data through food, drug, and other retail outlets in 79 countries. Flagship service is U.S.-based Scan-Track, which provides weekly data on packaged-goods sales, market shares, and retail prices from UPC scanner-equipped supermarkets. Another service, Precision, tracks health and beauty aids product sales through drug and mass-merchandiser stores. In other countries, either scanning or audit-based methods are used to collect retail data.

Expert Systems Based on Single-Source Services

The rapid increase in the use of scanner technology has brought a peculiar problem to the marketing analyst. Although about a decade ago researchers were struggling to obtain data to conduct research, they now are faced with exactly the opposite problem. Users of scanner data have been overwhelmed with massive amounts of data. Therefore, suppliers of scanner data have created expert systems to give the data more utility for the managers. These expert systems are designed to cut the mass of scanner data down to actionable pieces of information. There are many expert systems that give solutions to specific problems. Both Aldata and Nielsen have developed a number of these expert systems to make the decision process easier. A partial list is provided below.

Aldata[13]

- **Apollo Space Management Software** provides suggestions for optimizing shelf allocations for each item in the section of a retail store. It analyzes scanner data from the InfoScan database to review the amount of shelf space, price, and profit components of product category shelf sets, such as dishwashing soaps or cereals. Apollo also can produce photo-quality schematics using its library of 120,000 product images and dimensions. Thus, the retailer gets a visual picture of what the shelf reallocation will look like.

Nielsen[14]

- **Promotion Simulator** is an easy-to-use software application that automatically simulates future promotion strategies. It uses historical Nielsen data to calculate the effect of the promotional plans on manufacturer and retailer profitability, given the price points and retail conditions in the plan.

- **Spotlight** is an expert system that runs through the database, calculating volume and share changes, and searching for the key merchandising and competitive factors that influence those factors. Then it summarizes the findings in a presentation-quality report.

- **Sales Advisor** automatically highlights need-to-know information and enables the sales force to add personal insights to presentation-quality output. Sales Advisor produces finished summaries and presentations of sales and marketing data.

Media-Related Standardized Sources

Another area in which there is a great deal of commercial information available for marketers relates to advertising and media. A number of services have evolved to measure consumer exposure to the various media and advertisements. For example, Nielsen Media Research unveiled its much-anticipated Nielsen/NetRatings Internet Measurement Service on March 22, 1999. According to a Nielsen spokesman, the NetRatings service uses data from 9,000 users on a real-time basis and will track movement on both websites and so-called banners, or Web-page ads that users click on to learn more information. Nielsen took on the help of Media Metrix, which has been the main company measuring consumer use of websites.[15] In addition to Nielsen, several media-related services are described below.

Nielsen Television Index

The Nielsen Television Index (NTI) is probably the best known of all the commercial services available in this category. As a system for estimating national television audiences, NTI produces a "rating" and corresponding share estimate. A *rating* is the percent of all households that have at least one television set tuned to a program for at least 6 of every 15 minutes that the program is telecast. *Share* is the percent of households that have a television set that is tuned to a specific program at a specific time.

From 1987 onward, Nielsen has been using "people meters" instead of the traditional diary to obtain this information. The *people meter*, which is attached to the television set, continuously monitors and records television viewing in terms of when the set was turned on, what channels were viewed, how long the channels were tuned in, and who in the household was watching that channel.[16] The data are stored in the people meter and later are transmitted via telephone lines to a central processing facility.

Nielsen National Television Index (NTI) is based on a national 5,000-household sample equipped with people meters, and reporting TV, cable, and home video viewing. At the market level, Nielsen Media Research (NMR) provides Nielsen Station Index (NSI), which uses set meters to measure TV audiences through weekly mail diary surveys in 211 local markets among

100,000-plus households. Nielsen Homevideo Index (NHI) measures cable and VCR audiences using a combination of NTI, NSI, and custom diaries. Data on syndicated programs in the Nielsen Syndication Service (NSS) come from the same sources. Two services, through people meters, measure Hispanic audiences for Spanish-language media across the United States (800 households) and in the Los Angeles market (200 households).

The Nielsen NTI-NAD data are used by media planners to analyze alternative network programs. Next, the cost efficiency of each program is calculated. Cost efficiency represents a television program's ability to deliver the largest target audience at the smallest cost. A cost per thousand (CPM) calculation is computed as

$$\frac{\text{Cost of a commercial}}{\text{Number of target audience delivered}} = \text{CPM}$$

Since 1994, Statistical Research Inc. (SRI)—a company known primarily for measuring national network ratio audiences—has made a priority of its pilot program for a new TV measurement system called SMART (Systems for Measurement and Reporting Television). SMART is known for its user-friendliness and the ability to count more viewers than Nielsen's People Meter. Media industry observers believe that SRI could have what it takes to topple Nielsen.

SRI's SMART grew out of the broadcast industry's dissatisfaction with Nielsen Media Research. Critics have complained that Nielsen does not measure enough viewers, charges too much, and takes too long to provide subscribers with data. On the other hand, the SMART setup consists of meters with sensors that can pick up signals from the air. The meters require no wire connection and the meters attach to television sets with a Velcro strip.

Despite SRI's potential, the company still faces an uphill battle against Nielsen. According to president and co-founder of SRI Gale Metzger, SMART was designed to respond to the industry's needs, and whether or not his company will beat out Nielsen depends on the industry.[17]

Major differences between the two systems are given in the chart below:

	SMART	People meter
Mechanics	No wire connection—sensors pluck signals from the air.	Wired directly to TV and VCR tuners.
Research Methods	Data are retrieved by reading embedded codes called Universal Television Program Codes (UTPC) in some program signals; a decoder attached to the back of the TV will be able to record the UTPC identifying the program used.	Telephone connections are used to return data.
Method of Data Collection	User logs in and out before and after watching TV with remote control device.	User punches numerical code into a data-entry device.
Reputation as:	Media measurement business serving the radio industry.	

Arbitron Diary Panel

Arbitron gathers information that describes consumers' demographic, socioeconomic, and lifestyle characteristics, as well as purchase intentions in 260 markets. Arbitron provides three qualitative services tailored to fit specific market size and marketing requirements: Scarborough caters to large markets, RetailDirect® is available in medium markets, and the Qualitative Diary Service is offered in smaller markets ranked 100+. Each service profiles a market, the consumers, and the media choices in terms of key characteristics. The three services cover the major retail and media-usage categories in almost any area.

There has been a lot of recent controversy over Nielsen television ratings. The networks claim that since Nielsen became a monopoly—all the other rivals dropped out—service has been unprofessional. The networks also have problems with Nielsen's sampling methodology. The networks charged that Nielsen bases its ratings on too few diaries, making its data less representative of what viewers watch. In response to this, Nielsen decided to send out 10 percent more paper diaries for viewers to note what they watch. By 1998, the number of diaries increased by 50 percent, which Nielsen claims is the largest increase in sample size in the history of TV audience measurement.

Arbitron, a subsidiary of Control Data, maintains both national and regional radio and TV panels. The panel members are chosen by randomly generated telephone numbers, to ensure that households with unlisted numbers are reached. Those household members who agree to participate when called are sent diaries in which they are asked to record their radio listening behavior over a short duration. Most radio markets are rated only once or twice a year; however, some larger ones are rated four times a year. The TV diary panel is supplemented with a sample of households that have agreed to attach an electronic meter to their television sets. Arbitron produces custom reports for clients. Typically, these are based on an interactive computer-based system called Arbitron Information on Demand (AID).

Starch Scores

The previous two sources of marketing data involve radio and television ratings, whereas Starch scores cover print media. The Starch Readership Service measures the readership of advertisements in magazines and newspapers.[18] Some 75,000 advertisements in 1,000 issues of consumer and farm magazines, business publications, and newspapers are assessed each year, using 100,000 personal interviews.

The Starch surveys employ the *recognition method* to assess a particular ad's effectiveness. Four degrees of reading are recorded:

1. *Nonreader:* A person who does not remember having seen the advertisement in the issue.

2. *Noted:* A person who remembers seeing the advertisement in the issue.

3. *Associated:* A person who not only "noted" the advertisement, but who also saw or read some part of it that clearly indicated the brand or advertiser.

4. *Read Most:* A person who read 50 percent or more of the written material in the ad.

Because newspaper and magazine space cost data are also available, a "readers per dollar" variable can be calculated. The final summary report from Starch shows each ad's (one-half page or larger) overall readership percentages, readers per dollar, and rank when grouped by product category.

Multimedia Services

Simmons Media/Marketing Services uses a national probability sample of some 19,000 respondents and serves as a comprehensive data source, allowing the cross-referencing of product usage and media exposure. Four different interviews are conducted with each respondent, so that magazine, television, newspaper, and radio can all be covered by the Simmons Service. Information is reported for total adults and also for males and females separately.

Media-mark Research also makes available information on exposure to various media and on household consumption of various products and services. Its annual survey of 20,000 adult respondents covers more than 250 magazines, newspapers, radio stations, and television channels, and over 450 products and services.

Applications of Standardized Sources of Data

Standardized data sources are used widely in a number of marketing research problems. We have already discussed the various sources of standardized data. In this section, we will look at some of the applications of standardized data. Table 6.2 gives a comprehensive framework of the types of sources used for different applications.

Measuring Product Sales and Market Share

A critical need in today's increasingly competitive environment is for firms to have an accurate assessment of their performance. Marketing performance typically is measured by the company's sales and market share. Firms can track their own sales through analyses of their sales invoices. An alternative source that can be used is the online bibliographic data sources. The measurement of sales to final customers historically has been done by the use of diary panels and retail store audits. Scanner data are now being widely used for this purpose.[19]

Measuring Advertisement Exposure and Effectiveness

With media costs rising exponentially, and the options for advertising increasing dramatically with the advent of cable television, measurement of advertising exposure and effectiveness, and program ratings has become critical. Advertising exposure and effectiveness in the print media are tested by Starch scores[20] and in the audio-visual media by Nielsen Television Services and Arbitron. Ratings of the various network and cable programs can be found in the Nielsen Television Index and those of the radio programs in the Arbitron panels. Multimedia services such as the Simmons Media/Marketing Services and Media-mark Research conduct research on overall media exposure and effectiveness. Scanner data also have been used extensively for modeling ad exposure and measuring ad effectiveness.[21]

Table 6.2 Applications of Standardized Data Sources

Measuring promotion effectiveness	Measuring ad exposure and effectiveness
1. Scanner data	1. Starch scores
2. Diary panels	2. NTI
	3. Arbitron
	4. Multimedia services
Measuring product sales and market share	**Estimation and evaluation of models**
1. Diary panels	1. Scanner data
2. Retail audits	2. Starch scores
3. Scanner data	3. Diary panels
4. Internal records	4. Internal records
5. NAICS	

Measuring Promotion Effectiveness

Only since the advent of scanner data have marketers begun to fathom the power of promotion in increasing product sales and market share. This is evident from the fact that the number of coupons, samples, displays, and features at the retail outlets have increased tremendously over the past few years. Before scanner data were introduced in a big way, promotion effectiveness was measured by diary panels of the NPD group. Since store-level scanner data and scanner panels were introduced by IRI and Nielsen, measurement of promotion effectiveness has been revolutionized. The effect of promotions now can be observed directly through scanner data.[22]

Estimation and Evaluation of Models

Models are essentially explanations of complex phenomena, expressed by symbols. They can be mathematical, verbal, graphical, or a figure. Marketing researchers build models to explain the various marketing phenomena and to draw managerial implications from them. The models can either be at the aggregate level or at the individual level. Scanner data are used to evaluate the efficacy of the model and estimate the response of the market to changes in the marketing-mix elements.[23] North American Industry Classification System (NAICS) codes and diary panels are used for this purpose.

SUMMARY

Between the generally available secondary sources (which are economical and quickly found but perhaps not relevant) and primary data (which are designed to be directly relevant but consume considerable time and money), there are various standardized information services. These exist whenever there are economies of scale in collecting data for a number of users with similar information needs. The most widely used services are still retail store audits and consumer panels. With recent developments in information technology, and especially the widespread adoption of store checkout scanners, the use of these services is quickly shifting to scanner audits. New capabilities for understanding consumer response by integrating measures of purchase behavior and communications exposure in single-source data are also changing the conduct of research very rapidly.

The remainder of this book will emphasize the collection and analysis of primary data, for it is here that the greatest problems and opportunities are found. Knowledge of the methods of primary data collection is also essential to informed usage of secondary sources.

QUESTIONS AND PROBLEMS

6.1 Which of these two, a product audit (such as the Audits and Surveys National Market Audit) or a store audit (such as the Nielsen Retail Index), would be more suitable for the following products:

  (a) peanut butter;

  (b) cameras;

  (c) engine oil additives;

  (d) chewing gum? Why?

6.2 The manager of a supermarket in Hoboken, New Jersey, has two local newspapers competing for weekly ads. The salesperson for newspaper A claims that although A's rates are significantly higher than newspaper B's, paper A has the best circulation in the market. Also, readership studies show that area residents really scrutinize the paper's pages. The salesperson for newspaper B concedes that the publication does not have the widest circulation, but points to readership studies showing that its ads are equally effective. "Why pay twice as much for an ad, when my paper can do as strong a job for less money?" This problem has been unresolved for some time. Recently, the store had nine scanner checkouts installed. The manager would like your advice on how to use the store's scanner sales data to compare the effectiveness of the two newspapers.

6.3 What combination of standardized services would you use to monitor the effects on your existing cereal brands when a new cereal brand is being introduced? Why? Would you use the different services to monitor trial and repeat purchases of the new cereal product in a test market?

6.4 The sales and market shares for the same brand in the same period are often different when they are measured by a scanner audit rather than a consumer panel. How would you account for the differences? What would you do about them?

6.5 Campbell Soup used BehaviorScan data to discover that viewers of two daytime serials had very good appetites. *Search for Tomorrow* viewers bought 27 percent more spaghetti sauce than average, but 22 percent less V8 vegetable juice. Viewers of *All My Children* bought 10 percent less spaghetti sauce than average, but purchased 46 percent more V8 than the norm for all viewers. How would you go about explaining the differences between these two programs that led to the consumption differences? What action would you recommend to Campbell Soup management?

6.6 Wash O'Well, a leading detergent company in Canada, is unable to explain the reason why its new zeolite-based detergent has not captured the anticipated market share since its launch in Minneapolis, Minnesota, in 1992. The company has decided to focus on point-of-sale activities: for example, which brands have distribution in which stores, what shelf location each brand occupies, the kinds of displays in effect, and so forth. The marketing manager has been instructed to recommend a suitable source of standardized data.

(a) What are the various data source alternatives available to Wash O'Well?

(b) Discuss the advantages and limitations of each of them and recommend the data source most suitable for Wash O'Well's needs.

6.7 **(a)** What are the two types of consumer panels used for gathering marketing research data?

(b) Which type of panel is most frequently used in the United States?

(c) What are the advantages and disadvantages of using a consumer panel?

END NOTES

1. S. Sudman and R. Ferber, *Consumer Panels*, Chicago: American Marketing Association, 1979.

2. *Source:* A.C. Nielsen.

3. S. Caminiti, "What the Scanner Knows About You," *Fortune*, December 3, 1990, pp. 51(2).

4. J. Sinkula, "Status of Company Usage of Scanner Based Research," *Journal of the Academy of Marketing Science*, Spring 1986, p. 17.

5. This example was adapted from L. M. Lodish and D. J. Reibstein, "New Gold Mines and Mine Fields in Marketing Research," *Harvard Business Review*, January–February 1986, pp. 168–182.

6. "Safeway Launches New StoreLab Testing Service," *Marketing News*, January 8, 1990, p. 45.

7. M. Sloane, "Technology May Alter Supermarket Checkout," *Houston Chronicle*, Wednesday, July 21, 1999, p. 11F.

8. The following articles give a good overview of the single-source systems: D. Curry, "Single Source Systems: Retail Management Present and Future," *Journal of Retailing*, Spring 1989, pp. 1–20; M. Prince, "Some Uses and Abuses of Single Source Data for Promotional Decision Making," *Marketing Research*, December 1989, pp. 18–22; "Futuristic Weaponry," *Advertising Age*, June 11, 1990, pp. 5–12.

9. J. Lipman, "Single Source Ad Research Heralds Detailed Look at Household Habits," Wall Street Journal, February 16, 1988, p. 35.

10. Examples of recent applications of scanner data include: P. S. Fader and L. McAllister, "An Elimination by Aspects Model of Consumer Response to Promotion Calibrated on UPC Scanner Data," *Journal of Marketing Research*, August 1990, pp. 322–332; E. Waarts, M. Carree, and B. Wierenga, "Full Information Maximum Likelihood Estimation of Brand Positioning Maps Using Supermarket Scanning Data," *Journal of Marketing Research*, November 1991, pp. 483–490.

11. The information on BehaviorScan is drawn from a pamphlet from Information Resources Incorporated.

12. A good article that compares the two single-sources suppliers is Leon Winters, "Home Scan vs. Store Scan Panels: Single Source Options for the 1990s," *Marketing Research*, December 1989, pp. 61–65. Also see "Now It's Down to Two Equal Competitors," *Superbrands 1991: A Supplement to Adweek's Marketing Week*, p. 28; and "IRI, Nielsen Slug It Out in Scanning Wars," *Marketing News*, September 2, 1991, p. 1.

13. *Source:* Information Resources Incorporated.

14. *Source:* A.C. Nielsen.

15. "Nielsen on the Net," *Wall Street Journal*, Friday, March 19, 1999.

16. W. R. Dillon, T. J. Madden, and N. H. Firtle, *Marketing Research in a Marketing Environment*, Boston: Irwin, 1990; and Soong Roland, "The Statistical Reliability of People Meter Readings," *Journal of Advertising Research*, February–March 1988, pp. 50–56.

17. M. Wirth-Fellman, "A SMART Move," *Marketing News*, September 14, 1998, pp. 1, 7.

18. *Starch Readership Report: Scope, Method and Use*, Mamaroneck, NY: Starch INRA Hooper, undated.

19. V. Kumar and T. Heath, "A Comparative Study of Market Share Models Using Disaggregate Data," *International Journal of Forecasting*, July 1990, pp. 163–174; F. J. Mulhern and R. P. Leone, "Implicit Price

Bundling of Retail Products: A Multiproduct Approach to Maximizing Store Profitability," *Journal of Marketing*, October 1991, pp. 63–76.

20. G. M. Zinkhan and B. D. Gelb, "What Starch Scores Predict," *Journal of Advertising Research*, August–September 1986, pp. 45–50.

21. G. J. Tellis, "Advertising Exposure, Loyalty, and Brand Purchase: A Two-State Model of Choice," *Journal of Marketing Research*, May 1988, pp. 134–144; V. Kumar and R. T. Rust, "Market Segmentation by Visual Inspection," *Journal of Advertising Research*, 1989, pp. 23–29.

22. S. Gupta, "Impact of Sales Promotions on When, What, and How Much to Buy," *Journal of Marketing Research*, November 1988,

pp. 342–355; V. Kumar and R. Leone, "Measuring the Effect of Retail Store Promotions on Brand and Store Substitution," *Journal of Marketing Research*, May 1988, pp. 178–185; R. C. Blattberg and S. A. Neslin, *Sales Promotion: Concepts, Methods, and Strategies*, Englewood Cliffs, NJ: Prentice Hall, 1990.

23. V. Kumar, A. Ghosh, and G. Tellis, "A Decomposition of Repeat Buying," *Marketing Letters*, 3(4), 1992, pp. 407–417; P. S. Fader, J. M. Lattin, and J. D. C. Little, "Estimating Nonlinear Parameters in the Multinomial Logit Model," *Marketing Science*, Fall 1992, pp. 372–385.

Case 6-1 || Promotion of Rocket Soups

Soups provide an interesting case history through which to examine the impact of sales promotion. Soups are sold primarily through food stores and frequently are promoted by both the manufacturer and the retailer. This case is based on 40 weeks of scanner sales history in one city. Please answer all of the questions at the end of the case.

Background

Soups are purchased by over 75 percent of all households. On average, the time between purchases is around 40 days. Sales promotion, including features, displays, and price reductions, is extremely important in this category, with around 55 percent of annual category sales moving with some sort of sales promotion. Shelf-price reductions, when they are used, average about 30 percent.

The major competitors in this category are

Brands	Share
Rocket	19.7
Stellar	40.3
Tasty	13.4
Lovely	3.5
Happy	18.1
Smile	5.0

The data for this case were collected from grocery store scanner installations in one market area and consist of

1. Weekly store sales by brand
2. Predominant price charged by brand by store
3. Occurrence of promotional activity by brand by store

The data have been summarized across all stores in the market on a weekly basis, for a total of 60 weeks. Table 6.3 is the week-by-week summary.

At the weekly level, Table 6.4 shows the data on the amount of volume moved by various promotions at various prices. However, since the stores in the market are of varying sizes, direct evaluation of promotional effects is difficult. Therefore, the sales effects are normalized (adjusting for store sizes statistically). Table 6.5 shows the normalized sales volume by promotional type. The commonly used methods for store-level scanner data are (1) brand volume per $1,000,000 total all commodity volume spending, and (2) brand volume per 1,000 register checkouts.

During the time of data collection, some extremely "hot" promotional activity occurred as the result of a Rocket promotional program. Some retailers decided to use Rocket soup as a "loss leader" in addition to the manufacturer promotions, and combined both. These activities resulted in substantial variations in price, volume, and share of Rocket.

This case was prepared by V. Kumar for the purpose of classroom discussion. For similar cases, refer to J. C. Totten and M. P. Block, Analyzing Sales Promotion, Chicago: Dartnell Corp., 1994.

Table 6.3 City Sales of Soup by Week (Price is Volume-Weighted Average)

Week	Rocket volume	Rocket dollars	Category volume	Category dollars	Rocket price	Rocket share	Competitive volume
1	306	250	5,984	4,356	0.82	5.1	5,678
2	345	384	14,288	9,780	1.11	2.4	13,943
3	873	694	6,201	4,893	0.79	14.1	5,328
4	900	715	5,657	4,447	0.79	15.9	4,757
5	4,404	2,772	7,673	5,453	0.63	57.4	3,269
6	456	388	5,027	4,196	0.85	9.1	4,571
7	444	395	5,570	4,687	0.89	8.0	5,126
8	513	507	11,519	8,305	0.98	4.5	11,006
9	483	441	4,661	3,917	0.91	10.4	4,178
10	615	548	4,803	4,381	0.89	12.8	4,188
11	624	571	5,038	4,632	0.91	12.4	4,414
12	16,113	705	19,633	3,982	0.04	82.1	3,520
13	1,056	811	4,476	3,967	0.76	23.6	3,420
14	381	375	3,863	3,599	0.98	9.9	3,482
15	534	526	5,014	4,677	0.98	10.6	4,480
16	1,821	870	6,487	5,257	0.47	28.1	4,666
17	390	384	3,642	3,350	0.98	10.7	3,252
18	405	398	3,743	3,441	0.98	10.8	3,338
19	1,152	1,012	5,042	4,865	0.87	22.8	3,890
20	348	342	4,733	4,248	0.98	7.4	4,385
21	378	372	3,862	3,448	0.98	9.8	3,484
22	5,319	5,129	8,352	7,839	0.96	63.7	3,033
23	2,280	1,691	7,086	5,311	0.74	32.2	4,806
24	1,194	962	5,931	4,878	0.80	20.1	4,737
25	1,020	837	5,708	4,666	0.82	17.9	4,688
26	342	336	7,780	5,849	0.98	4.4	7,438
27	1,509	1,378	5,385	5,191	0.91	28.0	3,876
28	420	413	7,352	5,533	0.98	5.7	6,932
29	528	520	7,516	5,661	0.98	7.0	6,988
30	942	676	6,416	5,461	0.71	14.7	5,474
31	957	711	15,599	7,578	0.74	6.1	14,642
32	1,014	738	4,937	4,294	0.72	20.5	3,923
33	1,059	990	5,664	5,213	0.93	18.7	4,605
34	351	385	9,045	7,302	1.09	3.9	8,694
35	384	418	5,435	4,932	1.09	7.1	5,051
36	4,122	3,084	8,672	7,699	0.74	47.5	4,550
37	9,108	4,466	13,165	8,694	0.49	69.2	4,057
38	498	542	5,643	5,103	1.09	8.8	5,145
39	459	500	5,555	5,150	1.09	8.3	5,096
40	486	529	4,485	4,285	1.09	10.8	3,999

Table 6.4 City Sales of Soup by Week (Price is Volume-Weighted Average Sales by Promotional Type)

Week	Volume with no promotion	Price with no promotion	Volume with display only	Price with display only	Volume with feature only	Price with feature only	Volume with feature and display	Price with feature and display
1	306	0.82	0	–	0	–	0	–
2	345	1.11	0	–	0	–	0	–
3	477	0.75	396	0.85	0	–	0	–
4	420	0.75	480	0.84	0	–	0	–
5	222	0.69	0	–	0	–	4,182	0.63
6	399	0.83	57	0.99	0	–	0	–
7	375	0.87	69	0.99	0	–	0	–
8	471	0.98	42	1.07	0	–	0	–
9	405	0.90	78	0.99	0	–	0	–
10	486	0.87	129	0.99	0	–	0	–
11	537	0.90	87	0.99	0	–	0	–
12	486	0.79	102	0.85	0	–	15,525	0.02
13	384	0.75	0	–	0	–	672	0.78
14	381	0.99	0	–	0	–	0	–
15	534	0.99	0	–	0	–	0	–
16	267	0.87	153	0.98	0	–	1,401	0.35
17	390	0.99	0	–	0	–	0	–
18	405	0.98	0	–	0	–	0	–
19	315	0.81	672	0.89	60	0.98	105	0.98
20	348	0.99	0	–	0	–	0	–
21	378	0.98	0	–	0	–	0	–
22	201	0.69	0	–	0	–	5,118	0.98
23	0	–	702	0.86	1,578	0.69	0	–
24	819	0.86	375	0.69	0	–	0	–
25	366	0.74	654	0.86	0	–	0	–
26	252	0.98	90	0.99	0	–	0	–
27	117	0.99	288	0.99	585	0.89	519	0.88
28	327	0.98	93	0.99	0	–	0	–
29	309	0.98	219	0.99	0	–	0	–
30	588	0.74	354	0.69	0	–	0	–
31	450	0.73	507	0.75	0	–	0	–
32	333	0.69	288	0.69	195	0.79	198	0.79
33	555	0.87	504	1.01	0	–	0	–
34	303	1.10	48	1.12	0	–	0	–
35	384	1.09	0	–	0	–	0	–
36	132	0.89	0	–	0	–	3,990	0.74
37	0	–	2,409	0.74	0	–	6,699	0.40
38	498	1.09	0	–	0	–	0	–
39	459	1.09	0	–	0	–	0	–
40	486	1.09	0	–	0	–	0	–

Table 6.5   City Sales of Soup by Week (Price is Volume-Weighted Average Normalized Volume Sales by Promotional Type)

Week	Normalized volume with no promotion	Price with no promotion	Normal volume with display only	Price with display only	Normal volume with feature only	Price with feature only	Normal volume with feature and display	Price with feature and display
1	0.21	0.82	0.00	–	0.00	–	0.00	–
2	0.20	1.11	0.00	–	0.00	–	0.00	–
3	0.45	0.75	0.66	0.85	0.00	–	0.00	–
4	0.50	0.75	0.63	0.84	0.00	–	0.00	–
5	0.60	0.69	0.00	–	0.00	–	3.94	0.63
6	0.33	0.83	0.32	0.99	0.00	–	0.00	–
7	0.24	0.87	0.36	0.99	0.00	–	0.00	–
8	0.31	0.98	0.27	1.07	0.00	–	0.00	–
9	0.30	0.90	0.34	0.99	0.00	–	0.00	–
10	0.36	0.87	0.50	0.99	0.00	–	0.00	–
11	0.41	0.90	0.41	0.99	0.00	–	0.00	–
12	0.50	0.79	0.45	0.85	0.00	–	3.95	0.02
13	0.38	0.75	0.00	–	0.00	–	1.14	0.78
14	0.25	0.99	0.00	–	0.00	–	0.00	–
15	0.26	0.99	0.00	–	0.00	–	0.00	–
16	0.34	0.87	0.65	0.98	0.00	–	2.05	0.35
17	0.25	0.99	0.00	–	0.00	–	0.00	–
18	0.27	0.98	0.00	–	0.00	–	0.00	–
19	0.70	0.81	1.85	0.89	0.15	0.98	0.48	0.98
20	0.21	0.99	0.00	–	0.00	–	0.00	–
21	0.27	0.98	0.00	–	0.00	–	0.00	–
22	0.57	0.69	0.00	–	0.00	–	4.79	0.98
23	0.00	–	0.64	0.86	3.77	0.69	0.00	–
24	0.65	0.86	0.98	0.69	0.00	–	0.00	–
25	0.55	0.74	0.80	0.86	0.00	–	0.00	–
26	0.21	0.98	0.28	0.99	0.00	–	0.00	–
27	0.43	0.99	0.82	0.99	1.55	0.89	0.79	0.88
28	0.26	0.98	0.29	0.99	0.00	–	0.00	–
29	0.24	0.98	0.67	0.99	0.00	–	0.00	–
30	0.48	0.74	1.15	0.69	0.00	–	0.00	–
31	0.45	0.73	0.95	0.75	0.00	–	0.00	–
32	0.55	0.69	0.93	0.69	0.96	0.79	0.55	0.79
33	0.52	0.87	0.88	1.01	0.00	–	0.00	–
34	0.22	1.10	0.36	1.12	0.00	–	0.00	–
35	0.25	1.09	0.00	–	0.00	–	0.00	–
36	0.37	0.89	0.00	–	0.00	–	2.98	0.74
37	0.00	–	1.92	0.74	0.00	–	18.61	0.40
38	0.29	1.09	0.00	–	0.00	–	0.00	–
39	0.26	1.09	0.00	–	0.00	–	0.00	–
40	0.29	1.09	0.00	–	0.00	–	0.00	–

CASE QUESTIONS

Question 1

According to Table 6.3, weeks 5, 12, 22, 23, 36, and 37 were highly important sales weeks for Rocket. Weeks 2, 8, and 31 were important sales weeks for the competition. If data on promotional activity are not known, its presence is usually inferred by abnormally high sales of the brand or category, a cut in price, or both. Reviewing these weeks, and nearby weeks, discuss the effects on Rocket and its competitors on:

1. Total category volume
2. Total category dollar spending
3. Each other's volume (Rocket's and competitors')
4. Sales in the weeks following high volume movement

Question 2

Table 6.4 shows overall promotional activity. Sales during week 12 were at an average price near zero. This typically arises out of a retail promotion of the type: "Free box of Rocket given with total purchases of $10.00 or more." Table 6.5 shows sales levels adjusted for the percentage of stores in each class, and for their relative sizes. Discuss any difficulties you see in assessing the impact of the week 12 promotion on:

1. Incremental volume to Rocket
2. Promotional volume borrowed from future sales

Question 3

Using Table 6.5, plot only the nonpromoted sales versus the nonpromoted price. Discuss the probable percent impact on Rocket sales from a 10 percent increase or decrease in price.

Question 4

Using Table 6.5, plot the relationship between sales on display only, and display-only price. What similarities and differences in sales levels and response to price do you see in comparing the display-only response to the nonpromotional response?

Case 6-2 ||| Kerry Gold Products, Ltd.

In late May of 1996, the research manager for Kerry Gold Products met with the product manager for margarine to review the company's first experience with Nielsen scanner data. A year-long test in a single chain organization, which began in April 1995, had been completed recently.

The first purpose of their review was to interpret the findings. They decided to concentrate on the results of the first 18 weeks of the tests, which are summarized in Figure 6.4. The size of the bars represents the weekly unit sales for Kerry Gold brand and the three competing brands also sold by the chain organization. In addition to the weekly data, there were summary data on share of total sales for the first and second halves of the year. This distinction was important because Kerry Gold had spent relatively little on promotion in the second half of the year. Since Nielsen had full records of all sales, they were also able to examine their share of sales during weeks when no brands offered price-reduction promotions. These data are shown in the two right-hand columns in Table 6.6.

While reviewing these results, the research manager also was wondering whether scanner data would be useful for other grocery products sold by Kerry Gold. Many of them were as heavily promoted as margarine. Judgments on the desirability of consumer promotions for these products usually were based on a combination of store audit data plus periodic controlled experiments.

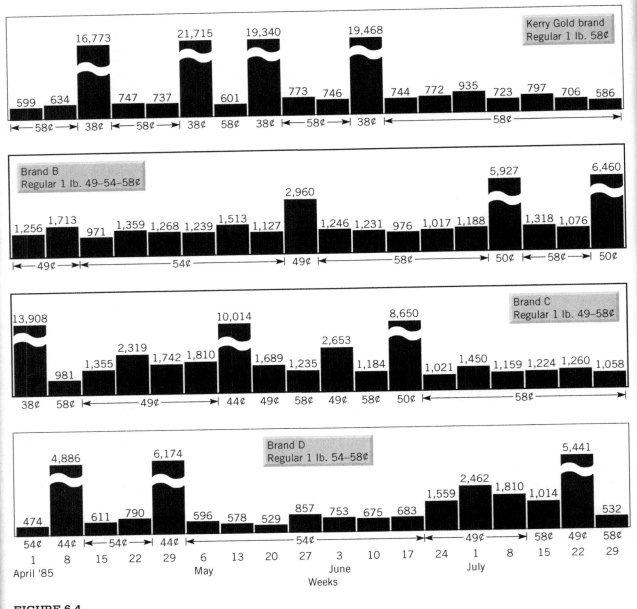

FIGURE 6.4
Unit Sales Per Week (and Prevailing Price for the Brand During the Week).

Table 6.6   Semi-Annual Share by Brand

Brand	Share of total sales (%)				Share of sales in nonpromotional weeks (%)	
	1st $\frac{1}{2}$ yr		2nd $\frac{1}{2}$ yr		1st $\frac{1}{2}$ yr	2nd $\frac{1}{2}$ yr
Kerry Gold	39	(34)[a]	13	(7)	18.9	19.3
B	17	(8)	42	(35)	30.4	30.3
C	29	(13)	28	(18)	33.1	33.9
D	15	(11)	17	(12)	17.6	16.5
		(66)	100	(72)	100	100

[a]Figures in parentheses are deal merchandise shares of market. In the first half of the year, 66 percent of total unit sales in the category were on deal.

Additional Case for this Chapter is available on the Web:

Web Case 6-1	Paradise Foods

7 Marketing Research on the Internet[1]

LEARNING OBJECTIVES

- Discuss past and current developments of the Internet.
- Describe the components of the Internet.
- Discuss current commercial research applications.
- Discuss the current use of the Internet as a marketing research tool.
- Discuss the outlook of future developments.

The Internet is arguably an immensely important tool that has added a new dimension to traditional marketing research intelligence. With volumes of relevant information available at the click of a mouse, decision making has assumed a new perspective. The number of Internet users around the world is constantly growing. According to data published by Internet World Stats, the Internet currently reaches 3.09 billion people worldwide. The highest growth percentages over the past year comes from countries in Africa including Zimbabwe, Uganda, and Angola (17 percent).[2]

At the start of the new century, 55 million of us were shopping to our hearts' content at home. Shopping online, and researching products online, has increased since 2000. In 2000, while 22 percent of Americans had bought a product online, this rate grew to 90 percent in 2013. For product-related research, 35 percent had used the Internet in 2000, and 91 percent in 2007.[3] According to a sales forecast conducted by Forrester Research Inc., total retail online spending in general merchandise will increase from $263 billion in 2013, up to $414 billion in 2018.[4] Those numbers exclude online ticket sales projected by Forrester at $9.4 billion in 2010, up from $4.3 billion in 2004. Further, the report projects additional online sales of about $155.5 billion in 2010 from the combined category of automobiles and auto parts, food and beverages and travel, up from $65.6 billion for the category in 2004.

Shopping on the Internet has increased significantly in recent years. In 2014, U.S. retail sales amounted to USD297.4 billion and this number is predicted to continue to increase. The U.S. retail e-commerce spending summary for the period between 2006 and 2014 is given in Table 7.1, along with the percentage change every year.

Current Trends in Web Usage

National trends of Internet usage have increased with improved education, income, and the advancements in smart phones and tablets. According to a report titled "Computer and Internet Use in the United States: 2013" released by the U.S. Census Bureau, an estimate 78.1 percent of

Table 7.1 U.S E-Commerce Sales (USD Mn.), 2006–2014

Year	E-Commerce sales (millions of dollars)	Percent change from prior year
2006	113,015	—
2007	136,205	17.03%
2008	142,137	4.17%
2009	145,090	2.04%
2010	169,335	14.32%
2011	198,623	14.75%
2012	228,552	13.10%
2013	259,857	12.05%
2014	297,418	12.63%

Source: "Quarterly Retail E-commerce Sales – 2nd Quarter 2015," U.S. Census Bureau, August 17, 2015. Accessed from http://www.census.gov/retail/mrts/www/data/pdf/ec_current.pdf

people in American households had a high-speed Internet connection in 2013.[4] Further, data from the Pew Internet and American Life Project revealed that 87 percent of American adults were found to use the Internet in January 2014, up from 73 percent in January 2006. It further reported that 13 percent of American adults do not use the Internet, as of January 2014.[5]

Advertisers are taking advantage of increased Internet use, with Internet advertising revenue at $42.78 billion in FY2013, more than double the amount from 2007, according to a report published by the Interactive Advertising Bureau. The report also found that contributions from the mobile advertising revenues more than doubled to 7.1 percent in 2013, up from 3.4 percent in 2012, indicating the strong impact of the mobile medium.[6] As more customers rely on the Internet for their daily transactions, analysis of this becomes essential for businesses in order to determine the profile of customers, customer lifetime value, and effectiveness of promotional campaigns, among others. The Internet usage today is witnessing a change among the older users. The Pew Report states that in 2014, 88 percent of individuals in the United States aged between 50 and 64 use the Internet, compared to 57 percent of those aged 65 and older.[7] While a majority of the e-commerce market is yet to design senior-specific sites, some pharmaceutical and financial sites have developed websites usable by everyone and particularly catering to older people. Pfizer Inc. has websites that are specifically designed to aid older people by providing information on senior citizen products. Financial companies such as Fidelity Investments and Charles Schwab Corp. have also incorporated usability features for seniors on its websites.[8]

The prominence of the Internet is being increasingly witnessed in developing countries as well. According to Internet World Stats, North America is home to about 10 percent of world Internet users, with a penetration rate of 87.7 percent. However, it recorded the lowest usage growth of 187.1 percent between 2000 and 2014. During the same period, the highest usage growth of 6,499 percent was registered in Africa. The Middle East was second, recording over 3,303 percent growth. The Latin America/Caribbean region was in third place with 1,672 percent growth.[9]

Language too plays an important role in Internet usage. According to Internet World Stats, Internet users by native speakers were found to be English—28.6 percent, Chinese—23.2 percent, Spanish—7.9 percent, Arabic—4.8 percent, Portuguese—4.3 percent, Japanese—3.9 percent, Russian—3.1 percent, German—2.9 percent, French—2.8 percent, and Malaysian—2.7.[10] With such a wide variety of users taking to the Internet, marketers are incorporating language selections in their home pages to cater to all speakers.

It is quite evident that as the Web usage continues to grow, it provides marketers with a whole variety of options in terms of reaching a wider audience and better exposure to the products or services that are offered. In this context, monitoring Web usage assists Web developers in developing a website that is accessible to a larger population.

The Internet offers real advantages to all firms, including small ones. Since the cost of constructing a website is reasonably low, a firm with less than a million dollars in sales is as accessible to potential customers worldwide as Nestle or French Telecom. The Internet can "level the playing field" for marketing to potential customers through efficient use of the medium. Examples abound of companies that have made it big through the use of the Internet. According to research conducted by Forrester Research, e-commerce transactions are expected to increase from $263 billion in 2013 to $414 billion in 2018. The estimates include mobile devices, typically the biggest e-commerce sales driver. It further estimates that by 2018, e-commerce will have a 9.5 percent compounded annual growth rate over six years.[11]

WWW Information for Marketing Decisions

Online Advertisements

With technological advancements and the rapid spread of the World Wide Web, advertising online provides instant access to the fastest growing media audience in the world. Online advertising provides an interactive element like no other traditional advertising medium. The origins of online advertising can be found in the banner advertisements first featured in the early 1990s. The forms of advertising soon expanded to opt-in e-mails, search engine advertising, floating animated pages, and audio and video streams among others. Since online advertising provides an interactive element, it enables advertisers to develop a one-to-one relationship with prospective and existing clients. With the advertisements carrying links to the advertiser's website, measurement and tracking of advertisements become easier.

One of the popular methods of online advertising is Search Engine Advertising. According to a research conducted in February 2012 by Pew Internet & American Life Project, nearly 91 percent of the viewers have had successful search experiences. It further says that 73 percent of Americans who are online have used search engines, and, on any given day, 59 percent of people online are using them.[12] With search sites becoming popular, search engine advertising can help advertisers reach their target audience in more ways than one. This type of advertising involves advertising on the Web by tracking keyword searches. In other words, when a viewer is searching for information on the Internet, the keywords used for the searches would lead the viewer to the advertiser's website, amid other search results. For this to be effective, the target audience must be properly identified and the keyword phrases used for searching must be placed strategically on the website.

Advertising in local media sources can be an effective way to overcome the targeting issue. According to a research report by BIA/Kelsey, the U.S. local media revenues are forecast to reach $139.3 billion in 2015, representing a growth of 1.6 percent from 2014.[13] Table 7.2 shows how online advertising spending has increased worldwide between 2012–2018.

A relatively new online advertising option is contextual advertising. This form of advertising goes one step further from search engine advertising. A contextual advertisement is similar to the advertisement that is displayed at the top of search results but is instead displayed on the content page that contains the relevant material.[14] For instance, social-networking website Facebook Inc. is working on a new advertising system that would let marketers target users with ads based on the information people reveal on the site about themselves. Eventually, it hopes to refine the system to allow it to predict what products and services users might be interested in even before they have specifically mentioned an area.[15]

Table 7.2   Digital Advertising Spending Worldwide, 2012–2018

Year	Digital ad spending worldwide (USD bn.)	Share in total media ad spending (in %)
2011	86.85	—
2012	104.57	20.8
2013*	120.05	23.3
2014*	140.15	25.7
2015*	160.18	27.9
2016*	178.45	29.5
2017*	196.05	30.9
2018*	213.89	32.3

Source: Printed with permission from "Global Ad Spending Growth to Double This Year," July 9, 2014, accessed from http://www.emarketer.com/Article/Global-Ad-Spending-Growth-Double-This-Year/1010997 on April 2, 2015
NOTES: *denotes estimates.
Digital ad spending includes spending on all advertising that appears on desktop and laptop computers as well as mobile phones and tablets, excluding SMS, MMS, and P2P messaging-based advertising.
Total media ad spending includes spending on digital (desktop/laptop and mobile), directories, magazines, newspapers, outdoor, radio, and TV.

In certain cases, participating content sites achieve high search engine rankings. Limiting the advertisements to these sites may not be guarantee maximum viewership. This is because; searchers may not click these search result sites. Hence, advertising in sites that fit the context of keyword may not only bring in more viewers but will also capture those who do not visit through a search engine.

Online Tracking Measurements

An average consumer through exposure to online advertisements consumes enough to call for study and monitoring. A true measurement of an advertisement's performance is thus essential for creating and retaining customers. Before the advent of the Internet, researchers relied primarily on telephone surveys to ascertain the advertisement recall rates by interviewing a sample. However, with the penetration of the Internet, online tracking of advertisements has become a viable option.

Online tracking is advantageous to researchers in many ways. First, Internet tracking offers researchers a means to test viewers' advertisement recognition by providing visual cues, unlike telephone surveys that only provide verbal cues. Second, online tracking yields faster results. This is because everyone in the sample is sent an invitation to fill out the response online. This saves a lot of time and energy as compared to the telephone version. Finally, not only is it now possible for researchers to know the viewer awareness of advertisement campaigns, they can also determine the degree of awareness of a campaign by comparing segments of the audience. With traditional telephone recall studies, only determining advertisement awareness was possible.[16]

In order to track online advertisements, new methods are being incorporated by large companies. For instance, Yahoo! and A.C. Nielsen are using a research methodology called Yahoo! Consumer Direct for measuring the impact of online advertisements on off-line retail purchases of consumer products. With the Internet undergoing change frequently, the profile of viewers changes accordingly. While new metrics for tracking online advertisements are being implemented, marketers do not have a "perfect metric" for tracking.[17] Thus, marketers will have to recognize the changing consumer profile and develop suitable tracking methods. Marketing Research in Action 7.1 presents a novel use of online tracking practices.

Some examples of firms involved in keeping track of online trends which can provide valuable information to companies for marketing decision making include the following.

Cyberatlas, a division of I/PRO, compiles and publishes public-domain information about Internet market size, growth, forecast, and demographics. In addition, Cyberatlas provides news on WWW markets such as advertising, finance, and search services, as well as normative data and industry benchmarking studies. The domain name market shows a strong rate of new registrations and a stabilizing base of domain names. According to "The Domain Name Industry Brief, April 2014" published by VeriSign, registered domain names have grown to a base of 271 million worldwide across all top-level domains. The domain name registrations have grown by 7.3 percent between 2012 and 2013.[18]

Forrester Research from Cambridge, Massachusetts, offers a service called New Media Research. One component of this project is Media & Technology Strategies, which focuses on new business media models for publishers, broadcasters, and information service providers. Research topics include, for example, how information will be priced in the electronic marketplace. This is critical information for corporations which do heavy advertising on the Web (such as IBM or Netscape) because they want an adequate return on their advertising spending. Many different proposals have been made for pricing ads on the Internet. Forrester found out that advertisers complain about pricing schemes based on cost per thousand and would rather see click-through (based on the number of clicks for the ads) pricing. Table 7.3 shows the Internet advertising revenues by major industry categories of 2013 and 2014.

Marketing Research in Action 7.1

■ TRACKING FLU—THE GOOGLE WAY

Ever wondered what happens to all the search words in a search box? Google, a leader in web search, has been tracking such key words and offering search related content apart from the search results. Google has extended this concept and launched the Google Flu Trends. This tool (www.google.org/flutrends) allows web users to see the flu activity across the United States. By tracking the search phrases related to "flu symptoms," Google has been able to detect the regional outbreaks of the flu a week to 10 days before they are reported by the U.S. Centers for Disease Control and Prevention. This tool analyzes the searches as they happen and creates graphs (both at a state and country level) that, ideally, will show where the flu is spreading.

Talking about the tool's predictive accuracy, Google says it witnessed a spike in the search data related to flu symptoms about two weeks prior to the flu report released by the Center for Disease Control (CDC). Since the CDC relies on the healthcare providers to provide information related to diseases and their outbreaks, valuable time is lost in data collection efforts. Google on the other hand, collects data as it happens and tracks the flu spread. This tool could help accelerate the response of doctors, hospitals, and public health officials; reduce the spread of the disease; and, potentially, save lives.

Source: M. Helft, "Google uses web searches to track flu's spread," New York Times, November 11, 2008.

Table 7.3   Internet Advertising Revenues by Major Industry Category, 2014 vs 2013

Industry	2014 (in $Billion)	2013 (in $Billion)	Percentage growth
Mobile Advertising	12.5	7.1	76%
Digital Video	3.3	2.8	17%
Social Media	7	4.5	57%
Search	19	18.4	3%
Display Ads	13.5	12.8	5%

Source: "U.S. Internet Ad Revenues Reach Record-Breaking $49.5 Billion in 2014, a 16% Increase Over Landmark 2013 Numbers, Marking Fifth Year in a Row of Double-Digit Growth for the Industry," April 22, 2015. Accessed September 8, 2015 from http://www.iab.net/about_the_iab/recent_press_releases/press_release_archive/press_release/pr-042215

Global online advertising expenditures in 2014 were $137.53 billion up from $119.84 in 2013.[19] The advantages of advertising on the Internet cannot be understated. First, a targeted audience can help not only to define the site's audience but also to produce customized ads to be shown on the next visit.

Table 7.4 shows how consumer preferences are helpful in designing effective online advertisements.

One problem in Web advertising is audience measurement. A firm would like to measure "eyeballs," that is, how many total exposures an ad receives. However, on a given site visit, customers often go back and forth rapidly between hypertext pages. Measuring the number of times a particular page is on the screen may not be the appropriate measure of exposure, as the screen

Table 7.4   Designing an Effective Online Ad

Survey responses show that the most effective ads. . .	
Give more personality to the brand	65%
Are more engaging	64%
Give consumers more control	60%
Are more informative	60%

Ads with these qualities. . .	
Attract more people's gazes	63%
for a longer period of time	500%
Generate higher interaction	34%
Are rated higher by consumers	17%
Generate Greater Brand Lift	30%
Produce Stronger Brand Recall	300%

Source: "IAB Display Rising Stars Outperform Traditional Display Ads Across Key Brand Effectiveness Metrics, According to In-Depth Research Study from IAB & C3Research." Press Release, Feb. 9, 2015. Accessed online September 8, 2015 at http://www.iab.net/about_the_iab/recent_press_releases/press_release_archive/press_release/pr-020915_risingstars

time may have been very brief. A minimum amount of time might be necessary before it can count as a "hit." Or the viewer may not scroll all the way down the screen. These issues confront the large number of companies interested in measuring site audiences.20 To address these problems, some new services are being developed.

AdCount by NetCount is a tracking service of Web users that attempts to measure the effect of Web ads. It promises not only to monitor how many Web cruisers see an ad but whether they click on it to be connected to the advertiser's own website. Such "click-through" rates are the true measure of whether an ad placement had an effect. For this purpose, special software is installed on the host computer. The software sends frequent updates of ad activity on the sites to a central computer from which the reports are generated. These reports usually comprise daily and weekly totals of ad impressions and click-throughs, daily and weekly totals of ad transfers (clicks on ads which successfully deliver the user to the advertiser's website), and advertiser summary reports with comparable statistics on each ad tracked.

Some good examples of how companies are using the Internet and the World Wide Web are the following (source: World Wide Web):

The Ford Motor Company is now offering an online store that allows users to buy cars of their choice online. Users can select the brand, model, and the features for the car. In short, they can *build* their car online and get the estimated cost. They could apply for a financial loan as well. (www.ford.com)

Amazon.com opened its virtual doors in July 1995 with a mission to use the Internet to transform book buying into the fastest, easiest, and most enjoyable shopping experience possible. Today, Amazon.com is the place to find and discover anything you want to buy online. It is the leading online shopping site, with 270 million people in more than 160 countries shopping with them. They have Earth's Biggest Selection™ of products, including free electronic greeting cards, online auctions, and millions of books, CDs, videos, DVDs, toys and games, and electronics. (www.amazon.com)

Google Maps is a leader in Advanced Mapping Solutions. Since 2005, Google Maps has been a leader in offering online, interactive maps, and driving directions for consumers across the world. Over the years, they have expanded their coverage of geographic areas and included route planning applications for users traveling by foot, car, bicycle, or with public transportation. The maps can also be embedded on third-party websites, thereby increasing the website's usage and adoption. The maps are also available on a wide range of devices such as desktops, laptops, smartphones, and tablets, among others. Other popular in-built applications on Google Maps include real-time traffic status, biking directions (in select cities), 360 degree panoramic street views, local business listings, and aerial views, among others (www.maps.google.com).

eBags is the world's largest online retailer of bags and accessories for business, sports, and travel. They carry a complete line of premium and popular brands, including Samsonite, JanSport, North Face, Eagle Creek, and Timberland. From backpacks and carry-ons to computer cases and adventure gear, eBags combines the best selection of products with unrivaled services and extremely competitive prices. It is five times larger than most department stores. eBags allows you to browse a huge selection of bags in a large variety of colors. Unlike most stores, eBags offers smaller specialty brands for those looking for something unique. In addition, eBags carries bags in every price range, ensuring that shoppers find the perfect bag at the perfect price (www.eBags.com).

The Internet and Marketing Research Today

Over the past few years, online research has become an important mode of quantitative market research. For instance, Forrester Research estimates indicate that business-to-business (B2B) marketers will increase their overall budgets by an average of 6 percent in 2015, of which nearly 13 percent will be in the online space.[21] This rise in online presence has been largely due to the wide acceptance of the Internet as a source of information. Other factors include the wide presence of Internet and the declining response rates of the telephone/computer aided telephone interview (CATI) method. While the online mode of research is clearly more cost effective than the traditional modes of research, the quality of online research results is still a topic for debate. The rapid advancement of the online mode has given rise to many market research innovations such as opt-in panels like Harris Interactive and Greenfield Online, self-service survey providers such as Zoomerang and SurveyMonkey.[22] Like any traditional information resource, the Internet has certain advantages and disadvantages. Besides this, the Internet is characterized by very dynamic technological developments, which in turn influence the information search process. This section looks at a variety of ways the Internet can be utilized for marketing research.

Primary Research

The Internet is now being used for collecting primary information for use in mainstream marketing, though with caution. The various ways of collecting information are briefly discussed.

E-mail Surveys

A familiar example for this is the use of electronic mail for survey research. This technique uses e-mail for the entire process of receiving, completing, and returning questionnaires. This type of survey technique has a number of advantages:

- Greater speed of delivering electronic mail over regular postal mail. Questionnaires are delivered, or redelivered if lost, in a matter of seconds.

- Higher speed of delivering responses and feedback.

- Cost-savings benefits over regular mail surveys.

- No intermediaries—e-mail messages are usually read only by the recipient.

- Asynchronous communication. Unlike telephone surveys, messages can be sent, read, and replied to at the convenience of the user.

While e-mail survey is an important and effective tool, it is not without its share of problems. Important among the drawbacks of e-mail surveys is spamming or sending unsolicited bulk messages. Spam in e-mail started to become a problem when the Internet was opened up to the general public in the mid-1990s. It grew exponentially over the following years, and today comprises a majority of all the email in the world. A market research firm, Radicati Group Inc. reports that the average number of e-mail messages sent daily in 2010 was around 294 billion, of which 89 percent are spam. Of these junk messages, nearly 50 percent were delivered. While mail filtering programs are being developed at a fast pace to curb the spam menace, spammers are finding newer ways to send messages to e-mail users.

Some of the less desirable properties of e-mail surveys are that the security of electronic mail is low in comparison to traditional media. Also, even though many researchers guarantee anonymity of participants, respondents may often not answer truthfully for fear that their identity might be revealed.

As the population of the Internet and online users increases, new research issues have arisen concerning the demographics and psychographics of the online user and the opportunities for a product or service. Marketing Research in Action 7.2 gives an example for how consumer surveys can be conducted on Google. The key issue is to provide a disclaimer that the firm seeks only composite data and that names and addresses will not be used for solicitation or sold to another vendor. This kind of survey can also be conducted by announcing it on appropriate lists and groups, and then, in response to a request, sending the survey out via e-mail.[23]

Interactive Forms

Primary data collection may also be performed through interactive forms which are filled out on the screen. For example, in order to gain specific demographic information and reading habits about Internet users, one company that provides access to newspapers and magazines ran a contest for those willing to fill out an online survey. A news release was put out to the net-happenings mailing list, announcing that the information was being made available on their Gopher.

Online Panels

Online panels are an effective way of conducting Internet research whereby groups of people agree to participate in surveys and exchange their views. Companies such as Harris Interactive and Synovate conduct online panels with participants from all over the world. The information collected from the members through these panels is used for developing business and marketing solutions. Apart from being cost effective and fast, online panels provide high-quality data acquired from willing, interested, and motivated participants. As they provide anonymity and

Marketing Research in Action 7.2

■ GOOGLE CONSUMER SURVEYS

Survey tools and their ease of access to the general public have grown drastically over the past few years. One such survey tool is the Google Consumer Survey. It is a market research tool that lets you create online survey in order to access high-quality content. Understanding the market's appetite for launching new ideas, market size, demand, brand perception across demographics, customer satisfaction are few of the many information Google Consumer Surveys can define. Some salient features of this tool are as follows:

- Survey questions can be in 10 different formats (such as multiple choice, star rating, and image selection)
- Surveys can be customized based on your business and narrow your audience using a screening question
- Survey questions are embedded directly into the content across a network of premium online news, reference, and entertainment sites

- On the Web, the questions should be answered in order to view the content (an alternative to subscribing or upgrading)
- Demographic data can automatically be garnered based on the users browsing history and IP address
- Tracking surveys that run for set time intervals can be chosen to measure insights such as brand awareness

There important advantages of using this tool are three-fold. First, the survey methodology has evolved from traditional methods to highly customized, audience defining, and easily accessible research tools. Data can be gathered with minimum amount of time and efforts. Second, high exposure sites capture significant portion of all the user activity. This helps in acquiring data from varied set of people. Finally, the new customization features provide an almost accurate data. Additionally, the demographics data collected automatically from the back end reduces the demographic surveys to be created.

Source: "Google Consumer Survey," https://support.google.com/consumersurveys/

convenience to the panel members, it provides a viable option for the marketers to research sensitive topics. Some of the other advantages of online panels include the possibility of covering a wide audience, the ability to conduct international research from one place, and the viability of electronic monitoring of respondents through log file analyses.

The quality of online panels is determined by recruitment, maintenance, and response rate standards.[24] The online panel recruitment can be broadly classified into two categories: actively recruited online panels and passively recruited online panels. In case of actively recruited online panels, participants are carefully selected and targeted, either off-line or online. Since this involves a selection procedure, it becomes a closed pool of participants. In passively recruited online panels, participants find their way to register themselves through the various links available on the Internet and in magazines. Since this does not involve any selection procedure, it functions as an open pool of participants. The recruitment of online panel members may also include employees and customers. The point to be noted here is that, recruiting members for the online panel based on the purpose of the online panel would yield better results from the subsequent surveys.

The maintenance of online panels is essential in conducting online research. This calls for a continuous monitoring of the panel members. Researchers, while monitoring the existing panel members, must also be on the lookout for new panel members to replace users who have left the panel. The existing panel members may also be replaced with new members because of their familiarity with research methods, which may lead to response bias. The process of recruiting new members is easier in online panels than in off-line panels, as researchers can stay in constant touch with the members and responses can be obtained instantly. Maintaining online panels also calls for communicating with panel members on a regular basis, ensuring the time relevance of collected data and satisfaction of panel members, as this would be a good indicator of panel quality.

Response rates perform an important part in online research by indicating the quality of survey research and in determining the cost of the project. When respondents "opt in" to the panel, they bring in a significant amount of information relating to demography and behavior. The information thus collected later helps in deciding the samples. Opt-ins typically lead to higher response rates as the questionnaire can be shorter. This is possible because the researcher would already have the basic information of the panel members and need not spend time and energy on collecting the information again. The response rates also depend on the length of online survey, the amount and type of incentives offered, and the technical equipment available to the respondents. Researchers have to be aware that having e-mail addresses or having a large panel does not translate into a higher response rate.

With business problems demanding attention, further limited by time, online panels offer researchers and marketers a way to obtain immediate results from the targeted consumers and at their convenience. Given the higher response rates, online panels are gaining popularity among researchers. When compared to other traditional methods such as telephone and mail studies, The Council for Marketing and Opinion Research reports that cooperation rates for Internet panel studies in 2010 were as high as 65 percent.

Online Focus Groups

Online focus groups are conducted entirely online—everything from recruitment and screening (which the recruiter does via e-mail) to moderation of the discussion itself. This method allows researchers to reach target segments more effectively. Online focus groups, while lacking the dynamics of a face-to-face discussion, provide a unique alternative to the traditional method. An online environment allows respondents to interact voluntarily "behind their computer screens" and therefore encourages them to respond with honest and spontaneous answers. Furthermore, all respondents, extroverted and introverted, get a fair chance to express their views, and "instant messaging" allows the key focus-group players to interact privately with each other. Although online respondents do not "hear" each others' answers, they can see them. Thanks to "emoticons" (the use of certain keys that, typed in combination, look like facial expressions), cyberspace allows online focus-group participants and moderators to express themselves.[25]

As the online population increases, the demographics broaden, enabling remote global segments to be reached, something not possible via traditional methods. One of the limitations to online research is that the results cannot be projected to the general population because not everyone has access to a computer, modem, and online service. Another difference between online and traditional qualitative research is that cyberspace is populated by trend leaders. Commonly targeted by marketers, advertisers, and product manufacturers, trend leaders are early adopters who try out new ideas, products, services, and technologies before these innovations reach popularity in the mass market.

Companies are increasingly collecting information from their website visitors. Especially for companies which sell over the Web, collecting information about potential customers who have Internet access is critical. This type of data collection can serve a number of purposes:

- Counting and describing website visitors in order to customize website content to suit their needs

- Collecting additional information for customer databases, which then may be used by product development, sales, marketing, or service departments

- Receiving questions or suggestions regarding the use of a product

- Receiving and answering complaints

It is surprising to see how many website visitors are willing to leave personal information (such as address, phone number, and e-mail number). In many cases, companies offer a small reward as a token for the complying visitor. For example, upon completing a questionnaire at the Campbell's Soup website, the company mails a number of coupons for their products to the customer. Other tokens from packaged-goods companies are good for product samples, price drawings, or sweepstakes.

I/PRO has launched a service called I/CODE that lets users submit information about themselves once; it then makes the data available to sites participating in the I/CODE scheme. The advantage to the user is being able to skip answering the same questions repeatedly, and I/CODE offers prizes as an incentive to register. Publishers and advertisers pay for the information, and in return can build a database of users and track their behavior. CINET gathers information about users without asking questions. Its servers can recognize each visitor's browser and computer type as well as their domain (.com, .edu, .org, etc.). It uses this information to deliver a "banner" (advertising) tailored to different types of users—for example, a Mac warehouse banner for a Mac user and a PC warehouse ad for a PC user.

Return on Investment (ROI) is becoming increasingly popular as a new technology in helping promote direct marketing. ROI tracks the consumers that are surfing online who click on the banner ads. The positive trend for ROI stems from the demand for quantifiable results from business investments made by executives and shareholders. This has resulted in an increasing number of firms to equip themselves with analytic software programs that measure ROI on a real-time basis. A recent report on marketing ROI and ROI measurement trends found that in 2005, 78 percent marketers felt their budgets for marketing analytics was underfunded. In 2006 that percentage had dropped to 64 percent.[26]

The click-through rates measure the type of consumer response by the amount of clicks produced. In counting returns, ROI becomes a key metric in evaluating the effectiveness of banner ads for some online advertising agencies. The calculation on the return of ad spending to track actual sales, software downloads, or user registration is done in the following way:

- A banner ad is served to an online viewer, who is tagged with an identification code stored in the browser's cookie

- The user will then click on the ad and is sent to the link promoted by the advertiser

- An ad-tracking firm serves a tiny pixel-sized image, which is posted on key pages of the website the advertiser wants to track. Such pages often begin software downloads or are the "thank you" pages that are shown after a consumer makes a purchase

- When the user clicks on the key page, identification information stored on the cookie is sent to a central server that tracks the pixel-sized image and the resulting consumer action

- Results logged at the central server are compared with overall investment in advertising to generate ROI results.[27]

User Generated Reviews

Listening to customer reviews is becoming an increasing source of vital marketing information. User generated information, especially product and site reviews, can be mined to devise marketing and advertising strategies. A Forrester research recently evaluated more than 4,000 product reviews belonging to the Electronics and Home & Garden categories of Amazon.com and found that (1) 76 percent of people use customer reviews for shopping, (2) 84 percent of product reviews were positive or neutral, and (3) despite negative product reviews consumers understood that not all products or experiences are perfect.[28]

Many companies have now included a user review web page in their websites. For instance, when CompUSA added a user generated review page along with the product search option, they saw conversion rates rise 60 percent and individual spend rising 50 percent. Similarly, Yahoo! estimates that 40 percent of the online buying population is a product advocate and have an enormous influence on buying habits and online communications patterns. Further, Bazaarvoice, a company that provides online brands with managed solutions to enable, encourage and monitor online customer ratings and reviews found that nearly 77 percent of all customers use reviews and 81 percent of shoppers who spend more than $500 online each month use product reviews when making buying decisions.[29]

Until recently, consumers were only talking among a small group of people. But with the emergence of social media, consumers now have a wider and a more receptive audience. By listening to such responses about product and user experiences, companies can generate a two-way conversation with the consumers and act on the reviews received. Such an exercise will boost loyalty among consumers.

Secondary Research

The main forte of the Internet is probably its advantages in researching secondary information. As the 2014 Pew Internet & American Life Project pointed out, 87 percent of online adults utilize the Internet for searching or gathering information. Additionally, 89 percent use it for making a purchase.

The Internet competes with several other online resources to satisfy the information needs of businesses and consumers. Businesses typically rely on professional databases such as Lexis/Nexis or Knight-Ridder. Consumers most often utilize commercial online services such as America Online or CompuServe. Although the latter also provide Internet access, they represent a comprehensive information resource in themselves. Table 7.5 depicts how the Internet compares against other online information sources.

Table 7.5   Comparison of Information Sources

	Internet (WWW, usenet)	Professional databases (e.g., Lexis/Nexis)	Commercial online services (e.g., CompuServe)
Speed[a]	Low to high	High	Low to high
Information structure	Structure not very good	Very well structured	Well structured
Information scope	Very broad	Depends on the database, mostly narrow	Medium to broad
Overall information quality	Low to high	High to very high	Medium to high
Search tools	Limited, not complete	Extensive, accurate	Mostly accurate
User support	Limited	Very good	Good
Cost	Low	High to very high	Medium

[a]Depending on modem, server, and database structure.

The main advantages of the Internet at this point are its very broad scope, covering virtually every topic, and its comparably low cost. These characteristics make it a very appealing medium to use for both consumers and businesses. Also, it is expected that the technical constraints of the Internet, such as low bandwidth, will be gradually resolved in the future, making it less cumbersome to use in terms of downloading times.

Finding out information about competitor activities is an important task for businesses. The Internet is a prime tool for this task, since it reduces the time spent and may increase substantially the quality of the information collected. Both product and financial information are probably suited best for competitive tracking. In particular, larger corporations display this information most often in their websites. On the other hand, pricing information might not be amenable to tracking readily, since it is not too common for businesses to display product prices (unless they actually sell over the Internet). Competitive promotion and distribution information is probably the least suited to tracking via the Internet. Information about products or companies can be obtained using search engines on the Web. However, search engines have certain limitations and hence do not guarantee that all relevant information has been obtained. For this purpose, there are providers of custom search services, who search for information for a fee.

Custom Search Service

A growing number of custom search services are becoming available that offer information tracking and forwarding for a fee. These services range from one-time custom searches to regular news deliveries. It is very common for these services to specialize in a particular area such as global telecommunication or food processing and then offer their search results in a regular electronic newsletter to subscribers. Depending on the service, the charges can be based on usage (one time or for the whole project), time frame (weekly, monthly, yearly), object (document fee, fee per researched publication), amount of text (number of characters), or any combination of these. For example, Acxiom Corporation provides customer and business information in the form of service data for various clients, with the intent of assisting them in targeting different advertising campaigns and scoring leads. With clients ranging from a variety of sectors including insurance, marketing, information services, health care to telecommunications, Acxiom's focus lies in strengthening the connection between businesses and their partners.

Agents

The use of intelligent agents in monitoring information is increasing rapidly. For illustrative purposes, let us consider a competitive analyst for a TV producer. The analyst needs constant information on the pricing of competitors' products. An intelligent agent would monitor websites of TV manufacturers and TV retailers, collect price and availability information, and deliver easy-to-skim summaries.

Agents function in many different ways. Some are available on the Internet and preprogrammed for particular search tasks, such as Bargain Finders. This commercial application will most likely gain tremendous significance in the near future. Other types of agents are a piece of software that is purchased by the user, who then has to specify downloading criteria. Most often searches are scheduled at night so they do not have to wait to download documents. Agent technology is on the verge of entering the mainstream of Web search, and the future is likely to bring many innovations in this area.

Leveraging Web Analytics for Marketing

With the ever-changing dynamics of the World Wide Web, the relationship between consumers and brands continues to evolve. Consumers are increasingly seeking avenues online to gather information about brands and to fulfill their need for products and services. As more consumers continue to navigate online to connect with brands and to make purchase decisions, it is only natural that marketers will seek to target them in this online space where time and convenience are on the side of the consumer.

For the first time in U.S. history, marketers are projected to spend more on online advertising than on advertising in print magazines and newspapers. As shown in Figure 7.1, online ad revenues are expected to continue to grow over the next few years with total online ad investment projected to hit $62 billion by 2016.[30]

With online advertising increasing exponentially, marketers are interested in utilizing resources to measure the effectiveness of their online communications in reaching consumers and encouraging interaction with their brands. A few examples of sources used to capture the online behavior of consumers and how people traverse through a site's content is Google Analytics and Amazon's Mechanical Turk.

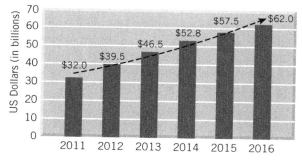

FIGURE 7.1

U.S. Online ad Spend 2011–2016.

Source: Printed with permission from "US Online Advertising Spending to Surpass Print in 2012," January 19, 2012. Accessed from http://www.emarketer.com/Article/US-Online-Advertising-Spending-Surpass-Print-2012/1008783.

What Is Google Analytics?

Google Analytics is a free website statistics solution that gives rich insights into Web traffic and marketing effectiveness. It is the most widely used website statistics service with 60 percent of the 10,000 most popular websites using the service.[31] It allows businesses to see (1) how people find their site, (2) how they navigate through that site, and (3) how they ultimately become customers. The tool allows marketers to monitor sales, conversion rates, and site engagement by generating detailed statistics about the visitors to a website. This tool can also track site visitors from all sources including search engines, advertising, e-mails, and digital links.

Google Analytics offers tracking of campaign elements such as e-mail, banner ads, and offline ads to measure reach and effectiveness. The service is integrated with Adwords, an advertising product that offers pay-per-click (PPC) advertising, cost-per-thousand (CPM) advertising, and site-targeted advertising for text, banner, and rich-media ads. Subscribing to Adwords allows businesses to display their ads on Google and its advertising network. Google Analytics can be used to optimize the performance of Adwords by providing post-click data on keywords, search queries, match type, and other ad components.

In terms of e-commerce, Google Analytics tracks sales activity and performance from products and services sold online. The tool can trace *transactions to campaigns* and *keywords* to show which site content is generating the most revenue. In addition, the tool displays loyalty and latency metrics for purchases on the site. Purchase latency, the number of days between purchase events, can be monitored to increase customer retention and revenues. Google Analytics can create a detailed overview of how often customers in different segments are using the site's products and services.

Additionally, the tool can also be used to track user interaction with websites and applications accessed from a mobile device. Traffic coming from smart phones can be tracked by device or carrier and usage of apps can be tracked in the same way as a website.

How Do You Access It?

Access to Google Analytics is easily obtained by signing-up for an account and adding custom Java script provided by Google to each website page to be tracked.

Known as tracking code, the code collects visitor data and sends it to the Google server. The data are then compiled by Google into a Dashboard with charts and graphs that display an overview of the site's performance. Figure 7.2 provides a screenshot of a typical Google Analytics Dashboard. The dashboard is customizable to user specifications. When users login to their account, they are able to view visitor activity based on traffic, content, usage, location, e-commerce, and other parameters selected by the user.

How Can It Be Used For Marketing Purposes?

Google Analytics makes it possible for advertisers, publishers, and website owners to improve their online results. Through this tool, marketers can design targeted ads and strengthen their online marketing activities (such as online campaigns). Marketing Research in Action 7.3 shows how Nissan used Google Analytics to increase its bottom line. Some of the marketing implications of using such a tool are described below.

Targeting consumers: By tracking the source of Web traffic (such as search engine ads, e-mail, and referrals), marketers can better target consumers with marketing messages and ad placement that is customized accordingly. This would eliminate the all too common mass advertising in the online space. One can also create custom segments based on the most profitable groups of customers who visit the website.

Manage online advertising: With the ever-increasing relevance of online advertising, marketers (through Web analytics tools such as Google Analytics) can make informed decisions on search engine advertising decisions (through Google Adwords), web page banner ad placement, and

FIGURE 7.2
Google Analytics Dashboard.
Google and Google logo are registered trademarks of Google Inc., used with permission.

online campaign management. Valuable metrics such as revenue per click, ROI, and margin can be tracked across various campaigns, thereby allowing marketers to manage online campaigns from the dashboard. Figure 7.3 is a screenshot of how managers can manage online campaigns on the Google Analytics dashboard. Marketers can evaluate several campaigns simultaneously against several key variables including *visits, impressions, clicks, ROI,* and *margin.*

Understand regional distribution of visitors: In addition to understanding how visitors navigate through the website, marketers (especially working with MNCs) would be interested to know *where* their customers/visitors are located. Google Analytics also provides marketers with a mapping tool to describe the regional distribution of visitors (by continent, country, region, state, and city) to the website. This information can assist marketers in creating local search advertising or off-line ads/promotions in a specific region.

What is Amazon's Mechanical Turk?

Amazon's Mechanical Turk, also known as MTurk, is a crowdsourcing Internet marketplace that allows businesses and individuals a chance to align the use of human intelligence to perform tasks that computers are unable to do. Furthermore, a business is given access to a diverse, on-demand,

Marketing Research in Action 7.3

■ GOOGLE ANALYTICS IN ACTION: REAL-WORLD IMPLEMENTATION

Nissan, a Japanese automotive company with a worldwide presence, owns a network of websites around the globe helping consumers decide the vehicle they would like to purchase. These sites provide information on their products and services, localized versions of promotional materials, and a test drive reservation. Apart from tracking e-commerce activity, Nissan wanted to track their non-e-commerce activity like user preferences on the car type, model, and color to allocate inventory accordingly in their respective local markets.

This was achieved through Google Analytics' flexible profile setting and custom reporting by requesting customers to fill a form every time they book a test drive. This form, along with contact details, prompted customers to specify the vehicle category, model, and color they were interested in. This data was available not only to the Global Marketing Strategy Division but also to the country managers to assess the popularity in their specific region at one glance.

As a result, Nissan has been able to decentralize access to their different market operations. This has been a significant advantage for Nissan. Although from the Google Analytics traditional model, user experiences were reported, the customization helped Nissan view market/global based product popularity. This dramatically reduced the time to summarize and analyze multiple reports, document the findings and share the same. Ultimately, Google Analytics provided Nissan with timely information that resulted in accurate decision making with respect to inventory and website optimization.

Source: Adapted from case study titled "Nissan Motor Company gains deep insights into users' product preferences with Google Analytics e-commerce," (2010) http://static.googleusercontent.com/media/www.google.com/en/us/analytics/customers/pdfs/nissan.pdf

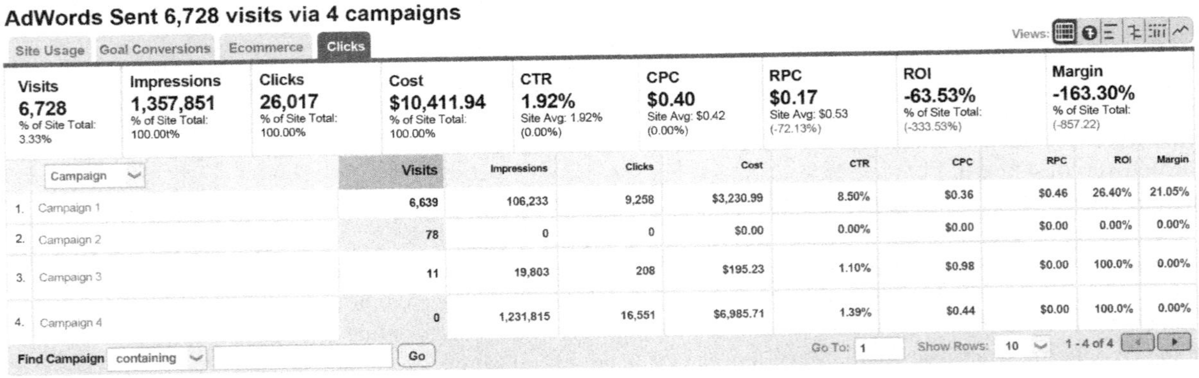

AdWords Sent 6,728 visits via 4 campaigns

Site Usage | Goal Conversions | Ecommerce | **Clicks**

	Visits	Impressions	Clicks	Cost	CTR	CPC	RPC	ROI	Margin
	6,728	1,357,851	26,017	$10,411.94	1.92%	$0.40	$0.17	-63.53%	-163.30%
	% of Site Total: 3.33%	% of Site Total: 100.00t%	% of Site Total: 100.00%	% of Site Total: 100.00%	Site Avg: 1.92% (0.00%)	Site Avg: $0.42 (0.00%)	Site Avg: $0.53 (-72.13%)	% of Site Total: (-333.53%)	% of Site Total: (-857.22)

Campaign ∨	Visits	Impressions	Clicks	Cost	CTR	CPC	RPC	ROI	Margin
1. Campaign 1	6,639	106,233	9,258	$3,230.99	8.50%	$0.36	$0.46	26.40%	21.05%
2. Campaign 2	78	0	0	$0.00	0.00%	$0.00	$0.00	0.00%	0.00%
3. Campaign 3	11	19,803	208	$195.23	1.10%	$0.98	$0.00	100.0%	0.00%
4. Campaign 4	0	1,231,815	16,551	$6,985.71	1.39%	$0.44	$0.00	100.0%	0.00%

Find Campaign [containing ∨] [_____] [Go]   Go To: 1   Show Rows: 10 ∨ 1 - 4 of 4 ◄ ►

FIGURE 7.3

Campaign Tracking in Google Analytics.

Google and Google logo are registered trademarks of Google Inc., used with permission.

scalable workforce, and allows workers the opportunity to complete a variety of tasks based on convenience. The device was initially created by Peter Cohen, for Amazon to use internally and find duplicates in its web page with regard to product description. After being launched in late 2005, the product experienced great success and within its first five years of existence had over 500,000 users in over 190 countries. Before the development of MTurk, these tasks were typically performed by temporary workers who were hired for the specific task.

How Does it Work?

The rationale behind its MTurk's creation and development is based on the belief that there are several tasks out there that humans are capable of performing in a far more effective and efficient manner than computers. There are two critical components to MTurk: the Requesters and the Workers. The Requesters are allowed to post Human Intelligence Tasks (HIT's), which can range from identifying the artist on a particular music record, selecting a particular object in a photo/video, or writing product descriptions. On the other hand, Workers, who can also be called Providers, are able to search among the existing tasks/objectives and then complete them for compensation at an amount set by the Requester.

What are Certain Applications?

- Missing Person Search: MTurk has been extremely helpful in assisting with the search of missing individuals. When computer scientist Jim Gray disappeared, Satellite Data were used along with photography of his last location, to attempt to find his whereabouts. This search was unsuccessful.

- Research with regard to Education and Arts: MTurk's ability to crowdsource has allowed artists to create certain works that collaborate several individual drawings.[32]

International Marketing Research

The Internet, as a global medium, increases the scope of communication tremendously. Even though the globe-shrinking experience is already prevalent, the Internet's ability to communicate across borders will have a dramatic impact. Marketing Research in Action 7.4 discusses

Marketing Research in Action 7.4

ATTRACTING ONLINE CUSTOMERS WITH CONTENT APPEAL

Developing up and promoting a site is one thing; getting prospective customers to visit is another. A well-known online vacation rentals around the world, Airbnb, was founded in 2008. The company now has over 550,000 listings in 33,000 cities and 192 countries. Their creative digital marketing strategy helped them touch international waters but not without few challenges.

Airbnb in Germany was faced with competitors who were in the industry from twentieth century. To overcome this competition, Airbnb applied content strategy techniques to their digital marketing by rating appealing spaces higher, offering beneficial services to the professional photos, and letting users control their web pages. Lower quality content created by the users was hard to find which forced the users to create high-quality appealing content. This optimized the search engine listings, enabling the best listings to rise to the top. Professional photos created by the users added value to the content visuals and made it more attractive for the users. Users control on the company's web pages saves time and money that needs to be spent by the company on creating the content.

This mode of business development is echoed by the comment made by Brian Chesky, the CEO of Airbnb, "...we're living in a world where people can become businesses in 60 seconds."

Source: D. Wheeler, "4 Digital Marketing Strategies: An Airbnb Case Study," Search Engine Journal, March 25, 2014, accessed on April 21, 2015 from http://www.searchenginejournal.com/4-digital-marketing-strategies-airbnb-case-study/95007/; and Gregory Ferenstein, "Airbnb CEO spells out the end game for the sharing economy, in 7 quotes," July 2, 2014, accessed on April 21, 2015 from http://venturebeat.com/2014/07/02/airbnb-ceo-spells-out-the-end-game-for-the-sharing-economy-in-7-quotes/

how one Web retailer has used a compelling tactic to capture new online consumers. Marketing Research in Action 7.5 gives an illustration on the power of the Internet for international marketing research.

Marketing Research in Action 7.5

■ INTERNATIONAL MARKETING RESEARCH ON THE INTERNET

Reeno, Inc., a chemical company based in Minneapolis, Minnesota, operates worldwide in the area of agricultural inputs such as fertilizer, pesticides, and seeds. In the early 2000s, the company developed a new product line of agricultural seeds for improved cotton, rice, and corn varieties. After these products became an initial success in the home market, Reeno saw a tremendous potential for these products in countries such as India and China. These countries have a large and growing population, and they have to satisfy a constantly growing demand for food. Therefore, making agricultural output more efficient is a high priority in these countries.

However, Reeno knew from their past operation that introducing a new product in a country with a completely different culture is not an easy task. They felt a need for more information regarding the purchase behavior and decision making of rural farmers in these countries. Reeno's new line of seeds differed considerably from existing products, but the advantages of the new seed varieties had to be communicated properly. They appointed Innovative Marketing Consultants (IMC), a Houston-based marketing research company, to do this research project. The task for IMC was to conduct secondary research on the agricultural commodity markets in India and China. Also, IMC was to provide a report on decision-making behavior of Indian and Chinese farmers.

The Internet was the natural first stop for Dr Werner, the project supervisor at IMC. He based his secondary research on the following four important types of information that were available.

- Data from trustworthy sites such as the Indian government website Agmarknet, which contains national-, state-, and district-level data on Integrated Schemes for Agricultural Marketing (ISAM), current prices, future predictions, new project sanctions, organic and AGMARK certification programs, guidelines for funds and grants, market, and commodity profile were obtained. Data on China's agricultural commodity that provided spot and future prices of the agricultural products and Bulk Commodity Index (BCI) to monitor China's macro economy was collected from the website SunSirs. These country-specific data sources helped him analyze the trends and demands of the market. Also, U.S. government websites and the World Bank provided information on agricultural imports/exports and a number of interesting facts about farmers' practices in emerging markets.

- The local and international media coverage on the topic of research was intense and very helpful to Dr Werner. The Internet archive of *The Hindu*, India's national newspaper (Madras), offered all farming-related stories within the last five years. The National Bank for Agricultural and Rural Development, India, as an alternative also provides an all-in-one site with press releases and ongoing projects on agriculture. *China Daily USA* and *Shanghai Daily.com*, leading online newspapers in English, served as a reference to Dr Werner on his research with respect to China.

- Reports published by consulting groups were another source that Dr Werner looked into. Despite the language and access barriers to Chinese websites, Dr Werner could research on China's agricultural information based on the consulting group's annual/monthly reports. Consulting groups such as McKinsey, UNCTAD, Oxfam, and so on provided qualitative and quantitative analyses on the agricultural markets across the world. These articles and publications provided Dr Werner an in-depth knowledge of the country's stand with respect to agricultural growth and its supporting industries.

- Rural sociology research papers readily available on the Web assisted Dr Werner with another standpoint. These papers provided him with aggregated data on agricultural topics that have been referred from multiple sources.

All in all, within less than a day Dr Werner was able to gather an impressive amount of qualified information on the subject. Even more impressive was the fact that he did this without even leaving his office desk. He collected useful information in a fraction of the time he would have spent in libraries or collecting other secondary resources. Also, he was able to pinpoint his search much more quickly than he used to with printed resources.

Table 7.6   The Far-Reaching Web

Country	Internet users	1 year growth (%)	Total population	Penetration (% of pop. with internet)
China	641,601,070	4	1,393,783,836	46.03
United States	243,198,922	14	1,267,401,849	19.19
India	109,252,912	8	126,999,808	86.03
Japan	107,822,831	7	202,033,670	53.37
Brazil	84,437,793	10	142,467,651	59.27
Russia	71,727,551	2	82,652,256	86.78
Germany	67,101,452	16	178,516,904	37.59
Nigeria	57,075,826	3	63,489,234	89.90
United Kingdom	55,429,382	3	64,641,279	85.75
France	50,923,060	7	123,799,215	41.13
Mexico	45,314,248	8	49,512,026	91.52
South Korea	42,258,824	9	252,812,245	16.72
Indonesia	40,311,562	10	83,386,739	48.34
Egypt	39,772,424	9	92,547,959	42.97
Vietnam	39,470,845	10	100,096,496	39.43
Philippines	36,593,969	2	61,070,224	59.92
Italy	35,358,888	3	75,837,020	46.62
Turkey	35,010,273	3	47,066,402	74.38
Spain	33,000,381	7	35,524,732	92.89
Canada	25,666,238	2	38,220,543	67.15

Source: Used with permission from "Internet Users by Country (2014)," accessed on April 2, 2015 from http://www. internetlivestats.com/internet-users-by-country/

Particularly for businesses that are involved in international activities, the collection of intelligence from international resources will become natural. Also, databases such as STAT-USA are available that are built and maintained by U.S. government agencies. These offer information to companies entering the growing international trade market at no cost. Further, the most common Internet language is English. Table 7.6 shows how the World Wide Web has penetrated the entire world and where the largest number of users are located.

The Internet and Marketing Research Developments

The time when one could keep up with the information on the World Wide Web is already ancient history. With the Web growing dramatically, it becomes impossible to track even a small and well-defined segment of the Web. Therefore, the market researcher has even more difficulty finding the information he or she seeks. The purpose of this section is to point out some developments of the Internet which are most likely to happen in the near future and which will affect the way a market researcher utilizes the Web.

Intranets

Intranets are internal company networks. While corporations are looking for ways and means of communicating to consumers through the World Wide Web, it is apparent that intranets are the building blocks for successful commercial activity. These internal networks start off as ways for employees to connect to company information. Intranets may also incorporate connections to the company's various suppliers. According to many industry experts, the advent of total commercial integration is fairly close—employees, suppliers, and customers will soon operate in a totally seamless environment. The advantage for an intranet user is that he or she can connect to the Internet easily, whereas Internet users cannot access intranets without appropriate security codes.

The utilization of intranets will aid in the communication and distribution of information inside large corporations. This is especially crucial for firms where information and know-how is mission-critical, such as management consultants or software developers. Once information is gathered, it is stored in internal databases so that it can be accessed from any company location in the world. By researching internal databases in the first place, the danger of duplicating information search procedures in separate locations is minimized, and therefore, the return on information is maximized. For example, IBM maintains a large internal database to which every consultant worldwide has access. When starting on a new project, the associate can research the database to find out if a similar project has been worked on before (by IBM) and what types of information are already available.

Thus, the Web can become an integral part of the information system of a corporation. "Firewalls" can protect from outside intrusion into the intranet. Sales, marketing, and communication applications can combine internal and external information resources smoothly. Recently, networks between two companies have been set up to access information from both firms, and these are termed as "Extranet."

Speed

There are a number of promising technologies on the horizon which all have a common objective: to increase the bandwidth of the Internet. The demand for high-speed connections is huge, since more and more large data files such as multimedia applications are sent over the Internet. Backbone operators such as MCI and Sprint are starting to switch to fiber-optic networks, which can accommodate transmission of full-screen motion pictures. Marketing researchers will gain tremendously from this development. For example, focus groups can be conducted from remote locations, and participants who are thousands of miles apart can participate effectively. This will allow market researchers to discuss special topics with professionals or researchers who otherwise could not be brought together due to time and travel constraints.

Work is currently being done in the area of photonic switching—switching light waves without converting light in to electrical energy. This work eventually will enable networks to take the next leap to speeds not even dreamed of today.

Issues and Concerns

Even as the use of the Internet gains rapid momentum worldwide, users and content providers have to be aware of certain issues and concerns that go hand in hand with the various advantages of Web usage.

Identity Theft[33]

As the Internet grows to reach a wider audience, it brings with it the problem of identity theft. According to the Federal Trade Commission, identity theft occurs when a person obtains personal information of others without permission to commit fraud or other crimes. The type of information prone to theft includes details such as Social Security number (SSN), credit card number, and driver's license number among others pieces of identification. Victims are left with a tainted reputation and the complicated task of restoring their good names. The Federal Trade Commission released a report which identifies that in 2015 nearly 9.9 million Americans were victims of identity theft, and the cost incurred due to identity theft is estimated at $52.6 billion.[34] There are four types of identity theft crime.[35]

1. *Financial ID theft*—Here the focus is on the victim's name and SSN. The imposter may apply for telephone service, credit cards, or loans, buy merchandise, and lease cars or apartments.

2. *Criminal ID theft*—If stopped by law enforcement, the imposter in this case provides the victim's information over his/her own. Eventually when the warrant for arrest is issued, it is in the name of the person issued the citation—the victim.

3. *Identity cloning*—In this case, the imposter uses the victim's information to establish a new life. Examples: Illegal aliens, criminals avoiding warrants, and people hiding from abusive situations or becoming a "new person" to leave behind a poor work and financial history.

4. *Business or commercial identity theft*—Businesses are also victims of identity theft. Typically, the perpetrator gets credit cards or checking accounts in the name of the business. The business finds out when unhappy suppliers send collection notices or their business rating score is affected.

In addition to conventional methods such as stealing wallets, dumpster diving, or theft of paper mail, imposters also employ sophisticated means like accessing credit report information by impersonating an employer, a family member, or a friend; getting hold of names and SSNs from personnel files in the workplace, "shoulder surfing" in order to capture PIN numbers while waiting at ATM machines and phone booths, and browsing the Internet to identify information by locating public records sites and fee-based information broker sites. Some people even steal personal information through e-mail or phone by posing as legitimate companies and claiming that you have a problem with your account. This practice is known as "phishing" online, or pretexting by phone. In fact, more than 20 percent of all cases involve telecommunications and the Internet.

Thus, while several precautions are advised, the key to reduce the risk due to fraud lies in closely guarding personal information, checking online accounts regularly to check for any fraudulent transactions, and monitoring credit history regularly. At the same time, online marketers and researchers have to reassure customers and participants that their personal information will be closely guarded and will not be misused in any way.

Privacy Issues[36]

In this digital era, the Internet has become an important part of daily life. An increasing number of everyday activities are now being performed with the help of the Internet. This means that, given the amount of data being exchanged every minute and the dearth of federal laws in the United States governing disclosure of information to website visitors, the issue of online privacy is assuming great significance.[37] This affects individuals, companies, and societies as a whole.

People would want to maintain their privacy by controlling the information received about them by others. According to the Pew Research Center findings, 61 percent of adults "disagree" or "strongly disagree" with the statement: "I appreciate that online services are more efficient because of the increased access they have to my personal data."[38]

A major cause of concern in dealing with online privacy is about regulating the information collected by companies that involve online transactions. The practice of placing files called "cookies" and Web bugs by online companies in the user's computer during a visit is quite common. These files capture information during an exchange between client and server. This trail of bread crumbs may then be used to gather personal information about the user without their knowledge. Typically, information such as time spent online, length of visits, type and name of search engine accessed, products purchased, responses to promotions, and the navigation history are collected through these cookies.

While privacy issues are preventing some users from shopping online, more experienced Internet users recognize data collection and have embraced it in some respects. A recent Gallup study indicates that online consumers are more quite willing to share personal information with e-marketers. The results from the study are listed in Table 7.7.

Personalization is one of the reasons customers are willing to share their information online. Further, consumers are more likely to supply data such as birthday, household composition, or phone numbers when the data are used to create personalized content and pages. Another reason for customer cooperation in sharing personal information is the customer choice of contact.

Thus, the response toward online privacy remains divided between users who refrain from shopping online due to privacy concerns and those who do not mind providing their personal information in return for benefits. A study by Accenture that surveyed 2,000 U.S. and U.K. consumers found that while 86 percent surveyed were concerned that their data were being tracked, 49 percent surveyed said that they trusted brands tracking the data in return for a personalized shopping experience. This clearly indicates that while personalization is preferred by most consumers, the privacy fears associated with that continue to grow.[39] Between these conflicting groups of consumers are companies who are not really clear about the privacy policies. Hence, to better address this issue, it is essential for companies to develop and manage their customers' privacy by taking a comprehensive and holistic outlook.

Table 7.7   Percentage of Net Users Would Trust

Banks and Credit card companies	39%
Health insurance companies	26%
Cellphone carriers	19%
E-mail providers	16%
Retail stores	14%
State government agencies	14%
Federal government agencies	12%
Online retailers	6%
Social networking sites or applications	2%

Source: Used with permission from J. H. Fleming and E. Kampf, "Few Consumers Trust Companies to Keep Online Info Safe," June 6, 2014, accessed on April 2, 2015 from http://www.gallup.com/poll/171029/few%E2%80%90consumers%E2%80%90trustcompanies%E2%80%90keep%E2%80%90online%E2%80%90info%E2%80%90safe.aspx

The Future of the Internet

With wireless connectivity so widespread, the Internet has become an integral part of daily life. This is more so in the developed countries, where broadband adoption and broadband speed provide instant access to the Internet. For example, there are more than a billion users in the Asia/Pacific region, with an Internet penetration rate of 34.7 percent as of June 2014.[40] With the rise of the Internet, an increasing number of services are gaining popularity.

Communication devices such as cell phones and PDAs are changing the face of Internet-enabled devices with the ability to send and receive e-mail and access the Web. Through the widespread use of blogs, dramatic changes have happened to the media and publishing world.[41] The Internet has also advanced the quality of human life by facilitating cutting edge technology. For instance, Electrolux, best known for its vacuum cleaners, has developed the Screen-Fridge.[42] It is an Internet icebox that manages the pantry, among other things. It e-mails a shopping list to the local supermarket and coordinates a convenient delivery time according to the schedule.

The Internet is thus one of the important sources of information. The speed, reliability, and coverage of information are what make the Internet a fascinating medium. It has grown tremendously from a predominantly communication medium to a much larger and wider application. Its presence can be felt from daily, routine activities to specialized research activities. The Internet also has a flip side to it. The advancement of the Internet has given rise to Internet-based crimes such as identity thefts, privacy right violations, cyber stalking, and many more. As soon as one crime is brought under control, another crime, bigger and much larger in size, comes up. Despite the contrasting sides to it, the Internet continues to provide a viable option for information for marketers and consumers alike.

SUMMARY

The Internet is a worldwide network of computers originally designed by the U.S. government to provide an alternative communications network. Today, the Internet is a network of home and business users, libraries, universities, organizations, and others. The Internet uses a common computer language, and there are numerous communication services (for example, the World Wide Web) available for exploring the Internet. The Internet can level the playing field for marketing to potential customers through efficient use of the medium. Both commercial and academic ventures have explored the characteristics of users of the Internet as well as uses for the Internet.

Collection of primary information on the Internet is increasing, as evidenced by the use of e-mail for survey research. Other forms of primary data collection are performed primarily through interactive forms which are filled out on the screen. Online focus groups are conducted entirely online—everything from recruitment and screening to moderation of the discussion itself. Secondary information about products or companies can be obtained using search engines on the Web. The power of the Internet for international marketing research cannot be underestimated.

QUESTIONS AND PROBLEMS

7.1 John Smith has to make an unscheduled trip this coming weekend to New York from his home town, Houston. He searched on the Internet for the lowest-price offering and bought his ticket. Demonstrate the search process that John used to get his ticket.

7.2 Assume that your family is interested in visiting the NASA Space Center in Houston. They would like to gather more facts about the place before they embark on a trip. How can you assist them in this process?

7.3 Design a customer satisfaction questionnaire and e-mail it to your friends. Ask them to respond to your survey by filling out the questionnaire and e-mailing it back to you.

7.4 You are hired as an intern in the marketing research department of a chemical plant in the United States. The firm is interested in expanding its worldwide operations and is interested in country-specific information regarding land use for agriculture. How will you obtain this information on the Internet?

7.5 Pick any company of your choice, and

(a) Identify its website

(b) Browse through the website

(c) List the type of information that is available through the website

END NOTES

1. Although most of the Internet sites listed in this chapter are current and updated, it is possible that some of them might have been changed or linked with another site. You should go through the search procedure (for example, Net Search in Netscape) for current information on relevant websites or visit http://www.wiley.com for an index of updated links.

2. Internet Users By Country, http://www.internetlivestats.com/internet-users-by-country/, Retrieved on April 2, 2015.

3. E. Burns, "E-Commerce Equals Convenience, Risk to Consumers," February 15, 2008, http://www.clickz.com/clickz/stats/1705925/e-commerce- equals-convenience-risk-consumers, Retrieved on January 18, 2007.

4. "Nearly 8 in 10 Americans Have Access to High-Speed Internet," Press Release, November 13, 2014, U.S. Census Bureau, accessed from http://www.census.gov/newsroom/press-releases/2014/cb14-202.html, Retrieved on April 2, 2015.

5. Pew Research Center, "Internet User Demographics," accessed from http://www.pewinternet.org/data-trend/internet-use/latest-stats/, Retrieved on April 2, 2015.

6. IAB Internet Advertising Revenue Report, April 2014, accessed from http://www.iab.net/media/file/IAB_Internet_Advertising_Revenue_Report_FY_2013.pdf, Retrieved on April 2, 2015.

7. Pew Research Center, "Internet User Demographics," accessed from http://www.pewinternet.org/data-trend/internet-use/latest-stats/, Retrieved on April 2, 2015.

8. J. Saranow, "Memo to Websites: Grow Up!" *The Wall Street Journal*, November 2004, p. R.14.

9. "World Internet Users and 2014 Population Stats," Internet World Stats, accessed from http://www.internetworldstats.com/stats.htm, Retrieved on April 2, 2015.

10. "Internet World Users by Language," Internet World Stats, accessed from http://www.internetworldstats.com/stats7.htm, Retrieved on April 2, 2015.

11. A. Enright, "U.S. online retail sales will grow 57% by 2018," accessed from https://www.internetretailer.com/2014/05/12/us-online-retail-sales-will-grow-57-2018, Retrieved on April 2, 2015.

12. Pew Internet & American Life Project, "Search Engine Use 2012," accessed from http://www.pewinternet.org/2012/03/09/search-engine-use-2012/, Retrieved on April 2, 2015.

13. BIA/Kelsey, "U.S. Local Media Revenues to Reach $139.3 Billion in 2015," accessed from http://www.biakelsey.com/Company/Press-Releases/140922-U.S.-Local-Media-Revenues-to-Reach-$139.3-Billion-in-2015.asp, Retrieved on April 2, 2015.

14. F. Marckini, "Contextual Advertising," October 6, 2003, http://www.clickz.com/clickz/stats/1715611/contextual-advertising-part.

15. V. Vara, "Facebook Gets Personal With Ad Targeting Plan," *Wall Street Journal*, August 2007.

16. D. Bruzzone and P. Shellenberg, "Track the Effects of Advertising Better, Faster and Cheaper Online," July 2000, http://www.quirks.com/articles/a2000/20000713.aspx?searchID=21438461&sort=5&pg=1.

17. R. E. Bruner, "The Decade in Online Advertising—1994–2004," April 2005, http://static.googleusercontent.com/external_content/untrusted_dlcp/www.google.com/en/us/doubleclick/pdfs/DoubleClick-04-2005-The-Decade-in-Online-Advertising.pdf.

18. "The Domain Name Industry Brief," The Verisign Domain Report, Volume 11, Issue 1, April 2014, accessed from http://www.verisigninc.com/assets/domain-name-report-april2014.pdf, Retrieved on April 2, 2015.

19. "Digital Ad Spending Worldwide to Hit $137.53 Billion in 2014—See more at: http://www.emarketer.com/Article/Digital-Ad-Spending-Worldwide-Hit-3613753-Billion-2014/1010736#sthash.iyIF93fK.dpuf".

20. D. R. Lehman and R. S. Winer, *Product Management*, Chicago, IL: Irwin, 1997.

21. Forrester Research Inc., "B2B Marketers' Budget Allocations in 2015," January 23, 2015, accessed from https://www.marketingcharts.com/traditional/b2b-marketers-budget-allocations-in-2015-50732/, Retrieved on April 2, 2015.

22. G. Gelb, "Online Options Change Biz a Little—and a Lot," *Marketing News*, November 1, 2006, pp. 23–24.

23. J. H. Ellsworth and M. V. Ellsworth, *The Internet Business Book*, New York: John Wiley, 1996.

24. Online Panels, Globalpark, http://www.globalpark.com/market-research/online-panel.html.

25. *Marketing Report,* July 22, 1996, p. 4.

26. A. Enright, "Real-time Analytics Boost ROI, Accountability," *Marketing News*, October 1, 2006, pp. 20 & 24.

27. S. V. Haar, "ROI Shows Marketers the Money," *Inter@ctive Week*, 6(12), March 1999, p. 35.

28. B. Kardon, "They're Saying Nasty Things," *Marketing News*, December 15, 2007, p. 30.

29. E. Burg, "Leverage User-Generated Content To Boost Brands," http://www.mediapost.com/publications/index.cfm?fa=Articles.showArticle&art_aid=56933. Retrieved on September 17, 2008.

30. IAB Internet Advertising Revenue Report, accessed from http://www.iab.net/media/file/IAB_Internet_Advertising_Revenue_Report_FY_2013.pdf, Retrieved on April 2, 2015.

31. "Google Analytics Usage Trends," BuiltWith, February 12, 2012, http://trends.builtwith.com/analytics/GoogleAnalytics

32. Amazon MTurk, accessed from https://www.mturk.com/mturk/help?helpPage=overview, Retrieved on April 2, 2015.

33. For more information, please visit https://www.ftc.gov/news-events/media-resources/identity-theft-and-data-security

34. "Identity Theft Facts," http://www.transunion.com/personal-credit/identity-theft-and-fraud/identity-theft-facts.page.

35. For more information, please visit http://www.idtheftcenter.org/.

36. Adapted with permission from Michael Pastore, "Consumers Fear for Their Online Privacy," November 1999, http://www.clickz.com/clickz/stats/1701261/consumers-fear-their-online-privacy.

37. R. Frost, "Who Is Securing Your Identity Online?" September 2003, http://www.brandchannel.com/features_effect.asp?pf_id=177.

38. M. Madden, "Public Perceptions of Privacy and Security in the Post-Snowden Era," November 12, 2014, accessed from http://www.pewinternet.org/2014/11/12/public-privacy-perceptions/, Retrieved on April 2, 2015.

39. "Today's Shopper Preferences: Channels, Social Media, Privacy and the Personalized Experience," Accenture Interactive, November 2012, accessed from http://www.accenture.com/SiteCollectionDocuments/PDF/Accenture-Interactive-Survey-Results.pdf on April 2, 2015.

40. "Internet Usage in Asia," http://www.internetworldstats.com/stats3.htm.

41. S. Fox, J. Q. Anderson, and L. Rainie, *The Future of the Internet.* Washington D.C.: Pew Internet & American Life Project, 2005.

42. "Linux community touched by the touchscreen on Electrolux fridge," accessed from http://www.electroluxgroup.com/en/linux-community-touched-by-the-touchscreen-on-electrolux-fridge-8873/ on April 2, 2015.

Case 7-1 ‖ Caring Children's Hospital

Mary Beth, President of Caring Children's Hospitals (CCH), always looked forward to New Years. New Years were meant for family reunions and holidays for her. But this New Year had something totally different in store for her. The previous year had not been good for the hospital revenues. The number of patients served by the hospital had gone down, and the costs of health care were rising. The balance sheet presented a very sorry picture to her. But there was a glimmer of hope in the gloomy balance sheet.

About two years ago, Mary had started a small division within CCH that provided health care for disabled children in their houses. This division resembled a home health-care facility, but Mary was wary about developing this division into a full-fledged home health-care organization within CCH. This division had been doing well for the past two years. It was the only division in CCH with a positive picture in the balance sheet. Mary decided to develop the home health-care division in the hospital to get around the problems facing the hospital's financial situation.

But there were a lot of issues to be addressed, such as the kind of expansion plan to adopt, the kind of services to be provided by the home health-care facility, the kind of insurance plans that the patients would be able to use, and the type of publicity to use. Mary decided to use the services of Innovative Marketing Consultants (IMC), a top-notch local marketing consulting firm, for addressing these issues and suggesting an expansion plan. A meeting was set up with Dr K, president of IMC, to discuss the issues involved and to explain the details of a home health-care program. Dr K suggested using the Internet to analyze the scope for a new player in the industry, the trends in the industry, the common modes of payment available, the costs involved per patient, the profit margins possible, and the kinds of diseases requiring home health care. The Internet was selected for secondary data analysis because of its speed and availability of up-to-date information.

Dr. K used several search engines available in the Internet, such as Lycos, Infoseek, and AltaVista, to get a wide and varied coverage of the Internet. The information collected from the Internet suggested that the home health-care industry was booming and that pediatric home health care had a significant share in the market. The results also suggested that given a choice, people would prefer to receive the needed care in their homes. Also, the cost involved in serving patients at their houses was significantly less and it was fully covered by Medicare. Home health care was also found to be the fastest growing health-care segment in the nineties. The diagnoses most often referred to home health care were found to be favorable to CCH. These results formed the base for conducting primary research in the market. The use of the Internet allowed Dr K to analyze a wide range of issues within a short time frame.

Questions for Discussion

1. Use the Internet to corroborate the findings of Dr K.

2. Prepare a report based on the information that you have collected.

3. What are your recommendations to Mary based on your findings?

The case was prepared by V. Kumar and Rajkumar Venkatesan for the purpose of classroom discussion.

8

Information Collection: Qualitative and Observational Methods

LEARNING OBJECTIVES

- Discuss the need for qualitative research.
- Describe the different types of qualitative research methods.
- Discuss in-depth interviews, focus group, and projective techniques in detail.
- Discuss various observational methods.
- Describe recent applications of qualitative and observational methods.

This chapter shifts the focus from the utilization of already available secondary data to the collection of primary data for a specific purpose. Seldom is enough known about a marketing problem or situation for the researcher to be able to proceed directly to the design of a structured study that would yield representative and quantifiable results. The type of research one should do is driven by the information needed. Marketing research can use either primary or secondary data, and it can also be either qualitative or quantitative.

Qualitative data collection is done to obtain a basic feel for the problem before proceeding to the more analytical portion of the study.

A variety of qualitative methods can be used for such exploratory purposes. Specifically, we will discuss individual and group interviews and case studies. The category of qualitative methods includes projective techniques that are used when self-reports are likely to be misleading. Although projective techniques are utilized during exploratory research, they are also used for primary data collection.

Observational methods are also discussed in this chapter. The observation of ongoing behavior is a widely used exploratory method, as well as an effective way to collect quantitative information when direct questioning is not possible.

Need for Qualitative Research

The purpose of qualitative research is to find out what is in a consumer's mind. It is done in order to access and also get a rough idea about the person's perspective. It helps the researcher to become oriented to the range and complexity of consumer activity and concerns. Qualitative data are collected to know more about things that cannot be directly observed and measured. Feelings, thoughts, intentions, and behavior that took place in the past are a few examples of those things that can be obtained only through qualitative data collection methods. It is also used to identify likely methodological problems in the study and to clarify certain issues that were not clear in the problem. Sometimes, it may not be possible or desirable to obtain information from respondents by using fully structured or formal methods. Qualitative data collection methods are used in such situations. People may be unwilling to answer some questions when confronted with them directly. Questions that they perceive as invasion of privacy, that they think will embarrass them, or that may have a negative impact on their ego or status will not be answered. Examples of such sensitive questions could be: "Are you a compulsive drinker of alcohol? Do you use drugs to relieve stress or anxiety?" Sometimes, accurate answers will not be forthcoming because they are part of the subconscious mind and cannot be tapped into directly. They are disguised from the outer world through the mechanism of ego defenses, such as rationalization. For example, a person may have purchased an expensive sports car to overcome a feeling of inferiority. However, if asked, "Why did you purchase this sports car?" he or she may say, "I got a great deal," or "My old car was falling apart." It has been shown that information of this sort can be better obtained from qualitative methods, such as focus-group discussions or projective techniques, than through a formal, structured-survey method of data collection.

The basic assumption behind qualitative methods is that an individual's organization of a relatively unstructured stimulus indicates the person's basic perceptions of the phenomenon and his or her reaction to it.[1] The more unstructured and ambiguous a stimulus is, the more subjects can and will project their emotions, needs, motives, attitudes, and values. The structure of a stimulus is the degree of choice available to the subject. A highly structured stimulus leaves very little choice: The subject has unambiguous choice among clear alternatives. A stimulus of low structure has a wide range of alternative choices. If it is ambiguous, the subjects can "choose" their own interpretations.

Qualitative Research Methods

Collectively, these methods are less structured and more intensive than standardized questionnaire-based interviews. There is a longer, more flexible relationship with the respondent, so the resulting data have more depth and greater richness of context—which also means a greater potential for new insights and perspectives. The numbers of respondents are small and only partially representative of any target population, making them preludes to, but not substitutes for, carefully structured, large-scale field studies. There are three major categories of acceptable uses of qualitative research methods:

1. Exploratory

   • Defining problems in more detail.

   • Suggesting hypotheses to be tested in subsequent research.

   • Generating new product or service concepts, problem solutions, lists of product features, and so forth.

   • Getting preliminary reactions to new product concepts.

   • Pretesting structured questionnaires.

2. Orientation

   • Learning the consumer's vantage point and vocabulary.

   • Educating the researcher to an unfamiliar environment: needs, satisfactions, usage situations, and problems.

3. Clinical

   • Gaining insights into topics that otherwise might be impossible to pursue with structured research methods.

The range of possible applications of these methods can be seen from the following examples:

1. A telephone equipment supplier wanted to know what features to incorporate in an answering device located in a telephone substation (rather than in the home or office). From several group discussions came ideas for many features such as variable-length messages and accessibility from any telephone. Specific features and price expectations were tested in a subsequent survey.

2. In 2002, the photovoltaic (PV) solar electric system was installed in the state of Oregon. The PV technology uses the sun's energy to make electricity, unlike a solar hot water system which uses the sun's energy to heat water. The Oregon Office of Energy was interested to find out about the issues concerned with acquiring a PV resource. For this purpose, individuals who had been directly involved with the PV industry in Oregon were chosen to participate in focus groups.

   The focus groups concentrated on the delivery, education, and installation of the PV solar electric system in the state. In particular, issues relating to the major barriers as perceived by the industry, the market opportunities, and the requirements to develop a grid-tied PV market in Oregon were discussed. Results from the focus groups revealed the significant difference in opinions about market development for PV systems. The complaints and comments relating to the types of incentives, equipment performance, standards for equipment, and installer guarantees were then used in subsequent decisions such as consumer education, training, and easing the buying process of PV systems for the consumer.[2]

3. General Motors uses consumer and dealer focus groups,[3] as well as extensive questionnaires, to identify the best features of their own and of competitors' automobiles. These give insight on "world-class" elements they want to meet or exceed. For example, the design of air-filter covers for the GM10 line of cars was inspired by Mazda; the seat adjustment was made by a long bar under each front seat; and electrical fuses were put in the glove box—an idea used by Saab.

Among the heaviest users of qualitative data are Japanese firms. They prefer "soft data" collected by managers during visits to dealers and customers, because it gives them a much better feel for a market's nuances. Talks with dealers who know their customers result in realistic, context-specific information. These talks relate directly to consumer attitudes, or the way the product has been or will be used, rather than being remote from actual behavior.[4] If Japanese firms do conduct surveys, they interview only people who have actually experienced the product or service, rather than asking a random sample about general attitudes. When Toyota wanted to learn what Americans preferred in small, imported cars, they asked groups of Volkswagen Beetle owners what they liked and disliked about that particular car.

Use of Computers in Qualitative Research

Four major perceived constraints have traditionally mitigated the use of qualitative research:

1. Volume of data

2. Complexity of analysis

3. Detail of clarification record

4. Time-consuming nature of the clerical efforts required.

Computer technology has helped alleviate most of these problems and has helped to increase the use of qualitative research. The role of computer applications in the various tasks of qualitative data analysis is briefly described as follows:

Transcribing—Data has to be transcribed into text. A popular program used for qualitative analysis is Hyper TRANSCRIBE (www.researchware.com).

Storing—With the use of computer data, storage becomes very easy. It also brings more sophistication in the organization of data. The researcher can access the material quickly and precisely.

Coding—Codes have to be assigned by the researcher. Codes are labels assigned to data segments to enable taxonomic organization of the data. Once codes have been assigned, the computer can recall and print out all material belonging to a specific code. Each extracted piece is logged with its source so that the researcher can easily see from where it was extracted. The software can be used for complex, multiple coding. Coding systems can be reused much more easily and researchers can collaborate directly with each other by working in parallel on the data analysis of one text, as some programs (e.g., Atlas/Ti and NVivo9 (www.qsrinternational.com)) support the concept of multiauthoring for code systems.

Searching and retrieving—Researchers use not only standard Boolean operations (and, or, not) but also various kinds of more complex search requests. For example, it is possible to request the computer to perform a search such as "produce a list of quotations relating to code 'acceleration of a car' as described by single men."

Building relationships—The computer can be used to assist in the complex tasks of building relationships between the data segments as part of the theory development process. In some programs (e.g., Atlas/Ti, Infination, and NVivo9), the relationship between data segments can then be visualized as a network with annotated lines linking codes, memos, or quotations.

Matrix building—Matrixes are cross-tabulation of variables, codes, or dimensions of the data which help the researcher see how certain elements of the data interact. Many programs (e.g., XSIGHT from qsrinternational) feature a special matrix-building function that speeds up this task.

Another perceived constraint slowing down the use of qualitative research is the comparatively higher expenses associated with the collection of qualitative data.

Individual In-Depth Interviews

Individual in-depth interviews are interviews that are conducted face to face with the respondent, in which the subject matter of the interview is explored in detail. There are two basic types of in-depth interviews. They are nondirective and semistructured, and their differences lie in the amount of guidance the interviewer provides. Marketing Research in Action 8.1 explores the reasons why one-on-one in-depth interviews should be considered more often by researchers.

Nondirective Interviews

In nondirective interviews, the respondent is given maximum freedom to respond, within the bounds of topics of interest to the interviewer. Success depends on (1) establishing a relaxed and sympathetic relationship; (2) the ability to probe in order to clarify and elaborate on interesting responses, without biasing the content of the responses; and (3) the skill of guiding the discussion back to the topic outline when digressions are unfruitful, and (4) always pursuing reasons behind the comments and answers. Such sessions normally are one to two hours long and may be tape recorded (always with the permission of the respondent) for later interpretation.

Marketing Research in Action 8.1

■ TAKE A QUALITATIVE APPROACH TO QUALITATIVE RESEARCH

In-depth interviews are a method that provides more information for less money without many of the limitations focus groups can impose. One-on-one in-depth interviews should be considered more often by researchers for a number of critical reasons:

1. More quality

Unlike in focus groups, one-on-one interviews can avoid responses that are influenced by other people. Interviewers may ask respondents directly and find out their personal thoughts on the product; this enhances the quality of information.

2. More quantity

Researchers can receive twice the amount of information per respondent in an in-depth interview, where the interviewer speaks at most 20 percent of the time, as in a typical 10-member focus group.

3. More depth

In-depth interviews capture all the relevance and salience of the qualitative information of focus groups.

Every word the respondent speaks can be taped and transcribed and used in multiple ways. Well-designed surveys can go beyond surface answers and produce a rich database of interviews to produce analyst reports, identify broad themes, and understand the ranges and depths of reactions.

4. More representation

In-depth interviews allow a much more representative approach as respondents are carefully selected to represent the marketplace as accurately as possible.

5. More efficiency

Participants may be interviewed via a 15- to 45-minute phone conversation. Incentives of food and money used in focus groups are not necessary for in-depth interviews.

6. More value

One-on-one interviews can double or triple the number of minutes that the respondent is talking, and that is the true goal of research: understanding your consumers better.

For more interesting articles on marketing research visit http://www.marketingpower.com.
Source: M. B. Palmerino, "Take a Qualitative Approach to Qualitative Research," Marketing News, June 7, 1997.

Semistructured or Focused Individual Interviews

In semistructured or focused individual interviews, the interviewer attempts to cover a specific list of topics or subareas, and the respondent has less freedom to extend the bounds of the topics. The timing, exact wording, and time allocated to each question area are left to the interviewer's discretion.

This mode of interviewing is especially effective with busy executives, technical experts, and thought leaders. Basic market intelligence, such as trends in technology, market demand, legislation, competitive activity, and similar information are amenable to such interviews. The open structure ensures that unexpected facts or attitudes can be pursued easily.

This type of interview is extremely demanding, and much depends on the interviewer's skill. First, the interviewer must be sufficiently persuasive to get through the shield of secretaries and receptionists around many executives, in order to get an appointment. The major challenge is to establish rapport and credibility in the early moments of the interview and then maintain that atmosphere. For this, there is no substitute for an informed, authoritative person who can relate to respondents on their own terms. This can be achieved by asking the respondent to react to specific information provided by the interviewer. Care should be taken to avoid threatening questions. A good opener might be, "If you had to pick one critical problem affecting your industry, what would it be?" Cooperation sometimes can be improved by offering a *quid pro quo*, such as a summary of some of the study findings.

A difficult problem with these interviews is the matter of record keeping. Some executives dislike tape recorders, so it may be necessary to use a team of interviewers who alternate between asking questions and note taking. To keep the interview as short as possible, it is usually best to leave behind a structured questionnaire for any specific data that are wanted, and this can sometimes be assigned to staff for answering. Finally, since the appropriate respondents for these studies are often difficult to identify and may represent many parts of an organization, it is always advisable to ask for recommendations about which other people it might be useful to interview.

Individual in-depth interviews are also used in consumer markets to identify key product benefits and trigger creative insights. Three techniques are being widely used now. In the first technique, *laddering*,[5] questioning progresses from product characteristics to user characteristics. A good starting point is with a repertory (sometimes called *Kelly's triad*). If the topic were airlines, respondents might be asked to compare one airline in a set of three to the other two: How do airlines A and B differ from C? How do A and C differ from B? And so on. Each attribute, such as "a softer seat," is then probed to see why it is important to the respondent; then that reason is probed, and so on. The result might be the following kind of dialogue:

Interviewer:	"Why do you like wide bodies?"
Respondent:	"They're more comfortable."
Interviewer:	"Why is that important?"
Respondent:	"I can accomplish more."
Interviewer:	"Why is that important?"
Respondent:	"I will feel good about myself."

Notice that the dialogue has moved from a very tangible aspect of an airline to its contribution to self-esteem.

The second technique is called *hidden-issue* questioning. In hidden-issue questioning, the focus is not on socially shared values but rather on personal "sore spots"—not on general lifestyles but on deeply felt personal concerns. The third technique, *symbolic analysis*, attempts to analyze the symbolic meaning of objects by comparing them with their opposites. For example, the following question could be asked: "What would it be like if you could no longer use airlines?" Responses such as "Without planes, I would have to rely on long-distance calls and letters" may be received. This would suggest that one of the attributes that can be highlighted in an ad campaign for an airline could be face-to-face communication. Sometimes an interviewer may have to go outside his country to interview people or may have to design questionnaires that are to be administered in other parts of the world. Issues that an interviewer commonly faces when interviewing in another culture are described in Marketing Research in Action 8.2.[6]

Telephone depth interviewing and online interviewing using software like Skype are starting to gain greater acceptance among consumers and has proven to be more beneficial than focus groups. When information is needed from business decision makers, strategically designed and well-executed phone interviews may well turn out to be more successful than focus groups. For one thing, phone interviews involve less time and expenditure of money. Also, interacting with customers on an individual basis is more likely to elicit more detailed and useful information than in a focus-group setting. Of course, the catch lies in employing experienced and intelligent interviewers who are well briefed about the company, research objectives, and terminology likely to be encountered. These interviewers should also be intelligent enough to sustain the interest of the interviewees and come up with probing, open-ended questions, at the same time taking care to avoid espousing personal judgments. The interviewers should also be well trained to listen and record responses verbatim. Listening has been the hallmark of many successful product managers and CEOs. The idea is to establish a personal rapport with interviewees that encourages them to talk freely and without inhibition. The most important step in phone interviews is capturing the data in a software program that can code and tabulate responses

Marketing Research in Action 8.2

■ QUALITATIVE INTERVIEWING IN THE INTERNATIONAL CONTEXT

Evaluation has become an international activity. International and cross-cultural short-term evaluation site visits are much more subject to misinterpretations and miscommunications than traditional, long-term anthropological fieldwork. The data from interviews are words. It is tricky enough to be sure what a person means when using a common language, but words can take on a very different meaning in other cultures. In Sweden, I participated in an international conference discussing policy evaluations. The conference was conducted in English, but I was there for two days, much of the time confused, before I came to understand that their use of the term *policy* corresponded to my American use of the term *program*. I interpreted policies, from an American context, to be fairly general directives, often very difficult to evaluate because of their vagueness. In Sweden, however, policies are very specific programs.

The situation becomes more precarious when a translator or interpreter must be used because of language differences. Using an interpreter when conducting interviews is fraught with difficulty. Special and very precise training of translators is critical. It is important that questions be asked precisely as you want them asked and that full and complete answers be translated. Interpreters often want to be helpful by summarizing and explaining responses. This contaminates the interviewee's actual response with the interpreter's explanation to such an extent that you can no longer be sure whose perceptions you have—the interpreter's or the interviewee's.

There are also words and ideas that simply can't be translated. People who regularly use the language come to know the unique cultural meaning of special terms, but they don't translate well. One of my favorites from the Caribbean is "liming." It means something like hanging out, just being, doing nothing—guilt free. In conducting interviews for a program evaluation, a number of participants said they were just "liming" in the program. But that was not meant as a criticism. Liming is a highly desirable state of being, at least to participants. Funders might view the situation differently.

The high esteem in which science is held has made it culturally acceptable in Western countries to conduct interviews on virtually any subject in the name of science. Such is not the case worldwide. Evaluation researchers cannot simply presume that they have the right to ask intrusive questions. Many topics may be taboo. I have experienced cultures where it is simply inappropriate to ask questions to a subordinate about a superordinate. Any number of topics may be taboo, or at least indelicate, for strangers—family matters, political views, who owns what, how people came to be in certain positions, and sources of income.

There are also different norms governing interactions. I remember with great embarrassment going to an African village to interview the chief. The whole village was assembled. Following a brief welcoming ceremony, I asked if we could begin the interview. I expected a private, one-on-one interview. He expected to perform in front of and involve the whole village. It took me a while to understand this, during which I kept asking to go somewhere else so we could begin the interview. He did not share my concern about preference for privacy. What I expected to be an individual interview soon turned out to be a whole village focus-group interview! In many cultures, it is a breach of etiquette for an unknown man to ask to meet alone with a woman. Even a female interviewer may need the permission of a husband, brother, or a parent to interview a village woman.

Source: M. Q. Patton, Qualitative Evaluation and Research Methods, 2nd ed., Thousand Oaks, CA: Sage, 1990.

---

from open-ended questions. This step could also be done manually, but using suitable software enhances credibility by capturing the responses *verbatim* and also making them available for future use.[7] More telephoning is being used in qualitative research because of the following factors as well: The telephone has become a standard medium of communications, clients are more receptive to saving time and therefore money, and studies can be conducted in remote areas that other qualitative methods, such as focus groups, cannot access.

Technology is chipping in by helping with the analysis of individual in-depth interviews. Here's how it works: A topic guide is entered into the computer in advance; the interviewer, with a headset on for comfortable, hands-free interviewing, types answers directly into the program. Comments of any length can be accommodated, wherever they occur, and skip patterns are easily handled. Afterward, a printout shows all responses to each open-ended question, either for the full sample or by subgroup (male/female, age group, heavy users, former subscribers, etc.). Individual interviews and interview summaries of each interview can also be printed out. The program provides frequency counts and averages on the closed ends.[8]

Focus-Group Discussions

A focus-group discussion is the process of obtaining possible ideas or solutions to a marketing problem from a small group of respondents by discussing it. The emphasis in this method is on the results of group interaction when focused on a series of topics a discussion leader introduces. Each participant in a group of five to nine or more persons is encouraged to express views in each topic and to elaborate on or react to the views of the other participants. The objectives are similar to unstructured in-depth interviews, but the moderator plays a more passive role than an interviewer does.

In conducting focus groups, it is very important to position focus-group observers by spending time to brief them before the groups start and debrief them afterward. Positioning client observers behind one-way viewing windows can avoid problems of misinterpretation of results in the future, and prepare observers to gain a better understanding of what they will be seeing and hearing. Observers are less prone to assume that the opinions of one or two participants are somehow representative of any group of people other than the focus-group participants themselves. Some of the issues that need to be addressed in the briefing session are

1. Outlining the intended direction of the group

2. Explaining how participants were recruited

3. Reeducating observers on the concepts of random selection, statistical reliability, and projectability of research results.[9]

The **focus-group discussion** offers participants more stimulation than an interview; presumably this makes new ideas and meaningful comments more likely.[10] Among other advantages, it is claimed that discussions often provoke more spontaneity and candor than can be expected in an interview. Some proponents feel that the security of being in a crowd encourages some participants to speak out. Marketing Research in Action 8.3 illustrates two scenarios of focus-group discussion. The following photo shows a typical focus-group room.

@Marmaduke St. John/Alamy

A Focus Group in Progress with Researchers Observing the Group Discussion Through a One-Way Mirror.

Marketing Research in Action 8.3

■ A TALE OF TWO FOCUS GROUPS

It's Wednesday evening, and the first focus group of the night at a New Jersey facility is winding up a session paid for by a mid-sized Eastern city that wants nothing more than to become a bonafide tourist destination. This group, composed entirely of people over 50 who already have visited the destination, seems reluctant to have the session end. The city in question is an important site in African-American history, and several well-informed black women are relishing their reminiscences of it. One very animated woman seems pleased that she knows a number of facts that the moderator doesn't.

She mentions that the city is also the site of an annual basketball playoff for African-American colleges. A white man wonders whether people who are not African-American would hesitate to visit the city were it to advertise its connection to that event. A heated discussion breaks out, and the other participants agree that the man is off the mark.

After the moderator ends the session—which went 10 minutes past its 90-minute time slot—several of the members of this well-informed group shake hands and say how much they've enjoyed meeting each other.

Now it's time for the 6:00–7:30 P.M. session. A decidedly tired-looking group of men and women, all parents between the ages of 30 and 45, plop down in their chairs. Maybe it's because the participants haven't had dinner yet, or miss their kids, or had tough days, or intimidate each other, or have lackluster personalities, but this crowd is much less expressive. They also don't seem as well-informed. Several seem as if they'd probably criticize just about anything on general principle.

A mother of two, friendly and eager to please, says she found the city's history fascinating and she believes others

would, too. The man next to her—a naysayer if ever there were one—says he ended up in the city by accident and found nothing much of interest there. Several minutes later, the woman unaccountably switches her mind and says that she doesn't think the city's history would interest many people. A heavy atmosphere settles over the room. Everyone looks drained and no one ventures a strong view.

Interestingly, given the differences in the two panels, both groups were chosen through random phone surveys conducted by the facility personnel. The panelists were asked their ages, number of children, and familiarity with the city. They also were asked if they had participated in similar sessions. In recent years, the industry has been plagued by "focus-group junkies" who show up repeatedly. Recently, annoyed sponsors have begun demanding fresh blood.

Both panels were asked to give reactions to eight possible slogans for the city. Surprisingly, both groups chose the same three slogans, each of which underscored the city's diverse attractions, such as restaurants, shopping, and children's amusements. The participants' consensus was that a broad-based pitch would attract the largest number of tourists. Similarly, they rejected several slogans playing up the city's role in history, concluding that such a focus would be too narrow.

Client John Boatwright, who owns a Virginia tourism consulting group called Boatwright & Co., says it is occurrences like very different groups arriving at identical results that give him confidence in focus groups. Clients tend to conclude they are on the right track when such coincidences take place, he says. "If you do four to six groups and get a consensus, you can conclude that if you did exponentially more groups, you would get the same results," he explains.

For more articles from Forecast Magazine visit http://adage.com/section/american-demographics/195.
Source: L. Wines, "A Tale of Two Focus Groups," Forecast Magazine, July/August 1995, p. 27.

Types of Focus Groups

Focus groups can be classified into three types. **Exploratory focus groups** are commonly used at the exploratory phase of the market research process to aid in defining the problem precisely. They can also be viewed as pilot testing: Exploratory groups can be used to generate hypotheses for testing or concepts for future research.

Clinical focus groups involve qualitative research in its most scientific form. The research is conducted as a scientific endeavor, based on the premise that a person's true motivations and feelings are subconscious in nature. The moderator probes under the level of the consumer's consciousness. Obviously, clinical groups require a moderator with expertise in psychology and sociology. Their popularity is less because of the difficulty of validating findings from clinical groups and because unskilled operators sometimes attempt to conduct clinical groups.

The reality in the kitchen or supermarket differs drastically from that in most corporate offices. **Experiential focus groups** allow the researcher to experience the emotional framework in which the product is being used. Thus, an experiencing approach represents an opportunity to "experience" a consumer in a natural setting.

Carmen Sandoes, marketing manager for the Bronx Zoo, says the nonprofit institution used focus groups to test various appeals to increase the number of zoo visitors. Participants were divided evenly between those who had and had not been to the zoo. They were asked to pick animal concepts—such as "Great Snakes Day" and "Big Bears Week"—which could be used as special-events themes. These themes—promotional tools—would feature exotic snakes for a day or display grizzly and polar bears for a week. Using the focus group helped Sandoes and her staff to find which animals aroused the most interest and to implement their discovery in the form of future special events.

There are no hard-and-fast rules for choosing focus groups rather than individual in-depth interviews for qualitative studies. The comparison in Table 8.1 may help you to make the choice.[11]

Table 8.1   Comparison of Focus Groups and Individual In-Depth Interviews

	Focus groups	Individual in-depth interviews
Group interactions	Group interaction is present. This may stimulate new thoughts from respondents.	There is no group interaction. Therefore, stimulation for new ideas from respondents comes from the interviewer.
Group/peer pressure	Group pressure and stimulation may clarify and challenge thinking.	In the absence of group pressure, the thinking of respondents is not challenged.
	Peer pressure and role playing may occur and may be confusing to interpret.	With one respondent, role playing is minimized and there is no peer pressure.
Respondent competition	Respondents compete with one another for time to talk. There is less time to obtain in-depth details from each participant.	The individual is alone with the interviewer and can express thoughts in a noncompetitive environment. There is more time to obtain detailed information.
Influence	Responses in a group may be "contaminated" by opinions of other group members.	With one respondent, there is no potential for influence from other respondents.
Subject sensitivity	If the subject is sensitive, respondents may be hesitant to talk freely in the presence of several other people.	If the subject is sensitive, respondents may be more likely to talk.
Interviewer fatigue	One interviewer can easily conduct several group sessions on one topic without becoming fatigued or bored.	Interviewer fatigue and boredom are problems when many individual interviews are needed and they are conducted by one interviewer.
Amount of information	A relatively large amount of information can be obtained in a short period of time at relatively modest cost.	A large amount of information can be obtained, but it takes time to obtain it and to analyze the results. Thus, costs are relatively high.
Stimuli	The volume of stimulus materials that can be used is somewhat limited.	A fairly large amount of stimulus material can be used.
Interviewer schedule	It may be difficult to assemble 8 or 10 respondents if they are a difficult type to recruit (such as very busy executives).	Individual interviews are easier to schedule.

Source: Adapted from *Focus Groups: Issues and Approaches.* New York: Advertising Research Foundation, 1985..

Key Factors for Focus-Group Success

As a rule, three or four group sessions usually are sufficient. The analyst invariably learns a great deal from the first discussion. The second interview produces much more, but less is new. Usually, by the third or fourth session, much of what is said has been heard before, and there is little to be gained from additional focus groups. Exceptions to this rule occur if there are distinct segments to cover, such as regional differences in tastes, the differences between women working in the home and outside the home, or the differences between married or unmarried women.

A focus group is not an easy technique to employ. Further, a poorly conducted or analyzed focus group can yield very misleading results and waste a good deal of money.[12] The recruitment costs, payments to participants, space rental, moderation, and analyst fees easily are in the range of $5,000–$7,500 per focus group for consumer studies.[13] Ten tips for running successful focus groups are presented in Marketing Research in Action 8.4.

Planning the Agenda

Planning starts by translating the research purpose into a set of managerially relevant questions, which ensures that client and moderator agree on specific objectives before the study begins. From these questions, the group moderator can prepare a discussion guide to serve as a checklist of the specific issues and topics to be covered. However, this list is strictly for general guidance; it is not desirable to read formal questions to the group.

An important issue is the order in which the moderator introduces topics. Usually, it is best to proceed from a general discussion to increasingly specific questions, for if the specific issue is addressed first it will influence the general discussion. It is also easier for respondents to relate to a specific issue when it has been preceded by general discussion. For example, Mother's Cookies was interested in concept-testing a new fruit-filled cookie, and a proposed introductory promotion involved tickets to a circus performance. The moderator started with a general discussion about snacks and then moved to the use of cookies as snacks and the question of buying versus making cookies. Only after this general discussion was the more specific topic addressed.

Marketing Research in Action 8.4

■ TEN TIPS FOR RUNNING A SUCCESSFUL FOCUS GROUP

1. You can never do too much planning for a focus group. Developing the discussion guide with the topics to be covered is critical.
2. Manage the recruitment process actively to be sure to get the right people in the groups.
3. Don't prejudge the participants based on physical appearance.
4. The best focus-group moderators bring objectivity and expertise in the process to a project.
5. Achieving research objectives does not guarantee a successful focus-group project.
6. The moderator and the client should coordinate their efforts at all stages of the process for the research to achieve its objectives.
7. Most client organizations conduct more focus groups than are necessary to achieve the research objectives.
8. One of the most important services a moderator can provide is a fast report turnaround.
9. Client observers should be thoroughly briefed about the research objectives before the sessions start.
10. The most valuable service a moderator can provide is objective conclusions based on the interpretation of the research, without regard for what the client wants to hear.

Source: T. Greenbaum, "10 Tips for Running Successful Focus Groups," Marketing News, September 14, 1998.

The set of topics covered may change after each focus-group experience. The moderator and client may decide that a question is not generating useful, nonrepetitive information, and drop it from the remaining focus groups. Or a new, interesting idea may emerge, and reactions to that idea may be sought from subsequent groups.[14]

Recruitment

When recruiting participants, it is necessary to provide for both similarity and contrast within a group. However, as a rule, it is undesirable to combine participants from different social classes or stages in the life cycle because of differences in their perceptions, experiences, and verbal skills.[15]

Within an otherwise homogeneous group, it may be helpful to provide for a spark to be struck occasionally, by introducing contrasting opinions. One way to do this is to include both users and nonusers of the product or service or brand. If the product carries social connotations, however, this mixing up may suppress divergent opinions; for example, buyers of large life insurance policies may believe that nonbuyers are irresponsible. Some moderators believe that having conflicting opinions within a group may invite either a "rational" defense or a "withdrawal" of those who think their opinions are in a minority.

One controversial source of participants is the "experienced" panel, whose members have been trained in ways that contribute to the dialogue in the group. Those who oppose this practice feel that "professional" respondents who show up repeatedly are so sensitized by the interview experience that they are no longer representative of the population.[16]

Although groups of 8–12 have become customary, smaller groups may be more productive.[17] With 12 panelists, for example, after subtracting the time it takes to warm up (usually about 3 minutes) and the time for the moderator's questions and probes, the average panelist in a 90-minute focus group has 3 minutes of actual talking time. The experience becomes more like a group survey than an exploration of experiences, feelings, and beliefs. It is also a very expensive form of survey, so cutting group size makes sound economic sense.

The Moderator

Effective *moderating* encourages all participants to discuss their feelings, anxieties, and frustrations as well as the depth of their convictions on issues relevant to the topic, without being biased or pressured by the situation.[18] The following are critical moderating skills:

- Ability to establish rapport quickly by listening carefully, demonstrating a genuine interest in each participant's views, dressing like the participants, and avoiding the use of jargon or sophisticated terminology that may turn off the group.

- Flexibility observed by implementing the interview agenda in a way the group finds comfortable. Slavish adherence to an agenda means the discussion loses spontaneity and degenerates into a question-and-answer session.

- Ability to sense when a topic has been exhausted or is becoming threatening and to know which new topic to introduce to maintain a smooth flow in the discussion.

- Ability to control group influences to avoid having a dominant individual or subgroup that might suppress the total contribution.

Common techniques for conducting successful focus-group interviews include the chain reaction, devil's advocate, and false termination. In the **chain reaction** technique, the moderator builds a cumulative effect by encouraging each member of the focus group to comment on a prior idea suggested by someone else in the group, by adding to or expanding on it. When playing *devil's advocate*, the moderator expresses extreme viewpoints; this usually provokes reactions from focus-group members and keeps the discussion moving forward in a lively manner. In *false termination*, the moderator falsely concludes a focus-group interview, thanks group members for participating, and inquires whether there are any final comments. These "final comments" frequently lead to new discussion avenues and often result in the most useful data obtained.

Analysis and Interpretation of the Results

Analysis and interpretation of the results is complicated by the wealth of disparate comments usually obtained, which means that any analyst can find something that agrees with his or her view of the problem. A useful report of a group session is one that captures the range of impressions and observations on each topic and interprets them in the light of possible hypotheses for further testing. When reporting comments, it is not sufficient merely to repeat what was said without putting it into a context, so that the implications are more evident.

Several features of group interactions must be kept in mind during the analysis. An evaluation of a new concept by a group tends to be conservative; that is, it favors ideas that are easy to explain and not necessarily very new. There are further problems with the order of presentation when several concepts, products, or advertisements are being evaluated. If group participants have been highly critical of one thing, they may compensate by being uncritical of the next. Marketing Research in Action 8.5 discusses Procter and Gamble's experience with focus groups while developing new products.

Trends in Focus Groups

A growing number of focus groups have migrated from the real to the virtual world over the past few years. Given the cheaper costs, speed, and new technologies that will facilitate Web-based communication, the number of virtual focus groups will keep increasing but will never entirely replace their real-world counterparts.[19] Marketing Research in Action 8.6 points out the advantages and disadvantages of online versus traditional focus groups. The number of focus groups being conducted is growing at a rapid pace. There may be over 50,000 focus groups conducted annually. The quality of focus groups' facilities have also become better. Instead of tiny viewing rooms with small oneway mirrors, plush two-tiered observation areas that wrap around the conference room to provide an unobstructed view of all the respondents are being used. Telephone focus groups have emerged recently. This technique has been developed for respondents who are difficult to recruit, such as doctors. These focus groups use the conference calling facility to conduct

Marketing Research in Action 8.5

■ THE SWEET SMELL OF SUCCESS

When Procter & Gamble Co. were researching to build a better air freshener, they decided that they would ask the consumers about their "desired scent experience." Through this exercise, researchers at P&G found out that many people seemed to adjust to a scent after about half an hour and could not smell it anymore. They also learnt that most air-freshener scents do not spread evenly across a room and people felt many scents smell artificial.

After considering all these views, P&G developed Febreze Scentstories, a scent "player" that looks like a CD player and plays one of five alternating scents every 30 minutes. Priced at $34.99, the player contained a tiny fan inside that circulated the scent throughout the room. Along with this player, P&G offered five different disks holding a variety of scents with trademarked names.

Source: D. Ball, S. Ellison, and J. Adamy, "Just What You Need!," The Wall Street Journal—Marketplace, October 28, 2004.

Marketing Research in Action 8.6

▉ ONLINE FOCUS GROUP

An online focus group is very similar to a traditional focus group, but it takes place on the Web rather than in a physical location. The sessions have a moderator, and the participants interact via chatlike interfaces. With technology advancing by the day, researchers are increasingly attracted to online focus groups. They started off just as modified chat rooms, but their capabilities have grown to include access to multiple people, who can view the session as it unfolds. Viewers can even make comments to the moderators without alerting participants. In short, online focus groups have been transformed into sophisticated research environments. Online qualitative research is especially good for some of the following situations:

- Studies in potentially sensitive or confidential areas where anonymity is essential.
- B2C studies with a widely dispersed (including rural areas) audience.
- Studies where it is not economically feasible to bring respondents together under the same roof because of small numbers involved.
- Studies related to information technology that involve feedbacks on related topics and website evaluations.
- Studies where professionals are involved and time is a constraint (e.g., B2B customers).

In the situations mentioned above, online focus groups can perform as well as or better than traditional focus groups. But they may not always work best. The following are situations for which online focus groups may not be the best approaches:

- When capturing body language or facial expressions is vital.
- When you need to show prototypes or three-dimensional models.
- When products need to be handled—that is, when hands-on usage is critical or touching/feeling experience is mandatory.
- When conducting taste-testing, commercial testing, or testing of ads with extensive copy.
- When the client material or the topic is highly confidential.

Most researchers who have used online focus groups agree that online respondents tend to be more candid and direct. Generally, respondents compose their answers before reading others' postings and express only their own opinions, avoiding the peer pressure sometimes experienced in traditional groups. Respondents also seem to express their opinions without the tempering sometimes seen in traditional groups. For example, respondents feel more comfortable giving you negative or controversial feedback.

Source: M. Zinchiak, "Online Focus Group FAQs," Quirk's Marketing Research Review (*www.quirks.com*), July 2001.

the discussion. Marketing Research in Action 8.7 discusses three identifiable periods of qualitative research of women, as they have become increasingly involved in focus groups over the decades.

In cities where focus-group facilities are not available, a focus group can be conducted in church basements, in restaurants, and in a variety of hotel meeting rooms. One of the most successful groups was held in what the hotel called its boardroom. This was an elegant room containing a handsome conference table seating 12, with very plush executive-style chairs, deep pile carpeting, and subdued lighting. Through the hotel, valet parking was arranged for the participants, as well as a gourmet meal, a cash honorarium, and (perhaps the most unexpected touch) having all their cars lined up and waiting as the focus group ended. Client reps watched and listened to the group through a video feed to an adjoining meeting room. While this lacked some of the immediacy and intimacy of viewing through a mirror, it still gave the client the sense of being there. And the participants, the CFOs of area hospitals, enthusiastically responded with a candid and lively discussion of the key issues.[20] Marketing Research in Action 8.8 shows how Internet technology serves the traditional focus group by reducing costs and facilitating greater participation from people.

Marketing Research in Action 8.7

■ FOCUS ON WOMEN: THREE DECADES OF QUALITATIVE RESEARCH

There are three identifiable periods for qualitative research of women:

1. The early 1970s—the end of the traditional era
   - Focus groups were done during the day (assuming all women were housewives).
   - Women were paid less than men for attending: $7.50 vs. $10.00.
2. The late 1970s through late 1980s—the discovery of the new working woman

- Market researchers started including women in studies for "nontraditional" products (for example, air travel, investments, and cars).
3. The late 1980s to the present—the end-of-the-century woman
   - Researchers now routinely include women in what previously had been all-male groups.
   - Women hold their own mixed-gender focus groups on such nontraditional categories as technology, financial management, and sports.

For more interesting articles on marketing research visit http://www.marketingpower.com.
Source: J. Langer, Marketing News, *September 14, 1998, p. 21.*

Marketing Research in Action 8.8

■ INTERNET TECHNOLOGY HELPS TRADITIONAL FOCUS GROUPS

Focus group, one of marketing's favorite research tools, has now been made even more attractive and user-friendly. Video-streaming technology now means that focus groups can be observed "live" from one's desk, while the focus-group technique itself remains unchanged. Participants gather at a location to discuss and talk under the guidance of a group facilitator. However, observers no longer need to be on-site, behind the mirror, to view the proceedings. A camera captures all the action close-up, including facial expressions, and broadcasts the action via video streaming to an unlimited number of viewers who can watch in real time from the comfort of their desktop computers at any time, in any place. Once the focus-group session is complete, the data are saved to a server, where it can be viewed again by the client on demand. Major benefits of the technology are reduced travel costs and an expanded viewing audience.

Source: A. Nucifora, "Internet Revolutionizes Focus Groups," American City Business Journal, September 2000.

Recently, marketers have begun including creativity, in addition to the principles of marketing science, in the spectrum of focus groups. Creative moderating processes augment questioning, thus better engaging the group's thinking and concentration and resulting in a more in-depth and revealing feedback. Marketing Research in Action 8.9 lists three of the most effective interactive exercises.

Another emerging trend is in **two-way focus groups**.[21] This allows one target group to listen to and learn from a related group. In one application, physicians viewed a focus group of arthritis patients discussing the treatment they desired. A focus group of these physicians was then held to determine their reactions. A new focus-group television network called the Focus Vision Network may represent a third trend. Instead of flying from city to city, clients can view the focus groups in their offices. Live focus groups are broadcast by video transmission from a nationwide network of independently owned focus facilities. The cost of this option, of course, is quite high.[22]

Marketing Research in Action 8.9

▓ EFFECTIVE INTERACTIVE FOCUS-GROUP EXERCISES

Focus-group interactive exercises are not only instrumental in eliciting in-depth feedback based on the perceptions and emotions of respondents; they are also useful in improving their thinking and concentration. In addition, interactive exercises may uncover issues that respondents had been previously unable to verbalize or had been unaware of. Such exercises must be in line with the research objectives and should be relevant to the respondent base. The following are three effective interactive focus-group exercises:

- **Product sort:** This exercise presents the respondents with a sample of products that are to be sorted into groups that make sense to them. They are then asked to give each group a name that describes why those items have been put together. Thus, this exercise provides key insights into the segmentation process through visual simulation and active discussion.

- **Storytelling:** Here the moderator describes a scenario (related to the product or brand) and then asks the respondents to tell a story related to that setting. The process of weaving a story around the product or brand reveals the perceived cues, images, and biases of the respondents. This exercise is helpful in understanding the attitudes of the consumer.

- **Sticker allocation:** This exercise provides the respondents with a short list of choices, such as product concepts or flavors. They are then asked to assign 10 stickers or purchase coupons according to their preferences. Though the data from this exercise might not be statistically significant, the discussions during the exercise might throw more light onto customer preferences.

These dynamic interactive exercises not only stimulate lively discussions but also increase consumer learning.

Source: H. M. O'Neill, "Interactive Exercises Better Engage Groups," Marketing News, March 3, 2003, p. 55.

Focus Vision also plans to unveil an international network of focus facilities. Thus, global focus groups will be possible in the near future.[23]

Using Projective Techniques in Qualitative Research

The central feature of all projective techniques is the presentation of an ambiguous, unstructured object, activity, or person that a respondent is asked to interpret and explain.[24] The more ambiguous the stimulus, the more respondents have to project themselves into the task, thereby revealing hidden feelings and opinions. These techniques often are used in conjunction with individual nondirective interviews.

Projective techniques are used when it is believed that respondents will not or cannot respond meaningfully to direct questions about (1) the reasons for certain behaviors or attitudes, or (2) what the act of buying, owning, or using a product or service means to them. People may be unaware of their own feelings and opinions, unwilling to make admissions that reflect badly on their self-image (in which case they will offer rationalizations or socially acceptable responses) or are too polite to be critical to an interviewer.

Originally, projective techniques were used in conjunction with clinical "motivation research" studies. One such study was done on Saran Wrap, a plastic food wrap, when it was first introduced. Because it was very clingy, it was effective in sealing food, but it was also quite difficult to handle. As a result, strong negative attitudes toward the product became evident. To clarify the reasons for this dislike, a series of in-depth, nondirective clinical interviews was conducted. During the 1950s, there were many homemakers who disliked or even hated their role of keeping house and cooking. At that time, prior to the resurgence of the women's movement, there was no acceptable outlet among women for this dislike. It could not be verbalized openly, and many women were too inhibited to admit it to themselves. The study concluded that many homemakers found an outlet for this dislike by transferring it to Saran Wrap. The frustrations they had with the use of the product came to symbolize their frustrations with their role and lifestyle. As a result of the study, the product was made less clingy, and nonkitchen uses were stressed.

The underlying assumption of the clinical approach is that people often cannot or will not verbalize their true motivations and attitudes. They may be embarrassed to reveal that they dislike cooking. Alternatively, they may have suppressed this dislike and not even be conscious of it.[25] They simply may believe that their dislike is caused by the plausible judgment that Saran Wrap is awkward to use. The difficulty with clinical research is that true motivations are seldom clear. Indeed, two different clinical analysts working from different theoretical backgrounds may arrive at totally different interpretations. These problems have brought considerable disrepute to motivation research. At present, this type of research is relegated to a distinctly secondary role; however, projective techniques for asking indirect questions, when direct questions may not provide valid answers, are used more extensively. The following categories of projective techniques will be discussed: (1) word association, (2) completion tests, (3) picture interpretation, (4) third-person techniques, (5) role playing, and (6) case studies.

Word Association

The **word-association** technique asks respondents to give the first word or phrase that comes to mind after the researcher presents a word or phrase. The list of items used as stimuli should include a random mix of neutral items such as "chair," "sky," and "water," interspersed with the items of interest, such as "shopping downtown," "vacationing in Greece," or "Hamburger Helper." An interviewer reads the word to the respondents and asks them to mention the first thing that comes to mind. The list is read quickly to avoid allowing time for defense mechanisms to come into play. Responses are analyzed by calculating (1) the frequency with which any word is given as a response, (2) the amount of time that elapses before a response is given, and (3) the number of respondents who do not respond at all to a test word within a reasonable period of time.

New products tend to come from existing products; new technologies are applied to make them faster, healthier, less expensive, and easier to use. In fact, many researchers argue that there is no such thing as a really new product "function" because consumer needs are relatively permanent; that is, new engineering solutions or technologies periodically address the same ongoing consumer problems. Many years ago, people cleaned their hair with water; today they do it with some new shampoo technology. Either way, the basic function—cleaning hair—remains unchanged.

The role played by marketing research in a really new product development is limited. Consumers simply cannot describe needs for products that do not exist. Fifty years ago, for example, how could marketing researchers have identified the huge demand among drivers for automatic transmissions?

Traditional marketing research methods have been largely confined to asking people about problems with current products, watching them use these products, and giving them new prototypes for extended-use tests.

Researchers Jeffrey Durgee, Gian Colarelli O'Connor, and Robert Veryzer describe a new method for identifying new consumer or industrial product functions. They asked consumers to rate "mini-concepts," novel verb-object combinations that describe possible new functions for products. (A new function for a vacuum cleaner, for example, might be "deodorize rug.")

Whether the technology is available to perform these new functions is immaterial. The aim of the mini-concepts method is simply to generate interesting, "really new" function ideas and assess buyer responses.

The authors tested the mini-concept method among 30 middle-aged mothers regarding needs and opportunities for new food-related products. Their results indicated latent needs for products that would educate them about food, enhance their enjoyment of food, and enable them to prepare foods that have healing and energizing properties.

Using this method, marketing researchers can identify opportunities for really new functions in any product category. Current technologies can then be applied—or new technologies developed—to address and fulfill these needs.

Their study describes a new method for addressing this traditional limitation of marketing research. Asking consumers to rate novel verb-object combinations generated a number of interesting really new function ideas and allowed researchers to assess buyer responses.

Using the method, they elicited potential new functions for food-processing technology. Top scorers included "spend less money on food," "alert to spoiling food," "learn more about food," and "calculate calories of food."[26]

The result of a word-association task often is hundreds of words and ideas. To evaluate quantitatively the relative importance of each, a representative set of the target segment can be asked to rate, on a five-point scale, how well the word fits the brand, from "fits extremely well" to "fits not well at all." It is also useful to conduct the same associative research on competitive brands. When such a scaling task was performed for McDonald's on words generated from a word-association task, the strongest associations were with the words Big Macs, Golden Arches, Ronald, Chicken McNugget, Egg McMuffin, everywhere, familiar, greasy, clean, food, cheap, kids, well-known, French fries, fast, hamburgers, and fat. In the same study, Jack-in-the-Box had much lower associations with the words everywhere, familiar, greasy, and clean, and much higher associations with tacos, variety, fun, and nutritious.[27]

The word-association technique has also been particularly useful for obtaining reactions to potential brand names. Consumers associate a brand with (1) product attributes, (2) intangibles, (3) customer benefits, (4) relative price, (5) use/application, (6) user/customer, (7) celebrity/person, (8) lifestyle personality, (9) product class, (10) competitors, and (11) country/geographic area.[28] This technique is being used extensively to explore these associations. Word association has also been used to obtain reactions to and opinions about advertising slogans. For example, Bell Telephone found that one theme for advertising, "The System Is the Solution," triggered negative, "Big Brother is watching you" reactions among some people.

Completion Tests

The simplest **completion test** involves giving a respondent an incomplete and ambiguous sentence, which is to be completed with a phrase. The respondent is encouraged to respond with the first thought that comes to mind. Sentences are usually in the third person ("The average person considers television _____." "People drawing unemployment compensation are _____.") but may refer directly to the object or activity ("Insurance of all kinds is _____.") The completion test can be expanded readily to involve the completion of a story presented as an incomplete narrative or simply as a picture or photograph.

Picture Interpretation

The **picture interpretation** technique is based on the Thematic Apperception Test (TAT). The respondent is shown an ambiguous picture in the form of a line drawing, illustration, or photograph, and asked to describe it. This is a very flexible technique, for the pictures can be adapted readily to many kinds of marketing problems. An example of picture interpretation was a study that showed the respondents two scenes.[29] One involved a break after a daytime hike on a mountain; the other showed a small evening barbecue with close friends. During the scene, the beer served was either Coors or Lowenbrau.

Respondents were asked to project themselves into the scene and indicate, on a five-point scale, the extent to which they would feel "warm," "friendly," "healthy," and "wholesome."

The study was designed to test whether the advertising of Coors and Lowenbrau had established associations with their use-contexts—Coors with hiking, wholesomeness, and health, and Lowenbrau with a barbecue-type setting, friends, and warmth. The results showed that Coors was evaluated higher in the mountain setting and Lowenbrau in the barbecue setting, as expected, but that the other (word) associations were not sensitive (related) to the setting. For example, in the hiking context, Coors was higher on the "warm" and "friendly" dimensions, as well as on "healthy" and "wholesome."

Third-Person Techniques

By asking how friends, neighbors, or the average person would think or react in the situation, the researcher can observe, to some extent, the respondents projecting their own attitudes onto this **third person**, thus revealing more of their own true feelings. Magazines use this technique to identify which articles to feature on the cover, to stimulate newsstand sales. Direct questioning as to the articles of greatest interest to the respondent tends to be confounded by socially desirable responses. For example, articles on complex issues of foreign affairs are rated highly interesting to the respondent during direct questioning but are not thought to be of interest to the neighbors.

Another variant of this technique provides a shopping list or a description of a person's activities and asks respondents to describe the person. The respondents' attitudes toward the activities or items on the list will be reflected in their descriptions of the person. Usually, two lists are prepared and presented to matched sets of respondents; these could be grocery shopping lists, in which all items are identical except that Nescafe instant coffee on the first list is replaced by Maxwell House (drip grind) coffee on the second list[30]; or the contents of a billfold, which differ only in the inclusion of a Bank Americard on one list. Differences in the descriptions attributed to the two lists can reveal the respondents' underlying attitudes toward the product or activity that is being studied.

Role Playing

In **role playing**, a respondent assumes the role or behavior of another person, such as a salesperson in a store. This person then can be asked to try to sell a product to consumers, who raise objections. The method of coping with objections may reveal the respondents' attitudes, if they project themselves fully into the role playing without feeling uncomfortable or embarrassed.

Another technique with similar expressive objectives is the *role rehearsal* procedure used as part of a focus-group discussion. The participants in a focus group are encouraged, by offering them an incentive, to alter their behavior pattern in some extreme way. Abelson describes a study in which homemakers were asked to serve chicken to their families three times a week for a year, in return for $15.00 a week and an agreement not to tell the family about the arrangement.[31] The reaction of the participants to this offer, as they "rehearsed" the problems and objections they would likely encounter, gave useful insights into their own attitudes toward chicken. This technique is used toward the end of the focus-group session, and when the exercise is finished, respondents must be told that the offer was fictional.

Case Studies

A **case study**, in the research sense, is a comprehensive description and analysis of a single situation. The data for a case study usually are obtained from a series of lengthy, unstructured interviews with a number of people involved in the situation, perhaps combined with available secondary and internal data sources.

Case studies are very productive sources of research hypotheses. This approach was used by a food company to suggest the attributes that might characterize successful district sales managers.

Marketing Research in Action 8.10

■ A CASE FOR CASE STUDIES

Which would you rather bet your company's strategy on: what consumers say or what they do? Surveys, focus groups, and mall intercepts attempt to develop an understanding of customers' motivations by collecting reactions to researchers' questions. The major criticism of these methods is that what they gather are mere opinion statements that don't reveal actual behavior. Instead of gathering poorly considered opinion statements, the case-study approach builds insight into marketing behavior by pursuing—and verifying—the stories behind specific recent purchases in a given product category. It builds the full stories of how 50 supermarket shoppers selected their peanut butter last

Tuesday, or how 25 companies replaced their PBX systems last month.

Key arguments for the case-study approach are

- Case studies uncover motivations through demonstrated actions, not through statements of opinions.
- They're conducted in the surroundings where a product is bought or used to achieve greater immediacy (and accuracy) of response.
- They use observation and documentation to stimulate questions and corroborate responses.
- They access multiple decision makers.
- They require the talents of "marketing detectives" rather than "census takers."

Source: "Study What People Do, Not What They Say," Marketing News, *January 6, 1992, pp. 15, 32.*

A successful and an unsuccessful manager from otherwise similar territories (i.e., the territories had similar market structure, potential, and competitive situations) were studied closely for two weeks. They were interviewed, observed during sales calls and trips with their salespeople, and given a series of personality tests. The differences were used to develop a series of surveys that were administered to all the managers.

In some circumstances, a case study may be the only way to understand a complex situation. For example, the decision-making processes in large organizations may be imperfectly understood by a single participant. This problem makes it difficult to understand the sequence of decisions leading to, for example, the choice of a telephone service that customers use to call for reservations or information, or to place purchase orders. A telecommunications manager may be simply a technical consultant on the telephone system for the using company and not know how the system is used in the business. The functional managers in marketing or operations actually may make the decision to offer the service to customers but not know the intricacies of the switching network. To get a picture of the company's use of the service, all parties must be interviewed. Marketing Research in Action 8.10 makes a case for case studies.

Other Projective Techniques

Many other projective techniques have been developed and used in recent years. BBDO Worldwide has developed a trademarked technique called Photo Sort. Consumers express their feelings about brands through a specially developed photo deck showing pictures of different types of people, from business executives to college students. Respondents connect the people with the brands they think they use. Another photo-sort technique called the Pictured Aspirations Technique (PAT) has been created by Grey Advertising. This device attempts to uncover how a product fits into consumers' aspirations. Consumer drawings are used to unlock motivations or express perceptions. Researchers ask consumers to draw what they are feeling or how they perceive an object. An example of how Internet technology is used to elicit the inner feelings, not simply the top-of-mind reactions of consumers, is given in Marketing Research in Action 8.11.

Most people make rational, conscious, purchase decisions and can accurately report the reasons for their decisions when asked. However, many decisions appear to result from preconscious drives that can be either expressed or repressed. When a drive is repressed, a consumer may not be able to access the reason for a particular purchase decision. A technique called the *implicit model* provides a solution to this type of a problem.

In one study, a respondent, discussing the brand of interest, had only positive comments regarding the brand. Then a set of animal photographs was presented and the respondent was asked to select the animal that best represented this brand. A very different picture was painted of the brand. The photo chosen was described as a sly, wily, cunning, and even sneaky animal. In other words, this animal was a pretty, nice, neat-looking animal that was really a fairly mean, predatory creature stealing its prey in the night.[32]

Marketing Research in Action 8.11

■ FOCUS-GROUP PROJECTIVE TECHNIQUES

When conducting a focus group, one goal for the moderator is to get to deeper feelings, emotions, and values. Companies are seeking the elements that drive consumers in order to create successful marketing communication programs. The following are some projective techniques that are often used to elicit findings beyond the top-of-mind reactions of focus-group members:

- **Animal exercise:** In order to discover their underlying feelings about a product, company, or person, researchers often ask people to think of the item as an animal and have them write down the animal's name and why they selected it. For example, people may think of a nonprofit organization as a Labrador than as simply a dog because of the animal's personality traits, such as loyalty, caring, and intelligence.
- **Mindmapping:** Researchers often ask respondents to write down all the key words that come to mind when thinking of the central idea and then have them connect the key words in complete sentences. When done within a time limit, this technique can produce results quickly and generate discussion topics for the focus group.
- **Projective drawing:** Researchers often ask participants to draw anything they want so as to gather visual insights about their underlying thoughts about an issue. People

generally start drawing with a simple figure and then fill in details about that figure's life, such as name, age, facial features, clothing, and family. Researchers then ask the participants questions such as: What is his daily life? What are the impressions she conveys to people? What does his family think of him? This technique can be used to elicit consumers' perception of a certain product (such as Miller Lite or Bud Light).

- **Picture sort:** Similar to the animal exercise, researchers display pictures that represent a range of emotions. These pictures could be images of animals, people, or landscapes. Participants select the picture that reminds them of the issue and then are asked why they selected that picture and what impression they get from it.
- **Debate session:** Researchers can use debates to research products or organizations, especially when they are connected to highly emotional topics such as war or environmental issues. Participants are divided into two groups and assigned one side of the issue. Each group is given a certain amount of time to develop its best arguments. The moderator then has each group appoint a spokesperson but allows any group member to chime in during the debate. In addition, the moderator asks questions, directs the debate, and listens for each group's key messages to determine their underlying values or feelings about a certain issue.

Source: B. Dalbec, "Stage an Intervention for the Focus Group," Marketing News, February 2001, p. 46.

Limitations of Qualitative Methods

Most of the limitations of these qualitative methods stem from the susceptibility of the results to misuse, rather than their inherent shortcomings. There is a great temptation among many managers to accept small-sample exploratory results as sufficient for their purposes, because they are so compelling in their reality. The dangers of accepting the unstructured output of a focus group or a brief series of informal interviews are twofold. First, the results are not necessarily representative of what would be found in the population, and hence cannot be projected. Second, there is typically a great deal of ambiguity in the results. The flexibility that is the hallmark of these methods gives the moderator or interviewer great latitude in directing the questions; similarly, an analyst with a particular point of view may interpret the thoughts and comments selectively to support that view. In view of these pitfalls, these methods should be used strictly for insights into the reality of the consumer perspective and to suggest hypotheses for further research.

Observational Methods[33]

Observational methods provide a researcher with information on current behavior. Too often, this limitation becomes an excuse for not considering observational methods; because many researchers do not use these methods, they may not appreciate their considerable benefits. Nevertheless, there are strong arguments for considering the observation of ongoing behavior as an integral part of the research design. Some of these are the following:

- *Casual observation* is an important exploratory method. Managers continually monitor such variables as competitive prices and advertising activity, the length of lines of customers waiting for service, and the trade journals on executives' desks, to help identify problems and opportunities.

- *Systematic observation* can be a useful supplement to other methods. During a personal interview, the interviewer has the opportunity to note the type, condition, and size of the residence, the respondent's race, and the type of neighborhood with regard to mixed types and qualities of homes and apartments. Seldom is this data source adequately exploited in surveys.

- Observation may be the least expensive and most accurate method of collecting purely behavioral data such as in-store traffic patterns or traffic passing a certain point on a highway system. Thus, people's adherence to pedestrian safety rules before and after a safety campaign can be measured most easily by counting the number of people who cross against the light or outside the crosswalks.

- Sometimes observation is the only research alternative. This is the case with physiological phenomena or with young children who cannot articulate their preferences or motives. Thus, the Fisher Price Company operates a nursery school in a residential area as a means of field-testing potential new toys.

Direct Observation

Direct observation is frequently used to obtain insights into research behavior and related issues, such as packaging effectiveness. One firm uses an observer, disguised as a shopper, to watch grocery store shoppers approach a product category; to measure how long they spend in the display area, and to see whether they have difficulty finding the product; and whether the package is read, and if so, whether the information seemed hard to find. This kind of direct observation can be highly structured, with a detailed recording form prepared in advance, or very unstructured. When making an unstructured observation, the observer may be sent to mingle with customers in the store and look for activities that suggest service problems. This is a highly subjective task, because the observer must select a few things to note and record in varying amounts of detail. This inevitably will draw subjective inferences from the observed behavior. For example, just what was meant by the frown on the face of the shopper waiting at a cash register?

Regardless of how the observation is structured, it is desirable that the respondents not be aware of the observer.[34] Once conscious of being observed, people may alter their behavior, but in very unpredictable ways. One-way mirrors, disguises, and cameras are some of the common solutions. Care should be taken, however, that there is not an invasion of privacy. Marketing Research in Action 8.12 explains Procter & Gamble's experience in observational methods in developing new products.

Marketing Research in Action 8.12

■ P&G SWEEPING UP A MARKET

When Procter & Gamble launched its Swiffer mop in 1999, it was introduced as a dry mop to replace the traditional mop and bucket. However, with roughly 75 percent of American homes being covered with carpet, P&G now hopes to push the popular Swiffer mop onto the carpets of American homes, sidelining the traditional vacuum. Following this, studies were conducted to identify the tasks that consumers found unpleasant when it comes to cleaning their homes. For this purpose, visits were made to consumer homes during October 2003 to identify the disagreeable, awkward, or inconvenient issues faced by consumers about cleaning. The study included observing carefully how consumers cleaned the floor, dusted their furniture, and vacuumed the carpet. Even dirt was scattered around the living room rugs to see how consumers dealt with it.

The studies threw light on various aspects of cleaning for P&G. Their research showed that three out of every four times a consumer pulled out a vacuum cleaner, it was to tackle a little debris on a small portion of the carpet—things like leaves, grass, and nail clippings that do not require the full force of a traditional vacuum. Further, they noticed that a certain portion of the population was allotting less time to one big weekly cleaning session and instead were cleaning in a piecemeal fashion during the week, in between other errands or tasks. They identified several "compensating behaviors" that consumers adopted in order to tackle the inconvenience of vacuuming. Some left their vacuum cleaner in a corner of the room, always plugged in, to avoid the hassle of putting the machine away and getting it out again.

Others bought several vacuums, one for each level of the house, to avoid carrying the machine up and down the stairs. Yet another group simply avoided the task altogether by buying carpets that did not show much dirt. P&G concluded that "the setup and breakdown time" of the traditional vacuum cleaner was one of the things that kept people from cleaning.

Based on the results of these studies, P&G planned to launch a cordless carpet sweeper in August 2005. The Swiffer CarpetFlick, their seventh major Swiffer brand extension, is designed to clean up small patches of dirt, grass, and debris spilled on carpets, and keep consumers from dragging out their traditional vacuum cleaners for the small jobs. The new CarpetFlick resembles an old-fashioned manual sweeper, but operates on a different principle. The plastic on the base of the Swiffer CarpetFlick pushes down on crumbs or dirt, and then flicks the particles up through an opening in the sweeper into a cavity that contains a sticky adhesive sheet, where the debris is captured. The adhesive is double-sided, and the bottom side helps pick up fuzz and lint that is not "flicked" into the body. Like other Swiffer products, the adhesive is disposable, and replaceable. The new Swiffer has a tinted orange window through which consumers can see the debris they are collecting. The tinting keeps the refuse from being too visible but allows people to keep track of how much dirt is stuck to the adhesive sheet. This way, consumers need not have to deal with the "bagful of dirt." At the same time, as they can see the dirt they are collecting, it provides consumers with a signal that they are getting the floor cleaned.

Procter & Gamble hopes the new device can extend the run of the Swiffer brand, which has benefited from consumers who are lazy in their cleaning habits. The "Quick-clean" products have become the fastest-growing category of the $3 billion-plus cleaning-products market. Procter & Gamble estimates the niche, which includes products like the Swiffer, Clorox Co.'s Toilet Wand, and S.C. Johnson & Son

Inc.'s Pledge Grab-it, at $800 million, and is growing at about 7 percent a year. Since, most of the products in this category have replacement cleaning elements that can be thrown away once they are dirty, consumers now need not bother about dealing with dirty appliances. They're also appealing to manufacturers, who can charge a premium for the refills.

Source: Adapted with permission from S. Ellison, "Studying Messy Habits to Sweep up a Market," The Wall Street Journal, July 14, 2005.

Contrived Observation

Contrived observation can be thought of as behavioral projective tests; that is, the response of people placed in a contrived observation situation will reveal some aspects of their underlying beliefs, attitudes, and motives. Many direct-mail offers of new products or various kinds of books fall into this category, as do tests of variations in shelf space, product flavors, and display locations. The ethics of such offers can be very dubious, as in the example where a manufacturer decides to produce a product only after receiving an acceptable number of orders from a direct-mail advertisement.

A variant of this method uses buying teams, disguised as customers, to find out what happens during the normal interaction between the customer and the retailer, bank, service department, or complaint department. This method has provided useful insights into the discriminatory treatment of minorities by retailers, and the quality of public performance by employees of government agencies, banks, and airlines. One is hard pressed to think of other ways of finding out about the knowledgeability, helpfulness in meeting customers' needs, and efficiency of the staff. Clouding this picture are some serious, unresolved questions of ethics.

Content Analysis

Content analysis is an observation technique used to analyze written material into meaningful units, using carefully applied rules.[35] It is defined as the objective, systematic, and quantitative description of the manifest content of communication. It includes observation as well as analysis. The unit of analysis may be words, characters, themes, space and time measures, or topics. Analytical categories for classifying the units are developed, and the communication is broken down according to prescribed rules. Marketing research applications involve observing and analyzing the content or message of advertisements, newspaper articles, television and radio programs, and the like. For example, a study hypothesized that because of the growing number of elderly Americans, advertisers would use more elderly models in their promotions. After a content analysis of all the advertisements, the researchers found that the use of elderly people in advertisements has indeed increased.

Physical Trace Measures

Physical trace measures involve recording the natural "residue" of behavior. These measures are rarely used because they require a good deal of ingenuity and usually yield a very gross measure. When they work, however, they can be very useful.[36] For instance, (1) the consumption of alcohol in a town without liquor stores has been estimated from the number of empty bottles in the garbage[37]; (2) an automobile dealer selected radio stations to carry his advertising by observing the most popular dial settings on the radios of cars brought in for servicing; (3) one magazine readership research method employs small glue spots in the gutter of each page spread of a magazine, so broken glue spots are used as evidence of exposure; and (4) a museum gauges the popularity of individual exhibits by measuring the rate of wear on the floor tiles in front of the exhibit and by the number of nose smudges on the glass of the case around the exhibit.

The **home audit approach** to purchase panels (described in Chapter 6) is yet another type of physical trace measure. The auditor describes the inventory in several prespecified categories. This method is not very useful if used on a one-shot basis, for it then requires a very tenuous assumption that possession indicates purchase and usage. However, if the inventory is made over an extended period and supplemented with a record of cartons and wrappers, an indication of the rate of purchase is possible.

Empathic Interviewing[38]

Empathic interviewing is an exploratory form of research that draws from the wisdom of sociology, psychology, market research, and anthropology to help researchers probe beneath generalizations and identify the social factors that influence consumer behavior. In understanding how complex decisions and behaviors emerge, empathic interviewing can supplement or replace traditional research methods. Some guidelines in conducting empathic interviews are as follows:

1. Imagine yourself in the person's situation.

2. Avoid self-referencing.

3. Gently challenge generalizations by asking for specific examples.

4. Ask open-ended, nonleading questions that start with *how, what*, and *why*.

Humanistic Inquiry

Humanistic inquiry is a controversial research method that relies heavily on observation but is now being used in marketing with increasing frequency.[39] The humanistic approach advocates immersing the researcher in the system under study rather than as in the traditional scientific method, in which the researcher is a dispassionate observer. Throughout the immersion process, the humanistic researcher maintains two diaries, or logs. One is a theory construction diary that records in detail the thoughts, premises, hypotheses, and revisions in the researcher's thinking. The second set of notes the researcher maintains is a methodological log. Detailed and time-sequenced notes are kept on the investigative techniques used during the inquiry, with special attention to biases and distortions a given technique may have introduced. To access whether the interpretation is drawn in a logical and unprejudiced manner from the data gathered and the rationale employed, humanistic inquiry relies on the judgment of an outside auditor or auditors. Marketing Research in Action 8.13 illustrates humanistic inquiry research.

Behavior-Recording Devices

Various **behavior-recording devices** have been developed to overcome particular deficiencies in human observers. The most obvious example is the traffic counter, which operates continuously without getting tired and consequently is cheaper and probably more accurate than humans. For the same reasons, as well as for unobtrusiveness, cameras may be used in place of human observers. Someone still has to interpret what is recorded on the film, but the options exist of sampling segments of the film, slowing the speed, or having another observer view it for an independent judgment.

Marketing Research in Action 8.13

■ CONSUMPTION VALUES AND LIFESTYLES OF WASPS

The objective of the study was to interpret the consumption values and lifestyles of WASP (White, Anglo-Saxon, Protestant) consumers. Since this group of consumers is very large, the researcher decided to narrow down his scope geographically to communities along the eastern seaboard. The researcher made field trips to such locales as Richmond, Virginia; Charleston, North Carolina; Connecticut; and Maine. During these trips, observations were made in residential neighborhoods, shopping areas, and other places. Whenever the researcher had personal contact in the community, he lived in the local household observing and participating in their daily rounds; attending church services and community meetings; and engaging in shopping activities and meeting and talking with other residents. After every meeting or contact episode, the researcher made a note of the thinking, transformation, and conclusion he made regarding WASPs' consumption values and lifestyle in his theory construction diary, while he made a note of the happenings, the time and date when a certain event occurred in his methodological log. After 18 months of participating in the WASP lifestyle and meticulous record keeping, a pattern began to emerge. The pattern was formed around the central values that WASP consumers had expressed verbally to the researcher in several contexts and other documentary evidence. The researcher was suddenly able to grasp that the same core values (practicality, conservatism, individual responsibility, self control, etc.) were expressed in all aspects of the consumers' lifestyle—from clothing and automobile preference to leisure activities.

Source: E. C. Hirschman, "Humanistic Inquiry in Marketing Research: Philosophy Method and Criteria," Journal of Marketing Research, August 1986, pp. 237–249.

Of the mechanical devices that do not require respondents' direct participation, the A.C. Nielsen "people meter" is best known. The *people meter* is attached to a television set to record continually to which channel the set is tuned. It also records who is watching. Arbitron recently developed a pocket people meter that is no larger than an electronic pager and can recognize the unique code that broadcasters embed in the soundtrack of radio or television programs.[40] The latest trend is to develop "passive people meters." These meters will record an individual's broadcast viewing and listening without his or her intervention. Mediacheck has introduced one such system. It has two units: a set-top meter that detects audio codes to identify programming being watched or listened to, and a device such as a pendant or a wristwatch worn by the person being measured. The main drawback of this system is that it requires that all programming carry a nonintrusive audio code that can be recorded by the meter system. Nielsen is also developing its own passive people meter. It will recognize a person entering the room and also keep track of the person's activities while he or she watches TV. Technological advances such as the Universal Product Code (UPC) have had a major impact on mechanical observation. The UPC system, together with optical scanners, allow for mechanical information collection regarding consumer purchases, by product category, brand, store type, price paid, and quantity.

Some types of observation are beyond human capabilities. All physiological reactions fall into this category. Therefore, devices are available to measure changes in the rate of perspiration as a guide to emotional response to stimuli (the psychogalvanometer), and changes in the size of the pupils of subjects' eyes, which are presumed to indicate the degree of interest in the stimulus being viewed (the pupilometer). These devices can be used only in laboratory environments, and often yield ambiguous results.

Marketing Research in Action 8.14

■ TRACKING SHOPPERS VIRTUALLY

Kimberly-Clark Corp. has developed a new tool that tracks retina movements and records every glance of the consumer. Using the tool, virtual shopping aisles were created wherein consumers are requested to shop for products. The shopping behavior was then captured by the devices and the observations are used for understanding consumer behavior.

Kimberly-Clark hopes these virtual shopping aisles will help it better understand consumer behavior and make the testing of new products faster, more convenient and more precise. The mobile testing unit is usually based in a new

high-tech studio that Kimberly-Clark completed in May 2007 in Appleton, Wisconsin. The room also features a U-shaped floor-to-ceiling screen that re creates in vivid detail interiors of the big retailers that sell the company's products—a tool that the company will use in presentations to executives in bids to win shelf space. A separate area is reserved for real replicas of store interiors, which can be customized to match the flooring, light fixtures and shelves of retailers such as Target Corp. and Wal-Mart Stores Inc. Kimberly-Clark uses the data from its virtual-reality tests with consumers to tout how products in development perform.

Source: E. Byron, "A Virtual View of the Store Aisle," Wall Street Journal, October 3, 2007.

Experience with *eye-movement recorders* has been more successful. This device records the experience of viewing pictures of advertisements, packages, signs, or shelf displays, at a rate of 30 readings per second. The recorded eye movements show when the subjects starts to view a picture, the order in which the elements of the image were examined and reexamined, and the amount of viewing time given each element. One application is for testing the visual impact of alternative package designs. An example of how technology can help in data collection using eye-movement recorders is provided in Marketing Research in Action 8.14.

Voice-pitch analysis examines changes in the relative vibration frequency of the human voice to measure emotion.[41] In voice analysis, the normal or baseline pitch of an individual's speaking voice is charted by engaging the subject in an unemotional conversation. The greater the deviation from the baseline, the greater is said to be the emotional intensity of the person's reaction to a stimulus. For example, voice-pitch analysis has been used in package research, to predict consumer brand preference for dog food.[42] An example of how technology can help in data collection through direct link is provided in Marketing Research in Action 8.15.

Limitations of Observational Methods

The vast majority of research studies use some form of questionnaire. Observation methods, despite their many advantages, have one crucial limitation: They cannot observe motives, attitudes, or intentions, which sharply reduces their diagnostic usefulness. To be sure, these cognitive factors are manifested in the observed behavior, but so are many other confounding factors. For example, the Zippo Lighter Company seemingly has a valuable measure of advertising effectiveness in the volume of its lighters sent in for repair. Despite the mention of the free repair privilege in the advertising, it is questionable whether such a measure can unambiguously test for impact.

Observational methods suffer other limitations as well. They are often more costly and time-consuming and may yield biased results if there are sampling problems or if significant observer subjectivity is involved. However, these biases usually are very different in character from those that affect obtrusive questionnaire methods. This is one of the underexploited strengths of observation methods: they help to increase our confidence in questionnaire measures if they yield similar results when used as a supplement.

Marketing Research in Action 8.15

■ NEW TECHNOLOGY COLLECTS MEDIA BEHAVIOR DATA

Systems for measuring radio and TV audiences haven't improved much over the past few decades. Audiences are measured by small, representative panels. TV panels use set-top boxes. Radio panelists are asked to record listening habits in a diary. Researchers use highly refined methods to create a small sample of individuals whose behaviors and attitudes represent everyone. The problem is understanding the media habits of the panel members: to accurately determine what they watch and listen to, when, and for how long.

Germany's largest market research company, GFK, presented a new technology to measure what TV and radio shows a person watched or listened to by using a wristwatch named Radiocontrol. Several thousand panel members are given watches to wear for two weeks. The watch takes a four-second "fingerprint" of ambient sound every minute. At the end of two weeks, the watch is returned and the sound fingerprint is matched against a database of radio and TV programming to determine *exactly* what a person watched or listened to. The sample is then projected out to a national audience.

The watch is a highly sophisticated instrument, containing a motion detector and a thermostat to determine whether it is worn at any given moment. It's sleek and stylish but automatically stops telling time after two weeks, which prompts the wearer to return it to the research company.

The ability to accurately track people's real-world behaviors is of tremendous interest to marketers. When this type of technology is married with attitudes and purchase behavior, marketers will have a direct link between what people think and buy and the advertising they're exposed to. It promises to create enormous advertising efficiencies.

Source: J. Graham, "Tracking Moves Offline," http://www.clickz.com/clickz/column/1711679/tracking-moves-offline, November 27, 2002.

Recent Applications of Qualitative and Observational Methods

In recent years, many companies, across various industry verticals, have applied qualitative and observational techniques to acquire vital information about marketing problems. Here are a few examples of companies who have adopted these techniques. Marketing Research in Action 8.16 describes a brand that used observational techniques to identify a new market.

- Maritz Marketing Research, Inc. (St. Louis), says its Virtual Customers system for evaluating service quality goes beyond typical mystery shopping programs because of its integrated approach, customer certification process, and high-tech project management system. Virtual customers (e.g., mystery shoppers) receive job-specific training and periodic updates during the certification process, said Al Goldsmith, director of virtual customer research at Maritz. The emphasis on training is needed because "without it, each person would be unlikely to role-play adequately enough to obtain reliable data." Maritz uses a high-tech project management system to track the skill level and demographic information on each virtual customer. A database shows each person's shopping performance and other pertinent information to ensure that the right people are assigned to each project. The same system can produce real-time feedback on the status of the project, the number of locations visited, and current ratings compared with ratings of previous visits.

- On-site observation is an underutilized method that has tremendous potential for helping marketers understand consumers' thinking. It is as valuable as traditional qualitative techniques such as focus groups and in-depth interviews. On-site observation gives researchers

Marketing Research in Action 8.16

■ BERTOLLI—NOW SERVING

In 2007, Unilever's Bertolli brand that includes pasta sauces and olive oils, zeroed in on a market segment that did not have their presence—the prepared meals segment consisting of frozen meals. Market research reports identified that with the growth of average work hours by 26 percent in 2006, the frozen meals that Americans eat have increased by 47 percent. A majority (75 percent) of this $5.7 billion market comprised single-serve options and about 20 percent of the market was made up of multi-serve frozen entrées and dinner. It was this 20 percent that Bertolli was interested in as this market was growing at an impressive 16 percent between 2003 and 2005.

Bertolli had some questions that helped them identify their brand strategy—Is it a big space or a growing space, or both? Do we have a brand that can play and compete in that space? And, if so, what difference can we make? Based on the findings, Bertolli decided to compete in complete meal solutions market and the result was the launch of "Dinner for Two" line of products.

Before launching this product line, Bertolli turned to ethnographic research in 2000 to help design meals that would stand out from competitors—that would mark its products as an upscale, luxurious end to a busy day, not just a convenience. They conducted observational studies which had researchers accompanying participating families to grocery stores to observe their shopping habits and, watching them cook and eat frozen meals. This helped them identify areas of complaint and dissatisfaction. They learnt that polybag meals already on the market had mushy pasta and did not taste fresh. Participants also complained that the packaging was unappealing and seemed downscale. Meanwhile, other researchers visited traditional Italian restaurants in and popular Italian chain restaurants to see what kinds of ingredients chefs used in their dishes.

With the market research complete, Bertolli then concentrated on the packaging of the meals. Designers placed a photograph of the cooked entrée against a sepia-toned background of the hills of Tuscany. There's also a glass of wine on the package, meant to underscore the idea that the food inside is on par with a restaurant meal.

The efforts paid off for Unilever. Since launching nationwide in January 2005, Bertolli-brand frozen entrees have garnered a 38.6 percent share of the multi-serve polybag market, outperforming both Stouffer's and Birds Eye. In U.S. grocery stores, Bertolli accounts for 8 of the top 11 best-selling polybag dinners, according to AC Nielsen. Meanwhile, the line has become a new growth driver for Unilever with sales rising more than 185 percent, from $70 million in its first year to a projected $200 million plus in 2007.

Source: J. Borden, "Bertolli's Big Bite," Marketing News, October 1, 2007.

the chance to observe and learn about consumer purchasing decisions as they are being made. Observing consumer decisions as they choose products from a shelf or casually asking them to explain their preferences can lead to a wealth of qualitative information. The best approach in conducting on-site observation is by placing researchers in a supermarket and letting them present themselves as shoppers who need advice from other shoppers in making a purchasing decision. The shoppers in question will give spontaneous responses on the product that are noteworthy for marketing analysis.

A skilled researcher can do about 35 interviews a day in several supermarkets with minimal overhead costs and an excellent yield for qualitative work. It requires individuals who are outgoing and are able to *listen*—not just hear what people say. A person with these traits can then be taught how to obtain relevant answers, absorb information, evaluate responses, and avoid asking leading questions. Field observations also require tremendous patience, discipline, and enthusiasm.[43]

SUMMARY

Exploratory research is an essential step in the development of a successful research study. In essence, this kind of research is insurance that major elements of the problem or important competing hypotheses will not be overlooked. It further ensures that both the manager and the researcher will see the market through the consumer's eyes. Fortunately, research design is an iterative and not a sequential process, so major initial oversights are not necessarily irreversible. In particular, the exploratory technique of semistructured interviews should be reemployed later when the structured study is pretested. Properly handled, a pretest should provide opportunities for respondents to express their frustrations with the specific questions, as well as identify deficiencies in the scope of the questions.

In this chapter, we also discussed observational methods. These are useful during the exploratory stage of the research design but are even more valuable as a data collection method. The advantages of observational methods will become even more apparent in Chapter 9, as we examine the errors that are inherent when an interviewer starts to interact with a respondent.

QUESTIONS AND PROBLEMS

8.1 What are the significant differences between nondirective and semistructured individual interviews? In what circumstances would a nondirective interview be more useful than a semistructured interview?

8.2 You have conducted two group meetings on the subject of telephone answering devices. In each group, there were seven prospective users of such devices, and in the two groups, there were four users of telephone answering services. (These services use an operator to intercept calls and record messages.) When the client's new-product development manager heard the tapes and read the transcripts of the two meetings, the first reaction was, "I knew all along that the features I wanted to add to our existing model would be winners, and these people are just as enthusiastic. Let's not waste any more research effort on the question of which features are wanted." What do you say?

8.3 There have been a number of complaints in your city that minorities are discriminated against by local major appliance retailers (with respect to prices, trade-ins, sales assistance, and credit). How would you use the techniques described in this chapter to study this question?

8.4 A local consumer organization is interested in the differences in food prices among major stores in the area. How should it proceed in order to obtain meaningful comparisons?

8.5 Toothpaste manufacturers have found consistently that if they ask for detailed information on the frequency with which people brush their teeth and then make minimal assumptions as to the quantity of toothpaste used on each occasion, as well as spillage and failure to squeeze the tube empty, the result is a serious overstatement of toothpaste consumption. How would you explain this phenomenon? Would it be possible to design a study to overcome these problems and obtain more accurate estimates of consumption? Describe how such a study could be conducted.

8.6 The school board of St. Patrick's High School is concerned about the rise of student violence involving guns during the past two months. During an emergency meeting, Father Hennessy, the school's principal, insisted that steps be taken to return student behavior to its traditionally exemplary level. He suggested that this rise in the level of violence was for reasons beyond the experience of most of the school board members, and recommended that they needed to gather some background information on the situation in order to address the problem knowledgeably. The school board agreed with his proposal and decided to commission a market research study to question students on whether they carried guns and their underlying motivation for doing so. The research firm, Church and Associates, has decided to use focus groups or individual in-depth interviews to obtain the required information.

(a) Which of the above-mentioned techniques is suitable for this purpose? Give reasons.

(b) Church and Associates has recommended separate focus-group discussions involving the faculty. How can the moderator effectively encourage all the participants to discuss their feelings on the topic?

(c) What possible questions could be asked in an in-depth interview?

8.7 What difficulties might be encountered when conducting a qualitative interview in an international context?

8.8 When would you recommend observational methods? Why?

8.9 How can a pretest add to the quality of a marketing research study?

8.10 For each of the following scenarios, indicate whether qualitative or quantitative research is more appropriate. Also recommend a specific technique for each and justify your answer.

(a) A manufacturer of herbal teas wants to know how often and for what purposes consumers use herbal tea products.

(b) A political campaign manager wants to identify ways of sharply increasing the amount of contributions from the population.

(c) An amusement park is nearing the final stages of designing two new rides. It wants to measure the reactions of the public and their potential enthusiasm for the new rides.

(d) A company that manufactures potato chips has two alternative package designs for the product and wants to determine which design will yield higher sales.

END NOTES

1. F. N. Kerlinger, *Foundations of Behavioral Research*. 3rd ed., New York: Holt, Rinehart and Winston, 1986.

2. http://www.energytrust.org, October 22, 2002.

3. D. Kiley, "At Long Last, Detroit Gives Consumers the Right of Way," *Adweek*, June 6, 1988, pp. 26–27.

4. J. K. Johansson and I. Nonaka, "Market Research the Japanese Way," *Harvard Business Review*, May–June 1987, pp. 16–22.

5. J. F. Durgee, "Depth-Interview Techniques for Creative Advertising," *Journal of Advertising Research*, January 1986, pp. 29–37.

6. M. Q. Patton, *Qualitative Evaluation and Research Methods*. Newbury Park, CA: Sage, 1990. For additional discussion of cross-cultural research and evaluation, see M. Q. Patton, *Culture and Evaluation: New Directions for Program Evaluation*. San Francisco: Jossey-Bass, 1985; W. J. Lonner and J. W. Berry, *Field Methods in Cross Cultural Research*. Newbury Park, CA: Sage, 1986.

7. B. Eisenfeld, "Phone interviews may garner more data," *Marketing News*, March 3, 2003; A. Foden, "Customer-Focused Efforts Require Listening," *Marketing News*, March 3, 2003.

8. J. Langer, "Telephone Time: In-Depth Interviews via Phone Gain Greater Acceptance," *Marketing Research Forum*, Summer 1996, p. 6.

9. M. Garee and T. R. Schori, "Position Focus Group Observers for Best View," *Marketing News*, September 14, 1998, p. 29.

10. M. Lautman, "Focus Groups: Theory and Method," *Advances in Consumer Research 9*, October 1981, p. 54.

11. See T. Greenbaum, "Focus Groups vs. One-on-Ones: The Controversy Continues," *Marketing News*, September 2, 1991, p. 16.

12. P. Tuckel, E. Leppo, and B. Kaplan, "Focus Groups under Scrutiny: Why People Go and How It Affects Their Attitudes towards Participation," *Marketing Research*, 12, June 1992.

13. For a comprehensive listing of the providers of focus group facilities, see "1992 Marketing News Directory of Focus Group Facilities and Moderators," *Marketing News*, January 6, 1992.

14. D. W. Stewart and P. N. Shamdasani, *Focus Groups: Theory and Practice*, Newbury Park, CA: Sage, 1990.

15. N. E. James and N. Frontczak, "How Acquaintanceship and Analyst Can Influence Focus Group Results," *Journal of Advertising*, 17, 1988, pp. 41–48.

16. W. Hayward and J. Rose, "We'll Meet Again . . . Repeat Attendance at Group Discussions—Does it Matter?" *Journal of the Advertising Research Society*, July 1990, pp. 377–407.

17. For more discussion, see E. F. Fern, "The Use of Focus Groups for Idea Generation: The Effects of Group Size, Acquaintanceship, and Moderator on Response Quantity and Quality," *Journal of Marketing Research*, 19, February 1982, pp. 1–13.

18. N. R. Henderson, "Trained Moderators Boost the Value of Qualitative Research," *Marketing Research*, June 1992, p. 20.

19. R. X. Weissman, "Online or Off Target," *American Demographics*, November 1998.

20. D. Prince, "Handling the Unexpected during Focus Group," *Marketing News*, September 23, 1996, p. 29.

21. M. Silverstein, "Two Way Focus Groups Can Provide Startling Information," *Marketing News*, January 4, 1988, p. 31.

22. "Network to Broadcast Live Focus Groups," *Marketing News*, September 3, 1990, pp. 10, 47.

23. C. Miller, "Anybody Ever Hear of Global Focus Groups?" *Marketing News*, May 27, 1991, p. 14.

24. H. H. Kassarjian, "Projective Methods," in R. Ferber, ed., *Handbook of Marketing Research*. New York: McGraw-Hill, 1974, pp. 3–87; S. J. Levy, "Dreams, Fairy Tales, Animals, and Cars," *Psychology and Marketing*, 2, Summer 1985, pp. 67–82.

25. R. K. Schnee, "Quality Research: Going Beyond the Obvious," *Journal of Advertising Research*, 28, February–March 1988.

26. B. Ordini, "A Novel Idea for Market Researchers," *Insights from MSI*, Marketing Science Institute, Cambridge, MA, Fall 1997.

27. D. A. Aaker, *Managing Brand Equity: Capitalizing on the Value of a Brand Name*. New York: Macmillan, 1991.

28. D. A. Aaker, *Managing Brand Equity: Capitalizing on the Value of a Brand Name*. New York: Macmillan, 1991.

29. D. A. Aaker and D. M. Stayman, "Implementing the Concept of Transformational Advertising," *Psychology and Marketing*, May–June 1992, pp. 237–253.

30. This was the design of the classic study by M. Haire, "Projective Techniques in Marketing Research," *Journal of Marketing*, 14, 1950, pp. 649–656. However, recent validation studies have found that differences in the two descriptions are also influenced by the relationship of the two test products to the items in the shopping list, so the interpretation is anything but straightforward. See also J. C. Andersen, "The Validity of Haire's Shopping List Projective Technique," *Journal of Marketing*, 15, November 1978, pp. 644–649.

31. H. Abelson, "A Role Rehearsal Technique for Exploratory Research," *Public Opinion Quarterly*, 30, 1966, pp. 302–305.

32. C. B. Raffel, "Vague Notions," *Marketing Research*, Summer 1996, pp. 21–23.

33. The analysis of secondary records, as discussed in the previous chapter, is an observational method. In this chapter, however, we are restricting ourselves to the observation of ongoing behavior.

34. C. Scott, D. M. Klien, and J. Bryant, "Consumer Response to Humor in Advertising: A Series of Field Studies Using Behavioral Observation," *Journal of Consumer Research*, 16, March 1990, pp. 498–501.

35. An excellent summary article of content analysis is R. Kolbe and M. Burnett, "Content Analysis Research: An Examination of Applications with Directives for Improving Research Reliability and Objectivity," *Journal of Consumer Research*, September 1991, pp. 243–250. Other examples of content analysis are M. Zimmer and L. Golden,

"Impressions of Retail Stores: A Content Analysis of Consumer Images," *Journal of Retailing*, Fall 1988, pp. 265–293; and T. Shimp, J. Urbany, and S. Camlin, "The Use of Framing and Characterization for Magazine Advertising of Mass Marketed Products," *Journal of Advertising*, January 1988, pp. 23–30.

36. For a fuller discussion, see S. Lee, *New Directions for Methodology of Behavior Science: Unobtrusive Measurement Today*. San Francisco: Jossey-Bass, 1979.

37. J. A. Cote, J. McCullough, and M. Reilly, "Effects of Unexpected Situations on Behavior-Intention Differences: A Garbology Analysis," *Journal of Consumer Research*, 12, September 1985, pp. 188–194.

38. P. Lawless, *Marketing News*, January 4, 1999.

39. E. Hirschman, "Humanistic Inquiry in Marketing Research: Philosophy, Method and Criteria," *Journal of Marketing Research*, August 1986, pp. 237–249. For more detailed information, see Y. Lincoln and E. Guba, *Naturalistic Inquiry*. Beverly Hills, CA: Sage, 1985.

40. "Arbitron to Develop 'Pocket People Meter,'" *Marketing News*, January 4, 1993.

41. N. Nighswonger and C. Martin, Jr., "On Voice Analysis in Marketing Research," *Journal of Marketing Research*, August 1981, pp. 350–355.

42. G. Brickman, "Uses of Voice Pitch Analysis," *Journal of Advertising Research*, April 1980, pp. 69–73.

43. W. B. Helmreich, "Louder Than Words," *Marketing News*, March 1, 1999, p. 13.

APPENDIX

Myths of Qualitative Research: It's Conventional, but Is It Wisdom?

Myth	Fact
Focus groups should never have more than six or seven respondents, so each one gets more "air time."	The ideal number of respondents depends on the type of respondents, the subject, and the moderator's style.
Qualitative researchers should approach each study with a clean-slate mentality. Past research by other companies, information about the clients' hunches, or internal political battles concerning the current study will only bias the researcher.	Background on a project's real objectives and past learning is an important part of the moderator briefing. The information could certainly bias the moderator but a good researcher knows what to look for. The moderator can probe responses that do not fit hypotheses, touching more briefly on what confirms well-accepted knowledge.
Many good ideas die in focus groups because consumers are not ready to accept new concepts.	Qualitative research offers researchers the opportunity to probe what underlies consumers' reactions. If an idea meets immediate respondent rejection, a good researcher explores the reasons why, whether the product might fit a real need, and what, if anything, could change the respondent's mind.
Focus groups should be demographically homogeneous.	Most research budgets cannot afford the luxury of focus groups that differ demographically, with one group per type in each market. Some diversity may actually prove to be beneficial. The rule of thumb is that the respondents must feel comfortable with one another talking about the subject.

It is a mistake to ask respondents "why" they do or feel something.

Usually the problem is not in asking the questions, but in how the questions are formed. The questions should not be intimidating and must show genuine interest and a desire to understand.

Qualitative research should rely mainly on projective techniques (such as collages, drawings, photographs, and role-playing). These bring out thoughts and feelings that consumers either are not in touch with or are uncomfortable acknowledging publicly.

Projective methods are excellent tools but they should not take the place of direct questions. In many areas, straightforward, nonjudgmental questions about respondents' feelings successfully uncover respondents' emotions.

Focus groups at 8 P.M. are not a good idea because everyone is tired.

Focus groups at 6 P.M. and 8 P.M. are necessary because most people work during the day. The energy level of a focus group is more indicative of the chemistry of respondents and their interest in the topic than the time.

The sign of a good moderator is that he or she says very little in a focus group.

The moderator's role should be active, responsive, and creative. That role includes guiding the group dynamics. Moderators should offer nonleading feedback by reflecting back to respondents what the moderator picks up and probing further.

Recruiting is fairly easy when the client provides lists of customers to be interviewed for focus groups and in-depth interviews.

Recruiting from a list is not necessarily easy. Lists typically take longer to produce than expected, which doesn't allow sufficient time for recruiting. Many lists lack telephone numbers, requiring additional time and expense for phone lookups.

Sending notes to the moderator during the focus group enables clients to be involved in the process, ensuring that the research provides answers to their questions.

Notes brought into the interviewing room can be quite disrupting. Notes can be a reminder that the respondents are being observed and hence will make them self-conscious. Also, repeated notes raise questions in respondents' minds about whether the observers trust the moderator, creating a tense and awkward situation.

Focus groups should be used rarely since there is usually a strong personality who dominates the discussion.

In many groups, respondents all contribute to the discussion, although some people are more talkative or articulate than others. Instead, other respondents may distance themselves from that person, feeling free to disagree. A strong personality may speak up confidently yet not dominate. Experienced moderators have a variety of techniques for dealing with respondents.

The topic guide and materials shown in a series of focus groups should be kept the same throughout for consistency.

Qualitative research should be dynamic; new ideas may come up, which should alter the topic guide during the study. Changes usually mean that learning has taken place and the topic should not constantly remain the same. The purpose of the qualitative study is to help the client move toward ideas that work, not to "quantify" that an idea doesn't work.

Qualitative research studies should always be followed by quantitative research to test the hypotheses.

At times, due to budget constraints, qualitative studies are sufficient for marketing research. In terms of quality of research, if the research of a sizeable qualitative study is consistent and has a "commonsense validity," then it is unnecessary to do quantitative research.

A discussion guide for focus groups is referred to by some clients as a "script," a term that implies that the moderator should follow it pretty much verbatim.

A topic guide should be just that—a general *guide* to the topics that should be covered and the order in which they should be covered, and some ideas on possible probes or techniques the moderator might use. The sequence is merely a guideline when there is no significant research reason for holding off on a subject until another one has been discussed.

Qualitative research must be done in person and through in-depth interviews to develop rapport between interviewer and respondent

Rapport can be just as strong or stronger in telephone interviews. Not being able to see the interviewer can be an advantage. To build rapport on the phone, we ease into the interview with simple usage or attitude questions rather than the icebreakers often asked in focus groups.

Source: J. Langer, *Marketing News*, 33(5), March 1, 1999, p. 13.

Quant-Qual Combo in Understanding Customers

Recent thinking among subject-matter specialists is focused toward integrating qualitative and quantitative methodologies in an attempt to understand customer behavioral patterns. For quite some time now, it has been realized that neither qualitative nor quantitative research is sufficient in perfectly describing behavioral patterns. Quantitative methods, in their effort to provide more "objective" results, tend to overlook a multitude of factors that may actually have been influential in decision making. Most such research, based on quantitative analysis, is done using oversimplified linear models, which make a lot of unwarranted and unrealistic assumptions. Such assumptions tend to distort facts because dimensions like self-identity could have played major roles in channeling customer behavior. In such cases, qualitative analysis tools like ethnographies (an anthropological tool that studies human behavior in perspective of cultures), case studies, and histobiographies (biographies in historical context) would provide a better understanding. Using both quantitative and qualitative analyses in tandem would be the best way to understand customer needs and how to appropriately market to these needs.

Source: D. Estrin, "Quant-Qual Combo Aids Audience Understanding," Marketing News, March 3, 2003, p. 56.

Case 8-1 | Mountain Bell Telephone Company

Jim Martin, marketing research manager for Mountain Bell, studied the final research design for the hospital administrator study that had been prepared by Industrial Surveys, a marketing research firm in Denver. He realized that he needed to formulate some recommendations with respect to some very specific questions. Should individual personal interviewers be used as suggested by Industrial Surveys, or should a series of one to six focus-group interviews be used instead? Was the questionnaire satisfactory? Should individual questions be added, deleted, or modified? Should the flow be changed? Exactly who should be sampled, and what should the sample size be?

Research Setting

About 20 field salespeople at Mountain Bell Telephone Company were involved in sales of communication equipment and services to the health-care industry. Because of job rotations and reorganizations, few salespeople had been in their present positions for more than three years. They were expected to determine customer needs and problems and to design responsive communication systems. In addition, there was a health-care industry manager, Andy Smyth, who had overall responsibility for the health-care industry marketing effort at Mountain Bell, although none of the sales personnel reported directly to him. He prepared a marketing action plan and worked to see that it was implemented. The marketing action plan covered:

Sales objective by product and by segment

Sales training programs

Development of sales support materials and information

Andy Smyth was appointed only recently to his current position, although he had worked in the health-care market for several years while with the Eastern Bell Telephone Company. Thus, he did have some first-hand knowledge of customer concerns. Further, there was an AT&T marketing plan for the health-care industry which included an industry profile; however, it lacked the detailed information needed, especially at the local level. It also lacked current information as to competitive products and strategies.

Mountain Bell had long been a quasi-monopoly, but during the past decade had seen vigorous aggressive competitors appear. Andy Smyth thought it imperative to learn exactly what competitive products were making inroads, in what applications, and the basis of their competitive appeal. He also felt the need for some objective in-depth information as to how major Mountain Bell customers in the health-care industry perceived the company's product line and its sales force. He hypothesized that the sales force was generally weak in terms of understanding customers' communication needs and problems. He felt that such information would be particularly helpful in understanding customers' concerns and in developing an effective sales training program. He hoped that the end result would be to make the sales force more customer oriented and to increase revenues from the health-care market.

While at Eastern Bell, Andy Smyth had initiated a mail survey of hospital administrators that had been of some value. Several months before, he had approached Jim Martin with the idea of doing something similar at Mountain. Jim's reaction was that the questionnaire previously used was too general (that is one question was: What basic issues confront the health-care area?) or too difficult to answer (How much do you budget monthly for telecommunications equipment or service? 0–$1,000; $1,000–$2,000; etc.) Further, he felt that in-depth individual interviews would be more fruitful. Thus, he contacted Industrial Surveys, which, after considerable discussion with both Jim and Andy, created the research design. They were guided by the following research objectives:

1. What are the awareness and usage levels of competitive telecommunications products by the hospital?

2. What is the perception of Mountain Bell's sales force capabilities as compared to other telecommunications vendors?

3. What is the decision-making process as it pertains to the identification, selection, and purchase of telecommunications equipment?

4. What concerns/problems impact most directly upon the hospital's (department's) daily operations?

5. What are the perceived deficiencies and suggestions for improvement of work/information flow?

Research Design

Research interviews will be conducted in seven Denver area hospitals with the hospital administrator and, where possible, with the financial officer and the telecommunications manager. A total of 14 interviews are planned. Interviews will be held by appointment, and each respondent will be probed relative to those questions that are most appropriate for his or her position and relevant to the study's overall objectives. The cost will be from $6,500 to $8,500, depending on the time involved to complete the interviews. The questionnaire to be used follows.

A. Awareness and Usage of Competitive Telecommunications Equipment

   1. What departments presently use non-Bell voice communications equipment (paging, intercom, message recording, etc.)? What were the main considerations in selecting this equipment?

   2. What departments use non-Bell data terminals (CRTs)? What are the major functions/activities that this equipment is used for? What were the main considerations in selecting this equipment?

   3. How do you view the capabilities of Bell System voice-communications equipment to meet your operations needs?

   4. How do you view the capabilities of Bell System data terminals to meet your records- and information-retrieval needs?

   5. What do you feel are Mountain Bell's main strengths and/or weaknesses in meeting your hospital's overall telecommunications needs?

B. Perceptions of the Mountain Bell Sales Force

   1. What should a telecommunications specialist know about the hospital industry in order to adequately address your voice-communications and data-processing needs?

   2. Have you ever worked with any Mountain Bell marketing people in terms of your communications needs? If so, how knowledgeable do you perceive the Mountain Bell sales force to be with respect to both the health-care industry and their telecommunications equipment? How do they compare to non-Bell vendors of such products?

C. Purchasing Decision

   1. What is the standard procedure for selecting and authorizing a telecommunications purchase? Is this based primarily on the dollar amount involved or type of technology?

   2. Who has the greatest input on the telecommunications decision (department manager, administrator, physicians, and so on)?

   3. What are the most important considerations in evaluating a potential telecommunications purchase (equipment price, cost-savings potential, available budget, and so on)?

   4. What supplier information is most important in facilitating the purchasing decision? How effective has the Mountain Bell sales force been in providing such information?

D. Specification of the Most Important Problems or Concerns Relating to Effective Hospital Management

   1. What are the most important problems or concerns confronting you in managing the hospital?

   2. What type of management data is required in order to deal effectively with these problems or concerns?

   3. How are these data presently recorded, updated, and transmitted? How effective would you say your current information-retrieval system is?

4. Do you have any dollar amount specifically budgeted for data or telecommunications improvements in 2004–2005? What specific information or communication functions are you most interested in upgrading?

E. Achieving Maximum Utilization of Hospital Facilities

1. Do you experience any problems in obtaining accurate, up-to-date information on the availability of bed space, operating rooms, or lab services?

2. Do you see _____ hospitals as competing with other area hospitals or HMOs in the provision of health-care services? If so, with which hospitals? Do you have a marketing plan to deal with this situation?

F. Efficient Use of Labor Resources

1. How variable is the typical daily departmental workload, and what factors most influence this variance?

2. How do you document and forecast workload fluctuations? Is this done for each hospital department?

3. To what extent (if any) do you use outside consulting firms to work with you in improving the delivery of hospital services?

G. Reimbursement and Cash Flow

1. Which insurer is the primary provider of funds? How is reimbursement made by the major insurers?

2. What information do you need to verify the existence and type of insurance coverage when an individual is being processed for admission or outpatient hospital services? What, if any, problems are experienced in the verification and communication of insurance information?

Source: This case was prepared by D. Aaker and J. Seydel as a basis for class discussion.

Case 8-2 | U.S. Department of Energy (A)

Judy Ryerson, the head of the windmill power section of the U.S. Department of Energy, was considering what types of qualitative marketing research would be useful to address a host of research questions.

The U.S. Department of Energy was formed to deal with the national energy problem. One of its goals was to encourage the development of a variety of energy sources, including the use of windmill power. One difficulty was that almost nothing was known about the current use of windmill power and the public reaction to it as a power source. Before developing windmill power programs, it seemed prudent to address several research questions to obtain background information and to formulate testable hypotheses.

Current Use of Windmills in the United States

How many power-generating windmills are there? Who owns them? What power-generating performance is being achieved? What designs are being used? What applications are involved?

Public Reaction

What are the public attitudes to various power sources? How much premium would the public be willing to pay for windmill power sources, both in terms of money and in terms of "visual pollution?" What is the relative acceptance of six different windmill designs ranging from the "old Dutch windmill" design to an egg-beater design?

ASSIGNMENT

Design one or more qualitative research designs to address the search questions and to develop hypotheses for future testing. If focus-group interviews are considered, provide a set of questions to guide the moderator.

Case 8-3 | Hamilton Beach Conducts Primary Research in Mexico and Europe

Hamilton Beach is well-known in the United States as a maker of small kitchen appliances like blenders, toasters, and mixers. However, the brand is not so familiar in other countries. When the firm decided to expand into Europe and Mexico with a new product line, they wanted to assess the brand awareness in these markets. Based on the assumption that the Mexican consumer is slightly more prone to buying U.S. products, the firm wanted to confirm that there was better brand awareness in Mexico.

A mixture of qualitative and quantitative research techniques were used in Mexico. Through the study, the firm was looking to determine what features were to be included in the product and the retail environment through which they were going to sell. They also wanted to find out the acceptance level for the brand and whether the features of the product fit in well with consumer needs. They found that the brand awareness was high in Mexico, and considering the proximity to the United States and the similar taste preferences due to exposure to the same types of products, they were optimistic in going ahead with the product launch. The initial results were promising and indicated success. Then Hamilton Beach changed its focus to the European market.

The research in Europe involved focus groups with the participants being asked to look at and touch the products. After the participants had an opportunity to examine the products, they were asked to come back and talk about them in general, spontaneous terms. The discussion showed that European consumers were much more focused on design than American consumers. They seemed to like colors, rounded shapes, and good-looking appliances, especially those they plan to leave out on their kitchen counters. European consumers also did not appear to be as interested in product features. For example, while an American consumer perceives an 18-speed blender as definitely added value, the European consumer seemed to perceive it as confusing and therefore as something negative.

The research also highlighted the differences in how Hamilton Beach product designers and consumers define a product line. To the designers, uniformity of things like the color of knobs on the appliances and the fonts used in the instructions make a group of products into a product line. But European consumers felt product attributes like color and shape defined a product line. Hamilton Beach decided to change the whole European line to suit the consumer preferences and go back and do the same kind of research, before launching the product on a large scale.

Questions for Discussion

1. Do you think the focus group research conducted in Europe was representative of the population in terms of:

   • Brand awareness and acceptance

   • Desired product features

   • Distribution channels

2. As a market research analyst, is there an alternate way to design the research process in Europe to address the issues?

Source: Adapted with permission from Joseph Rydholm, "Seeking the Right Mix," November 2001, http://www.quirks.com/articles/a2001/20011105.aspx?searchID=218469119&sort=9

MINI PROJECT

The mini project is a group activity designed for students wherein they are required to see video clips from websites (e.g., www.pbs.org and www.leaduser.com). The topics of the clips include narrowcasting, narrowing boundaries between content and advertising, science of selling, and lead-users and innovation. The students are then asked to present the topic in class and be prepared to answer questions related to the topics discussed. Grading for the presentation is based on the students' ability to clearly define the concept assigned, explanation of the concept using relevant examples, and incorporation of their relation to contemporary marketing research issues. Students are also encouraged to refer to other relevant sources in designing the content of the presentation. This project is aimed at giving students a real-world look at both qualitative marketing research and data analytics issues. Additional information on this project including the URLs for the topics is available at http://www.drvkumar.com/MR12.

Information from Respondents: Issues in Data Collection

9

LEARNING OBJECTIVES

- Discuss the different kinds of information that are collected through surveys.
- Discuss the errors that occur while conducting a survey.
- Discuss in-depth interviews, focus group, and projective techniques in detail.
- Discuss the various factors that influence the selection of the survey method to use.
- Discuss the ethical issues involved in collecting data from respondents.

The survey is the overwhelming choice of researchers for collecting primary data. The methods already discussed—qualitative and observational research, secondary data analysis, and secondary data research on the Internet—are more likely to be used to improve or supplement the survey method than to take its place.

The principal advantage of a survey is that it can collect a great deal of data about an individual respondent at one time. It is perhaps only stating the obvious to say that for most kinds of data the respondent is the only, or the best, source. The second advantage of this method is versatility; surveys can be employed in virtually any setting with any group—whether among teenagers, old-age pensioners, or sailboat owners—and are adaptable to research objectives that necessitate either a descriptive or causal design.

These advantages are not easy to achieve. Effective implementation requires considerable judgment in the choice of a survey method, whether a personal or telephone interview or a self-administered survey such as an email, mail, or fax questionnaire. There are also some distinct disadvantages to surveys that stem from the social interaction of interviewer and respondent. Indeed, a survey cannot be developed or interpreted properly without a knowledge of the errors that may bias the data during this interaction. These and other related issues are discussed in this chapter as a prelude to the analysis of the methods of collecting survey data, the principal focus of the next chapter.

Information from Surveys

Surveys can be designed to capture a wide variety of information on many diverse topics and subjects. Attitudes are very often the subject of surveys. Information on attitudes frequently is obtained in the form of consumers' awareness, knowledge, or perceptions about the product; its features, availability, and pricing; and various aspects of the marketing effort. Surveys can also capture the respondents' overall assessment and the extent to which the object is rated as favorable or unfavorable. Information can be obtained about a person's image of something. Each person tends to see things a little differently from others, so no two images are apt to be exactly alike. Decisions are also the topic of research, but the focus is not so much on the results of decisions in the past but more on the *process* by which respondents evaluate things. Those seeking survey information are often keenly interested in those aspects of the decision process that people use to choose actions. Marketers are often concerned with *why* people behave as they do. Most behavior is directed toward satisfying one or more human needs. Thus, the answer to the question of "why" is often obtained by measuring the relationship between actions and needs, desires, preferences, motives, and goals.

Measuring behavior usually involves four related concepts: what the respondents did or did not do; where the action takes place; the timing including past, present, and future; and the frequency or persistence of behavior. In other words, it often means assessing *what*, *where*, *when*, and *how often*. Surveys can also be conducted to determine respondents' lifestyles. Groupings of the population by lifestyle can be used to identify an audience, constituency, target market, or other collections of interest to the sponsor. Social contact and interaction are often the focus of survey research or bear heavily on other issues relevant to the survey. So the family setting, memberships, social contacts, reference groups, and communications of respondents frequently are measured or assessed within the survey research process. Demographic factors often obtained through surveys include such variables as age, sex, marital status, education, employment, and income, among others. Personality reflects consistent, enduring patterns of behavior, and it is more deeply rooted than lifestyle. Personality can be measured using rating methods, situational tests, projective techniques, and inventory schemes. Motivation and knowledge are also frequently measured using surveys.

Sources of Survey Error

The process by which respondents are questioned appears deceptively simple. The reality, however, is closer to Oppenheim's opinion that "questioning people is more like trying to catch a particularly elusive fish, by hopefully casting different kinds of bait at different depths, without knowing what is going on beneath the surface."[1]

The problem of getting meaningful results from the interview process stems from the need to satisfy reasonably the following conditions:

- Population has been defined correctly.

- Sample is representative of the population.

- Respondents selected to be interviewed are available and willing to cooperate.

- Respondents understand the questions.

- Respondents have the knowledge, opinions, attitudes, or facts required.

- Interviewer understands and records the responses correctly.

These conditions often are not satisfied because of interviewer error, ambiguous interpretation of both questions and answers, and errors in formulating responses. These types of errors are shown in Figure 9.1 as filters or screens that distort both the question and response. Ambiguity, usually a consequence of poor question wording, is covered in Chapter 12. In this section, we will deal with the factors that influence prospective respondents' willingness to cooperate and provide accurate answers to whatever questions are asked.

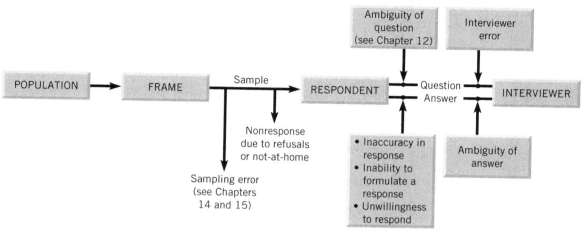

FIGURE 9.1
Sources of Error in Information from Respondents.

Nonresponse Due to Refusals

Refusal rates are highly variable. They can be as low as 3–5 percent of those contacted for a short interview on a street corner or at a bus stop, to 80 or 90 percent and higher for lengthy personal and telephone interviews or mail questionnaires, which are of little interest to most subjects. High refusal rates can be a major source of error if those who refuse to be interviewed are very different from those who cooperate. People cooperate for a number of reasons, such as trying to be friendly and helpful, to interact socially when they are lonely or bored, to know more about the subject, or to experience something novel. Many people also cooperate when they expect a reward or a direct benefit.

People refuse to answer survey questions for a number of reasons. Fear is the main reason for refusal.[2] Others might be that some may think of surveys as an invasion of privacy; the subject matter may be sensitive (such as death, sexual habits); or there may be hostility toward the sponsor.[3] Refusal rates can be reduced if the reason for refusals is related to a phenotypic source. A **phenotypic source of refusals** refers to characteristics of the data collection procedure (which questions are asked, how they are asked, the length of the interview, and so on). These elements vary from study to study and can be controlled to a certain extent. But if the source of refusals is genotypic, then it is difficult to control for them. A **genotypic source** refers to the indigenous characteristics of respondents (such as age, sex, and occupation). One avenue to reducing this type of refusal is to try to interview respondents in ways that are less intrusive in their lives.[4] Other methods, such as multiple callbacks (mailings), guarantee of anonymity, increasing surveyor credibility, incentives for completed responses, randomized responses, and shortening the survey through matrix designs, can increase response rates.[5] An example of the effect of nonresponse errors is given in Marketing Research in Action 9.1.

Inaccuracy in Response

Respondents may be *unable* to give any response, or *unwilling* to give a complete and accurate response.

Marketing Research In Action 9.1

■ NONRESPONSE BIAS LEADS TO WRONG PREDICTION IN PRESIDENTIAL OPINION POLL

An example of significant bias as a result of low response to mail questionnaires is the often-cited *Literary Digest* presidential poll in 1936. The two candidates were A. E. Landon of the Republican Party and Franklin D. Roosevelt of the Democratic Party. The *Literary Digest* conducted a mail survey and predicted a victory for Landon in the election. But Roosevelt won by a big margin in a landslide victory for the Democrats. The story is told that the sample was drawn from telephone books, and the Republicans (Landon's party) were more likely to have telephones in 1936. Hence, this biased the sample toward Republicans. In addition, the failure of the poll to predict correctly was attributed to non-response; only a minority of those asked to return questionnaires did so. As is typical of mail surveys, those who returned the questionnaire wanted the underdog Landon to win. The Landon supporters were particularly likely to want to express their views, whereas the Roosevelt supporters, since they were the majority, did not bother to respond to the survey.

Source: M. Bryson, "The Literary Digest Poll: Making of a Statistical Myth," American Statistician, November 1976, pp. 184–185.

Inability to Respond

Respondents may not know the answer to a question because of ignorance or forgetting or may be unable to articulate it. All three problems create further errors when respondents contrive an answer because they do not want to admit that they don't know the answer or because they want to please the interviewer. Respondents are likely to be ignorant when asked some questions. For example, a husband and wife may not be equally aware of the financial status of the family (such as insurance, investment, and benefits), so depending on who you survey you will get a different answer.

The likelihood of forgetting an episode, such as a visit to a doctor, a purchase, and so forth, depends on both the recency of the occurrence and the importance of the event, as well as on what else was happening at the same time.[6] Ideally, questions should be asked only about recent behavior. If retrospective questions are required, the accuracy of recall can be improved by questioning the respondent about the context in which an event occurred. Memories may be sharpened by **aided-recall techniques**. These attempt to stimulate recall with specific cues, such as copies of magazines, pictures, or lists. It is always preferable to ask about specific occasions of an activity.

It is essential to keep in mind that most respondents want to be cooperative; when in doubt, they prefer to give too much rather than too little information. Memory distortions compound this source of error by *telescoping* time, so that an event is remembered as occurring more recently than it actually did.[7] Another common memory error is **averaging**, whereby something is reported as more like the usual, the expected, or the norm. This is a particular problem for researchers trying to study the exceptions to the ordinary. General Foods' researchers interested in homemaker's variations in evening meals found it very difficult to overcome the respondent's tendency to say "It was Sunday, so it must have been roast beef." In studies of evening meals at General Foods, researchers reduced the averaging problem by asking respondents a series of questions that helped them to reconstruct the event. A third memory pitfall is called **omission**, where a respondent leaves out an event or some aspect of an experience. Respondent fatigue and poor interviewer rapport are demotivating and result in increased omitting. The use of graphic aids to recall or recognition measures will help to reduce omission.

Finally, respondents may be unable to respond because they cannot formulate an adequate answer. This is especially true of direct questions about motivations. Many choice decisions are made without conscious consideration of the reasons. So when people are asked why they responded to a charitable appeal, bought a particular brand of analgesic, or watched a certain television program, the reasons they give are likely to be incomplete and superficial. An alternative is to use indirect methods such as the projective techniques described in Chapter 8.

One technique that is being used to judge the probability of response inaccuracies is to measure the time it takes for the respondent to answer a question. Studies show that a too-slow response may mean that the question is too difficult to understand, whereas an immediate response probably means that it was either misunderstood or not well thought out.

Unwillingness to Respond Accurately

During the interview, a number of **response bias** factors may come into play to subvert the positive motivations that were present when the respondent agreed to participate. Questionnaires that are lengthy and boring are especially vulnerable to these biases.

1. *Concern about invasion of privacy.* Although most respondents don't regard a survey, per se, as an invasion of privacy, their tolerance may not extend to detailed personal questions. As many as 20 percent of the respondents in a telephone or personal interview survey may refuse to answer an income question, and others may distort their answer. To some extent, assurances of confidentiality and full explanations of the need for the data will reduce this problem.

2. *Time pressure and fatigue.* As a lengthy interview proceeds, the accuracy of responses is bound to decline. Those respondents who initially were reluctant to participate because they were busy become anxious about the time that seems to be required. Not surprisingly, they may decide that giving abrupt answers and avoiding requests for clarification are the best ways to terminate the interview quickly. Even those who respond willingly and fully to all questions will become fatigued eventually if the interview is too long. The resulting bias is most likely random but is sometimes in a consistent direction if the respondent decides to retaliate by grouping all answers about some point on a scale.[8]

3. *Prestige seeking and social desirability response bias.* There is mounting evidence that respondents will distort their answers in ways that (they believe) will enhance their prestige in the eyes of the interviewer and will not put them at variance with their perception of the prevailing norms of society. Consequently, questions that have implications for prestige—such as income, education, time spent reading newspapers, tastes in food, or even place of residence—may be biased subtly in ways that reflect well on the respondent.

4. *Courtesy bias.* There is a general tendency to limit answers to pleasantries that will cause little discomfort or embarrassment to the interviewer or to avoid appearing uncooperative. We have seen already how this bias can inflate responses to aided-recall questions. It also is encountered in concept-testing situations when a respondent gives a "courtesy endorsement" to the description of a new idea, even though he or she may have little interest in the idea.[9]

5. *Uninformed response error.* Simply asking someone a question implies that the interviewer expects the respondent to have an answer. This expectation, plus a desire to appear cooperative, may induce respondents to answer a question despite a complete lack of knowledge about the topic. When a sample of the general public was asked a question about a fictitious organization, the National Bureau of Consumer Complaints, an astonishing 75 percent of those who returned the questionnaire expressed an opinion about the effectiveness of the organization in obtaining relief for consumers.[10]

6. *Response style.* Evaluative questions requiring a good-bad, positive-negative judgment are afflicted by systematic tendencies of certain respondents to select particular *styles or categories of response* regardless of the content of the question. For example, there is an acquiescence response set, which is the tendency to favor affirmative over negative responses. This is different from "yea saying," which is a tendency to give exaggerated responses; that is, good becomes very good and bad becomes very bad. For example, Wells found that yea-sayers consistently gave higher ratings to favorably evaluated advertisements and were more likely to exaggerate self-reports of product purchases.[11]

Interviewer Error

Interviewers vary enormously in personal characteristics, amount of previous experience, style of interviewing, and motivation to do a thorough job. The differences among interviewers also mean a great deal of variability in the way interviews are conducted.

Respondent's Impression of the Interviewer

For most respondents, a personal interview is a sufficiently novel experience that the interviewer becomes a major source of clues to appropriate behavior. The interviewer must be seen as a person who is capable of understanding the respondent's point of view and of doing so without rejecting his or her opinion. This kind of rapport is most likely to be established quickly when respondent and interviewer share basic characteristics such as sex, age, race, and social class.

The attitudes the interviewer reveals to the respondent during the interview can greatly affect their level of interest and willingness to answer openly. Especially important is a sense of assurance and ease with the task. Communication will be inhibited further if the interviewer appears flippant or bored, constantly interrupts the person when speaking, or is too immersed in note taking to look up.[12] Obviously, proper selection of interviewers, coupled with good training, can reduce many of these problems.

Questioning, Probing, and Recording

The way an interviewer asks a question and follows up by probing for further details and clarification will be colored by (1) the interviewer's own feelings about the "appropriate" answer to the questions and (2) expectations about the kind of answers that "fit" the respondent. For example, when interviewing a person with limited education, the interviewer might shift unconsciously from a question worded, "Have any of your children attended college?" to "I don't imagine any of your children have gone to college. Have they?" In one study, it was found that one interviewer obtained 8 percent while another interviewer obtained 92 percent choosing the same option.[13]

Perhaps the most common interviewer error is insufficient probing. The respondents may not be expected to have much to say about the subject or may have given an answer that the interviewer thinks is "right."

Fraud and Deceit

Modest interviewer compensation and the problem of monitoring the activities of personal interviewers out in the field, or telephone interviewers calling from their home, provide ample incentive for cheating. This may be as serious as outright fabrication of an entire interview or judicious filling in of certain information that was not obtained during the interview. Because it is such a serious potential source of error, most commercial research firms validate 10–15 percent of the completed interviews. This entails interviewing a sample of those who were reported to have been interviewed, to verify that an interview actually took place and that the questions were asked.

Table 9.1   Sources of Error in Interview Surveys

1. Nonresponse errors due to refusals
   a. Fear of the consequences of participation
   b. Resentment of an invasion of privacy
   c. Anxiety about the subject

2. Inaccuracy in responses
   a. Inability to give a response
      i.   Don't know the answer
      ii. Memory problems
      iii. Problems in formulating an answer
   b. Unwillingness to respond accurately
      i.   Concern about invasion of privacy
      ii. Time pressure and fatigue
      iii. Desire to enhance prestige
      iv. Desire to appear cooperative
      v.   Biased response style
      vi. Interviewer forcing the respondent to have an answer

3. Errors caused by interviewers
   a. Provision of clues to "appropriate" responses
   b. Inadequate questioning and probing
   c. Fraud and deceit

Improving Interviewer Quality

New approaches to improving data collection quality are being constantly tried in order to overcome some of the interview problems that have been mentioned. Field briefings can be improved by preparing videotaped briefings to show to interviewers, to ensure a consistent message to all interviewers prior to data collection. Actual interviews can be recorded by camera at a particular site, and all interviewers can be rotated through that site to check on the quality of interviewing. Finally, if electronic quality checks are too expensive, research firms can hire independent field personnel to check quality.

The array of problems and sources of error, summarized in Table 9.1, have the greatest effect on the personal interview method. The best solution by far is to minimize the problems by proper recruiting, selecting, training, motivation, and control of interviewers. Yet the potential for poor-quality interviews is enormous.[14]

While other methods of data collection are less prone to interview error, they have offsetting problems, as we will see in Chapter 10.

Methods of Data Collection

The choice of a data collection method is a critical point in the research process. The decision is seldom easy, for there are many factors to be considered and many variations of the three basic **survey methods**: (1) personal interview, (2) telephone interview, and (3) self-administered survey (e.g., mail, email, fax). In this section, we will look briefly at the different methods of data collection and the factors affecting the choice of method.

Because each research problem will have a different ranking of importance, and no data collection method is consistently superior, few generalizations can be made. Much depends on the researcher's skill in adapting the method to the circumstances. Overall, however, the telephone and the self-administered survey methods are the dominant methods for conducting surveys. In the 1990 Walker Industry Image Study, it was found that 69 percent of the respondents had

Table 9.2   Basic Survey Methods and Their Characteristics

Survey method	Characteristics
Personal interviews	The interviewer interviews the respondent in person.
	There is direct contact between the interviewer and the respondent.
	The environment (mood of the respondent and the interviewer, the time and place of the interview, etc.) affects the data collection process to a large extent.
	Costliest, and the most time-consuming form of data collection.
Telephone interviews	The interviewer interviews the respondent over the telephone.
	The interviewer has only verbal contact with the respondent.
	The environment plays a relatively minor role in the data collection process.
	Data collection cost is in between that of a personal interview and a mail survey.
Self-administered surveys (mail, email, web-based, and fax)	The questionnaire is completed by the respondent.
	The interviewer has no contact with the respondent.
	The environment plays no role in the data collection process.
	The least expensive form of data collection.

participated in mail surveys, 68 percent had participated in telephone surveys, 32 percent in mall intercept surveys, and 15 percent in door-to-door interviews. However, both in academic and business environment, email and web-based surveys are being used increasingly. The characteristics of each survey method are explained briefly in Table 9.2.

Factors Affecting the Choice of a Survey Method

One of the most important decisions a researcher must make is the way in which the data will be collected. The decision to choose among the various survey methods already discussed is affected by a number of factors.[15] Some of them are described in the paragraphs that follow.

Sampling

The way a researcher plans to draw a sample is related to the best way to collect the data. Certain kinds of sampling approaches make it easier or more difficult to use one or another data collection strategy. If one is sampling from a list, the information on the list matters. Obviously, if a list lacks either good mailing or email addresses or good telephone numbers, trying to collect data by mail, phone, or mail/email is complicated. Random-digit dialing has improved the potential of telephone data collection strategies by giving every household with a telephone a chance to be selected.

Of course, it is possible to use random-digit dialing strategies, which are explained in Chapter 10, merely to sample and make initial contact with households, followed by collecting data using some other mode. Once a household has been reached, one can ask for a physical or email address, to permit either a mail or email questionnaire to be sent or an interviewer to visit. Such designs are particularly useful when one is looking for a rare population, because both the sampling and the screening via telephone are relatively less expensive than doing the same task with a personal interviewer.

Another sampling issue to consider is designating a respondent. If the sample frame is a list of individuals, any procedure, including mail, is feasible. Many surveys, however, entail designating a specific respondent at the time of data collection. If a questionnaire is mailed to a household or organization, the researcher has little control over who actually completes it. Therefore, the involvement of an interviewer is a critical aid if respondent designation is an issue.

Type of Population

The reading and writing skills of the population and its motivation to cooperate are two salient considerations in choosing a mode of data collection. Self-administered approaches to data collection place more of a burden on the respondent's reading and writing skills than do interviewer procedures. Respondents who are not very well educated, whose reading and writing skills in English are less than facile (but who can speak English), people who do not see well, and people who are somewhat ill or tire easily will find an interviewer-administered survey easier than filling out a self-administered form. Another problem for self-administered surveys is getting people to return a completed questionnaire. People who are particularly interested in the research problem tend to be most likely to return self-administered questionnaires.[16]

Question Form

Generally speaking, if one is going to use one of the self-administered questionnaire methods, it is best to use closed-end questions—that is, questions that can be answered by simply checking a box or circling the proper response from a set provided by the researcher. Second, and more important, self-administered open-ended questions often do not produce useful data. With no interviewer present to probe incomplete answers for clarity and to meet consistent question objectives, the answers are not often comparable across respondents, and they will be difficult to code.

There are question forms (including those with complex descriptions of situations or events and those requiring pictures or other visual cues) that cannot be adapted to the telephone. If such measurement is a critical part of a survey, some form other than the telephone survey probably is needed.

Question Content

Researchers have argued persuasively that one or another of the strategies should have an advantage when dealing with sensitive topics. Self-administered surveys are thought to be best, because the respondent does not have to admit directly to an interviewer a socially undesirable or negatively valued characteristic or behavior. Others have argued that telephone surveys lend an air of impersonality to the interview process that should help people report negative events or behaviors. Moreover, random-digit dialing at least provides the option of having a virtually anonymous survey procedure because the interviewer need not know the name or location of the respondent. Still others argue that personal interviews are the best way to ask sensitive questions because interviewers have an opportunity to build rapport and establish the kind of trust that is needed for respondents to report potentially sensitive information.

An entirely different aspect of question content that may affect the mode of data collection is the difficulty of the reporting task. In some surveys, researchers want to ask about events or behaviors that are difficult to report with accuracy because they extend over a period of time or are quite detailed. In such cases, reporting accuracy may benefit from a chance to consult records or to discuss the questions with other family members. The standard interview is a quick question-and-answer process that provides little such opportunity; this is especially true for telephone interviews. Self-administered procedures provide more time for thought, for checking records, and for consulting with other family members.

Response Rates

The rate of response is likely to be much more salient than other considerations in the selection of a data collection procedure. Obviously, one of the strengths of group-administered surveys, when they are feasible, is the high rate of response. Generally speaking, when students in classrooms or workers in job settings are asked to complete questionnaires, the rate of response can approach 100 percent.

There is no doubt that the problem of nonresponse is central to the use of self-administered surveys. If one simply mails questionnaires to a general population sample without an appropriate follow-up procedure, the rate of return is likely to be less than 10 percent. In cases of short and well-formatted questionnaires, email surveys can be an efficient way to collect information in a short period of time. It would be relatively easy for a participant to fill in the questionnaire, and email it back to the surveyor, resulting in quicker responses than mail surveys. It would also be economical to email reminders, which would help increase response rates. However, fax surveys would perform better when Internet penetration is low.

The effectiveness of telephone strategies in producing high response rates depends in part on the sampling scheme. Response rates in some urban areas benefit from using the telephone, whereas suburban and rural rates are usually lower for telephone surveys than when a personal interviewer is used. Using the telephone permits better coverage of units in buildings with security systems and neighborhoods where interviewers are reluctant to go in the evening.

As discussed earlier, the issue of nonresponse bias may appear more pertinent for surveys with low response rates. This is especially true in the international context. The key to addressing the nonresponse bias is in ensuring the representativeness of the responding sample. Even surveys with relatively high response rates (e.g., 70–80 percent) may be just as susceptible to nonresponse bias as those with relatively low response rates (e.g., 30–40 percent). Therefore, understanding the nature of potential nonresponse bias should be considered to be of importance while conducting surveys. Table 9.3 provides the response rates for various countries.

Costs

The great appeal of mail or email and telephone survey procedures is that in most cases they cost less than personal interviews. Survey costs depend on a multitude of factors. Some of the more salient factors are the amount of professional time required to design the questionnaire, the questionnaire length, the geographic dispersion of the sample, the availability and interest of the sample, the callback procedures, respondent selection rules, and the availability of trained staff. Although on the surface mail survey costs might appear to be lowest, the cost of postage, of clerical time for mailing, and of printing questionnaires turns out not to be trivial. Moreover, if there are telephone follow-ups, the expense gets higher. Email and web-based surveys can cost the least since no long-distance telephone charges are present and there are minimal administrative costs. Further, there is no need to reproduce the questionnaires.

Available Facilities

The facilities and staff availability should be considered in choosing a data collection mode. Developing an interviewing staff is costly and difficult. Attrition rates are generally high for newly trained interviewers. Many new interviewers are not very good at enlisting the cooperation of respondents, producing high refusal rates at the start. In addition, people who are good at training and supervising interviewers are not easy to find. Thus, one very practical consideration for anyone thinking about doing an interviewer-conducted survey is the ability to execute a professional data collection effort.

Table 9.3 Response Rates for a Sample of Countries

Country	Survey and response rate (effective sample size)
United Kingdom: Confederation of British Industry	Industry 45% (2,000), Retail 22% (1,000), Investment 19% (2,000), Services 20% (1,000).
South Africa: Bureau for Economic Research	40–45% across retail/wholesale, manufacturing, motor trade and contractors (building related). Total sample of around 3,000.
Canada: Statistics Bureau	Business conditions for manufacturing (55%).
Finland: Statistics Bureau	Consumer Survey 74% (2,200).
Austria: WIFO	Manufacturing 30%, Construction 30%, Services 34%. These are panel response rates; response rates of recruits are lower.
France: INSEE	Industry 81% (4,000), Investment 77% (4,000), Retail 82% (5,000), Services 76% (4,500), Construction 84% (5,000).
Netherlands: Statistics Office	Industry 90%.
Slovenia: Statistics Office	Consumer Survey 68% (1,500), Industry 91% (600), Construction 92% (300), Services 92% (520), Retail 82% (800).
Japan: Central Bank	Whole economy: TANKAN survey 95%.
Germany: IFO	Manufacturing 90%, Construction 70%, Overall including other sectors 80%.
Slovak Republic: Statistics Office	Industry 75% (500), Construction 85% (420), Retail 60% (420), Services 63% (500).
Statistics Norway	Business Tendency Survey for Manufacturing, Mining and Quarrying 85% (700).
China	Whole economy 95%.

Source: OECD Report on "Assessing and minimising the impact of non-response on survey estimates," OECD Statistics Directorate, November 2005.

The available facilities are a crucial factor in the choice of a survey method in the international context. The question that has to be evaluated is whether local researchers must be used in conducting the survey or whether to use foreign researchers. In considering whether to use local researchers or import foreign researchers with specific skills, a number of factors need to be evaluated. This question arises particularly in the context of developing countries, where research staff with specific skills, such as the ability to conduct in-depth interviews or focus groups, or skills in research design and analysis, may not be readily available.

The major advantage of using local researchers for qualitative research or in research design is that they will know the local culture and people, as well as the language, and hence be best able to understand local cultural differences.

On the other hand, local researchers may have more limited research experience than foreign staff and may not have the same specialist skills. In interviewing, they may have difficulties in adopting a neutral or objective stance relative to respondents or may lack familiarity with the design of a sophisticated research instrument. In some cases, there may be a scarcity of local researchers with even the minimum required skills, thus necessitating consideration of importing foreign researchers.

A second issue is that of training field interviewers. This is particularly critical in cases where a pool of experienced interviewers is not readily available. In political and social surveys conducted in developing countries, extensive training programs have been developed for interviewing. Upscale individuals in leadership positions, such as village headmen, teachers, and prefects, have been found to be good interviewers in these situations.

Duration of Data Collection

The time involved in data collection varies by mode. Mail surveys usually take two months to complete. A normal sequence involves mailing the questionnaires and waiting for the responses. If the response rate is poor, then some more questionnaires are mailed and, finally, some telephone or in-person follow-up is done if the second wave of mailing also does not produce a good response rate. At the other extreme, it is quite feasible to do telephone or email surveys in a few days. Surveys done in a very short period of time pay a cost in nonresponse because some people cannot be reached during any short period. However, telephone and email surveys can be done more quickly than mail or personal interview surveys of comparable size.

Ethical Issues in Data Collection

Survey research is an objective process and therefore has explicit guidelines and principles. However, it takes place in a subjective context and thus is vulnerable to distortion by its producers and perceivers. Misrepresentation of the research itself through the use of inadequate sampling procedures or volunteers to obtain the so-called "survey" information will be discussed in Chapter 14.

Misrepresentation of the data collection process stems from two principal sources. The first is the representation of a marketing activity other than research, as research. The second is the abuse of respondents' rights during the data collection process under the rationale of providing better quality research.

Consumers expect to be sold and to be surveyed, and they expect to be able to tell the difference without great difficulty. When a selling or marketing activity uses the forms and language of survey research in order to mask the real nature of the activity being performed, it violates the public trust. Classic examples of this type of practice are the following:

1. *The use of survey techniques for selling purposes.* In this case, a person answers a few questions only to find him/herself suddenly eligible to buy a specific product or service. The misuse of the survey approach as a disguise for sales canvassing is a widespread practice that shows no signs of abating.

2. *The use of survey techniques to obtain names and addresses of prospects for direct marketing.* These efforts are usually conducted by mail. Questionnaires about products or brands are sent to households, and response is encouraged by the offer of free product samples to respondents. The listing firms compile the information by implying to the prospective customer that he or she has been interviewed in a market study.[17]

In both of these cases, the consumer is not told that the company conducting the survey is in a business other than research. The harm caused by this practice is that legitimate research is given a bad name in the eyes of consumers. Both response rates and response quality are jeopardized.

Even companies that practice legitimate research can violate the rights of respondents by deliberately engaging in a number of practices such as:

- Disguising the purpose of a particular measurement, such as a free draw or free product choice question.

- Deceiving the prospective respondent as to the true duration of the interview.

- Misrepresenting the compensation in order to gain cooperation.

- Not mentioning to the respondent that a follow-up interview will be made.

- Using projective tests and unobtrusive measures to circumvent the need for a respondent's consent.

- Using hidden tape recorders to record personal interviews (or recording phone conversations without the respondent's permission).

- Conducting simulated product tests in which the identical product is tried by the respondent except for variations in characteristics, such as color, that have no influence on the quality of a product.

- Not debriefing the respondent.[18]

Many of these practices cannot be condoned under any circumstances, and others present the conscientious researcher with a serious dilemma. Under certain circumstances, disguising the nature of the research hypotheses may be the only feasible method to collect the necessary data. Yet these practices have the potential to create biased data and suspicion or resentment that later may be manifested in a refusal to participate in subsequent studies.

Both the misrepresentation of research and the abuse of respondents' rights during the legitimate research interviewing process involve consumer deception. This has two implications. From a business perspective, if public willingness to cooperate with the research process is adversely affected, the long-term statistical reliability of marketing research is jeopardized. From a social perspective, consumer deception violates basic business ethics. The responsibility of business to society rests on a fundamental concern for the advancement of professional business practices. Marketing research depends on mutual trust and honesty between the business community and society. Deception undermines the trust by using people as mere instruments to accomplish unstated purposes.

Other ethical issues in data collection arise even when the respondent is not being deceived. One of the most important is invasion of privacy. A basic criterion of good research is respect for the privacy of the individual, yet legitimate research is always to some extent intrusive in nature. Excessive interviewing in certain metropolitan areas, especially in those popular for test markets, can be perceived by consumers as violating their basic right to privacy. A recent telephone survey with 300 respondents found that 57 percent had been interviewed at some time in the past and 50 percent had been interviewed during the past year. This type of overinterviewing may result in consumers feeling resentful and less willing to cooperate fully. If they suspect that participation in one interview leads to further requests for interviews, they will be more likely to refuse.

Ethics in Online Data Collection

With more people taking to the Internet, online data collection has become an attractive option for all types of research. People flock to "chat rooms" and message boards to share experiences or thoughts or ideas with "virtual" strangers, thus making an abundance of social and behavioral information available on the 'Net. The Internet thus offers an ideal medium for collecting data from widely dispersed populations at relatively low cost and in less time than similar efforts in the physical world.[19] While offering the comfort of data collection from a single physical location, the Internet does raise concerns about the ethical and legal dimensions of such research. Even when respondents choose to remain anonymous, privacy issues and the unclear distinction between public and private domains make it possible for researchers to record their online interactions without the knowledge or consent of the respondents.

This is all the more important when it comes to social and behavioral research where the confidentiality of the respondents may not be maintained. For instance, in a study about sexually abused survivors,[20] researchers had collected and analyzed information from an online support group on condition of anonymity. Though the published report did not disclose the names of the participants, it quoted the text of the participant's postings as they were, making it possible for the respondents to identify themselves. Also for a determined reader of the report, it would be easy to trace the message back to the participant, if the name of the studied group were known.

Thus, while the Internet does offer logistical comforts in data collection, it raises serious questions about interpretation and applicability guidelines governing online data collection.

SUMMARY

There are bound to be a number of errors when surveys are conducted, some of which can be controlled and others of which cannot be controlled. A researcher should know all the potential sources of errors and should try to reduce their impact on the survey findings. This is a good research practice and will lead to more robust results.

The choice of a survey method, that is, whether to use self-administered, or telephone or personal interviews, is determined by a number of factors. A knowledge of these factors will make it easier for the researcher to decide among the various methods. The most important factors are the sampling plan to be employed, the type of population to be surveyed, the response rates required, the budget for the survey, and the available resources. A number of factors may be important for the choice of survey method other than those discussed here. It depends on the particular study, but the factors listed in the text are the most common ones.

All data collection methods are susceptible to misrepresentation by the researchers. Two principal sources of this misrepresentation are disguising the true purpose of a marketing activity, such as selling, by calling it marketing research, or abusing respondents' rights during a legitimate data collection process. Both of these practices involve a disregard of professional business ethics. Maintaining high standards of business ethics while collecting data is the obligation of all responsible researchers.

QUESTIONS AND PROBLEMS

9.1 How would you overcome some of the problems you might anticipate in designing a survey to establish the kind of paint used by the "do-it-yourself" market when the members of this sample last redecorated a room?

9.2 How would you balance the requirements of improving the quality of interviews against any ethical considerations that may arise?

9.3 Is the biasing effect of an interviewer more serious in a personal or telephone interview? What steps can be taken to minimize this biasing effect in these two types of interviews?

9.4 People tend to respond to surveys dealing with topics that interest them. How would you exploit this fact to increase the response rate in a survey of attitudes toward the local urban transit system, in a city where the vast majority of people drive to work or to shop?

9.5 If you were a marketing research manager, would you permit the following if they were important to the usefulness of a study?

(a) Telling the respondent the interview would take only two or three minutes when it usually took four minutes and a follow-up 10-minute interview was employed.

(b) Telling the respondent the questionnaire would be anonymous but coding it so that the respondent could be identified (so that additional available information about the respondent's neighborhood could be used).

(c) Secretly recording (or videotaping) a focus-group interview.

(d) Saying the research was being conducted by a research firm instead of your own company.

9.6 You are product manager for Brand M butter, a nationally known brand. Brand M has been declining in absolute level of sales for the last four consecutive months. What information, if any, that could be obtained from respondents would be useful for determining the cause or causes of this decline?

9.7 What are the general advantages and disadvantages associated with obtaining information by questioning and by observation? Which method provides more control over the sample?

9.8 Innovative Marketing Consultant has been contracted to conduct a job-satisfaction survey among the 2,470 employees of United Machine Tools, Inc., Dayton, Ohio. The management insists that the questionnaire be comprehensive and incorporate all the views of the respondent in order to improve the work environment.

(a) What factors should Innovative Marketing Consultant consider in choosing the survey method to be used?

(b) Which question form would be most likely to supply management with the information it has requested?

(c) Design a sample questionnaire that Innovative Marketing Consultant will use in conducting the job-satisfaction survey.

(d) What possible sources of survey error might be encountered?

(e) United Machine Tools, Inc., has a wholly owned subsidiary in Madras, India. What additional factors must Innovative Marketing Consultant consider in choosing the survey method to assess the job-satisfaction levels of the employees at the Madras plant?

9.9 Mark Hirst, a high school student in Sydney, Australia, developed an innovatively shaped surfboard that radically increased the number of maneuvers a surfer could perform in low surf. In his enthusiasm to research the market, he developed a comprehensive seven-page questionnaire to be completed by customers and distributed it among surf supply stores.

(a) How will the length of the questionnaire affect the response rate?

(b) What possible biases could arise from Mark's sampling method?

9.10 Families for the Future, a nonprofit organization formed to promote a return to the family values of the 1950s in the United States, is conducting a mail survey to determine the level of domestic violence and its causes. The organization plans to survey families in urban areas in four cities across the United States.

(a) What are the possible sources of survey error in this study?

(b) How might the study be redesigned to eliminate these errors?

END NOTES

1. A. N. Oppenheim, *Questionnaire Design and Attitude Measurement.* New York: Basic Books, 1966.

2. G. S. Day, "The Threats to Marketing Research," *Journal of Marketing Research*, 12, November 1975, pp. 462–467.

3. F. Wiseman and M. Schafer, "If Respondents Won't Respond, Ask Nonrespondents Why," *Marketing News*, September 9, 1977, pp. 8–9; S. Kraft, "Who Slams the Door on Research?," *American Demographics*, September 1991, p. 14.

4. A. Ossip, "Likely Improvements in Data Collection Methods—What Do They Mean for Day-to-Day Research Management?," *Journal of Advertising Research*, Research Currents, October/November 1986, pp. RC9–RC12.

5. A. Saltzman, "Improving Response Rates in Disk-by-Mail Surveys," *Marketing Research*, 5, Summer 1993, pp. 32–39.

6. C. F. Cannel, L. Oksenberg, and J. M. Converse, "Striving for Response Accuracy: Experiments in New Interviewing Techniques," *Journal of Marketing Research*, 14, August 1977, pp. 306–315.

7. W. Cook, "Telescoping and Memory's Other Tricks," *Journal of Advertising Research*, 87, February–March 1987, pp. 5–8.

8. J. Julbert and D. R. Lehmann, "Reducing Error in Question and Scale Design: A Conceptual Framework," *Decision Sciences*, 6, January 1975, pp. 166–173.

9. B. Iuso, "Concept Testing: An Appropriate Approach," *Journal of Marketing Research*, 12, May 1975, pp. 228–231.

10. D. I. Hawkins and K. A. Coney, "Uninformed Response Error in Survey Research," *Journal of Marketing Research*, 13, August 1981, pp. 370–374.

11. W. D. Wells, "The Influence of Yea Saying Response Style," *Journal of Advertising Research*, 1, June 1963, pp. 8–18.

12. D. P. Warwick and C. A. Lininger, *The Sample Survey: Theory and Practice.* New York: McGraw-Hill, 1975, pp. 198, 203.

13. J. Freeman and E. W. Butler, "Some Sources of Interviewer Variance in Surveys," *Public Opinion Quarterly*, Spring 1976, pp. 84–85.

14. Good discussions of what can be found in Warwick and Lininger are in R. Ferber, ed., *Hand book of Marketing Research.* New York: McGraw-Hill, 1974, pp. 2.124–2.132, 2.147–2.159.

15. This section is adapted from F. J. Fowler, Jr., *Survey Research Methods.* Newbury Park, CA: Sage, 1993.

16. T. Heberlein and R. Baumgartener, "Factors Affecting Response Rates to Mailed Questionnaires: A Quantitative Analysis of the Published Literature," *American Sociological Review*, 43(4), 1978, pp. 447–462.

17. ARF Position Paper, "Phony or Misleading Polls," *Journal of Advertising Research*, Special Issue, 26, January 1987, pp. RC3–RC8.

18. G. S. Day, "The Threats to Marketing Research," *Journal of Marketing Research*, 12, November 1975, pp. 462–467.

19. M. S. Frankel and S. Siang, "Ethical and Legal Aspects of Human Subjects Research in Cyberspace. A Report of a Workshop. June 10–11, 1999." American Association for the Advancement of Science, November 1999, http://shr.aaas.org/projects/human_subjects/cyber-space/report.pdf.

20. J. Finn and M. Lavitt, "Computer Based Self-Help Groups for Sexual Abuse Survivors," *Social Work with Groups*, 17, 1994, pp. 21–46.

Case 9-1 ||| Essex Markets

Essex Markets was a chain of supermarkets in a medium-sized California city. For six years, it had provided its customers with unit pricing of grocery products. The unit prices were provided in the form of shelf tags that showed the price of the item and the unit price (e.g., the price per ounce). The program was costly. The tags had to be prepared and updated. Further, because they tended to become dislodged or moved, considerable effort was required to make sure that they were current and in place.

A study was proposed to evaluate unit pricing. Among the research questions in the study were the following:

- What percentage of shoppers was aware of unit pricing?
- What percentage of shoppers used unit pricing?
- With what frequency was unit pricing in use?
- What types of shoppers used unit pricing?
- For what product classes was it used most frequently?
- Was it used to compare package sizes and brands or to evaluate store-controlled labels?

It was determined that a five-page questionnaire completed by around 1,000 shoppers would be needed. The questionnaire could be completed in the store in about 15 minutes, or the respondent could be asked to complete it at home and mail it in.

Source: Prepared by B. McElroy and
D. A. Aaker as a basis for class discussion.

Questions for Discussion

1. Specify how the respondents should be approached in the store.
2. Write out the exact introductory remarks that you would use.
3. Should the interview be in the store, or should the questionnaire be self-administered at home and mailed in, or should some other strategy be employed?
4. If a self-administered questionnaire is used, write an introduction to it.
5. What could be done to encourage a high response rate?

Case 9-2 ||| More Ethical Dilemmas in Marketing Research

The following scenarios are similar to those you saw in Chapter 1, but bear directly on the rights of respondents in a research study. As before, your assignment is to decide what action to take in each instance. Be prepared to justify your decision.

1. Your company is supervising a study of restaurants conducted for the Department of Corporate and Consumer Affairs. The data, which have already been collected, included specific buying information and prices paid. Respondent organizations have been promised confidentiality. The ministry demands that all responses be identified by business name. Their rationale is that they plan to repeat the study and wish to limit sampling error by returning to the same respondents. Open bidding requires that the government maintain control of the sample.

What action would you take?

2. You are a project director on a study funded by a somewhat unpopular federal policing agency. The study is on marijuana use among young people in a community and its relationship, if any, to crime. You will be using a structured questionnaire to gather data for the agency on marijuana use and criminal activities. You believe that if you reveal the name of the funding agency and/or the actual purposes of the study to respondents, you will seriously depress response rates and thereby increase nonresponse bias.

What information would you disclose to respondents?

3. You are employed by a market research company. A manufacturer of female clothing has retained your firm to

conduct a study for them. The manufacturer wants you to know something about how women choose clothing, such as blouses and sweaters. The manufacturer wants to conduct group interviews, supplemented by a session which would be devoted to observing the women trying on clothing, in order to discover which types of garments are chosen first, how thoroughly they touch and examine the clothing, and whether they look for and read a label or price tag. The client suggests that the observations be performed unobtrusively by female observers at a local department store, via a one-way mirror. One of your associates argues that this would constitute an invasion of privacy.

What action would you take?

4. You are the market research director in a manufacturing company. The project director requests permission to use ultraviolet ink in precoding questionnaires on a mail survey. Although the accompanying letter refers to a confidential survey, the project director needs to be able to identify respondents to permit adequate cross-tabulation of the data and to save on postage costs if a second mailing is required.

What action would you take?

Source: Provided with the permission of Professor C. Weinberg, University of British Columbia.

10 Information from Respondents: Survey Methods

LEARNING OBJECTIVES

- Discuss the different types of survey methods.
- Discuss the process involved using each method.
- Discuss the advantages and disadvantages of the survey method.
- Discuss future trends in survey methods.
- Discuss the problems that the researcher faces in conducting international surveys.

The importance of reliable and timely data for marketing intelligence can be gauged if we realize how an uncertain future could make the plans of a corporation go haywire. It is thus extremely important that the survey methods used be very reliable. There are as many survey methods as there are different forms of communication technology. As the technology for communication progresses, the number of survey methods also proliferates. The web and recent advances in PDA technology have introduced many new possibilities for conducting error-free surveys. Hence, a researcher has to know the mechanics of each method clearly and also how it performs compared to the other methods. The choice among different survey methods is never an easy one. The factors affecting the choice of a survey method were discussed in Chapter 9, but without a thorough knowledge of the various methods, it will always be difficult to choose among them. In this chapter, the three most prevalent methods of conducting surveys—personal interviews, telephone interviews, and self-administered surveys—are discussed in detail. The latest trends in survey methods are also discussed. Conducting international surveys leads to a number of new problems that are not encountered in domestic research. These problems and possible solutions are also discussed briefly.

Collecting Data

Recent studies have revealed that only about 10–15 percent of consumers contacted at home will participate in a survey. American consumers are confronted by about 250 surveys (telephone, email, and self-administered surveys) a year. One approach to offset such an adverse reaction to surveys is the relationship survey, a customer satisfaction survey that not only measures a vendor's competency with the customer but also provides a closed-loop feedback process for sharing the results with participants. The customer satisfaction survey can be turned into a relationship-building process, and to pursue this opportunity, one must be prepared to deliver the survey results in a detached, professional manner. Below are some guidelines for doing so:

1. *Reviewing data*—Carefully read the results of the survey, review all comments, and note any common or consistent areas of dissatisfaction or satisfaction. Look at the information objectively.

2. *Getting started*—Create a list of the "good" and "bad" aspects of the survey results. Revise your list as you see fit.

3. *Setting the feedback objective*—Before preparing the feedback vehicle, create a clear objective statement.

4. *Customer presentation*—There are four basic ways the information can be shared with the participants: by newsletter, with a letter from the company, with a group presentation, and with one-on-one presentations.

5. *Sharing responsibility*—Emphasize the joint-planning aspect as you get and keep the customers involved. A joint effort will lead to better solutions.

6. *Handling issues you cannot fix*—Be honest with customers, and point out that if many customers have the same complaint, the problem will be immediately investigated as thoroughly as possible.

7. *Working the issue resolution with your account*—Try to resolve any issues that have developed, but remember to keep your promises realistic.[1]

Personal Interviewing

The different methods of conducting personal interviews can be classified based on the respondents to be contacted and on the means of contacting them. In this section, the different types of personal interview methods are discussed, as well as their advantages and limitations.

Process

The personal interviewing process is characterized by the interaction of four entities: the researcher, the interviewer, the interviewee, and the interview environment. Each of the three participants has certain basic characteristics, both inherent and acquired. Each also has general research knowledge and experience, which vary a great deal among them. Collectively, these characteristics influence the interviewing process and, ultimately, the interview itself. During a personal interview, the interviewer and the interviewee interact and simultaneously influence one another in an interview environment. The choice of an interview environment is made by the researcher, depending on the type of data to be collected. A brief discussion of the various personal interview methods, classified according to interview environment, follows.

At Home or Work Interviewing

The **at home or work interview**, in which consumers are interviewed in person in their homes or at their office, has traditionally been considered the best survey method. This conclusion was based on a number of factors. First, the door-to-door interview is a personal, face-to-face interview with all the attendant advantages—feedback from the respondent, the ability to explain complicated tasks, the ability to use special questionnaire techniques that require visual contact to speed up the interview or improve data quality, the ability to show the respondent product concepts and other stimuli for evaluation, and so on. Second, the consumer is seen as being at ease in a familiar, comfortable, secure environment.

The door-to-door interview remains the only viable way to do long, in-depth, or detailed interviews and certain in-home product tests. In addition, the door-to-door survey is the only way currently available to obtain anything approaching a probability sample in a study that involves showing concepts or other stimuli to consumers.

Executive Interviewing

The term *executive interviewing* is used by marketing researchers to refer to the industrial equivalent of door-to-door interviewing. This type of survey involves interviewing business people at their offices concerning industrial products or services.

This type of interviewing is very expensive. First, individuals involved in the purchase decision for the product in question must be identified and located. Once a qualified person is located, the next step is to get that person to agree to be interviewed and to set a time for the interview.

Finally, an interviewer must go to the particular place at the appointed time. Long waits are frequently encountered; cancellations are not uncommon. This type of survey requires the very best interviewers because frequently they must conduct interviews on topics about which they know very little.

Mall Intercept Surveys

Shopping-center interviews are a popular solution when funds are limited and the respondent must see, feel, or taste something. Often, they are called shopping **mall intercept surveys**, in recognition of the interviewing procedures. Interviewers, stationed at entrances or selected locations in a mall, randomly approach respondents and either question them at that location or invite them to be interviewed at a special facility in the mall. These facilities have equipment that is adaptable to virtually any demonstration requirement, including interview rooms and booths, kitchens with food preparation areas, conference rooms for focus groups, closed-circuit television and sound systems, monitoring systems with one-way mirrors, and online video-screen interviewing terminals.

Since interviewers don't travel and respondents are plentiful, survey costs are low. However, shopping center users, who are not representative of the general population, visit the center with different frequencies and shop at different stores within the center.[2] These problems can be minimized with the special sampling procedures described in Chapter 14. The number of people who agree to be interviewed in the mall will increase with incentives.[3]

Mall intercept surveys, known for their low cost, have recently been plagued by cost/quality issues. The desire to provide "better," "faster," and "cheaper" service has cost the research/opinion industry money, quality, and efficiency of item and resources, and the satisfaction of the customer.

In situations where significantly low incidence levels are expected or when the data collected must meet special parameters for analysis or modeling, small bases (number of interviews in a given location) are appropriate. However, key players are mistakenly choosing smaller bases (and therefore, more locations on a single project), assuming that it will lead to faster completion of the interviewing process and save money.

If purchasers of data collection services consider larger base sizes whenever possible, the research process can be positively affected in the following ways:

- Consistency in the number of quality interviewers working on the project.

- Increased sample representatives at individual mall locations.

- Decreased "real" costs—such as shipping, travel, phone, facsimile, and production of concepts, prototypes, and videos—associated with more markets.

- More efficient use of the available respondent pool at the mall.

- Decreased briefing time necessary to train interviewers properly on each project.[4]

Purchase Intercept Technique[5]

The **purchase intercept technique (PIT)** is different from, but related to, the mall intercept approach. This technique combines both in-store observation and in-store interviewing to assess shopping behavior and the reasons behind that behavior. Like a mall intercept, the PIT involves intercepting consumers while they are in a shopping environment; however, the PIT is administered at the time of an observable, specific product selection, as compared to consumers in a mall location. The researcher unobtrusively observes the customer make a purchase in a particular product category; then the researcher intercepts the customer for an interview as soon as the purchase has been made.

The major advantage of the PIT is that it aids buyer recall. Interviewing at the point of purchase minimizes the time lapse between the purchase and data collection and can provide a neutral set of memory cues for the respondent while the purchase is still salient. Apart from difficulties in gaining access to stores, the principal disadvantage of the PIT is that it samples only purchasers and not anyone else who might be influencing the decision on what to buy or where to shop.

Omnibus Surveys

Omnibus surveys are regularly scheduled (weekly, monthly, or quarterly) personal interview surveys with questions provided by a number of separate clients. The questionnaires, based on which the interviews are conducted, will contain sequences of questions on different topics. Each sequence of questions is provided by one client, and the whole questionnaire is made up of such sequences of questions, on diverse topics, from different clients.

There are impressive advantages to the omnibus approach whenever only a limited number of personal interview questions is needed. The total costs are minimized, since the rates are based on the number of questions asked and tabulated, and the cost of the survey is shared by the clients. The results are available quickly because all the steps are standardized and scheduled in advance. The regularity of the interview schedule and the assurance that the independent samples are matched make this a suitable base for continuous "tracking" studies and before–after studies. Some omnibus operators offer split-run facilities, so that half of the sample receives one stimulus (one version of a question or concept) and the other, matched half, gets another version. Also, by accumulating over several waves of interviews, it is possible to conduct studies of low-incidence activities, such as the extent of salt-free diets and shortwave transmitter ownership.

Advantages

An interviewer, face to face with a respondent, can do a great deal to arouse initial interest and thereby increase the rate of participation and continuing rapport. To reduce the likelihood of a respondent refusing to finish the interview with an interviewer, it is also feasible to ask complex questions and enhance their meaning with pictorial and mechanical aids, clarify misunderstandings, and probe for more complete answers. For these reasons, the **personal interview** usually is preferred when a large amount of information is required and the questions are complex or involve tasks such as sorting cards into ordered piles or evaluating visual cues such as pictures of product concepts or mock-ups of advertisements.

The personal interview questionnaire has a high degree of flexibility. For example, if the answer to "Have you ever heard of (a community agency)?" is "yes," the interviewer asks questions A and B, but if the answer is "no," the interviewer asks about the next agency.

Generalizations about the **accuracy** of personal interview responses are hazardous. On one hand, interviewer probes and clarifications maximize respondent understanding and yield complete answers, especially to open-ended questions. Possibly offsetting these advantages are the problems of prestige seeking, social desirability, and courtesy biases discussed earlier. In relative terms, it seems that for questions about neutral topics, all three methods are equally satisfactory, whereas for embarrassing topics, the personal interview is at a disadvantage.

Finally, there is an advantage to having a personal interview when an explicit or current list of households or individuals is not available. The interviewer can be assigned to specific census tracts, blocks, or residences as defined by census data. Once a residence is chosen, the researcher can control who is interviewed and how much assistance is obtained from others in the household.

Limitations

Personal interview studies are time consuming, administratively difficult, and costly. The time requirements are understandable in light of the need to travel between interviews, set up appointments, and perhaps schedule return visits to complete interrupted interviews. Only 30–40 percent of an interviewer's time on the job is devoted to interviewing itself. One can use more interviewers to reduce the elapsed time, but then problems of quality control increase. Because of the time and administrative problems, the cost per completed personal interview tends to be higher than it is for mail or telephone surveys. Direct comparisons of the costs of different methods are difficult, in part, because of the wide variability in the implementation of each method.

Table 10.1 provides some approximate indices of the direct cost of a completed interview, to help compare data collection methods. In 1996, an index value of 1.0 corresponded to a cost of $20.00. Thus, in 1996, one could expect a 40- to 60-minute personal interview on a national basis, with one callback and 10 percent validation, to cost between $50 ($2.5 \times $20.00) and $70.00 ($3.5 \times $20.00). This cost assumes that the study is conducted by a commercial research supplier and a general population is interviewed. If the sample to be interviewed consists of a particular segment, such as physicians, then a 40- to 60-minute interview would cost close to $200 per interview.

Until recently, it was thought that the personal interview method was always the best way to reduce nonresponse bias. Interviewers can track down hard-to-find respondents and minimize refusals by being physically present at the door. Unfortunately, the costs of the callbacks needed

Table 10.1   Comparative Indices of Direct Costs per Completed Interview (Including Travel and Telephone Charges, Interviewer Compensation, Training, and Direct Supervision Expenses)

Data collection method	Index of cost[a]
1. **Email and Mail Survey** (costs depend on return rate, incentives, and follow-up procedure)	0.3–0.8
2. **Telephone interviews**	
a. Seven-minute interview with head of household in metropolitan area	0.5–0.8
b. Fifteen-minute interview with small segment of national population from a central station	1.3–1.7
3. **Personal interviews**	
a. Ten-minute personal interview in middle-class suburban area (1 call back and 10 percent validation)	1.5–1.8
b. Forty- to 60-minute interview of national probability sample (1 call back and 10 percent validation)	2.5–3.5
c. Executive (VIP) interviews	4.0–15.0+

[a]In 1997, an index value of 1.0 corresponded to a cost of $20.00.

to achieve high response rates are becoming excessive. This is especially a problem in inner-city areas, which interviewers are reluctant to visit and may refuse to enter at night even when they work in teams.

Screening questions are used in marketing research to find people with particular behavioral, attitudinal, or demographic characteristics. Screening questions are usually asked first to minimize fieldwork costs or to enhance a study's cost-effectiveness. Unfortunately, this could cause self-selection bias because the respondents receive clues as to what the researchers want to know and they have the option to refuse to participate. "To the point" screening questions can offer a signal as to who qualifies for the survey and who doesn't.

Although a screener saves time and money by asking screening questions at the beginning of the survey, as soon as self-selection bias occurs the survey is no longer random or representative. From the results of many studies involving funerals, careers, pets, and night clubs, it was determined that it is wise to begin by working with a sample frame that will minimize the number of screening questions needed. When that is not practical, researchers should use more buffer questions and write less obviously worded screeners to minimize self-selection bias. Although this may increase costs, the findings will be more accurate and the research more valuable. Ignoring the problem will cause survey validity along with confidence in the work to deteriorate.[6]

Telephone Interviewing

The telephone interview gradually has become the dominant method for obtaining information from large samples, as the cost and nonresponse problems of personal interviews have become more acute. At the same time, many of the accepted limitations of telephone interviewing have been shown to be of little significance for a large class of marketing problems.

Process

The telephone interviewing process generally is very similar to personal interviewing. Only certain unique aspects of telephone interviewing, such as selecting the telephone numbers, the call outcomes, the introduction, when to call, and call reports, are described below.

Selecting Telephone Numbers

There are three basic approaches to obtaining telephone numbers when selecting study participants for telephone interviews. A researcher can use a prespecified list, a directory, or a random dialing procedure. Prespecified lists—membership rosters, customer lists, or lists purchased from commercial suppliers of telephone numbers—are sometimes used for selected groups of people. This use, however, is not widespread in marketing research.

The traditional approach to obtaining numbers has been to use a directory, one provided by either a telephone company or a commercial firm (for instance, the Polk crisscross directory). However, a directory may be inadequate for obtaining a representative sample of consumers or households. On the average, about 25 percent of the U.S. households that have telephones are not included in telephone directories. People who are voluntarily not listed in a telephone directory tend to have characteristics somewhat different from those listed.

To overcome telephone directory nonrepresentativeness, many researchers now use **random-digit dialing** when they interview consumers by telephone. In its most general form, complete random-digit dialing is a nondirectory procedure for selecting all 10 (area code, prefix or exchange, suffix) telephone number digits at random. Although this approach gives all households with telephones an approximately equal chance of being called, it has severe limitations. It is costly to implement, both in dollars and time, since not all possible telephone numbers are in service, and therefore many telephoning attempts are to nonexistent numbers. Additionally, complete random-digit dialing does not discriminate between telephone numbers in which a researcher is interested and those of no interest (numbers outside the geographic study area and those of business or government). Further, all the prefixes in the United States are distributed across the regular land lines (78 percent), cellular (10.5 percent), paging (4.6 percent), shared wireless (3.3 percent), and other (4 percent).[7]

A variation of the random-digit dialing procedure is *systematic random-digit dialing* (SRDD). In SRDD, a researcher specifies those telephone area codes and exchanges, or prefixes, from which numbers are to be selected. Thus, government, university, business, or exchanges not of interest (outside the geographic study area) are avoided. The researcher determines a starting number (seed point) plus a sampling interval—a constant number added systematically to the starting number and subsequent numbers generated, to obtain the list of telephone numbers to be called. For metropolitan areas, it is necessary to generate approximately four times as many telephone numbers as completed interviews desired because of not-in-service numbers and the like. An illustration of the SRDD process is described in Marketing Research in Action 10.1.

SRDD has several advantages. Because there is a random starting point, each telephone number has an equal chance of being called. Second, since telephone exchanges tend to cover specific geographic areas, a spatial focus is possible. Third, if the same number of telephone calls is attempted from each exchange studied, the resulting sample tends to have the same geographic dispersion as the original population. Finally, SRDD can be incorporated into a standard computer program.

Another version of random-digit dialing is **plus-one dialing**, a directory-assisted, random-digit-dialing telephone number selection procedure. Plus-one dialing consists of selecting a random sample of telephone numbers from one or more telephone directories, then adding the constant "1" to the last four digits of each number selected. This procedure increases the chances of an existing telephone number being obtained and also allows unlisted numbers to be included in the sample.

Call Outcomes

Once the telephone numbers have been selected, a call is made. Once a call has been attempted, eight possible outcomes can occur. The possible outcomes of a call attempt are as follows: The telephone number is not in service, the number dialed is busy, no one answers the phone, the number called is a fax number, an answering machine responds, the call is answered by someone other than the person to be contacted, the call results in contacting a person outside the sampling frame (the telephone line was given to someone else when the respondent relocated), and, finally, the call is answered by the actual respondent. Table 10.2 discusses the various call outcomes and the method to handle each outcome.

Marketing Research in Action 10.1

■ AN ILLUSTRATION OF THE SRDD PROCESS

Suppose an interviewer wants to poll a thousand ($n = 1,000$) respondents on the eve of the presidential election in a particular area (with the area code prefix as 743). There are a total of ten thousand ($k = 10,000$) numbers with the prefix 743, that is, 743-0000 to 743-9999. The first step in the SRDD process is to compute the sampling interval (I) given by

k/n, which in this case is equal to 10. The interviewer then randomly chooses a telephone number in the interval 743-0000 to 743-0010. Once a number is chosen (say, 743-0005), then, to generate additional numbers, the value of I is added to each of the previously selected numbers. In other words, the telephone numbers to call would be $743 - 0005, 743 - (0005 + I), 743 - (0005 + 2I), \ldots, 743 - [0005 + (n-1)I]$.

Table 10.2   Call Outcomes and Recommendations to Deal With Them

Call outcome	Recommendation
The telephone is not in service.	Eliminate the number from further consideration.
The number dialed is busy.	Call the number again later, because the characteristics of the people whose lines are busy will be different from those whose lines are not.
No one answers the call.	Call the number back later, because the characteristics of the people who are not at home will be different from those who are at home.
The number called is a fax number.	Send a fax to the respondent requesting his or her time to conduct the interview, and get his or her telephone number.
An answering machine comes on.	Leave a message on the answering machine saying who you are and the purpose of your call. Call the number again after some time.
The call is answered by someone other than the respondent.	Find out when the respondent will be available and call back at that time.
The person contacted is not in the sampling frame.	Eliminate the number from further consideration.
The call is answered by the person to be contacted.	Conduct the interview.

The Introduction

One of the most important aspects of telephone interviewing, and the key to a successfully completed interview, is the introduction. For the interview to be completed successfully, the interviewer must gain immediate rapport with potential study participants. Gaining rapport requires a pleasant telephone voice (being male or female does not seem to matter) and a good introduction. It is important that the introduction introduces the topic of study and be brief. An overly long introduction tends to decrease cooperation and elicit refusals to participate.

When to Call

To efficiently obtain a representative sample of study participants, telephone interviews should be attempted at times when prospective interviewees will most likely be available. For consumer interviews, telephone interviews should probably be attempted between 6 P.M. and 9 P.M. on weekdays, and 10 A.M. to 8 P.M. on weekends. Calling before 6 P.M. on weekdays decreases the chances of reaching working individuals, and calling after 9 P.M. incurs the wrath of those who are early to bed. On the other hand, the best time to reach homemakers or contact individuals at work is between 9 A.M. and 4:30 P.M.

Call Reports

A **call report** is a form that has telephone numbers to be called and columns for interviewers to document their telephoning attempts—what day and time the call was made, the outcome, the length of the call, and so forth. Call reports provide records of calling experiences and are useful for managing data collection.

Advantages

Telephone interviews may be conducted either from a central location, at prescribed hours under close supervision, or from the interviewer's home, unsupervised and at his or her own hours. The former is preferred because problems can be isolated quickly and greater uniformity is possible. Supervisors can double-record interviews by listening on an extension and can gradually weed out incompetent interviewers.

Regardless of how the telephone interviews are conducted, the obvious advantages are the same: (1) More interviews can be conducted in a given time period because no time is lost in traveling and locating respondents; (2) more hours of the day are productive, especially the evening hours when working women and singles are likely to be at home and apartment doors are locked; and (3) repeated callbacks at different times of the day can be made at very low cost. The key to the low costs for the latter surveys is the *wide-area telephone service (WATS)*, which provides unlimited calls to a given zone in Canada or the United States for a fixed monthly charge.

Overall, the telephone method dominates the personal interview with respect to speed, absence of administrative problems, and cost per completed interview. As we saw in Table 10.1, the costs of a telephone survey seldom will exceed two-thirds of the comparable costs of a personal interview.[8] Costs can be reduced further with omnibus surveys.

For better or worse, the telephone is an "irresistible intruder." A ringing telephone literally compels us to answer. Long-distance calling brings a further dimension of urgency and importance to reaching the desired respondent. This tends to counteract the fact that it is easier for a person to terminate midway through a telephone interview. The telephone is a particularly effective method for gaining access to hard-to-reach people such as busy executives. The receptionist who thwarts the personal interviewer will readily connect a telephone interview request. Thus, Payne found that 94 percent of the interviews attempted with responsible persons in the 600 largest companies were completed successfully.[9] The intrusiveness of the telephone, plus the ease of making callbacks, means that there should be less sample bias due to nonresponse.

For most topics, there is likely to be little difference in the accuracy of responses between telephone and personal interviews. The Survey Research Center (University of Michigan) found that similar aggregate results were obtained by the two methods in their quarterly interview of consumer intentions. However, less differentiated responses were obtained over the telephone.[10]

During the telephone interview, the respondent's only impression of the interviewer is that conveyed by the voice. The lack of rapport is offset to a degree by lessened interviewer bias and greater anonymity of the situation. However, the research on whether the respondent will reply with greater candor to personal questions (such as alcohol consumption) is mixed.

Limitations

Relatively few of the problems with the telephone method are completely insurmountable. The most obvious problem is the inability to employ visual aids or complex tasks. For example, it does not appear feasible to ask respondents to retain in their minds the names of nine department stores and then ask them to choose one store. There have been solutions to this problem, including separate mention of individual stores and asking the respondent to treat the telephone pushbuttons as a 10-point rating scale (from "1" for *like it very much* to "0" for *don't like it at all*). A related problem with the telephone is that the interviewer must rely solely on verbal cues to judge the reaction and understanding of respondents.

There is some controversy about the amount of information that can be collected in a telephone interview. Most telephone interviews are kept as short as 5–10 minutes because of the belief that a bored or hurried respondent will be likely to hang up the phone. However, there is a tendency for respondents to underestimate the length of time spent on a telephone call. Therefore, 20- to 30-minute interviews are increasingly frequent and successful, but only with interesting topics and capable interviewers.

A further limitation of telephone interviewing is the potential for sample bias, which is a consequence of some people being without phones, having unlisted phones, and telephone directories being unable to keep up with a mobile population. A subsequent chapter (Chapter 14) on sampling will discuss some of the solutions to these sampling problems, as well as the use of callbacks to reduce the frequency of not-at-homes.

Finally, a recent National Health Interview Survey explored the efficacy of random digit dialing.[11] During the first half of 2006, nearly 12.5 percent of American households did not have a landline phone. Among these people, 84 percent had at least one wireless phone; and for some other segments, wireless is the primary mode of communications. For instance, in targeting consumers aged between 18 and 24, nearly 25 percent have only a wireless phone. This means that a random digit dialing program would not be able to reach these consumers. Similarly, 44 percent of the swinging singles consumer segment uses cell phones. These new findings have wide implications on targeting consumers.

Self-Administered Surveys

The third major survey method is the **self-administered survey**. This type of survey can be emailed, mailed, faxed, or simply handed to the respondent. In the *self-administered interview* method, no interviewer is involved. Even though this reduces the cost of the interview process, this technique has one major disadvantage: There is no one present to explain things to the respondent and clarify responses to open-ended questions. This results in the answers to most of the open-ended questions being totally useless. Some have argued, however, that the absence of an interviewer results in the elimination of interviewer bias.

Self-administered interviews are often used in malls or other central locations where the researcher has access to a captive audience. Airlines frequently use this technique to get information about their services; the questionnaires are administered in flight. Many hotels, restaurants, and other service businesses provide brief questionnaires to patrons, to find out how they feel about the quality of service provided.

The Process

Using a self-administered survey consists of identifying and locating potential study participants, deciding on the best way to get the questionnaire to those participants, and waiting for completed questionnaires to be returned. Substantively, the process is a series of distinct and often difficult decisions regarding the identification of study participants and the interview package. For example, for a mail survey you would need an outgoing envelope, cover letter, questionnaire, return envelope, and the incentives, if any, to be used.

Unlike personal and telephone interviews, self-administered interviews require at least broad identification of the individuals to be sampled before data collection begins. Therefore, an initial task is to obtain a valid mail or email address, fax number, or location to distribute the questionnaire to the study participants. This information can be obtained from customer lists, association or organization membership rosters, telephone directories, publication subscription lists, or commercial "list houses." Regardless of its source, the information must be current and relate closely to the group being studied. As might be expected, obtaining a useful list is especially difficult when a list that is representative of the general population is desired.

Decisions must also be made about the various elements to be contained in a self-administered survey. Although many of these decisions involve relatively mechanical elements, each decision influences both the response rate and the response quality. Some decisions that are to be considered are

Method of addressing

Cover letter

Questionnaire length, content, layout, color, and format

Method of notification; should there be a follow-up?

Incentive to be given.

One decision area is method of notification. In both preliminary and follow-up notification, a researcher communicates with potential self-administered interview respondents more than once. Preliminary notification may also be used to screen, or qualify, individuals for study inclusion. This communication may be by postcard, letter, email, or telephone. Follow-up communication methods include sending potential study participants postcards or letters, or telephoning them a few days after they receive the questionnaire to remind them to complete and return it as soon as possible.

Advantages

The most likely reason for choosing a mail survey is cost, but there are other reasons also, as illustrated by the decision of the Census Bureau to switch from a personal interview to a census by mail to gain "better results, including a shortening of the period for collecting the data and more reliable answers supplied directly by respondents instead of through a more-or-less inhibiting intermediary, the enumerator."[12] This approach worked well for the 2010 census, when forms were mailed to over 90 percent of American households, of which 90 percent were completed voluntarily. More recent tests, to larger segments of the population, have not been so encouraging.

There is consistent evidence that self-administered surveys yield more accurate results—among those completing the survey. Because the questionnaire is answered at the respondent's discretion, the replies are likely to be more thoughtful and others can be consulted for necessary information. Self-administered surveys generally are superior when sensitive or potentially embarrassing topics, such as sexual behavior and finances, are covered (so long as the respondent is convinced that the answers will be kept in confidence). For example, a study of Boston residents, which compared the three basic methods of data collection, found that each of them gave equivalent results for neutral topics. On sensitive topics, however, where socially undesirable responses were possible, there were large differences. On the question of legalizing abortion, 89 percent of mail survey respondents were in favor compared to 62 and 70 percent of telephone and personal interview respondents, respectively.[13]

Limitations

The absence of an interviewer means that a large number of variables are controlled inadequately, including the following:

- The identity of the respondent (Was it the addressee who answered, or someone else?).

- Whom the respondent consults for help in answering questions.

- The speed of the response. (The usual time lag before receipt of a questionnaire delays the study and makes the responses vulnerable to external events taking place during the study.)[14]

- The order in which the questions are exposed and answered. (The respondent can look ahead to see where the questions are leading, so it is not possible to funnel questions from the general to the specific, for example.)

- Respondent understanding of the questions. (There is no opportunity to seek clarification of confusing questions or terms, so many respondents return their questionnaire partially completed.)

One consequence of these problems is that long questionnaires with complicated questions cannot be used without diminishing the response rate. As a rule of thumb, six to eight pages is the upper limit on topics of average interest to respondents.[15]

Self-administered surveys are limited to situations where a list (mailing addresses, email addresses, fax numbers, etc.) is available and the cost of the list is not prohibitive. Unfortunately, there are a number of possible flaws in all such lists: obsolescence, omissions, duplications, and so forth. This makes it difficult to find the ideal list, which consists entirely of the type of person to be contacted, and also represents all of those who exist. Great care must be taken at this stage to ensure that the study objectives can be achieved without excessive compromise.

If the benefit of self-administered surveys is cost, then the bane is *response rates*. The response rate gives an indication of the number of questionnaires that have been returned. The Council of American Survey Research Organizations defines response rates as the ratio of the number of completed interviews with responding units to number of eligible responding units in the sample.[16] Implementing the definition may be simple or complex, depending on the methods used to select the sample.[17] The problem is not that acceptable response rates cannot be achieved, but rather that the rate is hard to forecast and there is substantial risk that an acceptable rate may not be achieved. Marketing Research in Action 10.2 illustrates how refusal rates are calculated.

Marketing Research in Action 10.2

■ RESPONDENT COOPERATION: AUDIT UPDATE YIELDS WAYS TO IMPROVE RESULTS

In early 1997, CMOR undertook a project to update refusal rate information. Forty CASRO and CMOR member firms were recruited to keep track of all their phone research for April 1997. This yielded 385 surveys with a total base of 243,597 interviews for which sample disposition data and some basic facts were provided about the subject matter and purpose of the survey, length of interview, client identification, type of samples, and use of incentives. Refusal rate was calculated using the industry-accepted definition as follows:

$$\text{Refusal Rate} = \frac{\text{Total Refused}}{\text{Total Contacts}}$$

Total Refused = Initial Refusals + Breakoffs
+ Qualified Refusals

Total Contacted = Total Refused + Eligible Respondents
Not Available + Language Barrier
+ Completed Interviews

The result was that keeping the interview length short improves cooperation:

Interview	Refusal rate (%)
5 minutes or less	32
10 minutes	45
15 minutes	46
20 minutes	56
Over 20 minutes	57

Disclosing the length of the interview in the "intro" seems to improve cooperation regardless of the length of the interview (the base sizes for disclosed are small):

Interview	Refusal rate (%)	
	Length disclosed	Length not disclosed
5 minutes or less	18	38
6–10 minutes	35	46
11–15 minutes	41	47
16 minutes or more	42	55

Honest disclosure of facts during interview introduction has a positive effect on cooperation:

	Refusal rate (%)
Interview Length Disclosed	34
Length Not Disclosed	52
Client Identified	29
Client Not Identified	54
Subject Matter Disclosed	43
Subject Not Disclosed	61

However, providing reassurance in the interview introduction of whether the survey is confidential or a sales pitch did not appear to improve cooperation:

	Refusal rate (%)
Not a Sales Attempt	51
No Mention of Sales	43
Responses Confidential	48
Confidentiality Not Mentioned	46

Source: P. Humbaugh, Opinion—The News Magazine of CMOR, 1(1), Winter 1998.

Marketing Research in Action 10.3

▨ ETHICS IN SURVEYS

Millions of Americans find in the welter of junk mail they receive items labeled "survey," usually in oversized envelopes, sent by political or other advocacy groups. They usually include a brief questionnaire, perhaps half a dozen questions worded to encourage "yes" answers if the group is for something or "no" answers if it is against. Most consumers can detect the manipulative nature of these surveys and do not respond. Consumer nonresponse represents a threat to legitimate marketing research.

Though many marketing groups have spoken out against the unethical behavior of the causes and candidates, public

relations (PR) is most effective in stopping the distribution of advocacy surveys. After authorizing a sound PR budget, mass media should be used to send the message about how surveys are fooling the public by misrepresenting responses and asking for contributions under false pretenses. Clients, the users of survey research information, should be made aware that discouraging the phony-survey practice is crucial to them. These "surveys" are likely to undermine the reliability of the marketing research data they depend on by further discouraging consumer response. Their support will be useful for the campaign against advocacy surveys.

Source: T. T. Semon, "Advocacy Surveys Threaten Marketing Research," Marketing News, April 24, 1995, p. 9.

Many factors combine to influence the response rate, including (1) the perceived amount of work required, which in turn depends on the length of the questionnaire and the apparent ease with which it can be completed; (2) the intrinsic interest of the topic; (3) the characteristics of the sample; (4) the credibility of the sponsoring organization; (5) the level of induced motivation; and (6) increased unethical use of marketing research to sell products. (See Marketing Research in Action 10.3 for an example.) A poorly planned mail survey on a low-interest topic may achieve only a 10–15 percent response rate. Under the right circumstances, 90 percent response rates are also possible.

Coping with Nonresponse to Self-administered Surveys

Nonresponse is a problem, because those who respond are likely to differ substantially from those who do not respond. The best way to protect against this bias is to improve the response rate. The most consistently effective methods for achieving high response rates involve some combination of monetary incentives and follow-ups or reminders.[18] The inclusion of a dollar bill in the mailing, which is the usual reward, has been found to improve response rates by increments of 18–27 percent when compared to returns when no incentive is used. Comparable improvements have been obtained from the single or multiple follow-up letter. Although each follow-up brings additional responses, the optimum number seems to be two. It is a moot point whether it is worthwhile to include another questionnaire in the follow-up letter. Other techniques for improving response rates, such as having a persuasive cover letter, appear to have a lesser but still worthwhile effect. Surprisingly, there is no clear evidence that personalization of the cover letter or email, promises of anonymity, color, and methods of reproduction make much difference.

Another approach to the nonresponse problem is to determine the extent and direction of bias by studying the differences between those who respond and those who do not. This sometimes can be done by taking a subsample of the nonrespondents and using a variety of methods to get a high response rate from this group. Of course, when the questionnaire is anonymous or time is short, this cannot be done. In this situation it may be possible to compare the results of the survey with "known" values for the population, using such variables as age and income. Alternatively, one can use extrapolation methods, which assume that those who respond less readily are more

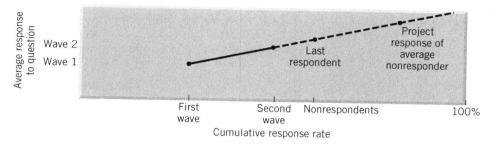

like nonrespondents.[19] "Less readily" can be defined as either being slower than average in answering a simple mailing or responding to the extra prodding of a follow-up mailing. With data from two waves of mailings, a trend can be established in the pattern of answers; nonrespondents can be assumed to be like either the last respondent to the second wave or like a projected respondent at the midpoint of the nonresponse group. This is represented graphically in the response rate chart.

Panels

A **panel** is a representative national sample of people who have agreed to participate in a limited number of surveys each year. Some panels mail surveys to participants, others have web-based portals that participants use to answer survey questions. A number of these panels are operated by firms such as Market Facts, Home Testing Institute, and National Family Opinion, Inc. The latter firm, for example, offers a number of panels that contain 130,000 people. The major advantage is the high response rate, which averages 75–85 percent.

A typical mail panel is the Conference Board Survey of Consumer Confidence. Each quarter, a large sample, drawn from the National Family Opinion Panel, is sent a questionnaire in the card format shown in Figure 10.1. This card is sent with cards from as many as 10 other studies, which spreads the costs of the survey across a number of companies. Since the questions and the sampling procedures are the same every quarter, the Conference Board has a standard measuring stick for tracking fluctuations in consumer attitudes and buying intentions.

Panels are recruited to match the general population with respect to geographic location, city size, age of homemaker, family income, and so on. Hence, it is possible to draw special samples of particular occupation groups (such as lawyers), age categories (such as teenagers), and geographic areas. Large samples can be obtained quickly in test-market areas, for example. Inevitably, those people who agree to serve on such panels will be different from the rest of the population—perhaps because they are more interested in such research, have more time available, and so forth. Little is known about the impact of such differences on questionnaire responses.

Web Surveys[20]

Web-based marketing research studies fundamentally and permanently are changing the role marketing research will play in future businesses. Web-based surveys have many advantages over traditional methods: they can be of high quality, fast, and inexpensive.

There are no interviewers involved, thereby eliminating interviewer error and bias. Web-based surveys give researchers much more control over data quality. Logic checks can be built into the survey so that contradictory or nonsensical answers are not allowed, eliminating the need for data cleaning and editing. With a Web-based survey, the questionnaire is posted on a secure website where clients can instantaneously view results as soon as any respondent has completed the interview. Web-based marketing can also reduce data collection costs to zero; this could be done by

Answer This Side First

1. How would you rate the present general business conditions in your area?
   - ☐ GOOD   ☐ NORMAL   ☐ BAD
   a. SIX MONTHS from now do you think they will be:
   - ☐ BETTER?   ☐ SAME?   ☐ WORSE?

2. What would you say about available jobs in your area right now?
   - ☐ PLENTY   ☐ NOT SO MANY   ☐ HARD TO GET
   a. SIX MONTHS from now do you think there will be:
   - ☐ MORE?   ☐ SAME?   ☐ FEWER?

3. How would you guess your total family income to be SIX MONTHS from now?
   - ☐ HIGHER   ☐ SAME   ☐ LOWER

4. Does anyone in your household plan to buy a house in the next SIX MONTHS?
   - ☐ YES   ☐ NO   ☐ MAYBE
   a. If YES: ☐ NEW?   ☐ LIVED IN?   ☐ DON'T KNOW?

5. Does anyone in your household plan to buy a car in the next SIX MONTHS?
   - ☐ YES   ☐ NO   ☐ MAYBE
   a. If YES: ☐ NEW?   ☐ USED?   ☐ DON'T KNOW?

   MAKE? _____ ☐ DON'T KNOW?

   CONTINUE →

Answer Other Side First

6. Please check which, if any, of the items you plan to buy in the next SIX MONTHS, and which *brand* you are most likely to choose:

   BRAND PREFERENCE

Item		
Refrigerator	01 ☐	_____
Washing Machine	02 ☐	_____
Black/White TV	03 ☐	_____
Color TV	04 ☐	_____
Vacuum Cleaner	05 ☐	_____
Range	06 ☐	_____
Clothes Dryer	07 ☐	_____
Air Conditioner	08 ☐	_____
Dishwasher	09 ☐	_____
Microwave Oven	10 ☐	_____
Sewing Machine	11 ☐	_____
Carpet (over 4′ × 6′)	12 ☐	_____
NONE OF THESE	☐	

7. Do you plan to take a vacation *away from home* between NOW and the next SIX MONTHS?
   - ☐ YES   ☐ NO   ☐ UNDECIDED
   a. Where will you spend *most* of your time while on vacation?
   - ☐ HOME-STATE   ☐ OTHER STATE(S)   ☐ FOREIGN COUNTRY
   b. How will you mainly travel?
   - AIRPLANE ☐   CAR ☐   TRAIN ☐   BOAT ☐   BUS ☐

FIGURE 10.1
Conference Board Mail Panel Survey of Consumer Confidence.

posting invitation banners on company websites that receive high traffic from target customers. These website visitors would click on the banner and immediately be sent to a secure website to conduct a brief interview. Afterward, respondents are automatically returned to their point of departure.

On the other hand, the validity of online surveys depends on the sample selection, survey design, response tendencies, and technology challenges.

In e-research, the choice of sampling units is in the form of e-mail addresses, electronic subscription groups, and heavily visited websites. Unfortunately, people change their e-mail addresses very often, thus creating problems in obtaining well-defined samples. Another problem is the poor translation of well-designed surveys into electronic versions. This results in lower response rates for the surveys, which in turn lower their statistical value and validity.

Therefore, Web-based surveys need continuous monitoring to determine their direction, appropriate use, and long-term effectiveness. Research is being transformed by the online medium; however, and increasing numbers of people are opting for fast and efficient Web-based surveys.[21] Web-based marketing research will greatly increase the amount of customer feedback on which managers base critical business decisions.

Combinations of Survey Methods

Since each of the basic methods of data collection has different strengths and weaknesses, it is sometimes desirable to combine them and retain the best features of each while minimizing the limitations. Some of the feasible combinations (or sequences) are illustrated below:

1. Telephone appointment ———→ Personal interview ———→ Leave behind a self-administered questionnaire to be mailed later

2. Telephone request ———→ Mail survey for permission to mail a questionnaire ———→ Telephone follow-up (optional)

3. Personal interview ———→ Telephone pre-interview (as part of a panel study or verification)

4. Mail survey ———→ Telephone follow-up

5. Telephone or personal ———→ Self-administered questionnaire delivered by "interviewer" ———→ To be either picked up or mailed in

6. Telephone request for permission to fax questionnaire ———→ Fax survey telephone (optional) ———→ Follow-up

   With the exception of the reinterview panel design of sequence 3, each of the above combinations has proven very effective in increasing the response rate. Indeed, sequence 1 is virtually mandatory for personal interviews with executives, as we noted in the previous chapter. The virtues of the other sequences are not quite so obvious. Marketing Research in Action 10.4 describes a study that included a combination of survey methods, namely a mail survey with a telephone follow-up.

Marketing Research in Action 10.4

■ USE OF MAIL SURVEY WITH TELEPHONE FOLLOW-UP

A study was conducted to determine the effect on response rates when mail and telephone survey methods were used. The survey also included a prepaid $2.00 cash incentive. The survey drew samples from Medicaid enrollees, who were stratified by race and ethnicity.

The sampling was performed in two stages. While the first stage consisted of a simple random sample (SRS) of Medicaid enrollees, the second stage consisted of randomly drawn samples from American Indian, African-American, Latino, Hmong, and Somali enrollees. A total of 8,412 enrollees were assigned randomly to receive a mail survey with no incentive or a $2.00 bill.

The response rate within the SRS following the mailing portion of the survey was found to be 54 percent in the incentive group and 45 percent in the nonincentive group. After telephone follow-ups, the incentive SRS response rate increased to 69 percent, and the nonincentive response rate increased to 64 percent. It was seen that the inclusion of the $2.00 incentive had similar effects on response rates.

Source: T. Beebe, M. Davern, D. McAlpine, K. Call, and T. Rockwood. "Increasing Response Rates in a Survey of Medicaid Enrollees: The Effect of a Prepaid Monetary Incentive and Mixed Modes (Mail and Telephone)," Medical Care, 43(4), April 2005, pp. 411–414.

The *telephone prenotification approach* is essentially a phone call to ask permission to mail or fax a questionnaire. The key is the telephone presentation, which must not only gain agreement to participate but also make sure that the prospective respondent is serious about cooperating. In one study in which 300 households were phoned, 264 households (88 percent) agreed to the mailing and 180 (60 percent) returned usable questionnaires.[22] If the return rate is not acceptable, a follow-up phone call can be made.

The **lockbox approach** is designed to circumvent the screens that receptionists and secretaries set around busy executives. The mail is used to deliver a small locked metal box containing a questionnaire and other interviewing materials such as flashcards, exhibits, and pictures. A covering letter, attached to the box, explains the purpose of the survey and tells the prospective respondent that an interviewer will conduct a telephone interview in a few days. The letter also tells the respondent that the box is a gift but that the combination to the lock will not be provided until the time of the interview. Ostensibly, this is so the respondent will not be biased by seeing the interview materials in advance. However, it is clear that the value of the gift depends on participation in the survey. Also, the locked box stimulates respondent curiosity. As a result, the originator of this technique has been able to obtain response rates of 50–70 percent, even with notoriously difficult respondents such as attorneys in private practice, who sell time for a living and are loath to participate in "free interviews."[23]

The **drop-off approach** is an illustration of sequence 5, which is particularly well suited to studies within compact geographic areas. For public transit studies, the questionnaire can be hand delivered to sampling points, such as every 25th house within areas that have access to a transit line. It also can be used for subjects living in designated political precincts or within a given radius of a specific retail outlet or other service. The major advantages are that (1) only lightly trained interviewers are required to gain the cooperation of the respondents, deliver the questionnaires, and arrange a return visit; (2) response rates are high, generally between 70 and 80 percent, in part because of the initial commitment to cooperate, coupled with the realization that the person who dropped the survey will be returning to pick up the completed questionnaire; (3) several questionnaires can be left in each household, if all adults are part of the sample; (4) lengthy questionnaires can be used without affecting the response rate; and (5) it is a very cost-effective method.[24]

Table 10.3 presents a comprehensive set of advantages and disadvantages of the various methods discussed above.

Prepaid phone cards are now being pitched as a way to get consumers to participate in surveys for marketing research. MHA Communications of Illinois has designed a system for gathering consumer information through an interactive voice response (IVR) system linked to a phone card.

Certain consumers are given prepaid phone cards worth about 10 minutes by a client company. Once they call the 800 number, the callers are offered additional free phone time in exchange for answering a few survey questions. One advantage of IVR phone card research is flexibility and convenience for its customers; they can call whenever they like. IVR is also flexible enough to allow companies to alter survey questions and substitute new ones. But for consistency, only data from the new questions should be measured, and data from ineffective questions dropped.[25]

Trends in Survey Research

Surveys will continue to dominate as a method of data collection for marketing research, at least for the next few decades. Rapid advancement in technology, however, is changing the very nature of data collection and survey methods. Computers and interactive technology are revolutionizing the way surveys are conducted. This section will look into some survey methods that have become popular in the last few years and also the future of survey research.

Table 10.3   Advantages and Disadvantages of Survey Methods

Type of survey method	Advantages	Disadvantages
Personal interviewing	• There are sample designs that can be implemented best by personal interview (e.g., area probability samples). • Personal interview procedures are probably the most effective way of enlisting cooperation. • Advantages of interview questions—probing for adequate answers, accurately following complex instructions or sequences—are realized. • Multimethod data collection, including observation, visual cues, and self-administered sections, are feasible. • Rapport and confidence building are possible (including any written reassurances that may be needed for reporting very sensitive material). • Probably longer interviews can be done in person.	• It is likely to be more costly than alternatives. • A trained staff of interviewers that is geographically near the sample is needed. • The total data collection period is likely to be longer than for most procedures. • Some samples (those in high-rise buildings or high-crime areas, elites, employees, and students) may be more accessible by some other mode.
Telephone interviewing	• Lower costs than personal interviews. • Random-digit-dialing (RDD) sampling of general population. • Better access to certain populations, especially as compared to personal interviews. • Shorter data collection periods. • The advantages of interviewer administration (in contrast to mail surveys). • Interviewer staffing and management easier than personal interviews—smaller staff needed, not necessary to be near sample, supervision and quality control potentially better. • Likely better response rate from a list sample than from mail.	• Sampling limitations, especially as a result of omitting those without telephone. • Nonresponse associated with RDD sampling is higher than with interviews. • Questionnaire or measurement constraints, including limits on response alternatives, use of visual aids, and interviewer observations. • Possibly less appropriate for personal or sensitive questions if no prior contact.
Self-administration (mail, email, fax, drop-off, etc.)	• Ease of presenting questions requiring visual aids (in contrast to telephone interviews). • Asking questions with long or complex response categories is facilitated. • Asking batteries of similar questions is possible. The respondent does not have to share answers with an interviewer. • Relatively low cost. • Can be accomplished with minimal staff and facilities. • Provides access to widely dispersed samples and samples that for other reasons are difficult to reach by telephone or in person. • Respondents have time to give thoughtful answers, look up records, or consult with others.	• Especially careful questionnaire design is needed. • Open questions usually are not useful. • Good reading and writing skills are needed by respondents. • The interviewer is not present to exercise quality control with respect to answering all questions, meeting questions objectives, or the quality of answers provided. • Ineffective as a way of enlisting cooperation (depending on group to be studied). • Various disadvantages of not having interviewer involved in data collection. • Need for good mailing addresses for sample.

Computer-Assisted Telephone Interviewing (CATI)

Computers are being used increasingly to control the administration and sequence of questions asked by an interviewer seated at a terminal. This use of computers provides researchers with a way to prevent many interviewer errors, such as choosing the wrong respondent in a household, failing to ask a question that should be asked, or asking a series of questions that is not appropriate for a particular respondent. If the respondent selection procedure or the skip patterns in a questionnaire are complicated, these interviewer errors are more likely to happen. When control of the question sequence is turned over to the computer, the interviewer theoretically is free to concentrate fully on reading the questions, recording the answers, and establishing rapport with the respondent.

There are some limitations to computer-controlled telephone interviewing. It is generally more expensive to use the computer than to administer the traditional paper-and-pencil questionnaire. For that reason, use of a computer-controlled system is recommended when a large number of surveys must be done or when the questionnaire will be used many times in a tracking study.

A second limitation relates to the problems involved in using a mechanical system and to human error in its programming and operation. A program must be written and carefully debugged for each questionnaire. The computer system must be able to handle the demands of a large number of interviewers. At the worst, several days of interviewing may pass before someone notices that a mistake has been made and the questionnaire program is incorrectly skipping over a crucial series of questions. Valuable interviewing time and money may be lost if the computer system becomes overloaded and "crashes."

At its best, computer-controlled telephone interviewing can produce faster, more complete, data to the researcher.

Computer Interactive Interviewing

In computer interactive interviewing, the respondent interacts directly with the computer. The respondent is asked to sit before the computer and to answer the questions as they appear on the screen. This type of interview is being widely used in malls. Customers are intercepted and qualified in the mall and then brought to a test facility in the mall. They are seated at a computer terminal, given some instruction on what to do, and the administrator enters the sequence to start the interview. The interview then proceeds in the same manner as the CATI described earlier, the only difference being that the information is input directly into the computer by the respondent. Computer interactive interviewing has resulted in better responses from respondents and, in some instances, 30–40 percent cost savings.[26] Marketing Research in Action 10.5

Marketing Research in Action 10.5

■ HERSHEY RESEARCH SEES NET GAIN

Integrating old and new research without losing any is important to any company that puts work into gathering the information. While moving toward 'Net research, firms are not going to throw away 10 years of testing and start over from scratch. In 1999 and 2000, Hershey Food Corp. moved its all-important new-product testing online, along with all of its historical testing data, in one king-sized commitment to 'Net research. The move cut the time spent on the new product development process by two-thirds, a key strategic advantage in mature markets, and simultaneously ensured that a wealth of institutional knowledge remained on hand even as the company's roster of research professionals changed over the years.

While the company's mail testing results might not come back for six weeks, online results can be garnered in two.

Although Hershey took a giant step into online research, the company took small steps at first to ensure that the transfer would go smoothly. The first task was validation testing. With more than half of the U.S. population becoming more representative of the national population every day, Hershey had to make sure that the results would be the same regardless of the method its researchers used. The correlation between the two sets of tests was about 0.9 on a scale of 1.

With the online collection of data, Hershey has an easily accessible and searchable database. With this new system, there are fewer man-hours spent collecting the information, less human error, and greater cost-effectiveness than with the old system. What Hershey has is a special application for companies that wish to preserve their vast investment in past off-line research.

Source: "Hershey Research Sees Net Gain," Marketing News, November 25, 2002, p. 17.

gives an example of how and why Hershey converted its survey process in to a computer interactive one—but without losing old research information. Thus, Hershey succeeded in preserving its vast investment in past off-line research while reaping the advantages of online methods.

Recent Developments in Software and Hardware.[27]

Many recent developments in both hardware and software have helped researchers to use computers more effectively. A few of them are discussed here:

- *GRiDPAD* is a pen computer that has an 8-in.-by-10-in. screen with a wand attached. Respondents use the wand to touch answer categories that appear on the screen (no more keyboards, no more mice). Advanced Data Research (ADR) produces software that can be used with GRiDPAD. Auto manufacturers were among the first to take advantage of the new system.

- *FormPro* enables the researcher to create a custom-made, scannable questionnaire using standard paint and drawing tools. The finished questionnaire is then printed by a laser printer using special scanning paper.

- *ScanPro* reads forms from FormPro as well as those not made with FormPro. ScanPro, together with an optical mark reader, enables the researcher to scan a questionnaire and produce a standard ASCII file for later use with statistical software packages, spreadsheets, databases, and so on.

- *ScanPhone* is a high-tech telephone that enables consumers to scan and transmit bar codes. This may offer new opportunities to researchers because in the future even questionnaires may be scanned.

Internet-Based Surveys

Although Web-based surveys have become quite popular and can be advantageous, many problems remain, including choosing the right 'Net service provider and 'Net software from a variety of choices available in the market. There is also the problem of the selection bias, which occurs when the sample universe is composed of individuals with the technical skills to use the 'Net and the income to own a PC. This is not a random cross-section of the general population. Another problem is attracting potential respondents to participate in the survey.

Some issues should be noted when conducting Internet-based surveys:

1. Check responses carefully. See if they are logically correct and acceptable; respondents may provide false data.

2. Limit the number of characters allowed in the fill-ins.

3. Watch out for LANs. LAN servers may collect responses from several stations and send them to Internet servers in bursts.

When these considerations have been taken care of, Internet-based surveys prove to be very efficient and practical, and most important, they provide fast results.[28] Marketing Research in Action 10.6 gives an example of wireless marketing surveys conducted through cell phones using Internet technology, which succeed in overcoming many limitations of traditional survey modes.

Figure 10.2 and Table 10.4 illustrate previously described data collection methods with new computerized methods.

Computer-Assisted Data Collection Methods

BENEFITS	Personal Computer-assisted personal interviewing	On-site Computer-assisted self-interviewing	On-site Fully automated self-interviewing	Telephone Computer-assisted telephone interviewing	Telephone Fully automated telephone interviewing	Web-based Fully interactive
Respondents need not have any computer-related skills	✓		✓	✓	✓	
Allows respondents to choose own schedule for completing survey		✓	✓			✓
Can easily incorporate complex branching questions into survey	✓	✓	✓	✓	✓	✓✗
Can easily use respondent-generated words in questions throughout the survey	✓	✓	✓	✓		✓✗
Can accurately measure response times of respondents to key questions	✓	✓	✓	✓	✓	✓✗
Can easily display a variety of graphics and directly relate them to questions	✓	✓	✓			✓✗
Eliminates need to encode data from paper surveys	✓	✓	✓	✓	✓	✓
Errors in data less likely, compared to equivalent manual method	✓	✓	✓	✓	✓	✓
Speedier data collection and encoding, compared to equivalent manual method	✓	✓	✓	✓	✓	✓

FIGURE 10.2

Computer-Assisted Data Collection Methods.

Source: S. G. Dacko, "Data Should Not Be Manual Labor," *Marketing News,* August 28, 1995, p. 31.

Marketing Research in Action 10.6

■ CELL PHONES—REVOLUTIONIZING MODE OF MARKETING RESEARCH

Study of consumer behaviors in their natural environment is the key to better consumer research. Though very expensive, new research technologies and methods, such as the ethnographic method, enable researchers to study consumers' natural behavior, thus providing new insights to researchers. Wireless marketing surveys address the expense issue while broadening and deepening the entire study of consumer behavior.

Wireless marketing surveys are a data collection technique that uses standard wireless phones (cell phones) to conduct marketing surveys either in text-based, voice-based, or a multimodal format. The technical aspects of implementing these kind of surveys are delegated to specialized companies, while the researchers focus on interaction with the respondents in real time.

The ability to deliver instant responses anywhere, anytime, and anyplace makes this technique unique. At the same time, wireless surveys reflect consumer behavior better than other methods because they record consumers' experiences and feelings at the moment of purchase or consumption. This feature helps researchers overcome the weakness of retrospective methods, which rely on the respondents' biased and distorted memories. In addition, it not only helps respondents answer questions such as "Why did I buy this product?" or "How do I feel about it?" (affective heuristic factors) but also accurately measures customer satisfaction, interpersonal influences, and advertising effectiveness. This technique also helps researchers keep track of individual respondents (longitudinal behavior) and study location-sensitive topics in depth. From the consumers' point of view, wireless surveys are nonintrusive because they—to fill out the survey. All it takes is an Internet-enabled cell phone, application service provider, and text-based short questions. Wireless surveys will definitely open big doors in marketing research. Of course, the success of this mode will depend on the cost of completed surveys versus the response rate.

Source: "Calling Customers—Wireless Technology Ideal to Study Behavior," Marketing News, January 20, 2003, P. 19.

Table 10.4 Eight Methods of Computerized Data Collection Available to Marketing Researchers

Survey methods	Characteristics
Computer-assisted personal interviewing	A method in which the researcher conducts in-person interviews, reads questions to the respondent off a computer screen, and keys the respondent's answers directly into the computer.
Computer-assisted self-interviewing	An on-site member of the research team intercepts and directs willing respondents to nearby computers. Each respondent reads questions off a computer screen and keys his or her answers directly into a computer.
Fully automated self-interviewing	Respondents independently approach a centrally located computer station or kiosk, read questions off a screen, and key their answers directly into the station's computer.
Computer-assisted telephone interviewing	Members of the research team telephone potential respondents, ask questions of respondents from a computer screen, and key the answers directly into a computer.
Fully automated telephone interviewing	An automated voice asks questions over the telephone, and respondents use keys on their touch-tone telephones to enter their replies.
Web-based survey	Using batch-type electronic mail, researchers send emails to potential respondents with weblink. Potential respondents go to the link that contains an interactive survey. Respondents access the survey and enter their answers.

Choice of Survey Methods for HMO Study

The HMO study described in earlier chapters successfully used a modification of the drop-off method. The changes were made so that advantage could be taken of the availability of a complete address list of all faculty, staff, and married students. This population was scattered over an area with a 20-mile radius, so it was not practical for the survey assistant to make unannounced personal visits. The specific procedure was as follows:

1. A telephone contact was made with each household named in the sample to determine the head of the household and obtain that person's agreement to participate. To minimize non-response bias, at least five telephone callbacks were made.

2. During the telephone call, arrangements were made to deliver the questionnaire, and a pick-up time was set.

3. Before the pick-up, a reminder phone call was made to see if the questionnaire had been completed.

4. If the questionnaire was not ready at the promised time, arrangements were made for a second pick-up time.

Only 3 percent of the sample of 1,500 persons refused to participate on the first contact. Fourteen percent were ineligible, not at home after calls, or had disconnected phones. Another 9 percent refused to complete the questionnaire they had received, usually citing lack of time (this is not surprising, as the questionnaire had 14 pages and more than 200 variables). The overall response rate of 74 percent reflected the interest of most respondents in the subject and the subtle pressure to respond from the knowledge that someone was calling to pick up the questionnaire.

Surveys in the International Context

While conducting surveys for international research, a number of differences between the domestic and the international environment have to be taken into account. In this section, the differences between domestic and international research and the problems faced by the researcher in conducting international research are discussed briefly for the three major survey methods. Often, surveys in the international context involve the use of translators and interpreters. Correct use of the local language in a research instrument is critical to successful research design. Owing to cross-national variances, the meaning of survey responses may get lost during translation and interpretation into other languages. Marketing Research in Action 10.7 provides a few tips for effective interpretations in international surveys.

Personal Interviews

Personal interviewing tends to be the dominant mode of data collection outside the United States.[29] Lower wage costs imply that personal procedures are cheaper than in the United States. On the other hand, use of personal interviewing requires the availability of field staff fluent in the relevant language.

Often, however, given the lack of a pool of trained interviewers in other countries, companies with local research units or international research organizations may train and develop their own field staffs. This provides greater control over the quality of the interviewing conducted in different countries. This is in marked contrast to the practice of "buying field and tab services" from an outside organization that is common in the United States. These interviewers are not necessarily

Marketing Research in Action 10.7

■ TIPS FOR EFFECTIVE INTERPRETATIONS

Language is perhaps the most important barrier when researching international markets. Therefore, irrespective of the research instrument being used, ensuring exact interpretations is vital in deriving insightful results. The following tips would be of help to researchers using interpreters.

1. *An interpreter is different from a translator!*

   While it may seem obvious, people generally use one for the other. Therefore, it is critical to understand their terminologies. A translator is someone who works with the written word and translates a written text in one language into a written text in another language. In contrast, an interpreter works with the spoken word or oral communication and is used for real-time communication in a foreign country.

2. *It's all about the meaning*

   Interpreters do not translate. Rather, they communicate what researchers mean in the listener's language. There are plenty of examples of marketing gaffes that have relied heavily on literal translations and have produced erroneous and often embarrassing results. Therefore, it is not about the literal translation—it's the appropriate rendering of your meaning in the other language.

3. *A pause goes a long way*

   If you speak for too long without a pause, the interpreter will find it more difficult to render your meaning and your listeners will get bored or lose focus. Therefore, a pause helps the interpreter to collect, assimilate and effectively interpret the message into the foreign language.

4. *Go easy on the slangs*

   The focus should be on the message that has to be communicated. This calls for easy and straight talk that does not involve slangs, humor, pun, or play with words. This helps the interpreter to concentrate on interpreting the message correctly.

5. *Look at your counterpart, not the interpreter!*

   In the most ideal setting, the interpreter should be invisible, with only the interpreted messages going back and forth. This is possible only if the researcher focuses his attention on the counterpart, and using the ears only with the interpreter. Such an approach also helps the researcher to pick up the nonverbal cues from the counterpart.

Source: A. Orban, "Qualitatively Speaking: Ten tips for using interpreters in international research," Quirk's Marketing Research Review, November 2005, p. 20. http://www.quirks.com/articles/a2005/20051112.aspx?searchID-249352105.

required to work exclusively for a given research supplier, though often they may do so of their own choice.

The ease with which the cooperation of respondents can be obtained may vary, however, from one country or culture to another. In Latin countries, and particularly in the Middle East, interviewers are regarded with considerable suspicion. In Latin countries, where tax evasion is more prevalent, interviewers are often suspected of being tax inspectors. In the Middle East, where interviewers are invariably male, interviews with housewives often have to be conducted in the evenings when husbands are at home.

Telephone Interviews

In international marketing research, the advantages of these telephone interviews are not always as evident. Low levels of telephone ownership and poor communications in many countries limit the coverage provided by telephone surveys. In addition, telephone costs are often high, and volume rates may not be available. Again, this depends on the specific country and the target population. Consequently, the desirability of conducting a telephone survey will depend to a large extent on the nature and purpose of the survey.

In industrial international marketing research, the use of telephone surveys may be quite effective. Most businesses, other than some small or itinerant retailers or craftspersons, are likely to have telephones.

With the decline of international telephone costs, multicountry studies can also be conducted from a single location. This significantly reduces the time and costs associated with negotiating and organizing a research project in each country, establishing quality controls, and so on. Although the additional costs of making international telephone calls are incurred, these may not be highly significant when a centralized location is used.[30]

International calls also obtain a higher response rate. Results obtained using this technique have been found to be highly stable. Interviewer and client control is considerably greater. The questionnaire can be changed and modified in the course of the survey, and interviewing can be extended or stopped to meet the client's requirements. It is necessary to find interviewers fluent in the relevant languages, but in most European countries, this is rarely a problem.

In consumer research, the feasibility of using telephone surveys depends on the level of private telephone ownership in a country, and the specific target population. In countries such as India, telephone penetration is very low. According to the Ministry of Communications and Information Technology in 2004, India's rural telephone penetration was 4.3 main lines per 100 populations and urban telephone density was 15.2 per 100 populations.[31] Even in relatively affluent societies such as Great Britain, telephone penetration is only 80 percent, and telephone interviewing is not widely used because many practitioners are still skeptical about it. In Britain and France, there are substantial declines in telephone response rates in large cities. However, these declines are not observed in Germany and Switzerland. In some of the Eastern European countries and some members of the Eastern European Commonwealth of Independent States which have poor telecommunication systems, conducting telephone surveys may not be a good idea.

Self-Administered Surveys

As in the case of telephone interviews, the advantages and limitations of self-administered surveys in international marketing research are not always clear. In many markets, the efficacy of self-administered surveys depends on the specific product market being investigated (i.e., industrial versus consumer) and also on the nature of the survey. For example, response rates are a problem in international mail surveys. Because of the absence of mailing lists, poor mail services, limited email use, limited web access, and high levels of illiteracy, when international mail surveys are conducted the response rates can be very low.

Self-administered surveys typically can be used effectively in industrial international marketing research. Mail and email lists such as those from Bottin International, or directories for specific industries, are generally available.

In consumer research, and particularly in developing countries, the use of self-administered surveys may give rise to some problems. Mailing addresses and email lists comparable to those in the domestic market may not be available, or not sold, and public sources such as telephone directories may not provide adequate coverage. Lists that are available, that is, magazine subscription lists or membership association lists, may be skewed to better-educated segments of the population. In addition, in some countries, the effectiveness of self-administered surveys is limited not only by low literacy levels but also by the reluctance of respondents to respond to them. As noted previously, levels of literacy are often less than 40 or 50 percent in some Asian and African markets, thus limiting the population that can be reached by mail or email. Even in countries where literacy levels and mail services make the use of mail surveys feasible, a tendency to regard surveys as an invasion of privacy may limit their effectiveness.

Thus, while mail surveys may be used effectively in industrial marketing research, in consumer research they may be appropriate only in industrialized countries where levels of literacy are high and mailing lists are generally available.

SUMMARY

The choice of a data collection method involves a series of compromises in matching the often conflicting requirements of the situation with the strengths and limitations of the available methods. While each situation is unique to some degree, the following represent the major constraints to be satisfied:

Available budget

Nature of the problem

Need for accuracy

The complexity of the required information

How quickly the results are needed.

Part of the skill of research design is adapting a basic data collection method, whether personal or telephone interview or self-administered survey, to those constraints. This process of adaptation means exploiting the advantages as well as blunting the limitations, which to some extent makes generalizations suspect. Nonetheless, it is useful to summarize the relative merits of the basic survey methods, as in Table 10.3, to put the methods into perspective. Of course, these summary judgments do not reflect the myriad special factors that may be influential in specific cases, such as the availability of a sampling frame, the need to ask sensitive questions, and the rarity of the population to be sampled.

The greatest potential for effective adaptation of method to situation lies with combinations of methods, or specialized variants of basic methods. The latter include omnibus surveys and mail panels, which are particularly good for tracking studies, or where limited responses from specific populations are required and budget constraints are severe. Some combinations of methods, such as the drop-off method, similarly confer impressive advantages by combining some of the advantages of personal interviews and mail surveys. As with specialized variants, however, their usefulness often is restricted to certain settings.

Survey research is bound to be the most dominant data collection method in the future. The future of survey research is exciting. With technology growing at such a tremendous pace, newer and better methods to conduct surveys, such as web-based surveying and email surveys, are becoming more common. Another trend in the survey research area is internationalization. This introduces a number of new challenges to the marketing researcher, who has to contend with language, cultural, and a host of other problems.

QUESTIONS AND PROBLEMS

10.1 What kind of data collection procedure would you recommend to research the question of why female shoppers choose a particular retail store at which to buy clothing?

10.2 Even with the use of expensive gifts and callbacks, all three interview methods produce low response rates, usually under 30 percent. What are some ways to increase these response rates?

10.3 What biases, if any, might be introduced by offering to give respondents $5.00 when they return a mail questionnaire? Would these biases be different if a gift with a retail value of $5.00 were included with the questionnaire?

10.4 What can an interviewer do during the first 30 seconds of an interview to maximize the cooperation rate of (a) a personal interview and (b) a telephone interview? Assume that the appropriate respondent is the head of the household.

10.5 What are the advantages of the telephone prenotification approach over a conventional mail survey?

10.6 Write a cover letter for a mail survey of householders that contains a number of questions regarding the utilization of various kinds of burglary-protection devices.

10.7 You are a senior analyst in the marketing research department of a major chemical company. Your company has accidentally stumbled upon a chemical that, when combined with plastic, gives it near metallic properties. You have been asked to find out various uses for this chemical and also forecast its total market potential.

(a) What information if any, that could be obtained from respondents would be useful for this research?

(b) What techniques are applicable for obtaining each item of information?

(c) Design a survey to obtain the information desired. Prepare all instructions, collection forms, and other materials required to obtain such information.

(d) Estimate the cost of conducting the survey you have designed.

10.8 You are a publisher of national repute and you would like to find the potential for an academic book. You have decided to conduct a survey among college professors for this purpose. What form of survey method would you use? What trend do you see in the future for this survey method?

10.9 What are the advantages and disadvantages of computer interactive interviewing compared to the traditional methods of surveying?

10.10 What are the problems faced by researchers when they are conducting research in developing countries?

10.11 You are the manufacturer of a major consumer product in the United States. You plan to enter the following countries with your products within the next two years: Russia, France, South Africa, Brazil, China, Japan, Mexico, Canada, India, and Germany. Based on the demographic data and the infrastructural data about these countries, determine the best survey method to be adopted in each of these countries.

10.12 Idaho Ideal Potatoes, Ltd., developed a new guacamole-flavored potato chip and wanted to ascertain the national sales potential for this unique product offering. However, the market researcher found the mail response rate to be extremely low (10 percent) and that many of the returned surveys had been completed incorrectly.

(a) How might the company have collected the relevant data more effectively?

(b) What are the advantages and disadvantages of using telephone surveys and focus groups for this kind of study? Due to stringent budget constraints, the marketing research director decided to limit the survey to residents of San Antonio, Texas.

(c) What possible biases could be reflected in the survey results?

(d) Idaho Ideal Potatoes, Ltd., has decided to offer their new potato chip simultaneously in foreign markets and wishes to survey potential sales demand for the product in the United Kingdom. How should the choice of survey method be altered to suit the company's research of foreign markets?

10.13 Judy Gomez, head of marketing for Wildlife Treasures, Inc., has been informed by the board of directors that they would like a marketing research study conducted to determine the cause of the plateau in sales performance over the past two years. The company is a producer of art and ornaments depicting African wildlife, and currently supplies specialty stores throughout the United States. A considerably restricted budget has been allocated to the project. Ms. Gomez is expected to survey all of these stores in order to determine how sales in the domestic market can be increased. The board of directors has been generous in its time allowance for the study, preferring a thorough marketing research effort to a hasty one.

(a) Suggest a suitable survey method for the study and justify your answer. Ms. Gomez believes that a possible remedy to the company's stagnant sales performance may be an entry into foreign markets. Because Wildlife Treasures has received some unsolicited inquiries from European tourists, she feels that a market may exist in Europe for its specialty goods.

(b) Given the restraints of the study, how can Ms. Gomez conduct a survey to determine potential markets across Europe?

(c) Ms. Gomez would like to utilize the company's recently updated computer system for the marketing research study. What features would need to be available in order to use the computer system for this purpose?

10.14 A museum of arts in a large city wants to conduct a study of museum patrons' attitudes concerning its collection of exhibits. What survey method would you suggest? Why?

END NOTES

1. S. Lewis, "Fear Not, We Come in Peace: You Can Convert Survey-Phobics into Lasting Relationships," *Marketing News*, 33(1), January 4, 1999, p. 18.

2. S. Sudman, "Improving the Quality of Shopping Center Sampling," *Journal of Marketing Research*, 17, November 1980, pp. 423–431.

3. F. Wiseman, Marianne Schafer, and Richard Schafer, "An Experimental Test of the Effects of a Monetary Incentive on Cooperation Rates and Data Collection Costs in Central-Location Interviewing," *Journal of Marketing Research*, November 1983, pp. 439–442.

4. S. M. McIntyre and S. D. F. G. Bender, "The Purchase Intercept Technique in Comparison to Telephone and Mail Surveys," *Journal of Retailing*, 62, Winter 1986, pp. 364–383.

5. E. Gregory, "Cost/Quality Issues Plague Mall Intercepts," *Marketing Research*, Summer 1996, pp. 46–47.

6. N. A. Glassman and M. Glassman, "Screening Questions: How Screening Questions Can Cause Self-Selection Bias," *Marketing Research*, Fall 1998, pp. 26–31.

7. "The Frame," published by Survey Sampling, Inc., September 1996.

8. S. L. Payne, "Data Collection Methods: Telephone Surveys," in R. Ferber, ed., *Handbook of Marketing Research*. New York: McGraw-Hill, 1974, pp. 2.105–2.123.

9. Payne, *Handbook of Marketing Research*. New York: McGraw-Hill, 1974, p. 2.116.

10. J. B. Lansing and J. N. Morgan, *Economic Survey Methods*, Ann Arbor, MI: University of Michigan, Institute of Social Research, 1971, pp. 203–243.

11. "So how good is RDD?" *Marketing Research*, Fall 2007, p. 5.

12. Quoted from Census Bureau sources by P. L. Erdos, "Data Collection Methods: Mail Surveys," in R. Ferber, ed., *Handbook of Marketing Research*. New York: McGraw-Hill, 1974, pp. 2–91.

13. Results from other comparative studies have not been so clear-cut. See, for example, W. Locander, S. Sudman, and N. Bradburn, "An Investigation of Interviewer Method, Threat and Response Distortion," *Journal of the American Statistical Association*, June 1976, pp. 262–275.

14. M. J. Houston and N. M. Ford, "Broadening the Scope of Methodological Research on Mail Surveys," *Journal of Marketing Research*, 13, November 1976, pp. 397–403.

15. Quoted from Census Bureau by P. L. Erdos, "Data Collection Methods: Mail Surveys," in R. Ferber, ed., *Handbook of Marketing Research*. New York: McGraw-Hill, 1974, pp. 2–91.

16. Council of American Survey Research Organizations, "On the Definition of Response Rates," Special Report, Port Jefferson, NY: CASRO, 1982.

17. F. Wiseman and M. Billington, "Comment on a Standard Definition of Response Rates," *Journal of Marketing Research*, August 1984, pp. 336–338.

18. L. Kanuk and C. Berenson, "Mail Surveys and Response Rates: A Literature Review," *Journal of Marketing Research*, 12, November 1975, pp. 440–453; J. M. James and Richard Bolstein, "The Effect of Monetary Incentives and Follow-up Mailings on the Response Rate and Response Quality in Mail Surveys," *Public Opinion Quarterly*, 54, Fall 1990, pp. 346–361.

19. J. S. Armstrong and T. S. Overton, "Estimating Nonresponse Bias in Mail Surveys," *Journal of Marketing Research*, 14, August 1977, pp. 396–402.

20. D. McCullough, "Web-based Market Research Ushers in New Age," *Marketing News*, September 14, 1998.

21. N. M. Ray and S. W. Tabor, "Cyber Surveys," *Marketing Research*, Spring 2003, pp. 35–37.

22. M. A. Jolson, "How to Double or Triple Mail-Survey Response Rates," *Journal of Marketing*, 41, October 1977, pp. 78–81.

23. D. Schwartz, "Locked Box Contains Survey Methods, Helps End Some Woes of Probing Industrial Field," *Marketing News*, January 27, 1978, p. 18.

24. C. H. Lovelock, R. Stiff, D. Cullwick, and I. M. Kaufman, "An Evaluation of the Effectiveness of Drop-off Questionnaire Delivery," *Journal of Marketing Research*, 13, November 1976, pp. 358–364.

25. G. Gaboda, "Phone Cards Help Researchers Reward Respondents," *Marketing News*, September 15, 1997, p. 14.

26. For more details on cost savings, refer to J. P. Liefeld, "Response Effects in Computer Administered Questioning," *Journal of Marketing Research*, 25, November 1988, pp. 405–409.

27. L. C. Winters, "Questionnaires in the 1990s: Wands and Scannable Forms Are 'In'," *Marketing Research*, June 1992, p. 46.

28. R. Hays, "Phone Cards Help Researchers Reward Respondents," *Marketing News*, April 13, 1998, p. 13.

29. D. Monk, "Marketing Research in Canada," European Research, November 1987, p. 274; J. J. Honomichl, "*Survey Results Positive*," Advertising Age, November 1984, p. 23.

30. M. De Houd, "International Computerized Telephone Research: Is It Fiction?," *Marketing Research Society Newsletter*, January 1982, pp. 14–15.

31. "Doing ebusiness in India," The Economist Intelligence Unit, The Economist, http://globaltechforum.eiu.com/index.asp?layout-newdebi &country_id=IN&title=Doing+ebusniess+in+India.

Case 10-1 ||| Roland Development Corp

Roland Development was a leading builder of homes in the western United States. Its emphasis was on condominiums and ownhouses, which were forecast to have an attractive future in these markets. These housing types lent themselves to standardization and cost-reduction possibilities. Further, rising land costs were causing the share of single-family detached houses to decline significantly. Meanwhile, the share of market for single-family attached houses (houses with common walls, floors, or roofs) was expected to double in the next five years. Roland was well positioned to exploit these trends by following a strategy that differed from competition in three areas:

- Market segmentation. Roland typically segmented the market more finely than other home builders and then designed homes to meet the specific needs of these groups.

- Direct selling. Shoppers in some department stores could find full-scale, fully furnished Roland homes on display.

- Low prices for a complete housing package (including all the furnishings and necessary financing).

The company had begun to expand its limited line of condominiums and townhouses to provide design and square-footage combinations that would appeal to higher-income households. The management was especially pleased with the elegance, convenience, and durability of the four new models they were planning to launch. Several problems remained to be solved. The first was the identification of a creative strategy that would position the new models and attract the largest number of purchases. That is, the company wanted to know what main ideas and themes should be used in the advertising of the new models. Another problem was to identify those segments of the market with the highest probability of purchasing the new models. The company asked the YKG Group, a large national research firm, to submit a written proposal for research which would provide Roland's management with information useful in solving these two problems. Their proposal is summarized below.

Research Proposal

The recommended research design would use a consumer panel and employ both telephone interviews and mail questionnaires. The research firm felt that the needed information could be obtained only from that very small proportion of the population who might buy such a home. Each of several different market segments would be studied to determine how they positioned the new models in relation to competing homes already on the market. The likelihood of purchasing a Roland model would also be determined during the study for each of the three market segments and also for each of several different advertising themes. This information would help Roland identify the most promising market segments for the new models, as well as the creative advertising strategy that would most appeal to them.

The proposed research design consisted of three phases: (1) The members of a large consumer mail panel would be screened to locate qualified prospects for the new models; (2) a relatively small sample of qualified prospects would be interviewed "in depth" to identify possible advertising themes; and (3) a large sample of qualified respondents would be surveyed by mail to test their response to alternative creative strategies.

Phase 1. The YKG Group maintained a bank of over 200,000 families who agreed to cooperate in research projects undertaken by the firm. Considerable information existed about each family, including geographic location, occupation and age of male and female heads of family, total family income, and presence and age of children. Roland managers felt that the four new models would most likely appeal to middle- and upper-income families of size two, three, or four, with a household head 30 years of age or over. For this reason, the first phase of the proposed research involved mailing a short questionnaire to all panel members with those characteristics. The questionnaire asked panel members to indicate the likelihood of their purchasing a home in the next two to three years and also to report their attitude toward buying a townhouse or condominium.

It was expected that this screening process would locate some 3,000–5,000 families who would be prospects to buy the new models over the next few years. To be considered a prospect,

a family had to report being likely to purchase a home in the next two to three years, as well as having a favorable attitude toward a condominium or townhouse. Among these prospects, three market segments would be identified. A high-income family would be a "very good" prospect if it was "very likely" to buy a home; a medium-income family would be a "good" prospect if it was "very likely" to buy a new home; and a high-income family would be a "fair" prospect if it was "somewhat" likely to buy a new home. All other responses were considered to indicate nonprospects.

Phase 2. In this phase about 200 qualified prospects would be interviewed using a combination of telephone and mail. These families would be mailed pictures, specifications, and line drawings of the company's new models of condos and townhouses, although they would not be identified by the Roland name. The line drawings would include front and rear views of each unit's exterior as well as sketches of each room. The specifications would include the number of square feet, wall thickness, heating and cooling equipment capacities, appliance brands and models, slab thickness, type of roof covering, and other features.

After reviewing these materials, respondents' reactions and impressions would be obtained through telephone interviews using open-ended questions. Interviewers would be told that the objective was to obtain qualitative data useful for ascertaining how potential buyers perceived the new models with respect to appearance, comfort, elegance, convenience, durability, ease and economy of maintenance, and other criteria. Interviewers would be instructed to record verbatim responses and were told that it was very important to do so because none of the responses would be tabulated or analyzed statistically. Responses to the open questions would then be studied to identify four or five ideas of themes that might be considered for use as creative strategies in advertising the new models.

Phase 3. This phase would be undertaken after four of the best advertising themes had been identified. Some 2,400 families would be selected from the list of prospects obtained from Phase 1—approximately 800 "very good" prospects, 800 "good" prospects, and 800 "fair" prospects.

All of the families in each of the three market segments would be sent pictures, line drawings, and specifications (including prices) of the new Roland models as well as those of major competing models, all identified by brand name. Each of these three groups of prospects would then be randomly divided into four subsamples of 200, each of which would receive one, and only one, of the four advertising themes identified for the new models. Thus, the study design would consist of three samples of 800 families each. In turn, each sample would be broken into four subsamples, each of which would receive a different advertising theme.

Analysis. The effect of each advertising theme on each prospect segment would be evaluated on three measures: the degree to which it (1) resulted in the new line being rated as "most appealing," (2) led respondents to request further information about the company's products, and (3) led respondents to indicate that they would be most likely to select one of the company's homes if they were to make such a purchase in the near future. For each advertising theme-prospect segment combination the research would yield three percentages. For example, for theme #1 and the "very good" prospects, the research might show that 38 percent of the respondents found a model in the new line "most appealing" among all the models reviewed; that 26 percent requested further information about the Roland models; and that 17 percent indicated that they "most likely

would purchase" one of the new Roland models. By comparing these three percentages for each advertising theme-prospect segment combination, it would be possible to identify the most promising combinations. These results could be weighed by the relative size of each prospect segment to decide which creative strategy would be most effective in generating sales interest in the new models.

Questions for Discussion

1. Would you recommend that Roland accept the YKG Group proposal?

2. If yes, what conclusions can be drawn from the data in Phase 3 of the research?

3. If the proposal is not accepted, what alternative designs should be considered?

11 Attitude Measurement

LEARNING OBJECTIVES

- Define attitudes.
- Discuss the concept of measurement and scaling in marketing research.
- Discuss the different scales in measurement.
- Describe the different types of scales used for measuring attitudes.
- Give a description of each of the well-known scales that are used to measure attitudes.
- Describe the guidelines for developing a multiple-item scale.
- List the limitations of attitude scales.
- Discuss how to select the most appropriate attitude scale.
- Discuss the concepts of reliability, validity, and generalizability.
- Describe issues using scales in cross-national research.

Most questions in marketing research surveys are designed to measure attitudes. The answers to these questions help decision makers in designing specific products or services to cater to the needs of segmented audiences. For example, each of the following situations involves the measurement of some aspect of a respondent's attitude:

1. An appliance manufacturer wants to know how many potential buyers are aware of a brand name. (What brand names do they think of in connection with dishwashers?)

2. Administrators concerned with formulating an energy policy want to know what proportion of voters agree that car buyers should pay an extra tax of several hundred dollars on cars that get poor gasoline mileage.

3. A food manufacturer is interested in the intentions of a sample of consumers to buy a possible new product after the concept has been described to them.

Common to each of these examples is a need to learn something about the basic orientation or attitude of present or prospective customers. Their attitudes are based on the information they have, their feelings (liking and disliking), and their intended behavior.

What management really wants to understand—and ultimately influence—is behavior. For many reasons, however, they are likely to use attitude measures instead of behavior. First, there is a widely held belief that attitudes are precursors of behavior. If consumers like a brand, they are more likely to choose that brand over one they like less. Second, it is generally more feasible to ask attitude questions than to observe and interpret actual behavior. Attitude measures offer the greatest advantage over behavior measures in their capacity for diagnosis or explanation. Attitude measures can be used to help learn which features of a new product concept are acceptable or unacceptable, as well as the perceived strengths and weaknesses of competitive alternatives. Insights can be gained into the process by which choice decisions are made: What alternatives are known and considered? Why are some rejected? What problems are encountered with the products or services that are used?

This chapter is concerned primarily with the measurement of attitudes. Some measurement approaches were encountered in earlier chapters. Projective techniques and physiological methods, discussed in Chapter 8, are indirect methods for inferring a person's attitude. By far the most popular approach is the direct self-report, in which the respondent is asked a series of questions. The two previous chapters described the survey methods appropriate for such self-reports. This chapter and the next are devoted specifically to attitude measurements, in recognition of their importance to marketing and of the special problems of specifying and identifying attitudes.

Attitudes

What is an *attitude?* How can it be measured for marketing research purposes? Attitudes are psychological constructs, and a way of conceptualizing the intangible. Attitudes can't really be observed or measured directly because their existence is inferred from their consequences. On the other hand, people's values and beliefs may dictate or affect their purchasing decisions. Values and beliefs in retrospect are influenced by a person's attitude; conversely, values are the determinants of attitudes and belief involves evaluation.

A person with more positive than negative beliefs toward a psychological object is judged to have a positive attitude. Attitude measurement techniques are generally systematic methods for abstracting the effective component of belief systems in order to generate an attitude score. Attitudes are the essence of the "human change agent" that all marketers strive to influence, but without the right tools to effectively measure attitude, attitudinal research has little to offer.[1]

Attitudes are mental states used by individuals to structure the way they perceive their environment and guide the way they respond to it. There is general acceptance that there are three related components that form an attitude: a cognitive or knowledge component, a liking or affective component, and an intentions or actions component. Each component provides a different insight into a person's attitude.

Cognitive or Knowledge Component

The **cognitive or knowledge component** represents a person's information about an object. This information includes awareness of the existence of the object, beliefs about the characteristics or attributes of the object, and judgments about the relative importance of each of the attributes.

Consider the knowledge people might bring to planning a ski vacation in the Rockies. They might remember the names of several ski areas without prompting: Aspen, Snowmass, Alta, and Park City, for example. This is **unaided-recall awareness**. The names of additional ski areas are likely to be remembered when the travel agent mentions them. This is **aided-recall awareness**.

Knowledge of ski areas is not limited to awareness, however. From the experience of friends, brochures, magazine articles, and other sources, a person will have formed beliefs or judgments about the characteristics or attributes of each of these ski areas. These attributes might range from the difficulty of the slopes to the type of social life and the cost of accommodations. Often, these beliefs incorporate explicit comparative judgments within a set, such as which ski area is the most difficult or the cheapest. Another kind of belief is an overall similarity judgment: Are Aspen and Snowmass more similar to each other than Aspen and Alta, for example?

Affective or Liking Component

The **affective or liking component** summarizes a person's overall feelings toward an object, situation, or person, on a scale of *like–dislike* or *favorable–unfavorable*. When there are several alternatives to choose among, liking is expressed in terms of preference for one alternative over another. Preferences can be measured by asking which is "most preferred" or the "first choice," which is the "second choice," and so forth. Affective judgments also can be made about the attributes of an object, such as a ski area. Someone may like all other aspects of an area but dislike the location because it requires too much traveling.

Intention or Action Component

The **intention or action component** refers to a person's expectations of future behavior toward an object. Is he or she "very," "somewhat," or "not at all" likely to go to Aspen for a ski week next winter? Intentions usually are limited to a distinct time period that depends on buying habits and planning horizons. The great advantage of an intentions question is that it incorporates information about a respondent's ability or willingness to pay for the object, or otherwise take action. One may prefer Aspen over all other ski areas in the Rockies but have no intention of going next year because of the cost.

The Concept of Measurement and Scaling

Measurement can be defined as a standardized process of assigning numbers or other symbols to certain characteristics of the objects of interest, according to some prespecified rules. Measurement often deals with numbers because mathematical and statistical analyses can be performed only on numbers, and they can be communicated throughout the world in the same form without any translation problems. For a measurement process to be a standardized process of assignment, two characteristics are necessary. First, there must be one-to-one correspondence between the symbol and the characteristic in the object that is being measured. Second, the rules for assignment must be invariant over time and the objects being measured.

    Scaling is the process of creating a continuum on which objects are located according to the amount of the measured characteristic they possess. An illustration of a scale that is often used in research is the dichotomous scale for sex. The object with male (or female) characteristics is assigned the number 1 and the object with the opposite characteristics is assigned the number 0. This scale meets the requirements of the measurement process in that the assignment is one to one and it is invariant with respect to time and object. Measurement and scaling are basic tools used in the scientific method and are used in almost every marketing research situation. The decision of what type of scale is critically important since the scale type will dictate the method(s) of analysis that you will be able to use to analyze the data collected. For example, if you want to be able to calculate the average satisfaction the scale for the question asked must have certain scale properties be either inverval or ratio. If you want to show that two constructs are correlated they each must be measured with an interval or ratio scale. Therefore, you should think about the analysis you want to perform as you design the scales you will use on your questionnaire.

Properties of Measurement Scales

The assignment of numbers is made according to rules that should correspond to the properties of whatever is being measured. The rule may be very simple, as when a bus route is given a number to distinguish it from other routes. Here, the only property is identity, and any comparisons of numbers are meaningless. This is a **nominal scale**. At the other extreme is the **ratio scale**, which has very rigorous properties. In between the extremes are **ordinal scales** and **interval scales**, as shown in Table 11.1.

Attitude variables, such as beliefs, preferences, and intentions, are also measured using rating scales. These scales provide respondents with a set of numbered categories that represent the range of possible judgments or positions. An attitude scale involves measurement in the same sense that a thermometer measures temperature or a ruler measures distance. In each of these cases, measurement means the assignment of numbers to objects or persons to represent quantities of their attributes. For example, the attributes of a person include his or her income, social class, attitude, and so forth. Therefore, it is very important to understand the differences among the types of scales and to be able to identify them in practice, for their properties put significant restrictions on the interpretation and use of the resulting measurements.

Nominal Scale

In a nominal scale, objects are assigned to mutually exclusive, labeled categories, but there are no necessary relationships among the categories; that is, no ordering or spacing is implied. If one entity is assigned the same number as another, they are identical with respect to a nominal variable. Otherwise, they are just different. Sex, zip code, occupation, and marital status are nominally scaled variables. The only arithmetic operation that can be performed on such a scale is a count of each category. Thus, we can count the number of automobile dealers in the state of California or the number of males seen on a given bus route in the past hour.

Table 11.1 Types of Scales and Their Properties

Types of measurement scale	Types of attitude scale	Rules for assigning number	Other typical marketing applications	Statistics/ statistical tests
Nominal	Dichotomous "yes" or "no" scale; "buy" or "not buy" scale	Objects are either identical or different	Classification (by sex, geographic area, social class)	Percentages, mode/chi-square
Ordinal or rank order	Comparative, rank order, itemized category, paired comparison	Objects are greater or smaller	Rankings (preference, class standing)	Percentile, median, rank-order correlation/Friedman ANOVA
Interval	Likert, Thurstone, Stapel, associative, semantic-differential	Intervals between adjacent objects are equal	Index numbers, temperature scales, attitude measures	Mean, standard deviation, product moment correlations/t-tests, ANOVA, regression, factor analysis
Ratio	Certain scales with special instructions such as a constant sum scale	There is a meaningful zero, so comparison of absolute magnitudes between objects is possible	Sales, incomes, units produced, costs, age	Geometric and harmonic mean, coefficient of variation

Ordinal Scale

An ordinal scale is obtained when objects are ranked or arranged in order with regard to some common variable. The question is simply whether each object has more or less of this variable than some other object. The scale provides no information as to how much difference there is between the objects.

Because we do not know the amount of difference between objects, the permissible arithmetic operations are limited to statistics such as the median or mode (but not the mean). For example, suppose a sample of 1,000 consumers ranked five brands of frozen mixed vegetables according to quality. The results for Birds Eye brand were as follows:

Quality rank	Number of respondents giving ranking to birds eye
First	150
Second	300
Third	250
Fourth	200
Fifth	100
Total	1,000

The "second" quality category is the mode; the "third" category is the median; however, it is not possible to compute a mean ranking because the differences between ordinal scaled values are not necessarily the same. The finishing order in a horse race illustrates this type of scale since while one would know the order they finished, the distance between the horses could be very different. Similarly, brands of frozen vegetables can be ranked according to quality, from highest to lowest.

Interval Scale

In an interval scale, the numbers used to rank the objects also represent equal increments of the attribute being measured. This means that differences can be compared. The difference between 1 and 2 is the same as between 2 and 3 but is only half the difference between 2 and 4. The location of the zero point is not fixed, and therefore zero does not denote the absence of the attribute. Fahrenheit and Celsius temperatures are measured with different interval scales and have different zero points. Interval scales have very desirable properties because virtually the entire range of statistical operations can be employed to analyze the resulting number, including addition and subtraction. Consequently, it is possible to compute an arithmetic mean from interval-scale measures.

A recurring question regarding most attitude measures is whether or not they are interval scales. Usually it is doubtful that the intervals between categories are exactly equal, but they may not be so different as to preclude treating the whole as an interval scale. A good example is a "willingness to buy" scale with 10 categories labeled from 1 to 10. If this were an interval scale, we could say that two people with scores of 2 and 4, respectively, differed by the same degree of "willingness" as two other people with scores of 8 and 10. Further, only ratios of the differences in scale values can be meaningfully interpreted, not ratios of the absolute scale values. For example, the difference between 8 and 10 is twice the difference between 2 and 3, but 6 on the "willingness" scale does not represent three times the value of 2 in terms of the degree of willingness. This is due to the fact that zero has no real meaning.

Ratio Scale

A ratio scale is a special kind of interval scale that has a naturally defined zero point. Examples would include weight, market share, or dollars in savings accounts. With a ratio scale it is possible to say how many times greater or smaller one object is than another. This is the only type of scale that permits us to make comparisons of absolute magnitude. For example, we can say that an annual income of $80,000 is two times as large as an income of $40,000.

There have been some contemporary efforts to adapt ratio scales to the measurement of social opinion. Some researchers have attempted to use magnitude estimation scales to overcome the loss of information that results when categories arbitrarily constrain the range of opinion. Magnitude scaling of attitudes has been calibrated through numeric estimation. The following is an example of numeric estimation of social opinion:[2]

> *I would like to ask your opinion about how serious you think certain crimes are. The first situation is, "A person steals a bicycle parked on the street." This has been given a score of 10 to show its seriousness. Use this situation to judge all others. For example, if you think a situation is 20 times more serious than the bicycle theft, the number you tell me should be around 200, or if you think it is half as serious, the number you tell me should be around 5, and so on.*

> *COMPARED TO THE BICYCLE THEFT AT SCORE 10, how serious is: A parent beats his young child with his fists. The child requires hospitalization. A person plants a bomb in a public building. The bomb explodes and 20 people are killed. . . .*

Magnitude scaling of this type has shown some interesting results, but there are problems with the technique. The researcher must be sure that the respondents have the competence to make these proportional judgments, which means that respondents must be allowed to practice before attempting the actual research questions.

Types of Attitude Rating Scales

There are many ways to present a respondent with a continuum of numbered categories that represent the range of possible attitude judgments. Figure 11.1 shows one of the ways the various attitudinal scales used in marketing research can be classified. They can be generally classified as single-item scales and multiple-item scales.

Single-Item Scales

As the name itself suggests, single-item scales are those that have only one item to measure a construct. Under the single-item scales, the itemized-category scale is the most widely used by marketing researchers. In some situations, comparative scales, rank-order scales, or constant-sum scales have advantages. Each of these major types of rating scales will be discussed in turn.

Itemized-Category Scales

The following scale from the Health maintenance organization (HMO) study (discussed in Chapter 3) is an **itemized-category scale**. There are four categories from which respondents can choose to indicate their overall level of satisfaction with their present health insurance plan:

_____ Very satisfied

_____ Quite satisfied

_____ Somewhat satisfied

_____ Not at all satisfied

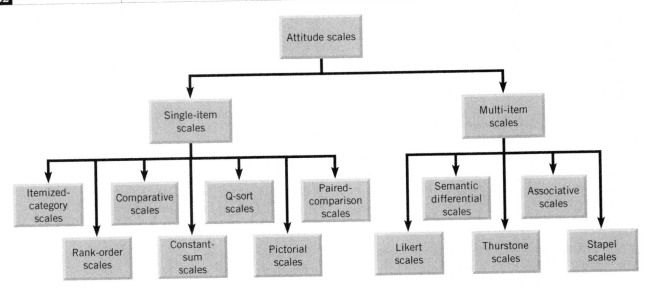

FIGURE 11.1
Classification of Attitude Scales.

This satisfaction scale has the following characteristics:

1. All categories are labeled.

2. The respondent is forced to make a choice; there is no provision for neutral opinion or "don't know" responses.

3. There are more favorable than unfavorable categories, so the scale is unbalanced.

4. There is no explicit comparison of the respondent's present plan with other health insurance plans.

The design of the satisfaction scale requires decisions along several dimensions, as shown in Figure 11.2. Note that for this scale there is no attempt to make the intervals between categories even approximately the same so this is an ordinal scale.

A quite different scale would have resulted had the decision been to label only the polar or end categories, balance the favorable and unfavorable categories, and provide an obvious neutral category.

1. Extent of category description	All categories labeled Polar categories labeled
2. Treatment of respondent uncertainty or ignorance	Forced choice (no neutral point) Neutral point Provision of "don't know" category
3. Balance of favorable and unfavorable categories	Equal Unbalanced
4. Comparison judgment required	Yes No

FIGURE 11.2
Types of Itemized Category Scales.

A numerical scaling of the response categories from +2 to −2, as presented in the following chart, could help to create a scale that can be treated as an interval scale. This would be referred to as a quasi-interval scale. While evidence is mixed, it appears that an adequate approximation of an interval scale can be achieved with this procedure.[3]

Very satisfied				**Very dissatisfied**
+2	+1	0	−1	−2

Yet another set of choices is illustrated by the following scale, which was used to ask respondents in the HMO study about the various medical services (including private clinics, private doctors, and an existing HMO), on a number of attributes, one of which was quality of care provided.

Q28... "we are interested in your opinions about the medical services offered in this area ... (a) Quality of medical care provided: (check one for each provider)"

	Excellent	**Very good**	**Average**	**Below average**	**Don't know**
Private doctors in area	☐	☐	☐	☐	☐
Private clinics	☐	☐	☐	☐	☐
Health organizations in the area	☐	☐	☐	☐	☐

The scale used for this question is unbalanced, with all categories labeled and a "don't know" category provided, and implies a comparison with other health-care providers. The decision to use an unbalanced scale was based on an assumption of positively skewed attitudes toward all health-care providers. This assumption was borne out by the results, which showed that only 15 percent rated private doctors as average or below average. However, 31 percent replied "don't know" to this question, indicating that they did not have sufficient experience to form a judgment. This could be thought of as a form of awareness question. In general, a "don't know" category should be provided whenever respondents may have insufficient experience to make a meaningful attitude judgment.

Comparative Scales

Another version of the preceding scale would label the categories "excellent," "very good," "good," "fair," and "poor," thereby eliminating the implicit comparison. The problem with a comparative scale is that the reference point is unclear and different respondents may use different reference points or standards. Are private doctors rated "excellent" or "very good" because they are superior to the existing alternatives, or because they measure up to an ideal form of medical care provider? In marketing studies where competitive alternatives are being evaluated, some form of explicit or implicit comparison should be built into the scale; for example:

Compared to private clinics in the area, the doctors in private practice provide a quality of medical care which is

Very superior		Neither superior nor inferior		Very inferior	
____	____	____	____	____	____

A recent review of research on the question of the appropriate number of response categories concluded:[4]

- "Scales with two or three response alternatives generally are inadequate in that they are incapable of transmitting very much information and they tend to frustrate and stifle respondents."

- There is little to be gained from using more than nine categories.

- An odd rather than an even number of categories is preferable when the respondent legitimately can adopt a neutral position.

Rank-Order Scales

Rank-order scales require the respondent to arrange a set of objects with regard to a common criterion: advertisements in terms of interest, product features in terms of importance, or new-product concepts with regard to willingness to buy in the future. The result is an ordinal scale with the inherent limitations of weak scale properties. Ranking is widely used in surveys, however, because it corresponds to the choice process occurring in a shopping environment where a buyer makes direct comparisons among competing alternatives (brands, flavors, product variations, and so on). An example of a rank-order scale is given below.

Please rank from 1 to 6 the following characteristics of the cellular phone service (1 is most important and 6 is least important, no ties allowed)

Characteristics	Rank
Total cost of service	⸻
Reception clarity	⸻
Low fixed cost of service	⸻
Reliability of service	⸻
24-hour customer service	⸻
Size of local coverage area	⸻

Rank-order scales are not without problems. Ranking scales are more difficult than rating scales because they involve comparisons and hence require more attention and mental effort. The ranking technique may force respondents to make choices they might not otherwise make, which raises the issue of whether the researcher is measuring a real relationship or one that is artificially contrived.

Due to the difficulties of rating, respondents usually cannot meaningfully rank more than five or six objects. The problem is not with the rankings of the first and last objects but with those in the undifferentiated middle. When there are several objects, one solution is to break the ranking task into two stages. With nine objects, for example, the first stage would be to rank the objects into classes: top three, middle three, and bottom three. The next stage would be to rank the three objects within each class.

When using paired comparisons, the objects to be ranked are presented two at a time, and the respondent has to choose between them according to some criterion such as overall preference or willingness to buy. Before a ranking of all objects can be obtained, all possible combinations of pairs have to be presented. This means that for n objects there are $[n(n-1)/2]$ comparisons. This is very manageable for five objects (10 comparisons), but with more objects the task can get out of hand. When 10 brands, for example, there are 45 paired comparisons. Paired-comparisons data have some potential analytical advantages, which will become apparent in Chapter 22, when we discuss multidimensional scaling. A serious problem, however, is that the comparison of two objects at a time is seldom the way choices are made in the marketplace; thus, an item may do well in a paired-comparison situation but perform poorly in an actual market situation.[5] Despite these limitations, however, rankings still have much to recommend them if a researcher is interested in how consumers rank alternatives.

Q-Sort Scaling

When the number of objects or characteristics that are to be rated or ranked is very large, it becomes rather tedious for the respondent to rank order or do a pairwise comparison. If the respondent is forced to do a rank ordering or a pairwise comparison, a number of problems and biases creep into the study. To deal with such a situation, the *Q-sort scaling process* is used. In Q-sort scaling, the respondents are asked to sort the various characteristics or objects that are being compared into various groups, such that the objects in each group are viewed as the most similar. Then the respondent can rank order the cards within each group which would be a much easier task. For example, let us take the case of a toy manufacturing company such as Toys "Я" Us developing a new product. After a marathon brainstorming session, the new-product team has come up with a hundred different products, each with minor variations in features, and wants to test and find out from consumers which feature combination is the most preferred and will generate the maximum sales. The best scaling procedure that can be used in this context is Q-sort scaling. The procedure the respondent is asked to use is as follows.

> *Each respondent is handed 100 cards, each containing a product with various features. The respondent is then asked to sort the cards into 12 different piles in such a way that one pile contains what they feel is the most preferred among the products that have been developed, and another pile contains the least preferred of the products that have been developed. The other 10 piles will contain cards with products that vary gradually from those with higher preference to those with lower preference. The number of cards in each pile is normally distributed as shown in Figure 11.3. In this particular case, only five cards can be placed in the most and the least preferred product piles. After placing all the cards in the piles, the respondent is asked to rank-order only those products in the most-preferred pile or in the top few sets of piles.*

In Q-sort scaling, a relatively large number of groups or piles should be used (10 or more). This increases the reliability or precision of the results.

Constant-Sum Scales

Constant-sum scales require respondents to allocate a fixed number of rating points (usually 100) among several objects, to reflect the relative preference for each object.[6] It is widely used to measure the relative importance of attributes, as in the following example.

> *Please divide 100 points among the following characteristics so the division reflects the relative importance of each characteristic to you in the selection of a health care plan.*

Ability to choose a doctor	_____
Extent of coverage provided	_____
Quality of medical care	_____
Monthly cost of the plan	_____
Distance to clinic or doctor from your home	_____
TOTAL	100

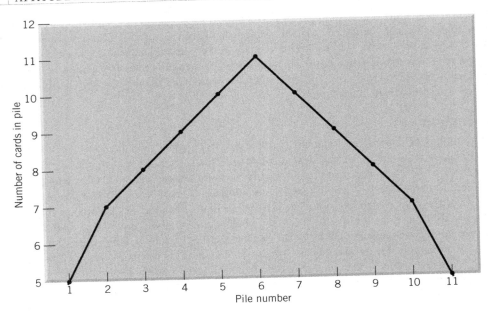

FIGURE 11.3
Plot of Number of Cards in Each Pile.

The most attractive feature of this scale is the quasi-interval nature of the resulting scale. However, just how close it comes to a true interval scale has not been fully established. The scale is limited in the number of objects or attributes it can address at one time. Respondents sometimes have difficulty allocating points accurately among more than a few categories.

Pictorial Scales

In pictorial scales, the various categories of the scale are depicted pictorially. The respondents are shown a concept or read an attitudinal statement and are asked to indicate their degree of agreement or interest by indicating the corresponding position on the pictorial scale. Therefore, in designing a format, it is of prime importance to design one that the respondent will comprehend and that will enable him or her to respond accurately. Commonly used pictorial scales are the *thermometer scale* and the *funny faces scale*. Pictorial scales are used mainly when the respondents are young children or with people who are illiterate.

Paired-Comparison Scales

The brands to be rated were presented two at a time, so each brand in the category was compared once to every other brand. In each pair, the respondents were asked to divide 10 points among the brands, on the basis of how much they liked one compared to the other. A score was then totaled for each brand. Although this scale performs well on the criteria, it is cumbersome to administer. Another possible limitation is that the frame of reference is always the other brands in the set being tested. These brands may change over time.

Several features are shared by all three of the most effective scales:

- They restrict the numbers of highly positive ratings that can be given, either by forcing a choice or by comparing brands directly.

- They provide a limited number of categories that have verbal anchors. Respondents prefer words to numbers, and especially avoid negative numbers. Also, including more than seven categories may actually reduce the scale's power to discriminate.

- The stimulus to the respondent is simple and unambiguous. One of the worst-performing scales presented a picture of a thermometer with 10 categories of liking; each was labeled by a number from 0 to 100, as well as an assortment of verbal anchors. For example, 80 was labeled "like very much" while 50 was "indifferent" and 30 was "not so good."

Although these issues are useful, and should be carefully considered, the best guidance still comes from carefully tailoring the scale to the research objectives, followed by thorough pretesting for comprehension and discrimination.

Issues in Designing Single-Item Scales

Attitude rating scales are widely used to test the effectiveness of advertising copy or compare the performance of new product concepts and segment markets. Despite years of experience with these applications, the design of the rating scale is usually an ad hoc judgment based on the researcher's preferences and past experiences in similar situations. The various decisions that a researcher has to make regarding the form and structure of the scale while designing a scale are described briefly below:

1. *Number of scale categories.* Theoretically, the number of rating-scale categories can vary from two to infinity. A continuous rating scale has infinite categories, whereas the number of categories in a discontinuous scale depends on several factors, such as the capabilities of the scalers, the format of the interview, and the nature of the object.[4,7] For example, if the survey is done by telephone, the number of categories that a scale can have is very limited because the memory of the respondent is limited.

2. *Types of poles used in the scale.* All rating scales have verbal descriptors or adjectives that serve as end points or anchors. The scale can have a single pole or two poles. An example of a two-pole scale is "sweet . . . not sweet," and an example of a scale with a single pole is the Stapel scale, which is discussed later. The advantage of the single-pole scale over the scale with double poles is ease of construction, as one need not look for adjectives to achieve bipolarity. The disadvantage is that we do not know what each category represents in a single-pole scale.

3. *Strength of the anchors.* By strength of the anchor, we refer to the intensity of the adjective that is used to anchor the scale. A rating-scale anchor could vary from "extremely colorful" to "very colorful" to "colorful." Anchor strength has been found to shape scale-response distributions; the stronger the anchors, the less likely scalers are to use the extreme scale categories, so the resulting scale response distribution will be more peaked.

4. *Labeling of the categories.* Another decision that has to be made while developing scales is whether to label every category of the scale or to label only the extreme categories. Labeling all categories reduces the scale's ambiguity.[8] Evidence also shows that using such terms as "very" or "somewhat" markedly influences responses to scales.[9]

5. *Balance of the scale.* A related decision is whether category labels should be balanced or unbalanced. A balanced four-category scale to measure the smell of a perfume could be

The smell of Morning Dew is . . .

| _____ Very good | _____ Good | _____ Bad | _____ Very bad |

while a corresponding unbalanced scale might be expressed as

| _____ Superb | _____ Very good | _____ Good | _____ Average |

Generally, a balanced scale is preferred to an unbalanced scale in order to obtain meaningful results.

There is little argument on the criteria a rating scale ideally should satisfy. The results should be reliable and valid, and there should be a sharp discrimination among the objects being rated and a sensitivity to advertising or product stimuli. These criteria are seldom employed in practice. Part of the reason is the sheer variety of rating scales. The real problem is the absence of empirical evidence on the performance of the various rating scales on these criteria. However, one study of different scales did shed some useful light on the subject, and can help us narrow down the set of acceptable scales.[10]

Respondents in the study were given various subsets of the scales and asked to rate six brands in each of six package-goods categories such as coffee, analgesics, detergents, and toothpaste. Three criteria were used to compare the performance of the scales: (1) response distribution, which is the ability to avoid having responses pile up in the end categories; (2) discrimination among brands in the category; and (3) concurrent validity—how well the ratings related to current brand usage.

Two scales were found to be particularly attractive:

- **Brand Awareness Scale.** This question asked: When I mention detergents, what brand do you think of? Any others? Have you heard of (interviewer mentions other brands of interest that were not reported)?

  _____ First unaided mention
  _____ Second unaided mention
  _____ Other unaided mention
  _____ Aided recall
  _____ Never heard of

  This scale was consistently the best discriminator among brands and had high concurrent validity. By design, it yielded uniform distributions of responses.

- **Verbal Purchase Intent Scale.** The question asked: What is the chance of your buying (brand) the next time you purchase this product?

Definitely buy	Probably buy	Might buy	Probably not buy	Definitely not buy
____	____	____	____	____

  This balanced scale made efficient use of the five categories, distributing the responses quite uniformly. The labels were easy for the respondents to handle. On average it discriminated well.

Multiple-Item Scales

Attitudes toward complex objects such as health plans, automobiles, credit instruments, or transportation modes have many facets. Thus, it is often unrealistic to attempt to capture the full picture with one overall attitude-scale question. For example, the public appears to support the general idea of income tax reform but opposes the elimination of the most popular tax loopholes. While beliefs in any specific issue, aspect, or characteristic are useful indicators of the overall attitude, there may be unusual reasons that make the single belief unrepresentative of the general position.[11] To cope with this problem, a variety of methods have been developed to measure a sample of beliefs toward the attitude objects (such as agreement or disagreement with a number of statements about the attitude object) and combine the set of answers into some form of average score. The most frequently employed of these methods are _Likert_, _Thurstone_, and _semantic-differential_ scales. An adaptation of these methods, with particular relevance to marketing problems, is _associative scaling_.

Likert Scales

Likert scales require a respondent to indicate a degree of agreement or disagreement with a variety of statements related to the attitude or object. They are also called **summated scales** because the scores on the individual items are summed to produce a total score for the respondent. A Likert scale usually consists of two parts, the item part and the evaluative part. The item part is essentially a statement about a certain product, event, or attitude. The evaluative part is a list of response categories ranging from "strongly agree" to "strongly disagree." An important assumption of this scaling method is that each of the items (statements) measures some aspect of a single common factor; otherwise, the items cannot legitimately be summed. In other words, the resulting scale is *unidimensional*. The Likert scaling method, then, refers to the several steps in the procedure for culling out the items that do not belong. The result is a series of 5 to 20 or more statements and questions, of which those given below are illustrative.

	Agree strongly	Agree somewhat	Neither agree nor disagree	Disagree somewhat	Disagree strongly
1. There needs to be much improvement in the health insurance available for people like me.	☐	☐	☐	☐	☐
2. I have a variety of very good health plans from which to choose.	☐	☐	☐	☐	☐
3. I haven't heard of a health insurance plan that will protect me against a disastrous illness.	☐	☐	☐	☐	☐

Thurstone Scales

The procedure of **Thurstone scales** is also known as the method of **equal-appearing intervals**, since the objective is to obtain a unidimensional scale with interval properties.

The first step is to generate a large number of statements or adjectives reflecting all degrees of favorableness toward the attitude objects. Then, a group of judges is given this set of items (as many as 75 to 100 in all) and asked to classify them according to their degree of favorableness or unfavorableness. Usually, this is done with an 11-category bipolar scale, with "very favorable" at one end, "very unfavorable" at the other, and a neutral position in the middle. The judges are instructed to treat the intervals between categories as equal and to make evaluations of each item without expressing their own attitudes. The scale value of each item is the median position to which it is assigned by the judges. Items that have been placed in many different categories are discarded as ambiguous because there was no consensus among the judges. The resulting scale consists of 10 to 20 items that are distributed uniformly along the scale of favorability. The scale then is administered as part of a survey by asking each respondent to select those statements which best reflect his or her feelings toward the attitude object. The respondent's attitude score is the average of the scale scores of the chosen statements.

Because of the two-stage procedure, a Thurstone scale is both time consuming and expensive to construct; however, the scale itself is easy to administer and requires a minimum of instructions. Because there is not an explicit response to each item in the scale, it does not have as much diagnostic value as a Likert scale. Thurstone scales also have been criticized because the scale values themselves may depend on the attitudes of the original judges. This seems to be a problem only with topics that elicit strong feelings, such as abortion or school integration.

Semantic-Differential Scales

Semantic-differential scales are used widely to describe the set of beliefs that comprise a person's image of an organization or brand. The procedure is also an insightful procedure for comparing the images of competing brands, stores, or services.[12] Respondents are asked to rate each attitude object in turn on a number of five- or seven-point rating scales, bounded at each end by polar adjectives or phrases. Some researchers prefer unipolar scales, while others use bipolar scales. In either case, the respondent chooses the end point only if that adjective is closely descriptive of that object. However, the midpoint of the scale has two different meanings, depending on the type of scale. With unipolar scales, the midpoint is simply a step on the scale from "sweet" to "not sweet," whereas on a bipolar scale it is a neutral point.

Low price	_____	_____	_____	_____	_____	High price
Consistent quality	_____	_____	_____	_____	_____	Spotty quality
Tangy	_____	_____	_____	_____	_____	Smooth
Bitter	_____	_____	_____	_____	_____	Not bitter

There may be as many as 15 to 25 semantic-differential scales for each attitude object. The scales in the preceding chart were used in a beer-brand image study in a U.S. regional market. (Only 4 of a total of 10 scales are shown.) Each of 10 brands was evaluated separately on the same set of 10 scales, for comparison.

This set of scales is characteristic of most marketing applications of the semantic differential:

1. The pairs of objects or phrases are selected carefully to be meaningful in the market being studied and often correspond to product or service attributes.[13] Exploratory research generally is required to ensure that important attributes are represented and described in words that are familiar to respondents.[14]

2. The negative or unfavorable pole is sometimes on the right side and sometimes on the left. This rotation is necessary to avoid the halo effect, in which the location of previous judgments on the scale affects subsequent judgments because of respondent carelessness.

3. The category increments are treated as interval scales, so group mean values can be computed for each object on each scale. As with Likert scaling, this assumption is controversial, but is adopted because it permits more powerful methods of analysis to be used.

The semantic differential also may be analyzed as a summated rating scale. Each of the seven scale categories is assigned a value from -3 to 3 or 1 to 7, and the scores across all adjective pairs are summed for each respondent. Individuals then can be compared on the basis of their total scores. Summation is not usually advisable, however, for a good deal of specific information is lost in the aggregate score, which may be distorted if there are several scales that measure roughly the same thing.

Profile Analysis

Profile analysis is an application of the semantic-differential scale. Visual comparisons of the images of different objects can be aided by plotting the mean ratings for each object on each scale. To show what can be done, Figure 11.4 compares the ratings for two well-known national brands of beer and a regional brand, on 6 of the 10 scales. Even with three brands and only 6 of 10 attributes, the interpretation of the profiles is not easy. With more brands and attributes, the overall comparisons of brands are even harder to grasp. A second difficulty is that not all attributes are

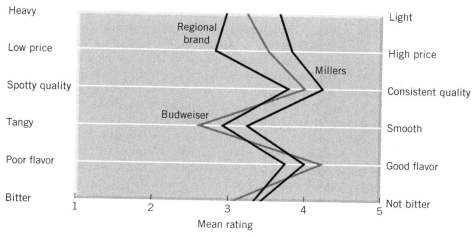

FIGURE 11.4
Profile Analysis of Three Beer Brands.

independent; that is, several of the attributes may be measuring approximately the same dimension. For example, to most beer drinkers, there is not likely to be much difference in the meaning of the "tangy–smooth" and "bitter–not bitter" scales. This is borne out by the similarity of the scores of the three brands on these two scales in Figure 11.4. Fortunately, there are several procedures using multidimensional scaling techniques that can deal effectively with these problems and yield easily interpreted spatial maps that describe the overall image of a brand. These are discussed in detail in Chapters 21 and 22, which deal with methods for analyzing interdependencies among variables.

Stapel Scales

Stapel scales are simplified versions of semantic-differential scales, which use only one pole rather than two. Respondents are asked to indicate the object by selecting a numerical response category. The higher the positive score, the better the adjective describes the object. A typical format for this scale is shown for Coors beer as it would be adapted to the measurement of beer brand attitudes.

The main virtue of this scale is that it is easy to administer and construct because there is no need to provide adjectives or phrases to assure bipolarity.[15]

Coors Beer

	+3		+3		+3
	+2		+12		+2
	+1	Consistent	+11	Tangy	+1
Heavy	−1	quality	−1		−1
	−2		−2		−2
	−3		−3		−3

Associative Scaling

Although the semantic-differential and Stapel scales are used widely for image studies, they have substantial limitations in markets where the average respondent is likely to be knowledgeable only about a small subset among a large number of choice alternatives. They also can be cumbersome and time consuming to administer when there are a number of attributes and alternatives to consider. An alternative approach, **associative scaling**, designed to overcome these limitations, asks the respondent simply to associate one alternative with each question. The questions in Figure 11.5 illustrate how this approach is employed in a telephone survey of retail-store images.

The technique is argued to be particularly appropriate to choice situations that involve a sequential decision process. For example, supermarkets have to be within a reasonable distance to be considered, and within that set the choice is made on the basis of which chain is best in satisfying customers' needs. Of course, the technique does not answer the questions of how consumers make trade-offs when there are several important dimensions and no alternative is superior across the board. Thus, the benefits of low cost and ease of telephone administration are purchased at a possible cost of reduced validity in representing the market structure. For this reason, the associative technique is best suited to market tracking, where the emphasis is on understanding shifts in relative competitive positions.

General Guidelines for Developing a Multiple-Item Scale

Multiple-item scales very often are used in social sciences research to measure abstract constructs. The characteristic that is to be measured is generally referred to as the *construct*. Most of the well-known scales that measure constructs, such as IQ, consumer confidence, and so on, are multiple-item scales. Developing a multiple-item scale is a complex procedure and requires quite a lot of technical expertise. Figure 11.6 presents the various steps in the development of a multiple-item scale. The stages of development are discussed below.

1. *Determine clearly what it is that you want to measure.* The scale should be well grounded in theory. Relevant social science theories should always be considered before developing the scale. The construct to be measured and the scale itself should be specific. The meaning and the definition of the construct should be clearly distinguishable from other constructs.

2. *Generate as many items as possible.* Items essentially are statements that are relevant to the construct. The content of each item should reflect primarily the construct of interest. If items are being written anew, they should be written with as much creativity as possible. The greater the number of initial items generated, the better the final scale will be. The items that are developed should not be too long, nor should they pose any reading difficulty to the respondent.

3. *Ask experts to evaluate the initial pool of items.* Experts are people who have worked or are currently working on the phenomenon that is being studied. They can be either business managers or academics who are doing research on that particular phenomenon. Having experts review the item pool can confirm or invalidate the definition of the construct. Experts can also give inputs on the relevancy, clarity, and conciseness of the items. Based on the experts' evaluation, the initial pool of items is modified. Some items are dropped while others are added, and a few of the existing ones are changed.

4. *Determine the type of attitudinal scale to be used.* The next step in the multiple-item scaling process is to decide on the type of scale to be employed. The various scales such as the Likert scale, semantic-differential scale, Thurstone, and associative scales have already been discussed. In fact, the type of attitudinal scale to be used has to be decided quite early, because the wording of the items varies with each scale format.

5. *Include validation items in the scale.* Certain items are added to the scale in order to improve the scale's validity and also to detect certain flaws in it. An example of items that can be included in the scale to increase the validity of the results is those that are socially desirable.

Which store	Eaton's store or catalog	The bay	Simpsons	Sears store or catalog	Horizon	Sayvette	Towers	Woolco	Zellers	Any other	None DK	More than one answer
1. Has the lowest overall prices?	1	2	3	4	5	6	7	8	9	0	B	X
2. Has the highest overall prices?	1	2	3	4	5	6	7	8	9	0	B	X
3. Is the easiest one to get to from your home?	1	2	3	4	5	6	7	8	9	0	B	X
4. Has the most knowledgeable, helpful sales clerks?	1	2	3	4	5	6	7	8	9	0	B	X
5. Has the highest-quality products?	1	2	3	4	5	6	7	8	9	0	B	X
6. Has the lowest-quality products?	1	2	3	4	5	6	7	8	9	0	B	X
7. Gives you the best overall value for the money?	1	2	3	4	5	6	7	8	9	0	B	X
8. Gives you the worst overall value for the money?	1	2	3	4	5	6	7	8	9	0	B	X
9. Has the best advertising?	1	2	3	4	5	6	7	8	9	0	B	X
10. Is the best for the latest, most fashionable merchandise?	1	2	3	4	5	6	7	8	9	0	B	X
11. Has the largest overall merchandise selection or assortment?	1	2	3	4	5	6	7	8	9	0	B	X
12. Do you shop at most often?	1	2	3	4	5	6	7	8	9	0	B	X

FIGURE 11.5
Retail-Store Image Questions (Telephone Questionnaire).

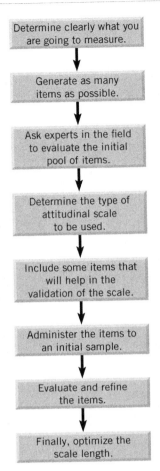

FIGURE 11.6
Steps in Multiple-Item Scale Development.

Some respondents answer in a certain fashion because they want to be perceived as socially desirable. In order to weed out such answers, items of social desirability are added to the scale. Those responses that correlate highly with social desirability are then dropped.

6. *Administer the items to an initial sample.* Once it has been determined which construct-related items are to be included in the scale, the next step is to administer the scale to an initial sample. This is done to check the validity of the items. This will yield the best results if the sample size is large and the sample is representative of the population.

7. *Evaluate and refine the items of the scale.* The ultimate quality that is sought in an item is high correlation with the true score of the latent variable that is being measured. The properties that the items of a scale should possess are high intercorrelation, high item scale correlation, high item variances, a mean close to the center of the range of possible scores, and a high coefficient alpha. The items in the scale are then evaluated on the basis of these criteria.

8. *Optimize scale length.* The larger the scale, the greater the reliability, but shorter scales are easier for the respondent to answer. Hence, a balance has to be struck between brevity and reliability, and the optimal scale length has to be determined. Certain items in the scale are dropped or modified, then the final scale is ready to be administered to the respondent.

Interpreting Attitude Scales

Conclusions obtained from attitude-scale measurements are strictly limited by the properties of the scale that is used. Failure to recognize these limits can lead to serious misinterpretation, as we see from Marketing Research in Action 11.1. The problem was created by assuming a ratio scale where there was really only an interval scale.

Marketing Research in Action 11.1

■ INTERPRETING ATTITUDE SCALES: A PROBLEM FOR THE ADVERTISING REVIEW BOARD

The Phoenix Drug Co. currently sells the leading brand of tranquilizers, known as Restease. A competitor, Montfort Drug Co., recently announced a tranquilizer brand called Calm, which they claim to be 50 percent more effective in reducing tension than the leading brand.

As product manager for Restease you are concerned and also angry, because you don't believe there is a significant difference in effectiveness. Your first action is to complain to the National Advertising Review Board (NARB), an advertising industry-sponsored body that investigates advertising claims and can put considerable pressure on advertisers to change their claims.

As part of the investigation of your complaint, the research director from Montfort Drug is asked by the NARB to present the research findings that support the claim. Among the findings are the results of an apparently well-designed comparison test with large sample sizes. In the test, one group of product users was given Restease capsules. After a month, each user was asked to rate the effectiveness of the brand as follows:

For easing tension I found Restease to be:

Very effective	Effective	Neither effective nor ineffective	Ineffective	Very ineffective
☐	☐	☐	☐	☐

Another group of product users, identical in all respects to the first group, was given Calm capsules and asked to rate the effectiveness of this brand on the same scale.

The research director for Montfort Drug coded the scale with a +2 for "very effective," +1 for "effective," 0 for "neither effective nor ineffective," −1 for "ineffective," and −2 for "very ineffective." The director correctly points out that this is a well-accepted coding convention. When the data for the two groups are summarized, the average response for the Calm user groups is calculated to be +1.2, while the average for Restease is +0.8. Because the 0.4 difference is 50 percent more than the +0.8 level achieved by Restease, the director concludes that the claims of superior effectiveness are valid.

While you are listening to this argument, the research director from your company has taken the same data and calculated that Calm is only 10.5 percent more effective, rather than 50 percent as claimed. Immediately you examine the figures. The only difference is that the "very effective" category has been coded +1, and "very ineffective" assigned +5, with the middle category assigned +3. It is argued that this is an equally acceptable coding procedure. The two different coding schemes are as follows:

Very effective	Effective	Neither effective nor ineffective	Ineffective	Very ineffective
☐	☐	☐	☐	☐
+2	+1	0	−1	−2
+1	+2	+3	+4	+5

Soon you will be asked to present the basis of your complaint to the Review Board. What do you say about the capacity of the data presented by your competitor to support its claim of superiority?

Source: Adapted from B. Venkatesh, "Unthinking Data Interpretation Can Destroy Value of Research," Marketing News, January, 1978, pp. 6, 9.

Choosing an Attitudinal Scale

The choice of an appropriate scale is complicated by two problems:

1. There are many different techniques, each with its own strengths and weaknesses.

2. Virtually any technique can be adapted to the measurement of any one of the attitude components.

While these problems are significant impediments to broad generalizations, it is also true that all techniques are not equally suitable for all purposes. Table 11.2 summarizes some useful rules of thumb as to which scale types are likely to be best suited to the various components of attitudes. What is most evident from this table is the versatility of the itemized-category scale, which itself has many variations. Ultimately, the researcher's choice will be shaped by (1) the specific information that is required to satisfy the research objectives, (2) the adaptability of the scale to the data collection method and budget constraints, and (3) the compatibility of the scale with the structure of the respondent's attitude.

The value of careful selection and adaptation of scales will be demonstrated by a study of attitudes toward automobile dealers. The data came from a mail survey of people who had purchased a new car from an automobile dealer between one and two years earlier.[16] Each respondent rated 14 attributes of the dealer's service department, on two separate scales. The first scale asked how *important* the attribute was (on a four-point scale ranging from "extremely important" to "not important"). The second scale asked how well the service department *performed* (on a four-point scale from "excellent" to "poor"). Each attribute was located in the grid shown in Figure 11.7, according to its median score on the two scales.

To illustrate how the grid can be used, quadrant A includes those attributes, such as "low prices on service" (attribute 10), which are very important, and where performance is rated only fair. By contrast, in quadrant B, customers place a high value on "courteous and friendly service" (attribute 6) and "prompt warranty work" (attribute 3), and are pleased with the dealer's performance. In quadrant C, the dealer's performance is rated low in terms of providing courtesy buses and rental cars, but fortunately these are not perceived as important services.

Table 11.2   Appropriate Applications of Various Attitude Scales

Attitude component	Type of scale				
	Itemized category	Rank order	Constant sum	Likert	Semantic differential
Knowledge					
awareness	a				
attribute beliefs	a	b	b	b	a
attribute importance	a	b	a	b	
Affect or liking					
overall preferences	a	b	a	b	b
specific attributes	a	b	b	b	a
Action					
intentions	a	b	a	b	

a = Very appropriate
b = Sometimes appropriate

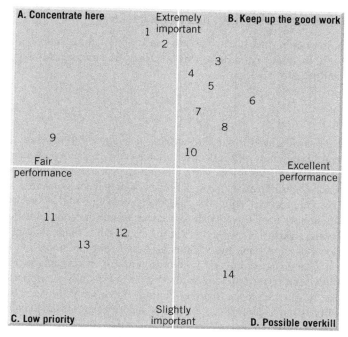

FIGURE 11.7
Importance–Performance Grid.

While the importance–performance grid yields useful insights, this application suffered from the inability of the four-point rating scale to discriminate. Ten of the 14 attributes had median ratings between 3.3 and 3.8 on this scale, where 4 means "extremely important" and 3 is "important." A constant-sum scale, on the other hand, might have resulted in sharper distinctions among attributes, as shown in Table 11.3 giving two possible patterns of responses of service customers thinking hard about which of six attributes were really important.

Table 11.3   Comparison of Two Rating Techniques

Attribute	Median importance rating	Illustrative constant-sum scale	
		Customer A	Customer B
1. Job done right the first time	3.8	35	25
2. Fast action on complaints	3.6	15	20
3. Prompt warranty work	3.6	10	15
4. Able to do any job needed	3.6	10	10
5. Service available when needed	3.4	15	20
6. Courteous and friendly service	3.4	15	10
		100	100

Accuracy of Attitude Measurements

Attitude measures, in common with all measures used in marketing, must be both accurate and useful. In this section, the focus is on those aspects of attitude measures that contribute to accuracy: validity, reliability, and sensitivity.

Validity

An attitude measure has validity if it measures what it is supposed to measure. If this is the case, then differences in attitude scores will reflect differences among the objects or individuals on the characteristic being measured. This is a very troublesome question; for example, how is a researcher to know whether measured differences in the attitudes of managers, consumer activists, and consumers toward marketing practices, regulation, and the contribution of the consumer movement are true differences? There have been three basic approaches to this question of validity assessment.

Face, or **consensus, validity** is invoked when the argument is made that the measurement so self-evidently reflects or represents the various aspects of the phenomenon that there can be little quarrel with it. For instance, buyers' recognition of advertisements is usually accepted at face value as an indication of past ad exposure. This faith typically is supported by little more than common sense, despite evidence that recognition scores are influenced by reader interest.

Criterion validity is more defensible, for it is based on empirical evidence that the attitude measure correlates with other "criterion" variables. If the two variables are measured at the same time, **concurrent validity** is established. Better yet, if the attitude measure can predict some future event, then **predictive validity** has been established. A measure of brand preference or buying intentions is valid if it can be shown through sales records to predict future sales. This is the most important type of validity for decision-making purposes, for the very nature of decisions requires predictions of uncertain future events.

While face, concurrent, and predictive validity provide necessary evidence of overall validity, often they are not sufficient. The characteristic of these three approaches is that they provide evidence on **convergent validity**. That is, an attitude measure can adequately represent a characteristic or variable if it correlates or "converges" with other supposed measures of that variable. Unfortunately, an attitude measure may converge with measures of other variables in addition to the one of interest. Thus, it is also necessary to establish **discriminant validity** through low correlations between the measure of interest and other measures that are supposedly not measuring the same variable or concept. Advertising recognition measures often fail this second test. While they correlate or converge with past ad exposure, which is what we want, they also are correlated with number of magazines read and product interest.

Construct validity can be considered only after discriminant and convergent validity have been established.[17] It is achieved when a logical argument can be advanced to defend a particular measure. The argument aims first to define the concept or construct explicitly and then to show that the measurement, or operational definition, logically connects the empirical phenomenon to the concept. The extreme difficulty of this kind of validation lies in the unobservable nature of many of the constructs (such as social class, personality, or attitudes) used to explain marketing behavior. For example, is occupation a good operational definition of social class, or does it measure some other characteristic? One way to assess construct validity is to test whether or not the measure confirms hypotheses generated from the theory based on the concepts. Since theory development is at a youthful stage in marketing, the theory itself may be incorrect, making this approach hazardous. This is one reason why little construct validation is attempted in marketing. A more significant reason is the lack of well-established measures that can be used in a variety of circumstances. Instead, marketing researchers tend to develop measures for each specific problem or survey and rely on face validity.

Reliability

So far we have been talking about systematic errors between an observed score (X_o) and a true score (X_t), which will determine whether a measure is valid. However, the total error of a measurement consists of this systematic error component (X_s) and a random error component (X_r). Random error is manifested by lack of consistency (unreliability) in repeated or equivalent measures of the same object or person. As a result, any measurement can be expressed as a function of several components:

$$X_o = X_t + X_s + X_r$$
Observed score = true score + systematic error + random error

To interpret this equation, remember that a valid measure is one that reflects the true score. In this situation, $X_o = X_t$ and both X_s and X_r are zero. Thus, if we know the measure is valid, it has to be reliable. The converse is not necessarily true. A measure may be highly reliable, $X_r = 0$, and still have a substantial systematic error that distorts the validity. If the measure is not reliable, then it cannot be valid since at a minimum we are left with $X_o = X_t + X_r$. In brief, reliability is a necessary but not a sufficient condition for validity.

Although **reliability** is less important, it is easier to measure, and so receives relatively more emphasis. The basic methods for establishing reliability can be classified according to whether they measure stability of results over time or internal consistency of items in an attitude scale.[18]

Stability over time is assessed by repeating the measurement with the same instrument and the same respondents at two points in time and correlating the results. To the extent that random fluctuations result in different scores for the two administrations, this correlation and hence the reliability will be lowered. The problems of this test-retest method are similar to those encountered during any pretest–posttest measurement of attitudes. The first administration may sensitize the respondent to the subject and lead to attitude change. The likelihood of a true change in attitude (versus a random fluctuation) is increased further if the interval between the test and the retest is too long. For most topics, this would be more than two weeks. If the interval is too short, however, there may be a carryover from the test to the retest: attempts to remember the responses in the first test, boredom or annoyance at the imposition, and so forth. Because of these problems, a very short interval will bias the reliability estimate upward, whereas longer periods will have the opposite effect.

The equivalence approach to assessing reliability is appropriate for attitude scales composed of multiple items that presumably measure the same underlying unidimensional attitude. The *split-half method* assumes that these items can be divided into two equivalent subsets that then can be compared. A number of methods have been devised to divide the items randomly into two halves and compute a measure of similarity of the total scores of the two halves across the sample. An average split-half measure of similarity—coefficient alpha—can be obtained from a procedure that has the effect of comparing every item to every other item.

Sensitivity

The third characteristic of a good attitude measure is **sensitivity**, or the ability to discriminate among meaningful differences in attitudes. Sensitivity is achieved by increasing the number of scale categories; however, the more categories there are, the lower the reliability will be. This is because very coarse response categories, such as "yes" or "no," in response to an attitude question can absorb a great deal of response variability before a change would be noted using the test-retest method. Conversely, the use of a large number of response categories when there are only a few distinct attitude positions would be subject to a considerable, but unwarranted, amount of random fluctuation.

Generalizability

Generalizability refers to the ease of scale administration and interpretation in different research settings and situations.[19] Thus, the generalizability of a multiple-item scale is determined by whether it can be applied in a wide variety of data collection modes, whether it can be used to obtain data from a wide variety of individuals, and under what conditions it can be interpreted. As in the case of reliability and validity, generalizability is not an absolute but rather is a matter of degree.

Relevancy

Relevancy of a scale refers to how meaningful it is to apply the scale to measure a construct. Mathematically, it is represented as the product of reliability and validity:

$$\text{Relevance} = \text{Reliability} * \text{Validity}$$

If reliability and validity are evaluated by means of correlation coefficients, the implications are

- The relevance of a scale can vary from 0 (no relevance) to 1 (complete relevance).

- If either reliability or validity is low, the scale will possess little relevance.

- Both reliability and validity are necessary for scale relevance.

Scales in Cross-National Research

The previous sections of this chapter discussed the various types of scales that are typically used in domestic marketing research. The question remains whether the same scales can be administered to respondents all over the world.[20] Low educational or literacy levels in some countries will have to be taken into account when the decision is made to administer the same scale. Literacy and educational levels influence the response formats of the scales employed. Moreover, culture in a country can also affect the responses and may induce some cultural biases.

Research has been conducted to find out whether there is a pan-cultural scale. The semantic-differential scale seems to come closest to being a truly pan-cultural scale. It consistently gives similar results in terms of concepts or dimensions that are used to evaluate stimuli, and also accounts for a major portion of the variation in response when it is administered in different countries. An alternative approach that has been attempted is to apply techniques that use a base referent, a self-defined cultural norm. This type of approach is likely to be particularly useful in evaluating attitudinal positions where evidence exists to suggest that these are defined relative to the dominant cultural norm.

Another issue that is important in international research is whether response formats, particularly their calibration, need to be adapted for specific countries and cultures. For example, in France a 20-point scale is commonly used to rate performance in primary and secondary schools. Consequently, it has been suggested that 20-point scales should also be used in marketing research. In general, verbal scales are more effective among less educated respondents, but a more appropriate procedure for illiterate respondents would be scales with pictorial stimuli. For example, in the case of lifestyle, pictures of different lifestyle segments may be shown to the respondents, and they may be asked to indicate how similar they perceive themselves to be to the one in the picture. Some other devices such as the funny faces and the thermometer scale are also used among less educated respondents.

Therefore, based on the type of research and the attribute that is being measured, the type of scale can be used accordingly. Ultimately, the researcher's choice will be shaped by (1) the specific information that is required to satisfy the research objectives, (2) the adaptability of the scale to the data collection method and budget constraints, and (3) the compatibility of the scale with the structure of the respondent's attitude. While in domestic marketing research the issues with respect to scales may not be high, in an international marketing research, researchers have to face an important issue—the issue of equivalence. Specifically, this issue arises when there is a need to compare results across countries.

SUMMARY

This chapter has dealt with attitudes, defined as the mental orientation of individuals that structures the way they respond to their environment. This concept is useful to marketers only to the extent that the various components of attitudes can be measured "accurately."

Measurement was defined here as the assignment of numbers to objects or persons to represent quantities of their attributes. The problem is to establish how to assign numbers. This leads to an examination of the properties of different scales of measurement—nominal, ordinal, interval, ratio—and establishes a useful basis for

evaluating various attitude scales, including itemized-category, rank-order, semantic-differential, Thurstone, and Likert scales. Each of these methods involves a direct self-report, which means that they should be supplemented with the behavioral and indirect measures discussed in Chapter 8.

To this point we have not been explicit as to what is meant by an "accurate" measurement of any kind. Intuitively it means freedom from error. More formally, an accurate measure is both valid and reliable.

QUESTIONS AND PROBLEMS

11.1 Advertising is an expenditure that ultimately must be justified in terms of its effect on sales and profits, yet most evaluations of advertising are in terms of the effects on attitudes. How do you account for this apparent mismatch?

11.2 What is measurement? What are the scales of measurement and what information is provided by each?

11.3 For each of the following, identify the type of scale and justify your answer.

(a) During which season of the year were you born?
_____ Winter _____ Spring
_____ Summer _____ Fall

(b) How satisfied are you with the Ford Taurus that you have bought?
_____ Very satisfied
_____ Neither satisfied
        nor dissatisfied
_____ Dissatisfied
_____ Satisfied
_____ Very dissatisfied

(c) On average, how many cigarettes do you smoke in a day?
_____ Over 1 pack
_____ ½ pack to 1 pack
_____ Less than ½ pack

(d) Rank the following according to your preference:
_____ Tide _____ Bold
_____ Wisk _____ Cheer
_____ Surf

11.4 One trend that is expected to have a large impact on marketing is the aging of the baby-boom population. This aging will likely result in changing consumer attitudes in a variety of areas. What types of attitude changes would be of most interest or concern to a product manager for a branded food product?

11.5 How would you select a set of phrases or adjectives for use in a semantic-differential scale to evaluate the image of banks and other consumer financial institutions? Would the procedure differ if you were going to use a Likert scale?

11.6 Develop a battery of attitude scales to predict whether or not people who currently smoke will try to quit smoking within the next year.

11.7 Suppose that paired-comparison choices of most-preferred brand were made among three brands (A, B, and C) by a sample of 100 respondents. The results of 25 choosing A and 75 choosing B would be represented as $A_{25}B_{75}$. One possible set of results from the three paired comparisons might be $A_{50}B_{50}$, $B_{50}C_{50}$, and $A_{50}C_{50}$. Is this set of results consistent with any one of the following results of the choice of most preferred brand from an array of the three brands? Why?

$$A_{25}B_{25}C_{50}$$
$$A_{33}B_{33}C_{33}$$
$$A_{50}B_{0}C_{50}$$

11.8 Under what circumstances can attitude measures be expected to be good predictors of subsequent behavior? Is there any value to measuring attitudes in situations where attitudes are likely to be poor predictors?

11.9 Explain the concepts of reliability and validity in your own words. What is the relationship between them?

11.10 Develop a multiple-item scale to measure students' attitudes toward the present system of grading. How would you assess the reliability and validity of this scale?

11.11 In March 1977 (during an "energy crisis",) the U.S. Federal Energy Administration (FEA) conducted a personal interview survey of a sample of homes where there was a heating load (that is, the outside temperature was below 65°F). The average indoor temperature of these homes, as measured by a calibrated thermometer, was 70°F + or −2°F during the day and 69°F + or −2°F at night. This represented little or no change from the previous two years; yet, during an independent telephone survey, the FEA found that people said they were keeping their homes at 66°F during the day and 64°F at night.

(a) What are some of the possible hypotheses for this difference between stated and actual temperatures?

(b) What questions would you ask during a telephone survey to clarify the stated house temperature and learn about people's attitudes toward reducing the house temperature?

11.12 In February 1975, the Gallup poll asked, "Do you approve or disapprove of the way Ford is handling his job as president?" and found that 55 percent approved and 28 percent disapproved. A Harris poll at the same time asked, "How do you rate the job President Ford is doing as president—excellent, pretty good, only fair, or poor?" Forty-six percent gave "positive" responses (excellent or pretty good), and 52 percent were negative (only fair or poor). How do you explain the differences? What are the implications of your explanation for public opinion polls as guides to political leaders?

11.13 It has been said that for decisional research purposes, the investigator is interested in predictive validity, to the exclusion of reliability or any other kind of validity. Do you agree? Explain.

11.14 Carter Toys, the U.S.-based manufacturer of the popular PollyDolly, feels that a strong sales potential exists for the doll in foreign markets. The management has identified the selection of suitable foreign country markets as being its first priority. Worldwide Research Corp. has been employed to conduct a survey of the three countries that are currently under consideration: The United Kingdom, Japan, and Kenya.

(a) Can the same questionnaire be used to survey all three countries? Give reasons for your answer.

(b) What factors must be considered in selecting a suitable scale to be used in each country?

(c) Recommend the most suitable scale for use in each country.

11.15 Ben Gatsby is a jewelry craftsman who specializes in high-quality religious artifacts. Recently, he has received a growing number of requests from customers for nonreligious artifacts and is considering expanding his product line to meet this new demand. Mr Gatsby has decided to contact a local marketing research company to solicit help in formulating a marketing strategy for the new product development. They inform him that the first task is to establish whether an unmet demand exists for the nonreligious items. They suggest that in order to evaluate consumers' jewelry purchase behavior, an attitudinal study should be undertaken. Mr Gatsby does not understand why attitudes have to be measured when he is interested only in the consumers' behavior. Imagine you are the marketing research consultant and explain to Mr Gatsby the rationale behind this research method.

11.16 **(a)** How are attitude rating scales most commonly applied in marketing research?

(b) What decisions must a researcher make in designing a single-item scale for these purposes?

END NOTES

1. S. E. Ballou, "Effective Research Requires a Good (Measurement of) Attitude," *Marketing News*, 31, September 1997, p. 15.

2. M. Lodge, *Magnitude Scaling: Quantitative Measurement of Opinions*, Beverly Hills, CA: Sage, 1981.

3. C. E. Osgood, G. Suci, and P. Tannenbaum, *The Measurement of Meaning*, Urbana, IL: University of Illinois Press, 1957.

4. E. P. Cox, "The Optimal Number of Response Alternatives for a Scale: A Review," *Journal of Marketing Research*, 17, November 1980, pp. 407–422.

5. A. B. Blankership, "Let's Bury Paired Comparisons," *Journal of Advertising Research*, 6, March 1966, pp. 13–17.

6. J. P. Guilford, *Psychometric Methods*, New York: McGraw-Hill, 1954.

7. M. M. Givon and Z. Shapira, "Response to Rating Scales: A Theoretical Model and Its Application to the Number of Categories Problem," *Journal of Marketing Research*, 21, November 1984, pp. 410–419.

8. H. H. Friedman and J. R. Leefer, "Label versus Position in Rating Scales," *Journal of the Academy of Marketing Science*, 9, Spring 1981, pp. 88–92; R. I. Haley and P. B. Case, "Testing Thirteen Attitude Scales for Agreement and Brand Discrimination," *Journal of Marketing*, Fall 1979, pp. 20–32.

9. See, for instance, N. Bradburn and C. Miles, "Vague Quantifiers," *Public Opinion Quarterly*, 43, Spring 1979, pp. 92–101.

10. R. I. Haley and P. B. Case, "Testing Thirteen Attitude Scales for Agreement and Brand Discrimination," *Journal of Marketing*, 43, Fall 1979, pp. 20–32.

11. C. A. Moser and G. Kalton, *Survey Method in Social Investigation*, 2nd ed., London: Heinemann, 1971.

12. N. K. Malhotra, "A Scale to Measure Self-Concepts, Person Concepts and Product Concepts," *Journal of Marketing Research*, 18, November 1981, pp. 456–464.

13. The scale was developed originally by Osgood et al. (see Note 04) as a method for measuring the meaning of an object to an individual. They explored a wide variety of adjective pairs that were sufficiently general to be applicable to diverse concepts and objects. From their results they identified three dominant dimensions along which judgments are made, and labeled them the evaluative, potency, and activity dimensions.

14. Several methods for eliciting attribute descriptors are described by J. Dickson and G. Albaum, "A Method for Developing Tailor-Made Semantic Differentials for Specific Marketing Content Areas," *Journal of Marketing Research*, 14, February 1977, pp. 87–91.

15. D. Menezes and N. F. Elbert, "Alternative Semantic Scaling Formats for Measuring Store Image: An Evaluation," *Journal of Marketing Research*, 16, February 1979, pp. 80–87.

16. J. A. Martilla and J. C. James, "Importance–Performance Analysis," *Journal of Marketing*, 41, January 1977, pp. 77–79.

17. F. M. Andrews, "Construct Validity and Error Components of Survey Measures," *Public Opinion Quarterly*, 48, Summer 1984, p. 432.

18. J. P. Peter, "Reliability: A Review of Psychometric Basis and Recent Marketing Practices," *Journal of Marketing Research*, 16, February 1979, pp. 6–17.

19. For a discussion of *generalizability* theory and its applications in marketing research, see J. O. Rentz, "Generalizability Theory: A Comprehensive Method for Assessing and Improving the Dependability of Marketing Measures," *Journal of Marketing Research*, 24, February 1987, pp. 19–28.

20. Most international research studies conducted use different kinds of scales in their research. A few recent examples are D. C. Fieldman and D. C. Thomas, "Career Management Issues Facing Expatriates," *Journal of Business Studies*, Second Quarter 1992; E. Naumann, "Organizational Predictors of Expatriate Job Satisfaction," *Journal of Business Studies*, First Quarter 1993, 24, pp. 61–81.

Case 11-1 ||| National Kitchens

For several years the management of National Kitchens, a diversified packaged-foods manufacturer, had been watching the rapid growth in sales of microwave ovens. They were particularly interested in the prospects for ready-to-eat soup in glass jars. The attraction of glass packaging was that the soup could be heated in a microwave oven in its original container. However, a single-serving, ready-to-eat soup in a glass jar was expected to cost $1.10 as compared to $0.90 for a comparable canned soup. While the price premium for glass was thought to be excessive, there were some new data on the acceptability of this price premium that had just been provided by a glass manufacturer.

The Research Study

The glass manufacturer had designed a brief questionnaire to evaluate consumer attitudes to glass packaging for a variety of microwave-oven cooking jobs. This questionnaire was mailed to 600 names obtained from the warranty cards returned to one microwave oven manufacturer. The results had just been tabulated and were being shown to National Kitchens.

The questionnaire obtained information on microwave usage. Two key questions addressed the issue of ready-to-eat soup in glass directly:

15. Would you purchase ready-to-eat soup in a single-serving container (approximately 10 ounces) that could be put directly into your microwave oven and poured into a bowl after heating? Assume the same price per serving as canned soup.

    ☐ Yes About how many individual servings per month

    _____

    ☐ No Why not? _____

16. Please review question 15 and indicate below whether or not you would be willing to pay 20 cents more per individual serving for the product.

    ☐ Yes

    ☐ No

Of the 600 questionnaires, 312 were returned. The responses to questions 15 and 16 that related to soup in glass are summarized in Table 11.4.

Table 11.4 Summary of Question Responses

Number of servings per month	Q. 15: No. of responses	Q. 16: No. responding that they would pay 20 cents more per serving
0 ("No")	103	185 = would not pay 20 cents more
2	12	7
3	5	3
4	26	19
5	9	6
6–10	31	14
11–15	19	9
16–20	56	38
21–30	11	9
31–40	17	8
41–50	14	10
50+	1	1

Questions for Discussion

1. What have you learned about the potential market for soup in glass jars?

2. What else would you like to know?

3. How else would you assess people's attitudes toward this concept?

Designing the Questionnaire

LEARNING OBJECTIVES

- Discuss the concept of questionnaire design.
- Describe how to format question.
- Discuss how to deal with sensitive questions.
- Discuss how the sequence and layout decisions impact ease of use and order bias.
- Discuss the issues of questionnaire design in an international context.

The ultimate and most important effect of marketing intelligence is reflected in business decision making. To get the right information to make the right decision, one has to ask the right questions to the right audience. Questionnaire construction is properly regarded as a very imperfect art. There are no established procedures that will lead consistently to a "good" questionnaire. One consequence is that the range of potential error contributed by ambiguous questions may be as much as 20 or 30 percentage points.[1] Fortunately, such extreme errors can be reduced sharply by common sense and insights from the experience of other researchers. A major objective of this chapter is to present systematically the "rules of thumb" that have been acquired with experience.

A good questionnaire accomplishes the research's objectives. Surveys must be custom-built to the specification of given research purposes, and they are much more than a collection of unambiguous questions. A number of constraints are imposed on the development of an appropriate questionnaire. For example, the number, form, and ordering of the specific questions are partly determined by the data collection method. The respondent's willingness and ability to answer, discussed in Chapter 9, also influences the final questionnaire format. That wording and sequence of questions can facilitate recall and motivate more accurate responses.

Although each questionnaire must be designed with the specific research objectives in mind, there is a sequence of logical steps that every researcher must follow to develop a good questionnaire:

1. Plan what to measure.

2. Formulate questions to obtain the needed information.

3. Decide on the order and wording of questions and on the layout of the questionnaire.

4. Using a small sample, test the questionnaire for omissions and ambiguity.

5. Correct the problems (and pretest again, if necessary).

We will use this sequence to organize the remainder of this chapter. Figure 12.1 gives a flowchart for this process.

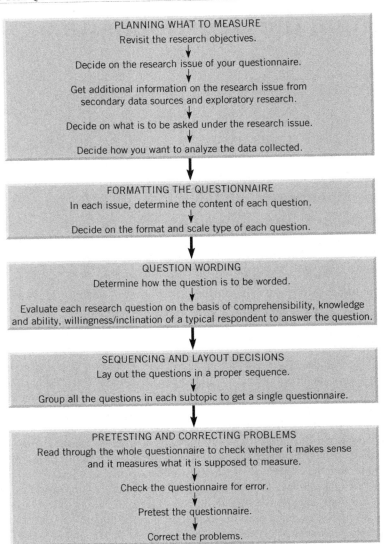

FIGURE 12.1
The Process of Questionnaire Design.

Planning What to Measure

The most difficult step is specifying exactly what information is to be collected from each respondent. Poor judgment and lack of thought at this stage may mean that the results are not relevant to the research purpose or that they are incomplete. Both problems are expensive and may seriously diminish the value of the study.

To combat the lack of relevance problem, it is necessary to ask constantly, "How will this information be used?," and ultimately to anticipate the specific analyses that will be made. It is also important to have a clear idea of the target population. Questions that are appropriate for college students may not be appropriate for homemakers. Understanding is related to respondent socioeconomic characteristics.[2]

When a questionnaire is sent into the field that is incomplete in important aspects, the error is irreversible. To avoid this awful situation, careful thought is required; this is facilitated by the following:

1. Clear research objectives, which describe as fully as possible the kind of information the decision maker needs, the hypotheses, and the scope of the research

2. Exploratory research, which will suggest further relevant variables and help the researcher absorb the vocabulary and point of view of the typical respondent

3. Experience with similar studies

4. Pretesting of preliminary versions of the questionnaire

Translating Research Objectives into Information Requirements

At the end of Chapter 4, we saw how the research objectives for the HMO study were established. These objectives are summarized in Table 12.1. Before individual questionnaire items can be written, these objectives have to be translated into specific information requirements. Here is where the hypotheses play an especially important role. Since hypotheses suggest possible answers to the questions implied by the research objectives, there must be questionnaire items that could elicit those possible answers. For example, the HMO study included specific hypotheses as to which characteristics or features of a health plan would influence the choice of plan. Each of these characteristics needed to be represented by a question, so that the hypotheses could be tested. The questions also need to be of the appropriate scale type in order to do the desired type of analysis. For example, if the goal is to see whether satisfaction with the plan is correlated with overall evaluation, both questions would need to be asked using at least an interval scale. From the information requirements specified on the right-hand side of Table 12.1, one can see how the process advances.

Table 12.1   Research Objectives for HMO Study

Research objectives	Information requirements
1. What is the probable demand for the proposed HMO?	1. General attitudes and awareness with respect to health care and the concept of prepaid plans; and specific attitudes and knowledge regarding existing health plans.
2. Which market segments will be most interested in the proposed HMO?	2. Process by which the present plan was selected; sources of information and influences.
3. What will be the probable rate of utilization of medical services by the most interested segment?	3. Satisfaction with present plan (a) overall (b) with respect to specific characteristics of the plan, and (c) intentions to change.
4. Which aspects of health plans have the greatest influence on the choice process?	4. Reaction to proposed HMO design a. overall evaluation b. evaluation of specific characteristics c. preference, compared to present plan d. likelihood of adoption e. influence of changes in price and benefits
	5. Classification variables including demographics; distance from HMO; time in area; expected stay in area; and utilization of medical services by individual family members.

Formatting the Question

Before specific questions can be phrased, a decision has to be made as to the degree of freedom to be given to respondents in answering the question. The alternatives are (1) open-ended with no classification, where the interviewer tries to record the response verbatim; (2) open-ended, where the interviewer uses precoded classifications to record the response; or (3) the closed, or structured, format, in which a question or supplementary card presents the responses the respondent may consider.[3] These options can be illustrated by the following brief sequence of questions from a personal interview survey:

Q10   Is there any particular type of information about life insurance that you would like to have, that you do not now have, or don't know enough about?

Q11   What kind of information?

PROBE   What else?

The first question uses a precoded classification, since a "yes" or "no" answer is strongly implied. The second question is completely open-ended, and the goal is to achieve an exact transcription. Only 20 percent of a national sample said "Yes" to question 10, and 44 percent of these responded only in very general terms to the follow-up question. This meant that only 11 percent of the total sample said they had a need for specific information, such as rates, or family benefits in case of disability or accident. It is likely that different results would have been obtained if either Q10 or Q11 had been converted to a closed-ended response, such that respondents were handed a card describing many different kinds of information and asked to indicate which they would like to have or didn't know enough about.

Open-Response Questions

There are advantages and disadvantages to **open-response** (or **unstructured) questions**. The advantages stem from the wide range of responses that can be obtained and the lack of influence in the responses from prespecified categories. Respondents often appreciate this freedom, as illustrated by the surprising frequency with which people write marginal comments in mail surveys when they don't feel the response categories capture their feelings adequately. Because of these advantages, open-ended questions are useful in the following circumstances:

- As an introduction to a survey or to a topic. A question such as, "In general, how do you feel about (color TV, this neighborhood, the bus service in this area)," will acquaint the respondent with the subject of the survey, open the way for more specific questions, and make the respondent more comfortable with the questioning process.

- When it is important to measure the salience of an issue to a respondent. (Asking "What do you think is the most important problem facing this country today?" will give some insight into what currently is bothering the respondent.)

- When there are too many possible responses to be listed, or they cannot be foreseen; for example, "What were some of the reasons why you decided to pay cash (for a major appliance purchase?)" or "What do you especially like about living in this neighborhood?"

- When verbatim responses are desired to give the flavor of people's answers or to cite as examples in a report.

- When the behavior to be measured is sensitive or disapproved (such as estimates of drinking or sexual activities). Reported frequencies are higher on an open format where there are no prespecified response categories. When respondents are given a choice of a low-frequency category on a closed format, they are less willing to admit to higher frequencies.[4]

The disadvantages of open-response or open-ended questions are numerous. The major problem is that variability in the clarity and depth of responses depends to a great extent on (1) the articulateness of the respondent in an interview situation, or the willingness to compose a written answer to a mail survey, and (2) the personal or telephone interviewer's ability to record the verbatim answers quickly—or to summarize accurately—and to probe effectively. A third area arose in Chapter 9, where we saw that the interviewer's expectations will influence what is selected for recording or when to stop probing. Open-ended questions are also time consuming, both during the interview and during tabulation. Classifications must be established to summarize the responses, and each answer must be assigned to one or more categories. This involves subjective judgments that are prone to error. To minimize this source of error it may be desirable to have two editors independently categorize the responses and compare their results. This adds further to the cost.

Another problem that occurs frequently in an open-ended question is that the answer given to it expands or contracts, depending on the space or time available for it. When students are given a full page for a question, they have a tendency to fill up the whole page. If only half a page is left, they will write the answer in the space available. Open-ended questions must be designed so that the available answer space and time coincide with question importance.

In addition, respondents may not always use the same frame of reference when answering an open-ended question, and these different frames of reference may not be readily discernible by the researcher. This problem is illustrated in the results of an experiment on work values that compared the following two questions:[5]

Q1 People look for different things in a job. What would you most prefer in a job?

Q2 People look for different things in a job. Which one of the following five things would you most prefer in a job?

1. Work that pays well

2. Work that gives a sense of accomplishment

3. Work where there is not too much supervision and you make most decisions by yourself

4. Work that is pleasant and where the other people are nice to work with

5. Work that is steady with little chance of being laid off

In the open-response format, many respondents said that pay was the most important aspect of a job. There was evidence that some of them meant "high pay," whereas others meant "steady pay." Since both answers were expressed in the same words, it was impossible to separate the two different frames of reference. Answers to the closed-response format did not have this problem, since "work that pays well" and "work that is steady" were two distinct options. Open-response questions run the risk that the researcher may not always be able to tap differences among respondents accurately.

In view of the disadvantages and the lack of convincing evidence that open-ended questions provide more meaningful, relevant, and nonrepetitive responses, it is advisable to close up as many questions as possible in large-scale surveys.

Closed-Response Questions

There are two basic formats for **closed-ended** (or **structured**) **questions**. The first asks respondents to make one or more choices from a list of possible responses. The second is a rating scale like those discussed in Chapter 11 where the respondent is given a continuum of labeled categories that represents the range of responses. Research organizations, such as McCollum/Spielman, use both formats to ask diagnostic questions about commercials—both the message (theme, basic idea, and unique selling point) and the presentation (setting, demonstration devices, music, etc.). The following sample of ad testing questions illustrates what can be done.

Choice from a List of Responses
Which one of the following words or phrases best describes the kind of person you feel would be most likely to use this product, based on what you saw and heard in this commercial?

_____ *Young*	_____ *Single*
_____ *Old*	_____ *Married*
_____ *Modern*	_____ *Homemaker*
_____ *Old-fashioned*	_____ *Career woman*

Appropriate Single-Choice Rating on a Scale
Please tell us your overall reaction to this commercial.

_____ *A great commercial, would like to see it again*

_____ *A pretty good commercial*

_____ *Just so-so, like a million others*

_____ *Another bad commercial*

Based on what you saw and heard in this commercial, how interested do you feel you would be in buying the product?

_____ *Definitely would buy*

_____ *Probably would buy*

_____ *May or may not buy*

_____ *Probably would not buy*

_____ *Definitely would not buy*

Here is a statement about world peace. "World leaders are basically working to establish peace between countries." Do you agree, disagree, or do you not have an opinion about that?

_____ *Definitely agree*

_____ *Moderately agree*

_____ *Neither agree nor disagree*

_____ *Moderately disagree*

_____ *Definitely disagree*

_____ *No opinion*

Regardless of the type of closed-response format, the advantages are the same. Such questions are easier to answer, in both an interview and a mail survey; they require less effort by the interviewer; and they make tabulation and analysis easier. There is less potential error due to differences in the way questions are asked and responses recorded. Normally, a closed-response question takes less time than an equivalent open-ended question. Perhaps the most significant advantage of these questions in large-scale surveys is that the answers are directly comparable from respondent to respondent (assuming each interprets the words the same way). Comparability of respondents is an essential prelude to the use of any analytical methods.

There are significant limitations to closed-response questions. There is considerable disagreement among researchers on the type of response categories that should be listed. One area of controversy is whether middle alternatives should be included in the questions. It is not unusual for 20 percent of respondents to choose a middle alternative when it is offered, although they would not have volunteered this answer had it not been mentioned. Hence, if one wants to design questions that will help make a clear, actionable decision, it is best not to include the neutral category in the question.

One way of handling this problem is to include a "don't know" alternative, so that respondents are not forced to choose one opinion. Another way of handling this distortion of responses is by providing a scale that captures intensity of a respondent's feeling about a particular question.[6] The measurement of intensity is useful as a follow-up not only for items with logical middle positions but for attitude questions generally. Strength of feeling has been shown to predict both attitude stability and attitude consistency. Two of the most commonly used intensity indicators are the Likert and semantic-differential scales.

Another potential limitation of the closed-response question arises from the fact that an answer will be received for a question, no matter how irrelevant the question is in that context.[7] Hence, if a large number of categories are included in the closed-response question, all the categories will receive a certain percentage of responses. This may not produce meaningful results. Therefore, care should be taken to include only relevant categories. A N/A choice should also be included.

An extreme form of the closed-ended question is the dichotomous question. A dichotomous question has only two response categories. For example,

Sex:

_____ *Male*   _____ *Female*

Dichotomous questions are used mainly to collect demographic and behavioral data when only two answers logically exist. They are not used to collect psychological data because they tend to provide oversimplified, often forced, answers. Dichotomous questions are also prone to a large amount of measurement errors; because alternatives are polarized, the wide range of possible choices between the poles is omitted.

A researcher must constantly strive to overcome the many limitations of closed-response questions. First, good questions are hard to develop, and exploratory work is necessary to ensure that all potentially important response alternatives are included. In one experiment, respondents were first asked who should manage company benefit funds, the company, the union, or government. When these three alternatives were given, only 15 percent of the respondents suggested combinations. However, when the combinations were mentioned explicitly, the number choosing these alternatives jumped to 52 percent.[8] Second, the very nature of rigid closed responses provides fewer opportunities for self-expression or subtle qualifications, and they are not nearly so involving for the respondent.

Finally, the list of alternative response categories provides answers that respondents might not have considered. In this situation, the respondent might choose a "responsible" alternative. The respondent may also try to avoid a difficult choice or judgment by selecting the easiest alternative, such as "don't know." Where there is a distinct possibility of such biasing occurring in a personal or telephone interview survey, it may be desirable to precede the closed-response question with an open-response question. This is done often in brand-name awareness studies. The respondent is asked first what brands are associated with the product (unaided recall) and then is given a list of brands and asked to choose those that are known (aided recall).

Number of Response Categories

The number of categories can range from a two-point scale all the way to a 100-point scale. Some questions—especially those dealing with points of fact—admit only two possible answers: Did you purchase a new car in the past year? Did you vote in the last election? However, in most situations, a dichotomous question will yield misleading results. Sometimes an either/or choice is not possible, and the correct answer may be both. In a survey of shaving habits, the question was asked, "Do you shave with an electric razor or a safety razor?" Some people apparently use both, the specific choice depending on the situation.[9] Attitudinal questions invariably have intermediate positions. A simple question such as "Are you considering changing your present health insurance plan?" revealed that 70 percent were not, 8 percent definitely were, and the remaining 22 percent were uncertain or might consider a change in the future. These subtleties are very important in interpreting such a question.

As a general rule, the range of opinion on most issues can be captured best with five or seven categories. Five categories are probably the minimum needed to discriminate effectively among individuals. One popular five-point scale is the Likert scale. This number of categories can be read by the interviewer and understood by the respondent. A seven- or nine-category scale is more precise but cannot be read to respondents with the assurance that they won't get confused.

Multiple-choice questions present special problems. Ideally, the response categories provided for such questions should be mutually exclusive and should exhaust the possibilities. Sometimes it is neither possible nor desirable to include all the possible alternatives. A listing of all the brands in a houseware's product category, such as hand mixers, might include 50 or more names if all distributor-controlled and import brands are included. Since this is impractical, only the top five or six are listed, and the rest are consigned to an "other" category, which is accompanied by a "please specify" request and a space to enter the brand name.

A common type of question requires numerical data in response: What is your annual income? How far is it to your work? How many stores did you visit? Usually, it is preferable to group the possible answers into categories; for example, under $4,000, $4,000 to $7,000, . . ., $20,000, and over. This is a somewhat less sensitive way of asking an income question and facilitates coding. If the numbers falling in the response categories are not known or it is important to know the exact number (of children, pets, etc.) for later analysis, this does not apply.

Order of Response Categories

The order of presentation of categories to respondents in personal or telephone interview situations sometimes can have a big influence on results. A classic study in 1974 provided clear evidence for this. One way of asking a person's income over the telephone is to start by asking "Is your income more than $2,000?" and increasing the figure in increments of $2,000 until the first "no" response. Alternatively, one can start with the highest income category and drop the figure until the first "yes" response. The study found that the median income when the first category was $2,000 was $12,711; however, when the income question started with the high category, $17,184 was the median income.[10] One explanation for this remarkable difference is that respondents find the question threatening and try to get it out of the way by making a premature terminal response. A much better approach is to begin with the median income figure and use a series of branching questions, such as, "Is it over (the median income)?" and if the answer is "No," then asking, "Is it under (half the median income)?" and so forth. This gives a relatively unbiased measure of income and the lowest proportion of refusals.

Another ordering problem is encountered with self-administered survey questions, in which respondents tend to select categories that are in the middle position of a range of values. This is especially prevalent with questions of fact, such as the number of checkouts at a local store. Respondents who do not know the answer will choose the center position as a safe guess. This also can happen with questions about information that is unique to the respondent, such as the distance to the nearest department store. When the question is constructed with multiple categories, with the middle category representing an estimate of the average distance, the natural tendency to choose the middle position may lead to inaccurate responses. One solution is to place the average or expected distance at various positions in the sequence of categories.[11]

Handling Uncertainty and Ignorance

One awkward question concerns the handling of "don't know" and neutral responses. There are many reasons why respondents do not know the answer to a question, such as not knowing, forgetting, or an inability to articulate. If an explicit "don't know" response category is provided, it is an easy option for those in the latter group. But often "don't know" is a legitimate response and may yield very important insights. Thus, the option always should be provided as a response to questions about knowledge or opinions when there is some likelihood of ignorance or forgetting. Sometimes, this response category is used by those who are unwilling to answer a question. In personal and telephone interviews, it may be advisable to provide the interviewer with an additional "no answer" category to identify these people correctly. A neutral response category such as "not sure" or "neither like nor dislike" also may be desirable for those people who genuinely can't make a choice among specific opinion statements. In certain cases, an N/A category should be included.

If there is likelihood of both ambivalence and ignorance, then both a neutral category and a "don't know" category are appropriate.

Using Both Open-Response and Closed-Response Questions

The choice between open- and closed-response questions is not necessarily an either/or distinction. Open-response questions can be used in conjunction with closed-response questions to provide additional information. Using an open-response question to follow up a closed-response question is called a *probe*. Probes can efficiently combine some advantages of both open and closed questions. They can be used for specific prechosen questions or to obtain additional information from only a subset of people who respond to previous questions in a certain way. A common example of the latter is to ask respondents who choose "none of the above" a follow-up question to expand on their answer.

There are two general purposes for the use of probes in a questionnaire. The first is to pinpoint questions that were particularly difficult for respondents. Adequate pretesting of questions reduces this need to use probes. The second purpose is to aid researcher interpretation of respondent answers. Answers to open-response follow-ups can provide valuable guidance in the analysis of closed-response questions.

Question Wording: A Problem of Communication

The wording of particular questions can have a large impact on how a respondent interprets them. Even small changes in wording can shift respondent answers, but it is difficult to know in advance whether or not a wording change will have such an effect. Our knowledge of how to phrase questions that are free from ambiguity and bias is such that it is easier to discuss what not to do than it is to give prescriptions. Hence, the following guidelines are of greatest value in critically evaluating and improving an existing question.

1. *Is the vocabulary simple, direct, and familiar to all respondents?* The challenge is to choose words that can be understood by all respondents, regardless of education level, but that do not sound patronizing. The most common pitfall is to use technical jargon or specialized terms. Many respondents will not be able to identify their "marital status," but they can say

whether they are married, single, divorced, and so forth. Special care must be taken to avoid words that have different meanings for different groups. This can be readily appreciated in cross-cultural studies, where translation problems are profound, but it is also applicable within a country. One socioeconomic group may refer to the evening meal as dinner, while others call this meal supper and have their dinner at noon.

2. *Do any words have vague or ambiguous meanings?* A common error is not giving the respondent an adequate frame of reference, in time and space, for interpreting the question. Words such as "often," "occasionally," and "usually" lack an appropriate time referent, so respondents choose their own, with the result that answers are not comparable. Similarly, the appropriate space or locale often is not specified. Does the question, "How long have you lived here?" refer to this state, county, city, neighborhood, or particular house or apartment? Some words have many interpretations; thus, a respondent might interpret income to mean hourly pay rate, weekly salary, or monthly income, either before or after taxes and deductions, and could include or exclude sources of income other than wages and the incomes of other family members.

3. *Are any questions "double-barreled"?* There are questions in which a respondent can agree with one part of the question but not the other, or cannot answer at all without accepting a particular assumption. In either case, the answers cannot be interpreted. For example, what can be learned from such questions as, "Do you plan to leave your job and look for another one during the coming year?" or, "Are you satisfied with the cost and convenience of this (service)?" The second type of error is a bit more elusive to find, as the following example from a Harris poll demonstrates. The question was, "Have you often, sometimes, hardly ever, or never felt bad because you were unfaithful to your wife?" One percent said often, 14 percent said sometimes or hardly ever, and 85 percent said they never felt bad because of this.

4. *Are any questions leading or loaded?* A leading question is one that clearly suggests the answer or reveals the researcher's (or interviewer's) opinion. This can be done easily by adding "don't you agree?" or "wouldn't you say?" to a desired statement. A loaded question introduces a more subtle bias. A common type of loading of possible responses is through failure to provide a full range of alternatives—for example, by asking, "How do you generally spend your free time—watching television, or what?" Another way to load a question is to provide the respondent with a reason for one of the alternatives: "Should we increase taxes in order to get more housing and better schools, or should we keep them about the same?" A second form of loading results from the use of emotionally charged words. These are words or phrases such as "fair profits," "radical," or "luxury items," which have such strong positive or negative overtones that they overshadow the specific content of the question. Organizations and groups also have emotional associations, and using them to endorse a proposition will certainly bias the response: "A committee of experts has suggested . . .; Do you approve of this, or do you disagree?" For this reason, it is also risky to reveal the sponsor of the study. If one brand or company is identified as the sponsor, the respondents will tend to exaggerate their positive feelings toward the brand.

   Questions that involve appeals or threats to the respondent's self-esteem may also be loaded.[12] A question on occupations usually will produce more "executives" if the respondent chooses from one of a small number of occupational categories rather than being asked for a specific job title.

5. *Are the instructions potentially confusing?* Sheatsley[13] counsels against lengthy questions that explain a complicated situation to a respondent and then ask for an opinion. In his experience, "If the respondent is not aware of these facts, you have probably confused or

biased him more than you have enlightened him, and his opinion won't mean much in either case." The question should be directed more toward measuring the respondent's knowledge or interest in the subject.

6. *Is the question applicable to all respondents?* Respondents may try to answer a question even though they don't qualify to do so or may lack an opinion. Examples of such questions are "What is your present occupation?" (assumes respondent is working), "Where did you live before you moved here?" (assumes a prior move), or "For whom did you vote in the last election?" (assumes that respondent voted). The solution to this is to ask a qualifying or filter question and limit further questioning to those who qualify.

7. *Are the questions of an appropriate length?* It is not always the case that shorter questions are better, although one common rule of thumb is to keep the number of words in any question under 20. Under certain circumstances, a question may have to be long in order to avoid ambiguity, but this should be the exception rather than the rule. A questionnaire filled with long questions is more fatiguing to answer and more difficult to understand.

Whenever there is doubt as to the appropriate wording, it is desirable to test several alternatives. For instance, the responses to a question may vary with the degree of personalization. The question, "Do you think there should be government-run off-track betting in this state?" is different from "Is it desirable to have government-run off-track betting in this state?" Sometimes the choice can be resolved by the purpose of the study; the impersonal form being preferred if the study aims at measuring the general tenor of public sentiment. Where the choice is not obvious, the best solution is to use one version in half of the questionnaire and the second version in the remaining half. This is known as a *split-ballot technique.* Any significant differences in the results can be helpful in interpreting the meaning of the question.

Asking Sensitive Questions

One can virtually guarantee meaningless responses by directly asking such questions as, "Have you ever defaulted on a credit account?," "Do you smoke pot at least once a week?," or "Have you ever been involved in an unreported automobile accident?" Sometimes, however, a research question will involve sensitive areas. Marketing Research in Action 12.1 gives an idea as to how to probe for confidential information from customers. A variety of approaches can be used to attempt to get honest answers. For example, long, open-ended questions with familiar wording have been found effective when asking threatening questions that require quantified responses. The only limit is the creativity of the researcher. Alan Barton made this point best when in 1958 he composed a parody on ways to ask the question, "Did you kill your wife?"[14] His approach has been adapted to a different situation. Here the respondent is a responsible adult who is being questioned about his or her consumption of Kellogg's Frosted Flakes (a potentially embarrassing situation).

1. *The casual approach:* "Have you eaten Frosted Flakes within the last week?"

2. *The numbered card:* "Would you please read off the number on this card that corresponds to what you had eaten for breakfast in the last week?"
(Hand card to respondent.)

   1. Pancakes
   2. Frosted Flakes
   3. Other (what)?

(GET CARD BACK FROM RESPONDENT BEFORE PROCEEDING!)

Marketing Research In Action 12.1

■ HOW TO ASK SENSITIVE QUESTIONS

An environment of mutual trust is necessary if respondents are to be forthcoming with personal and intimate details. The interviewer should be given relevant training and should have sufficient time to make the respondents comfortable. Care should also be taken to populate the questions with noncontroversial words.

A casual and natural approach to asking sensitive questions, such as ones involving personal financial information, is necessary to elicit honest responses from respondents. Interviewers who themselves are not comfortable with such questions end up transmitting their own concerns to respondents, increasing the likelihood of indifferent or nonchalant answers.

The question of trust plays an even more important role in Web surveys. Participants will not respond if they have even the slightest suspicion that their information may not be secure. It often boils down to the respondent's perception of the integrity of the person/institution asking the questions. Clarity in conveying the purpose for which the questions are asked also helps allay respondent fears. Relaying this important information in an unambiguous and clear manner is particularly relevant for Web-based surveys.

It is more realistic and less controversial to collect certain types of information from mystery shopping projects or from secondary sources like the Internet. For example, it might be unrealistic to expect respondents to share information about their deposits with your competitor and the interest rates they are getting, even though the information may be being collected for neutral third parties. This is because in an e-mail or on an Internet-based survey, respondents are often unaware of the identity of the organization and its country of operation and the confirmation that their information is being stored. Respondents are aware that there is no directory of e-mail addresses.

For instance, it's unrealistic to expect customers to share with an interviewer the details of pricing arrangements they might have in place with your competitors, even if the information is being collected by a neutral third party. You can sometimes gather this type of information from a mystery shopping project, combined with secondary research from websites, for instance, rather than from individuals. A marketing research questionnaire gives the interviewer the flexibility to ask almost any question. But there is still one question that is totally taboo. Respondents should never get the impression that the organization is trying to sell them its product/service. Questions about whether respondents would allow a sales representative to call on them have to be avoided. These would give respondents the feeling of being cheated into answering. Consequently, the image of the brand or organization drops in their esteem. Such a feeling can also lower their opinion of legitimate marketing research.

Source: G. Humphreys and J. McNeish, "Designing a Questionnaire That Dives Beneath the Surface," Quirk's Marketing Research Review, November 2001, Article 0722.

3. *The everybody approach:* "As you know, many people have been eating Frosted Flakes for breakfast. Do you eat Frosted Flakes?"

4. *The "other people" approach:*
   a. "Do you know of any adult who eats Frosted Flakes?"
   b. "How about yourself?"

5. *The sealed ballot technique:* In this version, you explain that the survey respects people's right to anonymity with respect to their eating habits and that they themselves are to fill out the answer to the question, seal it in an envelope, and drop it in a box conspicuously labeled "sealed ballot box" that is carried by the interviewer.

6. *The Kinsey technique:* Stare firmly into respondent's eyes and ask in simple, clear-cut language such as that to which the respondent is accustomed, and with an air of assuming that everyone has done everything, "Do you eat Frosted Flakes for breakfast?"

Hornik, Zaig, and Shadmon report high rates of refusal to answer questions about sexual behavior, personal income, use of drugs, criminal behavior, and so on. It is suggested that the foot-in-the-door (FITD) technique and the low-ball (LB) technique are both effective in enhancing compliance to requests for information about sensitive topics. However, a combination of these two techniques is more effective than either alone. In the combined technique, subjects first commit to responding to a survey (LB), and then are asked, "While we are on the phone, could you please respond to three short questions concerning personal matters?" (FITD).[15]

Randomized Response Technique

There is good evidence that accurate answers to sensitive questions sometimes can be obtained using the randomized response technique. The respondent is asked to answer one or two randomly selected questions without revealing which question has been answered. One of the questions is sensitive; the other is innocuous, such as, "Does your birthday occur during the month of October?" The respondent selects which of the two questions to answer by flipping a coin or by looking at the last number of his or her driver's license or Social Security card to see if it is odd or even. Since the interviewer records a "yes" or "no" answer without knowing which question has been answered, the respondent feels free to answer honestly.[16]

Suppose a sample of 1,000 respondents has been given a card with two possible questions:

A. Have you smoked marijuana during the past year?
B. Is the last digit of your driver's license equal to seven?

After flipping a coin to choose which question to answer, 30 percent, or 300, respond "yes." How can the proportion who responded "yes" to question A be determined from this information? First, we know that each question has an equal probability of being chosen, because a coin flip was used. Therefore p(question A is chosen) p(question B is chosen) $= 0.5$. In other words, 0.5 times (total sample of 1,000) 500 respondents answered question A, and 500 answered question B. We also can estimate that 10 percent of those answering question B would have said "yes," because they would have had a seven as the last digit of their license. This also means that only 50 of those choosing question B would have answered yes, since 0.10 times 500 = 50. This formula is presented in the following table.

Question	Estimated Sample Size	*	Estimated Percentage "Yes"	=	Estimated Response "Yes"
A. Have you smoked marijuana during the past year?	500	*	?	=	?
B. Is the last digit of your driver's license equal to seven?	500	*	10	=	50
The total population	1,000	*	30	=	300

We also know, however, that 300 respondents actually answered "yes." In order for this to have happened, there must have been 250 respondents who answered "yes" to the sensitive question. Thus we can estimate that 250 / 500 = 50 percent of the sample had smoked marijuana in the past year. To summarize, the unknown proportion, x, answering "yes" to a sensitive question can be determined from the following formula:

$$p\,(\text{yes}) = p(\text{question A is chosen}) * p(\text{yes answer to question A})$$
$$+ \, p(\text{question B is chosen}) * p(\text{yes answer to question B})$$

Therefore,

$$0.30 = (0.50)\,(x) + (0.50)\,(0.10)$$
$$0.50x = 0.30 - 0.05 = 0.25$$
$$x = 0.25\,/\,0.50 = 0.50$$

Sequence and Layout Decisions

The order, or sequence, of questions will be determined initially by the need to gain and maintain the respondent's cooperation and make the questionnaire as easy as possible for the interviewer to administer. Once these considerations are satisfied, attention must be given to the problem of **order bias**—the possibility that prior questions will influence answers to subsequent questions.

The basic guidelines for sequencing a questionnaire to make it interesting and logical to both interviewer and respondent are straightforward.

1. Open the interview with an easy and nonthreatening question. This helps to establish rapport and builds the confidence of the respondent in his or her ability to answer.[17] For most routine interviewing, it is better to start this way than to offer a lengthy explanation of the survey. It may even be desirable to design a throwaway question for this purpose: "We're doing a survey on medical care. The first question is, what do you usually do when you have a cold?"

2. The questionnaire should flow smoothly and logically from one topic to the next. Sudden shifts in topic are to be avoided, as they tend to confuse respondents and cause indecision. When a new topic is introduced, a transition statement or question should be used, explaining how the new topic relates to what has been discussed previously or the purpose of the study.

3. For most topics, it is better to proceed from broad, general questions to the more specific. Thus, one might ask, "What are some of the things you like about this community? What things don't you like?," and proceed to "How about the transportation facilities generally?," and finally to "Should they add another bus or widen the highway?" This funnel approach helps the respondent put the specific question in a broader context and give a more thoughtful answer.

4. Sensitive or difficult questions dealing with income status, ability, and so forth, should not be placed at the beginning of the questionnaire. Rather, they should be introduced at a point where the respondent has developed some trust and confidence in the interviewer and the study. In short interviews, they can be postponed until the end of the questionnaire.

The physical layout of the questionnaire also will influence whether the questionnaire is interesting and easy to administer. For self-administered questionnaires, the quality of the paper, the clarity of reproduction, and the appearance of crowding are important variables. Similarly, the job of the interviewer is considerably eased if the questionnaire is not crowded, if precise instructions are provided, and if flow diagrams with arrows and boxes are used to guide the interviewer through filter questions. The manner in which a typical questionnaire is organized is given in Table 12.2.

Table 12.2 Organization of a Typical Questionnaire

Location	Type	Function	Example
Starting questions	Broad, general questions	To break the ice and establish a rapport with the respondent	Do you own a VCR?
Next few questions	Simple and direct questions	To reassure the respondent that the survey is simple and easy to answer	What brands of VCR did you consider when you bought it?
Questions up to a third of the questionnaire	Focused questions	Relate more to the research objectives and convey to the respondent the area of research	What attributes did you consider when you purchased your VCR?
Major portion of the questionnaire	Focused questions; some may be difficult and complicated	To obtain most of the information required for the research	Rank the following attributes of a VCR based on their importance to you
Last few questions	Personal questions that may be perceived by the respondent as sensitive	To get classification and demographic information about the respondent	What is the highest level of education you have attained?

Order Bias: Does the Question Create the Answer?

We have indicated already that it is usually preferable to ease a respondent into a subject by beginning with some general, orienting questions. However, when the topic is unfamiliar to the respondents—or their involvement with the subject is low or little—the nature of the early questions will significantly affect subsequent answers.

A new-product concept test is the most prevalent example of research on an unfamiliar subject. Respondents typically are given a description of the new product and asked to express their degree of buying interest. As one study showed, however, this interest will depend on the sequence of the preceding questions.[18] The new product was described as a combination pen-and-pencil selling for 99 cents. Four different types of questions were asked of four matched sets of respondents before the buying-interest question was asked:

Questions Preceding Buying-Interest Question	Percentage of Respondents "Very Much Interested" in Buying New Product
1. No question asked	2.8
2. Asked only about advantages	16.7
3. Asked only about disadvantages	0.0
4. Asked about both advantages and disadvantages	5.7

The nature of the preceding questions definitely establishes the frame of reference to be used by the respondent. The issue for the questionnaire designer is to decide which is the most valid frame of reference, that is, which corresponds most closely to the type of thinking that would precede an actual purchase decision in this product category. The same problem confronts survey researchers dealing with social issues that are not of immediate relevance to the respondent. The "cautionary tale" by Charles Raymond in Marketing Research in Action 12.2 shows how questions create answers in these settings.

Marketing Research In Action 12.2

■ WHEN QUESTIONS CREATE ANSWERS

Suppose I were to call you on the telephone as follows: "Hello, this is Charles Raymond of the XYZ Poll. We are trying to find out what people think about certain issues. Do you watch television?"

Whatever your answer, the next question is, "Some people say that oil tankers are spilling oil and killing the fish and want to pass a law against this; do you agree or disagree?" Your answer is duly recorded and the next question is, "Have you ever read or heard anything about this?"

Again, your answer is recorded, and finally I ask, "Do you think anyone should do anything about this? Who? What?"

And now the main question, "I'd like you to rate some companies on a scale from minus five to plus five, minus five if you totally dislike the company, plus five if you totally like it, and zero if you are in between or indifferent. First, U.S. Steel." You give a number and I say, "The gas company." You give another number and I say, "Exxon."

You see what is happening. Or do you? Suppose I now tell you that this form of questioning is given only to a random half of a large sample called the experimental group. To the control group, the interview is as follows:

"Hello, this is Charles Ramond from XYZ Poll. We are trying to find out what people think about certain things. Do you ever watch TV?" You answer and then I ask, "Now I'd like you to rate some companies on a scale from minus five to plus five. . . ." And the difference in the average rating between the experimental and control group can be attributed to them having thought about tankers spilling oil and killing the fish, for that is the only difference in the way the two groups were treated.

Questions Shape the Attitudes

I think you can see for yourselves, merely by following this interview pattern, how you might very well rate companies differently after having rehearsed your "attitude" toward oil pollution than without having done so. In case it is difficult for you to imagine how you would respond under these two conditions, I can assure you that random halves of well-drawn samples of certain elite publics rated large companies very differently, depending on whether they were in the experimental or control group. They did so in survey after survey, consistently over time, thereby showing the reliability of the phenomenon.

Source: C. Raymond, "When Questions Create Answers," Speech to the Annual Meeting, Advertising Research Foundation, New York, May 1977.

Order bias is also a concern when the answer to one question has an obvious implication for the answer to another. Thus, fewer people say their taxes are too high after being asked a series of questions about whether government spending should be increased in various areas.[19] This may be explained in a number of different ways. Respondents may attempt to maintain consistency in their answers. Another explanation is that earlier questions may make some experiences or judgments more salient to the respondent than they would otherwise be. For example, in a study dealing with pricing questions, it is observed that greater price sensitivity is found when individuals are asked to respond to a low price first, followed by successively higher prices. In contrast, the reverse order (i.e., high price to low) results in considerably less price sensitivity. This effect has been seen with all popular data collection modes.

The difficulty with this type of order bias is that even where context is shown to have an effect, it is frequently unclear that one order is better than another. Instead, each order may reveal a different facet of the issue being studied.

Pretesting and Correcting Problems

The purpose of a **pretest** is to ensure that the questionnaire meets the researcher's expectations in terms of the information that will be obtained. First drafts of questionnaires tend to be too long, often lack important variables, and are subject to all the hazards of ambiguous, ill-defined, loaded, or double-barreled questions. The objective of the questionnaire pretest is to identify and correct these deficiencies.

Effective pretesting demands that the researcher be open to criticism and be willing to pursue the deficiencies. Thus, a good starting point is for the researcher to take the respondent's point of view and try to answer the questions.

Pretest Design

Because a pretest is a pilot run, the respondents should be reasonably representative of the sample population. However, they should not all be "typical," for much can be learned from those at the extremes of the sample. Will the questions work with those with a limited education, strong negative opinions, or little understanding of the subject? Only small samples are necessary—15 is sufficient for a short and straightforward questionnaire, whereas 25 may be needed if the questionnaire is long and complex, with many branches and multiple options. Even when the field survey will be done by mail, the pretest should be done with a personal or telephone interview to get direct feedback on problems. Only the best, most insightful, and experienced interviewers should be used for this work.

A personal interview pretest can use either a debriefing or a protocol approach. In the debriefing approach, the questionnaire is administered first, just as it would be in the full-scale study. For example, a mail survey would be filled out without assistance from the interviewer; however, the interviewer should be instructed to observe and note reactions of confusion, resistance, or uneasiness. When the interview is completed, the interviewer should debrief the respondent by asking what he or she was thinking about when forming each answer, whether there were any problems of understanding, and whether any aspects of the subject were not covered by the questions.

In the protocol method, the subject is asked to "think aloud" as he or she is filling out the questionnaire. The interviewer records these thoughts, and at the end of the pretest asks for further clarification of problems where necessary. The latter approach seems to work better when the pretest is being done by telephone rather than face to face. Respondents offer more frequent and extensive comments over the telephone because they lack nonverbal means of communication.

Pretesting Specific Questions

There are some very specific reasons for pretest questions. Four common tests for specific questions are as follows:[20]

1. *Variation.* Testing items for an acceptable level of variation in the target population is one of the most common goals of pretesting. The researcher is on the lookout for items showing greater variability than will be useful in detecting subgroups of people. Very skewed distributions from a pretest can serve as a warning signal that the question is not tapping the intended construct.

2. *Meaning.* This is probably the most important pretesting purpose. The intended meaning of the questions for the investigators may not be the meaning the respondents interpret it to be, for two important reasons. The first is that respondents may not necessarily hear or even see every word in a question. This can result in a distortion of the meaning of the question, as when, for example, the "im" is missed from the word "impossible." The second reason for problems with meaning is that a respondent is likely to modify a difficult question in a way that makes it easier for him or her to respond. This can happen in several ways: People may pay more attention to the part of the question they think is more sensible and answer only that part; or they may take the parts of the question that are meaningful to them and assemble a different question and answer that. Studies have shown that respondents often transform obscure questions into ones that seem sensible to them in order to minimize the amount of effort required.

3. *Task difficulty.* A meaningful and clear question can still be difficult to answer if the question requires that a respondent make connections or put together information in unfamiliar ways. A question such as "How many pounds of laundry detergent have you consumed this past year?" is likely to be too difficult for most respondents to answer, since they probably do not total up their consumption of laundry detergent by the pound or even by the year.

4. *Respondent interest and attention.* This is an area of pretesting that is often overlooked by researchers. Excessive repetition within a question or use of the same format within a question can reduce the amount of attention paid to questions by respondents. Researchers should at least make note of questions that respondents found especially interesting and especially dull.

Pretesting the Questionnaire

Some research concerns about the questionnaire as a whole, such as the order of questions, have already been mentioned. Other concerns that should be pretested are the following.

1. *Flow of the questionnaire.* Testing the "flow" of the questionnaire is often a matter of intuitive judgment. Since respondents do not know what the next question will be, questions must appear in a logical sequence and be part of a coherent flow. Transitions from one topic to another must also be pretested to ensure that they are clear and logical.

2. *Skip patterns.* Many questionnaires have instructions on what questions to skip, depending on the answer to a previous question. Whether the skip patterns are to be followed by the respondent (as in a mail survey) or by the interviewer (as in a personal interview), they must be clear and well laid out. In this context, a questionnaire is a little like a road map with signs. Researchers who have been involved with the questionnaire design may not spot any inconsistencies or ambiguities in the skip patterns simply because they already know the "road map."

3. *Length.* Each section of the questionnaire should be timed to ensure that none of them is too long. While respondents are willing to spend more time on questionnaires when they have a personal interest in the topic, there is an upper limit to the duration that is considered reasonable. Unless the length is pretested, the research may experience problems with respondent fatigue, interview break-off, and initial refusal if respondents know in advance the expected length.

4. *Respondent interest and attention.* Capturing and maintaining the interest of a respondent throughout the entire questionnaire is a major design challenge. Often, the answering task is varied throughout the questionnaire, to engage a respondent's active attention. The extent to which this is successful can and should be pretested.

Role of the Pretest

There are limits to how well a pretest can detect errors. One study found that pretest respondents were virtually unable to detect loaded questions, and most did not recognize when response alternatives were missing or questions were ambiguous.[21] For example, less than 10 percent of a pretest sample pointed out the ambiguity of the following question: "Do you think things will be better or worse next summer than they are now?" Five response options were provided, ranging from much better to much worse.

Although it requires only one perceptive or confused respondent to identify problems or improvements, respondents are not the only source of insights. Interviewers are equally important to the pretesting process. Once the interviewers have reported their experiences, they also

Marketing Research In Action 12.3

■ DO-IT-YOURSELF RESEARCH SURVEYS

With the increasing use of online survey websites such as www.surveymonkey.com and www.zoomerang.com, many companies are undertaking the do-it-yourself survey option of conducting surveys. However, designing surveys with the do-it-yourself tools can be tricky and can lead to unusable results, if adequate care in designing questions is not undertaken. The following checklist helps marketing researchers and other professionals design their own surveys:

- Is there a clear understanding of the goals and objectives of the survey?
- Is the selected sample size appropriate to conclude a specific outcome of the survey? Is the sample representative of the population? Do we generate an in-house respondent list or buy one from panel companies?
- Does the questionnaire start with general questions and then proceed into specific questions?
- Since actions speak louder than words, does the questionnaire ask about behaviors and not attitudes?
- Since open-ended questions are harder to analyze, does the questionnaire have more of close-ended questions?
- Can the respondent complete the survey in a short period of time, say 5–10 minutes?
- Has the questionnaire gone through a pilot run to check for typos, jargon or confusing questions?

Source: N. Hopewell, "Surveys By Design," Marketing Research, December 2008.

should be asked for their suggestions. There is a danger that some interviewers will make changes in the field on their own initiative if they believe it will make their job easier. This can create serious problems if some interviewers make the change and others do not.

Finally, the pretest analysis should return to the first step in the design process. Each question should be reviewed once again and asked to justify its place in the questionnaire. How will the answer be used in the analysis? Is the pattern of answers from the pretest sensible, or difficult to interpret? Does the question add substantial new information, or unnecessarily duplicate the results from another question? Of course, the last step in the process may be another pretest, if far-reaching changes have been necessary.

Marketing Research in Action 12.3 provides a novel way of conducting surveys.

Questionnaire Design for International Research

Choosing the Question Format for Cross-National Research

The issue of question format is an important one when constructing a questionnaire for cross-cultural or cross-national research.[22] The researcher may lack experience with purchasing behavior or relevant determinants of response in another country or cultural context. Use of open-ended questions may thus be desirable in a number of situations. Since they do not impose any structure or response categories, open-ended questions avoid the imposition of cultural bias by the researcher. Furthermore, they do not require familiarity with all the respondents' possible responses.

In addition, differences in levels of literacy may affect the appropriateness of using open-ended questions as opposed to closed questions. Since open-ended questions require the respondent to answer on his or her own terms, they also require a moderate level of sophistication and comprehension of the topic on the part of the respondent; otherwise, responses will not be meaningful. Open-ended questions will therefore have to be used with care in cross-cultural and cross-national research, in order to ensure that bias does not occur as a result of differences in levels of education.

Another consideration is whether direct or indirect questions should be utilized. Direct questions avoid any ambiguity concerning question content and meaning. On the other hand, respondents may be reluctant to answer certain types of questions. Similarly, they may tend to provide responses perceived as socially desirable or those they feel are desired by the interviewer. Use of indirect questions may aid in bypassing such biases. In this case, rather than being stated directly, the question is posed in an indirect form.

For example, respondents might be asked to indicate, rather than their own preferences, those they would anticipate from the majority of respondents, neighbors, or other relevant reference groups. Thus, the decision to use a direct or an indirect format for a particular question depends on the respondent's perception of the topic. If the topic is perceived as sensitive by the respondent, then it is better to use an indirect format than a direct one. The sensitivity of a topic may vary from culture to culture. Hence, a direct question in one country may have to be asked as an indirect one in a different country.

Another important consideration in instrument design is the extent to which nonverbal, as opposed to verbal, stimuli are utilized in order to facilitate respondent comprehension. Particularly where research is conducted in countries or cultures with high levels of illiteracy, as, for example, Africa and the Far East, it is often desirable to use nonverbal stimuli such as show cards. Questionnaires can be administered orally by an interviewer, but respondent comprehension will be facilitated if pictures of products, concepts, or test packs are provided.

Various types of nonverbal stimuli may be used in conjunction with questionnaires, including show cards, product samples, or pictures. It should be noted that nonverbal stimuli are often used in other data collection techniques. The main focus here, however, is on their use in surveys in order to ensure that respondents understand verbal questions, relevant products, and product concepts.

Problems Faced in Wording Questions for International Research

When conducting cross-national research, the wording of questions has to be changed according to the country in which the questionnaire is being administered. Certain categories, such as sex and age, are the same in all countries or cultures, and hence, equivalent questions can be posed. Somewhat greater difficulties may be encountered with regard to other categories, such as income, education, occupation, or the dwelling unit, since these are not always exactly comparable from one culture or country to another. In addition to the fact that in some countries men may have several wives, marital status can present problems, depending on how the question is put. The growing number of cohabiting couples, especially those who are divorced, creates a particular problem in this regard. What is included in the category of income may vary from country to country, and incomes vary considerably within countries.

Similarly, with regard to education, types of schools, colleges, or universities are not always comparable from one country to another. Also, certain occupational categories may not be comparable from one country to another. In general, however, the major distinctions or broad categories tend to be the same, that is, farm workers, industrial workers, blue-collar workers, office or white-collar workers, self-employed persons, lower and upper management, and professionals. Alternatively, comparable social hierarchies can be identified. Another category where differences may occur is in the dwelling unit. In the major Western societies, dwelling units are primarily apartments or multistory houses. In African countries, however, dwelling units may be huts, whereas in Far Eastern countries many homes are one-story units.

In developing questions related to purchase behavior and consumption or usage behavior, and to specific product markets, two important issues need to be considered. The first concerns the extent to which such behavior is conditioned by a specific sociocultural or economic environment and hence is likely to vary from one country or cultural context to another. Each culture, society, or social group has its own particular conventions, rituals, and practices relating to behavior in social situations, such as entertaining family or friends on festive occasions—for example, graduation or Christmas. Rules relating to the exchange of gifts and products are, for example, governed by local cultural conventions. Thus, in some cultures wine may be an appropriate gift for a dinner host or hostess, whereas in others, flowers are preferred. Consequently, questions relating to the gift market, and products positioned as gifts, will need to be tailored to these specific behavior patterns. Significant differences also occur in the retail distribution network. In many developing countries, for example, there are few self-service outlets or supermarkets, except in major cities, and most purchases are made in small Mom-and-Pop-type stores. Such shopping patterns affect the formulation of questions relating to the location and timing of purchasing, as well as the importance of investigating the salesperson's influence on purchase decisions.

In addition to such differences in usage and purchase behavior, relevant product class boundaries or competing and substitute products vary from one country to another. For example, washing machines and other household appliances may be competing with domestic help and professional washerwomen, as well as with other brands of washing machines.

The most significant problems in drawing up questions in multicountry research are likely to occur in relation to attitudinal, psychographic, and lifestyle data. Here, as has already been pointed out, it is not always clear that comparable or equivalent attitudinal or personality constructs—such as aggressiveness, respect for authority, and honor—are relevant in all countries and cultures. Even where similar constructs exist, it is far from clear whether they are most effectively tapped by the same question or attitude statement. Marketing Research in Action 12.4 is a list of pointers that should be addressed when conducting research in international markets.

Marketing Research In Action 12.4

▉ AN INTERNATIONAL RESEARCH QUESTIONNAIRE DESIGN CHECKLIST

A checklist has been put together to help marketing researchers and other professionals navigate the rough seas:

- Has the questionnaire/discussion guide been translated into the local language by personnel who currently speak the local language day to day and who are therefore up-to-date on current meanings, usages, slang, and so on?

- Has the local language questionnaire/discussion guide version been back-translated to English, again by personnel who are current speakers of both the local language and English?

- Is your study benefiting from consulting help from your local in-market research firms at the stages of determining local study methodology, questionnaire/discussion guide design, and again during analysis of results?

- If there are study requirements that include the need for certain water temperatures or for amounts of different items such as in a recipe, are these requirements expressed in understandable terms for all countries included in the study (e.g., Fahrenheit vs Celsius, metric vs English measurements, etc.)?

- If you are conducting a multicountry study, have you designed the questionnaire so that different brand lists can be fielded in each country and so that identical brands can be easily identified and tabulated across all countries where they are found?

- Have you considered the need to create more than one questionnaire per country, depending on the number of regional dialects or even indigenous languages that may exist?

Source: K. Hamilton, "An International Marketing Research Checklist," Quirk's Marketing Research Review, November 1998, Article 0376.

SUMMARY

As with most steps in the research process, the design of the questionnaire is highly iterative. Because it is an integral part of the research design, the objective is to seek consistency with the other elements of the design, notably the research purpose, the budget, and the methods of analysis. Additional constraints are imposed by the data collection method and the respondent's ability and willingness to answer questions about the subject.

Within these constraints, the questionnaire writer practices this art through the adroit choice of wording, response format, sequencing of questions, and layout of the questionnaire. Success in this activity comes from experience, an ability to look at the subject and the wording of the questions from the respondent's perspective, and a good understanding of the objectives of the research.

The difficulties in designing a good questionnaire have encouraged researchers to use previously published survey questions wherever possible. There are many published compilations of survey questions that can be consulted to save time and effort. This does not mean, however, that only previously published questions can or should be used, since it is the specific research purpose that ultimately determines the questionnaire design.

Guidelines for writing and organizing questionnaires have been presented here. Since they are a distillation of the experience of many researchers, adherence to these principles will narrow the range of problems. Ultimately, a good questionnaire is one that has been thoroughly pretested. There can be no substitute for this step in the process.

Even though the process of designing questionnaires for international research is essentially the same, there are certain key differences that have been discussed earlier. A classic trade-off situation exists with respect to the use of closed- versus open-response format in international research. While closed-response questions will lead to an imposition of the researcher's cultural biases on the respondent, open-response questions require a certain level of education and familiarity with the subject, which may not be present among respondents in many countries. Another area where a researcher is likely to encounter problems in cross-cultural research is in question wording. Words that represent a construct in one culture may turn out to be totally different in another culture when they are translated or, worse, a particular construct may not have a word at all in the language of that culture. A researcher conducting cross-cultural research has to overcome many such problems in questionnaire design.

QUESTIONS AND PROBLEMS

12.1 Critique the questionnaire in Figure 12.2, which is from an appliance manufacturer whose objective is to collect information on the reasons for purchasing their product, the buyer's demographic, and lifestyle activities.

12.2 A researcher investigating the general happiness of respondents in a particular age and socioeconomic group is considering using the following two questions in a questionnaire:

(a) All things considered, how happy would you say you were these days? Would you say that you were very happy, pretty happy, or not too happy?

(b) All things considered, how would you describe your marriage? Would you say your marriage is very happy, pretty happy, or not too happy?

What are some concerns you might have about the order in which these questions might be asked? Which order would you suggest?

12.3 "Questionnaire design for descriptive research is more difficult than for exploratory research." Discuss this statement.

12.4 "As long as a question pertains to at least one of the research objectives, it must be included in the questionnaire." Do you agree or disagree with this statement? Explain your answer.

12.5 Open-response questions sometimes are used to establish the salience or importance of issues such as irritation from clutter due to excessive advertisements and station announcements during TV programs. Why would you want

IMPORTANT!   IMPORTANT!   IMPORTANT!

10 - 94   <u>Please complete and return within 10 days.</u>

1. Mr. ❏ 2. Mrs. ❏ 3. Ms. ❏ 4. Miss ❏   22A

First Name: Initial: Last Name:

Address: (Number and Street)   Apt #:

City: State: Zip:

Date of Purchase: Phone Number:

Month   Day   Year

Model #:_____   Product Type/Name:_____
(Located on bottom of product)

Store Name:

Is This Product: 1. ❏ a replacement   2. ❏ first time purchase?

If this is a replacement purchase, was your previous brand a Holmes? 1. ❏ Yes 2. ❏ No

Purchase Price: .00   Date of <u>Your</u> Birth:
                                Month   Day   Year

I purchased this Holmes Air product because of (please check top <u>two</u> (2) reasons):
1. ❏ Style/Appearance   4. ❏ Price/Value   7. ❏ Packaging Information
2. ❏ Holmes Reputation   5. ❏ Sale/Promotion   8. ❏ Warranty
3. ❏ Good Housekeeping Seal   6. ❏ Special Features

<u>Excluding yourself</u>. What are the ages of the other people (in years) in your household?
❏ I Live Alone

Male Female Age   Male Female Age   Male Female Age
❏   ❏   ❏   ❏   ❏   ❏

Male Female Age   Male Female Age   Male Female Age
❏   ❏   ❏   ❏   ❏   ❏

Which group best describes your family income?
1. ❏ Under $15,000   3. ❏ $25,000–$34,999   5. ❏ $50,000–$75,000
2. ❏ $15,000–$24,999   4. ❏ $40,000–$49,999   6. ❏ Over $75,000

Education: (Please check which category applies)
1. ❏ High School   3. ❏ Completed College
2. ❏ Some College   4. ❏ Graduate School

In the last six (6) months have you or your spouse:
1. ❏ Purchased clothes through the mail?   3. ❏ Worked in your garden?
2. ❏ Purchased gifts through the mail?   4. ❏ Traveled on a vacation?

Thank you for filling out this questionnaire. We value your answers and input. Please check here ❏ if you would prefer not to obtain information on new and interesting opportunities.

FIGURE 12.2
Appliance Manufacturer Survey.

to use this type of response format rather than a closed-response question?

12.6 How do the responses from an unaided-recall question on brand awareness compare to those from an aided-recall question?

12.7 Use the formula for the randomized response model to estimate the percentage of respondents who indicated they did not report all of their income to the federal tax authorities in a survey in which a total of 16 percent answered "yes." Also, 10 percent of the sample were estimated to have their birthdays in June (and so would have answered "yes" to the innocuous question), and a coin toss was used to choose which of the two questions to answer.

12.8 What can a researcher do to make the request for information seem legitimate?

12.9 Evaluate the following questions and suggest improvements.

(a) Please check the following activities in which you participate as a private citizen interested in politics.

_____ Read books and articles on the subject
_____ Belong to political party
_____ Attend political rallies
_____ Write letters to legislators, newspapers, or government officials
_____ Other (please specify)

(b) When you eat dinner out, do you sometimes eat at the same place?

_____ Yes   _____ No

(c) Is the current level of government regulation on environmental protection adequate or inadequate?

_____ Adequate   _____ Inadequate

(d) Where do you buy most of your clothes?

(e) Do you think that Con Edison is doing everything possible to reduce air pollution from their electricity-generating stations?

_____ Yes   _____ No

(f) Please indicate how much of an average issue of *Sunset* magazine you usually read:

1. _____ Less than ⅓

2. _____ ⅓ to ½

3. _____ Over ¼

(g) List the magazines you read regularly ("read" means read or look at; "regularly" means almost as often as the magazine is published).

(h) What kind of hobbies do you have?

(i) Everybody knows that teenagers and their parents have lots of arguments. What are some of the things you and your parents have argued about lately?

12.10 A large automobile manufacturer has asked you to develop a questionnaire to measure owners' satisfaction with the servicing of their vehicles. One sequence of questions will deal with satisfaction with the design, construction, operating costs, performance, and amount of service required. In order to interpret these results, it has been decided to ask further questions to isolate the responsibility for car problems. That is, do car owners tend to blame the manufacturers, the service work by the dealer, or poor upkeep and driving habits of car owners? What kind of questions would you ask to determine this information?

12.11 Based on the following list of research questions, determine the research objective(s) of this questionnaire. Are any of the questions unnecessary; if so, why?

(a) How many hours per week do you work, on average?

(b) What type of magazines do you read?

(c) Do you feel you have enough "free time" away from work?

(d) What kind of hobbies do you have?

(e) Would you describe yourself as a well-rounded person?

12.12 Develop three double-barreled questions related to eating habits and restaurant preferences. Also develop correct versions of each question.

12.13 What are some recommended ways by which one can ask sensitive information? Where in the questionnaire should one ask for sensitive information?

12.14 A research company has decided to pretest a personal interview questionnaire prior to collecting the actual data. Interviewers will conduct the pretest interviews. Design a separate questionnaire containing from 5 to 10 questions that you feel the interviewer should fill out after each pretest interview. The objective of this separate questionnaire is to provide the research company with sufficient information to evaluate any problems with the personal interview questionnaire.

12.15 The Student Disciplinary Committee of Clint State University is extremely concerned about the increasing incidence of cheating in both in-class and out-of-class student assignments. They have approached a marketing research class to conduct a survey of Clint State students. They wish to know:

(i) How predominant this behavior is campus-wide

(ii) Whether it occurs most frequently among freshman, sophomores, juniors, or seniors

(iii) Some of the reasons for this behavior

(iv) Possible solutions to the problem

(a) What are the information requirements for the study?

(b) How should the questions be formatted? (Hint: consider the topic of the study.) Give reasons for your answer.

(c) How could order bias affect the results of this survey?

(d) It has been decided that the questionnaire should be pretested.

(i) What are the reasons for pretesting a questionnaire?

(ii) Suggest a suitable group of respondents for the pretest.

As part of its assimilation in the present global environment, the marketing research class is paying close attention to research techniques for international markets. To meet this objective, the professor has instructed the students to undertake a similar study among students of a university in France.

(e) What is the most appropriate question format for this research?

(f) What are the possible problems that may be encountered by the class in the international research project?

12.16 The finance committee of St. Dunstan's Church has reported a fall in the level of donations to the church at Sunday services, despite the fact that attendance has not declined. In an effort to boost donations, the committee has decided to conduct personal interviews of all church members in their homes to determine each member's habits regarding donations to the church.

(a) How might this survey method bias the results of the study? Each member of the committee has been given a questionnaire from which to conduct the personal interviews. The first four questions are as follows:

(i) How often do you attend Sunday services per year?

(ii) Do you realize that the church's only form of income is the donations from its members?

(iii) Do you donate to the church every Sunday?

(iv) How much, on average, do you donate?

(b) How would the following factors affect the results of this study?

(i) Question order

(ii) Question wording

(iii) Subject matter

(iv) Interviewer's affiliation to the church

12.17 Two consumers were considering buying a lawnmower. Bill's wife suggested brand B, and after shopping for a good price, Bill bought brand B at a discount store. Jake, however, consulted *Consumer Reports*, and found repair trouble reported with brands A, C, D, F, and H, and unwanted features in brands M, E, and G. Therefore, he decided on brand B as well. Jake can respond accurately to the question of why he did not buy brand M. Bill cannot because he had no reason for not buying brand M, and may not even have been aware of the product. Both, however, can easily explain why they bought brand B.

Meanwhile, at Markmix Co., the owner pondered over the low sales record for heavily promoted brand M and decided to conduct a survey to find out why his product was not being bought. However, if this question were asked directly in a survey, a problem of focus would appear. Company M's focus is on the product, but the consumer's is not. In Bill's case, the reason for not buying brand M does not concern brand M, or brands A, C, D, E, F, G, and H, for that matter. There was no decision to buy brand M, only a positive reason to buy brand B.

Design a questionnaire (10 questions) that will open doors to the reasons for not buying Markmix Co.'s brand. Consider carefully the process described in Figure 12.1. (Hint: How would you approach: (1) the question regarding the reason for buying the product, (2) the uncertainty and ignorance of the respondent, and (3) the buying-interest question—indirectly or directly?)[23]

12.18 A Korean digital camera manufacturer is planning to enter the United States by changing its image of a technology, feature-led company to one focusing on fashion and brand value. You have been asked to assist them in this venture by developing a questionnaire suitable to survey the American consumers. The proposed study is to be done through telephone interviews. To help you in this, a previously conducted Korean market segmentation study is provided as a model. The questions asked in the Korean market segmentation study were largely based on perception of popular brands, camera usage, camera specifications, and demographics.

(a) Design a questionnaire containing 5 to 10 questions that you feel would be necessary to bring out the required information?

(b) How will you ensure that the result is effectively communicated and understood in the context of the Korean market?

END NOTES

1. S. L. Payne, *The Art of Asking Questions*. Princeton, NJ: Princeton University Press, 1951.

2. J. Singh, R. D. Howell, and G. K. Rhoads, "Adaptive Designs for Likert-Type Data: An Approach for Implementing Market Surveys," *Journal of Marketing Research*, 27, August 1990, pp. 304–321.

3. G. J. Spagna, "Questionnaires: Which Approach Do You Use?," *Journal of Advertising Research*, 24, February–March 1984, pp. 67–70.

4. J. M. Converse and S. Presser, *Survey Questions, Handcrafting the Standardized Questionnaire*, Sage University Paper, Series on Quantitative Applications in the Social Sciences, 07-063, Beverly Hills, CA: Sage, 1986.

5. H. Schuman and S. Presser, *Questions and Answers in Attitude Surveys: Experiments in Question Form, Wording and Context*, New York: Academic Free Press, 1981.

6. G. F. Bishop, "Experiments with the Middle Response Alternatives in Survey Questions," *Public Opinion Quarterly*, Summer 1987, pp. 220–232.

7. G. F. Bishop, A. J. Tuchfarber, and R. W. Oldendick, "Opinions on Fictitious Issues: The Pressure to Answer Survey Questions," *Public Opinion Quarterly*, Summer 1986, pp. 240–250.

8. S. L. Payne, *The Art of Asking Questions*. Princeton, NJ: Princeton University Press, 1951, p. 87.

9. Boyd, Westfall, and Stasch, *Marketing Research*, 4th ed., Homewood, IL: R. D. Irwin, 1980.

10. W. B. Locander and J. P. Burton, "The Effect of Question Form on Gathering Income Data by Telephone," *Journal of Marketing Research*, 13, May 1976, pp. 189–192.

11. N. J. Blunch, "Position Bias in Multiple-Choice Questions," *Journal of Marketing Research*, 21, May 1984, pp. 216–220, has argued that position bias in multiple-choice questions cannot be eliminated by rotating the order of the categories.

12. Such questions are vulnerable to the prestige seeking and social-desirability-response bias discussed in Chapter 8.

13. P. B. Sheatsley, *Questionnaire Design and Wording*. Chicago: National Opinion Research Corporation, 1969.

14. A. J Barton, "Asking the Embarrassing Question," *Public Opinion Quarterly*, 22, Spring 1958, pp. 67–68.

15. J. Hornik, T. Zaig, and D. Shadmon, "Reducing Refusals in Telephone Surveys on Sensitive Topics," *Journal of Advertising Research*, 31, 1991, pp. 49–56.

16. C. Campbell and B. L. Joiner, "How to Get the Answer without Being Sure You've Asked the Question," *American Statistician*, 27, December 1973, pp. 119–231; and J. E. Reinmuth and M. D. Guerts, "The Collection of Sensitive Information Using a Two-Stage Randomized Response Model," *Journal of Marketing Research*, 12, November 1975, pp. 402–407.

17. R. L. Kahn and C. F. Cannell, *The Dynamics of Interviewing*, New York: John Wiley, 1957.

18. E. J. Gross, "The Effect of Question Sequence on Measures of Buying Interest," *Journal of Advertising Research*, 4, September 1964, p. 41.

19. C. F. Turner and K. Krauss, "Fallible Indicators of the Subjective State of the Nation," *American Psychologist*, 33, September 1978, pp. 456–470.

20. J. M. Converse and Stanely Presser, Survey Questions, Handcrafting the Standardized Questionnaire, Sage University Paper, Series on Quantitative Applications in the Social Sciences, 07-063. Beverly Hills, CA: Sage, 1986.

21. S. Hunt, R. D. Sparkman, and J. B. Wilcox, "The Pretest in Survey Research: Issues and Preliminary Findings," *Journal of Marketing Research*, 19, May 1982, pp. 269–273.

22. E. D. Jaffe and I. D. Nebenzahl, "Alternative Questionnaire Formats for Country Image Studies," *Journal of Marketing Research*, 21, November 1984, pp. 463–471.

23. T. T. Semon, "Why Didn't You Buy Brand C?," *Marketing News*, 17, July 1996, p. 13.

Case 12-1 | Wine Horizons

Wine Horizons was a medium-sized New York State winery that emphasized sparkling wines. The company was not known to the public as a producer of good-quality domestic champagne because all of their output was sold to well-known hotels and restaurants, which put their own labels on the bottles. However, their still (nonsparkling) wines were sold under the Wine Horizons label and were moderately well known.

The management of the company had been planning for some time to launch a line of champagnes under their own brand name. They were seriously considering whether the launch should be based on a packaging innovation. The specific proposal was to package their champagne in six-packs of 7-ounce bottles in an easy-to-carry container, at a retail price of approximately $9.00. The 7-ounce quantity was chosen because it was the equivalent of two average-sized champagne glasses, thus making one bottle a convenient serving for one or two people. This size and price were expected to make the champagne an attractive alternative to imported beers in a variety of social situations.

Before a decision could be made, the management team had to be satisfied that there was an adequate market for the new packaging. They also wanted to know the occasions during which the target market would be likely to use the product, and whether these people would expect to find it in the imported beer or wine section of their retail outlet. To answer these questions, the firm Ritchey and Associates was retained to conduct a market study. A meeting to review their attitude questionnaire was just beginning.

Developments in the Wine Industry

The wine industry had enjoyed significant growth in recent years. The growth of white wines had been especially strong, but sparkling wines had also experienced an upward trend. Champagne sales had grown, but less than sparkling wines in general. The reason for the increased popularity of white wines was not known, but many in the industry believed it was due to a general trend toward "lightness" on the part of consumers, as reflected in their increased use of light beers, light wine, bottled mineral water, health foods, and low-tar cigarettes. Whatever the reason, wine was being chosen more frequently as a beverage alternative to beer and liquor in various formal and informal social situations. It was also believed that champagne was not sharing in wine's growth because of the difficulty in keeping champagne fresh after the bottle was opened—a large, opened bottle of champagne would lose all its carbonation in a few hours and "go flat."

Two wineries had recently begun test-marketing wine in small packages. One winery was offering chablis, rosé, and burgundy in six-packs of cans, with each can containing six ounces of wine. Another winery was test-marketing chablis in six-packs of 6.5-ounce bottles. The new packaging seemed to be selling reasonably well in test areas, and retailers reportedly had a favorable attitude toward the new packaging. Compared with "single" small bottles or cans of wine—which were considered a nuisance—retailers felt that the six-packs were more profitable and more convenient to stack and display.

The Research Study

The objectives of the study were to (1) measure consumers' acceptance of wine in six-packs, (2) identify the type of person who was a potential purchaser and user of champagne in six-packs, (3) determine where in the store he or she would expect to find such champagne, and (4) determine the size of the potential market. The sample would be champagne drinkers who were 21 years of age or older. Also, the research would be limited to markets where the six-packs of wine were already being tested. It was further decided that the data would be collected with personal interviews using a shopping mall intercept method. This would permit the interviewer to show a picture of the proposed six-pack and to use cards to list answer categories in complex questions. Only malls that contained liquor stores would be selected. The interviewers would be located in the vicinity of the liquor store and would attempt to interview adults leaving the stores.

A six-part questionnaire (see Marketing Research in Action 12.5) was designed to obtain the desired information. The major issues to be resolved were whether this questionnaire and the mall intercept design would identify potential users and yield a valid estimate of the potential market for the six-packs.

Questions for Discussion

1. Will the proposed questionnaire and research design achieve the research objectives?

2. What alternative questions could be used to assess attitudes and intentions-to-buy? Which approach would yield the most valid responses?

Marketing Research in Action 12.5

Hello! My name is _____. I'm an interviewer with the marketing research firm of Ritchey and Associates, and we are conducting a study concerned with certain alcoholic beverages. Would you please take a few minutes to answer some questions? I assure you that your answers will be kept *completely confidential.*

1. Are you 21 years of age or older? (ASK ONLY IF NECESSARY)

   _____ Yes   _____ No (TERMINATE)

2. Do you drink any alcoholic beverages?

   _____ Yes   _____ No (TERMINATE)

3. What different kinds of alcoholic beverages do you drink?

   _____ Beer   _____ Liquor (any kind)

   _____ Wine   _____ Other

   _____ Champagne (to Q5)

4. Do you drink champagne?

   _____ Yes   _____ No (TERMINATE)

5. About how often do you drink champagne? (CLARIFY RESPONSE IF NECESSARY)

   _____ Once a week or more often   _____ About once in 2–3 months

   _____ About twice a month   _____ About twice a year

   _____ About once a month   _____ About once a year

                                          _____ DK

6. On what types of occasions do you drink champagne?

   _____ Dinner for two   _____ Picnics

   _____ Small dinner party   _____ After athletic activities

   _____ Parties   _____ Just relaxing

   _____ Special holidays   _____ Other (specify) _____

   _____ Dinner

7. Do you consider champagne to be an appropriate beverage to serve at informal occasions, or is it only for formal occasions?

   _____ Appropriate for informal occasions

   _____ Only for formal occasions   _____ For both occasions

   EXPLAIN: I'm now going to ask you some questions about wine, not champagne. These are questions about some new packaging that has recently been used by some brands of wine.

8. Are you aware that some wine is now being sold in packages consisting of six small cans and bottles, each containing about 6 ounces?

   _____ Yes   _____ No (to Q10)   _____ DK (to Q10)

9. Have you ever purchased wine sold in such packaging or drank wine from one of these small containers?

   _____ Purchased   _____ Both

   _____ Drank   _____ Neither

10. Do you think it's a good idea to sell wine in packages consisting of six small cans or bottles—that is, are you in favor of it?

    _____ A good idea, in favor of   _____ Indifferent (to Q12)

    _____ Not a good idea   _____ Undecided (to Q12)

11. Why?

    EXPLAIN: Wine Horizons is one of the largest private-label bottlers of champagnes in the United States. For example, it supplies well-known hotel chains and restaurants with their own brand of champagne. Wine Horizons is planning to market this package (SHOW PICTURE) of six small bottles of champagne.

12. Do you think it's a good idea to sell champagne in packages consisting of six small bottles—that is, are you in favor of it?

    _____ A good idea, in favor of (to Q14)   _____ Indifferent (to Q14)

    _____ Not a good idea   _____ Undecided (to Q14)

13. Why not?

14. Would you consider purchasing such a package of champagne at the retail price of $9.00?

    _____ Yes (to Q16)   _____ No

    _____ Maybe, possibly (to Q16)   _____ DK

15. Why not?

16. For what kinds of occasions would you use these small bottles of champagne?

    _____ Dinner for two   _____ Picnics

    _____ Small dinner party   _____ After athletic activities

    _____ Parties   _____ Just relaxing

    _____ Special holidays   _____ Other (specify)_____

    _____ Dinner

17. Would you use them for any of the occasions shown on this list? (SHOW CARD)

_____ Dinner for two   _____ Picnics

_____ Small dinner party   _____ After athletic activities

_____ Parties   _____ Just relaxing

_____ Special holidays

_____ Dinner

18. In what types of retail stores would you expect to find this product being sold?

_____ Liquor stores   _____ Other (specify) _____

_____ Supermarkets

19. In what section of the store would you expect to find this package of champagne, that is, what other products would you expect to find alongside it?

_____ Other champagnes   _____ Beer

_____ Wine   _____ Other (specify) _____

Case 12-2 ‖ Smith's Clothing (A)

John Simpson, the head of Simpson Research, was attempting to design a marketing research study that would address the research questions posed by Jim Andrews, the president of Smith's Clothing, during their morning meeting. The research questions seemed rather well defined:

1. Which women's clothing stores compete with Smith's?

2. What is the image of Smith's, and how does this image compare with that of its competitors? In other words, how is Smith's positioned with respect to its competitors?

3. Who is the Smith customer and how does she differ from that of Smith's competitors?

Although no final judgment had been made, Andrews was leaning toward an in-home, self-administered questionnaire. He was not certain, however, whether a questionnaire could be developed that would be responsive to the research questions. The population of interest was operationally defined to be those women whose family income exceeded the median income. Simpson's immediate task was to draft a questionnaire and to develop a tentative sampling plan.

Smith's was a six-store chain of women's clothing stores located in Bayview, a large, growing city in the southwestern United States. The chain had provided fine clothing for the upper class of Bayview for over 40 years. Twenty years previously, Smith's had opened its first suburban store. Having closed its downtown store 10 years ago, it now had five suburban stores and one in a nearby community of 60,000 people. Smith's had avoided trendy fashions over the years, in favor of classic, lasting designs. During the last 10 years a set of five or six aggressive, high-fashion retailers had expanded into or within Bayview. Thus, despite the fact that the market for fine women's clothes had expanded enormously during the past decade, the competition had grown much more intense.

Andrews was justifiably concerned about the performance of his stores. Profits at five of the six stores had fallen during each of the past four years. The sixth store had been opened only 18 months before and had not achieved its target growth rate. Although the chain was still profitable, if the existing trend continued it would soon be losing money.

This performance had stimulated Andrews to engage in serious reappraisal of the whole operation. In particular, he was reviewing the chain's rather conservative policy toward the product line, advertising, store decor, and store personnel. He felt that it might be time to consider stocking some trendy fashions and attempting to increase the store's appeal to women in their teens and twenties. A working hypothesis was that Smith's had a higher appeal relative to other stores to women over 40 and was less attractive to younger women. He realized that any such move was risky in that it would jeopardize the existing customer franchise without any guarantee that new customers would compensate. Before making any such move he felt that it was critical to learn exactly how Smith's was now positioned. He also felt that he needed a much more reliable fix on the current Smith customers in terms of their age, the stores in which they shop, their preferences, and their purchase profile. With such information he would be in a much better position to identify alternatives and evaluate them.

ASSIGNMENT

Develop a research design including:

1. The type of survey to be employed

2. A questionnaire

Appendix for this Chapter is available on the Web.

Additional Cases for this Chapter are available on the Web:

Web Case 12-1 ‖	Compact Lemon

| Web Case 12-2 ‖ | Project DATA: An Urban Transportation Study |

13 Experimentation

LEARNING OBJECTIVES

- Define experimentation and discuss the distinction between experiments and other types of research approaches.
- Discuss the concept of causality and the conditions required to infer causality.
- Describe the distinction between laboratory and field experiments.
- Discuss the concept of validity as applied to experimental research and distinguish between internal and external validity.
- Discuss the different threats to validity that are controlled by each type of design.
- Discuss the basic issues and terminologies involved in experimental research.
- Describe the distinction between classical designs and statistical designs.
- List guidelines for conducting experimental research and discuss the limitations of experimental research.
- Discuss the advantages and limitations of the different types of experimental designs.

A utility company wants to encourage people to insulate their homes. It is recognized that insulation will conserve energy, reduce utility bills, improve living comfort, and retard fires. A decision is needed as to which of these appeals should be used in the campaign. More particularly, an advertisement using both the utility bill and comfort appeals has been developed, and a decision is needed as to whether the advertisement should be the basis of a statewide promotion.

Several research approaches have been discussed in previous chapters, such as the use of secondary data, small-sample interviewing, observation, and surveys. All these can provide helpful insights in answering these questions and others. However, they are useful primarily as elements of exploratory or descriptive research efforts. They are not well suited to making definitive judgments about which appeal, if any, will work, or about how much impact an advertisement will have. To determine the answer to these more demanding causal questions, experimentation, the subject of this chapter, is employed.

Experiments are defined as studies in which conditions are controlled so that one or more independent variable(s) can be manipulated to test a hypothesis about a dependent variable. In other words, in experimental research, the researcher manipulates the independent/experimental variable(s) and then measures the effect of this manipulation on the dependent variable(s). Thus, experiments are research investigations in which implementation involves an active intervention by the observer beyond that required for measurement. In the case of the utility company, the simplest experiment would be to run the advertisement and then measure its impact. The act of running the advertisement would be the experimental intervention or treatment. Ultimately, there is no substitute for actually trying the advertisement to see how it works. As we shall see, however, such a simple experiment has limitations, and it is usually useful and worthwhile to consider other research designs.

This chapter provides an overview of the basic concepts and issues relating to experimentation. We will discuss a few of the most often used experimental designs and some marketing applications that use experiments to obtain causal inferences.

Descriptive versus Experimental Research

The key principle of experimental work is **manipulation** of a treatment variable (say, X), followed by observation of a response variable (say, Y). If a change in X causes Y to change in the hypothesized way, then we are tempted to say that X causes Y. However, this causal inference rests on soft ground unless the experiment has been properly designed to *control* for other variables.[1] As discussed in Chapter 4, though descriptive research can show that two variables are related or associated, this is not sufficient to establish a causal inference. Of course, evidence of a relationship or an association is useful; otherwise, we would have no basis for even inferring that causality might be present. To go beyond this inference, however, we must have reasonable proof that one variable precedes the other and that no other causal factors could have accounted for the relationship.

What Are Causal Relationships?

Marketing intelligence is primarily about causal relationships between a host of independent variables and their effect on dependent variables. A concern with causality appears throughout marketing decision making. For example,

- What effect have recent price increases had on product class sales?

- Does the number of sales calls per month affect the size of the order placed?

Underlying the research questions just given is the need to understand the **causal relationships** between an action and a probable outcome. These could be actions taken in the past (if we are in an evaluative or problem-solving mode) or predictions about future actions. If the focus is on the future, then the primary interest is in comparing the potential outcomes of decision alternatives.

Limitations of Descriptive Designs

Why can't a descriptive research design answer these needs for causal insights? In the first place, most descriptive research does exactly as it says—it provides a "snapshot" of some aspect of the market environment at a specific point in time. Thus we use surveys, store audits, observation studies, analyses of financial records, and so on, to give us information about such variables as brand shares, distribution coverage, and the demographic characteristics of heavy buyers. In general, causal insight that can be obtained from such data are rare. Under some circumstances, however, descriptive information can be used to infer—though rarely to establish—the presence of causal relationships.

The first step toward establishing causality usually is a calculation of the strength of association between two or more variables measured during the descriptive study. If a causal link exists between two variables, they may be expected to be associated. Thus, we might find that a high quality of service is associated with health maintenance organizations that have small staffs.

Another way is to measure association with data over time. For example, historical data may show an association between advertising expenditures and sales. Does this finding mean that advertising causes sales? Unfortunately, this question is not easily answered. There is still the possibility of a third causal variable, such as distribution, being involved. Increased distribution might require more advertising support and may generate sales. There is also a direction-of-causation issue. It could be that the advertising expenditures are budgeted as a fixed percent of sales. Thus, a forecast of sales increases may lead to increases in advertising expenditures, so a more correct model might be

Sales change *causes* advertising expenditure change

instead of

Advertising expenditure change *causes* sales change

Clearly, what is needed is some idea of the time sequence of events; that is, did the change in advertising activity actually precede the observed change in sales? With a positive answer to this question, we get closer to the characteristics of a proper causal design.

The following quotation provides a clear distinction between experimental research and other research approaches.

> *Experimentation differs from alternative methods of marketing research in that in experimentation the researcher manipulates the independent variable or variables before measuring the effect upon the dependent variable. For example, the effect of price changes on sales volume of a particular product can be examined by actually varying the price of the product. A nonexperimental approach would be to ask consumers whether they would buy more of the product if its price were lowered. The manipulation of independent variables, together with procedures of controlling extraneous variation . . . forms the basis of the power of experimental research relative to other research techniques. The better the researcher's control over the experimental variables and extraneous variations, the more confident the researcher can be that he [or she] is in fact determining cause and effect relationships.*[2]

Hence, of all the various types of research approaches that may suggest causality between two variables, the greatest assurance that a causal inference is sound stems from experimental research.[3] Specifically, experimentation consists of manipulating levels or amounts of selected independent variables (causes) to examine their influence on dependent variables (effects).

Although theoretically a completely controlled experiment can indicate 100 percent causality, in practice, causal inference can seldom be established conclusively. Because experimental design is concerned with detecting and quantifying causal relationships, it is appropriate and indeed necessary to discuss what constitutes causality and what the conditions are for valid causal inferences.

What Constitutes Causality?

Causation, strictly speaking, means that a change in one variable will produce a change in another. In this context, the definition will be broadened somewhat to include the concept of a precondition influencing a variable of interest. For example, we could conceive that credit card usage is determined partly by a person's sex. In this case, sex could be conceptualized as causal in nature, despite the fact that it would be impossible to take a group of people and change their sex to observe if a change in credit card usage was "produced." The weaker term "influence" often will be used when it is more appropriate than the term "cause," but the logic of the analysis normally will remain the same.

Given the causation concept, that a change in one variable will produce a change in another, it is reasonable to conclude that if two variables are causally linked, they should be **associated**. If association provides evidence of causation,then, conversely, the lack of association suggests the absence of causation. Thus, an association between attitude and behavior is evidence of a **causal relationship:**

Attitude → behavior

Direction of Causation Issue

If a causal link between two variables is thought to exist, a reasonable question is which variable is the causal (or independent) variable and which is the "caused" (or dependent) variable.

One approach to determining the direction of causation is to draw on logic and previous theory. In this context, it is useful to observe whether one of the variables is relatively fixed and unalterable. Variables such as sex, age, and income are relatively permanent. If, for example, an association is found between age and attendance at rock concerts, it would be unrealistic to claim that attendance at rock concerts causes people to be young. In this case, age could not be a "caused" variable, because it is fixed in this context. However, it could be that age is an important determinant of who attends rock concerts.

A second approach is to consider the fact that there is usually a time lag between cause and effect. If such a time lag can be postulated, the causal variable should have a positive association with the effect variable lagged in time.

Conditions for Valid Causal Inferences

As the preceding discussion on competing explanations indicates, the concept of causality is complex. The scientific notion of causality is very different from the commonsense, everyday notion.[4] The following table summarizes the difference between the commonsense and the scientific notions of causality.

Commonsense notion	Scientific notion
• There is a single cause of an event; that is, X is the only cause of Y.	• There can be more than one cause; that is, X may be only one of the multiple causes of Y.
• There is a deterministic relationship between X and Y.	• There is only a probabilistic relationship between X and Y.
• The causal relationship between X and Y can be proved.	• The causal relationship can never be proved; we can only infer that X is a cause of Y.

Thus, the scientific notion holds that causality is inferred; it is never demonstrated conclusively.[5] Then what kind of evidence can be used to support causal inferences?

The following types of evidence are relevant to evaluating causal relationships:

- *Condition of concomitant variation*
  —Evidence that a strong association exists between an action and an observed outcome.

- *Condition of time order of occurrence*
  —Evidence that the action preceded the outcome.

- *Absence of competing causal explanations*
  —Evidence that there is no strong competing explanation for the relationship—that a high level of internal validity exists.

In addition, if the resulting causal inference is to be useful to management, it should be

- Generalizable beyond the particular setting in which it was found; that is, it should have a high level of external validity.

- Persistent in that it will hold long enough to make management action worthwhile.

As discussed earlier, even if the above-mentioned conditions are fulfilled—that is, there is evidence of concomitant variation, time order of occurrence, and absence of competing explanations—scientifically, the presence of a causal relationship can never be proved. The presence of strong evidence only increases our confidence in inferring the presence of a causal relationship. The results from controlled experimental research studies, conducted in different environmental settings, increase the reliability of our inference.

Laboratory and Field Experiments

Experimental research can also be broadly divided into two main categories: laboratory experiments and field experiments. The first, laboratory experiments, as the name suggests, are experiments in which the experimental treatment is introduced in an artificial or laboratory setting. In this type of research study, the variance of all or nearly all of the possible influential independent variables not pertinent to the immediate problem of the investigation is kept to a minimum. This is done by isolating the research in a physical situation apart from the routine of ordinary living and by manipulating one or more independent variables under rigorously specified, operationalized, and controlled conditions. For example, a shopper might be exposed to a new product in a simulated supermarket, or two groups of hospital users might be asked to react to two different pricing plans for the delivery of medical services.

The second, field experiments, are conducted in the "field." A field experiment is a research study in a realistic situation in which one or more independent variables are manipulated by the experimenter under carefully controlled conditions as the situation will permit.[6] For example, one television advertisement is run in Omaha and another in Dayton. The next day viewers in the two cities are called to determine their response. A **field experiment** is the experimental treatment or intervention introduced in a completely natural setting. The respondents usually are not aware that an experiment is being conducted; thus, the response tends to be *natural*.

The **laboratory experiment** tends to be *artificial*. Furthermore, there is a *testing effect*, in that respondents are usually aware of being in a test and therefore are sensitized and tend not to respond naturally. Thus, the question always arises: What will happen outside the laboratory? Are the results projectable to the real world? Does the result have external validity? **External validity** refers to the applicability of the experimental results to situations external to the actual experimental context. Field experiments tend to have much greater external validity than laboratory experiments. Laboratory experiments, however, tend to be much less costly and allow the experimenter greater control over the experiment, thus reducing alternative explanations of the results and increasing internal validity. **Internal validity** refers to the ability of the experiment to show relationships unambiguously. For example, a large response to the Omaha advertisement might be caused by the number of people in Omaha, the weather when the advertisement was run, or the scheduling of civic activities. Although it is possible, by improving the experimental design, to reduce the number of competing explanations of the results of field experiments, they still tend to have less internal validity than laboratory experiments.

The purpose of an experiment usually is to detect or confirm causal relationships and to quantify them. The validity issue is thus extremely important. Of course, enhanced validity has associated costs and, as with other research approaches, the goal is not to maximize validity, regardless of cost. The goal, rather, is to make the appropriate trade-off between validity and cost. The design of an experiment allows considerable room for making such trade-offs.

Threats to Experimental Validity[7]

An experiment is intended to provide information regarding the causal influence of an experimental treatment on the measure of interest. The *internal validity* of the experiment depends on the extent to which competing explanations for the results are avoided. The *external validity* of the experiment refers to the extent that the causal inferences can be generalized from the experimental environment to the environment of the decision maker.

Threats to Internal Validity[8]

The major source of threat to internal validity comes from eight different classes of extraneous variables, which if not controlled might produce effects confounded with the effects of the experimental stimulus.

1. *History:* Events external to the experiment that affect the responses of the people involved in the experiment.

2. *Maturation:* Changes in the respondents that are a consequence of time, such as aging, getting hungry, or getting tired.

3. *Testing:* The effects of taking a test on the results of a subsequent test.

4. *Instrumentation:* The measuring instrument may change, as when different interviewers are used.

5. *Statistical regression:* Operates where groups have been selected on the basis of their extreme scores.

6. *Selection bias:* An experimental group is systematically different in some relevant way from the population being studied.

7. *Mortality:* Respondents dropping out of the experiment while the experimental research is in progress.

8. *Selection–maturation interaction:* In certain experimental designs, the selection–maturation interaction effect might be mistaken for the effect of the experimental variable.

Threats to External Validity[9]

Laboratory experiments have the greatest external validity problem because of the *artificiality* of the setting and arrangements. The exposure to an experimental treatment, such as a mock-up of a new product in a laboratory, can be so different from conditions in the real world that projections become very difficult and risky. Consider the plight of a researcher seeking to design a laboratory experiment to yield quick feedback on the effect of a company rebuttal to adverse publicity.

An example is a government report on Alka-Seltzer, which contended that because it contained aspirin it was damaging to some of the stomach conditions it was designed to treat. Since "bad news" is thought to have superior attention-getting ability, a valid laboratory experiment would provide for selective exposure, attention, or perception of the attack and the rebuttal. This problem has defeated several ingenious researchers.

In addition to the problem of artificiality in laboratory experiments, most of the previous list of eight internal validity threats also apply to external validity. In particular, selectivity bias can be very serious. In field experiments, the test market site, the stores chosen to test, and the people interviewed as part of the experiment are sometimes not representative of the entire market or population. In a laboratory experiment, the respondents are often not a good representation of the population, especially if the experiment requires considerable effort and if self-selection is involved. As Seymour Banks notes: "The greater the demand upon respondents in terms of either the effort expended or the period of time covered by the experiment, the greater the likelihood that the subject who cooperates throughout the study is atypical."[10]

Also, a significant before-measure effect may diminish external validity. If the before measure increases respondent sensitivity to the treatment, then the results will not be typical of the "real world." This problem can be severe in experiments that ask respondents to record purchases in a diary. These consumer panel members invariably pay closer attention to the choices in the categories being recorded, and they may buy larger-than-usual quantities in order to have something to record. The novelty does wear off, and purchase behavior is thought to return to normal, but that can occur after the experiment is over.

In general, the major factors that jeopardize external validity of the experiment are as follows:

1. *The reactive or interaction effect of testing*, in which a pretest might increase or decrease the respondent's sensitivity or responsiveness to the experimental variable, and thus make the results obtained for a pretested population unrepresentative of the effects of the experimental variable for the unpretested universe from which the experimental respondents were selected.

2. *The interaction effect of selection biases and the experimental variable.*

3. *Reactive effects of experimental arrangements*, which would preclude generalization about the effect of the experimental variable on persons being exposed to it in nonexperimental settings.

4. *Multiple treatment interference*, likely to occur whenever multiple treatments are applied to the same respondents, because the effects of prior treatments usually are not erasable.

This enumeration of sources of invalidity is bound to be incomplete. Some threats are too specific to a given setting to be generalized easily. The sources of invalidity (internal and external) that are still a potential threat for classical experimental designs are provided in Table 13.1. For example, the likelihood that competitors will distort the results of market tests (by aggressive promotional activity, additional sales force effort, or even doing nothing when they certainly would take action if the new product were launched into a regional or national market) is an ever-present "history" problem in this particular setting.

What is important is not the completeness of the checklist of threats but a heightened sensitivity to the possibility of threats so that

1. The extent and the direction of the bias in results can be considered when it becomes time to use the relationship obtained from the experiment to make a decision.

2. The possibility of design improvements can be anticipated.

3. Other methods of measurement with different restraints on validity can be employed. The virtue of multiple measures or approaches to the same phenomena is that the biases of each may cancel each other.

Table 13.1 Sources of Invalidity

	Internal								External			
	A	B	C	D	E	F	G	H	I	J	K	L
Preexperimental designs:												
1. One group, after-only design	–	–				–	–				–	
2. One group, before–after design	–	–	–	–	?	+	+	–	–	–	?	
3. Nonmatched control group design	+	?	+	+	+	–	–	–		–		
4. Matched control group design	+	?	+	+	+	+	–	–				
True experimental designs:												
5. Two group, before–after design	+	+	+	+	+	+	+	+	–	?	?	
6. Solomon four-group design	+	+	+	+	+	+	+	+	?	?	?	
7. Two group, after-only design	+	+	+	+	+	+	+	+	?	?	?	
Quasi-experimental designs:												
8. Time-series design	–	+	+	?	+	+	+	+		?	?	

Source: Adapted from Donald T. Campbell and Julian C. Stanley, *Experimental and Quasi-Experimental Designs for Research*, Chicago: Rand McNally, 1963.

A = history **B** = maturation **C** = testing **D** = instrumentation
E = statistical regression **F** = selection **G** = mortality
H = interaction of selection and maturation, etc.
I = reactive or interaction effect of testing
J = interaction of selection biases and the experimental variable
K = reactive effect of experimental arrangements
L = multiple treatment interference

(−) Indicates a definite weakness   (+) Indicates that the Factor is controlled
(?) Indicates a possible source of concern   ( ) Indicates that the Factor is not relevant

Issues in Experimental Research

Experimental research involves decision making on three major issues:

1. What type of experimental design should be used?

2. Should the experiment be performed in a "laboratory" setting or in the "field"?

3. What are the internal and external threats to the validity of the experiment, and how can we control for the various threats to the experiment's internal and external validity?

We will discuss the various types of experimental designs and how these designs take care of the threats to experimental validity. Table 13.2 introduces the basic terminologies that are often used in experimental design.

Basic Symbols and Notations[11]

We introduce six notations that are commonly used while conducting experiments. First are observation (O) and exposure (X).

O denotes a formal **observation** or measurement of the dependent variable that is made as part of the experimental study. Symbols O_1, O_2, and so on, will be used when two or more measurements of the dependent variable are involved during the experiment.

Table 13.2   Basic Concepts and the Language of Experimental Design

Independent variable: The variable that can be manipulated, changed, or altered by the experimenter, independently of each other variable. The independent variable is hypothesized to be the causal influence.

Dependent variable: The variable whose value is dependent on the experimenter's manipulations. It is the criterion or the standard by which the results of the experiment are judged. Changes in the dependent variable are presumed to be the effect of changes in the independent variable.

Test unit: A subject or entity whose responses to experimental treatments are being observed and measured.

Manipulation: Creating different levels of the independent variable is known as manipulating the variable. In the experiment, the independent variable is manipulated, and the effect of each level of manipulation on the dependent variable is observed.

Experimental treatments: Experimental treatments are the alternative manipulations of the independent variable being investigated. For example, low exposure level, medium exposure level, and high exposure level might be experimental treatments in an advertising experiment.

Experiment: Studies in which conditions are controlled so that one or more independent variables can be maintained to test a hypothesis about a dependent variable. In other words, in experimental research, the researcher manipulates the independent/experimental variable(s) and then measures the effect of this manipulation on the dependent variable(s).

Experimental group: The group of subjects exposed to the experimental treatment is termed the experimental group.

Control group: The group of subjects not exposed to the experimental treatment is termed the control group.

Extraneous variable: Variables other than the manipulated variable that affect the response of the test units and hence the results of the experimental research. These variables interfere with the changes in the dependent variable and thus confound the results of the experiment. Hence they are also known as **confounding variables**.

Selection bias: If an experimental group is systematically different in some relevant way from the population being studied, it invalidates the results of the experiment. This is known as selection bias. Also, if the subjects assigned to the experimental group differ systematically from the subjects assigned to the control group, then the result of the experiment could be attributed to the differences between the groups rather than to the experimental manipulations.

Randomization: A procedure in which the assignment of subjects and treatments to groups is based on chance. Randomization ensures control over extraneous variables and increases the experiment's reliability.

Blocking: Even after adopting random assignments of subjects and treatments to groups, it is possible at times for the experimental groups to differ in a systematic manner on some relevant variable. Blocking is a procedure by which a nonmanipulated variable is introduced into the experiment to ensure that the groups are equalized on that variable.

Matching: Matching is a procedure for the assignment of subjects to groups that ensures each group of respondents is matched on the basis of pertinent characteristics. Matching helps reduce the experimental error that arises out of selection bias.

Treatment effect: Conducting the experiment by itself can alter the effects of the manipulations and thus affect the results of the experiment. This is known as treatment effect.

Hawthorne effect: A form of treatment effect wherein the results of the experimental research are altered unintentionally by the subjects being aware that they are participating in an experiment.

Demand characteristics: Another type of treatment effect, which refers to design procedures that unintentionally alert the subject about the experimenter's hypothesis. If participants recognize the experimenter's expectation or demand, they are likely to act in a manner consistent with the experimental treatment, and this introduces error in the experiment's results.

Experimental design: A set of procedures that guide an experimental study by specifying (1) what independent variables are to be manipulated, (2) what dependent variables are to be measured, (3) what levels of the experimental treatment are to be used, (4) how to select test units and assign them to different groups, (5) how to control for selection bias, and (6) how to minimize the influence of extraneous variables on the results of the experiment.

X denotes *exposure* of test units participating in the study to the experimental manipulation or treatment. Symbols X_1, X_2, and so forth, will be used when the test units are exposed to two or more experimental treatments.

Note: The ordering of O's and X's from left to right will represent the time sequence in which they occur.

EG denotes an **experimental group** of test units that are exposed to the experimental treatment. Symbols EG_1, EG_2, and so on, will be used when the experiment has more than one experimental group.

CG denotes a **control group** of test units participating in the experiment but not exposed to the experimental treatment. Symbols CG_1, CG_2, and so on, will be used when the experiment involves more than one control group.

R denotes *random* assignment of test units and experimental treatments to groups. Randomization ensures control over extraneous variables and increases the reliability of the experiment.

M denotes that both the experimental group and the control group are **matched** on the basis of some relevant characteristics. Matching helps reduce the experimental error that arises out of selection bias.

Types of Experimental Designs

Experimental designs can be broadly categorized into two groups: classical designs and statistical designs. The basic difference between these two types of experimental designs is that classical designs consider the impact of only one treatment level of an independent variable at a time. On the other hand, statistical designs allow for examining the impact of different treatment levels of an independent variable and also the impact of two or more independent variables.[12] Figure 13.1 provides a detailed classification of the more commonly used experimental designs.

Classical Designs

Classical designs can be further categorized into three groups: preexperimental, true experimental, and quasi-experimental designs.

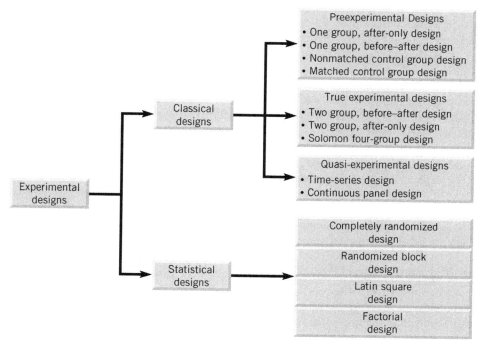

FIGURE 13.1
A Classification of Experimental Designs.

Preexperimental Designs

Preexperimental designs, as the name suggests, are somewhat exploratory types of studies that have almost no control over the influence of extraneous factors on the results of the experiment. In the strict sense of the term, preexperimental studies cannot be classified under experimental research, as they have little or no value in establishing causal inferences. But preexperimental studies can lead to hypotheses about causal relationships, and this is precisely the reason we discuss these designs. Once the basic hypotheses about causal relationships between variables are developed, additional research can be performed to establish causality with greater confidence.

The most commonly used preexperimental designs are (1) one group, after-only design; (2) nonmatched control group design; (3) matched control group design; and (4) one group, before–after design.

One Group, After-Only Design

The simplest experiment is simply to apply the experimental treatment to a subject or group and measure the results. The utility company might run a two-week advertising campaign in Modesto, California, during January, advocating insulation. They then might measure the number of requests for price quotations that insulation firms received. A large number of requests would serve to justify the advertising expenditure and support a decision to expand it to other cities. This experimental design can be described with the following notation:

$$EG \quad X \quad O$$

That is, an observation is made after an experimental group has been exposed to an experimental treatment.

One problem with this design is that it leaves open the possibility that the results could be explained by events external to the design. For example, insulation requests might arise from the fact that California was unseasonably cold during the test period, that utility bills are always high during January and high bills prompt interest in insulation, or that *Time* magazine ran a cover story on energy during the period. Such a possibility of confounding effects that are external to the design are termed **history effects**.[13] In marketing studies, a prime source of history effects are the actions of competitors, retaliatory, or otherwise. In some situations, competitors deliberately run special promotions in markets in which others are experimenting, to foul them up. The longer the time period involved, the greater is the likelihood that history will account for the observed results. A one-year trial run of a marketing program in a single city probably would generate many history effects.

Another problem analogous to history is **maturation**,[14] which refers to changes within respondents that are a consequence of time, including aging, growing tired, or becoming hungrier. For example, suppose the experimental treatment is a one-year delinquency-prevention program. At the year's end, the program is evaluated by measuring the number of subjects who have jobs and the incidence of crime. If 18-year-olds are more likely than 17-year-olds to hold jobs and avoid crime, then the findings may be the result of the young people maturing during the year, and not because of the delinquency program.

Nonmatched Control Group Design

One approach to control for history and maturation effects is to introduce a control group. Data on insulation requests might be readily available for Reading, California. Thus, the number of requests obtained in Reading could be compared with that of Modesto. This design would be

$$\begin{array}{ccc} EG & X & O_1 \\ \hline CG & & O_2 \end{array}$$

The top line refers to the Modesto group and the bottom line to the Reading group, which, of course, receives no experimental treatment. The results of interest would then be $O_1 - O_2$. A dotted horizontal line means that the groups are separate, and that the experimental treatment does not reach the control group. If people in Modesto read the Reading newspaper, such would not be the case.

Another major problem that existed in the first design and is not solved by the second is termed **selection bias**.[15] It may be that the response to the experiment is strictly a function of the city selected, Modesto. Modesto has many characteristics that could influence the experiment, including its location, its income, the quality of its insulation firms, and its climate. If two, three, or more test cities and a like number of control cities were used, the selection bias very likely would be reduced, but it still would be there. Perhaps all of the test cities would be in the northern part of the state and the control cities in the southern part.

Selection bias is particularly severe when self-selection occurs, as when the test group consists of those who volunteered to participate in a program or research study. For example, suppose a group of students agreed to participate in a physical fitness program. To evaluate the program, the number of push-ups that the group can do is compared to the number possible by those who did not volunteer to be part of the experimental group. Those who did volunteer are likely to be in better condition before the program, and the results simply might reflect this selection bias.

Matched Control Group Design

One approach to reducing selection bias is to match the experimental and control groups. Thus, if average temperature is expected to affect a community's reaction to insulation advertising, cities are matched as to their average temperature. A control city is picked that is similar to Modesto in terms of temperature. Of course, another city may be found that matches Modesto in other dimensions besides temperature, such as the percentage of homes not insulated, or demographic variables. This design can be denoted as

$$EG \quad M \quad X \quad O_1$$
$$CG \quad M \quad \quad O_2$$

where M indicates that the two groups are matched with respect to some variable of interest.

The use of matched control groups is very beneficial when the sample design and cost considerations limit the size of the sample. It is very costly to run a test marketing program with subsequent measurement in a city or a small group of cities, and the researchers are often constrained to a single test city or at most two or three. In such cases, attempting to match the control city or cities with the test city or cities might be appropriate.

One Group, Before–After Design

The designs considered thus far have been "after-only" designs because they had no "before" measures. Another approach to improving the control is to add a *before measure*:

$$EG \quad O_1 \quad X \quad O_2$$

The *before measure* acts as a control, because if the city is large the O_1 measure also will be large. The interest is then in the change from O_1 to O_2, correcting for seasonal patterns.

The *before measure* can be added to any design already presented. It will enhance sensitivity by adding another method to control for confounding variables. When the observation is obtrusive, several potential threats to internal validity emerge. Consider, for example, a laboratory experiment to test an advertisement aimed at reducing the incidence of smoking among teenage women. Attitudes and perceptions toward smoking are measured, the group is exposed to the advertisement, and the attitudes are measured again, immediately or perhaps after several days. The *before measure* in such an experiment may produce the following validity threats:[16]

1. *Before-measure effect.* The before-measure effect may alert the respondents to the fact that they are being studied. The result can be a tendency to give more socially desirable responses and behavior, such as reducing the claimed and actual smoking frequency. Further, the before-measure effect can stimulate or enhance an interest in the subject of the study. It can therefore generate heightened curiosity and attention and even lead to discussing the topic with friends and changing the behavior. Thus, the mere fact that a prior measurement was taken can have an effect on any measurement taken after the treatment.

2. *Mortality effect.* This is due to the possibility that some subjects may stop participating in the experiment or may not respond when sought out for a follow-up interview. This dropout, or mortality, effect usually is not uniform across the sample being studied. Busy people, high-income households, and urban-area residents are always more difficult to reach.

3. *Instrumentation effect.* This is the result of a change in the measuring instrument. An instrumentation effect may be as simple as a change in question wording between interviews or the use of a different interviewer for the follow-up interview. A more subtle problem is a consequence of interviewers changing as they gain experience and virtually becoming different instruments.

True Experimental Designs

Most of the problems mentioned above to a large extent can be controlled by adopting a *random assignment* procedure. Randomization means assigning members of a universe to experimental treatments in such a way that, for any given assignment to a treatment, every member has an equal probability of being chosen for that assignment.[17] The basic purpose of random assignment is to assign subjects to treatments so that individuals with varying characteristics are spread equally among the treatments, in an effort to neutralize the effect of extraneous variables. Experimental designs that adopt the random assignment procedure are called **true experimental designs**, and those designs are generally far superior to preexperimental designs in making causal inferences with confidence. Thus, the defining feature of the true experimental design is the random assignment procedure.[18]

True experimental designs have two key features that enable researchers to exercise tight control over extraneous influences: the presence of one or more control groups and, more important, the random assignment of test units to various experimental and control groups. Random assignment, however, is not a panacea; it is merely a procedure for minimizing the odds of systematic differences between groups at the start of an experiment. However, the ability of random assignment to lower those odds depends on the number of units available for assignment. The larger the initial sample size, the more successful random assignment will be in achieving equivalence across groups. For most marketing applications, complete random assignment may not always be practical, even if a sufficiently large sample of units is available. Studies conducted under these circumstances cannot employ experimental designs that are strictly true, and hence their findings must be interpreted with caution.[19]

The more commonly used true experimental designs are (1) two group, before–after design, (2) two group, after-only design, and (3) the Solomon four-group design.

Two Group, After-Only Design

In the matched control group design (a preexperimental design), we saw that matching helps in reducing selection bias and thus provides relatively more control in the experiment. The problem with matching is that test units cannot be matched on all relevant dimensions. They can be matched on one, two, and sometimes several dimensions, but in most contexts, there are many dimensions that potentially could influence the results. Further, some or even most of these might be unknown or ones for which information is not available. For example, response to insulation might be due to people's attitude toward home improvement. If there is no information about people's attitudes, it is not possible to develop sets of matched cities on this dimension.

Randomly assigning test units or subjects to test and control groups provides a mechanism that, when the sample size is sufficient, serves to match test and control groups on all dimensions simultaneously. Suppose we had 50 cities to use in our test. We randomly assign 25 to the test condition and use the remaining 25 as a control. Because of the randomization, it would be unlikely that the test cities are larger, colder, or of higher income than the control cities. All of these factors should tend to average out. Of course, as the sample size increases, the degree of matching achieved by randomization also increases.

A randomized, two group, after-only design can be denoted as

$$
\begin{array}{cccc}
EG & R & X & O_1 \\
\hline
CG & R & & O_2
\end{array}
$$

where R indicates that the test units are randomly assigned to the test and control groups. Randomization is particularly appropriate whenever the sample size is large enough that the randomization will result in the test and control groups being similar.

An advantage of this design over the two group, before–after design is that the interaction effect of testing that is present in the earlier design is absent in this design, because there are no pretest measurements.

Two Group, Before–After Design

The addition of a control group in the randomized case of the one group, before–after design (a preexperimental design) generates the following true experimental design:

$$
\begin{array}{ccccc}
EG & R & O_1 & X & O_2 \\
\hline
CG & R & O_3 & & O_4
\end{array}
$$

This design provides a control group that helps control for history and maturation effects and, in addition, controls for the reactive effect of O_1 on O_2 (part of the before-measure effect). The output of interest is the difference obtained by subtracting O_2 from O_1 and O_4 from O_3. However, the design fails to control for the effect of the *before measure* on X, the experiment treatment (the other part of the before-measure effect). It may be that the *before measure* will sensitize the respondents so that their reaction to the experimental treatment will be distorted. After giving their attitudes about smoking, the teenage women subjects might react quite differently to an antismoking advertisement than if they had not given their attitudes. Marketing Research in Action 13.1 describes how Campbell Soup used these types of design for some experiments.

Solomon Four-Group Design[20]

A possible solution to the problem in the two group, before–after design is to augment the design with an after-only design as follows:

$$
\begin{array}{ccccc}
EG & R & O_1 & X & O_2 \\
\hline
CG & R & O_3 & & O_4 \\
\hline
EG & R & & X & O_5 \\
\hline
CG & R & & & O_6
\end{array}
$$

Marketing Research in Action 13.1

■ THE CAMPBELL SOUP EXPERIMENTS

The Campbell Soup Company conducted a series of 19 before–after, randomized control group experiments in the 1970s to evaluate alternative advertising strategies for many of its products, including Campbell's condensed soups, Soup for One soups, Chunky soups, Franco American Pasta, Swanson frozen dinners, and V-8 cocktail vegetable juice. The studies tested increased advertising, shifts to different media, shifts to different markets, and new creative approaches.

One yearlong experiment for Campbell's Chunky soups evaluated the shift of 25 percent of the spot TV budget to outdoor in two test markets, Indianapolis and Houston. Sales were measured for each four-week period using warehouse withdrawals as reported by the SAMI system, during the experiment and for the prior three years. Prior sales were used to adjust sales for seasonal variations (caused in part by regular seasonal promotions) and for any trend over time. An increase in sales of 8 percent was found after eight months, an increase that was attributed to outdoor-reached people not exposed to TV advertising.

Several conclusions emerged from the experiments. First, in five tests of increased advertising expenditures, consumers did not respond to being told the same thing more often. Second, three of five experiments, including the Chunky soup experiment, in which the test advertising reached more people, did result in increased sales. Third, improved creative efforts did result in increased sales in three of five experiments that tested new advertising. Fourth, in the experiments where significant sales increases occurred, they usually occurred within a relatively short time period, three or four periods.

For more information on the Campbell Soup Company go to http://www.campbellsoup.com.
Source: J. O. Eastlack, Jr., and Ambar G. Rao, "Conducting Advertising Experiments in the Real World: The Campbell Soup Company Experience," Marketing Science, 5(3), Winter 1989, pp. 245–259.

This design is usually prohibitively expensive, but it does provide the power to control for the before-measure effect of O_1 on both X and O_2. This design provides several measures of the experimental effect [that is, $(O_2 - O_4)$, $(O_2 - O_1) - (O_4 - O_3)$, $(O_6 - O_5)$]. If there is agreement among these measures, the inferences about X can be much stronger. If there is no agreement, it is still possible to measure directly the interaction of the treatment and before-measure effects [$(O_2 - O_4) - (O_5 - O_6)$].

Quasi-Experimental Designs

Quasi-experimental designs offer the researcher some degree of control (more than preexperimental designs), but there is no random assignment of subjects as there is for true experimental designs. Nevertheless, quasi-experimental designs usually provide more measurements and more information than a typical preexperimental design. The most popular and most frequently used quasi-experimental designs are the time-series designs.

Time-Series Designs

Time-series designs are similar to the one group, before–after design except that a series of measurements is employed during which an experimental treatment occurs. Symbolically, time-series designs can be shown as

$$EG \quad O_1 \quad O_2 \quad O_3 \quad O_4 \quad X \quad O_5 \quad O_6 \quad O_7 \quad O_8$$

There are two variants of this design, depending on whether the measurements are all from the same sample or from separate samples.

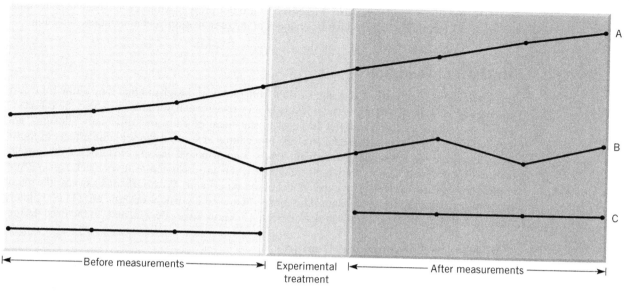

FIGURE 13.2
A Time-Series Design.

Trend studies are measures over time that come from a succession of *separate* random samples from the same population and yield much of the basic information on which marketing decisions are made.

The data from trend studies can be analyzed only in the aggregate form in which they are collected. The question is whether the measures following the experimental treatment are a continuation of earlier patterns or whether they mark a decisive change. In Figure 13.2, a decisive change is apparent only in case C.

The insights from trend studies can be expanded considerably if several trends can be analyzed simultaneously. For example, an estimate of the price elasticity of demand for a product can be obtained if parallel trends of prices and market shares or sales are available.

The availability of data spanning a number of time periods means that *maturation* is unlikely to be a possible cause of the observed effect. *History* and *instrument* changes remain as possible threats to validity. Of the two threats, the possibility that a simultaneous event produced the change is clearly the most difficult to rule out. If one is to use this design, there must be continuing sensitivity to plausible competing explanations.[21] Ideally, this should be done prior to the experimental treatment, so that the data needed to confirm or disconfirm the competing hypotheses are available. This may entail recording the weather, prices of related products, and so forth.

Continuous Panel Studies[22]

These collect a series of measurements on the same sample of test units, over an extended period of time. They offer insights into choice behavior that cannot be obtained from any other source. Each person, whose behavior or attitude changed, can be identified, instead of the information being buried in the aggregation of a time series. This is especially important in product categories where stable sales often obscure large, but compensating, gains and losses of individual buyers.

Since panel data normally are collected directly from an individual, there is a significant threat to internal validity from the before-measure effect. When a person is asked about a subject and knows that further interviews will be made, the result is an unusual degree of awareness and sensitivity. Fortunately, this seems to decay over time, and within three to five months the preceding interview usually is forgotten. Also, these threats are not present while using scanner panel data. Other threats to validity include history, changes in instrumentation, and nonrandom selection.

Statistical Designs

As mentioned earlier, statistical designs differ from classical designs in that they allow for examining the effects of different treatment levels of an experimental variable, and also the effects of two or more independent variables. In general, statistical designs are "after-only" designs, and they require relatively complex data analysis procedures to sort out the separate effects of multiple independent variables and/or treatment levels. Two principal aspects of statistical designs are (1) the experimental layouts by which treatment levels are assigned to test objects, and (2) the techniques that are used to analyze the results of the experiment. We briefly discuss now the major types of layouts used to obtain data. The most often used statistical designs are (1) completely randomized design, (2) randomized block design, (3) Latin square design, and (4) factorial design.

Completely Randomized Design

The **completely randomized design** is the simplest type of statistical design. In this design, the experimental treatments are assigned to test units on a random basis. Any number of treatments can be assigned by a random process to any number of test units. Direct-mail tests of advertising appeals are an ideal setting for this design. The mailing list can be sampled randomly to obtain the experimental and control groups. Suppose, for example, that three different promotion pieces for a series of plays are to be tested. The question is which will deliver the most orders. A mailing list of 20,000 people is available. A random sample of 1,200 is selected and divided randomly into three groups of 400 each. The experiment would appear as

$$
\begin{array}{cccc}
EG_1 & R & X_1 & O_1 \\
EG_2 & R & X_2 & O_2 \\
EG_3 & R & X_3 & O_3
\end{array}
$$

where the X_1 refers to the first experimental treatment "level," namely, on the first of the three promotional pieces; X_2 refers to the second level; and so on. Here there is no separate control group. Each of the three treatments acts as a control for the others. The point of the experiment is to compare the three experimental treatments.

A variant of this design combines the treatment and the observation in the same questionnaire. In fact, this is the preferred method of obtaining reactions to different marketing options using surveys. For example, a study was conducted to determine the demand for a bus service at various price levels. One approach would have been to ask prospective patrons if they would ride the bus if the fare was 25 cents, 50 cents, or $1. However, it might have been unrealistic to ask a respondent to make a judgment on a 50-cent fare after he or she has just considered a 25-cent fare. To avoid this problem, each respondent was given only one price. Each pricing alternative was presented to a randomly chosen third of a representative sample from the service area of the new bus route. The modified design then was

$$
\begin{array}{ccc}
EG_1 & R & (X_1, O_1) \\
EG_2 & R & (X_2, O_2) \\
EG_3 & R & (X_3, O_3)
\end{array}
$$

Once the nature of the service and the fare level were described to each respondent, a measure of intentions or preferences relative to existing modes of transportation was obtained.

Randomized Block Design

A randomized control group design employs the randomization process for all variables, since there should be no tendency for an experimental group to differ systematically from the others on any dimension. However, there will be differences as long as the sample size is not extremely large. For example, even with 1,200 in the sample, the group that received the first promotion piece might happen to be wealthier, more interested in the plays selected, or more urban than suburban. Thus, it could be argued that a superior performance by the first promotional piece actually could have been caused by those characteristics of the sample. Matching ensures that on the matched variable or variables there is/are no difference(s) between test samples. Randomization controls for all variables, not just the matched ones, but ensures only that the groups will tend to be similar.

Randomization and matching are combined in the **randomized block design.** The research identifies which one of the variables is the most important and controls for it by adding a block effect. This means that the control variable is used to define groups and the randomized experiment is conducted within each group. Symbolically, the randomized block design might be

$$
\begin{array}{cccc}
EG_1 & R & X & O_1 \\
CG_1 & R &   & O_2 \\
EG_2 & R & X & O_3 \\
CG_2 & R &   & O_4 \\
\end{array}
$$

The solid line separates the two experiments.

For example, suppose that the urban respondents are expected to react more favorably than suburban respondents to a promotion for subscriptions to a series of plays. It is important to ensure that the experimental groups do not differ on this dimension. When a *block effect* is added, the experiment simply is repeated for both urban respondents and suburban respondents. Thus, 600 randomly selected urban respondents are divided randomly into three test groups who are shown three different types of promotions. The subscripts refer to the three different test groups. Similarly, 600 randomly selected suburban subjects are divided randomly into three groups. This experiment could be represented as follows:

$$
\begin{array}{ccccc}
 & EG_1 & R & X_1 & O_1 \quad n = 200 \\
\text{Urban} & EG_2 & R & X_2 & O_2 \quad n = 200 \\
 & EG_3 & R & X_3 & O_3 \quad n = 200 \\
 & EG_1 & R & X_1 & O_1 \quad n = 200 \\
\text{Suburban} & EG_2 & R & X_2 & O_2 \quad n = 200 \\
 & EG_3 & R & X_3 & O_3 \quad n = 200 \\
\end{array}
$$

The results might be presented in the form of a table as shown here:

	Percentage who ordered tickets		
Treatment	Urban	Suburban	Means
A	11	4	7.5
B	24	11	17.5
C	24.5	15.5	20
Means	20	10	15

If, in the original experiment, which did not block the urban–suburban factor, the group that received promotion B happened to have a higher percentage of urban respondents than the other group, promotion might appear superior to treatment C. However, when the blocked design is used, treatment C is superior.

The results provide evidence that treatment C is the best; however, it is not much better than treatment B. The difference is small enough that it might be due to chance. The treatment C respondents might just happen to be better prospects, and if the sample size was increased 10-fold, promotions B and C actually might be the same. Hypothesis testing provides precise answers to such considerations and will be discussed later.

Another separate motivation for matching on the urban–suburban dimension might be to see if there are differences in reaction to the three promotions. Perhaps a segmentation strategy might emerge that would indicate that one promotion is best for urban dwellers and another for suburbanites. The analysis of such **interaction effects** will be presented in a later section, when factorial designs are discussed. It should be emphasized that this motivation is completely distinct and different from the experimental design motivation, to ensure that the respondents' location does not confound the results.

There is no reason why several control variables cannot be used. To the urban–suburban control variable, a prior-attendance control variable (attended frequently, attended, did not attend) and an age-control variable (older, middle-aged, and younger) could be added. The experiment then simply is repeated for each cell. For example, a group of respondents who are urban, have attended frequently in the past, and are middle-aged, is divided into three groups, and the three experimental treatments are applied to each group. The problem is, of course, that as the number of control variables increases, so does the number of cells and the required sample size. In our example there are $2 \times 3 \times 3$, or 18 cells. The usual solution to this problem is the Latin square design.

Latin Square Design

The **Latin square design** is a method to reduce the number of groups involved when interactions between the treatment levels and the control variables can be considered unimportant. We will use a laboratory nutritional labeling experiment to describe and illustrate the Latin square design.[23]

The goal of the experiment was to contribute to the judgment of those proposing and evaluating several public-policy nutritional labeling alternatives. In particular, the research goal was to determine the effect of variations in nutritional information on canned peas labels on shopper perceptions and preferences. Four levels of information were tested. The first provided only a simple quality statement. The second listed some major nutrient components and indicated whether the product was high or low on them. The third provided the amounts of each nutrient. The fourth listed all nutritional components and was the most complete.

There were two control or block variables, the store and the brand. Four brands of canned peas, each with associated prices, were used. Four locations, each adjacent to a supermarket, were used, and 50 shoppers were interviewed in each. It was felt that interactions among the nutritional information treatments and the brands or stores would be insignificant, so the Latin square could be used. The design is shown in Figure 13.3. Note that treatment level I appears with each store once and only once, and with each brand once and only once. Thus, the results for treatment level I should not benefit from the fact that one of the brands is rated higher than the others or that shoppers from one of the stores are more sensitive to nutrition.

Each respondent was exposed to four cans of peas. For example, at store 1, respondents were exposed to Private Brand A at 21 cents with the treatment III label information, to Private Brand B at 22 cents with treatment II, and so on. After being exposed to the four cans, the respondents were asked to evaluate each on six different nine-point scales. Thus, this experiment illustrates the use of multiple measures of the results. The mean score for each treatment level is shown in

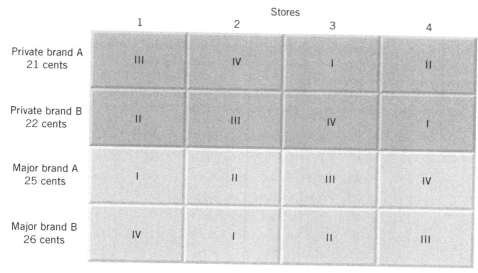

FIGURE 13.3

A Latin Square Design: The Treatment Levels I, II, III, and IV.

Source: Adapted from E. H. Asam and L. P. Bucklin, "Nutritional Labeling for Canned Goods: A Study of Consumer Response," *Journal of Marketing,* 37, April 1973, p. 36.

the following table. Again, the issue as to whether the results are "statistically significant" will be deferred until later chapters.

In a randomized block design, each cell would require four experimental groups, one for each treatment level. In the Latin square design, each cell requires only one treatment level, so a minimum of 16 groups is required instead of 64. The Latin square normally has a separate sample for each cell. In this study, the same 50 respondents from store 1 were used for all the cells in the first column. Each respondent reacted to four brands. Thus, the store block served effectively to control not only for the store but for many other characteristics of the sample. As a result, the experiment was more sensitive. However, the experience of rating one brand may have had a carryover effect on the task of rating another, which could generate some bias.

Mean Scores for Attitudes and Preference Scales for Four Different Levels of Nutritional Information on Can Labels

Nutritional treatment	Scale					
	Like	Good buy	Tasty	Tender	Wholesome	Preference
Level I	4.73	4.88	5.05	5.78	4.86	2.47
Level II	4.49	4.38	4.87	5.39	4.90	2.28
Level III	4.63	4.71	4.87	5.65	5.13	2.55
Level IV	4.86	4.91	5.07	5.99	5.32	2.69

The Latin square design allows one to control two variables without requiring an expanded sample. It does require the same number of rows, columns, and treatment levels, so it does impose constraints in that respect. Also, it cannot be used to determine interaction effects. Thus, if nutritional information has a different effect on private-label brands than major brands, this design would not discern such differences.

Factorial Designs

In the statistical designs discussed so far, only one experimental variable was involved. In **factorial designs**, two or more experimental variables are considered simultaneously. Each combination of the experimental treatment levels applies to randomly selected groups.

Suppose that a consumer product is to be tested in 36 cities. Three levels of advertising are to be tested: a high level, a low level, and no advertising. In addition, two price levels are to be considered, a high price and a low price. The resulting factorial experiment could be denoted as

$$
\begin{array}{ccccc}
EG_1 & R & X_1\left(\text{High Adv, High Price}\right) & O_1 & n = 6 \\
EG_2 & R & X_2\left(\text{High Adv, Low Price}\right) & O_2 & n = 6 \\
EG_3 & R & X_3\left(\text{Low Adv, High Price}\right) & O_3 & n = 6 \\
EG_4 & R & X_4\left(\text{Low Adv, Low Price}\right) & O_4 & n = 6 \\
EG_5 & R & X_5\left(\text{No Adv, High Price}\right) & O_5 & n = 6 \\
EG_6 & R & X_6\left(\text{No Adv, Low Price}\right) & O_6 & n = 6
\end{array}
$$

The output of the experiment will provide not only the effects of advertising but also the effects of the price variable. Suppose the findings are as shown in the following table.

Thus, in one experiment, the effects of two variables are determined. The real power of a factorial design, however, is that it provides the ability to determine interactive effects.

Sales in an Experiment Involving Advertising and Price

	High price	Low price	Average sales
High advertising	105	133	119
Low advertising	103	124	113.5
No advertising	101	112	106.5
Average sales	103	123	113

Interaction Effects

Figure 13.4a shows the results in graphical form. The judgment about advertising can be refined now. When the product is priced high, the advertising effect almost disappears, whereas when the product is priced low the advertising effect is much larger. This illustrates an interaction effect between two experimental variables. The effect of the advertising level is termed a *main effect*, the main effect due to advertising. Similarly, the effect of price is termed the **main effect of price**. Thus, the main effect is distinguished from the interactive effect.

In Figure 13.4a, there is a price effect because the low-price results are higher on the average than the high-price results. There is also an *advertising effect*, as the average results for the various advertising levels differ. As has been noted already, there is also an *interaction effect*. Figure 13.4b is an example of the case where there is both an advertising and price effect but no interaction. The two main effects are additive here. Figure 13.4c shows a case where there is a price main effect but no advertising main effect. The average sales for each level of advertising are the same. There is, however, an interactive effect between advertising and price, an even more pronounced effect than the one observed in Figure 13.4a.

The factorial design could be expanded to include three or more variables. Each then would generate a main effect and each pair would generate a possible interactive effect. Of course, there needs to be an experimental group for each combination of experimental treatment levels. Thus, if three levels of advertising, two levels of price, and two promotion alternatives are

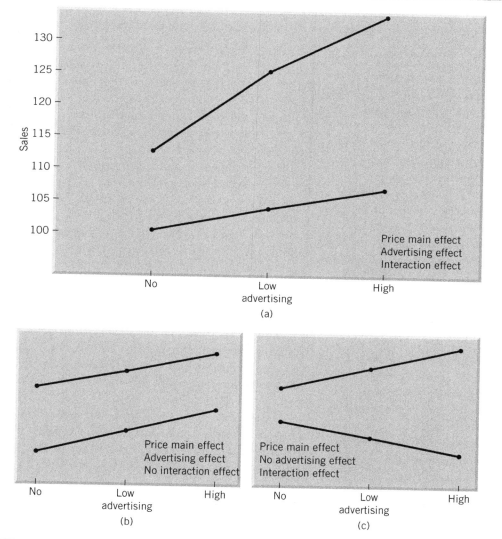

FIGURE 13.4
Interactive Effects.

involved, a total of 12 possible conditions will have to be tested. That will require a sample size of at least 12, which might be expensive if test cities are involved. Further, if each cell is to provide a reliable estimate of that treatment combination, several test cities might be desired. If the respondents are people instead of cities, several hundred might be required in each experimental group. Thus, one of the problems of factorial designs is that the number of experimental groups can get large rather quickly. Of course, the Latin square concept can be employed to reduce the number somewhat, if interactions can be neglected.

Factorial designs also can be expanded to include block effects. Thus, the advertising and price experiment could be duplicated, once for large cities and once for small ones, for example. Furthermore, factorial designs can be created using matching instead of randomization to develop the experimental groups. An example of a factorial experiment is given in Marketing Research in Action 13.2.

Marketing Research in Action 13.2

■ THE BATTLE FOR SHELF SPACE

It has been a general belief among retailers and manufacturers that shelf space in retail outlets shares a positive relationship with product sales, and that product displays attract the attention of potential buyers and thus stimulate their demand for goods. Based on this notion, manufacturers yearn for more shelf space for their products in the hope that it will help maximize their brands' revenue and profit. On the other hand, the retailer is interested in maximizing the store profits and not necessarily the profits of any particular brand. With the growing power of the retailer, this conflict in interests has led to what is known in the industry as the "battle for shelf space." Manufacturers are forced to pay "slotting allowances" to retailers for them to carry their brands.

A field experiment was conducted to determine whether there is really a positive correlation between shelf space and product sales. The objective of the study was to determine whether there exists a relationship between shelf space, location of store (located either in a low-, middle-, or high-income area), and product sales; and if so, whether the location of the store (located either in a low-, middle-, or high-income area) moderates the relationship between shelf space and product sales. Because this was a field experiment, controlling for other factors or variables was a must to ensure the validity and reliability of the research results.

The cooperation of the store managers of a major retail chain was sought. Any variations from differences in retail chains were eliminated by conducting the experiment in outlets controlled by the same retail chain. Seasonality was controlled for by carrying out the experiment within a two-month time period when no major holidays occurred. Also, the experiment was repeated in another time period and the data resulting from replication was also analyzed. This was done to see whether the observed effect was consistent over different time periods. During this time period, we ensured that there were no promotions for the brand under study. Promotional activities of competing brands were also monitored, and no major competing brands were fixed at their normal levels. To account for factors such as differences in sizes of the stores, the data analysis involved not only analyzing the actual sales data but the data were also adjusted by the product category sales and the all commodity volume (ACV) sales of each store. Also, to account for any change in sales of this product category for reasons other than change in shelf space, the product category sales in six other stores (control group) was monitored during the period of the experiment.

The cooperation of the store manager and the dairy manager of each of the six stores was personally solicited in executing the prescribed shelf treatments to the brand under study. The shelf facings for the chilled orange juice brand were varied each week. Since the normal number of shelf facings in this market for orange juice was three facings (as confirmed by the manufacturers and the store managers), we decided to study the effect of two, three, and four shelf facings (one below the normal and one above the normal); there seemed to be a realistic assumption that they would perform, given the constraints. The stores were closely monitored every day of the week to ensure proper execution of the shelf treatments. Any irregularity in the shelf treatments was brought to the notice of the dairy managers and was immediately rectified.

A 3×3 factorial design was used, with shelf facings and store location (neighborhood type) being the major factors. The experiment was carried out over a three-week period and was replicated over another three-week period. The shelf facings in each store were randomly assigned so that no two stores in the same income level had the same number of shelf facings in any given time period. The research results revealed that there is a distinct positive relationship between shelf space and product sales and that this effect is independent of location. This study provides more evidence for the belief that shelf space is positively related to product sales. Although the research findings were conclusive in that they were consistent over time and place, these results cannot be generalized to encompass all the product categories in the supermarket. Also, because the shelf treatments for the orange juice brand under study were altered only between 2, 3, and 4 facings, it is not possible to predict the relationship for greater than 4 facings or for less than 2 facings.

Source: Excerpts of an experimental study conducted by V. Kumar and K. K. Cox, University of Houston, Houston, Texas, 1992–1993.

Guidelines for Conducting Experimental Research[24]

To design and analyze an experiment, it is necessary that everyone involved in it have a clear idea in advance of exactly what is to be studied, how the data are to be collected, and at least a qualitative understanding of how these data are to be analyzed. An outline of the recommended procedure is as follows:

1. *Recognition of and statement of the problem.* This may seem to be a rather obvious point, but in practice it is often not simple to realize that a problem requiring experimentation exists, nor is it simple to develop a clear and generally accepted statement of this problem. A clear statement of the problem often contributes substantially to a better understanding of the phenomena and the final solution of the problem.

2. *Choice of factors and levels.* The experimenter must choose the factors to be varied in the experiment, the ranges over which these factors will be varied, and the specific levels at which runs will be made. Thought must be given to how these factors are to be controlled at the desired levels and how they are to be measured.

3. *Selection of the response variable.* In selecting the response variable, the experimenter should be certain that this variable really provides useful information about the process under study.

4. *Choice of experimental design.* If the first three steps are done correctly, this step is relatively easy. Choice of design involves the consideration of sample size (number of replicates), the selection of a suitable run order for the experimental trials, and the determination of whether or not blocking or other randomization restrictions are involved.

5. *Performing the experiment.* When running the experiment, it is vital to monitor the process carefully to ensure that everything is being done according to plan. Errors in experimental procedure at this stage will usually destroy experimental validity.

6. *Data analysis.* Statistical methods should be used to analyze the data so that results and conclusions are objective rather than judgmental in nature. If the experiment has been designed correctly and if it has been performed according to the design, then the statistical methods required are not elaborate. (Data analysis is covered in great detail in Part III of the text.)

7. *Conclusion and recommendations.* Once the data have been analyzed, the experimenter must draw practical conclusions about the results and recommend a course of action. Graphical methods are often useful in this stage, particularly in presenting the results to others. Follow-up runs and confirmation testing should also be performed to validate the conclusions from the experiment.

Common Misuses of Experimental Research in Marketing[25]

Experimental and quasi-experimental design approaches have their own uses, methodological sets, benefits, and pitfalls. Each family of techniques is highly appropriate for specific uses, but neither is amenable to slavish application for all marketing purposes. Some examples of the most common misuses include:

- Concluding from a test of two media spending levels that sales are inelastic with regard to media and that advertising can be turned off entirely.

- Observing that a 10 percent price increase has no impact, so sales are not responding to price, and the price can be increased by 25 percent.

- Deciding that an umbrella display for a number of brands won't work because a similar display that was tested for a single brand didn't pay off.

Limitations of Experiments

Experimentation is a powerful tool in the search for unambiguous relationships that we hope may be used to make valid predictions about the effects of marketing decisions and to develop basic theories. The laboratory experiment is the preferred method because of its internal validity; however, because of acute external validity problems in the laboratory setting, managers are reluctant to rely on it. Unfortunately, the field experiment is beset by a number of problems whose net effect has been to limit the vast majority of marketing experiments to short-run comparisons across stores, home placements of product variations, and so forth. Relatively few large-scale experiments with social programs, marketing programs, or advertising campaigns are conducted in any given year. What are the reasons?

Cost

Cost and time pressures are the first hurdle. Even "simple" in-store tests require additional efforts to gain cooperation; to properly place the display, price, or promotion; to measure the uncontrolled variables; and then to audit the resulting sales differences. The measurement costs alone are often substantial. When larger interventions, such as comparing alternative advertising themes in multiple geographic areas, are contemplated, management may be very wary that the costs will exceed the benefits. These costs are likely to be considerable if any amount of reinterviewing or special manipulation of advertising, product, or other controllable variables is required.

Another cost is the fact that the research delays management decisions. For some experiments, the effect of the experimental treatment can extend over a long time period, as much as a year or even longer. Consider the Budweiser advertising experiments, which were run for a full year. The researcher is often placed in a difficult position. If the experiment, especially the *after observation*, is not allowed sufficient time, the validity of the results might suffer. On the other hand, if the experiment is too lengthy, the resulting delays in making and implementing policy might be unacceptably long. One way to avoid the constraint of time pressure is to conduct an ongoing program of experimentation in anticipation of recurring decisions. Thus, some companies are building up data files of responses to marketing programs in a variety of contexts.

Security

Still another cost is security. A field experiment naturally involves exposing a marketing program in the marketplace, so it is difficult to hide from competitors, who are in contact with their own field sales force, store personnel, research suppliers, and trade sources. For example, one consumer-products company constructed product displays in several stores in one city for one eight-hour period on one Friday. At the end of the day, all traces of the test had been removed. By Monday, however, the major trade magazine and most competitors knew of the test and the details of the test product.

Implementation Problems

Implementation problems abound in the conduct of experiments. First, it may not be easy to gain cooperation within the organization. Regional managers resist proposals to experiment with varying the size and call frequency of a sales force. They do not want to subject their market area to a reduced sales effort. Administrators of social programs may resist efforts to assign people randomly to treatments. They want to decide the assignments according to who can benefit most from the service and which service is most suitable. A second problem to which experiments involving market areas are especially susceptible is *contamination* because of an inability to confine the treatment to the designated experimental area. Buyers from one geographic area may visit an adjacent area or receive media messages that overflow from that area. It is seldom possible to partition geographic market areas so that the sales measurements and treatments exactly coincide.

Experiments involving people as test units may become contaminated because people in the control group associate with people assigned to the program and learn what they have been doing. A third problem is that the variability in behavior across test units can be so large that it is difficult to detect the effects of the experiment. Of course, some of the variability can be removed by *blocking* or by *matching*, but it will not be eliminated. The question is: Can it be reduced enough so that the experimental effects can be discerned?

The ultimate problem, however, is that there may be no person or geographic area available to serve as a control. This is the case with industrial markets composed of a few large buyers who communicate among each other or who are geographically dispersed. Any effort to limit a new-product introduction to a subset of such a market would be unsuccessful. The same problem occurs in attempting to assess the effects of federal legislation, which goes into effect in all parts of the country at the same time. Also, practitioners may be unwilling to deny access to a social program because they believe that to do so is counter to their professional obligation.

Uncertain Persistency of Results

A final category of the problems that limit the acceptance and usage of field experiments is uncertain persistency of results. For an experimental result to be useful, it must hold long enough to be acted on to advantage. The two factors most damaging to an assumption of persistency are high rates of technological, economic, or social change in the market environment and aggressive competitive behavior. During the experiment, the competition may elect to monitor the test independently and learn as much as possible—or take unusual action, such as a special consumer promotion, to confound the results. Similarly, when the test is expanded to a regional or national market, the competitors may either do nothing or retaliate. This means that there are at least four combinations of circumstances, each with different implications for the nature of the causal relationship being studied:

Possible Competitive Responses

	After experiment	
	No response	Retaliation
No response	1	3
Retaliation	4	2

The persistency, and hence the value of the experimental results, will be uncertain to the degree that the decision maker cannot assess (1) the probability of each of the four possible events; (2) the magnitude of the retaliatory action, if any; or (3) the number of direct competitors taking action.

Simulated Test Marketing

To overcome some of the limitations posed by experiments such as test marketing in terms of cost, time involved, and sabotage or imitation by competition, many marketing research firms resort to simulated test marketing (STM). STMs are used to estimate sales volume of new products prior to market launch by utilizing information gathered from responses of consumers, manufacturers' promotional spending plans, and other forecasting models. This method of testing enables firms to screen new ideas during the early phases of development and channel resources to maximize the potential for success. The STMs are further made use of when the new product initiative progresses, by providing estimates of sales, marketing plan optimization, and additional findings that assist the company's launch decision.[26]

STMs are now being widely used by the packaged-goods industry as an aid for effective business planning. For instance, the launching of Heinz ketchup in plastic bottles instead of glass bottles was preceded by an STM conducted by Yankelovich to assess the acceptance of the new packaging. When compared with the traditional test market method, STMs score on account of speed, economy, and accuracy with respect to their forecasting ability. Some companies involved in STM research are BASES, ASSESSOR, and Yankelovich.

SUMMARY

Experiments are defined as studies in which conditions are controlled so that one or more independent variables can be manipulated to test a hypothesis about a dependent variable. The key principle of experimental work is *manipulation* of a treatment variable (say, X), followed by observation of response variable (say, Y). If a change in X causes Y to change in the hypothesized way, then we are tempted to say that X causes Y. However, this causal inference rests on soft ground unless the experiment has been properly designed to *control* for other extraneous or spurious variables. Hence, to establish causality between two variables, the following types of evidence are required: (1) *condition of concomitant variation*, (2) *condition of time order of occurrence*, and (3) *absence of competing causal explanations*.

Experimental designs can be broadly categorized into two groups, classical designs and statistical designs. The basic difference between these two types of experimental designs is that classical designs consider the impact of only one treatment level of an independent variable at a time. On the other hand, statistical designs allow for examining the impact of different treatment levels of an independent variable

and also the impact of two or more independent variables. The types of classical design discussed in this chapter include preexperimental designs, true experimental designs, and quasi-experimental designs. The statistical designs include completely randomized design, randomized block design, Latin square design, and factorial design.

Experimental research can be broadly divided into two main categories, laboratory experiments and field experiments. Laboratory experiments are often relatively inexpensive and provide the opportunity to exercise tight control. In a laboratory, for example, an exposure to a concept can be controlled, whereas in the more realistic field context, many factors can distort an exposure, such as weather, competitive reactions, and family activities. However, the laboratory experiment suffers from the testing effect and from the artificiality of the situation. Thus, the external validity (the ability to generalize from the experiment) is limited. Field experiments have greater external validity but are more costly to run (in expense, time, and security), are difficult to implement, and lack the tight control possible in the laboratory. As a result, their internal validity is often a problem.

QUESTIONS AND PROBLEMS

13.1 How is experimental research different from descriptive research?

13.2 What is a spurious association? How do you distinguish between spurious association and the existence of an intervening variable?

13.3 When does association imply causation? Under what conditions? Could there ever be a causal relationship without association present?

13.4 Explain the following terms:

(a) Experimental treatments

(b) Manipulation

(c) Extraneous variable

(d) Selection bias

(e) Randomization

(f) Blocking

(g) Matching

13.5 In a laboratory experiment (designed to test a new brand), people are exposed to advertisements for a new brand and then are asked to buy a brand from that product class from a supermarket aisle that has been set up as realistically as possible. After they use the brand, they are asked if they would like to repurchase it. When would such an experiment be preferred over a field experiment?

13.6 Distinguish between the internal and external validity of an experiment. List the various threats to internal validity and briefly describe each of these threats.

13.7 A blind taste test was responsible in part for the decision by Coca-Cola to introduce the "new Coke," a product that ran into resistance from those loyal to "old Coke" (now Coke Classic). On a blind taste test, unlabeled colas would be tasted and the respondent would report taste preferences. Evaluate the validity of this experiment.

13.8 Contrast the following pairs of concepts by defining and illustrating each:

(a) History versus instrumentation effects

(b) Maturation versus mortality effects

(c) Testing versus before measure effects

(d) Selection bias versus self-selection

13.9 NuSystems, Inc., a computer software distributing company, has recently completed an innovative sales training program in order to boost recently lagging sales. The head of the marketing department is interested in discovering how effective this new training has been in improving the performance of sales personnel and increasing sales.

(a) Would experimental or descriptive research methods be most suitable for this purpose? Give reasons for your answer.

(b) What kind of association exists between the variables?

13.10 In an effort to identify the reasons for the rise in teenage violence in the United States, Concerned Citizens of America (CCA) has decided to examine the relationship between exposure to rap music and incidents of teen violence. They have decided to utilize an experimental technique to establish whether a relationship exists.

(a) Suggest how such an experiment could be undertaken. Include a description of how the experiment would be conducted, from the problem statement to the conclusion.

(b) What are the possible limitations of this type of research?

13.11 (a) In the preceding question, suggest ways in which this experiment could be conducted as:

(i) A field experiment

(ii) A laboratory experiment

(b) Which type of experiment would best serve the purpose of the study? Give reasons for your answer.

13.12 Which type of experimental design offers the most effective control of internal sources of validity?

13.13 A group of known smokers are sent literature on the harmful effects of smoking on a weekly basis for one year. At the end of the year, a poll is taken to see how many of the smokers stopped smoking during the year. The results are used to establish the effectiveness of this literature campaign in encouraging smokers to stop smoking.

(a) This is an example of what kind of experiment design?

(b) What are the potential hazards in drawing the above conclusion from this type of experiment?

13.14 A leading manufacturer of ladies' lingerie has maintained its high share in the pantyhose market over the past five years but has experienced a dramatic decrease in sales. This has led Cheryl Martin, the VP of marketing, to conclude that the market for pantyhose as a whole must be shrinking. In an effort to determine whether a shift in women's attitudes or lifestyles is responsible for the shrinkage of the market for pantyhose, she has decided to conduct a nation-wide telephone survey of women across the country.

(a) How can the adoption of a random assignment procedure help maintain the internal validity of the experiment?

(b) Suggest a randomization technique that would be appropriate for this study.

13.15 (a) What are the possible threats to the validity of a trend analysis?

(b) How can these threats be eliminated by the experimental design process?

13.16 A profile group wanted to test the effectiveness of anti-gun ownership commercial. Two random samples, each of 250 respondents, were recruited in Houston. One group was shown the anti-gun ownership commercial. Then, attitudes toward gun ownership were measurement for respondents in both groups.

(a) Identify the independent and dependent variables in this experiment.

(b) What type of design was used?

(c) What are the potential threats to internal and external validity in this experiment?

END NOTES

1. S. R. Brown and L. E. Melamed, *Experimental Design and Analysis.* Newbury Park, CA: Sage, 1990.

2. K. K. Cox and B. M. Enis, *Experimentation for Marketing Decisions.* Scranton, PA: International Textbook, 1969, p. 5.

3. A. Parasuraman, *Marketing Research.* Reading, MA: Addison-Wesley, 1986, p. 267.

4. D. A. Kenny, *Correlation and Causality.* New York: Wiley, 1979.

5. G. A. Churchill, Jr., *Marketing Research: Methodological Foundations,* 5th ed. New York: Dryden, 1991, pp. 167–168.

6. Ibid., p. 369.

7. Adapted from D. T. Campbell and J. C. Stanley, *Experimental and Quasi-Experimental Designs for Research*, Chicago: Rand McNally, 1963.

8. Source: D. T. Campbell and J. C. Stanley, *Experimental and Quasi-Experimental Designs for Research*, Chicago: Rand McNally, 1963; and T. D. Cook and D. T. Campbell, *Quasi-Experimentation: Design and Analysis Issues for Field Settings*, Boston: Houghton Mifflin, 1979.

9. Ibid.

10. S. Banks, *Experimentation in Marketing.* New York: McGraw-Hill, 1965, p. 33.

11. This system of notation was introduced by D. T. Campbell and J. C. Stanley, *Experimental and Quasi-Experimental Designs for Research*. Chicago: Rand McNally, 1963.

12. E. P. Green, S. D. Tull, and G. Albaum, *Research for Marketing Decisions*, 5th ed. Englewood Cliffs, NJ: Prentice-Hall, 1988.

13. Refer to our discussion on the threats to experimental validity in this chapter.

14. Ibid.

15. Ibid.

16. Ibid.

17. F. N. Kerlinger, *Foundations of Behavioral Research.* New York: Holt, Rinehart and Winston, 1973, p. 114.

18. L. H. Kidder and S. Wrightsman, *Cook's Research Methods in Social Relations.* New York: Holt, Rinehart and Winston, 1981, p. 18.

19. Adapted from A. Parasuraman, *Marketing Research.* Reading, MA: Addison Wesley, 1991.

20. This design is named after R. L. Solomon, who first proposed it in his article, "An Extension of Control Group Design," *Psychological Bulletin*, 46, 1949, pp. 137–150.

21. For a stimulating discussion of this method of strength in causal inferences, see E. J. Webb, D. T. Campbell, R. D. Schwarz, and L. Lechrest, *Unobtrusive Measures: Nonreactive Research in the Social Sciences*, Chicago: Rand McNally, 1966.

22. The term "panel" sometimes refers to a consumer jury, whose members provide a reaction to some proposed product on a one-shot basis.

23. Adapted from E. H. Asam and L. P. Bucklin, "Nutritional Labeling for Canned Goods: A Study of Consumer Response," *Journal of Marketing*, 37, April 1973, p. 36.

24. Adapted from D. C. Montgomery, *Design and Analysis of Experiments.* New York: Wiley, 1991, pp. 9–11.

25. J. L. Carefoot, "Modeling and Experimental Designs in Marketing Research: Uses and Misuses," *Marketing News*, June 1993, p. H19.

26. http://www.nielsen.com/us/en/practices/product-innovation-renovation.html

Case 13-1 ||| Evaluating Experimental Designs

A description of a variety of experimental designs follows. For each design: (1) indicate the type of experiment that is being used, (2) briefly discuss the threats to *internal* and *external* *validity* and identify those you regard as the most serious, and (3) describe how you would improve the design to overcome the problems you have identified.

1. In the Bayer deceptive advertising case, an issue was whether people were influenced by some Bayer advertisements to believe that Bayer was more effective than other aspirins in relieving pain. In an experiment designed to address that issue, a Bayer print advertisement was shown to 428 people projectable to the U.S. adult population, and two television advertisements were shown to 240 people recruited from local organizations (which received $1.00 for each participant) in nine communities in Massachusetts, Missouri, and Georgia. After being exposed to the advertisements, respondents were asked to identify the main points of the advertisement, what the advertisement meant by its major claim, and whether the advertisement suggested that Bayer is more effective at relieving pain than any other brand of aspirin. The percentage of respondents were tabulated who, in response to the open-ended questions, said (1) that Bayer is best and (2) that Bayer is better than other aspirins. Whether the respondents made explicit reference to effectiveness also was noted. These percentages were used to address the issue. For example, across all surveys it was found that 10 percent felt that a main point of the advertisement was that Bayer is best or better than other aspirins *in effectiveness*. Also across all surveys, 71 percent felt that the advertisement suggested that Bayer works better than any other aspirin.

2. In 1982, the instrument group of National Chemical decided to change from a modest advertising effort aimed at generating leads for its sales force to a more substantial program aimed at increased awareness and preference. A major vehicle for this campaign was *Chemical Process Instrumentation*, a leading trade magazine. To evaluate the advertising, a survey was made of the readers of that magazine before and after the one-year campaign. In each case, a systematic sample of 2,500 readers was sent questionnaires. Responses were obtained from 572 for the before sample and 513 for the after sample. Among the questions were

   - List the companies you consider to be the leading manufacturers of the following products.
   - Check the one manufacturer (for each product) that you would first consider when purchasing the item.

   The results showed

	Before	After
Percentage aware of National Chemical	23	46
Percentage prefer National Chemical	8	11

   The results were averaged across the major products carried by National Chemical.

3. An account executive notices that a client is sponsoring a program that will be shown on about three-fourths of the network's station lineup. This provides a possibility for testing the effectiveness of the new commercials being used. The executive's letter to the research supervisor reads, in part: "What if we picked several markets that will receive the program and several that won't? Then within each of these we can measure attitudes and purchasing among a randomly selected group of consumers. After the broadcast we can interview other randomly selected groups on the same questions."

4. A manufacturer of products sold in food stores wished to find out whether a coupon good for 10 cents off the purchase price of its product could win new users. Coupons were mailed to half the households in the city's upper-80-percent income groups. Ten days before mailing, phone interviews were conducted with 200 randomly selected households scheduled to receive the coupon and 200 randomly selected who would not receive it. Whoever answered the phone was questioned about brand awareness and past purchasing within the product category. One month later, callbacks were made to 400 households. Of the original group, 165 coupon receivers and 160 nonreceivers were asked the awareness and purchase questions again. In addition, 100 coupon recipients and 100 nonrecipients who were not previously questioned were interviewed on this occasion. The latter also were picked randomly from the receiver and nonreceiver populations.

Case 13-2 | Barrie Food Corporation

Al Blankenship (of Carter-Wallace) has just given an enthusiastic account of a new technique for evaluating television commercials. Your boss—the marketing research manager for a large food manufacturer—who is in the audience with you, wants you to analyze the technique carefully and make a recommendation on the use of the technique. The transcript of Blankenship's remarks follows:

Jim stopped in my office one day early this year, bursting with an idea he had to test the effectiveness of television commercials. He told me that in fall, 1976, WCAU-TV had telecast a program which discussed the pros and cons of the proposed roofed-over sports stadium for the city. Viewers were asked to telephone their reactions to a special number to indicate whether they were in favor of or opposed to the sports palace. Jim and his group had been assigned the job of keeping a running total of the vote.

He had become intrigued, he said, that this sort of approach might be used to measure the effectiveness of television commercials. In a balanced experiment, you could have an announcer, immediately following the test commercial, ask people to telephone in to request a sample of the product. Differences in rate of response between different commercials would measure their effectiveness.

My reaction was immediate and positive. This was really getting close to a behavioral measurement of response to advertising. But it lacked a crucial control. How could you be sure that the same number of people had been exposed to each commercial? The technique required a measurement of the size of audience exposed to each test commercial.

In this situation, I thought of C. E. Hooper, since one of Hooper's specialties is measurement of audience size. If audience size could be built in as a control, it seemed to me that the technique was solid. I got Jim together with Bruce McEwen, Executive Vice President of Hooper. Bruce was just as excited as I had been.

However, following our discussion, I began to cool off. I was afraid that the audience size measurement made the whole thing too cumbersome, and that the cumbersomeness might somehow introduce error. There was something a bit sloppy about the methodology. I did not warm up to the idea, the more

I thought about it, that the viewer was going to get a free sample merely by a telephone call. This was not real life. I was afraid that the free offer bit would result in such a high level of response that it would be impossible to differentiate between commercials.

Several weeks later it hit me. What we needed was an easy method of controlling audience size and who received the special offer, and a way to make the viewer pay at least something for his [or her] product. Couponing, properly designed, could provide the solution.

A simple method was devised, and pretesting was conducted on the couponing aspects to make sure that the price level was right. The entire test procedure required four steps: a screening telephone call, a coupon mailout, a telephone postcall, and measurement of coupon redemption.

The precall is made within a stated time period in advance of the television show that is to carry the test advertising. The respondent is asked about his or her viewing plans for the forthcoming period. The last brand purchased of each of several product groups is asked about. The product group for the brand of the test commercial is included.

Immediately following screening, each person stating that he or she intended to watch the test vehicle is sent a special coupon, good for the product advertised at a special, low price. This coupon is sent in the manufacturer's envelope, and so far as the recipient knows, has no connection with the survey. This is not a store coupon. To be redeemed, it must be sent to the manufacturer. However, it is made as easy as possible to redeem. A postage-paid return envelope is included, and all the recipient must do is insert the proper coins in a card prepared for this purpose, which includes his name and address. The coupon has an expiration date of one week from date of mailing, to prevent responses that are meaningless trickling in over a long time period. The procedure makes it possible to consider coupon responses only from those who viewed the program, which is crucial.

The day following the telecast, a call is made to each person who has said that he or she expected to view the particular program. The only purpose of the call is to determine whether the person has actually viewed the particular show. No question about advertising or about brands is asked.

Sampling Fundamentals

14

LEARNING OBJECTIVES

- Describe the distinction between a census and a sample.
- Describe the differences between sampling and nonsampling errors.
- Describe the sampling process.
- Describe probability sampling procedures.
- Describe nonprobability sampling procedures.
- Discuss determining sample size with ad hoc methods.
- Discuss sampling in the international context.

Marketing intelligence often involves the estimation of a characteristic of some population of interest. For instance, the average level of usage of a park by community residents might be of interest; or information might be needed on the attitudes of a student body toward a proposed intramural facility. In either case, it would be unlikely that all members of the population would be surveyed. Contacting the entire population—that is, the entire census list—simply would not be worthwhile from a cost–benefit viewpoint. It would be both costly and, in nearly all cases, unnecessary, since a sample usually is sufficiently reliable. Further, it often would be less accurate, since nonsampling errors, such as nonresponse, cheating, and data-coding errors, are more difficult to control. A **population** can be defined as the set of all objects that possess some common set of characteristics with respect to a marketing research problem.

Sample or Census

A researcher typically is interested in the characteristics of a population. For example, if the proportion of people in a city watching a television show has to be determined, then the information can be obtained by asking every household in that city. If all the respondents in a population are asked to provide information, such a survey is called a **census**. The proportion of television viewers generated from a census is known as the **parameter**. On the other hand, a subset of all the households may be chosen and the relevant information could be obtained from that. Information obtained from a subset of the households is known as the **statistic** (from sample). Researchers then attempt to make an inference about the population parameter with the knowledge of the relevant sample statistic. A critical assumption in the process of inference is that the sample chosen is representative of the population. Estimation procedures and hypotheses tests are the types of inferences that link sample statistics and the corresponding population parameters.

When a Census Is Appropriate

A census is appropriate if the population size itself is quite small. For example, a researcher may be interested in contacting all the firms in the petroleum industry to obtain information on the use of a particular software. A census also is conducted if information is needed from every individual or object in the population. For example, if the researcher is interested in determining the number of foreign students enrolled in a university, it is necessary to get information from all the departments in the university because of possible variations within each department. Further, if the cost of making an incorrect decision is high or if sampling errors are high, then a census may be more appropriate than a sample.

When a Sample Is Appropriate

Sampling may be useful if the population size is large and if both the cost and time associated with obtaining information from the population is high. Further, the opportunity to make a quick decision may be lost if a large population must be surveyed. Also, with sampling, in a given time period, more time can be spent on each interview (personal), thereby increasing the response quality. Additionally, it is easy to manage surveys of smaller samples and still exercise quality control in the interview process.

Sampling may be sufficient in many instances. For example, if a company is interested in obtaining reactions to installing a check-cashing operation within the premises, a sample of employees may be adequate. If the population being dealt with is homogeneous, then sampling is fine. Finally, if taking a census is not possible, then sampling is the only alternative. For example, if a researcher is interested in obtaining consumer response from all over the world to a new advertising theme for Coca-Cola, a census is not possible.

Error in Sampling

Execution of a research project always introduces some error in the study. As stated in Chapter 4, the total error in a research study is the difference between the true value (in the population) of the variable of interest and the observed value (in the sample). The total error in the study has two major components: sampling and nonsampling errors. If the difference in value (error) between the population parameter and the sample statistic is only because of sampling, then the error is known as **sampling error**. If a population is surveyed and error is observed, this error is known as a **nonsampling error**. Nonsampling errors can be observed in both a census and a sample.[1] Some of the common sources of nonsampling errors include measurement error, data-recording error, data analysis error, and nonresponse error. The sources of nonsampling errors are discussed in greater detail in Chapter 4.

Sampling error can be minimized by increasing the sample size. However, as sample size is increased, the quality control of the research study may become more difficult. Consequently, nonsampling errors can increase (e.g., the number of nonresponses can go up), thereby setting up a classic trade-off between sampling and nonsampling errors. Since nonsampling errors can occur from various sources, it is difficult to identify and control them. Therefore, more attention should be given to reducing them.

Sampling Process

When a decision is made to use a sample, a number of factors must be taken into consideration. The various steps involved in the sampling process are given in Figure 14.1. The major activities associated with the sampling process are (1) identifying the target population, (2) determining the sampling frame, (3) resolving the differences, (4) selecting a sampling procedure, (5) determining the relevant sample size, (6) obtaining information from respondents, (7) dealing with the nonresponse public, and (8) generating the information for decision-making purposes.

Determining the Target Population

Sampling is intended to gain information about a population. Thus, it is critical at the outset to identify the population properly and accurately. If the population is defined fuzzily, the results will also be fuzzy. If the population is defined improperly, the research probably will answer the wrong question. For example, if some research questions involve prospective car buyers and the population includes all adults with driver's licenses, the research output will be unlikely to provide the relevant information.

A target population for a toy store can be defined as "all households with children living in Houston." The ambiguities with this definition are many:

- How do you define children? Are they below 10 years, 13 years, or 16 years?

- How do you define Houston? Does it include only the metropolitan area, or are suburbs also included?

- Who in the household is going to provide the information?

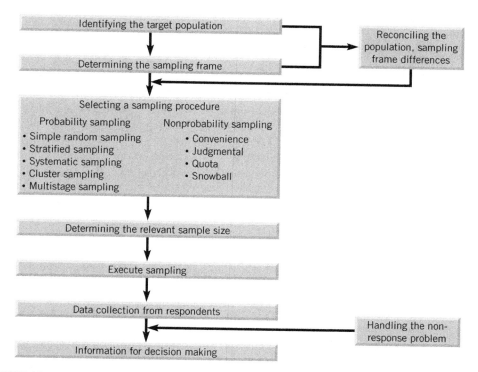

FIGURE 14.1
The Sampling Process.

Therefore, the definition of a target population should contain information on sampling elements (children or parent), sampling units (households with children), and area of coverage [Standard Metropolitan Statistical Area (SMSA) or greater Houston].

Although the definition of the *target population* is important, it is often neglected because it seems obvious and noncontroversial. Devoting effort to identifying the target population usually will pay off. The following guidelines should be considered.

Look to the Research Objectives

If the research objectives are well thoughtout, the target population definition will be clear as well. Recall from Chapter 3 that the research objectives include the research question, the research hypothesis, and a statement of the research boundaries. Each of these elements contributes to refining the definition of the target population. For example, the research question might involve how business firms in Chicago would react to a particular pricing method for advertising in the Yellow Pages of the telephone directory. The hypothesis might indicate that retailers of different types need to be sampled. Consideration of the research boundary could restrict the population to metropolitan Chicago. Thus, the target population would be retail business firms in metropolitan Chicago.

Consider Alternatives

It is rare to find a study for which there are no alternative, reasonable, target population definitions. The task really is to identify and evaluate several of the alternatives instead of simply assuming that the first one mentioned is appropriate. For example, suppose the task is to determine the relative importance of such features as compactors, saunas, and patios in medium-priced homes. The target population could be present owners of medium-priced homes, shoppers in middle-income shopping centers, those who might upgrade their homes, or clients of real estate firms. The choice will depend on the research objectives. The key point is to recognize that alternative definitions exist.

Know Your Market

If the research objective is to learn about the market response to some element of the marketing program, it is necessary to know something about the market. One may hope that some previous research will provide this type of information. Without it, the population definition will have to be unnecessarily broad and, therefore, will lead to an unnecessary increase in research expenses. For example, if a shopping center management is considering whether restaurants should be added to the center, the opinions of customers and potential customers will be desired. A key question for the population definition, especially if potential customers are to be reached, is from how large an area the shopping center draws. If previous studies show, for instance, that the center draws from a 3-mile radius, that information will help in defining the target population.

Consider the Appropriate Sampling Unit

The target population consists of sampling units. A **sampling unit** may contain people, stores, households, organization transactions, products, or whatever. One task is to specify which sampling unit is appropriate. Is the interest in museums or in museum directors? Sometimes the choice is not clear. Should a study of banking activity or of leisure-time activities use individuals or households? The choice will depend on the purpose of the study and perhaps on some judgments about consumer behavior. For example, if decisions about banking or leisure activities are thought to be family decisions, then the household might be the appropriate sampling unit. A respondent would report for the family. The assumption would be that family members are enough alike that responses within a family would tend to be similar. If, however, the decisions are assumed to be relatively independent among household members, then the sampling unit would be individuals instead of households.

Specify Clearly What Is Excluded

The specification of the target population should make clear what is excluded. A study of voting intentions on certain candidates and issues might restrict the sampling population to those of voting age and even to those who intend to vote or to those who voted in the last election. If the election were in Cook County, for instance, it would be reasonable to restrict the population to those eligible to vote in Cook County.

Don't Overdefine

The population, of course, should be compatible with the study purpose and the research questions; however, the researcher should not arbitrarily overdefine the population. For example, a population of working wives between the ages of 25 and 30 earning more than $15,000 may be artificially restrictive. Such a restrictive population can generate a very costly design because so many people need to be screened out to obtain the desired sample.

Should Be Reproducible

The population definition should be not so restrictive that it may not be reproducible at a later point in time. For example, if a researcher defines population as "all households living in the Kleine school district as of June 4, 1994," it would be hard to reproduce at a later date because of the time factor in the population definition. However, in certain studies, the time period may be a critical factor in the population definition.

Consider Convenience

When there is a choice, preference should be given to populations that are convenient to sample. Suppose that the population was to include those who are bothered by airplane noise. One population compatible with the research purpose might be those who live within one mile of an airport. This population would be easy and convenient to sample. Of course, the population should not be distorted for the sake of creating a convenient sample. A population of subscribers to *Sports Illustrated* may be convenient to sample but may not be appropriate for the research purpose.

Determining the Sampling Frame

It is important to distinguish between the population and the sampling frame. The **sampling frame** is a list containing all or a random selection of population members used to obtain a sample. It might be a list of magazine subscribers, retail hardware stores, or college students that represent the overall population of interest;even a geographical area such as a zip code or census track can serve as a "list."[2] Actually, the description of a sampling frame does not have to enumerate all population members. It may be sufficient to specify the procedure by which each sampling unit can be located. For instance, a member of a probability sample of school children could be obtained by randomly selecting a school district, a school, a classroom, and, finally, a pupil. The probability of picking any given pupil could be determined, even if a physical list were not created that included all students in the population.

Creating Lists

The biggest problem in simple random sampling is obtaining appropriate lists. R. R. Donnelley Company maintains a list drawn from telephone directories and automobile registrations, which contains around 88 percent of U.S. households. Such a list can be used to obtain a national sample for a mail survey. Within a community, the local utility company will have a fairly complete list of households.

The problem, of course, is that lists do not exist for specialized populations. For example, there is no list of high-income people, mothers, tennis players, or cyclists. A solution for this problem that is usually unsatisfactory is just to use a convenient list. For example, for tennis players, a list of subscribers to *Tennis World* or membership lists in tennis clubs might be available. Obviously, neither would be representative of the entire tennis-playing population but still might be useful for some purposes. When lists that do not match the population are used, biases are introduced that should be considered. For instance, readers of *Tennis World* will be much more involved and knowledgeable than the average tennis player. A list of residents of a given community will not include new arrivals nor people living in dwellings built since the list was created. Thus, whole new subdivisions can be omitted. If such omissions are important, it can be worthwhile to identify areas of new construction and design a separate sampling plan for them.

Sometimes, several lists are combined in the hope of obtaining a more complete representation of the population. For example, subscribers to *Tennis World* and *Tennis Today* might be combined with a list of those who had purchased tennis equipment through a mail-order catalog. This approach, however, introduces the problem of duplication. Those appearing on several lists will have an increased chance of being selected. Removing duplication can be expensive and must be balanced against the bias that is introduced.

Another problem with lists is simply that of keeping them current. Many industrial firms maintain lists of those who have expressed interest in their products, and these are used in part for the mailing of promotional material. Similarly, many organizations, such as charities, symphony groups, and art galleries, have lists of various types, but these lists can become outdated quickly as people move and change jobs within an organization.

Many special populations, such as ethnic and religious groups or high-income households, are not spread evenly across the United States but are found in a limited number of geographic areas. Therefore, if traditional sampling procedures are employed in such cases, a large number of contacts in many segments are made that yield no eligible respondents. If these segments (with no special populations) can be determined in advance from census data or other sources, and can be eliminated from the sample, substantial cost savings are possible. If those segments are not known in advance, it is still possible to make substantial savings by the use of a modified Waksberg procedure. This procedure requires that initially a single member be screened (usually by telephone) within a geographic segment. If that member belongs to a special population, additional screenings are conducted in the segment until a predetermined segment size is reached. If that member does not belong to the special population, no additional screenings are made. This eliminates all the segments with no special population, after a single call.

Creating Lists for Telephone Interviewing

As might be expected, telephone directories are used extensively as a basis for generating a sample. The concern with the use of directories is that population members may be omitted because they have changed residences, requested an unlisted number, or simply do not have a telephone.[3]

The incidence of unlisted numbers is extensive and poses a challenge to the use of telephone directories for sampling purposes. Over 20 percent of all fixed-line phone numbers and 98 percent of wireless numbers are currently unlisted in the United States. As of October 2003, over 51 million telephone numbers or just over 50 percent of landlines in the United States have been registered on the national Do-Not-Call registry.[4] Table 14.1 lists the 10 metropolitan areas with the highest levels of unlisted numbers. Nationally, 29.6 percent of the phones were unlisted in 1997, up from 21.8 percent in 1984 and 10 percent in 1965.

Table 14.1   Top 10 Unlisted Markets (of the Top 100 Metropolitan Areas)

MSA rank based on percentage of unlisted households	MSA name	Percent estimated phone households unlisted
1	Sacramento, CA	71.6
2	Oakland, CA PMSA	71.4
3	Fresno, CA	71.1
4	Los Angeles-Long Beach PMSA	69.8
5	San Diego, CA	68.9
6	San Jose, CA PMSA	68.9
7	Orange County, CA PMSA	67.0
8	Riverside-San Bernardino, CA PMSA	65.5
9	Bakersfield, CA	64.8
10	San Francisco, CA PMSA	64.4

Source: http://www.census.gov/compendia/statab/cats/population/estimates_and_projections—states_metropolitan_areas_cities.html

The preference for being unlisted varies across states. While slightly more than a third of Americans nationally have unlisted home numbers, about half the people in California, Nevada, Arizona, Oregon, and Washington choose not to be listed. Americans residing in areas of Michigan, Arkansas, and Wisconsin are willing to pay up to $5 per month to have them unlisted. According to Survey Sampling International, 93 percent of households in Vermont and 90 percent of households in Maine have listed numbers. The Cellular Industry Trade Association estimates that nearly 10 percent of the nation's 165 million cell phone users have no land line.[5] A research released nationally in August 2003 shows that 7.5 million Americans have shifted to mobile phones from land lines. In-Stat/MDR reports that the percentage is expected to more than double by 2008 to nearly 30 percent.[6]

About 20 percent of the unlisted numbers comprise people who have moved and have not had a chance to get a number listed. The other 80 percent (unlisted by choice) are people motivated to avoid crank or prank callers, telemarketers, bill collectors, or other unwanted callers. Those with unlisted numbers differ from other telephone subscribers. Demographically, these households tend to be younger, more urban, and less likely to own single-family dwelling units. Households that are unlisted by choice tend to have a higher-than-average income. Households that are unlisted by circumstance tend to be lower-income. Lower-income households own fewer automobiles, are less educated, and tend to be nonwhite. One study showed that of those requesting unlisted telephones, 42 percent were female, whereas 32 percent of the other subscribers were female.

One way to reach unlisted numbers, dialing numbers randomly, can be very costly because many of the numbers will be unassigned or will be business numbers.[7] A variant starts from a sample of listed telephone numbers. The number called is then the number drawn from the directory, plus some fixed number such as 10. Of course, this method still will result in reaching some nonworking numbers. A study using this approach, conducted in two Colorado communities (Sterling and Boulder), resulted in 10 percent nonworking numbers in Sterling and 29 percent in Boulder.[8]

The method of adding a fixed number to a listed telephone number will not include those who are in a new series of numbers being activated by the telephone company. Seymour Sudman of The Survey Research Laboratory of the University of Illinois, a researcher long interested in sampling issues, therefore suggests that the last three digits in a listed telephone number be replaced by a three-digit random number. He indicates that the coverage will then increase and that half of the resulting numbers generally will be nonworking numbers.[9]

Another approach is to buy lists from magazines, credit card firms, mail-order firms, or other such sources. One problem is that each such list has its own type of biases.

Sometimes it is possible to define the population to match the sampling frame exactly. Usually, however, an exact match is not possible and the task is to consider what portions of the population are excluded by the sampling frame and what biases are therefore created. For example, a list of a city's residents will exclude those in new housing developments. The questions are how many are in this category, and whether their responses to the survey will be different from the others. The existence of such biases usually will not affect the study's usefulness, as long as the biases are identified and the interpretation of the results takes that into consideration.

Dealing with Population Sampling Frame Differences

When a sampling frame is not representative of the population, three types of problems arise that result in **frame error**: the subset problem, the superset problem, and the intersection problem. A *subset* problem occurs when the sampling frame is smaller than the population. In other words, some of the elements in the population will not be present in the sampling frame. For example, if a researcher is using the Dun & Bradstreet small-business list for contacting all firms with less than 1,000 employees, then a subset problem occurs. The D&B small-business list contains names of firms with less than 500 employees. To deal with the subset problem, a researcher may have to redefine the population in terms of sampling frame or get information from other sources to match up with population.

A *superset* problem occurs when the sampling frame is larger than the population but contains all the elements of the population. For example, a researcher may be interested in contacting the buyers of Revlon lipstick. However, if the sampling frame contains a list of buyers of all Revlon cosmetics, then a superset problem occurs. To deal with a superset problem, a researcher may pose a filter question such as "Do you buy Revlon lipsticks"; if "yes," that person will be included in the sample.

Finally, the most serious of these types of problems, an *intersection problem*, occurs when some elements of the population are omitted from the sampling frame, and when the sampling frame contains more elements than the population. Assume that a researcher is interested in contacting small-business owners with at least $4 million in sales. If the researcher uses the American Business list, which contains all businesses (not strictly small businesses) with over $5 million in sales, an intersection problem results. To deal with such problems, a researcher may not only have to redefine the population but also may have to pose a better question.

As noted previously, a famous example of a biased frame was that used by the *Literary Digest* to predict the 1936 Presidential election. This frame consisted of subscribers to the magazine, automobile owners, and households with telephones, at a time when many people had neither cars nor phones. The *Literary Digest* predicted a victory for Republican Alf Landon, but the actual result was a landslide for President Franklin D. Roosevelt.

Selecting a Sampling Procedure

There are many ways of obtaining a sample and many decisions associated with generating a sample. A researcher should first choose between using a Bayesian procedure and a traditional sampling procedure. Next, a decision is made to sample with or without replacement. Most marketing research projects employ a traditional sampling method without replacement because a respondent is not contacted twice to obtain the same information. Among traditional sampling procedures, some are informal or even casual. Passers-by may be queried as to their opinions about a new product. If the response of everyone in the population is uniform—they all either love it or hate it—such an approach may be satisfactory. If you want to determine whether the water in a swimming pool is too cold, it is not necessary to take a random sample; you just have to test the water at any one place because the temperature will be constant throughout.

In most cases, however, the situation is more complex. There are several questions to be answered and a wide variability in responses. It is then necessary to obtain a representative sample of the population consisting of more than a handful of units. It is possible, even necessary in some cases, to obtain a sample representative of the population just by using judgment and common sense. The preferred approach, however, is to use probability sampling (where some randomization process is used) to obtain a representative sample. In **probability sampling**, all population members have a known probability of being in the sample. In most probability sampling procedures, a sampling frame is needed and information on objects/sampling units is necessary prior to employing the sampling process.

Probability sampling has several advantages over nonprobability sampling. First, it permits the researcher to demonstrate the sample's representativeness. Second, it allows an explicit statement as to how much variation is introduced because a sample is used instead of a census of the population. Finally, it makes possible the more explicit identification of possible biases.

In the next two sections, probability sampling will be described first, followed by a description and comparison of nonprobability sampling methods.

Probability Sampling

Probability sampling involves four considerations. First, the target population—the group about which information is being sought—must be specified. Second, the method for selecting the sample needs to be developed. Third, the sample size must be determined. The sample size will depend on the accuracy needs, the variation within the population, and the cost. Finally, the nonresponse problem must be addressed.

Selecting the Probability Sample

Various methods can be used to select a probability sample. The simplest, conceptually, is termed **simple random sampling**. It not only has practical value, it is a good vehicle for gaining intuitive understanding of the logic and power of random sampling.

Simple Random Sampling

Simple random sampling is an approach in which each population member, and thus each possible sample, has an equal probability of being selected.

This can be accomplished by using a table of random numbers. A *random-number table* is a long list of numbers, each of which is computer-generated by randomly selecting a number from 0 to 9. It has the property that knowledge of a string of 10 numbers gives no information about what the 11th number will be. Suppose that a sample is desired from a list of 5,000 opera season-ticket holders. A random-number table might provide the following set of numbers:

7659 / 0783 / 4710 / 3749 / 7741 / 2960 / 0016 / 9347

Using these numbers, a sample of five would be created that would include these ticket holders:

0783 / 4710 / 3749 / 2960 / 0016

The numbers above 5,000 are disregarded because there are no season-ticket holders associated with them.

If the original list of season-ticket holders were randomly arranged, a result equivalent to the computer-generated list could be obtained by taking the first ticket holders in the list. However, there is always the danger that the list may have some subtle deviations from random order. Perhaps it was prepared according to the order in which the tickets were purchased; thus, the more interested and organized patrons would be early on the list. The use of random numbers eliminates such concerns.

Accuracy–Cost Trade-off

The trade-off between the cost of employing a probability sampling procedure and the resulting accuracy can best be described by the term **sampling efficiency**, or **efficiency of sampling**, which is defined as the ratio of accuracy over cost. In general, the higher the cost, the higher is the accuracy. The simple random sampling process has some sampling efficiency associated with it. Researchers are always interested in increasing the sampling efficiency, and the various attempts to increase it have resulted in different probability sampling techniques. The feasible ways to increase the sampling efficiency include (1) holding the accuracy constant and decreasing the cost, (2) holding the cost constant and increasing the accuracy, (3) increasing the accuracy at a faster rate than the rate of cost increase, and (4) decreasing the accuracy at a slower rate than the rate of cost decrease. The subsequent probability sampling procedures are the result of the attempts to increase the sampling efficiency in the above-described ways.

Stratified Sampling

In simple random sampling, a random sample is taken from a list (or sampling frame) representing the population. Often, some information about subgroups within the sample frame can be used to improve the efficiency of sampling. **Stratified sampling** improves the sampling efficiency by increasing the accuracy at a faster rate than the cost increase. The rate of increases of both accuracy and cost depends on the variable(s) used to form the groups and the strength of association between the measure of interest (for example, attitudes) and the variable(s) used to form the groups.

Suppose that information is needed on the attitudes of students toward a proposed new intramural athletic facility. Let us assume that there are three groups of students in the school: off-campus students, dormitory dwellers, and those living in fraternity and sorority houses. Assume, further, that those living in fraternities and sororities have very homogeneous attitudes toward the proposed facility; that is, the variation, or variance, in their attitudes is very low. Suppose also that the dormitory dwellers are less homogeneous and that the off-campus students vary widely in their opinions. In such a situation, instead of allowing the sample to come from all three groups randomly, it will be more sensible to take fewer members from the fraternity/sorority group and draw more from the off-campus group. We would separate the student-body list into the three groups and draw a simple random sample from each of the three groups, resulting in stratified sampling.

The sample size of the three groups will depend on two factors. First, it will depend on the amount of attitude variation in each group. The larger the variation, the larger the sample. Second, the sample size will tend to be inversely proportional to the cost of sampling. The smaller the cost, the larger the sample size that can be justified. (Sample-size formulas for stratified sampling are introduced in Chapter 15.)

In developing a sample plan, it is wise to look for natural subgroups that will be more homogeneous than the total population. Such subgroups are called *strata*. Thus, there will be more homogeneity within the strata compared to between the strata. In fact, the accuracy of stratified sampling is increased if there are dissimilarities between the groups, and similarities within the groups, with respect to the measure of interest.

The major difference among the different types of stratified sampling processes is in the selection of sample sizes within each group. The different types of stratified sampling are described below.

Proportional Stratified Sampling

In this type of sampling procedure, the number of objects or sampling units chosen from each group is proportional to the number in the population. **Proportional stratified sampling** can further be classified as *directly proportional* and *inversely proportional stratified sampling*. Examples of both types of proportional stratified sampling are provided here.

Directly Proportional Stratified Sampling

Assume that a researcher is evaluating customer satisfaction for a beverage that is consumed by a total of 600 people. Among the 600 people, 400 are brand-loyal and 200 are variety-seeking. Past research indicates that the level of customer satisfaction is related to consumer characteristics, such as being either brand-loyal or variety-seeking. Therefore, it should be beneficial to divide the total population of 600 consumers into two groups of 400 and 200 each, and randomly sample from within each of the two groups. If a sample size of 60 is desired, then a 10 percent directly proportional stratified sampling is employed.

Consumer type	Group size	10 percent directly proportional stratified sample size
Brand-loyal	400	40
Variety-seeking	200	20
Total	600	60

Inversely Proportional Stratified Sampling

Assume, now, that among the 600 consumers in the population, say 200 are heavy drinkers and 400 are light drinkers. If a researcher values the opinion of the heavy drinkers more than that of the light drinkers, more people will have to be sampled from the heavy drinkers group. In such instances, one can use an inversely proportional stratified sampling. If a sample size of 60 is desired, a 10 percent inversely proportional stratified sampling is employed.

Consumer type	Group size	10 percent inversely proportional stratified sample size
Heavy drinkers	200	40
Light drinkers	400	20
Total	600	60

In inversely proportional stratified sampling, the selection probabilities are computed as follows:

Denominator $\Rightarrow 600/200 + 600/400 = 3 + 1.5 = 4.5$

Heavy drinkers proportional sample size $\Rightarrow 3/4.5 = 0.667; 0.667 \times 60 = 40$

Light drinkers proportional sample size $\Rightarrow 1.5/4.5 = 0.333; 0.333 \times 60 = 20$

Disproportional Stratified Sampling

In stratified sampling, when the sample size in each group is not proportional to the respective group sizes, it is known as **disproportional stratified sampling**. When multiple groups are compared and their respective group sizes are small, a proportional stratified sampling will not yield a sample size large enough for meaningful comparisons, and disproportional stratified sampling is used. One way of selecting sample sizes within each group is to have equal group sizes in the sample. In the example of heavy and light drinkers, a researcher could select 30 people from each of the two groups.

In general, stratified sampling is employed in many research projects because it is easy to understand and execute.

Cluster Sampling

In **cluster sampling**, the sampling efficiency is improved by decreasing cost at a faster rate than accuracy. Like stratified sampling, cluster sampling is a two-step process. Unlike stratified sampling, the process of cluster sampling involves dividing the population into subgroups, here termed *clusters* instead of strata. This time, however, a random sample of subgroups or clusters is selected and all members of the subgroups are interviewed. Even though cluster sampling is very cost effective, it has its limitations. Cluster sampling results in relatively imprecise samples, and it is difficult to form heterogeneous clusters because, for example, households in a block tend to be similar rather than dissimilar.[10]

Cluster sampling is useful when subgroups that are representative of the whole population can be identified.

Suppose a sample of high school sophomores who took an English class is needed in a Midwestern city. There are 200 English classes, each of which contain a fairly representative sample with respect to student opinions on rock groups, the subject of the study. A cluster sample randomly selects a number of classrooms, say 15, and includes all members of those classrooms in the sample. The big advantage of cluster sampling is lower cost. The subgroups or clusters are selected so that the cost of obtaining the desired information within the cluster is much smaller than if a simple random sample were obtained. If the average English class has 30 students, a sample of 450 can be obtained by contacting only 15 classes. If a simple random sample of 450 students across all English classes were obtained, the cost probably would be significantly greater. The big question, of course, is whether the classes are representative of the population. If the classes from upper-income areas have different opinions about rock groups than classes with more lower-income students, then the assumption underlying the approach would not hold. The differences between stratified sampling and cluster sampling are striking. A comparison between the stratified sampling process and the cluster sampling process is given in Table 14.2.

Table 14.2   A Comparison of Stratified and Cluster Sampling Processes

Stratified sampling	Cluster sampling
Homogeneity within group	Homogeneity between groups
Heterogeneity between groups	Heterogeneity within groups
All groups are included	Random selection of groups
Sampling efficiency improved by increasing accuracy at a faster rate than cost	Sampling efficiency improved by decreasing cost at a faster rate than accuracy

Systematic Sampling

Another approach, termed **systematic sampling**, involves systematically spreading the sample through the list of population members. Thus, if the population contains 10,000 (= N) people and a sample size of 1,000 (= n) is desired, every tenth (= I, sampling interval) person is selected for the sample. A starting point could be randomly chosen between the first name and the Ith name initially, and then every Ith name is chosen. Although in nearly all practical examples such a procedure will generate a sample equivalent to a simple random sample, the researcher should be aware of regularities in the list. Suppose, for example, that a list of couples in a dance club routinely places the female's name first. Then selecting every tenth name will result in a sample of all males.

In general, the sampling efficiency of systematic sampling is improved by lowering costs while maintaining accuracy relative to simple random sampling. However, the sampling efficiency of systematic sampling depends on the ordering of the list.

If the list of elements in the sampling frame is arranged in a random order (say, alphabetical), then the accuracy of systematic sampling may be equal to that of simple random sampling. If the elements (firms) are arranged in a monotonic order (say, increasing sales revenues), then the accuracy of systematic sampling will exceed that of a simple random sampling, because the sample will be representative (include firms from low to high sales revenues) of the population. Finally, if the elements are arranged in a cyclical order (say, days of the week) and a sampling interval of 7 is selected, then a researcher studying the consumer visits to a theater will be collecting data from the same day of the week, resulting in a lower accuracy than simple random sampling.

One situation in which systematic sampling is risky is the sampling of time periods. Suppose the task is to estimate the weekly traffic flow on a certain street. If every twelfth 10-minute period is selected, then the sampling point will be the same each day, and periods of peak travel or low usage easily could be missed.

A common use of systematic sampling is in telephone surveys. A number such as 17 could be obtained from a random-number table. Then the seventeenth name on each page of a telephone directory is a sample member. (Actually, a random number of inches from the top of the page would be used, so that names would not have to be counted.) Of course, more than one name could be selected from each page if a larger sample is needed, or every other (or every third or fourth) page could be used if a smaller sample is desired.

Multistage Design

It is often appropriate to use a **multistage design** in developing a sample. Perhaps the most common example is in the case of area samples, in which a sample of some area such as the United States or the state of California is desired.

Suppose the need is to sample the state of California. The first step is to develop a cluster sample of counties in the state. Each county has a probability of being in the cluster sample proportionate to its population. Thus, the largest county—Los Angeles County—will much more likely be in the sample than a rural county. The second step is to obtain a cluster sample of cities from each county selected. Again, each city is selected with a probability proportionate to its size. The third step is to select a cluster sample of blocks from each city, again weighting each block by the number of dwellings in it. Finally, a systematic sample of dwellings from each block is selected, and a random sample of members of each dwelling is obtained. The result is a random sample of the area, in which each dwelling has an equal chance of being in the sample. Note that individuals living alone will have a greater chance of being in the sample than individuals living in dwellings with other people.

Table 14.3 Cities in Ajax County

City	Population	Cumulative population
Concord	15,000	1–15,000
Mountain view	10,000	15,001–25,000
Filmore	60,000	25,001–85,000
Austin	5,000	85,001–90,000
Cooper	2,000	90,001–92,000
Douglas	5,000	92,001–97,000
Rural area	3,000	97,001–100,000

To see how a cluster sample of cities is drawn so that the probability of each being selected is proportionate to its population, consider the following example. Suppose there are six cities in Ajax County. In Table 14.3, the cities, plus the rural areas, are listed together with their population sizes and the "cumulative population." The cumulative population serves to associate each city with a block of numbers equal in size to its population. The total population of Ajax County is 100,000. The task is to select one city from the county, with the selection probability proportionate to the city population. The approach is simply to obtain a random number between 1 and 100,000. Let us assume that the random number selected is 89,701. The selected city would be the only one with a cumulative population corresponding to 89,701: Austin. Clearly, the largest city, Filmore, would have the best chance of being drawn (in fact, a 60 percent chance), and Cooper the smallest chance (only 2 percent).

Large marketing research firms develop a set of clusters of dwellings after each U.S. Census. The clusters may be counties or some other convenient grouping of dwellings. Perhaps 100 to 300 such areas are selected randomly. Each area will have a probability of being selected that is proportional to the population within its boundaries. This set of clusters may then be used by the marketing research firm for up to 10 years for their national surveys. For each area, data are compiled on blocks and on living units within blocks. For rural areas, these firms hire and train interviewers to be available for subsequent surveys. Respondents from each area are selected on the basis of a sampling scheme such as stratified sampling or on the basis of a multistage scheme.

Nonprobability Sampling

In probability sampling, the theory of probability allows the researcher to calculate the nature and extent of any biases in the estimate and to determine what variation in the estimate is due to the sampling procedure. It requires a sampling frame—a list of sampling units or a procedure to reach respondents with a known probability. In **nonprobability sampling**, the costs and trouble of developing a sampling frame are eliminated, but so is the precision with which the resulting information can be presented. In fact, the results can contain hidden biases and uncertainties that make them worse than no information at all. These problems, it should be noted, are not alleviated by increasing the sample size. For this reason, statisticians prefer to avoid nonprobability sampling designs; however, they often are used legitimately and effectively.

Nonprobability sampling typically is used in situations such as (1) the exploratory stages of a research project, (2) pretesting a questionnaire, (3) dealing with a homogeneous population, (4) when a researcher lacks statistical knowledge, and (5) when operational ease is required. It is worthwhile to distinguish among four types of nonprobability sampling procedures: judgmental, snowball, convenience, and quota sampling.

Judgmental Sampling

In **judgmental sampling** an "expert" uses judgment to identify representative samples. For example, patrons of a shopping center might serve to represent the residents of a city, or several cities might be selected to represent a country.

Judgmental sampling usually is associated with a variety of obvious and not-so-obvious biases. For example, shopping center intercept interviewing can oversample those who shop frequently, who appear friendly, and who have extra time. Worse, there is no way of really quantifying the resulting bias and uncertainty, because the sampling frame is unknown and the sampling procedure is not well specified.

There are situations where judgmental sampling is useful and even advisable. First, there are times when probability sampling is either not feasible or prohibitively expensive. For example, a list of sidewalk vendors might be impossible to obtain, and a judgmental sample might be appropriate in that case.

Second, if the sample size is to be very small—say, under 10—a judgmental sample usually will be more reliable and representative than a probability sample. Suppose one or two cities of medium size are to be used to represent 200 such cities. Then it would be appropriate to pick judgmentally two cities that appeared to be most representative with respect to such external criteria as demographics, media habits, and shopping characteristics. The process of randomly selecting two cities could very well generate a highly nonrepresentative set. If a focus-group interview of eight or nine people is needed, again, a judgmental sample might be a highly appropriate way to proceed.

Third, sometimes it is useful to obtain a deliberately biased sample. If, for example, a product or service modification is to be evaluated, it might be possible to identify a group that, by its very nature, should be disposed toward the modification. If it is found that they do not like it, then it can be assumed that the rest of the population will be at least as negative. If they like it, of course, more research probably is required.

Snowball Sampling

Snowball sampling is a form of judgmental sampling that is very appropriate when it is necessary to reach small, specialized populations. Suppose a long-range planning group wants to sample people who are very knowledgeable about a specialized new technology, such as the use of lasers in construction. Even specialized magazines would have a small percentage of readers in this category. Further, the target group may be employed by diverse organizations, such as the government, universities, research organizations, and industrial firms. Under a snowball design, each respondent, after being interviewed, is asked to identify one or more others in the field. The result can be a very useful sample. This design can be used to reach any small population, such as deep-sea divers, people confined to wheelchairs, owners of dunebuggies, families with triplets, and so on. One problem is that those who are socially visible are more likely to be selected.

Convenience Sampling

To obtain information quickly and inexpensively, a **convenience sample** may be employed. The procedure is simply to contact sampling units that are convenient—a church activity group, a classroom of students, women at a shopping center on a particular day, the first 50 recipients of mail questionnaires, or a few friends and neighbors. Such procedures seem indefensible, and, in an absolute sense, they are. The reader should recall, however, that information must be evaluated not "absolutely," but in the context of a decision. If a quick reaction to a preliminary service concept is desired to determine if it is worthwhile to develop it further, a convenience sample may be appropriate. It obviously would be foolish to rely on it in any context where a biased result could have serious economic consequences, unless the biases can be identified. A convenience sample often is used to pretest a questionnaire.

Quota Sampling

Quota sampling is judgmental sampling with the constraint that the sample includes a minimum number from each specified subgroup in the population. Suppose that a 1,000-person sample of a city is desired and it is known how the population of the city is distributed geographically. The interviewers might be asked to obtain 100 interviews on the east side, 300 on the north side, and so on.

Quota sampling often is based on demographic data such as geographic location, age, sex, education, and income. As a result, the researcher knows that the sample "matches" the population with respect to these demographic characteristics. This fact is reassuring and does eliminate some gross biases that could be part of a judgmental sample; however, there are often serious biases that are not controlled by the quota sampling approach. The interviewers will contact those most accessible, at home, with time, with acceptable appearance, and so forth. Biases will result. Of course, a random sample with a 15 to 25 percent or more nonresponse rate will have many of the same biases. Thus, quota sampling and other judgmental approaches, which are faster and cheaper, should not always be discarded as inferior.

In order to meet the quotas, researchers using quota sampling sometimes overlook the problems associated with adhering to the quotas. For example, the researcher may match the marginal frequencies but not the joint frequencies. Assume that an oil company is interested in finding out if women assume responsibility for vehicle maintenance. The company is interested in interviewing women aged below 35 and with age equal to and above 35, as well as working women and nonworking women. Suppose the distribution of the population of women in a city ($N = 1,000$) is as follows:

	Population characteristics			
	<35 years	35 years and above	Total	Percentage
Working women	300	200	500	50
Nonworking women	200	300	500	50
Total	500	500	1,000	100
Percentage	50	50	100	

Assume that the researcher is interested in interviewing 100 women from this city and develops a quota system such that 50 percent of the sample should be working women and 50 percent of the sample should also be under 35 years old. A quota matrix can be developed for a sample size of 100.

	Sample characteristics			
	<35 years	35 years and above	Total	Percentage
Working women	50	0	50	50
Nonworking women	0	50	50	50
Total	50	50	100	100
Percentage	50	50	100	

In the above illustration, although the marginal frequencies (50 percent and 50 percent) in the sample match those of the population, the joint frequencies (in each cell, 30, 20, 20, 30 percent) do not match. Researchers should take precautions to avoid making such errors when using quota sampling.

Determining the Sample Size

How large should the sample be? This question is simple and straightforward, but to answer it with precision is not easy. Statistical theory does provide some tools and a structure with which to address the question, which will be described in more detail in Chapter 15.

Web-Based Samples

The use of volunteer Internet samples has grown rapidly and is now widely used among government agencies, academic institutions, advertising agencies, consumer goods manufacturers, and media companies for a variety of applications. The popularity of Web research is due to the benefits offered in terms of speed, flexibility, and economy. With overall spending for online research increasing, established market research methods are being replaced by Web-based methods of research.[11]

Clients and marketing research suppliers are convinced that online research is not representative based on the fact that the majority of consumers do not access the Internet, but this is not necessarily true. In traditional research, random-digit dialing telephone samples are considered representative of the universe of telephone subscribers. Studies conducted in malls are viewed as representative of the demographics of those locations. Similarly, online research samples are representative of the universes from which they are drawn depending on the methodology used to create them. As with many types of surveys, Web-based surveys increase participation by offering incentives: sweepstakes, prizes, or cash. Evidence also shows that online and traditional research methods often yield similar results, both in quantitative and qualitative studies. The Web, like any central location, simply serves as a meeting place. It can be used to study people who would otherwise be too expensive to survey.[12]

Nonresponse Problems

The object of sampling is to obtain a body of data that are representative of the population. Unfortunately, some sample members become nonrespondents because they (1) refuse to respond, (2) lack the ability to respond, (3) are not at home, or (4) are inaccessible.

Nonresponse can be a serious problem. It means, of course, that the sample size has to be large enough to allow for nonresponse. If a sample size of 1,000 is needed and only a 50 percent response rate is expected, then 2,000 people will need to be identified as possible sample members. Second, and more serious, is the possibility that those who respond differ from nonrespondents in a meaningful way, thereby creating biases.

The seriousness of **nonresponse bias** depends on the extent of the nonresponse. If the percentage involved is small, the bias is small. Unfortunately, however, as the discussion in Chapter 9 made clear, the percentage can be significant. For example, a review of 182 telephone studies found a refusal rate of 28 percent.[13] Further, this level is likely to increase with the increase in the use of telemarketing, and the problem is generally more severe in home personal interviews and worse in mail surveys, where nonresponse of 90 percent is not uncommon.

The nonresponse problem depends on how the nonrespondents differ from the respondents, particularly on the key questions of interest. The problem is that the very act of being a nonrespondent often implies a meaningful difference. Nonrespondents to in-home interviews tend to be urban dwellers, single or divorced, employed, and from the higher social classes. A comparison of 100 nonrespondents to a telephone interview with 100 respondents revealed that responses were associated with older age, lower income, nonparticipation in the workforce, interest in the question, and concern with invasion of privacy.[14] Clearly, the nonresponse problem can be substantial and significant in many studies, although its impact will depend on the context.

What can be done about the nonresponse problem? A natural tendency is to replace each nonrespondent with a "matched" member of the sample. For example, if a home is included in the sample but the resident is not at home, a neighbor may be substituted. The difficulty is that the replacement cannot be matched easily on the characteristic that prompted the nonresponse, such as being employed or being a frequent traveler. Three more defensible approaches are (1) to improve the research design to reduce the number of nonresponses, (2) to repeat the contact one or more times (callbacks) to try to reduce nonresponses, and (3) to attempt to estimate the nonresponse bias.

Improving the Research Design

In Chapter 9, the problem of refusals was discussed in some detail, along with suggestions on how to improve the research design to reduce the incidence of refusals. The challenge in personal and telephone interviewing is to gain initial interest and to generate rapport through interviewer skill and the design and placement of questions. In mail surveys, the task is to motivate the respondent to respond, through incentives and other devices. The number of not-at-homes can be reduced by scheduling calls with some knowledge of the respondents' likely activity patterns. For example, midday is obviously a bad time to reach employed homemakers. Sometimes it is useful to make a telephone appointment for an in-home interview, although this tactic may tend to increase the refusal rate.

Callbacks

Callbacks refer to overt new attempts to obtain responses. The use of callbacks is predicated on the assumption that they will generate a useful number of additional responses and that the additional responses will reduce meaningfully a nonresponse bias. If the nonresponse is due to refusals or the inability to respond, callbacks may not reduce significantly the number of nonrespondents. They are most effective for the not-at-home nonrespondent. For some surveys, it may be worthwhile to use as many as six callbacks to reduce the number of nonrespondents to acceptable levels, although the first and second callbacks are usually the most productive.[15] The efficiency of the callbacks will be improved by scheduling them at different times of the day and week.

In a mail survey, the callback is particularly important because the nonresponse level can be high. As was noted in Chapter 9, it is common practice to remind nonrespondents at regular intervals.

Estimating the Effects of Nonresponse

One approach is to make an extra effort to interview a subsample of the nonrespondents. In the case of a mail survey, the subsample might be interviewed by telephone. In a telephone or personal survey, an attractive incentive, such as a worthwhile gift, might be employed to entice a sample of the nonrespondents to cooperate. Often, only some of the critical questions thought to be sensitive to a nonresponse bias are employed in this stage. The Politz approach is based on the fact that not-at-homes can be predicted from a knowledge of respondents' frequency of being away from home.[16] The respondents are asked how many evenings they are usually at home (if the interviewing is to be done in the evening). This information serves to categorize them into groups that can serve to represent the not-at-home respondents. For instance, if a respondent usually is at home only one night a week, it might be assumed that there are six more similar ones among the nonrespondents. On any given night, there would be only one chance in seven of finding one home. Thus, on the average, six homes with people with this tendency to be away would have to be contacted to find one person at home. This respondent is therefore assumed to represent six of the nonrespondents. There are uncertainties introduced by this approach, but it does provide a way to proceed, especially when callbacks are costly.

Shopping Center Sampling

Shopping center studies in which shoppers are intercepted present some difficult sampling problems. As noted in Chapter 9, over 32 percent of all questionnaires completed or interviews granted were store intercept interviews.[17] One limitation with shopping center surveys is the bias introduced by the methods used to select the sample. In particular, biases that are potentially damaging to a study can be caused by the selection of the shopping center, the part of the shopping center from which the respondents are drawn, the time of day, and the fact that more frequent shoppers will be more likely to be selected. Sudman suggests approaches to minimize these problems and, in doing so, clarifies the nature of these biases.[18]

Shopping Center Selection

A shopping center sample usually will reflect primarily those families who live in the area. Obviously, there can be great differences between people living in a low-income neighborhood and those in a high-income, professional neighborhood. It is usually good policy to use several shopping centers in different neighborhoods, so that differences between them can be observed. Another concern is how representative the cities used are. When possible, several diverse cities should be used.

Sample Locations within a Center

The goal usually is to obtain a random sample of shopping center visits. Because of traffic routes and parking, one entrance may draw from very different neighborhoods than another. A solution is to stratify by entrance location and to take a separate sample from each entrance. To obtain an overall average, the resulting strata averages need to be combined by weighting them to reflect the relative traffic that is associated with each entrance.

Suppose that a survey is employed to determine the average purchase during a shopping trip. Assume that there are two shopping mall entrances. Entrance A, which draws from a working-class neighborhood, averages 200 shoppers per hour; while entrance B, which draws from a professional suburb, averages 100 shoppers per hour. Thus, 67 percent of shoppers use entrance A and 33 percent of shoppers use entrance B. Assume further that the entrance A shoppers spend $60 on the average, while the entrance B shoppers average $36. These statistics are tabulated as follows.

The estimate of the average dollar amount of the purchase made by a shopping center visitor is the entrance A average purchase plus the entrance B average purchase, weighted by the proportion of shoppers represented, or

$$(0.67 * 60) + (0.33 * 36) = \$52$$

Sometimes it is necessary to sample within a shopping center because the entrances are inappropriate places to intercept respondents. The location used to intercept shoppers can affect the sample. A cluster of exclusive women's stores will attract a very different shopper than the Sears store at the other end of the mall. A solution is to select several "representative" locations, determine from traffic counts about how many shoppers pass by each location and then weight the results accordingly.

A major problem is that refusals can increase if respondents are asked to walk a specific distance to an interviewing facility. The cost of increasing nonresponse may outweigh any increase in the sample's representativeness.

Time Sampling

Another issue is the time period. For example, people who work usually shop during the evening, on weekends, or during lunch hours. Thus, it is reasonable to stratify by time segments—such as weekdays, weekday evenings, and weekends—and interview during each segment. Again, traffic counts can provide estimates of the proportion of shoppers that will be in each stratum, so the final results can be weighted appropriately.

Sampling People versus Shopping Visits

Obviously, some people shop more frequently than others and will be more likely to be selected in a shopping center sample. If the interest is in sampling shopping center visits, then it is appropriate to oversample those who shop more. If the goal is to develop a sample that represents the total population, however, it becomes important to adjust the sample so that it reflects the infrequent as well as the frequent shoppers.

One approach is to ask respondents how many times they visited the shopping center during a specified time period, such as the last four weeks. Those whose current visit was the only one during the time period would receive a weight of 1. Those who visited two times would have a weight of $\frac{1}{2}$; those who visited three times would have a weight of $\frac{1}{3}$; and so on.

One industry researcher measured the effect of weighting results by the frequency of visiting a shopping center on the analysis of four commercial studies.[19] He found that the weighting procedure did not affect either the demographic profiles or the values of the key questions in each study. He concluded that a frequent-shopper bias should be a problem warranting the use of a weighting procedure only where there is some reason to suspect that the bias will affect a key question. For example, if a test of a Sears commercial is conducted in a mall with a Sears store, there could be a problem.

Another approach is to use quotas, which serve to reduce the biases to levels that may be acceptable. One obvious factor to control is respondents' sex, since women shop more than men. The interviewers can be instructed simply to sample an equal proportion of men and women. Another factor to control is age, as those aged 25 to 45 tend to make more visits to shopping centers than do either younger or older shoppers.[20] Still another is employment status, as unemployed people spend more time shopping than do those who are employed.[21] The quotas would be set up so that the number sampled is proportional to the number of the population. If 55 percent of the people are employed, then the quota should ensure that 55 percent of the sample is employed.

Sampling in the International Context

Sampling in the international context requires certain special care and is seldom an easy task. The major problems here are the absence of information on sampling frames in other countries and one of sampling equivalence. The procedure to be followed when sampling for an international research is described briefly below.

Selecting the Sampling Frame

In domestic research, in order to determine the sampling frame, one has to first decide on the target population. Once the target population has been determined, the availability of a list of population elements from which the sample may be drawn should be assessed. In the international context, this frequently presents difficulties because of the paucity of information available in other countries. Even when sampling frames such as municipal lists, directories, and telephone books are available, they do not provide adequate coverage, particularly in less developed countries, and hence give rise to frame error.

Another point of difference between sampling in the domestic and international contexts is that sampling in the international context may take place at a number of geographic levels. The most aggregate level is the world, the next being regions such as the Pacific Rim or Europe, following which are the country-level units and then the subunits within each country. The level at which the sample is drawn will depend to a large extent on the specific product market, the research objectives, and the availability of lists at each level. Table 14.4 gives a few examples of lists for different levels of the sampling frame.

Once the sampling frame has been determined, the next step is to determine the specific respondents to be interviewed. The specific respondents in each country have to be identified, as they may vary from country to country. For example, in some cultures (such as the Oriental cultures), parents buy toys without even consulting the children, whereas in some other cultures (Western cultures), the child is the decider. Hence, when conducting research about toys, in some countries, the respondent will be adults, whereas in some it will be children.

Sampling Procedure

The next step in the sampling process is to determine the appropriate sampling procedure. In international research, the first decision that has to be taken in this context is whether research has to be conducted in all countries or whether results and findings are generalizable from one

Table 14.4   The Different Levels of Sampling Frames

Levels	Examples of sampling lists
World	Bottin International
	Kelly's Manufacturers and Merchants Directory
	Financial Times, International Business and Company Yearbook
Regions	Directory of European Associations
	Europa Yearbook
	Regional Associations
Countries	National Associations
	Banking Associations
	Population Lists
	Telephone Listings
Cities	Municipal Lists
	Church Organizations
	List of Government Organizations
	Public Administration

Source: S. P. Douglas and S. C. Craig, *International Marketing Research*, Upper Saddle River, NJ: Prentice Hall, 1983.

country to another. Ideally, it is best if research is conducted in all the countries where marketing operations are planned. Given the high costs of multicountry research, however, there is a trade-off between the number of countries in which the research can be conducted and the cost of the research project. In many cases, findings in one country can be used as a proxy for findings in another. For example, the market response pattern in Denmark will be similar to those in the other Scandinavian countries.

Once the number of countries or other sample units and the sequence in which they are to be investigated have been determined, the next step is selecting the appropriate sampling technique. The most appropriate sampling technique for domestic research is that of random or probabilistic sampling, but this may not always be true in the international context. Random sampling is a good technique only if there are comprehensive lists available of the target population. If such information does not exist, then conducting random sampling will lead to errors in sampling. Hence, probabilistic sampling techniques may not be best for international research.

Researchers facing a paucity of information have two options open to them. Either they can obtain the required information themselves and construct a sampling list from which they can randomly sample, or they can adopt a nonprobability sampling technique. In the international context, nonprobability sampling techniques are used more frequently than probability sampling techniques because of lack of information. Techniques such as convenience sampling, judgmental sampling, and quota sampling are used. One technique that is very popular in international research is the snowball sampling technique. In this technique, the initial respondents are selected at random and additional respondents are selected based on information given by the initial respondents. Two-phase sampling procedures also are frequently employed in order to reduce costs. In two-phase sampling, the data collection process is done in two stages. In the first phase, data is collected from the customers on certain characteristics such as purchase behavior, demographic variables, and so forth. Based on this information, a sampling frame is developed, and then a second sample is drawn from this frame.

A related issue that a researcher in the international context faces is whether to use the same sampling procedure across countries. Sampling procedures vary in reliability across countries. Therefore, instead of using a single sampling procedure in all the countries, it may be preferable to use different methods or procedures that have equivalent levels of accuracy or reliability. Further, costs of different sampling procedures may also differ from country to country. Hence, cost savings can be achieved by choosing the cheapest method in that country. Cost savings also can be achieved by using the same method in many countries, so that the cost of analysis, coding, and so on may be reduced because of economies of scale. Hence, the researcher has to weigh all these issues and make a decision.

Another important decision facing an international researcher concerns sample size. Given a fixed budget, the researcher has to decide on the number of countries he or she has to sample and also on the number of respondents in each country. To estimate sample sizes statistically, some measure of population variance is required. Since this may not be available, in many instances, the researcher determines the sample size on an ad hoc basis.

SUMMARY

There are two methods by which one can obtain information on the population of interest. Census is the process of obtaining information about the population by contacting every member in the population. Sampling is the process of estimating a population parameter by contacting only a subset of the population. Sampling is adopted because of the limitations of time and money. In some cases, a census may not be possible and sampling may be the only alternative.

The first step in the sampling process is to define the target population. The target population has to be defined in such a manner that it contains information on sampling elements, sampling units, and the area of coverage. In order to define the target population, certain simple rules of thumb should be adopted, such as looking to the research objectives, reproducibility, and convenience.

The next step is to determine the sampling frame. The sampling frame is usually a convenient list of population members that is used to obtain a sample. A number of biases will result if the sampling frame is not representative of the population. Hence, care should be taken to choose an appropriate list. There is extensive use of telephone directories as a basis for generating lists, but problems such as changed residences, unlisted numbers, and so forth, introduce biases in the sample.

Next, the mechanism for selecting the sample needs to be determined. There are essentially two different methodologies for sample selection. In probability sampling, probability theory is used to determine the appropriate sample. Simple random sampling, cluster sampling, stratified sampling, systematic sampling, and multistage designs are among the various available choices in probability sampling.

Nonprobability sampling methods, such as judgmental sampling, snowball sampling, and quota sampling, are appropriate in the right context, even though they can be biased and lack precise estimates of sampling variation. Shopping center sampling is used widely, in part because it is relatively inexpensive. Biases in shopping center samples can be reduced by adjusting the samples to reflect shopping center characteristics, the location of the shoppers within the shopping center, the time period of the interviewing, and the frequency of shopping.

The fourth consideration in the process is determining the sample size. In Chapter 15, we will examine the various approaches to determining sample size.

The final consideration is nonresponse bias. Nonresponse bias can be reduced by improving the research design to reduce refusals and by using callbacks. Sometimes the best approach is to estimate the amount of bias and adjust the interpretation accordingly.

Sampling in international research poses some special problems. The absence of reliable sampling lists brings in a number of biases into the study. Moreover, adopting the same sampling method in different countries may not yield the best results. Even if one adopts the same sampling procedure across all countries, sampling equivalence will not necessarily be achieved.

QUESTIONS AND PROBLEMS

14.1 Develop a population list or sampling frame for an attitude study when the target population is

(a) All those who rode on a public transit system during the last month

(b) Retail sporting goods stores

(c) Stores that sell tennis rackets

(d) Watchers of evening television

(e) High-income families

(f) Adults over 18 years of age in California

(g) Dwelling units with compactors

(h) Users of unit pricing during the past week

14.2 For question 1, consider how the various populations might be stratified.

14.3 A manufacturer wanted to get opinions from 4,000 hardware store managers on a new type of lawn mower. An associate provided a list of such stores, divided into 400 large and 3,600 small stores. He drew a random sample of 200 stores and was disappointed to find only 19 large stores in the sample, since they represented more than 30 percent of the potential volume. A friend suggested that he draw a second sample. What do you recommend? What other pieces of information would you like to have?

14.4 A telephone survey is planned to determine the day-after recall of several test commercials to be run in Fargo, North Dakota. Design a telephone sampling plan.

14.5 The owners of a seven-store drugstore chain want to sample shoppers of their chain and shoppers of a competing chain so that they can administer a 10-minute questionnaire. Develop alternative sampling plans. Recommend one and defend your recommendation.

14.6 A town planning group is concerned about the low usage of a library by its citizens. To determine how the library could increase its patronage, they plan to sample all library-card holders. Comment.

14.7 Assume that you have a list of 80 managers of research and development departments, who are numbered from 1 to 80. Further, you want to talk to a random sample of seven of them. Use the following random numbers to draw a sample of seven. Draw four additional samples. Calculate the average number in each case.

60311428243730443968059455937559496776391450608085041765794444744128820

14.8 A concept for a new microcomputer designed for use in the home is to be tested. Because a demonstration is required, a personal interview is necessary. Thus, it has been decided to bring a product demonstrator into the home. The city of Sacramento has been selected for the test. The metropolitan area map has been divided into a grid of 22,500 squares, 100 of which have been selected randomly. Interviewers have been sent out to call on homes within the selected square until five interviews are completed. Comment on the design. Would you make any changes?

14.9 The U.S. Department of Energy would like a census of power-generating windmills. How could such a census be obtained?

14.10 Use a set of random numbers to select a city from those listed in Table 14.3. You can even roll a dice to randomly select one.

14.11 A shopping center sample was used to evaluate a new product. Given the data in Table 14.5, what is your estimate of the proportion of people who say they will buy the product?

14.12 Discuss the differences between stratified sampling and cluster sampling.

14.13 Briefly describe the concept of sampling efficiency and discuss the ways in which it could be improved.

14.14 The sampling efficiency of systematic sampling can be greater than, less than, or equal to single random sampling. Discuss.

14.15 Identify a situation where you would be in favor of using a nonprobability method over a probability sampling method.

14.16 Discuss the differences between proportionate and disproportionate stratified sampling.

14.17 Pete Thames, the general manager of the Winona Wildcats, a minor league baseball team, is concerned about the declining level of attendance the team's games in the past two seasons. He is unsure whether the decline is due to a national decrease in the popularity of baseball or to factors that are specific to the Wildcats. Having worked in the marketing research department of the team's major league affiliate, the New Jersey Lights, Thames is prepared to conduct a study on the subject. However, because it is a small organization, limited financial resources are available for the project. Fortunately, the Wildcats have a large group of volunteers who can be used to implement the survey. The study's primary objective is to discover the reasons why Winona residents are not attending games. A list of 1,200 names, which includes all attenders for the past two seasons, is available as a mailing list.

(a) What is the target population for this study?

(b) What is the appropriate sampling frame for this study of the attitudes of both attenders and nonattenders?

(c) Which kind of sample would provide the most efficient sampling?

(d) Why would this method of sampling be the most efficient in this situation?

14.18 **(a)** How does the sampling procedure employed in an international environment differ from that used domestically?

(b) What issues are relevant to a researcher's decision to use the same sampling procedure across countries?

14.19 Jane Walker is the founder and CEO of Sport Style, a sporting goods manufacturing company based in Louisville, Kentucky, that specializes in leather goods. The company currently is under contract as exclusive supplier of Sport Style accessories for one of the leading

Table 14.5

Time period	Location of shopping center	Normal store traffic	Sample size	Proportion of sample saying they will buy it
Weekdays	A	500	100	50
Evenings	A	200	100	25
Weekends	A	400	100	20
Weekdays	B	600	100	60
Evenings	B	250	100	30
Weekends	B	550	100	35

sporting goods companies. This large multinational company markets the products under its own label as part of its "Made in the USA" promotional campaign. Sport Style has expanded its product line to include golf gloves; premium quality leather grips for tennis, squash, racquetball, and badminton rackets; and sports bags. The contract for exclusive supply will expire within the next year.

Ms. Walker has recently felt that Sport Style specialized products may not be best served by this method of distribution, and she believes that her company's sales revenue could be increased drastically if Sport Style were to market its goods under its own label as specialty goods. This would allow the company to eliminate the intermediary and its

portion of the selling price. The specialty goods could be offered at the same prices as are currently being asked, but without the intermediary Sport Style would get a larger proportion of the final retail sales price. Ms. Walker has decided to undertake a marketing research study to determine whether a market exists among retail outlets and sporting goods distributors for these specialty items, under the Sport Style brand name.

(a) Define the target population for this study.

(b) Suggest a suitable sampling frame.

(c) Recommend a sampling procedure for this study and support your answer.

END NOTES

1. Assael and J. Keon, "Non Sampling vs. Sampling Errors in Sampling Research," *Journal of Marketing*, 46, Spring 1982, pp. 114–123.

2. E. Blair, "Sampling Issues in Trade Area Maps Drawn from Shopper Surveys," *Journal of Marketing*, 47, Winter 1983, pp. 98–106.

3. For a comparison of directory-based sampling with other methods of sampling, see R. Czaja, J. Blair, and J. P. Sebestik, "Respondent Selection in a Telephone Survey: A Comparison of Three Techniques," *Journal of Marketing Research*, 19, August 1982, pp. 381–385.

4. K. A. Pierz, The Pierz Group, October 2003, http://www.telecom writing.com/Pierz/A-PrivacyTreatise.pdf

5. May Wong, "Cell Phone Directory Makes Some Nervous," June 2004, http://msnbc.msn.com/id/ 5236101/#.TplebN61mxo

6. R. Greenspan, "Callers Hanging Up on Wireline Phones," February 27,2004,http://www.clickz.com/clickz/stats/1714687/callers-hanging-up-wireline-phones

7. C. L. Rich, "Is Random Digit Dialing Really Necessary?," *Journal of Marketing Research*, 14, August 1977, pp. 301–304.

8. E. L. Landon Jr., and S. K. Banks, "Relative Efficiency and Bias of Plus-One Telephone Sampling," *Journal of Marketing Research*, 14, August 1977, pp. 294–299.

9. S. Sudman, *Applied Sampling*. New York: Academic Press, 1976, p. 65.

10. Geographic clustering of rare populations, however, can be an advantage. See Seymour Sudman, "Efficient Screening Methods for the Sampling of Geographically Clustered Special Populations," *Journal of Marketing Research*, 22, February 1985, pp. 20–29.

11. V. Pineau and D. Slotwiner, "Probability Samples vs. Volunteer Respondents in Internet Research: Defining Potential Effects on Data and Decision-Making in Marketing Applications," November 19, 2003, http://www.knowledgenetworks.com/insights/docs/Volunteer%20white%20paper%2011-19-03.pdf

12. A. J. Yoffie, *Marketing News*, April 13, 1998, p. 16.

13. F. Wiseman and P. McDonald, *The Nonresponse Problem in Consumer Telephone Surveys*. Cambridge, MA: Marketing Science Institute, 1978.

14. J. M. Struebbe, J. B. Kernan, and T. J. Grogan, "The Refusal Problem in Telephone Surveys," *Journal of Advertising Research*, 26, June/July 1986, pp. 29–37.

15. In the late 1960s the Survey Research Center, University of Michigan, found that when they made six or more calls, they reached 25 percent of the final sample on the first call, 33 percent on the first callback, and 17 percent on the second callback. The remaining 25 percent were reached on subsequent callbacks. W. C. Dunkelberg and G. S. Day, "Nonresponse Bias and Call-Backs in Sample Surveys," *Journal of Marketing Research*, 10, May 1973, pp. 160–168.

16. A. N. Politz and W. R. Simmons, "An Attempt to Get 'Not-At-Homes' into the Sample without Callbacks," *Journal of the American Statistical Association*, 44, March 1949, pp. 9–31, and 45, March 1950, pp. 136–137.

17. "Shoppers Grant 91 Million Interviews Yearly," *Survey Sampling Frame*, Spring 1978, p. 1.

18. S. Sudman, "Improving the Quality of Shopping Center Sampling," *Journal of Marketing Research*, 17, November 1980, pp. 423–431.

19. T. D. DuPont, "Do Frequent Shoppers Distort Mall-Intercept Results?," *Journal of Advertising Research*, 27, August/September 1987, pp. 45–51.

20. Seymour Sudman, "Improving the Quality of Shopping Center Sampling," *Journal of Marketing Research*, 17, November 1980, p. 430.

21. Ibid., p. 430.

Case 14-1 ||| Exercises in Sample Design

In each of the following situations, make recommendations as to the type of sample to be used, the method of selecting the sample, and the sample size.

1. The manager of the appliance department of a local full-line department store chain is planning a major one-day nonprice promotion of food processors, supported by heavy advertising in the two local newspapers. The manager asks you to recommend a method of sampling customers coming into the department. The purpose is to assess the extent to which customers were drawn by the special advertisement, and the extent to which the advertisement influenced their intentions to buy. A pretest of the questionnaire indicates that it will take about 3 minutes to administer. The manager is especially interested in learning whether there are significant differences in the response to the questionnaire among (a) males versus females, (b) gift buyers versus other buyers, and (c) age groups.

2. A major airline wants to run a preliminary study on the attitudes of university students toward air travel. The company's research director already has submitted an interview plan and has estimated that, on average, each interview will require between an hour and an hour-and-a-half to administer. It is estimated that the cost of interviewing and interpreting the interview will be roughly $75.00 per respondent.

3. A small Caribbean island relies heavily on tourist income. There is a need to develop a study so that an estimate can be provided each month as to

   a. The number of tourists
   b. The length of stay
   c. Their activities
   d. Their attitudes toward some programs and activities

   The plan is to conduct a short interview with each respondent and to leave with them a short questionnaire to be completed and mailed after returning home.

   Several sampling plans are being considered. One is to generate a random sample of hotel rooms and to interview each occupant. Another involves sampling every nth person that passes a predetermined point in the city. Still another is to sample departing planes and ships. About six planes and three ships depart each day. Design a sampling plan so that each month 500 tourists are obtained in the sample.

4. A sample of homeowners in the state of Illinois is desired for a major segmentation study conducted by a large financial institution. A lengthy personal interview lasting over 1 hour will be conducted with each respondent. A sample size of 3,000 is targeted.

Case 14-2 ||| Talbot Razor Products Company

One of the products marketed by Talbot Razor Products Company is an after-shave lotion called Enhance. This brand is sold through drugstores, supermarkets, and department stores. Sales exceed $30 million per year but are barely profitable because of advertising expenses that exceed $9 million. For some time the company and its advertising agency have felt the need to undertake a study to obtain more data on the characteristics of their users as contrasted to those of other leading brands. Both the company and the agency believe that such information would help them find better ways to promote the Enhance brand.

Preliminary discussions between the advertising department and the research department of the advertising agency resulted in the following study objectives.

1. To determine the characteristics of Enhance users versus competitors by such factors as age, income, occupation, marital status, family size, education, social class, and leisure-time activities.

2. To determine the image of the Enhance brand versus competitors on such attributes as masculinity, expensiveness, and user stereotypes (such as young men,

factory workers, young executives, and men living in small towns).

3. To discover the meaning to consumers of certain words that were used to describe after-shave lotions.

4. To examine the media habits of users by television programs, magazines, and newspapers.

In discussing the sampling universe, the advertising manager thought the study results should be broken down by heavy versus light users of Enhance. In the manager's opinion, as few as 15 to 20 percent of the users might account for 60 percent of the total purchases. It was not clear how many containers a user would have to buy during a specified time period to qualify as a heavy or a light user. The research director and the advertising manager disagreed on a definition of user: The research director thought that anyone who had used the Enhance product within the past year should qualify as a user and therefore be included in the study, while the advertising manager thought that a user should be defined as one who had purchased the product within the past three months. In fact, the advertising manager went on to say, "I am really interested only in those people who say that the Enhance brand is their favorite brand or the brand that they purchase more than any other."

After much discussion about what constituted or should constitute a user, the research director pointed out that the advertising manager was being unrealistic about the whole sampling problem. A pilot study was conducted to determine how many qualified users could be obtained out of every 100 persons interviewed in Sacramento, California. While the findings were not completely representative, they did provide a crude estimate of the sampling problem and the costs that would result from using any kind of a probability sample. The research director said:

> In the Sacramento study we were interested only in finding out how many males 18 years of age or older used after-shave, what brands they had purchased during the past year and the past three months, and what brand they bought most frequently. All interviewing took place during the evening hours and the weekend. The findings revealed that only about 70 percent of the male respondents were at home when the interviewer made the call. Of those who were home and who agreed to cooperate, only 65 percent were users of after-shave: that is, affirmatively answered the question: "Do you ever use after-shave?" Of those who used after-shave, only 7 percent had purchased the

> Enhance brand within the past three months, while 15 percent reported having purchased it within the past year. The costs of the Sacramento job figured out to about $6.00 per contact including the not-at-homes, refusals, and completed interviews, all as contacts. The sample size for the Sacramento pilot study was 212 male respondents, and the field costs were $1,272. These costs will be increased substantially if the sample includes smaller towns and farm interviews.

The research director believed that the best sample size they could hope for would be one that provided about 100 interviews with Enhance users plus 100 interviews with users of other brands in each of 10 to 15 metropolitan areas. This would provide a total sample size of 2,000 to 3,000 and would require contacts with between 40,000 and 50,000 respondents. The research director indicated that this size sample would permit breakdown of the results for the United States by heavy versus light users.

The advertising manager, who did not think this would be an adequate national sample, said:

> I can't present these results to my management and tell them that they are representative of the whole country, and I doubt if the sample in each of the 10 to 15 metropolitan areas is big enough to enable us to draw reliable conclusions about our customers and noncustomers in that particular area. I don't see how you can sample each metropolitan area on an equal basis. I would think that the bigger areas such as New York and Chicago should have bigger samples than some of the smaller metropolitan areas.

The research director explained that this way of allocating the sample between areas was not correct since the size of the universe had no effect on the size of the sample. According to the director:

> If we do it the way you are suggesting, it will mean that in some of the big metropolitan areas we'll end up with 150 to 200 interviews, while in some of the smaller ones, we'll have only 50 or 75 interviews. Under such conditions it would be impossible to break out the findings of each metropolitan area separately. If we sample each area equally, we can weigh the results obtained from the different metropolitan areas so as to get accurate U.S. totals.

When the discussion turned to costs, the advertising manager complained:

> *I can't possibly tell my management that we have to make 40,000 to 50,000 calls in order to get 2,000 to 3,000 interviews. They're going to tell me that we're wasting an awful lot of money just to find users. Why can't we find Enhance users by selecting a sample of drugstores and offering druggists some money for getting names and addresses of those men who buy after-shave? We could probably locate Enhance users for maybe 35 to 50 cents each.*

The research director admitted that this would be a much cheaper way, but pointed out that it is not known what kind of sample would result, and therefore it would be impossible to tell anything at all about the reliability of the survey. The advertising manager thought management would provide no more than $30,000 for the study. The research director estimated that the results could be tabulated, analyzed, a report written, and the results presented to management for about $7,000, thus leaving around $23,000 for fieldwork.

Questions for Discussion

1. How should the sampling universe be defined?

2. How large a sample should be collected?

3. How should the sample be distributed geographically?

Sample Size and Statistical Theory

15

LEARNING OBJECTIVES

- Discuss some ad hoc methods of determining sample size.
- Discuss the concepts of population characteristics.
- Discuss the concepts of sample statistics.
- Discuss sample reliability.
- Discuss confidence intervals and interval estimation.
- Describe how to calculate sample size for a simple random sample.
- Discuss the formulas used for estimating proportions.
- Discuss when to use the coefficient of variation.
- Describe how to calculate sample sizes for stratified sample designs.
- Describe how to calculate sample sizes for multistage designs.
- Describe the concept of sequential sampling.

A practical question in marketing research often involves determining sample size. A survey cannot be planned or implemented without knowing the sample size. As we saw in earlier chapters, the right sample size yields valuable information, which can be used for intelligent decision making. Further, the sample size decision is related directly to research cost and therefore must be justified.

This chapter presents several practical approaches to obtaining sample size. These approaches are extremely sensible, will lead to reasonable sample size decisions, and, in fact, often are used in marketing research. There is, however, a formal approach to determining sample size using statistical theory. It is useful to understand this formal approach for several reasons. First, in some contexts, it can be applied directly to make more precise sample size decisions. Second, it can provide worthwhile guidance even when it may not be easy to apply the statistical theory. Finally, the discussion serves to introduce some important concepts and terms of sampling that, together, will generate a deeper understanding of the process. Among these terms and concepts are *population characteristics, sample characteristics, sample reliability*, and *interval estimation*. Each of them will be introduced, and then the question of *sample size* will be considered.

Determining the Sample Size: Ad Hoc Methods

The size of a sample can be determined either by using statistical techniques or through some ad hoc methods. Ad hoc methods are used when a person knows from experience what sample size to adopt or when there are some constraints, such as budgetary constraints, that dictate the sample size. This section discusses a few common ad hoc methods for determining sample size.

Rules of Thumb

One approach is to use some rules of thumb. Sudman suggests that the sample should be large enough so that each group or subset of respondents you want to study will have a minimum sample size of 100 or more.[1]

Suppose that the opinions of citizens regarding municipal parks are desired. In particular, an estimation is to be made of the percentage who felt that tennis courts are needed. Suppose, further, that a comparison is desired among those who (1) use parks frequently, (2) use parks occasionally, and (3) never use parks. Thus, the sample size should be such that each of these groups has at least 100 people. If the frequent park users, the smallest group, are thought to be about 10 percent of the population, then under simple random sampling a sample size of 1,000 would be needed to generate a group of 100 subjects.

In almost every study, a comparison between groups provides useful information and is often the motivating reason for the study. It is therefore necessary to consider the smallest group and to make sure that it is of sufficient size to provide the needed reliability.

In addition to considering comparisons between major groups, the analysis might consider subgroups. For example, there might be an interest in breaking down the group of frequent park users by age, and comparing the usage by teenagers, young adults, middle-aged persons, and senior citizens. Sudman suggests that for such minor breakdowns the minimum sample size in each subgroup should be 20–50.[2] The assumption is that less accuracy is needed for the subgroups. Suppose that the smallest subgroup of frequent park users, the senior citizens, is about 1 percent of the population and it is desired to have 20 in each subgroup. Under simple random sampling, a sample size of about 2,000 might be recommended in this case.

If one of the groups or subgroups of the population is a relatively small percentage of the population, then it is sensible to use **disproportionate sampling**. Suppose that only 10 percent of the population watches educational television, and the opinions of this group are to be compared with those of others in the population. If telephone interviewing is involved, people might be contacted randomly until 100 people who do not watch educational television are identified. The interviewing then would continue, but all respondents would be screened, and only those who watch educational television would be interviewed. The result would be a sample of 200, half of whom watch educational television.

Budget Constraints

Often there is a strict *budget constraint*. A museum director might be able to spare only $2,500 for a study, and no more. If data analysis will require $500 and a respondent interview is $25, then the maximum affordable sample size is 80. The question then becomes whether a sample size of 80 is worthwhile, or if the study should be changed or simply not conducted.

Comparable Studies

Another approach is to find similar studies and use their sample sizes as a guide. The studies should be *comparable* in terms of the number of groups into which the sample is divided for comparison purposes. They also should have achieved a satisfactory level of reliability.

Table 15.1 Typical Sample Sizes for Studies of Human and Institutional Populations

Number of subgroup analyzes	People or households		Institutions	
	National	**Regional or special**	**National**	**Regional or special**
None or few	1,000–1,500	200–500	200–500	50–200
Average	1,500–2,500	500–1,000	500–1,000	200–500
Many	2,500+	1,000+	1,000+	500+

Source: S. Sudman, *Applied Sampling*, New York: Academic Press, 1976, p. 87.

Table 15.1, which is based on a summary of several hundred studies, provides a very rough idea of typical sample size. Note that the typical sample size tends to be larger for national studies than for regional studies. A possible reason is that national studies generally address issues with more financial impact and therefore require a bit more accuracy. Note, also, that samples involving institutions tend to be smaller than those involving people or households. The reason is probably that institutions are more costly to sample than people.

Factors Determining Sample Size

Sample size really depends on four factors. The first is the size of the population number of groups and subgroups within the sample that will be analyzed. The second is the value of the information in the study in general, and the accuracy required of the results in particular. At one extreme, the research need not be conducted if the study is of little importance. The third factor is the cost of the sample. A cost-benefit analysis must be considered. A larger sample size can be justified if sampling costs are low than if sampling costs are high. The final factor is the variability of the population. If all members of the population have identical opinions on an issue, a sample of one is satisfactory. As the variability within the population increases, the sample size also will need to be larger.

Population Characteristics/Parameters

Let us assume that we are interested in the attitudes of symphony season-ticket holders toward changing the starting time of weekday performances from 8:00 P.M. to 7:30 P.M. The population comprises the 10,000 symphony season-ticket holders. Their response to the proposal is shown in Figure 15.1. Of these ticket holders, 3,000 respond "definitely yes" (which is coded as +2). Another 2,000 would "prefer yes" (coded as +1), and so on. The needed information is the average, or **mean**, response of the population (the 10,000 season-ticket holders), which is termed $\propto$:

$$\mu = \text{population mean} = 0.3$$

This population mean is one population characteristic of interest. Normally, it is unknown, and our goal is to determine its value as closely as possible, by taking a sample from the population.

Another population characteristic of interest is the population **variance**, σ^2, and its square root, the population **standard deviation**, σ. The population variance is a measure of the population dispersion, the degree to which the different season-ticket holders differ from one another in terms of their attitude. It is based on the degree to which a response differs from the population

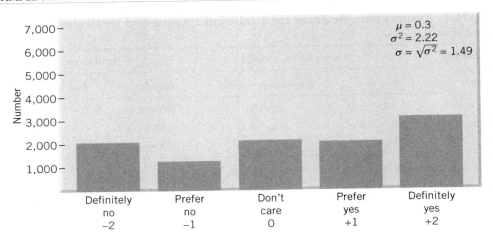

FIGURE 15.1
The Population Opinion on Symphony Starting Time (7:30 P.M. on Weekdays).

average response, $\propto$. This difference is squared (making all values positive) and averaged across all responses.[3] In our example, the population variance is

$$\sigma^2 = \text{population variance} = 2.22$$

and

$$\sigma = \text{population standard deviation} = 1.49.$$

Sample Characteristics/Statistics

The problem is that the population mean is not known but must be estimated from a sample. Assume that a simple random sample of size 10 is taken from the population. The 10 people selected and their respective attitudes are shown in Figure 15.2.

$$\bar{X} = \frac{1}{10}\sum_{i=1}^{10} X_i = 0.5$$

$$S^2 = \frac{1}{n-1}\sum_i (X_i - \bar{X})^2 = \frac{14.50}{9} = 1.61$$

$$S = \sqrt{s^2} = 1.27$$

Just as the population has a set of characteristics, each sample also has a set of characteristics. One sample characteristic is the sample average, or mean:

$$\bar{X} = \frac{1}{n}\sum_{i=1}^{n} X_i = 0.5$$

Two means now have been introduced, and it is important to keep them separate. One is the *population mean* ($\propto$), a population characteristic. The second is the *sample mean* ($\bar{X}$) a sample

Attitude

1.	John T.	$X_1 = +1$
2.	Lois M.	$X_2 = +2$
3.	Steve K.	$X_3 = +2$
4.	Paul A.	$X_4 = 0$
5.	Carol Z.	$X_5 = +1$
6.	Judy D.	$X_6 = +1$
7.	Tom E.	$X_7 = -1$
8.	Sharon P.	$X_8 = +1$
9.	Jan K.	$X_9 = -2$
10.	Ed J.	$X_{10} = 0$

FIGURE 15.2
A Sample of Symphony Season-Ticket Holders.

characteristic. Because $\overline{X}$ is a sample characteristic, it will change if a new sample is obtained. The sample mean ($\overline{X}$) is used to estimate the unknown population mean (∞).

Another sample characteristic or statistic is the sample variance (s^2), which can be used to estimate the population variance (σ^2). Under simple random sampling, the sample variance is

$$s^2 = \text{sample variance} = \frac{1}{n-1}\sum_{i=1}^{n}(X_i - \overline{X})^2 = 1.61$$

Note that s^2 will be small if the sample responses are similar, and large if they are spread out. The corresponding sample standard deviation is simply[4]

$$s = \text{sample standard deviation} = \sqrt{s^2} = 1.27$$

Again, it is important to make a distinction between the population variance (σ^2) and the sample variance (s^2).

Sample Reliability

Of course, all samples will not generate the same value of $\overline{X}$ (or s). If another simple random sample of size 10 were taken from the population, $\overline{X}$ might be 0.3 or 1.2 or 0.4, or whatever. The point is that $\overline{X}$ will vary from sample to sample.

Intuitively, it is reasonable to believe that the variation in $\overline{X}$ will be larger as the variance in the population σ^2 is larger. At one extreme, if there is no variation in the population, there will be no variation in $\overline{X}$. It also is reasonable to believe that as the size of the sample increases, the variation in $\overline{X}$ will decrease. When the sample is small, it takes only one or two extreme scores to substantially affect the sample mean, thus generating a relatively large or small $\overline{X}$. As the sample size increases, these extreme values will have less impact when they do appear, because they will be averaged with more values. The variation in $\overline{X}$ is measured by its **standard error**,[5] which is

$$\sigma_{\overline{x}} = \text{standard error of } \overline{X} = \sigma_x \sqrt{n} = 1.49/\sqrt{10} = 0.47$$

(σ_x can be written simply as σ). Note that the standard error of $\overline{X}$ depends on n, the sample size. If n is altered, the standard error will change accordingly, as Table 15.2 shows.

Table 15.2   Increasing Sample Size

Sample size	σ_x	$\sigma_{\bar{x}} = \sigma_x / \sqrt{n}$
10	1.49	0.470
40	1.49	0.235
100	1.49	0.149
500	1.49	0.067

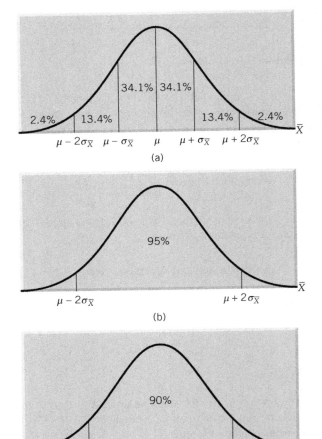

FIGURE 15.3
The Normal Distribution of $\bar{X}$. (a) Area Contained within 1 Standard Error and 2 Standard Errors of a Normal Distribution. (b) 95% Confidence interval; +/− 2 Standard Errors. (c) 90% Confidence Interval; +/−1.67 Standard Errors.

The variable X has a probability distribution, as reflected in Figure 15.1. The sample mean, $\bar{X}$, also has a probability distribution. It is customary to assume that the variation of $\bar{X}$ from sample to sample will follow the normal distribution.[6] Figure 15.3 shows the familiar bell-shaped normal probability distribution. In other words, it indicates that $\bar{X}$ usually will be close to the population mean (∞)

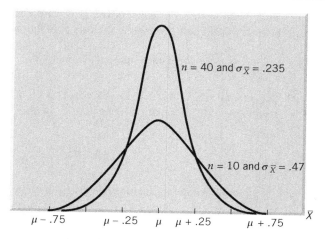

FIGURE 15.4
The Effect of Increasing Sample Size on the Normal Distribution of $\bar{X}$.

and that it is just as likely to be larger than $\propto$ as smaller. Figure 15.3a shows how the area under the normal curve is divided. The area corresponds to probability; that is, the area under the curve between two points is the probability that $\bar{X}$ will be between those two points. For example, in Figure 15.3b, 95 percent of the area is shown. Thus, the probability that $\bar{X}$ lies within 2 of the population mean ($\propto$) is 0.95. Similarly, Figure 15.3c shows 90 percent of the area under the normal curve. Its interpretation is that the probability is 0.90 that $\bar{X}$ is within $5/3 \, \sigma_{\bar{x}}$ of the population mean ($\propto$).[7]

Thus, the concept of a standard error now can be illustrated in the context of Figure 15.3a-c. There is a 0.95 probability that $\bar{X}$ will fall within ± 2 standard errors of the population mean. In our symphony example from Figure 15.1, suppose we drew 100 different samples of 10 people. About 95 percent of the resulting sample means ($\bar{X}$) will be within ± 2 standard errors ($\sigma_{\bar{x}} = 0.47$) of the population mean ($\mu = 0.3$). Figure 15.3a-c is sometimes called a *sampling distribution*, since it indicates the probability of getting a particular sample mean.

Table 15.2 illustrates how the standard error of $\bar{X}, (\sigma_{\bar{x}})$, decreases as the sample size gets larger. Thus, with a large sample, $\bar{X}$ will tend to be close to $\propto$, and the distribution of $\bar{X}$ will change accordingly. Figure 15.4 shows the effect of sample size change from 10 to 40 on the distribution of $\bar{X}$. If the sample size were increased further, the $\bar{X}$ probability distribution would get taller and narrower.

A source of confusion is the fact that two probability distributions are being discussed. It is very important to keep them separate. The first is the distribution of response over the population, as illustrated by Figure 15.1. The population standard deviation, σ, reflects the dispersion of this distribution. The second is the distribution of $\bar{X}$, illustrated by Figures 15.3a-c and 15.4 (the dispersion of which is reflected by $\sigma_{\bar{x}}$). To conceptualize the X distribution (distribution of the sample), it is necessary to conceive of many replications of the sample.

Interval Estimation

The sample mean, $\bar{X}$, is used to estimate the unknown population mean ($\propto$). Because $\bar{X}$ varies from sample to sample, it is not, of course, equal to the population ($\propto$). There is a sampling error. It is useful to provide an interval estimate around $\bar{X}$ that reflects our judgment of the extent of this sampling error:

$$\bar{X} \pm \text{sampling error} = \text{the interval estimate of } \mu$$

The size of the interval will depend on the confidence level. If it were necessary to have a 95 percent confidence level, the interval estimate containing the true population mean would be

$$\bar{X} \pm 2\sigma_{\bar{x}} = \bar{X} \pm 2\sigma_x / \sqrt{n} = 95\% \text{ interval estimate of } \mu$$

(recall that $\sigma_{\bar{x}} = \sigma_x / \sqrt{n}$). The interval size is based on $2\sigma_{\bar{x}}$ because, as Figure 15.3a-c shows, the probability that X will be within $2\sigma_{\bar{x}}$ of the population mean is 0.95. In our example, the interval would be

$$\bar{X} \pm 2\sigma_{\bar{x}} = 0.5 \pm 2 \times 0.47 = 0.5 \pm 0.94$$

since $\sigma_{\bar{x}} = \sigma_X / \sqrt{n} = 0.47$. Note that this interval includes the true population mean (recall from Figure 15.1 that $\mu = 0.3$). About 95 percent of samples will generate an interval estimate that will include the true population mean.

If the desire were to have a 90 percent confidence level, then the interval estimate containing the true population mean would be

$$\bar{X} \pm 5/3 \left(\sigma_{\bar{x}} \right) = \bar{X} \pm (5/3)\sigma_x / \sqrt{n} = 90\% \text{ interval estimate of } \mu$$

Again, the interval is based on $5/3(\sigma_{\bar{x}})$ because, as shown in Figure 15.3a-c, there is a 0.90 probability that $\bar{X}$ is within $5/3(\sigma_{\bar{x}})$ of the true population mean, $\propto$. In our example, the 90 percent interval estimate is

$$\bar{X} \pm 5/3 \left(\sigma_{\bar{x}} \right) = 0.5 \pm 5/3(0.47) = 0.5 \pm 0.78$$

Note that the interval is smaller, but that we are less confident that it would include the true population mean.

If the population standard deviation ($\sigma_x = \sigma$) is not known, it is necessary to estimate it with the sample standard deviation, s.[8] Thus, the 95 percent interval estimate would be

$$\bar{X} \pm 2s / \sqrt{n} = 95\% \text{ interval estimate with } \sigma \text{ unknown}$$

In our example, it would be

$$0.5 \pm 2(1.27 / \sqrt{10}) = 0.5 \pm 0.80$$

since, from Figure 15.2, s was determined to be 1.27.

To summarize, the interval estimate of the population mean, $\propto$, can be written as

$$\bar{X} \pm \text{sampling error, or } \bar{X} \pm z\sigma_x / \sqrt{n}$$

where

$z = 2$ for a 95 percent confidence level

$z = 5/3$ for a 90 percent confidence level

$\sigma_x = $ population standard deviation $\left(s \text{ is used if } \sigma_x \text{ is unknown} \right)$

$n = $ the sample size

Thus, the size of the interval estimate will depend on three factors. The first is the confidence level. If we are willing to have a lower confidence level for the interval estimate to include the true unknown population mean, then the interval will be smaller. The second factor is the population standard deviation. If there is little variation in the population, then the interval estimate of the population mean will be smaller. The third is the sample size. As the sample size gets larger, the sampling error is reduced and the interval gets smaller.

Sample Size Question

Now we are finally ready to use these concepts to help determine sample size. To proceed, the analyst must specify

1. Size of the sampling error that is desired

2. Confidence level; for example, the 95 percent confidence level

3. Expected variance

This specification will depend on a trade-off between the value of more accurate information and the cost of an increased sample size. For a given confidence level, a smaller sampling error will "cost" in terms of a larger sample size. Similarly, for a given sampling error, a higher confidence level will "cost" in terms of a larger sample size. These statements will become more tangible in the context of some examples.

Using the general formula for the interval estimate (recall that, $< \sigma$ and σ_x are the same),

$$\bar{X} \pm \text{sampling error, or } \bar{X} \pm z\sigma/\sqrt{n}$$

We know that

$$\text{Sampling error} = z\sigma/\sqrt{n}$$

Dividing through by the sampling error and multiplying by $\sqrt{n}$,

$$\sqrt{n} = z\sigma/(\text{sampling error})$$

and squaring both sides, we get an expression for sample size:

$$n = z^2\sigma^2/(\text{sampling error})^2$$

Thus, if we know the required confidence level, and therefore z, and also know the allowed sampling error, then the needed sample size is specified by the formula.

Let us assume that we need to have a 95 percent confidence level that our sampling error in estimating the population mean does not exceed 0.3. In this case, sampling error = 0.3, and, since the confidence level is 95 percent, $z = 2$. In our example from Figure 15.1, the population standard deviation is 1.49, so the sample size should be

$$n = 2^2 (1.49)^2/(0.3)^2 = 98.7 \approx 99$$

Changing the Confidence Level

If the confidence level is changed from 95 percent to 90 percent, the sample size can be reduced, because we do not have to be as certain of the resulting estimate. The z term is then 5/3 and the sample size is

$$n = (z\sigma)^2/(\text{sampling error})^2 = (5/3)^2 (1.49)^2/(0.3)^2 = 68.5 \approx 69$$

Changing the Allowed Error

If the allowed error is increased, the sample size will also decrease, even if a 95 percent confidence level is retained. In our example, if the allowed error is increased to 0.5, then the sample size is

$$n = (z\sigma)^2 / (\text{sampling error})^2 = 4(1.49)^2 / (0.5)^2 = 35.5 \approx 36$$

Population Size

It should be noted that the sample size calculation is independent of the size of the population. A common misconception is that a "good" sample should include a relatively high percentage of the sampling frame. Actually, the size of the sample will be determined in the same manner, whether the population is 1,000 or 1,000,000. There should be no concern that the sample contain a reasonable percentage of the population. Of course, if the population is small, the sample size can be reduced.[9] Obviously, the sample size should not exceed the population.

Determining the Population Standard Deviation

The procedure just displayed assumes that the population standard deviation is known. In most practical situations it is not known, and it must be estimated by using one of several available approaches.

One method is to use a sample standard deviation obtained from a previous comparable survey or from a pilot survey. Another approach is to estimate σ subjectively. Suppose the task is to estimate the income of a community. It might be possible to say that 95 percent of the people will have a monthly income of between $4,000 and $20,000. Assuming a normal distribution, there will be four population standard deviations between the two figures, so that one population standard deviation will be equal to $4,000.

Another approach is to take a "worst-case" situation. In our example, the largest population variance would occur if half the population would respond with a +2 and the other half with a −2.[10] The population variance would then be 4, and the recommended sample size, at a 95 percent confidence level and a 0.3 allowable error, would be 178. Note that the sample size would be larger than desired, and thus the desired accuracy would be exceeded. The logic is that it is acceptable to err on the side of being too accurate.

Proportions

When proportions are to be estimated (the proportion of people with negative feelings about a change in the symphony's starting time, for example), the procedure is to use the sample proportion to estimate the unknown population proportion, π. Because this estimate is based on a sample, it has a population variance, namely,

$$\sigma_p^2 = \pi(1-\pi)/n$$

where

π = population proportion
p = sample proportion (corresponding to $\bar{X}$), used to estimate the unknown
σ_p^2 = population variance of p

The formula for sample size is then

$$n = z^2 \pi(1-\pi)/(\text{sampling error})^2$$

As Figure 15.5 shows, the worst case (where the population variance is at its maximum) occurs when the population proportion is equal to 0.50:

$$\pi(1-\pi) = 0.25$$
$$\pi = 0.50$$

Because the population proportion is unknown, a common procedure is to assume the worst case. The formula for sample size then simplifies to

$$n = z^2(0.25)/(\text{sampling error})^2$$

Thus, if the population proportion is to be estimated within an error of 0.05 (or 5 percentage points) at a 95 percent confidence level, the needed sample size is

$$n = 2^2(0.25)/(0.05)^2 = 400$$

since z equals 2, corresponding to a 95 percent confidence level, and the allowed sampling error equals 0.05. Figure 15.6 summarizes the two sample size formulas.

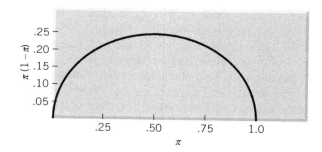

FIGURE 15.5
A Graph of $\pi(1-\pi)$.

In general
  Sample size $= n = z^2\sigma^2 \div (\text{sampling error})^2$

where
  $z = 2$ for a 95 percent confidence level
  $z = \frac{5}{3}$ for a 90 percent confidence level
  σ = population standard deviation

and
  sampling error = allowed sampling error

For proportions,
  Sample size $= n = z^2(0.25) \div (\text{sampling error})^2$

FIGURE 15.6
Some Useful Sample Size Formulas.

Coefficient of Variation

Sampling error (also known as *accuracy* or *precision error*) can be defined in relative rather than absolute terms. In other words, a researcher might require that the sample estimate be within plus or minus G percentage points of the population value. Therefore,

$$D = G\mu$$

The sample size formula may be written as

$$n = \sigma^2 z^2 / (\text{sampling error})^2$$
$$n = \sigma^2 z^2 / D^2$$
$$= c^2 z^2 / G^2$$

where

$$c = (\sigma / \mu)$$

which is known as the *coefficient of variation*.

If a researcher has information on the coefficient of variation, the required confidence level, and the desired precision accuracy level, then the estimation of sample size can be readily obtained from the chart in Marketing Research in Action 15.1. One has to locate a number corresponding to the desired information level and read the sample size. For example, if $c = 0.30$, the confidence level = 95 percent and the desired precision = 0.034, then the required sample size, n, is equal to 300. On the other hand, if desired precision is 0.70 and $c = 0.60$, then the line connecting the two will intersect at a sample size of about 300 for 95 percent confidence level and a sample size of about 500 for about 99 percent confidence interval.

Several Questions

A survey instrument or an experiment usually will not be based on just one question. Sometimes hundreds can be involved. It usually will not be worthwhile to go through such a process for all questions. A reasonable approach is to pick a few representative questions and determine the sample size from them. The most crucial ones with the highest expected variance should be included.

Stratified Sampling

In **stratified sampling** the population is divided into subgroups or strata and a sample is taken from each. Stratified sampling is worthwhile when one or both of the following are true:

1. The population standard deviation differs by strata.

2. The interview cost differs by strata.

Suppose we wanted to estimate the usage of electricity to heat swimming pools. The population of swimming pools might be stratified into commercial pools at hotels and clubs and private home swimming pools. The latter might have a small variation and thus would require a smaller sample. If, however, the home-pool owners were less costly to interview, that would allow more of them to be interviewed than if the two groups involved the same interview cost.

Marketing Research in Action 15.1

CALCULATION OF SAMPLE SIZE

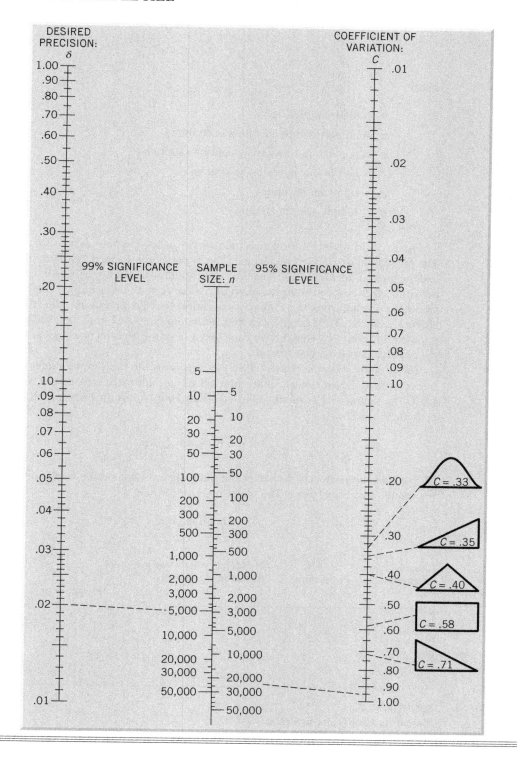

How does one determine the best allocation of the sampling budget to the various strata? This classic problem of sampling was solved in 1935 by Jerzy Neyman.[11] His solution is represented by the following formula:

$$n_i = \frac{\pi_i \sigma_i / \sqrt{c_i}}{\sum \left(\pi_i \sigma_i / \sqrt{c_i} \right)} n$$

where

n = total sample size

π_i = proportion of population in stratum i

σ_i = population standard deviation in stratum i

c_i = cost of one interview in stratum i

$\sum_i$ = sum over all strata

n_i = sample size for stratum i

Figure 15.7 presents information on a survey of the monthly usage of bank teller machines. The population is stratified by income. The high-income segment has both the highest variation and the highest interview cost. The low- and medium-income strata have the same interview cost but differ with respect to the standard deviation of bank teller usage. The column at the right shows the breakdown of the 1,000-person sample into the three strata. Note that the high-income stratum is allocated 235 people. If a simple random sample of size 1,000 had been taken from the population, about 200 would have been taken from the high-income group, since 20 percent of the population is from that stratum.

The formula shows how to allocate the sample size to the various strata; however, how does one determine the sample size in the first place? One approach is to assume that there is a budget limit. The sample size is simply adjusted upward until it hits the budget limit. The budget should be figured as follows:

$$\text{Budget} = \sum_i c_i n_i$$

The second approach is to determine the sampling error and decide whether it is excessive. If so, the sample size is increased. The sampling error formula is

$$\text{Sampling error} = z \sigma_{\bar{x}}$$

Income stratum (i)	Proportion (π_i)	Standard deviation (σ_i)	Interview cost (c_i)	$\pi_i \sigma_i / \sqrt{c_i}$	n_i
Low	.3	1	25	.06	177
Medium	.5	2	25	.20	588
High	.2	4	100	.08	235
				$.34 = \sum \pi_i \sigma_i \div \sqrt{c_i}$	$1,000 = n$

FIGURE 15.7
Allocating Sample Size to Strata.

and is based on the standard error of $\bar{x}$, which is found as follows:

$$\text{Standard error of } \bar{X} \text{ or } \sigma_{\bar{x}} = \sqrt{\left(\sum_i \pi_i \sigma_i / n_i\right)}$$

It is based on the variances of the individual strata. In the example given in Figure 15.7,

$$\sigma_{\bar{x}} = 0.7$$

As was illustrated in the last chapter, the estimate of the population mean under stratified sampling is a weighted average of the sample means found in each stratum sample:

$$\text{Estimate of the population mean} = \sum_i \pi_i \bar{X}_i$$

where

$$\bar{X}_i = \text{the sample mean for stratum } i$$

Multistage Design

If other sampling designs are employed, the logic used to generate the optimal sample size will still hold; however, the formula can get complicated. For example, in an area design, the first step might be to select communities at random. Then the procedure could be to select census tracts, then blocks, and finally households. In such a design, the expression for determining the standard error of X becomes hopelessly complex. The solution is to replicate the entire sampling plan and obtain two, three, or four independent estimates of $\bar{X}$. These different estimates can be used to estimate the standard error of $\bar{X}$.

Sequential Sampling

Sometimes a researcher may want to take a modest sample, look at the results, and then decide if more information, in the form of a larger sample, is needed. Such a procedure is termed **sequential sampling**. For example, if a new industrial product is being evaluated, a small probability sample of potential users might be contacted. Suppose it is found that their average annual usage level at a 95 percent confidence level is between 10 and 30 units, and it is known that for the product to be economically viable the average has to be 50 units. This is sufficient information for a decision to drop the product. If, however, the interval estimate from the original sample is from 45 to 65, the information is inadequate for making that decision, and an additional sample might be obtained. The combined samples then would provide a smaller interval estimate. If the resulting interval is still inadequate, the sample size could be increased a third time. Of course, although sequential sampling does provide the potential of sharply reducing costs, it can result in increased costs and a delayed decision.

The concept of sequential sampling is useful because it reminds the researcher that the goal of marketing research is providing information to help in decision making. The quality of the information must be evaluated in the decision-making context. Too often, information tends to be evaluated absolutely (it is intellectually comfortable to be "certain"). Instead, it should be judged with respect to its use.

SUMMARY

This chapter began by discussing some ad hoc methods of determining sample size and then introduced some useful concepts and applied them to the problem of determining sample size. A population characteristic, such as the attitude of symphony season-ticket holders, is to be estimated by the sample. A sample statistic, such as the average attitude of a sample of season-ticket holders, is used to estimate the population characteristic. The sample statistic will have a variance (it will not be the same each time a sample is drawn), and this will be a measure of its reliability. The estimate, based on the sample statistic, has an interval associated with it that reflects its variance and the confidence level of the researcher. The sample size then is determined by the confidence level desired, the allowed estimate error, and the variance of the population by the following formula:

$$n > (z\sigma)^2 / (\text{sampling error})^2$$

In stratified sampling, the sample size of each stratum will depend on the variance and the interviewing cost within each stratum.

QUESTIONS AND PROBLEMS

15.1 A group of 25,000 design engineers was asked a series of questions concerning the importance of various attributes of a milling machine. The group had the following response to the question: "How important is it that the machine be capable of working with both hard and soft metals?"

(a) What is the average response of this population?

(b) What are the variance and standard deviation? (See end note 1.)

(c) A sample of size 25 yielded the following numbers: 4, 4, 1, 2, 3, 5, 4, 2, 3, 3, 3, 4, 4, 4, 1, 1, 5, 5, 4, 1, 3, 4, 4, 5, 2. Determine the sample mean, the sample variance, and the sample standard deviation.

(d) Calculate the standard error of the sample mean, $\sigma_{\bar{x}}$. How would your calculation change if the sample size were 100 instead of 25? Why? Estimate $\sigma_{\bar{x}}$ using s instead of σ.

(e) Repeat parts (a) and (b) assuming that half the population of 25,000 engineers responded "extremely important" and half responded "of no consequence."

15.2 A sample of size 100 was taken from the population represented in Figure 15.1. The results showed that

$$\bar{X} = 0.52$$
$$s^2 = 2.62$$

(a) Determine a 90 percent interval estimate for $\propto$. (Recall from Figure 15.1 that $\sigma = 1.49$.)

(b) Determine a 95 percent interval estimate for $\propto$.

(c) Repeat (a) and (b) using s^2 instead of σ^2.

(d) What sample size would be needed to reduce the sampling error to 0.10 if a confidence level of 95 percent were desired? Use the fact that $\sigma = 1.49$.

Scale	Description	Frequency	Percentage
5	Extremely important	5,000	20
4	Important	8,000	32
3	Desirable	6,000	24
2	Only a small plus	2,000	8
1	Of no consequence	4,000	16
		25,000	100

15.3 If the proportion of people who intend to vote Democratic were to be estimated at a 95 percent confidence level, what sample size should be taken

(a) If the accuracy is to be ±0.01 (or one percentage point)?

(b) If the accuracy is to be ±0.03?

(c) If the accuracy is to be ±0.06?

(d) Repeat the above for a 90 percent confidence level.

15.4 A promotion campaign is being planned to encourage people to reduce heat in their houses at night. In order to measure the campaign's impact, we want to determine the proportion of people who reduce their heat at night, $\neq$. A telephone sample will be taken before and after the campaign.

(a) What sample size is required if an accuracy of ±0.03 is desired at a 90 percent confidence level?

(b) At a 95 percent confidence level?

(c) How would your answer to part (b) change if you knew that the proportion would not exceed 0.3? What if it would not exceed 0.1?

(d) Assume that a "before" measure was taken with a sample size of 400 and the sample proportion was 0.3. Generate a 90 percent confidence-level estimate for the population proportion. (Hint: Recall that $\sigma_p^2 = [\pi(1-\pi)/n]$.)

15.5 A new consumer product is proposed. It is thought that 25 percent of the population will buy it. A critical question is how frequently buyers will use it. A judgment has been made that 95 percent of them will use it between one and 17 times per month. On that basis, the population standard deviation is estimated to be 4.

(a) Explain how the standard deviation estimate was obtained.

(b) What sample size is required if an accuracy of ±1 is needed at the 90 percent level? At the 95 percent level? (The sampling error should not exceed 1.)

(c) Repeat (b) for an accuracy of ±0.4.

(d) What considerations should be introduced in selecting the confidence level and desired accuracy?

15.6 The problem is to estimate the sales for the coming year for a maker of industrial equipment. The forecast is based on asking customers how much they are planning to order next year. To use the research budget efficiently, the customers are stratified by the size of their orders during the past year. The following is some relevant information based on the past year:

Strata customer size	Proportion (π_i)	Standard deviation (σ_i)	Interview cost (c_i)
Large	0.1	40	64
Medium	0.2	3	64
Small	0.7	2	64
Number of customers: 5,000			

(a) Assume that a total of 300 interviews are to be conducted. How would you allocate those interviews among the three strata?

(b) If a simple random sample of size 300 were obtained from the population, about 10 percent, or 30 interviews, would be from the large-customer stratum. Why did you recommend in part (a) that more than 30 interviews be conducted from this stratum?

(c) The survey was conducted, and the average values (in thousands) for each stratum were as follows:

$$\bar{X}_1 = 100$$
$$\bar{X}_2 = 8$$
$$\bar{X}_3 = 5$$

What would your estimate be of the population mean, the average sales that will be received from all customers next year?

(d) Given the context of part (c), what would be the variance of your estimate of the population mean? Do you think that this variance would be larger or smaller than the variance of your estimate of the population mean if you had taken a simple random sample of size 300 from the total population? Why?

(e) What is the total interviewing cost, given a cost per interview of $64, and 300 interviews?

(f) Assume now that it has been decided that the small customers can be contacted by telephone, making their cost per interview only $9 each. Repeat the analysis that you did for part (a). How would you allocate 300 interviews now?

(g) Now, under part (f), what is the total interviewing cost?

(h) How many interviews could you conduct, assuming that you had the same amount of money determined under part (e), that you allocated the interviews according to your answer in part (f), and that the costs were as in part (f)?

15.7 In the Winona Wildcats study presented in Chapter 14 (question 17), Pete Thames, the team's general manager, has decided to use a stratified sample. One sample group includes only those who attended Wildcats games during the past two years. The other sample group represents nonattenders. The Wildcats hope to draw fans from Winona and surrounding areas, which have a combined population of 144,000.

(a) What proportion of those included in the sample should be in the stratum of nonattenders, assuming that a directly proportional method of stratification will be used?

(b) What is the actual number of people in the nonattender sample?

(c) What will be the size of the entire sample used in the study?

15.8 The owner of Galaxy Pizza, a pizza delivery business in Mercury, South Dakota (population 100,000), believes that there may be a demand for a service that provides customers with their choice of movie videos along with the pizza delivery. Galaxy Pizza currently delivers only to customers within a 10-mile radius of the store, but guarantees delivery within 30 minutes.

(a) What sampling frame would the owner use to establish how many households lie within this delivery area?

It was found that 1,000 households are within the current delivery area, which is 5 percent of the total number of households in Mercury. The owner wants to conduct this study throughout the city and has decided to collect a random sample of 2,000 households.

(b) What percentage of the total population will be represented in the sample?

(c) Recommend a sampling method that is most suitable for this study, and support your answer.

END NOTES

1. S. Sudman, *Applied Sampling*. New York: Academic Press, 1976, p. 50.

2. Ibid., p. 30.

3. Here follows one method for calculating the population mean and variance. Note the responses (R) are weighted by the response frequency (f). Thus, the response +1 is weighted by 0.20 because it occurs 0.20 of the time in the population. For a further discussion, see any introductory statistics book.

4. The term $n - 1$ appears in the expression for the sample variance so that s^2 will be an unbiased estimate of the population variance. The reader need not be concerned about this fact; it has little practical significance. If the population size, termed N, is small relative to the sample size, n, a "finite population correction factor" of $N - n / N - 1$ should be added. Thus, if N is 1,000 and n is 100, the correction factor would be 0.9. If N is more than 10 times the sample size, the correction factor is rarely significant.

5. We also could use the term *population standard* error of $\bar{x}$. The word "population" is omitted in this context to make the discussion less cumbersome.

6. Such an assumption is not as extreme as it may seem. The $\bar{x}$ distribution will be normal if the distribution of the underlying population is normal, or if the sample size gets large. The last condition is due to the central-limit theorem. In practice, if the population distribution is fairly symmetrical in appearance, a "large" n can be 30, 20, or even smaller, depending on the accuracy required by the situation. Even with an n of 10, the error introduced by assuming that $\bar{x}$ is distributed normally is often not of practical importance, and the reality is that there is often no practical alternative.

7. Actually, the numbers 2 and 5/3 are approximations. The correct numbers from a normal distribution table are as follows:

Number of σ_x	Probability
2.575	0.99
1.96	0.95
1.64	0.90
1.282	0.80

8. Actually, the use of s adds a bit more uncertainty to the interval estimate. If the sample size is small, and if it is important to be extremely precise in the confidence-interval estimate, this uncertainty can be accounted for explicitly by replacing the normal distribution with the t-distribution, which makes the interval larger. For example, using the t-distribution, the 95 percent interval estimate would involve a factor of 2.23 for a sample size of 10, a factor of 2.06 for a sample size of 20, and a factor of 2.00 for a sample size of 60. As n gets larger, the t-distribution approaches the normal distribution.

Response (R)	Response frequency (f)	Weighted average (Rf)	Population mean (μ)	(R − μ)	(R − μ)²	(R − μ)²f
+2	0.3	0.6	0.3	1.7	2.89	0.87
+1	0.2	0.2	0.3	0.7	0.49	0.10
0	0.2	0	0.3	0.3	0.09	0.02
−1	0.1	−0.1	0.3	1.3	1.69	0.17
−2	0.2	−0.4	0.3	2.3	5.29	1.06
Total		$0.3 = \mu$				$2.22 = \sigma^2$

9. When sampling with relatively small populations, the standard error of $\bar{x}$ is

$$\left(\sigma / \sqrt{n} \right) \sqrt{\frac{N - n}{N - 1}}$$

where N is the size of the population. If the sample size is a meaningful percentage of N (such as 30 to 50 percent), then it might be worthwhile to reduce the sample size.

10. The population variance would be $0.5 (2 - 0)^2 + 0.5(-2 - 0)^2 = 0.5 \times 4 + 0.5 \times 4 = 4$, since 0.5 of the population responded with a +2, and the population mean, or average, would be zero. See end note 1 for a calculation formula.

11. J. Neyman, "On the Two Different Aspects of the Representative Method: The Method of Stratified Sampling and the Method of Purposive Selection," *Journal of the Royal Statistical Society*, 1934, Vol 97, pp. 97, 558–606.

Cases for Part II

Data Collection

Dr Karen Anderson, Manager of Planning for Century Bank of Los Angeles, settled down for an unexpected evening of work in her small beach apartment. It seemed that every research project Century had commissioned in the last year had been completed during her 10-day trip to Taiwan. She had brought three research reports home that evening to try to catch up before meeting with the bank's Executive Planning Committee the next day.

Possibly because the currency exchange facilities had been closed at the Taiwan Airport when she first arrived, Dr Anderson's attention turned first to a report on a project currently under consideration by one of Century Bank's wholly owned subsidiaries, Currency Concepts International (CCI). The project concerned the manufacture and installation of currency exchange automatic teller machines (ATMs) in major foreign airports.

CCI had been responsible for the development of Century Bank's very popular ATM ("money machine"), now installed in numerous branches of the bank, as well as in its main location in downtown Los Angeles. The current project was a small part of CCI and Century Bank's plan to expand electronic banking services worldwide.

As she started to review the marketing research effort of Information Resources, Inc., she wondered what she would be able to recommend to the Executive Planning Committee the next day regarding the currency exchange project. She liked her recommendations to be backed by solid evidence, and she looked forward to reviewing results of the research performed to date.

Activities of Information Resources, Inc

Personnel of Information Resources, Inc., had decided to follow three different approaches in investigating the problem presented to them: (1) review secondary statistical data; (2) interview companies that currently engage in currency exchange; and (3) conduct an exploratory consumer survey of a convenience sample.

Secondary Data

The review of secondary data had three objectives:

1. To determine whether the number of persons flying abroad constitutes a market potentially large enough to merit automated currency exchange

2. To isolate any trends in the numbers of people flying abroad

3. To determine whether the amount of money that these travelers spend abroad is sizeable enough to provide a potential market for automated currency exchange

The U.S. Department of Transportation monitors the number of people traveling from U.S. airports to foreign airports. These statistics are maintained and categorized as follows: citizen and noncitizen passengers, and civilian and military passengers. Since this study was concerned only with Americans who travel abroad, only citizen categories were considered. Furthermore, since American military flights do not utilize the same foreign airport facilities as civilian passenger flights, the military category was also excluded. The prospect that non-Americans might also use these facilities

Marketing Research in Action II.1

■ AMERICAN CITIZENS FLYING ABROAD IN 2001 TO MAJOR FOREIGN PORTS OF ENTRY

Region/country	Number of travelers (in thousands)
Mexico	17,153
Canada	15,561
Europe	11,438
Caribbean	4,141
South America	2,247
Central America	1,414
Africa	505
Middle East	1,010
Asia	4,318
Oceania	1,187

Source: U.S. Department of Commerce, International Trade Administration, Office of Travel and Tourism Industries, January 2003.

[1] This case is printed with permission of the author, grady D. Bruce of the California State University, Fullerton.

Marketing Research in Action II.2

■ MOST FREQUENTED FOREIGN COUNTRIES OF ENTRY FROM ALL AMERICAN PORTS IN 2000 AND 2001

Country	2000 travelers (in thousands)	Percent change	2001 travelers (in thousands)
Mexico	18,849	−9%	17,153
Canada	15,188	2%	15,561
U.K.	4,189	−19%	3,383
France	2,927	−10%	2,626
Italy	2,148	−10%	1,944
Germany	2,309	−18%	1,894
Dominican Republic	779	72%	1,338
Jamaica	886	48%	1,313
Japan	1,262	−16%	1,060
Spain	1,262	−20%	1,010

Source: U.S Department of Commerce, International Trade Administration, Office of Travel and Tourism Industries, January 2003.

causes the statistics to be somewhat conservative. The figures for 2001 were summed for each foreign airport; the results by geographic area are shown in Marketing Research in Action II.1. The top 10 gateway countries from all American ports are shown in Marketing Research in Action II.2.

The second objective, to determine any growth trends in air travel, was addressed by studying the number of Americans flying abroad in the last five years. Marketing Research in Action II.3 shows the number of American travelers flying to various geographic areas and the associated growth rates in each of those areas. Europe clearly has the greatest number of travelers. Generally, the growth rates in overseas air travel have been negative since 2000 due to the slowing economy and terrorist attacks.

In order to address the third objective, whether the amount of money spent by American travelers abroad constitutes a potential market, per-capita spending was examined. Marketing Research in Action II.4 shows per-capita spending, by geographic area, for 1997–2001 as well as yearly percentages of growth. These figures indicate that Americans are spending increasing amounts of money abroad; even when inflation is taken into consideration, these figures are positive.

Information Resources, Inc., concluded, therefore, that Europe holds the greatest market potential for the new system. As Dick Knowlton, coordinator of the research team, said, "Not only are all of the statistics for Europe high, but the short geographic distances between countries can be expected to provide a good deal of intra-area travel."

Company Interviews

In an attempt to better understand the current operations of currency exchange in airports, four major firms engaged in these activities were contacted. While some firms were naturally reluctant to provide information on some areas of their operations, several were quite cooperative. These firms, and a number of knowledgeable individuals whose names surfaced in initial interviews, provided the information that follows.

In both New York and Los Angeles, there is only one bank engaged in airport currency exchange: Deak-Perera. American Express, Bank of America, and Citibank, as well as Deak-Perera, are engaged in airport currency exchange in a variety of foreign locations. Approval of permits to engage in airport currency exchange activity rests with the municipal body that governs the airport, and is highly controlled. It appears that foreign currency exchange is a highly profitable venture. Banks make most of their profits on the spread in exchange rates, which are posted daily.

Both Citibank and Bank of America indicated that they attempt to ensure their facilities' availability to all flights. The more profitable flights were found to be those that were regularly scheduled, rather than chartered. The person more likely to use the facilities was the vacationer rather than the businessperson. Neither bank could give an exact figure for the average transaction size; estimates ranged from $85 to $100.

It was the opinion of bank/Deak employees, who dealt with travelers on a daily basis, that the average traveler was somewhat uncomfortable changing money in a foreign country. They also believed it to be particularly helpful if clerks at the exchange counter converse with travelers in their own language. A number of years ago Deak attempted to use a type of vending machine to dispense money at Kennedy Airport. This venture failed; industry observers felt that the absence of human conversation and assurance contributed to its lack of success.

Most of the exchanges performed the same types of services, including the sale of foreign currency and the sale of travelers checks. The actual brand of travelers checks sold varies with the vendors.

American Express has recently placed automated unmanned travelers check dispensers in various American

Marketing Research in Action II.3

■ GROWTH IN NUMBERS OF U.S. CITIZENS FLYING ABROAD 1997–2001 (IN THOUSANDS)

Regions	1997	Percent change 1997–1998	1998	Percent change 1998–1999	1999	Percent change 1999–2000	2000–2001	Percent change 2000–2001	2001
Europe	10,099.50	8.90%	10,995.40	6.10%	11,665.80	12%	13,121.67	−7%	12,137.83
Caribbean	4,108.10	1.50%	4,170.40	8.70%	4,533.50	3%	4,681.87	−5%	4,432.90
Asia	3,399.60	1.80%	3,459.50	5.10%	3,635.60	10%	4,000.62	−5%	3,819.87
South America	1,681.50	8.50%	1,824.20	−0.60%	1,812.80	4%	1,879.96	0%	1,873.43
Central America	1,104.00	19.90%	1,323.80	10.80%	1,466.80	10%	1,606.71	0%	1,601.55
Oceania	613.5	8.80%	667.6	22.00%	814.6	9%	885.9	−8%	816.79
Middle East	449.8	−3.90%	432.2	2.90%	444.9	0%	446.59	−25%	334.55
Africa	177.9	10.30%	196.2	4.50%	205	12%	230.04	1%	232.12
Total overseas	21,633.90	6.60%	23,069.20	6.50%	24,579.10	9%	26,853.35	−6%	25,249.03
Mexico	4,333.50	2.50%	4,442.60	7.80%	4,788.60	4%	4,992.49	−2%	4,909.34
Canada	3,192.40	13.50%	3,622.80	5.10%	3,806.70	2%	3,871.89	−3%	3,767.08
Grand total	29,159.80	6.80%	31,134.60	6.60%	33,174.40	−3%	32,123.15	5%	33,625.45

Source: U.S. Department of Commerce, International Trade Administration, Office of Travel and Tourism Industries.

Marketing Research IN Action II.4

■ PER-CAPITA SPENDING BY AMERICANS TRAVELING ABROAD 1997–2001 (US$)

Region	1997	Percent change	1998	Percent change	1999	Percent change	2000	Percent change	2001
Europe	63	15%	73	3%	75	2%	76.6	2%	78
Latin America	30	85%	56	6%	59	1%	59.6	1%	60
South and Central America	-	-	41	3%	43	2%	43.7	2%	45
Asia and Pacific	-	-	42	3%	44	0%	43.6	0%	43
Overseas total	142	12%	158	6%	167	0%	167.0	0%	167
Canada	17	17%	20	7%	22	3%	22.4	3%	23
Mexico	23	−1%	23	−9%	21	8%	22.2	7%	24
Total	182	10%	201	5%	210	1%	211.6	1%	214

Source: U.S. Department of Commerce, International Trade Administration, Office of Travel and Tourism Industries, January 2003.

airports. This service is available to American Express card holders and the only charge is 1 percent of the face value of the purchased checks; the purchase is charged directly to the customer's checking account. As yet, the machines have not enjoyed a great deal of use, although American Express has been successful in enrolling its customers as potential users.

Methods of payment for currency purchases are similar at all exchanges. Accepted forms of payment include actual cash, travelers checks, cashier checks drawn on local banks, and MasterCard or Visa cards. When using a credit card to pay for currency purchases, there is a service charge added to the customer's bill, as with any cash advance.

Traveler Interviews

To supplement and complement the statistical foundation gained by reviewing secondary data sources, the consumer interview portion of the study was designed to elicit qualitative information about travelers' feelings toward current and future forms of exchanging currency. Approximately 60 American travelers were interviewed at both the San Francisco and Los Angeles International Airports, due to the accessibility of these locations to Information Resources' sole location. An unstructured, undisguised questionnaire was developed to assist in channeling the interview toward specific topics (see Appendix A). Questions were not fixed and the question order was dependent on the respondent's answers. Basically, the guide served to force the interview conversation around the central foreign currency exchange theme. The interviews were conducted primarily in the arrival/departure lobbies of international carriers and spanned over four weeks. A deliberate attempt was made to include as many arriving as departing passengers to neutralize the effect of increasing holiday traffic. Additionally, to reduce interviewer bias, three different interviewers were used. Interviews were intentionally kept informal. And Dick Knowlton cautioned the interviewers to remain objective and "not let your excitement over the product concept spill over into the interview and bias the responses."

The interviews were divided almost evenly between those who favored the concept and those who did not. Those who did perceive value in the concept tended also to support other innovations such as the automated teller machine and charging foreign currency on credit cards. Those who would not use the currency exchange terminals wanted more human interaction and generally did not favor automation in any form; a fair proportion also had had previous problems exchanging foreign currency. However, even those who did not favor the currency exchange idea did seem to prefer the system of having

24-hour availability of the machines, and of using credit cards to get cash under emergency situations.

The respondents represent a diverse group of individuals ranging in age from 18 to 80 years, holding such different positions as oil executive, photographer, housewife, and customs officer. Primarily bound for Europe, Canada, and Mexico, the interviewees were mainly split between pleasure-seekers and those on business. Only three individuals interviewed were part of tour groups, and of these three, only one had previously traveled abroad. The majority of the others had been out of the United States before and had exchanged currency in at least one other country. Many had exchanged currency in remote parts of the world, including Morocco, Brazil, Australia, Japan, Tanzania, and Russia. Only five individuals had not exchanged money in airports at one time or another. The majority had obtained foreign currency in airports and exchanged money in airports, primarily in small denominations for use in taxi cab fares, bus fares, phones, and airport gift shops, as well as for food, tips, and drinks. Most respondents agreed a prime motive for exchanging money in airports was the security of having local currency.

Exchanging currency can become a trying ordeal for some individuals. They fear being cheated on the exchange rate; they cannot convert the foreign currency into tangible concepts (e.g., "how many yen should a loaf of bread cost?"); they dislike lines and associated red tape; and many cannot understand the rates as posted in percentages. Most individuals exchange money in airports, hotels, or banks, but sometimes there are no convenient facilities at all for exchanging currency.

People like to deal with well-known bank branches, especially in airports, because they feel more confident about the rate they are receiving. However, major fears of individuals are that money exchange personnel will not understand English and that they will be cheated in the transaction. Furthermore, a few people mentioned poor documentation when they exchange currency in foreign airports.

The travelers were divided as to whether they exchange currency before or after they arrive in the foreign country, but a few said that the decision depended on what country they were entering. If a currency, such as English pounds, could easily be obtained from a local bank before leaving the United States, they were more likely to exchange before leaving. However, in no case would the traveler arrange for currency beyond a week in advance. Most preferred to obtain the foreign currency on relatively short notice—less than three days before the trip. Of the individuals on tours, none planned to obtain currency in the foreign airport. Apparently, the tour guide had previously arranged for the necessary transportation from the airport to the hotels, and there would be only enough time to gather one's luggage and find the bus before it would depart, leaving no time to enjoy the facilities of the airport that required foreign currency. All three tour individuals did mention that they planned to obtain foreign currency once they arrived at the hotel. All individuals mentioned that they had secured their own foreign currency, but a few of the wives who were traveling with their husbands conceded that their spouses usually converted the currency in the foreign airport.

Very few of the interviewees had actually used an automated teller machine, but the majority had heard of or seen the teller machines on television. Those who had used the automated machines preferred their convenience and were generally satisfied with the terminal's performance. Many of those who had not used the automated teller machines mistrusted the machine and possible loss of control over their finances. Concerns about security and problems with the machines breaking down were also expressed. One woman described the teller machines as being "convenient, but cold." Apparently, many people prefer having human interaction when their money is concerned.

As noted earlier, approximately 30 of the respondents would favor the exchange terminals over their normal airport currency exchange routine, while the same number would have nothing to do with the machines. However, the majority of potential users qualified their use by such features as competitive rates, knowing the precise charges, or knowing they could get help if something went wrong. Individuals who indicated no preference were included in the favorable category, simply because they would not refuse to try the machine. Most of the indifferent people seemed to indicate they would try such a machine if some type of introductory promotional

offer was included, such as travel information, currency tips, or a better rate.

With virtual unanimity, the respondents felt that 24-hour availability made the currency exchange machines more attractive, yet that alone would not persuade the dissenters to use the terminals. Some individuals felt that a machine simply could not give the travel advice that could be obtained at the currency exchange booths.

The opportunity to charge foreign currency against a major credit card, such as MasterCard or Visa, was a definite plus in the minds of most respondents. One individual clearly resented the idea, however, feeling that he would "overspend" if given such a convenient way to obtain cash. Respondents offered a number of suggestions concerning implementations of the product concept and a number of specific product features:

1. Add information about the country.
2. Provide small denominations, and include coins.
3. Have it communicate in English.
4. Put in travelers checks to get cash.
5. Put in cash to get foreign currency.
6. Post rates daily.
7. Keep rates competitive and post charges.
8. Have television screen with person to describe procedure.
9. Place the machines in hotels and banks.
10. Have a change machine nearby that can convert paper money.
11. Place machine near existing currency exchange facilities for convenience when normal lines become long.
12. Demonstrate how to use the machine.
13. Use all bank credit cards.

APPENDIX A

Interview Guide for International Travelers (U.S. Citizens)

These interviews should remain as informal as possible. The object is not to obtain statistically reliable results, but to get ideas that will help to stimulate research. These questions are not fixed; the order, however, is sometimes dependent on answers the respondents give.

Introduce yourself

1. Are you going to be traveling to a foreign country? Arriving from a foreign country? A U.S. resident?

2. Where is/was your final destination?
3. Why are you traveling (business, pleasure, a tour)?
4. How often do you travel outside of the United States?
5. Have you ever exchanged currency in a foreign country? (If no, go to #6.) Where? Does anything in particular stand out in your mind when you exchanged currency?
6. Have you ever changed money in an airport? (If no, go to #7.)

7. Where do you plan to exchange currency on this trip?

8. Where do you change money normally?

9. Have you ever had any problems changing currencies? Explain circumstances.

10. Normally, would you change money before entering a country or after you arrive? If before, how long in advance? Where? (Probe.)

11. Are you familiar with automated teller machines that banks are using? (If not, explain.) Have you used one of these machines?

12. What are your feelings toward these machines?

13. If a currency exchange terminal, similar to an automated teller machine, was placed in your destination airport, would you use the machine or follow your normal routine?

14. Would 24-hour availability make the currency exchange machines more attractive? Would you use the terminals at night?

15. None of the currency exchange machines currently exists. What features or services could be provided so that you might choose to use a terminal rather than other currency exchange facilities?

16. If you could charge the foreign currency received to a major credit card, such as MasterCard or Visa, would you be more likely to use the machine?

17. Demographics—Age range (visual) Occupation?
    Sex?
    Traveling alone?

Fundamentals of Data Analysis

16

LEARNING OBJECTIVES

- Discuss the need for preliminary data preparation techniques such as data editing, coding, and statistically adjusting the data where required.

- Describe the various statistical techniques for adjusting the data.

- Discuss the significance of data tabulation.

- Discuss the factors that influence the selection of an appropriate data analysis strategy.

- Discuss the various statistical techniques available for data analysis.

The HMO study introduced in Chapter 4 resulted in a survey from which 1,145 usable questionnaires were obtained. This represents a stack of paper literally over 10 feet high. Data analysis plays an important role in turning this quantity of paper into defensible, actionable sets of conclusions and reports, thereby unleashing the potential of marketing intelligence. It is actually a set of methods and techniques that can be used to obtain information and insights from the data.

An understanding of the principles of data analysis is useful for several reasons. First, it can lead the researcher to information and insights that otherwise would not be available. Second, it can help avoid erroneous judgments and conclusions. Third, it can provide a background to help interpret and understand analysis conducted by others. Finally, a knowledge of the power of data analysis techniques can constructively influence research objectives and research design.

Although data analysis can be a powerful aid to gaining useful knowledge, it cannot rescue a badly conceived marketing research study. If the research purpose is not well conceived, if the research questions are irrelevant, or if the hypothesis is nonviable or uninteresting, the research will require an abundance of good fortune to be useful. Further, data analysis rarely can compensate for a bad question, an inadequate sampling procedure, or sloppy fieldwork.

Data analysis has the potential to ruin a well-designed study. Inappropriate or misused data analysis can suggest judgments and conclusions that are at best unclear and incomplete, and at worst erroneous. Thus, it can lead to decisions inferior to those that would have been made without the benefit of the research. One important reason for studying data analysis, therefore, is to avoid the pitfalls associated with it.

The purpose of Parts III and IV of this book is to describe data analysis techniques, so that when the appropriate situation arises, the researcher can draw on them. Another goal is to provide an understanding of the limitations of the various techniques, to minimize the likelihood that they will be misused or misinterpreted. The techniques and approaches revealed in this chapter are used routinely in nearly all descriptive and causal research. It is therefore important for the reader to understand them.

The type of data analysis required will be unique to each study; however, nearly all studies involving data analysis will require the editing and coding of data, will use one or more data analysis techniques, and will have to be concerned with presenting the results effectively.

In this chapter, some preliminary data preparation techniques, such as data editing, coding, and statistically adjusting the data for further analysis, will be discussed. Basic ways to tabulate individual questions from a questionnaire (one-way tabulation) then will be developed. The discussion on tabulation will also include graphical representation of tabulated data. Next, the focus will turn to the question of tabulation among sample subgroups (cross-tabulation). Further, we will provide a discussion of the various factors that influence the selection of an appropriate data analysis strategy. This chapter will also present an overview of the various statistical techniques that a researcher can use in analyzing data.

Preparing the Data for Analysis

The raw data obtained from the questionnaires must undergo preliminary preparation before they can be analyzed using statistical techniques. The quality of the results obtained from the statistical techniques and their subsequent interpretation depend to a great degree on how well the data were prepared and converted into a form suitable for analysis. The major data preparation techniques include (1) data editing, (2) coding, and (3) statistically adjusting the data (if required).

Data Editing

The role of the editing process is to identify omissions, ambiguities, and errors in the responses. It should be conducted in the field by the interviewer and field supervisor, as well as by the analyst just prior to data analysis. Among the problems to be identified are the following.

Interviewer error	Interviewers may not be giving the respondent the correct instructions.
Omissions	Respondents often fail to answer a single question or a section of the questionnaire, either deliberately or inadvertently.
Ambiguity	A response might not be legible or it might be unclear (which of two boxes is checked in a multiple-response system).
Inconsistencies	Sometimes two responses can be logically inconsistent. For example, a respondent who is a lawyer may have checked a box indicating that he or she did not complete high school.
Lack of cooperation	In a long questionnaire with hundreds of attitude or image questions, a respondent might rebel and check the same response (in an agree–disagree scale, for example) in a long list of questions.
Ineligible respondent	An inappropriate respondent may be included in the sample. For example, if a sample is supposed to include only women over 18, others should be excluded.

When such problems are identified, several alternatives are available.[1] The preferred alternative, where practical, is to contact the respondent again. This is often quite feasible and should be done by the interviewer if the questions involved are important enough to warrant the effort. Another alternative, to throw out the whole questionnaire as not usable, might be appropriate if it is clear that the respondent either did not understand the survey or was not cooperating. A less extreme alternative is to throw out only the problem questions and retain the balance of the questions. Some respondents will bypass questions such as income or age, for example, and cooperate fully with the other questions. In the parts of the analysis involving income or age, only those respondents who answered those questions will be included, but in the rest of the analysis all respondents could be included. Still another alternative is to code illegible or missing answers into a category such as "don't know" or "no opinion." Such an approach may simplify the data analysis without materially distorting the interpretation. Alternatively, for any respondent, one can input missing values for certain variables through the use of mean profile values, or infer the values by matching the respondent's profile to that of another, similar respondent.

A by-product of the editing process is that it helps in evaluating and guiding the interviewers; an interviewer's tendency to allow a certain type of error to occur should be detected by the editing process.

Coding

Coding the closed-ended questions is fairly straightforward. In this process, we specify exactly how the responses are to be entered. Figure 16.1 is an example of an auto maintenance questionnaire, and Figure 16.2 illustrates the corresponding coding mechanism. The survey was mailed to 500 participants, and 150 responded.

As shown in Figure 16.2, the first three columns are used for identifying the respondents. The column reference is synonymous with variable identification; the questionnaire number is also indicated to provide a direct link between the question number, the variable identification, and the column numbers. Each question is described briefly in a separate column, and the range of permissible values provides the key information of the value to be entered for the particular type of response.

Once the response values are entered into a spreadsheet, a statistical software program can be employed to generate diagnostic information. However, before any data analysis is performed, the data have to be checked for any error that might have come from the process of data entry. Once the data are error free, statistical adjustments to the data can be made.

Coding for open-ended questions is much more difficult. Usually a lengthy list of possible responses is generated and then each response is placed into one of the list items. Often the assignment of a response involves a judgment decision if the response does not match a list item exactly. For example, a question such as "Why did you select your instrument from Ajax Electronics?" might elicit literally hundreds of different responses, such as *price, delivery, accuracy, reliability, familiarity, doesn't break down, can get it repaired, features, includes spare parts, a good manual, appearance, size*, and *shape*. Decisions must be made about the response categories. Should "reliability" and "doesn't break down" be in the same category, or do they represent two different responses? The difficulty of coding and analyzing open-ended responses provides a reason to avoid them in the questionnaire whenever possible.[2]

Statistically Adjusting the Data

Many adjustments can be made to the data in order to enhance its quality for data analysis. The most common procedures for statistically adjusting data are as follows:

Weighting

Weighting is a procedure by which each response in the database is assigned a number according to some prespecified rule. Most often, weighting is done to make the sample data more representative of a target population on specific characteristics. Categories underrepresented in the sample are given

---

Directions: Please answer the questions below by placing a check mark (√) in the appropriate boxes or, where applicable, by writing your response in the place provided.

1. Are you solely responsible for taking care of your automotive maintenance needs?
   ☐ Yes   ☐ No
   If you answered "no" to question No. 1, who is and what is that person's relationship to you?
   _____

2. Do you perform simple auto maintenance yourself? (for example, *tire pressure, change wiper blades, change air filter, etc.*)
   ☐ Yes   ☐ No
3. If you answered "no" to question No. 2, where do you take your car for servicing?
   _____

4. How often do you either perform maintenance on your automobile or have it serviced?
   ☐   Once per month
   ☐   Once every three months
   ☐   Once every six months
   ☐   Once per year
   ☐   Once (*please specify*) _____
5. When do you handle maintenance-related automobile problems?
   ☐   Through scheduled maintenance
   ☐   As problems arise
   ☐   Postpone as long as possible
   ☐   Other (*please specify*) _____
   ☐   I do not keep track of it
6. If scheduled maintenance is done on your automobile, how do you keep track of what has been done?
   ☐   Auto dealer or mechanic's records
   ☐   Personal records
   ☐   Mental recollection
   ☐   Other (*please specify*) _____
   ☐   I do not keep track of it
7. Please rank the following list of car maintenance activities in order of importance. (*1 = most important; 2 = second most important; 3 = third most important; etc.*)

   _____ Tire maintenance

   _____ Oil change

   _____ Brake maintenance

   _____ Check belts and hoses

   _____ Check spark plugs

8. Are there any other maintenance activities that should be included in the above list?
   _____
   _____
   _____

AUTO MAINTENANCE QUESTIONNAIRE

FIGURE 16.1
Auto Maintenance Questionnaire.

higher weights, while overrepresented categories are given lower weights. For example, this would be necessary if the sample was taken using non-proportional stratified sampling. Weighting also is done to increase or decrease the number of cases in the sample that possess certain characteristics.

Weighting may also be used for adjusting the sample so that greater importance is attached to respondents with certain characteristics. For example, if a study is conducted to determine the

Column number	Column reference	Question number	Question description	Range of permissible values
1–3	A		ID No. of Questionnaire	001–150
4	B	1	Responsible for maintenance	0 = no, 1 = yes, 9 = blank
5	C	1	Who is responsible	0 = husband, 1 = boyfriend, 2 = father, 3 = mother, 4 = relative, 5 = friend, 6 = other, 9 = blank
6	D	2	Perform simple maintenance	0 = no, 1 = yes, 9 = blank
7	E	3	Where for service	
8	F	4	How often is maintenance performed	Once per: 0 = month, 1 = three months, 2 = six months, 3 = year, 4 = other, 9 = blank
9	G	4	Other for "how often"	
10	H	5	When are problems handled	0 = scheduled maintenance, 1 = as problems arise, 2 = postpone as long as possible, 3 = other, 9 = blank
11	I	5	Other for "when problems handled"	
12	J	6	How maintenance is tracked	0 = not tracked, 1 = auto dealer/ mechanic's records, 2 = personal records, 3 = mental recollection, 4 = other, 5 = doesn't keep track, 9 = blank
13	K	6	Other for "how maintenance is tracked"	
14	L	7	Rank in order of importance: tire	0 = blank, 1 = most important, 2 = second most important, 3 = third, 4 = fourth, 5 = fifth
15	M	7	Rank in order of importance: oil	0 = blank, 1 = most important, 2 = second most important, 3 = third, 4 = fourth, 5 = fifth
16	N	7	Rank in order of importance: brake	0 = blank, 1 = most important, 2 = second most important, 3 = third, 4 = fourth, 5 = fifth
17	O	7	Rank in order of importance: belts	0 = blank, 1 = most important, 2 = second most important, 3 = third, 4 = fourth, 5 = fifth
18	P	7	Rank in order of importance: plugs	0 = blank, 1 = most important, 2 = second most important, 3 = third, 4 = fourth, 5 = fifth
19	Q	8	Any that should be included in No. 7	

FIGURE 16.2
Coding Instructions for the Auto Maintenance Questionnaire.

market potential of a new sports drink, the researcher might want to attach greater weight to the opinions of the younger people in the market, who will be the heavy users of the product. This could be accomplished by assigning weights of 2.0 to persons in the sample who are under age 30 and 1.0 to respondents over 30. Weighting should be applied with caution, and the weighting procedure should be documented and made a part of the project report.[3]

Variable Respecification

Variable respecification is a procedure in which the existing data are modified to create new variables, or in which a large number of variables are collapsed into fewer variables. The purpose of this procedure is to create variables that are consistent with the study's objectives. For example, suppose the original variable represented the reasons for purchasing a car, with 10 response categories. These might be collapsed into four categories: performance, price, appearance, and service. Respecification also includes taking the ratio of two variables to create a new variable, taking square root and log transformations, and using dummy variables.

Dummy variables are used extensively for respecifying categorical variables. They are also called **binary, dichotomous, instrumental**, or **qualitative** variables. The general rule is that if there are m levels of the qualitative variable, we use $m-1$ dummy variables to specify them. The reason for using only $m-1$ dummy variables is that only $m-1$ levels (or categories) are independent, and the information pertaining to the mth level can be obtained from the existing $m-1$ dummy variables. A product could have been purchased in either the first half or the second half of the year (a qualitative variable with two levels). The purchase time could be represented by a single dummy variable.[4] It will take a value of 1 if it was bought in the first half of the year, and 0 if it was bought in the second half.

Scale Transformation

Yet another common procedure for statistically adjusting data is scale transformation. **Scale transformation** involves the manipulation of scale values to ensure comparability with other scales. In the same study, different scales may be employed for measuring different variables. Therefore, it would not be meaningful to make comparisons across the measurement scales for any respondent. Even if the same scale is employed for all the variables, different respondents may use the scale differently. Some respondents may consistently use the lower end of a rating scale, whereas others may consistently use the upper end. These differences can be corrected by appropriately transforming the data.[5]

One of the most common scale transformation procedures is standardization. *Standardization* allows the researcher to compare variables that have been measured using different types of scales. For example, if sales are measured in actual dollars, and price in cents, then the actual value of the variance for the sales variable will be higher compared to price, because of the units of measurement. To compare the variances, both variables can be brought down to a common unit of measurement. This can be achieved by forcing the variables, by standardization, to have a mean of zero and a standard deviation of one. Mathematically, this is done by first subtracting the mean, $\bar{X}$ from each score and then dividing by the standard deviation, s_x. Standardization can be done only on interval or ratio-scaled data. The formula for standardized score, z_i, is

$$z_i = \left(X_i - \bar{X}\right)/s_x$$

Strategy for Data Analysis

Usually the first step in data analysis, after data preparation, is to analyze each question or measure by itself. This is done by tabulating the data. Tabulation consists simply of counting the number of cases that fall into the various categories. Other than aiding in "data cleaning" aspects, such as identifying the degree of omissions, ambiguities, and errors in the responses, the primary use of tabulation is in (1) determining the empirical distribution (frequency distribution) of the variable in question and (2) calculating the descriptive (summary) statistics, particularly the mean or percentages.

Next, the data are subjected to cross-tabulations to assess if any association is present between two (typically) nominal variables. If the variables are measured as interval or ratio, they can be transformed to nominally scaled variables for the purpose of cross-tabulation. For example, the income of a household can be rescaled to <$30,000 and >$30,000 to cross-tab with another nominally scaled variable. For analyzing relationships between two or more interval or ratio variables, *multivariate analysis* (discussed later) can be performed.

Tabulation: Frequency Distribution

A **frequency distribution** simply reports the number of responses that each question received, and is the simplest way of determining the empirical distribution of the variable. A frequency distribution organizes data into *classes*, or groups of values, and shows the number of observations from the data set that falls into each of the classes. Figure 16.3 provides a frequency distribution for two of the questions from the HMO study. A key question is the enrollment plan question in which the respondents are asked if they would enroll in the described plan. The number of people in each response category is shown. Thus, 124 responded "Yes, I would enroll." The figure shows two other methods of presenting the frequency distribution. One is the percentage breakdown of the various categories; the percentage often is easier to interpret than the actual numbers (rounding errors cause the percentage total to differ from 100 percent). The other is a visual bar-graph presentation known as a histogram.

A *histogram* is a series of rectangles, each proportional in width to the range of values within a class and proportional in height to the number of items falling in the class. If the classes we use

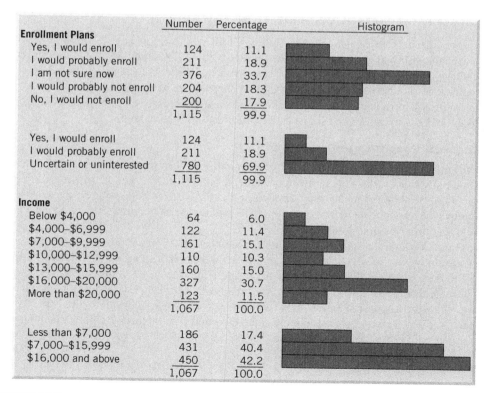

FIGURE 16.3
Frequency Distribution.

in the frequency distribution are of equal width, the vertical bars in the histograms are also of equal width. The height of the bar for each class corresponds to the number of items in the class. The actual distribution of the variable can be visualized easily through the histogram. The actual distribution can then be compared to some theoretical distribution to determine whether the data are consistent with a prior model.

For many questions, it is useful to combine some of the question categories. For example, in Figure 16.3, the enrollment question is shown with three of the responses combined into an "uncertain or uninterested" category. The logic is that a response of "I am not sure now" probably means that the respondent will not enroll. Responses to a new concept usually need to be discounted somewhat to correct for initial curiosity and a desire to please the survey sponsor. Decisions to combine categories should be supported by some kind of logic or theory. The resulting combinations also should result in categories that contain a worthwhile number of respondents. Usually, it is not useful to work with categories with only a few respondents. In fact, one purpose of combining categories is to develop larger respondent groups. Note that the two lowest income categories had relatively small respondent groups before they were combined.

Why not start with only three categories in each case? The questionnaire then would be shorter and easier to complete. One reason for not doing so is that before the study is conducted there may be no knowledge as to how the respondents are distributed. If too few categories are planned, all the respondents may end up in one of them and none in the others. Furthermore, extra categories might make responses more realistic. In the enrollment plan question in Figure 16.3, if there were not five responses available, people might have a greater tendency to check the "I would probably enroll" category.

Tabulation: Descriptive Statistics

Descriptive statistics are statistics normally associated with a frequency distribution that helps summarize the information presented in the frequency table. These include (1) measures of central tendency (mean, median, and mode), (2) measures of dispersion (range, standard deviation, and coefficient of variation), and (3) measures of shape (skewness and kurtosis).[6] This requires the data to be collected using either interval or ratio scaled questions. Here we restrict our discussion to the more commonly used statistics, the mean and the percentage.

Means and Percentages

In some situations, it is desirable to use a single number to describe the responses to a question. In such circumstances, the sample mean or percentage is used. The sample **mean** is simply the average number, obtained by dividing the sum of the responses to a question by the sample size (the number of respondents to that question). The *percentage* is the proportion who answered a question a certain way, multiplied by 100.

Table 16.1 illustrates a study of the reaction of members of a community to a transit system. As part of the study, four lifestyle and attitude questions were asked, using a 7-point, agree–disagree scale. The first column of Table 16.1 gives the mean or average score among the 62 respondents. They indicate that the sample in general is concerned with gasoline costs and is not excited about jogging. When the response is based on two alternatives, or when a single alternative is the focus of the analysis, the percentage is used. For example, Question 5 in Table 16.1 reports that 36 percent of the shoppers live close to a transit station. The balance of Table 16.1 will be discussed shortly.

When to Use What

Descriptive statistics can provide accurate, simple, and meaningful figures by summarizing information in a large set of data. The summary measures can sometimes communicate the information in an entire distribution. There is an obvious trade-off between the use of the frequency distribution and the use of a single number. The frequency distribution can be unwieldy but does provide more

Table 16.1   Rapid Transit User

	Mean score	Transit system		Difference between sample means, $\bar{X}_u - \bar{X}_H$
		User,[a] $\bar{X}_u$	Nonuser,[b] $\bar{X}_H$	
Agreement on a 7-point scale (7 is strongly agree; 1 is strongly disagree) to the statements:				
1. I dislike driving.	3.7	4.3	2.9	1.4
2. I like to jog.	3.9	3.8	4.0	−0.2
3. I am concerned about gasoline costs.	5.3	6.1	4.4	1.7[c]
4. I am concerned about air pollution.	4.6	4.6	3.9	0.7
Percentage who answer affirmatively to the question:				
5. Do you live within 3 miles of a transit station	36%	50%	25%	25%[d]
Sample size	62	28	34	

[a]Average score over the 28 respondents using the transit system.
[b]Average score over the 34 respondents not using the transit system.
[c]Significant at the 0.01 level.
[d]Significant at the 0.10 level.

Table 16.2   A Question Response[a]

		Response	Frequency	Percentage
	Disagree	−3	300	30
		−2	120	12
I prefer abstract art exhibitions to nonabstract art exhibitions		−1	50	5
		0	50	5
		+1	100	10
		+2	300	30
	Agree	+3	80	8

[a]Mean response = −0.3.

information. For example, Table 16.2 shows the response to an attitude question. The average response indicates that the sample is fairly neutral about abstract art. Underlying that mean response, however, is the frequency distribution that indicates that a substantial group likes abstract art, a larger group dislikes it, and, in fact, very few people actually are neutral. In situations where the population is not likely to be clustered around the mean, the frequency distribution can be useful.

When nominal scales are involved, frequency distributions must be employed. Recall that a *nominal scale* is one in which numbers merely label or identify categories of objects. For example, suppose respondents were asked if they lived in an urban area, a suburban area, or a rural area. There would be no way to determine an average number to represent that sample (although the percentage who live in rural areas could be used).

Difference between Means or Percentages

The second step in most data analysis procedures is to repeat the analysis of a single question for various subgroups of the population. Thus, the interest might be in the heavy user, and the analysis would be done for this group. More likely, it would be done for the heavy user, the light user, and the nonuser; then the results would be compared. Responses often are more meaningful and useful when a comparison is involved. For instance, in this case, it might be of interest to determine how those who use the transit system differ from those who do not use it.

Table 16.1 presents the sample means of the five questions for the users and the nonusers. The sample percentages answering positively to the location question also are presented for each group. The differences between the responses for the two groups provide some interesting insights. The difference between the sample means for Question 1, for example, indicates that the transit user tends to dislike driving more than the transit nonuser. The Question 2 difference indicates that the user shows only a small tendency to enjoy jogging more than the nonusers. The other comparisons suggest that the user is more concerned about gasoline costs and air pollution and lives closer to a transit station.

The difference between means is concerned with the association between two questions, the question defining the groups (transit usage in this case) and another question (Question 1, on disliking driving, for example). In terms of the scale definitions, the question defining the groups would be considered a *nominally scaled question* and the question on which the means are based would be considered an *intervally scaled question*. Of course, the analysis could use three, four, or more groups instead of just two. For example, comparisons could be made among nonusers of the transit system, light users, medium users, and heavy users.

A variety of variables besides usage can be used to identify subgroups of interest. For example, in a segmentation study we might focus on

- Loyal buyers versus nonloyal buyers

- Those interested in abstract art versus those not interested

- Customers of a competing store versus others

- Those aware of our art gallery versus others

- High-income versus moderate-income versus low-income groups

If our initial analysis involved means (or percentages), the focus would turn to the difference between means (or percentages). If the initial analysis involved frequency distributions, then cross-tabulation, the subject of the next section, would be the focus.

Cross-Tabulations

The appropriate statistical analysis technique for studying the relationships among and between nominal and/or ordinal variables is termed **cross-tabulation**. It also is called cross-tabs, cross-classification, and **contingency table analysis**. In cross-tabulation, the sample is divided into subgroups in order to learn how the dependent variable varies from subgroup to subgroup. Cross-tabulation tables require fewer assumptions to construct, and they serve as the basis of several statistical techniques such as chi-square and log-linear analysis. Percentages are computed on each cell basis or by rows or columns. When the computations are by rows or columns, cross-tabulation tables usually are referred to as contingency tables, because the percentages are basically contingent on the row or column totals.

Figure 16.4 illustrates cross-tabulation with two examples from the HMO study. The focus here is on the question of enrollment intentions. Often, a usage or intentions question is the key question in a study.

To illustrate cross-tabulations in a probability framework, if the above data (intentions to enroll, by income) were representative of U.S. households (they are not), the probability of a

INTENTIONS TO ENROLL—BY INCOME

	Less than $7,000	$7,000–$15,999	$16,000 and above	
Most interested	20.4% (38)	11.6% (46)	7.6% (37)	11.3% (121)
Moderately interested	19.4% (36)	11.9% (47)	17.9% (87)	16.0% (170)
Uncertain or uninterested	60.2% (112)	76.5% (302)	74.5% (362)	72.5% (776)
	100% (186)	100% (395)	100% (486)	100% (1,067)

(The differences between income groups are significant at 0.01 level.)

INTENTIONS TO ENROLL—BY AGE

	Under 30 years	30–40 years	Over 40 years	
Most interested	14.0% (60)	12.5% (40)	6.6% (24)	11.1% (124)
Moderately interested	21.9% (94)	20.0% (64)	14.5% (53)	18.9% (211)
Uncertain or uninterested	64.1% (276)	67.5% (216)	78.9% (288)	70.0% (780)
	100% (430)	100% (320)	100% (365)	100% (1,115)

(The differences between age groups are significant at 0.01 level.)

FIGURE 16.4
Cross-Tabulations—the HMO Study.

household most interested in enrolling is 0.11 (121/1,067). However, the probability of a household most interested in enrolling, given that the household's income is less than $7,000, is 0.20 (38/186).

We wish to determine if various income groups differ in their intentions. One way to define groups is by using the income question, or variable. The top of Figure 16.4 shows an intentions-by-income cross-tabulation. It presents the frequency distribution breakdown for the degree of intentions within each of the three income groups. If the three groups were similar, each of their frequency distributions should be expected to be similar to that of the total sample (marginal frequencies shown at the right). The results do not support this view. In fact, the higher-income people are less likely to be interested than the middle-income groups, and the low-income group is the most interested. More than 20 percent of the low-income group was classified as "most interested," as contrasted with only 7.6 percent of the high-income group. When the intentions by income cross-tabulated data are subjected to statistical analysis to evaluate the association between income groups and degree of intentions, the results indicate that there are differences among the three income groups in the degree of intentions to enroll.

The bottom of Figure 16.4 shows the intentions, by age cross-tabulation. Again, the frequency distribution within each of the subgroups must be compared to the frequency distribution for the total sample, shown at the right. The youngest group has somewhat more interest than the middle group, and both have considerably more interest than the older group.

Cross-tabulation is the analysis of association between two variables that are nominally scaled. Of course, any interval-scaled variable can be used to define groups and therefore form a nominally scaled variable. For example, income and age are fundamentally intervally scaled (actually, ratio scaled), but in the context of Figure 16.4, when they are used to define categories they are ordinally scaled. Most marketing research studies go no further than cross-tabulation, and even those studies that do use more sophisticated analytical methods still use cross-tabulation as an important component. Hence, along with the data-preparation techniques, understanding, developing, and interpreting cross-tabulation are the fundamental needs of data analysis.[7]

Chapters 17 through 22 will discuss in detail the various statistical tests and techniques that can be used to analyze the data obtained from questionnaires. Before we launch a formal discussion of these sophisticated statistical techniques, it will be beneficial to discuss the various factors that influence the choice of an analysis technique. This will help us to identify the appropriate technique(s) based on our needs. Finally, we will end this chapter with an overview of the various statistical techniques that are available to the researcher and a brief discussion on how these techniques are classified.

Factors Influencing the Choice of Statistical Technique

Data analysis is not an end in itself. Its purpose is to produce information that will help to address the problem at hand. Several factors influence the selection of the appropriate technique for data analysis. These include (1) type of data, (2) research design, and (3) assumptions underlying the test statistic and related considerations.[8]

Type of Data

The type of data plays a central role in the choice of a statistical technique to be employed in data analysis. As pointed out already, a useful classification of data involves nominal, ordinal, interval, and ratio scales of measurement. The **nominal scale type** of data are the most primitive form of data from the perspective of data analysis. They are just numbers assigned to objects, based only on the fact that the objects belong to particular categories. Very few formal statistical analyses can be done on nominal data, and the only meaningful measure of central tendency is the mode.

The **ordinal scale** represents a higher level of measurement than the nominal, because the numerals assigned to reflect order also serve to identify the objects. The *median* and *mode* are now both legitimate measures of central tendency. Most nonparametric tests can be performed on ordinal data. Even though parametric tests cannot be used on ordinal data, in many research studies, one sees them being used erroneously.

Interval and **ratio-scaled** data (also called *metric data*) are the best from the perspective of data analysis. A wide range of both parametric and nonparametric tests can be performed on these types of data. The mean, the median, and the mode are now legitimate measures of central tendency. Measures of dispersion and measures of shape are meaningful only on these types of data. Hence, researchers should always try to collect interval or ratio-scaled data.

Research Design

A second consideration that affects the choice of analysis technique is the research design used to generate the data. Some of the decisions the analyst has to face involve the dependency of observations, the number of observations per object, the number of groups being analyzed, and the control exercised over the variables of interest.

Sample Independence

The type of statistical test that can be done depends on whether the research design uses dependent or independent samples. Let us clarify this statement with the following example. Suppose that you were interested in determining the effectiveness of an advertisement. Also, assume that the measure of effectiveness was attitudes toward the product advertised, and that an interval or ratio scale was used to measure attitude, and, in particular, that the research design was

$$X \quad O_1$$
$$O_2$$

where O_1 represents the attitudes of those who saw the advertisement and O_2 the attitudes of those who did not see the advertisement. In this case, the samples are independent. The O_2 measures do not depend on the O_1 measures. An appropriate test of significance would allow for the independence of the samples. In this case, the t-test for the difference in two means would be appropriate.

Consider another research design that is represented by

$$O_1 \quad X \quad O_2$$

Again, there are two sets of observations, O_1 and O_2. However, now they are obtained from the same individuals, before and after seeing the advertisement. The measurements are not independent, and the observations must be analyzed in pairs. The focus is on differences in attitudes per individual before and after exposure to the advertisement. A paired difference t-test should be used in this case.

Number of Groups

The choice of a statistical method for data analysis also depends on the number of groups that are in the experimental design. Suppose that you were interested in the relative effectiveness of two different advertisements, and you decided to explore the question through a controlled experiment. In the experiment, some respondents receive X_1, others get X_2, and a third group receives neither. The design can be represented as

$$X_1 \quad O_1$$
$$X_2 \quad O_2$$
$$O_3$$

This design parallels that for the single advertisement, except for the addition of the alternative advertisement X_2. Now, however, there are three groups or three means to be compared (two experimental and one control), whereas previously there were two (one experimental and one control). The t-test for the difference in two means is no longer applicable; the problem is best handled through analysis-of-variance procedures.

Number of Variables

The number of variables in the study (measurements per object) also affects the analysis procedure. Let us consider the single advertisement example again. Previously, we used attitudes toward the advertised product as the measure of the advertisement's effectiveness. In order to check on the validity of this measure, we now wish to contrast the "exposed" and "unexposed" groups, not only in terms of their differences in attitude, but also in terms of the sales of the product to each group. The design has not changed. It is still represented as

$$X \quad O_1$$
$$O_2$$

only now O_1 and O_2 represent measures of both sales and attitudes.

A univariate technique cannot be applied in this case because it will lead to erroneous conclusions. We need to have some means of looking at the differences among groups when several characteristics are considered simultaneously. This type of problem is handled using multivariate statistical procedures.

Variable Control

Another important factor that affects the choice of technique for analysis involves the control of variables in the design, which can affect the result. Let us consider the one-advertisement design again,

$$X \quad O_1$$
$$O_2$$

in which the emphasis is on the differences in attitudes between the two groups. This attitudinal difference between the two groups can be the result of some variable other than exposure to the advertisement. One variable that would certainly seem to determine attitudes is previous usage of the product. If so, in the experimental design, the analyst would like to control for prior usage, to minimize its effect. A good way of doing this would be to make the experimental and control groups equal with respect to prior usage, by matching, by randomization, or by some combination of these approaches. If this control procedure is followed, the t-test for analyzing the difference in two means can legitimately be employed. If the control is not affected but if attitudes do depend on prior use of the product, the conclusions produced using the t-test will be in error, to the extent that the two groups differ in their previous use of the product.[9]

Assumptions Underlying Test Statistic

The assumptions underlying the test statistic also affect the choice of a statistical method of analysis. For example, the assumptions of a two-sample t-test are as follows:

1. The samples are independent.

2. The characteristics of interest in each population have normal distribution.

3. The two populations have equal variances.

The t-test is more sensitive to certain violations of these assumptions than others. For example, it still works well with respect to violations of the normality assumption but is quite sensitive to violations of the equal-variance assumption. When the violation is too severe, the conclusions drawn are inappropriate. Hence, if the assumptions on which a statistical test is based are violated or are not met, those tests should not be performed, because they will give meaningless results. If the samples are not independent or have unequal variances, a modified t-test can still be employed. Ultimately, the researcher's knowledge about statistical techniques does matter in the selection of the technique for data analysis.

An Overview of Statistical Techniques

The entire gamut of statistical techniques can be broadly classified as univariate and multivariate techniques, based on the nature of the problem. *Univariate techniques* are appropriate when there is a single measurement of each of the n sample objects, or when there are several measurements of each of the n observations but each variable is analyzed in isolation. On the other hand, *multivariate techniques* are appropriate for analyzing data when there are two or more measurements of each observation and the variables are to be analyzed simultaneously.

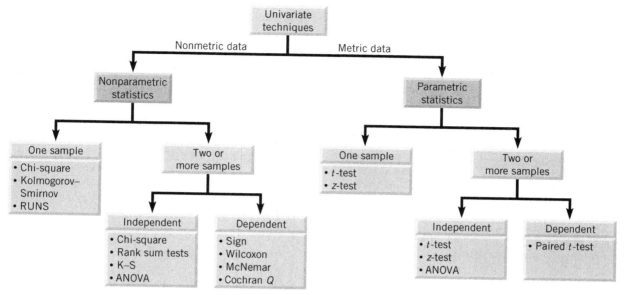

FIGURE 16.5
Classification of Univariate Statistical Techniques.

Univariate techniques can be further classified based on the type of data—whether they are *nonmetric* or *metric*. As mentioned earlier, nonmetric data are measured on a nominal or ordinal scale, whereas metric data are measured on an interval or ratio scale. Nonparametric statistical tests can be used to analyze nonmetric data. Nonparametric tests do not require any assumptions regarding the distribution of data.

For both nonmetric and metric data, the next level of classification involves determining whether a single sample or multiple samples are involved. Further, in the case of multiple samples, the appropriate statistical test depends on whether the samples are independent or dependent. Figure 16.5 provides an overview of the univariate analysis techniques.

For metric data, *t*-tests and *z*-tests can be used for one or two samples. For more than two samples, the analysis of variance (ANOVA) is used. For nonmetric data with a single sample, chi-square, Kolmogorov–Smirnov (K–S), and RUNS tests can be used. For two or more independent samples, chi-square, rank sum tests, K–S, and ANOVA (Kruskal–Wallis ANOVA) should be used. For two or more dependent samples, a sign test, a Wilcoxon test, a McNemar test, or Cochran *Q*-tests can be used. A detailed discussion of nonparametric statistics is beyond the scope of this book.[10]

Multivariate statistical techniques can be broadly defined as "a collection of procedures for analyzing the association between two or more sets of measurements that were made on each object in one or more samples of objects." If only two sets of measurements are involved, the data typically are referred to as *bivariate*.[11] The multivariate techniques can be classified based on the following logic.

- Can the data be partitioned into dependent and independent variable sets? If so, classify according to the number of variables in each set. If not, classify the technique as an interdependence technique.

- In the case of interdependence techniques, classification is done based on the principal focus of the analysis. Is the focus on the object (person/thing/event) or is it on the variable?

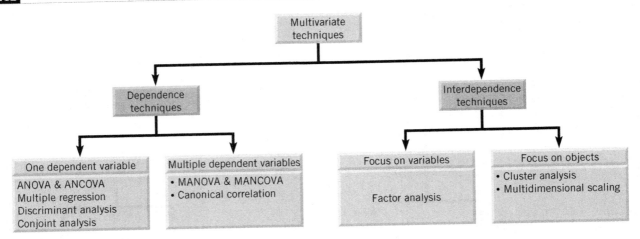

FIGURE 16.6
Classification of Multivariate Statistical Techniques.

Based on the first factor, the multivariate techniques can be broadly classified as **dependence techniques** or **interdependence techniques**. Dependence techniques are appropriate when one or more variables can be identified as dependent variables and the remaining as independent variables. The appropriate choice of dependence techniques further depends on whether there are one or more dependent variables involved in the analysis.

In interdependence techniques, the variables are not classified as dependent or independent; rather, the whole set of interdependent relationships is examined. The interdependence techniques can be further classified as focusing on variables or objects; that is, as variable interdependence or interobject similarity techniques. Figure 16.6 provides an overview of the various multivariate analysis techniques.

Subsequent chapters will discuss in detail most of the techniques represented in Figures 16.5 and 16.6. The chi-square tests for independence and goodness-of-fit will be discussed in Chapter 12, and the hypothesis testing (t-test and z-test) and the analysis of variance (ANOVA) will be discussed in Chapter 18. Chapter 19 will focus on correlation and regression analysis. Chapters 20 through 22 will very briefly describe the various multivariate techniques that are available to the marketing researcher.

Why use multivariate analysis, anyway? Clearly, substantial information can be obtained without using such complex techniques; however, there are several reasons why multivariate analysis is useful.

Multiple Linear Regression

A manager is interested in determining which factors predict the dollar value of the firm's personal computer sales. Aggregate data on population size, income, educational level, proportion of population living in metropolitan areas, and so on, have been collected for 30 areas. As a first step, a multiple linear regression equation is computed, where dollar sales is the outcome factor and the other factors are considered as candidates for predictor factors. A linear combination of the predictor factors is used to predict the outcome or response factor.

ANOVA

Suppose that a retail chain is interested in determining whether it should run a quarter-page, half-page, or a full-page advertisement for a product. In order to choose the size of the ad that will bring in the most store traffic, the chain decides to conduct an experiment to determine the ad's effect on store traffic. The number of customers visiting the store on three different occasions (when each of the different-sized ads is used) can be collected for all the stores belonging to the chain, and ANOVA can be performed to see if there are any differences in the store traffic across ad length.

Discriminant Analysis

A large sample of consumers over 50 years of age from a small city has been contacted to see if they had a proper retirement savings plan. A survey was conducted to obtain information on the respondents' savings behavior, and psychographic and demographic variables. The investigator would like to determine a linear function of these and possibly other measurements that would be useful in predicting who would and who would not have a proper (adequate) retirement savings plan. That is, the investigator wishes to derive a classification (discriminant) function that would help determine whether or not a middle-aged consumer is likely to have a proper retirement savings plan.

Canonical Correlation

A psychiatrist wishes to correlate measures of market orientation with marketing performance, from data obtained from a number of firms. This problem is different from a multiple linear regression example because more than one outcome factor is being predicted. The investigator wishes to determine the linear function of the market orientation variables such as interdepartmental conflict, interdepartmental connectedness, and concern for the ideas of other departments that is most highly correlated with a linear function of marketing performance variables: profit, sales, sales growth, market share, and so on. After these two linear functions, called *canonical variables*, are determined, the investigator will test to see whether there is a statistically significant (canonical) correlation between scores from the two linear functions, and whether a reasonable interpretation can be made of the two sets of coefficients from the functions.

Factor Analysis

An investigator has asked each respondent in a survey whether he or she strongly agrees, agrees, is undecided, disagrees, or strongly disagrees with 15 statements concerning attitudes toward inflation. As a first step, the investigator will do a factor analysis on the resulting data, to determine which statements belong together, in sets that are uncorrelated with other sets. The particular statements that form a single set will be examined to obtain a better understanding of attitudes toward inflation. The scores derived from each set or factor will be used in subsequent analysis to predict consumer spending.

Cluster Analysis

Investigators have made numerous measurements on a sample of consumers who have been classified as being brand-loyal. They wish to determine, on the basis of their measurements, whether these consumers can be classified by type of brand loyalty. That is, is it possible to determine distinct types of brand-loyal consumers by performing a cluster analysis on measures of purchase behavior on various purchase occasions?

Unlike the investigator of consumers who do or do not have a proper retirement savings plan, these investigators do not have a set of individuals whose type of brand loyalty can be known before the analysis is performed. Nevertheless, they want to separate the consumers into separate groups and to examine the resulting groups to see whether distinct types do exist and, if so, what their characteristics are.

Multidimensional Scaling (MDS)

It might be useful to determine how schools are perceived—which ones are perceived as similar and which ones are considered different. Is Stanford more like the University of California at Berkeley because of location and educational quality, or is Stanford perceived as being more like Harvard or MIT, two private schools? The general problem of positioning objects such as universities in an interpretable, multidimensional space is termed **multidimensional scaling (MDS)**. The resulting locations or positions on the relevant perceptual dimensions serve to define new dimensions.

Conjoint Analysis

Conjoint analysis is an analysis-of-dependence technique. The dependent variable is the preference judgment a respondent makes about a new concept. The independent variables are the attribute levels that were specified. Thus, one motivation is prediction: What sales or usage level will a new concept achieve? A second motivation is understanding relationship: What is the effect on preference of changing one of the attribute levels?

Simultaneous Equation Regression Analysis

Consider a regression model with price, advertising, and perceived product quality (the three independent variables) influencing sales (the dependent variable). Suppose that sales also influenced advertising, because the advertising budget was in part set as a percentage of sales, and that advertising (which emphasized quality) and price also affected perceived product quality. Instead of a single regression equation, it would then be more appropriate to work simultaneously with three regression equations and three associated dependent variables (sales, advertising, and product quality). A single regression equation, for example, would not reflect the indirect impact of advertising through its impact on product quality, and would confuse the sales-to-advertising influence with the advertising-to-sales influence.

Unobservable Variables in Regression Analysis

In single or simultaneous regression analysis, there could be several indicators of one of the key variables; for example, the performance of salespeople, the dependent variable, could be based on supervisor ratings, customer ratings, sales gain over the last year, and sales gain over plan. The question is, how to combine the four indicators (the observables) to provide a measure of salesperson performance (the unobservable). The answer, provided by the model, is to weight each indicator according to its relationship to the independent variables.

If there is only one regression equation involved, and the unobservable variable is the dependent variable, the approach is termed canonical correlation (defined earlier). In the more usual case, in which multiple dependent variables and thus multiple equations are involved, the approach often is termed *causal modeling*, since the interest is in causal relationships, or LISREL analysis. LISREL is the name of the computer program that is used to estimate the parameters of such models.

Information on the choice of a statistical package to perform the statistical analysis is given in the appendix of this chapter.

Presenting the Results

Eventually, the researcher must develop some conclusions from the data analysis and present the results. The presentation, whether oral, written, or both, can be critical to the ultimate ability of the research to influence decisions. We will address this in Chapter 23, where we provide several guidelines that will lead to effective presentations and where we also offer some special tips for making written and oral presentations.

SUMMARY

The first phase in data analysis involves editing, coding, and statistically preparing the data for analysis. Editing involves identifying omissions, ambiguities, inconsistencies, lack of cooperation, and ineligible respondents. Coding involves deciding how the responses are going to be entered. There are several techniques that can be used to statistically adjust the data. These include (1) weighting, (2) variable respecification, and (3) scale transformation.

A variety of data analysis techniques are available. The most basic is to analyze each question by itself. A frequency distribution provides the most complete information and often leads to decisions to combine response categories. Several descriptive statistics such as the mean, median, mode, standard deviation, and variance can be obtained from these distributions. In most marketing research applications, only the sample means and/or percentages are reported.

Responses at times are much more meaningful and useful when a comparison is made. The usual step is to tabulate questions among subgroups, and this involves two of the questions from the questionnaire. Thus, the sample mean or the frequency distribution is obtained for subgroups such as transit users and transit nonusers, and they are compared to identify the differences. Guidelines are developed for selecting the appropriate statistical techniques. A discussion on the overview of statistical analysis is provided.

QUESTIONS AND PROBLEMS

16.1 A poll of just over 1,000 Californians selected by an area sampling plan were asked early in Governor Jerry Brown's tenure whether they felt that Governor Brown was doing a good, fair, or poor job as governor. They were then asked why they held those opinions. The results were coded into 35 response categories. Each respondent's answer was coded in from one to six of the categories. A total of 1,351 responses were coded. The most frequently used categories (besides "No answer," given by 135 of the respondents) were the following:

   (i) Not bad or good; OK so far; Too soon to tell (253)

   (ii) Doing his best (123)

   (iii) Trying to help people; cares about people (105)

   (iv) Cutting down government expenses (88)

   (v) Like or agree with his ideas (69)

   (vi) Not afraid to take a stand (61)

Do you think the responses are being analyzed properly? A respondent who gives a lengthy reply that includes as many as six coded responses will have more weight than a respondent who gives a short direct response that is coded into only one category. Is that appropriate? Are there any alternatives? Code the following responses, using the above categories.

   (a) I like his position on welfare. It's probably the most critical problem facing the state. On the other hand, he is not helping the business climate. All the regulations are making it impossible to bring in industry. It's really too soon to make a judgment, however.

   (b) He's reducing unemployment, improving the economy. I like his ideas about welfare and cutting down government expense. However, I don't like his position on the smog device bill. On balance, he's doing okay.

   (c) He's too much of a politician. He will swing with the political currents. He has started some needed government reorganization, however.

   (d) I dislike his stand on education. He is really not interested in education, perhaps because he has no children. He's young and immature. He takes strong stands without getting his facts straight.

   (e) He's concerned about the farm workers. He's doing a good job. I like him.

16.2 Analyze Figure 16.4. What conclusions can you draw? What are the implications? What additional data analysis would you recommend, given your conclusions?

16.3 In the HMO study the "Intentions to enroll" by "Intentions to have more children" cross-tabulation is shown in Table 16.3. Interpret it in the context of Figure 16.4.

Table 16.3 Intentions to Enroll by Intentions to Have More Children

	Yes, intend to have children		Not sure		Do not intend to have children		Total	
Most interested	14.1%	(39)	14.9%	(97)	9.1%	(13)	11.1%	(121)
Moderately interested	25.6%	(71)	17.6%	(114)	16.8%	(25)	18.9%	(170)
Uncertain or uninterested	60.3%	(167)	67.5%	(438)	74.1%	(110)	70.0%	(776)
	100%	(277)	100%	(649)	100%	(148)	100%	(1,067)

END NOTES

1. See N. K. Malhotra, "Analyzing Marketing Research Data with Incomplete Information on the Dependent Variable," *Journal of Marketing Research*, 24 (February 1987), pp. 74–84.

2. For a more detailed discussion on coding, see P. S. Sidel, "Coding," in R. Ferber, ed., *Handbook of Marketing Research*, New York: McGraw-Hill, 1974; P. L. Alreck and R. B. Settle, *The Survey Research Handbook*. Homewood, IL: Richard D. Irwin, 1985, pp. 254–286; J. Pope, *Practical Marketing Research*. New York: AMACOM, 1981, pp. 89–90.

3. For more information on weighting, see T. Sharot, "Weighting Survey Results," *Journal of the Marketing Research Society*, 28, July 1986, pp. 269–284.

4. See L. B. Bowerman and R. T. O'Connell, *Linear Statistical Models: An Applied Approach*. Boston: PWS-Kent, 1990.

5. See R. E. Frank, "Use of Transformations," *Journal of Marketing Research*, August 1966, pp. 247–253.

6. The biggest advantage of the standard deviation is that it enables us to determine, with a great deal of accuracy, where the values of a frequency distribution are located in relation to the mean. This can be done using *Chebyshev's theorem*, which states that regardless of the shape of the distribution, at least 75 percent of the values will fall within plus and minus two standard deviations from the mean of the distribution, and at least 89 percent of the values will lie within plus and minus three standard deviations from the mean. If the distribution is a symmetrical, bell-shaped curve, then, using Chebyshev's theorem, we can say that:

- About 68 percent of the values in the population will fall within plus and minus one standard deviation from the mean.

- About 95 percent of the values will fall within plus and minus two standard deviations from the mean.

- About 99 percent of the values will fall within plus and minus three standard deviations from the mean.

For a detailed discussion on fundamental statistics, see R. I. Levin, *Statistics for Management*. Upper Saddle River, NJ: Prentice Hall, 1987, or any business statistics textbook.

7. See O. Hellevik, *Introduction to Causal Analysis: Exploring Survey Data by Cross-Tabulation*. Beverly Hills, CA: Sage, 1984.

8. Adapted from G. A. Churchill, Jr., *Marketing Research: Methodological Foundations*. Orlando, FL: Dryden Press, 1991.

9. See P. E. Green and D. S. Tull, "Covariance Analysis in Marketing Experimentation," *Journal of Advertising Research*, 6, June 1966, pp. 45–53.

10. For a detailed discussion of nonparametric tests, refer to W. W. Daniel, *Applied Nonparametric Statistics*. Boston: PWS-Kent, 1990.

11. P. E. Green, *Analyzing Multivariate Data*. Hinsdale, IL: Dryden Press, 1978.

APPENDIX

Choice of a Statistical Package

Whether the investigator decides to use a PC or a mainframe, there is a wide choice of statistical packages available. Unlike the situation for word processing where a handful of packages have captured a large share of the market, numerous statistical packages are available, some written for a particular area of application (such as survey analysis) and others quite general. One feature that distinguishes among the statistical packages is whether they were originally written for mainframe computers or for PCs. Packages written for mainframe computers tend to be more general and comprehensive. They also take more computer memory to store and are often more expensive. Originally, the programs written for the mainframe computers were just adapted for PCs, but recent versions include more interactive features and menu-driven options. The cost of a PC package is less of a factor if a site license is purchased by the school, business, or governmental unit where one works, in which case the cost can be shared by a number of users.

SAS and SPSS are the two commonly used statistical packages for marketing research analysis. Additional information on these can be found at the respective websites listed here.

SAS:

http://www.sas.com.

SPSS:

www-01.ibm.com/software/analytics/spss/.

Hypothesis Testing: Basic Concepts and Tests of Associations

17

LEARNING OBJECTIVES

- Discuss the logic behind hypothesis testing.
- Describe the steps involved in testing a hypothesis.
- Discuss the concepts basic to the hypothesis-testing procedure.
- Discuss the significance level of a test.
- Describe the difference between Type I and Type II errors.
- Describe the chi-square test of independence and the chi-square goodness-of-fit test.
- Discuss the purpose of measuring the strength of association.

When an interesting, relevant, empirical finding emerges from data analysis based on a sample, a simple, yet penetrating hypothesis test question should occur to every manager and researcher as a matter of course: Does the empirical finding represent only a sampling accident? For example, suppose that a study is made of wine consumption. Data analysis reveals that a random sample of 100 California residents consumes more wine per family than a random sample of 100 New York residents. It could be that the observed difference was caused only by a sampling error; in actuality, there may be no difference between the two populations. If the difference found in the two samples could be caused by sampling fluctuations, it makes little sense to spend additional time on the results or to base decisions on it. If, on the other hand, the results are not caused simply by sampling variations, there is a reason to consider the results further.

Hypothesis testing begins with an assumption, called a **hypothesis**, that is made about a population parameter. Then, data from an appropriate sample are collected, and the information obtained from the sample (sample statistics) is used to decide how likely it is that the hypothesized population parameter is correct. The hypothesis test question is thus a screening question. Empirical results should pass this test before the researcher spends much effort considering them further.

The purpose of hypothesis testing is not to question the computed value of the sample statistic but to make a judgment about the *difference* between two sample statistics or the sample statistic and a hypothesized population parameter. For example, in many marketing research situations, the need arises to test an assumption regarding a certain value for the population mean. To test the assumption's validity, data from a sample are gathered and the sample mean is calculated. Then the difference between the sample mean and the hypothesized value of the population mean is calculated. The smaller the difference is, the greater is the likelihood that the hypothesized value for the population mean is correct. The larger the difference is, the smaller is the likelihood.

Unfortunately, the difference between the hypothesized population parameter and the actual sample statistic is more often neither so large that the hypothesis automatically is rejected nor so small that it is not rejected just as quickly. In hypothesis testing, as in most significant real-life decisions, clear-cut solutions are the exception, not the rule. The mechanism that is adopted to make an objective decision regarding the hypothesized parameter forms the core of hypothesis testing.

A primary objective of this chapter is to provide a real understanding of the logic of hypothesis testing. The hope is that the reader will become conditioned to asking whether the result just happened by chance. Just thinking of the question at the appropriate time is winning half the battle. Further, an effort will be made to help the reader think in terms of a model or set of assumptions (such as that there is no difference between California and New York in per-capita wine consumption) in very specific terms. Hypothesis testing provides an excellent opportunity to be rigorous and precise in thinking and in presenting results.

In the first section, the logic of hypothesis testing is developed in the context of an example. This is followed by sections describing the steps in the hypothesis-testing process and the concepts basic to the hypothesis-testing procedure. The final section presents the hypothesis tests used in cross-tabulations. Here the chi-square statistic, which is useful in interpreting a cross-tabulation table, is developed. Also, the two major applications of the chi-square test—as a goodness-of-fit measure and as a test of independence—are discussed.

The Logic of Hypothesis Testing

An Illustrative Example

To guide the development and control of wilderness areas and national parks, a large-scale survey was conducted. A total of nearly 10,000 people participated and answered a series of questions about their usage of wilderness areas and their opinions on public policy alternatives regarding them. One key question was how to control the number of people asking to use some of the popular rafting rivers. At one extreme, a very restrictive policy was proposed, using a permit system that would preserve the wilderness character of the parks but that would also deprive many people of the opportunity to use them as a national resource. At the other extreme, there would be unrestricted access. One question asked for opinions about this policy spectrum as it applied to several wilderness areas. The scale was as follows:

Highly restrictive   No restrictions

    0   1   2   3   4   5   6   7   8   9

The average response of the 10,000 respondents was 5.6.

The researcher who conducted this survey wanted to test the theory that those who did white-water rafting would favor fewer restrictions. To test this hypothesis, 35 such people were identified in the study, which had an average response of 6.1. Thus, the evidence directionally supports the contention that those engaging in white-water rafting did tend to support a no-restrictions policy more than did the rest of the population.

But how convincing is the evidence? After all, the opinions of a sample of only 35 rafters is known. The difference between 5.6 (the 10,000 respondent average) and 6.1 (the white-water rafters' average) might be more a random finding than proof that the white-water rafters had different opinions. The extent to which the statement about the population is believable depends on whether the sample from which the information was generated is large or small (other things being equal).

If the average response rate of the 35 white-water rafters was, say, 8.6, then the hypothesis that those who did white-water rafting favor fewer restrictions cannot be rejected. On the other hand, if the average response of rafters was 2.7, then without any hesitation, the hypothesis can be rejected. With an average response rate of 6.1, however, we can neither accept nor reject the hypothesis with absolute certainty; a decision about the hypothesis has to be taken based not on intuition, but on some objective measure. To what extent the statement about the population parameter is believable depends on whether the information generated from the sample is a result of few or many observations. In other words, evidence has to be evaluated statistically before arriving at a conclusion regarding the hypothesis. *This is the logic behind hypothesis testing.*

Steps in Hypothesis Testing

The steps involved in the process of hypothesis testing are illustrated in Figure 17.1. As shown in the figure, problem definition leads to the generation of hypotheses. The relevant probability distribution is then chosen. The corresponding critical value is determined from the information

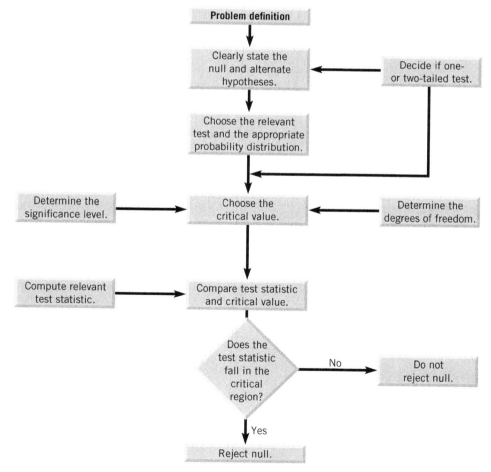

FIGURE 17.1
Hypothesis-Testing Process.

on the significance level, degrees of freedom, and one- or two-tailed test. The appropriate test statistic (calculated from the sample data) is then compared with the relevant critical value, and if the test statistic falls in the critical region (i.e., in general, when the test statistic equals or exceeds the critical value), the null hypothesis is rejected.

Basic Concepts of Hypothesis Testing

The Null and Alternative Hypotheses

Let us continue with the wilderness survey example. To test the theory that people who did white-water rafting would be in favor of fewer restrictions, the researcher has to formulate—just for argument—the **null hypothesis**[1] that the opinions of white-water rafters do not differ from those of the general population (the 10,000 respondents); and that if all the white-water rafters were contacted, their average response would be 5.6 instead of 6.1. This null hypothesis (represented mathematically as H_0) will be tested against the **alternative hypothesis** (represented mathematically as H_a); that is, the contention that people who did white-water rafting would favor fewer restrictions. This would be a one-tailed test.

As mentioned earlier, the purpose of hypothesis testing is not to question the computed value of the sample statistic but (for example) to make a judgment about the difference between that sample statistic and the hypothesized population parameter.

Choosing the Relevant Statistical Test and the Appropriate Probability Distribution

The next step in hypothesis testing is selecting the appropriate probability distribution. The choice of an appropriate probability distribution depends on the purpose of the hypothesis test. The purpose could vary, from comparing sample and population to comparing two sample characteristics such as means, proportions, and variances. Table 17.1 provides the conditions under which various statistical tests can be used for different purposes. For a given purpose, a particular form of a statistical test may or may not be appropriate, depending on the sample size and whether or not the population standard deviation is known. In marketing research applications, typically, we deal with large samples ($n \geq 30$), which allows us to draw valid conclusions.

Hence, the next logical step, after stating the null and alternative hypotheses, is to decide upon the criteria (for choosing the critical or the table values for a statistical test) to use for making the decision whether to accept or reject the null hypothesis. (Strictly speaking, one should use the terminology "not reject" instead of "accept"; however, for simplicity's sake, we use the term "accept.") The three criteria referred to are (1) the **significance level**, (2) the number of **degrees of freedom**, and (3) *one- or two-tail test*.

Choosing the Critical Value

Significance Level

Say that the hypothesis is to be tested at the 10 percent level of significance. This means that the null hypothesis will be rejected if the difference between the sample statistic and the hypothesized population parameter is so large that this or a larger difference would occur, on the average, only 10 or fewer times in every 100 samples (assuming that the hypothesized population parameter is correct). In other words, assuming the hypothesis to be true, *the significance level indicates the percentage of sample means that is outside the cutoff limits*, also called *the critical value*.[2]

Table 17.1   Hypothesis Testing and Associated Statistical Tests

Hypothesis testing	Number of groups/ samples	Purpose	Statistical test	Assumptions/comments
Frequency	One	Goodness of fit	χ^2	
distributions	Two	Tests of independence	χ^2	
Proportions	One	Comparing sample and populations proportions	Z	If σ is known, and for large samples
		Comparing sample and populations proportions	t	If σ is unknown, and for small samples
	Two	Comparing two sample proportions	Z	If σ is known
		Comparing two sample proportions	t	If σ is unknown
Means	One	Comparing sample and population mean	Z	If σ is known
		Comparing sample and population mean	t	If σ is unknown
	Two	Comparing two sample means	Z	If σ is known
		Comparing two sample means (from independent samples)	t	If σ is unknown
		Comparing two sample means (from related samples)	t	If σ is unknown
	Two or more	Comparing multiple sample means	F	Using analysis of variance framework (discussed in Chapter 18)
Variance	One	Comparing sample and population variances	χ^2	
	Two	Comparing sample variances	F	

Legend : σ = population standard deviation.

There is no single rule for selecting a significance level, called alpha (α). The most commonly chosen levels in academic research are the 1-percent level, the 5-percent level, and the 10-percent level. Although it is possible to test a hypothesis at any level of significance, bear in mind that the significance level selected is also the risk assumed of rejecting a null hypothesis when it is true. *The higher the significance level used for testing a hypothesis, the greater is the probability of rejecting a null hypothesis when it is true.* This is called **Type I error**.

Alternately, not rejecting a null hypothesis when it is false is called **Type II error**, and its probability is represented as β (beta). Whenever a choice of the significance level for a test of hypothesis is made, there is an inherent trade-off between these two types of errors. The probability of making one type of error can be reduced only if the manager or researcher is willing to increase the probability of making the other type of error.

Figure 17.2 provides a graphical illustration of this concept.[3] From this figure, it can be seen that as the significance level increases, the acceptance region becomes quite small (.50 of the area under the curve in Figure 17.2c). With an acceptance region this small, rarely will a null hypothesis be accepted when it is not true; but at a cost of being this sure, the probability that a null hypothesis will be rejected when it is true will increase. In other words, in order to lessen the probability of committing a Type II error, the probability of committing a Type I error necessarily has to be increased.

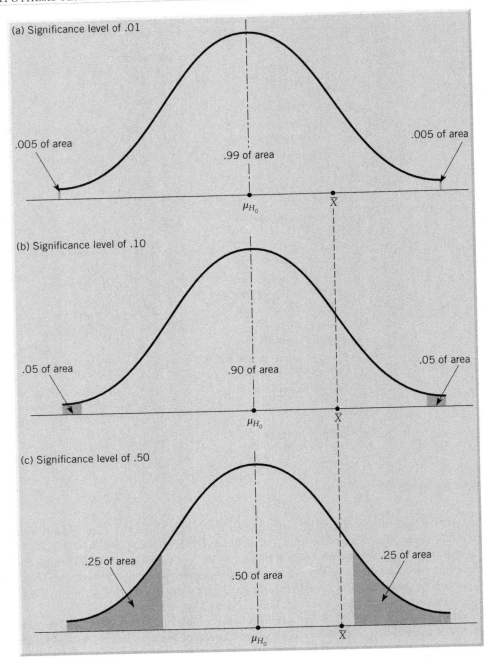

FIGURE 17.2
Relationship Between Type I and Type II Errors.

To deal with this trade-off, researchers decide the appropriate level of significance by examining the costs or penalties attached to both types of errors. For example, if making a Type I error (rejecting a null hypothesis when it is true) involves taking the time and trouble to reexamine the batch of packaged-food products that should have been accepted, but making a Type II error (accepting a null hypothesis when it is false) means taking a chance that the consumers purchasing the product may suffer from food poisoning, obviously the company management will prefer a Type I error to a Type II error. As a result, it will set high levels of significance in its testing. Likewise, if the cost of committing a Type I error is overwhelming when compared to the cost of committing a Type II error, the researcher will go for low values of α.

The Power of a Hypothesis Test

Ideally, a good test of a hypothesis ought to reject a null hypothesis when it is false. In other words, β (the probability of accepting a null hypothesis when it is false) should be as low as possible, or $1 - \beta$ should be as high a value as possible (preferably close to 1.0). A high value of $1 - \beta$ indicates that the hypothesis test is working very well. Since the value of $1 - \beta$ provides a measure of how well the test works, it is also known as the *power of the hypothesis test*.

Thus, the power of a statistical test of a null hypothesis is the probability that it will lead to the rejection of the null hypothesis; that is, the probability that it will result in the conclusion that the phenomenon exists. The power of a statistical test depends on three parameters: the significance level of the test, the reliability of the sample results, and the "effect size" (i.e., the degree to which the phenomenon exists).[4]

Degrees of Freedom

Degrees of freedom (df) refers to the number or bits of "free" or unconstrained data used in calculating a sample statistic or test statistic.

Degrees of freedom is traditionally represented as $n - k$, where n is the total number of information bits available and k is the number of linear constraints or restrictions required when calculating a sample statistic or test statistic. In a simple random sample of n observations, there are n degrees of freedom if no restrictions are placed on the sample. A sample mean X has n degrees of freedom, since there are no constraints or restrictions applied to the sample when calculating its value. However, there are $(n-1)$ degrees of freedom associated with a sample variance, because 1 degree of freedom is "lost" due to the restriction that it is necessary to calculate a mean before calculating the variance. Stated somewhat differently, the first $n-1$ observations in a sample can be selected freely, but the nth value must be chosen so that the constraint of an identical mean value is satisfied. In general, the more degrees of freedom there are, the greater is the likelihood of observing differences or relationships among variables.

One- or Two-Tail Test

When conducting a one-sided hypothesis test, the researcher determines whether a particular population parameter is larger or smaller than some predefined value. In this case, only one critical value (and region) of a test statistic is used. In a two-sided hypothesis test, the researcher determines the likelihood that a population parameter is within certain upper and lower bounds. Depending on the statistical technique applied, one or two critical values may be used.

The next section discusses the statistical test used to measure associations.

Cross-Tabulation and Chi-Square

Chapter 16 presented the data analysis technique of cross-tabulating two questions. Recollect that Figure 16.4 illustrated cross-tabulation with the focus on the enrollment-intention question. In this case, the appropriate null hypothesis would be that there was no relationship between the respondents' enrollment intention and the income group to which they belong. Such a hypothesis can be tested based on a measure of the relationship between the questions of the cross-tabulation table, termed the *chi-square statistic*. In this section the chi-square and its associated test will be introduced formally. Typically, in marketing research applications, the chi-square statistic is employed either as a *test of independence* or as a *test of goodness of fit*.

A *test of statistical independence* is employed when the manager or the researcher wants to know whether there are associations between two or more variables in a given study. On the other hand, in situations where the manager needs to know whether there is a significant difference between an observed frequency distribution and a theoretical frequency distribution, the *goodness-of-fit test* is employed. In this section we will discuss each of these applications of the chi-square statistic in detail.

Before introducing the chi-square statistic as a test of independence, however, it is useful to develop and illustrate the notion of *statistical independence*. The concept of independence is really central not only to the chi-square statistic but to all association measures.

The Concept of Statistical Independence

Two variables are *statistically independent* if a knowledge of one would offer no information as to the identity of the other. Consider the following experiment, illustrated in Table 17.2. Suppose that in a repeated-choice task conducted in New York City, a product was preferred in such a manner that it would yield a choice share of .40 (4 of 10 individuals would choose the product). Suppose, further, that we have a group of consumers in Los Angeles that has 20 percent loyals, 30 percent variety seekers, and the rest deal-prone consumers. The experiment consists of executing the choice task and drawing a consumer from the group. The outcome of the choice task is independent of the draw from the group of consumers. Before the experiment begins, the chance of getting a loyal consumer is .20. After the choice task, the probability of getting a loyal is still .20. The knowledge of the outcome of the choice task does not affect our information as to the outcome of the consumer draw; therefore, the choice task is statistically independent of the consumer draw.

Expected Value

If the previous experiment were repeated many times, we would expect 20 percent of the outcomes to include a loyal consumer. The number of "loyal" outcomes that we would expect would be $.20n$, where n is the number of experiments conducted. In each experiment, we would expect 40 percent of consumers to choose the product and 60 percent not to choose the product. Then the number of experiments resulting in drawing a loyal consumer and choosing the product would be "expected" to be $[(.40) * (.20n)]$.

Table 17.2   An Experiment and Its Expected Outcome?

| | | Choice task in New York | | Outcomes expected | Probability |
		Choose	Not choose		
	Loyal	$E_1 = 16$ [a]	$E_2 = 24$	40	.20
	Deal prone	$E_3 = 40$	$E_4 = 60$	100	.50
Drawing a customer in Los Angeles	Variety seeking	$E_5 = 24$	$E_6 = 36$	60	.30
	Outcome expected	80	120	200	
	Probability	0.40	0.60		

[a] E_1 = expected cell size under independence.

If n is equal to 200 and E_i is the number of outcomes expected in cell i, then for cells 1, 2, and 3 we have

$$E_1 = (.40)*(.20n) = 16$$
$$E_2 = (.60)*(.20n) = 24$$
$$E_3 = (.40)*(.50n) = 40$$

The reader should determine E_4, E_5, and E_6. The expected number of outcomes in cell i, E_i, is the number that would be expected, on average, if the experiments involving independent variables were repeated many times. Of course, cell 1 will not have 16 entries; sometimes it will have more and sometimes fewer. However, on average, it will have 16.

Chi-Square as a Test of Independence

Consider Table 17.3, which shows the results of a survey of 200 opera patrons who were asked how frequently they attended the symphony in a neighboring city. The frequency of attendance was partitioned into the categories of never, occasionally, and often; thus it became a nominally scaled variable. The respondents also were asked whether they regarded the location of the symphony as convenient or inconvenient. The resulting cross-tabulation shows the percentage breakdown of attendance in each location category. The observed number of respondents in cell i, termed O_1, also is shown. Thus, 22 people in cell 1 attended the symphony often and felt that the location was convenient ($O_1 = 22$).

The row totals and column totals and the proportions (p_A and p_L) are tabulated in the margin. Note that they are the frequency distribution for the respective variables. For example, the column total indicates that 80 respondents (.40 of all the respondents) felt the location was convenient and 120 (.60 of all the respondents) felt it was inconvenient.

Table 17.3 A Cross-Tabulation of Opera Patrons

		Location (L)			
		Convenient	Not convenient	Row total	p_A
		1	2		
	Often (more than 6 times a season)	27.5% $O_1 = 22$	15% $O_2 = 18$	20% (40)	.20
		3	4		
Attendance at symphony (A)	Occasionally	60% $O_3 = 48$	43.3% $O_4 = 52$	50% (100)	.50
		5	6		
	Never	12.5% $O_5 = 10$	41.7% $O_6 = 50$	30% (60)	.30
				100%	1.00
	Column total,	100% (80)	100% (120)	(200)	
	p_L	.40	.60	1.00	

$$\chi^2 = \sum \frac{(O_i - E_i)^2}{E_i} = 20$$

Note: E_i equals the expected cell values and O_i equals the observed cell values.

The null hypothesis associated with this test is that the two (nominally scaled) variables are statistically independent. The alternative hypothesis is that the two variables are not independent. Formally,

Null hypothesis H_0: attendance at symphony is independent of the location

Alternative hypothesis H_a: attendance at symphony is dependent on the location

The Chi-Square Distribution

If the variables are not independent—that is, if the null hypothesis is true—then the sampling distribution of the chi-square statistic can be closely approximated by a continuous curve known as a chi-square distribution. The *chi-square distribution* is a probability distribution and, therefore, the total area under the curve in each chi-square distribution is 1.0. As in the case of the t-distribution, different chi-square distributions are associated with different degrees of freedom. The chi-square distribution is one of the statistical distributions that is completely determined by its degree of freedom. The mean of the distribution is equal to v, the number of degrees of freedom, and the variance of the chi-square distribution is equal to $2v$. The chi-square values based on the distribution are given in Appendix Table A-2.

The number of degrees of freedom, v, for the chi-square test of independence is obtained using the formula $v = (r-1) * (c-1)$, where r is the number of rows in the contingency table and c is the number of columns. For large values of v, the distribution is approximately normal.

The Chi-Square Statistic

The **chi-square statistic** (χ^2) is a measure of the difference between the actual numbers observed in cell i, termed O_i, and the number expected if the null hypothesis were true, that is, under the assumption of statistical independence, E_i. The chi-square statistic is defined as

$$\chi^2 = \Sigma_{i=1}^{k} \frac{(O_i - E_i)^2}{E_i}$$

with $(r-1)(c-1)$ degrees of freedom,

where

     O_i = observed number in cell i

     E_i = number in cell i expected under independence

     r = number of rows

     c = number of columns

If the two variables (location and attendance) are independent, then the expected frequencies in each cell will be

$$E_i = p_L * p_A * n$$

where p_L and p_A are proportions defined in Table 17.3. Thus, for the data in Table 17.2,

$$E_i = .40 * .20 * 200 = 16$$

The appropriate χ^2 statistic is computed as

$$\chi^2 = \frac{(22-16)^2}{16} + \frac{(18-24)^2}{24} + \frac{(48-40)^2}{40} + \frac{(52-60)^2}{60} + \frac{(10-24)^2}{24} + \frac{(50-36)^2}{36} = 20.03$$

The number of degrees of freedom in this case is given by (rows – 1) ∗ (columns – 1), which is (3 – 1) ∗ (2 – 1) = 2, and if the test is done at a significance level $\alpha = 0.05$, the table value of χ^2 can be found to be 5.99. Since the calculated value of χ^2 (20.03) is greater than the table value (5.99), the *null hypothesis* is rejected. The researcher can thus conclude that the attendance at the symphony is dependent on the location of the symphony. Figure 17.3 shows a graphical description of the chi-square test.

Interpreting the Chi-Square Test of Independence

The chi-square test of independence is valid only if the sample size is large enough to guarantee the similarity between the theoretically correct distribution and the χ^2 sampling distribution. If the expected frequencies are too small, the value of χ^2 will be overestimated and will result in too many rejections of the null hypothesis. *As a general rule, the results of the chi-square test are valid only if the value of expected frequency in each cell of the contingency table is at least 5.* If the table contains more than one cell with an expected frequency of less than 5, the chi-square test can still be used by combining these in order to get an expected frequency of 5 or more. In doing this, however, the number of degrees of freedom is reduced and thus will yield less information from the contingency table.

Although the rejection rule in a chi-square hypothesis test is to reject the null hypothesis if the computed chi-square value is greater than the table value and vice versa, if the computed chi-square value is zero, we should be careful to question whether *absolutely no difference* exists between observed and expected frequencies. If the manager or researcher has reasons to believe that some difference *ought* to exist, he or she should examine either the way the data were collected or the manner in which measurements were taken, or both, to be certain that existing differences had not been obscured or missed in collecting sample data.

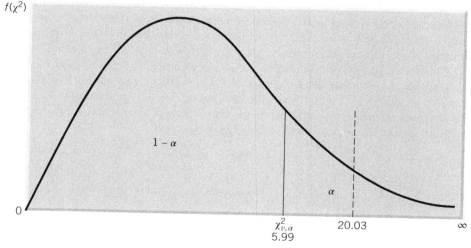

FIGURE 17.3
Cutoff Points of the Chi-Square Distribution Function.

Strength of Association

The strength of the association can be measured by the contingency coefficient (C). This index is also related to chi-square, as follows:

$$C = \sqrt{\frac{\chi^2}{\chi^2 + n}}$$

The contingency coefficient varies between 0 and 1. The 0 value occurs in the case of no association (i.e., the variables are statistically independent), but the maximum value of 1 is never achieved. Rather, the maximum value of the contingency coefficient depends on the size of the table (number of rows and number of columns). For this reason, it should be used only to compare tables of the same size. The value of the contingency coefficient for our example is

$$C = \sqrt{\frac{20.03}{20.03 + 200}}$$
$$= .30$$

Limitations as an Association Measure

The chi-square statistic provides a measure of association between two variables, but it has several limitations. First, it is basically proportional to the sample size, which makes it difficult to interpret in an absolute sense (free from the effect of sample size) and to compare cross-tabulations with different sample sizes. However, in a given analysis, it is often necessary to compare different cross-tabulations with the same sample size. Second, it has no upper bound; thus, it is difficult to obtain a feel for its value. Furthermore, the chi-square value does not indicate how the two variables are related. A further discussion of the use of chi-square as an association measure and some alternatives are presented next. Chapter 19 presents a detailed discussion of the more commonly used measures of association, such as the correlation and regression analysis.

Measures of Association for Nominal Variables

We saw earlier in this chapter that the chi-square statistic is seriously flawed as a measure of the association of two variables. The essence of the problem is that the computed value of chi-square can tell us whether there is an association or a relationship but gives us only a weak indication of the strength of the association. The principal purpose of this section is to describe a measure, Goodman and Kruskal's tau, which overcomes many of the problems of chi-square. First we look at some efforts to correct the problems of the chi-square measure. To illustrate these measures we return to Table 17.3. According to the chi-square test ($\chi^2 = 20$), the relationship between location and attendance in Table 17.3 is highly significant. That is, there is a probability of less than .001 that the observed relationship could have happened by chance. Now we wish to know whether there is a sufficiently strong relationship to justify taking action.

		Location		Row total
		Convenient	Not convenient	
	Often	22	18	40
	Occasionally	48	52	100
Attendance at symphony (Y)	Never	10	50	60
	Column total	80	120	200

Measures Based on Chi-Square

The most obvious flaw of chi-square is that the value is directly proportional to the sample size. If the sample in the previous table were 2,000 rather than 200, and if the distribution of responses were the same (i.e., all cells were 10 times as large), the chi-square would be 200 rather than 20. Two measures have been proposed to overcome this problem; they are the contingency coefficient (C), which was discussed earlier, and phi-squared (ϕ^2).

$$\text{Phi-squared}: \phi^2 = \frac{\chi^2}{n} = \frac{20.03}{200} = .10$$

Other measures include Cramer's V, which is a modified version of the phi-squared coefficient and is used for larger tables (greater than 2×2).

$$V = \sqrt{\frac{\phi^2}{\min(r-1)(c-1)}}$$

$$= \sqrt{\frac{\chi^2/n}{\min(r-1)(c-1)}}$$

$$= \sqrt{\frac{.10}{2}}$$

$$= .223$$

While the phi-squared correlation has no upper limit for larger tables, Cramer's V adjusts ϕ^2 by the minimum of the number of columns or rows in the table. This adjustment results in V ranging from 0 to 1, and a higher value indicates a stronger association. For a 2×2 table, Cramer's V is identical to the coefficient phi (ϕ).

Both measures are easy to calculate but, unfortunately, are hard to interpret. On the one hand, when there is no association they are both zero. When there is an association between the two variables, there is no upper limit against which to compare the calculated value. In a special case, when the cross-tabulation has the same number of rows r and columns c, an upper limit of the contingency coefficient can be computed for two perfectly correlated variables as $(r-1)/r$.

Goodman and Kruskal's Tau

Goodman and Kruskal's tau is one of a class of measures that permits a *proportional reduction in error* interpretation. That is, a value of tau between zero and one has a meaning in terms of the contribution of an independent variable, such as location, to explaining variation in a dependent variable such as attendance at the symphony.

The starting point for the calculation is the distribution of the dependent variable. Suppose we were given a sample of 200 people and, without knowing anything more about the people, were given the task of assigning them to one of three categories, as follows:

		Number in category	
Attendance at symphony (Y)	1. Often	40	(20%)
	2. Occasionally	100	(50%)
	3. Never	60	(30%)
Total		200	

The only way to complete the task is to randomly draw 40 from the 200 for the first category and then 100 for the second category, and so forth. The question is, how many of the 40 people who actually belong in the first category would wind up in that category if this procedure were followed? The answer is 40 times (40/200), or 8 people. This is because a random draw of any size from the 200 will on average contain 20 percent who attend the symphony often.

For the purpose of computing tau, our interest is in the number of errors we would make by randomly assigning the known distribution of responses. For the first category this is $40-8=32$ errors; similarly, for the second ("occasionally") category, we would make $100 (100/200) = 50$ errors; and for the third category, there would be $60 (140/200) = 42$ errors. Therefore, we would expect to make $32 + 50 + 42 = 124$ errors in placing the 200 individuals. Of course, we do not expect to make exactly 124 errors, but this would be the best estimate if the process were repeated a number of times.

The next question is whether knowledge of the independent variable will significantly reduce the number of errors. If the two variables are independent, we expect no reduction in the number of errors. To find out, we simply repeat the same process we went through for the total sample *within each category of the independent variable* (i.e., within each column). Let us start with the 80 people who said the location of the symphony was convenient. Again we would expect an average, when randomly assigning 22 people from the "convenient location" group to the "often attend" category, to have $22 (58/80) = 16$ errors. In total, for the "convenient location" group we would expect $16 + 48 (32/80) + 10 (70/80) = 44$ errors. We next take the 120 in the "not convenient" group and randomly assign 18 to the first category, 52 to the second category, and 50 to the third category of the dependent variable. The number of errors that would result would be

$$18 (102/120) + 52 (68/120) + 50 (70/120) = 74 \text{ errors}$$

With knowledge of the category of the independent variable X to which each person belongs, the number of errors is $44 + 74 = 118$. This is six errors fewer than when we didn't have that knowledge. The tau measure will confirm that we have not improved our situation materially by adding an independent variable, X:

$$tau = \frac{(\text{number of errors not knowing } X) - (\text{number of errors when } X \text{ is known})}{\text{number of errors not knowing } X}$$

$$= \frac{124 - 118}{124} = .05$$

We now have a measure that is theoretically more meaningful, since a value of 0 means no reduction in error and a value of 1.0 indicates prediction with no error. However, a value of 1.0 can be achieved only when all cells but one in a column are empty, and such a condition is often impossible, given the marginal distributions. Thus, most tables have a ceiling on tau that is less than 1.0. For example, for the tables on symphony attendance, the best relationship we would expect to get—given the table's marginal distributions—is as follows:

		Location (X)		
		Convenient	Not convenient	Total
	Often	40	0	40
Y	Occasionally	40	60	100
	Never	0	60	60
	Total	80	120	200

The tau for this table is 0.19. The ceiling value of 0.19 for tau, in a table that satisfies the known marginals, indicates that there is little basis for expecting a strong relationship in this table. This value helps to put our calculated value in perspective.

The Chi-Square Goodness-of-Fit Test

In marketing, there are situations when the manager or researcher is interested in determining whether a population distribution corresponds to a particular form such as a normal or a Poisson distribution. Also, there are situations where the manager wants to know whether some observed pattern of frequencies corresponds to an "expected" pattern. In such situations, the chi-square test can be used as a goodness-of-fit test to investigate how well the observed pattern fits the expected pattern.

For example, an automobile manufacturer, planning the production schedule for the next model year, is interested in knowing how many different colors of the car should be produced, and how many in each of the various shades. Past data indicate that red, green, black, and white are the fast-moving shades and that for every 100 cars, 30 red, 25 each of green and black, and 20 white cars are sold. Also, of the 2,500 current-year model cars sold to date, 680 were red, 520 were green, 675 were black, and the remaining 625 were white. Based on this sample of 2,500 cars, the production manager feels there has been a substantial shift in consumer preference for color and that the next model year production should not follow the 30:25:25:20 ratio of the previous years. The manager wants to test his hypothesis at an α level of .05. The purchases are independent and fall into 4 ($= k$) mutually exclusive categories. Therefore, the chi-square goodness-of-fit test can be employed to test this hypothesis. Formally,

H_0: The observed color preference coincides with the expected pattern

H_a: The observed color preference does not coincide with the expected pattern

$\alpha = .05$

The chi-square statistic is calculated using the formula

$$\chi^2 = \sum_{i=1}^{k} \frac{(O_i - E_i)^2}{E_i}$$

where

O_i = observed number in cell i

E_i = number in cell i expected under independence

k = number of mutually exclusive categories

The number of degrees of freedom for this test is determined to be $v = (k-1) = 3$. The expected value for each category is calculated using $E_i = p_i * n$. For the case of the red cars, this will be $0.3 * 2,500 = 750$. Hence, the chi-square statistic can be calculated to be

$$\chi^2 = \frac{(680-750)^2}{750} + \frac{(520-625)^2}{625} + \frac{(675-625)^2}{625} + \frac{(625-500)^2}{500} = 59.42$$

The chi-square at $\alpha = .05$ for 3 degrees of freedom is obtained from the tables as 7.81. Since the calculated value of χ^2 (59.42) is greater than the table value (7.81), the *null hypothesis is* rejected. The production manager can thus conclude that consumer preference for colors has definitely changed.

As mentioned earlier, the results of the chi-square goodness-of-fit test are valid only if the expected number of cases in each category is five or more, although this value can be less for some cells. Also, in the case of problems where the researcher is interested in determining whether the population distribution corresponds to either a normal or Poisson or binomial distribution, certain additional restrictions might be imposed on the calculations of the degrees of freedom. For example, if we have six categories, v is calculated to be $6 - 1 = 5$. If, however, the sample mean is to be used as an estimate for the population mean, an additional degree of freedom has to be sacrificed. Also, if the sample standard deviation is to be used as an estimate for the population standard deviation, another degree of freedom has to be sacrificed. In this case v will be equal to 3. The rule of thumb to determine the degrees of freedom for the goodness-of-fit test is *first* to employ the $(k - 1)$ rule and *then* subtract an additional degree of freedom for each population parameter that has to be estimated from the sample data.

SUMMARY

Hypothesis testing begins with an assumption, called a *hypothesis*, that is made about a population parameter. Then data from an appropriate sample are collected, and the information obtained from the sample (sample statistics) is used to decide how likely it is that the hypothesized population parameter is correct. The purpose of hypothesis testing is not to question the computed value of the sample statistic but to make a judgment about the *difference* between (1) the sample statistics and (2) the sample statistic and a hypothesized population parameter. There are several points worth remembering about hypothesis testing.

1. Hypothesis testing is a screening test. If the evidence does not pass this test, it may not be worth much attention. If it does pass this test, then it might at least be worth further analysis.

2. Hypothesis testing really measures the effect of sample size. A large sample has a tendency to always yield "statistically significant" results, whereas a small sample will not. Thus, the test really does no more than provide a measure of sample size.

3. Hypothesis testing does not establish whether the null hypothesis is true or false; it only quantifies how persuasive

the evidence is against it. A low p value indicates impressive evidence, and a high p value indicates that the evidence is not impressive.

It is common to test a hypothesis concerning a single mean or proportion and the difference between means (or proportions) in data analysis, particularly when experimentation is involved. The hypothesis-testing procedure for differences in means differs, depending on the following criteria:

1. Whether the samples are obtained from different or related samples

2. Whether the population standard deviation is known or not known

3. If the population standard deviation is not known, whether or not they can be assumed to be equal

4. Whether it is a large sample ($n \geq 30$) or not

A cross-tabulation has associated with it a chi-square test of the relationship between the two variables. A goodness-of-fit test can also be performed with the chi-square analysis.

QUESTIONS AND PROBLEMS

17.1 A study was conducted to determine the relationship between usage of a library and age of users. A sample of 400 was polled and the following cross-tabulation was generated. The numbers in parentheses are the observed cell sizes (O_i).

(a) Complete the table.

(b) Interpret the term $E_1 = 17.8$.

(c) Calculate the χ^2 value.

(d) Is the χ^2 value significant? At what level? What exactly is the null hypothesis?

(e) This data set proves that the usage of the library differs by age. True or false? Why?

		Age of library users			Row total	Proportion
		Under 25	25–45	Over 45		
Library usage	Heavy	26.2% (21) $E_1 = 17.8$	19.5% (41) $E_4 =$	24.5% (27) $E_7 =$	22.3% (89)	.223
	Medium	32.5% (26) $E_2 =$	18.1% (38) $E_5 =$	31.8% (35) $E_8 =$		
	Light	41.3% (33) $E_3 =$	62.4% (131) $E_6 =$	43.6% (48) $E_9 =$		
	Column total	100% (80)			100% (400)	1.00
	Proportion	.20			1.00	

17.2 P&G sampled 400 people to determine their cereal purchase behavior on a particular trip to the store. The results of the study are as follows:

	Brand			
Purchaser	A	B	C	D
Buys the brand	45	50	45	60
Doesn't buy the brand	55	50	55	40

Are preferences and brands related?

17.3 It is known that on a particular high school campus, 62 percent of all students are juniors, 23 percent are seniors, and 15 percent are freshmen and sophomores. A sample of 80 students attending a concert was taken. Of these sample members, 74 percent were juniors, 17 percent were seniors, and 9 percent were freshmen and sophomores. Test the null hypothesis that the distribution of students attending the concert was the same as the distribution of students on campus.

17.4 An admissions dean has noted that, historically, 70 percent of all applications for a college program are from in state, 20 percent are from neighboring states, and 10 percent are from other states. For a random sample of 100 applicants for the current year, 75 were from in state, 15 were from neighboring states, and 10 were from other states. Test the null hypothesis that applications in the current year follow the usual pattern.

17.5 The accompanying table shows, for independent random samples of boys and girls, the numbers who play for more or less than 2.5 hours per day. Test at the 10-percent level the null hypothesis of no relationship between a child's sex and the hours of play.

	Number of hours of play per day	
	Less than 2.5	2.5 or more
Boys	18	10
Girls	17	13

END NOTES

1. The term *null hypothesis* arises from earlier agricultural and medical applications of statistics. In order to test the effectiveness of a new fertilizer or drug, the tested hypothesis (the null hypothesis) was that it had *no effect*; that is, there was no difference between treated and untreated samples.

2. For a more detailed description of significance tests, see A. G. Sawyer and P. J. Peter, "The Significance of Statistical Significance Tests in Marketing Research," *Journal of Marketing Research*, May 1982, pp. 122–131.

3. See R. I. Levin, *Statistics for Management*, Englewood Cliffs, NJ: Prentice-Hall, 1987.

4. For a more detailed discussion on the power of a test, see J. Cohen, "The Concept of Power Analysis," Chapter 1, *Statistical Power for the Behavioral Sciences*, New York: Academic Press, 1969, pp. 1–16.

Case 17-1 | Medical Systems Associates: Measuring Patient Satisfaction[1]

Between 1975 and 1994, per-capita consumer expenditures for nursing home services grew at a faster rate than any other health-service category. During this period, serious doubts were raised as to the quality of nursing-home care and service. These concerns were confirmed by the U.S. Department of Health, Education and Welfare (HEW) investigation in 1996 that led to substantial adverse publicity. Ray Baxter, of Medical Systems Associates (MSA), felt that most of the problems stemmed from the "product orientation" of the nursing homes; that is, they were "more concerned with selling the services and facilities they had than with providing a service mix designed to satisfy the needs and wants of the patients." A study grant was received from HEW to test this broad proposition, and in particular (1) to study the process by which patients chose nursing homes and (2) to identify the determinants of patient satisfaction. In early 1997 Baxter had completed the fieldwork and was wondering what he could conclude about the latter objective from the relationships he had observed in the data.

Study Design

The primary vehicle for data collection was a 12-page personal interview questionnaire containing more than 200 variables. The questionnaire was generally divided into six major conceptual areas as follows:

1. Socioeconomics

2. Lifestyle measures (past and present)

3. Attitudes, interests, and opinions

4. Nursing-home selection process

5. Evaluation of nursing-home environment

6. Perceived health

Questionnaire development required considerable trial and revision. Questions had to be worded to be compatible with low educational levels because the median school grade attained by patients was under eight years. Five-point rating scales did not work, because the respondents rejected the supplied category descriptions and substituted broader descriptions of favorable, neutral, and negative. Standard projective techniques did not work well, apparently because many of the respondents were highly introspective.

The final questionnaire was administered in late 1996 to a stratified random sample of 122 patients in 16 nursing homes in Wisconsin. These homes were selected from a universe of 93 homes. The sampling plan was designed to insure representativeness along the following dimensions:

1. Type of ownership (individual, partnership, corporate, and nonprofit)

2. Level of care (skilled, limited, and personal)

3. Type of assistance approval (Medicare and Medical Assistance, Medical Assistance only, and no assistance)

4. Size (small—less than 100 patients; medium—100 to 200 patients; and large—more than 200 patients)

In order to maintain approximate proportionate representativeness of the sample with the universe, the number of patients randomly selected from each sample-member nursing home was based on the size of the home.

Prior to the contact of respondents by the field interviewers, telephone calls or visits were made to the administrators of each nursing home in the sample, eliciting their cooperation. In general, administrators proved to be highly cooperative.

In contacting respondents, the interviewer was provided with a prearranged random sampling procedure, which he or she was instructed to follow. Upon completion of the basic interview, the interviewer requested that the respondent sign two "release forms" permitting the researchers subsequently to obtain financial data and to discuss medical details with the respondent's doctor.

Analysis

The issue of the measurement of patient satisfaction and identification of determining variables was complicated by the special nature of the respondents. As Baxter noted, "Very few persons not in nursing homes want to be in a nursing home. And how satisfied are people with nursing homes when they have given up an established lifestyle because they now need services they would prefer not to need? Most persons, in and out of nursing homes, would opt for good health and independence. Because a nursing home represents an undesired portion of a life cycle, the problem, then, is to measure the satisfaction level of people who are, in an important sense, dissatisfied."

Three approaches were used to measure "conditional satisfaction," as it was termed. One was the *acceptance* of the necessity of entering a nursing home. The second was their *adjustment* to the disruption of established routines. The third was the patients' direct *evaluation* of their physical (medical), attitudinal, and environmental satisfaction. Each of the elements in the evaluation measure was represented by a separate index, based on combinations of responses to various questions, as follows:

1. An Environmental Rating Index (ERI) was based on answers to 14 questions involving satisfaction with such aspects of the nursing home as room size, physical layout, staff courtesy, medical care, cleanliness of facilities, food preparation, and so forth.

2. A Psychological Adjustment Index was based on a series of attitudinal questions involving such issues as perceived self-usefulness, self-perceived level of activity, perceived lifestyle change, self-perceived reaction of others to nursing-home patients, perceived difficulty in adjusting to nursing-home life (upon arrival), desire to relocate, and so on.

3. A Physical Well-Being Validity Index was based on a comparison of patients' self-perceived level of health with that indicated by medical records.

The focus of the initial analysis was on the determinants of the Environmental Rating Index (ERI). Cross-classification analyses with chi-square tests of significance were run for combinations of many variables with the ERI. Only three of the variables showed any statistical significance. (These variables, and the strength of the relationships, are summarized in Table 17.4.)

None of the other variables, such as the modernity of the home, size of the home, reasons for being in the nursing home, selection process, or patient mobility, were found to be significantly associated with the ERI. As Ray Baxter reviewed these results, he was wondering what conclusions he could draw, and whether other analyses would be required to examine the basic "product orientation" hypothesis with the ERI.

Question for Discussion

1. How can you help Ray Baxter develop some implications based on the analyses?

Table 17.4 Cross-Classification Results: Environmental Rating Index versus Selected Variables[a]

Variable	Environmental rating index		
	Low	Medium	High
Nursing home religious affiliation			
Church-supported	15.8%	34.1%	45.9%
Nonsectarian	84.2	65.9	54.1
	100.0	100.0	100.0
Sample size	(19)	(41)	(61)
"Have you made any new friends here?"			
Yes	84.2	71.8	96.7
No	15.8	28.2	3.3
	100.0	100.0	100.0
Sample size	(18)	(39)	(60)
Number of friends			
"Just a couple"	31.2	21.4	5.1
"Just a few"	31.2	14.3	20.3
"Quite a few"	37.6	64.3	74.6
	100.0	100.0	100.0
Sample size	(16)	(28)	(59)

[a]All variables are associated with the ERI at a level of .05 or greater using the χ^2 test of significance.

18 Hypothesis Testing: Means and Proportions

LEARNING OBJECTIVES

- Discuss the more commonly used hypothesis tests in marketing research—tests of means and proportions.

- Describe the relationship between confidence interval and hypothesis testing.

- Discuss the use of the analysis of variance technique.

- Describe one-way and n-way analyses of variance.

- Discuss the probability-values (p-values) approach to hypothesis testing.

- Describe the effect of sample size on hypothesis testing.

Suppose a brand manager is interested in making a marketing intelligence decision. He would want to determine whether the company's brand is preferred over a competing brand. The manager chooses two cities, Houston and Philadelphia, in which to obtain preference ratings from a sample of 100 consumers of that product category in each city. The mean preferred ratings for that brand and the competing brand were computed as 4.2 and 4.4, respectively. The question is whether 4.4 is better than 4.2—in statistical terms, whether 4.4 is significantly different from 4.2, given the information on respective sample sizes, standard deviations, and the significance level.

In another scenario, 77 percent of the 280 consumers surveyed in Los Angeles favored Lay's potato chips, and 84 percent of the 260 consumers surveyed in New York favored Lay's. An important question facing the brand manager is whether these two proportions are different from one another—in statistical terms, are these two proportions significantly different from each other, given the sample information and significance level?

These examples are just two illustrations of the many questions that face all businesses. Managers resort to using hypothesis testing of means and proportions, described next. The first section discusses the commonly used hypothesis tests in marketing research. The next section describes the probability-value (p-value) approach to hypothesis testing. The section that follows discusses the relationship between confidence interval and hypothesis testing. Also, in this chapter, we discuss another important statistical technique that is commonly used in experimental studies: the analysis of variance, or ANOVA. The analysis of variance is a statistical technique that allows the researcher to test for statistically significant differences between treatment means and to estimate the differences between the means. Here, we will discuss in detail both one-factor and n-factor analysis of variance.

Commonly Used Hypothesis Tests in Marketing Research

Testing Hypothesis about a Single Mean

One of the most commonly occurring problems in marketing research is the need to make some judgment about the population mean. This can be done by testing the hypothesized value of the population mean. A discussion on the hypothesis test of the mean will not be complete until we clarify a few issues pertaining to the test. Table 17.1 described the factors that influence the choice of the appropriate probability distribution. Broadly speaking, the choice of the distribution depends on (1) the purpose of hypothesis testing, (2) the size of the sample, and (3) whether or not the population standard deviation is known. When the population standard deviation (σ) is known, the sample size does not really matter because the normal distribution and the associated z-tables can be used for either of the cases. When the population standard deviation is not known, the size of the sample dictates the choice of the probability standard distribution. Hence, this section discusses applications pertaining to both the z- and the t-distributions. Also, it was mentioned earlier that the test could be either a two-tailed test or a one-tailed test, depending on the nature of the hypothesis. Examples of both tests will be presented in this section.

Samples with Known σ

Two-Tailed Test Superior Shields, a manufacturer of automobile windshields, is faced with a problem. The company has to manufacture windshields that can obtain a quality rating of 5,000 points (the average of the competition). But any further increase in the ratings raises production costs significantly and will result in a competitive disadvantage. Based on past experience, the manufacturer knows that the standard deviation of the quality rating is 250. To check whether this company's windshields meet the competitive standards for quality, the management picks a random sample of 100 industrial customers and finds that the mean quality rating from the sample is 4,960. Based on this sample, the management of Superior Shields wants to know whether its product meets the competitive standards and is neither higher nor lower. Management wants to test its hypothesis at a .05 level of significance.

Statistically, the data in this case can be presented as follows:

Null hypothesis	$H_0: \mu = 5{,}000$	Hypothesized value of the population mean (competitive standards)
Alternative hypothesis	$H_a: \mu \neq 5{,}000$	The true mean value is not 5,000
Sample size	$n = 100$	
Sample mean	$\bar{x} = 4{,}960$	
Population standard deviation	$\sigma = 250$	
Significance level	$\alpha = .05$	

Since the population standard deviation is known, and the size of the sample is large enough to be treated as infinite, the normal distribution can be used. The first step, then, is to calculate the standard error of the mean. This is done using the formula

$$\text{Standard error of mean } \sigma_{\bar{x}} = \frac{\sigma}{\sqrt{n}}$$

$$= \frac{250}{10} = 25$$

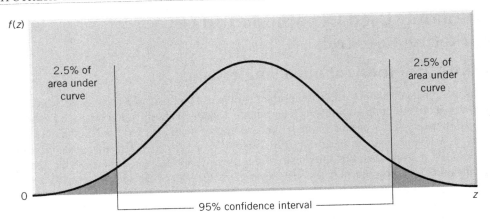

FIGURE 18.1
The Normal Distribution.

Because this is a two-tailed test with a significance level α of .05, using the normal distribution table, the Z-value for .975 $[1 - (0.05/2)]$ of the area under the curve is found to be 1.96. The calculated Z-score is

$$Z = \frac{\bar{x} - \mu}{\sigma_{\bar{x}}} = \frac{(4,960 - 5,000)}{25} = -1.6$$

Figure 18.1 provides a graphical description of the hypothesis test. The rejection rule is to reject the null hypothesis in favor of the alternative hypothesis if $|Z_{calc}| > Z_{\alpha/2}$. Because $1.6 < 1.96$, the management of Superior Shields is convinced that its windshields meet the competitive standards of a quality rating of 5,000 points.

One-Tailed Test

Mr James Ginter, the purchase manager of a big automobile manufacturer, wants to buy windshields that have quality ratings of *at least* 5,000 points, and he doesn't mind paying the price for a good-quality windshield. But Mr Ginter is skeptical about the claims of Superior Shields that its windshields meet the competitive level. To convince Mr Ginter, Superior Shields offers to pay for the survey of a sample of 50 consumers. The quality ratings from the sample reveal a mean of 4,970 points. The problem facing Mr Ginter now is whether to accept the claims of Superior Shields based on the sample mean. Also, Mr Ginter wants the probability of a Type II error occurring (accepting the null hypothesis when it is false) to be as low as possible; hence, he wants the test to be done at a .01 level of significance.

Statistically, the new data can be presented as follows:

Null hypothesis	$H_0: \mu \geq 5,000$	Hypothesized value of the population mean
Alternative hypothesis	$H_a: \mu < 5,000$	The true mean value is less than 5,000
Sample size	$n = 50$	
Sample mean	$\bar{x} = 4,970$	
Population standard deviation	$\sigma = 250$	
Significance level	$\alpha = .01$	
Standard error of mean	$\sigma_{\bar{x}} = \sigma/\sqrt{n}$	
	$= 250/7.07 = 35.36$	

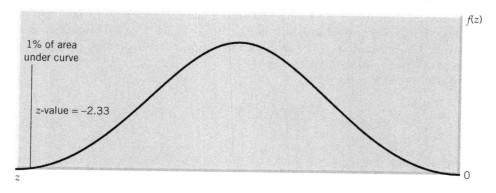

FIGURE 18.2
The Normal Distribution.

Since this is now a one-tailed test (left-tailed test) with a significance level α of .01, using the normal distribution table, the Z-value for .990 $(1-.01)$ of the area under the left or right tail of the curve can be found to be 2.33. The calculated Z-score is

$$Z = \frac{\bar{x}-\mu}{\sigma_{\bar{x}}} = \frac{(4,970-5,000)}{35.36} = -0.85$$

Figure 18.2 provides an illustration of this test. The rejection rule for a left-tailed test is to reject the null hypothesis in favor of the alternative hypothesis if $Z_{\text{calc}} < -Z_{\alpha}$. Since $-0.85 > -2.33$, we fail to reject the null hypothesis.

Samples with σ Not Known

Now assume that Superior Shields provided Mr. Ginter with a sample of only 25 consumers for the previous example and that the mean quality ratings from the sample were 4,962 points. Also, assume that Superior Shields did not have prior knowledge of the population standard deviation, and the sample standard deviation was found to be 245.

Statistically, the data can now be presented as follows:

Null hypothesis	$H_0: \mu \geq 5,000$	Hypothesized value of the population mean
Alternative hypothesis	$H_a: \mu < 5,000$	The true mean value is less than 5,000
Sample size	$n = 25$	
Sample mean	$\bar{x} = 4,962$	
Sample standard deviation	$s = 245$	
Significance level	$\alpha = .01$	

Because the population standard deviation is not known, the sample standard deviation can be used as an estimate of the population standard deviation. Also, since an estimate for the population standard deviation is being used, the standard error of the mean will also be an estimate, given by

$$s_{\bar{x}} = \frac{s}{\sqrt{n}} = \frac{245}{\sqrt{25}} = 49$$

As discussed earlier, if σ is not known, the appropriate probability distribution will be the t-distribution. The appropriate t-distribution will have $n-1$ (in our case 24) degrees of freedom. The table value can be obtained by looking at the t-table under the .01 column for the 24 degrees of freedom row. The t-value thus obtained is 2.492.

The calculated t-value is given by

$$t_{calc} = \frac{\bar{x} - \mu}{s_{\bar{x}}} = \frac{(4,962 - 5,000)}{49} = -0.78$$

The rejection rule for a left-tailed t-test is to reject the null hypothesis in favor of the alternative hypothesis if $t_{calc} < -t_{\alpha}^{n-1}$. Here, $-0.78 > -2.492$; hence, Mr Ginter again will fail to reject the null hypothesis that the mean quality rating of Superior Shields' windshields is greater than or equal to 5,000 points.

Relationship Between Confidence Interval and Hypothesis Testing

In the white-water rafter example in Chapter 17, can one determine whether the white-water rafters' average response of 6.1, which will be termed $\bar{X}$ (the sample mean), is the same as the population mean response of 5.6?

$$H_0: \mu = 5.6$$
$$H_a: \mu \neq 5.6$$

To answer this question, an estimate of the sample standard error $\bar{X}$ of has to be obtained using the formula

$$S_{\bar{x}} = \frac{S}{\sqrt{n}} = \frac{2.5}{\sqrt{35}} = 0.42$$

where s, the standard deviation of the sample, was determined to be 2.5 in this example. Although the population standard deviation is not known, the normal distribution can be used because we have an estimate based on the sample standard deviation. The appropriate Z-value for $\alpha = .05$ can be obtained from the z-table (Appendix A-1) and is found to be 1.96. Now the critical values or the cutoff limits can be calculated using the formula

$$\mu_0 \pm 1.96 s_{\bar{x}} = 5.6 \pm (1.96 * 0.42) = (4.78, 6.42)$$

Because 6.1 falls within the limits, *we fail to reject* the null hypothesis. Figure 18.3 provides a graphical illustration of the hypothesis test. From the z-table, it can be determined that 95 percent of all the area under the curve is included in the interval extending $1.96\sigma_{\bar{x}}$ on either side of the hypothesized mean. In 95 percent of the area, then, there is no significant difference between the sample statistic and the hypothesized population parameter. If the sample statistic falls into the shaded area under the curve, representing 5 percent of the total area (2.5 percent in each tail), then we would reject the null hypothesis.

The term "fail to reject" is used instead of "accept" because even though the sample statistic falls within the critical values, this does not prove that the null hypothesis is true; *it simply does not provide statistical evidence to reject it.*

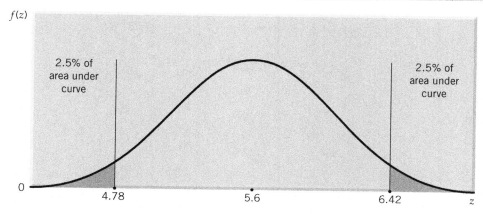

FIGURE 18.3
The Normal Distribution.

Alternatively, acceptance or rejection of the hypothesis can be done without the need for calculating the critical values. This is done by calculating the Z-statistic. The Z-statistic is obtained using the formula

$$Z = \frac{\bar{X} - \mu}{s_{\bar{x}}} = \frac{6.1 - 5.6}{0.42} = 1.19$$

Then one should apply the rejection rule, which states: For a two-tailed test (for which the alternative hypothesis would be $H_a: \mu \neq c$, the hypothesized value), the rejection rule is to reject the null hypothesis if $|Z_{calc}| > Z_{\alpha/2}$; for a right-tailed test of hypothesis, reject the null hypothesis if $Z_{calc} > Z_\alpha$ (where Z_α is obtained from the z-tables). There are similar rules for a left-tailed test: For a left-tailed test (for which the alternative hypothesis would be $H_a: \mu < c$, the hypothesized value), the rejection rule is to reject the null hypothesis if $Z_{calc} < -Z_\alpha$.

Analysis of Variance (ANOVA)

Consider the following pricing experiment. Three prices are under consideration for a new product: 39 cents, 44 cents, and 49 cents. To determine the influence the various price levels will have on sales, three samples of five supermarkets are randomly selected from the geographic area of interest. Each sample is assigned one of the three price levels. Figure 18.4 shows the resulting sales levels in both graphic and tabular forms. The 39-cent stores, the first row, had sales of 8, 12, 10, 9, and 11, and averaged 10 units. The 44-cent stores, the second row, averaged 8 units; and the 49-cent stores, the third row, averaged 7 units. Obviously, determining the optimal price will require an extensive analysis involving a host of considerations. However, before the analysis begins, it is appropriate to consider the basic concepts of experiment analysis.

In experimental design, the dependent variable is called the *response variable* and the independent variables are called **factors**. The different levels of a factor are called *treatments*. The purpose of most statistical experiments is (1) to determine whether the effects of the various treatments on the response variable are different, and (2) if so, to estimate how different they are. In our pricing experiment, the response variable is sales, the factor being the price, and the treatment being the three levels of the price—39 cents, 44 cents, and 49 cents.

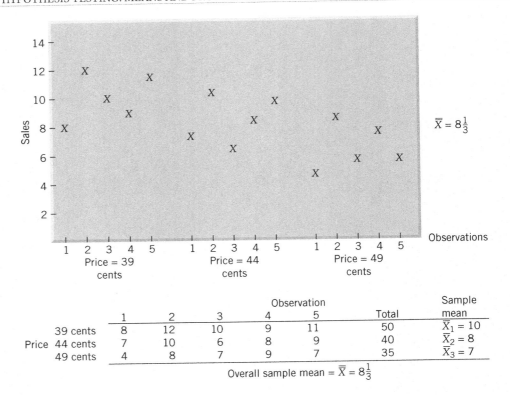

			Observation				Sample
	1	2	3	4	5	Total	mean
39 cents	8	12	10	9	11	50	$\bar{X}_1 = 10$
Price 44 cents	7	10	6	8	9	40	$\bar{X}_2 = 8$
49 cents	4	8	7	9	7	35	$\bar{X}_3 = 7$

Overall sample mean = $\bar{\bar{X}} = 8\frac{1}{3}$

FIGURE 18.4
A Pricing Experiment.

One-Factor Analysis of Variance

Suppose that we wish to study one qualitative factor with levels 1, 2, . . . , r. (In the case of the pricing experiment, the number of levels is 3.) That is, we wish to study the effects of these r treatments on a response variable (in this case sales). The ANOVA of a one-factor model is sometimes called a *one-way analysis of variance*. As a preliminary step in one-way ANOVA, we wish to determine whether or not there are any statistically significant differences between the treatment means μ_1, μ_2, μ_3, . . ., μ_r (μ_r being the mean value of the population of all possible values of the response variable that could potentially be observed using treatment r). To do this, we test the null hypothesis,

$$H_0: \mu_1 = \mu_2 = \mu_3 = \cdots = \mu_r$$

(this hypothesis says that all treatments have the same effect on the mean response) against the alternative hypothesis,

$$H_a: \text{at least 2 of } \mu_1, \mu_2,...,\mu_r \text{ are different}$$

(This hypothesis says that at least two treatments have different effects on the mean response.)

Essentially, in the case of the pricing experiment, the null hypothesis will be that the price levels have no effect on sales. The differences between sample means could be caused by the fact that a sample of only five was employed for each price level. The alternative hypothesis is that there is a price effect—sales would not be the same for each of the price levels if they were applied to all stores.

To test these hypotheses, we need to compute the ratio between the "between-treatment" variance and "within-treatment" variance. Here, we define **between-treatment variance** as the variance in the response variable for different treatments. On the other hand, **within-treatment variance** is defined as the variance in the response variable for a given treatment. If we can show that "between" variance is significantly larger than the "within" variance, then we can reject the null hypothesis.

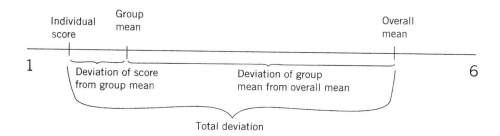

As illustrated above, the within-group variance can be represented by the deviation of an individual's score from his/her group mean, the between-group variance as the deviation of the group mean from the overall mean, and the total variance as the deviation of the individual's score from the overall mean.

Variation among Price Levels

Consider the pricing experiment illustrated in Figure 18.4. To test the null hypothesis, first focus on the variation among price levels ($\bar{X}_1 = 10$, $\bar{X}_2 = 8$, and $\bar{X}_3 = 7$). Then consider the variation within price levels (e.g., the stores with the 39-cent price level had sales of 8, 12, 10, 9, and 11). Under the null hypothesis that price levels have no effect on sales, each of these estimates should be similar. If the estimate based on variation among stores of different price levels is inflated, doubt will be cast on the null hypothesis.

The "between" variance estimate is based on the variation between the sample mean values of each row (price level), which is calculated using the formula

$$SS_r = \sum_{p=1}^{r} n_p \left(\bar{X}_p - \bar{\bar{X}} \right)^2$$

where

SS_r = sum of squares between price levels (rows), also called the treatment sum of squares or the variation explained by the price level

$\bar{X}_p$ = mean sales at price level p (e.g., $\bar{X}_1 = 10$)

$\bar{\bar{X}}$ = overall mean (in this case = $8\frac{1}{3}$)

n = number of observations at each price level ($n = 5$)

p = treatment or price level ($p = 1, 2, 3$)

r = number of treatments or price levels ($r = 3$)

Hence, in this example, the treatment sum of squares can be calculated to be

$$SS_r = 5\left[\left(10 - \tfrac{25}{3}\right)^2 + \left(8 - \tfrac{25}{3}\right)^2 + \left(7 - \tfrac{25}{3}\right)^2 \right] = 23.3$$

Clearly, as the difference between means gets larger, so will the treatment sum of squares. The "between" variance estimate is termed MSS_r (the mean sum of squares between price levels and is an estimate of the variance among stores) and is obtained by dividing the SS_r by its associated degree of freedom (df), which here is the number of treatments (rows) less one. Thus,

$$MSS_r = \frac{SS_r}{r-1}$$

$$= \frac{23.3}{2} = 11.65$$

Variation within Price Levels

The "within" variance estimate is based on the variation within each price level (row), which is calculated using the formula

$$SS_u = \sum_{i=1}^{n_p} \sum_{p=1}^{r} \left(X_{ip} - \bar{X}_p \right)^2$$

where

SS_u = sum of squares unexplained by the price level (row), also called the error sum of squares or the variation within the price levels

X_{ip} = sales of observations (stores) i at price level p

n_p = number of observations at each price level ($n_p = 5$ for all p's)

p = treatment or price level ($p = 1, 2, 3$)

r = number of treatments or price levels ($r = 3$)

Hence, in this example, the error sum of squares (or unexplained variations) can be calculated to be

$$SS_u = (8-10)^2 + (12-10)^2 + \cdots + (7-7)^2$$

$$= 34$$

The "within" variance estimate is termed MSS_u (the mean sum of squares unexplained by the price level, an estimate of the variance within stores) and is generated by dividing SS_u by its associated degrees of freedom,[1] which is here equal to $r(N-1)$ or 12 for equal group sizes only. For equal or unequal group sizes, it is equal to total sample size (N) minus the total number of treatment levels (r). Thus,

$$MSS_u = \frac{SS_u}{N-r}$$

$$= \frac{34}{12} = 2.8$$

Having calculated the variation explained by the treatment (price level) and the variation unexplained by it, an addition of these two factors would give the total variation or the sum of squares total (SS_t). Thus,

$$SS_t = SS_r + SS_u$$

$$= 23.3 + 34 = 57.3$$

ANOVA Table

The expressions derived above are summarized in Table 18.1, which presents an *analysis of variance* and is termed an *ANOVA* table. The ANOVA table is a conventional way to present a hypothesis test regarding the difference between several means. The table indicates, at the left, the source of the variation. The first row summarizes the determination of MSS_r, which is based on the variation between rows (the explained variation, or the variation explained by the price level). The second row summarizes the determination of MSS_u, which is based on the within-row variation (variation unexplained by the price levels). The third row represents the total variation based on the deviations of the individual sales results from the overall mean. All the variation is thus accounted for.[2]

F-Statistic and *p*-Value

We now consider the ratio of the two estimates of the variance (the "between" and "within") of the store sales. This ratio is termed an *F*-*ratio* or *F*-*statistic*:

$$F = \frac{MSS_r}{MSS_u}$$
$$= \frac{11.65}{2.8} = 4.16$$

If the null hypothesis that price levels have no effect on sales is true, then our variance estimates using the difference between the sample means, MSS_r, should be the same as those based on the within-row (price-level) variations. The *F*-ratio should then be close to 1. If, however, the hypothesis is not true and the different price levels generate different sales levels, the MSS_r term will have two components. One component will reflect the variance among stores; the other will reflect the different price effects. As a result, the *F*-ratio will tend to become large.

The *p*-value is the probability that the *F*-ratio would be larger than 4.16, given the null hypothesis. To generate the *p*-value, the *F*-probability distribution is used. Associated with each *F*-ratio are the numerator (MSS_r) degrees of freedom (2) and the denominator (MSS_u) degrees of freedom (12).

Table 18.1   Price Experiment ANOVA Table

Source of variation	Variation, sum of squares (SS)	Degrees of freedom (df)	Variance estimate, mean sum of squares (MSS)	F-Ratio
Between price levels explained variation	$SS_r = \sum_{p=1}^{r} n_p \left(\bar{X}_p - \bar{\bar{X}} \right)^2$ $= 23.3$	$r - 1 = 2$	$MSS_r = \frac{SS_r}{2} = 11.65$	$\frac{MSS_r}{MSS_u} = 4.16$
Within price levels unexplained variation	$SS_u = \sum_{i=1}^{5} \sum_{p=1}^{3} \left(X_{ip} - \bar{X}_p \right)^2$ $= 34$	$N - r = 12$	$MSS_u = \frac{SS_u}{12} = 2.8$	
Total	$SS_t = \sum_{i=1}^{5} \sum_{p=1}^{3} \left(X_{ip} - \bar{X}_p \right)^2$ $= 57.3$	$N - 1 = 14$		

Knowing this pair of degrees of freedom, a table of the F-distribution (Table A-3 at the back of the book) can be used to determine, at least approximately, the p-value. The F-distribution table provides the following p-values for our case, in which the degrees of freedom are 2 and 12.

F-statistic	p-value
1.56	.25
2.81	.10
3.89	.05
6.93	.01

Thus, the p-value associated with 4.16 is not in the table but would be about .04. If the null hypothesis were true, there would be a .04 probability of getting an F-statistic of 4.16 or larger. Therefore, the evidence that the null hypothesis is not true is fairly substantial. The observed difference between sample means could have occurred by accident even if the null hypothesis were true, but the probability is low (1 chance in 25). Since the p-value is less than .05, we can say that the F-statistic is significant at the .05 level. *Note: The ANOVA approach and the regression approach to one-factor analysis of variance give the same value for the F-statistic.*

Strength of Association

A good descriptive statistic for measuring the strength of association is to compute ρ (rho), the ratio of the sums of squares for the treatment (SS_r) to the total sums of squares (SS_t). Rho is a measure of the proportion of variance accounted for in the sample data. In our example, $\rho = 23.3/57.3 = .407$. In other words, 40.7 percent of the total variation in the data is explained by the treatment (price levels). However, since the sample value (ρ) tends to be upward-biased, it is useful to have an estimate of the population strength of association (ω^2, omega squared) between the treatment and the dependent variable. A sample estimate of this population value can be computed as

$$\hat{\omega}^2 = \frac{SS_r - (r-1)MSS_u}{SS_t + MSS_u} = \frac{23.3 - 2(2.8)}{57.3 + 2.8} = .295$$

In other words, 29.5 percent of the total variation in the data is accounted for by the treatment.

Expanding the ANOVA Table

In Chapter 13, we saw how an experiment involving a treatment variable such as price could be expanded. It is possible to control experimentally for one or more variables, such as store size or city, by adding one or more *block effects*. In essence, the experiment is repeated for each block (i.e., large stores and small stores). It is also possible to add more treatment variables. In either case, more than one nominally scaled variable is introduced, and there are several *difference between sample means* relationships. To handle such experiments, the ANOVA table is expanded.

To illustrate, consider the experiment Keith Hunt conducted on corrective advertising, which is advertising required by the Federal Trade Commission (FTC) to "correct" a previous advertisement deemed deceptive.[3] The advertisement in question introduced F-310, a gasoline additive. The FTC claimed, in part, that the product did not significantly reduce pollution as claimed and that the demonstration involving a balloon attached to the exhaust emissions of two cars was rigged, in that one car had a dirty engine and the other emitted invisible pollutants. The effect of various "corrective advertisements" had policy implications for the FTC, which wanted a fair and effective remedy for deceptive advertising but did not want to be harsh and punitive.

Three types of corrective advertisements were tested:

1. *Explicit.* A specific statement explicitly pointing out the deceptive characteristics of the advertisement in question.

2. *General.* A general statement about the deception of the advertisement.

3. *No corrective advertisement.* A bland statement by the FTC on gasoline additives with no mention of the company.

Prior to being exposed to one of the corrective advertisements, the respondents were exposed to one of three "inoculation" advertisements. An inoculation advertisement is hypothesized to mitigate the effect of the corrective advertising, either by giving high levels of support *(support-ive inoculation)* or by giving weak doses of the corrective advertisement, which are refuted *(refu-tational inoculation).* Three inoculation treatments were used:

1. *Refutation.* This advertisement warned of the upcoming corrective ad and refuted it. "If every motorist used F-310 for 2,000 miles, air pollutants would be reduced by thousands of tons per day. The FTC doesn't seem to think that is significant. We think it is."

2. *Supportive.* This contains no mention of the FTC or the upcoming corrective advertisement but does restate the positive arguments.

3. *No inoculation.* This advertisement makes no mention of the positive arguments.

A 3×3 factorial design was used, as outlined in Table 18.2. Each of the nine cells had 22 respondents, each of whom was exposed to the "deceptive" advertisement, the inoculation treat-ment, and the corrective advertisement. The criterion measure was the degree of agreement or disa-greement, on a 28-point scale (where larger numbers indicate greater agreement), with the statement "I like Chevron with F-310." Table 18.2 shows the sample mean for each of the rows and columns. The hypothesis test involves determining the probability of obtaining the observed differences between the sample means, under the hypothesis that the population means were the same.

The expanded ANOVA table is shown in Table 18.3. Notice that each of the two treatments, inocu-lation and corrective advertising, now has an associated variation (sum of squares) and variance esti-mate (mean sum of squares). Consider first the inoculation treatment. The F-ratio for inoculation is

$$F\text{-ratio} = \frac{MSS_{inoculation}}{MSS_{unexplained}}$$

$$= \frac{35.2}{34.4} = 1.02$$

Table 18.2 A Factorial Design

Type of inoculation	Type of corrective advertising			
	Explicit	General	Advertising no corrective	Sample means
Refutational inoculation	(1)	(2)	(3)	16.7
Supportive inoculation	(4)	(5)	(6)	16.9
No inoculation	(7)	(8)	(9)	15.4
Sample means	10.1	18.2	20.4	

Cell size = 22

Table 18.3   Expanded ANOVA Table

Source of variation	Variation (SS)	Degrees of freedom (df)	Mean sum of squares (MSS)	F-Ratio	p-Value less than
Inoculation	70.5	2	35.2	1.02	.36
Corrective advertising	3,882.4	2	1,941.2	56.43	.001
Interaction between treatments	503.7	4	125.9	3.66	.007
Unexplained variation	6,496.6	189	34.4		
Total	10,953.2	197			

The associated p-value would be approximately .36. Thus, the evidence against the null hypothesis of no inoculation effect is not impressive. The evidence is the fact that the three sample means found in Table 18.2 (16.7, 16.9, and 15.4) are not equal. However, although they are not equal, they are close enough so that we cannot reject the null hypothesis that the population means are equal.

Consider next the corrective advertising. The F-ratio is calculated for the corrective advertising treatment in the same manner:

$$F\text{-ratio} = \frac{MSS_{\text{corrective advertising}}}{MSS_{\text{unexplained}}}$$

$$= \frac{1,941.2}{34.4} = 56.43$$

The associated p-value is less than .001. Thus, the evidence is extremely impressive against the null hypothesis that there is no corrective advertising effect. The evidence is the fact that the three sample means found in Table 18.2 (10.1, 18.2, and 20.4) are not equal. Thus, the null hypothesis that there is no corrective advertising effect can be rejected at the .001 level. A closer look at the three sample means in Table 18.2 reveals that it is the explicit corrective advertising that is effective at changing attitudes. This finding is potentially important in designing remedies for deceptive advertising.

There is an advantage to analyzing the two treatments in the same analysis of variance table. By including both, the unexplained variation is reduced, as is the associated mean sum of squares (MSS_u). As a result, there will be less "noise" in the data, the results will be more sensitive, and the F-ratios will be larger.

Interaction

There is a third term in Table 18.3, the interaction between the two treatments. An **interaction effect** means that the impact of one treatment, such as inoculation, will not be the same for each condition of the other treatment. Figure 18.5 shows the results graphically. Note that inoculation affects the attitude created by explicit corrective advertising, but it really has little effect under the "no corrective advertising" and the "general corrective advertising" conditions. There is thus an *interaction effect* present. If there was no interaction, the shape (slope) of the three lines shown in Figure 18.5 would be the same. Their levels would differ, but their shapes would be the same.

The hypothesis of no interaction can be tested in the ANOVA table given in Table 18.3 by determining the appropriate F-ratio for interaction.

$$F\text{-ratio} = \frac{MSS_{\text{interaction}}}{MSS_{\text{unexplained}}}$$

$$= \frac{125.9}{34.4} = 3.66$$

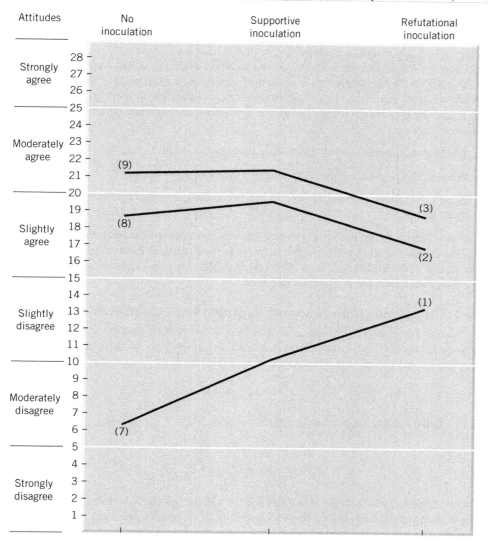

FIGURE 18.5
Attitude Toward Chevron with F-310.
Source: Adapted from H. K. Hunt, "Effects of Corrective Advertising," *Journal of Advertising Research*, 13, October 1973, pp. 15–22.

The associated *p*-value is approximately .007. Thus, the evidence against the null hypothesis of no interaction is very impressive.[4]

Hypothesis Testing for Differences between Means

As discussed in Chapter 17, often in business research, the manager or the researcher is more interested in making a statement regarding the difference between two population means or proportions. Testing differences in two or more means is commonly used in experimental research. The statistical technique used when testing more than two means is called the *analysis of variance* or, more commonly, *ANOVA* (discussed later in this chapter). This section will explore the hypothesis tests pertaining to differences in two means and proportions.

For example, the mayor of a city wants to test whether the daily wages received by the male and female employees of large organizations in that city are the same for the same job description. To test this hypothesis, a random sample of 400 male and 576 female employees is selected and the average wages recorded. The mean and standard deviation of the wages for the males are $105.70 and $5.00, respectively, whereas for the females, the corresponding numbers are $112.80 and $4.80. A significance level of .01 is desired. As was the case in the hypothesis testing of a single mean, the hypothesis-testing procedure for differences in means differs depending on the following criteria:

1. Whether the samples are obtained from unrelated or related samples

2. Whether the population standard deviations are known or not known

3. If the population standard deviations are not known, whether they can be assumed to be equal or not

The logic behind the hypothesis tests and the basic concepts of the tests remains the same for all the above-mentioned conditions. What varies is the statistical formula used to compute the standard error of the difference between the means. Also, for small sample sizes in the testing of means and proportions, the t-distribution is used.

Case 1: Unrelated (Independent) Samples with Unknown σ

In the "salary comparison" example, the null hypothesis will be that the mean salary of male employees is equal to the mean salary of the female employees of the same job description. Hence, in this case $\mu_1 - \mu_2 = 0$. Thus, the null hypothesis will be

$$H_0: \mu_1 - \mu_2 = 0$$

For a two-tailed test, the alternative hypothesis will be

$$H_a: \mu_1 - \mu_2 \neq 0$$
$$\text{Reject } H_0 \text{ if } |Z_{calc}| > Z_{\alpha/2}$$

Since we use large sample sizes, we can use the sample standard deviation as an estimate for the population standard deviation. The standard error of difference in means

$$S_{\bar{X}_1 - \bar{X}_2} = \sqrt{\frac{s_1^2}{n_1} + \frac{s_2^2}{n_2}} = \sqrt{\frac{(5.00)^2}{400} + \frac{(4.80)^2}{576}} = \$0.32$$

where

s_1 = standard deviation of sample 1
s_2 = standard deviation of sample 2
n_1 = size of sample 1
n_2 = size of sample 2

and the calculated value of Z is

$$Z_{calc} = \frac{(\bar{x}_1 - \bar{x}_2) - (\mu_1 - \mu_2)}{s_{\bar{X}_1 - \bar{X}_2}} = \frac{(105.70 - 112.80) - 0}{0.32} = -22.19$$

where

$(\bar{x}_1 - \bar{x}_2)$ = difference between sample means

$(\mu_1 - \mu_2)$ = difference between the population means

For $\alpha = .01$ and a two-tailed test, the z-table value is 2.58. Since the $|Z_{\text{calc}}|$ is greater than $Z_{\alpha/2}$, the null hypothesis is rejected. This means that the mean daily wages of males and females are not equal.

If the null hypothesis is $H_0: \mu_1 - \mu_2 \leq 0$, the alternative hypothesis will be

$$H_a: \mu_1 - \mu_2 > 0$$
$$\text{Reject } H_0 \text{ if } Z_{\text{calc}} > Z_\alpha$$

If the null hypothesis is $H_0: \mu_1 - \mu_2 \geq 0$, the alternative hypothesis will be

$$H_a: \mu_1 - \mu_2 < 0$$
$$\text{Reject } H_0 \text{ if } Z_{\text{calc}} < -Z_\alpha$$

For unknown σ, whether or not it is assumed to be equal across the two samples, the t-distribution is used. Table 18.4 gives information on the computation of the test statistic, degrees of freedom (df), and standard error.

Case 2: Related (Dependent) Samples Test

Instant Fit, a health club, advertises that on average its clientele lose at least 20 pounds within the first 30 days of joining the club. A health-conscious chief executive of an organization wants to provide his employees with free memberships to Instant Fit as part of the organization's employee

Table 18.4   Procedure for Testing of Two Means

Unknown σ assumed to be equal	Unknown σ not assumed to be equal
Compute	Compute
$t = \dfrac{(\bar{x}_1 - \bar{x}_2) - (\mu_1 - \mu_2)}{s_{\bar{x}_1 - \bar{x}_2}}$	$t = \dfrac{(\bar{x}_1 - \bar{x}_2) - (\mu_1) - (\mu_2)}{s_{\bar{x}_1 - \bar{x}_2}}$
where	where
$s_{\bar{x}_1 - \bar{x}_2} = s_p \sqrt{\dfrac{1}{n_1} + \dfrac{1}{n_2}}$	$s_{\bar{x}_1 - \bar{x}_2} = \sqrt{\dfrac{s_1^2}{n_1} + \dfrac{s_2^2}{n_2}}$
where	where
$s_p^2 = \dfrac{(n_1 - 1)s_1^2 + (n_2 - 1)s_2^2}{n_1 + n_2 - 2}$	$g = \dfrac{s_1^2/n_1}{\left(s_1^2/n_1\right) + \left(s_2^2/n_2\right)}$
and	and
$df = n_1 + n_2 - 2 \, (\text{degrees of freedom})$	$df = \dfrac{(n_1 - 1)(n_2 - 1)}{(n_2 - 1)g^2 + (1 - g)^2(n_1 - 1)}$

The rejection rule is the same as before.

benefit program, but the chief finance officer is rather skeptical about Instant Fit's advertising claims. In an effort to satisfy the finance officer, Instant Fit provides him with "before and after" weight data for 10 of its clients. The finance officer wants to test the claim at a significance level of .05. Formally, the data can be presented as

Null hypothesis	$H_0: \mu_1 - \mu_2 \geq 20$
Alternative hypothesis	$H_a: \mu_1 - \mu_2 < 20$
Significance level	$\alpha = .05$

In this case, the t-test for differences between means is not appropriate because the test assumes that the samples are independent. Conceptually, Instant Fit has not provided two independent samples of before and after weights, inasmuch as the weights of the same 10 persons were recorded twice. The appropriate procedure for this case is to obtain the mean and standard deviation of the "difference"; that is, the data have to be viewed as *one sample of weight losses*.

This can be done by defining a variable D, which is the difference between the before and after weights of each individual in the sample. Assume that the data provided by Instant Fit are as follows:

Before:	237	135	183	225	147	146	214	157	157	144
After:	153	114	181	186	134	166	189	113	188	111
Then D:	84	21	2	39	13	−20	25	44	−31	33

Let $\bar{D}$ be the mean of the difference variable D and let $s_{\bar{D}}$ be the standard deviation of the difference. Now:

Null hypothesis	$H_0: \bar{D} \geq 20$
Alternative hypothesis	$H_a: \bar{D} < 20$

The appropriate test statistic is

$$t = \frac{\bar{D} - d}{s_{\bar{D}} / \sqrt{n}}$$

where

d = hypothesized valued difference, in our case $d = 20$
n = sample size (10)

Then

$$\bar{D} = \frac{1}{n} \sum_{i=1}^{n} D_i = \frac{210}{10} = 21$$

$$s_D^2 = \frac{1}{n-1} \left(\sum_{i=1}^{n} D_i^2 - n\bar{D}^2 \right) = \frac{1}{9}\left[14,202 - 10(21)^2 \right] = 1,088$$

$$s_{\bar{D}} = 32.98$$

Thus,

$$t = \frac{21-20}{32.98 / \sqrt{10}} = 0.96$$

The rejection rule is the same as before.

If $\alpha = .05$, for 9 (i.e., $n-1$) degrees of freedom and a one-tail test, the critical t-value is -1.833. Because the calculated t-value of $0.096 \geq -1.833$, the null hypothesis is not rejected. Therefore, Instant Fit's claim is valid.

Hypothesis Testing of Proportions

There are instances in marketing research where the management is concerned not with the mean but with proportions. Consider, for example, the quality assurance department of a light bulb manufacturing company. The manager of the department, based on his experience, claims that 95 percent of the bulbs manufactured by the company are defect-free. The CEO of the company, a quality-conscious person, checks a random sample of 225 bulbs and finds only 87 percent of the bulbs to be defect-free. The CEO now wants to test the hypothesis (at the .05 level of significance) that 95 percent of the bulbs manufactured by the company are defect-free.[5]

The data for this test can be described statistically as

$p_0 = .95$: hypothesized value of the proportion of defect-free bulbs
$q_0 = .05$: hypothesized value of the proportion of defective bulbs
$p = .87$: sample proportion of defect-free bulbs
$q = .13$: sample proportion of defective bulbs

Null hypothesis	$H_0: p = 0.95$
Alternative hypothesis	$H_a: p \neq 0.95$
Sample size	$n = 225$
Significance level	$\alpha = 0.05$

The first step in the hypothesis test of proportions is to calculate the standard error of the proportion using the hypothesized value of defect-free and defective bulbs; that is,

$$\sigma_{\bar{p}} = \sqrt{\frac{p_0 q_0}{n}} = \sqrt{\frac{.95 * .05}{225}} = .0145$$

The two-tailed test of proportions is graphically illustrated in Figure 18.6. Since np and nq are each larger than 5, the normal approximation of the binomial distribution can be used. Hence, the appropriate Z-value for .975 of the area under the curve can be obtained from the z-tables as 1.96. Thus, the limits of the acceptance region are

$$p_0 \pm 1.96\sigma_{\bar{p}} = .95 \pm (1.96 * .0145) = (.922, .978)$$

Inasmuch as the sample proportion of defect-free bulbs, .87, does not fall within the acceptance region, the CEO should reject the quality assurance manager's claims (the null hypothesis). A one-tailed test of hypothesis of proportions can be performed similarly.

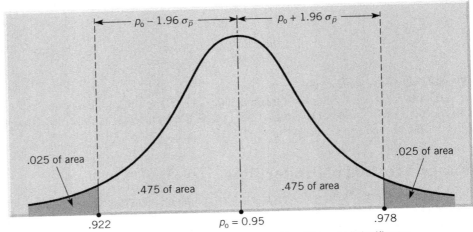

Two-tailed hypothesis test of a proportion at the .05 level of significance

FIGURE 18.6
The Normal Distribution.

Hypothesis Testing of Difference between Proportions

John and Linda, sales executives for a big computer company, have been short-listed as the final-
ists in their company's annual sales competition. John and Linda have identical track records, and
the winner of the competition will be selected based on his or her "conversion ratio" (i.e., the
number of prospects converted into sales). The sales manager randomly picks 100 of John's prospects and finds that 84 of them have been converted to customers. In Linda's case, 82 of her
sample of 100 prospects have been converted. The sales manager needs to know (at $\alpha = .05$)
whether there is a difference in the conversion ratio, based on the sample proportions. Statistically,
the data in this case can be represented as

$p_j = .84 =$ John's conversion ratio based on his sample of prospects
$q_j = .16 =$ Proportion that John failed to convert
$n_1 = 100 =$ John's prospect sample size
$p_L = .82 =$ Linda's conversion ratio based on her sample of prospects
$q_L = .18 =$ Proportion that Linda failed to convert
$n_2 = 100 =$ Linda's prospect sample size

Null hypothesis	$H_0: p_J = p_L$
Alternative hypothesis	$H_a: p_J \neq p_L$
Significance level	$\alpha = .05$

As in the case of the pooled variance estimate of difference in means, the best estimate of p (the
proportion of success), if the two proportions are hypothesized to be equal, is

$$\hat{p} = \frac{\text{Total number of successes in the two samples weighted by the respective sample sizes}}{\text{Total number of observations in the two samples}}$$

$$\hat{q} = 1 - \hat{p}$$

In this example,

$$\hat{p} = \frac{(n_1 p_J) + (n_2 p_L)}{n_1 + n_2} = \frac{(100 * .84) + (100 * .82)}{200} = .83$$

$$\hat{q} = .17$$

Now an estimate of $\sigma_{p_J - p_L}$ can be obtained using

$$\hat{\sigma}_{p_J - p_L} = \sqrt{\frac{\hat{p}\hat{q}}{n_1} + \frac{\hat{p}\hat{q}}{n_2}}$$

$$= \sqrt{\frac{(.83)(.17)}{100} + \frac{(.83)(.17)}{100}}$$

$$= .053$$

The Z-value can be calculated using

$$Z_{calc} = \frac{(pJ - pL) - (0)}{\hat{\sigma}_{p_J - p_L}} = \frac{.02}{.053} = .38$$

The Z-value obtained from the table is 1.96 (for $\alpha = .05$). Hence, we fail to reject the null hypothesis.

The Probability-Values (*p*-Values) Approach to Hypothesis Testing

In the hypothesis tests discussed so far, the manager or researcher tested the null hypothesis at a prespecified level of significance α. While discussing Type I and Type II errors, it became clear that the choice of α will depend on the manager's concern for reducing either of these errors. In other words, there is a trade-off involved between the cost of each of these two kinds of errors, and the managers' choice of the significance level α will be guided by this cost-benefit analysis. However, knowledge of the nature of this trade-off still does not provide the manager with a foolproof method of selecting the appropriate α. The *p*-value, or the probability-value, approach provides the manager or researcher with an alternative method of testing a hypothesis without having to prespecify α. The *p*-value can be defined as the largest significance level at which we would accept H_0.

Difference between Using α and *p*-Value

In hypothesis testing where α is prespecified, the researcher is trying to answer the question, "Is the probability of what has been observed less than α?" and reject or fail to reject accordingly. Alternatively, by using the *p*-values, the researcher can answer the question, "How unlikely is the result that has been observed?" Once the probability value for the test is reported, the decision maker can weight all the relevant factors and decide whether to accept or reject H_0, *without being bound by a prespecified significance level.*

For example, in a hypothesis test of a population mean, let the data be as follows:

Null hypothesis	$H_0: \mu = 25$
Alternative hypothesis	$H_a: \mu \neq 25$
Sample size	$n = 50$
Sample mean	$\bar{x} = 25.2$
Standard deviation	$\sigma = .7$

The standard error of mean can be calculated using

$$\sigma_{\bar{x}} = \frac{\sigma}{\sqrt{n}} = \frac{.7}{\sqrt{50}} = .1$$

The Z-statistic can be calculated using

$$Z = \frac{\bar{x} - \mu}{\sigma_{\bar{x}}} = \frac{(25.2 - 25)}{.1} = 2.0$$

From the z-table, the probability that Z is greater than 2.0 can be found to be .0228 (value corresponding to $Z = 2.0$).

Since this is a two-tailed test the p-value $= 2 \times 0.0228 = 0.0456$. In other words, the p-value of 0.0456 is precisely the largest significance level at which we fail to reject the null hypothesis. For any other value of $\alpha > 0.0456$, we will reject H_0.

If, instead, the hypothesis testing is done using a prespecified value of α, then

at $\alpha = .05$ the researcher will reject the null hypothesis, and

at $\alpha = .01$ the researcher will fail to reject

In general, the smaller the p-value, the greater is the researcher's confidence in the sample findings.

Effect of Sample Size and Interpretation of Test Results

Sample size is important to the interpretation of hypothesis tests. The p-value generally is sensitive to sample size, in that if the sample size increases, the p-value usually will become smaller. In the example discussed in Chapter 17, suppose that the white-water rafter sample size was 900 instead of 35 and that the average response was 5.8. The p-value then would be less than 0.01.[6] Thus, it could be concluded that the white-water rafters' response was indeed significantly higher (at the .01 level) than 5.6.

However, it may well be of no interest if the response of white-water rafters differs only slightly from the response of others. The hypothesis test does not provide information as to whether the evidence put forth is meaningful—only whether it is likely to have been a statistical accident. If the sample size becomes large, the probability of getting "lucky" or "unlucky" with the sample becomes small. Conversely, if the sample size is small, the probability of a statistical accident will be higher. The p-value can be conceived as a mechanism to report the impact of the sample size on the reliability of the results. If the sample size is large, a low p-value should be expected; if the sample size is small, a high p-value is more likely.

If more than two groups are involved, differences in means across multiple groups can be analyzed through a procedure called the **analysis of variance (ANOVA)**.

SUMMARY

The chapter discussed the more commonly used hypothesis testing of means and proportions. It proposed the use of various statistical tests, depending on factors such as whether one or two groups are involved and whether the population or sample standard deviation is used. It also discussed the probability value approach to hypothesis testing and the relationship between confidence interval and hypothesis testing. Finally, for comparison of multiple group means, it proposed an analysis of variance framework.

The goal of one-factor ANOVA is to estimate and compare the effects of the different treatments on the response variable. The purpose of most statistical experiments is (1) to determine whether the effects of the various treatments on the response variable are different, and (2) if so, to estimate how different they are. The ANOVA table can be expanded to accommodate n-factor or n-way analysis of variance.

QUESTIONS AND PROBLEMS

18.1 In Table 16.1, the statement concerning gasoline costs generated a larger difference (1.7) than the other three statements. Could you therefore conclude that it was the statement that best distinguished the unit-price user from the unit-price nonuser? What assumptions are involved in that conclusion?

18.2 The Consumer Fraud Council claims that Skippy Foods does not put the required weight of peanut butter in its 10-ounce jar. For evidence, a sample of 400 jars is selected randomly, weighed, and found to average 9.9 ounces. The p-value, .07, is associated with the hypothesis that the population mean (μ) is usually 10 ounces and the production process is not generating "light" bottles. Has the council proved the point? Evaluate the evidence. Is the evidence statistically significant at the .10 level? At the .05 level? Should the Consumer Fraud Council recommend a boycott?

18.3 A new product was tested in Fresno with a 25-cent coupon and in Tulsa with a 50-cent coupon. A sample of 100 people was contacted in each test city. A total of 40 percent of those contacted in Tulsa had tried the new product, whereas only 30 percent of those contacted in Fresno had tried it, a 10 percent difference. Prior to making the decision as to which coupon to use in the marketing program, a hypothesis was suggested.

(a) What should the null hypothesis be?

(b) What should the alternative hypothesis be?

(c) The probability of obtaining this result under the null hypothesis, namely, that the trial level in Tulsa was 10 percent higher than that in Fresno, was determined to be 0.06. What is the p-value?

(d) Is the result significant at the .10 level? At the .05 level? Would you reject the null hypothesis at the .10 level? At the .05 level?

(e) Does the hypothesis show that there will be more trials with a 50-cent coupon? Do you feel that a 50-cent coupon should be used?

18.4 A manufacturer claims that through the use of a fuel additive, automobiles should achieve, on average, an additional 5 miles per gallon of gas. A random sample of 100 automobiles was used to evaluate this claim. The sample mean increase in miles per gallon achieved was 4.4, and the sample standard deviation was 1.8 miles per gallon. Test the null hypothesis that the population mean is at least 5 miles per gallon. Find the p-value of this test, and interpret your findings.

18.5 A beer distributor claims that a new display, featuring a life-size picture of a well-known athlete, will increase product sales in supermarkets by an average of 40 cases a week. For a random sample of 25 supermarkets, the average sales increase was 31.3 cases and the sample standard deviation was 12.2 cases. Test, at the 5 percent level, the null hypothesis that the population mean sales increase is at least 40 cases, stating any assumption you make.

18.6 Of a sample of 361 owners of retail service and business firms which had gone into bankruptcy, 105 reported having no business experience prior to opening the business. Test the null hypothesis that at most 25 percent of all members of this population had no business experience before opening the business.

18.7 In a random sample of 400 people purchasing state lottery tickets, 172 sample members were women. Test the null hypothesis that half of all purchasers are women.

18.8 A random sample of 200 members of the American Marketing Association was asked which continuing professional education course had most appeal. Of these sample members, 70 opted for international marketing research-related courses. Test the null hypothesis that 45 percent of all members of the association hold this view against the alternative that the true percentage is lower.

18.9 A questionnaire was designed to compare the level of students' familiarity with two types of product. For a random sample of 120 students, the mean familiarity level with burglar alarms was found to be 3.355, and the sample standard deviation was 2.03. In an independent random sample of 100 students, the mean familiarity level for television was 9.5, and the sample standard deviation was 2.1. Assuming that the two population distributions are normal and have the same variance, test the null hypothesis that the population means are equal.

18.10 A random sample of consumers is taken, and their mean preference for visiting a sports event is found to be 5.1 (on a 1 to 7 scale, where 7 denotes most preferred). In the previous surveys, the mean preference has always been 5.0. Has the mean preference changed now? (Use $\alpha = .10$ and $\sigma = .1$.)

18.11 In a test-marketing study, the average sales for a new brand of shampoo in 9 stores is 1.95 units (each unit is 100 bottles). The retail management was expecting to sell on the average 2.0 units. Was the management's expectation realized? (Use $\alpha = .05$ and $\sigma = .06$.)

18.12 An experiment was conducted to determine which of three advertisements to use in introducing a new personal computer. A total of 120 people who were thinking of buying a personal computer was split randomly into three groups of 40 each. Each group was shown a different advertisement and each person was asked his or her likelihood of buying the advertised brand. A scale of 1 (very unlikely) to 7 (very likely) was used. The results showed that the average likelihood of purchase was

Advertisement A: 5.5
Advertisement B: 5.8
Advertisement C: 5.2

The ANOVA table was as follows:

Source of variation	SS	df	MSS	F-Ratio	p-Value
Due to advertisements	12	2	6.0		
Unexplained	234	117	2.0		
Total	246	119			

(a) What is the appropriate null hypothesis? The alternative hypothesis?

(b) What is the F-ratio? The p-value?

(c) Is the result significant at the .10 level? The .05 level? The .01 level?

(d) Are there any differences among the impacts of the three advertisements?

18.13 Using Question 12, assume that each of the three groups of respondents had been divided into two groups: younger (under 30) and older (over 30). The revised ANOVA table was as follows:

Source of variation	SS	df	MSS	F-Ratio	p-Value
Due to advertisements	12	2	6.0		
Due to age	24	1	24.0		
Unexplained	210	116	1.81		
Total	246	119			

(a) What are the F-ratio and p-value associated with the hypothesis test that there is no advertisement effect? Why is it different from that in Question 6? Notice that the total SS and the advertisement SS have not changed.

(b) Test the hypothesis that there is no age effect.

END NOTES

1. For a more detailed description of the analysis technique, see G. Kepel, *Design and Analysis: A Researcher's Handbook*, Englewood Cliffs, NJ: Prentice-Hall, 1973.

2. The reader also might note that the total degrees of freedom, which is the total sample size of 15 less one, or 14, is equal to the sum of the degrees of freedom associated with the first two rows of the ANOVA table.

3. H. K. Hunt, "Effects of Corrective Advertising," *Journal of Advertising Research*, 13, October 1973, pp. 15–22.

4. For a more detailed discussion on the analysis of experimental designs, see D. C. Montgomery, *Design and Analysis of Experiments*, New York: John Wiley, 1991.

5. Companies practicing total quality management (discussed in Chapter 25) usually go for zero defects, or six sigma quality, rather than 5 percent defects used in this example.

6. If the sample standard error again was found to be 2.5, then

$$t = \frac{(\bar{x} - u)}{s_{\bar{x}}/\sqrt{n}} = \frac{(5.8 - 5.6)}{2.5/\sqrt{900}} = 2.4$$

A t-value of 2.4 would have associated with it a p-value less than .01.

The American Conservatory Theater (ACT), a major repertory theater located in San Francisco, was completing its tenth season. The management team at ACT decided to conduct a major research study, intended to help their planning effort. A questionnaire was developed and mailed to their approximately 9,000 season subscribers. A return rate of 40 percent was obtained. A sample of 982 of these returned questionnaires was selected for analysis.

One of the major interests of ACT management was in developing an understanding of the dynamics of the process whereby individuals became ACT subscribers. To assist in this process, the sample was divided into four groups according to their behavior pattern over the past five seasons:

1. Continual subscribers (32 percent)—subscribed all 10 seasons
2. Gradual subscribers (31 percent)—one or more seasons of attendance followed by becoming a subscriber
3. Sudden subscribers (21 percent)—became a subscriber without attending prior performances
4. Miscellaneous patterns (16 percent)

The existence of a substantial "sudden subscriber" group was surprising and ran counter to conventional belief among theater managers that people were first enticed to attend a few performances at a particular theater and only after they had had some positive experiences with this theater would they become subscribers.

The next step in the research study was to attempt to identify characteristics of the continual, gradual, and sudden subscriber groups that might be of use in understanding the segment differences and as inputs in the development of audience building and retention programs. Five variables appeared to be useful in this regard:

1. Years resident in the San Francisco Bay Area, measured on a scale ranging from 1 = two years or less to 5 = more than 20 years.
2. Age of subscriber, measured on a scale ranging from 1 = 25 years old or less to 5 = more than 65 years old.
3. Household income, measured on a scale ranging from 1 = $15,000 per year or less to 4 = more than $50,000 per year.
4. Whether the subscriber spent more than 20 hours a week watching TV, measured as a dummy variable: 1 if yes, 0 if no.
5. Attendance at six other cultural institutions (that is, ballet, Civic Light Opera, DeYoung Museum, Museum of Modern Art, opera, and symphony) in San Francisco. The attendance score is the number of the six different activities that the respondent attended at least once in the previous year.

Table 18.5 shows the differences between the mean scores for the three groups for these five variables.

Each respondent was asked which two benefits from a list of eight were the best reasons for purchasing a subscription. One of the benefits listed was the subscription price discount (ACT offered subscribers seven plays for the price of six). The percentage of each subscriber group that mentioned each benefit is shown in Table 18.6.

Table 18.5 Subscriber Groups

	Mean scores		
	Continual	Gradual	Sudden
Years resident (1 to 5 scale)[a]	4.32	3.68	3.53
Age (1 to 5 scale)[a]	3.34	2.74	2.86
Income (1 to 4 scale)	2.54	2.39	2.38
Cultural activities (0 to 6 scale)[a]	2.84	2.95	2.08
Twenty hours of TV (0 to 1 dummy variable)	0.31	0.26	0.38
Sample size	314	304	206

[a]Indicates that the differences between means are significant at the .01 level.

Table 18.6 Benefits Obtained by Subscribing to ACT

Subscriber group	Benefit[a]								
	Ease of ordering (%)	Guaranteed ticket (%)	Price discount (%)	Priority seating (%)	Discount on special plays (%)	More certain to attend (%)	New play series (%)	Support for art (%)	Total mentions
Continual subscriber	7.5	16.4	12.4	22.0	1.1	25.9	2.9	11.8	549
Gradual subscriber	8.2	16.5	12.5	22.2	1.1	28.5	3.0	7.9	558
Sudden subscriber	11.0	13.9	10.4	25.7	1.6	30.7	1.6	5.1	374
Total sample	8.6	15.8	12.0	23.0	1.2	28.1	2.6	8.6	1,481

[a]Each respondent could check a maximum of two benefits. Percentages are based on total number of benefits checked.

Questions for Discussion

1. Does it surprise you that there are so many "sudden subscribers"? Why would a person subscribe (at a cost that could be as high as $50 per person) instead of first trying it out? After reviewing Table 18.5, in what aspects would you say that such a person differed from other subscribers? Interpret the footnote in Table 18.5.

2. What does Table 18.6 say about the difference between the three groups? What are the other implications of Table 18.6 for ACT?

Prepared by Adrian B. Ryans,
Charles B. Weinberg, and David A. Aaker as
a basis for class discussion.

Case 18-2   **Apple Appliance Stores**

An experiment using a randomized design was conducted by the Apple Appliance chain of 300 retail stores. Four levels of advertising provided the experimental treatment: none, low, medium, and high. In addition, the stores were divided by store size into small, intermediate, and large. A random sample of eight stores was taken from each of the three store-size groups. Each set of eight stores was divided randomly into four groups of two stores for the experimental treatment, as summarized in Table 18.7.

Stores sales were measured during the six-month period after the experiment started. Sales also were determined during the same period in the previous year. The difference between the sales during the two periods was the variable of interest. A plot of the sales change is shown in Figure 18.7.

In Table 18.8, an analysis of variance is shown. Exactly what statistical questions are answered by the table? What additional, unanswered questions may be of interest?

Table 18.7 Research Design

		Store size			
		Small	Medium	Large	Total
Advertising level	None	2	2	2	6
	Low	2	2	2	6
	Medium	2	2	2	6
	High	2	2	2	6
	Total	8	8	8	

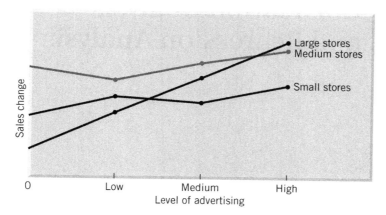

FIGURE 18.7
Effect of Advertising on Sales.

Table 18.8   Analysis of Variance of Sales Changes

Source of variation	Sum of squares	Degrees of freedom (df)	Mean sum of squares	F-ratio
Advertising	360	3	120	3.0[a]
Store size	88	2	44	1.1
Interaction	984	6	164	4.1[b]
Unexplained variation	480	12	40	
Total	1,912	23		

[a]Significant at the .10 level.
[b]Significant at the .05 level.

The following additional materials for Part III of the book are available on the Web:

| *Web Case III-1* | The Vancouver Symphony Orchestra |

| *Web Case III-2* | Popular Pizzas Identifying Consumer Preferences |

19 Correlation Analysis and Regression Analysis

LEARNING OBJECTIVES

- Discuss the use of correlation as a measure of association and describe the distinction between simple correlation and partial correlation.
- Discuss the objectives of regression analysis.
- Discuss the application of regression analysis.

Oftentimes in business research, the researcher is interested in determining whether there is any association (relationship) between two or more variables and, if so, the researcher would like to know the strength of the association and the nature of the relationship. The significance of this cause–effect relationship between two or more variables will be important in helping the manager make intelligent decisions. For example, if the researcher finds that there is no significant cause–effect relationship between advertising and sales in a particular location, the manager may decide to spend less on advertising. Previously we discussed the chi-square goodness-of-fit test as a measure of association. We also discussed the limitations of the chi-square test as an association measure. In this chapter, we will discuss the more commonly used measure of association—the *correlation coefficient*. *Correlation analysis* involves measuring the strength of the relationship between two variables. For example, the correlation coefficient provides a measure of the degree to which there is an association between two variables (X and Y).

Regression analysis is a statistical technique that is used to relate two or more variables. Here, a variable of interest, the *dependent* or *response* variable (Y) is related to one or more *independent* or *predictor* variables (X's). The objective in regression analysis is to build a regression model or a prediction equation relating the dependent variable to one or more independent variables. The model can then be used to *describe, predict*, and *control* the variable of interest on the basis of the independent variables. For example, when a new product or concept is being explored, one of the key variables of interest is usually the respondent's attitude or intentions toward it. Is it something that the respondent would consider buying and/or using? The goal may be to predict the ultimate usage of the product or concept under a variety of conditions. Another goal might be to understand what causes high intentions to purchase so that when the product does emerge, the marketing program can be adjusted to improve the success probability.

In this chapter, we will discuss in detail the most simple form of regression analysis, the *bivariate* analysis. We will study how, in the bivariate analysis, the variable of interest is related to *one* independent variable. Regression analysis that involves more than one independent variable is called *multiple regression analysis*.

Correlation Analysis

The **Pearson correlation coefficient** measures the degree to which there is a linear association between two intervally scaled variables. A positive correlation reflects a tendency for a high value in one variable to be associated with a high value in the second. A negative correlation reflects an association between a high value in one variable and a low value in the second variable. If the database includes an entire population, such as all adults in California, the measure is termed the *population correlation* (p). If it is based on a sample, it is termed *sample correlation* (r).

If two variables are plotted on a two-dimensional graph, called a **scatter diagram**, the sample correlation reflects the tendency for the points to cluster systematically about a straight line rising or falling from left to right. The sample correlation r always lies between 1 and -1. An r of 1 indicates a perfect positive linear association between the two variables, whereas if r is -1 there is perfect negative linear association. A zero correlation coefficient reflects the absence of any linear association.

Figure 19.1 illustrates five scatter diagrams. In Figure 19.1a, there is a rather strong tendency for a small Y to be associated with a large X. The sample correlation is .80. In Figure 19.1b, the pattern slopes from the lower left to the upper right, and thus the sample correlation is .80. Figure 19.1c is an example of a sample correlation of 1. It is a straight line running from the lower left to the upper right. Figure 19.1d is an example in which there is no relationship between X and Y. Figure 19.1e shows a plot in which there is a clear relationship between the two variables, but it is not a linear or straight-line relationship. Thus, the sample correlation is zero.

Simple Correlation Coefficient

The concept of simple or bivariate correlation can be best understood by following the methodology for calculating it. First, the points are plotted in a scatter diagram. In the sample shown in Figure 19.2, the Y-axis indicates the sales in thousands of dollars per day of six stores in a retail chain, and the X-axis indicates the distance in travel time to the nearest competing store corresponding to each of the six stores. Six stores are located on the scatter diagram. A reasonable measure of association between the two variables is the covariance between the two variables:

$$\text{Cov}(x, y) = \sum \left(X_i - \bar{X}\right) * \left(Y_i - \bar{Y}\right)$$

Points in quadrants I and III suggest a positive association, so large values of X will be associated with large values of Y. For store E, for example, the $(X_i - \bar{X}) * (Y_i - \bar{Y})$ term equals 5 times 6, or 30. Table 19.1 provides a summary of this calculation.

If the data point had been higher (farther away from Y) or farther to the right (farther from X), then the value of the $(X_i - \bar{X}) * (Y_i - \bar{Y})$ term for store E would have been greater. On the other hand, a point near one of the dotted axes would contribute little to the association measure. Store D is located on the X line and, as shown in Table 19.1, contributes zero to the association measure. Similarly, points in quadrants II and IV suggest a negative association. Thus, store B, which is in quadrant II, has a negative contribution to the association measure. Table 19.1 shows this contribution to be -2.

The second step of the method for calculating the sample correlation is to divide the association expression by the sample size:

$$\frac{1}{(n-1)} * \sum (X_i - \bar{X}) * (Y_i - \bar{Y})$$

To ensure that the measure does not increase simply by increasing the sample size (one of the limitations associated with the use of chi-square as an association measure), it is divided by

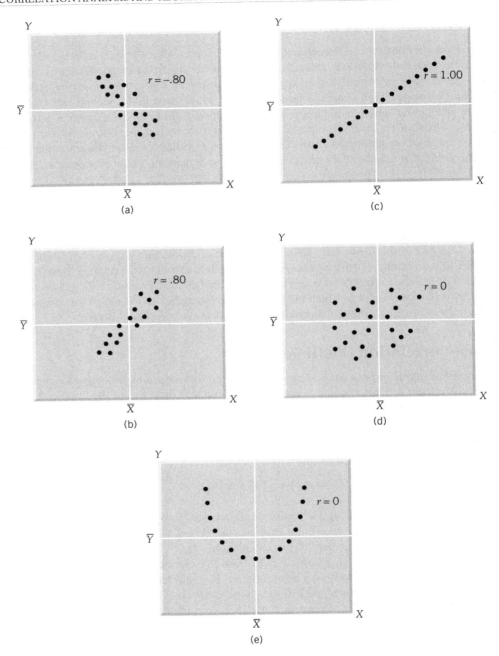

FIGURE 19.1
Scatter Plots Showing Different Levels of Correlation Between X and Y.

the sample size. The association between retail store sales volume and distance to competitive stores should not get larger simply because the association measure is calculated using data from 20 stores instead of 10. Thus, we divide by the sample size [strictly speaking, by $(n-1)$]. Table 19.1 shows that this association measure would then be 15.6. This expression is called the

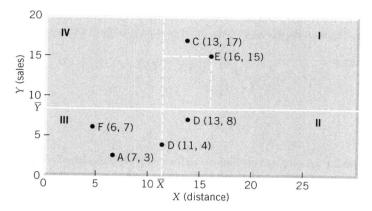

FIGURE 19.2
Store Sales versus Distance.

Table 19.1 Determining the Sample Correlation Coefficient

	Daily sales (thousands), Y_i	$Y_i - \bar{Y}$	Distance to nearest competing store (min), X_i	$X_i - \bar{X}$	$(X_i - \bar{X})(Y_i - \bar{Y})$
Store A	3	−6	7	−4	24
Store B	8	−1	13	2	−2
Store C	17	8	13	2	16
Store D	4	−5	11	0	0
Store E	15	6	16	5	30
Store F	7	−2	6	−5	10
Total	54	0	66	0	$78 = \sum_i (X_i - \bar{X})(Y_i - \bar{Y})$
Average	$\bar{Y} = 9$		$\bar{X} = 11$		$15.6 = \dfrac{1}{n-1}\sum_i (X_i - \bar{X})(Y_i - \bar{Y})$

$$r_{YX} = \frac{1}{n-1} \frac{\sum (X_i - \bar{X})(Y_i - \bar{Y})}{s_X s_Y} = \frac{78}{5\,(3.85)(5.76)} = .70$$

$$s_X = 3.85 = \sqrt{\frac{1}{n-1}\sum_i (X_i - \bar{X})^2}$$

$$s_Y = 5.76 = \sqrt{\frac{1}{n-1}\sum_i (Y_i - \bar{Y})^2}$$

sample *covariance*. Thus, the covariance between X and Y (denoted Cov_{XY}) measures the extent to which X and Y are related.

The size of the covariance measure could be changed simply by changing the units of one of the variables. For example, if sales are measured in dollars instead of thousands of dollars, then the association measure is 15.6 million instead of 15.6. Such a dependence on the units of measure makes the measure difficult to interpret. The solution is to divide the measure by the sample standard deviations for X and Y.[1] The result is the sample correlation coefficient, which will not be affected by a change in the measurement units of one or both of the variables:

$$r_{XY} = \frac{1}{(n-1)} \times \sum \frac{(X_i - \bar{X})}{s_X} \times \frac{(Y_i - \bar{Y})}{s_Y}$$

$$r_{XY} = \frac{\text{Cov}_{XY}}{s_X s_Y}$$

This expression for the sample correlation coefficient (r) is called the *Pearson product-moment correlation coefficient*. If the correlation coefficient is calculated for the entire population, it is denoted by ρ, the population correlation coefficient. Like the case of the sample mean being an estimator of the population mean, the sample correlation coefficient r is an estimate of the population correlation coefficient ρ.

The product-moment correlation coefficient has several important properties. First, as the methodology has demonstrated, it is independent of sample size and units of measurement. Second, it lies between -1 and $+1$. Thus, the interpretation is intuitively reasonable. Further, when regression analysis is discussed later in this chapter, a rather useful interpretation of the square of the sample correlation (r^2) will be presented that will provide additional insights into its interpretation.

Here it should be stressed that, even though the correlation coefficient (r) provides a measure of association between two variables, *it does not imply any causal relationship* between the variables. A correlation analysis or, for that matter, even a regression analysis can measure only the nature and degree of association (or covariation) between variables; it cannot imply causation. Statements of causality must spring from underlying knowledge and theories about the phenomena under investigation and not from mathematical measures of association.[2] Further, the sample correlation coefficient can be seriously affected by outliers or extreme observations.[3]

The correlation coefficient provides a measure of the relationship between two questions or variables. The underlying assumption is that *the variables are intervally scaled*, such as age or income. At issue is to what extent a variable must satisfy that criterion. Does a seven-point agree–disagree scale qualify? The answer depends in part on the researcher's judgment about the scale. Is the difference between -2 and -1 the same as the difference between $+2$ and $+3$? If so, it qualifies. If not, a correlation analysis may still be useful, but the results should be tempered with the knowledge that one or both of the scales may not be intervally scaled.

Testing the Significance of the Correlation Coefficient

As discussed earlier, the calculation of the correlation coefficient r assumes that the variables, whose relationship is being tested, are metric. If this assumption is not met either partially or completely, it affects the value of r. A simple test of hypothesis can be performed to check the significance of the relationship between two variables, measured by r. This involves testing

The null hypothesis	$H_0: \rho = 0$ against
The alternative hypothesis	$H_a: \rho \neq 0$

Consider the example presented in Table 19.1. Here, the relationship between the sales per day of stores in a retail chain and the distance in travel time to the nearest competing store is determined using the sample correlation coefficient r and is calculated to be .70. To test the significance of this relationship, the test statistic t can be computed using

$$t = r\sqrt{\frac{n-2}{1-r^2}}$$

In our example, $n = 6$ and $r = .70$. Hence,

$$t = .70\sqrt{\frac{6-2}{1-0.70^2}} = 1.96$$

If the test is done at $\alpha = .05$ with $n - 2 = 4$ degrees of freedom, then the critical value of t can be obtained from the tables to be 2.78. Since $1.96 < 2.78$, we fail to reject the null hypothesis.

What does this mean? The statistical test of significance reveals that the value of the sample correlation r (found to be .70) is not significantly different from zero. In other words, the strength of the relationship between store sales and the distance from competing stores at best can be attributed to a chance occurrence. If the same value of r (.70) had been obtained from a larger sample (say, $n = 50$), then one could possibly conclude that there is a systematic association between the variables.

As an exercise, retest the hypothesis that $\rho = 0$, assuming that the value of $r = .70$ was obtained from a sample size of 50. Do you still fail to reject the null hypothesis? Why not?

Partial Correlation Coefficient

The Pearson correlation coefficient provides a measure of linear association between two variables. When there are more than two variables involved in the relationship, partial correlation analysis is used. The **partial correlation coefficient** provides a measure of association between two variables after controlling for the effects of one or more additional variables. For example, the relationship between the advertising expenditures and sales of a brand is influenced by several other variables. For the sake of simplicity, let us assume that the relationship is affected by a third variable, the use of coupons. If the brand manager is interested in measuring the relationship between the dollar amount spent on advertisements (X) and the associated sales of the brand (Y), he or she has to control for the effect of coupons (Z). The partial correlation coefficient can thus be expressed as

$$r_{XY.Z} = \frac{r_{XY} - r_{XZ} * r_{YZ}}{\sqrt{\left(1 - r^2_{XZ}\right)} * \sqrt{\left(1 - r^2_{YZ}\right)}}$$

Although the correlation analysis provides a measure of the strength of the association between two variables, it tells us little or nothing about the nature of the relationship. Hence, *regression analysis is used to understand the nature of the relationship between two or more variables.*

Regression Analysis[4]

As mentioned earlier, **regression Analysis** is a statistical technique that is used to relate two or more variables. Here, a variable of interest, the *dependent* or *response variable* (Y), is related to one or more *independent* or *predictor* variables $(X's)$. The objective in regression analysis is to build a regression model or a prediction equation relating the dependent variable to one or more independent variables. The model can then be used to *describe, predict,* and *control* the variable of interest on the basis of the independent variables.

For example, consider the HMO study. In this study, the intention to enroll is one of the variables of interest. One motivation is prediction: to predict the enrollment if the plan is implemented. Thus, the intention question is analyzed to help predict the acceptance of the concept among the sample of respondents. However, it is desirable to determine how the intentions to enroll are related to the distance to the HMO. If such a relationship were known, it might be possible to predict intentions for neighborhood areas just by knowing the distance to the HMO. Similarly, if the relationship between enrollment intentions and the health plan now used were known, some knowledge would be available about the possible intentions of others just by knowing their health plan. Furthermore, if the relationship between the coverage of the HMO (what services are included) and people's intentions were known, the prediction could be adjusted, depending on the coverage actually used when the plan is implemented.

Prediction is not the only reason a knowledge of the relationship between intentions and other variables is useful in the HMO study. Another motivation is to gain an understanding of the relationship so that the marketing program can be adjusted. If the relationship between intentions and the distance to the HMO is known, then a decision as to where to focus the marketing program geographically can be made more intelligently. It makes little sense to expend marketing effort on groups with little potential. Further, the relationship of intentions to the health plan of participants might provide information as to what competitive health plans are most vulnerable, and could help guide the development of the marketing program. The relationship between intentions and an HMO characteristic, such as coverage, could influence the exact type of plan introduced. A "product feature" such as coverage should be specified, so that the costs of the feature can be balanced with its impact on enrollment.

Regression analysis provides a tool that can quantify such relationships. Further, unlike cross-tabulations and other association measures, which deal only with two variables, regression analysis can integrate the relationship of intentions with two, three, or more variables simultaneously. Regression analysis not only quantifies individual relationships, it also provides statistical control. Thus, it can quantify the relationship between intentions and distance while controlling statistically for the health plan and coverage variables.

Simple Linear Regression Model

The construction of a simple linear regression model usually starts with the specification of the dependent variable and the independent variable. Suppose that our organization, Midwest Stereo, has 200 retail stores that sell hi-fi and related equipment. Our goal is to determine the impact of advertising on store traffic, that is, the number of people who come into the store as a result of the advertising. More specifically, we are concerned with the number of people entering the store on a Saturday as a result of advertising placed the day before. The following regression model might be hypothesized:

$$Y_i = \beta_0 + \beta_1 X_i + \varepsilon_i$$

where

Y = the number of people entering the store on Saturday (dependent variable)

X = the amount of money the store spent on advertising on Friday (independent variable)

β_0 = a model parameter that represents the mean value of the dependent variable (Y) when the value of the independent variable X is zero (It is also called the Y intercept.)

β_1 = a model parameter that represents the slope that measures the change in the value of the independent variable associated with a one-unit increase in the value of the independent variable

ε_i = an error term that describes the effects on Y_i of all factors other than the value of X_i

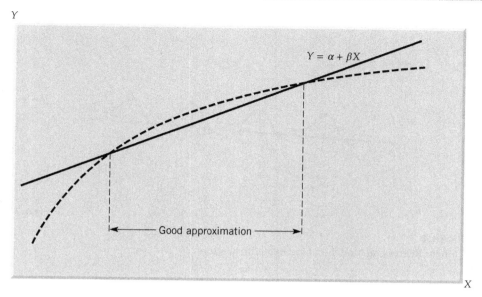

FIGURE 19.3
The Linear Approximation.

Several aspects of the model are worth emphasizing. First, the hypothesized relationship is linear; it represents a straight line, as shown in Figure 19.3. Such an assumption is not as restrictive as might first appear. Even if the actual relationship is curved, as illustrated by the dotted arc in Figure 19.3, the relationship still may be close to linear in the range of advertising expenditures of interest. Thus, a linear relationship still may be entirely adequate.[5]

The error term is central to the model. In reality, store traffic is affected by variables other than advertising expenditures; it is also affected by store size and location, the weather, the nature of what is advertised, whether the advertising is in newspapers or on radio, and other factors. Thus, even if advertising expenditures are known, and our hypothesized linear relationship between advertising expenditures and store traffic is correct, it will be impossible to predict store traffic exactly. There still will be a margin of error. The error term reflects the error explicitly. Several assumptions surrounding the error term are made when estimating the parameters of the model and during significance testing. These are called the *assumptions of the regression model*.

Assumptions of the Regression Model

There are five major assumptions associated with the simple linear regression model.[6]

- The error term is normally distributed (i.e., for each value of X, the distribution of Y is normal).

- The mean or average value of the error term is zero $[E(\varepsilon_i) = 0]$.

- The variance of the error term is a constant and is independent of the values of X.

- The error terms are independent of each other (the observations are drawn independently).

- The values of the independent variable X are fixed (e.g., by an experimenter).

- Figure 19.4 provides an illustration of the model.

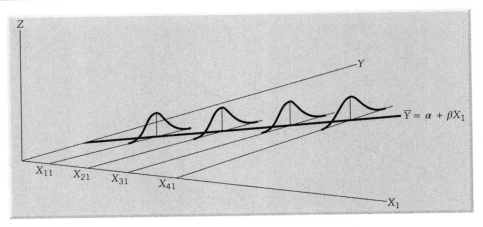

FIGURE 19.4
Simple Linear Regression Model—a Graphical Illustration.

Estimating the Model Parameters

The parameters, β_0 and β_1, that characterize the relationship between X and Y are of prime interest. One of the goals of the regression analysis is to determine what they are. Although we do not know the true values of the parameters β_0 and β_1, we can calculate point estimate b_0 and b_1 of β_0 and β_1. The procedure used is to obtain a random sample of stores and to use the information from it to estimate β_0 and β_1. For example, assume that a random sample of 20 stores was selected. For each store in the sample, the number of people entering the store on a given Saturday is determined. Further, for each store, the amount spent on advertising for the previous day is recorded. Table 19.2 presents the data for the 20 stores in our sample. The results are plotted in Figure 19.5.

The next step is to obtain a line that has the best "fit" to these points. Of course, a line could be drawn freehand; in practice, however, a computer program is used. The computer program generates a line with the property that the squared vertical deviations from the line are minimized. Such a line is termed a *least-squares* line and is denoted by the following expression:

$$\hat{Y}_i = b_0 + b_1 X_i$$

where $\hat{Y}_i$ is called the predicted value of Y_i.

The values of the least-squares estimates b_0 and b_1 are calculated using the formulas

$$b_1 = \frac{n \sum x_i y_i - \left(\sum x_i\right)\left(\sum y_i\right)}{n \sum x_i^2 - \left(\sum x_i\right)^2}$$

and

$$b_0 = \overline{y} - b_1 \overline{x}$$

where

$$\overline{y} = \frac{\sum y_i}{n} \quad \overline{x} = \frac{\sum x_i}{n}$$

Table 19.2 Advertising versus Store Traffic Data

No. of stores	Store traffic, Y_i	Advertising dollars, X_i	$X_i * Y_i$	X_i^2
1	90	40	3,600	1,600
2	125	75	9,375	5,625
3	320	100	32,000	10,000
4	200	110	22,000	12,100
5	600	190	114,000	36,100
6	450	200	90,000	40,000
7	400	300	120,000	90,000
8	700	310	217,000	96,100
9	800	380	304,000	144,400
10	810	410	332,100	168,100
11	1,000	480	480,000	230,400
12	1,170	500	585,000	250,000
13	1,200	520	624,000	270,400
14	1,500	550	825,000	302,500
15	1,000	560	560,000	313,600
16	900	580	522,000	336,400
17	700	690	483,000	476,100
18	1,000	700	700,000	490,000
19	1,300	710	923,000	504,100
20	1,350	800	1,080,000	640,000
Mean	780.75	410.25		
Sum	15,615	8,205	8,026,075	4,417,525

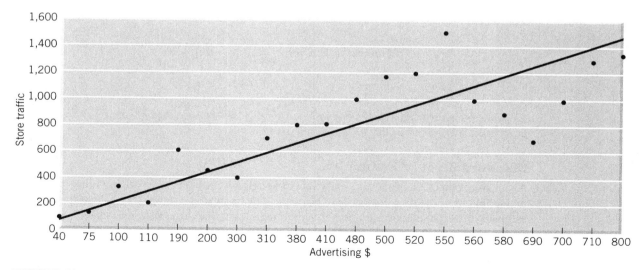

FIGURE 19.5
Advertising versus Store Traffic.

In this case, from Table 19.2, we can calculate b_0 and b_1 to be 148.64 and 1.54, respectively. In the case of the simple linear regression model involving one dependent and one independent variable, the parameter estimates and other model values easily can be hand-calculated. As the number of independent variables increases, however, the model becomes large, and hand computation is no longer feasible. In such situations, statistical packages such as SAS and SPSS normally are used. Subsequent sections and chapters, dealing with multiple regression analysis and other advanced multivariate techniques, provide the relevant SAS outputs along with the interpretations.

The value b_0 (148.64) is an estimate of the parameter β_0, and the value b_1 (1.54) is an estimate of the parameter β_1. These estimates are termed *regression coefficients* and are based on the random sample. The term $\hat{Y}$ (read "Y hat") indicates the points on the line and is an estimate of store traffic based on the regression model. For example, when X is 600, then $\hat{Y} = 148.64 + 1.54 * 600 = 1,073$ (approx). Thus, if advertising expenditures of 600 are planned, our estimated store traffic will be 1,073. In contrast, Y is the actual sales level. For example, for one store, the advertising expenditure (X) was 500, the store traffic (Y) was 1,170, and the store traffic estimate ($\hat{Y}$) was calculated to be 919. The difference between the actual and predicted values is called the *residual* and is an estimate of the error in the population.

If another random sample of 20 stores were to be obtained, undoubtedly it would contain different stores. As a result, the plot of X and Y would differ from Figure 19.5 and the regression coefficients, b_0 and b_1, would be different. Every random sample would have associated with it a different b_0 and b_1. In general, if any particular values of b_0 and b_1 are good point estimates of β_0 and β_1, they will, for $i = 1, 2, \ldots, n$, make $\hat{Y}_i$ fairly close to Y_i. Therefore, the ith residual,

$$e_i = y_i - \hat{y}_i$$
$$= y_i - (b_0 + b_1 x_i)$$

will be fairly small.

The regression coefficients can be estimated using a number of statistical techniques. Each of the techniques is based on some criterion to get the best measure of the population coefficients from the sample. One of the most commonly used techniques to estimate these coefficients is based on the *least-squares criterion*. According to this criterion, the regression coefficients are calculated so as to minimize the residual sum of squares. In mathematical form, this can be represented as

$$\text{Minimize:} \quad SSE = \Sigma e_i^2 = \left[\Sigma \left(y_i - \hat{Y}_i \right) \right]^2$$
$$= \Sigma \left[y_i - (b_0 + b_1 x_i) \right]^2$$

Thus, the point estimates, b_0 and b_1, *minimize the residual or error sum of squares (SSE)*. Hence, these estimates are called the *least-square estimates*.

Standard Error of Estimate

An examination of Figure 19.5 reveals that, although the least-squares regression line provides a reasonable fit of the data points, there are some deviations in the sample data about the line. An estimate of the population variation about the regression line provides a reasonable measure of goodness-of-fit of the model (called the *mean square error, MSE*) and can be calculated using the formula

$$S_{Y/X}^2 = \frac{SSE}{n-2} = \frac{\Sigma e_i^2}{n-2} = \frac{\Sigma \left(Y_i - \hat{Y}_i \right)^2}{n-2}$$

The square root of mean square error given by $s_{Y/X}$ (more commonly denoted simply as s) is called the **standard error of the estimate**. In our example, the standard error can be calculated to be 218.40.

The standard error of the estimate (s) is interpreted to mean that, for any given value of the independent variable X_i, the dependent variable tends to be distributed about the predicted value $\hat{Y}_i$, with a standard deviation equal to the standard error of the estimate. Hence, the smaller the standard error of the estimate, the better the fit. Further, the standard error of the estimate is the same for any given value of the independent variable. In other words, as the value of the independent variable X_i changes, the predicted value of $\hat{Y}_i$ will also change, but the standard deviation of the distribution of Y_i about $\hat{Y}_i$ remains a constant.

Interpretation of the Parameter Estimates

The parameter estimates have a very precise meaning. The parameter β_1 indicates that if the variable X is changed by one unit, the variable Y will change by β_1 units. Thus, if \$1 is added to the advertising budget, regardless of the level at which the budget is set, an extra β_1 customers will be expected to visit the store. Similarly, the parameter β_0 reflects the number of customers expected, on average, if no advertising is run the previous day. When understanding the phenomenon of interest is the motivation behind the data analysis, the prime interest is in b_1, the estimate of the β_1 parameter. The size of b_1 will be a reflection of the influence of advertising on store traffic.

Earlier we mentioned that the parameter estimates b_0 and b_1 vary from sample to sample. A measure of this variation of the parameter estimates is given by their standard errors. Thus, just as the sample mean, $\bar{X}$, has a standard error, which is estimated by s_x, b_0, and b_1 also each has a standard error associated with it. If the constant variance and independence assumptions of the simple linear regression model hold good, the standard error of b_1 can be shown to be

$$s_{b_1} = \frac{s}{\sqrt{\sum(x_i - \bar{x})^2}} = \sqrt{\frac{1}{n-2} * \frac{\sum\left(Y_i - \hat{Y}\right)^2}{\sum(x_i - \bar{x})^2}}$$

Similarly, the standard error of b_0 can be shown to be

$$s_{b_0} = s\sqrt{\frac{1}{n} + \frac{\bar{x}^2}{\sum(x_i - \bar{x})^2}}$$

In this example, the standard error of b_0 and b_1 can be calculated to be 100.10 and 0.21, respectively.

Testing the Significance of the Independent Variables

If β_1 is zero, there will be no effect of advertising on store traffic, and hence the model specified does not serve any purpose. Before using the model, it is useful to consider the hypothesis that β_1 is zero. If the evidence that β_1 is zero (namely, a nonzero estimate b_1) is impressive, we may want to discard the model.

As indicated previously, the estimate b_1 has a variation associated with it (measured by s_{b_1}) because it is based on a sample of stores. Thus, it could happen that b_1 is nonzero even if the parameter β_1 is zero. In fact, it would be highly likely that, even if there were no relationship between advertising (X) and store traffic (Y), any given random sample would produce a nonzero value for b_1. One way to evaluate the magnitude of b_1, taking into account its variation, is to use a statistical hypothesis test. The null hypothesis is that there is no linear relationship between the dependent and the independent variables. The hypothesis test can be represented formally as

Null hypothesis	$H_0: \beta_1 = 0$
Alternative hypothesis	$H_a: \beta_1 \neq 0$

The test statistic is given by

$$t = \frac{b_1 - \beta_1}{s_{b1}} = \frac{1.54 - 0}{.21} = 7.33$$

The calculated test statistic has a t-distribution. Hence, if we fix α as .05, the table value of t corresponding to $v = n - 2 = 18$ degrees of freedom is 2.10. Applying the rejection rule for a two-tailed test of hypothesis, we reject the null hypothesis that there is no linear relationship between the dependent and independent variables (since $t_{calc} > t_{table}$). Therefore, one can conclude that advertising expenditure affects store traffic.

In this example, the test of hypothesis resulted in the rejection of the null hypothesis. If it had resulted otherwise—that is, if the hypothesis test had failed to reject the null—this does not immediately indicate that the independent variable is not significant. It is perfectly possible that the dependent and independent variables are in fact related, albeit in a nonlinear manner. Also, before any hasty decision is made regarding the significance of the independent variable, the researcher needs to ascertain that a Type II error is not being committed.

Testing $H_0: \beta_1 = 0$ versus $H_1: \beta_1 \neq 0$ Using p-Values

The rejection rule is then: *Reject $H_0: \beta_1 = 0$ if $\alpha > p$-value*. In our case, the p-value (computed by SAS) was found to be .0001, resulting in the rejection of the null hypothesis. Hence, the smaller the p-value, the stronger is the evidence to reject H_0.

Predicting the Dependent

The regression model can also be used as a predictive tool. Given an advertising expenditure, the model will predict how much store traffic will be generated. For example, if an advertising expenditure level of $200 is proposed, a model-based estimated store traffic is

$$\hat{Y} = b_0 + b_1 X_{01} = 148.64 + (1.54 * 200) = 457$$

Two cautionary comments: *First*, prediction using extreme values of the independent variable (such as $X = 2,000$ in our example) can be risky. Recall Figure 19.3, which illustrates that the linearity assumption may be appropriate for only a limited range of the independent variables. Further, the random sample provides no information about extreme values of advertising. *Second*, if the market environment changes, such as if a competitive chain opens a series of stores, the model parameters probably will be affected. The data from the random sample were obtained under a set of environmental conditions; if they change, the model may well be affected.

How Good Is the Prediction?

A natural question is, "How well does the model predict?" Assume that we have n observed values of the dependent variable, but we do not have the n observed values of the independent variable X with which to predict Y_i. In such a case the only reasonable prediction of Y_i is

$$\bar{Y} = \frac{\sum Y_i}{n}$$

The error of prediction is then $Y_i - \bar{Y}$.

While adopting the simple linear regression model, we predict Y_i using the formula $\hat{Y}_i = b_0 + b_i x_i$. The error of prediction here is $Y_i - \hat{Y}_i$. Therefore, by using the independent variable, the error of prediction has decreased by an amount equal to

$$(Y_i - \bar{Y}) - (Y_i - \hat{Y}_i) = (\hat{Y}_i - \bar{Y})$$

It can be shown that, in general,

$$\Sigma\left(Y_i - \bar{Y}\right)^2 - \Sigma\left(Y_i - \hat{Y}_i\right)^2 = \Sigma\left(\hat{Y}_i - \bar{Y}\right)^2$$

Or by rearranging, it can be shown that the

$$\Sigma\left(Y_i - \bar{Y}\right)^2 = \Sigma\left(\hat{Y}_i - \bar{Y}\right)^2 + \Sigma\left(Y_i - \hat{Y}_i\right)^2$$

Total variation = explained variation + unexplained variation

where

Total variation (SST) = sum of squared prediction error that would be obtained if we do notuse X to predict Y.

Unexplained variation (SSE) = sum of squared prediction error that is obtained when we use X to predict Y.

Explained variation (SSM) = reduction in the sum of squared prediction errors that has been accomplished by using X in predicting Y. That is, the explained variation measures the amount of the total variation that can be explained by the simple linear regression model.

The measure of the regression model's ability to predict is called the *coefficient of determination* (r^2) and is the ratio of the explained variation to the total variation,

$$r^2 = \left(SST - SSE\right)/SST = SSM/SST$$

For our example, r^2 is equal to .74. Thus, 74 percent of the total variation of Y is explained or accounted for by X. The variation in Y was reduced by 74 percent by using X and applying the regression model.

The r^2 term is the square of the correlation between X and Y. Thus, it lies between zero and one. It is zero if there is no linear relationship between X and Y. It will be one if a plot of X and Y points generates a perfect straight line. Another way to interpret r, the sample correlation, is to interpret r^2 instead. A reduction or increase in r^2 can be interpreted as the percentage of reduction or increase in the explained variation.

So far, we have discussed the concepts and issues related to the simple linear regression model. When more than one independent variable is included in a single linear regression model, we get a **multiple linear regression** model.

Multiple Regression

Recall from our earlier discussion that the error term includes the effects on the dependent variable of variables other than the independent variable. It may be desirable to include explicitly some of these variables in the model. As predictions, their inclusion will improve the model's ability to predict and will decrease the unexplained variation; in terms of understanding, they will introduce the effect of other variables and therefore elaborate and clarify the relationships.

The general form of the multiple regression model can be expressed as

$$Y = \alpha + \beta_1 X_1 + \beta_2 X_2 + \cdots + \beta_i X_i + \varepsilon$$

where $\beta_1, \beta_2, \ldots, \beta_k$ are regression coefficients associated with the independent variables $X_1, X_2, \ldots, X_k$ and ε is the error or residual. The assumptions discussed in relation to simple linear regression apply equally to the case of multiple regression, except that instead of the one X used in the former, more than one X is used in the latter. As was the case in simple linear regression, a solution is sought for the constants (α and the β's) such that the sum of the squared errors of prediction ($\sum \varepsilon^2$) is minimized or that the prediction is optimized. It is worth noting that the equations cannot be solved if (1) the sample size, n, is smaller than or equal to the number of independent variables, k; or (2) one independent variable is correlated perfectly with another.

The prediction equation in multiple regression analysis is

$$\ddot{Y} = \alpha + b_1 X_1 + b_2 X_2 + \cdots + b_k X_k$$

where $\hat{Y}$ is the predicted Y score, and $b_1, \ldots, b_k$ are the partial regression coefficients.

To understand the meaning of a partial regression coefficient, let us consider a case in which there are two independent variables, so that

$$Y = \alpha + b_1 X_1 + b_2 X_2 + \text{error}$$

First, note that the relative magnitude of the partial regression coefficient of an independent variable is, in general, different from that of its bivariate regression coefficient. In other words, the partial regression coefficient, b_1, will be different from the regression coefficient, b_1, obtained by regressing Y on X_1 only. This happens because X_1 and X_2 usually are correlated. In bivariate regression, X_2 was not considered, and any variation in Y that was shared by X_1 and X_2 was attributed to X_1. In the case of multiple independent variables, however, this is no longer true.

The interpretation of the partial regression coefficient, b_1, is that it represents the expected change in Y when X_1 is changed by one unit, keeping X_2 constant or controlling for its effects. Similarly, b_2 represents the expected change in Y for a unit change in X_2, when X_1 is held constant. Therefore, b_1 and b_2 are called *partial regression coefficients*. It can also be seen that the combined effects of X_1 and X_2 on Y are additive. In other words, if X_1 and X_2 are each changed by one unit, the expected change in Y will be $(b_1 + b_2)$. Similar interpretation holds good for the case of k variables.

The regression coefficients will be unique to the random sample that happens to be selected. If another random sample were taken, the regression coefficients will be slightly different. This sampling variation in the regression coefficients is measured by the standard error (discussed in the previous chapter) associated with each of them. The procedure installed in most software packages calculates this standard error and provides it as one of the outputs.

Consider the following example, where a researcher did a survey of the CEOs of some small businesses to explore the firms' interest in exporting to foreign markets. The description of the variables and the associated scale values are presented in Table 19.3. Two hundred small businesses received the questionnaire, and 98 were returned. Eight instruments could not be used because of random responding and incomplete information. Of the 90 usable questionnaires (45 percent response rate), data for 60 firms were used for model estimation and the remaining 30 observations were held for model validation (discussed later in this chapter). The information obtained from the survey instrument is given in Table 19.4.

The estimated regression equation is

$$\widehat{\text{Will}} = 1.927 + .026 \text{ size (model 1)}$$

where

$$\widehat{\text{Will}} = \text{predicted value for Will}$$

Table 19.3 SPSS® Description of Variables

Variable description		Corresponding name in computer output	Scale values
Willingness to export	(Y_1)	Will	1 (definitely not interested) to 5 (definitely interested)
Level of interest in seeking government assistance	(Y_2)	Govt	1 (definitely not interested) to 5 (definitely interested)
Employee size	(X_1)	Size	Greater than zero
Firm revenue	(X_2)	Rev	In millions of dollars
Years of operation in the domestic market	(X_3)	Years	Actual number of years
Number of products currently produced by the firm	(X_4)	Prod	Actual number
Training of employees	(X_5)	Train	0 (no formal program) or 1(existence of a formal program)
Management experience in international operation	(X_6)	Exp	0 (no experience) or 1 (presence of experience)

Table 19.5 shows the results of this simple linear regression model (model 1).

The regression coefficient for size is .026 and is significant at the 10 percent level $(\alpha = .10)$. The amount of variance in "Will" explained by size is about 5.8 percent $(R^2 = .058)$. R^2 cannot decrease as more independent variables are added to the regression equation. Yet diminishing returns set in, so after the first few variables, the additional independent variables do not make much of a contribution. For this reason, R^2 is adjusted for the number of independent variables and the sample size. The adjusted R^2 (adjusted for the number of degrees of freedom) is .042 in this example and is computed from the following formula:

$$R^2 \text{ (adjusted)} = 1 - \left(1 - R^2\right)\frac{n-1}{n-k-1}$$

$$= 1 - \left(1 - .058\right)\frac{(60-1)}{(60-1-1)}$$

$$= .042$$

where

n = number of observations

k = number of parameters

Since the variation explained is low, the researcher might consider adding a few more independent variables to explain additional variation in the dependent variable. It might be that the researcher considers adding variables X_2, X_3, and X_4 to the original regression equation. The resulting model (model 2) is

$$Y = b_0 + b_1X_1 + b_2X_2 + b_3X_3 + b_4X_4 + \text{ error}$$

Table 19.4 SPSS® Export Data Set

Company	Willingness to export (Y_1)	Level of interest in seeking government assistance (Y_2)	Employee size (X_1)	Firm revenue (million) (X_2)	Years of operation in the domestic market (X_3)	Number of products (X_4)	Training of employees (X_5)	Management experience in international operations (X_6)
1	5	4	54	4.0	6.5	7	1	1
2	3	4	45	2.0	6.0	6	1	1
3	2	5	44	2.0	5.8	11	1	1
4	4	3	46	1.0	7.0	3	1	0
5	5	4	46	3.0	6.5	8	1	1
6	1	2	37	0.9	5.0	2	0	1
7	2	1	42	0.9	5.0	2	0	1
8	3	3	29	3.6	6.5	3	0	0
9	3	2	46	0.9	6.0	5	0	1
10	2	3	28	0.9	6.0	2	0	1
11	4	1	39	3.6	7.0	3	0	1
12	3	2	31	4.0	7.0	3	1	0
13	4	5	65	1.0	7.0	9	1	1
14	1	4	50	1.0	7.0	9	1	1
15	4	1	30	2.0	7.5	3	1	0
16	5	4	58	1.0	6.0	5	1	1
17	3	4	54	2.0	6.5	4	1	1
18	4	5	58	1.0	7.0	9	1	1
19	2	1	37	1.0	7.0	9	1	0
20	5	1	35	2.0	9.5	5	1	0
21	4	3	49	2.0	8.5	4	1	1
22	3	2	37	2.0	7.0	2	0	1
23	3	4	34	0.9	6.0	5	0	1
24	2	5	66	1.0	5.5	10	1	1
25	5	4	50	0.3	6.5	6	1	1
26	4	3	43	1.0	7.0	3	1	0
27	4	3	54	1.0	7.0	4	1	1
28	3	4	49	1.0	6.5	7	1	1
29	3	2	43	1.8	6.0	2	0	1
30	2	4	52	1.8	5.0	7	0	1
31	4	5	29	0.9	4.5	11	0	1
32	2	3	37	0.9	5.5	2	0	1
33	3	1	27	0.9	7.0	3	0	0
34	2	2	32	0.9	6.5	3	0	0
35	3	2	34	2.7	6.5	2	0	1
36	3	4	48	1.8	5.0	4	0	1
37	4	5	53	0.9	4.5	5	0	0
38	4	3	41	0.9	5.5	2	0	1

Table 19.4   (Continued)

Company	Willingness to export (Y₁)	Level of interest in seeking government assistance (Y₂)	Employee size (X₁)	Firm revenue (million) (X₂)	Years of operation in the domestic market (X₃)	Number of products (X₄)	Training of employees (X₅)	Management experience in international operations (X₆)
39	5	4	47	2.7	5.5	4	0	1
40	1	2	31	1.8	6.0	4	0	0
41	3	2	34	0.9	6.5	3	0	0
42	1	1	28	0.9	7.0	2	0	0
43	2	3	39	0.9	5.5	2	0	1
44	1	4	45	0.9	5.5	4	0	0
45	2	2	29	1.8	7.0	2	0	0
46	2	3	37	1.8	6.0	3	0	1
47	2	5	49	0.9	4.5	9	0	1
48	2	1	33	0.9	6.5	2	0	1
49	3	1	27	1.8	7.0	3	0	0
50	2	4	49	1.0	5.5	6	1	1
51	4	3	46	1.0	6.5	4	1	1
52	4	5	54	1.0	6.0	7	1	1
53	2	2	31	0.9	6.0	3	0	0
54	3	2	31	3.0	6.0	5	1	0
55	3	4	50	2.0	6.5	7	1	1
56	2	5	69	1.0	5.5	9	1	1
57	5	1	34	1.0	7.0	6	1	1
58	4	5	62	2.0	5.5	7	1	1
59	3	4	49	1.0	7.0	5	1	0
60	4	3	43	2.0	7.5	4	1	1

Parameter Interpretation in Multiple Regression

When the parameters of model 2 are estimated using the least-squares criterion, the result is

$$\widehat{\text{Will}} = -2.153 + 0.032 \, \text{size} + 0.344 \, \text{Rev} + 0.483 \, \text{years} + 0.042 \, \text{Prod}$$

Table 19.6 shows the results of model 2.

A major assumption of multiple regression is that the model includes all the important and relevant variables. If an important variable is omitted, the model's predictive power is reduced. Further, if the omitted variable is correlated with an included variable, the estimated coefficient of the included variable will reflect both the included variable and the omitted variable.[7] In our example, the coefficient of size in the simple linear regression model (model 1) is about 0.03, and in the multiple regression model (model 2), it remains around 0.03. This indicates that the additional variables (Rev, Years, and Prod) did not have large correlations with size and that the size coefficient remains unaffected to a large extent. From the results of model 2, one can interpret that the score on a firm's willingness to export would go up by 0.03 units for every one unit

Table 19.5   SPSS® Results of Model 1

Model: MODEL 1
Dependent variable: WILL

Analysis of variance

Source	df	Sum of squares		Mean square	F-Value	Prob > F
Model	1	4.601		4.601	3.595	0.0629
Error	58	74.248		1.280		
C total	59	78.850				
	Root MSE		1.131	R^2	0.058	
	Dep mean		3.050	Adj R^2	0.041	
	CV		37.096			

Parameter estimates

Variable	df	Parameter estimate	Standard error	t for H_0: parameter = 0	Prob > |t|	Standardized estimate
Intercept	1	1.927	0.609	3.161	0.002	0.000
Size	1	0.026	0.013	1.896	0.062	0.241

Table 19.6   SPSS® Results of Model 2

Model: MODEL 2
Dependent variable: WILL

Analysis of variance

Source	df	Sum of squares		Mean square	F-Value	Prob > F
Model	4	25.976		6.494	6.755	0.0002
Error	55	52.873		0.961		
C total	59	78.850				
	Root MSE		0.980	R^2	0.329	
	Dep mean		3.050	Adj R^2	0.280	
	CV		32.146			

Parameter estimates

Variable	df	Parameter estimate	Standard error	t for H_0: parameter = 0	Prob > |t|	Standardized estimate
Intercept	1	−2.153	1.131	−1.903	0.062	0.000
Size	1	0.032	0.014	2.215	0.030	0.298
Rev	1	0.344	0.140	2.442	0.017	0.279
Years	1	0.483	0.146	3.294	0.001	0.385
Prod	1	0.042	0.060	0.690	0.492	0.092

increase in the firm's size, keeping other variables (X_2, X_3, and X_4) at a constant/fixed value. Similar interpretations hold true for other variables.

Tests of Significance and Their Interpretations

Several tests of significance may be applied to the results of multiple regression analysis. Three of them are presented here: (1) test of R^2, (2) tests of regression coefficients, and (3) tests of increments in the proportion of variance accounted for by a given variable or a set of variables.

Test of R^2

Significance testing involves testing the significance of the overall regression equation as well as specific partial regression coefficients. The null hypothesis for the overall test is that the coefficient of multiple determination in the population, R^2_{pop}, is zero:

$$H_0: R^2_{pop} = 0$$

$$H_a: R^2_{pop} \neq 0$$

This is equivalent to the following null hypothesis:

$$H_0: \beta_1 = \beta_2 = \beta_3 = \cdots = \beta_k = 0$$
$$H_a: \text{not all } \beta's \text{ are equal to zero}$$

The overall test can be conducted by using an F-statistic:

$$F = \frac{R^2/k}{(1-R^2)(n-k-1)}$$

with k and $n-k-1$ degrees of freedom, where $k =$ number of independent variables and $n =$ sample size. For the data of Table 19.6, $R^2 = .329$, $N = 60$,

$$F = \frac{.329/4}{(1-.329)/(60-4-1)} = \frac{.0823}{.012} = 6.75$$

with 4 and 55 df, $p < .01$. The results clearly indicate that H_0 is rejected, meaning the independent variables do have a systematic association with the dependent variable in the model.

If the independent variables are statistically independent (uncorrelated), then R^2 will be the sum of bivariate r^2 of each independent variable with the dependent variable.

Test of Regression Coefficients

If the overall null hypothesis is rejected, one or more population partial regression coefficients has a value different from zero. To determine which specific coefficients (β_i's) are nonzero, additional tests are necessary. Testing for the significance of the β_i's can be done in a manner similar to that in the bivariate case, by using t-tests. The significance of the partial regression coefficient for size may be tested by the following equation:

$$t = \frac{b}{S_b}$$
$$= \frac{0.032}{0.014}$$
$$= 2.215$$

which has a t-distribution with $n-k-1$ degrees of freedom. If the significance level (α) is 0.05, then this t-value is significant. All the regression coefficients are significant at the 5 percent level, with the exception of Prod or Variable X4.

Tests of Increments in the Proportion of Variance Accounted for by Additional Variables

One of the typical questions that a manager asks is whether adding three more variables helped to explain more variation in the dependent variable. This can be learned by assessing the difference in R^2 between the larger (more variables) model and the smaller (fewer variables) model. In this example, the difference in R^2 amounts to .271 (.329 − .058), and suppose the question is: *Is this a significant difference at the 1 percent level?* One can use an F-statistic to evaluate the statistical significance of this difference:

$$F = \frac{R_l^2 - R_s^2}{1 - R_l^2} * \frac{d_l}{d_s - d_l}$$

where R_l^2 and R_s^2 are the total variance explained by the larger and smaller models and d_l and d_s are the degrees of freedom in the larger and smaller models, respectively,

$$F = \frac{(.329 - .058)}{(1 - .329)} * \frac{55}{(58 - 55)}$$
$$= 7.4$$

The table value for F at the 1 percent level of significance for 3 and 55 degrees of freedom is about 2.19. The computed F-value of 7.4 exceeds the table F-value of 2.19 (corresponding to $\alpha = .01$), and therefore the difference in R^2 is statistically significant at the 1 percent level. In other words, the larger model significantly explains more variation in the dependent variable than the smaller model.

Evaluating the Importance of Independent Variables

When regression analysis is used to gain understanding of the relationships between variables, a natural question is: *Which of the independent variables has the greatest influence on the dependent variable?* One approach is to consider the t-values for the various coefficients. The t-value, already introduced in the single-variable regression case, is used to test the hypothesis that a regression coefficient (i.e. β_1) is equal to zero and a nonzero estimate (i.e., b_1) was simply a sampling phenomenon.[8] The one with the largest t-value can be interpreted as the one that is the least likely to have a zero β parameter.

A second approach is to examine the size of the regression coefficients; however, when each independent variable is in a different unit of measurement (store size, advertising expenditures, etc.), it is difficult to compare their coefficients. One solution is to convert regression coefficients to "beta coefficients." Beta coefficients are simply the regression coefficients multiplied by the ratio of the standard deviations of the corresponding independent variable to the dependent variable.

$$\text{Standardized } \beta_i = b_i \left(\frac{\text{standard deviation of } X_i}{\text{standard deviation of } Y} \right)$$

The beta coefficients can be compared to each other: The larger the beta coefficient is, the stronger is the impact of that variable on the dependent variable. The beta coefficients are the partial regression coefficients obtained when all the variables $(Y, X_1, X_2, \ldots X_k)$ have been standardized to a mean of zero and a variance of one before estimating the regression equation. In Table 19.6, an analysis of the beta coefficients indicates that years (0.385) and firm size (0.298) have the most explanatory power, the same conclusion that the analysis of t-values showed. Comparing the unstandardized b directly does not achieve this result because of the different units and degrees of variability of the X variables. The regression equation itself should be reported for future use in terms of the unstandardized coefficients, so that prediction can be made directly from the raw X values.

The manager is quite excited about the ability to explain more variation in model 2 with the addition of some variables. In the interest of explaining some more variation, the manager adds the two remaining variables (X_5 and X_6) to the equation and then estimates the model (model 3). Table 19.7 shows the results of the OLS estimation of the model with all the six predictor variables.

An important thing to note in the latest results (model 3) is that the coefficient values of some predictor variables in model 2 have changed in model 3, and so have their levels of significance. This change of value can occur due to *multicollinearity*, which represents the correlations among the predictor variables. The problem of multicollinearity cannot be viewed as dichotomous (no or yes), but should be viewed as the degree of multicollinearity (in a continuous form). Since the two new variables, Train and Exp, are highly correlated with Size and Years (in the range of 0.4 to 0.5, obtained through computing correlation coefficients), the variation to be explained in the dependent variable probably is shared by all the correlated variables, resulting in changed

Table 19.7   SPSS® Results of Model 3

Model: MODEL 3
Dependent variable: WILL

Analysis of variance

Source	df	Sum of squares		Mean square	F-Value	Prob > F
Model	6	27.652		4.608	4.771	0.0006
Error	53	51.197		0.966		
C total	59	78.850				
	Root MSE		0.982	R^2	0.350	
	Dep mean		3.050	Adj R^2	0.277	
	CV		32.224			

Parameter estimates

Variable	df	Parameter estimate	Standard error	t for H_0: parameter = 0	Prob > |t|	Standardized estimate
Intercept	1	−1.824	1.578	−1.156	0.252	0.000
Size	1	0.019	0.018	1.062	0.293	0.181
Rev	1	0.344	0.155	2.220	0.030	0.257
Years	1	0.474	0.193	2.450	0.017	0.377
Prod	1	0.027	0.067	0.400	0.690	0.059
Train	1	0.216	0.417	0.518	0.606	0.094
Exp	1	0.409	0.328	1.248	0.217	0.166

coefficients, inflated standard errors, and lack of statistical significance for some of the variables in the model.

One simple way to check for multicollinearity is to examine the correlations among the X variables. If, for example, X_1 and X_2 are highly correlated (say greater than .95), then it may be simpler to use only one of them, inasmuch as one variable conveys essentially all of the information the other contains. In the current example, the coefficient for Size changed from 0.032 to 0.019 and, further, the significance level changed from 0.03 to 0.29 when variables X_5 and X_6 were added. If one comes to the conclusion that size is not an important predictor, one is wrong. Therefore, it is always necessary to check for multicollinearity in multiple regression analysis. The R^2 for this full model is .35, which is larger than the model with four predictors ($R^2 = .329$); however, the adjusted R^2 for the full model (.277) is less than that for the four-predictor model (.28). This implies that the addition of the two remaining variables did not add much to explaining the variation in "willingness to export."

One can also use *stepwise regression* to select, from a large number of predictor variables, a small subset of variables that account for most of the variation in the dependent or criterion variable. Here, the predictor variables enter or are removed from the regression equation one at a time. There are several approaches to stepwise regression.

> *Forward addition.* To start with, there are no predictor variables in the regression equation. Predictor variables are entered one at a time, only if they meet certain criteria specified in terms of F-ratio. The order in which the variables are included in the model depends on the contribution to the explained variation.

> *Backward elimination.* At the beginning, all the predictor variables are included in the regression equation. Predictors are then removed one at a time based on the F-ratio for removal.

> *Stepwise method.* The forward addition is combined with the removal of predictors that no longer meet the specified criterion at each step.

Interactions

Another issue in model fitting is to determine whether the X variables interact. If the effects of two variables X_1 and X_2 are *not* interactive, then they appear as $b_1 x_1 + b_2 x_2$ in the regression equation. In this case the effects of the *two* variables are said to be *additive*. On the contrary, if the effect of X_2 on Y depends on the level of X_1, then interaction of X_1 and X_2 is said to be present. This phenomenon can be observed in many situations. For example, the influence of shelf displays on product sales could depend on the price-reduction level. A commonly used practice is to add the product $X_1 X_2$ to the set of X variables to represent the interaction between X_1 and X_2. The model is

$$y = b_0 + b_1 x_1 + b_2 x_2 + b_3 x_1 x_2 + \text{error}$$

Analyzing Residuals

While high R^2 and significant partial regression coefficients are comforting, the efficacy of the regression model should be evaluated further by an examination of the residuals.

A *residual* is the difference between the observed value of Y_i and the value predicted ($\hat{Y}_i$) by the regression equation. Residuals are used in the calculation of several statistics associated with regression. In addition, scattergrams of the residuals, in which the residuals are plotted against the predicted values, $\hat{Y}_i$, time, or predictor variables, provide useful insights in examining the appropriateness of the underlying assumptions and the regression model fitted. Figure 19.6 provides illustrations of four plots (a through d) of residual analysis.

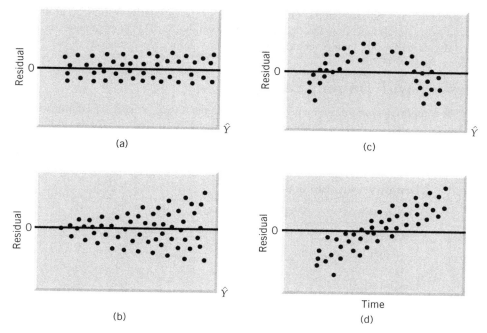

FIGURE 19.6
Residual Plots Showing Different Levels of Error Variance.

Figure 19.6a shows that the residuals are distributed randomly when plotted against the predicted value of Y, indicating no major violation of the assumption of constant variance. However, in Figure 19.6b, the residuals show an increasing pattern, with increasing values of $\hat{Y}$ indicating a nonconstant error variance. This problem is referred to as *heteroskedasticity*. A weighted least-squares procedure can be used to correct for this problem when estimating the parameters of the regression model. Figure 19.6c shows a nonlinear pattern of residuals, with $\hat{Y}_i$ indicating that possibly some nonlinear terms (basically nonlinear in variables such as X_1^2) should be included in the model. Finally, in Figure 19.6d, the plot of residuals with time shows a trend indicating the violation of independence of error/residual terms. This problem is referred to as *autocorrelation* and can be corrected for by using procedures such as the Cochrane–Orcutt procedure.

Predictive Validity

All multivariate procedures tend to capitalize on chance variations in the data. This could result in a model that is unduly sensitive to the specific data used to estimate the model. *Predictive validity* examines whether any model that is estimated with one set of data continues to hold good on comparable data that are not used in the estimation. Predictive validity can be assessed in many ways. The three most commonly used methods are as follows.

1. The data are split into the *estimation sample* and the *validation sample*. The estimation sample contains more than half of the total sample, and the coefficients from the two samples are compared.

2. The coefficients from the estimated model are applied to the data in the validation sample to predict the values of the dependent variable Y_i in the validation sample, and then the model fit is assessed.

3. The sample is split into halves. One half serves as the estimation sample, and the other is used as a validation sample in conducting cross-validation. The roles of the estimation and validation halves are then reversed, and the cross-validation is repeated.

Regression with Dummy Variables[9]

Nominal or categorical variables may be used as predictors if they are coded as dummy variables. The concept of *dummy variables* was introduced in Chapter 16. In that chapter, we explained how a categorical variable with four categories can be coded in terms of three dummy variables, D_1, D_2, and D_3, as shown:

Dummy-variable coding

Consumer types	Original variable code	D_1	D_2	D_3
Brand loyalty	1	1	0	0
Variety seeker	2	0	1	0
Impulse buyer	3	0	0	1
Rational buyer	4	0	0	0

Assume that the researcher is interested in running a regression analysis of the effect of consumer types on coupon redemption. The dummy variables D_1, D_2, and D_3 can be used as predictors. A *regression with dummy variables* would then be

$$Y_i = a + b_1D_1 + b_2D_2 + b_3D_3 + \text{ error}$$

Here the "rational buyer" has been chosen as the base level and has not been included directly in the regression equation. However, for the rational buyer group, D_1, D_2, and D_3 assume a value of 0, and the regression equation becomes

$$\hat{Y}_i = a$$

For brand-loyal consumers, $D_1 = 1$, and $D_2 = D_3 = 0$, and the regression equation becomes

$$\hat{Y}_i = a + b_1$$

Thus, the coefficient b_1 is the difference in predicted Y_i for brand-loyal as compared to rational buyers. The coefficients b_2 and b_3 have similar interpretations. The concept of dummy variable regression analysis is widespread in the use of another multivariate technique, conjoint analysis (see Chapter 22).

SUMMARY

In this chapter, we discussed two of the more commonly used data analysis techniques in business research: correlation analysis and regression analysis.

Correlation analysis involves measuring the strength of the relationship between two or more variables. Regression analysis is used (1) to predict the dependent variable, given knowledge of independent variables, and (2) to gain an understanding of the relationship between the dependent variable and independent variables.

Applications. Regression analysis is used (1) to predict the dependent variable, given knowledge of independent variable values, and (2) to gain an understanding of the relationship between the dependent variable and independent variables.

Inputs. The model inputs required are the variable values for the dependent variable and the independent variables.

Outputs. The regression model will output regression coefficients—and their associated beta coefficient and t-values—which can be used to evaluate the strength of the relationship between the respective independent variable and the dependent variable. The model automatically controls statistically for the other independent variables. Thus, a regression coefficient represents the effect of one independent variable when the other independent variables are held constant. Another output is the R^2 value, which provides a measure of the predictive ability of the model.

Statistical Tests. The hypothesis that a regression parameter obtained from the sample evidence is zero or not is based on the t-value.

Assumptions. The most important assumption is that the selected independent variables do, in fact, explain or predict the dependent variable and that no important variables have been omitted. In creating and evaluating regression models, the following questions are appropriate: Do these independent variables influence the dependent variable? Do any lack logical justification for being in the model? Are any variables omitted that logically should be in the model? A second assumption is that the relationship between the independent variables and the dependent variable is linear and additive. A third assumption is that there is a "random" error term that absorbs the effects of measurement error and the influences of variables not included in the regression equation.

Limitations. First, a knowledge of a regression coefficient and its t-value can suggest the extent of association or influence that an independent variable has on the dependent variable. However, if an omitted variable is correlated with the independent variable, the regression coefficient will reflect the impact of the omitted variables on the dependent variables. A second limitation is that the model is based on collected data that represent certain environmental conditions. If those conditions change, the model may no longer reflect the current situations and can lead to erroneous judgments. Third, the ability of the model to predict, as reflected by R^2, can become significantly reduced if the prediction is based on values of the independent variables that are extreme in comparison to the independent variable values used to estimate the model parameters. Fourth, the model is limited by the methodology associated with the data collection, including the sample size and measures used.

QUESTIONS AND PROBLEMS

19.1 A random sample of eight introductory marketing texts yielded the figures shown in the table for annual sales (in thousands) and price (in dollars):

Sales	12.2	18.6	29.2	15.7	25.4	35.2	14.7	11.1
Price	29.2	30.5	29.7	31.3	30.8	29.9	27.8	27.0

(a) Determine the sample correlation between sales and price.

(b) Test at the 5 percent level that the population correlation coefficient is zero.

19.2 A college administers a student evaluation questionnaire for all its courses. For a random sample of 12 courses, the accompanying table shows both the instructor's average student ratings (on a scale from 1 to 5) and the average grades that the students expected (on a scale from $A = 4$ to $E = 0$).

Instructor rating	2.8	3.7	4.4	3.6	4.7	3.5
Expected grade	2.6	2.9	3.3	3.2	3.1	2.8
Instructor rating	4.1	3.2	4.9	4.2	3.8	3.3
Expected grade	2.7	2.4	3.5	3.0	3.4	2.5

(a) Find the sample correlation between the instructor ratings and expected grades.

(b) At the 10 percent significance level, test the hypothesis that the population correlation coefficient is zero against the alternative that it is positive.

19.3 Some regression models are used to predict, some to gain understanding, and some to do both. Consider a product manager for Betty Crocker cake mix: Give an example of each of the three types of models in the context of this product manager.

19.4 If an estimated regression model $\hat{Y} = a + bX$ yielded an r^2 of .64, we could say (choose one):

(a) 64 percent of the variation in the dependent variable was explained by the independent variable.

(b) The sample correlation between Y and X was 0.80.

(c) 64 percent of the data points lie on the regression line.

(d) a and b only.

(e) None of the above.

19.5 A company sets different prices for a pool table in eight different regions of the country. The accompanying table shows the numbers of units sold and the corresponding prices (in hundreds of dollars).

Sales	420	380	350	400	440	380	450	420
Price	5.5	6.0	6.5	6.0	5.0	6.5	4.5	5.0

(a) Plot these data, and estimate the linear regression of sales on price.

(b) What effect would you expect a $150 increase in price to have on sales?

19.6 An attempt was made to evaluate the forward rate as a predictor of the spot rate in the Spanish trea-sury bill market. For a sample of 79 quarterly observations, the estimated linear regression,

$$\hat{Y} = .00027 + .7916x$$

was obtained,

where

$\hat{Y}$ = actual change in the spot rate

x = change in the spot rate predicted by the forward rate

The coefficient of determination was .1, and the estimated standard deviation of the estimator of the slope of the population regression line was .27.

(a) Interpret the slope of the estimated regression line.

(b) Interpret the coefficient of determination.

(c) Test the null hypothesis that the slope of the population regression line is zero against the alternative that the true slope is positive, and interpret your result.

(d) Test the null hypothesis that the slope of the population regression line is one, and interpret your result.

19.7 An analyst for an oil company has developed a formal linear regression model to predict the sales of 50 of their filling stations. The estimated model is

$$\hat{Y} = b_0 + b_1 X_1$$

where

$\hat{Y}$ = average monthly sales in gallons

X = square foot area of station property

$X_1 = X - \bar{X}$ (difference from the mean)

Some empirical results were

Variable	Mean	Range of data	Reg. coefficient	t-Value	t^2
Y		5,000–80,000 gal	$b_0 = 10,000$		
X	10,000	3,000–20,000 sq ft	$b_1 = 3.1$	2	.3

(a) What does r^2 mean?

(b) Interpret the parameter estimates b_0 and b_1.

(c) Is the X_1 variable significant? At what level?

(d) A new station is proposed with 30,000 sq. ft. What would you predict sales to be? What assumptions underlie the estimate?

19.8 Consider the problem of predicting sales for each store in a chain of 220 bookstores. The model will have two functions. First, it will be used to generate norms that will be used to evaluate store managers. Second, it will be used to evaluate new site locations. What independent variables would you include in the model? How would you measure them?

19.9 The following table represents two other regression analyses completed in the HMO study. The dependent value of the first is the respondent's overall evaluation of the proposed HMO. The independent variables were the response to the question: "How satisfactory does this plan appear to you with respect to the following factors?" The scale was 1 to 5. The second analysis was the same, except the focus was on the respondent's present plan instead of the HMO. Provide an interpretation of the results. What does a beta coefficient of .18 for the first variable mean? Interpret the table footnote. What do the two regressions show? What are the management implications?

Independent variables	Proposed HMO beta coefficient	Respondent's present plan beta coefficient
Ability to choose doctor	.18[a]	.02
Coverage provided	.21[a]	.45[a]
Distance to doctor or hospital	.12[a]	.01
Participation	.13[a]	.08[a]
Efficiency in operations	−.03	.15[a]
Quality of care	.28[a]	.17[a]
Personal attention	.04	.09[a]
r^2	.38	.47
Dependent variable	Overall evaluation of proposed HMO	Overall evaluation of respondent's present plan

[a] Significant at the .01 level.

19.10 Refer to Question 7. If two additional variables are now added to the model in that question, then

$$\hat{Y} = b_0 + b_1 X_1 + b_2 X_2 + b_3 X_3$$

where

$X_2 =$ average daily traffic flow, cars

$X_3 =$ number of competing filling stations

The empirical results now are

Variable	Variable mean	Variable range	Regression coefficient	t-Value
Y	10,000			
X	10,000	3,000–20,000	$b_1 = 4.0$	1.3
X_2	6,000	2,500–12,500	$b_2 = 4.0$	1.0
X_3	12	0–25	$b_3 = 21,000$	1.0
$r^2 = .45$			$b_0 = 10,000$	

(a) Which independent variable seems now to be the most significant predictor?

(b) Are X_1, X_2, and X_3 significant at the .05 level?

(c) How might you explain why b_1 is now larger?

(d) Interpret b_2.

(e) Provide a prediction of sales given the following inputs:

$$X_1 = 5,000$$
$$X_2 = 2,000$$
$$X_3 = 0$$

How might you qualify that prediction? What model assumptions may be violated?

(f) A skeptic in upper management claims that your model is lousy and cites as evidence a station in Crosby, North Dakota, where

$$X_1 = 5,000$$
$$X_2 = 2,000$$
$$X_3 = 0$$

Yet sales are 50,000, which is far more than predicted by the model. How would you answer this attack?

19.11 The following regression model was estimated to explain the annual sales from a direct marketing campaign:

$$S_t = 55 + 1.5P_t + 6.0M_t + 0.25C_t, \quad R^2 = 0.92$$
$$(2.1) \quad (0.5) \quad (0.55)$$

where

$S_t = \$$ sales in year t

$P_t = \$$ promotional expenditure in year t

$M_t = \$$ product mailing expenditures in year t

$C_t =$ Number of pamphlets distributed in year t

The estimated standard errors are given (in parentheses) corresponding to the coefficient estimates. The marketing director suggests that we should increase our mailing expenditures next year by sending more shipments first class, rather than via parcel post, since the mailing expenditure coefficient is "significant" in the regression. What would you advise?

END NOTES

1. Recollect that the sample standard deviation is obtained using the formula

$$S_x = \sqrt{\frac{\Sigma(X_i - \bar{X})^2}{n-1}}$$

2. See G. A. Churchill, Jr., *Marketing Research: Methodological Foundations*, 5th ed., Orlando, FL: Dryden, 1991, pp. 824–825.

3. A measure of correlation that is not susceptible to serious influence by extreme values and on which valid tests can be based for very general population distributions is obtained through the use of ranks. The ranks of x_i and y_i are used to compute the Spearman rank correlation (r_s), given by

$$r_s = 1 - \left[\frac{6\Sigma d^2}{n(n^2 - 1)} \right]$$

where

$d =$ difference in ranks

$n =$ sample size

4. For a more detailed and comprehensive discussion on regression, see B. L. Bowerman and R. T. O'Connell, *Linear Statistical Models: An Applied Approach*, Boston: PWS-Kent, 1990; or D. G. Kleinbaum, L. L. Kupper, and K. E. Muller, *Applied Regression Analysis and Other Multivariable Methods*, Boston: PWS-Kent, 1988; or any other advanced applied statistical textbook.

5. Further, a simple transformation of the independent variable can change some types of nonlinear relationships into linear ones. For example, instead of advertising, we might replace the advertising term with the logarithm of advertising. The result would be a model such as

$$Y_i = \beta_0 + \beta_1 \log X_i + \varepsilon_i$$

6. Violation of these assumptions can cause serious problems in applying and interpreting the regression model. For a more detailed discussion of the regression assumptions and remedies for violations of model assumptions, see Kmenta, *Elements of Econometrics*, 2nd ed., New York: Macmillan, 1986.

7. Recall the assumption that the error term is not correlated with the independent variables. If the error term includes an omitted variable that is correlated with an independent variable, this assumption will not hold.

8. Three qualifications. First, like any hypothesis test, the t-test is sensitive to the sample size. A small but nonzero regression parameter (i.e., β_1) can generate a low "p-level" if the sample size is large enough (and therefore s_b is small enough). Second, if the independent variables are intercorrelated (multicollinearity exists), the model will have a difficult time ascertaining which independent variable is influencing the dependent variable, and small t-values will emerge (the s_b terms will get large). Thus, small t-values can be caused by intercorrelated independent variables. Third, in addition to testing each independent variable using the t-test, it is possible to test (using an F-test) the hypothesis that all regression parameters are simultaneously zero. If such a hypothesis is not "passed," the entire model might be dismissed.

9. Adapted from N. K. Malhotra, *Marketing Research*, Upper Saddle River, NJ: Prentice-Hall, 1993; and V. Kumar, A. Ghosh, and G. Tellis, "A Decomposition of Repeat Buying," *Marketing Letters*, 3(4), 1992, pp. 407–417.

Case 19-1 | **The Seafood Grotto**

A study involving 158 families, selected randomly from a large New England city, was designed to help The Seafood Grotto, operators of several fine seafood restaurants, to determine who their customers were. Four segmentation variables were explored: age, income, social class, and life-cycle stage. Social class was determined using Warner's Index of Status Characteristics, which uses the variables of occupation, income source, house type, and dwelling area. Life cycle was based on four categories: under 40 without children, under 40 with children, 40 and over with children in the household, and 40 and over without children in the household.

Each segmentation variable was correlated with frequency-of-use descriptions of various entertainment activities, ranging from about once a year to more than once a week, and

Table 19.8 Correlation Coefficients for the Use/Nonuse and Frequency of Use of an Entertainment Activity

Entertainment activity	Use/nonuse				Frequency of use			
	Income	Social class	Age	Life cycle	Income	Social class	Age	Life cycle
Bowl	−.08	−.15[b]	.28[a]	.38[a]	.12	−.04	.35	.25[b]
Movies	.25[b]	.01	.38[a]	.46[a]	−.14	.35[a]	−.44[b]	−.49[a]
Ski	.18[b]	−.02	.27[a]	.36[a]	−.05	−.25[b]	−.08	−.07
Golf	.43[a]	.06	−.08	.04	.06	.32	.15	.15
In-state travel	−.20[a]	−.02	.26[a]	.25[a]	.09	.06	.14	.05
Out-of-state travel	−.24[b]	.10	−.07	.06	.13	−.05	−.03	−.07
Foreign travel	.14	.09	−.01	.01	—[c]	—[c]	—[c]	—[c]
Dine at expensive restaurant	.27[a]	.02	.08	.17[b]	.12	.23[a]	.13	.17[b]
Dine at moderately priced restaurant	−.22[a]	−.03	.17[b]	.20[a]	.19[b]	−.12	.17[b]	.08
Dine at inexpensive restaurant	−.14	−.16[b]	.25[b]	.31[a]	.10	−.25[a]	−.07	−.07
Nightclubs	.12	.08	.32[a]	.41[a]	.28[a]	.11	−.42[a]	−.34[a]
Cocktail parties	−.23[a]	.03	.03	.16[b]	.15	−.02	.05	.01
Professional athletic events	−.32[a]	.01	.21	.33[a]	−.13	.07	−.09	−.12
College/high school athletic events	−.25[a]	−.06	.11	.17[b]	.35[a]	.23[b]	−.12	−.22[b]

[a]Significant at 0.1 level or better.
[b]Significant at .05 level or better.
[c]Foreign travel was excluded from this part of the analysis because it rarely occurs more than once a year.

with a variable that simply noted whether the selected entertainment activities were used during the past year. Using Table 19.8, answer the following questions.

Source: Prepared by R. D. Histrich, M. P. Peters, and D. A. Aaker as a basis for class discussion.

Questions for Discussion

1. Can you say which segmentation variable is the most relevant for expensive restaurants?

2. Looking at the data across activities, which variables are the most relevant?

3. Explain the statistical test that is reported.

Case 19-2 | Election Research, Inc.

Election Research, a marketing research firm specializing in political campaigns, did an analysis on the 1996 California state legislature elections. Data were obtained for 72 districts and included the total number of registered voters by district, their party affiliation, the number of votes received by each candidate, the campaign expenditures of each candidate, and the identity of the incumbent, if one existed.

Of the 72 districts used, 27 had Republican winners and 45 had Democratic winners. There were 55 incumbent winners and 17 nonincumbent winners. The winners received an average of 66.6 percent of the votes cast and incurred 63.2 percent of the advertising expenses. The winner's advertising expenditure averaged $18,031 per district ($22,805 without an incumbent and $10,710 with an incumbent).

The following are the results of three regression runs (the numbers in parentheses are the *t*-values):

All districts:

$$WSV = 0.240 + 0.174WSTE\,(4.82) + 0.414WSRV\,(4.60)$$
$$+ 0.751\,(7.01)$$
$$r^2 = .535$$
$$N = 72$$

Incumbent districts:

$$WSV = 0.329 + 0.157WSTE\,(3.67) + 0.409WSRV\,(6.07)$$
$$r^2 = .440$$
$$N = .55$$

Nonincumbent districts:

$$WSV = 0.212 + 0.234WSTE\,(3.39) + 0.399WSRV\,(3.21)$$
$$r^2 = .615$$
$$N = 17$$

where

WSV = winner's share of total votes cast

$WSTE$ = winner's share of total advertising expenditures

$WSRV$ = proportion of registered voters that are registered to the winner's political party

I = winner's incumbency dummy variable. A dummy variable is a 0–1 variable. In this case $I = 1$ for an incumbent district and $I = 0$ for a nonincumbent district.

Questions for Discussion

1. Interpret the regression coefficients. For all districts, what exactly does the coefficient 0.174 mean? Interpret the coefficients 0.414 and 0.75 as well. Why is the coefficient for the *WSTE* variable different in the three equations?

2. Explain exactly what the *t*-value means. Determine the *p*-value associated with each. Interpret r^2. Why is r^2 different for each equation?

3. Why does the incumbency dummy variable appear only in the first equation?

4. Could this model be used productively to predict? What insights could a candidate get from the model?

Source: Prepared by S. Vitell and D. A. Aaker of the University of California at Berkeley as the basis for class discussion.

Additional Case for this Chapter is available on the Web:

Web Case 19-1 | Ajax Advertising Agency

20 Discriminant, Factor, and Cluster Analysis

LEARNING OBJECTIVES

- Discuss the concept of discriminant analysis.
- Discuss the concept of multiple discriminant analysis.
- Discuss how to interpret the results of the discriminant and multiple discriminant analysis techniques.
- Discuss the concept of factor and cluster analyses.
- Describe business applications of factor analysis.
- Discuss the potential limitations (through violations of the assumptions) of the factor analysis technique.
- Describe business applications of cluster analysis.
- Discuss the potential limitations (through violations of the assumptions) of the cluster analysis technique.

Discriminant Analysis

Discriminant analysis techniques are used to classify individuals into one of two or more alternative groups (or populations) on the basis of a set of measurements. It is used to identify variables that discriminate between two or more naturally occurring groups. For example, an educational researcher may want to identify variables that discriminate between high school graduates who decide (1) to go to college, (2) to attend a trade or professional school, or (3) to seek immediate careers rather than continuing their education. The researcher would collect relevant data before the students graduate and then use *discriminant analysis* to identify variables that predict the students' next step. Discriminant analysis also has numerous applications in the business world. It is a valuable intelligence tool that helps managers in business decision making. The populations are known to be distinct, and each individual belongs to one of them. These techniques also can be used to identify which variables contribute to making the classification. Thus, prediction and description, as in regression analysis, are the two major uses of discriminant analysis.

As an example, consider a mortgage company loan officer who wishes to decide whether to approve an applicant's mortgage loan. This decision is made by determining whether the applicant's characteristics are more like those of persons in the past who repaid loans successfully than like those of persons who defaulted. Information on these two groups, available from past records, would include factors such as age, income, marital status, outstanding debt, and ownership of certain durable goods. Similarly, a researcher interested in business failures may be able to group firms according to whether they eventually failed or did not fail, on the basis of independent variables such as location, financial ratios, or management changes. The challenge is to find the discriminating variables to use in a predictive equation that will produce better-than-chance assignment of the individuals to the two groups.

Objectives

Discriminant analysis has four major objectives[1]:

- Determining linear combinations of the predictor variables to separate the groups by maximizing between-group variation relative to within-group variation (objects in different groups are maximally separated).

- Developing procedures for assigning new objects, firms, or individuals, whose profiles but not group identity are known, to one of the two groups.

- Testing whether significant differences exist between the two groups, based on the group centroids.

- Determining which variables count most in explaining intergroup differences.

Basic Concept

Suppose that an individual may belong to one of two populations. We begin by considering how individuals can be classified into one of these populations on the basis of a measurement of one characteristic—say, X. Suppose that we have a representative sample from each population, enabling us to estimate the distribution of X and the means. Typically, these distributions can be represented as shown in Figure 20.1.

From the figure, it is intuitively obvious that a low value of X will lead us to classify an individual into population II, and a high value will lead us to classify an individual into population I. To define what is meant by *low* or *high*, we must select a dividing point. If we denote this dividing

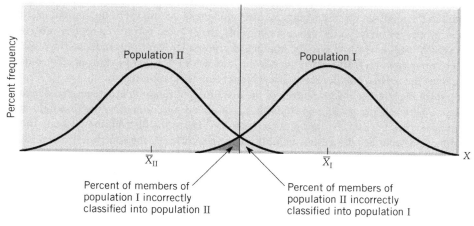

FIGURE 20.1
Distribution of Two Populations.

point by C, then we can classify an individual into population I if $X > C$. For any given value of C, we incur a certain percentage of error. If the individual came from population I but the measured X were less than C, we would incorrectly classify the individual into population II, and vice versa. These two types of errors are illustrated in Figure 20.1. If we can assume that the two populations have the same variance, then the usual value of C is

$$C = \frac{\bar{X}_I + \bar{X}_{II}}{2}$$

where $\bar{X}_I$ and $\bar{X}_{II}$ are the mean values for the two groups, respectively. This value ensures that the two probabilities of error are equal. In actual applications, a researcher is faced with more than one predictor variable and therefore needs to develop a linear combination of the predictor variables.

Methodology

Discriminant analysis involves deriving the linear combination of the two (or more) independent variables that will discriminate best between the a priori defined groups. This is achieved by the statistical criteria of maximizing the between-group variance relative to the within-group variance. The linear combination (known as the discriminant function or axis) for a discriminant analysis is derived from an equation that takes the form

$$Z = b_1 X_1 + b_2 X_2 + b_3 X_3 + \ldots + b_n X_n$$

where

Z = discriminant score
b = discriminant weights
X = predictor (independent) variables

Discriminant analysis (and ANOVA) are the appropriate statistical techniques for testing the hypotheses that the group means of two or more groups are equal. In discriminant analysis, one multiplies each independent variable by its corresponding weight and adds these products together (see the preceding equation). The result is a single composite discriminant score for each individual in the analysis. By averaging the discriminant scores for all of the individuals within a particular group, we arrive at the group mean. This group mean is referred to as a **centroid**. The number of centroids corresponds to the number of groups. The centroids indicate the most typical location of an individual from a particular group, and a comparison of the group centroids shows how far apart the groups are along the discriminant function being tested.

The test for the statistical significance of the discriminant function is a generalized measure of the distance between the group centroids. It is computed by comparing the distribution of the discriminant scores for two or more groups. If the overlap in the distribution is small, the discriminant function separates the groups well; if the overlap is large, the function is a poor discriminator between the groups.

Figure 20.2 is a scatter diagram and projection that shows what happens when a two-group discriminant function is computed. Let's assume that we have two groups, A and B, and two measurements, X_1 and X_2, on each member of the two groups. We can plot in a scatter diagram the association of variable X_1 with variable X_2 for each member of the two groups. Group membership is identified by the use of large dots and small dots. In Figure 20.2, the small dots represent the variable measurements for the members of group B, and the large dots represent the variable measurements for group A. The ellipses around the large and small dots would enclose

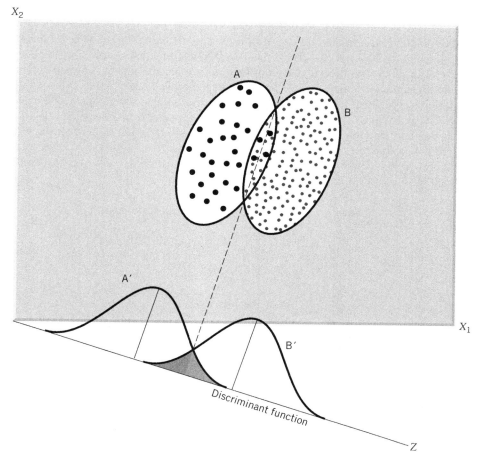

X_2

A

B

A'

B'

X_1

Discriminant function

Z

FIGURE 20.2
A Graphical Illustration.

some prespecified proportion of the points, usually 95 percent or more in each group. If we draw a straight line through the two points where the ellipses intersect and then project the line to a new Z-axis, we can say that the overlap between the univariate distributions A' and B' (represented by the shaded area) is smaller than would be obtained by any other line drawn through the ellipses formed by the scatter plots.[2]

The important thing to note about Figure 20.2 is that the Z-axis expresses the two-variable profiles of groups A and B as single numbers (discriminant scores). By finding a linear combination of the original variables X_1 and X_2, we can project the result as a discriminant function. For example, if the dots and circles are projected onto the new Z-axis as discriminant Z-scores, the result condenses the information about group differences (shown in the X_1X_2 plot) into a set of points (Z-scores) on a single axis. The mean value for the discriminant Z-scores for a particular category or group is the *centroid*. A two-group discriminant analysis has two centroids, one for each of the groups. When the analysis involves two groups, the percentage of cases classified correctly (the *hit ratio*) is determined by computing a single cutoff score. Those entities whose Z-scores are below this score are assigned to one group, while those whose scores are above it are classified in the other group.

Group Assignment

The effects of equal and unequal sample sizes on the classification rule can be better understood by examining Figures 20.3 and 20.4. The critical cutoff point for equal sample sizes in each group is shown in Figure 20.3. The effect of one group being larger than the other is shown in Figure 20.4. Figure 20.4 illustrates both the weighted and unweighted critical cutoff points. The *cutoff score* is the criterion (score) against which each individual's discriminant score is judged to determine into which group the individual should be classified. It is apparent from Figure 20.4 that if group A is much smaller than group B, the optimal cutoff score will be closer to the centroid of group A than to the centroid of group B. Note also that if the difference in sample sizes is ignored, then use of the unweighted cutoff point results in perfect classification in one group (group B), but substantially misclassifies members of the other group (group A).

For equal group sizes	For unequal group sizes
$Z_{cutoff} = \dfrac{\bar{Z}_A + \bar{Z}_B}{2}$	$Z_{cutoff} = \dfrac{n_B \bar{Z}_A + n_A \bar{Z}_B}{n_A + n_B}$

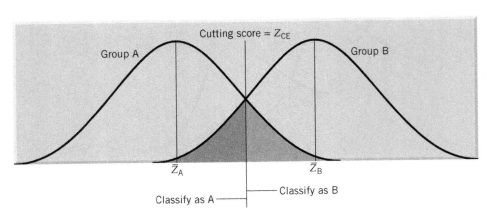

FIGURE 20.3
Equal Group Sizes.

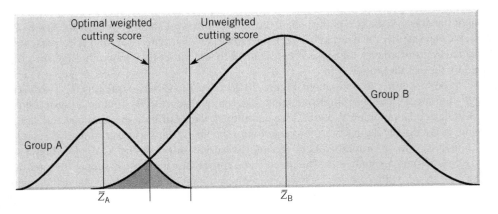

FIGURE 20.4
Unequal Group Sizes.

Comparing Regression and Discriminant Analysis

First, recall that in regression analysis the assumption is that the dependent variable Y is normally distributed and the independent variables are fixed. In discriminant analysis, the situation is reversed: the independent variables are assumed to be normally distributed, and the dependent (i.e., grouping) variable is fixed, with values of zero or one. Second, the objective of regression analysis is to predict the mean population value of the dependent variable on the basis of the known and fixed values of the independent variables. In contrast, the objective in discriminant analysis is to find a linear combination of the independent variables that maximizes the discrimination between the two groups and minimizes the probability of misclassifying individuals or objects into their respective groups. In **regression analysis**, certain assumptions are made in order to generate parameter estimates that have desirable statistical properties. **Discriminant analysis** invokes a strategy for finding a means of accurately classifying individuals or objects into groups. Thus, these two techniques, though computationally similar, are conceptually different.

Application

In the export data set (see Chapter 19, Tables 19.3 and 19.4), one can create a nonmetric or categorical dependent variable by rescaling the "willingness to export" (Y_1) variable. A new variable "export interest" (EI) can be formed from the original (Y_1) variable. In other words, the EI variable will assume a value of 2 if one includes all the companies that responded with a value of 4 or 5 on the "willingness to export" scale. The EI variable will assume a value of 1 if one includes all the companies that responded with a value less than or equal to 3 on the "willingness to export" scale. Now that the two groups with export interest = high (2) and export interest = low (1) have been formed, one can perform the discriminant analysis. The independent variables for the discriminant analysis are the workforce size (X_2), the firm's revenues (X_4), its years of operation in the domestic market (X_5), and number of products currently produced by the firm (X_6). With two ($m = 2$) levels for the dependent variable and four ($p = 4$) independent variables, the number of discriminant functions that can be generated is given by the minimum of the number of levels in the dependent variable minus one and the number of predictor variables [denoted by $\text{Min}(m - 1, p)$], which is one in this example.

Estimation

The *direct method* involves estimating the discriminant function so that all the predictors are included simultaneously. In this case, each independent variable is included, regardless of its discriminating power. This method is appropriate when the researcher has a priori reasons for the discrimination to be based on all the predictors. The parameters of the discriminant function are estimated subject to maximizing the between-group variation relative to the within-group variation. In other words, the discriminant weights are described such that the discriminant function provides maximum separation of groups (see Figure 20.2). Because there are two groups, only one discriminant function is estimated. Table 20.1 shows the results of the discriminant analysis for the export data. The canonical correlation (just like multiple R in regression analysis) associated with this function is .483. The square of this correlation, $(.483)^2 = .233$, indicates that 23.3 percent of the variance in the dependent variable (export interest) is explained or accounted for by this model. The next step is determination of significance.

Table 20.1   SPSS® Results of Two-Group Discriminant Analysis for Export Data

Canonical discriminant analysis

60 observations	59 df total
4 variables	58 df within classes
2 classes	1 df between classes

Class level information

Export interest	Frequency	Weight	Proportion
High	22	22.000	0.366
Low	38	38.000	0.633

Multivariate statistics and exact F-statistics

$S = 1$	$M = 1$	$N = 26.5$

Statistic	Value	F	Num df	Den df	Prob > F
Wilks' λ	0.766	4.192	4	55	0.004

Test of H_0: The canonical correlations in the current row and all that follow are zero

	Likelihood ratio	F	Num df	Den df	Prob > F
1	0.76632980	4.192	4	55	0.004

Pooled-within discriminant loadings

	DIS1
Size	0.585
Rev	0.249
Years	0.541
Prod	0.358
Canonical correlation = 0.483	

Table 20.1   (continued)

Total-sample standardized
discriminant coefficients

	DIS1
Size	0.825
Rev	0.196
Years	0.824
Prod	0.156

Raw canonical coefficients

Size	0.077
Rev	0.300
Years	0.895
Prod	0.061

Class means on
discriminant variables

Export interest	CAN1
High	0.713
Low	−0.413

Classification summary using linear discriminant function; number
of observations and percent classified into export interest (*EI*)

From *EI*	High	Low	Total
High	16	6	22
	72.73	27.27	100.00
Low	9	29	38
	23.68	76.32	100.00
Total	25	35	60
Percent	41.67	58.33	100.00
	Hit ratio: (16 + 29) / 60 = 75%		

Determination of Significance

The null hypothesis, namely, that in the population the group means of the discriminant function ($H_0: \mu_A = \mu_B$) are equal, can be tested statistically. In testing for significance in the export example (see Table 20.1), it may be noted that the Wilks' λ (defined as the ratio of within-group variance to the total variance) associated with the function is .766, which corresponds to an F-value of 4.1927 with 4 numerator degrees of freedom and 55 denominator degrees of freedom. This is significant beyond the .05 level. Wilks' λ assumes a value between zero and one. Larger values of λ indicate that group means do not appear to be different, and vice versa. If the null hypothesis is rejected, indicating significant discrimination, one can proceed to interpret the results.

Interpretation[3]

The interpretation of the discriminant weights, or coefficients, is similar to that in multiple regression analysis. The value of the coefficient for a particular predictor depends on the other predictors included in the discriminant function. The signs of the coefficients are arbitrary, but they indicate which variable values would result in large and small function values and associate them with particular groups. Generally, predictors with relatively large standardized coefficients contribute more to the discriminating power of the function than do predictors with smaller coefficients.

The relative importance of the predictors also can be obtained by examining the structure correlations, also called *canonical loadings* or *discriminant loadings*. These simple correlations between each predictor and the discriminant function represent the variance that the predictor shares with the function. We use these correlations for substantive interpretations (e.g., to name the underlying constructs that the discriminant function represents). Like the standardized coefficients, these correlations must be interpreted with caution. Unless the sample size is large relative to the number of predictors, both the standardized coefficients and the loadings are very unstable. In other words, the results in one sample will not likely hold good in another sample from the same population. It is advised that the ratio of the number of observations to the predictors be at least 20:1.

Based on examination of the standardized discriminant function coefficient for the predictor variables, we can conclude that workforce size (.83) and years of operation in the domestic market (.82) are the two most important discriminating variables of the level of export interest. This indicates that the larger the workforce size and the more years of operation in the domestic market, the more likely it is for the firm to have a greater interest in exporting. The unstandardized (or raw) discriminant function coefficients are given also. These can be applied to the raw values of the variables in the data set for classification purposes.

The group means or centroids based on the discriminant function for each group are 0.713 for the high-export interest group and −0.413 for the low-export interest group. Given that the two groups have unequal sizes, the cutoff score on the discriminant function for classifying companies into one of the two groups is computed to be

$$\frac{38(0.713)+22(-0.413)}{60}=0.3$$

In terms of assigning firms to one of the two groups, if a firm has a Z-score greater than 0.3, then that firm belongs to the high-export-interest group. If the firm's score is below 0.3, then it belongs to the low-export-interest group.

Classification and Validation[4]

Validation of the discriminant function is necessary to avoid any sample or data-specific conclusions, in which case the results are not generalizable. The results should hold good for other samples from the same population.

The *holdout method* splits the total sample in two. One subsample is used to construct the classification rule, and the other is used for validation. A **classification matrix** is a matrix containing numbers that reveal the predictive ability of the discriminant function. The numbers on the diagonal of the matrix represent correct classifications, and the off-diagonal numbers are incorrect classifications (see Table 20.1). The **hit ratio**, or the percentage of cases classified correctly, can then be determined by summing the diagonal elements and dividing by the total number of cases. For validation, the discriminant weights, estimated by using the estimation sample, are multiplied by the values of the predictor variables in the holdout sample to generate discriminant scores for the cases in the holdout sample. The cases are then assigned to groups, based on their discriminant scores and an appropriate decision rule. For example, in two-group discriminant analysis, a case is assigned to the group whose centroid is the closest. A variation of this method is to split the sample into K randomly chosen pairs of sets of equal size.

The **U-method**, or **cross-validation**, makes use of all of the available data without serious bias in estimating error rates. Frequently, it is inaccurately referred to as a jackknife procedure. Originally proposed by Lachenbruch (1967),[5] it holds out one observation at a time, estimates the discriminant function based on $n_1 + n_2 - 1$ observations, and classifies the held-out observation. This process is repeated until all observations are classified. If we denote by m_1 and m_2 the numbers of sample observations misclassified in G_1 (Group 1) and G_2 (Group 2) respectively, then the estimated classification error rates are given by $P_1 = m_1/n_1$ and $P_2 = m_2/n_2$.

Most discriminant analysis programs estimate a classification matrix based on the estimation sample. Because they capitalize on chance variation in the data, such results are invariably better than the classification obtained on the holdout sample. The hit ratio, or the percentage of cases classified correctly, is $(16 + 29)/60 = 0.75$, or 75 percent for the estimation sample. One might suspect that this hit ratio is artificially inflated, as the data used for estimation are also used for validation. Conducting classification analysis on an independent hold-out set of data (with 60 additional observations) results in a classification matrix with a hit ratio of $(16 + 29)/60 = 0.75$, or 75 percent. If the chance classification is based on the size of the largest group, then it is called a *maximum chance criterion*. Given two groups of unequal sizes, if everyone is assigned to the larger group (to maximize the percentage classified correctly), then the maximum chance criterion is $38/60 = 63.3$ percent. The *proportional chance criterion* (where the members are assigned to groups based on the original proportions) is given by $(22/60)^2 + (38/60)^2 = 53.5$ percent. The hit ratio in our example exceeds both criteria, and thus it is probably worthwhile to pursue the discriminant analysis.

In summary, the following steps are to be taken in conducting discriminant analysis:

1. Form groups

2. Estimate discriminant function

3. Determine significance of the function and the variables

4. Interpret the discriminant function, and

5. Perform classification and validation

Multiple Discriminant Analysis

In **multiple discriminant analysis**, the goal is much the same, in that we wish to find an axis with the property of maximizing the ratio of between-group to within-group variability of projections onto this axis. A complicating feature in the case of three or more groups is that a single axis may not distinguish the groups satisfactorily, and much discrimination potential still remains. In general, with m groups and P predictor variables, there are min $(p, m-1)$ (i.e., the minimum of the number of predictors and the number of groups minus one) possible discriminant axes (i.e., linear combinations). In most applications, since the number of predictor variables far exceeds the number of groups under study, at most $m-1$ discriminant axes will be considered. However, not all of these axes may show statistically significant variation among the groups, and fewer than $m-1$ discriminant functions actually may be needed. Thus, in such cases, a good deal of parsimony will have been achieved.

Application

In the export data set, the original dependent variable can be split into three levels of export interest (EI). The EI variable will assume a value of 3 (high) if "willingness to export" exceeds 3; $EI = 2$ (medium) if the value = 3; and $EI = 1$ (low) if "willingness to export" is less than 3. Thus, a three-group discriminant analysis can be performed. Since there are three groups and four predictor variables, two discriminant functions will be generated. Table 20.2 shows the results of the multiple discriminant analysis.

Discussion of Results

If several functions are tested simultaneously (as in the case of multiple discriminant analysis), the Wilks' λ statistic is the product of the univariate λ for each function. In this export example, the Wilks' λ is .636 (as shown in Table 20.2) and is significant at the .05 level. Among two discriminant functions, the first function is significant at the .05 level of significance. Note that the second function is not significant at the prespecified level ($\alpha = .05$). However, the process of interpretation remains the same for both the functions.

As in the two-group discriminant analysis, the discriminant loadings (pooled within) can be interpreted. For example, in the pooled-within discriminant loadings, "Years" has the highest correlation (.649) and "Prod" has the lowest correlation (.171) with the first discriminant function. However, the second function exhibits higher correlation with "Size" and "Rev." Since only the first function is significant, we interpret only the results of the first discriminant function. The standardized and the raw discriminant coefficients can be interpreted similarly to the two-group discriminant analysis.

In two-group discriminant analysis, the members are classified to a particular group based on their discriminant score being above or below the cutoff score. The group assignment in multiple discriminant analysis becomes complicated when there are multiple discriminant functions and multiple groups. In such cases, a classification function is used to assign each object or individual to one of the three groups. This classification function is based on the concept of Mahalnobis distance (Euclidean distance adjusted with the variance–covariance matrix—a matrix containing variances in the diagonal and covariances in the off-diagonal). A score is obtained on each of three classification functions for an object, and the object is assigned to the group that yields the maximum score.

The classification matrix yields a hit ratio of $(15+14+8)/60 = 61.7$ percent on the estimation sample and 60 percent on the hold-out sample. The maximum chance criteria for the three groups (of sizes 22, 21, and 17) is $(22/60) = 36.6$ percent, and the proportional chance criteria is $(22/60)^2 + (21/60)^2 + (17/60)^2 = 33.7$ percent. The hit ratio for the three-group discriminant analysis in our example far exceeds the *maximum-chance* and the *proportional-chance criteria* by providing a significant improvement of at least 68.5 percent $(61.7 - 36.6)/(36.6)$.

Table 20.2   SPSS® Results of Multiple Discriminant Analysis for Export Data

Canonical discriminant analysis

60 observations	59 df total
4 variables	57 df within classes
3 classes	2 df between classes

Class level information

Export interest	Frequency	Weight	Proportion
High	22	22.000	0.366
Medium	17	17.000	0.283
Low	21	21.000	0.350

Multivariate statistics and F approximations

$S = 2$	$M = 0.5$	$N = 26$

Statistic	Value	F	Num df	Den df	Prob > F
Wilks' λ	0.636	3.418	8	108	0.001

Test of H_0: the canonical correlations in the current row and all that follow are zero

	Likelihood ratio	Approx. F	Num df	Den df	Prob > F
1	0.636	3.414	8	108	0.001
2	0.903	1.965	3	55	0.129

Pooled-within discriminant loadings

	DIS1	DIS2
Size	0.352	−0.741
Rev	0.510	−0.698
Years	0.649	−0.208
Prod	0.171	0.585

Table 20.2   (continued)

Total-sample standardized discriminant coefficients

	DIS1	DIS2
Size	0.676	0.547
Rev	0.511	−0.677
Years	0.851	0.140
Prod	0.032	0.323

Raw discriminant coefficients

	DIS1	DIS2
Size	0.063	0.051
Rev	0.300	−0.400
Years	0.925	0.152
Prod	0.012	0.127

Class means on canonical variables

Export interest	DIS1	DIS2
High	0.688	0.233
Medium	0.091	−0.505
Low	−0.795	0.164

Classification Function

	Export interest		
	High	**Low**	**Mid**
Constant	−58.540	−44.319	−50.858
Size	0.749	0.651	0.673
Rev	0.002	0.001	0.002
Years	11.637	10.254	10.972
Prod	0.222	0.194	0.120

Classification summary using linear discriminant function; number of observations and percent classified into export interest

From export interest	High	Medium	Low	Total
High	15	3	4	22
	68.18	13.64	18.18	100.00
Medium	4	8	5	17
	23.53	47.06	29.41	100.00
Low	4	3	14	21
	19.05	14.29	66.67	100.00

SUMMARY OF DISCRIMINANT ANALYSIS

Application. Discriminant analysis is used primarily to identify variables that contribute to differences in the a priori defined groups with the use of discriminant functions. The analysis is also used for classifying objects into one or more groups that are already defined.

Inputs. The model requires variable values for the independent variables and the dependent variable (nonmetric).

Outputs. Discriminant analysis will provide the characteristics of the discriminant function, such as the variables that contribute to each discriminant function (through discriminant loadings). The significance of the function is also given. The raw and the standard discriminant weights are given to assist in the classification of objects. Finally, the usefulness of the discriminant analysis for classification is evaluated through the hit ratio.

Statistical Tests. The significance of the discriminant function (through Wilks' λ) and the variables are evaluated through an F-statistic.

Assumptions Underlying the Discriminant Function

1. The p independent variables must have a multivariate normal distribution.

2. The $p \times p$ variance–covariance matrix of the independent variables in each of the two groups must be the same.

Limitations. Some of the limitations are similar to that of regression analysis, such as intervariable correlations in the model, correlation of variables with the omitted variables, and change of environment condition. The assumption of the discriminant analysis has to be tested and it is often possible that the assumption of equal variance–covariance matrixes of the independent variables in each group is not met. In such cases, we have to resort to alternative techniques such as logit analysis (beyond the scope of this book).

Factor and Cluster Analysis

Factor analysis and cluster analysis are techniques that serve to (1) combine questions or variables to create new factors and (2) combine objects to create new groups, respectively. Often these are termed the **analysis of interdependence** techniques because they analyze the interdependence of questions, variables, or objects. The goal is to generate understanding of the underlying structure of questions, variables, or objects and to combine them into new variables or groups. These two techniques can be illustrated by the following simple example.

Suppose we are interested in determining how prospective students select universities. The first step might be to determine how prospective students perceive and evaluate institutions. To generate relevant questions, students might be asked to talk informally about schools. More particularly, the students could be asked why they prefer one school or why they regard two as similar. The result could be 100 or more items, such as *large, good faculty, expensive, good climate, dormitories, facilities, athletic program, social aspects, impersonal*, and so on. A second step might be to ask a group of prospective students to evaluate how important each of these attributes is to them. At this point, the analysis could get bogged down simply because there are too many attributes or variables. Furthermore, many of the attributes are redundant, really measuring the same construct. To determine which are redundant and what they are measuring, the analyst can turn to factor analysis. One result will be a set of new variables (or factors) created by combining sets of school attributes.

In another phase of the study, groups of students might be identified by what they are looking for in a college. We might hypothesize that one group is concerned about individual attention; another, low cost; another, proximity to home; and still another, quality education. If such groups exist and can be identified, it might be possible to isolate several, describe them, and develop a communication program—tailored to their interests—that could be directed toward them. **Cluster analysis** can be used to identify such groupings. It is used to identify people, objects, or variables that form natural groupings or clusters. A new variable is defined by cluster membership.

HMO enrollment intentions, for example, were based on a single question. However, it often will be theoretically and practically desirable to combine several questions, thereby creating a new variable that is based on more than one question. The fact that some constructs require more than one question to represent them generates a need to combine questions or variables. Social class, for example, often is represented best by a set of questions including income, education, and occupation. The need to combine questions also is due partially to the fact that sets of questions measuring complex areas such as lifestyle or image often are redundant. If questions on lifestyle or if image question sets were not combined, the analysis will be very unwieldy and confused. A variable that is based on a combination of questions, of course, can be tabulated, just as the original questions or variables can (and are).

Factor Analysis

Purpose

Researchers can use **factor analysis** for two primary functions in data analysis. One is to identify underlying constructs in the data. Thus, the variables "impersonal" and "large" in our school study actually may be indicators of the same theoretical construct.

A second role of factor analysis is simply to reduce the number of variables to a more manageable set. In reducing the number of variables, factor analysis procedures attempt to retain as much of the information as possible and make the remaining variables meaningful and easy to work with.

Methodology

The two most commonly employed factor analytic procedures in marketing applications are **principal component** and **common factor** analysis. When the objective is to summarize information in a larger set of variables into fewer factors (our second purpose), principal component analysis is used. On the other hand, if the researcher is attempting to uncover underlying dimensions surrounding the original variables (first purpose), common factor analysis is used. So the researcher's objective dictates which procedure will be used. Conceptually, principal component analysis is based on the total information in each variable, whereas common factor analysis is concerned only with the variance shared among all the variables.

In general, factor analysis can be summarized as a method of transforming the original variables into new, noncorrelated variables, called *factors*. Each factor is a linear combination of the original variables. One measure of the amount of information conveyed by each factor is its variance. For this reason, the factors are arranged in order of decreasing variance. Thus, the most informative factor is the first, and the least informative is the last. In other words, the objective of the principal components is to generate a first factor that will have the maximum explained variance. Then, with the first factor and its associated loadings fixed, the principal components will locate a second factor that maximizes the variance it explains. The procedure continues until there are as many factors generated as there are variables or until the analyst concludes that the number of useful factors has been exhausted. How to determine the number of factors to include will be considered shortly.

A Geometric Perspective

It often is helpful to consider a geometric interpretation of factor analysis. Principal components analysis, normally the first step in a factor analysis, will be described from a geometric perspective in the context of an example. Suppose that a group of prospective students rated, on a −5 to +5 scale, the importance of "good faculty" and "program reputation" in their decision as to which school to attend. Thus, a −5 rating would mean that the individual does not really care if the school has a good faculty (or rather, she or he might be more concerned about the athletic program). The respondents

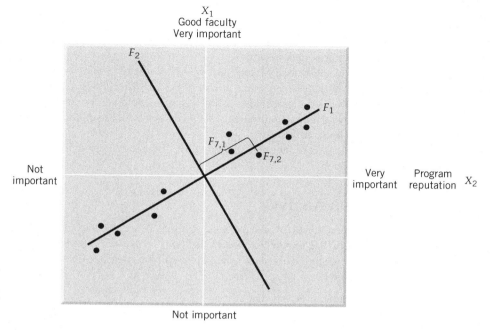

FIGURE 20.5
A Factor Analysis Solution.

are plotted with respect to their ratings on the X_1 (good faculty) scale and on the X_2 (program reputation) scale. At this point, two questions arise. First, are there really two dimensions operating or are both variables really measuring the same thing? If people value a good faculty, it seems likely that they also would value program reputation. Thus, these two dimensions might be measuring the underlying construct of overall quality. Second, there is the practical question of whether the number of variables could be reduced from two to one without sacrificing information.

Principal components analysis provides an approach to these questions. It will generate a new dimension, shown as F_1 in Figure 20.5, which retains as nearly as possible the interpoint distance information, or variance, that was contained in the original two dimensions. The new axis is termed F_1, or the first factor. It also is termed the *first principal component* or the *first principal factor*. Each person has a "score" or projection on the new dimension, just as he or she had on the original X_1 and X_2 dimensions. For example, in Figure 20.5, person 7 has a coordinate on factor 1 that is shown to be $F_{7,1}$. This projection is termed the **factor score** for person 7 on factor 1.

An important statistic is the percentage of the original variance that is included in the first factor. The original variance is the variance on the X_1-axis plus the variance on the X_2-axis. In this case, the variance of the factor scores on factor 1 might be 90 percent of the total original variance. This statistic indicates how well the factor serves to represent the original data.

In Figure 20.5, the points do not all lie exactly on the line represented by the first factor. There is variation about the first factor. To capture this variation, a second factor, F_2, is added perpendicular to F_1. The two factors together represent the data completely. They account for all the variation along the two axes, X_1 and X_2. Just as there were factor scores for the first factor, there also will be factor scores or projections on the second. The projection for factor 2 for person 7 is shown in Figure 20.5.

In Figure 20.5, since there are only two dimensions, the second factor is positioned automatically. However, if a third dimension such as "school size" is added to the original analysis (it would be shown coming out of the page), the position of the second factor has to be determined. It could be a dimension tilted at any angle to the figure and still be perpendicular to the first factor. With three original variables, the second factor is selected so that the variance of the factor scores on the second factor is maximized.

The analysis can continue to select factors until the process is stopped (using one of the rules of thumb) or until the number of factors equals the number of original variables. Each factor will have a statistic associated with it—the percentage of the variance explained by that factor. After factors have been generated by principal components, they can be rotated using one of the many rotation schemes, such as **varimax rotation**.

Assume for the moment that data reduction is the objective. In that case, principal component analysis is used for data reduction.

Principal Component Analysis

A (hypothetical) study was conducted by a bank to determine if special marketing programs should be developed for several key segments. One of the study's research questions concerned attitudes toward banking. The respondents were asked their opinion on a 0-to-9, agree–disagree scale, on the following questions:

1. Small banks charge less than large banks.

2. Large banks are more likely to make mistakes than small banks.

3. Tellers do not need to be extremely courteous and friendly; it's enough for them simply to be civil.

4. I want to be known personally at my bank and to be treated with special courtesy.

5. If a financial institution treated me in an impersonal or uncaring way, I would never patronize that organization again.

For illustrative purposes, assume that a pilot study was conducted using 15 respondents. An actual pilot study probably would have a sample size of 100–400 respondents. Table 20.3 shows the pilot study data and the correlations among the variables. The correlation matrix shown in Table 20.3 has unities in the diagonal, implying that the researcher is interested in the total variance as opposed to the shared variance. A factor analysis program usually starts by calculating the variable-by-variable correlation matrix. In fact, it is quite possible to input the correlation matrix directly, instead of the raw data. In any case, the factor analysis program will provide the correlation matrix as one of its outputs. It is a good idea to examine these correlations to see what information and hypotheses can be obtained. Which correlations are the largest? What does this imply?

Since the objective of factor analysis is to represent each of these variables as a linear combination of a smaller set of factors, we can express this as

$$x_1 = I_{11}F_1 + I_{12}F_2 + \ldots + I_{15}F_5 + e_1$$
$$x_2 = I_{21}F_1 + I_{22}F_2 + \ldots + I_{25}F_5 + e_2$$
$$\vdots$$
$$x_5 = I_{51}F_1 + I_{52}F_2 + \ldots + I_{55}F_5 + e_5$$

where x_1 through x_5 represent the standardized scores, F_1 through F_5 are the standardized factor scores, $I_{11}, I_{12}, \ldots, I_{55}$ are the factor loadings, and e_1–e_5 are the error variances. The maximum number of factors possible equals the number of variables. However, a small number of factors (two in this example) may alone be sufficient for retaining most of the information in the original variables.

Table 20.3 SPSS® Principal Component Analysis

	Input = Variable values					Output = Factor scores	
Obs	X1	X2	X3	X4	X5	Factor 1	Factor 2
1	9	6	9	2	2	−0.91581	1.03767
2	4	6	2	6	7	0.93263	−0.00767
3	0	0	5	0	0	−1.05059	−1.94294
4	2	2	0	9	9	1.64856	−1.03405
5	6	9	8	3	3	−0.44159	1.04045
6	3	8	5	4	7	0.44671	0.30815
7	4	5	6	3	6	−0.00002	−0.03933
8	8	6	8	2	2	−0.80081	0.80036
9	4	4	0	8	8	1.44238	−0.39930
10	2	8	4	5	7	0.69027	0.09916
11	1	2	6	0	0	−1.10436	−1.35569
12	6	9	7	3	5	−0.11766	1.03863
13	6	7	1	7	8	1.27690	0.50694
14	2	1	7	1	1	−1.01006	−1.23345
15	9	7	9	2	1	−0.99654	1.18107

Correlation analysis

	X1	X2	X3	X4	X5
X1	1.00000	0.60980	0.46870	−0.01795	−0.09642
X2		1.00000	0.23048	0.18969	0.31863
X3			1.00000	−0.83183	−0.77394
X4				1.00000	0.92732
X5					1.00000

Principal component analysis; prior communality estimates: one eigenvalue of the correlation matrix: total = 5; average = 1

	1	2	3	4	5
Eigenvalue	2.754602	1.774869	0.377091	0.064964	0.028474
Difference[a]	0.979733	1.397778	0.312127	0.036491	
Proportion[b]	0.5509	0.3550	0.0754	0.0130	0.0057
Cumulative[c]	0.5509	0.9059	0.9813	0.9943	1.0000

Two factors will be retained by the MINEIGEN criterion.

	Factor pattern			Rotated factor pattern: rotation method: varimax		
	Factor 1	Factor 2	Communalities	Factor 1	Factor 2	Communalities
X1	−0.29	0.85	0.81	−0.17	0.89	0.81
X2	0.05	0.92	0.83	0.17	0.90	0.83
X3	−0.94	0.28	0.94	−0.89	0.41	0.94
X4	0.95	0.23	0.94	0.97	0.09	0.94
X5	0.94	0.27	0.96	0.97	0.13	0.96

Table 20.3 (continued)

Variance explained by each factor		Variance explained by each factor	
Factor 1	Factor 2	Factor 1	Factor 2
2.754602	1.774869	2.735	1.794

	Standardized scoring coefficients	
	Factor 1	Factor 2
X1	−0.03915	0.49096
X2	0.08936	0.51083
X3	−0.31526	0.20227
X4	0.35929	0.07915
X5	0.35906	0.10182

[a]Difference represents the difference in eigenvalues between that factor and the subsequent factor.
[b]Proportion denotes the amount of variance explained by the factor relative to the total variance.
[c]Cumulative indicates the total proportion of variance explained by all the factors. For example, the first two factors explain a total of 90.59 percent of all the variations in the original variables.

What Is a Factor?

To interpret the balance of Table 20.3, it is first necessary to understand the concept of a factor. The input variables very likely will contain redundancies. Several variables may be measuring in part the same underlying construct. This underlying construct is what is termed a factor. A **factor** is thus simply a variable or construct that is not directly observable but that needs to be inferred from the input variables. It also might be viewed as a grouping of those input variables that measure or are indicators of the factor. In the factor model, just as in the regression model, there is a small set of independent variables, here termed *factors*, which are hypothesized to explain or cause the dependent variable. The regression coefficients, here termed **factor loadings**, link the factors to the variables and are used to help interpret the factors. In this context, the factor loadings are the correlations between the factors and the variables. The error term in both the factor and regression models absorbs measurement error and variation in the dependent variable that are not caused or explained by the factors. The *source* of the unexplained variation in the dependent variable is an important concept in both factor analysis (percentage of variance explained and communality) and regression analysis (R^2).

How Many Factors?

Since factor analysis is designed to reduce many variables to a smaller number of underlying factors or constructs, a central question is: *How many factors are involved in the model?* It is always possible to keep generating factors until there are as many factors as original variables, but that would defeat one of the primary purposes of the technique.

Theoretically, the answer to the question is clear. There is a certain number of constructs that the input variables are measuring. These constructs are identified before the analysis, from theory and our knowledge of the situation; then the data are factor analyzed until these constructs emerge as factors. Unfortunately, the theory is rarely that well defined. We therefore add some rules of thumb to the theoretical answer.

The rule of thumb we rely on most heavily in factor analysis studies is that all included factors (prior to rotation) must explain at least as much variance as an "average variable." In Table 20.3 the average variable would explain one-fifth, or 20 percent, of the variance. Actually, the second factor explains 36 percent, and the third factor, which is not shown, explains only 7 percent of the variance. The logic is that if a factor is meaningful and capable of representing one or more of the variables, it should absorb at least as much variance as an average original input variable.

Just because a lot of variance is explained, of course, does not mean that a factor is valid or meaningful or useful. If an irrelevant scale or question is repeated many times, each with a small modification, a factor underlying that question will explain much of the variance, but will not be a very interesting construct because the questions on which it was based are not very interesting.

A related rule of thumb is to look for a large drop in the variance explained between two factors (in the principal components solution). For example, if the variances explained by five factors (before rotation) are 40 percent, 30 percent, 20 percent, 6 percent, and 4 percent, there is a drop in variance explained in the fourth factor. This drop might signal the introduction of meaningless, relatively unimportant factors. A brief description of other criteria is provided next.

Eigenvalue Criteria

An **eigenvalue** represents the amount of variance in the original variables that is associated with a factor. Here, only factors with eigenvalues greater than 1.0 are retained; the other factors are not included in the model. In other words, the sum of the square of the factor loadings of each variable on a factor represents the eigenvalue, or the total variance explained by that factor. Hence, only factors with eigenvalues greater than 1.0 are included. A factor with an eigenvalue less than 1.0 is no better than a single variable, since, due to standardization, each variable has a variance of 1.0. Therefore, a factor should explain at least the amount of variance in one variable; otherwise it is better to have the original variable.

Scree Plot Criteria

A **scree plot** is a plot of the eigenvalues against the number of factors, in order of extraction (see Figure 20.6). The shape of the plot is used to determine the number of factors. Typically, the plot has a distinct break between the steep slope of factors with large eigenvalues and a gradual trailing off associated with the rest of the factors. This gradual trailing off is referred to as the "scree." Experimental evidence indicates that the point at which the scree begins denotes the true number of factors. Based on Figure 20.6, one would choose three factors. However, the third factor has a very low eigenvalue, which makes it impractical. Therefore, we would retain two factors.

Percentage of Variance Criteria

In this approach the number of factors extracted is determined so that the cumulative percentage of variance extracted by the factors reaches a satisfactory level. The level of variance that is satisfactory depends on the problem. However, a criterion of factors explaining at least 70 percent of the variance is not uncommon.

Significance Test Criteria

It is possible to determine the statistical significance of the separate eigenvalues and retain only those factors that are statistically significant. A drawback is that with large samples (sizes greater than 200) many factors are likely to be statistically significant, although, from a practical viewpoint, many of these account for only a small proportion of the total variance.

Perhaps the most appropriate rule is to stop factoring when the factors stop making sense. Eventually, the smaller factors will represent random varimax rotation and should be expected to be uninterpretable. Clearly, the determination of the number of factors, like the interpretation of individual factors, is very subjective.

Factor Scores

Although a factor is not observable like the other five variables, it is still a variable. One output of most factor analysis programs is the values for each factor for all respondents. These values are termed *factor scores* and are shown in Table 20.3 for the two factors that were found to

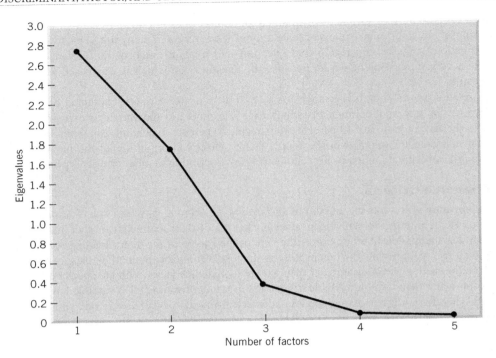

FIGURE 20.6
Scree Plot.

underlie the five input variables. Thus, each respondent has a factor score on each factor, in addition to the respondent's rating on the original five variables. In subsequent analysis, it may be convenient and appropriate to work with the factor scores instead of the original variables. The factor scores might be preferred because they have simply fewer factors than variables and (if the analyst is lucky) the factors are conceptually meaningful.

The factor is a derived variable in the sense that the factor score is calculated from a knowledge of the variables associated with it. Factors themselves can be represented as linear combinations of the original variables. For example,

$$F_j = b_{j1}x_{s1} + b_{j2}x_{s2} + \cdots + b_{jk}x_{sk}$$

where

F_j = standardized factor scores for the jth factor
b_j = standardized factor score coefficients on the jth factor
x_{sk} = kth variable (standardized)

Table 20.3 provides the factor score coefficients for the bank example. For instance, the first subject's factor 1 score is computed as

$$-0.91 = -0.039x_{s1} + 0.089x_{s2} - 0.315x_{s3} + 0.359x_{s4} + 0.359x_{s5}$$

These computed factor scores can be used as predictor variables in regression, discriminant, or other statistical analysis.

Factor Interpretation

How is the factor interpreted if it is unobservable? Interpretation is based on *factor loadings*, which are the correlations between the factors and the original variables.[6] The factor loadings for our bank study are shown at the bottom of Table 20.3. For example, the correlation between variable 1 and factor 1 is .29. The factor loadings thus provide an indication of which original variables are correlated with each factor, and the extent of the correlation. This information then is used to identify and label the unobservable factors subjectively.

Clearly, variables 3, 4, and 5 combine to define the first factor, which might be labeled a "personal" factor. This is so because the variables 3, 4, and 5 stress the "personal" aspects of the transaction in the banks. A larger value for variable 3 might indicate that the customers agree that the tellers need not be courteous. However, variable 3 has a high negative loading on factor 1, which indicates that customer do care about courteous service. Both variables 4 and 5 load positive on the first factor stressing the personal nature of the business.

The second factor is correlated most highly with variables 1 and 2. It might be termed a "small bank" factor, because both variables 1 and 2 have a positive loading on the second factor, and a high value on these variables indicates that the statements hold true for small banks.

Communality

Each of the five original input variables has associated with it a variance that reflects the differences among the 15 respondents. The amount of the variable 1 variance that is explained or accounted for by the factors is the communality of variable 1 and is shown in Table 20.3 to be 81 percent. **Communality** is the percentage of a variable's variance that contributes to the correlation with other variables or is "common" to other variables. In Table 20.3, variables 3, 4, and 5 have higher communalities; therefore, their variation is represented fairly completely by the two factors, whereas variable 1 has a lower communality. Just over 80 percent of the variance of variable 1 is due to the two factors.

Variance Explained

The percentage of variance explained is a summary measure indicating how much of the total original variance of all five variables the factor represents.[7] Thus, the first factor explains 55 percent of the total variance of the five variables and the second factor accounts for 36 percent more variance. The percentage-of-variance-explained statistic can be useful in evaluating and interpreting a factor, as will be illustrated shortly.

Factor Rotation

Factor analysis can generate several solutions (loadings and factor scores) for any data set. Each solution is termed a particular **factor rotation** and is generated by a *factor rotation scheme*. Each time the factors are rotated, the pattern of loadings changes, as does the interpretation of the factors. Geometrically, rotation means simply that the dimensions are rotated. There are many such rotation programs, such as *varimax rotation* (for orthogonal rotation) and *promax* (for oblique rotation). In varimax rotation, each factor tends to load high (1 or 1) on a smaller number of variables and low, or very low (close to zero), on other variables, to make interpretation of the resulting factors easier. In other words, the variance explained by each unrotated factor is simply rearranged by the rotation. The total variance explained by the rotated factors still remains the same. Here, the first rotated factor will no longer necessarily account for the maximum variance. The amount of variance each factor accounts for has to be recalculated. In *oblique rotation*, the factors are rotated for better interpretation, such that the orthogonality is not preserved anymore. Examples of both orthogonal and oblique rotation are provided in Figure 20.7a,b.

In Figure 20.7a, before the rotation, variables 1 and 2 have a high positive loading on both factors. Variables 3, 4, and 5 load positive on factor 1 and negative on factor 2. After the orthogonal

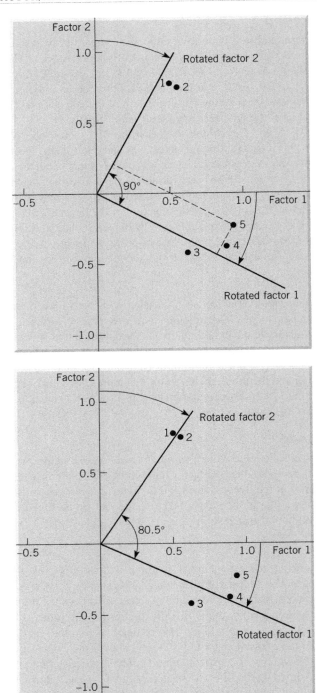

FIGURE 20.7
Factor Rotations. (a) Orthogonal Rotation. (b) Oblique Rotation.

rotation, variables 1 and 2 load high only on factor 1, and the remaining variables load high only on factor 2, thus facilitating easier interpretation of the factors. If the original factors are subjected to an oblique rotation, the results obtained will be similar to those of the orthogonal rotation (in this example); however, the two rotated factors will be correlated. In oblique rotation, we sacrifice orthogonality of factors for better interpretation.

In the bank example, the unrotated factor loadings themselves provide somewhat clearer interpretation. When the orthogonal varimax rotation is employed, the overall interpretation of the two factors does not change much; however, individual loadings do change to some extent. Table 20.3 shows both the unrotated and the rotated factor loadings for the bank example.

Why Perform Factor Analysis on Data?

One reason to perform factor analysis on data is to obtain insights from the grouping of variables that emerge. In particular, it often is possible to identify underlying constructs that might have practical and theoretical significance. Another reason is to reduce the number of questions or scales to a manageable number. This variable reduction can be accomplished in either of the two following ways:

1. Select one, two, or more of the input variables to represent each factor. They should be selected on the basis of their factor loadings and a judgment as to their usefulness and validity. In the example in Table 20.3, question 2 might be selected to represent the second factor. If the factor analysis is based on a pilot study, the larger study to follow then will have fewer questions to include. A set of 100 questions in a pilot study might be reduced to a group of 20 to 30 in the larger study.

2. Replace the original input variables with the factor scores. In the example represented by Table 20.3, the result would be two interpretable factors replacing five variables. In a larger problem, 50 input variables might be replaced by eight or nine factors. Subsequent data analysis would become easier, less expensive, and have fewer interpretation difficulties.

Common Factor Analysis

As stated earlier, if the purpose is to recover underlying factors in the original variables, then common factor analysis is used. The factor extraction procedure is similar to that of principal component analysis except for the input correlation matrix. Communalities, or shared variance, are inserted in the diagonal instead of unities in the original variable correlation matrix. Communalities are defined as the amount of variance a variable shares with all the other variables. Since common factor analysis focuses on shared variance (to recover the underlying construct), communalities are used in the diagonal of the correlation matrix rather than inserting "1's." Therefore, the total amount of variance that can be explained by all the factors in common factor analysis is the sum of the diagonal elements in the correlation matrix. Table 20.4 shows the results of common factor analysis.

The total amount of variance (eigenvalue) to be explained in the principal component analysis was 5, and it is 4.28 for the common factor analysis. Overall, the results of common factor analysis do not seem to vary from those of principal component analysis. However, this need not always be true, because the output of common factor analysis depends on the amount of shared variance. If the shared variance is high among the variables, then the two procedures will yield similar solutions. Otherwise, differences can be observed between principal component and common factor analysis.

Table 20.4   Common Factor Analysis

Obs	Input = variable values					Output = factor scores	
	X1	X2	X3	X4	X5	Factor 1	Factor 2
1	9	6	9	2	2	−0.84037	1.09086
2	4	6	2	6	7	0.88018	−0.19022
3	0	0	5	0	0	−1.09151	−2.00037
4	2	2	0	9	9	1.74028	−0.61231
5	6	9	8	3	3	−0.43271	1.04976
6	3	8	5	4	7	0.40098	0.32186
7	4	5	6	3	6	−0.02497	−0.15184
8	8	6	8	2	2	−0.77007	0.72030
9	4	4	0	8	8	1.43499	−0.46909
10	2	8	4	5	7	0.64349	0.13451
11	1	2	6	0	0	−1.14897	−1.44074
12	6	9	7	3	5	−0.14974	0.93232
13	6	7	1	7	8	1.19589	0.10743
14	2	1	7	1	1	−0.93920	−0.90774
15	9	7	9	2	1	−0.94820	1.11161

Correlation analysis

	X1	X2	X3	X4	X5
X1	0.75495	0.60980	0.46870	−0.01795	−0.09642
X2		0.72752	0.23048	0.18969	0.31863
X3			0.91853	−0.83183	−0.77394
X4				0.95004	0.92732
X5					0.92883

Principal factor analysis: prior communality estimates, SMC

X1	X2	X3	X4	X5
0.754955	0.727517	0.918529	0.950038	0.928834

Eigenvalues of the reduced correlation matrix: total = 4.27987218, average = 0.85597444

	1	2	3	4	5
Eigenvalue	2.682061	1.538428	0.165240	−0.039876	−0.065981
Difference[a]	1.143633	1.373187	0.205116	0.026105	
Proportion[b]	0.6267	0.3595	0.0386	−0.0093	−0.0154
Cumulative[c]	0.6267	0.9861	1.0247	−1.0154	1.0000

Two factors will be retained by the NFACTOR criterion.

Table 20.4 (continued)

	Factor pattern			Rotated factor pattern: rotation method, varimax		
	Factor 1	Factor 2	Communalities	Factor 1	Factor 2	Communalities
X1	−0.26	0.79	0.69	−0.16	0.82	0.69
X2	0.05	0.84	0.78	0.16	0.82	0.78
X3	−0.92	0.30	0.94	−0.87	0.42	0.94
X4	0.95	0.20	0.94	0.97	0.09	0.94
X5	0.93	0.25	0.93	0.96	0.13	0.93

Variance explained by each factor		Variance explained by each factor	
Factor 1	Factor 2	Factor 1	Factor 2
2.68	1.54	2.66	1.56

Standardized scoring coefficients		
	Factor 1	Factor 2
X1	−0.04508	0.30071
X2	0.01872	0.27600
X3	−0.16960	0.82512
X4	0.48129	0.51197
X5	0.36845	0.23793

[a]Difference represents the difference in eigenvalues between that factor and the subsequent factor.

[b]Proportion denotes the amount of variance explained by the factor relative to the total variance.

[c]Cumulative indicates the total proportion of variance explained by all the factors. For example, the first two factors explain a total of 98.61 percent of all the variations in the original variables.

SUMMARY OF FACTOR ANALYSIS

Application. Factor analysis is used to identify underlying dimensions or constructs in the data and to reduce the number of variables by eliminating redundancy.

Inputs. The input to factor analysis is usually a set of variable values for each individual or object in the sample. It is possible instead to input the matrix of correlations between the variables.[8] Actually, any type of square matrix whose components provide a measure of similarity between variables could be factor analyzed. The similarity measure does not have to be a correlation, although most often it is.

Outputs. The most important outputs are the factor loadings, the factor scores, and the variance-explained percentages. The factor loadings—that is, the correlations between the factors and the variables—are used to interpret the factors. Sometimes an analyst will pick one or two variables that load heavily on a factor to represent that factor in subsequent data collection or analysis. It also often is appropriate and useful to calculate the factor score and use that as a variable in the subsequent data analysis. The percentage-of-variance explained and other criteria help to determine the number of factors to include and how well they represent the original variables.

Key Assumption. The most important assumption is that there are factors underlying the variables and that the variables completely and adequately represent these factors. In practical terms, this assumption means that the list of variables should be complete; that is, each factor among them is measured at least once and, hopefully, several times from several different perspectives. If for some reason the variables list is deficient from the beginning, it will take a large dose of luck to emerge with anything very useful.

Limitations of Factor Analysis. The greatest limitation of factor analysis is that it is a highly subjective process. The determination of the number of factors, their interpretation, and the rotation to select (if one set of factors displeases the analyst, rotation may be continued indefinitely) all involve subjective judgment.

A related limitation is that no statistical tests are regularly employed in factor analysis.[9] As a result, it is often difficult to know if the results are merely accidental or really reflect something meaningful. Consequently, a standard procedure of factor analysis should be to divide the sample randomly into two or more groups and independently run a factor analysis of each group. If the same factors emerge in each analysis, then one may be more confident that the results do not represent a statistical accident.

Cluster Analysis

All scientific fields have the need to cluster or group similar objects. Botanists group plants, historians group events, and chemists group elements and phenomena. It should be no surprise that when marketing managers attempt to become more scientific, they need procedures for grouping objects. Actually, the practical applications in marketing for cluster analysis are far too numerous to describe; however, it is possible to suggest by example the scope of this basic technique. *Cluster analysis* is a technique for grouping individuals or objects into unknown groups. It differs from discriminant analysis in that the number and characteristics of the groups derived from the data in cluster analysis usually are not known prior to the analysis.

One goal of marketing managers is to identify similar consumer segments so that marketing programs can be developed and tailored to each segment. Thus, it is useful to cluster customers. We might cluster them on the basis of the product benefits they seek. Thus, students could be grouped on the basis of the benefits they seek from a college. We might group customers by their lifestyles. The result could be one group that likes outdoor activities, another that enjoys entertainment, and a third that likes cooking and gardening. Each segment may have distinct product needs and may respond differently to advertising approaches.

We might want to cluster brands or products to determine which brands are regarded as similar and therefore competitive. Brands or products also might be grouped with respect to usage. If two brands or products are found to be bought by the same group of people, a tie-in promotion might be possible. If a test-market experiment is planned, it might be useful to identify similar cities so that different marketing programs can be compared by trying them out in different cities. To identify similar cities, we might cluster them on the basis of variables that could contaminate the test, such as size or ethnic composition. In marketing-media decisions, it often is helpful to know which media appeal to similar audiences and which appeal to different audiences.

In general, while employing any cluster analytic procedure, the user should be cautious about the following[10]:

- Most cluster analysis methods are relatively simple procedures that usually are not supported by an extensive body of statistical reasoning.

- Cluster analysis methods have evolved from many disciplines, and the inbred biases of these disciplines can differ dramatically.

- Different clustering methods can and do generate different solutions to the same data set.

- The strategy of cluster analysis is structure-seeking, although its operation is structure-imposing.

As with other techniques, the first step in performing cluster analysis is defining the problem. After defining the problem, a researcher should decide on an appropriate similarity measure. Next, decisions on how to group the objects are made. Later, the number of clusters must be decided. When groups, or clusters, are formed, the researcher should then attempt to interpret, describe, and validate them for managerial relevance.

Problem Definition

Let us consider the bank example once again. Assume we are interested in grouping individuals based on their similarity of responses to questions x_1 through x_5.

Measures of Similarity

In order to group objects together, some kind of similarity or dissimilarity measure is needed. Similar objects are grouped together and those farther apart are put in separate clusters. The commonly used measures for cluster analysis are (1) distance measures, (2) correlation coefficients, and (3) association coefficients.

The most popular distance measure is the Euclidean distance. The formula for squared Euclidean distance is

$$d_{ij}^2 = \sum_{m=1}^{p} \left(X_{im} - X_{jm} \right)^2$$

where X_{im} and X_{jm} represent the standardized (to mean zero and unit standard deviation) values of the m th attribute for objects i and j and d_{ij}, the Euclidean distance.

Inasmuch as the variables in a data matrix often are measured in different units, the formula above usually is applied *after* each variable has been standardized to zero mean and unit standard deviation. Standardization can remove the influence of the unit of measurement; however, it can also reduce the differences between groups on variables that may best discriminate clusters. Observations with extreme values (outliers) should be removed. A major drawback of the distance measures is that variables with both large size differences and standard deviations can essentially swamp the effects of other variables with smaller absolute sizes and standard deviations.

Correlation coefficients (see Chapter 19) can also be computed between the five variables and input into cluster analysis. A major problem with the use of correlation coefficients is their sensitivity to the pattern of ups and downs across the variables at the expense of the magnitude of differences between the variables.

Association coefficients are used to establish similarity between objects when binary (1–0) variables are used. Suppose we want to create association coefficients between two brands (A and B) based on the presence or absence of eight attributes for each brand.

	A1	A2	A3	A4	A5	A6	A7	A8
Brand A	1	1	0	1	1	0	1	1
Brand B	1	0	0	0	1	1	1	0

One measure of a simple matching or association coefficient, s, is given by

$$s = \frac{a+d}{a+b+c+d}$$

where

   a = number of attributes possessed by brands A and B
   b = number of attributes possessed by brand A but not by brand B
   c = number of attributes possessed by brand B but not by brand A
   d = number of attributes not possessed by both the brands

In this illustration,

$$s = \frac{3+1}{3+3+1+1} = \frac{4}{8} = 0.5$$

This measure has received little attention in our literature so far because of its exclusion from many software packages.

Clustering Approach

There are two approaches to clustering, a hierarchical approach and a nonhierarchical approach. **Hierarchical clustering** can start with all objects in one cluster and divide and subdivide them until all objects are in their own single-object cluster. This is called the "top-down," or decision, approach. The "bottom-up," or agglomerative, approach, in contrast, can start with each object in its own (single-object) cluster and systematically combine clusters until all objects are in one cluster. When an object is associated with another in a cluster, it remains clustered with that object.

A **nonhierarchical clustering program** differs only in that it permits objects to leave one cluster and join another as clusters are being formed, if the clustering criterion will be improved by doing so. In this approach, a cluster center initially is selected, and all objects within a pre-specified threshold distance are included in that cluster. If a three-cluster solution is desired, three cluster centers are specified. These cluster centers can be random numbers or the cluster centers obtained from the hierarchical approach.

Each approach has advantages. Hierarchical clustering is relatively easy to read and interpret. The output has the logical structure that theoretically always should exist. Its disadvantage is that it is relatively unstable and unreliable. The first combination or separation of objects, which may be based on a small difference in the criterion, will constrain the rest of the analysis. In doing hierarchical clustering, it is sound practice to split the sample into at least two groups and do two independent clustering runs to see if similar clusters emerge in both runs. If they are entirely different, there is an obvious cause for caution.

The advantage of nonhierarchical clustering is that it tends to be more reliable; that is, split-sample runs will tend to look more similar than those of hierarchical clustering. If the program makes a close decision early in the analysis that subsequently proves wrong with respect to the clustering criterion, it can be remedied by moving objects from cluster to cluster. The major disadvantage is that the series of clusters is usually a mess and very difficult to interpret. The fact that it does look messy is sometimes good in that the analysis does not convey a false sense of order when none exists. But the fact remains, it can be very difficult to work with. Further, we have to choose the number of clusters a priori, which could be a difficult task.

Actually, both approaches can be used in sequence. First, a hierarchical approach can be used to identify the number of clusters and any outliers, and to obtain cluster centers. The outliers (if any) are removed and a nonhierarchical approach is used with the input on the number of clusters and the cluster centers obtained from the hierarchical approach. The merits of both approaches are combined, and hence the results should be better.

Hierarchical Clustering

There are several methods for grouping objects into clusters under both the hierarchical and the nonhierarchical approach. In the hierarchical approach, the commonly used methods are single linkage, complete linkage, average linkage, Ward's method, and the centroid method. Figure 20.8 illustrates the different methods of hierarchical clustering.

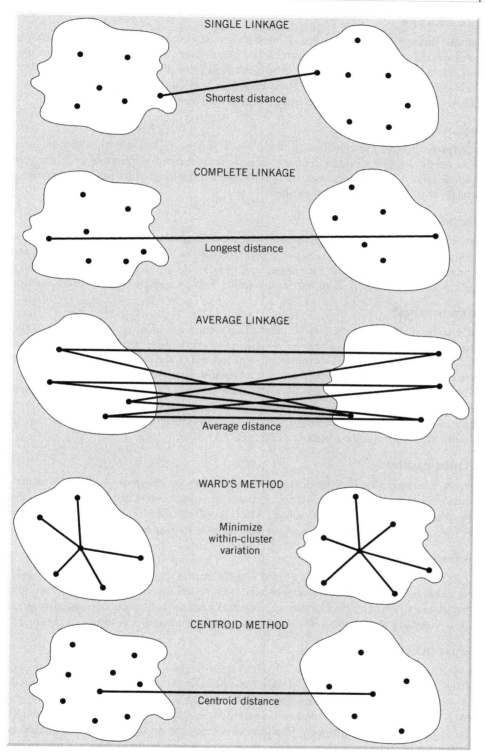

FIGURE 20.8
Hierarchical Clustering Methods.

Single linkage

The **single linkage** procedure is based on the shortest distance. It finds the two individuals (objects) separated by the shortest distance and places them in the first cluster. Then the next shortest distance is found, and either a third individual joins the first two to form a cluster or a new two-individual cluster is formed. The process continues until all individuals are in one cluster. This procedure is also referred to as the *nearest-neighbor* approach.

Complete linkage

The **complete linkage** procedure is similar to single linkage except that the clustering criterion is based on the longest distance. For this reason, it is sometimes referred to as the *farthest-neighbor* approach. The distance between two clusters is the longest distance from a point in the first cluster to a point in the second cluster.

Average linkage

The **average linkage method** starts out the same as single linkage and complete linkage, but the clustering criterion is the average distance from individuals in one cluster to individuals in another. Such techniques do not use extreme values, as do single linkage or complete linkage, and partitioning is based on all members of the clusters rather than on a single pair of extreme members.

Ward's method

Ward's method is based on the loss of information resulting from grouping objects into clusters, as measured by the total sum of squared deviations of every object from the mean of the cluster to which the object is assigned. As more clusters are formed, the total sum of squared deviations (known as the error sum of squares) increases. At each stage in the clustering procedure, the error sums of squares (ESS) is minimized over all partitions (the complete set of disjoint or separate clusters) obtainable by combining two clusters from the previous stage. This procedure tends to combine clusters with a small number of observations. It is also biased toward producing clusters with approximately the same number of observations.

Centroid method

The *centroid method* measures the distance between the group centroids (the centroid is the point whose coordinates are the means of all the observations in the cluster). If a cluster has one observation, then the centroid is the observation itself. The process continues by combining groups according to the distance between their centroids, the groups with the shortest distance being combined first.

An example

Table 20.5 shows the results of using Ward's hierarchical clustering method on the bank data. Fifteen individuals are clustered hierarchically, and the results show what objects are grouped together at each step. The ESS (clustering criteria) associated at each step are also given. An elegant hierarchical arrangement of clusters known as a *dendrogram* is shown in Figure 20.9.

Interpretation of Table 20.5

The objective of the analysis in Table 20.5 is to identify clusters among the 15 objects. To start with there are 15 clusters. As shown in the table, objects 1 and 8 are combined first to produce a cluster, since those two objects are the closest to each other among other pairs of objects. However, objects 6 and 10 are also close (in fact, the same distance apart as objects 1 and 8), and they form another cluster. Now only 13 clusters are left, with no significant loss of information. As the process of forming clusters evolves, the ESS increases. A substantial increase in the ESS is observed when we try to go from a four-cluster solution to a three-cluster solution, and a big increase in ESS when a two-cluster solution is obtained (see Figure 20.10). Therefore, an analyst would probably decide to stop with either a four-cluster or a three-cluster solution. As discussed

Table 20.5 Hierarchical Cluster Analysis

Number of clusters	Clusters	Joined	Frequency of new cluster	Error sums of squares	Tie
14	OB1	OB8	2	0.002	T
13	OB6	OB10	2	0.002	
12	CL14	OB15	3	0.003	
11	OB5	OB12	2	0.004	T
10	OB11	OB14	2	0.004	
9	OB2	OB13	2	0.006	
8	OB3	CL10	3	0.008	
7	OB4	OB9	2	0.008	
6	CL13	OB7	3	0.018	
5	CL9	CL7	4	0.038	
4	CL12	CL11	5	0.042	
3	CL5	CL6	7	0.105	
2	CL4	CL8	8	0.297	
1	CL2	CL3	15	0.463	

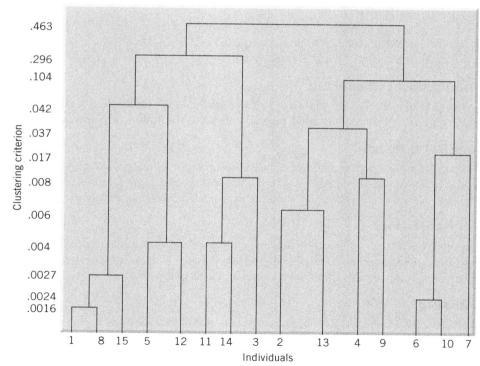

Not drawn to scale.

FIGURE 20.9
A Dendrogram for Hierarchical Clustering of Bank Data.

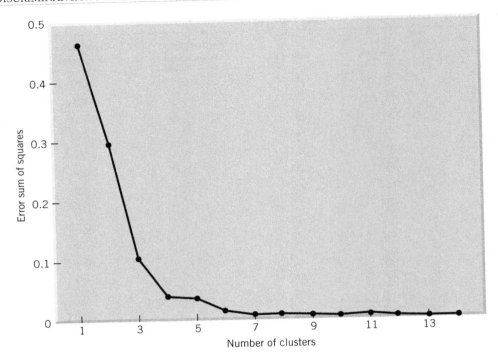

FIGURE 20.10
Plot of Error Sums of Squares.

earlier, the bias of Ward's method to produce equal-size clusters can be seen clearly in the two-cluster solution (with sizes of 8 and 7, respectively).

Nonhierarchical Clustering

In nonhierarchical methods (also known as *iterative partitioning*), the three most commonly used approaches are the sequential threshold, parallel threshold, and optimizing procedures.

Sequential threshold

In this case, a cluster center is selected and all objects within a prespecified threshold value are grouped. Then a new cluster center is selected and the process is repeated for the unclustered objects, and so on. Once objects enter a cluster, they are removed from further processing.

Parallel threshold

This method is similar to the preceding one except that several cluster centers are selected simultaneously, and objects within the threshold level are assigned to the nearest center; the threshold levels can then be adjusted to admit fewer or more objects to the cluster.

Optimizing

This method modifies the previous two procedures in that objects can later be reassigned to clusters by optimizing some overall criterion measure, such as the average within-cluster distance for a given number of clusters.

An example

The results of the nonhierarchical clustering for the bank data are shown in Table 20.6. The number of clusters is specified to be three, and the initial cluster seeds for the three clusters in the

Table 20.6 Nonhierarchical Cluster Analysis

Nonhierarchical procedure

Replace = FULL	Radius = 0	Maxclusters = 3	Maxiter = 6	Converge = 0.02	
Cluster	X1	X2	X3	X4	X5
1	6.00	9.00	7.00	3.00	5.00
2	2.00	2.00	0.00	9.00	9.00
3	0.00	0.00	5.00	0.00	0.00

Minimum distance between seeds = 12.4499

	Change in cluster seeds		
Iteration	1	2	3
1	1.960	3.921	1.795
2	0.867	1.138	0
3	0.925	0.909	0
4	0	0	0

Cluster listing

Obs	Cluster	Distance from seed
1	1	2.82
2	2	0.99
3	3	1.79
4	2	5.38
5	1	2.30
6	2	4.54
7	1	4.96
8	1	1.91
9	2	3.16
10	2	3.69
11	3	1.10
12	1	3.05
13	2	2.99
14	3	1.69
15	1	3.21

Cluster summary

Cluster	Frequency	RMS std. deviation	Maximum distance from seed to observation	Nearest cluster	Centroid distance
1	6	1.5642	4.9638	2	9.1591
2	6	1.8239	5.3826	1	9.1591
3	3	0.8563	1.7951	1	9.3853

Table 20.6   (continued)

Cluster	Frequency	RMS std. deviation	Maximum distance from seed to observation	Nearest cluster	Centroid distance

Cluster means

Cluster	X1	X2	X3	X4	X5
1	7.00	7.00	7.83	2.50	3.16
2	3.50	5.83	2.00	6.50	7.66
3	1.00	1.00	6.00	0.33	0.33

Cluster standard deviations

Cluster	X1	X2	X3	X4	X5
1	2.00	1.67	1.16	0.55	1.94
2	1.51	2.40	2.09	1.87	0.81
3	1.00	1.00	1.00	0.57	0.57

Distance between cluster means

Cluster	1	2	3
1	.	9.1591	9.3853
2	9.1591	.	11.7225
3	9.3853	11.7225	.

original variable space are selected. Through iterative partitioning, the objects are reassigned to different clusters until no individual moves from one cluster to the other. The cluster listing indicates which individual belongs to what cluster.

Interpretation of Table 20.6

As shown in Table 20.6, a three-cluster solution is sought. The initial cluster centers, or seeds, are given for the three clusters on the five variables. These initial cluster centers may be random numbers or may be obtained from the hierarchical approach for a three-cluster solution. The distance of an object from each of the three cluster centers is compared and the object is assigned to the closest cluster. Each object is thus assigned to one of the three clusters. After all the objects have been assigned, the cluster seeds are recomputed. Then the assignment process begins all over again. In this example, four iterations are required to converge on a solution.

The cluster listing identifies the cluster members and their distances from the cluster seeds. Descriptive information such as cluster means and standard deviations is provided.

Number of Clusters

A central question in cluster analysis is how to determine the appropriate number of clusters. There are several possible approaches. First, the analyst can specify in advance the number of clusters. Perhaps, for theoretical and logical reasons, the number of clusters is known. Or the analyst may have practical reasons for specifying the number of clusters, based on the planned use of the clusters. Second, the analyst can specify the level of clustering with respect to the clustering criterion.

If the clustering criterion is easily interpretable, such as the average within-cluster similarity, it might be reasonable to establish a certain level that would dictate the number of clusters.

A third approach is to determine the number of clusters from the pattern of clusters the program generates. The distances between clusters at successive steps may serve as a useful guideline, and the analyst may choose to stop when the distance exceeds a specified value or when the successive distances between steps make a sudden jump. These distances are sometimes referred to as *error variability* measures. Figure 20.10 shows the plot of ESS with the number of clusters, using the Ward's method. Based on the large jump from four to three clusters, one would probably choose four clusters. However, based on the relative increase in ESS, a three-cluster solution also appears possible.

Fourth, the ratio of total within-group variance to between-group variance can be plotted against the number of clusters. The point at which an elbow or a sharp bend occurs indicates an appropriate number of clusters. Increasing the number of clusters beyond this point probably is not useful, and decreasing the number can result in combining apples and oranges.

Whatever approach is used, usually it is useful to look at the total cluster pattern, such as those illustrated in Figures 20.9 and 20.10. It can provide a feel for the quality of the clustering and for the number of clusters that emerge at various levels of the clustering criterion. Usually more than one clustering level is relevant, and in the bank example it is clearly evident that three or four clusters are possible. Although cluster analysis can be used for identifying segments, a density estimation procedure may be a worthwhile alternative.[11]

Evaluating and Profiling the Clusters

Once clusters are developed, the analyst still faces the task of describing them. One frequently used measure is the **centroid**—the average value of the objects in the cluster on each of the variables making up each object's profile. If the data are interval-scaled and clustering is performed in the original variables space, this measure appears quite natural as a summary description. Table 20.6 provides the cluster means and standard deviations on the original five variables for a three-cluster solution. The mean scores should help to describe or profile the clusters.

If the data are standardized or if the cluster analysis is performed using factor analysis components (component factors), the analyst must go back to the raw scores for the original variables and compute average profiles using these data.

Often, it is helpful to profile the clusters in terms of variables that were not used for clustering.[12] These may include demographic, psychographic, product usage, media usage, and other variables. For example, the clusters may have been based on benefits sought. Further profiling may be done in terms of demographic and psychographic variables, to target marketing efforts for each cluster. The variables that significantly differentiate between clusters can be identified via discriminant analysis and one-way analysis of variance.

Statistical Inference

Despite attempts to construct various tests of the statistical reliability of clusters, no fully defensible procedures currently are available. The lack of appropriate tests stems from the difficulty of specifying realistic null hypotheses.

Despite the formidable problems associated with statistical inference in cluster analysis, analysts might try a few ad hoc procedures to provide rough checks on the clustering results. For example, they might apply two or more different clustering routines to the same data or perform cluster analysis on the same data using different distance measures and compare results across algorithms and distance measures. Or they may wish to split the data randomly into halves, perform separate clustering, and then examine the average profile values of each cluster across subsamples. Alternatively, analysts may delete various columns (variables) in the original profile data, compute dissimilarity measures across the remaining columns, and compare these results with the clusters found by using the full set of columns (variables).

We also recommend another approach to validation. Use simulation procedures that employ random-number generators to create a data set with the properties matching the overall properties of the original data but containing no clusters. Use the same clustering methods on both the real and the artificial data, and compare the resulting solutions.

Finally, when you use cluster analysis in a research study, the study should provide:

- An unambiguous description of the clustering method

- The similarity measure used in the study

- The computer program used

- The procedure used to determine the number of clusters

- Adequate evidence of the validity of cluster analysis solution

SUMMARY OF CLUSTER ANALYSIS

Application. Cluster analysis is used to group variables, objects, or people. For example, people can be grouped into segments.

Input. The input is any valid measure of similarity between objects, such as correlations. It also is possible to input the number of clusters or the level of clustering.

Output. The output is a grouping of objects into clusters. Groupings are provided, such as those shown in Figure 20.9. Associated with each set of clusters will be the value of the clustering criterion. Some programs also output diagnostic information associated with each object. For example, they may provide the distance from each object to the center of its cluster and to the center of the next closest cluster. This information can help determine in more depth the cluster cohesion and the level of association between an object and a cluster.

Key Assumptions. The most important assumption is that the basic measure of similarity on which the clustering is based is a valid measure of the similarity between the objects. A second major assumption is that there is theoretical justification for structuring the objects into clusters. As with other multivariate techniques, there should be theory and logic guiding an underlying cluster analysis.

Limitations. Usually, it is difficult to evaluate the quality of the clustering. There are no standard statistical tests to ensure that the output is not purely random. The value of the criterion measure, the reasonableness of the output, the appearance of a natural hierarchy (when a nonhierarchical method is used), and the split-sample reliability tests all provide useful information. However, it is still difficult to know exactly which clusters are very similar and which objects are difficult to assign. Usually, it is difficult to select a clustering criterion and program on any basis other than availability.

QUESTIONS AND PROBLEMS

20.1 A researcher wishes to perform a three-group multiple discriminant analysis and is interested in using information from the three variables that she collected during the study. How many discriminant functions are possible? Do you need all of them?

20.2 Are discriminant loadings better than discriminant weights for interpretation purposes?

20.3 If you have only one sample of 30 observations and use all of them to estimate the coefficients of the discriminant function, how can you validate the results?

20.4 If you violate the assumptions of the linear discriminant analysis, what other alternatives do you have in terms of statistical analysis?

20.5 Your consulting firm is approached by a leading consumer-products manufacturer, General Mills, which has just introduced a new brand of cookie in a test-market city. General Mills would like your company to use a discriminant analysis to see if it is possible to predict the people who will try a new brand, compared to those who will not try the new brand. You know that the market share of the new brand is only 10 percent, and observe that you can predict 90 percent of the population correctly by simply assuming that each person did not try the new brand. This assumes that the market share of the new brand should be zero. From past experience, you know that it is difficult to predict 90 percent correctly with a discriminant analysis model, so you are reluctant to suggest such an investigation. Can anything possibly come out of the discriminant analysis research that might justify the cost of the investigation? Why?

20.6 How is a factor loading interpreted?

20.7 What is communality? What is the implication of low communality for a few of the variables?

20.8 How does principal components analysis differ from varimax rotation?

20.9 Why are factors rotated?

20.10 Identify a situation where you would expect the first factor to have high loadings on all variables and to account for almost all the variance.

20.11 Suppose five variables were factor analyzed and the percentage of variance explained was 80 percent, 12 percent, 5 percent, 2 percent, and 1 percent. How many factors would you include? What if the first three factors were interpretable and relevant?

20.12 Suppose you are conducting a large, 2,000-respondent study for a bank. Among other elements, the study includes:

(a) A 28-item image rating for three commercial banks, two savings and loans banks, and an "ideal" financial institution

(b) A 75-item lifestyle question set

(c) A 30-item set of questions to determine whether the respondents are opinion leaders, sources of product information, and so on

(d) A 40-item set of questions on the importance of bank services

(e) A set of questions on usage of 35 bank services. Specifically, how would factor analysis be employed in this study?

20.13 What labels would you attach to the varimax rotated factors in Table 20.3? Do you believe the varimax rotations are more valid than the principal components factors? More interesting?

20.14 Interpret and address factor loadings, factor scores, and factor score coefficients in Table 20.4.

20.15 Suppose similarity ratings for beer were cluster analyzed and three distinct clusters were found. How might those clusters differ? On what dimensions? On what characteristics?

20.16 When might hierarchical clustering be preferred over non-hierarchical clustering?

20.17 Respondents in a study were asked to indicate their activities (such as playing tennis, attending plays, attending dinner parties, etc.) on a 7-point scale (from 1 = never to 7 = frequently). A correlation between respondents was obtained. Cluster-analyze these respondents.

	1	2	3	4	5	6	7	8	9	10	11	12
1.	—	.32	−.10	−.10	−.30	.01	.50	−.12	−.40	.22	−.07	.32
2.		—	.02	.02	−.45	.12	.82	.05	−.10	.32	−.15	.15
3.			—	−.60	.16	.35	.50	.87	.01	−.15	.44	.20
4.				—	.34	.71	.35	.42	−.10	.19	.49	.26
5.					—	.40	−.01	−.12	.51	.49	−.11	.35
6.						—	.08	.26	.11	.09	−.46	−.01
7.							—	−.17	.20	.03	.07	.16
8.								—	.09	.33	.32	.32
9.									—	.16	.01	−.12
10.										—	.03	.11
11.											—	.40
12.												—

END NOTES

1. P. E. Green, D. Tull, and G. Albaum, *Research for Marketing Decisions*. Englewood Cliffs, NJ: Prentice-Hall, 1988.

2. This section is drawn from J. Hair et al., *Multivariate Data Analysis with Readings*. New York: Macmillan, 1992.

3. C. J. Huberty, "Issues in the Use and Interpretation of Discriminant Analysis," *Psychological Bulletin*, 95, 1984, pp. 156–171; W. D. Perreault, D. N. Behrman, and G. M. Armstrong, "Alternative Approaches for Interpretation of Multiple Discriminant Analysis in Marketing Research," *Journal of Business Research*, 7, 1979, pp. 151–173.

4. M. Crask and W. Perreault, "Validation of Discriminant Analysis in Marketing Research," *Journal of Marketing Research*, 14, February 1977, pp. 60–68.

5. P. A. Lachenbruch, "An Almost Unbiased Method of Obtaining Confidence Intervals for the Probability of Misclassification in Discriminant Analysis," *Biometrics*, 23, 1967, pp. 639–645.

6. Actually, the factor loadings will be correlations only when (1) the input variables are standardized [each variable has its mean subtracted and is divided by its standard deviation $(x - \overline{x}) / \sigma_r$], and (2) the factors are perpendicular or independent, two conditions that normally are present. As noted previously, most factor analysis programs begin by calculating a correlation matrix, a process that standardizes the variables. If neither condition is present, the factor loadings, although not correlations, still can be interpreted as indicators of the association between the variables and the factors. Further, a matrix of variable-factor correlations, termed a *factor structure matrix*, is provided as an output of the factor analysis program. When the variables are standardized, the factor coefficients become "beta coefficients" in the regression context. Unlike regression analysis, where the independent variables usually are correlated, the factors are independent. That is why a factor loading is here a correlation, whereas a beta coefficient in the regression context is not a correlation.

7. The percentage of variance explained is proportional to the sum of squared loadings associated with that factor. Thus, a factor's percent of explained variance depends in part on the number of variables on which the factor has high loadings. A variable's communality actually is equal to the sum of the squared factor loadings of that variable.

8. Factor analysis could be conducted on a correlation matrix between people or objects instead of a between-variable correlation matrix. The resulting factors would then represent groups of people instead of groups of variables. This approach is called Q-factor analysis. The more common focus on relationships between variables is termed R-factor analysis.

9. D. W. Stewart, "The Application and Misapplication of Factor Analysis in Marketing Research," *Journal of Marketing Research*, 18, February 1981, pp. 51–62.

10. M. S. Aldenderfer and R. K. Blashfield, *Cluster Analysis*. Beverly Hills, CA: Sage, 1984.

11. V. Kumar and R. Rust, "Market Segmentation by Visual Inspection," *Journal of Advertising Research*, 29(4), August/September 1989, pp. 23–29.

12. G. Punj and D. W. Stewart, "Cluster Analysis in Marketing Research: Review and Suggestions for Application," *Journal of Marketing Research*, 20, May 1983, pp. 134–148.

Case 20-1 | Southwest Utility

In view of the problem of pollution from energy sources, it was felt that a need existed for an in-depth baseline study of consumer attitudes and perceptions of energy-related issues. As a result, a study was conducted in February 1994 (at the peak of the pollution problems) on a variety of energy-related issues.

A mail questionnaire was sent to 2,500 residents of three medium-sized cities. A total of 922 respondents returned the questionnaire. A sample of 574 of the respondents was selected for the initial analysis. One key question asked if the respondent would be willing to give up degrees of heat in the home in order to achieve less air pollution, assuming that such a trade-off were possible. One analysis was to determine how those willing to give up some heat in their homes differed from those who were not willing. Accordingly, the two groups are profiled in Table 20.7 on the basis of 10 variables.

The table shows the mean values for each group, the *F*-ratio, which reflects the statistical significance of the difference between the means, and the standardized discriminant coefficients.

Interpret the table elements. What is the appropriate interpretation of each term? Which variables are the most helpful in identifying the characteristics of the group? What are the appropriate hypothesis tests to be used in the analysis?

Source: Prepared by David J. Barnaby, Richard C. Reizenstein, and David A. Aaker as a basis for class discussion.

Table 20.7   Discriminant Analysis for Two Home Heat Preference Groups

Variable[a]	F-ratio	Group 1 Prefer less heat $n = 171$ mean (standard deviation)	Group 2 Prefer same heat $n = 378$ mean (standard deviation)	Standardized discriminant coefficients
Family member 15–19 years	5.87	0.39 (0.69)	0.25 (0.58)	.35
Paid family members	3.81	2.16 (1.31)	1.93 (1.28)	.28
Education	14.34	4.05 (1.30)	3.55 (1.48)	.31
Income	5.67	3.64 (1.59)	3.28 (1.66)	−.08
Television	4.42	2.64 (1.04)	2.43 (1.09)	.14
Magazines	7.08	2.05 (1.16)	1.76 (1.20)	−.03
Civic clubs	7.68	1.44 (1.22)	1.14 (1.16)	.28
Spouse	4.80	1.27 (1.14)	1.04 (1.14)	.18
Amount each family should pay	16.94	3.55 (2.87)	2.57 (2.42)	−.05
Amount family is willing to spend	18.29	3.98 (3.13)	2.89 (2.61)	.12
Mean discriminant score (significant at .001 level)		0.44	−.20	

[a]Nonsignificant (at the .05 level) variables include the following demographics: sex, marital status, family size, age distribution of persons 0–14 and over 20 living at home, mobility, race, age (of respondent), and length of time as area resident. Only variables with an F-ratio included at the .05 level of significance are displayed.

Case 20-2 ‖ Store Image Study

Table 20.8 shows the output of a factor analysis conducted on the ratings of 82 respondents who were asked to evaluate a particular discount store using 29 semantic-differential, seven-point scales. The same respondents were asked to evaluate a supermarket. A second factor analysis was conducted on the supermarket data, and the results are shown in Table 20.9.

Source: Based on a study by John Dickson and Gerald Albaum, "A Method for Development of Tailormade Semantic Differentials for Specific Marketing Content Areas," *Journal of Marketing Research*, 8, February 1977, pp. 87–91.

Questions for Discussion

1. Label the factors. Compare these factors with those found in the discount store analysis of Table 20.8. Why should they be different? Hint: It isn't because a discount store is different from a supermarket.

2. Analyze the communalities. Which are low? What are the implications? Contrast with Table 20.8.

Table 20.8   Factor Loadings for a Discount Store (Varimax Rotation)

Scale	I	II	Factor III	IV	V	Communality
1. Good service	.79	−.15	.06	.12	.07	.67
2. Helpful salespersons	.75	−.03	.04	.13	.31	.68
3. Friendly personnel	.74	−.07	.17	.09	−.14	.61
4. Clean	.59	−.31	.34	.15	−.25	.65
5. Pleasant store to shop in	.58	−.15	.48	.26	.10	.67
6. Easy to return purchases	.56	−.23	.13	−.03	−.03	.39
7. Too many clerks	.53	−.00	.02	.23	.37	.47
8. Attracts upper-class customers	.46	−.06	.25	−.00	.17	.31
9. Convenient location	.36	−.30	−.02	−.19	.03	.26
10. High quality products	.34	−.27	.31	.12	.25	.36
11. Good buys on products	.02	−.88	.09	.10	.03	.79
12. Low prices	−.03	−.74	.14	.00	.13	.59
13. Good specials	.35	−.67	−.05	.10	.14	.60
14. Good sales on products	.30	−.67	.01	−.08	.16	.57
15. Reasonable value for price	.17	−.52	.11	−.02	−.03	.36
16. Good store	.41	−.47	.47	.12	.11	.63
17. Low pressure salespersons	−.20	−.30	−.28	−.03	−.05	.18
18. Bright store	−.02	−.10	.75	.26	−.05	.61
19. Attractive store	.19	.03	.67	.34	.24	.66
20. Good displays	.33	−.15	.61	.15	−.20	.57
21. Unlimited selections of products	.09	.00	.29	−.03	.00	.09
22. Spacious shopping	.00	.20	.00	.70	.10	.54
23. Easy to find items you want	.36	−.16	.10	.57	.01	.49
24. Well-organized layout	−.02	−.05	.25	.54	−.17	.39
25. Well-spaced merchandise	.20	.15	.27	.52	.16	.43
26. Neat	.38	−.12	.45	.49	−.34	.72
27. Big store	−.20	.15	.06	.07	−.65	.49
28. Ads frequently seen by you	.03	−.20	.07	.09	.42	.23
29. Fast checkout	.30	−.16	.00	.25	−.33	.28
Percentage of variance explained	16	12	9	8	5	
Cumulative variance explained	16	28	37	45	50	

Possible Factor Interpretations:

Factor I	Good service—friendly	Factor IV	Spaciousness
Factor II	Price level	Factor V	Size
Factor III	Attractiveness		

Table 20.9 Factor Loadings for a Supermarket (Varimax Rotation)

Scale	I	II	Factors III	IV	V	Communality
1. Well-spaced merchandise	.73	.10	−.11	.02	.12	.57
2. Bright store	.63	−.08	.45	−.11	.06	.62
3. Ads frequently seen by you	−.04	.08	−.02	−.12	.58	.36
4. High-quality products	.50	.32	.24	.01	−.03	.41
5. Well-organized layout	.70	.08	.05	.00	.12	.51
6. Low prices	−.09	.64	−.02	.19	.18	.49
7. Good sales on products	.27	.73	.00	−.10	−.01	.62
8. Pleasant store to shop in	.63	.36	.09	.12	.01	.55
9. Good store	.73	.37	.26	.19	−.06	.78
10. Convenient location	.18	.01	.59	−.10	.36	.52
11. Low pressure salespersons	−.15	.05	.40	−.06	−.11	.20
12. Big store	.08	−.02	.42	.00	.14	.20
13. Good buys on products	.35	.73	.04	.18	−.10	.70
14. Attractive store	.68	.28	.38	.10	−.10	.70
15. Helpful salespersons	.43	.16	.34	.34	.45	.64
16. Good service	.60	.19	.21	.35	.01	.56
17. Too many clerks	−.06	.03	−.01	.62	−.08	.40
18. Friendly personnel	.48	.11	.17	.47	.36	.62
19. Easy-to-return purchases	.39	.10	.01	−.10	.43	.36
20. Unlimited selection of products	.10	.09	.48	.17	−.18	.31
21. Reasonable prices for value	.24	.71	.04	.01	.13	.58
22. Neat	.87	.00	.11	.07	.04	.78
23. Spacious shopping	.72	.02	−.26	−.01	.18	.62
24. Attracts upper-class customers	.38	−.37	−.17	−.06	.06	.32
25. Clean	.83	.11	.16	.12	.03	.74
26. Fast checkout	.22	.12	−.07	.68	−.13	.55
27. Good displays	.73	.19	.07	.14	.13	.61
28. Easy to find items you want	.57	.23	−.08	.03	−.01	.39
29. Good specials	.37	.62	.08	.06	.32	.63
Percentage of variance explained	26	11	6	5	5	
Cumulative variance explained	26	37	43	48	53	

Additional Case for this Chapter is available on the Web:

Web Case 20-1	Behavioral Research

21

Multidimensional Scaling and Conjoint Analysis

Multidimensional Scaling

Multidimensional scaling (MDS) addresses the general problem of positioning objects in a perceptual space. Much of marketing management is concerned with the question of positioning. With whom do we compete? How are we compared to our competitors? On what dimensions? What positioning strategy should be followed? These and other questions are addressed by MDS.

MDS basically involves two problems. First, the dimensions on which customers perceive or evaluate objects (organizations, products, or brands) must be identified. For example, students must evaluate prospective colleges in terms of their quality, cost, distance from home, and size. It would be convenient to work with only two dimensions, since the objects could then be portrayed graphically. However, this is not always possible, because additional dimensions sometimes are needed to represent customers' perceptions and evaluations. Second, objects need to be positioned with respect to these dimensions. The output of MDS is the location of the objects on the dimensions and is termed a **perceptual map**.

There are several approaches to MDS. They differ in the assumptions they employ, the perspective they take, and the input data they use. Figure 21.1 categorizes the major approaches in terms of the input data and the methods used to produce perceptual maps. One set of approaches involves object attributes. If the objects were colleges, the attributes might be faculty, prestige, facilities, cost, and so on. MDS then combines these attributes into dimensions such as quality. Another set of approaches bypasses attributes and considers similarity or preference relationships between objects directly. Thus, two schools could be rated as to how similar they are or how much one is preferred over the other, without regard to any underlying attribute. This chapter will first describe the attribute-based approaches. An application of MDS based on nonattribute data will follow. Finally, we will discuss the ideal-object concept.

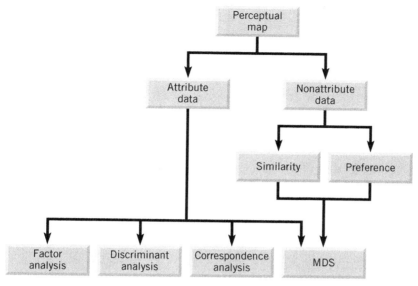

FIGURE 21.1
Approaches to Creating Perceptual Maps.

Attribute-Based Approaches

An important assumption of attribute-based approaches is that we can identify attributes on which individuals' perceptions of objects are based. Let us start with a simple example. Suppose that the goal is to develop a perceptual map of the nonalcoholic beverage market.[1] Suppose further that exploratory research has identified 14 beverages that seem relevant and nine attributes that are used by people to describe and evaluate these beverages. A group of respondents is asked to rate each of the beverages on the nine attributes, on a 7-point scale. An average rating of the respondent group on each of the nine attributes, termed profile analysis in Chapter 11, would be of interest. However, it would be much more useful if the nine attributes could be combined into two or three dimensions, or factors. Two approaches—**factor analysis** and **discriminant analysis**—usually are used to reduce the attributes to a small number of dimensions.

Factor Analysis

Since each respondent rates 14 beverages on nine attributes, he or she ultimately will have 14 factor scores on each of the emerging factors, one for each beverage. The position of each beverage in the perceptual space, then, will be the average factor score for that beverage. The perceptual map shown in Figure 21.2 illustrates this. Three factors, accounting for 77 percent of the variance, serve to summarize the nine attributes. Each beverage is then positioned on the attributes. Since three factors or dimensions are involved, two maps are required to portray the results. The first involves the first two factors, while the second includes the first and third. For convenience, the original attitudes also are shown on the maps as lines or vectors. The vectors are obtained based on the amount of correlation the original attitudes possess with the factor scores (represented as factors). The direction of the vectors indicates the factor with which each attribute is associated, and the length of the vector indicates the strength of association. Thus, on the left map the "filling" attribute has little association with any factor, whereas on the right map the "filling" attribute is strongly associated with the "refreshing" factor.

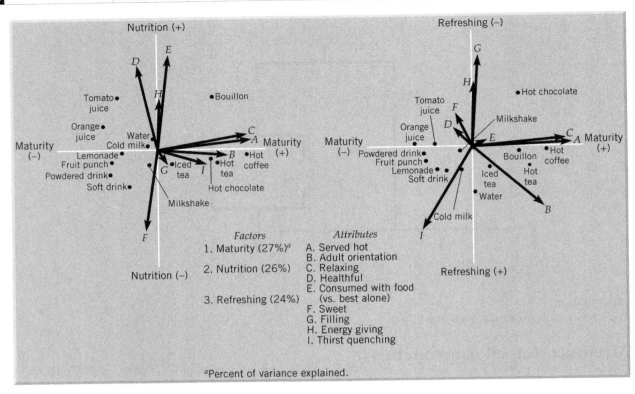

FIGURE 21.2
Perceptual Maps of a Beverage Market.

Discriminant Analysis

Whereas the goal of factor analysis is to generate dimensions that maximize interpretability and explain variance, the goal of discriminant analysis is to generate dimensions (termed **discriminant function factors**) that will discriminate or separate the objects as much as possible. As in factor analysis, each dimension is based on a combination of the underlying attributes. However, in **discriminant analysis**, the extent to which an attribute will tend to be an important contributor toward a dimension depends on the extent to which there is a perceived difference among the objects having that attribute.

Comparing Factor and Discriminant Analysis

Each of the approaches has advantages and disadvantages. *Discriminant analysis* identifies clusters of attributes on which objects differ. If all objects are perceived to be similar with respect to an attribute (such as an airline's safety), that attribute should not affect preference (such as the choice of an airline). Following that logic, the discriminant analysis objective of selecting attributes that discriminate between objects seems sensible. A second useful characteristic of discriminant analysis is that it provides a test of statistical significance. The null hypothesis is that two objects actually are perceived identically. The test will determine the probability that the between-object distance is due simply to a statistical accident. A third quality of discriminant analysis is that it will identify a perceptual dimension even if it is represented by a single attribute.

In contrast, *factor analysis* groups attributes that are similar. If there are not several attributes representing a dimension, it will tend not to emerge in the factor analysis solution. Factor analysis is based on both perceived differences between objects and differences between people's perceptions of objects. Thus, it tends to provide a richer solution, use more of the attributes, and result in more dimensions. All perceptual dimensions are included, whether they discriminate between objects or not. Hauser and Koppelman conducted a study of shopping centers in which they compared several approaches to MDS.[2] They found that factor analysis dimensions provided more interpretive value than did those of discriminant analysis.

Introducing Importance Weights

Both factor analysis and discriminant analysis ignore the relative importance of particular attributes to customers. Myers and Tauber suggest that the attribute data be multiplied by importance weights and then be subjected to a factor analysis.[3] As a result, the attributes considered more important will have a greater tendency to be included in a factor analysis solution. Myers and Tauber presented a factor analysis perceptual map for snack food that included the dimensions of "convenience" and "nutrition." When that study was repeated, this time with importance weights introduced, a "child likes" dimension replaced the "convenience" dimension.

Correspondence Analysis

In both factor analysis and discriminant analysis, the variables are assumed to be intervally scaled, continuous variables. A 7-point Likert scale (agree–disagree) would usually be used. However, often it is convenient to collect binary or zero–one data. Respondents might be asked to identify from an attribute list which ones describe a brand. The result will be a row of zeros and ones for each respondent. Or the respondent could be asked to pick three (or k) attributes that are associated with a brand, or two (or k) use occasions that are most suitable for a brand. The result is again a row of zeros and ones for each respondent and each brand.

When the data consist of rows of zeros and ones reflecting the association of an attribute or other variable with a brand or other object, the appropriate MDS technique is termed **correspondence analysis**.[4] Correspondence analysis generates as an output a perceptual map in which the elements of attributes and brands are both positioned.

Binary judgments are used in several contexts. First, if the number of attributes and objects is large, the task of scaling each object on each attribute may be excessive and unrealistic. Simply checking which attributes (or use occasions) apply to a given object may be a more appropriate task. Second, it may be useful to ask respondents to list all the attributes they can think of for a certain brand or to list all the objects or brands that would apply to a certain use occasion. For example, what snacks would you consider for a party given to watch the Super Bowl? In that case, binary data would result, and correspondence analysis would be the appropriate technique.

Basic Concepts of MDS

MDS uses proximities among different objects as input. A proximity is a value that denotes how similar or different two objects are, or are perceived to be, or any measure of this type. MDS then uses these proximities data to produce a geometric configuration of points (objects), in a two-dimensional (preferably) space as output. Attribute-based data such as objects' X attributes (profile matrix) and nonattribute-based data, including similarity and preference data, can be used to obtain proximities data. The Euclidean distances (derived) between objects in the two-dimensional space are then computed and compared with the proximities data.

A key concept of MDS is that the derived distances (output) between the objects should correspond to the proximities (input). If we make the rank order of derived distances between objects/brands correspond to the rank order of the proximities data, the process is known as *nonmetric MDS*. On the contrary, if the derived distances are either multiple or linear functions of the proximities, then it is known as *metric MDS*. Nonmetric MDS assumes that the proximities data are ordinal but metric MDS assumes that they are metric. However, in both cases, the output (derived distances) is metric.

Evaluating the MDS Solution

The fit between the derived distances and the proximities in each dimension is evaluated through a measure called *stress*. In MDS, the objects can be projected onto two, three, four or even higher dimensions. Since visual inspection is possible only with two, or possibly three, dimensions, we always prefer lower dimensions. Usually, the stress value increases when we decrease the number of dimensions. The appropriate number of dimensions required to locate the objects in space can be obtained by plotting the stress values against the number of dimensions. As with factor analysis (scree plot) and cluster analysis (error sums of squares plot), one chooses the appropriate number of dimensions, depending on where the sudden jump in stress starts to occur. Sometimes we directly seek a two-dimensional representation, since managers always prefer that because it is easier to interpret.

Determining the Number of Dimensions

Figure 21.3 plots the stress values against the number of dimensions. As you can see, higher dimensions are associated with lower stress values and vice versa. The plot indicates that probably two dimensions are acceptable, since there is a large increase in the stress values from two dimensions to one.

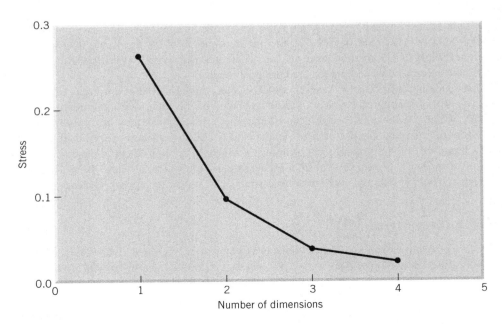

FIGURE 21.3
Plot of Stress versus Dimensionality.

Labeling the Dimensions

To label the dimensions, one can correlate the object's attribute ratings with the dimension to determine which dimensions correlate highly with what attributes and, accordingly, name the dimensions. Multiple regression is used with dimensional coordinates as the criterion variables and the attribute ratings as the predictor variables. Table 21.1 is an example of naming the dimensions for a perceptual map of shopping locations.

The regression weights indicate that the first dimension be labeled "variety" because attributes such as variety of merchandise, "specials," store availability, and so forth, are associated with it. Similar interpretation for the second dimension yields the label "Quality versus Price."

Interpreting the Dimensions

The perceptual map in Table 21.1 gives the location of the various shopping areas in Chicago. As you can see, the Chicago Loop location is the only one that offers a good value (quality/price) and variety. To the contrary, Korvette City offers low value and less variety. This location has a major opportunity to reposition and can decide to move toward the origin by increasing both value and variety. It is evident that different shopping locations are perceived to be different from one another.

Once the dimensions are appropriately labeled, the locations of the objects/brands are evaluated and an appropriate strategy is implemented to either repo-sition (if necessary) or maintain that location in the eyes of the consumers.

MDS can also be used on attribute data to produce perceptual maps. When MDS is used on the attribute data, it is known as the *attribute-based MDS*. However, the attribute/profile data that usually are represented as an objects × attributes matrix (e.g., see Table 21.1) are transformed to an object × object correlation/distance matrix (as in cluster analysis). For practical purposes, the transformed data appear similar to the similarity/dissimilarity data that could be collected directly from the respondents.

Table 21.1   Perceptual Map of Shopping Locations (Hauser and Koppelman Study)

		Variety	Quality versus price
1.	Layout of store	.217	.497
2.	Return and service	.318	.122
3.	Prestige of store	.297	.804
4.	Variety of merchandise	.929	.360
5.	Quality of merchandise	.295	.811
6.	Availability of credit	.880	−.085
7.	Reasonable price	.485	−.853
8.	"Specials"	.786	−.594
9.	Free parking	−.294	−.550
10.	Center layout	−.447	.036
11.	Store atmosphere	−.199	.452
12.	Parking available	−.463	−.478
13.	Center atmosphere	−.099	.480
14.	Sales assistants	−.052	.411
15.	Store availability	.872	.429
16.	Variety of stores	.921	.385

Attribute-based MDS has the advantage that attributes can have diagnostic and operational value and the dimensions can be interpreted in terms of their correlations with the attributes. Further, the Hauser and Koppelman study concluded that attribute data were easier for respondents to use and that dimensions based on attribute data predicted preference better than did dimensions based on nonattribute data.[5]

However, attribute data also have several conceptual disadvantages. First, if the list of attributes is not accurate and complete, the study will suffer accordingly. Generating an attribute list can be difficult, especially when possible differences among people's perceptions are considered. Second, it may be that people simply do not perceive or evaluate objects in terms of underlying attributes. An object may be perceived or evaluated as a whole that is not decomposable in terms of attributes. Finally, attribute-based models may require more dimensions to represent them than would be needed by more flexible models, in part because of the linearity assumptions of factor analysis and discriminant analysis. These disadvantages lead us to use nonattribute data, namely, similarity and preference data.

Application of MDS with Nonattribute Data

Similarity Data

Similarity measures simply reflect the perceived similarity of two objects in the eyes of the respondents. For example, each respondent may be asked to rate the degree of similarity in each pair of objects. The respondent generally is not told what criteria to use to determine similarity; thus, the respondent does not have an attribute list that implicitly suggests criteria to be included or excluded. In the following example, the respondent judged Stanford to be quite similar to Harvard.

		Pair number 1					
		Stanford	Harvard				
Extremely similar							**Extremely dissimilar**
	−	−	−	−	−	−	−
	1	2	3	4	5	6	7

The number of pairs to be judged for degree of similarity can be as many as $n(n-1)/2$, where n is the total number of objects. With 10 brands, there could be 45 pairs of brands to judge (although fewer could be used).

Although at least seven or eight objects should be judged, the approach is easier to illustrate if only four objects are considered. First, the results of the pairwise similarity judgments are summarized in a matrix, as shown in Figure 21.4. The numbers in the matrix represent the average similarity judgments for a sample of 50 respondents. Instead of similarity ratings, the respondents could be asked simply to rank the pairs from most to least similar. An average rank-order position then would replace the average similarity rating matrix. It should be noted, however, that rank ordering can be difficult if 10 or more objects are involved.

A perceptual map could be obtained from the average similarity ratings; however, it is also possible to use only the ordinal or "nonmetric" portion of the data. Thus, the knowledge that objects A and C in Figure 21.4 have an average similarity of 1.7 is replaced by the fact that objects A and C are the most similar pair. Figure 21.4 shows the conversion to rank-order information.

Objects	Average similarity ratings			
	A	B	C	D
A				
B	3.2			
C	1.7	3.9		
D	5.1	3.3	4.7	

Objects	Rank by degree of similarity			
	A	B	C	D
A				
B	2			
C	1	4		
D	6	3	5	

FIGURE 21.4
Similarity Judgments.

Ordinal or nonmetric information often is preferred, for several reasons. First, it actually contains about the same amount of information in that the output usually is not affected by replacing intervally scaled or "metric" data with ordinal or nonmetric data. Second, the nonmetric data often are thought to be more reliable.

Next, a computer program is employed to convert the rankings of similarity into distances in a map with a small number of dimensions, so that similar objects are close together and vice versa. The computer will be programmed to locate the four objects in a space of two, three, or more dimensions, so that the shortest distance is between pair (A, C), the next shortest between pair (A, B), and the longest between pair (A, D). One possible solution that satisfied these constraints in two dimensions is the following:

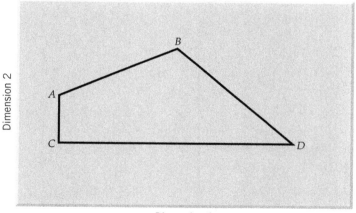

The reader might be able to relocate the points differently and still satisfy the constraints so that the rankings of the distances in the map correspond to the rankings of the pairwise similarity judgments. This is because there are only a few points to move in the space and only six constraints to satisfy. With 10 objects and 45 constraints, the task of locating the points in a two-dimensional space is vastly more difficult, and requires a computer. Once a solution is found (the points are located in the space), it is unlikely that there will be a significantly different solution that still satisfies the constraints of the similarities matrix. Thus, we can argue that the intervally scaled nature of the distances between points really was hidden in the rank-order input data all the time.

The power of the technique lies in its ability to find the smallest number of dimensions for which there is a reasonably good fit between the input similarity rankings and the rankings of distance between objects in the resulting space. Usually, this means starting with two dimensions and, if this is not satisfactory, continuing to add dimensions until an acceptable fit is achieved. The determination of "acceptable" is a matter of judgment, although most analysts will trade-off some degree of fit to stay with a two- or three-dimensional map, because of the enormous advantages of visual interpretations. There are situations where more dimensions are necessary. This happened in a study of nine different types of sauces (mustard, catsup, relish, steak sauce, dressing, and so on). Most respondents perceived too many differences to be captured with two or three dimensions, in terms of either the types of foods with which the sauces would be used or the physical characteristics of each sauce.[6]

A sample of 64 undergraduates provided similarity judgments for all 45 pairs of 10 drinks including Coke, Diet Coke, 7-Up, Calistoga Natural Orange, and Slice. They were asked to rate the similarity of each pair such as Slice–Diet Coke, on a nine-point scale. The two-dimensional solution is shown in Figure 21.5. Note that Slice is considered closer to Diet 7-Up than to 7-Up, and Schweppes and Calistoga are separated even though they are very similar.

Interpreting the resulting dimension takes place "outside" the technique. Additional information must be introduced to decide why objects are located in their relative positions. Sometimes, the location of the objects themselves can suggest dimensional interpretations. For example, in Figure 21.2, the location of the objects suggests dimension interpretations even without the attribute information. Thus, the fruit punch versus hot coffee object locations on the horizontal axis suggest a maturity dimension. In Figure 21.5, the objects on the horizontal axis indicate a cola–noncola dimension. The vertical axis seems to represent a diet–nondiet dimension, because in both the cola group and the noncola group, the nondiet drinks tend to be higher than the diet drinks.

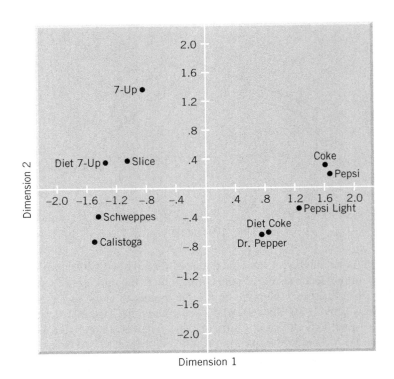

FIGURE 21.5
Perceptual Map Using Similarity Data.

The concept of an ideal object in the space is an important one in MDS because it allows the analyst to relate object positioning to customer likes and dislikes. It also provides a means for segmenting customers according to their preferences for product attributes.

Preference Data

An **ideal object** is one that the customer would prefer over all others, including objects that can be conceptualized in the space but do not actually exist. It is a combination of all the customers' preferred-attribute levels. Although the assumption that people have similar perceptions may be reasonable, their preferences are nearly always heterogeneous—their ideal objects will differ. One reason to locate ideal objects is to identify segments of customers who have similar ideal objects.

There are two types of ideal objects. The first lies within the perceptual map. For example, if a new cookie were rated on attribute scales such as

Very sweet . . . . Not at all sweet
Large, substantial . . . . Small, dainty

a respondent might well prefer a middle position on the scale.

The second type is illustrated by a different example. Suppose attributes of a proposed new car included

Inexpensive to buy . . . . Expensive to buy
Inexpensive to operate . . . . Expensive to operate
Good handling . . . . Bad handling

then respondents would very likely prefer an end point on the scale. For instance, the car should be as inexpensive as possible to buy and operate. In that case, the ideal object would be represented by an ideal vector or direction rather than an ideal point in the space. The direction would depend on the relative desirability of the various attributes.

There are two approaches to obtaining ideal-object locations. The first is simply to ask respondents to consider an ideal object as one of the objects to be rated or compared. The problem with this approach is that conceptualizing an ideal object may not be natural for a respondent, and the result may therefore be ambiguous and unreliable.

A second approach is indirect. For each individual, a rank-order preference among the objects is sought. Then, given a perceptual map, a program will locate the individual's ideal objects such that the distances to the objects have the same rank order (or as close to it as possible) as the rank-order preference. The preferred object should be closest to the ideal. The second most preferred object should be farther from the ideal than the preferred, but closer than the third most preferred, and so on. Often, it is not possible to determine a location that will satisfy this requirement perfectly and still obtain a small number of dimensions with which an analyst would like to work. In that case, compromises are made and the computer program does as well as possible by maximizing some measure of "goodness-of-fit."

Issues in MDS

Perceptual maps are good vehicles through which to summarize the position of brands and people in attribute space and, more generally, to portray the relationship among any variables or constructs. It is particularly useful to portray the positioning of existing or new brands and the relationship of those positions to the relevant segments. There is a set of problems and issues in working with MDS:

1. When more than two or three dimensions are needed, the usefulness is reduced.

2. Perceptual mapping has not been shown to be reliable across different methods. Users rarely take the trouble to apply multiple approaches to a context to ensure that a map is not method-specific.

3. Perceptual maps are static snapshots at a point of time. It is difficult from the model to know how they might be affected by market events.

4. The interpretation of dimensions can be difficult. Even when a dimension is clear, it can involve several attributes, and thus the implications for action can be ambiguous.

5. Maps usually are based on groups that are aggregated with respect to their familiarity with products, their usage level, and their attitude. The analysis can, of course, be done with subgroups created by grouping people according to their preferences or perceptions, but with a procedure that is ad hoc, at best.

6. There has been little study of whether a change in the perception of a brand, as reflected by a perceptual map, will affect choice.

Kumar and Leone suggest the use of nonlinear mapping technique, an alternative to MDS, to overcome some of the problems associated with the use of MDS.[7]

SUMMARY OF MDS

Application. MDS is used to identify dimensions by which objects are perceived or evaluated, to position the objects with respect to those dimensions, and to make positioning decisions for new and old products.

Inputs. *Attribute-based* data involve respondents rating the objects with respect to specified attributes. *Similarity-based* data involve a rank order of between-object similarity that can be based on several methods of obtaining similarity information from respondents. *Preference* data also can provide the basis for similarity measures and generate perceptual maps from quite a different perspective.

Ideal points or directions are based either on having respondents conceptualize their object, or by generating rank-order preference data and using the data in a second stage of analysis to identify ideal points or directions.

Outputs. The output will provide the location of each object on a limited number of dimensions. The number of dimensions is selected on the basis of a goodness-of-fit measure (such as the percentage of variance in factor analysis) and on the basis of the interpretability of the dimensions. In attitude-based MDS, attribute vectors may be included to help interpret the dimensions. Ideal points or directions may be an output in some programs.

Key Assumptions. The overriding assumption is that the underlying data represent valid measures. Thus, we assume that respondents can compare objects with respect to similarity or preference of attributes. The meaning of the input data is generally straightforward; however, the ability and motivation of respondents to provide it often is questionable. A related assumption is that the respondents use an appropriate context. Some could base a rank-order preference of beer on the assumption that it was to be served to guests. Others might assume the beer was to be consumed personally.

With attribute-based data, it is assumed that the attribute list is relevant and complete. If individuals are grouped, it is assumed that their perceptions are similar. The *ideal object* introduces additional conceptual problems. Another basic assumption is that the interpoint distances generated by a perceptual map have conceptual meaning that is relevant to choice decisions.

Limitations. A limitation of the attribute-based methods is that the attributes have to be generated. The analyst has the burden of making sure that the attributes represent the respondents' perceptions and evaluations. With similarity and preference data, this task is eliminated. However, the analyst then must interpret dimensions without the aid of such attributes, although attribute data could be generated independently and attribute-dimension correlations still obtained.

Conjoint Analysis

Before examining the technique of **conjoint analysis**, we first will take a look at three examples of the kind of management problems for which conjoint analysis is extremely well suited:

1. Modifying a credit card

2. Identifying land-use attitudes

3. Revamping an industrial product line

Modifying a Credit Card[8]

A firm wanted to improve the benefits of its credit card to retailers, to get more of them to honor the card. Changes could be made to any of the following attributes:

- Discount rate (percentage of billings deducted by the credit card company for providing the service); the alternatives were 2.5 percent versus 6 percent.

- Speed of payment after receipt of week's vouchers (1 day vs. 10 days).

- Whether card authorization was by computer terminal or toll-free billing number.

- Extent of the support payment for local advertising by the retailers (either 1.0 percent or 0.75 percent of billings).

- Provision of a rebate of 15 percent of charges on all billings in excess of the retailer's quota (which would be set at 25 percent more than the previous year's sales).

Because there are two levels for each of the five factors, 32 possible combinations of credit cards could be offered. The best combination would be both attractive to the retailers and profitable to the company.

Identifying Residential Land-Use Attitudes[9]

Most suburban land development follows a "spread" or "urban sprawl" pattern, with large home lots and uniformly low population densities. Is this what home buyers want, or do they accept this alternative because it is the only one that land developers offer? Specifically, would buyers be willing to sacrifice some elements of private space to gain a better view from their yard? More important, would they accept cluster developments—groups of small lots—surrounded by large areas of open land that might be scenically valuable or ecologically vulnerable? The answer to these questions depends on the importance that potential home buyers attach to attributes such as the view from the back or front yard, versus measures of lot size such as backyard size, distance between houses, and distance to the front sidewalk.

Revamping an Industrial Product Line[10]

The Brazilian subsidiary of the Clark Equipment Company was considering replacing their largest-selling forklift truck with two new models. One new model was to have slightly less per-for-mance than the current model but would sell at a 5 percent lower price. The other new model would offer an automatic transmission for the first time, plus better performance and reliability, but at a 5 percent higher price. For this move to be profitable, the company would have to gain and hold an additional 3 percent market share.

Overview of Conjoint Analysis

Conjoint analysis is an extremely powerful and useful analysis tool. Its acceptance and level of use have been remarkably high since its appearance around 1970. One study concluded that over 400 conjoint studies for commercial applications were undertaken annually in the 1980s.[11]

As the previous examples indicate, a major purpose of conjoint analysis is to help select features to offer on a new or revised product or service; to help set prices; to predict the resulting level of sales or usage; or to try out a new-product concept. *Conjoint analysis* provides a quantitative measure of the relative importance of one attribute as opposed to another. Chapter 11 introduced other methods to determine attribute importance weights. The most direct was simply to ask people which attribute is important. The problem is that respondents usually indicate that all attributes are important. In selecting a car, they want good gas mileage, sporty appearance, lots of room, a low price, and so forth. In conjoint analysis, the respondent is asked to make trade-off judgments. Is one feature desired enough to sacrifice another? If one attribute had to be sacrificed, which one would it be? Thus, the respondent provides extremely sensitive and useful information.

Some characteristics of situations where conjoint analysis has been used productively are:

1. Where the alternative products or services have a number of attributes, each with two or more levels (e.g., automatic versus manual transmission).

2. Where most of the feasible combinations of attribute levels do not presently exist.

3. Where the range of possible attribute levels can be expanded beyond those presently available.

4. Where the general direction of attribute preference probably is known (travelers want less noise, faster travel, more comfort, etc.).

The usual problem is that preferences for various attributes may be in conflict (a large station wagon cannot get into small parking spaces), or there may not be enough resources to satisfy all the preferences (a small price tag is not compatible with certain luxury features). The question usually is to find a compromise set of attribute levels.

The input data are obtained by giving respondents descriptions of concepts that represent the possible combinations of levels of attributes. For example, some of the credit card concepts for retailers to evaluate might be:

1. Discount rate of 6 percent.

2. Payment within 10 days.

3. Credit authorization by telephone.

4. 0.75 percent of billings to support payments for local retailer advertising.

5. No rebates.

Respondent retailers then evaluate each concept in terms of overall liking, intentions to buy, or rank order of preference compared to other concepts. Paired comparison judgments also can be obtained to provide the degree of preference of one profile over the other. However, ratings data are used in more than 50 percent of the commercial applications of conjoint analysis.

The computer program then assigns values or "utilities" for each level (also known as *part-worth utilities*) of each attribute. When these utilities are summed for each of the concepts being considered, the rank order of these total value scores should match the respondents' rank ordering of preference as closely as possible. This process can be illustrated with the utilities from the

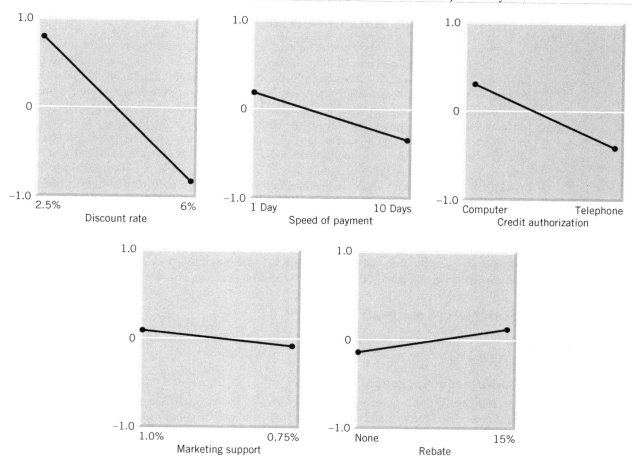

FIGURE 21.6
Utilities for Credit Card Attributes (Each Separate Interval Scale Measured in Terms of a Common Unit).
Source: P. E. Green, "A New Approach to Market Segmentation," *Business Horizons*, February 1977, pp. 61–73.

credit card study shown in the following table as well as in Figure 21.6. The combination with the highest total utility should be the one that originally was most preferred, and the combination with the lowest total utility should have been least preferred.

Attribute	Combination		Combination	
	Level	Utility	Level	Utility
Discount rate	2.5%	0.9	6%	−0.9
Speed of payment	1 day	0.2	10 days	−0.3
Credit authorization	Computer	0.3	Telephone	−0.3
Marketing support	1.0%	0.05	0.75%	−0.05
Rebate	15.0%	0.1	None	−0.1
Total utility for combination		1.55		−1.65

Interpreting Attribute Importance

The greater the difference between the highest- and the lowest-valued levels of an attribute, the more important is the attribute. Conversely, if all the possible levels have the same utility, the attribute is not important, for it has no influence on the overall attitude. In the credit card study, the size of the discount was clearly the most important attribute. While this is not a surprising finding, it should be kept in mind that the magnitude of the difference in utilities for the two discount levels is strongly influenced by the choice of extreme levels. Had the chosen discount levels been 2.5 percent and 4 percent, the difference in utilities would have been much less. For this reason, it is often desirable to use three or even four levels of a complex attribute. For example, in Figure 21.6, the relative importance of the discount rate is obtained as 56.25 percent $[(1.8)/(1.8+0.5+0.6+0.1+0.2)]$, where 1.8 is the difference in partworth utilities between the discount-rate levels. Similarly, the other numbers in the denominator represent the difference in utilities between the levels of the remaining attributes.

Usually, the measures of attribute importance obtained from a trade-off study are only a means to an end. The real payoff comes from using the results to identify optimal combinations of attribute levels for new products, services, or policies. To see how this is done, we first need to look more closely at the way the trade-off data are collected from respondents, analyzed, and interpreted.

Collecting Trade-off Data

Respondents can reveal their trade-off judgments by either considering two attributes at a time, or by making an overall judgment of a full profile of attributes.

Full-Profile Approach

In a **full-profile approach**, respondents are given cards that describe complete product or service configurations. For example, two possible full-profile descriptions of package tour holidays are shown in Figure 21.7. Not all possible combinations of attribute levels have to be presented in order to estimate the utilities. For example, in Figure 21.7, even with six attributes, each described at three levels, there are 18 profiles to compare.[12] Respondents can be asked either to rank-order the profiles in order of preference, or assign each of the 18 cards to a category of a rating scale

Card 1	Card 2
Water temperature Just warm enough to swim	**Water temperature** Comfortably warm
Hotel location Five-minute walk to beach	**Hotel location** Facing beach
Size of nearest town Fishing village	**Size of nearest town** Major country town
Flight schedule Weekend	**Flight schedule** Weekday
Local entertainment Bars	**Local entertainment** Bars, nightclubs, theaters
Price $250	**Price** $300

FIGURE 21.7

Product Descriptions.

Source: This illustration is adapted from D. Westwood, T. Lunn, and D. Bezaley, "The Trade-off Model and Its Extensions," paper presented at the *Annual Conference of the British Market Research Society*, March 1974.

measuring overall preference or intentions to buy. The advantage of the rating scale is that it can be administered by mail, whereas a ranking task usually entails a personal interview.

Trade-off Approach (Considering Two Attributes Simultaneously)

Respondents in a **trade-off approach** are asked to rank each combination of levels of two attributes, from most preferred to least preferred. The matrix shown in Figure 21.8 illustrates this approach, with the numbers in the cells representing one respondent's rankings. In this matrix, there are nine possible alternatives to be ranked. The best and the worst alternatives are obvious. The interesting evidence is that the respondent doing the ranking in this example is willing to walk five minutes to find comfortably warm water. However, there are six attributes in all, so potentially there could be

$$\frac{n(n-1)}{2} = \frac{6(5)}{2} = 15$$

such matrixes for each respondent to fill in. Fortunately, it is not necessary to present all pairs in order to extract statistically the utilities without confusing the contributions of the various attributes.

Comparing Data Collection Approaches[13]

The arguments in favor of the full-profile approach are that (1) the description of the concepts is more realistic, since all aspects are considered at the same time; (2) the concept evaluation task can employ either a ranking or rating scale; and (3) the respondent has to make fewer judgments than if the two-attribute trade-off approach is used. Unfortunately, as the number of attributes increases, the task of judging the individual profiles becomes very complex and demanding. With more than five or six attributes, there is a strong possibility of information overload, which usually leads respondents to ignore variations in the less important factors. To get the flavor of this problem, look at Figure 21.8 and see how difficult it is to choose one package holiday over another.

The pairwise trade-off approach is not a panacea either. Because more judgments are required, the task can be tedious and time consuming. Consequently, respondents may lose their place in the matrix or develop a standardized response pattern just to get the job done. Since only two attributes are being considered, there is a potential loss of realism. This problem is most troublesome when there is substantial environmental correlation among attributes for technological or other reasons. For example, the 0-to-55 mph acceleration time, gas mileage, horsepower rating, and top speed of an automobile are not independent attributes. When only two of these four attributes are being considered, respondents may be unclear as to what should be assumed about the others. This problem also is encountered with price because it may be used as an indicator of quality. Of course, if environmental correlations are high, it may be possible to create a composite factor. This means losing information about the component attributes.

		Facing beach	5 minutes walk to beach	More than 5 minutes walk to beach
	Comfortably warm	1	2	5
Water temperature	Just warm enough to swim	3	4	6
	Too cold to swim	7	8	9

FIGURE 21.8
Trade-Off Approach.

Studies comparing the two methods typically show that the estimated utilities are roughly similar and that, for large numbers of factors that are not environmentally correlated, the trade-off approach yields somewhat higher predictive validity. In part because it is difficult to find factors that are not correlated, the full-profile approach is increasingly preferred. Almost 60 percent of recent studies used the full-profile approach, and another 10 percent used a combination of full-profile and two factors at a time. Only 6 percent of the studies used the trade-off approach.[14]

Analyzing and Interpreting the Data

The analysis of conjoint or trade-off studies, like all other marketing research, is guided by the research purpose. As an illustration, a manufacturer of automobile batteries that carry a lifetime guarantee wanted to know how much emphasis to place on the fact that the batteries never need water. A conjoint study was conducted in which respondents were asked to evaluate full-concept profiles made up of combinations of three attributes and three levels:

Attribute	Levels
Price	$30, $45, $60
Length of guarantee	Lifetime, 60 months, 48 months
Maintenance required	No water needed, add water once a year, add water as needed

The preference ranking of these stimulus profiles was input to the analysis. The first problem in the data analysis is to estimate a set of utilities (or partworths) for the nine attribute levels, such that

1. The sum of the attribute level utilities for each specific profile equals the total utility for the profile.

2. The *derived* ranking of the stimulus profiles, based on the sum of estimated attribute level utilities, corresponds as closely as possible to the respondent's *original* ranking.

Although the details of the techniques used to achieve this are beyond the scope of this discussion, the elements are straightforward. The partworth utilities can be obtained with an iterative procedure that starts with an arbitrary set of utilities and systematically modifies them until the total utility of each profile correlates maximally to the original ranks. The procedure continues until no change in the utility of an attribute level will improve the correlation. As a practical matter, most analysts use regression analysis (Chapter 19) to obtain the attribute weight utilities, because it provides very similar results and is much easier and cheaper to use than an iterative procedure.[15]

Once the utilities are estimated, they are displayed, and the relative importance of each attribute is determined. In the case of automobile batteries, the following graph displays the results:

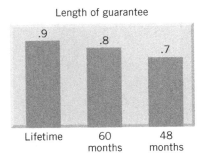

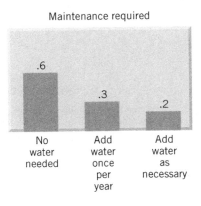

According to these utility values, both price and length of guarantee are more important than the maintenance attribute. However, the relative difference in the total utility from a change in the level of maintenance $(0.6 - 0.2 = 0.4)$ is greater than for a change in the length of guarantee $(0.9 - 0.7 = 0.2)$. Clearly, the fact that the battery does not need water should be emphasized as an advertising appeal, especially if potential buyers are not aware of this benefit.

Validity Issues

The conjoint model assumes that preference can be modeled by adding the utilities associated with attribute levels, and that these utilities can be estimated from either full-profile or trade-off data. There are several indications that the model has a substantial level of validity.

A bottom-line validity test is the remarkable acceptance of conjoint analysis in industry. The technique, introduced in 1971, was estimated to have had over 5,000 applications during its first 17 years. It now is used routinely by many market research firms and their clients.

The conjoint model has been found to predict the market share of transportation modes between two cities and the type of fare in North Atlantic air travel.[16] At the individual level, a conjoint model involving eight factors (including salary, location, need to travel, etc.) predicted subsequent job choice by MBA students, with an impressive 63 percent hit rate. Another study used a conjoint model successfully to predict the acceptance of 13 new products introduced into supermarkets.

The reliability of conjoint analysis has been the subject of several studies. In general, reliability has been found to be high. One study, exploring both the full-profile and the trade-off approach using five product classes, found that the output was not sensitive to which five of six attributes were included or whether three or five levels were used on the price attribute.[17] Another study concluded that reliability fell when the number of attributes was increased.[18] As in other multivariate techniques, the reliability of the profile evaluations or the partworth utilities can be assessed by the test-retest procedure. The internal validity can be evaluated through the hold-out sample and the external validity can be assessed through observing respondents' behavior in the actual marketplace.

Application Issues

Four areas of application appear especially promising. First, the insights that are gained into how consumers make choices within an existing market,[19] coupled with information on the perceptions of the competitive alternatives, are valuable for guiding communications programs. Second, the analysis can suggest new product or service configurations with significant consumer appeal compared to alternatives. Finally, the utility measurements can be used to develop strategic marketing simulations.[20] These are used to evaluate the volume and profit implications of changes in marketing strategies. The following is a typical application, taken from Kumar and Gaeth[21]:

> As a case in point, a study of consumer evaluations of color televisions was conducted in which consumer utilities were developed for 5 different attributes such as brand name, quality, warranty, serviceability, price, and their interactions. Moreover, each utility function was developed using both object data and ratings data as dependent variables.
>
> As might be expected, the utility function for each of the various types of airline service differed according to the length and purpose of the flight. However, in addition to obtaining consumers' evaluations of service profiles, the researchers also obtained information concerning their perceptions of each airline (that is, for the ones they were familiar with) on each of the service factors for which the consumers were given a choice.

The Reserves have been facing declining strength because of an inability to attract and retain people. The question was, What actions should be taken to modify the "product" or the "communications" to increase enlistments among civilians as well as the likelihood of reenlistment?

The overall objective of the study was to examine in detail motivational factors in enlistment and retention. More specific objectives were to (1) measure young men's propensity to serve or reenlist, (2) determine current perceptions of the Reserves, (3) determine the relative importance of the 12 key job attributes that may provide the basis for influencing young men to join and remain in the Reserves, and (4) indicate what configurations of job characteristics, benefits, and incentives will enhance accessions and reenlistment intentions among various target groups.

These objectives were tailor-made for a trade-off analysis. Separate samples of 17- to 26-year-old men without prior service and current reservists were studied. A computer-based interactive interview was used, with subjects responding on a keyboard to questions presented on a cathode-ray tube. The trade-off questions were in the form of preferences for pairs of attributes. A typical question appeared as follows:

"Which would you prefer . . . "

A 4-year enlistment term and a $1000 bonus	OR	A 6-year enlistment term and a $3000 bonus

Other attributes investigated included starting pay, educational assistance, hair regulations, retirement benefits, and hours of meeting each month.

The output of the study included the measurement of the relative importance of various attributes, and estimates of actual recruitment levels that would occur given any change in the attributes of the military "job."

FIGURE 21.9
Trade-Off Analysis.

These two major pieces of information provided the principal basis for developing a simulation of airline services over all major traffic routes. The purpose of the simulation was to estimate the effect on market share that a change in the service configuration of the sponsor's services would have, route by route, if competitors did not follow suit. Later, the sponsor used the simulation to examine the effect of assumed retaliatory actions by its competitors.

Although most applications have been in the private sector, conjoint and trade-off analyses also are well suited to conducting cost–benefit analyses of public policy decisions. An application (see Figure 21.9) to the problem of recruiting for the Armed Forces Reserves shows what can be done.[22]

There are constraints on applications, however. The most useful applications have been in complex, expensive, or risky product or service categories, such as remote computer terminals, transportation modes, and major appliances; or with problems such as retail-branch site selection. Even in these categories, the requirement that each attribute be divided into discrete levels is a potential limitation. The difficulty is with such attributes as durability or styling, which are difficult to divide sensibly into levels because there are no objective standards to define "very safe" or "smart styling." The value of trade-off analysis is limited further when used with products or services having only one or two important attributes or where little explicit attention is paid to trade-offs because the costs or risks are low. Kumar and Gaeth illustrate some problems that may occur with the use of conjoint analysis.[23]

SUMMARY OF CONJOINT ANALYSIS

Applications. Conjoint analysis is used to predict the buying or usage of a new product that still may be in concept form. It also is used to determine the relative importance of various attributes to respondents, based on their making trade-off judgments. One motivation is prediction. What sales or usage level will a new concept achieve? A second is understanding relationships. How does changing one of the attribute levels affect preference?

Inputs. The *dependent variable* is the preference judgment a respondent makes about a new concept. The *independent variables* are the attribute levels that need to be specified. Respondents make judgments about the concept either by considering two attributes at a time (trade-off approach) or by making an overall judgment of a full profile of attributes (full-profile approach).

Outputs. A value of relative utility is assigned to each level of an attribute. Each respondent will have her or his own set of utilities, although an average respondent can be created by averaging the input judgments. The percentage of respondents who would most prefer one concept from among a defined set of concepts can be determined.

Assumptions. The basic assumption is that people evaluate concepts by adding up their evaluations of the concept's individual attribute levels. It is assumed that the individual attributes are not excessively redundant and that there are no interactions between attributes.

Limitations. In the trade-off approach, the problem is that the task is too unrealistic. It's difficult to make trade-off judgments about two attributes while holding all the others constant. In the full-profile approach, the task can become very demanding, even for a motivated and conscientious respondent. There is a very real limit on the number of attributes that can be used, especially in the full-profile approach.

QUESTIONS AND PROBLEMS

21.1 Suppose an MDS study was to be made among high school seniors for use by the University of Indiana. The goal was to see how Indiana was positioned with respect to the 10–20 colleges with which it competes and to determine how students evaluate colleges.

(a) How would you determine which colleges should be the object of the MDS study?

(b) Generate a list of attributes that you feel should be included in the study. What methods did you use to generate the list?

(c) Detail 10 different ways to generate between-object similarities. Which one would you use in the study?

(d) Do you think the perceptual map would be different if preference data were used? Can you illustrate any hypothesized difference with an example?

21.2 How might a perceptual map like the one in Figure 21.2 be used to suggest a new-product concept? Be specific. How might the concept be developed? How might it be tested?

21.3 The claim is made that MDS is of little help in new-product planning, because most of the dimensions are "psychological" dimensions and not really actionable. Predicting psychological reactions to physical changes is very difficult. Furthermore, it is questioned, how much guidance do we gain from hearing that we need a "sportier" car or a more "full-bodied" beer? Comment.

21.4 How would you go about introducing ideal objects into Figure 21.2?

21.5 It is argued that people are not consciously aware of which dimensions they are employing to make similarity or even preference judgments. Further, respondents may base judgments on attributes to which they are unwilling to admit. The use of nonattribute data in MDS is, thus, rather like motivation research in that it allows the researcher to make judgments about information unavailable by direct methods. Comment.

21.6 Suppose, given Figure 21.5, an advertising objective was to reposition Pepsi as being more fun, light, active—closer to 7-Up. How could MDS be used to test proposed copy and evaluate the results of a campaign? Can you think of any possible problems with this kind of use of MDS?

21.7 An exciting use of correspondence analysis is using scanner data to generate maps. Scanner data provides information on which brands a family did and did not buy. Such a set of binary data can be used to generate a map positioning the brands in a space. Brands that are close will tend to be purchased by the same families, whereas brands that are far apart tend not to be purchased by the same family. Comment.

21.8 A relevant issue is whether respondents can provide directly similarity judgments that are meaningful. In particular,

(a) Do consumers commonly make overall similarity judgments? If not, will their judgment be meaningful?

(b) Does the perceptual map represent the internal cognitive structure, or does the nature of the task and memory limitation inhibit all the relevant dimensions from being recovered?

(c) Do respondents share the same concept of what is meant by "similarity?"

21.9 Attempt to label the dimensions of Figure 21.2 using only the object location information.

21.10 Describe why cluster analysis might be appropriate both before and after an MDS study.

21.11 In either the full-profile or the trade-off approach, the respondent can rank-order the alternative choices or can arrange them on some scale, such as extremely desirable, very desirable, desirable, neutral, and undesirable. What are the advantages and disadvantages to using a rank-order approach?

21.12 Explain how conjoint analysis is used to determine attribute importance. Is the resulting attribute importance sensitive to the selection of levels for an attribute? Illustrate by using Figure 21.6.

21.13 Compare the full-profile approach to the trade-off approach. What are the advantages of each? Which would you use in the example of automobile batteries? If price were one of the attributes, would you be more likely to use the full-profile approach?

21.14 Do purchasers of major appliances, such as refrigerators and room air conditioners, treat price as an attribute in an additive model of preference that underlies conjoint analysis? That is, do they arrive at an overall judgment by summing the evaluative rating of each attribute (including price)? How would you test whether this model applied to this situation?

21.15 Do the following:

(a) Reflect on the last airplane flight you took. What attributes did you consider in your choice of airline?

(b) To learn more about the trade-offs you made in your choice of airline, conduct a trade-off analysis on yourself. Start with the attributes and then establish two or three feasible levels for each attribute. Prepare trade-off matrices of 10 or more possible pairs of attributes, and fill in the cells according to a criterion that seems appropriate. What have you learned?

21.16 Interview the manager of a local "quick copy" shop or an individual who recently bought or specified a copying machine, to learn which attributes were used to choose it. Can the buyer describe on which features trade-off were made? Are there logical levels to the attributes that were used?

END NOTES

1. This example is based on research reported in T. P. Hustad, C. S. Mayer, and T. W. Whippie, "Consideration of Context Differences in Product Evaluation and Market Segmentation." *Journal of the Academy of Marketing Science*, 3, 1975, pp. 34–47.

2. J. R. Hauser and F. S. Koppelman, "Alternative Perceptual Mapping Techniques: Relative Accuracy and Usefulness," *Journal of Marketing Research*, 16, November 1979, pp. 495–506. Hauser and Koppelman conclude that factor analysis is superior to discriminant analysis; however, many other experienced researchers prefer discriminant analysis for the reasons noted herein.

3. J. H. Myers and E. Tauber, *Market Structure Analysis*. Chicago: American Marketing Association, 1977, pp. 48–55. The authors call this technique a *weighted covariance analysis*.

4. D. L. Hoffman and G. R. Franke, "Correspondence Analysis: Graphical Representation of Categorical Data in Marketing Research," *Journal of Marketing Research*, August 1986, pp. 213–227; M. J. Greenacre, "The Carroll-Green-Schaffer Scaling in Correspondence Analysis: A Theoretical and Empirical Appraisal," *Journal of Marketing Research*, 26, August 1989, pp. 358–365.

5. Hauser and Koppelman, op. cit.

6. J. H. Myers and E. Tauber, *Market Structure Analysis*. Chicago: American Marketing Association, 1977, p. 38.

7. V. Kumar and R. P. Leone, "Nonlinear Mapping: An Alternative to Multidimensional Scaling for Product Positioning," *Journal of the Academy of Marketing Science*, 19(3), 1991, pp. 165–176.

8. P. E. Green, "A New Approach to Market Segmentation," *Business Horizons*, February 1977, pp. 61–73.

9. R. L. Knight and M. D. Menchik, "Conjoint Preference Estimation for Residential Land Use Policy Evaluation," Institute for Environmental Studies, University of Wisconsin, July 1974.

10. D. Clarke, "*Clark Material Handling Group—Overseas: Brazilian Product Strategy* (A)," Boston: HBS Case Services, 1981.

11. D. R. Wittink and P. Cattin, "Commercial Use of Conjoint Analysis: An Update," *Journal of Marketing*, 53(3), 1989, pp. 91–96.

12. In fact, there are (333,333) 729 possible combinations. Fortunately, it is possible to use an experimental design, known as an *orthogonal array*, in which a small set of combinations is selected such that the independent contributions of all six factors are balanced, to reduce this to 18 combinations. See P. E. Green, "On the Design of Choice Experiments Involving Multifactor Alternatives," *Journal of Consumer Research*, 1, September 1974, pp. 61–68.

13. This section draws on P. E. Green and V. Srinivasan, "Conjoint Analysis in Consumer Research: Issues and Outlook," *Journal of Consumer Research*, 5, September 1978, pp. 103–123; P. E. Green and V. Srinivasan, "Conjoint Analysis in Marketing: New Developments with Implications for Research and Practice," *Journal of Marketing*, 54(4), 1990, pp. 3–19.

14. Wittink and Cattin, op. cit.

15. In the regression approach, the rank ordering is the dependent variable and the independent variables are 0–1 variables for each level on an attribute, less one. Thus, for the price attribute there would be a 0–1 variable for $45 (coded as "1" only if the profile has a $45 price) and a 0–1 variable for $60 (coded as a "1" only if the profile has a $60 price). The profile with a $30 price would be the reference level and therefore would not have its own 0–1 variable. If the $45 variable is coded "0" and the $60 variable is coded "0," then the level must be $30.

16. The predictive studies are reviewed in D. B. Montgomery, "Conjoint Calibration of the Customer/Competitor Interface in Industrial Markets," in Backhaus and D. Wilson, eds., *New Developments in Industrial Marketing*. New York: Springer-Verlag, 1985.

17. D. Reibstein, J. E. G. Bateson, and W. Boulding. "Conjoint Analysis Reliability: Empirical Findings," *Marketing Science*, Summer 1988, pp. 271–286.

18. N. K. Malhotra, "Structural Reliability and Stability of Nonmetric Conjoint Analysis," *Journal of Marketing Research*, 19, May 1982, pp. 199–207.

19. P. E. Green and A. M. Krieger, "Segmenting Markets with Conjoint Analysis," *Journal of Marketing*, 55(4), 1991, pp. 20–31; R. Kohli and V. Mahajan, "A Reservation-Price Model for Optimal Pricing of Multiattribute Products in Conjoint Analysis," *Journal of Marketing Research*, 28(3), 1991, pp. 347–354.

20. P. E. Green, J. D. Carrol, and S. M. Goldberg, "A General Approach to Product Design Optimization via Conjoint Analysis," *Journal of Marketing*, 45, Summer 1981, pp. 17–37.

21. V. Kumar and G. Gaeth, "Attribute Order and Product Familiarity Effects in Decision Tasks Using Conjoint Analysis," *International Journal of Research in Marketing*, 8, 1991, pp. 113–124.

22. Public Sector Research Group of Market Facts, Inc., "Conjoint Analysis of Values of Reserve Component Attributes," a report prepared for the Department of Defense. Washington, D.C.: U.S. Government Printing Office, November 1977.

23. Kumar and Gaeth, op. cit.

Case 21-1 ‖ Nester's Foods

Nester's Foods is evaluating a group of concepts for new diet products. To evaluate the positioning of these new products, an MDS study was conducted. The respondents, women who were on a diet, were asked to group 38 food products, including 10 of the new diet concepts. The output of the MDS, based on these similarity ratings, is shown in Figure 21.10. "L.C." stands for low calorie, and "M/S" stands for meal substitute.

Questions for Discussion

1. Label the dimensions.

2. Group the products into clusters visually and describe the different clusters. What are the positioning implications?

3. What other information would you collect, and how would you use it in the analysis?

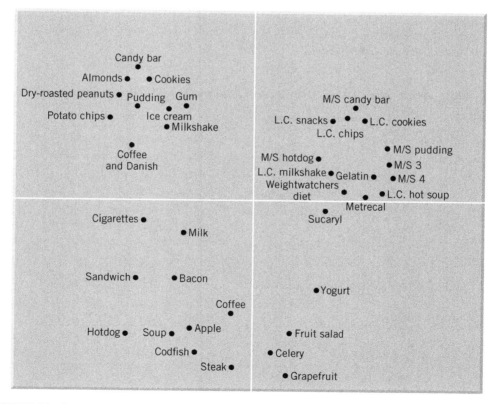

FIGURE 21.10

Two-Dimensional Perceptual Configuration of 38 Food Products.

Source: Adapted from Y. Wind and P. J. Robinson, "Product Positioning: an Application of Multidimensional Scaling," in R. L. Haley, ed., *Attitude Research in Transition*, Chicago: American Marketing Association, 1972.

Case 21-2	The Electric Truck Case

John Hirsch of Central Utility was attempting to develop conclusions from a conjoint analysis study of electrically powered trucks. The study objectives were (1) to determine the number of commercial applications that were compatible with the limitations of electric vehicles, and (2) to assess the perceived importance of those technical requirements as compared to other vehicle characteristics, such as initial costs and pollution levels.

In the first phase of the study, a sample of truck owners was interviewed and the nature of their applications was determined. They found that 11 percent of commercial truck applications could get along with the electric vehicle limitations of a 4-mile range, a maximum of 40 stops, a load limit of 1,500 pounds payload, and "seldom" freeway travel. The most sensitive dimension was freeway travel. If that limitation were removed, the electric vehicle could be used for 19 percent of applications. In the second phase of the study, people responsible for purchases of commercial trucks were invited to an "electric vehicle seminar at which an operating electric truck was available for inspection and test driving." During the seminar they discussed the advantages and disadvantages of electric vehicles and participated in a conjoint analysis study.

As Table 21.2 indicates, the conjoint study involved five attributes, each of which had two levels associated with it. For example, the initial price was either $5,000 or $8,000. The respondents were those attending the electric vehicle seminars. Each respondent was asked to rank 16 alternative truck designs, based on the attributes shown in Table 21.2. The rankings of the respondents were averaged and provided the inputs to a conjoint analysis program. The output utilities also are shown in Table 21.2.

Questions for Discussion

Evaluate the study. Do you feel the attributes and the attribute levels were well selected? Interpret Table 21.2.

1. What information does it contain?

2. What are the underlying assumptions?

3. What additional analysis might be useful to do?

Source: Prepared by George Hargreaves, John D. Claxton, Frederick H. Siller, and David A. Aaker as a basis for class discussion.

Table 21.2   Relative Utilities of Conventional versus Electric Vehicles

Attribute	Conventional vehicle	Utility	Electric vehicle	Utility
Speed and range	Unlimited	+1.426	40 mph and 40 miles	−1.426
Operating costs	Standard: 20 cents/mile	−0.928	Reduced: 10 cents/mile	+0.928
Initial price	Standard: $15,000	+0.901	Premium: $18,000	−0.901
Pollution levels	Standard: Gasoline engine	−0.544	Zero	+0.544
Propulsion system	Conventional: Gasoline engine	−0.019	New propulsion system	+0.019
	Net utility	+0.836	Net utility	−0.836

Additional Cases for this Chapter are available on the Web:

Web Case 21-1	Pepsi-Cola

Web Case 21-2	Fargo Instruments

Presenting the Results

22

LEARNING OBJECTIVES

- Discuss the fundamentals of research presentation.
- Discuss how to prepare the research report.
- Discuss issues related to successful oral presentation.
- Discuss the importance of continued relationship with the client.

It is difficult to exaggerate the importance of the role that communication skills play in effective management. Along with the related skill of working with and motivating people, the ability to communicate effectively is undoubtedly the most important attribute a manager can have. There is also little doubt that managers are dissatisfied with the present level of communication skills. Business schools are criticized routinely and justifiably for focusing on techniques and neglecting communication skills. Further, managers frequently make harsh judgments about themselves and their colleagues with respect to communication skills. A senior advertising executive concluded that "advertising people are bright, presentable, usually articulate—but most of them are duds when it comes to making presentations."[1] A special *Business Week* report said, "So appalling is the quality of written reports in some companies that senior executives are sending their managers through writing courses, to try to put some point back into the reports that cross their desks and eliminate the extraneous material that increasingly obscures the point."[2]

Effective communication between research users and research professionals is extremely important to the research process. The formal presentation usually plays a key role in the communication effort. Generally, presentations are made twice during the research process. First, there is the research proposal presentation, discussed in Chapter 4, when the client must decide to accept, change, or reject it. Second, there is the presentation of the research results, when decisions associated with the research purpose are addressed and the advisability of conducting further research often is considered. This chapter will focus on the pre-sentation of research results, but much of the material will apply to the original research proposal presentation as well.

Guidelines for Successful Presentations

The purpose of this chapter is to help readers avoid making presentations that are ineffective because they are dull, confusing, or irrelevant. Have you been exposed lately to any that hit the jackpot—that were all three? Presentations can be written, oral, or both. Later in the chapter, we will offer some tips on making both written and oral presentations. First, however, here are some guidelines that apply to both types of presentations. In general, a presenter should:

1. Communicate to a specific audience.

2. Structure the presentation.

3. Create audience interest.

4. Be specific and visual.

5. Address validity and reliability issues.

Each of these guidelines will be discussed in turn.

Communicate to a Specific Audience

The first step is to know the audience, its background, and its objectives. Most effective presentations seem like conversations, or memos to a particular person as opposed to an amorphous group. The key to obtaining that feeling is to identify the audience members as precisely as possible.

Know your audience

- Who are you addressing?
- What is their background?
- What are their time constraints?
- How technical can you get without losing your audience?
- Can you involve the audience by asking questions?

Audience identification affects presentation decisions such as selecting the material to be included and the level of presentation. Excessive detail or material presented at too low a level can be boring or seem patronizing. However, the audience can become irritated or lost when material perceived as relevant is excluded or the material is presented at too high a level. In an oral presentation, the presenter can ask audience members whether they already know some of the material.

Frequently, a presentation must be addressed to two or more different audiences. There are several ways to deal with such a problem. In a written presentation, an executive summary at the outset can provide an overview of the conclusions for the benefit of those in the audience who are not interested in details. The presentation should respect the audience's time constraints. An appendix also can be used to reach some people selectively, without distracting the others. Sometimes the introduction to a chapter or a section can convey the nature of the contents, which certain audiences may bypass. In an oral presentation, the presence of multiple audiences should be recognized with a statement such as, "I need to provide some information on instrumentation next. You engineers in the audience can help by making sure that I don't miss anything." Such an acknowledgment probably will please the engineers so that they will be helpful rather than bored and restless.

Structure the Presentation

Each piece of the presentation should fit into the whole, just as individual pieces fit into a jigsaw puzzle. The audience should not be muttering, "What on earth is this person talking about?" or "How does this material fit in?" or "I'm lost." The solution is to provide a well-defined structure. As Figure 22.1 illustrates, the structure should include an introduction, a body, and a summary.

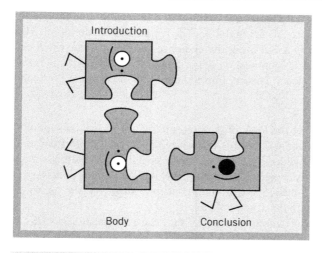

FIGURE 22.1
The Presentation Structure.

Further, each of the major sections should be structured similarly. The precept is to tell the audience what you are going to say, say it, and then tell them what you said. Sometimes you want to withhold the conclusion, to create interest. In that case the audience could be told, "The objective here will be to come to a recommendation as to whether this new product should go into test market and, if so, with what type of pricing strategy." Further, use nontechnical definitions as much as possible to present the report in simple language. For example, critical path could simply be stated as "the list of activities that must be completed on time."

Introduction

The *introduction* should play several roles. First, it should provide audience interest, a task that will be discussed in detail in the next section. A second function is to identify the presentation's central idea or objective. Third, it should provide a road map to the rest of the presentation so that the audience can picture its organization and flow. Sometimes the only way to develop such a road map is to say something like, "This presentation has four parts. The research purpose and objectives will be discussed first. The second section will describe the research design. . . ." However, with a little effort and luck it is sometimes possible to develop and use a flowchart that will convey the structure in a more interesting way. For example, in this book, such a structural role was played by Figures 1.1, 3.1 and 4.2. (The reader should attempt to identify other figures so used.) When such a device is used, the audience should be clear when each section will be addressed. The label for the section should use identical wording throughout, and the start of the section should be made clear: "Having finished the second section, we now move to the third."

Body

Usually, it is best to divide the *body* of the presentation (or the major section) into between two and five parts. The audience will be able to absorb only so much information. If that information can be aggregated into chunks, it will be easier to assimilate. Sometimes the points to be made cannot be combined easily or naturally. In that case, it is sometimes necessary to use a longer list: "There are 12 problems in this new product concept." However, the presentation should never drift through the body with no structure at all.

One way to structure a presentation is by the research questions: "This research was conducted to address four research questions. Each of these will be considered in turn." Another method that is often useful when presenting the research proposal is to base it on the research process, as was illustrated in Chapter 4.

The most useful presentations will include a statement of implications and recommendations relevant to the research purpose. However, when the researcher lacks information about the total situation because the research study addresses only a limited aspect of it, the ability to generate recommendations may be limited.

Summary

The purpose of the *presentation summary* is to identify and underline the important points of the presentation and to provide some repetition of their content. The summary should support the presentation communication objectives by helping the audience to retain the key parts of the content. The audience usually will perk up when they realize the end is near and an overview of the presentation is coming, so the summary section should be signaled clearly. A section summary has the additional task of providing a transition to the next section. The audience should feel that there is a natural flow from one section to the next.

Create Audience Interest

The audience should be motivated to read or listen to the presentation's major parts and to the individual elements of each section. Those in the audience should know why the presentation is relevant to them and why each section was included. A section that cannot hold interest probably should be excluded or relegated to appendix status.

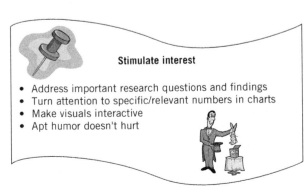

Stimulate interest

- Address important research questions and findings
- Turn attention to specific/relevant numbers in charts
- Make visuals interactive
- Apt humor doesn't hurt

The research purpose and objectives are good vehicles to provide motivation. The research purpose should specify decisions to be made and should relate to the research questions. A presentation that focuses on those research questions and their associated hypotheses will naturally be tied to relevant decisions and hold audience interest. In contrast, a presentation that attempts to report on *all* the questions that were included in the survey and in the cross-tabulations often will be long, uninteresting, and of little value.

The researcher should point out those aspects of the results that are important and interesting. Suppose a chart is used that contains 10 descriptors of customers in 13 different markets. The presenter should circle three or so of those 130 numbers and be prepared to say, "Look at this number. We had hypothesized it to be higher than the others and it actually is lower. Let's look at the possible reasons and implications." The presenter should not feel compelled to wade through every detail of the questionnaire and the analysis.

As the analysis proceeds and the presentation is being prepared, the researcher should be on the lookout for results that are exceptionally persuasive, relevant, interesting, and unusual. Sometimes the deviant respondent with the strange answers can provide the most insight if his or her responses are pursued and not discarded. For example, in Figure 16.4, more respondents answered the age question than the income question. Of the 48 respondents who did not answer the income question, almost all of them were "moderately interested" in the new health plan. Why? Are there any implications? Sometimes a few or even one deviant respondent can provide useful ideas and insights.

The best way to provide interest is to make the content so relevant that the audience will be interested; however, they may not always be absorbing the content. Especially in those cases, it is very useful to make the presentation a lively and interesting experience. One way is to interject humor. The best humor is that tied to the subject matter or to the presentation, as opposed to memorized jokes that really do not fit. It is good to reward the audience periodically, however, and humor often works. Another tactic is to change the pace of the presentation. Break up the text with graphs, pictures, or even cartoons. In an oral presentation, try a variety of visual aids and some audience-involvement techniques. For example, the audience may be asked a question periodically and given a chance to talk and become involved.

Be Specific and Visual

Avoid talking or writing in the abstract. If different members of the audience have different or vague understandings of important concepts, there is a potential problem. Terms that are ambiguous or not well known should be defined and illustrated or else omitted. Thus, in a segmentation study, an "active saver" might be unambiguously defined as one who added at least $500 to savings in each of the last two years.

Project important numbers clearly

Market				174480
Broucher	Sales Revenue	$174,480		26172
POS				148,308
Flower	Costs	$ 26,172		20,000
Direct	**Profit**	$148,308		128,308
Premium				0
Total	61030	19424 93	Net Profit	128,308

Be creative with visuals
focus-group findings on a student discount card

✓ Marketing efforts directed to parents

✓ Flyers with clear and concise information

👎 E-mail from unfamiliar third parties

👎 "Buzz" words on marketing materials

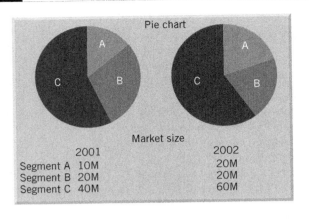

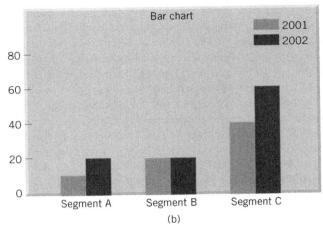

(a)   (b)

FIGURE 22.2
Graphically Portrayed Data. (a) Pie Chart. (b) Bar Chart.

The most interesting presentations usually use specific stories, anecdotes, studies, or incidents to make points. They will be much more interesting and graphic than a generalization, however accurate and scientific. Instead of "studies have shown that. . .," it is more effective to say, "In the Topeka test market the 69-cent price had far less trial than the 89-cent price for product X when the bright blue package was used." In other words, give concrete examples. A utility company conducted a focus-group study to learn homeowners' motivations to conserve energy and their attitudes toward adding insulation. The marketing research director, in presenting the results to top management, played a 20-minute edited videotape recording of the focus groups, in which the key segments were illustrated graphically. The impact on the audience was greater than otherwise would have been possible. They actually heard specific customers, representative of the emerged segments, forcefully put forth their views. The adage, "A picture is worth a thousand words," applies to both written and oral presentations. A mass of data often can be communicated clearly with graphs. A wide variety is available, such as bar graphs, line graphs, and pie charts (see Figure 22.2a,b). Color can be employed to add interest, to highlight findings, and to help deal with complexity. Also, use short, "crisp" titles as opposed to longer titles (see Table 22.1).

Table 22.1   **Title of Tables/Figures**

	Hypothetical, longer, more explanatory titles typical of many presentations	**Short, "crisp" titles**
Example 1	Median incomes for families, by type of community, for 1940 through 1980	Family incomes by area (1940–1980)
Example 2	Projected incomes for families, by type of community, for 1990 through 2020	Income predictions: the next 30 years
Example 3	Critical path analysis, tasks, and slack time for 12-month work program	Next year's work program
Example 4	Effectiveness–cost ratios for alternative development projects for fiscal year 1989–90	Project recommendations for next year
Example 5	Unemployment rates and frequencies for major industries and communities for six-county area	Regional unemployment statistics

Source: Adapted from L. P. Witzling and R. C. Greenstreet, *Presenting Statistics*, New York: John Wiley, 1992, p. 224.

Address Issues of Validity and Reliability

The presentation should help the audience avoid misinterpreting the results. Throughout Part II of this book, countless potential research design issues were raised that can affect the validity and interpretation of the results. The wording of the questions, the order in which they are asked, and the sampling design are among the design dimensions that can lead to biased results and misinterpretations. The presentation should not include an exhaustive description of all the design considerations. Nobody is interested in a textbook discussion of the advantages of telephone over mail surveys, or how you located homes in an area sampling design. However, when the wording of a question or some other design issue can affect an interpretation and ultimately a research conclusion, that issue should be raised and its possible effect on the interpretation discussed. For example, in a product-concept test, the method of exposing respondents to the concept may be crucial. Some discussion of why the method used was selected and its effect on the interpretation may be very useful. Try to identify those design issues that will affect interpretation and raise them in the context of the interpretation.

The presentation should include some indication of the reliability of the results. At a minimum, it always should be clear what sample size was involved. The key results should be supported by more precise information in the form of interval estimates or a hypothesis test. The hypothesis test basically indicates, given the sample size, what probability exists that the results were merely an accident of sampling. If the probability (or significance level) of the latter is not low, then the results probably would not be repeated. Do not imply more precision than is warranted. If 15 out of 52 respondents answered positively, do not give the percentage as 28.846. Rather, use 29 percent, or "nearly 30 percent." Consider the following exchange:

Speaker:	27.273 percent favored version B of the product.
Audience Member:	What was the sample size?
Speaker:	Around 11.
Audience Member:	Really? As large as that!

Written Report

The general guidelines discussed so far are applicable to both written reports and oral presentations. However, it is important to generate a research report that will be interesting to read. Most researchers are not trained in effective report writing. In their enthusiasm for research, they often overlook the need for a good writing style. In writing a report, long sentences should be reconsidered and the critical main points should stand out. Here are some hints[3] for effective report writing.

- Use main heading and subheadings to communicate the content of the material discussed.
   Main Heading: Probability Sampling
      Subheading: Statistical Issues in Probability Sampling—Systematic Sampling

- Use the present tense as much as possible to communicate information.
   "Most of the consumers prefer Brand A to Brand B"

- Whether the presentation is written or oral, use active voice construction to make it lively and interesting. Passive voice is wordy and dull.
   Active voice: Most consumers prefer Brand A.
   Passive voice: Brand A is preferred by most of the consumers.

- Use computer-generated tables and graphs for effective presentation. Figures 22.3 and 22.4 are examples of graphical illustration, and Table 22.2 shows the results for a sample of questions in a table form.

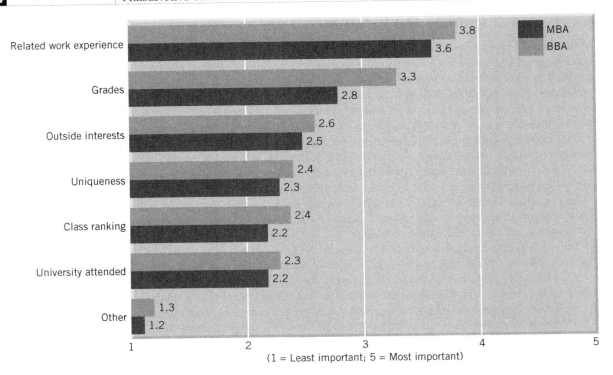

FIGURE 22.3
Ranking of Resume Screening Factors.

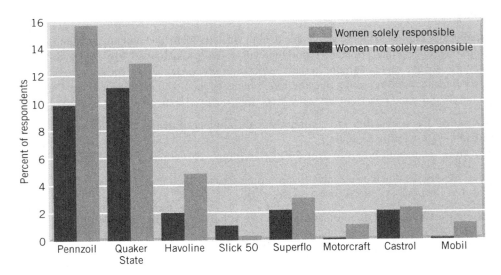

FIGURE 22.4
Unaided Recall of Brand Name.

Table 22.2 Descriptive Information on the Responses

		Statistic				
	Question	Mean	Median	Min	Max	Standard deviation
M A R K E T I N G R E S E A R C H	Need for external marketing research great?[a]	2.68	2.50	1	5	1.04
	Importance of need for external marketing research[b]	2.50	2.50	1	5	1.18
	Duration too long?[a]	2.90	3.00	2	5	1.01
	Duration too short?[a]	2.45	3.00	1	4	0.85
	Importance of duration[b]	2.09	2.00	1	4	1.06
	Frequency good?[a]	2.72	3.00	1	4	1.07
	Importance of frequency[b]	2.13	2.00	1	4	0.99
	Price good?[a]	2.90	3.00	1	5	1.15
	Importance of Price[b]	2.68	3.00	1	5	1.17
	Results confidential?[a]	4.04	5.00	2	5	1.55
	Importance of confidentiality[b]	3.90	4.00	1	5	1.41
	Benefits to UH great?[a]	4.00	4.00	2	5	0.81
	Importance of UH benefits[b]	2.45	2.00	1	5	1.14
	Sponsor time too long?[a]	2.27	2.00	1	4	0.82
	Sponsor time too short?[a]	2.90	3.00	2	4	0.68
	Importance of sponsor time[b]	2.27	2.00	1	4	0.88
	Value of project?[a]	3.18	3.00	1	5	1.05
	Importance of value[b]	3.50	3.00	1	5	1.10

[a] 1 = Strongly disagree, 2 = Disagree, 3 = Neither agree nor disagree, 4 = Agree, 5 = Strongly agree.
[b] 1 = Of no importance, 2 = Moderately important, 3 = Important, 4 = Very important, 5 = Extremely important.

- Use informative headings:
  "Brand Quality is the Key Factor in Product Selection," not "Outcomes of Product Selection Analysis."

- Use verbatims to communicate respondents' comments. Many times the way a customer expresses himself or herself means a lot to the brand manager.

- Use double-sided presentation if possible. For example, tables or graphs could be presented on the left side of an open report and their descriptions on the right side.

The Organization of the Report

A report can be organized in many ways since no single format is suitable for all purposes. The nature of the topic, the type of study, and the nature of the audience will dictate the report's format. A general format for presenting a research report is given in Table 22.3.

Table 22.3   General Format for a Research Report

I.   Cover Page

II.   Executive Summary

III.   Table of Contents

IV.   Introduction

V.   Methodology

VI.   Findings

VII.   Limitations

VIII.   Conclusions and Recommendations

IX.   Appendixes

Table 22.4   Table of Contents of a Research Report

Cover Page:	The cover page should provide information on the title of the study, the date prepared, for whom it is prepared, and the researcher(s)' names and organization.
Executive Summary:	This must be brief, crisp, and informative, since most of the time executives pay attention only to this section. Present the research objectives and goals, findings, conclusions, and recommendations.
Table of Contents:	This includes complete details of all the major sections and subsections and gives the associated page numbers. Table 22.4 is an example of a table of contents for a research report.
Introduction:	This section should describe the nature of the problem, clearly state the research objectives and research questions, and give an overview of the report's organization.
Methodology:	Describe the methodology used to conduct the study. All technical details should be presented in the appendix.
Findings:	The results of the study usually occupy the bulk of the report. Describe the findings in detail along with the necessary tables and graphs. This is the place to give the managerial implications of the study results.
Limitations:	Usually assumptions are made while conducting a research study. This section should describe the limitations of the assumptions and any problems that may have arisen during the data collection, sampling, or survey process.
Conclusions and	Here, you should clearly state the conclusions of the study and give Recommendations: possible recommendations. These recommendations would involve either suggesting a strategy or presenting ideas for implementing strategies, and so forth.
Appendixes:	These contain all technical details of the study such as copies of questionnaires, coding instructions, data, sampling, plan, and so on.

Finally, you should include a cover letter with the report. This cover letter provides details on the enclosed material—the research report, who is responsible for the project, and which people are receiving copies of the report. It should also communicate that the researcher will be happy to answer any questions that may arise from the report.

Oral Presentation

The ability to communicate orally is extremely important to effective management in general and to the marketing research functions in particular. What can be done to ensure that the oral presentation is as effective as possible? The following five suggestions will be discussed in this section:

1. Don't read.
2. Use visual aids.
3. Make sure that the start is positive.
4. Avoid distracting the audience.
5. Involve the audience.

Don't Read

Not everyone will agree with this first suggestion; however, these authors firmly believe that the risks and disadvantages of reading outweigh the advantages. The biggest problem with reading is that it usually is boring for the reader and for the audience. Very few can make a script sound interesting, and those few usually do even better without a script. Further, it is necessary to develop the ability to communicate orally in front of a group without a script, to prepare for those occasions when there is no time to prepare a script or when the presenter must adapt to new developments in the middle of a presentation. If you rely too heavily on a script and use it in what may be limited opportunities to give presentations, you will not develop this important capability.

The advantages of reading from a written report are that the time of the presentation and the choice of words are not left to chance, and you are protected from an attack of stage fright. The alternative is good preparation, a set of notes, and rehearsal. The notes should provide (1) an outline so that the proper flow is maintained, and (2) a list of items that should be included. You may want to consult the notes occasionally to make sure you have not omitted anything. More detailed notes can be consulted more frequently. To avoid distraction, keep the notes on a lectern or on cards or a clipboard, positioned so that you can manage them easily with one hand. Especially when the length of the presentation needs to be carefully controlled, rehearsal is essential. Often, five or more rehearsals can be worthwhile. It is even better if feedback is available in the form of a practice audience or a videotape. You can combat stage fright with deep breathing, pauses, and experience. There is no substitute for experience.

Use Visual Aids

Visual aids perform several functions. First, they give impact to the information and focus attention on important points. Second, ideas that are extremely difficult to express in words often can be communicated easily with visual aids. Finally, they help to give the presentation variety. Visual aids include computer-assisted (e.g., PowerPoint) presentations, transparencies, charts, handouts, slides, videotapes, films, samples, demonstrations, and role-playing. Transparencies, charts, slides, and hand-outs are probably the most widely used. However, computer-assisted presentations are increasingly being used when appropriate facilities are available.

Computer-assisted presentations provide many advantages, including high-quality pictures, ability to focus on a point-by-point basis (bulletin method), the ease of going forward/backward during the presentation, and opportunity to tie in with the Internet. This method of presentation requires computer hardware and appropriate software (e.g., PowerPoint, Corel), along with a projector. Portable devices are expensive and therefore the use of this method is not very common. Since most medium- to large-size companies have the required material, it is becoming the norm to use the computer-assisted presentation method when dealing with these companies.

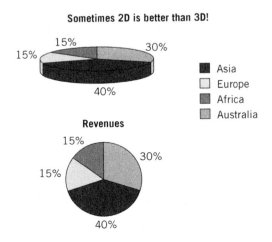

Sometimes screenshots speak louder than words!

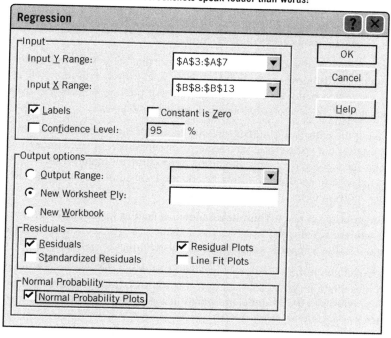

Transparencies are easy to make and can be carried in a folder. They have the advantage of controlling the audience's attention. The transparency can be exposed one line at a time by covering the rest with a piece of paper. The audience thus focuses on what is being uncovered at the moment and does not wander ahead of the presentation. You can write on the transparency to make a point during the presentation. The key to successful use of transparencies is using readable, large type, and minimizing the number of words or numbers used. Experienced and skilled users of transparencies often use only five or fewer lines per transparency, with each line containing only a few words or numbers. One rule of thumb is that a single transparency should contain no more then 30 words or items of data.

Similar guidelines apply to charts and slides, which share most of the characteristics of transparencies. Charts are more versatile than transparencies but are less convenient to make and carry. Slides are better for large audiences, since they can be seen more easily, but they require time to prepare and are not easily modified. Thus, they are not suitable for a presentation that is still being developed and refined.

The use of hand-outs provides the audience with something to take notes on and to take with them. As a result, the audience burden of taking notes is greatly reduced. Sometimes, when transparencies are used, the audience's note-taking task is so difficult that it becomes distracting. Hand-outs free listeners to attend to and participate more fully in the presentation. Their disadvantages are that they must be prepared beforehand and the audience is tempted to look ahead. Further, there is always the distraction of making sure everyone is on the right page, although numbering the pages helps.

The start should be positive in tone, confident, and involving. Sometimes a period of silence can be used effectively to get attention. It is useful to stimulate and involve the audience immediately, perhaps by a provocative question or statement. Absolutely never apologize at the outset, even in jest. If you tell the audience you are nervous, unprepared, or unknowledgeable, even in the context of a humorous line, the audience will tend to believe you.

Avoid Distracting the Audience

The presenter needs to be aware that the audience is easily distracted. The following do's and don'ts address some common causes of distraction.

1. Take everything out of your pockets and make sure that there is nothing on the lectern other than your notes. Remove pens, pointers, keys, and clips—everything. It often happens, without your even being aware of it, that you will pick up objects and manipulate them until the audience is severely distracted, if not driven bananas.

2. Try to avoid the extremes of either obvious pacing or hiding behind a lectern. It can be as distracting to see a speaker clutch a lectern for support as to see someone pace back and forth. The speaker's movements should be purposeful and natural, such as stepping aside to point to a chart, standing or sitting beside the lectern, or moving closer to the audience for a short portion of the presentation.

3. Maintain good eye contact. This allows audience feedback, stimulates trust and confidence in what you are saying, and involves the audience. A speaker who avoids eye contact by looking up or down or somewhere else risks distracting the audience.

4. Be concerned about the sound of your voice. Listen to a tape of your presentation if possible. A presentation can be distracting if it is too soft, loud, fast, slow, or monotoned. Be sure to use pauses to break up the presentation and to allow the audience time to digest the material.

Involve the Audience

An involved audience will be more interested. An effective technique is to intersperse questions throughout. If time does not permit a discussion, a pause at least gives the audience members a chance to reflect. Sometimes it is useful to ask each person to write down his or her opinion on a piece of paper—for example, a personal judgment on a key value in the data analysis. Another technique is to refer to the ideas of people in the audience, saying, for example, "As John mentioned last week. . . ."

The question-and-answer part of the presentation is particularly important. This often concludes the talk, but it can be permitted to occur during the presentation. Pause and make sure that the question is understood; then, if possible, give a short positive or negative response and as compact an explanation as possible. If you do not know, say so, adding (if appropriate) that you will get the answer by the next day. A good technique is to write the question down so you do not forget it. Equally important, those in the audience see that you are taking them seriously. Anticipate questions beforehand, and rehearse the answers. Sometimes it is even effective to leave things out of the presentation if they can be covered more effectively during the question-and-answer period.

Relationship with the Client

It is important to work with the client or at least be available to clarify or interpret the research results when the findings are implemented. This continued relationship not only helps researchers to evaluate the project's usefulness, it gives them a sense of confidence about the quality of their work. Since most marketing research projects are obtained through word-of-mouth referrals, not through advertising, it is important to satisfy the client. It may be useful for the researcher to sit with the client and get feedback on various aspects of the research project.

SUMMARY

Communication skills are important to the marketing research process; this includes the presentation of both the research proposal and the research results. An effective presentation involves several elements. The audience should be clearly identified so that the presentation will be on target. It should include an introduction with an overview of the presentation structure, a body, and a summary. Motivation can be provided by relating the presentation to the research objectives and purpose, by focusing on the most interesting findings, and by having an interesting presentation style. The use of specific examples and visual material can help you communicate more effectively and interestingly. You should discuss those elements of methodology that affect interpretation.

Several guidelines can help improve both written reports and oral presentations. Reading a report tends to be boring and should be avoided. Visual aids such as computer-assisted presentations, transparencies, and hand-outs can add punch and improve communication. Make sure the start is positive. Try to involve the audience, and avoid distracting mannerisms.

QUESTIONS AND PROBLEMS

22.1 By what criteria would you evaluate a written report? Develop an evaluation form. Would it differ depending on whether the research proposal or the research results were being presented?

22.2 By what criteria would you evaluate an oral presentation? Develop an evaluation form.

22.3 Observe three specific oral presentations outside of class. Consider the following:

(a) Were there any distracting mannerisms?

(b) What did the presenters do with their hands?

(c) How was the audience involved, if at all?

(d) Evaluate the visual aids used. Would you recommend the use of other visual aids?

(e) Did you ever become confused or bored? Was there anything the presenter could have done differently to counteract that tendency?

END NOTES

1   R. Hoff, "What's Your Presentation Quotient?" *Advertising Age*, January 16, 1978, p. 93.

2   "Teaching the Boss to Write," *Business Week*, October 25, 1976, p. 56.

3   Adapted from H. L. Gordon, "Eight Ways to Dress a Research Report," *Advertising Age*, October 20, 1980, p. S-37.

Case for Part IV is available on the Web:

SPSS® Web Case IV-1	NewFood

23

Marketing-Mix Measures

LEARNING OBJECTIVES

- Describe some major applications of marketing research.
- Discuss the applications of marketing research in pricing of a product.
- Discuss the various distribution decisions that require marketing research inputs.
- Describe the techniques used in the actual industry to obtain the measures used to evaluate advertisements.
- Describe the concept of total quality management.
- Describe the methodologies used to measure the different dimensions of total quality management.

Now that we have considered the various steps in the marketing research process in detail, it is time to think about what to do with it. In Part V, we again talk briefly about the various applications of marketing research, which can be applied to every stage of the marketing process. Traditionally, marketing decisions have been divided into 4P's—product price, promotion, and place (henceforth, distribution) decisions. In this chapter of Part V, we discuss the information needs for the 4P decisions and the various techniques available in the industry to obtain that information. The next chapter in this part deals with marketing research applications for contemporary issues such as total quality management (TQM), brand equity, and customer satisfaction. The last chapter focuses on the use of marketing research for emerging applications such as direct marketing, database marketing, and relationship marketing, along with some discussion of forecasting methods.

A strategy that companies have begun to adopt is **total quality management (TQM)**. To decide on and implement this strategy, managers require dramatically different information than they need for making marketing-mix decisions. Hence, marketing research has to rise to the challenge and provide managers with the requisite information. Moreover, tremendous advances in the field of statistics and computational capabilities have led market researchers to adopt more and more sophisticated techniques.

This chapter deals with product price, distribution, and promotion decisions. The main product decisions that need to be considered are the physical design of the product and its demand potential. Many companies spend millions of dollars on R&D in order to come up with a new product that will satisfy consumer needs. The various information requirements and techniques used for this purpose are covered in the section called "New-Product Research." The other major decision regarding new products is how to forecast sales potential. Various methods of forecasting are discussed in the appendix to Chapter 25. Once the product is available, its price must be determined.

We also discuss two methods of pricing and their informational requirements. The distribution decisions that are discussed here are (1) the number and location of warehouses and retail outlets, and (2) the number and location of salespersons (territory allocation decisions). The section on promotional research briefly discusses sales promotion research. Then, various methods of copy testing and the research required for other media decisions are described, as well as TQM.

New-Product Research

New products development is critical to the life of most organizations as they adapt to their changing environment. Since, by definition, new products contain unfamiliar aspects for the organization, there will be uncertainty associated with them. Thus, it is not surprising that a large proportion of marketing research is for the purpose of reducing the uncertainty associated with new products.

New-product research can be divided into four stages, as shown in Figure 23.1. The first stage is generating new-product concepts; the second is evaluating and developing those concepts; the third is evaluating and developing the actual products; finally, the product is tested in a marketing program.

Concept Generation

There are two types of concept generation research. The first might be termed **need identification research**. The emphasis in need research is on identifying unfilled needs in the market. The second is termed *concept identification*. Here, an effort is made to determine concepts that might fill an identified need.

Need Identification

Marketing research can identify needs in various ways. Some are qualitative and others, such as segmentation studies, can be quantitative. Following are some examples:

- **Perceptual maps**, in which products are positioned along the dimensions by which users perceive and evaluate, can suggest gaps into which new products might fit. Multidimensional scaling typically is used to generate these perceptual maps.

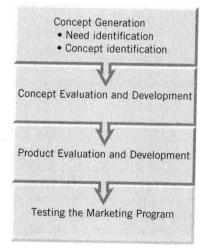

FIGURE 23.1
Phases in New-Product Research.

- Social and environmental *trends* can be analyzed. For instance, a trend away from low-calorie foods was the reason that Pizza Hut introduced the Big Foot Pizza and McDonald's reintroduced the Quarterpounder.

- An approach termed **benefit structure analysis** has product users identify the benefits desired and the extent to which the product delivers those benefits, for specific applications. The result is an identification of benefits sought that current products do not deliver.[1]

- Product users might be asked to keep a diary of a relevant portion of their activities. Analyzing such diaries can provide an understanding of unsolved problems associated with a particular task.

- In focus-group interviews, product users might discuss problems associated with product-use situations. Thus, office managers might, for example, discuss problems they have experienced with shipping services.

- **Lead user analysis** is another approach that many companies now use more often. In this approach, instead of just asking users what they have done, their solutions are collected more formally. First, lead users are identified. *Lead users* are those who face needs early that later will be general in a marketplace; they are positioned to benefit significantly by solving problems associated with these needs. Once a lead user is identified, the concepts that company or person generates are tested.

The advertising agency BBDO, which relies heavily on "problem detection" to generate new-product concepts and ideas for advertising campaigns, has developed a procedure for rating problems.[2] The agency asks each respondent who is a potential prospect to rank each problem as to whether it

- is important,

- occurs frequently,

- has a solution.

A "problem score" is obtained by combining these ratings, and the score is used to screen ideas. Using this technique, BBDO found that buyers of a dog food felt that it

- smelled bad,

- cost too much,

- did not come in different sizes for different dogs.

Subsequently, the company developed products that were responsive to the criticisms.

Concept Identification

There are various ways to identify concepts. Some are neither user-based nor follow from identification of unfilled needs. For example, a technological breakthrough can suggest concepts, as when the freeze-dry process suggested freeze-dried fruit in cereal; or competitors may introduce a new product that represents either a threat to or an opportunity for an organization. One role of marketing research is to monitor the environment systematically to learn of technological or competitive developments that may suggest new concepts.

During the new-product development process, there is usually a point where a concept is formed but there is no tangible usable product that can be tested. The concept should be defined well enough so that it is communicable. There may be simply a verbal description, or there may be a rough idea for a name, a package, or an advertising approach. The role of marketing research at this stage is to determine if the concept warrants further development and to provide guidance on how it might be improved and refined. Conjoint analysis typically is used to obtain an ideal combination of the concept's various features. Thus, research questions might include the following:

- Are there any major flaws in the concept?

- What consumer segments might be attracted to it?

- Is there enough interest to warrant developing it further?

- How might it be altered or developed further?

Some approaches to concept testing do not involve obtaining reactions from relevant people. One is to attempt to identify a set of similar products and to learn what the market response to them has been. Thus, a new crossword puzzle aid might be partly evaluated by determining the sales of similar products such as crossword puzzle dictionaries or of such complementary products as crossword puzzle magazines.

Most concept testing, however, involves exposing people to the concept and getting their reactions. In exposing people to the concept, the market researcher needs to address a series of questions:

- How are the concepts exposed?

- To whom are the concepts exposed?

- To what are they compared?

- What questions are asked?

There will always be a trade-off between the timing of the concept test and the development of the marketing program. The whole point of concept testing is to determine if it is worthwhile to develop a marketing program, so it is not realistic to hold off concept testing until a marketing program exists. Still, there is always the danger that a missing element in the final marketing program could distort the test.

Normally, the concept is exposed through personal contact, either in the respondent's home, office, or plant, or in some central location such as a shopping center. Normally, respondents should include those who would be among the target segments. Since the goal of concept testing is to determine if a viable market exists, the researcher should be careful to avoid omitting a potential segment from the study.

Usually, the concept test explores several versions of a concept or several product concepts that respond to a user need. For example, in the mid-1960s, in response to an identified need for a household garbage disposal system, Whirlpool engineers tested four concepts: a disposable garbage can, a garbage compactor that would hold two weeks' worth of garbage, a built-in kitchen compactor, and a portable kitchen compactor.[3] The concept test showed the last two alternatives to be definitely superior.

For the evaluative aspects of concept testing, it is necessary to include some overall indication of attitudes, interest, and likelihood of purchase. The purchase likelihood, for example, could be scaled as

Definitely Buy	Probably Buy	Might or Might Not Buy	Probably Not Buy	Definitely Not Buy
___	___	___	___	___

Researchers must interpret the results cautiously, particularly when they are encouraging, since the exposure, even if presented in a relatively neutral way, will sensitize the respondent to the product. The result actually is then an exaggerated tendency to indicate that the respondent will buy the product.

Concept testing is particularly important for durable goods and many industrial products because they rarely employ testing or test markets. The Ford Taurus, Mitsubishi large-screen TV sets, or the Sony Camcorder were never in test markets, for example. The problem is that it is really not practical to develop or produce such equipment on a pilot basis. A major commitment is required, and it would not be realistic economically to withdraw the product after market-testing it.

The conventional approach to concept testing can be subject to various problems:

- Respondents may read the concept statements without considering the environment in which the new product will be used.

- Participants are usually presented with only a small amount of information.

- For some new products, consumers prefer to learn through trial rather than reading.

These limitations can be restrictive when testing really new products (RNPs). Since different people follow different information processing strategies, concept statements to some extent constrain respondents' information search and processing. To overcome these problems, the *information acceleration* (IA) technique was developed.[4] Respondents are placed in a virtual buying environment in which they are first accelerated into a future time period and then allowed to choose information sources they wish to use to evaluate a new product.[5]

Product Evaluation and Development

Product evaluation and development, or product testing, is very similar to concept testing in terms of both the objectives and the techniques. The aim is still to predict market response to determine whether or not the product should be carried forward.

Use Testing

The simplest form of **use testing** gives users the product, and, after a reasonable amount of time, asks their reactions to it, including their intentions to buy it. Researchers can contact respondents in shopping centers by personal visits to their homes or offices, or, initially, by telephone. Burlington Industries, producer of fabrics, calls randomly selected telephone numbers to locate adult women who make many of their own clothes and who would be willing to evaluate a new dress fabric.[6] The fabric then is sent by mail, and a second telephone interview two months later solicits their description of their experience with it. Now market researchers can use the latest in computer technology and can do *virtual product testing*, which is explained in Marketing Research in Action 23.1. IA and Visionary Shopper are product-oriented techniques that do not take account of the fact that it is difficult to evaluate a service until it is consumed. Thus, when testing services, another virtual reality model, SERVASSOR, is more appropriate.[7]

Several problems are associated with use tests. First, because of unclear instructions, a misunderstanding, or lack of cooperation, respondents may not use the product correctly and may therefore report a negative opinion. Or they may not use it at all and simply fabricate an opinion. Second, the fact that they were given a free sample and are participating in a test may distort their impressions. Third, even when repurchase opportunities are made available, such decisions may be quite different than when they are made in a more realistic store situation with special displays

Marketing Research in Action 23.1

■ VIRTUAL PRODUCT TESTING

Websites like www.Bell.com and www.landsend.com allow visitors to create products online by specifying features and choosing sets of components that better meet their individual requirements. This virtual product configuration process has generated valuable insights into how new technologies affect product development research. Participants start with a basic product and then add or subtract features as desired. The end result should be a product that is closest to the customer's ideal product, in terms of both features and price.

Imagine a customer going to a website on which he can build a laptop computer for himself. The customer begins by choosing an operating system, the screen size, or the weight. After choosing a certain size and weight combination, some other features might not be available for a certain combination—say, a built-in CD-ROM drive comes only with a flat screen or a light machine. If having that drive is more important than size or weight, the customer might have to trade off in order to get the drive. At the same time, the total price changes with features. Once the customer has completed the ideal laptop, he evaluates it against the price calculated for those specific options and makes a decision on how likely it is that he would actually buy the designed product.

Online researchers currently use this configuration process to simulate trade-offs between price and product features in many product categories. In addition to helping consumers reach a decision to buy or not to buy, the process of selecting and discarding features also produces valuable data and adds to the richness of the research findings. Because the web-based systems track the entire configuration process, a number of interesting data points can be collected. For example, which features customers focus on first and how long they spend selecting various options are both measures of importance and possibly of price sensitivity. Furthermore, the behavioral process may reveal important information about the hierarchy of choice. Researchers also can perform segmentation profiling and other multivariate statistical analyses to determine the similarity of certain demographic or firmographic groups' approaches to the product configuration process. They are asking whether certain groups consider one type of feature first or more frequently than others, or whether some groups are better targets for upgraded features, or whether some groups are more price-sensitive in some feature categories. Because new features can be added instantly to a virtual product design test site, ongoing changes can be studied more efficiently. New-product concepts, competitive initiatives, and service programs can be evaluated more quickly and cheaply using online methods than using traditional trade-off techniques such as conjoint analysis.

Source: B. MacElroy, "Computer Configuration Figures to Change MR," Marketing News, April 4, 2002, p. 23.

presenting the new brand and those of its competitors. Fourth, there is the issue of whether the users will accept the product over a long time period. This problem is especially acute when repurchase data cannot be or are not obtained. Finally, they may inflate their intention to buy. Consumers may say that they will buy the product but may end up not doing so.[8]

A particular type of use test is the **blind-use test**, which is most appropriate just after the product emerges from the R&D laboratory. Even though a product may be proved superior in the laboratory, the consumer may not perceive it to be superior. For example, one consumer product company developed a window cleaner that was a definite improvement over existing products. The new product, however, was clear in color, whereas existing products had a bluish tint. A blind-use test, however, showed that consumers preferred the existing products. One hypothesis was that the blue color of the existing products was the reason consumers preferred them over the new, clear product. To test this hypothesis, a blind-use test pitted the new product against blue-colored water. Over 30 percent of the respondents preferred the water. Thus, the color of the new window cleaner was identified as the problem in the blind-use tests and was addressed in subsequent product development.

Predicting Trial Purchase

Several models have been developed to predict trial levels of new, frequently purchased consumer products.[9] The model called ESP (estimating sales potential) is typical.[10] Data from 45 new-product introductions were obtained and used to estimate the model. Trial levels (the percentage of a sample of consumers who had purchased the product at least once within 12 months after launch) were predicted on the basis of three variables:

- Product class penetration (PCP)—the percentage of households purchasing at least one item in the product class within one year.[11]

- Promotional expenditures—total consumer-directed promotional expenditures on the product.

- Distribution of the product—percentage of stores stocking the product (weighted by the store's total sales volume).

Knowledge of these three variables enabled ESP to predict trial levels of the 45 new products extremely accurately. (The regression model explained 95 percent of the variance of the three variables.) Once the model is estimated, it can be applied to other new products. The manager simply estimates the percentage of households using the product class, the total promotional expenditures planned for the new product, and the expected distribution level. The model will then estimate the trial level that will be obtained.

Trial also can be estimated directly using controlled shopping experience. A respondent is exposed to the new product promotion and allowed to shop in a simulated store or in an actual store in which the product is placed. The respondents then have an opportunity to make a "trial" or first purchase of the product.

Pretest Marketing

Table 23.1 is an overview of a laboratory test design (a form of pretest marketing) called ASSESSOR.[12] Two approaches are used to predict the new brand's market share. The first is based on the preference judgments. The preference data are used to predict the proportion of purchases of the new brand that respondents will make given that the new brand is in their response set. These estimates for the respondents in the study are coupled with an estimate of the proportion of all people who will have the new brand in their response set, to provide an estimate of market share. A useful by-product of this approach is an analysis of the concomitant market share losses of the other brands. If the firm has other brands in the market, such information can be critical.

The second approach involves estimating trial and repeat purchase levels based on the respondent's purchase decisions and intentions-to-buy judgments. A trial estimate is based on the percentage of respondents who purchase the product in the laboratory, plus an estimate of the product's distribution, advertising (which will create product awareness), and the number of free samples to be given away. The repeat-purchase rate is based on the proportion of respondents who make a mail-order repurchase of the new brand and the buying-intentions judgments of those who elected *not* to make a mail-order repurchase. The product of the trial estimate and the repeat purchase estimate become a second estimate of market share. ASSESSOR has been modified and other models have also been proposed for pretest marketing.[13]

The method has a host of limiting assumptions and limitations. Perhaps the most critical assumption is that the preference data and the purchase and repurchase decisions are valid predictors of what actually would happen in the marketplace. The artificiality of the product exposure and such surrogates for purchase decisions in the marketplace is a problem common to all laboratory approaches. Another problem is related to the convenience-sampling approach and the fact that there will be attrition from the original sample (in one study, 16 percent of the respondents did not use the brand and another 16 percent could not be reached for the telephone interview).[14]

Table 23.1   The ASSESSOR Laboratory Test Market Research Design and Measurement[a]

Design	Procedure	Measurement
O_1	Respondent screening and recruitment (personal interview).	Criteria for target group identification (e.g., product class usage).
O_2	Premeasurement for established brands (self-administered questionnaire).	Composition of "relevant set" of established brands, attribute weights and ratings, and preferences.
X_1	Exposure to advertising for established brands and new brand.	
(O_3)	Measurement of reactions to the advertising materials (self-administered questionnaire).	Optional, (e.g., likability and believability ratings of advertising materials).
X_2	Simulated shopping trip and exposure to display of new and established brands.	
O_4	Purchase opportunity (choice recorded by research personnel).	Brand(s) purchased.
X_3	Home use/consumption of new brand.	
O_5	Postusage measurement (telephone interview).	New brand usage rate, satisfaction ratings, and repeat purchase propensity. Attribute ratings and preferences for "relevant set" of established brands plus the new brand.

[a] O = measurement; X = advertising or product exposure.

Source: Adapted from A. J. Silk and G. L. Urban, "Pre-Test-Market Evaluation of New Packaged Goods: A Model and Measurement Methodology," *Journal of Marketing Research*, 15, May 1978, p. 178.

Laboratory tests have a number of advantages too. First, compared with test markets, they are fast, relatively cheap, confidential, and flexible. A basic ASSESSOR test can be conducted in three months with a cost that starts around $75,000 (most tests will compare alternative tactics and cost more), much less than test markets. The time and lack of confidentiality of test markets can be damaging. Further, for a relatively modest incremental cost, a laboratory test market can evaluate alternative executions of elements in the marketing program such as packaging, price, advertising, product features, and location within the store. Also, the accuracy experience is impressive.

Test Marketing

Test marketing allows the researcher to test the impact of the total marketing program, with all its interdependencies, in a market context as opposed to the artificial context associated with the concept and product tests that have been discussed.

Test marketing has two primary functions. The first is to gain information and experience with the marketing program before making a total commitment to it. The second is to predict the program's outcome when it is applied to the total market.

There are really two types of test markets: the sell-in test market and the controlled-distribution scanner market. **Sell-in test markets** are cities in which the product is sold just as it would be in a national launch. In particular, the product has to gain distribution space. **Controlled-distribution scanner markets (CDSMs)** are cities for which distribution is prearranged and the purchases of a panel of customers are monitored using scanner data.

Sell-In Test Markets

Selecting the Test Cities

1. *Representativeness.* Ideally, the city should be fairly representative of the country in terms of characteristics that will affect the test outcome, such as product usage, attitudes, and demographics.

2. *Data availability.* It often is helpful to use store audit information to evaluate the test. If so, it would be important to use cities containing retailers who will cooperate with store audits.

3. *Media isolation and costs.* It is desirable to avoid media spill-over. Using media that "spill out" into nearby cities is wasteful and increases costs. Conversely, "spill-in" media from nearby cities can contaminate a test. Media cost is another consideration.

4. *Product flow.* It may be desirable to use cities that don't have much "product spillage" outside the area.

An important issue for sell-in test markets is the number of test cities to use.[15] A single test city can lead to unreliable results because of the variation across cities of both brand sales and consumer response to marketing programs.[16]

Implementing and Controlling the Test

A second consideration is to control the test by ensuring that the marketing program is implemented in the test area so as to reflect the national program. The test itself may tend to encourage those involved to enhance the effectiveness of the marketing program. Salespeople may be more aggressive. Retailers may be more cooperative. There is also the reaction of competitors. At one extreme, they can destroy the test by deliberately flooding the test areas with free samples or in-store promotions. More likely, however, they will experiment with retaliatory actions and also monitor the results themselves.

Timing

A third consideration is timing. If possible, a test market normally should be in existence for one year. An extended time period is needed for several reasons. First, there are often important seasonal factors that can be observed only if the test is continued for the whole year. Second, initial interest is often a poor predictor of a program's staying power. There is usually a fatigue factor that sometimes can take a long time to materialize.

Measurement

A crucial element of the test market is the measure used to evaluate it. A basic measure is sales based on shipments or warehouse withdrawals. Store audit data provide actual sales figures and are not sensitive to inventory fluctuations. They also provide variables such as distribution, shelf facings, and in-store promotional activity. These already have been discussed in detail in Chapter 6. Knowledge of such variables can be important in evaluating the marketing program and in interpreting the sales data.

Measures such as brand awareness, attitude, trial purchase, and repeat purchase are obtained directly from the consumer, either from surveys or from consumer panels. Such variables as brand awareness and attitude also serve as criteria for evaluating the marketing program and can help interpret sales data. The most useful information obtained from consumers, however, is whether they bought the product at least once, whether they were satisfied with it, and whether they repurchased it or plan to.

Costs of Test Marketing

In making cost–benefit judgments about test markets, all costs need to be considered. Many costs are relatively easy to quantify; these might be the development and implementation of the marketing program, preparation of test products, administration of the test, and collection of data associated with the test.

The costs and risks that may delay the launch of a new product are more difficult to quantify. If a new-product launch is delayed by six months or a year, an opportunity to gain a substantial market position might be lost.

Controlled-Distribution Scanner Markets (CDSMs)

These markets are termed *controlled-distribution* because there are generally agreements with retailers to allow new products under test to have access to shelf space. An example of a CDSM is IRI's BehaviorScan, which was discussed in Chapter 6.

CDSMs have four major advantages over test markets. First, they are less expensive. Although it is difficult to generalize, they probably cost from one-sixth to one-third the cost of a full test market. Second, there is the potential to do more experimenting with marketing variables in a CDSM. The advertising seen by panel members is controllable. Further, in-store activities such as promotions and pricing are under more control than they would be in a sell-in test market. Third, the scanner-based data probably are more accurate, timely, and complete than the data available in a sell-in test market. Fourth, there is the potential to provide accurate early estimates of the test market results using the consumer panel information.

The most obvious disadvantage of a CDSM is that it provides no test of the product's ability to gain shelf space, special displays, in-store promotions, and so on. However, recent research on the effectiveness of sales promotions has generated useful information for making efficient decisions. Since gaining distribution can be a crucial issue for some products, leaving it unaddressed can be troublesome. Another major CDSM disadvantage is the limited choice of test cities.

Projecting Trial, Repeat, and Usage Rates Using Panel Data

To estimate the ultimate trial level, the percentage of product class buyers who will try the new brand at least once is monitored over time. Each person who tries the new product is then monitored again, and the time between the first (trial) purchase and second purchase is noted. The market share estimate is thus the product of the percentage of people who tried and the percentage of people who repeat-purchased the product. Market share and sales projections made using this modeling logic can be very accurate.[17] Marketing Research in Action 23.2 gives an example of test marketing. At the same time, the Internet is proving to be a fast and cost-effective method of new-product testing. Marketing Research in Action 23.3 shows how P&G used the World Wide Web to successfully launch its new product, Crest Whitestrips.

Really New Products

RNPs normally take a long time (sometimes 15–20 years) from conception to national introduction. RNPs[18] are those that:

1. Create or expand a new category, thereby making cross-category competition the key (e.g., fruit teas versus soft drinks).

2. Are new to customers, for whom substantial learning is often required (i.e., what it can be used for, what it competes with, why it is useful).

3. Raise broad issues such as appropriate channels of distribution and organizational responsibility.

4. Create (sometimes) a need for infrastructure, software, and add-ons.

Marketing Research in Action 23.2

■ HOKEY POKEY SOFT LAUNCH

Hokey Pokey wanted to launch frozen stone ice cream parlors in the Indian marketplace. The aim was to introduce a new concept utilizing ice cream and mix-ins to create your own dessert concoction. They chose Mumbai, India, to begin the rollout and then gradually spread to other cities. Many critical components were in place: The production facility was operationally ready, three parlors completed construction, and the management had organized a grand press launch with a famous Indian movie director.

However, three fundamental issues remained unanswered. First off, ice cream was a relatively unorganized sector in India and market information was not readily available. As a result, management was not able to project the appropriate selection of flavors to stock as inventory. Secondly, evidence regarding the acceptance of newly introduced ice cream flavors by local Indian consumers was lacking. Traditionally, with respect to taste, Indians tend to have an affinity for sweetened items, therefore, would additional sugar be required? Thirdly, would the impatient Indian consumers be able to "make-their-own" ice cream creations or would they prefer pre-designed options?

Being pressed on time by the investors and the PR agency, management had to make a decision. They could use prior assumptions or take into account a research driven technique to obtain additional concrete evidence. The research driven technique was favored, and management had three options to consider for collecting the necessary decision making data. They could send out a questionnaire, conduct a focus group, or open doors with a soft launch. Since time was of the essence, only one option could be executed.

Utilizing the soft launch technique, management opened one of the parlors, the least prominent of the three initial locations. This location was opened for business without any signs and brand name. Local restaurants were given free coupons for their customers and flyers were handed out on nearby street corners. The soft launch lasted three weeks, and management received adequate data that allowed operations to forecast the appropriate inventory mix (respective amounts of chocolate, vanilla, strawberry, etc.), so as to not contribute to product spoilage. Additionally, it was determined that impatient Indian consumers preferred designated options rather than relying on their own judgment. This was evident in the fact that most consumers chose ready-made creations versus creating their own. More importantly, competitive and locally sold ice creams were also served during the soft launch to gauge the public's reaction on sugar levels. It was determined that additional sugar was required to satisfy the Indian taste bud.

Source: Hokey Pokey, Inc.

Marketing Research in Action 23.3

■ USING INTERNET FOR NEW-PRODUCT TEST MARKETING

Since beginning online research in 1998, Procter & Gamble has become the industry's most avid user of the Internet as a fast, cost-effective means of researching new products or ideas. The giant consumer-goods company constantly invites consumers online to sample and provide feedback on new prototype products, using this information to decide whether to bring the products to retail stores or end new-product development on them. It is already conducting 40 percent of its 6,000 product tests and other studies online.

The introduction of Crest Whitestrips was one of the most successful product launches in P&G's history. P&G began with an eight-month campaign offering the strips exclusively on P&G's http://www.3dwhite.com/. In August 2000, the new home tooth-bleaching kit sold for a steep $44 retail price. To promote the online sale, from August to May, P&G ran TV commercials and advertisements in lifestyle magazines, such as *People* and *Good Housekeeping*, as well as sending e-mails directly to customers. Within eight months, 144,000 whitening kits were sold online. Twelve percent of visitors who registered for product information made a purchase, a great conversion rate. With this sales data in hand, P&G was then in a very good position to persuade retailers to stock the product, even at the high price. Introduced in stores in May and backed by print and TV ad campaigns, Crest Whitestrips had nearly $50 million in sales by late July 2001, an unqualified success.

Source: J. Gaffney, "How Do You Feel about a $44 Tooth-Bleaching Kit?" Business 2.0, October 2001, p. 46.

Examples of RNPs include light beer, overnight air delivery, microwave ovens, and semiconductors. In terms of the research prescribed for slightly new products (e.g., multiple generations of computers, flavored drinks) earlier in this chapter, most of the methods suggested have to be modified for RNPs. Given the absence of a well-defined industry for a RNP, researchers have to rely on generic usage situations. Further, the competition is not clearly established. Marketing research plays a big role in getting ideas for RNPs by

1. Asking (or listening to) dissatisfied customers
2. Asking nonrepresentative customers
3. Using open-ended, qualitative (versus structured survey) procedures
4. Involving customers as co-developers (especially for industrial products)
5. Listening to scientists and newcomers rather than engineers and experts
6. Scanning the literature (especially the technical literature) for interesting possibilities.

In terms of concept testing, the *information acceleration* method (discussed earlier) can be used. However, it may be difficult for consumers either to imagine many years into the future or to think of the RNP in terms of purchase intention.

Pricing Research

Research may be used to evaluate alternative price approaches for new products before launch or for proposed changes in products already on the market. As in the case of test marketing, the question of "reality" applies, and it has been found that the sales response to products at different prices in actual stores produces far more discriminating results than the sales response in an artificial store.

There are two general approaches to pricing research. The first is the well-established Gabor and Grainger method.[19] In this method, different prices for a product are presented to respondents (often by using test-priced packs), who then are asked if they would buy. A "buy-response" curve of different prices, with the corresponding number of affirmative purchase intentions, is produced.

In a second approach, respondents are shown different sets of brands in the same product category, at different prices, and are asked which they would buy. This multibrand-choice method allows respondents to take into account competitors' brands, as they normally would outside such a test. As such, this technique represents a form of simulation of the point of sale.

Decisions regarding price ranges for new products have to be made early in the development stage. A product concept cannot be tested fully, for example, without indicating its price, so when the product is ready to be introduced, a decision must be made about its specific price. Decisions on price changes—*Should we change the price, and, if so, in which way and by how much?*—will then need to be made over the product's life cycle.

Either of two general pricing strategies can be followed. The first is a skimming strategy, in which the objective is to generate as much profit as possible in the present period. The other is a share-penetration strategy, whose objective is to capture an increasingly larger market share by offering a lower price. Pricing research for the two different approaches differs substantially in terms of the information sought.

Research for Skimming Pricing

The skimming pricing strategy is based on the concept of pricing the product at the point at which profits will be the greatest until market conditions change or supply costs dictate a price change. Under this strategy, the optimal price is the one that results in the greatest positive difference between total revenues and total costs. This implies that the researcher's major tasks are to forecast the costs and the revenues over the relevant range of alternative prices. The forecasting methods discussed in the appendix to Chapter 25 can be used for this purpose.

Research for Penetration Pricing

Penetration pricing is a strategy based on the concept that average unit production costs continue to go down as cumulative output increases. Potential profits in the early stages of the product life cycle are sacrificed in the expectation that higher volumes in later periods will generate sufficiently greater profits to result in overall profit for the product over its life. For some products, this reduction takes the form of an experience curve.

The pricing pattern that is adopted for increasing market share is to:

1. Offer a lower price (even below cost) when entering the market.

2. Hold that price constant until unit costs produce a desired percentage markup.

3. Reduce price as costs fall to maintain markup at the same desired percentage of costs.

The pricing pattern is illustrated in Figure 23.2.
The types of information required for this pricing method are:

1. The nature of the experience curve.

2. Breakeven points.

3. Cost of units sold to additional market segments.

4. Competitor costs.

5. Forecast of the "decline" stage of the product life cycle.

The research techniques that have already been described in this text can generate the information required for this type of pricing.

A simple typology of the various pricing strategies that are followed in practice and the informational requirements for these strategies is given in Table 23.2.[20]

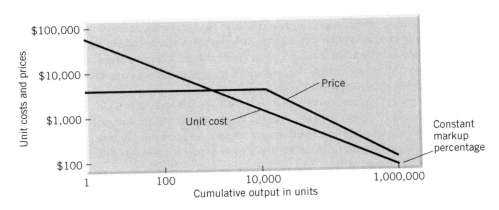

FIGURE 23.2
Share-Oriented Penetration Pricing.

Table 23.2   Informational Requirements for Pricing Strategies

Strategy	Description	Information requirements	Sources of information
Random discounting	If some consumers have heterogeneous search costs, firms discount their prices in a random manner to take advantage of those consumers. These consumers buy at the undiscounted price instead of searching for the lowest price, whereas consumers with low search costs will buy at the low price	Knowledge of consumer segments in the market Characteristics of consumers (their search costs, etc.) Product and cost information Information on legal constraints	Demographic consumer data Analysis of scanner data Internal records Legal data
Second-market discounting	If distinct markets exist and if the consumers in one market incur transaction costs to buy in another, the firm can discount its price in the other markets to below its average cost. In the international context, this is called dumping	Knowledge about the different markets and their characteristics Product and cost information Information on the legal aspects of the other markets Information on the transaction cost incurred by the consumer when he or she buys from the different market	Internal records Legal data Secondary data sources that give the demographic profile of the markets
Periodic discounting	When some consumers in the market have differential reservation prices, firms can start at high prices and periodically discount them in order to draw consumers with lower reservation prices	Information about the consumers' reservation prices Product and cost information	Internal records Survey research to determine the consumers' reservation price Legal data
Price signaling	When consumers in the market are willing to pay more for a product despite lack of knowledge regarding its quality, then price signaling can be used. Essentially the strategy is to produce an inferior product and sell it at the same price as the better-quality product another firm produces, in the belief that consumers will assume that the product is of high quality and buy it because of its high price	Information about your competitors' prices and costs Information about the legal constraints of price signaling Product and cost information	Internal records Secondary data on competitor prices Legal data Inferential information on competitor costs
Penetration pricing	Penetration pricing is used is situations similar to that in periodic discounting, except in this case competitors are also free to enter at the same price. Hence, the threat of competitive entry and price-sensitive consumers force the firm to price its products at a low price	Product and cost information Information about competitor prices and costs	Secondary data and inferential information on competitor prices and costs Internal records
Geographic pricing	Geographic pricing strategies are used by firms that sell in markets that are separated geographically. The difference in pricing is due to transportation costs rather than reservation prices or transaction costs	Information on the characteristics of the different markets Product and cost information Information on the transportation costs and about any legal aspects that may hinder this particular type of pricing strategy	Internal records Secondary data and inferential information on competitor prices and costs

(continued)

Table 23.2   (continued)

Strategy	Description	Information requirements	Sources of information
Premium pricing	This strategy and price signaling are very similar. The difference stems from the fact that in price signaling the firm produces only the inferior product and prices it high, whereas here the firm produces both the inferior and the better product and sells them at the same price to exploit the joint economies of scale	Product and cost information Information on the competitors' price and cost Information on the characteristics of the consumers (like the maximum price they are willing to pay for this product)	Secondary sources of legal data Internal records Secondary sources of information on markets and transportation costs
Price bundling	Bundling strategy is adopted when the products are nonsubstitutable, perishable, and there is an asymmetric demand structure for them. An example of this strategy is selling a car with the maximum number of options. The perishability in the case of durables is with regard to the purchase occasion	Information on the demand characteristics for the various components of the bundle Product and cost information Information on the consumer preferences for the various combinations of the bundle	Internal records Survey data on consumer characteristics and preferences Secondary sources of information on competitor costs and prices
Complementary pricing	Complementary pricing is the strategy used by firms to price complementary products. They usually price the main product at low price while the price of the complement is high. The classic example is Japanese pricing of their cars and the spare parts	Product and cost information	Internal records

Distribution Research[21]

Traditionally, the distribution decisions in marketing strategy involve the number and location of salespersons, retail outlets, warehouses, and the size of discount to be offered. The discount to be offered to the members in the channel of distribution usually is determined by what is being offered by existing or similar products, and also whether the firm wants to follow a "push" or a "pull" strategy. Marketing research, however, plays an important role in the number and location in decisions about numbers and locations. Marketing Research in Action 23.4 discusses the launch of Coke's C2 and its failure.

Warehouse and Retail Location Research

The essential questions to be answered before a location decision is made are: "What costs and delivery times would result if we choose one location over another?"

Simulation of scenarios is used to answer these questions. The simulation can be a relatively simple, paper-and-pencil exercise for the location of a single warehouse in a limited geographic area, or it can be a complex, computerized simulation of a warehousing system for a regional or national market.

Center-of-Gravity Simulation

The center-of-gravity method of simulation is used to locate a single warehouse or retail site. In this method, the approximate location that will minimize the distance to customers, weighted by the quantities purchased, is determined. The more symmetry there is in customer locations and

Marketing Research in Action 23.4

■ COKE'S C2 LAUNCH

In April 2004, Coca-Cola launched a new drink—C2. Around the same time, Pepsi launched another new drink called Edge. Both these new sodas had half of the sugar, calories, and carbohydrates of regular cola and were aimed at consumers who had cut back on or given up sodas due to weight or other health concerns. In particular, the dueling soft-drink giants were going after male consumers who normally shunned existing diet sodas either because of taste or the feminine image of those beverages.

New Coke launched by Coke in 1985 as a replacement for its regular soda had been rejected by customers, making Coke return to its traditional drink by marketing it as Classic Coke. C2 was designed to appeal to "people who would like less calories but don't want to compromise on taste." The introduction was backed by a U.S. marketing campaign with commercials using music from the Rolling Stones. Pepsi's idea was to keep its loyal customers and not have them drift into teas and juices or other competing drinks.

Neither C2 nor Pepsi Edge garnered much sales success, with market share for the new entrants remaining at very disappointing levels. Both companies dropped plans to expand the low-carb soft drinks into other markets.

Mistakes over C2 increased tensions between Coke and its biggest bottler, Coca-Cola Enterprises Inc., of Atlanta. For decades, Coke has sold its beverage concentrate to U.S. bottlers at a constant price, no matter what price the soft drinks would later command at retail. Thus, while Coke's revenue depends on selling higher volumes of soft-drink syrup to its bottlers and benefits when lower prices increase sales, bottler's profits were tied to margins. C2's pricing strategy was a bone of contention between Coke and its bottlers who set wholesale prices. Instead of costing only about 15 percent more than Coke's other colas, C2 sometimes cost 50–60 percent more than regular Coke—especially on weekends, when regular sodas are usually discounted. The high prices as well as complaints about taste turned off many customers who would otherwise have tried the new product.

---

weights, the more nearly the initial calculation approximates the optimal location. The location indicated by the first calculation can be checked to determine if it is optimal (or near-optimal) by using a "confirming" procedure. If it is not optimal, successive calculations can be made as necessary to "home in" on the best location.[22]

To illustrate the method, assume that five retail stores are located as shown in Figure 23.3. Stores 1 and 5 each buy, on average, 2 tons of merchandise per year, and stores 2, 3, and 4 each buy an average of 3 tons per year. We shall assume that straight-line distances (measured on the grid lines) are appropriate for estimating transportation costs and delivery times.

The procedure for determining the location that will give the minimum weighted average distance from the warehouse to the customers is as follows.

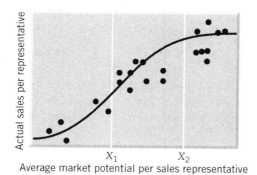

FIGURE 23.3
Center-of-Gravity Warehouse Location to Serve Five Retail Stores.

Step 1

Compute the weighted mean distance north (y coordinate) from the zero point for the stores. The weighted mean distance north $300/13 = 23.1$ miles. Then

$$\text{Distance} \times \text{weight} = \text{weighted distance}$$

Store 1 10 miles $\times$ 2 tons = 20 ton-miles
Store 2 30 miles $\times$ 3 tons = 90 ton-miles
Store 3 40 miles $\times$ 3 tons = 120 ton-miles
Store 4 10 miles $\times$ 3 tons = 30 ton-miles
Store 5 20 miles $\times$ 2 tons = 40 ton-miles

Step 2

Compute the weighted mean distance east (x coordinate) from the zero point for the stores. The weighted mean distance east = $470/13 = 36.2$ miles. Then

$$\text{Distance} \times \text{weight} = \text{weighted distance}$$

Store 1 10 miles $\times$ 2 tons = 20 ton-miles
Store 2 20 miles $\times$ 3 tons = 60 ton-miles
Store 3 40 miles $\times$ 3 tons = 120 ton-miles
Store 4 50 miles $\times$ 3 tons = 150 ton-miles
Store 5 60 miles $\times$ 2 tons = 120 ton-miles

Step 3

The location giving the minimum weighted average distance from the customers is the point for which the two weighted means are the coordinates. For the example, the location indicated is 36.2 miles east (x) and 23.1 miles north (y) of the zero point. The zero point can be chosen arbitrarily, but all of the initial calculations have to be made based on the selected zero point.

The confirmation procedure is as follows:

1. Calculate confirming coordinates x, y using the formulae

$$x = \frac{\sum_{i=1}^{n}\left(x_i M_i / N_i\right)}{\sum_{i=1}^{n}\left(M_i / N_i\right)} \quad y = \frac{\sum_{i=1}^{n}\left(y_i M_i / N_i\right)}{\sum_{i=1}^{n}\left(M_i / N_i\right)}$$

where x_j and y_j are the coordinates of the jth customer, M_j is the weight for that customer, and N_j is the distance of the customer from the point defined by the coordinates. N_j is computed from the center-of-gravity calculation and is calculated using the following equation:

$$N_i = \left[\left(x_i - x_g\right)^2 + \left(y_i - y_g\right)^2\right]^{1/2}$$

where x_g and y_g are the coordinates of the location of the store.

2. If the center-of-gravity coordinates and the confirmation model coordinates are the same (or nearly the same), no further calculations need be made. If they are not reasonably similar, replace the center-of-gravity coordinates with the initial confirmation model coordinates, and calculate a second set of confirmation coordinates.

3. Repeat step 2 as necessary until the new confirmation coordinates match those being confirmed.

Computerized Simulation Models

While the center-of-gravity method is an adequate method in most situations for locating a single warehouse, it is not designed to cope with the difficulties involved in determining how many warehouses should be used and where they should be located in an overall regional or national distribution system. A computer simulation approach is required to work on multiple warehouse location problems because of the large amounts of data that have to be processed for each of the many possible configurations of numbers and locations of warehouses.

The concept involved in simulations for this purpose is quite simple. Data that describe the customer characteristics (location of plants, potential warehouse, and retail sites) and distribution costs (costs per mile by volume shipped, fixed and variable costs of operating each warehouse, the effect of shipping delays on customer demand) are generated and input into the computer. The computer is then programmed to simulate various combinations of numbers and locations of warehouses and to indicate which one(s) gives the lowest total operating cost. Effective results have been achieved by using computer simulations to design distribution systems.

The role of marketing research in such simulations typically is to develop the data needed to operate it and then to validate the simulation model. The first step in the validation procedure should be to compare historical data with the model's predictions for some previous year. Warehouse locations, warehousing costs, transportation rates, and demand data for the year can be entered, and the model's predicted costs can be compared with actual costs. A second step is to run sensitivity analyses by making changes in the historical data (adding/subtracting a warehouse or a retail store, moving the location of a warehouse/retail outlet, and increasing the fixed cost of operating), such that the model outcomes are at least qualitatively predictable.

Trade-Area Analysis

Assume you manage a store in a regional shopping center. You are considering a direct-mail promotional campaign. How can you decide where to campaign materials? Trade-area data can be used to answer this question and for more purposes, such as creating mailing lists, evaluating a store's or shopping center's market positioning, measuring competitive customer bases, determining the potential of new locations, and evaluating regional retail chains and acquisition plans.[23]

Formal models have been developed that can be used to predict the trading area of a given shopping center or retail outlet based on relative size, travel time, and image.[24] A variety of other techniques can also be used to establish trading areas. An analysis of the addresses of credit card customers or the license plates of the cars (by plotting the addresses of the car owners) can provide a useful estimate of the trading area. Check-clearance data can be used to supplement this information.

The best, but also the most expensive, way of establishing trading-area boundaries is to conduct surveys to determine them. Shopping-center intercept surveys are commonly conducted for this purpose. When information on market potential and market penetration is desired, the shopping-center intercept survey needs to be supplemented by a survey of nonshoppers at the shopping center or store. The nonshopper surveys are often conducted by telephone, with screening to eliminate shoppers. To avoid selection bias when merging the two samples, appropriate weightings based on shopping frequencies must be used.[25]

Outlet Location Research

Individual companies and, more commonly, chains, financial institutions with multiple outlets, and franchise operations must decide on the physical location of their outlet(s).

Three general methods are in use for selecting specific store sites. The first is the *analogous location method*. This method involves plotting the area surrounding the potential site in terms of residential neighborhoods, income levels, and competitive stores. Regression models have been used for location studies for a variety of retail outlets, including banks, grocery stores, liquor stores, chain stores, and hotels.[26] Data for building the model and for evaluating new potential locations are obtained through secondary data analysis and surveys.

Multiple regression models can be used to generate a relationship between store sales and a range of store, population, and competitor characteristics. The advantage of multiple regression analysis is that the relationship between sales, as the dependent variable, and a range of independent variables can be assessed more systematically. Numerous variables, and even different forms of model, can be adopted and tested very quickly.

The multiple regression equation will take the following form:

$$Y = a + b_1 x_1 + b_2 x_2 + \cdots + b_m x_m + b_{m+1} x_{m+1} + \cdots + b_n x_n$$

$$\underbrace{\qquad\qquad\qquad}_{\substack{\text{Store} \\ \text{characteristics}}} \qquad \underbrace{\qquad\qquad\qquad}_{\substack{\text{Trade area} \\ \text{characteristics}}}$$

where Y is store sales and the x's are the independent variables, those concerned with the characteristics of each store (typically store size, car parking facilities, and so on) and those concerned with the characteristics of the trade area (population and competition). This approach can then be used in forecasting sales for a proposed store.

The *gravity model* has existed for a long time, and it has proved its worth in helping to explain certain types of human spatial behavior. Gravity theory holds that more people will travel from a particular origin to a given destination than will travel to a more distant destination of the same type and size. In more formal terms, it posits that preference to shopping in a store is directly proportional to store size and inversely proportional to the square of the distance of that store.

Number and Location of Sales Representatives

How many sales representatives should there be in a given territory? There are three general research methods for answering this question. The first, the sales effort approach, is applicable when the product line is first introduced and there is no operating history to provide sales data. The second involves the statistical analysis of sales data and can be used after the sales program is under way. The third involves a field experiment and is also applicable only after the sales program has begun.

Sales Effort Approach

A simple approach to estimating the number of sales representatives required for a given territory is as follows:

1. Estimate the number of sales calls required to sell to, and to service, prospective customers in an area for a year. This will be the sum of the number of visits required per year, Q_i, to each prospect/customer, C, in the territory, or

$$\sum_{i=1}^{n} Q_i C_i$$

where n is the number of prospects or customers.

2. Estimate the average number of sales calls per representative that can be made in that territory in a year, d.

3. Divide the estimate in step 1 by the estimate in step 2 to obtain the number of sales representatives required, M. That is,

$$M = \sum_{i=1}^{n} \frac{Q_i C_i}{d}$$

Statistical Analysis of Sales Data

Once a sales history is available from each territory, an analysis can be made to determine if the appropriate number of sales representatives is being used in each territory. An analysis of actual sales versus market potential for each sales representative may yield a relationship of the kind shown in Figure 23.4. If so, further analysis will very likely indicate those areas where the average market potential is less than X_1 per sales representative but that have too many representatives, and those with average market potential of more than X_2 but that have too few sales representatives.

Field Experiments

Experimenting with the number of calls made is another method of determining the number and location of sales representatives. This may be done in two ways: (1) making more frequent calls on some prospects or customers and less frequent calls on others in order to see the effect on overall sales (in this method, the number of sales representatives remains unchanged); and (2) increasing the number of representatives in some territories and decreasing them in others to determine the sales effect.

The design of the experiment(s), and the advantages and limitations of conducting them for determining the appropriate number of sales representatives for each territory, are very similar to those for conducting other experiments.

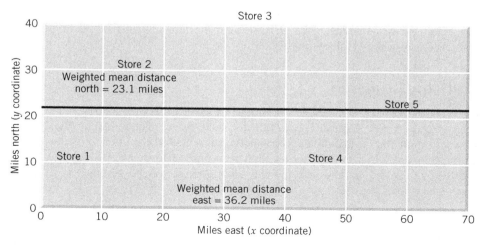

FIGURE 23.4
Actual Sales versus Market Potential Per Sales Representative.

Computerized Models of Sales Force Size and Allocation by Market and by Product Line

A number of computerized models, spreadsheet and others, can be used for determining sales force size and for allocating the sales force by market and by product line. Examples are CALLPLAN, which is an interactive salesperson's call planning system, and DETAILER, a decision calculus model for the question of sales force allocation. When management is considering using a formal model to assist in making sales force-related decisions, marketing research often becomes involved in many ways:

1. Determining what models are available and recommending which, if any, should be adopted.

2. Developing the data needed to operate the model selected (market potential) by product and by market, desirable call frequencies by class of customer, and so on.

3. Operating the model.

The model selected should be valid and should require data that can be obtained at a reasonable cost. An approach to testing the validity of a model is to run analyses with it under different conditions and see how it performs. A first step is to run the model with actual sales force data from the past two or three years and see if it replicates actual sales (and, depending on the model, by sales territory and product), at least reasonably accurately. After making any necessary calibrating adjustments, the model's "predictions" and the actual results ought to be fairly close. Following that, one should set up and run a range of cases that might actually occur. Examining the model's output for each of them and determining whether they seem reasonable will shed light on the model's predictive validity.

Promotion Research

This section focuses on the decisions that are commonly made when designing a promotion strategy. The decisions for the promotion part of a marketing strategy can be divided into (1) advertising and (2) sales promotion. Sales promotion affects the company in the short term, whereas advertising decisions have long-term effects. Companies spend more time and resources on advertising research than on sales promotion research because of the greater risk and uncertainty in advertising research. We first discuss the use of marketing research in advertising decisions and then talk briefly about the use of marketing research in sales promotion.

Advertising Research

Most promotion research companies concentrate on advertising because advertising decisions are more costly and risky than sales promotion decisions. Advertising research typically involves generating information for making decisions in the awareness, recognition, preference, and purchasing stages. Most often, advertising research decisions are about advertising copy. Marketing research helps to determine how effective the advertisement will be. Another area this section discusses relates to media decisions.

Criteria

What separates an effective advertisement from a dud? The criteria will depend, of course, on the brand involved and its advertising objective. However, four basic categories of responses are used in advertising research in general and copy testing in particular: (1) advertisement recognition, (2) recall of the commercial and its contents, (3) the measure of commercial persuasion, and (4) the impact on purchase behavior.

Recognition

One level of testing recognition is whether respondents can recognize the advertisement as one they have seen before. An example of recognition testing is the Bruzzone Research Company (BRC) tests of television commercials.[27] Questionnaires are mailed to 1,000 households. The sample is drawn from the Donnelley list of all households that have either a registered automobile or a listed telephone. Interest in the subject matter and a $1 payment usually generate a response of 500. The recognition question is at the top of the questionnaire; at the bottom is the brand-association question, a critical dimension of most campaigns.

Starch has been measuring printed-advertisement recognition since 1923. In the Starch survey, respondents are asked to read a magazine and, for each advertisement, are asked if they saw it in the issue. The noted score, usually the measure of recognition, is the percentage who answer affirmatively.

Recall

The **day-after recall (DAR) measure** of a television commercial, first used in the early 1940s by George Gallup, then by Young & Rubicam, is closely associated with Burke Marketing Research.[28] The procedure was to telephone 150–300 program viewers the day after a television commercial appears. They are asked if they can recall any commercials the previous day for a particular brand. They are then asked if they can recall anything about the commercial: what was said, what was shown, and what the main idea was. DAR is the percent of those in the commercial audience who were watching the show, before and after the commercial was shown, who remembered something specific about it, such as the sales message, the story line, the plot, or some visual or audio element.

The DAR is an "on-air" test in that the commercial exposure occurs in a natural, realistic, in-home setting. It is well established and has developed extensive norms over the years.

Gallup as well as Robinson, Mapes and Ross provide a similar measure for print media. They place a magazine with 150 of its regular readers and ask that it be read in a normal manner. The next day the readers are asked to describe ads for any brands of interest.

DAR scores have many limitations. First, their reliability is suspect. Extremely low test-retest correlations (below .30) have been found when commercials from the same product class are studied. Second, DAR scores are unduly affected by the nature of the program and whether viewers like the particular program. Third, of eight relevant studies, seven found practically no association between recall and the measure of persuasion it generated.

Persuasion

The **forced-exposure**, *brand-preference change* test measures the change in brand preference after watching an advertisement in a theater. Theater testing, pioneered by Horace Schwerin and Paul Lazarsfeld in the 1950s, is now done by McCollum/Spielman, ASI, and ARS.[29]

The McCollum/Spielman test uses a 450-person sample, spread over four geographically dispersed locations.[29] Forced-exposure tests recruit respondents by telephone and ask them to come to a central location to preview television programming. Seated in groups of 25 in front of television monitors, they respond to a set of demographic and brand/product-usage questions that appear on the screen. The respondents view a half-hour variety program featuring four professional performers. At midpoint in the program seven commercials, including four test commercials, are shown in a pattern like the one diagrammed here:

Performer	Performer	T	C	T	C	T	C	T	Performer	Performer
P	Q	1		2		3		4	R	S

C = constant commercials   T = test commercials

After the audience expresses its reactions to the program, an unaided brand-name-recall question is asked that forms the basis of the **clutter/awareness** score (the percentage who recalled that the brand was advertised). The clutter/awareness score (C/A) for 30-second commercials averages 56 percent for established brands and 40 percent for new brands.[30] The four test commercials are then exposed a second time, surrounded by program material, in the following pattern:

Program	T		T		T		T	
Intro.	1	Program	2	Program	3	Program	4	Program

T = test commercials

An *attitude-shift (AS)* measure is obtained. For frequently purchased package goods, such as toiletries, the preexposure designation of the brand purchased most often is compared with the postexposure brand selection in a market-basket-award situation. The respondents are asked to select brands they would like included if they were winners of a $25 basket of products. In product fields with multiple-brand usage, such as soft drinks, a constant-sum measure (i.e., a total of 10 points is allocated to brands, which are apportioned according to audience preference) is employed before and after exposure. For durables and services, the pre- and postpreferences are measured.

Finally, diagnostic questions are asked. Some of the areas that are frequently explored include the following:

- Comprehension of message or slogan.

- Communication of secondary copy ideas.

- Evaluation of demonstrations, spokesperson, message.

- Perception of brand uniqueness or brand differentiation.

- Irritating or confusing elements.

- Viewer involvement.

The ASI and ARS have similar tests to obtain a measure of persuasion.

Customized Measures of Communication/Attitude

Standardized-copy test measures are useful because they come with norms, sometimes based on thousands of past tests. Thus, the interpretation of a test becomes more meaningful. Some objectives, particularly communication objectives, necessarily are unique to a brand, and may require questions tailored to that brand. Customized measures of communication or attitude have to be developed for such applications.

On-Air Tests Brand-Preference Change

In the Mapes and Ross on-air test, commercials are aired on a radio station in a preselected prime-time position in each of three major markets. Prior to the test, a sample of 200 viewers

(150 if the target audience is all male) are contacted by phone and asked to participate in a survey and a cash-award drawing that requires viewing the test program. During the telephone interview, respondents provide unaided brand-name awareness and are questioned about their brand preferences for a number of different product categories. The day following the commercial exposure, the respondents again answer brand-preference questions as well as DAR questions. The key Mapes and Ross measure is pre- and post-brand-preference change. There are also other measures of brand-preference change, such as the one done by ASI Apex System, which differs slightly from the Mapes and Ross test.[30] Marketing Research in Action 23.5 is a sample proposal for a Mapes and Ross on-air test.

Purchase Behavior

Coupon-Stimulated Purchasing

In the Tele-Research approach, 600 shoppers are intercepted in a shopping center location, usually in Los Angeles, and randomly assigned to test or control groups. The test group is exposed to five television or radio commercials or six print ads. About 250 subjects in the test group complete a questionnaire on the commercial. Both groups are given a customer code number and a packet of coupons, including one for the test brand, which can be redeemed in a nearby cooperating drugstore or supermarket, depending on the product. The selling-effectiveness score is the ratio of purchases by viewer shoppers divided by the purchases by control shoppers. Purchases are tracked by scanner data. While the exposure context is highly artificial, the purchase choice is relatively realistic in that real money is spent in a real store.

Split-Cable Tests

Information Resources, Inc.'s (IRI) BehaviorScan is one of several **split-cable testing** operations (Burke and Nielsen being two others). BehaviorScan was described in part in Chapter 6. BehaviorScan monitors the purchases of panel members as well as in-store information such as special prices, features, and displays.

An additional capability of split-cable testing makes it extremely important in advertising research. Panelists have a device connected to their TV sets that not only allows the channel selection to be monitored but also allows the advertiser to substitute one advertisement for another in what are called "cut-ins." Thus, a host of tests can be conducted, such as the impact of specific commercials, sets of commercials, advertising budget levels, the time of day or the program in which the ad appears, the commercial length, or the interaction with promotion programs.

Tracking Studies

When a campaign is running, its impact often is monitored via a **tracking study**. Periodic sampling of the target audience provides a time trend of measures of interest. The purpose is to evaluate and reassess the advertising campaign, and perhaps also to understand why it is or is not working. Among the measures that often are traced are advertisement awareness, awareness of elements of the advertisement, brand awareness, beliefs about brand attributes, brand image, occasions of use, and brand preference. Of particular interest is knowing how the campaign is affecting the brand, as opposed to how the advertisement is communicating the message. The Eric Marder firm provides an approach to obtaining tracking data without doing customized studies.[31] On a continuous basis, they maintain a panel of women from whom they obtain the various measures just described. Table 23.3 gives a comprehensive view of the measures of advertisement effectiveness and the various tests the industry uses to obtain them.

Marketing Research in Action 23.5

▉ MAPES AND ROSS 24-HOUR-RECALL MARKETING RESEARCH PROJECT PROPOSAL

Project:	**Mapes and Ross on-air test**
Brand:	Diet Coke
Research Objectives:	The agency has changed the slogan used in the commercials to a new one. The objectives of this test will be
	(a) To measure the new slogan's effectiveness in generating attention (related recall)
	(b) To measure the new slogan's communication effectiveness

Research Design: The traditional Mapes and Ross on-air test method will be used. The sample will consist of 400 male and female respondents, aged 18 and older, in the program audience. The sample specifications will follow recent Mapes and Ross on-air tests. The data will be broken out by the age group 18–34, 35–49, and 50–65-year-olds, as they fall naturally in the program audience.

The commercial will be shown in Houston, Kansas City, and Chicago on UHF television channels, using movie programs. There will be one exposure. In each of the three metropolitan areas, interviewers will telephone a sample of men, age 18 and over, and invite them to view the test program that night.

The follow-up telephone interviews the next day will probe whether the prerecruited respondents watched the program. Then the respondents will be asked what commercials they recall and what they recalled about the Diet Coke commercial, followed by a measure of liking of the slogan.

Information to Be Collected:
1. Total commercial recall
2. Slogan recall
3. A measure of liking for the slogan

Evaluation Standard: The new slogan will be compared to the original slogan and the Mapes and Ross norms on the following measures:

Old Slogan	
Total commercial recall	18%
Percent recalling the slogan	35
Measure of liking for the new slogan on a 5-point scale	3.8

If the new slogan scores below the above scores for the original slogan, we will not move forward with the test slogan. Additionally, if new slogan scores lower than old slogan on the measure of liking in the 18–34 age group, we will not move forward with the new commercial.

Schedule: The time schedule for this research will be

1½ weeks to set up test/insert commercial into UHF movie programs
1 day field work
1 week top-line
2 weeks computer tabulations
2 weeks final report
7½ weeks total

Cost: The cost for this research will be $11,250 ± 10

Table 23.3 Measures and Tests of Ad Effectiveness

Measure of advertising effectiveness	Test used in the industry
Recognition	1. BRC tests of television commercials 2. Communicus recognition measures of radio and television advertisements 3. Starch scores
Recall	1. DAR measure by Young and Rubicam 2. Gallup & Robinson and Mapes and Ross provide similar measure for the print media
Persuasion	1. Forced Exposure Brand Preference Change tests done by McCollum/Spielman, ASI and ARS 2. On-air tests of brand preference change done by Mapes and Ross and ASI Apex system 3. Customized measures
Purchase behavior	1. Coupon-stimulated purchasing done by Tele-Research 2. Split-cable testing by IRI (BehaviorScan)
Tracking studies	1. Customized studies 2. Eric Marder's TEC audit

Diagnostic Testing

A whole category of advertising research methods is designed primarily not to test the impact of a total ad but rather to help creative people understand how the parts of the ad contribute to its impact. Which are weak and how do they interact? Most of these approaches can be applied to mock-ups of proposed ads as well as finished ads.

Copy Test Validity

Copy Test Validity

Refers to the ability to predict advertising response. Figure 23.5 is an overview of some of the important ways in which copy tests can differ. Each dimension involves validity issues and trade-offs with cost. Hence, each of these issues has to be considered carefully before a copy test can be designed.

Qualitative Research

Focus-group research is widely used at the front end of the development of an advertising campaign. In such groups, people will discuss their opinions about the product and the brand, their use experiences, and their reaction to potential advertisement concepts and actual advertisements.[32]

Audience Impressions of the Ad

Many copy test approaches append a set of open-ended questions designed to tap the audience's impressions of what the ad was about, what ideas were presented, interest in the ideas, and so on. One goal is to detect potential misperceptions. Another is to uncover unintended associations that may have been created. If too many negative comments are elicited, there may be cause for concern.

Adjective Checklist

The BRC mail questionnaire includes an adjective checklist that allows the advertiser to determine how warm, amusing, irritating, or informative the respondent thinks the ad is. Several of the phrases tap an empathy dimension: "I can see myself doing that," "I can relate to that," and so on. Some believe that unless advertisements can achieve a degree of empathy, they will not perform well.

Advertisement Used
  Mock-up
  Finished advertisement

Frequency of Exposure
  Single-exposure test
  Multiple-exposure test

How It's Shown
  Isolated
  In a clutter
  In a program or magazine

Where the Exposure Occurs
  In a shopping center facility
  At home on TV
  At home through the mail
  In a theater

How Respondents Are Obtained
  Prerecruited forced exposure
  Not prerecruited/natural exposure

Geographic Scope
  One city
  Several cities
  Nationwide

Alternative Measures of Persuasion
  Pre/post measures of attitudes or behavior
  (that is, pre/post attitude or behavior shifts)
  Multiple measures
  (that is, recall/involvement/buying commitment)
  After-only questions to measure persuasion
  (that is, constant sum brand preference)
  Test market sales measures
  (that is, using scanner panels)

Bases of Comparison and Evaluation
  Comparing test results to norms
  Using a control group

FIGURE 23.5
Alternative Methods of Copy Testing.

Eye Movement

Eye movement devices, such as those used by Perception Research and Burke, record the point on a print ad or package where the eye focuses, 60 times each second. An analysis can determine what the reader saw, what he or she "returned to" for reexamination, what point was "fixed on."

Physiological Measurement

Of particular interest in advertisements that are intended to precipitate emotional responses is the use of measures that reflect physiological arousal that the respondent normally cannot control. Among the measures used are galvanic skin response (GSR), skin resistance, heart beat, facial expressions, muscle movement, and voice pitch analysis. The difficulty is in the interpretation because a variety of reactions can stimulate arousal.[33] Brain-wave analyses of consumer response to advertising can also be used.[34]

Budget Decision

Arriving at analytical, research-based judgments as to the optimal advertising budget is surprisingly difficult. However, there are research inputs that can be helpful. Tracking studies that show advertising is either surpassing or failing to reach communication objectives can suggest that the budget should be either reduced or increased. Forced-exposure testing of multiple exposures can suggest the optimal number of exposures per month for an audience member. Such a number can help guide advertising budget expenditures. More direct approaches include regression analysis of internal sales and advertising data, field experimentation, and split-cable experimentation. Recent research has shown that advertising and promotion expenditure as a percent of sales for a firm is correlated with its market share and market growth.[35]

Media Research

In evaluating a particular media alternative such as *Time* magazine or *Dynasty*, it is necessary to know how many advertising exposures it will deliver and what will be the characteristics of the audience. A first cut of the vehicle's value is the cost per thousand (circulation), the advertisement insertion cost divided by the size of the audience.

Measuring Print-Vehicle Audiences

Print-vehicle circulation data are easily obtained, but they neglect pass-along readers both inside and outside the home. Thus, to measure a vehicle's audience, it is necessary to apply approaches such as recent-reading, reading-habit, and through-the-book methods to a randomly selected sample.

In the **recent-reading method**, respondents are asked whether they looked at a copy of a weekly publication within the past week, or during the last month if it is a monthly publication.[36]

The **reading-habit method**, which asks respondents how many issues out of the last four they personally read or looked at, is also sensitive to memory difficulties. In particular, it is difficult to discriminate between reading the same issue several times and reading several issues. The **through-the-book** method attempts to reduce the problem resulting from faulty memory. Respondents' readership is ascertained only after they are shown a specific issue of a magazine, asked whether they read several articles, and if they were interesting. The approach, which requires an expensive personal interview, is sensitive to the age of the issue.

Measuring Broadcast-Vehicle Audiences

Television audience size is estimated by a people meter and a diary. The people meter is attached to a television set and monitors the set's activity 24 hours a day, recording any change or activity that lasts over 30 seconds.

Nielsen, in its national ratings estimates, supplements the people meter with a matched-sample **diary panel**. A diary household notes viewing activity, including who is doing the watching. A clocklike meter keeps track of how long the set is on so that Nielsen can make sure that the diary is complete. Using the diary information, Nielsen can break down the audience estimates by age, sex, and geographic area. Mediamark and Simmons are two other major audience-measuring services.[37]

Consumer-Generated Media

While controlled media such as television, print ads, and direct mail assist marketers in designing media campaigns, consumer-generated media (CGM) is emerging as an important channel that can impact marketing initiatives. Shoppers are increasingly using CGM for researching products and learning about other consumers' opinions when making buying decisions. According to McConnell and Huba, CGM refers to anything created by a citizen marketer (typically an amateur)—a blogpost, a podcast, an animation, a video—that is posted on the Web and spread by social media.[38] They divide the citizen marketers into four categories—filters, fanatics, facilitators, and firecrackers.

Filters: Filters are people who set up aggregated news sites about a brand, a product, or a company. They constantly search for stories on the Web about a company and its products that interest them and the readers. An example of this is Starbucks Gossip website (http://www.starbucksgossip.com/) maintained by a professional journalist as a part-time hobby.

Fanatics: Fanatics are people who live and breathe a brand. They can be viewed like "a parent guiding a child brand in the right direction." The blog on McDonalds (http://mcchronicles.blogspot.com) is a good example of this demographic of citizen marketers.

Facilitators: Facilitators use online forums and bulletin boards to build a community around a product or brand. Such portals are typically independent sites and provide online support to the users of a specific product. The site that supports Apple iPod products (http://www.ilounge.com/) acts as a facilitator for the users of Apple iPod.

Firecrackers: Firecrackers are people who become one-hit wonders by making their work create buzz and die out pretty quickly. A good example of this is a teen named Melody who goes by the screen name of Bowiechick. She posted videos on YouTube about the features of Logitech QuickCam. Logitech observed spikes in sales of Web cams when Melody's videos appeared. They quickly formed a partnership with YouTube to capitalize on this buzz.

Sales Promotion Research

There are three major types of sales promotion: consumer promotions, retailer promotions, and trade promotions. Figure 23.6 depicts the major agents involved in sales promotion. In general, the consumer, or end user, is the ultimate target of all sales promotion activities. In consumer promotion, manufacturers offer promotions directly to consumers, whereas retail promotions involve promotions by retailers to consumers. Trade promotions involve manufacturers offering promotions to retailers or other trade entities. Trade entities can also promote to each other. For example, a distributor can offer a steep temporary price cut to retailers in order to sell excess inventory. We call these *trade promotions*, since the recipient of the promotion is a marketing intermediary.

Sometimes several manufacturers or several retailers combine in one promotion. These are called *cooperative promotions* or *promotion partnerships*. Partnership promotions often "tie in" a sample or other promotion for one product with the purchase of another. For example, a

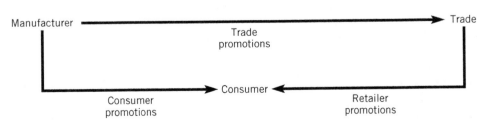

FIGURE 23.6
A Schematic Framework of the Major Types of Sales Promotion.

Marketing Research in Action 23.6

■ SPACE WARS

With consumers exposed to over 100,000 different items in supermarkets, household-goods companies are now forced to increase their shelf space and product visibility if they want to survive in the market. This demand has forced companies to take their battle to the supermarket floors. The companies are concentrating more on deals with retailers to garner shoppers, even as they spend huge amounts on advertising. According to Cannondale Associates, in-store promotions accounted for 17.4 percent of sales in 2003, up from 14 percent in 1999. According to Bain & Co., the share of volumes sold under promotion is as follows:

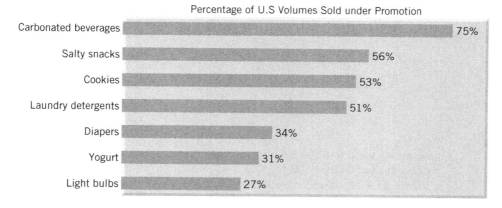

Percentage of U.S Volumes Sold under Promotion

Carbonated beverages — 75%
Salty snacks — 56%
Cookies — 53%
Laundry detergents — 51%
Diapers — 34%
Yogurt — 31%
Light bulbs — 27%

Source: Bain & Company

The promotion activities include buy-one-get-one-free deals and sample giveaways among others. For instance, when Unilever launched Axe men's deodorant spray in the United States in late 2002, it hired squads of female perfume models in Wal-Mart and Costco stores. The launch helped Axe's global sales growth to reach 22 percent in the first half of 2004 as compared to the 6 percent gain posted in 2001 over 2000. Similarly, during Procter & Gamble's launch of new version of Tide detergent containing Downy fabric softener in fall 2004, deals were made with big retailers like Wal-Mart and Kroger to set up in-store displays with pillows, posters, and balloons.

Though the actual costs of these promotions are not disclosed, industry analysts estimate the cost of new product launches in the United States to top $50 million between traditional ads and in-store promotions. On the promotion splurge by the manufacturers, says Cyrus Jilla, head of European consumer-goods practice at Bain, "In an ideal world, they wouldn't do so much promotion. But if they don't, the danger is that retailers will decrease their shelf space."

Source: Adapted with permission from D. Ball, "Consumer-Goods Firms Duel for Shelf Space," The Wall Street Journal—Market Place, October 22, 2004, p. B2.

snack-food company that offers coupons for a soda brand on its package is engaging in a tie-in consumer promotion. Marketing Research in Action 23.6 discusses the sales promotions undertaken by companies at various retail stores.

Strategically, trade promotions and the resultant retailer promotions are elements of the "push" component of a manufacturer's marketing effort, whereas consumer promotions are part of the "pull" effort. It is important that the push and pull elements of sales promotion strategy work hand in hand with the push and pull elements of a firm's marketing strategy. For example, trade

Table 23.4   Specific Sales Promotional Tools

Retailer promotions	Trade promotions	Consumer promotions
Price cuts	Case allowances	Couponing
Displays	Advertising allowances	Sampling
Feature advertising	Display allowances	Price packs
Free goods	Trade coupons	Value packs
Retailer coupons	"Spiffs"	Refunds
Contests/premiums	Financing incentives	Continuity programs
	Contests	Financing incentives
		Bonus packs
		Special events
		Sweepstakes
		Contests
		Premiums
		Tie-ins

promotions often must be coordinated with sales activity, whereas consumer promotions often are coordinated with advertising.

Table 23.4 lists some specific retailer, trade, and consumer promotions. This list is by no means exhaustive. The most commonly researched sales promotions are coupons, trade allowances, and retailer promotions. Even among retailer promotions, only recently have researchers begun to distinguish among price cuts, displays, and features, and even now, those are often subsumed under one "promotion" or "deal offer" variable.

Unfortunately, much of the research on sales promotion has concentrated on only a few types or has considered promotion only more generically. For example, couponing by far is the most researched form of consumer promotion. In one sense this is appropriate, since coupons are clearly the most important consumer promotion for packaged-goods marketers.[39] Catalina, Inc., has recruited over 10,000 retail stores to dispense coupons for brands that consumers did not buy in that product category. This kind of targeted couponing is becoming a useful approach. However, contests and sweepstakes, continuity offers, price packs, and premiums are clearly underresearched. Rebates, which are the durable-goods analog of couponing, have received very little attention. The use of premiums and financing incentives in a durable-goods context is also vastly underresearched.

With scanner data so easily and widely available, most of the information requirements for decisions on sales promotions can be readily acquired. Both Nielsen and IRI have installed scanner-based information-collection systems (both store and panel) to cover all the markets in the country, so researchers will have a wealth of information to rely on. They also have a number of ready-to-use expert systems, some of which were discussed in Chapter 6, which provide information such as sales and market share in that store in the week there was a promotion, so managers can easily find out whether the promotion was effective.

Total Quality Management

Recent years have witnessed a renewed emphasis on delivering superior-quality products and services to customers.[40] With foreign competition steadily eating away the profitability and the market shares of American companies, more and more of them are adopting **TQM** to become

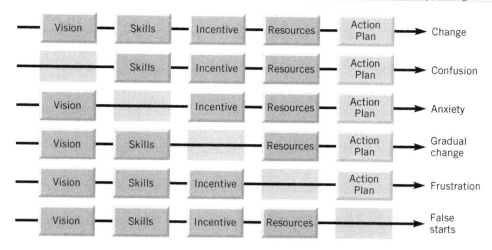

FIGURE 23.7
Managing Complex Change.
Source: American Productivity Council.

more competitive.[41] TQM is a process of managing complex changes in the organization with the aim of improving quality. In Figure 23.7, the process of managing complex change and the effects when one of the links in the chain is missing are depicted.

The TQM concept essentially is a business philosophy that was used by the Japanese to gain competitive advantage. It is now being discovered and used by American organizations. TQM can be defined as a systematic effort at continuous quality improvement of all processes, products, services, and human resources throughout the organization, undertaken with an objective of improving customer satisfaction. The characteristics of an organization that has successfully implemented TQM are as follows:

- A TQM company strives for a continuous improvement in quality. To achieve this continuous improvement process (CIP), everyone in the organization must be trained and educated continuously.

- Teams and teamwork are another cornerstone of the TQM organization. Cross-functional teams must be formed, and they must work together. The teams must be inherently motivated and should be empowered to set their own objective.

- Quantifiable measures of progress must be established, and rewards should be based on these measures. One of the most commonly used tools to set quantifiable measures is *benchmarking*. Competitive benchmarking means comparing the company's processes, practices, and products to the world's best, including those in other industries.

- TQM companies use a number of formal tools, techniques, and processes to ensure the quality of their products/services and processes. Almost all of them use some form of *statistical quality control* and *statistical process control*. TQM companies aim at zero defects. The most commonly used tools in a TQM company are *flowcharting, cause-and-effect diagrams, Pareto charts, control charts*, and *scatter diagrams*. Techniques such as *Taguchi methods, quality function deployment (QFD), Poka-Yoke*, and *Robust designs* are commonly employed. *Just-in-time processing*, the *plan-do-check-act* cycle, and *activity-based costing* are also frequently used in TQM companies.

The federal government has recognized the need for a quality imperative and has recently introduced the Malcolm Baldrige Award for Quality. Adoption of TQM is one of the prerequisites for competing for the award. The number of companies competing for this award has increased at a rapid pace since its inception.

Information Requirements for Total Quality Management

The first things on which a TQM company should decide are the guiding principles behind its data choices. Why these data, and not those data? As usual, the best rationale usually refers back to the bedrock of customer satisfaction. There should be a clear link between the kinds of data collected and maintained and the quality values of the company.[42] If short-term financial measurements drive the company, measures such as market value to book value and price-to-earnings multiples will dominate management reports and meetings. If, on the other hand, quality lies at the center of business strategy and planning, a larger share of the measurement and reporting will focus on quality issues. When companies are truly committed to quality values, many data issues resolve themselves.[43]

Many companies struggle with how to develop measures in order to plan, control, and implement their TQM program. Most of the Baldrige award winners have explicit methodologies and measures for their TQM programs. Honeywell created a guide to TQM for its managers.[44] The manual identifies the following "Principles of Measurement":

1. Measurement must be specific. You need to know exactly what you want to measure.

2. Measure the outputs of highest value to the customer. This entails converting customer information into measures, which means you must first know exactly what your customers expect.

3. Measures can be applied to all performance dimensions, external as well as internal. It is not enough to achieve an internal goal if you fail to meet customers' expectations or your competitors' performance.

4. Understand the game before you decide how you will keep score. Tracking the wrong measure will not improve your quality.

5. Measure process as well as results. If you just measure results, you will always be fixing mistakes instead of preventing them.

6. You can't hit tomorrow by shooting at yesterday. You can't even hit tomorrow by shooting at today. The science of anticipating future customer and process requirements is called "leading the duck."

7. There is no single perfect measure. First identify the indicators for your objective, then measure all those indicators.

Federal Express uses specific measurements to track events that negatively affect a customer as they happen, using their service quality indicator (SQI). Twelve types of events are weighted by degree of importance to the customer. FedEx's goal is an SQI score of zero. SQI results are broadcast weekly over the company's private television network. Identifying actual failure creates an intense focus on the relatively few service breakdowns. Marketing Research in Action 23.7 gives the details about Federal Express Service Quality Indicator.

The kind of data a company should collect also depends on the nature of its business. Accounting firms, for example, do not need extensive data on worker safety; their workers are not

Marketing Research in Action 23.7

■ SERVICE QUALITY INDICATORS: HOW FEDEX MEASURES ITS PERFORMANCE

Customers are the best judges of the quality of services. That's why, in developing a composite quality indicator, Federal Express looked for factors reflecting its customers' view of performance. It identified 12 components as key elements in successfully delivering what customers want. Some failures have much more impact than others. Losing or damaging a package, for example, is much more serious than simply delivering one a few minutes late. Therefore, the company assigns weighting factors according to the customer's perception of their importance.

The SQI is the weighted sum of the average daily failure points for the 12 components, and it is reported weekly and summarized monthly. Some 60 million weighted

opportunities for error exist each day, yet SQI scores have steadily dropped until they now run about 0.4 of 1 percent. The company now calculates a similar SQI figure for the international delivery service. The purpose of the SQI is to help Federal Express identify and eliminate causes of failures but not to place blame. If courier mislabeling of packages was found to be a cause for wrong-day-late failures, for example, the SQI team would work on creating effective methods for preventing miscoding at the source rather than on developing an elaborate and expensive expediting system. Finding out what dissatisfies customers is a first step, but then a cooperative effort within the context of all the goals of the organization is needed to find optimum solutions to any problems—so that employees do the right things right.

Following are the SQI components:

Failure	Weight	Description
Right day late	1	Delivery after the commitment time but the right day.
Wrong day late	5	Delivered the wrong day.
Traces unanswered by COSMOS	1	Number of proof of performance requests by customers where exception information, proper scans, or proof of delivery (POD) data are not in COSMOS.
Complaints reopened by customers	5	Includes customer complaints on traces, invoice adjustments, missed pickups, etc., reopened.
Missing proof of performance	1	Billing documents that don't match a POD in COSMOS or from the field POD queue on a timely basis, including prepaid and metered packages as well as those that are invoiced.
Invoice adjustment requested	1	Packages on which customers request an invoice adjustment, including those not granted because a request indicates the customer perceives a problem.
Missed pick-ups	10	Complaints from customers recorded as missed pick-ups.
Damaged packages	10	Includes packages with either visible or concealed damage and weather and water damage. Also includes contents spoiled or damaged due to a missed pick-up or late delivery.
Lost packages	10	Includes both packages missing and those with contents missing due to pilferage.
Overgoods	5	Packages received in Lost & Found (no label or identifying data inside package).
Abandoned calls	5	Any call to FedEx that is not answered, which is any call in which caller hangs up without speaking to an agent after 20 seconds from receipt of call.
International	1	Includes components from the performance measurement of international operations.

Source: R. Haavind, The Road to the Baldrige Award. Stoneham, MA: Butterworth-Heinemann, 1992, p. 76.

usually in physical danger. Chemical or mining companies, however, cannot afford to ignore that kind of data. Data and information relating to customers, employees, and suppliers should be collected. External, independent contractors, such as market research companies, law firms, and insurance providers, all qualify as suppliers. The company must control and monitor the quality of its goods and services. Data on support functions such as accounting and internal legal services are also important and should be collected.

The presentation of data is also important in a TQM company. The data should be grouped into categories, such as customer-related data, data on internal operations, supplier data, and so on, giving brief, thumbnail descriptions explaining the use and relevance of each database. The data can also be labeled according to whether they are generated by the company itself or by outside vendors.

Analysis of Data in a TQM Company

Analysis is the second phase of the data-and-information-gathering and problem-solving/quality-improvement process. The aim of analysis is to comb through the raw data you have collected and to turn it into useful information for such functions as planning, performance review, design of products and services, and quality-improvement projections. The key questions in data analysis are

- Who performs the analysis?

- What analytical techniques are used?

- Which data are analyzed and at what level of detail?

- How are data aggregated, and how are relations between data groups cross-referenced?

- How does the company improve its analytical capabilities? (This last question relates to continuous improvement.)

In responding to these questions, applicants should concentrate on how analysis, as it is performed for each major function, affects evaluation and decision making, especially at the corporate level.

Choosing the Right Analytical Method

TQM companies typically employ a handful of sophisticated analytical techniques, including formal statistical analyses, as well as informal tools such as "lessons learned." The analysis should be performed systematically, and problems should be analyzed efficiently and effectively. The idea here is to identify a problem in one operating area, and then to see if that problem is occurring elsewhere. The company must determine what, if any, connection there is between the two problems; if there is a connection, chances are there is a basic system flaw. A large, widespread system problem would trigger additional, more comprehensive analyses. Analyzing data in ways like this, which allow identification of system issues from among seemingly different sets of operating-group data, is the hallmark of organizations that have learned to effectively analyze information.

Managing and Maintaining the Data

Once the analyses are performed and the databases are assembled, the TQM companies have well-developed methods for managing and maintaining them. In particular, these companies have specific methods and techniques that they use to ensure the quality of data and their rapid assimilation throughout the company.

Data Quality

Data quality is measured in terms of validity, reliability, consistency, timeliness, and standardization. Periodic audits of the *processes* used to collect, analyze, and report data are a good way to ensure that the data are fundamentally sound. Some companies use cross-functional teams whose express responsibility is data-and-information management and measurement control. Outside, independent reviewers can be used to perform audits to corroborate internal findings. Because information and analysis is such a critical function, though, such audits should be aggressively monitored by senior management.

Comparisons and Benchmarks

Competitive and benchmark data are so absolutely critical to quality improvement that companies adopting TQM devote special attention to them. Vigorous benchmarking is a key indicator of external focus and an integral element in the strategic management of quality.[45]

Broadly speaking, *benchmarking* is the practice of searching outside one's company for new ideas for improvement of processes, products, and services. Benchmarking involves "either adopting the practices or adapting the best features, and implementing them to obtain the best of the best." Benchmarking also means establishing numerical operating targets for particular functions, based on the best possible industry or out-of-industry practices. This concept is very new for most companies and stands in contrast to their current practices, which project the future from the company's own past trends, without any reference to what competitors and other leading companies are doing. In addition, benchmarking validates and adds credibility to the goal-setting process by its concentration on best practices. The key questions in this item are

- What elements do you compare, and how do you select information for comparison?

- What is the full scope of comparison data?

- How do you get reliable information from the companies or the industry you have selected?

- How do you use benchmark information to encourage new ideas and innovation?

- How do you improve the benchmarking capabilities you already have?

The Xerox benchmarking model has been held up as the global standard against which other companies ought to benchmark *their* benchmarking. This version requires 10 steps:[46]

1. *Identify what is to be benchmarked.* A team selects a product, a service, a process, or a practice; even a level of customer satisfaction. The goal is to determine whether the area of interest is managed in the best way possible.

2. *Identify comparative companies.* Benchmarking partners can be other operating units within Xerox, Xerox competitors, or noncompetitors who are judged the leaders in the area to be benchmarked.

3. *Determine data collection method, and collect data.* In true "apples-to-apples" fashion, teams determine what measurements will be used in the benchmarking process. Then a trip is often made to the selected company, and face-to-face exchanges are conducted with principals of both firms. Often, a tour of the benchmarked area is included.

4. *Determine current performance levels.* Once the team has gathered the necessary data and compared them with current performance levels, the results are analyzed. Generally, they reveal a negative or positive performance gap.

5. *Project future performance levels.* The benchmarking team forecasts the expected improvement by the company under study and sets the new Xerox goals based on this forecast of the benchmark. This step ensures that the Xerox goals will still equal or perhaps exceed the performance of the studied organization after whatever time it takes to implement the team's findings.

6. *Communicate benchmark findings, and gain acceptance.* The team presents its methodology, findings, and proposed strategies to senior management. This information is also communicated to employees who will be asked to help implement the new strategies.

7. *Establish functional goals.* After concurrence, the team then presents final recommendations on ways in which the organization must change, based on benchmark findings, to reach the new goals.

8. *Develop action plans.* The team develops specific action plans for each objective, and develops strategies for obtaining full organizational support.

9. *Implement specific actions, and monitor progress.* The plans are put into place. Data on the new level of performance are collected. Adjustments to the process are made if the goals are not being met, and problem-solving teams may be formed to investigate.

10. *Recalibrate benchmarks.* Over time, the benchmarks are reevaluated and updated to ensure that they are based on the latest performance data from the benchmarked company.

Quality Function Deployment

The power of measurements is clearly visible in applications of *QFD*, a Japanese import used to make product designs better reflect customer requirements. In QFD, a multifunctional team measures and analyzes in great detail both customer attitudes and product attributes. Marketing research plays a crucial role at this stage of the process. Then the team creates a visual matrix in order to find ways to modify product attributes (engineering characteristics) so as to improve the product on the customer-based measures of product performance. Along the way, the team must develop a series of measures of several different types. Here is how it works.[47]

Step 1

Attributes that the customer looks for in the product (CAs) are defined. These are descriptions of what the customer wants, often in the customers' own words and phrases. There may be dozens of them, and it may be expedient to organize them into groups of related attributes. CAs are also given relative importance weightings, often through trade-off (conjoint) analysis and other forms of survey research. (Usually, weightings are in relative percents such that they total 100 percent.)[48]

Step 2

Customer evaluations of competing products are obtained for each of the customer attributes determined in step 1. (Usually, survey research is needed.) Competitive position is often measured on a relative scale where 1 = worst and 5 = best. These comparative data help product engineers and managers understand how to best achieve competitive advantage through their work on the attributes.

Step 3

Engineering characteristics (ECs) that may affect the attributes are listed. Usually the design team does this after reviewing attributes in detail (in order to help them develop descriptors that are meaningful from the customer's perspective). Some engineering characteristics affect more than one of the attributes. Some of the proposed ECs will not appear to affect any attributes, which means either that they may be unnecessary or that there may be a flaw in the customer research. ECs are described quantitatively: weight, length, number, and so forth. This exercise presents a good opportunity for rethinking both the design and the existing quality measures for it.

Step 4

The extent of the impact of each EC on each CA is determined or estimated. This is often done on a four-point scale in the body of the matrix, such as

1. Strong positive impact

2. Medium positive impact

3. Medium negative impact

4. Strong negative impact

Step 5

All this information is summarized in a chart, often called the *house of quality*. (The reason is obvious when you look at Figure 23.8.) The chart shows customer attributes on the horizontal and engineering characteristics on the vertical dimension. The resulting grid is filled in with the relationship scores from step 4.

Step 6

The impact of changes in any engineering characteristic on other ECs is evaluated. (A scale such as the one in step 4 can be applied to this step.) Interactions among ECs in which changes in one EC have an impact on another are represented in a "roof" diagram above the matrix. A simplified "house of quality" is shown in Figure 23.8.

Step 7

As the team develops the measures and fills in the matrix, its members naturally begin to focus on customer attributes in which the product appears weak and also begin to develop ideas concerning how to improve various engineering characteristics. Now that the matrix is complete, the team turns its attention completely to the task of redesign, using the house of quality diagram as a guide. Because the diagram integrates a great many measures having to do with customer perception, competitive position, and engineering characteristics, the team is far better able to keep all these considerations in mind during redesign than its members could without this tool.

A brief example helps make the benefits of QFD more tangible. Here is one from two professors who described the method in an academic journal when it was first introduced to the United States:

> Consider the location of an emergency brake lever in an American sporty car. Placing it on the left between the seat and the door solved an engineering problem. But it also guaranteed that women in skirts could not get in and out gracefully. In contrast, Toyota improved its rust prevention record from one of the worst to one of the best by coordinating design and production decisions to focus on the customer concern. Using the house of quality, designers broke down "body durability" into 53 items covering everything from climate to modes of operation. They obtained customer evaluations and ran experiments on nearly every detail of production, from pump operation to temperature control and coating composition. Decisions on sheet metal details, coating materials, and baking temperatures were all focused on those aspects of rust prevention most important to customers.[18]

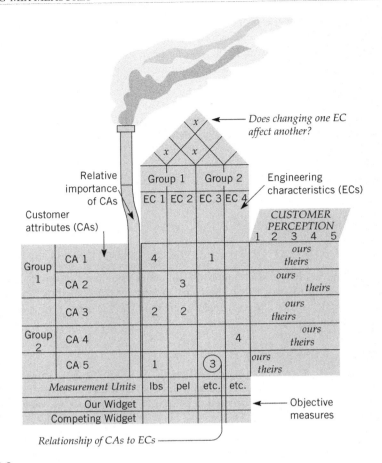

FIGURE 23.8
House of Quality.
Source: A. Hiam, *Closing the Quality Gap: Lessons from America's Leading Companies.* Englewood Cliffs, NJ: Prentice-Hall, 1992.

Marketing Research in QFD

Marketing research is an invaluable part of QFD. Customer attributes are obtained through conjoint analysis or through other forms of survey research. Customer evaluations of competing products are also obtained through survey research. Hence, a thorough knowledge of marketing research is required.

SUMMARY

The first stage in new-product research is *concept generation*, which involves research, first to identify needs, and second to identify concepts that will be responsive to those needs. The second stage is *concept evaluation and development*—getting relevant people's reactions to concepts. The purposes usually are to help make a judgment as to whether to proceed and to suggest some directions in the subsequent development phase. The third stage is *product evaluation and development*, where more realistic product exposure is possible because the product and much of the marketing program have been developed. In particular, the product will be available for use tests, in which potential customers try it and provide reactions. The laboratory test market, where respondents are exposed to the product and then given the opportunity to make a trial purchase in a simulated supermarket, is used for product trials. The fourth stage is the *test market*, where the product and the marketing program actually are implemented in the field.

In a *sell-in test market*, the product is sold just as it would be in a national launch. In a *controlled-distribution scanner market* (CDSM) test, distribution is prearranged and purchases are monitored using scanner data.

There are two approaches to pricing research. One is to present respondents with the product at different prices and ask them to buy. The second is to show respondents different sets of brands in the same product category, at different prices, and ask them which they would buy. The information to be obtained by pricing research depends on whether a skimming or a penetration strategy will be adopted.

The distribution decisions that typically require a lot of information from outside the firm are those that deal with the number and location of warehouses, retail outlets, and salespersons. Marketing research aids managers in making these decisions by providing the necessary information. The *center-of-gravity method, computerized simulation, trade-area analysis*, and *outlet location research* are some of the more commonly used analytical tools that managers use in this area of decision making. Marketing research also helps in conducting field experiments, statistical analysis of sales data, and setting up of computerized models for determining sales-force size and allocation of sales amounts.

Criteria used in copy testing can be usefully grouped into four types: recognition, recall, persuasion, and behavior. BRC uses mail questionnaires to measure television commercial recognition and brand-name association. Communicus (for television) and Starch (for print ads) use personal interviews. DAR is widely used but controversial because of its inability to predict persuasion or behavior, especially for emotional appeals. Persuasion has been measured in forced-exposure or on-air contexts, by change in brand preference, change in prize-list brand preference, comparison of its effect on brand preference with a nonexposed control group, measures of advertisement involvement and brand commitment, and measures tailored to particular advertising objectives. Behavior measures include coupon-stimulated buying after a forced exposure to an ad, and scanner-based monitoring of panelists in a split-cable testing operation.

Copy test validity concerns usually focus on the naturalness of the exposure, the reactive effect of being in an experiment (especially when the exposure setting is not natural and when an attitude measure is required), the representativeness of the sample, and the appropriateness and validity of the response measure. A tracking study provides measures of advertising impact over time by taking periodic (monthly, quarterly, or yearly) surveys of audience response. *Diagnostic testing*, to evaluate the advertisement content at all stages of the process, includes qualitative research, audience and impressions, adjective checklists, eye movement, physiological measures, and monitoring audience response during the commercial. *Media research* includes measuring vehicle audiences by asking people about their reading habits, and using audimeters connected to television sets.

There are different ways by which a product/service can be promoted. *Couponing* is the most common way of sales promotion, and most marketing research has concentrated on coupon promotion. Scanner data can provide most of the informational requirements for sales promotion decisions.

The most acclaimed strategy that is emerging in this decade is *total quality management*.[49] A brief description of this strategy is given, including the various data requirements necessary for managers trying to implement this strategy, and the methodologies to be adopted to obtain the necessary data.

QUESTIONS AND PROBLEMS

23.1   Develop a research design to provide a demand estimate for the following new products:

(a) A plastic disposable toothbrush that comes in a cylinder $\frac{5}{8}$ inches in diameter and 3 inches in length. Its unique, patented quality is that the toothpaste already has been applied.

(b) A lemon condiment. Lemon enhances the flavor of many foods, including corn on the cob, fish, and melons. The lemon condiment would be in a crystallized form that would capture the essence of lemon and be served in a "lemon shaker" that would complement salt and pepper shakers.

(c) A clear plastic umbrella attachment for bicycles, which folds away behind the handlebars when not in use.

(d) A vibrator secretarial chair, which contains a gentle vibrator device designed to provide relaxation and blood circulation for people who must sit for long periods of time.

(e) A battery-powered, two-passenger automobile with a top speed of 40 mph and a range of 120 miles.

23.2   In benefit structure analysis, 500 or so respondents are asked to react to a large number (75–100) of specific product benefits and to many product characteristics. The reactions are in terms of both the desire for and perceived deficiencies in current brands with respect to each benefit and characteristic. The focus is on a specific use occasion. For example, if a household cleaner were involved, the respondent would focus on a single cleaning occasion. The brand used also would be asked. How would you generate the list of benefits and product characteristics? Develop a sampling plan. What data analysis would you conduct?

23.3   In evaluating a new-product idea, what criteria should be used? What role should marketing research play in evaluating the idea against each of the criteria?

23.4 How would you find a name for a new brand of soda that is a "natural drink" made out of carbonated apple juice with some ginger and lemon added?

23.5 Identify five new products. Consider a concept test for each. Which could be exposed via a mail questionnaire? Via a phone interview? Via cable television? Which, if any, of these products would you take directly to market, bypassing a test market? Why?

23.6 How can the bias of a purchase-intention question in a concept test be measured?

23.7 What are the key assumptions of the ASSESSOR laboratory test market? What changes could you make to improve its validity?

23.8 Compare and contrast CDSMs with sell-in test markets. What are the advantages and disadvantages of each? When would you want to use a sell-in test market?

23.9 Beecham sued the research firm Yankelovich Clancy Shulman (YCS) when its laboratory test market prediction for a new product, Delicare, proved to be wrong. Beecham argued that one of the model inputs, the percentage of households using fine-fabric detergents, was assumed by YCS to be 75 percent when it was actually 30 percent. In general, should a research firm be held liable for an inaccurate prediction based on a market research study if the model

(a) Had an incorrectly entered key number?

(b) Had a structure that was found to be faulty (for example, a new-product model that failed to take into account that distribution might not be widespread)?

(c) Used a sample that was not representative of the market to be served by the new product?

23.10 When is periodic discounting preferred to random discounting? Is one better than the other?

23.11 A major airline announced that it was reducing its fares by 30 percent for off-peak travel. (Off-peak travel is defined as travel times between 8:00 P.M. and 8:00 A.M. on weekdays, and all weekend.) Do you consider this as price-signaling or second-market discounting?

23.12 The top management of your company has come up with a concept they think is exciting and has tremendous potential. Management wants to find out the demand for this product. Market skimming is planned if the demand for the product is high. You have been given the responsibility to design a prototype and determine the demand. You have also been asked to find out whether skimming would be the best pricing strategy to adopt. What information will you require to answer these questions, and how will you obtain it?

23.13 Why measure recognition anyway? Why would it ever be of value to have an audience member recognize an ad when he or she could not recall it without being prompted and could not recall its content? Why not just measure recall?

23.14 Compare the BRC recognition method with the Communicus method. What are the relative strengths and weaknesses?

23.15 Is DAR widely used? Why? Would you use it if you were the product manager for Lowenbrau? For American Express? Under what circumstances would you use it?

23.16 Review the validity problems inherent in the McCollum/Spielman theater testing approach. Compare these to

(a) Mapes and Ross method

(b) Apex method

(c) Tele-Research approach

(d) Sherman BUY test

(e) BehaviorScan approach

23.17 Why conduct tracking studies? Why not just observe sales?

23.18 How will adjective checklists help a creative group? What about eye-movement data?

23.19 DuPont conducted a field experiment for an improved version of Teflon several years after they first introduced Teflon. Four cities received 10 day-time commercial minutes per week during the fall months, five cities received 5 minutes per week, and four cities (the control group) received no advertising. Cities were randomly assigned to each of the three test conditions. The sales measure was a purchase of Teflon cookware as reported by telephone interviews with 1,000 housewives in each of the test cities. The total purchases turned out to be about 30 percent higher in the heavy-advertising cities than in those cities with no or low advertising, but there was no real difference between the low and no-advertising groups. Critique this test. What validity problems do you see? What changes would you make? Would you conduct the same test if the product change had been out for three years?

23.20 Mediamark estimated the total adult readers of *Family Circle* magazine as 32.1 million, while Simmons estimated it as 18.3 million. Why the difference? Which is right?

23.21 In a survey of homemakers, the readership of *Harper's* was exaggerated and the readership of *Modern Romance* seemed much less than circulation figures indicated. Why would respondents incorrectly report their readership in this manner? Can you think of ways to avoid this bias?

23.22 What are the weaknesses of the people meter? Of the diary? If cost was not a problem, do you believe a camera in the room would be a reasonable solution? Identify and evaluate other alternatives.

23.23 You are the sales manager for a firm that sells photocopying machines, laser printers, and fax machines. Design a system for finding the number and location of the salespersons in your company. Describe clearly the input, the method(s) of calculation, and the output of your system.

23.24 What is the significance of "trade area"? How does one decide the trading area for a retail store?

23.25 Conduct research on the computerized models that are available for locating warehouses and salespersons. Give

a detailed report on their capabilities, advantages, and disadvantages.

23.26 You are a startup entrepreneur who employs about 100 people. You supply mainly grade items (such as nuts, bolts, etc.) to a big NASA contractor. The contractor has threatened to cancel its future orders until you adopt TQM in your company. The contractor wants you to establish specific, tangible measures to achieve TQM in your company. Specify some of the measures you will have to show your contractor to convince him or her that you have adopted TQM, and also describe the informational requirements for these measures.

END NOTES

1. J. H. Meyers, "Benefit Structure Analysis: A New Tool for Product Planning," *Journal of Marketing*, 40, October 1976, pp. 23–32.

2. E. E. Norris, "Your Surefire Clue to Ad Success: Seek Out the Consumer's Problem," *Advertising Age*, March 17, 1975, pp. 43–44.

3. E. P. McGuire, *Evaluating New-Product Proposals*. New York: The Conference Board, 1973, p. 47.

4. G. L. Urban, B. D. Weinberg, and J. R. Hanser, "Premarket Forecasting of Really New Products," *Journal of Marketing*, 60(1), 1996, pp. 47–60.

5. P. J. Rosenberger III and L. de Chernalony, "Virtual Reality Techniques in NPD Research," *Journal of the Marketing Research Society*, 37(4), 1995, pp. 345–355.

6. McGuire, *op. cit.*, p. 58.

7. Rosenberger and de Chernalony, *op. cit.*

8. J. W. Taylor, J. J. Houlahan, and A. C. Gabriel, "The Purchase Intention Question in New Product Development: A Field Test," *Journal of Marketing*, 40, January 1975, pp. 90–92.

9. H. J. Claycamp and L. E. Liddy, "Prediction of New Product Performance: An Analytical Approach," *Journal of Marketing Research*, 6, November 1969, pp. 414–420; G. Assmus, "NEW-PROD: The Design and Implementation of a New Product Model," *Journal of Marketing*, 39, January 1975, pp. 16–23.

10. G. J. Eskin and J. Malec, "A Model for Estimating Sales Potential Prior to the Test Market," in *1976 Educators Proceeding*. Chicago: American Marketing Association, 1976, pp. 230–233.

11. In situations where no definition of the product class exists, a product appeal measure obtained from a concept test is used to estimate the size of the relevant product class for that particular product.

12. As discussed in Chapter 13, the symbols $O1$, $O2$, etc., refer to a measure or observation and $X1$, $X2$, etc., refer to experimental treatments.

13. G. L. Urban, J. R. Hauser, and J. H. Roberts, "Prelaunch Forecasting of New Automobiles: Models and Implementation," *Management Science*, 36(4), April 1990, pp. 401–421; G. L. Urban, J. S. Hulland, and B. D. Weinberg, "Premarket Forecasting of New Consumer Durables: Modeling Categorization, Elimination, and Consideration Phenomena," *Journal of Marketing*, 57, April 1993.

14. Ibid., p. 12.

15. For a listing of the most representative test market cities, refer to J. Waldrop, "All American Markets," *American Demographics*, January 1992, p. 27.

16. V. Appel, "Why a Single Pair of Markets Is Still Not Enough," ARF Advertising Heavy Spending Tests Workshop, April 1985.

17. J. H. Parfitt and B. J. K. Collins, "Use of Consumer Panels for Brand Share Prediction," *Journal of Marketing Research*, 5, May 1968, pp. 131–145.

18. D. R. Lehmann and R. S. Winer, *Product Management*. Chicago: Richard D. Irwin, 1997.

19. A. Gabor and C. Grainger, "Price as an Indicator of Quality," *Economics*, 33, 1966, pp. 43–70.

20. Table 23.2 was adapted from G. J. Tellis, "Beyond the Many Faces of Price: An Integration of Pricing Strategies," *Journal of Marketing*, 50(4), 1986, pp. 146–160.

21. This section is drawn with permission from L. Moutinho and M. Evans, *Applied Marketing Research*. Reading MA: Addison-Wesley, 1992.

22. S. V. Auken, "The Centroid Locational Model: A Study in Situational Dependency," *Logistics and Transportation Review*, 2, 1974, pp. 149–163.

23. J. A. Paris and L. D. Crabtree, "Survey License Plates to Define Retail Trade Area," *Marketing News*, 19, 1985, p. 12.

24. D. L. Huff and R. R. Batsell, "Delimiting the Areal Extent of a Market Area," *Journal of Marketing Research*, 14, 1977, pp. 581–585.

25. E. Blair, "Sampling Issues in Trade Area Maps Drawn from Shoppers Surveys," *Journal of Marketing*, 14, 1983, pp. 98–106.

26. C. S. Craig, A. Ghosh, and S. McLafferty, "Models of the Retail Location Process: A Review," *Journal of Retailing*, 60, 1984, p. 22.

27. M. F. Goodchild, "ILACS: A Location-Allocation Model for Retail Site Selection," *Journal of Retailing*, 60, pp. 84–100.

28. D. E. Bruzzone, "The Case for Testing Commercials by Mail," presented at the 25th Annual Conference of the Advertising Research Foundation, New York, October 23, 1979.

29. B. Lipstein, "An Historical Perspective of Copy Research," *Journal of Advertising Research*, 24, December 1984, pp. 11–15.

30. *AC-T Advertising Control for Television*. New York: McCollum/Spielman Research, no date.

31. Descriptive material from Mapes and Ross.

32. TEC audit. New York: TEC Measures.

33. B. Lipstein and J. P. Neelankavil, "Television Advertising Copy Research: A Critical Review of the State of the Art," *Journal of Advertising Research*, 24, April/May 1984, pp. 19–25.

34. R. Rust, L. Price, and V. Kumar, "Brain Wave Analysis of Consumer Responses to Advertising," in J. Olson et al. eds., *Advertising and Consumer Psychology*. New York: Praeger, 1986.

35. D. A. Aaker, D. M. Stayman, and M. R. Hagerty, "Warmth in Advertising: Measurement, Impact and Sequence Effects," *Journal of Consumer Research*, March 1986, pp. 365–381.

36. W. S. Blair, "Observed vs. Reported Behavior in Magazine Reading: An Investigation of the Editorial Interest Method," *Proceedings of the 12th Annual Conference of the Advertising Research Foundation*, New York, 1967.

37. "ARB and NSI Defend Their TV Diaries," *Media Decisions*, October 1973, pp. 72–74.

38. B. McConnell and J. Huba, *Citizen Marketers: When People are the Message*. Chicago, IL: Kaplan Publishing, 2007.

39. R. C. Blattberg and S. A. Neslin, *Sales Promotion: Concepts, Methods and Strategies*. Englewood Cliffs, NJ: Prentice Hall, 1990.

40. M. J. Bitner, "Evaluating Service Encounters: The Effects of Physical Surroundings and Employee Responses," *Journal of Marketing*, 54,

April 1990, pp. 69–82; A. Parasuraman, V. A. Zeithaml, and L. L. Berry, "A Conceptual Model of Service Quality and Its Implications for Future Research," *Journal of Marketing*, 49, Fall 1985, pp. 41–50; J. R. Hauser and D. Clausing, "The House of Quality," *Harvard Business Review*, May–June 1988, p. 64.

41. Special Report, "Quality—Small and Midsize Companies Seize the Challenge—Not a Moment Too Soon," *Business Week*, November 30, pp. 66–74.

42. A. C. Hyde, "Rescuing Quality Measurement from TQM," *Bureaucrat*, 19, Winter 1990–1991, pp. 16–20.

43. C. E. Bogan and C. W. L. Hart, *The Baldrige*. New York: McGraw-Hill, 1992.

44. *The Honeywell Quality Improvement Owner's Manual*.

45. S. George, *The Baldrige Quality System*. New York: John Wiley, 1992; R. Camp, *Benchmarking: The Search for Industry Best Practices That Lead to Superior Performance*. Milwaukee: Quality Press, 1989.

46. *Competitive Benchmarking: What It Is and What It Can Do for You*. New York: Xerox Corporate Quality Office, 1987, p. 17.

47. A. Hiam, *Closing the Quality Gap*. Englewood Cliffs, NJ: Prentice-Hall, 1992.

48. A. Griffin and J. Hauser, "The Voice of the Customer," *Marketing Science*, 12, Winter 1993, pp. 1–27.

49. For an understanding of how to implement TQM, read V. Kumar and V. Subramaniam, "Customers' Role in the Continuous Quality Improvement Process," *Australian Journal of Market Research*," 3, July 1995, pp. 3–14.

Case 23-1 ‖ **National Chemical Corporation**

The Tiger-Tread spray product designed to free cars stuck in ice or snow had been delayed due to problems with packaging. In the summer of 1996, the problems were solved and the product was ready to go. There were, however, a host of basic decisions that needed to be made, and Charley Omsrud was considering the value of delaying a national introduction of the product and running a test market.

One issue involved the amount of production capacity to plan both for the 5-oz can (good for two or three use occasions) and the 10-oz can (good for four to six use occasions). Although the 200 people from the Toledo lab that tried product samples did not seem to have problems using it, there was always the lingering concern that unanticipated product problems could materialize in a broader test.

An issue that had recently emerged was whether the market should be restricted to fleets of cars. A colleague of

Charley Omsrud, the marketing manager, had observed that for every fleet car there were well over 10 other potential customers. If a consumer effort were mounted, the nature of the marketing program needed to be decided. In the test market used in 1970, extensive information on advertising and distribution was obtained. Charley felt that a middle course might make sense. His idea was to distribute the product through service stations and support it with point-of-purchase display stands and brochures. After all, the consumer did rely on the service station to provide antifreeze and other winterization services.

Charley was evaluating a proposal from a local marketing research firm to conduct a test market through the coming winter in a snowbelt city of around two million people. The plan was to reach fleet owners with the existing sales force and to reach individual car owners through service stations supported by point-of-purchase advertising. The cost would be

$500,000 for running the test and evaluating the results. Among the outputs would be:

1. The percentage of households that
   - Were aware of the product
   - Purchased the product
   - Made a repeat purchase
2. The number and size of fleets that
   - Were aware of the product
   - Were aware but did not order the product
   - Ordered the product
   - Ordered the product and made repeat purchases
3. The type and incidence of any product problem

Questions for Discussion

1. What will be learned from the test?
2. What would you add or change about the test?
3. What else would you like to know before making a decision about the test?

Case 23-2 | Hokey Pokey is Born in India

It was a foggy Monday morning in early February 2008. As Rohan walked into the breakfast cafe of the Leela Hotel in Bangalore, he was deep in thought about the email he had just received from his boss back in the United States. He had been in Bangalore, India for a week and was conducting due diligence for an investment in a recycling factory in the outskirts of town. He gazed at the email on his laptop. The email and an attached report were from Raj, The Ross Group's Chief Operating Officer and Rohan's boss: "Please pack up and get on the next flight to Mumbai."

> To: Rohan
> From: Raj
> Subject: *Hokey Pokey ice cream*
>
> As a private investment group, you know that we have been actively looking to pick up a stake in the Indian Food & Beverage (F&B) sector. I went through the research report on the Indian F&B sector compiled by our colleagues in Mumbai. The team had also analyzed a business plan by a local Indian Chef's new start-up company that would focus on opening up ice cream parlors all over the nation. The goal is to establish outlets throughout a metropolitan city and then rapidly expand all over India. I see this as a valuable opportunity to enter this segment. I'm sure this opportunity to enter into the F&B sector would not only provide an excellent ROI possibility, but also enable us to diversify into the other product categories within the F&B sector. As of now, the recycling project in Bangalore has been put on hold. Please pack up and get on the next flight to Mumbai. I'll expect a memo with concrete suggestions within a week.

Even in his previous job, Rohan had always wanted to see how new products are developed and launched. With The Ross Group being one of the leading private equity firms in India, and with operations across several countries, he got hooked onto this challenge as he knew this would be a good canvas to see how things work. However, he didn't know where to get started from. He then turned his attention to the attached report.

Food & Beverage Industry Background

The Indian Food & Beverage sector is an estimated Rs. 4.66 trillion market (US$105 billion), of which the ice cream industry is an estimated Rs. 22 billion market (US$500 million) growing at a rate of 12 percent since 2001. Ice cream consumption in India is much lower than other countries with a yearly per capita consumption of 0.12 liters. However, the majority of growth is attributed to an emerging middle class equipped with spending power.

The industry is divided into an unorganized and organized sector with 50 percent attributed to each. Within the industry, there are two types of models, wholesale boxed and parlor retail, of which wholesale boxed makes up the majority of the organized sector. Amul, Kwality, and Vadilal are the three brands that dominate the fragmented wholesale boxed sector, which has yet to see an international player successfully enter. The parlor retail model is divided amongst neighborhood parlors like Bachelor's ice cream in Mumbai, comprising the unorganized sector and international chains such as Baskin Robbins. Pricing in the parlor retail model varies drastically as the unorganized parlors tend to price their product at a very cheap price due to lower quality in the range of 10–15 Rupees. On the other end of the spectrum, offering higher priced items due to better quality are gelato parlors, some of which are organized chains, and Baskin Robbins. Initially, when Baskin Robbins entered the marketplace, their price point was averaging 80 Rupees. However, due to lack of success, they have revamped their pricing structure to now average 55 Rupees.

Key Product Attributes

Product quality was a key focus and the goal was to make super premium ice cream locally. Ice cream quality is primarily characterized by the percentage of fat content and percentage of overrun that exists. Overrun is defined as the amount of air that is trapped within the ice cream during the production process. When more air is trapped, there is more overrun and the quality of ice cream is lower. The four main categories of ice cream quality are economy, standard, premium, and super-premium. Economy brands tend to have minimal fat content, in the range of 8–12 percent fat, and very high overrun (larger amount of trapped air), around 120 percent. On the other end, super premium brands have average fat content in the range of 15–18 percent and overrun that ranges from 25–40 percent.

The Business Plan

The business plan stated that there was great potential for growth in the Indian ice cream industry, specifically in retail parlor outlets. The USP (unique selling proposition) was to offer high grade super premium ice cream in a distinct fashion from the way it had been traditionally served in the country. The ice cream would be mixed at the parlors on a frozen stone with mix-ins (assortments of nuts, candy bars, cookies, brownies, fudge, etc.) and customers would have the option to design their own creations. This concept had seen success in international markets such as the United States and even other countries with similar spending habits, such as the United Arab Emirates and Singapore. Additionally, the concept would be served in a new age "lounge-like" atmosphere. During the recent growth in the economy, Indian consumers have spent more of their disposable income towards eating out than ever before. "Lifestyle concept" eateries such as coffee shops were gaining in popularity and catered to the new emerging middle class. The business plan focused on creating lifestyle parlors where a family or group of young adults

could "hang-out." This type of lifestyle parlor did not exist in a multi-chain format.

The Product Launch

The business plan called for the parlors to launch in Mumbai and then rollout to the rest of the country. As part of a brand building exercise, the cosmopolitan city of Mumbai was chosen due to its significance as the source of trendy and high quality products in India. Many brands are viewed upon as favorable when they have success in Mumbai. Therefore, it was imperative that the brand be "born" in Mumbai. Hokey Pokey was selected by the Chef in a brief survey he did with industry peers. He came up with a list of numerous names and asked his network of associates within the F&B sector to vote. The winner was "Hokey Pokey," inspired by a slang term used in several areas of the United States and parts of Great Britain in the 19th and early-to-mid 20th centuries, to describe ice cream sold by street vendors. Ice cream street vendors were colloquially referred to as "Hokey Pokey Men."

As Rohan sat wondering about the efficacy of the business plan, a lot of questions emerged. For his memo to Raj he knew he needed answers to the following questions.

Questions for Discussion

1. Is there a market for ice cream in India? How can I identify the market for a combined product—lifestyle and ice cream? Is the industry growth viable?

2. What is the current competition in the Indian ice cream industry? Is this an industry that can be penetrated?

3. What is the scope for lifestyle eateries, will the Indian audience be receptive to such a concept? How can I assess the opportunity?

4. What other cities within India should I looking at as a market for this product?

5. Is Hokey Pokey a good brand name for this venture? Is the Chef's process of selecting the brand name correct? What other product names can I suggest to Raj?

This case was prepared
by Rohan Mirchandani
for the purpose of classroom discussion.

Additional Case for this Chapter is available on the Web:

Web Case 23-1 ||| Brown Microwave

Brand and Customer Metrics

24

LEARNING OBJECTIVES

- Discuss the agenda for marketing research in the twenty-first century.
- Discuss the concept of competitive advantage and the various ways of measuring it.
- Discuss brand equity and the various techniques used to measure it.
- Discuss customer satisfaction and the different methods of operationalizing it.
- Discuss the importance of a customer satisfaction measurement process.
- Describe the concept of the "Wheel of Fortune Strategies."
- Discuss the strategies to maximize customer profitability.

Companies operate in a constant state of flux. With the environment characterized by increasing dynamism and uncertainty, firms have to innovate continuously to remain competitive. To survive in the twenty-first century, firms must not only provide goods and services to the consumer efficiently but should also possess sustainable competitive advantage. Hence, there has been a shift of focus in marketing, from delivering goods and services to consumers (satisfying their needs) to achieving a competitive advantage. Companies are embracing new tools, techniques, and strategies in order to remain competitive. This has resulted in a new agenda for marketing research in the new millennium.

This chapter discusses various new methods of operationalizing well-established constructs such as competitive advantage, brand equity, and customer satisfaction. Then it enumerates the informational requirements to implement this strategy. This chapter also briefly touches upon various techniques and methods that marketing research companies use to satisfy these informational requirements. The chapter concludes with a discussion of various strategies that companies can use to maximize customer profitability.

Competitive Advantage

The notion that achieving superior performance requires a business to gain and hold an advantage over competitors is central to contemporary strategic thinking. Businesses seeking advantage are exhorted to develop distinctive competencies at the lowest delivered cost or to achieve differentiation through superior value. The promised payoff is market share dominance and above-average profitability. Michael Porter's pioneering text on competitive strategy changed the way many companies think about their competition.[1] Porter identified five forces that shape competition: current competitors, the threat of new entrants, the threat of new substitutes, the bargaining power of customers, and the bargaining power of suppliers.

Assessing Competitive Advantage[2]

Assessing competitive advantage can be done in a number of ways. The methods can be broadly classified as market-based assessment and process-based assessment. **Market-based assessment** is direct comparison with a few target competitors, whereas **process-based assessment** is a comparison of the methods employed by the competitors in achieving their distinctive advantage. The different methods of assessing competitive advantage are given in Table 24.1.

Market-Based Assessment

Market Share   Market share is measured as a percentage of total industry sales over a specified time period. In terms of Porter's typology, market share is one of the measures used to assess current competition. About 70 percent of the companies in the 1990 Conference Board study tracked their competitors' market share, because market share identifies who the major players are, and changes in market share identify who has become more or less competitive in the marketplace (that is, who gained share from whom).

Clearly, there are problems in assessing competitive advantages using market share. A company's market share can change dramatically depending on whether the market is defined as global, a particular export market, the U.S. market, a region of the United States, a city, or a segment of users, or is based on product usage. The scope of the market normally is specified by a realistic assessment of company resources and by company growth objectives. Operationally, the market often is specified by the way market researchers are able to collect sales and market share information.

The change in market share over time is a vital indicator of competitive dynamics, particularly during the growth stage of a product or market. It indicates whether a firm is ahead, abreast of, or behind the market's total growth rate. Part of the reason that Japanese companies are concerned about gaining market share is that they often compete in high-growth markets, and they understand that this is the crucial time to develop brand loyalty. For example, the Japanese production of calculators grew 200 times during the 1970s. A firm had to expand its sales by this multiple just to keep its market share; Casio raced ahead of its rivals and increased its market share from 10 percent to 35 percent.[3]

Table 24.1 **Methods of Assessing Competitive Advantage**

Market-based	Process-based
Market share	Marketing skills audit
Recall share	Comparison of relative costs
Advertising share	Comparison of winning versus losing competitors
R&D share	Identifying high-leverage phenomena

Recall Share   Recall share is the percentage of customers who name the brand when they are asked to name the first brand that comes to mind when they consider buying a particular type of product. This indicates the consumer's top-of-mind brand awareness and preferences and gives a measure of advantage to that brand over others in the market.

Advertising Share   Advertising share is the percentage of media space or time a brand has of the total media share for that industry, often measured simply as dollars spent on advertising. This is likely to lead to a change in recall share. Advertising share is another measure of the current competition that a firm faces.

R&D Share   R&D share is a company's research and development expenditure as a percentage of total industry R&D expenditures. This is a long-term predictor of new-product development, improvements in quality, cost reductions, and hence market share. It is a very important measure of future competitiveness in many high-technology markets. All of the above share measures can be obtained from either survey data or secondary data.

Process-Based Assessment

Marketing Skills Audit   Skills are "the most distinctive encapsulation of the organization's way of doing business." One vehicle for assessing skills is the *marketing audit*. This is a comprehensive, systematic, independent, and periodic examination of a business unit's marketing environment, objectives, strategies, and activities. The audit should be based on customer orientation or focus on customer satisfaction as its overriding theme. The audit is simply a marketing research project whose objective is to critically evaluate the way the firm performs in its environment.

Comparison of Relative Costs   Another measure of advantage is a comparison of the firm's costs versus those of competitors. The company gains a cost advantage when its cumulative costs are lower than its competitors'. Competitors' costs can be estimated from public data or interviews with suppliers and distributors. Secondary data can be used to obtain such data. Techniques such as "reverse engineering" are also used to obtain competitors' costs.

Comparison of Winning Versus Losing Competitors   Key success factors can be inferred by analyzing differences in performance among competitors. For this approach to yield useful insights, three difficult questions must be answered. First, which competitors should be included in the comparison set? Second, which criteria should be used to distinguish the winners from the losers (e.g., profitability, growth, market share, creation of markets)? Third, what are the reasons for the differences in performance? This procedure is a good place to start to determine a competitive advantage. Secondary sources or qualitative research methods can provide this information.

Identifying High-Leverage Phenomena   Ideally, these are causal relationships that describe how controllable variables such as plant scale, production-run length, and sales force density affect outcomes such as manufacturing and sales costs per unit. The analysis task is formidable because a myriad of potential relationships must be examined, but only a few will be found to have significant leverage. The researcher determines the current position of each leading competitor for each significant relationship and estimates how these competitors will change their positions. Marketing research can play a very useful role in gathering this information.

Brand Equity

Brand equity is defined as a set of assets and liabilities linked to a brand that add to or subtract from the value of a product or service to a company and/or its customers.[4] The assets or liabilities that underlie brand equity must be linked to the name and/or symbol of the brand. The assets and liabilities on which brand equity is based will differ from context to context. However, they can be usefully grouped into five categories:

1. Brand loyalty

2. Name awareness

3. Perceived quality

4. Brand associations in addition to perceived quality

5. Other proprietary brand assets: patents, trademarks, channel relationships, and so on.

Brands captivate customers, which is a prime reason that relationships develop between customer and brand. The more enduring this relationship becomes, the more valuable it is for the company. To retain and build on this relationship, conscious effort has to be made to elevate the product/service from being looked at in a functional or transactional perspective. A consistently positive experience results in loyal customers.

The use of the mass media to create brands is no longer considered the correct way to build them because today's consumers are bombarded with so many distracting stimuli. It is believed that, in a day, consumers experience more stimuli than their counterparts a hundred years ago would have received in their entire lifetimes. This underlines the importance of customer-centric marketing that would build mutually beneficial relationships over time using all points of interaction.[5]

Marketing intelligence increases the potential value of customers who have had a positive experience with customer service. "Customer delight" takes customer satisfaction a step further. Delighted customers cost less to service, stay loyal longer, and buy more. They do not need an incentive to repurchase a product or service and become a free ambassador among their contacts.

The concept of brand equity is summarized in Figure 24.1, which shows the five categories of assets that are the basis of brand equity. The figure also shows that brand equity creates value for both the customer and the firm.

Research Questions under Brand Equity

An appraisal of the brand based on the five dimensions involves addressing and obtaining answers to the questions that follow. Marketing research can help to provide answers to these questions.

Brand loyalty. What are the brand-loyalty levels, by segment? Are customers satisfied? What do "exit interviews" suggest? Why are customers leaving? What is causing dissatisfaction? What do customers say are their problems with buying or using the brand? What are the market share and sales trends?

Awareness. How valuable an asset is brand awareness in this market? What is the company's brand awareness level as compared to that of competitors? What are the trends? Is the brand being considered? Is brand awareness a problem? What can be done to improve brand awareness?

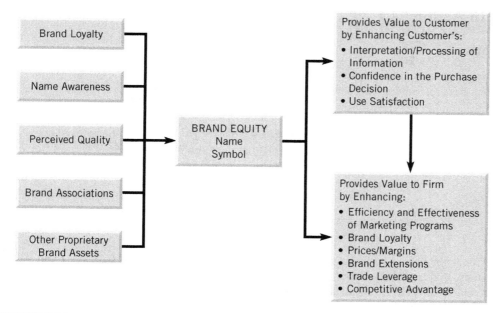

FIGURE 24.1
Brand Equity.
Source: D. A. Aaker, *Managing Brand Equity*. New York: The Free Press, 1994.

Perceived quality. What drives perceived quality? What is important to the customer? What signals quality? Is perceived quality valued—or is the market moving toward a commodity business? Are prices and margins eroding? If so, can the movement be slowed or reversed? How do competitors stack up with respect to perceived quality? Are there any changes? In blind-use tests, what is our brand name worth? Has it changed over time?

Brand associations. What mental image, if any, does the brand stimulate? Is that image a competitive advantage? Does it have a slogan or symbol that is a differentiating asset? How are the brand and its competitors positioned? Evaluate each position with respect to its value or relevance to customers and how protected or vulnerable it is to competitors.

Other brand assets. Are sustainable competitive advantages attached to the brand name that are not reflected in the other four equity dimensions? Is there a patent or trademark that is important? Are there channel relationships that provide barriers to competitors?

Typically, marketing research is used to obtain answers to these questions.

Measuring Brand Equity

It is important to develop approaches that place a value on a brand, for several reasons. First, since brands are bought and sold, a value must be assessed by both buyers and sellers. Which approach makes the most sense? Second, investments to enhance brand equity need to be justified, as there always are competing uses for funds. A bottom-line justification is that the investment will enhance the value of the brand. Thus, some "feel" for how a brand should be valued may help managers address such decisions. Third, the valuation question provides additional insight into the brand-equity concept.

Marketing Research in Action 24.1

■ ALL IN A BRAND NAME

When Andersen Consulting was told by a judge that the name *Andersen* would be retained by the parent company, Arthur Andersen, it had to do some quick decision making to reinforce itself. It had very little time to transfer the brand equity of the name *Andersen* to the new brand name, *Accenture*, and thereby retain its market. Because Andersen was a firm with a global brand name, the new look had to make sense worldwide. Extensive research was done to make sure that the look worked well in Europe as well as the United States.

The new look consisted of metal rings, arched panels, wood tones, and bright colors in order to represent Accenture's creative and future-oriented attitude. The look was such that customers and prospects around the world would form a distinct impression of Accenture.

Source: Tradeshow Week, April 23, 2001, p. 6.

What is the value of a brand name? Consider Compaq, Boeing, Betty Crocker, Ford, Weight Watchers, Bud, and Wells Fargo. What would happen to those firms if they lost their brand name but retained the other assets associated with the business? How much would they have to spend to avoid damage to their business if the name were lost? Could any expenditure avoid a loss of business, perhaps permanently? Marketing Research in Action 24.1 provides an example of a firm that tried to create and maintain brand value.

At least four general approaches have been proposed to assess the value of brand equity. One is based on the excess price that the name can command in the marketplace. The second looks at how much it would cost to replace the brand with a new one. The third is based on the stock price. The fourth focuses on a brand's earning power. Many other methods have also been proposed to measure brand equity.[6] We shall now consider these in the order listed.

Excess-Price Approach   Brand-equity assets such as name awareness, perceived quality, associations, and loyalty all have the potential to provide a brand with a price premium. The resulting extra revenue can be used (e.g.,) to enhance profits, or to reinvest in building more equity.

Observation   One way to measure the excess price a brand can support is simply to observe the price levels in the market. What are the differences, and how are they associated with different brands? For example, what are the price levels of comparable automobiles? How much are the different brands depreciating each year? How responsive is the brand to a firm's own price changes, or to competitors' price changes? These observations inform the manager about the brand's equity. With the emergence of scanner technology, observing price levels of different products has become relatively easy. In fact, both IRI and A.C. Nielsen sell syndicated products giving the prices of various products over a period of time.

Customer Research   Price premiums can also be measured through customer research. Customers can be asked what they would pay for various features and characteristics of a product (one characteristic would be the brand name).[7] Termed a **dollarmetric scale**, this survey provides a direct measure of the brand name's value. Using a variant of the dollarmetric measure, American Motors tested a car (then called the Renault Premier) by showing an "unbadged" (unnamed) model of it to customers and asking them what they would pay for it.[8] The same question was then asked with the car identified by various names. The price was around $10,000 with no name, and about $3,000 more with the Renault Premier name on it.

Obtaining buyer-preference or purchase-likelihood measures for different price levels furnishes additional insight. Such studies can gauge buyer resistance to competitors' price decreases, and determine consumer response to one's own company's decrease in price. A high-equity brand will lose little share to a competitor's lower price, and (up to a point) can gain share when its own relative price is decreased.

Trade-Off Analysis   Trade-off (conjoint) analysis is another approach. Here, respondents are asked to make trade-off judgments about brand attributes. For example, suppose that a computer's attributes included on-site service (supplied vs not supplied), price ($2,200 vs $1,700), and name (Compaq vs Circle). A respondent would prefer on-site service, low price, and an established brand name. To determine the relative value of each, the respondent would be asked to choose between:

Circle at $1,700 versus Compaq at $2,200
Service at $1,700 versus No Service at $2,200
Compaq with No Service versus Circle with Service

The output of trade-off analysis is a dollar value associated with each attribute alternative. The dollar value of the brand name is thus created in the context of making judgments relative to other relevant attributes of the product class. Given that a price premium can be obtained, the value of the brand name in a given year is that price differential multiplied by the unit sales volume. Discounting these cash flows over a reasonable time is one approach to valuing the brand.

Impact on Customer Evaluation   Considering the price premium for a brand may not be the best way to quantify brand equity, especially for product classes such as cigarettes and air travel, for which prices are fairly similar. An alternative is to consider the impact of the brand name on the customer evaluation of the brand, as measured by preference, attitude, or intent to purchase. What does the brand name do to the evaluation?

The value of the brand is then the marginal value of the extra sales (or market share) that the brand name supports. Suppose, for example, it is believed that sales would be 25 percent less if the brand name were discarded, or sales would decline 25 percent over a five-year period if the advertising support for the name were eliminated. The profits on the lost marginal sales would represent the value of the brand.

The size of any price premium and the preference rating of a brand can both be measured and tracked over time using survey research. However, this approach is static, in that it looks at the brand's current position—a view that does not necessarily take into account the future impact of changes (such as improvements in quality).

Replacement-Cost Approach   Another perspective is the cost of establishing a comparable product that can bring in the same amount of business. If it is believed that it would cost $200 million to develop and introduce a product and that the chance for success is 25 percent, on average four products costing a total of $800 million will need to be developed to ensure one winner. A firm should thus be willing to pay $800 million for an established brand with prospects comparable to those being developed. Hence, the equity of the brand can be valued at $800 million.

Stock-Price Approach   Another approach, suggested by financial theory, is to use stock price as a basis on which to evaluate the value of a firm's brand equities.[9] The argument is that the stock market will adjust the price of a firm to reflect the future prospects of its brands.

The approach starts with the market value of the firm, which is a function of the stock price and the number of shares, from which the replacement costs of the tangible assets (such as plant and equipment, inventories, and cash) are subtracted. The balance, intangible assets, is apportioned into three components: the value of brand equity, the value of nonbrand factors (such as R&D and patents), and the value of industry factors (such as regulation and concentration). Brand equity is assumed to be a function of the age of a brand and its order of entry into the market (an older brand has more equity), the cumulative advertising (advertising creates equity), and the current share of industry advertising (current advertising share is related to positioning advantages).

The problem with this approach is that if a firm has more than one brand, it is difficult to evaluate the value of each brand to the firm. The internal records of the company are sufficient to evaluate brand equity by this method.

Future-Earnings Approach   The best measure of brand equity would be the discounted present value of future earnings attributable to brand-equity assets.[10] The problem is how to provide such an estimate.

Discounting the Future Profit Stream   One approach is simply to discount the profit stream that is projected for the brand. Such a plan should take into account brand strengths and their impact on the competitive environment. One firm that uses the brand's plan to provide a value for brand equity adjusts the manufacturing costs to reflect the industry average rather than the actual costs. The logic is that any above- (or below-) average efficiency should be credited to manufacturing and not to brand equity. Scenario analysis is done to ascertain the most likely scenario that will occur. Based on this scenario, the profit stream is projected for the brand. Marketing research helps in building credible scenarios and deciding which is the most likely.

Applying an Earnings Multiplier   Another approach that researchers can use, even when a brand profit plan is unavailable or unsuitable, is to estimate current earnings and apply an earnings multiplier. The earnings estimate could be current earnings, with any extraordinary charges backed out. If the current earnings are not representative because they reflect a downward or upward cycle, then some average of the past few years might be more appropriate. If the earnings are negative or low due to correctable problems, an estimate based on industry norms of profit as a percent of sales might be useful.

The earnings multiplier provides a way to estimate and place a value on future earnings. To obtain a suitable earnings multiplier range, the historical price earnings (P/E) multipliers of firms in the involved industry and in similar industries should be examined. For example, a multiplier range for a brand might be 7 to 12 or 16 to 25, depending on the industry.

The use of an industry-based P/E ratio provides a judgment that stock-market investors have placed upon the industry prospects—its growth potential, the future competitive intensity from existing and potential competitors, and the threat of substitute products. The question remains, which P/E multiplier within the identified range should be used for the brand?

To determine the actual multiplier value within that range, an estimate of the competitive advantage of the brand is needed. Will the brand earnings strengthen over time and generally be above the industry average, or will they weaken and be below average? The estimate should be based on a weighted average of a brand appraisal on each of the five dimensions of brand equity.

In evaluating brand equity, one also needs to deal with the problem of evaluating other firm assets. First, some part of the discounted present value of a business is due to tangible assets such as working capital, inventory, buildings, and equipment. What portion should be so attributed? One argument is that such assets are book assets that are being depreciated, and their depreciation charge times an earnings multiplier will reflect their asset value. Another method is to focus on cash flow instead of earnings and estimate such assets by using book value or market value. This estimate is then subtracted from the estimate of discounted future earnings.

Evaluation of Brand Extensions   It is difficult to estimate the earnings streams from **brand extensions** (the use of the brand name to enter new product classes—for example, Kellogg's bread products, or Hershey's ice cream). Usually, the value of potential brand extensions has to be estimated separately.

Marketing Research in Action 24.2

▪ ESTIMATION OF BRAND EQUITY OF COKE

Financial World (FW) determined, for example, that the Coca-Cola brand family had 1992 worldwide sales of $49 billion. According to the best estimates of consultants and beverage experts, Coke enjoys an operating margin of around 30 percent, so operating profits for the Coke brand were $2.8 billion.

Coke's elaborate bottling and distribution system generated another $27 billion in revenues and operating profits of $3 billion. But *FW* did not take these numbers into consideration in valuing the Coca-Cola name, because to some extent that would be an overvaluation. We include only the value added by Coke directly, not the value added by the bottlers or distributors. "It is important to recognize that not all of the profitability attributed to a brand should be used in the calculation of brand value to avoid overvaluation and double counting," says Noel Penrose, executive vice president of the Interbrand Group.

Even if Coca-Cola's bottling and distribution network does contribute to brand image, it will be reflected in higher sales and margins of the product itself. The value of the distribution system, though significant, is not the value of the brand. Were we to include the bottling and distribution system, we would have added another $40 billion to our value of Coca-Cola.

Which brings us to the next step: Once product-related profits have been determined, we deduct from a brand's operating profit an amount equal to what would be earned on a basic, unbranded, or generic version of the product. To do this, we estimate the amount of capital it takes to generate a brand's sales. On average, analysts believe that it requires 60 cents worth of capital, which is generally a little higher than net property, plant and equipment plus net-working capital, to produce each dollar of sales. Using that yardstick, the capital used in production in Coke's case comes to $5.5 billion. Second, we assume that a 5 percent net return on employed capital after inflation can be expected from a similar nonbranded product. So we deduct 5 percent of Coke's capital employed ($273 million) from the $2.7 billion in operating profits to obtain the profit attributable to the brand name alone.

For Coke, that leaves an adjusted operating profit figure of $2.4 billion. We then make a provision for taxes, and the remainder is deemed to the net brand-related profits. Finally, we assign a multiple based on brand strength as having seven components: leadership, or the brand's ability to influence its market; stability, the ability of the brand to survive; market, the brand's trade environment; internationality, the ability of the brand to cross geographic and cultural borders; trend, the ongoing direction; support, effectiveness of the brand's communications; and protection, the brand owner's legal title. Obviously, the stronger the brand, the higher the multiple applied to earnings. This year, we used multiples ranging from 9 to 20. Coke was assigned the highest multiple, which results in a brand value of $33.4 billion.

Source: A. Ourusoff, "How the Brand Values Were Assigned," Brand Week, August 1993, p. 27.

The extension value will depend on the attractiveness of market area of any proposed extension, its growth and competitive intensity, and the strength of the extension. The extension strength will be a function of the relevance of the brand association and perceived quality, the extent to which they could translate into a sustainable competitive advantage, and the extent to which the brand will fit the extension.

The methodology followed by *Financial World* to measure the brand equity of Coca-Cola during its annual evaluation of global brands is given in Marketing Research in Action 24.2.

Customer Satisfaction

In recent years, American business has become increasingly committed to the idea of *customer satisfaction* and *product/service quality*. The measurement of customer satisfaction and its link to product/service attributes is the vehicle for developing a market-driven quality approach.[11] In this section we discuss customer satisfaction research. Marketing Research in Action 24.3 lists the customer satisfaction scene in the United States. Figure 24.2 shows the growth in customer satisfaction measurement.

Customer satisfaction research has been around for a long time, but it has become a fixture at most large corporations only in recent years. The growth in the popularity of customer satisfaction research is, of course, a corollary to the quality movement in American business. The idea

Marketing Research in Action 24.3

■ CUSTOMER RAGE

Many studies have found that effective customer complaint handling is crucial to customer satisfaction. When today's consumers get mad, they have more of a chance to get even—through the online medium of blogs, message boards, and websites. Consider the case of Casey Neistat who took his case to cyberspace when his iPod died in September 2003. Apple told him to buy a new iPod as they didn't offer a replacement battery. Instead, he and his brother Van Neistat—both professional filmmakers—made a short video including Casey's phone conversation with an Apple customer service representative. They posted it at iPodsdirtysecret.com and e-mailed 40 friends about the site, which has now received more than 1.5 million hits. Apple now has a battery replacement program for the iPod.

A survey of customer households by the Customer Care Alliance in 2004 in collaboration with Arizona State University found that an increasing number of Americans (73 percent of those with a product or service problem) are extremely upset about how "serious" complaints are being handled by companies. In fact, the CCA has termed this dissatisfaction as "customer rage." On the other hand, only 16 percent felt completely satisfied or received more than they asked for. Though product and service quality have improved in general over the past decades, customer rage is on the rise. Why? Because it takes customers an average of 4.3 contacts (referred to as ping-ponging) to get their issue resolved. According to the study, the most common reaction was negative word of mouth: 85 percent of customers shared their story with friends and other people. When people are unhappy with how their complaints are handled, they tell 15 people about their experience, whereas those who are satisfied only tell six people. However, the report added that a majority of complainants did not want a free product or service from companies, nor did they want compensation for their troubles. Apart from getting the problem fixed, all they wanted was an explanation or apology, a chance to vent their frustrations, and an assurance that the problem would not occur again. The survey attests to the idea customers don't become dissatisfied because of problems, but by the way problems are handled by the firm's representatives.

Source: http://wpcarey.asu.edu/csl/knowledge/2004-National-Customer-Rage-Study.cfm

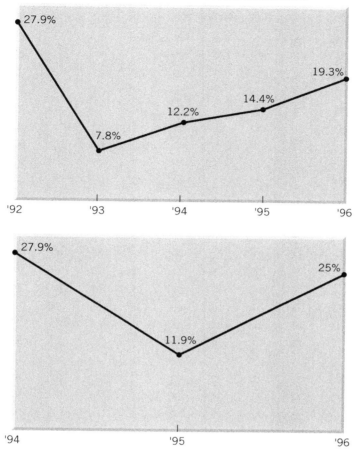

Annual growth in customer satisfaction measurement

FIGURE 24.2

Annual Growth in Customer Satisfaction Measurement.

Percentages are satisfaction research spending commissioned by research firms based on an annual sample of about a dozen research houses in (a) United States and (b) Europe.
Source: K. T. Higgins, "Coming of Age," *Marketing News*, 31(22), October 27, 1997, p. 1.

that the customer defines quality should not be new to marketers. However, its recognition in the Baldridge criteria has given this idea a credibility that was previously lacking.

Satisfaction research, like advertising tracking research, should be conducted at planned intervals so as to track satisfaction over time. Thus, satisfaction research can be put in the context of an interrupted, time-series, quasi-experimental design. Over time, management will do various things to improve customer satisfaction, take measurements following these changes, and evaluate the results to see if the changes that were implemented had a positive effect on customer satisfaction. This approach requires a sequential research design that uses the results from each research phase to build and enhance the value of subsequent efforts. During this process, it is imperative to study customers who were lost, to determine why they left. This issue must be addressed early in the system design.

A useful step is to provide management with a framework for understanding, analyzing, and evaluating the status of customer satisfaction in the firm. A sequential design provides some level of comfort, because it allows for the luxury of making critical decisions after you have sufficient data to reduce the risk of error inherent in establishing a customer satisfaction system.

Table 24.2   ACSI Scores by Industry, 2000–2011

Industry name	2000	2001	2002	2003	2004	2005	2006	2007	2008	2009	2010	2011
Airlines	63	61	66	67	66	66	65	63	62	64	66	65
Apparel	79	79	80	80	79	81	80	82	80	82	83	80
Automobiles & Light Vehicles	80	80	80	80	79	80	81	82	82	84	82	83
Banks	70	72	74	75	75	75	77	78	75	75	76	75
Department & Discount Stores	72	75	74	76	74	75	74	73	74	75	76	76
Electronics (TV/BD/DVD)	83	81	81	84	82	81	80	83	83	83	85	85
Express Delivery	81	78	79	79	81	81	83	81	82	82	83	84
Fixed Line Telephone Service	72	70	71	72	71	70	70	70	73	72	75	73
Food Manufacturing	81	82	81	81	81	82	83	81	83	83	81	81
Hospitals	69	68	70	73	76	71	74	77	75	77	73	77
Hotels	72	71	71	73	72	73	75	71	75	75	75	77
Life Insurance	75	78	79	77	75	75	79	78	78	79	80	80
Major Appliances	85	82	82	81	82	80	81	82	80	81	82	81
Motion Pictures	68	71	70	71	73	71	73	70	70	74	76	73
Network/Cable TV News	64	62	65	68	66	68	69	67	69	71	74	77
Newspapers	68	68	63	64	68	63	63	66	64	63	65	65
Personal Care & Cleaning Products	84	83	81	84	83	83	84	85	85	85	83	83
Personal Computers	74	71	71	72	74	74	77	75	74	75	78	78
Property & Casualty Insurance	79	79	77	78	77	78	78	80	81	80	80	83
Soft Drinks	86	82	85	84	83	83	84	84	83	85	84	85
Specialty Retail Stores	76	73	74	74	75	74	75	75	76	77	78	79
Supermarkets	73	75	75	74	73	74	75	76	76	76	75	76
U.S. Postal Service	72	70	73	72	74	73	71	73	74	74	71	74

Source: The American Customer Satisfaction Index, www.theacsi.org

In order to establish a customer satisfaction system, it would be helpful for companies to track and measure the existing level of satisfaction. In this regard, the American Customer Satisfaction Index (ACSI) measures the customer satisfaction scores at the national level for major industries and reports scores on a 0–100 scale. In addition to the company-level satisfaction scores, ACSI produces scores for the causes and consequences of customer satisfaction and their relationships. Using this index as a base, companies can effectively plan for a system that would manage customer satisfaction. Table 24.2 provides the satisfaction scores by industry in the United States from 2000 to 2011.

Customer Satisfaction Measurement Process

It is believed that 96 percent of dissatisfied customers never complain; 60 to 90 percent of these "silent" dissatisfied customers will not buy from you again; 90 percent of those who do complain will not buy from you again. Therefore, it is important that every firm should have a customer satisfaction program. A "no-frills" customer satisfaction program involves the following.[12]

Define Goals and How Information Will Be Used   A common failure of customer satisfaction research is lack of clear, comprehensive, and measurable goals. Given the strategic nature of the quality improvement process, key parts of a company must be involved in setting objectives for customer satisfaction measurement and management. This helps to clarify the needs of various users of the information, creates a sense of ownership of the process, and identifies how various levels of a company may have to cooperate to plan action.

Equally important is determining how the information will be used once it is developed. Careful analysis of strategic and tactical organizational applications will ensure that issues of design, sample, analysis, reporting, and deployment are structured to provide customer-focused information that can be acted on most effectively.

Discover What Is Important to Customers and Employees   This discovery phase of data collection is intended to identify, in customers' and employees' own language, the attributes that compose their perceptions and expectations for quality and satisfaction. This information is gathered through various qualitative techniques, notably, depth interviews with senior managers and focus groups or on-site interviews with customers and customer-contact personnel.

The research will generate a comprehensive list of everything that customers and employees consider important. It is now necessary to use similar associative techniques, to group related or redundant attributes, and to agree on candidates for subsequent measurement as key drivers of satisfaction.

Measure Critical Needs   Measuring the relative importance of the attributes identified in qualitative discovery and a company's competitive performance on those attributes is accomplished through critical-needs assessment. This phase uses in-depth telephone, mail, or personal interviews with a representative sample of customers, lost customers, and competitors' customers to gather quantitative information. Using trade-off techniques, instead of traditional importance scaling, provides improved discrimination on the relative importance of attributes.

This phase should provide a broad array of actionable information. It should include the relative importance of key drivers of satisfaction; competitive performance on these critical attributes; site-specific performance, depending on sample size; cross-market segments with specific service needs; value-adding performance relative to expectations; and specific gaps between importance and performance.

Act on the Information   Action planning organizes activity to improve customer satisfaction by operationally defining and functionally deploying customer requirements. This makes it possible to establish cross-functional quality improvement teams. Using techniques such as quality function deployment, flowcharts, check sheets, Pareto charts, and cause-and-effect diagrams, teams can improve processes based on external customer needs, internal chains of customers, work-flow analysis, and work-process analysis.

Measure Performance over Time   Periodic measurement of how a company and its competitors perform on the key drivers of satisfaction reveals the rate at which customer satisfaction is improving or declining. Using the same sample criteria and interviewing techniques applied in critical-needs assessment, measurement should involve a brief interview on current performance and include an opportunity for open-ended comments. The frequency of measurement should be determined by market dynamics and should allow sufficient time for change to become measurable.

Marketing Research in Action 24.4

■ FROM PERCEPTION TO DELIVERY

Customer service is what a business provides for its customers and customer satisfaction describes the mindset of the customer after receiving the service or lack thereof. Both the level of customer service and degree of satisfaction are defined by the perceptions of the customer. Four factors that determine a customer's perception of service and satisfaction are

- *Customer's knowledge of the product or service.*
- *Customer's past experience.* Perceptions are formed when inquiring about purchasing, using, or maintaining a specific product or service.
- *Customer's expectations about a product.* People who have high expectations are the most demanding, judgmental, and vocal customers. They are also the best customers, pushing the company to excel with every customer encounter.

- *Customer's encounter with a company and its employees.* Customers can tell if people care about them or about doing business with them. Visually, verbally, and environmentally, customers consciously and subconsciously search for clues that a business values them.

In every organization, customer satisfaction starts at the very top, not at the bottom, as most managers like to believe. Customer satisfaction is also a direct derivative of employee satisfaction. If an organization has an employee morale problem, it will never be capable of delivering good customer service with the consistency required for succeeding in competitive markets. An organization that consistently delivers poor customer service need not look further for the cause than its chief executive. Achieving ultimate customer satisfaction ensures repeat business, positive word-of-mouth promotion, and a competitive edge.

Source: J. F. O'Malley, Marketing News, October 27, 1997, p. 20.

Consideration also should be given to periodic qualitative monitoring to provide information on changes in environment. Using the model described in the preceding paragraph to improve and measure customer satisfaction requirements can greatly enhance existing total quality management and other quality improvement programs. It also can stand alone as a first step in focusing an organization on improved customer satisfaction as the key to improved market share and financial performance.

In either case, success ultimately is determined by the organization's top-down commitment to meet and exceed the customers' requirements in the marketplace. For example, knowing that customers want "quick service" is helpful; knowing that "quick service" means having their problems solved in less than 5 minutes is actionable. Marketing Research in Action 24.4 illustrates how customers determine their perception of service and satisfaction.

Issues in Questionnaire Design and Scaling in Satisfaction Research   Each customer-satisfaction study utilizes questions that are, to some degree, unique. However, as in the other types of studies discussed in this chapter, certain general types of information are collected in most customer-satisfaction studies.

- *Screening questions.* The question begins with screening questions to make sure that the person contacted falls into the target group. If the goal is to interview current customers, and current customers are defined to include those individuals who have patronized Wendy's in the last 30 days, the questionnaire will begin with a series of questions designed to determine whether the particular individual meets these requirements.

- *Overall ratings.* Some experts argue that it is important to get an overall satisfaction rating from respondents very early in the interview. This might be done by asking, "Please indicate your overall satisfaction with Wendy's on a scale of 1 to 10, where 1 is poor and 10 is excellent." This rating can be the dependent variable in the regression analysis.

- *Performance ratings.* The researchers are interested in measuring customer perceptions of Wendy's performance on a number of specific aspects of the product or service. The specific aspects are the key satisfaction factors discussed previously. The researcher will use a numerical rating scale to gauge the satisfaction with each element.

- *Intent to use or purchase product or service in the future.* Satisfaction surveys usually include some measurement of customer likelihood to do business with the firm in the future. This provides a basis for determining whether to purchase or use the product or service. The researcher would hypothesize that the higher the satisfaction level, the higher the likelihood to do business with the organization in the future.

- *Category or brand usage information.* This information will be used for classification purposes in cross-tabulation analysis. For example, does the respondent also patronize McDonald's, Burger King, Arby's, or Little Caesar's?

- *Demographic and lifestyle information.* This information is used for classification purposes. The researcher often is interested in determining whether any particular demographic or lifestyle group is more or less satisfied than Wendy's average customer.

    A few of the scales used in satisfaction research are given below.

- *Asking customers whether they agree or disagree that Luby's Cafeteria serves them satisfactorily.* For example:

Overall, I am extremely satisfied with the service I receive from Luby's Cafeteria.

Strongly agree	Somewhat agree	Neither agree nor disagree	Somewhat disagree	Strongly disagree
_____	_____	_____	_____	_____

- *Having the customer rate the performance of a company from excellent to poor.* For example:

Overall, how would you rate the service you receive from Luby's Cafeteria? Would you say

Excellent	Very good	Good	Fair	Poor
_____	_____	_____	_____	_____

- *Asking customers how satisfied they are with the food quality.* For example: Are you

Very satisfied	Somewhat satisfied	Neither satisfied nor dissatisfied	Somewhat dissatisfied	Very dissatisfied
_____	_____	_____	_____	_____

- *Having customers interpret their satisfaction based on a 5- or 10-point scale.* For example:

Using a 10-point scale, where 10 means extremely satisfied, how satisfied are you with Luby's Cafeteria overall? _____

To measure satisfaction with a service encounter, instruments such as SERVQUAL can be used. This can be modified and adapted to retailing and other settings. The SERVQUAL survey is composed of questions in five categories: tangibles (four questions on dimensions such as appearance of facilities and personnel), reliability (five questions), responsiveness (four questions), assurance (four questions on dimensions such as competence, courtesy, credibility, and security), and empathy(five questions on dimensions such as access or ease of contact, communication, and customer understanding). Each customer surveyed completes one questionnaire measuring expectations of each of the 22 questions and then one for each company or product to measure competitor performance. The SERVQUAL score for a product is the difference between the perception of the dimension and the expectation. A company can then determine its quality of service on each of the five dimensions by taking the average across the questions for that dimension and calculating an overall score. A weighted SERVQUAL score can also be calculated by asking the customer to give importance weights (summing to 1) on each of the five dimensions. All of these scales attempt to pinpoint a quantitative interpretation of the customer's feelings and attitudes in response to their experiences with a company's products and/or services.

Scale selection for customer satisfaction research usually follows considerations similar to those found in product and attitude testing. More specifically, selection is guided by the properties inherent in each of four different levels of measurement: nominal, ordinal, interval, and ratio.

For most behavioral marketing research, interval scales typically are the best measurements. From the standpoint of the marketing researcher, commonly used descriptive statistics (arithmetical mean, standard deviation) and tests of significance (t-tests, ANOVA) assume that the customer satisfaction data are at least interval-scaled.

There are advantages and limitations to scales with respect to at least four other aspects: (1) respondent interpretation and understanding, (2) appropriateness and ease of administration, (3) statistical analysis and description, and (4) ease and meaningful interpretation of results.[13]

Contemporary Applications of Marketing Intelligence

Buyer-Centricity: Emerging from Marketing Intelligence

As marketing intelligence tools come of age, *buyer-centricity* is becoming a key buzz word. But, to date, the business environment remains overwhelmingly *seller-centric*. It is populated by seller-centric companies, which flourish by making things (namely, products and services) and selling them. It is our argument that the wealth of meaningful information about customers' behavior patterns not only helps seller-centric customers maximize value for corporations but also that intelligent companies can help maximize value propositions for the customer by using information mined through marketing intelligence tools.

Seller-centric companies are usually concerned with (1) maximizing the efficiency, productivity, and marketable value of corporate assets such as money, property, raw materials, technology, skills, and know-how and (2) realizing the maximum possible value generated by these assets in the marketplace, for example, by closing more sales with more customers at the highest possible margins.

This seller-centric view of the world is extremely limiting with respect to consumers. It leaves consumers feeling that the products/services do not enhance the quality of their lives. So, in terms of value proposition, such products/services may end up being unnecessary for consumers. The forms of value as defined by sellers do not always appeal to buyers. Efforts to maximize the efficiency and value of corporate assets do not always translate into corresponding value addition for consumers.

What Is Buyer-Centricity?

The process of wealth creation and value maximization can be looked at from two perspectives—from the corporate side and from the consumer side. Buyer-centric companies look at both the above processes from the consumers' view. Such companies help consumers maximize the value they realize within the marketplace by doing the following:

1. Provide services that help customers make informed decisions on buying better and cheaper products more easily

2. Help buyers to buy rather than help sellers to sell

3. Help consumers maximize the efficiency, productivity, and marketable value of their personal assets such as money, time, information, attention, and emotional commitment

4. Present offerings that are relevant to the buyer's unique individual characteristics and that recognize what customers currently seek to achieve

Consumer take center stage, and creating value for them is of prime importance.

Note: Terms that seemingly mean the same thing do not necessarily do so. Similarly, *buyer-centric* and *customer-centric* actually have the opposite meanings. Seller-centric companies almost always talk about "customer focus" and "customer-centricity." But, according to many experts, customer-centricity actually reflects seller-centricity. Seller-centric companies want to "understand" customers in order to serve their own ends—to make more "in-demand" products, to sell them, and to make profits. On the other hand, buyer-centric companies use sellers as a means to achieving buyer-centric objectives.

Who Gains from Buyer-Centricity?

In contrast to popular perceptions, buyer-centricity aids not only consumers but also sellers. The advantages stem from a range of sources mentioned below that include new growth sectors, increased value, lower costs, and building of trust and closer relationships. The opportunities it can open up are tremendous and the following look at them in detail.

Growth Markets New buyer-centric services—which help consumers maximize the productivity and value of their own personal assets and help buyers to buy—represent a huge new growth sector. Any company capable of deploying corporate assets as a tool in the hands of the buyers—not only to provide valued products and services, but to save consumers time, money, or hassle, to streamline consumer processes or provide enriched consumer understanding and information and so on—can benefit from the rise of buyer-centricity.

Beyond Revenue Implications Consumers have always provided more value than just increased profits and increased revenues. But, traditionally, sellers have targeted consumers, keeping them in mind only for their money value. The other dimensions of consumer value have hitherto been untapped. Buyer-centric companies bring these other dimensions like consumer information, consumer attention, and emotional commitment to the fore.

Fewer Bucks for More Bang In traditional seller-centric marketing, buyers have the realization that the content of advertising is self-centered and about the effort aimed to bias choice between brands. In buyer-centric marketing, buyers take center stage and are heard. Buyers spell out their needs, thereby circumventing the need for expensive market research. Also, since it is a process done by buyers for their benefit, it catches the attention of other buyers. In short, it is a win-win situation in terms of lesser bucks for more bang for both sides.

Trust The aim of all marketers has been to win the trust of consumers. Database marketing, one-to-one marketing, CRM, and so on are used as tools toward this purpose. But, the very fact that these concepts/tools end up being used for seller-centric purposes defeats the concept of trust. Buyer-centric approach is the way to secure trust. Relationships built this way last.

Of course, there will be losers. Some sellers do lose—but not all of them. Only those sellers who now rely on their ability to flex their advertising and brand muscle, who bank on consumer inertia, ignorance about products, processes, quality, or simply market confusion and complexity for their profits, lose. Sellers with a good in-demand product who are willing to lend an ear to the consumers benefit.

Why Now?

The concept of buyer-centricity was all along waiting to take wings and it is now doing so because of a lot of reasons. With increased education and awareness, today's consumers are a sophisticated lot. Increased pressure at work and correspondingly less time available for disposal is leading to more demanding customers. Markets are maturing and power is shifting from the seller to the buyer. Traditional seller-centric marketing is leading to diminishing returns. Emergence of new technologies is also widening the scope of possible services. The impact of these trends can vary dramatically by consumer segment. But the trends themselves are long term, and inexorable. The pressure for buyer-centricity is mounting and won't go away.

Maximizing Customer Profitability

As discussed in the previous section, companies are now moving away from seller-centricity concept toward buyer-centricity concept. Meanwhile, companies are also looking at ways to maximize their profitability through implementing customer-centric strategies. In this section, we will look at strategies that companies can use to maximize customer profitability. Figure 24.3 provides a set of marketing strategies titled, "Wheel of Fortune Strategies"[14] that companies can use to maximize customer lifetime value (CLV). This set of strategies identifies ways for companies to target the right customers and allocate the right amount of resources in order to obtain the maximum profits from each customer. Specifically, this CLV maximization cycle is comprised of the following steps:

1. **Customer Selection.** This step involves selecting the right customers based on their estimated future profitability. This is a crucial step to ensure profitability maximization as the marketing budget of a company is always limited. Traditionally, companies select a preferred customer based on the customer's historical profitability, which might not be the best measure for the customer's future profitability. In this regard, the CLV model is proposed as a superior model for customer selection. This is because the CLV model incorporates forward-looking features of a customer's profitability, such as the probability of a customer making repeat purchases, the estimated profit margin earned from the customer's purchases, and the estimated marketing cost spent on the customer.

2. **Managing Loyalty and Profitability Simultaneously.** Companies need to be aware that (1) customers are not equally profitable, and (2) loyal customers are not necessarily profitable customers. Therefore, it's important for companies to have a good understanding of their customer segments based on the level of loyalty and profitability to the companies. Customers can be segmented into the following four groups: True Friends (profitable and loyal customers), Butterflies (profitable but not loyal), Barnacles (not profitable but loyal), and Strangers (neither profitable nor loyal, appear one time and are gone).[15] Segmenting customers into these four groups give companies guidance on how to devise optimal resource allocation strategies. For instance, companies should spend as few resources on Butterflies and Strangers as possible. At the same time, they should invest in True Friends and in some cases, Barnacles. For Barnacles, it is important that companies determine how to get them to buy more, more often, or when to let them go. For True Friends, companies

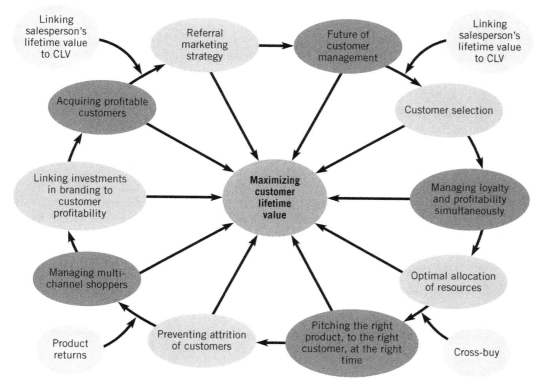

FIGURE 24.3

The Wheel of Fortune Strategies.

Source: Adapted and updated from V. Kumar, *Managing Customers for Profit, Strategies to Increase Profits and Build Loyalty*. New Jersey: Wharton School Publishing, 2008.

should be careful when using hard selling techniques or give them too much information as doing so can turn off even good customers.

3. **Optimal Allocation of Resources.** This means allocating the right amount of resources to the right customers. For instance, decisions such as how frequently a particular customer should be contacted, and what communication channels should be used to contact a customer are critical in ensuring a profitable customer relationship. As marketing resources of a company are limited, only those customers who are profitable and responsive should have priority in receiving communication from the company. In addition, when selecting the communication channel for each customer, companies should consider the cost-effectiveness of each channel. Companies should also take into account the type of services to offer to a customer when the customer is contacted such as up-selling or cross-selling.

4. **Pitching the Right Product to the Right Customer at the Right Time.** Research has shown that companies can maximize the profitability of a customer if they can estimate (1) what the customer is likely to purchase, (2) when the transaction is likely to occur, and (3) how much the customer is likely to spend. By understanding these three factors, companies will be able to deliver a sales message that is relevant to the product(s) or service(s) likely to be purchased in the near future. Companies thus will be able to minimize their marketing costs and increase their sales revenue concurrently.

5. **Preventing Customer Attrition.** Customer attrition can be prevented through understanding the quitting tendency of a customer and intervening at the right time. When a company identifies that a high-value customer is likely to churn, it is important from a retention viewpoint to create a value proposition that does not exceed the customer's future profit contribution. Such an approach is likely to retain profitable customers, thereby increasing future profitability.

6. **Managing Multi-level Shoppers.** This strategy essentially involves identifying customers who can be multi-level shoppers and devising strategies to encourage customers to become multi-level shoppers. Companies can also reduce marketing costs by migrating low-value customers to low-cost channels. As various shopping channels coexist, (e.g., online stores, catalog-based orders, physical stores, etc.) this strategy has become increasingly important for companies to manage their customer profitability. A study conducted in a B2B setting[16] shows that multi-channel shoppers are more profitable than single-channel shoppers. They buy more, have a deeper relationship, and are more likely to be active. Therefore, when a company identifies a customer as a multi-channel shopper buying predominantly through catalogs, it can significantly reduce the cost of servicing this customer by redirecting that customer to the company's online shopping services.

7. **Linking Investment in Branding to Customer Profitability.** This strategy allows a company to establish a link between the individual customer brand value (CBV) perceived by a customer and the customer's CLV. This enables companies to redesign their communication strategies towards achieving simultaneous growth in brand equity and customer profitability.

8. **Acquiring Profitable Customers.** This strategy involves acquisition and retention of the right prospective customers that are most likely to be profitable. The previous seven strategies enable companies to select the right customers, to manage them profitably and to allocate the right resources to retain them based on the CLV model. Companies now can re-apply this knowledge into identifying and acquiring prospective customers who are most likely to be profitable. This strategy also allows companies to decide which dormant customers should be invited to reactivate their relationship with the companies based on their profit potential. It is important for companies not to over-emphasize the short-term cost of acquiring a particular customer, nor under-emphasize the long-term gain that customer could bring to the companies. Studies show that some customers can be cheaper to acquire but not profitable, and vice versa, some customers may be expensive to acquire but will be profitable in the long run.[17] Therefore, only through efficient allocation of the marketing resources based on individual customer profile, companies can maximize their profitability.

9. **Referral Marketing Strategy.** There are two approaches to maximizing customer profitability: maximizing CLV and maximizing customer referral value (CRV). While CLV is the direct profits that a customer generates through making transaction with a company, CRV is the indirect profits that other customers, who are referred by that customer, generate with the company.[18] To maximize customer profitability, companies should consider maximizing both CLV and the referral behaviors (CRV) of their customers.

10. **The Future of Customer Management.** Looking ahead, the future of customer management is all about understanding each individual customer, and implementing the right marketing strategy for that particular customer. To do so, companies need to adopt an interactive marketing approach, and have the right customer information management system in place to constantly capture and process customer data in a timely and efficient manner.

In sum, to maximize customer profitability, companies should look at all the aspects of customer management, from acquisition to retaining, from managing CLV to managing CRV, from understanding customers' needs to implementing marketing strategies. Companies should also know that implementing these ten strategies is a dynamic process. The knowledge acquires today will be re-applied in the next cycle of acquiring and retaining customers. If the "Wheel of Fortune Strategies" are implemented in an appropriate manner, companies will be able to obtain sustainable maximized profitability.

SUMMARY

With the start of the twenty-first century characterized by burgeoning globalization and heightened competition among firms, the future seems to be more uncertain and unpredictable than ever before. The consumer has also undergone a dramatic transformation. Armed with more information and ever-increasing choices, today's consumer has become more and more demanding. With cheaper store brands invading the supermarkets, loyalty has become a scarce commodity in the marketplace. Marketing managers are trying many new strategies to cope with this uncertain environment and fickle consumers. A market researcher has to have thorough knowledge of these emerging strategies and concepts in order to survive. But the uncertainty in the environment has a rather fortunate consequence for the market researcher. Managers are turning increasingly to research to understand the complex global environment and the nature of the capricious consumer. Hence, marketing research has to rise to this challenge and provide the managers of the twenty-first century with the right kind of information to make their decisions.

This chapter has introduced some emerging concepts and strategies in marketing. Even though the concept of competitive advantage has been around for a long time, it is only in the last decade that it has received a lot of attention. More and more companies are trying to gauge their competitive advantage and trying to hold on to it. There are many ways of measuring competitive advantage, a few of which have been mentioned in this chapter. The term *brand equity*[19] has no clear definition nor a single methodology by which to measure it. A synthesis of the various definitions and measures of brand equity is given in the chapter. *Customer satisfaction* is another construct that has received a lot of attention. The basic methodology to measure customer satisfaction is discussed. Finally, the *"Wheel of Fortune Strategies"* mentioned in this chapter lists out various strategies that companies can use to maximize their customers' lifetime value and referral value and thus increase the overall profitability of the companies.

QUESTIONS AND PROBLEMS

24.1 What type of data need to be collected to build long-term relationships with your consumer if you are

  (a) A consumer-product company

  (b) An industrial-product firm

  (c) A service-oriented organization

24.2 Do you think the customer-satisfaction measurement methodology described in the text is a valid one? Why or why not? How will you check on the reliability and validity of your customer-satisfaction measurement?

24.3 The concept of brand equity is nebulous. Do you agree with the statement? Give reasons for your answers.

24.4 Why is measuring competitive advantage so important? Discuss the advantages and limitations of the various measures of competitive advantage given in the text.

24.5 You are the advertising agency for a retail store. You have talked about the concept of integrated marketing communications (IMC) to the top management of the retail store. Management does not want to implement IMC in its store because it feels that the costs of integrating outweigh the benefits. Conduct a cost-benefit analysis to convince your management that IMC is a worthwhile strategy to adopt.

END NOTES

1. M. E. Porter, *Competitive Strategy.* New York: The Free Press, 1980.

2. G. S. Day and R. Wensley, "Assessing Advantage: A Framework for Diagnosing Competitive Superiority,"*Journal of Marketing*, 52, April 1988, pp. 1–20.

3. S. N. Chakravarty, "Economic Darwinism," Forbes, October 6, 1986, pp. 52–56; J. W. Brittain and D. R. Wholey, "Competition Coexistence in Organizational Communities: Population Dynamics in Electronics Components Manufacturing," in Glenn R. Carrol (ed.), *Ecological Models of Organizations.* Cambridge, MA: Ballinger, 1988.

4. D. A. Aaker, *Managing Brand Equity.* New York: The Free Press, 1991.

5. For a good review, read V. Kumar and J. Ganesh, "State-of-the-Art in Brand Equity Research: What We Know and What Needs to Be Known," *Australian Journal of Market Research*, 3, January 1995, pp. 3–22.

6. W. A. Kamakura and G. J. Russell, "Measuring Brand Value with Scanner Data," *International Journal of Research in Marketing*, 10, March 1993, pp. 9–22; J. Swait, T. Erdem, J. Louviere, and C. Dubelaar, "The Equalization Price: A Measure of Consumer-Perceived Brand Equity," *International Journal of Research in Marketing*, 10, March 1993, pp. 23–45; K. L. Keller, "Conceptualizing, Measuring, and Managing Customer-Based Brand Equity," *Journal of Marketing*, 57, January 1993, pp. 1–22.

7. L. C. Winters, "Brand Equity Measures: Some Recent Advances," *Marketing Research: A Magazine of Management & Applications*, 4, December 1991, pp. 70–73.

8. A. L. Baldinger, "Marketing, Finance Must Work Together to Measure Brand Equity," *Marketing News*, 25, September 2, 1991, p. 36.

9. C. J. Simon and M. W. Sullivan, "The Measurement and Determinants of Brand Equity: A Financial Approach," *Marketing Science*, 12, Winter 1993, pp. 28–52.

10. B. G. Yovovich, "What Is Your Brand Really Worth?," *Adweek's Marketing Week*, August 8, 1988, pp. 18–24.

11. W. Boulding, A. Kalra, R. Staelin, and V. A. Zeithaml, "A Dynamic Process Model of Service Quality: From Expectations to Behavioral Intentions," *Journal of Marketing Research*, 30, February 1993, pp. 7–27.

12. J. M. Salter, "The Systematic Approach to Measuring Satisfaction," *Marketing News*, 25, February 4, 1991, p. 9.

13. R. A. Peterson and W. R. Wilson, "Measuring Customer Satisfaction: Fact and Artifact," *Journal of the Academy of Marketing Science*, 20, Winter 1992, pp. 61–71.

14. V. Kumar, *Managing Customers for Profit, Strategies to Increase Profits and Build Loyalty*. New Jersey: Wharton School Publishing, 2008.

15. W. Reinartz and V. Kumar (2002), "The Mismanagement of Customer Loyalty," Harvard Business Review, July 2002, pp. 86–97.

16. V. Kumar and R. Venkatesan, "Who are the Multichannel Shoppers and How do they Perform?: Correlates of Multichannel Shopping Behavior," *Journal of Interactive Marketing* 19(2), Spring 2005 pp. 44–62.

17. J. Thomas, W. Reinartz and V. Kumar, "Getting the Most out of All Your Customers," *Harvard Business Review*, July–August 2004, pp. 116–123.

18. For a good review on the concept of customer referral value, read V. Kumar, J. A. Peterson and R. P. Leone, "How Valuable Is The Word of Mouth", *Harvard Business Review*, October 2007, pp. 139–146; and V. Kumar, J. A. Peterson and R. P. Leone, "Driving Profitability by Encouraging Customer Referrals: Who, When, and How," *Journal of Marketing*, 74(5), January 2010, pp. 1–17.

New Age Strategies

25

LEARNING OBJECTIVES

- Describe the concept of database marketing research.
- Discuss the key elements of e-commerce.
- Discuss the key elements of mobile marketing.
- Discuss the key elements of social marketing.
- Discuss the key elements of experiential marketing.
- Discuss the role of marketing research in relationship marketing.
- Discuss recent applications of marketing intelligence.
- Discuss how market research can be used to measure word-of-mouth value.
- Discuss the importance of customer intelligence.

The creation of customers is only a first step in building a successful business. The next—and more important—step is to manage and retain these customers. Mail-order firms, faced with high up-front costs of printing and circulation, long ago adopted the concept of *lifetime value (LTV) of a customer* to guide marketing decision making. In the past, the nurturing of customer relationships has been difficult because of not knowing which customers came or went or why. Database technology has changed all that. Through database technology, an organization can at last identify its loyal customers, its repeat purchasers, and its one-time-only "triers," especially within well-defined market segments.

The power of database technology ties these three characteristics together. The database collects and analyzes customer information; it is able to target specific benefits to specific customers and it provides the means for accurately measuring results. With the advent of customer lists, direct marketing came into prominence. Direct marketing sales of products and services are expected to reach $1.798 trillion in 2010. Marketing Research in Action 25.1 illustrates the origin of direct marketing. (Source: *The Power of Direct Marketing*, 2009–2010 edition).

Product and service enterprises alike use the techniques and tools of direct marketing to create and retain customers. American Express builds continuing customer relationships with offers to its credit cardholders of a variety of insurance (life, accident, health, and credit card loss) and other financial services (investments, loans). Packaged-goods companies use database technology to harness the power of coupons. Whether coupons are mailed, inserted in newspapers, or distributed at the point of purchase, database technology is helping these companies to define, segment, and target markets. For many years, tax refund checks issued by the Internal Revenue Service have been accompanied by mail-order forms for U.S. Liberty Coins from nonprofit organization such as the U.S. Mint.

Marketing Research in Action 25.1

▆ THE SEARS STORY

Richard Warren Sears, a young railroad telegrapher in remote North Redwoods, Minnesota, acquired a shipment of unclaimed gold-filled pocket watches, timepieces of exceptional quality and accuracy. Sears reasoned that likely prospects for these fine watches would be railroad employees like himself. He just happened to have a "list" of 20,000 names and addresses, coupled with a database defining the railroad occupation of those on the list. Sears offered his fine watches, by mail order, to specific market segments. Obviously, he approached other railroad telegraphers before "testing" engineers, conductors, or station agents.

He quite likely used a form of direct marketing, a letter with a reply device. The information was probably simple, but most certainly it carried a benefit-oriented message that may have read like this:

Hey, I'm a telegrapher working for the railroad and so are you. I need an accurate timepiece and so do you. I just made an attractive purchase of unclaimed freight. And, I can personally vouch for the quality of these gold-filled watches. Do you want to buy one from me at a bargain price?

Sears sold his watches in no time at all.

Source: M. Baier, How to Find and Cultivate Customers through Direct Marketing, Lincolnwood, IL: NTC Business Books, 1996.

Considering the increasing popularity of direct marketing, it is important to note that the use of direct marketing should still be restricted under certain ethical and legal barriers. In 1993, a federal lawsuit filed in Sacramento, California, accused sweepstakes held by American Family Publishers, Publisher's Clearing House, Reader's Digest, and others of conducting illegal lotteries. The plaintiffs asserted that the companies relied on unfair business practices to entrap customers into using their services, buying their products, and entering the sweepstakes. The court dismissed these charges on a later verdict, stating that the common direct marketing practice of sending additional sweepstakes mailings to people who purchase products is legal. Had the judge ruled otherwise there would be two serious implications concerned. The first one would be the threat to the existence of customer-only promotions such as frequent-flyer programs and random prize drawings. This would jeopardize the relationship between a direct marketer and its customers. The second implication concerns the use of the "reasonable consumer" standard. This generally means that under the Federal Standard Commission's norms, direct marketers can distribute sweepstakes packages with enticing texts and graphics provided that a reasonable person would understand that these are simply means of generating excitement and not an indication of winning. The decision held by the judge is not a justification for the "deceptive" tactics used by direct marketers in attracting customers; rather it offers valuable guidance as to what is allowed in the usage of creative versus deceptive sweepstakes packaging.[1]

Database Marketing

What Is a Database?

A **database** is a customer list to which has been added information about the characteristics and the transactions of these customers. Businesses use it to cultivate customers and develop statistical profiles of prospects most like their present customers—as they seek new customers.

The Need for Databases

Database marketing is an important tool that has been with us long enough to draw significant conclusions about what works and what doesn't in marketing research. To understand database marketing, one should ask the following questions:

- *Who are my customers: Are my competitors' customers different from my own?*—It is important to know this in order to analyze and understand the demographic and behavioral profile of your customers.

- *How loyal are my customers?*—Determining a customer's loyalty can help you analyze your database better.

There are three interrelated dimensions that a company should probe to evaluate whether its current database marketing is effective: *attitudinal, behavioral*, and *financial*. In the area of attitudinal data, you should evaluate whether your program has had a real impact on consumer attitudes and opinions. Your measurement should include consumer awareness of your marketing program, including the advertising campaign; consumer likes and dislikes of your marketing campaign and an understanding of how, over time, your brand's image has been affected by your marketing program. Your analysis of behavioral data should address short-term issues such as (1) how much "trial" your marketing program has generated for a new product or for an established brand; (2) how much "new" penetration your program has caused, and in turn how much incremental business this has generated for your company. Other diagnostics should include a buyer profile of your company's brand as well as the program's financial efficiency in reference to other programs you might be running. The best way to test a program prior to rolling it out is with a test-group-versus-control-group design. To do so the following steps must be observed:[2]

1. Define your target group.

2. Go into your database.

3. Create a matched set.

4. Expose the test variable.

5. Minimize other marketing efforts while the test is going on.

6. Allow test program enough time to work.

7. Measure results by comparing the two groups' sales.

8. Take action. If the test results warrant going ahead with your plans, then

9. Implement it.

Further, a database (with the use of marketing models) can:[3]

- Match products or services to customers' wants and needs

- Help select new lists or use new media that fit the profile of existing customers

- Maximize personalization of all offers to each customer

- Provide for ongoing interaction with customers and prospects

- Pinpoint ideal timing and frequency for promotions

- Measure response and be accountable for results

Marketing Research in Action 25.2

■ DATA MINING AT KROGER FOR ITS COUPON PROGRAM

Only 1–3 percent of paper coupons are being redeemed by Americans. However, Kroger says its coupon redemption rate from regular customers is close to 50 percent! Surprised? The key to Kroger's success lie in its ability to mine data from its vast customer databases and provide coupons for products customers regularly buy. By ensuring that the coupons are for everyday, regular purchases, Kroger attains this high coupon redemption rate. This success tasted by Kroger shows that providing the right offers at the right places and at the right times makes it possible to improve coupon redemption rates.

In addition to mailing finely targeted coupons, Kroger uses the analyses from dunnhumby USA the data-mining and marketing operation Kroger co-owns with a London-based company, to guide strategies for promotions, pricing, placement, and even stocking variations from store to store.

Source: D. Sewell, "Data mining used in Kroger coupon program," Atlanta Journal Constitution, January 8, 2009.

- Help create the offers most likely to elicit responses from customers
- Help achieve a unique selling proposition (USP), targeted to appeal to your customers
- Integrate direct-response communication with other forms of advertising
- Demonstrate that *customers* are valuable assets

A marketing database can collect and manipulate information on customers, their individual characteristics and, most important, their response characteristics. With a database, marketers can use past actions by customers to predict their future preferences or profile prospective customers for effective market segmentation. With a database, marketers can project additional sales—through cross-selling and repeat purchases. At the same time, by collecting information and learning more about current customers' tastes and preferences, marketers can effectively target new customers with the same characteristics, and even predict the LTV of these newly acquired customers. In this way, the organization cannot just replace customers lost through attrition but can grow. Marketing Research in Action 25.2 provides an illustration of how one company targets its customers.

Elements of a Database

A database should attempt to create:[4]

- A unique identifier such as an ID or match code
- Name and title of individual and/or organization
- Mailing address, including Zip Code
- Telephone number
- Source of order, inquiry, or referral
- Data and purchase details of first transaction
- Recency/frequency/monetary transaction history by date, dollar amounts (cumulative) of purchase, and products (lines) purchased
- Credit history and rating (scoring)

- Relevant demographic data for consumer buyers, such as age, gender, marital status, family data, education, income, occupation, length of residence at address given, geodemographic cluster information, and similar data of value

- Relevant organization data for industrial buyers, such as standard industrial classification (SIC), size, revenues, number of employees, length of time in business, perhaps information about the area of the organization's economic or social location, and even information about the personality of individual buyers within the organization

Which data you include depends entirely on its future value in use. "Nice to know" or "we may need that somewhere down the line" are not valid reasons for accumulating data, even though today's technology encourages it. Information costs money, and that cost must return a value. Care must be taken to ensure accuracy, relevance, and currency of the information.

Using Marketing Databases for Marketing Intelligence

Your customers may have chosen you over your competitors for any of several reasons or even for a combination of items. Why is he or she your customer? Your customer may have come to you because he or she:

- Simply did not know your competitors' existence and/or their similar products and services. Perhaps he or she even thought you and what you sell were unique.

- Found you and your product or service superior in only one respect, but a respect that was important to him or her.

- Did not perceive any significant difference between you and your competitors but chose you by pure chance.

- Just found it more convenient to do business with you.

- Especially disliked something about your competitors and found you the best of several distasteful choices.

- Otherwise does not really know why or how he or she came to choose you.

This is obviously valuable information as input to your marketing planning of strategies and promotions. That the marketing database is a good key to gathering much information should come as no surprise.

Ways to Gather Consumer Data

There are many ways to gather consumer data. You may use such direct means as surveys, questionnaires, and application forms, but you may also get information from secondary sources, such as credit-reporting bureaus and published directories.

When you fill out an application for a rebate or a specially discounted or even free book or other item, you may wonder why some of the questions seem to be rather strange as far as the rebate or items are concerned. The firm is collecting personal data not normally available in any other medium. (Now you know!) Pace, the warehouse store, for example, furnishes brochures inviting customers to submit suggestions for additional items they would like to find in Pace outlets. This is a common practice, and many such brochures and pamphlets go well beyond simply asking for recommendations and pursue a wide range of facts and opinions from the customers.

If you apply for a free subscription to a trade publication, you generally must respond to a rather lengthy set of questions, but that, too, provides data not usually available otherwise.

You may use conventional advertising media to induce customers and prospective customers to call and write. One way to do this is to use a special form of inquiry advertising. And more than a few other companies are publishing free newsletters for customers today, encouraging letters from readers as an effective means for generating data for their databases.

The last time you signed onto the Internet, someone could have watched what you did, what you said, or what you bought and then shared the information with a curious marketer who wanted to know. Powerful computers and high-tech scanners now enable marketers to monitor closely how, where, and when you spend your money. These electronic transactions speak much louder than words because they reflect actual behavior. It no longer matters what consumers say they do; marketers can now track what they really do. Sometimes consumers know they are being watched. But consumers are becoming active in their quest to keep marketers out. Six out of ten people surveyed by the polling firm Louis Harris said they have refused to give information to a company they felt was being too nosy. Just a few years ago, only 4 in 10 had refused. And 80 percent agree that they have "lost all control" over how personal information about them is used by companies. On the other hand, while consumers fret about marketers digging up information behind their backs, the single most effective method by which marketers learn personal information about consumers is by asking. Procter & Gamble, for example, mails out questionnaires to as many as 20 million consumers annually. Even in this age of privacy concerns, millions willingly respond.[5]

Database marketers should be aware of less-sophisticated *guerilla marketers*, who might steal their business. The best targeting model is no substitution for great marketing fundamentals or creative thinking. Here are four guerilla tactics that smart small businesses use in capturing the big market:

1. *Get the product right.* Guerilla marketers reach broadly targeted customers with a preferred product.

2. *Use low-tech targeting and creative thinking.* Guerilla marketers reach a broader audience by adding different styles of questions that are not included in most survey and research questions. A guerilla marketer finds unconventional methods to reach the target audience based on collected consumer information. This type of creative thinking has led to many new media channels.

3. *Use other people's data (OPD) first.* Guerilla marketers are opportunistic and have no need to create every piece of data themselves. By using OPD, guerilla marketers move fast and inexpensively. Syndicated data are a traditional source of direct-mail campaign information that many database marketers now consider unfashionable. A variety of service providers will sell household-level data that can be presorted based on the guerilla marketer's request. This competitor will then use the syndicate's database and data-mining capability to create a basic targeting program.

4. *Buy new media.* Guerilla marketers tend to be brave and they invest in new, unproven media sources. They may capitalize on new media sources to leverage their often-superior targeting capabilities and introductory pricing.[6]

Types of Databases

Most firms want to have a customer database and a prospect database. The customer database can categorize customers as active or inactive customers and inquiries.

- *Active customers:* How recently have they purchased? How frequently have they purchased? How much did they spend? What are their product or service preferences? Identifying your most active customers can help you concentrate your resources on the most profitable segment of your customer list.

- *Inactive customers:* How long have prior customers been inactive? How long had they been active? What was their buying pattern while active? What offers have they received since? This information can help you design promotions that re-activate your inactive customers.

- *Inquiries:* From what media source did inquirers come? What was the nature and seriousness of the inquiry? Do you have any demographic or psychographic information on inquirers?

The prospect database is developed based on the characteristics similar to those of the customer database.

The objective of developing customer and prospect databases is to break down customers and the most likely prospects into groups identifiable by the kinds of appeals they find most persuasive. That is, we must learn what motivated each group to become our customers: Which were moved by the emotional content of our presentations? Which by our image as an old, reliable firm that cares about our customers? Which by our ironclad guarantees? Which by dissatisfaction with our competitor? Which by our TV commercials? Which by our direct-mail program? This means dividing up our customer population into small groups and targeting each group with the right promotion for that group to maximize response. The value of database marketing also depends directly on the quantity, accuracy, and relevancy of the information. Database marketing can prevent marketing disasters, which is as important a consideration or objective as increasing marketing successes.

Modeling customers serves several purposes or objectives:

- It helps us identify our most typical customers and so become more effective in our prospecting.

- It helps us identify our best customers, another aid to prospecting.

- It helps us identify niche markets to add to our marketing universe.

- It helps us develop more effective marketing tools (materials and media).

However, soliciting every member of the database can be quite costly. The break-even response rate a solicitation needs to be profitable is

$$\text{Breakeven response rate} = \frac{\text{cost of solicitation}}{\text{expected net revenue from a respondent}}$$

Hence, one rule is to solicit only those segments whose expected response rates are above the breakeven rate.

Value-Added Databases

Database enhancement can substantially increase the amount and quality of information you hold on each customer or prospect.

- In its simplest form, an enhancement might be the addition of age (from a driver's license record) or telephone number (from a directory record). Other possibilities include past transactions; demographic and psychographic data; credit experience, if pertinent; people on the move, evidenced by an address change; significant characteristics of a business; and a multiple of customer behavior and transaction data. For example, a home furnishings firm enhances its customer list with demographic and lifestyle information obtained from R. L. Polk Company.

- By overlaying multiple databases, you can eliminate duplication between and among the lists and identify "hotline names" (those who responded most recently) and "multi-buyers" (those who appear on more than one response list).

- Negative screening, such as a credit check, can be used to remove a record from a solicitation database. For an example, a major oil company screens all of its prospects for bad credit ratings before an offer solicitation is made.

Finally, your database is not just to collect transaction information and segment your list but also to aid decision making—both in marketing and in overall business planning. Using your database as an analytical tool involves the use of statistical techniques and findings of research as well as the results of testing. It also includes the models you build and the simulations you use to support your decisions.

Having assembled a list of consumers, the marketer then combines information from other sources. Research houses such as Donnelley, Metromail, and R. L. Polk collect vast amounts of data from public records—drivers' licenses, auto registrations, and mortgage-tax rolls. Even income, the most sensitive subject, can be estimated based on mortgages and automobile registrations. Such information isn't cheap, though. For instance, Ohio sold its drivers' license and car registration lists to TRW, Inc., for $375,000. Wittingly or unwittingly, consumers often offer plenty of data about themselves. Think of all those busybody questions on a warranty card: What's your age, income, occupation, education, and marital status? How many children? Do you hunt, fish, or play tennis? If you think none of that has much to do with the guarantee on that radio you just bought, you're right. But National Demographics & Lifestyles, Inc., based in Denver, collects those warranty cards and the precious information they reveal and then resells the information to database marketers.[7]

Heavy computing firepower isn't always necessary. For some efforts, all it may take is a few thousand dollars' worth of hardware and software. Using a Macintosh personal computer, Yuri Radzievsky has built a database of Russian, Polish, and Israeli immigrants to the United States. By combing lists of subscriptions to foreign-language newspapers and buyers of tickets to events such as tours by Russian entertainers, his YAR Communication has assembled lists of 50,000 Russians, 75,000 Poles, and 30,000 Israelis in the United States. Such information is of real value to telephone companies such as AT&T and Verizon—telephone service, after all, is one of the first things new arrivals want when they set up their households.

Using the lists, AT&T has mailed Hebrew- and Russian-language offers of discounts on calls home. "Every marketer's dream is to be able to target those little slices," says Sandra K. Shellenberger, district manager of diversified marketers and multicultural marketing communication for AT&T. Response rates for such database-directed offers sometimes run as high as 20 percent to 30 percent, she says, compared with the low single digits for broader, more conventional direct mail.[8]

Data Mining

Data mining is a word used for a class of database applications that look for hidden patterns in a group of data. Generally speaking, data mining is the process of analyzing data from different perspectives and summarizing it into useful information—information that can be used to increase revenue, cuts costs, or both. Data-mining software is one of a number of analytical tools for analyzing data.

A good example of data mining is a Midwest grocery chain that used the data-mining capacity of Oracle software to analyze local buying patterns. They discovered that when men bought diapers on Thursdays and Saturdays, they also tended to buy beer. Further analysis showed that these shoppers typically did their weekly grocery shopping on Saturdays. On Thursdays, however, they only bought a few items. The retailer concluded that they purchased the beer to have it available for the upcoming weekend. The grocery chain could use this newly discovered information in various ways to increase revenue. For example, they could move the beer display closer to the diaper display. And, they could make sure that beer and diapers were sold at full price on Thursdays.

Although data mining is a relatively new term, the technology is not. Companies have used powerful computers to sift through volumes of supermarket scanner data and analyze market research reports for years. However, continuous innovations in computer processing power, disk storage, and statistical software are dramatically increasing the accuracy of analysis while driving down the cost.

Identifying Most Profitable Customers

An essential tool for identifying your best customers is the recency/frequency/monetary (R/F/M) formula.[9] The exact R/F/M formulation for each direct marketer will vary according to the relative importance given each of the three variables:

- *Recency of purchase.* How often does the customer buy something from you?

- *Frequency of purchase.* How long has it been since this customer last placed an order with you?

- *Monetary value of purchase.* How much does the customer spend on a typical transaction?

Table 25.1 illustrates the use of the R/F/M formula in evaluating customers for an office products firm. In this hypothetical example, three customers (identified as John, Smith, and Mags) have a purchase history calculated over a 12-month period. Numerical points are assigned to each transaction, according to a historically derived R/F/M formula exclusive to this firm. Recency of purchase, frequency of purchase, and monetary value of purchase are given weights of 50 percent, 20 percent, and 30 percent, respectively. The resulting cumulative scores—249 for John, 112 for Smith, and 302 for Mags—indicate a potential preference for Mags. Based on Mags' R/F/M history, a greater number of promotion dollars (such as mailing a seasonal catalog) could be justified. While John sounds like a good prospect, mailing to Smith might be a misdirected marketing effort. Although recency of purchase has been given the greatest weight in this hypothetical example, each organization must determine through its own analysis the factors that influence purchases. As a rule of thumb, however, the buyer who has purchased most recently is the one likely to buy again.

Validating Prospect Profiles

Suppose, for example, that you have managed to identify a group of 4,000 individuals with attributes or characteristics that you believe identify them as unusually well-qualified prospects for what you sell. You estimate that marketing to the group by direct mail will produce a response of perhaps 15 percent to 20 percent. That is a fairly optimistic estimate by conventional standards, but possibly it is a realistic one under these special conditions of an unusually well-defined market. On the basis of what you sell and your own economic estimates—cost of the program/campaign versus net profitability—you see an almost assured breakeven and a good probability of a net profit even if you get as "little" as 8 percent to 10 percent response.

You can probably get a pretty good idea of how well your estimates hold up by testing about 25 percent, 1,000 names and addresses, of the group. For a group of 4,000, that ought to give you statistically significant results so you can get a good idea of the worst- and the best-case

Table 25.1 Evaluation of Customers by Recency, Frequency, and Monetary Values of Transactions (R/F/M)

Customer	Purchases (number)	Recency (months)	Assigned points	Weighted points (×5)	Frequency	Assigned points	Weighted points (×2)	Monetary	Assigned points	Weighted points (×3)	Total weighted points	Cumulative points
John	1	2	20	100	1	3	6	$40	4	12	118	118
	2	4	10	50	1	3	6	$120	12	36	92	210
	3	9	3	15	1	3	6	$60	6	18	39	249
Smith	1	6	5	25	2	6	12	$400	25	75	112	112
	1	2	20	100	1	3	6	$90	9	27	133	133
	2	4	10	50	1	3	6	$70	7	21	77	210
Mags	3	6	5	25	2	6	12	$80	8	24	61	271
	4	9	3	15	1	3	6	$40	4	12	37	308

For point:

Recency of transaction: 20 points if within past 2 months
                           10 points if within past 4 months
                           5 points if within past 6 months
                           3 points if within past 9 months
                           1 point if within past 12 months

Frequency of transaction: 3 points for each purchase within 12 months; Maximum = 15 points
Monetary value of transaction: 10 percent of the $ Volume of Purchase within 12 months; Maximum = 25 points
Relative weight   Recency   = 5
                               Frequency = 2
                               Monetary = 3

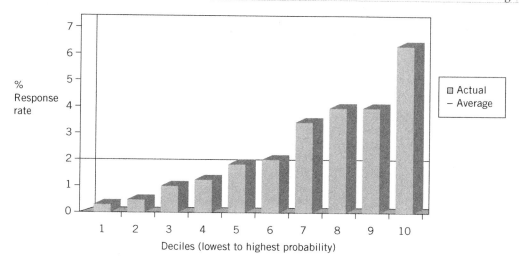

FIGURE 25.1
Decile–Response Rate Relationship.

probabilities. Figure 25.1 provides an illustration of how the rank ordering of prospects from the lowest to the highest probability of response and arranging by deciles affects the response rates. Whereas the average response rate is 2.1, the top four deciles yield a much higher response rate.

You want to develop a profile that defines the best prospect for what you sell. You have therefore somehow decided what the criteria and characteristics are that identify your customers. That information constitutes a model. If the model is a true representation and you can use it to build a list of prospects that matches the model, your response rate ought to skyrocket. On the other hand, because of this accelerated response rate, your marketing cost, the cost per order, ought to drop drastically. In substance, you will have the model to ensure continued marketing success in your business. You can now examine the characteristics and qualifications of every prospect in your general database to screen out those who do not conform to the model and make a first-priority list of those who do conform. This way, you can build a marketing database that represents a gold mine.[10]

Benefits of Database Marketing

Customers are Easier to Retain than Acquire

The first reason is that it takes five times the energy and budget to get a new customer as it does to keep an existing one. Also, a disproportionately small number of your customers generate a very large proportion of your income. The old 80/20 rule—that 80 percent of your business comes from 20 percent of your customers—is a remarkably accurate generalization. Therefore, the priority has changed to relationship building with the top 20 percent of your customers and working on the next 25 percent to upgrade them. A smaller effort should go into the following 25 percent, while final 30 percent are probably not worth bothering about.

Determine Their "Lifetime Value"

How do you assess the LTV of $50 for a monthly cellular phone bill? 93 cents for a can of cat food? $1.50 for a private bus fare? $40,000 for a new car? If you can keep the cellular phone customer's loyalty for 10 years, he or she is worth more than $6,000 to you. The cat-food buyer is worth at least $5,000 over the same period. The private-bus passenger, traveling both ways each day, has a 10-year value of $7,200. And the car buyer? With a new car every three years, plus

Marketing Research in Action 25.3

■ DO'S AND DON'TS IN DATABASE MARKETING

Do	**Don't**
• Use households' actual purchase data for identifying your target market whenever possible.	• Guess at what the right households are by substituting variables that might be related to your target group but aren't based on actual purchase behavior.
• Try to understand the quality of your buyers by understanding their loyalty behavior and switching patterns.	• Take the easy way out by identifying "prior brand buyers."
• Employ a true "experimental design" test-versus-control approach when-ever you conduct a test.	• Underutilize the real power of your database by running marketing events only as a test run. Make sure that there are adequate controls to ensure proper evaluation.
• Allow enough time for your test variable to work by taking into account category and brand purchase cycles.	• Execute a program and then measure it too quickly due to time constraints.
• Try to explore the reasons why a particular marketing outcome happened.	

Source: M. Hess and B. Mayer, "Test and Evaluate Your Way to Success," Marketing News, July 5, 1999, p. 12.

---

servicing, plus at least one second car, that could be $175,000 over 10 years. Once you start valuing your customers along these lines, the worth of each customer becomes an asset. And building a lasting relationship becomes the obvious way to a prosperous and profitable future.

Developing Relationships with Customers

Understanding your customers' tastes and preferences on an individual basis is the foundation for relationship marketing. Relationship marketing combines elements of general advertising, sales promotion, public relations, and direct marketing to create more effective and more efficient ways of reaching consumers.[11] It centers on developing a continuous relationship with consumers across a family of related products and services.

An important way of developing relationships with customers is through rewards program. A rewards program is the one that gives instant benefits such as cash back, or some price off for a future purchase, or a one-night off for a three-night stay at a hotel or a resort. This is often compared with loyalty programs. A loyalty program is the one that gives points for buying goods and services and something that can be accumulated over time and redeemed for a benefit in the future. While the loyalty program thanks past behavior, rewards program encourages future behavior. The best loyalty program is the one that not only thanks past behavior but also encourages future behavior.

Marketing Research in Action 25.3 displays a brief list of do's and don'ts in database marketing.

E-Commerce[12]

Online purchases have continued to increase dramatically in recent years[13] and the trend toward more and more people opting to buy products online continues to be up. Table 25.2 shows 2011 holiday sales compared to the corresponding days in 2010. Note the dramatic increase in each period including a 26 percent increase in Black Friday. Though price and convenience were the key drivers for online purchases, factors such as local pickup, later shipping deadlines, gift cards, and off-line product shortages increased online activity.[14] Table 25.3 lists the breakdown of online revenues for various categories.

Table 25.2   2011 Holiday Season to Date versus Corresponding Days[a] in 2010

	Millions		
	2010	**2011**	**Percent change**
November 1–December 26	$30,591	$35,274	15%
Thanksgiving Day (Nov. 24)	$407	$479	18%
Black Friday (Nov. 25)	$648	$816	26%
Thanksgiving Weekend (Nov. 26–27)	$886	$1,031	16%
Cyber Monday (Nov. 28)	$1,028	$1,251	22%
Green Monday (Dec. 12)	$954	$1,133	19%
Free Shipping Day (Dec. 16)	$942	$1,072	14%
Week Ending Dec. 25	$2,450	$2,831	16%

Non-Travel (Retail) Spending
Excludes Auctions and Large Corporate Purchases
Total U.S.—Home & Work Locations
Source: comScore, Inc.
[a]http://www.comscore.com/Press_Events/Press_Releases/2011/12/Final_Christmas_Push_Propels_U.S._Online_Holiday_Spending_to_35.3_Billion (This link has holiday sales numbers for both 2010 and 2011.)

Table 25.3   Top 5 Growing U.S. Retail E-Commerce Categories in 2010

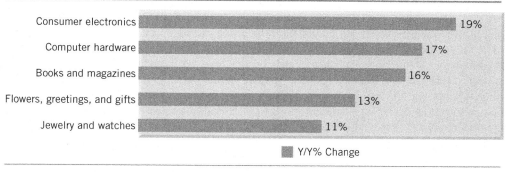

Source: comScore E-Commerce Measurement, 2010 vs. 2009

Time is precious when shopping, and Table 25.4 shows the reasons why shoppers prefer to shop online.[15] Better prices and wider selection were the other popular choices that drove many other shoppers online. Electronic commerce reinforces all aspects of online marketing. It provides a close connection between actions and profits. It dramatizes the problems of an organization and areas where improvements are needed. Moreover, it creates pressure to get closer to customers and do a better job of solving their problems.

To take a closer look at e-commerce, we must define its fundamentals:

- *E-commerce influence* is the impact of the 'Net on purchases made entirely off-line.

- *E-commerce ordering* captures the orders that are placed online but paid for later via telephone or in-store.

- *E-commerce buying* combines ordering and paying online.

The entertainment component of e-commerce is less developed than many of its functional aspects. This is partly due to technical reasons; currently most consumers' access speeds are too

Table 25.4   Reasons for Online Shopping Preference, July 2011

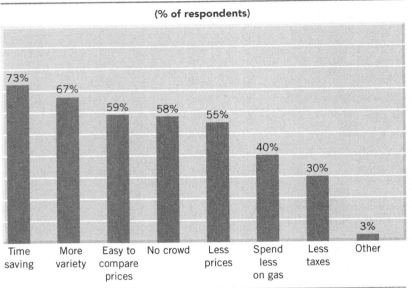

(% of respondents)

Reason	%
Time saving	73%
More variety	67%
Easy to compare prices	59%
No crowd	58%
Less prices	55%
Spend less on gas	40%
Less taxes	30%
Other	3%

Source: marketingcharts.com

slow for high-quality video and audio. With the arrival of high-speed modems and full-motion video, the Internet will be capable of a much higher entertainment quotient. Pay-per-view movies, interactive simulations, and near video on demand will blur the distinction between the Internet, television, and interactive video games. There is one notable exception to the lack of online media entertainment for pay. In 2004, *Forbes* magazine estimated that adult industry revenues amounted to $57 billion annually worldwide; $14 billion a year in the United States alone.[16]

Stores magazine surveyed 1,000 households to find the 100 largest retailers on the Web. They report results regarding online shoppers who have actually made purchases in 2004, how much they spent over a 12-month period, and how pleased they were with the experience. This is a treasure trove of data for researchers.[17]

Companies that do embrace electronic commerce must decide on the best channel structure. One method is to shift sales entirely to manufacturer direct. Some of the most successful companies of the 1990s, such as Dell Computer and Cisco Systems, follow this route. Channel conflict is one of the main concerns of companies as their e-commerce interests increase. Traditional distribution channels are threatened by online e-commerce. Threats come from final customers asking for direct extranet links to manufacturers, manufacturers launching e-commerce sites, and new online intermediaries with valuable information and innovative business models.

Electronic commerce is the challenge for retailers in the new century. Several responses from retailers are already emerging. Some seek to slow customer adoption of online commerce, some seek to differentiate physical retailers even more from online competitors, and still others seek to combine online efficiency with the benefits of a brick-and-mortar outlet. Among the retailer responses are

- Selective price discounts

- Concentrating attention on late adopters of technology

- Creating and staging experiences

- Partially adapting the Internet into a hybrid system

Marketing Research in Action 25.4

▓ MORE WOMEN ON THE WEB

As the popularity of e-commerce is growing, maximum sales growth was found not in categories traditionally dominated by men, but in products typically aimed at women. While sales of products like computer hardware and software slowed, sales of categories like cosmetics and fragrances and home goods aimed at female shoppers were brisk. This seems to indicate that more women are taking to the Internet for their purchases, who had initially showed a lesser interest than men.

According to a report published by Shop.org, online sales of cosmetics and fragrances witnessed the highest growth of 58 percent in 2004, with health and beauty care increasing by 34 percent and home products by 33 percent. Sales of computer hardware and software and auto parts grew by only 13 percent.

Source: E. Burns, "Online Retail Growth Robust," May 24, 2005, http://www.clickz.com/clickz/stats/1716977/online-retail-growth-robust#table1

Marketing Research in Action 25.4 shows the increasing presence of women on the Internet.

Consumer adoption of e-commerce will continue to accelerate. According to a new forecast by Forrester Research, Inc., U.S. online retail sales will rise from $172 billion in 2005 to $248.7 billion in 2014. The increase translates to a solid 7 percent compound annual growth rate over the next five years.[18] The other important predictions include the following:

- E-commerce will represent 8 percent of total U.S. retail sales in 2014.

- Travel will remain the largest online retail category, growing from $98 billion in 2009 to $144.7 billion in 2015.

- General merchandise (all retail categories excluding auto, food and beverage, and travel) will top $250 billion by 2014.

- An increase in the number of women shoppers will contribute to 14 percent of jewelry sales moving online by 2010. Online sales of health and beauty products will grow at an annual rate of 22 percent.

- Twenty-nine percent of small appliance sales will migrate online by the end of the decade as a generation that grew up with Internet access begins to get married and attend weddings.

Each of these approaches will have some success, and online retailers need to be aware of the power of incumbent retailers to learn and respond. A different e-commerce approach is through existing retailers and their websites. As more retailers adopt e-commerce, this strategy will grow in popularity. Some firms convinced of e-commerce benefits are moving their operations online and closing their traditional retail outlets.

This was the situation with Egghead Software when it closed its last store and went entirely online in February 1998. An online move allowed Egghead to stay in business and capitalize on its well-known brand name. It could expand into another region of the computer industry profit pool that was not feasible with a physical setting.

Continuous direct contact with customers is a requirement for effective real-time marketing. *Real-time marketing* is the marketing process of personally customizing goods or services that continuously update themselves to track changing customer needs, without intervention by corporate personnel, and often without conscious or overt input from the customer. Marketing Research in Action 25.5 is an example of how a software can help customers shop online. As the goal of real-time marketing is customization of the product both before and after the sale, a marketing organization must be able to maintain ongoing feedback with customers.

Marketing Research in Action 25.5

■ SHOPPING ON THE WEB

With increasing mobile penetration and speed of the Internet, mobile marketing is witnessing a tremendous change. Mobile phones equipped with cameras can now aid consumers in their shopping activities by recognizing bar codes and using that information to connect to websites. The new technology launched by PaperClick allows mobile users to link to any Web page in seconds by snapping a picture of a barcode or keying in a brand name. With just a click of a phone, the technology can provide useful information to the consumers regarding a purchase, best prices available, getting a coupon, or obtaining a rebate

instantly, apart from other normal features. This patented software, currently in development, is for use with 165 different models, including almost all of Nokia's and Motorola's makes.

Another company that developed the mobile phone shopping technology is Scanbuy Inc. Already 5,000 early adopters have visited the website to download a test version of the company's Scan Zoom technology, which lets them link bar codes on products to sites such as Amazon and Pricegrabber. They are also planning to release a software that offers driving directions to other stores where the same product is cheaper.

For more information on these products, check their websites at http://www.paperclick.com/ and http://www.scanbuy. com/.
Source: V. Hallett, "Ringing Up the Best Bargain," U.S. News & World Report, December 5, 2005.

Building a database of customer wants, needs, and preferences is valuable for several of the most widely used personalization systems. One of the incentives for online intermediaries is the ability to build a profile of customer choices based on a much wider array of business than a direct seller would acquire.

Building a customer profile leads to two very different incentives for data-driven intermediaries. These are *customer coalitions*, where customers join with intermediaries that protect their privacy while sharing appropriate knowledge with vendors that can personalize offerings based on data, and *seller scope*, which is how a multiproduct vendor can learn more about customers and use this information across its product categories.

Mobile Marketing

Over the past few years, mobile marketing is gradually arriving on the marketing spectrum. The reason it has not taken off in a big way is the variety of mobile phones in the market (around 700 mobile phone models in the United States alone). This has created an obstacle for a mobile developer.[19] Further, mobile phones are too slow and not user-friendly. However, with user-friendly phones such as the iPhone and increasing mobile marketing budgets in companies, analysts predict that mobile marketing is looking promising and is sure to open up as an effective means of marketing.

Mobile marketing is an important application that is poised to emerge as a medium that offers a quantifiable reach, rich experience as well as targeted marketing opportunities. The biggest advantage mobile marketing offers is that it can be used singularly or offered in conjunction with more traditional advertising channels. Some of the advantages of mobile phones are:

- *Wide presence:* Touted as the "third screen" after Internet and television, mobile phones have a wide presence. The mobile penetration in countries around the world is very high. According to Informa Telecoms & Media, mobile networks covered 90 percent of the global population by 2012. This implies that about 40 percent of the worldwide population are covered by a network but not connected and just 10 percent of the population is neither connected nor covered by a network.[20]

- *Interaction:* Mobile phones provide the opportunity of eliciting immediate responses and measuring the effectiveness of marketing campaigns. This helps in conducting customer satisfaction surveys and measuring quality control.

- *Impact:* Since mobile phones are very personal, they offer a wide scope for customizing marketing programs. It has a better impact than other traditional means of communication and can be a powerful medium of communication, especially with younger users.

- *Communication features:* Features such as SMS (short messaging service), MMS (multimedia messaging service), camera, WAP (wireless application protocol), and Internet access have changed the mobile phone usage. Users are increasingly using these services to be connected to latest trends, and these have important implications for marketing. In a recent survey of 1,800 mobile users between 13 to 65 years conducted by Mobile Marketing Association, nearly 70 percent of mobile phone owners used text messaging. Among these users, 44 percent used this service every day. A significant jump in consumer participation in mobile marketing programs was also reported in the survey. According to the survey, the consumer participation jumped from 8 percent in 2005 to 29 percent in 2006. Similarly, comScore Networks found that 23 percent of the Cellular Generation (ages 18 to 24 years old) and 29 percent of Transitioners (ages 25 to 34 years old) currently subscribe to Internet browsing feature on their mobile phones.[21]

An important implication of mobile phones for the mobile marketing efforts is the Opt-in feature. Opt-ins are a favorable way of attracting customers to the mobile marketing program. By participating in a mobile pull campaign, consumers essentially state that they want to participate in the call-to-action when they see the companies' print or TV advertisement. Such a program promotes mobile as an effective tool of marketing by carefully avoiding the issue of spamming. Further, opt-ins also enables quantifiable measurement of reach and impact of marketing programs. In a recent research conducted by Synovate, the number of U.S. mobile phone users who have participated in an opt-in mobile marketing campaign, by age, between 2005 and 2007 has increased. Table 25.5 provides the research results.

Mobile marketing is being implemented as an innovative way to extract maximum revenue from each customer. In order to do so, companies are moving forward to adopt a synoptic view

Table 25.5 Mobile Marketing Participation

Age category	2005 (n = 1,361)	2006 (n = 1,487)	2007 (n = 1,405)	2011 (forecast)
13–17 years	1%	4%	3%	42%
18–24 years	3%	3%	4%	42%
25–34 years	6%	3%	8%	58%
35–44 years	2%	4%	7%	40%
45–54 years	2%	1%	4%	40%
55+ years	2%	1%	3%	30%
18+ years subtotal	3%	2%	5%	n/a
Total 13+ years	**3%**	**2%**	**5%**	**n/a**

Source: 2007 Mobile Attitude and Usage Study, November 2007, Synovate, Chicago. http://mobilecommercedaily.com/2011/10/21/33pc-of-consumers-interested-in-joining-mobile-loyalty-program

of the total value of each customer. That means companies are trying to take a 360-degree view of each customer, to understand the various components of this value. Marketing research shows that each customer can generate both a direct value (direct contribution of sales revenue) and an indirect value to a company (additional profit contribution beside sales revenue, indirectly brought to the company by factors such as customer's influence, referral behaviors, feedback, and so on). These direct and indirect values are measured by the following indicators, namely:

- **Customer Lifetime Value (CLV)**[22]: measures the potential future profit contribution of each customer. We will discuss this concept in more detail subsequently in this chapter.

- **Customer Referral Value (CRV)**[23]: measures each customer's referral behavior by taking into account the average number of successful incentivized referrals that the customer has successfully made.

- **Customer Influence Value (CIV)**[24]: measures the monetized intrinsic value of each customer's influence on other existing or prospective customers in a social network.

- **Customer Knowledge Value (CKV)**[25]: measures the additional profits brought by a customer's ideas or feedback.

We can see that CLV is a direct measure, and the other three—CRV, CIV, and CKV—are indirect measures of customer value contribution to a company. In marketing research, all of these four measures are used together to evaluate the level of engagement of a customer with a company, termed as Customer Engagement Value (CEV). It is easy to see that when CLV, CRV, CIV, and CKV are maximized, CEV is also maximized, and so is the overall profitability of the company. That is also a reason why companies are looking at ways to enhance the total engagement of customers in effort to increase their overall profitability.

Mobile phones provide an excellent platform for companies to access the abovementioned measures of customer engagement (CLV, CRV, CIV, and CKV). The unique features of mobile marketing are that (1) it is an effective communication channel for companies to connect with each of their individual customers, and (2) it makes the communication process much faster and cost-effective.

Mobile marketing is thus being implemented widely to assess and enhance the total engagement of each customer. Fandango—a movie review and ticket selling site—provides mobile phone apps to allow its customer to send reviews on "what's in theaters." Many companies are using location-navigation technology to send out promotional text messages to attract customers once they are recognized as being a particular distance from the shop. Companies have also started using mobile marketing survey methods to collect customer data. For instance, the Standard Chartered Bank in Singapore sends out text messages to its customers to obtain feedback about the service quality they have received.

Companies are looking at creative ways to answer the above questions. However, in order for these companies to obtain the best results, thorough and systematic research is still required. For instance, while location-based texting technology is used by many companies to boost sales revenue, these companies still need to know the time and distance at which their text messages should be sent out in order to attract customers more effectively.

Below are potential development areas of mobile marketing research:

- **Enhancing Customer Knowledge Value (CKV).** Questions related to this research area deal with how companies implement mobile marketing to obtain customers' genuine feedback in order to generate creative product ideas. Many companies are doing so by promoting mobile-based blog postings—customers can share their reviews of the products and services they have used by posting them online via mobile phone. Other questions touch on how to measure the effectiveness of such implementations.

- **Enhancing Customer Referral Value (CRV) and Customer Influence Value (CIV).** Among possible research areas are how companies implement mobile marketing to enhance customer influence on social media, to promote referral behaviors among customers. More specific research questions may focus on how to identify a company's key influencers on popular social networking platforms and how to track their responses and impact thereof on the company's revenue.

- **Enhancing Customer Engagement Value (CEV).** Finally, potential research areas on this topic may touch on how mobile marketing helps companies reach out to individual customers and adopt an integrated approach to building a customized marketing strategy for each customer.

The mobile marketing research industry is currently at the beginning of its development, so it is still facing challenges. One main issue is privacy, as customers may not be comfortable with having their whereabouts tracked. Technical difficulties such as software compatibility issues, low data-transmission speeds, internet accessibility (or lack thereof), and low smartphone usage in certain markets are also barriers to mobile marketing research. Despite these challenges, given the current growth of mobile marketing, especially among 18- to 25-year-olds, the future of mobile marketing is expected to be promising.

Social Marketing[26]

As with other novel forms of marketing, social media marketing has gained momentum in recent years. The numbers of online social networks and blogs are expanding at a feverish pace, attracting consumers from a wide range of demographic segments. Internet users are turning to one another as trusted sources for everything from pie recipes to product reviews. Marketers have considered this ongoing/growing trend rather seriously. Online ad spending reached $32 billion, up from about $21.4 billion in 2007, according to eMarketer. Experts say a significant slice of that budget pie will be spent on social media. Table 25.6 provides the U.S. ad spending on social networking sites since 2006. Table 25.7 breaks down the estimated expenditures on social network advertising by type in 2011.

Table 25.6 U.S. Ad Spending on Social Networking Sites, 2006–2012

Year	Ad spending (in millions)
2006	$350
2007	$900
2008	$1,380
2009	$1,810
2010	$2,170
2011	$3,080
2012 (estimate)	$3,930

Source: eMarket, Jan 2011, http://www.emarketer.com/blog/index.php/tag/worldwide-social-network-ad-spending/.

Table 25.7   Ad Spending on Social Networking Sites by Type, 2011

Social networking site	2011 ad spending (in millions)
Facebook	$4,000
Twitter	$150
MySpace	$184
Social games	$274

Source: Businesswire, Feb 2011, http://www.businesswire.com/news/home/
20110216006308/en/Research-Markets-Worldwide-Social-Network-Ad-Spending

Social media covers all interactive media outlets in which customers can comment on or contribute to the medium's contents. Content can be submitted and updated quickly, and content providers can receive customer feedback in real time. Below are some of the popular social media channels:

- **Blogs:** online journals used to store information. Two popular types of blog are *corporate blogs*, such as Google Blog, Coca Cola Conversation, Delta Airlines—Under the Wing, and *micro blogs*, such as Twitter, Tumblr, Plurk. While corporate blogs are used to create consumer involvement with a company's marketing activities, micro blogs allow users to exchange small elements of content such as short sentences, individual images, or video links.

- **Social networks:** platforms that allow users to create and connect personal networks, such as Facebook, Myspace, LinkedIn.

- **Content Communities:** websites that store and share particular types of content such as Youtube, Google Video (video sharing), or Flickr (photo sharing).

- **Social Coupons:** websites that offer online daily deals and discounts, such as Groupon and Living Social.

The burgeoning of blogs has contributed largely to the popularity of this phenomenon. In the last two years, the number of blogs has increased nearly 15-fold to 164 million in July 2011. Each day, bloggers post more than 1.6 million entries, an 18-fold jump from 90,000 in 2005, according to Technorati, a San Francisco-based firm that collects information about blogs and other online "citizen media." Similarly, the value of diverse online communities to advertisers is also undeniable. Small online groups offer the chance to engage target audiences in conversation, while larger sites such as Facebook do it in a larger scale. Through Facebook's new ad programs, members can learn which advertisers their "friends" have indicated an interest in and get alerts detailing their friends' online purchases.

In this new consumer-driven format, quality of participation is key. While ineffective ads do not get any better or more effective on the Web, good messages resonate, even when the product is inherently sedate. For instance, in April 2007, H.J. Heinz Co. created www.topthistv.com, a Web site that let consumers create their own ketchup commercials. The site got more than 6,000 submissions in a four-month window and, attracted more than 3 million page views. The competition was so popular that Heinz started a second round up on the Web.

While the debate over consumers' privacy arises with ad targeting, marketing experts feel otherwise. With tracking consumers being an old practice since the usage of cookies, the latest iteration of the practice just needs time. Companies that have poured money into traditional Web

Marketing Research in Action 25.6

◼ GOVERNMENT AGENCIES TURNS ATTENTION TOWARD SOCIAL MEDIA

Government agencies are now experimenting with social media in disseminating information. They are using channels such as agency-run blogs, YouTube, Facebook, Twitter among others. This shift toward new media is due to a culture change, as agency leaders have begun to realize that when citizens search for information from the government, they want to use the same avenues they do in their everyday lives.

Of course, such experimentation is not without barriers. For instance, the social media sites require users to sign an agreement that allows advertising and establishes legal jurisdiction and indemnity, among other things. These agreements are in conflict with government users, who operate under their own rules and policies. Another barrier is the issue of security. While social media sites stand for free flow of information, sharing of sensitive content such as defense and intelligence information requires utmost scrutiny and protection.

However, there is optimism with the emergence of new media and their increasing role in everyday lives. Agency leaders believe that a firm approval from the government leaders would go a long way in the new media becoming accepted as a communication medium for dissemination government-related information.

For more information on these products, check their websites at http://www.govexec.com/dailyfed/0209/021909mag.htm?rss=getoday
Source: E. Newell, "Agencies test new waters in social media," February 19, 2009.

sites are finding that site visitors are scarce. As social networks grow, companies' marketing dollars would be better spent by planting a seed in an online community or featuring consumer-generated reviews on their Web sites. Marketing Research in Action 25.6 tracks the growing attention received by the social media.

More marketers are beginning to understand the power of social media in creating what viral marketing advocates call the Idea Virus. Despite criticisms, organizations such as Unilever, Blendec, and Nokia have reaped measurable growth both in terms of revenue as well as popularity from user generated content. Topping the list of ideal weapons in this media is Youtube, the user-generated video sharing Web site. However, with over a million videos being added every week, messages could easily get diffused in the crowd. At worst, active reply videos could turn the message against the organization itself.

Since popular videos bubble up to gain more exposure, a strong target base would quickly generate even more views. Once a video hits 10,000 hits, it is not unfathomable to predict a steeper ascent to 100,000, and from there to an even higher degree of exposure. Additionally, with users frequently linking to videos and discussing them in other social media frontiers such as blogs, forums, and networks, the spread of the video could increase exponentially.

A characteristic of most popular viral video channels is that they are high-concept ideas with low-fidelity execution, making them easily replicable. Additionally, ideas such as Dove's "Campaign for Real Beauty" instill a feeling of involvement amongst their customers by sponsoring a platform for them to create their own videos on the subject. However, bad products or messages, and unhappy customers turning the campaign around could be just as much, or even more viral. While social media must be handled with caution when using it as a marketing vehicle, marketers can no longer hide their head in the sand and pretend the viral wave will just go away. If organizations don't proactively take control, dissatisfied customers will.

To marketing researchers, social media is a new and powerful tool to increase customer values and company profitability. Firstly, it is a valuable data mining tool for you to obtain individual

Marketing Research in Action 25.7

■ THE CASE OF HOKEYPOKEY—CREATING A MEASURABLE SOCIAL MEDIA MARKETING STRATEGY

HokeyPokey is a chain of super premium ice cream retailers in India. With the goal to connect to their target customers and create an engaging brand experience, the company was looking for ways to develop an optimized social media strategy and measure the success of its marketing efforts. Through Facebook and Twitter, HokeyPokey implemented a seven-step framework to boost the value of customers' word-of-mouth and measure the corresponding increase in total sales. The company was eventually able to generate a share of 40 percent of the total increase in sales revenue, a 49 percent increase in brand awareness, and an 83 percent increase in return on investment.

The seven-step process was implemented in the following manner:

In the first three steps, to promote word-of-mouth for HokeyPokey, the company developed a systematic way to identify its "ideal influencers." Through monitoring conversations related to HokeyPokey on social media platforms such as Orkut.com, Twitter.com, Facebook.com, Foursquare.com, Gowalla.com, and so on these "ideal influencers" were identified as social media users who had (1) high message spread—the number of times a message was forwarded by the receivers, (2) high message influence—the number of times a message passed through to the receivers (friends of friends), and (3) high social impacts—the number of comments/replies received for each message.

In Step Four, based on a unique customer metric—Customer Influence Effect (CIE)—HokeyPokey identified all users on major social networks such as Facebook and Twitter who had similar characteristics with the "ideal influencers."

In Steps Five and Six, these identified "influencers" were invited to join two online social games to spread positive word-of-mouth about HokeyPokey. These games were called "Creation on the Wall" and "Share Your Brownies." The "Creation on the Wall" game allowed customers to create and name their ice cream creations with which they could identify themselves. The "Share Your Brownies" campaign allowed "influencers" to tweet their ice cream flavors/creations, and all winning creations were shared with all HokeyPokey parlors. These influencers were incentivized with "Brownie Points" when their followers or friends made a purchase of discussed the creation online.

In the final step, HokeyPokey's revenue from Facebook and Twitter was benchmarked against the previous three years' metrics. The final results showed that total sales increase attributed to conversations on Twitter and Facebook were 23 percent and 80 percent respectively. Positive word-of-mouth also increased by 33.5 times.

For more information on HokeyPokey's products, please visit their website at http://www.hokeypokey.in.
Source: V. Kumar, V. Bhaskaran, R. Mirchandani, and M. Shah, "Creating a Measurable Social Media Marketing Strategy for HokeyPokey: Increasing the Value and ROI of Intangibles and Tangibles", Working Paper, Atlanta: Georgia State University.

customer data/insights that are otherwise difficult or costly to obtain. If used appropriately, you will be able to mine honest and candid feedback from customers eager to voice their opinions. You will also be able to monitor customers' perceptions of your company's and your competitors' performance. Secondly, it is an effective and inexpensive way to reach out to a large number of customers almost instantly. Thirdly, it provides a two-way communication channel between a company and its customers, thus generating CEV for your company.

Implementing social media platforms can be a "double-edged sword" strategy. While many companies have been successful, not all can manage to translate this implementation into an increase in company profitability and customer values. If social media is not used appropriately, it might hurt rather than help the company. The two case studies below, presented in Marketing Research in Action 25.7 on HokeyPokey and 25.8 on Social Coupon, illustrate such a success and failure.

■ THE CASE OF SOCIAL COUPON AS A MARKETING STRATEGY: A MULTIFACETED PERSPECTIVE

Not all social media platforms can help companies generate immediate profitability and customer values. Social Coupon is one of those platforms. It is questionable whether Social Coupon can help small and medium businesses ensure long-term profitability. On one hand, social coupons have proved to be an excellent shopping tool. For customers, they provide heavily discounted deals, and incentives to try out various offerings at a lower price. For social coupon service providers, such as Groupon and LivingSocial, it means payment even before customers redeem the coupons, thus coverage of variable cost is guaranteed. For businesses that implement social coupons to their customers, it gives positive word-of-mouth effects to their businesses, and initial additions to their customer base. However, on the other hand, for these businesses, it also means deep discounts, higher redemption rates, extra payment to the social coupon providers, and low retention rate of customers. Many issues are worth looking into, such as:

Are social coupons helping or hurting the business?

Are social coupons profitable for the businesses offering them?

Can a tool that enables businesses to acquire and retain more customers also nurture profits?

Is there something fundamentally wrong with the current business model of social coupons and if so, how can it be fixed?

To adequately assess the issues above, a case study was conducted on three business models—an ethnic restaurant, a car wash service and a beauty salon. After the use of social coupons was launched in these businesses, their performance i n the following 12 months was tracked to ascertain the effectiveness of social coupons in three specific areas: customer acquisition, customer retention, and incremental profit generation.

The results showed an immediate impact on their profits right after the coupon launch. All three businesses suffered losses instead of making profits, and the magnitude of their losses were substantially high. Profits at the end of the month of the coupon launch fell between 1 and 3 times that of normal net profits earned before the launch. It would take several months for the businesses to recuperate the shortfalls in profits: 19 months in the case of the ethnic restaurant, 16 months for the car wash business, and 99 months for the beauty salon. This was provided that newly acquired customers would keep coming back within these periods.

The results showed that though all three businesses acquired new customers at the end of the first month the social coupons were launched, they were able to retain only 70 percent of those customers who first patronized the business due to the social coupon offer. With this retention rate, the ethnic restaurant would not have any new customers to retain in 19 months. However, by then, the restaurant would be able to recover only 12 percent of the shortfall in profit. The results also showed that many existing customers could use the coupons. Therefore, social coupons can cannibalize revenue earned from existing customers.

Given the short-term losses and the long break-even periods, it might not be worthwhile for these businesses to implement the social coupons in the first place.

The study went a step further to examine whether these businesses could influence the short-term profitability of a social coupon by changing relevant factors. A what-if analysis was run on three variables—number of new customers acquired, coupon discount rate, and percentage of existing customers using the coupon. Specifically, the analysis sought to answer how much the shortfall in profits would be changed if (1) the number of new customers increased by 1 person, (2) the coupon discount rate increased at 1 percent, and (3) the percentage of existing customers using the coupon increased by 1 percent. The results showed that when only one factor was changed, and the other two remained constant, the shortfall in profits would be minimized when the percentage of existing customers receiving the coupon reduced by 1 percent. However, when all three factors were variable factors, the shortfall in profits would be minimized when both the coupon discount rate and the percentage of existing customers receiving the coupon reduced by 1 percent. The bottom line is that if businesses have the flexibility and resources to alter all three variables, it is possible to identify the least shortfall in profits and decide whether they should implement social coupon strategy. The problem is finding out how businesses are able to have control over these variables.

In conclusion, while social coupons show certain superior benefits, further research needs to be conducted before they can be seen as a viable business strategy.

Source: V. Kumar, and B. Rajan, "Social Coupons as a Marketing Strategy: A Multifaceted Perspective", Journal of the Academy of Marketing Science, 40(1) (2012), pp. 120–136.

Experiential Marketing[27]

With novel marketing channels such as mobile marketing, podcasts, and viral marketing coming to the fray, the marketer's toolkit is becoming more tech savvy. However, as a means to stand out from the technological glitter, experiential marketing is gaining importance. By going back to the basics, marketers have discovered one-to-one communication all over again in experiential marketing. With an estimated yearly spending of $500 million to $1 billion and a growth rate of 15–20 percent over the past two years, this form of marketing is gaining traction among marketers.

Experiential marketing connects customers and brands in encounters designed to turn consumers into advocates. While experiential marketing may sound synonymous with word-of-mouth and event marketing, in reality, it is narrowly defined and aimed at niche audiences, generating a higher return on the investment. Procter & Gamble's Swash store is a prime example for this form of marketing.

Situated strategically near The Ohio State University, Columbus, the Swash store showcases P&G's new line of Swash products that remove stains and odors without a washing machine. Appropriately priced between $3 and $6, the initiative aims to stretch the visits to the local laundromat. In order to attract the student population, the store has a lounge area with free coffee, video games, computers, printers, and themed nights devoted to video games and movies. Other prominent experiential offerings are Delta's SKY360 lounge in New York and the Apple Store located in various cities across four continents. These initiatives show that marketers are ready to focus on specific target segments as against mass marketing.

Relationship Marketing

The Packaging Is the Message

It is important for today's product packaging to communicate the right message to the consumer in a dynamic and ever-changing selling environment, especially in the realm of e-commerce. It is still the last marketing opportunity to trigger a consumer response. When serving multiple geographic markets that may reach across two or three languages or dialects, the challenge is to communicate the right message to each. Icons or symbols are one of the most effective ways to overcome language barriers, but marketers must beware of unintended or mixed messages. One of the key advantages with symbols is that a symbol can be worth a thousand words. New interactive technology is driving changes in the way marketers are communicating with customers. Interactive opportunities for communicating brand equities in cyberspace are still in their infancy, but this could be the new frontier for marketers. Brand management will take on even greater importance. Recognizable logos, trademarks, and brand images will tell the story.[28]

The relationship marketing process incorporates three key elements:

1. Identifying and building a database of current and potential consumers, which records and cross-references a wide range of demographic, lifestyle, and purchase information

2. Delivering differential messages to these people through established and new media channels based on the consumers' characteristics and preferences

3. Tracking each relationship to monitor the cost of acquiring the consumer and the LTV of his or her purchases

Marketing Research in Action 25.9 talks about how Huggies and a few other companies used relationship marketing as a successful competitive strategy.

Marketing Research in Action 25.9

▧ RELATIONSHIP MARKETING IN PRACTICE

Huggies has spent over $10 million to set up a system that provides it with the names of over 75 percent of mothers in the United States. The names are obtained from doctors, hospitals, and childbirth trainers. During their pregnancies, the mothers-to-be receive personalized magazines and letters with ideas on baby care, thus building a bond between the mothers and Huggies.

When the baby arrives, a coded coupon is delivered that Huggies can track to know which mothers have tried the product. Later, as new technologies fall into place, Huggies will be able to know which mothers continue to purchase

Huggies. In this case, Huggies' parent, Kimberly Clark, is not only building diaper sales but also establishing relationships with mothers, which can be leveraged across other products. The cost of linking the consumer to the brand can be justified, since the per-baby consumption of single-use diapers averages more than $600 annually.

Other innovative programs include Kraft's "Cheese and Macaroni Club," which sends children a packet of goodies; MTV's custom magazine, which viewers get when they respond to MTV's 800 number; and Isuzu's personalized insets in *Time*, which list nearest dealerships and are redeemable for a premium.

Source: M. J. Wolf, "Relationship Marketing Positioning for the Future," Journal of Business Strategy, July/August 1990, pp. 16–21.

Three Keys to Relationship Marketing

There are strategic opportunities for companies on the leading edge of relationship marketing techniques.[29] Successfully addressing the trend will depend on a three-pronged effort as discussed below.

Identify and Build Marketing Databases of Present and Potential Purchasers

In the age of relationship marketing, the *customer database* will be as important a strategic asset for manufacturers as the brand itself. Advertisers will need the capability to use mass media and more targeted media channels as ways of prospecting for customers. Once potential customers have been identified, advertisers must capture their names and information on their lifestyles in a database for future communications.

It is important to keep in mind that not all consumers are appropriate targets for relationship marketing, and not all targets are customers. Consequently, the initial database must be carefully refined and segmented. Designed and developed properly, the marketing database will allow companies to expand their internal capabilities to include relationship marketing. Marketers leading the way include Procter & Gamble, which is using "800" telephone numbers in its ads for Cheer Free detergent to target people with sensitive skin; Porsche, which has created a database of 300,000 affluent prospective purchasers of its cars; and Citicorp, which is setting up a database of customer information collected from retail outlets for its own use and for sale to third-party marketers. Marketing research will play a crucial role in developing these databases. Most of these databases can be built using secondary data.

Deliver Differentiated Messages to Targeted Households

Advertisers must develop the ability to communicate with a defined audience of the existing and potential users of their products. The media choices they make must therefore offer the ability not only to broadcast the message to the entire circulation or audience but also to target precisely defined demographic slices. For advertisers, more precise targeting means greater impact.

Mass-circulation magazines are responding to advertisers' needs with selective binding and personalized inkjet printing. Applying these two technologies, an automobile manufacturer, for example, can send an ad for a high-end car to one household and an ad for a mid-range car to another household. In addition, the automobile manufacturer can add a personalized message to the ad with inkjet printing and even list the names of the nearest dealers.

Recently, MCI diverted money from its TV budget to pay for a subscriber-personalized ad in *Time*. Clearly, publishers can exploit mass reach with niche ads that provide more targeted messages.

Broadcast media are also relinquishing their positions as passive media. Telemarketing innovations will allow broadcast media to become increasingly interactive. At the same time, addressability will become an important factor in both cable and broadcast.

Track the Relationship to Make Media Expenditures More Effective and More Measurable

Common wisdom has it that half of all advertising dollars are wasted; the difficulty is knowing which half. The media innovations just described will allow advertisers to pinpoint what works and what doesn't. Consequently, relationship marketing's most important effect will be a shift in the way decisions are made about where to advertise. Traditionally, decisions have been based on various *ex ante* measures of exposure, such as cost-per-thousand, audience, or circulation. In the future, however, decisions will be made on *ex post* factors, such as evidence of penetration of the required target audience or even evidence of sales results.

In this new environment, the basis of measurement changes and emphasis will shift from cost-per-thousand to the value of reaching a target market. Advertisers must evaluate the cost of gaining and maintaining a customer relationship over several years. Once again, marketing research will play a significant role in this phase of the relationship marketing strategy. Tracking usually will be done by survey research. The various statistical tools necessary to process the information in the database are discussed in the data analysis chapters. The forecasting techniques generally used in database marketing are discussed in the online appendix to this chapter.

Recent Developments in Relationship Marketing

In today's marketing scenario, the customer has gained utmost importance. Identifying, acquiring and retaining the right customers are becoming the priority for marketers today. As the business outlook is transforming from a product-centric concept into a customer-centric one, it becomes increasingly important to assess the value of an individual customer to the firm. In such situations, the loyalty programs that are constituted by the firm are keenly studied and specific metrics are put in place to measure customer loyalty. A loyalty program is a marketing process that generates rewards to customers based on their repeat purchases. Consumers who enter a loyalty program choose to focus more of their buying on the focal company, thereby forgoing the free choice they had otherwise. In exchange for concentrating purchases, they accumulate assets (e.g., "points") that are exchanged for products and services, typically associated with the focal firm. Loyalty programs are certainly not a new instrument in the relationship marketer's toolkit. Sainsbury (UK) archives show how, in the 1930s, their managers wrote to customers who had not made their usual shopping trip in an effort to maintain patronage. Later, the store used Green Stamps that were well supported by customers, despite the need to paste them into many books.[30] The need for loyalty programs arises as consumers have varying degrees of loyalty associated to brands, stores, and companies.[31] It provides marketers an opportunity to retain customers by offering incentives.

Marketing Metrics to Manage Customer Loyalty

Today, marketers quantify how valuable each customer is to the firm. These metrics that measure customer value can be used to effectively manage customer loyalty. Some of the traditional metrics used to manage customer loyalty are provided in Table 25.8.

The Recency–Frequency–Monetary (RFM) Approach, as discussed earlier, assumes that past buying behavior is a good predictor of future purchasing patterns. It is based on three attributes, the recency, frequency, and monetary value of the purchase. The 'value' of the customer is ascertained using this metric and the resources are allocated to woo customers with a high RFM value. The Recency, Frequency, Monetary Value (RFM) model works well in a high volume business but can be applied to available historical customer data and not on data related to prospects.

The Past Customer Value (PCV) Approach is based on the assumption that the past performance of a customer is an indicator of the future level of customer profitability which is an extrapolation of existing buying trend. The PCV of a customer is his or her cumulative contribution toward firm's profits until the present period.

Share-of-Wallet (SOW) measures the amount of money that the customer is spending on a particular brand versus other brands, thereby indicating brand preference. Since SOW is a good predictor of a customer's preference it could also be an indicator of loyalty to a firm's brand. Being a measurement of consumption behavior, it is presumed to be more reliable than attitudinal measurements such as satisfaction.

However, when firms maximize share of wallet (SOW), the metric does not explain when a customer is likely to buy next and how profitable a customer will be in the future. Further, when firms use historical profits, they assume that the past spending behavior of the customer is going to continue in the future. Finally, the widely used Recency, Frequency and Monetary Value metric does not reveal any information about whether or not a customer is loyal, when a customer is likely to buy next, or how much profit a customer is likely to give. CLV overcomes these three issues by incorporating the probability of a customer being active in the future and the marketing dollars to be spent to retain the customer.

Table 25.8 Traditional Metrics

Metric	Description
Recency–Frequency–Monetary Value (RFM) Approach	Recency refers to how long it has been since a customer last placed an order with the company. Frequency refers to how often a customer orders from the company in a certain period. Monetary value denotes the amount that a customer spends on an average transaction.
Past Customer Value (PCV)	PCV extrapolates the results of past transactions into the future. In this model, the value of a customer is determined based on the total contribution (toward profits) provided by the customer in the past.
Share-of-wallet (SOW)	SOW refers to the proportion of category value accounted for by a focal brand or a focal firm within its base of buyers. SOW estimation can be done at the individual customer level or at an aggregate level.

Source: V. Kumar, "Customer Lifetime Value—The Path to Profitability," *Foundations and Trends in Marketing*, 2(1) (2007), pp. 1–96.

Customer Lifetime Value

CLV is very powerful and useful metric for customer analysis and strategy formulation. The CLV is calculated as the sum of cumulated cash flows—discounted using the weighted average cost of capital (WACC) or discount rate—of a customer over his or her entire lifetime with the company. CLV is a metric that assesses the customer as an individual and thereby assists the firm in treating each customer differently based on his/her contribution rather than treating all the customers same. The importance and relevance of CLV can be understood by the impact it makes on the following two issues:

- Calculating CLV helps the firm to know how much it can invest in retaining the customer so as to achieve a positive ROI. This is possible by knowing the cumulated cash flow of a customer over his or her entire lifetime with the company or the LTV of the customers.

- Once the firm has calculated the CLV of its customers, the framework is also the basis for selecting customers, selling the next best product/service to the customers, and deciding on the customer-specific communication strategies.

The CLV metric can be calculated at an individual or an aggregate level and as a result, provide managers with valuable information about the evolution of a client's LTV over time. In its general form, CLV can be expressed as:

$$CLV_i \sum_{t=1}^{T} = \frac{\left(\text{Future contribution margin}_{it} - \text{Future cost}_{it}\right)}{(1+d)^t}$$

where

i = customer index,

t = time index,

T = the number of time periods considered for estimating CLV,

d = discount rate.

If we add together the individual CLVs of all customers, we get the customer equity of the firm, which is the total economic worth of a firm's customer asset. Customer equity (CE) is defined as the total of the discounted LTV summed over all of firm's current and potential customers. CE can be computed by either using an aggregate-level (using firm-level or segment-level measures) or a disaggregate-level (using individual customer data) approach.

Depending on the approach used to compute CE, firms can develop various firm-level and customer-level strategies to enhance the firm performance.[32] When an aggregate-level approach is used, the measure of customer value is available only at the firm or segment level. Therefore we cannot develop customer-specific strategies. However, CE framework can be used to formulate firm/segment-level strategies concerning investments in acquisition, retention, and add-on selling. CE can also be used as a surrogate measure of the market worth of most firms and for comparing competing firms. On the other hand, CLVs of each customer are computed in a disaggregate-level approach. We can therefore formulate customer-specific marketing strategies such as (1) customer selection, (2) customer segmentation, (3) optimal resource allocation, (4) purchase sequence analysis, and (5) targeting profitable prospects based on CLV. A firm has limited resources and ideally wants to invest in those customers who bring maximum returns to the firm. Individual CLV is an appropriate measure of the future return of contribution from a customer and it helps the firm to identify customers who are profitable and deserve differential treatment.

Traditionally, firms used different customer selection metrics such as RFM, PCV, SOW, and relationship duration. Recent studies[33] have shown that CLV is a better metric for customer scoring and customer selection. CLV can also be used along with other customer value metrics such as historical profits and duration of relationship to identify customer segments and develop specific strategies for each segment so as to maximize returns from each segment.[34] In addition to selecting the right customers, firms are also interested to know how much to invest on them. By utilizing the customer value framework, Venkatesan and Kumar have now come up with models that will help a manager to know the extent to which he or she should use various contact channels to communicate to a customer and optimize the allocation of resources across channels of communication for each customer so as to maximize CLV. CLV framework is also the basis for purchase sequence analysis and for optimizing the timing of product offerings. A purchase sequence model developed by Kumar, Venkatesan, and Reinartz[35] offers a framework to analyze the purchase sequence and purchase timing of each customer. The model prioritizes customers by indicating the propensity to purchase different products at different time periods. Knowing the sequence and timing of purchases by individual customers will enable the firm to contact customers with time-specific and product-specific offerings rather than having to contact the customers with multiple product offerings in each time period. Finally, CLV is a powerful tool for profile analysis, which can be used to target prospects who exhibit the characteristics of profitable customers.

Word-of-Mouth Marketing

According to the Word-of-Mouth (WOM) Marketing Association, WOM marketing is defined as the art and science of building active, mutually beneficial consumer-to-consumer and consumer-to-marketer communications.[36] WOM marketing aids relationship marketing in generating a positive influence on the product for consumers. Using methods such as buzz, blog, viral, grassroots, social media marketing, and consumer-generated media, WOM is highly valued by product marketers. Since WOM includes the personal nature of the communications between individuals, it lends credibility to the message being communicated.

The concept of WOM is nothing new to us. Being social animals, the evolution of mankind, growth of societies and the rise of civilization are fairly entwined with WOM. Therefore this automatic, practically free and viral propaganda vehicle has become the mantra on the lips and minds of marketers. Generating and encouraging sustainable WOM by offering customers a platform to spread their opinions is the heart of the rising domain of Social Marketing. With the rise of online social media such as Twitter, Facebook, Friendfeed, and Youtube, spread of information is no longer limited by boundaries of demographics or even physical social circles. It is not uncommon for a trusting relationship to be formed online and for users to trust information from these sources as much, if not more than, that from real world sources. Whether organizations choose to post personal updates or keep their online presence as purely business, credibility, authenticity, influence, and relevance are vital in generating positive and sustainable WOM.

A recent example of WOM marketing is Burger King's Subservient Chicken (http://www.subservientchicken.com/pre_bk_skinned.swf). The Subservient Chicken is an advertising program created to promote Burger King's TenderCrisp chicken sandwich and their "Have it Your Way" campaign. The program featured a viral marketing Web site, television and print campaigns and a one-time pay-per-view program. This campaign generated a lot of word-of-mouth, but the word-of-mouth was about the marketing campaign instead of the product that was being marketed. Further, owing to the novelty "wear-out" effect, the WOM generated by the campaign was short lived.

Since this type of marketing involves personal communication and user reviews, it can be applied to a wide variety of industry verticals. For instance, in a recent research banks were found to have six times more positive WOM than negative. In the report titled "An Opportunity Missed? Insights on Word of Mouth About Banks" published by Keller Fay Group LLC in March 2007, conversations of more than 6,000 adults were monitored in a four-month period to gain insights about WOM information Americans pass along about banks. Table 25.9 provides the WOM

Table 25.9   Word-of-Mouth Conversations in Financial Categories

Financial category	Percentage of respondents citing most often in WOM conversations
Banks (including credit unions)	44%
Financial conglomerates	18%
Investment companies	14%
"Stock Talk" (companies, indexes)	10%
Credit cards	8%
Insurance companies	3%
Finance references	2%
Mortgage firms	1%

Source: Keller Fay Group LLC, New Brunswick, N.J., March 2008.

Marketing Research in Action 25.10

■ WHO ARE THE WORD-OF-MOUTH CHAMPIONS?

Consumers who are loyalty reward program members are far more likely to be WOM champions for their favorite brands than non-members. Further, the more active their program participation, the more likely they are to exhibit WOM behavior. This is according to a report published by COLLOQUY, a provider of loyalty marketing publishing, education and research. Some of their key findings are:

- Reward program members are 70 percent more likely to be WOM champions than the general population;
- Nearly 55 percent of reward program members are self-described WOM champions; as compared to only 32 percent of non-reward program members;

- Almost 68 percent of WOM champions in reward programs will recommend a program sponsor's brand within a year;
- Actively participating reward program members are over three times more likely to be WOM champions;
- Reward program members who have redeemed for experiential rewards are 30 percent more likely to be WOM champions than those who have redeemed for discounts.

Therefore, the challenge for companies is to find similar customers from their database and develop relationships that reward them for their profitable WOM activity.

For more information on these products, check their websites at http://digital50.com/news/72840.
Source: COLLOQUY Study Reveals Reward Program Members 70% More Likely to be Word-of-Mouth Champions than Non-Members.

conversations in financial categories. The report also reveals that while banks have strong WOM from consumers, recommendations are weak. This suggests that banks are not capitalizing on the positive WOM generated.

Recent research has identified conditions under which word-of-mouth communication is effective. Research also points to individuals being more inclined to believe WOM marketing than more formal forms of promotion methods. This is because the receiver of WOM referrals tends to believe that the communicator is speaking honestly and is unlikely to have an ulterior motive (i.e., they are not receiving an incentive for their referrals).[37] With the emergence of Web 2.0, social networking, and the increasing use of the Internet as a research and communications platform, WOM has become an even more powerful and useful resource for consumers and marketers. Marketing Research in Action 25.10 illustrates the linkage between WOM and reward programs.

Word-of-Mouth Marketing

So now we understand that it is important for companies to capitalize on positive WOM. But how can a company integrate positive WOM into its marketing strategy? How can a company identify and target customers that bring in most positive WOM? How can we measure that WOM value? Marketing Research in Action 25.11 describes how marketing research helps companies answer all of the above questions.

Marketing Research in Action 25.11

■ HOW VALUABLE IS WORD OF MOUTH?

This is a case study conducted on over 16,000 customers of two companies—a telecom and a financial service company—to identify customers who bring in the most referrals. The results of this study suggest several implications on how to capitalize on this knowledge.

- **Step 1: Measuring a customer's lifetime value (CLV) and referral value (CRV).**

As discussed in the earlier section, CLV of a customer refers to the net future profit contribution (operating margin minus the marketing cost) that the customer is likely to bring to a company. CRV of a customer, on the other hand, refers to the net profit contribution of customers brought in by that particular customer through successful referrals. The formulas to estimate CLV and CRV are presented below.

$$CLV_i = \frac{\text{Future contribution margin of the customer}}{\text{Discount Rate}}$$
$$- \frac{\text{Future cost spent on the customer}}{\text{Discount Rate}}$$

$$CLV_i = \sum_{y=1}^{T_i} \frac{CM_{i,y}}{(1+r)^{y/frequency_i}} - \sum_{l=1}^{n} \frac{\sum_m C_{i,m,l} * x_{i,m,l}}{(1+r)^l}$$

Where:

CLV_i	= lifetime value of customer i
$CM_{i,y}$	= predicted contribution to operating margin of customer i in purchase occasion y, measured in dollars
r	= discount rate for money
$frequency_i$	= predicted purchase frequency for customer i
$C_{i,m,l}$	= unit marketing cost for customer i in channel m in year l
$X_{i,m,l}$	= number of contacts to customer i in channel m in year l
n	= number of years to forecast
T_i	= predicted number of purchases made by customer i until the end of the planning period

$$CRV_i = \frac{\text{Value of customers who joined because of referral}}{\text{Discount Rate}}$$
$$+ \frac{\text{Value of customers that would join anyway}}{\text{Discount Rate}}$$

$$CRV_i = \sum_{t=1}^{T} \sum_{y=1}^{n_1} \frac{\left(A_{t,y} - a_{t,y} - M_{t,y} - ACQ1_{t,y}\right)}{(1+r)^t}$$
$$+ \sum_{t=1}^{T} \sum_{y=n_1}^{n_2} \frac{\left(ACQ2_{tn}\right)}{(1+r)^t}$$

Where:

CRV_i	= referral value of customer i
$A_{t,y}$	= contribution to operating margin by customer y who otherwise would not buy the product
$a_{t,y}$	= the cost of the referral for customer
$M_{t,y}$	= the marketing costs needed to retain the referred customers
$ACQ1_{t,y}$	= the savings in acquisition cost from customers who would not join without the referral
$ACQ2_{t,y}$	= the savings in acquisition cost from customers who would have joined anyway
T	= the number of time periods (years, for example) that will be predicted into the future
n_1	= the number of customers who would not join without the referral
$n_2 - n_1$	= the number of customers who would have joined anyway
r	= discount rate for money

- **Step 2: Identify the customers that have high CLV and CRV.**

After the CLV and CRV of all customers have been estimated, they were ranked order into 10 deciles, as presented in Table 25.10. From this table, we can see an interesting relationship between CLV and CRV. Firstly, customers who bought the most from the companies—had the highest CLV—might not be the best referrers. Secondly, the best referrers had remarkably low purchasing value.

- **Step 3: Analyze the results**

Based on the results presented in Table 25.10, customers were segmented into four groups based on their CLV and

(continued)

Table 25.10 Segmentation of customers according to CLV and CRV.

Deciles of customers	Average CLV after one year	Average CRV after one year
1	$1,933	$40
2	1,067	52
3	633	90
4	360	750
5	313	930
6	230	1,020
7	190	870
8	160	96
9	137	65
10	120	46

CRV, namely: (1) *The Champions*—who scored high on both CLV and CRV, (2) *The Affluents*—who had high CLV but low CRV, (3) *The Advocates*—who had high CRV, but low CLV, and (4) *The Misers*—who scored low on both measures.

- **Step 4: Apply the findings**

Once the two companies understood their customer segments, they went on applying this understanding to implementing marketing campaigns to maximize the CLV and CRV of each segment. Specifically, the companies look at ways to move Affluents and Advocates group to Champions group, and the Misers group into any of the other three.

- **Affluents.** Affluents group has high CLV but low CRV. To move Affluents group to Champions group, the companies looked at ways to encourage them to refer more new customers while maintaining their purchasing behaviors. Direct-mail communication was sent to those customers, followed by $20 referral incentives ($10 for the referring customer and $10 for the referred customers). After the campaign, the CRV of those Affluents group went up on average by $190, or increased by 388 percent. In total, 4 percent of the Affluents group was moved to the Champions group.

- **Advocates.** Advocates group had low CLV but high CRV. To move Advocates group to Champions group, the companies aimed to encourage them to buy/use more products and services without compromising their referral pattern. The implemented marketing campaigns focused on cross-selling, up-selling as well as offering attractive promotions to these customers through direct mailing and follow-up through phones. For instance, the telecom company sent out offers of bundled products, discount worth two months' subscription fees to customers signing a one-year contract. The campaign led to an average increase of approximately $110, or 96 percent, in CLV. In total, 5 percent of the Advocates were converted into Champions group.

- **Misers.** Misers group had both low CLV and low CRV. The companies aimed to move this group to either one of the other three groups by increasing either CLV, or CRV or both. Thus, the marketing campaign implemented for this group combined the features of the other two. Promotion of discounts on bundled products as well as referral incentives were offered to these customers via direct mail. Follow-up through phone calls was also made to answer any question regarding the additional services offered. As a result, CLV more than doubled, increased by $180 and CRV more than quadrupled, increased by $210.

This success was achieved through implementing marketing strategies on a sample of 16,000 customers. If the companies chose to adopt this marketing campaign on a larger set of customers, the resulting effects will be multiplied.

Source: V. Kumar, J. A. Petersen and R. P. Leone, "How Valuable is the Word of Mouth?", Harvard Business Review October (2007), pp. 139–146.

Customer Intelligence

The customer intelligence framework, shown in Figure 25.2, creates a nerve center that is able to send and receive messages and learn from experience, thus creating understanding and fostering relationships. According to Dr Jon Anton of the Purdue University Center for Customer Driven Quality, "Analysis is essential in order to understand what the customer is trying to tell us." The key step in this process is to identify customers. It is critical to know customers in as much detail

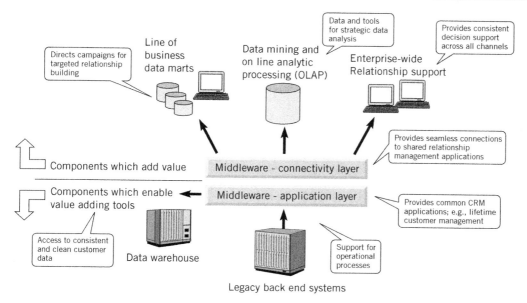

FIGURE 25.2
Customer Intelligence Framework
Source: http://www.crm-forum.com

as possible—not just names and addresses but also habits,preferences, and so forth. It would be most profitable if researchers were able to know these details across all critical points (through all media, across every product line, at every location, and in every division), not just at a snapshot.

Another application that is gaining importance today is *actionable customer intelligence*. This process requires companies to develop modeling and analysis capabilities to "mine" their raw data. This capability requires a combination of people, processes, and systems and needs to encompass a range of tools, such as customer profiling, customer segmentation, customer profitability, predictive modeling, event monitoring and triggering, "what-if" analysis, and so forth. Figure 25.3 shows the systems required to build a customer DNA.

Customer DNA

A recent trend in marketing research is to intelligently profile customers and assess the needs of each profile on a continuous basis. Just as DNA profiles have uncovered the secrets of life, researchers can now get under the skin of customers to discover the secrets of marketing success. Customer DNA is an approach to understanding and measuring customer needs and wants. Customer DNA generates a holistic appreciation of the brand and allows researchers to understand the fuller picture and identify exactly how to influence factors to improve customer retention and loyalty. The profile from a customer DNA model could look like Figure 25.4.

It is an interesting question whether the analysis should aim to identify what the customer wants to buy or to identify customers for what the supplier wants to sell. This brings into picture broader concepts like buyer-centricity and seller-centricity, which were discussed in Chapter 24. This type of question can be found lurking behind many analysis projects. The answer is both—and that these two views should become the same; they are, in fact, opposite sides of the same coin. Over time the product range offered by the supplier will match the demands of the customer base.

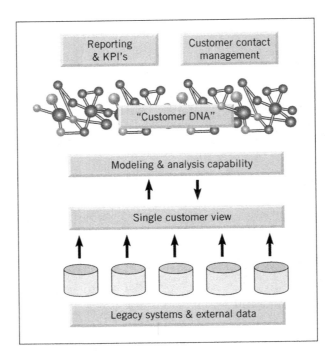

FIGURE 25.3
Customer DNA Model.
Source: http://www.gfk.com/

SEGMENT	LifeStage Segment X		
Card Segment—Macro	Credit Revolver		
Card Segment—Micro	High Balance to Credit Limit		
Profitability	High	Medium	Low
Current	—	✓	—
Potential	✓	—	—
Product Opportunity	Holds Product	Likely to Lapse	Likely to Buy
Product A	Yes	Low	—
Product B	Yes	Medium	—
Product C	No	—	High
Product D	No	—	Low
Product E	No	—	Low
Product F	No	—	High
Product G	No	—	Medium
Preferred Channels	High	Medium	Low
Mail	✓	—	—
Phone	—	—	✓
E-Mail	✓	—	—

FIGURE 25.4
Customer DNA Profile.
Source: http://www.gfk.com/

Customer Analysis

Customer analysis, in one way or another, always has to do with one of the following:

- Customer acquisition—finding new customers

- Customer cross-sell—making further sales to the same customers

- Customer up-sell—convincing customers to make greater use of the same product or service

- Customer retention—keeping customers loyal

Figure 25.5 presents the profitability distribution of a sample of customers. Figure 25.6 is a decile analysis, obtained by ranking the customers in the sample and dividing them into 10 equal groups by number. It groups together customers of similar profitability (or by whatever other measure is the subject of the analysis).

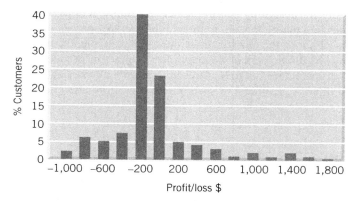

FIGURE 25.5
Profitability Distribution.

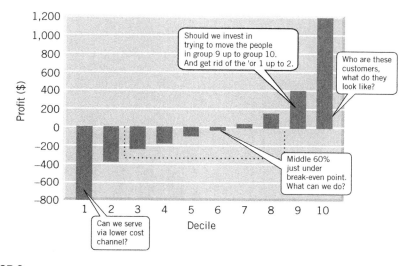

FIGURE 25.6
Decile Analysis.
Source: http://www.crm-forum.com/cgi-bin/form_to_mail.cgi.

Such groupings prompt a host of interesting questions to which the business—particularly the Marketing Department—would like to know the answers. For example,

- What does the profile of the most profitable customers look like in terms of demographics, geo-demographics, product holding, product usage, balances, transactions, and length of time as customers? What strategy should be adopted when dealing with them?

- What characteristics differentiate the least profitable customers from the most profitable?

- How much of marginal marketing dollars should go toward promoting customers up group levels?

- What strategy should be to adopted to maximize profitability from the middle range of customers?

The answers to these questions, which probably would not have come up but for the analysis, should pave the way for designing and implementing future actions. Some conclusions may seem really obvious, but the trick is not to jump to premature conclusions. Apparent and obvious conclusions need not be the most accurate ones. For example, the most profitable customers need not always be the holders of the maximum number of products. The least profitable customers could very well turn out to be well-organized money managers who take advantage of every available offer. A great deal of such interesting information is waiting as raw data to be mined.

Segmentation

All of these questions are really asking how the company's strategy should vary depending on the customer group in question. This is where analysis starts to become of value and starts to drive the strategy. The accompanying figure shows this in a simple yet powerful way. This segmentation profiles most and least profitable customers into groups, with the company needing to follow different strategic responses for each group. Such an understanding helps in identifying how to invest. This is a little glimpse into the immense potential of marketing intelligence.

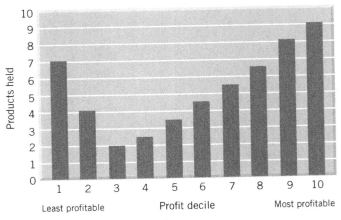

Source: http://www.crm-forum.com/

SUMMARY

As marketers move from mass marketing to customization, direct marketing is assuming increased importance. This is made possible by the availability of customer and prospect databases. A database is a source of information about individuals or organizations. A database can contain a wealth of information about customers' purchase history, demographics, and lifestyle, as well as firms' SIC codes, annual sales, employee size, and years of operation. Response models are built with the customer database to identify and target prospects. As transactions occur between a firm and the customer, a relationship is being developed. Relationship marketing focuses effectively on building and managing relationships with customers, with the purpose of retaining customers forever.

QUESTIONS AND PROBLEMS

25.1 Describe how AT&T can use direct marketing effort to promote its Universal Credit Card.

25.2 Identify sources/firms that supply mailing lists of prospects across industries. How would you assess the reliability of these mailing lists?

25.3 How can a manager use the information about his or her customers to identify prospects?

25.4 How often should a telecommunication firm offering cellular phone service update its database? Why?

25.5 When is it useful to model customer characteristics to identify prospects? What factors should one consider in the cost-benefit trade-offs?

25.6 Managers and researchers claim that modeling customer characteristics to identify prospects is not a one-shot deal but rather a continuous process. Do you agree or disagree? Why?

END NOTES

1. M. Zweig and B. Socolow, "Direct Marketers May Already Be Winners," *Marketing News*, 31(20), September 29, 1997, p.7.

2. M. Hess and B. Mayer, "Test and Evaluate Your Way to Success," *Marketing News*, July 5, 1999, p. 12.

3. M. Baier, *How to Find and Cultivate Customers through Direct Marketing*, Lincolnwood, IL: NTC Business Books, 1996.

4. M. Williams, *Interactive Marketing*, Englewood Cliffs, NJ: Prentice-Hall, 1994.

5. B. C. McCarthy, "Guerilla Targeters Win with Marketing Basics," *Marketing News*, July 5, 1999, p. 12.

6. B. Horovitz, "Marketers Tap Data We Once Called Our Own," *USA Today*, 1995.

7. "A Potent New Test for Selling: Database Marketing," *Business Week*, September 5, 1994.

8. Ibid.

9. A. M. Hughes, *The Complete Database Marketer*, 2nd ed. Chicago: Irwin, 1996.

10. H. Holtz, *Databased Marketing*. New York: John Wiley, 1992.

11. J. J. Harrison, "Transforming Data into Relationships," *National Underwriter*, 97, August 2, 1993, pp. 7, 12; D. Edelman, D. Schultz, and M. Winkleman, "Up Close and Personal," *Journal of Business Strategy*, 14, July/August 1993, pp. 22–31.

12. W. Hanson, *Principles of Internet Marketing*. Cincinnati, OH: South-Western College Publishing, 2000, pp. 357–396.

13. http://www.comscore.com/Press_Events/Press_Releases/2011/12/Final_Christmas_Push_Propels_U.S._Online_Holiday_Spending_to_35.3_Billion (This link has holiday sales numbers for both 2010 and 2011.)

14. We could not find totals, but this link shows the growth in each category. http://www.marketingcharts.com/direct/e-commerce-spending-grows-9-in-2010-16119/comscore-e-comerce-2010-growth-feb-2011jpg/

15. http://www.marketingcharts.com/direct/time-1-reason-for-shopping-online-18528/invesp-customer-preference-for-online-shopping-jul11gif/

16. Kathee Brewer, "A Bill in the Hand: Collecting the 'Uncollectible'," September 2005, http://www.avnonline.com.

17. https://nrf.com/resources/annual-retailer-lists/top-100-retailers

18. http://www.forrester.com/ER/Press/Release/0,1769,1033,00.html.

19. Daniel Honigman, "On the Verge," *Marketing News*, January 15, 2007, pp. 18–21

20. Mobile networks worldwide, http://blog.telecoms.com/mobile-networks-worldwide. Retrieved on January 18, 2008.

21. Allison Enright, "(Third) Screen Tests," *Marketing News*, March 15, 2007, pp. 17–18.

22. R. Werner, and V. Kumar, "The Impact of Customer Relationship Characteristics on Profitable Lifetime Duration," *Journal of Marketing*, 67(1), (2003), pp. 77–99.

23. V. Kumar, J. A. Peterson and R. P. Leone, "How Valuable is the Word of Mouth?", *Harvard Business Review* 85, October 2007, pp. 139–146.

24. V. Kumar, Vikram Bhaskaran, Rohan Mirchandani, and Milap Shah (2013), "Creating a Measurable Social Media Marketing Strategy:

Increasing the Value and ROI of Intangibles and Tangibles for Hokey Pokey," *Marketing Science*, 32(2), pp. 194–212 .

25. V. Kumar, L. Aksoy, B. Donkers, T. Wiesel, R. Venkatesan and S. Tillmanns, "Undervalued Customers: Capturing Total Customer Engagement Value", *Journal of Service Research*, 13(3), August 2010, pp. 297–310.

26. Elisabeth A. Sullivan, "Be Sociable," *Marketing News*, January 15, 2007, pp.12–16.

27. Jeff Borden, "The Marketing Tornado," *Marketing News*, January 15, 2007, pp. 22–26.

28. Howard Alport, "Global, Interactive Marketing Calls for Innovative Packaging," *Marketing News*, 31(1), January 6, 1997, p.30.

29. Regis McKenna, "Relationship Marketing," *Executive Excellence*, 9, April 1992, pp. 7–8; Jonathan R. Copulsky and Michael J. Wolf, "Relationship Marketing: Positioning for the Future," *Journal of Business Strategy*, July/August 1990, pp. 16–21.

30. J. Passingham (1998), "Grocery Retailing and the Loyalty Card," *Journal of the Market Research Society*, 40(1), pp. 55–67.

31. P. Kotler (2004), *Marketing Management* (11th edition), New York: Prentice Hall.

32. V. Kumar and Morris George (2007), "Measuring and Maximizing Customer Equity: A Critical Analysis," *Journal of the Academy of Marketing Science*, 35(2), pp. 157–171.

33. Rajkumar Venkatesan and V. Kumar, "A Customer Lifetime Value Framework for Customer Selection and Optimal Resource Allocation Strategy," *Journal of Marketing*, 68, October, 2004, pp. 106–125. Werner Reinartz and V. Kumar, "The Impact of Customer Relationship Characteristics on Profitable Lifetime Duration," *Journal of Marketing* 67, January, 2003, pp. 77–99 .

34. Werner Reinartz and V. Kumar , "The Mismanagement of Customer Loyalty," *Harvard Business Review*, 2002 July, 80(7): 86–94, 125.

35. V. Kumar, Rajkumar Venkatesan, and Werner Reinartz, "Knowing What to Sell When to Whom?," *Harvard Business Review*, 2006, pp. 131–137.

36. An Introduction to Word of Mouth Marketing, http://www.womma. org/wom101/. Retrieved on April 6, 2010.

37. Rajdeep Grewal, Thomas W. Cline, and Antony Davies (2003), "Early-Entrant Advantage, Word-of-Mouth Communication, Brand Similarity, and the Consumer Decision-Making Process," *Journal of Consumer Psychology*, 13(3), pp. 187–197.

Appendix for this chapter is available on the Web.

APPENDIX

A

Tables

A-1   Standard Normal, Cumulative Probability in Right-Hand Tail for Positive Values of z; Areas are Formed by Symmetry

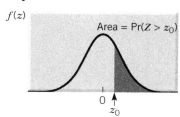

					Second decimal place of Z_0					
Z_0	.00	.01	.02	.03	.04	.05	.06	.07	.08	.09
0.0	.5000	.4960	.4920	.4880	.4840	.4801	.4761	.4721	.4681	.4641
0.1	.4602	.4562	.4522	.4483	.4443	.4404	.4364	.4325	.4286	.4247
0.2	.4207	.4168	.4129	.4090	.4052	.4013	.3974	.3936	.3897	.3859
0.3	.3821	.3783	.3745	.3707	.3669	.3632	.3594	.3557	.3520	.3483
0.4	.3446	.3409	.3372	.3336	.3300	.3264	.3228	.3192	.3156	.3121
0.5	.3085	.3050	.3015	.2981	.2946	.2912	.2877	.2843	.2810	.2776
0.6	.2743	.2709	.2676	.2643	.2611	.2578	.2546	.2514	.2483	.2451
0.7	.2420	.2389	.2358	.2327	.2296	.2266	.2236	.2206	.2177	.2148
0.8	.2119	.2090	.2061	.2033	.2055	.1977	.1949	.1922	.1894	.1867
0.9	.1841	.1814	.1788	.1762	.1736	.1711	.1685	.1660	.1635	.1611
1.0	.1587	.1562	.1539	.1515	.1492	.1469	.1446	.1423	.1401	.1379
1.1	.1357	.1335	.1314	.1292	.1271	.1251	.1230	.1210	.1190	.1170

A-1 (continued)

Z_0	.00	.01	.02	.03	.04	.05	.06	.07	.08	.09
				Second decimal place of Z_0						
1.2	.1151	.1131	.1112	.1093	.1075	.1056	.1038	.1020	.1003	.0985
1.3	.0968	.0951	.0934	.0918	.0901	.0885	.0869	.0853	.0838	.0823
1.4	.0808	.0793	.0778	.0764	.0749	.0735	.0722	.0708	.0694	.0681
1.5	.0668	.0655	.0643	.0630	.0618	.0606	.0594	.0582	.0571	.0559
1.6	.0548	.5037	.0526	.0516	.0505	.0495	.0485	.0475	.0465	.0455
1.7	.0446	.0436	.0427	.0418	.0409	.0401	.0392	.0384	.0375	.0367
1.8	.0359	.0352	.0344	.0336	.0329	.0322	.0314	.0307	.0301	.0294
1.9	.0287	.0281	.0274	.0268	.0262	.0256	.0250	.0244	.0239	.0233
2.0	.0228	.0222	.0217	.0212	.0207	.0202	.0197	.0192	.0188	.0183
2.1	.0179	.0174	.0170	.0166	.0162	.0158	.0154	.0150	.0146	.0143
2.2	.0139	.0136	.0132	.0129	.0125	.0122	.0119	.0116	.0113	.0110
2.3	.0107	.0104	.0102	.0099	.0096	.0094	.0091	.0089	.0087	.0084
2.4	.0082	.0080	.0078	.0075	.0073	.0071	.0069	.0068	.0066	.0064
2.5	.0062	.0060	.0059	.0057	.0055	.0054	.0052	.0051	.0049	.0048
2.6	.0047	.0045	.0044	.0043	.0041	.0040	.0039	.0038	.0037	.0036
2.7	.0035	.0034	.0033	.0032	.0031	.0030	.0029	.0028	.0027	.0026
2.8	.0026	.0025	.0023	.0023	.0023	.0022	.0021	.0021	.0020	.0019
2.9	.0019	.0018	.0017	.0017	.0016	.0016	.0015	.0015	.0014	.0014
3.0	.00135									
3.5	.000 233									
4.0	.000 031 7									
4.5	.000 003 40									
5.0	.000 000 287									

A-2 χ^2 Critical Points

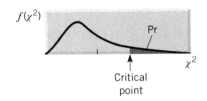

df \ Pr	.250	.100	.050	.025	.010	.005	.001
1	1.32	2.71	3.84	5.02	6.63	7.88	10.8
2	2.77	4.61	5.99	7.38	9.21	10.6	13.8
3	4.11	6.25	7.81	9.35	11.3	12.8	16.3
4	5.39	7.78	9.49	11.1	13.3	14.9	18.5

A-2 (continued)

df	Pr	.250	.100	.050	.025	.010	.005	.001
5		6.63	9.24	11.1	12.8	15.1	16.7	20.5
6		7.84	10.6	12.6	14.4	16.8	18.5	22.5
7		9.04	12.0	14.1	16.0	18.5	20.3	24.3
8		10.2	13.4	15.5	17.5	20.1	22.0	26.1
9		11.4	14.7	16.9	19.0	21.7	23.6	27.9
10		12.5	16.0	18.8	20.5	23.2	25.2	29.6
11		13.7	17.3	19.7	21.9	24.7	26.8	31.3
12		14.8	18.5	21.0	23.3	26.2	28.3	32.9
13		16.0	19.8	22.4	24.7	27.7	29.8	34.5
14		17.1	21.1	23.7	26.1	29.1	31.3	36.1
15		18.2	22.3	25.0	27.5	30.6	32.8	37.7
16		19.4	23.5	26.3	28.8	32.0	34.3	39.3
17		20.5	24.8	27.6	30.2	33.4	35.7	40.8
18		21.6	26.0	28.9	31.5	34.8	37.2	42.3
19		22.7	27.2	30.1	32.9	36.2	38.6	43.8
20		23.8	28.4	31.4	34.2	37.6	40.0	45.3
21		24.9	29.6	32.7	35.5	38.9	41.4	46.8
22		26.0	30.8	33.9	36.8	40.3	42.8	48.3
23		27.1	32.0	35.2	38.1	41.6	44.2	49.7
24		28.2	33.2	36.4	39.4	42.0	45.6	51.2
25		29.3	34.4	37.7	40.6	44.3	46.9	52.6
26		30.4	35.6	38.9	41.9	45.6	48.3	54.1
27		31.5	36.7	40.1	43.2	47.0	49.6	55.5
28		32.6	37.9	41.3	44.5	48.3	51.0	56.9
29		33.7	39.1	42.6	45.7	49.6	52.3	58.3
30		34.8	40.3	43.8	47.0	50.9	53.7	59.7
40		45.6	51.8	55.8	59.3	63.7	66.8	73.4
50		56.3	63.2	67.5	71.4	76.2	79.5	86.7
60		67.0	74.4	79.1	83.3	88.4	92.0	99.6
70		77.6	85.5	90.5	95.0	100	104	112
80		88.1	96.6	102	107	112	116	125
90		98.6	108	113	118	124	128	137
100		109	118	124	130	136	140	149

A-3   F Critical Points

$f(F)$

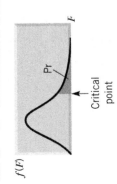

	Pr	df$_1$ = 1	2	3	4	5	6	7	8	9	10	12	15	20	24	30	40	60	∞
df$_2$ = 1	0.100	39.86	49.50	53.59	55.83	57.24	58.20	58.91	59.44	59.86	60.19	60.71	61.22	61.74	62.00	62.26	62.53	62.79	63.33
	0.050	161.45	199.50	215.71	224.58	230.16	233.99	236.77	238.88	240.54	241.88	243.91	245.95	248.01	249.05	250.10	251.14	252.20	254.31
	0.025	647.79	799.50	864.16	899.58	921.85	937.11	948.22	956.66	963.28	968.63	976.71	984.87	993.10	997.25	1001.41	1005.60	1009.80	1018.26
	0.010	4052.18	4999.50	5403.35	5624.58	5763.65	5858.99	5928.36	5981.07	6022.47	6055.85	6106.32	6157.29	6208.73	6234.63	6260.65	6286.78	6313.03	6365.86
2	0.100	8.53	9.00	9.16	9.24	9.29	9.33	9.35	9.37	9.38	9.39	9.41	9.42	9.44	9.45	9.46	9.47	9.47	9.49
	0.050	18.51	19.00	19.16	19.25	19.30	19.33	19.35	19.37	19.38	19.40	19.41	19.43	19.45	19.45	19.46	19.47	19.48	19.50
	0.025	38.51	39.00	39.17	39.25	39.30	39.33	39.36	39.37	39.39	39.40	39.41	39.43	39.45	39.46	39.47	39.47	39.48	39.50
	0.010	98.50	99.00	99.17	99.25	99.30	99.33	99.36	99.37	99.39	99.40	99.42	99.43	99.45	99.46	99.47	99.47	99.48	99.50
3	0.100	5.54	5.46	5.39	5.34	5.31	5.28	5.27	5.25	5.24	5.23	5.22	5.20	5.18	5.18	5.17	5.16	5.15	5.13
	0.050	10.13	9.55	9.28	9.12	9.01	8.94	8.89	8.85	8.81	8.79	8.74	8.70	8.66	8.64	8.62	8.59	8.57	8.53
	0.025	17.44	16.04	15.44	15.10	14.88	14.73	14.62	14.54	14.47	14.42	14.34	14.25	14.17	14.12	14.08	14.04	13.99	13.90
	0.010	34.12	30.82	29.46	28.71	28.24	27.91	27.67	27.49	27.35	27.23	27.05	26.87	26.69	26.60	26.51	26.41	26.32	26.13
4	0.100	4.54	4.32	4.19	4.11	4.05	4.01	3.98	3.95	3.94	3.92	3.90	3.87	3.84	3.83	3.82	3.80	3.79	3.76
	0.050	7.71	6.94	6.59	6.39	6.26	6.16	6.09	6.04	6.00	5.96	5.91	5.86	5.80	5.77	5.75	5.72	5.69	5.63
	0.025	12.22	10.65	9.98	9.60	9.36	9.20	9.07	8.98	8.90	8.84	8.75	8.66	8.56	8.51	8.46	8.41	8.36	8.26
	0.010	21.20	18.00	16.69	15.98	15.52	15.21	14.98	14.80	14.66	14.55	14.37	14.20	14.02	13.93	13.84	13.75	13.65	13.46
5	0.100	4.06	3.78	3.62	3.52	3.45	3.40	3.37	3.34	3.32	3.30	3.27	3.24	3.21	3.19	3.17	3.16	3.14	3.11
	0.050	6.61	5.79	5.41	5.19	5.05	4.95	4.88	4.82	4.77	4.74	4.68	4.62	4.56	4.53	4.50	4.46	4.43	4.37
	0.025	10.01	8.43	7.76	7.39	7.15	6.98	6.85	6.76	6.68	6.62	6.52	6.43	6.33	6.28	6.23	6.18	6.12	6.02
	0.010	16.26	13.27	12.06	11.39	10.97	10.67	10.46	10.29	10.16	10.05	9.89	9.72	9.55	9.47	9.38	9.29	9.20	9.02
6	0.100	3.78	3.46	3.29	3.18	3.11	3.05	3.01	2.98	2.96	2.94	2.90	2.87	2.84	2.82	2.80	2.78	2.76	2.72
	0.050	5.99	5.14	4.76	4.53	4.39	4.28	4.21	4.15	4.10	4.06	4.00	3.94	3.87	3.84	3.81	3.77	3.74	3.67

	Pr	$df_1 = 1$	2	3	4	5	6	7	8	9	10	12	15	20	24	30	40	60	∞
	0.025	8.81	7.26	6.60	6.23	5.99	5.82	5.70	5.60	5.52	5.46	5.37	5.27	5.17	5.12	5.07	5.01	4.96	4.85
	0.010	13.75	10.93	9.78	9.15	8.75	8.47	8.26	8.10	7.98	7.87	7.72	7.56	7.40	7.31	7.23	7.14	7.06	6.88
7	0.100	3.59	3.26	3.07	2.96	2.88	2.83	2.78	2.75	2.72	2.70	2.67	2.63	2.59	2.58	2.56	2.54	2.51	2.47
	0.050	5.59	4.74	4.35	4.12	3.97	3.87	3.79	3.73	3.68	3.64	3.57	3.51	3.44	3.41	3.38	3.34	3.30	3.23
	0.025	8.07	6.54	5.89	5.52	5.29	5.12	4.99	4.90	4.82	4.76	4.67	4.57	4.47	4.42	4.36	4.31	4.25	4.14
	0.010	12.25	9.55	8.45	7.85	7.46	7.19	6.99	6.84	6.72	6.62	6.47	6.31	6.16	6.07	5.99	5.91	5.82	5.65
8	0.100	3.46	3.11	2.92	2.81	2.73	2.67	2.62	2.59	2.56	2.54	2.50	2.46	2.42	2.40	2.38	2.36	2.34	2.29
	0.050	5.32	4.46	4.07	3.84	3.69	3.58	3.50	3.44	3.39	3.35	3.28	3.22	3.15	3.12	3.08	3.04	3.01	2.93
	0.025	7.57	6.06	5.42	5.05	4.82	4.65	4.53	4.43	4.36	4.30	4.20	4.10	4.00	3.95	3.89	3.84	3.78	3.67
	0.010	11.26	8.65	7.59	7.01	6.63	6.37	6.18	6.03	5.91	5.81	5.67	5.52	5.36	5.28	5.20	5.12	5.03	4.86
9	0.100	3.36	3.01	2.81	2.69	2.61	2.55	2.51	2.47	2.44	2.42	2.38	2.34	2.30	2.28	2.25	2.23	2.21	2.16
	0.050	5.12	4.26	3.86	3.63	3.48	3.37	3.29	3.23	3.18	3.14	3.07	3.01	2.94	2.90	2.86	2.83	2.79	2.71
	0.025	7.21	5.71	5.08	4.72	4.48	4.32	4.20	4.10	4.03	3.96	3.87	3.77	3.67	3.61	3.56	3.51	3.45	3.33
	0.010	10.56	8.02	6.99	6.42	6.06	5.80	5.61	5.47	5.35	5.26	5.11	4.96	4.81	4.73	4.65	4.57	4.48	4.31
10	0.100	3.29	2.92	2.73	2.61	2.52	2.46	2.41	2.38	2.35	2.32	2.28	2.24	2.20	2.18	2.16	2.13	2.11	2.06
	0.050	4.96	4.10	3.71	3.48	3.33	3.22	3.14	3.07	3.02	2.98	2.91	2.85	2.77	2.74	2.70	2.66	2.62	2.54
	0.025	6.94	5.46	4.83	4.47	4.24	4.07	3.95	3.85	3.78	3.72	3.62	3.52	3.42	3.37	3.31	3.26	3.20	3.08
	0.010	10.04	7.56	6.55	5.99	5.64	5.39	5.20	5.06	4.94	4.85	4.71	4.56	4.41	4.33	4.25	4.17	4.08	3.91
11	0.100	3.23	2.86	2.66	2.54	2.45	2.39	2.34	2.30	2.27	2.25	2.21	2.17	2.12	2.10	2.08	2.05	2.03	1.97
	0.050	4.84	3.98	3.59	3.36	3.20	3.09	3.01	2.95	2.90	2.85	2.79	2.72	2.65	2.61	2.57	2.53	2.49	2.40
	0.025	6.72	5.26	4.63	4.28	4.04	3.88	3.76	3.66	3.59	3.53	3.43	3.33	3.23	3.17	3.12	3.06	3.00	2.88
	0.010	9.65	7.21	6.22	5.67	5.32	5.07	4.89	4.74	4.63	4.54	4.40	4.25	4.10	4.02	3.94	3.86	3.78	3.60
12	0.100	3.18	2.81	2.61	2.48	2.39	2.33	2.28	2.24	2.21	2.19	2.15	2.10	2.06	2.04	2.01	1.99	1.96	1.90
	0.050	4.75	3.89	3.49	3.26	3.11	3.00	2.91	2.85	2.80	2.75	2.69	2.62	2.54	2.51	2.47	2.43	2.38	2.30
	0.025	6.55	5.10	4.47	4.12	3.89	3.73	3.61	3.51	3.44	3.37	3.28	3.18	3.07	3.02	2.96	2.91	2.85	2.73
	0.010	9.33	6.93	5.95	5.41	5.06	4.82	4.64	4.50	4.39	4.30	4.16	4.01	3.86	3.78	3.70	3.62	3.54	3.36
13	0.100	3.14	2.76	2.56	2.43	2.35	2.28	2.23	2.20	2.16	2.14	2.10	2.05	2.01	1.98	1.96	1.93	1.90	1.85
	0.050	4.67	3.81	3.41	3.18	3.03	2.92	2.83	2.77	2.71	2.67	2.60	2.53	2.46	2.42	2.38	2.34	2.30	2.21

	Pr	df₁ = 1	2	3	4	5	6	7	8	9	10	12	15	20	24	30	40	60	∞
	0.025	6.41	4.97	4.35	4.00	3.77	3.60	3.48	3.39	3.31	3.25	3.15	3.05	2.95	2.89	2.84	2.78	2.72	2.60
	0.010	9.07	6.70	5.74	5.21	4.86	4.62	4.44	4.30	4.19	4.10	3.96	3.82	3.67	3.59	3.51	3.43	3.34	3.17
14	0.100	3.10	2.73	2.52	2.39	2.31	2.24	2.19	2.15	2.12	2.10	2.05	2.01	1.96	1.94	1.91	1.89	1.86	1.80
	0.050	4.60	3.74	3.34	3.11	2.96	2.85	2.76	2.70	2.65	2.60	2.53	2.46	2.39	2.35	2.31	2.27	2.22	2.13
	0.025	6.30	4.86	4.24	3.89	3.66	3.50	3.38	3.29	3.21	3.15	3.05	2.95	2.84	2.79	2.73	2.67	2.61	2.49
	0.010	8.86	6.52	5.56	5.04	4.70	4.46	4.28	4.14	4.03	3.94	3.80	3.66	3.51	3.43	3.35	3.27	3.18	3.00
15	0.100	3.07	2.70	2.49	2.36	2.27	2.21	2.16	2.12	2.09	2.06	2.02	1.97	1.92	1.90	1.87	1.85	1.82	1.76
	0.050	4.54	3.68	3.29	3.06	2.90	2.79	2.71	2.64	2.59	2.54	2.48	2.40	2.33	2.29	2.25	2.20	2.16	2.07
	0.025	6.20	4.77	4.15	3.80	3.58	3.41	3.29	3.20	3.12	3.06	2.96	2.86	2.76	2.70	2.64	2.59	2.52	2.40
	0.010	8.68	6.36	5.42	4.89	4.56	4.32	4.14	4.00	3.90	3.81	3.67	3.52	3.37	3.29	3.21	3.13	3.05	2.87
16	0.100	3.05	2.67	2.46	2.33	2.24	2.18	2.13	2.09	2.06	2.03	1.99	1.94	1.89	1.87	1.84	1.81	1.78	1.72
	0.050	4.49	3.63	3.24	3.01	2.85	2.74	2.66	2.59	2.54	2.49	2.42	2.35	2.28	2.24	2.19	2.15	2.11	2.01
	0.025	6.12	4.69	4.08	3.73	3.50	3.34	3.22	3.12	3.05	2.99	2.89	2.79	2.68	2.63	2.57	2.51	2.45	2.32
	0.010	8.53	6.23	5.29	4.77	4.44	4.20	4.03	3.89	3.78	3.69	3.55	3.41	3.26	3.18	3.10	3.02	2.93	2.75
17	0.100	3.03	2.64	2.44	2.31	2.22	2.15	2.10	2.06	2.03	2.00	1.96	1.91	1.86	1.84	1.81	1.78	1.75	1.69
	0.050	4.45	3.59	3.20	2.96	2.81	2.70	2.61	2.55	2.49	2.45	2.38	2.31	2.23	2.19	2.15	2.10	2.06	1.96
	0.025	6.04	4.62	4.01	3.66	3.44	3.28	3.16	3.06	2.98	2.92	2.82	2.72	2.62	2.56	2.50	2.44	2.38	2.25
	0.010	8.40	6.11	5.19	4.67	4.34	4.10	3.93	3.79	3.68	3.59	3.46	3.31	3.16	3.08	3.00	2.92	2.84	2.65
18	0.100	3.01	2.62	2.42	2.29	2.20	2.13	2.08	2.04	2.00	1.98	1.93	1.89	1.84	1.81	1.78	1.75	1.72	1.66
	0.050	4.41	3.55	3.16	2.93	2.77	2.66	2.58	2.51	2.46	2.41	2.34	2.27	2.19	2.15	2.11	2.06	2.02	1.92
	0.025	5.98	4.56	3.95	3.61	3.38	3.22	3.10	3.01	2.93	2.87	2.77	2.67	2.56	2.50	2.45	2.38	2.32	2.19
	0.010	8.29	6.01	5.09	4.58	4.25	4.02	3.84	3.71	3.60	3.51	3.37	3.23	3.08	3.00	2.92	2.84	2.75	2.57
19	0.100	2.99	2.61	2.40	2.27	2.18	2.11	2.06	2.02	1.98	1.96	1.91	1.86	1.81	1.79	1.76	1.73	1.70	1.63
	0.050	4.38	3.52	3.13	2.90	2.74	2.63	2.54	2.48	2.42	2.38	2.31	2.23	2.16	2.11	2.07	2.03	1.98	1.88
	0.025	5.92	4.51	3.90	3.56	3.33	3.17	3.05	2.96	2.88	2.82	2.72	2.62	2.51	2.45	2.39	2.33	2.27	2.13
	0.010	8.19	5.93	5.01	4.50	4.17	3.94	3.77	3.63	3.52	3.43	3.30	3.15	3.00	2.93	2.84	2.76	2.67	2.49
20	0.100	2.97	2.59	2.38	2.25	2.16	2.09	2.04	2.00	1.96	1.94	1.89	1.84	1.79	1.77	1.74	1.71	1.68	1.61
	0.050	4.35	3.49	3.10	2.87	2.71	2.60	2.51	2.45	2.39	2.35	2.28	2.20	2.12	2.08	2.04	1.99	1.95	1.84
	0.025	5.87	4.46	3.86	3.51	3.29	3.13	3.01	2.91	2.84	2.77	2.68	2.57	2.46	2.41	2.35	2.29	2.22	2.09

	Pr	df₁ = 1	2	3	4	5	6	7	8	9	10	12	15	20	24	30	40	60	∞
	0.010	8.10	5.85	4.94	4.43	4.10	3.87	3.70	3.56	3.46	3.37	3.23	3.09	2.94	2.86	2.78	2.70	2.61	2.42
21	0.100	2.96	2.57	2.36	2.23	2.14	2.08	2.02	1.98	1.95	1.92	1.87	1.83	1.78	1.75	1.72	1.69	1.66	1.59
	0.050	4.32	3.47	3.07	2.84	2.68	2.57	2.49	2.42	2.37	2.32	2.25	2.18	2.10	2.05	2.01	1.96	1.92	1.81
	0.025	5.83	4.42	3.82	3.48	3.25	3.09	2.97	2.87	2.80	2.73	2.64	2.53	2.42	2.37	2.31	2.25	2.18	2.04
	0.010	8.02	5.78	4.87	4.37	4.04	3.81	3.64	3.51	3.40	3.31	3.17	3.03	2.88	2.80	2.72	2.64	2.55	2.36
22	0.100	2.95	2.56	2.35	2.22	2.13	2.06	2.01	1.97	1.93	1.90	1.86	1.81	1.76	1.73	1.70	1.67	1.64	1.57
	0.050	4.30	3.44	3.05	2.82	2.66	2.55	2.46	2.40	2.34	2.30	2.23	2.15	2.07	2.03	1.98	1.94	1.89	1.78
	0.025	5.79	4.38	3.78	3.44	3.22	3.05	2.93	2.84	2.76	2.70	2.60	2.50	2.39	2.33	2.27	2.21	2.15	2.00
	0.010	7.95	5.72	4.82	4.31	3.99	3.76	3.59	3.45	3.35	3.26	3.12	2.98	2.83	2.75	2.67	2.58	2.50	2.31
23	0.100	2.94	2.55	2.34	2.21	2.11	2.05	1.99	1.95	1.92	1.89	1.84	1.80	1.74	1.72	1.69	1.66	1.62	1.55
	0.050	4.28	3.42	3.03	2.80	2.64	2.53	2.44	2.37	2.32	2.27	2.20	2.13	2.05	2.01	1.96	1.91	1.86	1.76
	0.025	5.75	4.35	3.75	3.41	3.18	3.02	2.90	2.81	2.73	2.67	2.57	2.47	2.36	2.30	2.24	2.18	2.11	1.97
	0.010	7.88	5.66	4.77	4.26	3.94	3.71	3.54	3.41	3.30	3.21	3.07	2.93	2.78	2.70	2.62	2.54	2.45	2.26
24	0.100	2.93	2.54	2.33	2.19	2.10	2.04	1.98	1.94	1.91	1.88	1.83	1.78	1.73	1.70	1.67	1.64	1.61	1.53
	0.050	4.26	3.40	3.01	2.78	2.62	2.51	2.42	2.36	2.30	2.25	2.18	2.11	2.03	1.98	1.94	1.89	1.84	1.73
	0.025	5.72	4.32	3.72	3.38	3.15	2.99	2.87	2.78	2.70	2.64	2.54	2.44	2.33	2.27	2.21	2.15	2.08	1.94
	0.010	7.82	5.61	4.72	4.22	3.90	3.67	3.50	3.36	3.26	3.17	3.03	2.89	2.74	2.66	2.58	2.49	2.40	2.21
25	0.100	2.92	2.53	2.32	2.18	2.09	2.02	1.97	1.93	1.89	1.87	1.82	1.77	1.72	1.69	1.66	1.63	1.59	1.52
	0.050	4.24	3.39	2.99	2.76	2.60	2.49	2.40	2.34	2.28	2.24	2.16	2.09	2.01	1.96	1.92	1.87	1.82	1.71
	0.025	5.69	4.29	3.69	3.35	3.13	2.97	2.85	2.75	2.68	2.61	2.51	2.41	2.30	2.24	2.18	2.12	2.05	1.91
	0.010	7.77	5.57	4.68	4.18	3.86	3.63	3.46	3.32	3.22	3.13	2.99	2.85	2.70	2.62	2.54	2.45	2.36	2.17
26	0.100	2.91	2.52	2.31	2.17	2.08	2.01	1.96	1.92	1.88	1.86	1.81	1.76	1.71	1.68	1.65	1.61	1.58	1.50
	0.050	4.23	3.37	2.98	2.74	2.59	2.47	2.39	2.32	2.27	2.22	2.15	2.07	1.99	1.95	1.90	1.85	1.80	1.69
	0.025	5.66	4.27	3.67	3.33	3.10	2.94	2.82	2.73	2.65	2.59	2.49	2.39	2.28	2.22	2.16	2.09	2.03	1.88
	0.010	7.72	5.53	4.64	4.14	3.82	3.59	3.42	3.29	3.18	3.09	2.96	2.82	2.66	2.59	2.50	2.42	2.33	2.13
27	0.100	2.90	2.51	2.30	2.17	2.07	2.00	1.95	1.91	1.87	1.85	1.80	1.75	1.70	1.67	1.64	1.60	1.57	1.49
	0.050	4.21	3.35	2.96	2.73	2.57	2.46	2.37	2.31	2.25	2.20	2.13	2.06	1.97	1.93	1.88	1.84	1.79	1.67
	0.025	5.63	4.24	3.65	3.31	3.08	2.92	2.80	2.71	2.63	2.57	2.47	2.36	2.25	2.19	2.13	2.07	2.00	1.85
	0.010	7.68	5.49	4.60	4.11	3.79	3.56	3.39	3.26	3.15	3.06	2.93	2.78	2.63	2.55	2.47	2.38	2.29	2.10

	Pr	df₁ = 1	2	3	4	5	6	7	8	9	10	12	15	20	24	30	40	60	∞
28	0.100	2.89	2.50	2.29	2.16	2.06	2.00	1.94	1.90	1.87	1.84	1.79	1.74	1.69	1.66	1.63	1.59	1.56	1.48
	0.050	4.20	3.34	2.95	2.71	2.56	2.45	2.36	2.29	2.24	2.19	2.12	2.04	1.96	1.91	1.87	1.82	1.77	1.65
	0.025	5.61	4.22	3.63	3.29	3.06	2.90	2.78	2.69	2.61	2.55	2.45	2.34	2.23	2.17	2.11	2.05	1.98	1.83
	0.010	7.64	5.45	4.57	4.07	3.75	3.53	3.36	3.23	3.12	3.03	2.90	2.75	2.60	2.52	2.44	2.35	2.26	2.06
29	0.100	2.89	2.50	2.28	2.15	2.06	1.99	1.93	1.89	1.86	1.83	1.78	1.73	1.68	1.65	1.62	1.58	1.55	1.47
	0.050	4.18	3.33	2.93	2.70	2.55	2.43	2.35	2.28	2.22	2.18	2.10	2.03	1.94	1.90	1.85	1.81	1.75	1.64
	0.025	5.59	4.20	3.61	3.27	3.04	2.88	2.76	2.67	2.59	2.53	2.43	2.32	2.21	2.15	2.09	2.03	1.96	1.81
	0.010	7.60	5.42	4.54	4.05	3.73	3.50	3.33	3.20	3.09	3.01	2.87	2.73	2.57	2.50	2.41	2.33	2.23	2.03
30	0.100	2.88	2.49	2.28	2.14	2.05	1.98	1.93	1.88	1.85	1.82	1.77	1.72	1.67	1.64	1.61	1.57	1.54	1.46
	0.050	4.17	3.32	2.92	2.69	2.53	2.42	2.33	2.27	2.21	2.16	2.09	2.01	1.93	1.89	1.84	1.79	1.74	1.62
	0.025	5.57	4.18	3.59	3.25	3.03	2.87	2.75	2.65	2.57	2.51	2.41	2.31	2.20	2.14	2.07	2.01	1.94	1.79
	0.010	7.56	5.39	4.51	4.02	3.70	3.47	3.30	3.17	3.07	2.98	2.84	2.70	2.55	2.47	2.39	2.30	2.21	2.01
40	0.100	2.84	2.44	2.23	2.09	2.00	1.93	1.87	1.83	1.79	1.76	1.71	1.66	1.61	1.57	1.54	1.51	1.47	1.38
	0.050	4.08	3.23	2.84	2.61	2.45	2.34	2.25	2.18	2.12	2.08	2.00	1.92	1.84	1.79	1.74	1.69	1.64	1.51
	0.025	5.42	4.05	3.46	3.13	2.90	2.74	2.62	2.53	2.45	2.39	2.29	2.18	2.07	2.01	1.94	1.88	1.80	1.64
	0.010	7.31	5.18	4.31	3.83	3.51	3.29	3.12	2.99	2.89	2.80	2.67	2.52	2.37	2.29	2.20	2.11	2.02	1.81
60	0.100	2.79	2.39	2.18	2.04	1.95	1.87	1.82	1.77	1.74	1.71	1.66	1.60	1.54	1.51	1.48	1.44	1.40	1.29
	0.050	4.00	3.15	2.76	2.53	2.37	2.25	2.17	2.10	2.04	1.99	1.92	1.84	1.75	1.70	1.65	1.59	1.53	1.39
	0.025	5.29	3.93	3.34	3.01	2.79	2.63	2.51	2.41	2.33	2.27	2.17	2.06	1.94	1.88	1.82	1.74	1.67	1.48
	0.010	7.08	4.98	4.13	3.65	3.34	3.12	2.95	2.82	2.72	2.63	2.50	2.35	2.20	2.12	2.03	1.94	1.84	1.60
120	0.100	2.75	2.35	2.13	1.99	1.90	1.82	1.77	1.72	1.68	1.65	1.60	1.55	1.48	1.45	1.41	1.37	1.32	1.19
	0.050	3.92	3.07	2.68	2.45	2.29	2.18	2.09	2.02	1.96	1.91	1.83	1.75	1.66	1.61	1.55	1.50	1.43	1.25
	0.025	5.15	3.80	3.23	2.89	2.67	2.52	2.39	2.30	2.22	2.16	2.05	1.95	1.82	1.76	1.69	1.61	1.53	1.31
	0.010	6.85	4.79	3.95	3.48	3.17	2.96	2.79	2.66	2.56	2.47	2.34	2.19	2.03	1.95	1.86	1.76	1.66	1.38
∞	0.100	2.71	2.30	2.08	1.94	1.85	1.77	1.72	1.67	1.63	1.60	1.55	1.49	1.42	1.38	1.34	1.30	1.24	1.00
	0.050	3.84	3.00	2.60	2.37	2.21	2.10	2.01	1.94	1.88	1.83	1.75	1.67	1.57	1.52	1.46	1.39	1.32	1.00
	0.025	5.02	3.69	3.12	2.79	2.57	2.41	2.29	2.19	2.11	2.05	1.94	1.83	1.71	1.64	1.57	1.48	1.39	1.00
	0.010	6.64	4.61	3.78	3.32	3.02	2.80	2.64	2.51	2.41	2.32	2.19	2.04	1.88	1.79	1.70	1.59	1.47	1.00

A-4   Cut-Off Points for the Student's *t*-Distribution

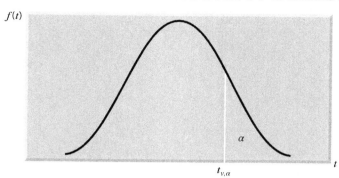

		α		
df(v)	.100	.050	.025	.010	.005
---	---	---	---	---	---
1	3.078	6.314	12.706	31.821	63.657
2	1.886	2.920	4.303	6.965	9.925
3	1.638	2.353	3.182	4.541	5.841
4	1.533	2.132	2.776	3.747	4.604
5	1.476	2.015	2.571	3.365	4.032
6	1.440	1.943	2.447	3.143	3.707
7	1.415	1.895	2.365	2.998	3.499
8	1.397	1.860	2.306	2.896	3.355
9	1.383	1.833	2.262	2.821	3.250
10	1.372	1.812	2.228	2.764	3.169
11	1.363	1.796	2.201	2.718	3.106
12	1.356	1.782	2.179	2.681	3.055
13	1.350	1.771	2.160	2.650	3.012
14	1.345	1.761	2.145	2.624	2.977
15	1.341	1.753	2.131	2.602	2.947
16	1.337	1.746	2.120	2.583	2.921
17	1.333	1.740	2.110	2.567	2.898
18	1.330	1.734	2.101	2.552	2.878
19	1.328	1.729	2.093	2.539	2.861
20	1.325	1.725	2.086	2.528	2.845
21	1.323	1.721	2.080	2.518	2.831
22	1.321	1.717	2.074	2.508	2.819
23	1.319	1.714	2.069	2.500	2.807
24	1.318	1.711	2.064	2.492	2.797
25	1.316	1.708	2.060	2.485	2.787
26	1.315	1.706	2.056	2.479	2.779
27	1.314	1.703	2.052	2.473	2.771
28	1.313	1.701	2.048	2.467	2.763

			α		
df(v)	.100	.050	.025	.010	.005
29	1.311	1.699	2.045	2.462	2.756
30	1.310	1.697	2.042	2.457	2.750
40	1.303	1.684	2.021	2.423	2.704
60	1.296	1.671	2.000	2.390	2.660
∞	1.282	1.645	1.960	2.326	2.576

For selected probabilities, α, the table shows the values $t_{v,\alpha}$ such that $P(t_v > t_{v,\alpha}) = \alpha$, where t_v is a student's t random variable with v degrees of freedom. For example, the probability is .10 that a student's t random variable with 10 degrees of freedom exceeds 1.372.

A-5 Procedures for Conducting Univariate and Multivariate Analysis in SPSS

Univariate Analysis

Chi-Square Tests

Data must be arranged in a special format for performing chi-square tests in SPSS. For example, we want to perform a chi-square test of whether two variables A and B are related to each other. Suppose A has 4 levels and B has 2 levels. The table of data needs to be arranged in a linear form in SPSS. In other words, three columns are necessary for performing the analysis: one column each for A and B, and the frequency of observed cases (say, count) for each combination of A and B. Once the data have been organized in this particular way, follow these steps:

Step 1. First we have to weight all the variables by the frequency (count). In our case, each level combination of A and B has an observed number of cases. The first step is to weight each unique combination of A and B by the frequency (count): (1) Choose the *Data* option from the main menu. (2) Choose the *Weight Cases* option. (3) Assign the count variable as the frequency variable by which to weight the cases.

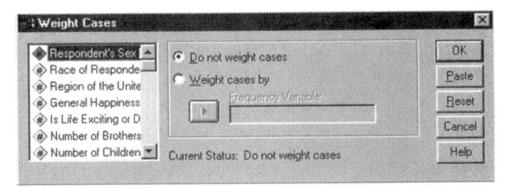

Step 2. Choose *Statistics* from the main menu. Then choose *Summarize->Crosstabs*. In the Crosstabs window, choose A and B as the row and column variables, respectively. Select the chi-square option in the statistics window.

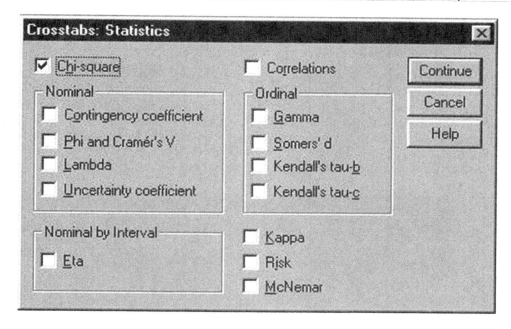

Hypothesis Tests

It is very simple to perform hypothesis tests in SPSS. Choose *Statistics* from the main menu, then choose the *Compare Means* option. Choose the appropriate hypothesis test you want to perform from this menu. Once the hypothesis test to be conducted is chosen, merely provide the variable that is being tested and the value under the null hypothesis.

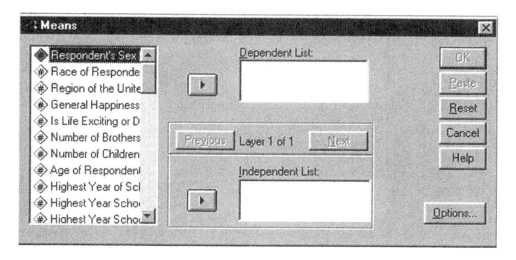

Multivariate Analysis

Multiple Regression

To perform multiple regression, arrange the dependent (y) and independent (x) variables in columns. From the *Statistics* option in the main menu, choose the *regression* option. Choose the linear estimation technique. The regression window will then ask you to specify the dependent and independent variables in the model you want to regress. If you want to include a constant in the model, click on the *Options* button in the regression window. Then check the *Include Constant in Equation* check box. The regression window also lets you decide on the procedure for doing multiple regression (i.e., stepwise, forward step, backward step, and enter or remove variables).

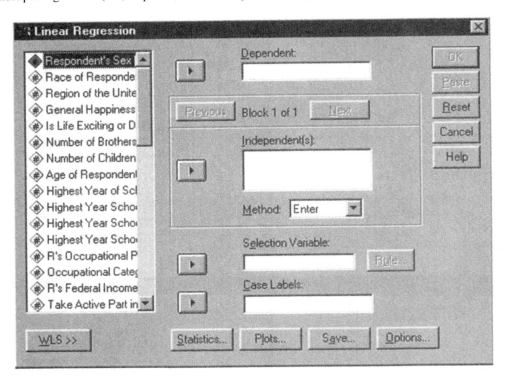

Factor Analysis

Factor analysis is performed by choosing *Statistics->DataReduction->Factor Analysis* from the main menu. In the factor analysis window, select the variables that you want to group in a cluster in the *Variables* window. The extraction button provides options for different techniques of factor extraction, such as principal component analysis. The type of rotation required for the factor analysis can be chosen from the rotation button.

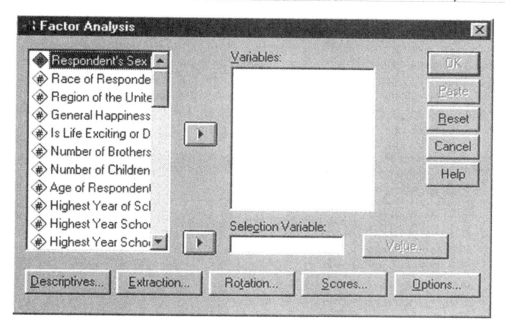

Cluster Analysis

Cluster analysis is performed by choosing *Statistics->Classify*. The appropriate clustering algorithm (hierarchical or nonhierarchical) is then chosen from the classify menu. In the cluster analysis window, select the variables that you want to cluster analyze in the *Variables* window. The other options in the cluster analysis window help you decide on the number of iterations, statistics, and plots required in the output and the cluster algorithm to be used.

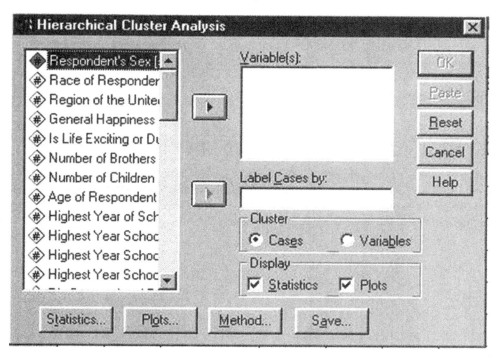

Discriminant Analysis

Discriminant analysis is performed by choosing *Statistics->Classify->Discriminant* from the menu. The discriminant analysis window provides slots for selecting the independent variables that compose the discriminant function and the variable that is predicted (grouping variable) based on the independent variables. The window also provides options for choosing the various statistics required in the output, the plots required, methods for choosing prior probabilities, and the structure of the variance–covariance matrix.

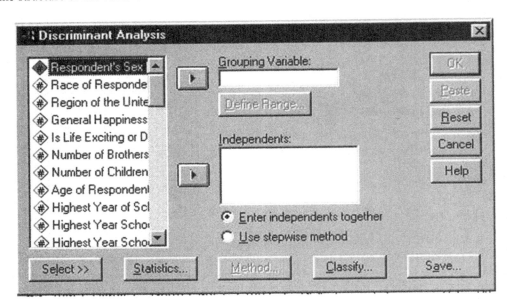

Multidimensional Scaling

Choose *Statistics->Scaling->Multidimensional* from the main menu. The multidimensional scaling window provides slots for selecting the variables that need to be scaled, the input type (variable attributes or distance matrix), and the algorithm to be used. There is also an option to plot the two-dimensional profile.

A-6   Output of Select Tables in SPSS

All of the analysis in this appendix has been performed with the entire export data set (all 120 observations), while the analysis in the book has been performed with only 60 randomly selected records from the export data set. The export data set along with the other data sets used in the book are available at the website www.imc-marketing.com/mr.

Table 19.5   Regression

Variables Entered/Removed[a]

Model	Variables entered	Variables removed	Method
1	SIZE[b]		Enter

[a]Dependent Variable: WILL.
[b]All requested variables entered.

Model Summary

Model	R	R square	Adjusted R square	Std. error of the estimate
1	.743[a]	.552	.548	.8651

[a]Predictors: (Constant), SIZE.

ANOVA[a]

Model		Sum of squares	df	Mean square	F	Sig.
1	Regression	108.683	1	108.683	145.226	.000[b]
	Residual	88.308	118	.748		
	Total	196.992	119			

[a]Dependent Variable: Will.
[b]Predictors: (Constant), SIZE.

Coefficients[a]

Model		Unstandardized coefficients		Standardized coefficients		
		B	Std. error	Beta	t	Sig.
1	(Constant)	−.900	.354		−2.542	.012
	SIZE	9.223E-02	.008	.743	12.051	.000

[a]Dependent Variable: Will.

Table 19.6 Regression

Variables Entered/Removed[a]

Model	Variables entered	Variables removed	Method
1	PRODUCTS, REV, YEARS, SIZE[b]		Enter

[a]Dependent Variable: WILL.
[b]All requested variables entered.

Model Summary

Model	R	R square	Adjusted R square	Std. error of the estimate
1	.850[a]	.723	.714	.6884

[a]Predictors: (Constant), PRODUCTS, REV, YEARS, SIZE.

ANOVA[a]

Model		Sum of squares	df	Mean square	F	Sig.
1	Regression	142.493	4	35.623	75.171	.000[b]
	Residual	54.498	115	.474		
	Total	196.992	119			

[a]Dependent Variable: WILL.
[b]Predictors: (Constant), PRODUCTS, REV, YEARS, SIZE.

Coefficients[a]

Model		Unstandardized coefficients		Standardized coefficients	t	Sig.
		B	Std. error	Beta		
1	(Constant)	1.792	.605		2.965	.004
	SIZE	6.394E-02	.007	.515	8.566	.000
	REV	.116	.069	.085	1.677	.096
	YEARS	−.395	.076	−.265	−5.167	.000
	PRODUCTS	.174	.031	.342	5.701	.000

[a]Dependent Variable: WILL.

Table 19.7   Regression

Variables Entered/Removed[a]

Model	Variables entered	Variables removed	Method
1	EXP, REV, TRAINING, YEARS, PRODUCTS, SIZE[b]		Enter

[a]Dependent Variable: WILL.
[b]All requested variables entered.

Model Summary

Model	R	R square	Adjusted R square	Std. error of the estimate
1	.851[a]	.724	.709	.6939

[a]Predictors: (Constant), EXP, REV, TRAINING, YEARS, PRODUCTS, SIZE.

ANOVA[a]

Model		Sum of squares	df	Mean square	F	Sig.
1	Regression	142.588	6	23.765	49.361	.000[b]
	Residual	54.404	113	.481		
	Total	196.992	119			

[a]Dependent Variable: WILL.
[b]Predictors: (Constant), EXP, REV, TRAINING, YEARS, PRODUCTS, SIZE.

Coefficients[a]

Model		Unstandardized coefficients		Standardized coefficients	t	Sig.
		B	Std. error	Beta		
1	(Constant)	1.993	.770		2.590	.011
	SIZE	6.191E-02	.009	.499	6.590	.000
	REV	.111	.071	.082	1.564	.121
	YEARS	−.418	.096	−.280	−4.337	.000
	PRODUCTS	.168	.034	.330	4.995	.000
	TRAINING	9.386E-02	.212	.034	.443	.658
	EXP	1.516E-02	.178	.005	.085	.932

[a]Dependent Variable: WILL.

Table 20.1 Discriminant

Analysis Case Processing Summary

Unweighted	Cases	N	Percent
Valid		120	100.0
Excluded	Missing or out-of-range group codes	0	.0
	At least one missing discriminating variable	0	.0
	Both missing or out-of-range group codes and at least one missing discriminating variable	0	.0
	Total	0	.0
Total		120	100.0

Group Statistics

EXPINT		Mean	Std. deviation	Valid N (listwise) Unweighted	Valid N (listwise) Weighted
1.00	Size	38.5167	7.8189	60	60.000
	REV	1.6150	.9282	60	60.000
	Years	6.7583	.9090	60	60.000
	Products	3.4500	1.4892	60	60.000
2.00	SIZE	51.6500	8.2294	60	60.000
	REV	1.7283	.9690	60	60.000
	YEARS	6.0400	.6463	60	60.000
	PRODUCTS	7.0667	1.9989	60	60.000
Total	SIZE	45.0833	10.3620	120	120.000
	REV	1.6717	.9466	120	120.000
	YEARS	6.3992	.8642	120	120.000
	PRODUCTS	5.2583	2.5255	120	120.000

Pooled Within-Groups Matrixes

		Size	REV	Years	Products
Correlation	SIZE	1.000	−.244	.103	.179
	REV	−.244	1.000	.248	−.038
	YEARS	.103	.248	1.000	.151
	PRODUCTS	.179	−.038	.151	1.000

Summary of Canonical Discriminant Functions

Eigenvalues[a]

Function	Eigenvalue	% of variance	Cumulative %	Canonical correlation
1	2.176[a]	100.0	100.0	.828

[a]First 1 canonical discriminant functions were used in the analysis.

Wilks' Lambda

Test of function(s)	Wilks' Lambda	Chi-square	df	Sig.
1	.315	134.041	4	.000

Standardized Canonical Discriminant Function Coefficients

	Function
	1
SIZE	.577
REV	.347
YEARS	−.562
PRODUCTS	.696

Structure Matrix

	Function
	1
PRODUCTS	.701
SIZE	.559
YEARS	−.311
REV	.041

Pooled within-groups correlations between discriminating
variables and standardized canonical discriminant functions.
Variables ordered by absolute size of correlation within function.

Functions at Group Centroids

	Function
EXPINT	1
1.00	−1.463
2.00	1.463

Unstandardized canonical discriminant
functions evaluated at group means.

Classification Statistics

Classification Processing Summary

Processed		120
excluded	Missing or out-of-range group codes	0
	At least one missing discriminating variable	0
Used in output		120

Prior Probabilities for Groups

		Cases used in analysis	
EXPINT	Prior	Unweighted	Weighted
1.00	.500	60	60.000
2.00	.500	60	60.000
Total	1.000	120	120.000

Classification Results[a]

			Predicted group membership		
		EXPINT	1.00	2.00	Total
Original	Count	1.00	58	2	60
		2.00	5	55	60
	%	1.00	96.7	3.3	100.0
		2.00	8.3	91.7	100.0

[a]94.2 percent of original grouped cases correctly classified.

Table 20.2 Discriminant

Analysis Case Processing Summary

Unweighted	Cases	N	Percent
Valid		120	100.0
excluded	Missing or out-of-range group codes	0	.0
	At least one missing discriminating variable	0	.0
	Both missing or out-of-range group codes and at least one missing discriminating variable	0	.0
	Total	0	.0
Total		120	100.0

Group Statistics

EXPINT		Mean	Std. deviation	Valid N (listwise) Unweighted	Valid N (listwise) Weighted
1.00	SIZE	34.3824	5.0693	34	34.000
	REV	1.7735	1.0148	34	34.000
	YEARS	6.6912	.0151	34	34.000
	PRODUCTS	3.5588	1.8780	34	34.000
2.00	SIZE	43.9231	7.5309	26	26.000
	REV	1.4077	.7715	26	26.000
	YEARS	6.8462	.7585	26	26.000
	PRODUCTS	7.3077	.7359	26	26.000
3.00	SIZE	51.6500	8.2294	60	60.000
	REV	1.7283	.9690	60	60.000
	YEARS	6.0400	.6463	60	60.000
	PRODUCTS	7.0667	1.9989	60	60.000
Total	SIZE	45.0833	10.3620	120	120.000
	REV	1.6717	.9466	120	120.000
	YEARS	6.3992	.8642	120	120.000
	PRODUCTS	5.2583	2.5255	120	120.000

Pooled Within-Groups Matrixes

		SIZE	REV	YEARS	PRODUCTS
Correlation	SIZE	1.000	−.208	.081	.221
	REV	−.208	1.000	.260	−.045
	YEARS	.081	.260	1.000	.155
	PRODUCTS	.221	−.045	.150	1.000

Summary of Canonical Discriminant Functions

Eigenvalues[a]

Function	Eigenvalue	% of variance	Cumulative %	Canonical correlation
1	2.240[a]	91.0	91.0	.831
2	.221[a]	9.0	100.0	.425

[a]First 2 canonical discriminant functions were used in the analysis.

Wilks' Lambda

Test of function(s)	Wilks' lambda	Chi-square	df	Sig.
1 through 2	.253	158.809	8	.000
2	.819	23.026	3	.000

Standardized Canonical Discriminant Function Coefficients

	Function	
	1	2
SIZE	.605	.816
REV	.325	−.253
YEARS	−.535	.348
PRODUCTS	.648	−.597

Structure Matrix

	Function	
	1	2
PRODUCTS	.684[a]	−.351
YEARS	−.301[a]	.256
SIZE	.638	.765[a]
REV	.030	−.305[a]

Pooled within-groups correlations between discriminating variables and standardized canonical discriminant functions. Variables ordered by absolute size of correlation within function.
[a]Largest absolute correlation between each variable and any discriminant function.

Functions at Group Centroids

EXPINT	Function	
	1	2
1.00	−1.671	−.519
2.00	−1.204	.797
3.00	1.469	−5.14 E-02

Unstandardized canonical discriminant functions evaluated at group means.

Classification Statistics

Classification Processing Summary		
Processed		120
excluded	Missing or out-of-range group codes	0
	At least one missing discriminating variable	0
Used in output		120

Prior Probabilities for Groups			
		Cases used in analysis	
EXPINT	Prior	Unweighted	Weighted
1.00	.283	34	34.000
2.00	.217	26	26.000
3.00	.500	60	60.000
Total	1.000	120	120.000

Classification Results[a]						
			Predicted group membership			
		EXPINT	1.00	2.00	3.00	Total
Original	Count	1.00	27	3	4	34
		2.00	6	20	0	26
		3.00	2	2	56	60
	%	1.00	79.4	8.8	11.8	100.0
		2.00	23.1	76.9	.0	100.0
		3.00	3.3	3.3	93.3	100.0

[a]85.8 percent of original grouped cases correctly classified.

Table 21.1a   Factor Analysis

Descriptive Statistics			
	Mean	Std. deviation	Analysis N
X1	4.400000	2.848559	15
X2	5.333333	2.919556	15
X3	5.133333	3.113718	15
X4	3.666667	2.794553	15
X5	4.400000	3.224903	15

Table 21.1a (continued)

Correlation Matrix

		X1	X2	X3	X4	X5
Correlation	X1	1.000	.610	.469	−.018	−.096
	X2	.610	1.000	.230	.190	.319
	X3	.469	.230	1.000	−.832	−.774
	X4	−.018	.190	−.832	1.000	.927
	X5	−.096	.319	−.774	.927	1.000

Communalities

	Initial	Extraction
X1	1.000	.815
X2	1.000	.849
X3	1.000	.956
X4	1.000	.954
X5	1.000	.956

Extraction method: Principal component analysis.

Total Variance Explained

	Initial eigenvalues			Extraction sums of squared load			Rotation sums of squared load		
Component	Total	% of variance	Cumulative %	Total	% of variance	Cumulative %	Total	% of variance	Cumulative %
1	2.755	55.092	55.092	2.755	55.092	55.092	2.736	54.711	54.711
2	1.775	35.497	90.589	1.775	35.497	90.589	1.794	35.878	90.589
3	.377	7.542	98.131						
4	96E-02	1.299	99.431						
5	47E-02	.569	100.000						

Extraction method: Principal component analysis.

Component Matrix[a]

	Component	
	1	2
X1	−.295	.853
X2	4.764E-02	.920
X3	−.938	.278
X4	.950	.228
X5	.940	.268

Extraction method: Principal component analysis.
[a]2 components extracted.

Table 21.1a (continued)

Rotated Component Matrix[a]

	Component	
	1	2
X1	−.173	.886
X2	.175	.904
X3	−.890	.405
X4	.972	9.340E-02
X5	.968	.134

Extraction method: Principal component analysis.
Rotation method: Varimax with Kaiser normalization.
[a]Rotation converged in three iterations.

Component Transformation Matrix

Component	1	2
1	.990	−.139
2	.139	.990

Extraction method: Principal component analysis.
Rotation method: Varimax with Kaiser normalization.

Component Score Coefficient Matrix

	Component	
	1	2
X1	−.039	.491
X2	.089	.511
X3	−.315	.202
X4	.359	.079
X5	.359	.102

Extraction method: Principal component analysis.
Rotation method: Varimax with Kaiser normalization.

Component Score Covariance Matrix

Component	1	2
1	1.000	.000
2	.000	1.000

Extraction method: Principal component analysis.
Rotation method: Varimax with Kaiser normalization.

Glossary

Accuracy a criterion used to judge whether a market research study is logical and presents correct information.

Administering Error error that occurs during the administration of a survey instrument to the respondent.

Advertising the nonpersonal communication of information, usually paid for and usually persuasive in nature about products, services, or ideas by identified sponsors through the various media.

Affective/Liking Component that part of attitude representing the person's overall feelings of liking or disliking the object, person, or event.

Aided Recall a questioning approach that attempts to stimulate a respondent's memory with clues about an object of interest.

Alternative Hypothesis the hypothesis that separates the effect which is opposite of the null hypothesis.

American Marketing Association the premier association of marketing practitioners and academicians in the United States, which publishes journals and organizes conferences for the dissemination of marketing knowledge.

Analysis of Dependence any multivariate analysis where one or more variables are predicted or explained by other variables.

Analysis of Interdependence any multivariate analysis where the interrelationships within a set of variables are examined and no variable is seen to be a dependent variable.

Analysis of Value an estimate of the benefits gained by undertaking a market research study.

Analysis of Variance (ANOVA) a method of testing a hypothesis regarding the difference between several means.

Artificiality the conditions that differ from the real world in experimental treatment so that projections become difficult and risky.

ASSESSOR a computer model for predicting market share of a new packaged good brand using laboratory test market data.

Associative Scaling a scale in which the respondent is asked to associate alternatives with each question.

Attitudes mental states used by individuals to structure the way they perceive their environment and to guide the way in which they respond. Apsychological construct comprised cognitive, affective, and intention components.

Attribute a characteristic or property of an object or person.

Average Linkage Method clustering approach that starts out the same as single linkage and complete linkage, but clustering criterion is the average distance from individuals in one cluster to individuals in another.

Averaging a memory error whereby something is reported as more like the usual, the expected, or the norm.

Bar Graph a graph of bars whose length indicates relative amounts of the variable.

Before Measure Effect the alerting of respondents to the fact that they are being studied, due to the presentation of a before measure, causing unnatural responses.

Behavior the past and present overt responses of subjects.

Behavior Recording Device a mechanical observation method, such as a traffic counter, that continuously monitors behavior, usually unobtrusively.

Benefit Structure Analysis has product users identify the benefits desired and the extent to which the product delivers those benefits, for specific applications.

Between-Treatment Variance defined as the variance in the response variable for different treatment levels.

Bibliographic/Reference Databases refer users to articles and news contained in other sources and provide online indices and abstracts.

Bipolar Scale a scale bounded at each end by polar adjectives that are antonyms.

Blind-Use Test a use test where consumers are asked to evaluate product alternatives without being aware of brand names.

Blocking a procedure by which a nonmanipulated variable is introduced into the experiment to ensure that the groups are equalized on that variable.

Bottom-Up Measurement a method of determining market potential that has as its starting point the identification of product use situations or applications.

Brand Equity the concept wherein the brand is considered an asset insofar as it can be sold or bought for a price. Apowerful brand is said to have high brand equity.

Brand Extension the use of a brand name to enter new product classes.

Call Report a form that has telephone numbers to be called and columns for interviewers to document their telephoning attempts.

CALLPLAN an interactive model designed to aid a salesperson in his or her call planning process. Its objective is to determine call-frequency norms for each client and prospect.

Case Study a comprehensive description and analysis of a single situation.

Causal Relationship a precondition influencing a variable of interest, or, more strictly, a change in one variable that produces a change in another variable.

Causal Research research having very specific hypotheses that is usually designed to provide the ultimate level of understanding—a knowledge that one construct under certain conditions causes another construct to occur or to change.

Census Data the demographic, economic, and social statistics of a population.

Census Tract a group of city blocks having a total population of more than 4000 and generally used to approximate neighborhoods.

Centroid the average value of the objects contained in the cluster on each of the variables making up each object's profile.

Chi-Square Statistic a measure of association between two nominally scaled variables.

City Block the smallest identifiable unit in the U.S. Census, being bounded by four streets or some other physical boundary.

Classification Matrix matrix containing numbers that reveal the predictive ability of the discriminant function.

Classification Variables used to classify respondents, such as demographic and socioeconomic measures.

Clinical Focus Groups focus groups where the moderator probes the subconscious of consumers. The moderator has to be proficient in sociology and psychology.

Closed-Response (or Structured) Question a question accompanied by the presentation of responses to be considered by the respondent.

Cluster Analysis a set of techniques for grouping objects or persons in terms of similarity.

Cluster Sampling a sampling method where a random sample of subgroups is selected and all members of the subgroups become part of the sample.

Clutter/Awareness the percentage who recalled a brand was advertised when exposed in a "clutter" of seven ads in a McCollum/Speilman test.

Coding the categorization and numbering of responses.

Cognitive/Knowledge Component that part of attitude representing the information a person knows about an object, person, or event.

Communality the proportion of a variable's variance explained by all of the factors in a factor analysis solution.

Comparative Scale a type of scale with some form of explicit or implicit comparison built into the scale.

Complementary Pricing the pricing strategy used by firms to price complementary products. They usually price the main product at a low price while the complement is charged at a higher price.

Complete Linkage linkage procedure similar to single linkage except that the clustering criterion is based on the longest distance.

Completely Randomized Design the simplest type of statistical design in which the experimental treatments are assigned to test units on a random basis.

Completion Test a projective technique in which the respondent is asked to complete a series of sentences.

Computer-Assisted Telephone Interviewing (CATI) telephone interviews conducted with the aid of computers, thus reducing interviewer error.

Computer Interactive Interviewing (CII) the respondent interacts directly with the computer.

Computer-Retrievable Databases secondary records accessible by a computer system.

Concept Test a test of a product concept where the concept is evaluated by a sample of the target segment.

Concurrent Validity criterion validity that is established by correlating the measurement score with the criterion variable, both measured at the same time.

Conjoint Analysis a method of obtaining the relative worth or value of each level of several attributes from rank-ordered preferences of attribute combinations.

Consensus/Face Validity is invoked when the argument is made that the measurement so self-evidently reflects or represents the various aspects of the phenomenon that there can be little quarrel with it.

Constant-Sum Scale a scale in which the respondent must allocate a fixed number of points among several objects to reflect the relative preference for each object.

Construct a concept, usually psychological such as attitudes and values, that is not directly observable.

Construct Equivalence deals with how the researcher and the subjects of the research see, understand, and code a particular phenomenon.

Construct Validity the ability of a measurement instrument to measure a concept or construct; construct validity is generally demonstrated by showing both convergent and discriminant validity.

Consumer-Direct a full service distribution channel that has its genesis in today's PeaPod and NetGrocer.

Content Analysis a technique used to study written material by breaking it into meaningful units, using carefully applied rules.

Contingency Coefficient a chi-square statistic corrected for sample size.

Continuous Panel Studies collect a series of measurements on the same sample of test units, over an extended period of time.

Continuous Purchase Panel a fixed sample of respondents who are measured on several occasions over a period of time.

Continuous Rating Scales respondents rate the objects by placing a mark at the appropriate position on a line that runs from one extreme of the criterion variable to the other.

Contrived Observation an observation method in which people are placed in a contrived situation so that their responses will reveal some aspects of their underlying beliefs, attitudes, and motives; examples are tests of variation in shelf space, product flavors, and display locations.

Control Group the group of subjects not exposed to the experimental treatment.

Controlled Distribution Scanner Markets (CDSM) distribution for new product test is prearranged and results are monitored with scanner data.

Convenience Sampling a sampling method in which convenient sampling units are contacted, such as church activity groups or student classes.

Convergent Validity the ability of a measurement instrument to correlate or "converge" with other supposed measures of the same variable or construct; the opposite of discriminant validity.

Copy Test Validity the ability to predict advertising response.

Correlation a number between +1 and −1 that reflects the degree to which two variables have a linear relationship.

Correspondence Analysis a technique for producing perceptual maps using binary data.

Cost–Benefit Analysis an analysis to determine the value of information sought from marketing research, by evaluating the cost required to collect the information and the benefit in dollar value provided by the information.

Criterion/Empirical Validity the validity of a measurement instrument as determined by empirical evidence that correlates the measurement instrument with other "criterion" variables.

Critical Path Method (CPM) a network approach that involves dividing the marketing research project into multiple components and estimating the time required to complete each component/activity.

Cross-Tabulation/Contingency Table Analysis the determination of a frequency distribution for subgroups.

Cross Validation/U-Method makes use of all the available data without serious bias in estimating error rates.

Customer Engagement Value is a measure of the level of engagement a customer shares with the firm, as evaluated using customer lifetime value, customer referral value, customer influence value, and customer knowledge value.

Customer Influence Value is a measure of the monetized intrinsic value of each customer's influence on other existing or prospective customers in a social network.

Customer Knowledge Value is a measure of the additional profits brought in by a customer's ideas or feedback.

Customer Lifetime Value the sum of cumulated cash flows—discounted using the weighted average cost of capital (WACC) or discount rate—of a customer over his or her entire lifetime with the company.

Customer Referral Value is a measure of each customer's referral behavior by taking into account the average number of successful incentivized referrals that the customer has successfully made.

Cyclical Indexes a representation of the effects of business cycle fluctuations in making a forecast.

Data unassimilated facts about the market.

Data Analysis Error errors that arise due to the faulty procedures employed in coding, editing, analyzing, and interpreting data.

Database an organized store of data, usually within a computer.

Data Editing identifies omissions, ambiguities, and errors in responses.

Day-after Recall (DAR) the percentage of the audience who can recall something specific about the commercial the next day.

Decision Support System (DSS) a collection of rules, procedures, and models for retrieving data from a database, transforming it into usable information, and disseminating it to users so that they can make decisions.

Degree of Freedom (df) the number of bits of "free" or unconstrained data used in calculating a sample statistic or test statistic.

Delphi Approach a group judgment method where each member makes an individual judgment and then each member is given an opportunity to revise his or her judgment after seeing the others' initial judgments, until, after several iterations, the group members reach their conclusion.

Demographic Shift changes in physical and socioeconomic characteristics of a population such as age, ethnicity, and income.

Dependence Techniques appropriate when one or more variables can be identified as dependent variables and the remaining as independent variables.

Descriptive Research research that usually is designed to provide a summary of some aspects of the environment when the hypotheses are tentative and speculative in nature.

DETAILER a decision calculus model for determining the sales force allocation by market and by product line.

Diary Panel the basic data-gathering instrument for local TV and radio ratings.

Direct Observation an observation method in which the researcher directly observes the person or behavior in question.

Discriminant Analysis a statistical technique for developing a set of independent variables to classify people or objects into one or more groups.

Discriminant Function the linear combination of variables developed by discriminant analysis for the purpose of classifying people or objects into one or more groups.

Discriminant Validity the ability of a measurement instrument not to correlate with supposed measures of other variables or constructs; the opposite of convergent validity.

Disproportionate Sampling best used when one of the groups or subgroups of the population is a relatively small percentage of the population.

Dollarmetric Scale survey that provides a direct measure of the brand name's value.

Door-to-Door Interviewing interviewing in which consumers are interviewed in person in their homes.

Drop-Off Approach the hand delivery of a questionnaire to sampling points.

Dummy/Binary/Dichotomous/Instrumental/Qualitative Variable a variable taking on the values of either 0 or 1, which is used to denote characteristics that are not quantifiable.

E-Commerce buying something electronically without talking to people or using invoices or any other paper to complete the business transaction.

Efficiency a criterion used to judge whether a market research study produces the maximum amount and quality of information for the minimum expenditure of time and money.

Eigenvalue represents the amount of variance in original variables that is associated with a factor.

Empathic Interviewing an exploratory way of research that draws from the wisdom of sociology, psychology, market research, and anthropology to help researchers probe beneath generalizations and identify the social factors that influence consumer behavior.

Evaluative Research is carried out to evaluate performance of programs, including tracking advertising recall, corporate and brand image studies, and measuring customer satisfaction with the quality of the product and service.

Expected Value the value obtained by multiplying each consequence by the probability of that consequence occurring and summing the products.

Experiment study in which conditions are controlled so that one or more independent variable(s) can be manipulated to test a hypothesis about a dependent variable.

Experimental Control the control of extraneous variables through experimental procedures such as randomization or block designs.

Experimental Error error that arises due to the improper design of the experiment.

Experimental Group the group of subjects exposed to the experimental treatment.

Experimental Treatments alternative manipulations of the independent variable being investigated.

Experiments studies that require the intervention by the observer beyond that required for measurement.

Exploratory Focus Groups focus groups commonly used at the exploratory phase of the market research process to aid in precise problem definition.

Exploratory Research research that usually is designed to generate ideas when the hypotheses are vague or ill-defined.

Exponential Smoothing in time-series extrapolations, the weighting of historical data so that the more recent data are weighted more heavily than less recent data, by exponentially decreasing sets of weights.

External Source a marketing data source found outside of the organization.

External Validity the applicability of experimental results to situations external to the actual experimental context.

Extraneous Variables variables other than the manipulated variable that affect the response of the test units and hence the results of the experiment; also known as the confounding variables.

Face/Consensus Validity the validity of a measurement instrument as determined entirely by subjective argument or judgment.

Factor an underlying construct defined by a linear combination of variables.

Factor Analysis a set of techniques for the study of interrelationships among variables, usually for the purposes of data reduction and the discovery of underlying constructs or latent dimensions.

Factor Loading the correlation (or sometimes the regression weight) of a variable with a factor.

Factor Rotation the generation of several factor analysis solutions (factor loadings and scores) from the same data set.

Factor Scores a respondent's score or value on a factor.

Factorial Design an experimental design in which two or more experimental variables are considered simultaneously by applying each combination of the experimental treatment levels to randomly selected groups.

Field Experiments experiments in which the experimental treatment is introduced in a completely natural setting.

Field Services these suppliers concentrate on collecting data for research projects.

Focus Group a group discussion focused on a series of topics introduced by a discussion leader; the group members are encouraged to express their own views on each topic and to elaborate on or react to the views of each other.

Forced Exposure respondents are exposed to an ad in a facility as opposed to an "on-air" test in the home.

Foreign Market Opportunity Analysis acquisition of information that would help the management to narrow the possibilities for international marketing activities. The aim of such an exercise is to gather information to aid in managerial decision making.

Frequency Distribution a report of the number of responses that a question has received.

F-Statistic the statistic used in the analysis of variance to test for differences in groups.

Full-Profile Approach a method of collecting data for trade-off analysis in which respondents are given cards that describe complete product or service configurations.

GANTT Charts a form of activity flowcharts that provide a schematic representation incorporating the activity, time, and personnel requirements for a given research project.

Genotypic Sources of Refusal these pertain to why survey respondents refuse to participate on account of their inherent characteristics such as age, sex, and occupation.

Goodman and Kruskal's Tau a measure of association for nominally scaled variables based on a proportional reduction in error.

Graphical Evaluation and Review Technique (GERT) essentially a second-generation PERT approach to scheduling, in which both the completion probabilities and activity costs to be built into a network representation are considered.

Hierarchical Clustering a method of cluster analysis that starts with each object in its own (single-object) cluster and systematically combines clusters until all objects are in one cluster.

History Effect any influence on subjects, external to an experiment, that may affect the results of the experiment.

Hit Ratio percentage of cases classified correctly.

Hold-Out Sample a sample used to test a model developed from another sample.

Home Audit a method of collecting continuous purchase panel data in which the panel members agree to permit an auditor to check their household stocks of certain product categories at regular intervals.

Humanistic Inquiry a method in which the researcher is immersed in the group or system under study.

Hypothesis is a possible answer to the research question.

Ideal Object the object the respondent would prefer over all others, including objects that can be conceptualized but do not actually exist; it is a combination of all the respondent's preferred attribute levels.

Independence in statistics, the property that the knowledge of one variable or event offers no information as to the identity of another variable or event.

Individual In-Depth Interview a qualitative research method designed to explore the hidden (deep) feelings, values, and motives of the respondent through a face-to-face interview with the researcher.

Industrial Market a market for goods and services composed of industrial firms, other businesses, government agencies, and organizations in general, rather than individual consumers.

Information data that have been transformed into answers for specific questions of the decision makers.

Information System a system containing marketing data and marketing intelligence.

Instrumentation Effect the effect of changes in the measuring instrument on the experimental results.

Integrated Marketing Communications a concept of marketing communications planning that recognizes the added value of a comprehensive plan that evaluates the strategic roles of a variety of communication disciplines and combines these disciplines to provide clarity, consistency, and maximum communication impact through the seamless integration of discrete messages.

Intention/Action Component the part of an attitude that represents the person's expectations of future behavior toward the object, person, or event.

Interactive Effect the case where the effect of one variable on another variable depends on the level of a third variable.

Interdependence Techniques the variables are not classified as dependent or independent; rather, the whole set of interdependent relationships is examined.

Interference Error error that occurs due to the failure of the interviewer to adhere to the exact procedure while collecting the data.

Internal Records a marketing data source found within the organization.

Internal Validity the ability of an experiment to show relationships unambiguously.

Internet a global network connecting millions of computers.

Interval Estimation the estimation of the interval in which an unknown population characteristic is judged to lie, for a given level of confidence.

Interval Scale a scale with the property that units have the same width throughout the scale (for example, thermometer).

Interviewer Error a source of error in personal interviews due to the impression the respondent has of the interviewer and the way the interviewer asks questions, follows up partial answers, and records the responses.

Intranets internal company networks.

Itemized Category Scale a scale in which the respondent chooses among one of several response options or categories.

Judgmental Sampling a nonprobability sampling method in which an "expert" uses judgment to identify representative samples.

Jury of Executive Opinion an efficient and timely qualitative research approach that combines the judgments of a group of managers about forecasts, most commonly used in consumer products and service companies.

Laboratory Experiment an experiment in which the experimental treatment is introduced in an artificial or laboratory setting.

Laboratory Test Market a procedure whereby shoppers are exposed to an ad for a new product and then taken on a simulated shopping trip in a laboratory facility.

Latin Square Design an experimental design that reduces the number of groups involved when interactions between the treatment levels and the control variables can be considered relatively unimportant.

Leading Indicators a variable that tends to predict the future direction of an object to be forecast.

Lead User Analysis an approach where instead of just asking users what they have done, their solutions are collected more formally.

Likert/Summated Scale a scale developed by the Likert method in which the subject must indicate his or her degree of agreement or disagreement with a variety of statements related to the attitude object and which then are summed over all statements to provide a total score.

Lockbox Approach the delivery by mail of a small, locked metal box containing a questionnaire and other interviewing exhibits.

Magnitude Scaling a technique for measuring opinions using a ratio scale instead of an interval scale.

Mail Diary Method a method of collecting continuous purchase panel data in which panel members record the details of each purchase in certain categories and return a completed mail diary at regular intervals.

Mail Panel a representative national sample of people who have agreed to participate in a limited number of mail surveys each year.

Mail Survey the mailing of questionnaires and their return by mail by the designated respondents.

Mall Intercept Surveys surveys conducted in malls by intercepting consumers who visit the mall.

Manipulation the creation of different levels of the independent variable is known as manipulating the variable.

Marketing activity, set of institutions, and processes for creating, communicating, delivering, and exchanging offerings that have value for customers, clients, partners, and society at large.

Marketing Decision Support System (MDSS) combines marketing data from diverse sources into a single database that line managers can enter interactively.

Marketing Intelligence the process of acquiring and analyzing information in order to understand the market (both existing and potential customers); to determine the current and future needs and preferences, attitudes, and behavior of the market; and to assess changes in the business environment that may affect the size and nature of the market in future.

Marketing Planning and Information System a system of strategic and tactical plans and marketing data and intelligence that provides overall direction and coordination to the organization.

Marketing Program Development the stage of the market planning process that deals with segmentation decisions, product decisions, distribution decisions, advertising and promotion decisions, personal selling decisions, and pricing decisions.

Marketing Research function that links the consumer, customer, and public to the marketer through information—information used to identify and define marketing opportunities and problems; generate, refine, and evaluate marketing actions; monitor marketing performance; and improve understanding of marketing as a process. Marketing research specifies the information required to address these issues, designs the method for collecting information, manages and implements the data collection process, analyzes, and communicates the findings and their implications.

Marketing Research Methodologist an individual who has a balanced and in-depth knowledge of the fields of statistics, psychometrics, marketing, and buyer behavior and applies that knowledge to describe and infer causal relationships from marketing data.

Market Potential the sales for the product or service that would result if the market were fully developed.

Market Segmentation the development and pursuit of marketing programs directed at subgroups or segments of the population that the organization could possibly serve.

Matching a procedure for the assignment of subjects to groups that ensures each group of respondents is matched on the basis of the pertinent characteristics.

Maturation during a research study, changes within respondents that are a consequence of time.

Mean the number obtained by summing all elements in a set and dividing by the number of elements.

Measurement the assignment of numbers by rules to objects in order to reflect quantities of properties.

Measurement Equivalence deals with the methods and procedures used by the researcher to collect and categorize essential data and information.

Measurement Error error that occurs due to the variation between the information sought by the researcher and the information generated by a particular procedure employed by the researcher.

Metropolitan Division A Metropolitan Statistical Area containing a single core with a population of at least 2.5 million may be subdivided to form smaller groupings of counties referred to as Metropolitan Divisions.

Metropolitan Statistical Areas urban areas that constitute counties containing a central city with populations of at least 50,000.

Mortality Effect the effect on the experimental results of respondents dropping out of an experiment.

Moving Average using the moving average of the last n data points (for example, the monthly averages for a year) to forecast.

Multiattribute Model any model linking attribute judgments with overall liking or affect.

Multidimensional Scaling (MDS) a set of techniques for developing perceptual maps.

Multiple-Item Scales scales used in social research to measure abstract constructs.

Multiple Linear Regression linear regression where more than one independent variable is used.

Mobile Marketing The use of wireless media as an integrated content delivery and direct response vehicle within a crossmedia or stand-alone marketing communications program. (Source: Mobile Marketing Association)

Multistage Designs a sampling procedure that consists of several sampling methods used sequentially.

Multivariate Analysis the simultaneous study of two or more measures on a sample of objects.

Need a want, an urge, a wish, or any motivational force directing behavior toward a goal.

Need Research/Identification a type of concept generation research with the emphasis placed on the identification of unfulfilled needs that exist in the market.

Nielsen Retail Index a retail store audit conducted by A.C. Nielsen for four major groups of stores: grocery products, drugs, mass merchandisers, and alcoholic beverages.

Nominal Scale a measurement that assigns only an identification or label to an object or set of objects.

Nondirective Interview a type of individual depth interview in which the respondent is given maximum freedom to respond, within the bounds of topics of interest to the interviewer.

Nonhierarchical Clustering Program permits objects to leave one cluster and join another as clusters are being formed, if the clustering criterion be improved by doing so.

Nonparametric Procedures analysis techniques that are applicable only if the data are nonmetric (nominal or ordinal).

Nonprobability Sampling any sampling method where the probability of any population element's inclusion is unknown, such as judgmental or convenience sampling.

Nonresponse Bias an error due to the inability to elicit information from some respondents in a sample, often due to refusals.

Nonresponse Error error that occurs due to nonparticipation of some eligible respondents in the study. This could be due to the unwillingness of the respondents to participate in the study or the inability of the interviewer to contact the respondents.

Nonsampling Error error that is observed when a population is surveyed.

Null Hypothesis the hypothesis to be tested.

Observation a data collection method where the relevant behaviors are recorded; examples are direct observation, contrived observation, physical trace measures, and behavior recording devices.

Omission a memory error where a respondent leaves out an event or some aspect of it.

Omnibus Survey a regularly scheduled personal interview survey comprised questions from several separate firms.

On-Air Test a test ad that is shown on a channel viewed at home.

Online Telephone Interview an interview where the interviewer (1) reads the questions from an online cathode-raytube (CRT) terminal that is linked directly to a computer and (2) records the answers on a keyboard for entry to the computer.

Open-Response/Unstructured Question a question with either no classification of responses or precoded classification of responses.

Optimizing (*in Cluster Analysis*) a nonhierarchical method of clustering wherein the objects can later be reassigned to clusters on the basis of optimizing some overall criterion measure.

Order Bias the bias of question responses due to the order of question presentation.

Ordinal Scale a measurement that assigns only a rank order (that is, "less than or greater than") to a set of objects.

Paired-Comparison Scale a scale in which the objects to be ranked are presented two at a time so that the respondent has to choose between them according to some criterion.

Parallel Threshold a nonhierarchical clustering method wherein several cluster centers are selected simultaneously and objects within the threshold level are assigned to the nearest center. Threshold levels can be adjusted to admit fewer or more objects to the cluster.

Parameter a number constant in each model considered but varying in different models.

Parametric Procedures analysis techniques that are applicable only if the data are metric (interval or ratio).

Partial Correlation Coefficient examining the association between a dependent and independent variable after satisfactorily factoring out the effect of other independent variables.

Partworth Utilities utilities associated with particular product or brand attributes that are added together to obtain an overall utility for a product or brand alternative in conjoint analysis.

Past Turning Point a point in time where a substantial change in growth rate can be identified by an environmental change; a forecast can be based on data since that point.

Pearson Correlation Coefficient measures the degree to which there is linear association between two intervally scaled variables.

Periodic Discounting strategy adopted by firms wherein the firms can start at a high price and periodically discount their prices in order to draw consumers with lower reservation prices. This is useful when markets have consumers with differential reservation prices.

Personal Interview a face-to-face interview between the respondent and the interviewer.

Phenotypic Source of Refusal these pertain to why survey respondents refuse to participate on account of the characteristics of the data collection procedure such as which questions are asked, how they are asked, length of the interview, and so on.

Phi-Squared a chi-square statistic corrected for sample size.

Physical Trace Measures an observation method, such as a home audit, in which the natural "residue" or physical trace of the behavior is recorded.

Pictorial Scales scales in which the various categories of the scale are depicted pictorially.

Picture Interpretation a projective technique based on the Thematic Apperception Test (TAT), in which the respondent is asked to tell a story on the presentation of a series of pictures.

Plus-One Dialing consists of selecting a random sample of telephone numbers from one or more telephone directories, then adding the constant "1" to the last four digits of each number selected.

Population Specification Error error that occurs when an inappropriate population is chosen for the study.

Population Standard Deviation true standard deviation of the population whose sample is being tested.

Potential Rating Index Zip Markets (PRIZM) the classification and grouping of residents of Zip Code areas based on demographic and lifestyle data derived from the Census.

Predictive Validity criterion validity that is established by correlating the measurement score with a future criterion variable.

Preexperimental Designs exploratory studies that have almost no control over the influence of extraneous factors on the results of the experiment.

Pretest the presentation of a questionnaire in a pilot study to a representative sample of the respondent population in order to discover any problems with the questionnaire prior to full-scale use.

Price Bundling the pricing strategy adopted for products that are nonsubstitutable, are perishable, and have an asymmetric demand structure. An example is pricing a car that includes many options.

Price Signaling the pricing strategy adopted when the consumers in the market are willing to pay more for a product despite lack of knowledge regarding a product's quality. The firm produces an inferior product and sells it at the same price as the better quality product produced by another firm, in the hope that customers will associate high quality with high price.

Primary Data data collected to address a specific research objective (as opposed to secondary data).

Principal Components/Principal Factor Analysis a type of factor analysis that seeks to explain the greatest amount of variance in a data set, thus providing data reduction.

Probability Sampling any sampling method where the probability of any population element's inclusion is known and is greater than zero.

Problem or Opportunity Definition a process of understanding the causes and predicting the consequences of problems or a process of exploring the size and nature of opportunities; the second phase of marketing program development.

Profile Analysis the comparison of evaluations of the alternatives in a consideration set, on the important and determinant attributes.

Program Evaluation and Review Technique (PERT) probability-based scheduling approach that recognizes and measures the uncertainty of project completion times.

Programmatic Research research performed to develop marketing options through market segmentation, market opportunity analysis, or consumer attitude and product usage studies.

Projective Techniques a set of presentation methods of ambiguous, unstructured objects, activities, or persons for which a respondent is asked to give interpretation and find meaning; the more ambiguous the stimulus, the more the respondent has to project himself or herself into the task, thereby revealing hidden feelings, values, and needs; examples are word association, role playing, completion tests, and picture interpretation.

Proportional Stratified Sampling sampling procedure in which the number of objects or sampling units chosen from each group is proportional to the number in the population.

Purchase Intercept Technique (PIT) a consumer survey technique for collecting data through personal interviews by in-store observation of purchase behavior and then interception of consumers in the shopping environment to determine the reasons behind that behavior.

Qualitative Research research designed primarily for exploratory purposes, such as getting oriented to the range and complexity of consumer activity, clarifying the problem, and identifying likely methodological problems; examples are individual and group interviews, projective techniques, and case studies.

Quasi-Experimental Design offers the researcher some degree of control, but there is no random assignment of subjects as there is for true experimental designs.

Quota Sampling a judgmental sampling method that is constrained to include a minimum from each specified subgroup in the population.

Random-Digit Dialing nondirectory procedure for selecting all 10 telephone number digits at random.

Random Error measurement error due to changing aspects of the respondent or measurement situation.

Randomization a procedure in which the assignment of subjects and treatments to groups is based on chance. Randomization ensures control over the extraneous variables and increases the reliability of the experiment.

Randomized Block Design an experimental design in which the test units are first grouped into homogeneous groups along some prespecified criterion and are then assigned randomly to different treatments within each block.

Rank-Order Scale a scale in which the respondent is required to order a set of objects with regard to a common criterion.

Ratio Scale a measurement that has a true or meaningful zero point, allowing for the specification of absolute magnitudes of objects.

Ratio-Scaled Data interval type data that has a distinct zero level.

Reading-Habit Method measuring print media exposure by asking how many issues of the last four you have read.

Recent-Reading Method measuring print media exposure by asking whether someone looked at a copy in the past week for a weekly or in the past month for a monthly.

Recording Error error that occurs due to the improper recording of the respondents' answers.

Refusal Rate a measure of any data collection method's ability to induce contacted respondents to participate in the study.

Refusals a source of nonsampling error caused by a respondent's refusing to participate in the study.

Regression Analysis a statistical technique that develops an equation that relates a dependent variable to one or more independent (predictor, explanatory) variables.

Relationship Marketing establishing, developing, and maintaining long-term, trusting relational exchanges with valued customers, distributors, suppliers, and dealers by promising and delivering high-quality services and products to the parties over time.

Relative Market Potential the market potential of one segment relative to other segments.

Relevance a criterion used to judge whether a market research study acts to support strategic and tactical planning activities.

Reliability the random error component of a measurement instrument.

Research Approach one of the following six sources of data—the information system, secondary and standardized data sources, qualitative research, surveys, observations, and experiments.

Research Boundary a delineation of the scope of the research study in terms of items such as population characteristics, locations, and product markets.

Research Design detailed blueprint used to guide a research study toward its objectives.

Research Objectives a precise statement of what information is needed, consisting of the research question, the hypotheses, and the scope or boundaries of the research.

Research Process the series of stages or steps underlying the design and implementation of a marketing research project, including the establishment of the research purpose and objectives, information value estimation, research design, and implementation.

Research Proposal a plan for conducting and controlling a research project.

Research Purpose the shared understanding between the manager and the researcher regarding the decision alternatives, the problems and opportunities to be studied, and who the users of the results shall be.

Research Question the statement(s) of what specific information is required for progress toward the achievement of the research purpose.

Research Tactics the development of the specific details of the research, including the research approach, sampling plan, and choice of research supplier.

Response Bias the tendency of respondents to distort their answers systematically for a variety of reasons, such as social desirability and prestige seeking.

Response Error error that occurs due to the respondents providing inaccurate information (intentionally or unintentionally). This might be due to the inability of the respondent to comprehend the question or a misunderstanding of the question due to fatigue or boredom.

Response Style the systematic tendency of respondents to select particular categories of responses regardless of the content of the questions.

Retail Store Audits audit data collected by research firms whose employees visit a sample of stores at fixed intervals for the purpose of counting stock and recording deliveries to estimate retail sales.

Role Playing a projective technique in which the respondent assumes the role or behavior of another person so that the respondent may reveal attitudes by projecting himself or herself fully into the role.

SAMI/Burke makes available standardized and recurrent marketing research reports to subscribers, usually manufacturers of frequently purchased consumer packaged goods.

Sample a subset of elements from a population.

Sampling process of surveying only a sample of the whole population to make inferences about the population.

Sampling Efficiency/Efficiency of Sampling ratio of accuracy over cost.

Sampling Equivalence deals with the question of identifying and operationalizing two comparable populations and selecting samples that are representative of other populations and that are comparable across countries.

Sampling Error error that occurs if the difference in value (error) between the population parameter and the sample statistic because of sampling.

Sampling Frame a listing of population members that is used to create a random sample.

Sampling Frame Error error that occurs when the sample is drawn from an inaccurate sampling frame.

Sampling Unit any type of element that makes up a sample, such as people, stores, and products.

Scale Transformation manipulation of scale values to ensure comparability with other scales.

Scanner Data the scanner is a device that reads the universal product code from a package as it is processed at a retailer's checkout stand. Scanner data include data on all transactions including size, price, and flavor. They also normally include in-store information such as special displays.

Scatter Diagram a two-dimensional plot of two variables.

Scree Plot used in factor analysis, a plot of the eigenvalues against the number of factors in order of their extraction. The shape of the plot is used to determine the number of factors.

Screening Sample a representative sample of the population being studied that is used to develop or pretest measurement instruments.

Seasonal Index a representation of the seasonal forecast.

Secondary Data data collected for some purpose other than the present research purpose.

Second Market Discounting a pricing strategy wherein the firm discounts its prices in the other markets below its average cost.

Selection Bias differences among subjects, prior to an experiment, that affect the experimental results.

Selection Error error that occurs in a nonprobability sampling method when a sample obtained is not representative of the population.

Selective Research research done to test different decision alternatives.

Self-administered Survey Any method where the respondent completes the survey on her own through the online or offline channels such as mail, Internet, and fax.

Sell-In Test Market the new product being tested must be sold to the retailer. Shelf space is not prearranged.

Semantic-Differential Scale a scale in which the respondent is asked to rate each attitude object in turn on a five- or seven-point rating scale bounded at each end by polar adjectives or phrases.

Semistructured/Focused Individual Interview a type of individual depth interview in which the interviewer attempts to cover a specific list of topics or subareas.

Sensitivity the ability of a measurement instrument to discriminate among meaningful differences in the variable being measured.

Sequential Sampling a sampling method in which an initial modest sample is taken and analyzed, following which, based on the results, a decision is made regarding the necessity of further sampling and analysis; this continues until enough data are collected.

Sequential Threshold a nonhierarchical clustering method wherein a cluster center is selected and all objects within a prespecified threshold value are grouped. Then a new cluster center is selected and the process is repeated. Once objects enter a cluster they are removed from further processing.

Significance Level the probability of obtaining the evidence if the null hypothesis were true.

Similarity/Judgment the judgment an individual makes about whether two objects are similar or different without specifying specific attributes.

Simple Random Sampling a sampling method in which each population member has an equal chance of being selected.

Single Linkage linkage procedure that is based on the shortest distance between objects to form clusters.

Single-Source Data data on product purchases and causal factors such as media exposure, promotion influence, and consumer characteristics that come from the same households as a result of advances in scanner and information technology.

Situation Analysis the stage of the market planning process that deals with understanding the environment and the market, identifying opportunities and threats, and assessing the firm's competitive position.

Snowball Sampling a judgmental sampling method in which each respondent is asked to identify one or more other sample members.

Social Marketing planning and implementation of programs designed to bring about social change using concepts from commercial marketing. (Source: Social Marketing Institute)

Split-Ballot Technique the inclusion of more than one version of a question in a questionnaire.

Split-Cable Testing exposing two or more groups of a cable system to different ads and monitoring their purchases.

Spurious Association an inappropriate causal interpretation of association due to an unmeasured variable influencing both variables.

Standard Deviation the square root of the variance.

Standard Error of Estimate in regression analysis, the standard deviation of the sampling distribution of the regression model parameter estimates.

Standard Industrial Classification (SIC) System a uniform numbering system developed by the U.S. Government for classifying industrial establishments according to their economic activities.

Standard Metropolitan Statistical Area (SMSA) census tracts that are combined in counties containing a central city with a population of at least 50,000.

Stapel Scale a 10-category unipolar rating scale with categories numbered from +5 to –5. It modifies the semantic differential by having the respondent rate how close and in what direction a descriptor adjective fits a given concept.

Statistic any of several characteristics of a sample.

Statistical Control the control of extraneous variables through statistical methods.

Statistical Designs designs that allow for examining the effects of different treatment levels of an experimental variable, and also the effects of two or more independent variables.

Strategic Plans plans that focus on strategic decisions of resource allocation with long-run performance implications, usually having time horizons of more than one year.

Stratified Sampling a sampling method that uses natural subgroups or strata that are more homogeneous than the total population.

Surrogate Information Error error that occurs due to the difference between the information that is required for a marketing research study and the information being sought by the researcher.

Survey Method a method of data collection, such as a telephone or personal interview, a mail survey, or any combination thereof.

Syndicated Services services from firms such as A.C. Nielsen and Information Resources Inc., where costs are shared by multiple client firms.

Systematic Error the measurement error due to constant aspects of the person or measurement situation.

Systematic Sampling sampling that involves systematically spreading the sample through the list of population members.

Test Marketing the introduction of the new product in selected test cities that represent the typical market, so that the results of the performance in these markets can be projected on a national basis.

Third-Person Techniques a technique of ascertaining the respondents' views by asking them to answer for a third person.

Through-the-Book measurement of exposure to print media by asking respondents if they recognized articles in an issue.

Thurstone/Equal-Appearing Interval Scale a scale developed by first having a group of judges categorize a set of items and then selecting those items that were similarly categorized; the scale is administered by having respondents choose those statements with which they agree.

Time-Series Design design in which a series of measurements is employed during which an experimental treatment occurs.

Total Quality Management (TQM) the concept of creation of value to the consumer through enhanced product and service quality, thereby enhancing customer satisfaction.

Tracking Studies monitoring the performance of advertising by regular surveys of the audience.

Trade-off Approach a method of collecting data for trade-off analysis in which the respondent is asked to rank each combination of levels of two attributes from most preferred to least preferred.

True Experimental Designs experimental designs that adopt the random assignment procedure.

Two-way Focus Groups One group watches another group and discusses the observed interactions and conclusions.

Type I Error rejecting a null hypothesis when it is true.

Type II Error accepting a null hypothesis when it is false.

Unaided Recall a questioning approach in which the respondent is asked to remember an object of interest without the assistance of clues from the researcher.

Uniform Resource Locator (URL) the address of a website on the World Wide Web or a general-purpose Internet addressing protocol in WWW (http).

Universal Product Code (UPC) a standard code assigned to each manufacturer's brand and pack size so that its purchases can be tracked through a store scanner system.

U.S. Bureau of the Census the federal agency that conducts the U.S. Census once every 10 years and compiles demographic statistics on the population. It also conducts one-shot surveys for other federal agencies.

Use Test a type of product evaluation where the product is given to consumers; after a reasonable period of time, the consumers are asked for their reactions to it.

Validity the ability of a measurement instrument to measure what it is supposed to measure.

Values and Lifestyle Survey (VALS) a survey conducted by the Stanford Research Institute, which classified the U.S. population into nine lifestyle segments based on individual values and lifestyles of survey respondents.

Variable Respecification a procedure by which existing data are modified to create new variables or a large number of variables are collapsed into fewer variables.

Variance a measure of dispersion based on the degree to which elements of a sample or population differ from the average element.

Varimax Rotation a rotation method that searches for simple structure; a pattern of factor loadings where some loadings are close to one, and some loadings are close to zero.

Ward's Method method based on the loss of information resulting from grouping objects into clusters, as measured by the total sum of squared deviations of every object from the mean of the cluster to which the object is assigned.

Warehouse Withdrawal Services syndicated services offered by firms such as SAMI/Burke in which periodic audits are done at the warehouse or wholesale level and reports are produced on product shipments made to retail stores served by those warehouses.

Weighting a procedure by which each response in the database is assigned a number according to some prespecified rule.

Wheel of Fortune Strategies a set of strategies based on the customer lifetime value metric that identifies ways for companies to target the right customers and efficiently manage their resources in order to obtain the maximum profits from each customer.

Within-Treatment Variance variance in the response variable within a single treatment level.

Word Association a projective technique in which the respondent is asked to give the first word that comes to mind on the presentation of another word.

Word-of-Mouth Marketing the art and science of building active, mutually beneficial consumer-to-consumer and consumer-to-marketer communications.

World Wide Web a graphical environment that provides point-and-click access to the Internet through a network of servers.

Index

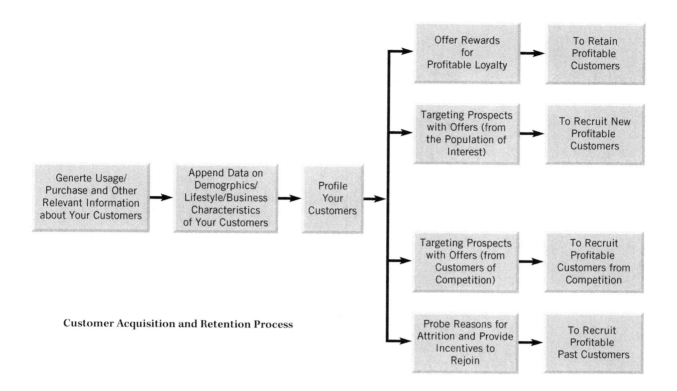

Customer Acquisition and Retention Process

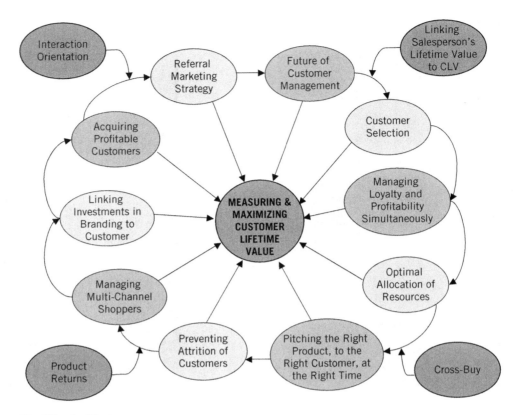

The Wheel of Fortune

Adapted and Updated from Kumar, V. (2008), *Managing Customers for Profits,* Upper Saddle River, NJ: Wharton School Publishing.

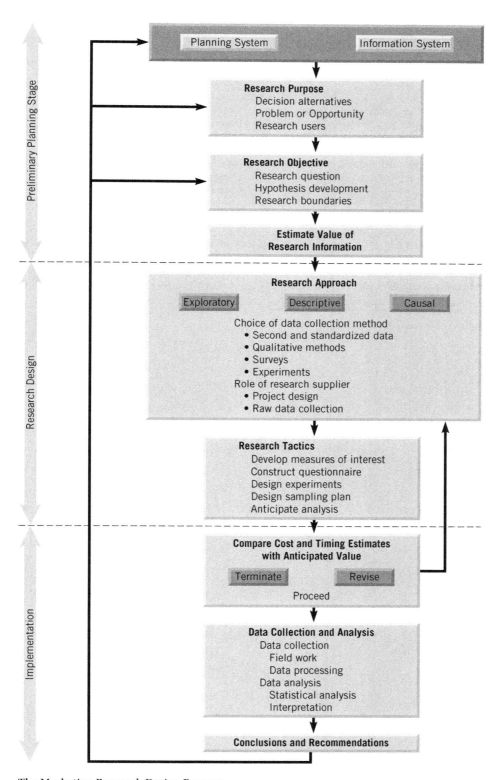

The Marketing Research Design Process

Do	Don't
■ Use households' actual purchase data for identifying your target market whenever possible.	■ Guess at what the right households are by substituting variables that might be related to your target group but aren't based on actual purchase behavior.
■ Try to understand the quality of your buyers by understanding their profitable loyalty behavior and switching patterns.	■ Take the easy way out by identifying "prior brand buyers."
■ Employ a true "experimental design" test-versus-control approach whenever you conduct a test.	■ Underutilize the real power of your database by running marketing events only as a test run. Make sure there are adequate controls to ensure proper evaluation.
■ Allow enough time for your test variable to work by taking into account category and brand purchase cycles.	■ Execute a program and then measure it too quickly due to time constraints.
■ Try to explore the reasons why a particular marketing outcome happened.	

Do's and Don'ts in Database Marketing.

CPSIA information can be obtained at www.ICGtesting.com
Printed in the USA
BVOW09s0806141016

464884BV00029B/19/P